HOW *to be* GAY

THE BELKNAP PRESS OF HARVARD UNIVERSITY PRESS

Cambridge, Massachusetts ★ London, England

HOW

to be

GAY

DAVID M. HALPERIN

First Harvard University Press paperback edition, 2014

Library of Congress Cataloging-in-Publication Data

Halperin, David M., 1952–
   How to be gay / David M. Halperin.
     p.   cm.
   Includes bibliographical references and index.
   ISBN 978-0-674-06679-3 (cloth : alk. paper)
   ISBN 978-0-674-28399-2 (pbk.)
   1. Gay men.   I. Title.
   HQ76.H2795   2012
   306.76'62—dc23   2012009043

for

Myra and Marie, Damon and Pier, Linda and Steven, Jill and Toby, Jean and Isabelle, Valerie and Gayle, Mark and Neil, Esther and Stephen, Gay and Randy, Rostom and Matthieu, Ume and Aaron, Peter and Andy, Jesse and Emily and Sarah, Nadine and Patsy, Michael and Martha, Paul and Zachary, Logan and Aric, David and Brent,

and for

John

CONTENTS

Let the pagans beget
and the Christians baptize.

PART ONE

∽ ∽ ∽

B+ Could Try Harder

DIARY OF A SCANDAL

The first hint of trouble came in the form of an e-mail message. It reached me on Friday, March 17, 2000, at 4:09 pm. The message was from a guy named Jeff in Erie, Pennsylvania, who was otherwise unknown to me. (He readily provided his full name and e-mail address, but I have suppressed them here, as a courtesy to him.)

At first, I couldn't figure out why Jeff was writing to me. He kept referring to some college course, and he seemed to be very exercised over it. He wanted to know what it was really about. He went on to suggest that I tell the Executive Committee of the English Department to include in the curriculum, for balance, another course, entitled "How To Be a Heartless Conservative." There was surely at least *one* Republican in the department, he supposed, who was qualified to teach such a course. But then Jeff made a show of coming to his senses. A conservative allowed in the English Department? The very idea was ridiculous. And on that note of hilarity, his message ended.

This was all very witty, to be sure. So far, though, it was not especially enlightening.

But soon it turned out that Jeff was not alone. A dozen e-mail messages, most of them abusive and some of them obscene, followed in quick succession. The subsequent days and weeks brought many more.

You may wonder, as I did myself, what I had done to deserve all this attention. Eventually, I realized that earlier on the same day, Friday, March 17, 2000, the Registrar's Office at the University of Michigan in Ann Arbor, where in fact I do teach English, had activated its course information website, listing the classes to be offered during the fall term of the 2000–2001 academic year. At virtually the same moment, unbeknownst to me, the website of the *National Review,* a conservative magazine of political commentary founded by William F. Buckley, Jr., had run a story in its series *NR Wire* called "How To Be Gay 101." Except for the heading, the story consisted entirely of one page from the University of Michigan's newly published course listings.

Staffers at the *National Review* may well be on a constant lookout for new material, but they are surely not so desperate as to make a habit of scanning the University of Michigan's website in eager anticipation of the exact moment each term when the registrar announces the courses to be taught the following semester.

Someone must have tipped them off.

It later emerged that there had indeed been a mole at work in the University of Michigan Registrar's Office. At least, someone with access to the relevant information had e-mailed it in early March to the *Michigan Review,* the conservative campus newspaper associated with the *National Review* and its nationwide network of right-wing campus publications. The *Michigan Review* had apparently passed the information on to its parent organization. Matthew S. Schwartz, a student at the University of Michigan who for two years had been editor-in-chief of the *Michigan Review,* coyly revealed in an article in the *MR* the next month that "a U-M conservative newspaper tipped off a *National Review* reporter" about the breaking story. After that, as Schwartz put it, "the wheels of dissemination were in motion. Word . . . trickled down through conservative circles, and the story was well on its way to mainstream media."[1]

So what was this story that was just too good for the *National Review* to keep under wraps for a single day? It had to do with an undergraduate English course I had just invented, called "How To Be Gay:

Male Homosexuality and Initiation." The course description had been made public that morning, along with the rest of the information about the class. The *National Review* website withheld all commentary, introducing the story thus: "What follows is the verbatim description from the University of Michigan's Fall 2000 course catalog. U. Michigan was ranked as the 25th best University in the United States in the most recent ratings by *US News and World Report*."

The next year, our national ranking went up.

Here is the course description, as it appeared (correctly, except for the omission of paragraph breaks) on the *National Review*'s website.

Just because you happen to be a gay man doesn't mean that you don't have to learn how to become one. Gay men do some of that learning on their own, but often we learn how to be gay from others, either because we look to them for instruction or because they simply tell us what they think we need to know, whether we ask for their advice or not. This course will examine the general topic of the role that initiation plays in the formation of gay identity. We will approach it from three angles: (1) as a sub-cultural practice—subtle, complex, and difficult to theorize—which a small but significant body of work in queer studies has begun to explore; (2) as a theme in gay male writing; (3) as a class project, since the course itself will constitute an experiment in the very process of initiation that it hopes to understand. In particular, we'll examine a number of cultural artifacts and activities that seem to play a prominent role in learning how to be gay: Hollywood movies, grand opera, Broadway musicals, and other works of classical and popular music, as well as camp, diva-worship, drag, muscle culture, style, fashion, and interior design. Are there a number of classically "gay" works such that, despite changing tastes and generations, ALL gay men, of whatever class, race, or ethnicity, need to know them, in order to be gay? What roles do such works play in learning how to be gay? What is there about these works that makes them essential parts of a gay male curriculum? Conversely, what is there about gay identity that explains the gay appropriation of these works? One aim of exploring these questions is to approach gay identity from the perspective of social practices and cultural identifications rather than from the perspective of gay sexuality itself. What can such an approach tell us about the sentimental, affective, or aesthetic dimensions of gay identity, including gay sexuality, that an exclusive focus on gay sexuality cannot? At the core of gay experience, there is not only identification but disidentification. Almost as soon as I learn how to be gay, or perhaps even before, I also learn how not to be gay. I say to myself, "Well, I may be gay, but at least I'm not like THAT!" Rather than attempting to promote one version of gay identity at the expense of others, this course will investigate the stakes in gay identifications and disidentifications, seeking ultimately to create the basis for a wider acceptance of the plurality of ways in which people determine how to be gay. Work for the class will include short essays, projects, and a mandatory weekly three-hour screening (or other cultural workshop) on Thursday evenings.

The *National Review* was right to think that no commentary would be needed. From the messages and letters I received, it was clear that a number of readers understood my class to be an overt attempt to recruit straight students to the gay lifestyle. Some conservatives, like Jeff from Erie, already believe that universities, and especially English Departments, are bastions of left-wing radicalism; others have long suspected that institutions of higher education indoctrinate students into extremist ideologies, argue them out of their religious faith, corrupt them with alcohol and drugs, and turn them into homosexuals. Now conservatives had proof positive of the last of those intuitions —the blueprint for homosexual world domination, the actual game plan—right there in plain English.

Well, at least the title was in plain English.

ᥫᩣ

The course description for my class actually said nothing at all about converting heterosexual students to homosexuality.[2] It emphasized, from its very first line, that the topic to be studied had to do with how men *who already are gay* acquire a conscious identity, a common culture, a particular outlook on the world, a shared sense of self, an awareness of belonging to a specific social group, and a distinctive sensibility or subjectivity. It was designed to explore a basic paradox: How do you become who you are?

In particular, the class set out to explore *gay men's characteristic relation to mainstream culture* for what it might reveal about certain structures of feeling distinctive to gay men.[3] The goal of such an inquiry was to shed light on the nature and formation of gay male subjectivity. Accordingly, the class approached homosexuality as a social rather than an individual condition and as a cultural practice rather than a sexual one. It took up the initiatory process internal to gay male communities whereby gay men teach other gay men how to be gay—not by introducing them to gay sex, let alone by seducing them into it (gay men are likely to have had plentiful exposure to sex by the time they take up residence in a gay male social world), but rather by showing them how to transform a number of heterosexual cultural objects and discourses into vehicles of gay meaning.

The course's aim, in other words, was to examine how cultural transmission operates in the case of sexual minorities. Unlike the members of minority groups defined by race or ethnicity or religion, gay men cannot rely on their birth families to teach them about their history or their culture. They must discover their roots through contact with the larger society and the larger world.[4]

As the course evolved over the years, it grew less concerned with adult initiation and became more focused on the kind of gay acculturation that begins in early childhood, without the conscious participation of the immediate family and against the grain of social expectations. The course's goal was to understand how this *counteracculturation* operates, the exact logic by which gay male subjects resist the summons to experience the world in heterosexual and heteronormative ways.

That is also the goal of this book.

⊙✕⊙

The course description indicated plainly that the particular topic to be studied would be gay *male* cultural practices and gay *male* subjectivity. The stated purpose of the course was to describe a gay male

perspective on the world and to explore, to analyze, and to understand gay male culture in its specificity. Male homosexuality often
gives rise to distinctive ways of relating to the larger society—to
forms of cultural resistance all its own—so there is good reason to
treat gay male culture as a topic in its own right. That is what I will
do here.

Women have written brilliantly about gay male culture. (So have a
few straight men.) Their insights played a central role in my class;
they also figure prominently in this book. Studying a gay male perspective on the world does not entail studying it, then, *from* a gay male
perspective. Nor does it entail excluding the perspectives of women
and others. Nonetheless, describing how gay men relate to sex and
gender roles, how they see women, and the place of femininity in gay
male cultural practices does mean focusing on gay male attitudes toward women, not on women themselves, their outlook or their interests. It is the gendered subjectivity of gay men—both gay male masculinity and gay male femininity—that is the topic of this book. The
fact that most of the women whose work I have depended on in order to understand gay male culture turn out to be gay themselves
does not diminish the usefulness of considering male homosexuality
apart from female homosexuality. (Since my topic is gay men, male
homosexuality, and gay male culture, the word "gay," as I use it here,
generally refers to males, as it did in the title of my course. When
I intend my statements to apply to gay people as a whole, to lesbians and gay men, or to queers more generally, I adjust my wording.)

ೲ

The project of studying gay male culture encounters an initial, daunting obstacle. Some people don't believe there is such a thing as gay
culture. Although the existence of gay male culture is routinely acknowledged as a fact, it is just as routinely denied as a truth.

To say that gay men have a particular, distinctive, characteristic relation to the culture of the larger society in which they live is to do
nothing more than to state the obvious. But despite how obvious

such a statement may be—and despite how often, how commonly it is made—it is liable to become controversial as soon as it is asserted as a claim. That is especially the case if the statement, instead of being casually tossed off with a knowing wink, is put forward in all seriousness as a sweeping generalization about gay men.

That gay men have a specific, non-standard attachment to certain cultural objects and cultural forms is the widespread, unquestioned assumption behind a lot of American popular humor.[5] No one will look at you aghast, or cry out in protest, or stop you in mid-sentence, if you dare to imply that a guy who worships divas, who loves torch songs or show tunes, who knows all of Bette Davis's best lines by heart, or who attaches supreme importance to fine points of style or interior design—no one will be horrified if you imply that such a man might, just possibly, not turn out to be completely straight. When a satirical student newspaper at the University of Michigan wanted to mock the panic of one alumnus over the election of an openly gay student body president, it wrote that the new president "has finally succeeded in his quest to turn Michigan's entire student body homosexual. . . . Within minutes . . . , European techno music began blaring throughout Central and North Campus. . . . The many changes . . . already implemented include requiring all incoming freshmen to take a mandatory three-credit course in post-modern interior design. . . . 94 percent of the school's curriculum now involves showtunes."[6]

Similarly, when a British tabloid wanted to dramatize the shocking case of a "typical, laddish, beer-swilling, sport-mad 20-something smitten with his fiancée" who became gay overnight as a result of an athletic injury, it recounted that the first warning signs took the form not of homosexual desire on the boy's part but of a sudden lack of interest in rugby scores, an inability to converse with his loutish mates, and a new tendency to be sarcastic. Only later did he start sleeping with men, quit his banking job, and become a hairdresser.[7] This is the stuff of popular stereotype.

Perhaps for that very reason, if you assert with a straight face that male homosexuality involves a set of non-standard cultural practices, not just some non-standard sexual practices; if you suggest that there is such a thing as gay male culture; or if you imply that there must be a connection of some kind between a specific sexual orientation and a fondness for certain cultural forms, it is likely that people will immediately object, citing a thousand different reasons why such a thing is impossible, or ridiculous, or offensive, and why anyone who says otherwise is deluded, completely out of date, morally suspect, and politically irresponsible. Which probably won't stop the very people who make those objections from telling you a joke about gay men and show tunes—even with their next breath.

My ambition in this book, then, is to try and occupy whatever gap I can manage to prise open between the acknowledged fact of gay male cultural difference and its disavowed truth.

☙❧

Happily for me, some large cracks have lately appeared in that fine line between casual acknowledgment and determined denial. (Complete obviousness combined with total unacceptability is typically what distinguishes every worthwhile idea.) At least since the success of such cable television series as *Queer Eye for the Straight Guy* and *RuPaul's Drag Race,* it has become commonplace to regard male homosexuality as comprising not only a set of specific sexual practices but also an assortment of characteristic social and cultural practices. According to this increasingly trendy way of thinking, male homosexuality somehow affords an unusual perspective on the world, along with a cluster of superior insights into life, love, and matters of taste in general. Being gay would seem to involve an entire attitude and set of values, an entire *cultural* orientation. It implies a refined sensibility, a heightened aesthetic sense, a particular sensitivity to style and fashion, a non-standard relation to mainstream cultural objects, a rejection of common tastes as well as a critical perspective on the straight world and a collectively shared but nonetheless singular vision of what really matters in life.[8]

That flattering image of gay culture—of gayness *as* culture—is not entirely new, even if its entry into the stock of received ideas that make up the common sense of straight society is relatively recent. That gay men are particularly responsive to music and the arts was already a theme in the writings of psychiatrists and sexologists at the turn of the twentieth century. In 1954 the psychoanalyst Carl Jung noted that gay men "may have good taste and an aesthetic sense."[9] By the late 1960s, the anthropologist Esther Newton could speak quite casually of "the *widespread belief* that homosexuals are especially sensitive to matters of aesthetics and refinement."[10] Many gay men, and a number of their straight friends and enemies, have long suspected that what makes gay men different from the rest of the world is something that goes well beyond sexual preference or practice.

Richard Florida, an economist and social theorist (as well as a self-confessed heterosexual), may have given that ancient suspicion a new, empirical foundation. In a widely discussed and often disputed series of sociological and statistical studies of what he has called the "creative class," Florida argues that the presence of gay people in a locality is an excellent predictor of a viable high-tech industry and its potential for growth.[11] The reason for this, Florida contends, is that high-tech jobs nowadays follow the workforce; the workforce does not migrate to where the jobs are—not, at least, for very long. (Florida used to teach in Pittsburgh.)

If cities and towns with lots of gay people in them are sure to prosper in the "Creative Age," that is not only because the new class of "creative" workers is composed of "nerds," oddballs, and people with "extreme habits and dress" who gravitate to places with "low entry barriers to human capital," where the locals are generally open and tolerant of unconventional folks. It is also because gay people, according to Florida and his collaborators, are the "canaries of the Creative Age." Gay people, in other words, can flourish only in a pure atmosphere characterized by a high quotient of "lifestyle amenities," coolness, "culture and fashion," "vibrant street life," and "a cutting-edge music scene." The presence of gay people "in large numbers is an indicator of an underlying culture that's open-minded and diverse—and thus conducive to creativity"; it also "signals an exciting place, where people can fit in and be themselves," where the "people climate" is good and "quality of place" represents an important community value.[12] All of which provides empirical confirmation, however flimsy, of the notion that homosexuality is not just a sexual orientation but a cultural orientation, a dedicated commitment to certain social or aesthetic values, an entire *way of being.*

☜

That distinctively gay *way of being,* moreover, appears to be rooted in a particular queer *way of feeling.* And that queer way of feeling—that queer *subjectivity*—expresses itself through a peculiar, dissident *way of relating* to cultural objects (movies, songs, clothes, books, works of art) and cultural forms in general (art and architecture, opera and musical theater, pop and disco, style and fashion, emotion and language). As a cultural practice, male homosexuality involves a characteristic way of receiving, reinterpreting, and reusing mainstream culture, of decoding and recoding the heterosexual or heteronormative meanings already encoded in that culture, so that they come to function as vehicles of gay or queer meaning. It consists, as the critic John Clum says, in "a shared alternative reading of mainstream culture."[13]

As a result, certain figures who are already prominent in the mass media become gay icons: they get taken up by gay men with a peculiar intensity that differs from their wider reception in the straight world. (That practice is so marked, and so widely acknowledged, that the National Portrait Gallery in London could organize an entire exhibition around the theme of *Gay Icons* in 2009.)[14] And certain cultural forms, such as Broadway musicals or Hollywood melodramas, are similarly invested with a particular power and significance, attracting a disproportionate number of gay male fans.

What this implies is that it is not enough for a man to be homosexual in order to be gay. Same-sex desire alone does not equal gayness. In order to be gay, a man has to learn to relate to the world around him in a distinctive way. Or, rather, *homosexuality itself, even as an erotic orientation, even as a specifically sexual subjectivity, consists in a dissident way of feeling and relating to the world.* That dissident way of feeling and relating to the world is reflected in gay male cultural practices.

On this account, "gay" refers not just to something you *are,* but also to something you *do.* Which means that you don't have to be homosexual in order to do it. Unlike the more arcane kinds of gay sex, gay culture does not appeal exclusively to those with a same-sex erotic preference. In principle, if not in actuality, anyone can participate in *homosexuality as culture*—that is, in the *cultural practice* of homosexuality. Gayness, then, is not a state or condition. It's a mode of perception, an attitude, an ethos: in short, it is a practice.

And if gayness is a practice, it is something you can do well or badly. In order to do it well, you may need to be shown how to do it by someone (gay or straight) who is already good at it and who can *initiate* you into it—by *demonstrating* to you, through example, how to practice it and by *training* you to do it right yourself.

Finally, your performance may be evaluated and criticized by other people, gay or straight, and it may invite suggestions for improvement from those who consider themselves to be experts.

Whence the common notion that there's *a right way* to be gay.

☙

Rather than dismiss that outrageous idea out of hand, I want to understand what it means. I want to figure out what on earth people have in mind when they subscribe to it. What exactly is at stake in different definitions or conceptions or ideals of *how to be gay?* What is the basis for determining the right way, or ways, to be gay? What are the larger implications of such judgments?

And what do people actually mean when they talk as if being sexually attracted to persons of the same sex were not enough to make you *really* gay? Or when they imply that there are certain things you need to know, or do, in order to make the grade and be *truly* gay? Or when they claim that some straight individuals are actually a lot gayer than many gay men? What picture, what understanding of male homosexual feeling and perception do such views reflect?

Take the example of some joker (straight or gay) who says to a gay man, "You're not really very gay, you know. If you don't watch out, they're going to revoke your license." Or consider the case of one gay man who says to another, "You really need to know about this movie, if you're going to be gay" or "I can't believe you've never heard of this designer: let me show you her work, I just know you'll absolutely love it!" What kinds of reasoning lie behind such remarks?

How about the friend who says to you, when he or she discovers that you are a great dancer or cook; that you love Cher or Madonna, Beyoncé or Björk, Whitney Houston or Kylie Minogue, Christina Aguilera or Mariah Carey, Tori Amos or Gwen Stefani (not to mention Lady Gaga); that you have a weakness for mid-century modern; that you would never dream of dressing for comfort; or that you drive a VW Golf or a Mini Cooper convertible or a Pontiac G6, "Gee, I guess you really *are* gay!"?[15] What does male homosexuality have to do with dancing, or cooking, or the music you like, or the car you drive, or the clothes you wear, or your attachment to period design? Are these just stereotypes about gay men? Are they expressions of a kind of sexual racism? Is there anything at all to these stereotypes, or anything behind them?

ೲ

It was because I believed all those questions were worth taking seriously that I decided to teach a class about "how to be gay." For I suspected that such questions registered—albeit in some socially encrypted way—a set of intuitions about the relation between sexuality, on the one hand, and cultural forms, styles of feeling, and genres of discourse, on the other. If that social code could be broken, and if those questions could be successfully addressed, the resulting insights would elucidate many aspects of gay male subjectivity. They would reveal, specifically, what makes it so *queer*—in the sense of both *homo-sexual* and *non-standard*—without producing an explanation couched in the language of ego psychology. We would thus recover a social mode of sexual analysis that escaped the individualizing, normalizing, essentially medical approach to sexuality that typifies our therapeutic society. Such a method could also evade the opposition between the normal and the pathological on which that medical, psychological approach relies—and on which modern homophobia depends.[16] We could then speak about gay male subjectivity, inquire into its specificity, and maybe even define the particular ways of feeling that constitute it, without worrying about whether our conclusions would make gay subjectivity look normal or abnormal, healthy or diseased.

Subjectivity without psychology. There must be ways of getting at the inner life of human subjects, and of gay men in particular, without delving into the peculiar psychic constitution of the individual. The study of social practices, aesthetic practices, styles, tastes, feelings—analyzed so as to disclose their internal structures, formal logic, cultural operation, meaning, and distribution—could provide an alternate and fresh approach to human subjectivity. In the case of gay male subjectivity, one way to depersonalize, deindividualize, and depsychologize it would be to ask how male homosexual desire connects with specific cultural forms, styles, modes of feeling, and kinds of discourse.

If we could figure that out, we would also be in a better position to understand the larger relations between sexuality and culture, between kinds of desire and conventions of feeling. We could measure the extent to which social practices and cultural forms themselves are both gendered and sexualized, and we could discover how they come to be imbued with specific sexual and gendered meanings. Finally, we might be able to apprehend an even more basic and defining feature of our world, an elementary structure of social meaning that until now has escaped sustained interrogation: *the sexual politics of cultural form.* So this entire project, trashy as it might seem at first, could actually help us get at something both elusive and profound.

ᏊᎧ

That was the point of departure for my class, as it is for this book. Precisely because the class focused on the *cultural practice* of male homosexuality, not on its *sexual practice,* its audience was not limited to gay men. (If the class had addressed itself solely to gay men, that would have meant it wasn't open on an equal basis to all qualified undergraduate students at the University of Michigan, and so it would have been unprofessional of me to teach it.) Gay culture, after all, is not something that you have to be gay in order to enjoy—or to comprehend. In fact, it turns out that being gay gives you no automatic intellectual advantage when it comes to appreciating, understanding, or analyzing gay culture. In my long experience of teaching the class, I found that women and non-gay male students routinely performed in it at least as well as gay men did, and sometimes a lot better.

Gay male culture coincides, admittedly, with lesbian culture at certain moments. Some mainstream cultural artifacts that have played significant roles in gay male culture also turn out to be lesbian classics—such as Hollywood movies featuring Marlene Dietrich or Greta Garbo, or the 1959 Doris Day–Rock Hudson comedy *Pillow Talk,* or Richard Strauss's opera *Der Rosenkavalier.* But even when the cultural objects are the same, the respective relations of gay men and lesbians to them are different, because lesbian and gay male audiences do not engage or identify with them in the same way. So the meaning that lesbians and gay men find in them is quite distinct.[17] It would also be mistaken to conceptualize lesbian culture's alternative reading of mainstream culture according to the gay male model I have described here, one that would consist in queering particular objects (such as power tools), icons (James Dean), and practices (softball). Lesbian culture often involves the appropriation of entire ethical categories from mainstream culture: honor, for example, or revenge, or ethics as a whole.[18] Which is another reason to study gay male culture independently.

That does not mean there is a *single* gay male culture. I do not claim there is one and only one gay culture, shared by all gay men—or that the cultural practice of male homosexuality is unitary, whole, autonomous, and complete in itself. There are many variations in the ways gay male culture is constituted, within individual gay communities no less than among gay communities belonging to different national and ethnic cultures in different parts of the globe. But there are also common themes that cross social and geographic divisions. Some international transpositions are easy to make. If there is a French equivalent, say, of Madonna or Kylie Minogue, it is probably Mylène Farmer, the very mention of whose name conjures up gay clichés—though it does that only in France, not in the rest of the world—just as Dalida does not signify much to American gay men, despite being a doomed and tragic personage reminiscent of Judy Garland, and an equally classic figure in the eyes of many French gay men of an earlier generation. Kylie herself is a more obvious gay icon in Great Britain and Australia than she is in the United States (which says a lot about how central she is to gay male culture in those other places). And Bollywood musicals may exercise the same queer appeal on the Indian subcontinent, or among the peoples of the Indian diaspora, or in other parts of the globe, that the Broadway musical does in North America.[19]

But many cultural practices that are characteristic of gay male communities in the United States do not exactly correspond to anything practiced elsewhere. There is no word for "camp" in French, German, or Chinese. Popular gay culture in Turkey, India, Indonesia, Thailand, the Philippines, China, and Japan, to mention only some of the most notable examples, may have many links with European and American gay culture—Lady Gaga is now a global gay male icon (no gay man comes anywhere close to rivaling her)—but gay male culture in those places also displays plenty of local, distinctive features.

The connections between transnational lesbian and gay male culture, on the one hand, and homegrown cultural practices in various corners of the world, on the other, are only starting to be described and understood.[20] And saying that does not even begin to confront the question of how far gayness itself is the same across national or linguistic boundaries, nor does it address the dynamic, complex nature of the relation between homosexuality and globalization. Although in choosing my material I glance occasionally at cultural contexts outside the United States, particularly at English culture, most of my observations refer consistently to American gay male life. (So the word "gay" in my text often implies "American" as well as "male.")

ᘓᗅᗒ

If "gay" can refer to a way of being, and to a distinctive cultural practice, that means gayness can be shared with others and transmitted to them. And to the extent that gay initiation involves learning how to queer heteronormative culture—how to decode heterosexual cultural artifacts and recode them with gay meanings—any undertaking, such as mine, that studies this procedure also necessarily exemplifies and performs it. If gay men circulate specific bits of mainstream culture among themselves, endowing them in the process with nonstandard meanings and consolidating a shared culture and sensibility on that basis, then a college course, for example, that involves circulating those specific items will also do the work of gay initiation, insofar as it introduces those students who have not yet encountered them to a wealth of possible gay significations latent in the surrounding culture.

In other words, a course that *surveys and examines* some of the materials on which gay men (both individually and in groups) have built a common culture, or cultures, will also be a course that *initiates* students, both straight and gay, into the *cultural practice* of male homosexuality, insofar as that practice consists precisely in the sharing and examining of such materials. My course was likely to expose students to non-gay works that had functioned in the past for some gay men as a means of acquiring and transmitting a common culture, a shared sensibility. Students, whether gay or straight, who hadn't encountered those particular materials before would in this way be "initiated" into gay male culture—in the specific sense that they would be *introduced* to it for the first time and given an opportunity to get to know, understand, experience, and identify with it. They would have the chance, *regardless of their sexual orientation,* to determine whether gay culture held out anything of value to them, whether it enhanced or enriched their perspective on the world, whether they wanted to participate in it and to make its distinctive outlook and attitudes their own. They would have the possibility of becoming *culturally* gay . . . or, at least, gayer.

Accordingly, the original course description emphasized that "How To Be Gay," the class itself, would function as "an experiment in the very process of initiation that it hopes to understand."

That got me into even deeper trouble.

ൟ

"We don't know what [Mr. Halperin] does in the classroom," darkly observed Gary Glenn, the president of the Michigan chapter of the American Family Association (AFA), but "it is outrageous that Michigan taxpayers are forced to pay for a class whose stated purpose is to 'experiment' with the 'initiation' of young men into a self-destructive homosexual lifestyle."[21]

In all the controversy that ensued, no one ever showed much concern about the female students enrolled in my class, who typically made up about half of it, or what effects my class might have on them.[22]

In any case, once the news about the class had leaked out, "the wheels of dissemination," to borrow Matthew Schwartz's grandiose formula, did not take long to start rolling. The story that the *National Review* posted to its website on Friday, March 17, 2000, was picked up by the *Washington Times,* which alerted a number of right-wing organizations. Within days, and certainly by Tuesday, March 21, 2000, the

American Family Association had added to its own website a link to the *National Review*'s online course description. On Wednesday, March 22, 2000, AFA-Michigan issued a long press release mentioning that Gary Glenn had e-mailed a written statement, calling for the cancellation of the class, to the governor of Michigan, to members of the Michigan House and Senate appropriations committees, and to the president of the University of Michigan, as well as to its elected Board of Regents.[23]

ᕱᕮᕲ

The next day, on Thursday, March 23, 2000, the *Sydney Star Observer* (*SSO*), the most popular gay newspaper in Sydney, published a scathing editorial about the class. The University of Michigan's campus newspaper, the *Michigan Daily*, had yet to pick up the story, but— thanks to the Internet—it was already news in Australia. Under the punning title, "B+ Could Try Harder," the *SSO*'s editorial treated the class as a laughable academic appropriation of a common gay male practice, implying that gay men hardly required any expert instruction in it, least of all from college professors—they could do perfectly well on their own, thank you very much.[24] The editorial was accompanied by a cartoon, which eloquently expressed the paper's attitude, and which merits further attention in its own right (Figure 1).

For in order to get the point of the cartoon, you need to understand the meaning of the line uttered by the teacher caricatured in it. And in order to do that, you need to have undergone a gay initiation yourself.

Here is the background you require. The line "What a dump!" was first pronounced by Bette Davis in a sublimely awful 1949 Hollywood movie, directed by King Vidor, called *Beyond the Forest*. Indolently filing her nails in one of the early scenes, Rosa Moline (played by Davis) descends a staircase in her large and comfortable house, greeting with that disgruntled exclamation her loving and long-suffering husband: an earnest, devoted, hardworking doctor (played by Joseph Cotten), who is coming home from a sleepless and emotionally draining night,

1 Editorial in the *Sydney Star Observer*, March 23, 2000 (with thanks to Jason Prior).

which he has spent in a desperate, heroic fight to save a patient's life. Looking disdainfully around her, Rosa remarks, "What a dump!"

More than a decade later, in 1962, Edward Albee's crypto-gay play *Who's Afraid of Virginia Woolf?* premiered on Broadway. In 1966 it was made into a brilliant black-and-white movie by Mike Nichols, with Elizabeth Taylor and Richard Burton in the leading roles. The film, like the play, opens with Martha, the character played by Elizabeth Taylor, doing her own drunken Bette Davis impersonation, citing Davis's now-classic line, vainly badgering her husband to remember the name of the obscure movie in which Davis originally uttered it, and trying—not very successfully—to recall the movie's plot. Here is how the scene unfolds in Albee's play.[25]

MARTHA *(Looks about the room. Imitates Bette Davis):* What a dump. Hey, what's that from? "What a dump!"

GEORGE: How would I know what . . .

MARTHA: Aw, come on! What's it from? *You* know . . .

GEORGE: . . . Martha . . .

MARTHA: What's it from, for christ's sake?

GEORGE *(Wearily):* What's what from?

MARTHA: I just told you; I just did it. "What a dump!" Hunh? What's that from?

GEORGE: I haven't the faintest idea what . . .

MARTHA: Dumbbell! It's from some goddamn Bette Davis picture . . . some goddamn Warner Brothers epic . . .

GEORGE: *I* can't remember all the pictures that . . .

MARTHA: Nobody's asking you to remember every single goddamn Warner Brothers epic . . . just one! One single little epic! Bette Davis gets peritonitis in the end . . . she's got this big black fright wig she wears all through the picture and she gets peritonitis, and she's married to Joseph Cotten or something . . .

GEORGE: . . . Some*body* . . .

MARTHA: . . . some*body* . . . and she wants to go to Chicago all the time, 'cause she's in love with that actor with the scar. . . . But she gets sick, and she sits down in front of her dressing table . . .

GEORGE: What actor? What scar?

MARTHA: *I* can't remember his name, for God's sake. What's the name of the *picture?* I want to know what the name of the *picture* is. She sits down in front of her dressing table . . . and she's got this peritonitis . . . and she tries to put her lipstick on, but she can't . . . and she gets it all over her face . . . but she decides to go to Chicago anyway, and . . .

GEORGE: *Chicago!* It's called *Chicago.*

MARTHA: Hunh? What . . . what is?

GEORGE: The picture . . . it's called *Chicago* . . .

MARTHA: Good grief! Don't you know *anything? Chicago* was a 'thirties musical, starring little Miss Alice *Faye.* Don't you know *any-thing?*

GEORGE: Well, that was probably before my *time,* but . . .

MARTHA: Can it! Just cut that out! This picture . . . Bette Davis comes home from a hard day at the grocery store . . .

GEORGE: She works in a grocery store?

MARTHA: She's a housewife; she buys things . . . and she comes home with the groceries, and she walks into the modest living room of the modest cottage modest Joseph Cotten has set her up in . . .

GEORGE: Are they married?

MARTHA *(Impatiently):* Yes. They're married. To each other. Cluck! And she comes in, and she looks around, and she puts her groceries down, and she says, "What a dump!"

GEORGE: (Pause) Oh.

MARTHA: (Pause) She's discontent.

GEORGE: (Pause) Oh.

MARTHA: (Pause) Well, what's the name of the picture?

GEORGE: I really don't know, Martha . . .

MARTHA: Well, think!

The scene itself reads like a failed attempt at gay initiation. It's actually a bit difficult to imagine a straight couple having that conversation, though it comes off plausibly enough on stage.

In any case, Bette Davis's line "What a dump!" already lent itself to exaggerated performance, or reperformance, in the United States by the early 1960s, at least on the evidence of Albee's dialogue. It was its own little mini-drama: a playlet within the play. "I just did it," says Martha, citing her own citation and identifying it as a demonstration. "'What a dump!'" had apparently become something you could *do.*

⊘⊘

The ability to perform such a line is treated by the cartoonist of the gay newspaper in Sydney as a standard part of the gay male repertoire, a typical piece of gay male theater, which is at home in gay male society but completely out of place in the classroom. It would be idiotic or absurd, the cartoon implies, to teach it to students, as if one were trying to instruct them all how to imitate Bette Davis or how to behave like gay men. Nor did I try to teach my students how to deliver the line, of course—my class was not a gay version of *Pygmalion* or *My Fair Lady,* and I was not some gay Professor Henry Higgins instructing the Eliza Doolittles of Ann Arbor how to pass muster in gay society—though I did end up teaching the cartoon and trying to draw out its implications, as I am doing here.

So what are those implications? Well, Bette Davis's infamous line clearly came to represent and express a certain specific attitude, a characteristic posture that would otherwise have been hard to capture in just three little words: a combination of vulgarity and hauteur, disdainful superiority, withering aesthetic judgment, upper-class-wannabe pretentiousness, and prissy, feminine dismissal of the selfless, sincere, manly values of middle-class respectability. The line got taken up at some point by gay male culture and made into a symbol, an economical way of encapsulating a dramatic pose so as to make it available for subsequent reenactment through citation. In particular, the line became a parody of extravagant disappointment, disenchantment, and disrespect, a vehicle for the theatrical expression of "bad attitude," a means of gleefully dismissing middlebrow American moralism as a contemptible aesthetic failure.

Once the line had been wrenched out of its original context and reappropriated, it could provide gay men with some elements of an alternative, collective stance, a style of resistance to the moral and gendered values of the dominant culture. And so it could contribute to the elaboration of a dissident, oppositional way of being and feeling.

"What a dump!" is thus a cardinal example of the practice I set out to study, an example that dramatizes how gay men have selectively appropriated, recoded, and recirculated certain bits, often quite obscure bits, of mainstream culture. That is why the *Sydney Star Observer*'s editorialist presented it (accurately enough) as typifying the curriculum of my class. But he assumed—in his superior, Bette Davis way—that my class was merely a simpleminded exercise, a literal attempt to teach my students how to be gay, instead of what it actually was: namely, an effort to inquire into the social and emotional logic behind the specific practices that constitute gay male culture.

But that's not what makes the cartoon interesting to me.

At the time the cartoon was published, the *SSO* had a circulation of about 25,000, consisting mostly of younger gay men in Sydney. If the editorialist intended the paper's readers to grasp the humorous point of the cartoon, he must have expected them to have no trouble picking up its various allusions to the gay male cultural curriculum that I have just reviewed.

Which in and of itself testifies to the phenomenon I have been calling *gay initiation*. Is there any other way to explain how young gay men in Australia in the year 2000 could be expected to get a joke that depends on a shared knowledge of obscure bits of American culture dating back to the late 1940s and early 1960s—references that virtually none of my own students has ever managed to recognize or identify? (Among my acquaintances, only the late Randy Nakayama could immediately pick up the allusion to *Beyond the Forest;* he is the one who first taught it to me.) Gay initiation clearly requires a critical mass of knowledgeable folk in a single location.

In other words, your degree of gay acculturation depends a lot on your social network. There is a big difference between living in a gay ghetto in a metropolitan center, such as Sydney, and growing up in a small town in the north of Michigan before going to school in Ann Arbor. The cartoonist for the *Sydney Star Observer* was operating within the horizons of a complex gay social world whose elaborately developed cultural infrastructure—including networks of friends and lovers, as well as popular and extensively stocked video stores in gay neighborhoods—appears to have been functioning actively and even to have been working overtime.

By now, many of those video stores in Sydney and other gay urban centers have gone out of business: the kind of social learning they once fostered has been taken over by the Internet and its social-networking sites. Whether these new electronic media perform their initiatory function as effectively as the older, more traditional social networks used to do, whether they expand or contract the available range of queer information, opening up new possibilities of literacy or reducing gay cultural references to a limited set of stereotypes—all that remains to be seen. In either case, the basic point is the same: gay culture doesn't just happen. It has to be made to happen. It requires material support, organization, and a queer public sphere.[26]

℘ↄ

The following week, back in the United States, another hostile account of my class appeared in a gay paper, this time in San Francisco.[27] The gay press did not seem to like the class any better than the American Family Association did. The reactions of some gay or gay-friendly individuals were supportive and enthusiastic, to be sure, but many others complained that I was being reckless and provocative, giving gay men a bad name, trading in stereotypes, implying that gay men are different from straight men, propounding the crazy idea that there is such a thing as gay culture and that it is distinct from straight culture, confirming the homophobic notion that gay men "recruit" straight men into the "gay lifestyle," or giving the religious Right a weapon to bash us with and thereby endangering the struggle for lesbian and gay civil rights. So the gay response was often antagonistic for one or more of those reasons. Still, I did receive strong expressions of support—which I want to acknowledge here, with heartfelt gratitude—from the Triangle Foundation, Michigan's statewide GLBT civil rights and advocacy organization, and its director, Jeffrey Montgomery; from students, colleagues, and administrators; and from numbers of previously unknown well-wishers, both gay and straight, at the University of Michigan, in the town of Ann Arbor, in the state of Michigan, and around the world.

Meanwhile, there was a storm of chatter on talk radio and in the national and international press. On Tuesday, May 23, 2000, eight Republican representatives in the Michigan state legislature sponsored an amendment to the yearly higher-education appropriations bill, requiring the state to set aside 10 percent of the annual sum allocated to the University of Michigan, and to distribute it to the fourteen other public universities in Michigan, if the university held a class "promoting or facilitating the participation in a sexual lifestyle or practices other than heterosexual monogamy." (Abstinence, for once, did not feature among the approved sexual lifestyles that the Republicans sought to promote.)

After a heated debate that "lasted well into the night," according to the *Michigan Daily*, a majority of the legislators voted for the measure, with 52 in favor and 44 against. But its passage required more than a simple majority, and its supporters came four votes short of the requisite number of 56. As state representative Valde Garcia (R-Clinton), a sponsor of the amendment, conceded, the proposal itself was a largely symbolic gesture: "I don't believe we should be spending taxpayer dollars to teach a class to teach someone to violate the law," he insisted, noting that homosexuality "is still against the law and it offends many people's deep-seated religious beliefs." At the same time, Garcia admitted that "he was not familiar with the actual content of the class." "We had some information about the class and that it exists," he told the *Daily*. "Beyond that, we don't know much about it."[28]

Since 2000 was an election year, the ripples from the vote in the state legislature continued to be felt throughout Michigan during the ensuing months. In some electoral districts, such as the 87th (comprising Barry and Ionia counties in west-central Michigan), the question of what line to take on the class became a central political issue in the Republican primary for state representative.[29] As November approached, election guides in the state of Michigan featured information about how individual lawmakers had voted on the budget amendment back in May. Outrage over the class led Auburn Hills mayor Tom McMillin, who had previously waged a successful campaign to defeat a gay rights ordinance in Ferndale, Michigan, to seek the Republican nomination for a vacant seat on the University's Board of Regents. He didn't get it, though the two Republicans who did also opposed the teaching of the class. They were both ultimately defeated in the general election in November, when Michigan tilted very slightly in favor of Al Gore.[30]

The Michigan branch of the American Family Association allegedly gathered 15,000 signatures on a petition urging "Gov. Engler, the Legislature, and the U-M Board of Regents to do everything possible to stop U-M officials from using my tax dollars to recruit teenage students into a class whose stated intention is to 'experiment' in the 'initiation' of students into a high-risk lifestyle of homosexual behavior that is immoral, illegal and a serious threat to personal and public health." Gary Glenn presented the petition to the Board of Regents of the University of Michigan on October 19, 2000.[31] Although it is remotely possible that the "homosexual behavior" in question—say, frequent viewing of films such as *Sunset Boulevard, All about Eve,* and *A Star Is Born*—might ruin your health, there is in fact no law against it, not even in Michigan, and I continued to teach the class without interference.

Three years later, with my course once again in the news, a bill was introduced into both houses of the Michigan legislature to amend the state constitution in order to give the state legislature veto power over course offerings at public universities in Michigan.[32] It caused a great deal of excitement in the media, on campus, and in the state capital, but it did not get very far.

೭✕೨

In order to make sense of all this, it helps to know that there had been a change of leadership in the Michigan branch of the American Family Association. Gary Glenn, who had formerly worked for an antiunion organization, the Idaho Freedom to Work Committee, as well as the Idaho Cattle Association, and who had made an unsuccessful run for U.S. Congress after serving as a Republican commissioner in Boise, moved to Michigan in 1998 to lobby for a school choice tuition tax credit, which later failed to be approved by the voters. He then took a job with the Mackinac Center for Public Policy, a conservative think tank in Midland, Michigan. In the fall of 1999, half a year before I came up with the bright idea of teaching a course on male homosexuality as a cultural practice, he had become head of the Michigan chapter of the AFA.[33]

That local chapter had proved to be a comparatively sleepy outfit, concerned mostly with pornography and obscenity issues, until Glenn took it over. Glenn made opposition to gay rights the focus of the AFA's mission. As Kim Kozlowski, a journalist with the *Detroit News,* put it in 2001, Glenn "gelled the group into Michigan's premier antigay organization." "'I've taken a leadership position in pro-family values when under assault by the homosexual agenda,' Glenn says. 'We have become the most high-profile, pro-family organization in the state and, quite frankly, one of the most high-profile in the country.'"[34] It was really Glenn, not I, who intended to proselytize. As a result, he and I found ourselves inadvertently collaborating on a kind of reciprocal membership drive, in which we made a successful if reluctant team. His organization increased its numbers, and my course got enrollments.

In fact, no one at the University of Michigan had paid any attention to my class before Glenn issued his press release on March 22, 2000. One University of Michigan undergraduate, who eventually enrolled in the class, first heard of it when a reporter from a local TV news team stuck a microphone in his face and asked him what he thought about it. After imperturbably expressing support for it, he raced off and signed up. So in the end, Glenn and I helped each other "recruit" new adherents to our respective "lifestyles." Never again would my class attract so many students.

Beyond that local skirmish, gay issues were starting to become a political obsession in the United States, occupying the forefront of the national news with some regularity. Civil unions in Vermont, boy scout organizations at the Supreme Court, the ordination of gay bishops by the Episcopal Church, the resignation of gay governors in New Jersey, the constitutionality of sodomy laws, gays in the military,

the rise of "wedge politics," gay marriage and a batch of state and
federal constitutional amendments redefining marriage, to say nothing of affirmative action, hate crimes, and the status of minorities: it
was all more than enough to make my class, which I continued to
teach every other year until 2007, a perennial and irresistible subject
of commentary, despite my best efforts to keep it out of the news. (I
wanted to shield the University of Michigan from hostile publicity.)
As late as January 7, 2008—when Mario Lavandeira, a gay blogger
better known by his pseudonym, Perez Hilton, belatedly caught up
with the class and posted a long out-of-date course description on his
celebrity gossip website—I was still studiously ignoring requests to
appear on *Hannity & Colmes, The O'Reilly Factor, Fox News,* CNN's
American Morning and *Headline News,* MSNBC's *Scarborough Country,*
ABC's *Good Morning America,* CBS's *The Early Show,* and NBC's *The
Today Show.*

Throughout all this time, the University of Michigan behaved im-
peccably. The course itself had been approved through the usual
channels and according to the usual bureaucratic process. Some people at the university may have disapproved of it when it got into the
news, and some may have been unhappy with me for proposing such
a course, but no one thought that politicians or pressure groups outside the University of Michigan should determine what its faculty
teach. So there was no opposition of any kind to my course from
within the University of Michigan.

The student newspaper editorialized eloquently in its favor, and
the student government unanimously passed a powerful resolution
supporting it. Even the *Michigan Review,* which made relentless fun of
it, argued in favor of my "right to free speech regardless of how repulsive and amoral it really is."[35] My colleagues, who had approved
the course, were generally enthusiastic about it. The university administration at all levels supported both the course and my right to
teach it. The English Department, the office of the Dean of the College, the president's office, and the office of the Alumni Association

uncomplainingly fielded hundreds of not especially friendly inquiries about it. The provost of the university issued a public statement on behalf of the president and the administration, saying, "We are completely in support of Professor Halperin's course and of his freedom to teach this course as he constructed it."

More remarkable, no one in the administration asked me to explain the rationale behind the course or justify what I was up to. The director of undergraduate studies in the English Department, the associate dean for undergraduate education (a professor of marine geochemistry), and the president of the university all issued public statements explaining and defending the course. But none felt the need to consult with me beforehand in order to seek advice about what to say or how to represent the thinking behind my admittedly novel approach to the analysis of gay male culture and gay male subjectivity. I would have been happy to offer them information that they might have used to defend the course in their public statements. They seemed, however, to feel a professional responsibility to inform themselves on their own, as if even to ask me to explain or justify myself would have been to subject me to possible indignity.

I found that quite extraordinary, especially as the university faced considerable criticism in the national media and in the state of Michigan on account of the course. Lesser schools, even fancy private institutions, might well have buckled under the pressure. I would therefore like to take this occasion to thank publicly, for their courage and intrepidity, John Whittier-Ferguson, who was director of undergraduate studies in the Department of English Language and Literature; Lincoln Faller, who was chair of the Department of English, and his successor in that position, Sidonie Smith; Robert Owen, who was the associate dean for undergraduate education in the College of Literature, Science, and the Arts (LSA); Terrence McDonald, who was associate dean for academic affairs in the College of LSA and later dean of the College; Nancy Cantor, who was provost and executive vice-president for academic affairs at the University of Michigan; Lee Bollinger, who was president of the University of Michigan; and the members of their offices and staffs.

❦

This book represents the explanation they never asked for.

It is an explanation that I feel I still owe them. I offer it, as well, to all those who defended and believed in my work. Most of all, I hope this book will serve to justify the value and seriousness of my course "How To Be Gay" to everyone who was skeptical, perplexed, offended, or outraged by it, who opposed it, or who criticized the University of Michigan because of it.

I don't expect to convince everybody who reads this book that my project is worthwhile, but I hope at least to make clear the genuineness of the intellectual stakes in my inquiry into gay male culture.

HISTORY OF AN ERROR

I found the unwanted publicity surrounding my class to be acutely embarrassing, for a number of reasons. Despite what some envious souls suggested at the time, I was not seeking celebrity and I had no wish to draw public attention to myself. Rather the opposite. I had joined the faculty of the University of Michigan only a few months before. I was grateful to the university for giving me a comfortable job, a constantly thrilling intellectual and cultural environment, and a new home. The last thing I wanted was to bring discredit on the university or on those who had just hired me.

Of course, I knew there was a chance that a class called "How To Be Gay" could raise eyebrows and attract unfavorable attention. Whatever the actual course content, the title itself was provocative: it might create misunderstanding or even invite deliberate misrepresentation. If I had called the class "Processes of Cultural Cross-Identification as Mechanisms of Sexual Sub-Cultural In-Group Community Formation in the United States," I doubt there would have been any trouble. But I believe in plain speaking and I am a big fan of truth in advertising. Although I despise provocation for its own sake, I like to avoid academic jargon if at all possible. I did not want to closet the class or to be deliberately, defensively obscure. I considered a tactic of concealment to be beneath my dignity. If, however, I had known then what I know now—namely, that the mere title of the course would end up costing the University of Michigan almost as much time and effort to defend as the university's continued support for affirmative action in its admissions policies—I certainly would have called it something else.

Once the controversy started, however, it was too late to change the course's name. To do so would have been to yield to the campaign of intimidation. It would have meant sacrificing academic freedom to public opinion and giving politicians or pressure groups the authority to determine what I could teach and how I could describe it. And that would have meant losing the precious right guaranteed to researchers in a free society: the right to follow their thinking wherever it may lead. After all, there's no point in having freedom if you can't use it. Freedom that you are not free to exercise isn't freedom.

So although I would have been no less happy to see the title "How To Be Gay" disappear from the course catalogue than from the media spotlight, and although I was eager to spare my colleagues the labor and annoyance of having to justify the class, I wasn't about to retitle the class or stop teaching it for those reasons alone. The class reflected my current research interests. It contributed meaningfully to the general project of higher education: it was interesting, well designed, thought-provoking, and rigorous. I got a lot of insight out of teaching it, and the students seemed to benefit from taking it. My thinking about male homosexuality as a cultural practice underwent a constant evolution during the years I taught it. I certainly found it gripping, as well as unsettling.

There was only one problem. I was the wrong person to teach it.

⚬⚬⚬

All my life, I've been told that I have no idea how to be gay. I am, apparently, utterly hopeless at it, a miserable failure as a gay man. That is a large part of the reason I found the publicity surrounding the class to be so embarrassing. It exposed me to the mockery of a number of my friends, both straight and gay. "Since when," they objected, "are *you* qualified to teach people how to be gay? What do you know about it? Why, just look at how you dress! *I* could do better than that. Come to think of it, I should be teaching this class." A number of students over the years have made similar observations, more gently at some times than at others.

But the point of my class was not to offer practical instruction in how to be a successful gay man, much less to provide a living exemplar. Nor is that the point of this book. Such instruction is abundantly available elsewhere. This book is not intended to compete, for instance, with Joel Derfner's *Swish: My Quest to Become the Gayest Person Ever and What Ended Up Happening Instead;* Donald Reuter's *Gaydar: The Ultimate Insider Guide to the Gay Sixth Sense;* Cathy Crimmins's *How the Homosexuals Saved Civilization: The True and Heroic Story of How Gay Men Shaped the Modern World;* Kevin DiLallo's *The Unofficial Gay Manual;* Judy Carter's *The Homo Handbook: Getting in Touch with Your Inner Homo: A Survival Guide for Lesbians and Gay Men;* Frank Browning's *The Culture of Desire: Paradox and Perversity in Gay Lives Today;* Daniel Harris's *The Rise and Fall of Gay Culture;* Bert Archer's *The End of Gay: And the Death of Heterosexuality;* or even Michael Bronski's classic survey, *Culture Clash: The Making of Gay Sensibility.* This book, like my class, is called *How To Be Gay* because that phrase names the topic, the phenomenon, the problem I want to explore and understand—namely, the very notion that there's a right way to be gay, that male homosexuality is not only a sexual practice but also a cultural practice, that there is a relation between sexuality and social or aesthetic form.

It's precisely because I've been told so often how bad I am at being gay, and how much I need to learn "how to be gay," that I find the thrust of those four little words so intriguing. I have long wanted to understand *exactly* what that mysterious imperative signified—what sense it might make to claim that there is a right way to be gay, a way that needs to be learned even (or especially) by gay men themselves.

Let me make it clear, then: I do not claim to possess some special, native insight that qualifies me to tell other people how to be gay. My relation to gay culture is that of a student, not an expert. I still feel like an outsider to it. Its workings aren't obvious to me; I don't find anything very intuitive about them. Gay male culture remains an enigma, whose obscure logic I continue to puzzle through. Some of my lesbian friends, and a number of my talented straight friends as well, have a much better grasp of it. And there are plenty of gay men, of various ages, who are deeply versed in gay male culture—who seem to have been born into it and who speak the language of gay sensibility as if it were their mother tongue. They are the ones who really ought to have invented my class. And they should be writing this book. I'm sure they'd do a much better job.

Or perhaps not. If in fact they're *not* doing this work themselves, it may be for a very good reason. After all, it's not as if they have nothing to say about gay male culture. In addition to the authors and books listed above, countless gay men have written learned, engaging, lovingly detailed studies of Hollywood cinema, the Broadway musical, grand opera, classical and popular music, style and fashion, interior decoration, and architectural design. But, with a few important exceptions (which I'll discuss in later chapters), they have said almost nothing about the *relation* between gay men and those aesthetic forms, about the gayness of those non-gay forms, or about the reasons for gay men's personal investment in them.[1] Because for them, no doubt, *gay male culture is not a problem*. It's not alien to them, and so they don't need to make an effort to understand it. They *already* understand it. Which is why they feel no particular impulse to explain it, either to themselves or to others.

Or, on those rare occasions when they do try to explain it, they tend to speak in a native language internal to the gay culture they are trying to explain, using indigenous concepts. They seldom advert to a critical language external to gay culture—that is, a meta-language. But if you don't use a critical meta-language, you just end up redescribing the culture in its own terms. Instead of accounting for its central features, you merely restate and reproduce them.

So I'm going to have to do the explaining.

☯

My explanation will be limited to a small number of examples. Like "What a dump!" each example requires extensive commentary to describe how it works. Under these conditions, a general survey of gay male culture is simply not an option, much as I would like to cover everything. So I won't be able to account for the gay male fascination with all the cultural forms I enumerated—Hollywood cinema, the Broadway musical, grand opera, classical and popular music, style and fashion, interior decoration, and architectural design—though I will touch on them. Instead, a great deal will be made of a very few cultural objects. For even ordinary cultural artifacts contain vast figural possibilities, and gay male cultural practices often consist in mobilizing the figural potential of seemingly unassuming, taken-for-granted objects.

My plan is to examine the figural and formal dimensions of some of the mainstream cultural objects that gay male culture appropriates and endows with queer value. I will seek *meaning* in *style* and I will look for queer *content* in *form* itself.[2] For that purpose, what I need is not a large quantity of empirical data, but a thorough, detailed understanding of how some typical and particularly expressive gay male cultural practices actually work. The goal is to make style speak, to make sense of gay aesthetics—of the peculiar, anti-social brand of aesthetics in which gay male culture specializes—and *to seize hold of social forms in all their specificity.*

Given the current state of queer cultural analysis, it is much too early to generalize about the meaning of divas, or melodramas, or musicals, or fashion and design. Instead, each individual object that gay male culture borrows from mainstream culture, each gay male cultural practice, demands to be considered with full attention to its particularity. That will involve an effort to arrive at a systematic grasp of the elusive, almost ineffable meaning of certain gestures, of specific attitudes, of particular perspectives, angles of vision, and styles of expression. The project is necessarily inductive: it begins with phenomena, not with theory (since it is not clear in advance what the right theoretical framework for understanding the phenomena would be), and it aims to extract a coherent and, ultimately, a unified comprehension of gay culture from a close examination of a few representative examples. For it is in those select examples that we'll find, condensed and encrypted, the information we are seeking about the meaning of gay style and about the sexual and gendered content of cultural forms.

We'll also discover that the great value of traditional gay male culture resides in some of its most despised and repudiated features: gay male femininity, diva-worship, aestheticism, snobbery, drama, adoration of glamour, caricature of women, and obsession with the figure of the mother.

☙

For a long time I found it ludicrous to suppose that a gay man, a man sexually attracted to men, a man who has sex with men, isn't "really" gay, simply because he lacks some specific bit of in-group knowledge or is ignorant of some particular item of gay cultural trivia. For me, personally, being gay has always been an erotic experience—not a matter of sensibility or cultural practice or even a preference for specific physical acts, but an experience of finding males sexually desirable. Period. I never thought that being gay, in and of itself, obligated me to be a certain way, to like certain things, or to enjoy certain activities. In the past, at least, I always insisted that being gay had absolutely nothing *necessarily* to do with anything at all besides gay sex.

In this, I think I was pretty typical of my generation—typical, that is, of gay men who came out in the mid-1970s, half a dozen years after the 1969 Stonewall riots, during the era of gay liberation which those riots ushered in and which saw the emergence in major cities of

new gay social worlds. Those events vastly expanded the available options for gay male sexual and social life, created a public, visible, open
gay male culture, and forged a dignified, habitable gay male identity,
thereby changing radically, and forever, the terms on which male homosexuality could be lived in the United States.

Gay men my age prided themselves on their generational difference. We were dimly aware that for a lot of gay men ten or twenty
years older than us, being gay had something to do with liking Broadway musicals, or listening to show tunes or torch songs or Judy Garland, or playing the piano, wearing fluffy sweaters, drinking cocktails,
smoking cigarettes, and calling each other "girlfriend." That was all
fine for them, no doubt, but it looked pretty pathetic to me—and distinctly unsexy. In fact, it seemed downright desperate: a feeble way of
compensating for being old, frustrated, effeminate, and hopelessly
unattractive. From my youthful perspective, which aspired fervently
to qualify as "liberated," those old queens were sad remnants from a
bygone era of sexual repression—victims of self-hatred, internalized
homophobia, social isolation, and state terror. (It did not occur to me
at the time that some lingering self-hatred or internalized homophobia of my own might be responsible for the righteous aversion I felt to
their self-hatred and homophobia, or what I took to be such.)[3]

In any case, if those sorts of queeniness and clannishness were
what gay culture was all about, I wanted no part of it. It certainly
wasn't *my* culture. I had already spent a certain amount of effort carefully cultivating my tastes, which I considered to be distinguished,
and which in my view expressed my particular relation to my historical moment, my chosen affiliation with certain movements or styles
in modern art and culture, and my political values. I liked to think—
naively, of course—that my tastes testified to my individual discernment and did not necessarily make me resemble other boys, other
Jews, other middle-class kids, other Americans, other intellectuals, or
even other classicists (I have a Ph.D. in classical Greek and Latin from
Stanford, which makes me part of yet another weird minority). I
didn't see why being gay should be any different—why I should sud-

denly have to adopt other people's tastes simply because my sexual practices identified me as a member of their group. Especially when their choices—in movies, say—seemed to be specific to a social class to which I did not see myself as belonging.

From time to time, George Cukor's 1939 film *The Women,* famous for its bevy of gorgeously costumed female Hollywood stars and for being a movie in which no male character ever appears except off-screen, would play at the Castro movie theater, in the heart of one of the gay districts of San Francisco. The audience would be full of gay men who knew the movie by heart and who would recite the lines out loud in unison with each other and the actresses. I was living in the San Francisco Bay Area at the time, but I deliberately stayed away. I found such performances profoundly distasteful and alienating. (I went to the Castro, in the company of straight friends, to see François Truffaut's *Day for Night*.) The whole experience was like being at Mass—or some exotic religious ritual rather less familiar to me than the Christian liturgy—where everyone except me knew the proper responses by heart. It made me feel like I had nothing in common with gay men. At least, nothing in common with *those* gay men.

For me, and for many gay men of my generation, gay culture was simply not a high priority. We certainly weren't much interested in what passed for gay culture at the time. After all, it didn't even focus on gay men like ourselves (who had yet to be visibly represented by the media). It didn't reflect our lives and it didn't help us to deal with the challenges we faced, as out, proud, young, masculine, sexually active gay men, trying to find our place in a homophobic society and struggling to reconcile our sex lives with our needs for love and loyalty and friendship. Instead, it featured female stars or divas whom older gay men identified with, apparently because those doomed, tragic figures reflected the abject conditions of their miserable lives and resonated with the archaic form of gay male existence that we ourselves had luckily escaped—that gay liberation had liberated us from.[4] Gay culture, as we knew it, was a vestige from a previous epoch. It didn't seem to be about us, to be *our* culture. It had nothing to offer us.

But there was another reason gay culture did not particularly appeal to us.

Culture itself, we thought, was pretty much beside the point. Why would we need gay culture anyway? After all, we had gay sex.[5] We had the real thing. *We were really doing it, not just dreaming about it.* What we wanted wasn't Somewhere over the Rainbow. It was Down on the Corner. (And it was starting to get impatient, so there was not a moment to lose.) For the first time in two thousand years, we could finally come out into the open, declare ourselves, and find quantities of people who wanted to have sex with us as much as we wanted to have sex with them. Also, thanks to gay liberation, we discovered it was possible to be gay without being effeminate. (Or so we imagined.) We therefore didn't see any resemblance between ourselves and those earlier generations of show queens, opera queens, and movie queens. We defined our generational difference by *rejecting* the gay culture of previous generations—by rejecting *gay culture* itself— as hopelessly anachronistic and out of touch, as a substitute for the real thing. And every gay generation, or half-generation, since ours has done exactly the same, all the while thinking it was the first gay generation to do so, the first gay generation in history to see nothing of interest or value in inherited, traditional gay culture.

Ever since the late 1970s, if not before, gay men have been in the habit of drawing invidious generational comparisons between gay boys in their teens and twenties—modern, liberated, enlightened, advanced, "utterly indistinguishable from straight boys . . . [and] completely calm about being gay" (as Andrew Holleran wrote in 1978), who fit into mainstream society just fine, have never experienced homophobia among their peers, don't see themselves as belonging to any gay community, and have no need of gay culture—and gay men in their thirties or forties (or even older), stuck in some fanatical allegiance to an outmoded, outdated brand of gay culture and convinced that it is the only gay culture there is, the obligatory culture of every-one who happens to be gay.[6]

That habit of thinking about gay life in terms of generational con-trasts is understandable to a certain degree. Social attitudes toward homosexuality have been changing rapidly over the past fifty years, and the social conditions in which gay kids grow up have changed as well. That gay culture, its appeal, and its audience should have evolved radically during the same period is only to be expected. At the same time, precisely because this process of historical change has been going on for decades now, the persistent assertion that younger gay men, unlike the half-generation of gay men before them, have no need of gay culture is starting to wear thin and to look downright suspicious—the result of systematic amnesia and collective denial.

In fact, it can't be perennially true. For those sorry gay men in their thirties, who supposedly cling to an old-fashioned and now passé ver-sion of gay male culture—a version of gay male culture that means nothing, and is of no use, to anyone in their teens and twenties—are obviously the very same people who, only a few years earlier, actually *were* those pioneering teenagers, taking their first innocent steps in a brave new world without homophobia, ignorant of gay culture and indifferent to it. From gay men who had no need of gay culture, they seem to become, in the twinkling of an eye, gay culture's stooges, its dreariest representatives. Which makes you wonder what happens to gay men in their mid- to late twenties that causes them suddenly to appear so tired, so superannuated, so culturally retrograde. Could it be gay initiation? Could gay male culture turn out to be not so irrele-vant to gay men after all, once they're gradually exposed to it? And once they accumulate a bit of experience, a bit of self-knowledge, and even perhaps a bit of humility?

Well, that might be one explanation. But there are also specific his-torical reasons why gay male culture constantly embarrasses its own subjects, why the previous gay generation's disavowal of gay culture is endlessly repeated by each new gay generation, why gay culture it-self always turns out to be—sometimes in the view of younger gay men and always in the view of those who speak for them—the exclusive property of the older guys, the queens, folks who in one way or another are simply past it: in short, *other people,* particularly other people whose real or imagined embrace of gay culture always ends up making them look both *effeminate* and *archaic.*

ᘒᘓ

Let us recall that homosexuality, as a distinctive classification of sexual behavior, sexual desire, and sexual subjectivity, was originally precipitated out of the experience and concept of gender inversion. The first psychiatric definitions of deviant sexual orientation, elaborated in the latter part of the nineteenth century, were definitions not of homosexuality but of sex-role reversal or transgenderism: Carl Friedrich Otto Westphal's "contrary sexual feeling" of 1869 and Arrigo Tamassia's "inversion of the sexual instinct" of 1878.[7] The pathological mental condition those terms referred to involved same-sex sexual desire but did not reduce to it. Instead, same-sex desire qualified as merely one symptom of a more profound reversal, or "inversion," of an individual's gender identity. Insofar as desire for a person of the same sex was opposite, or "contrary," to the individual's own sex, it pointed to a deeper and more pervasive gender disorder: an estrangement from one's actual sex and an identification with the opposite sex, which is to say a transgendered psychological orientation. It was this deviant orientation of the invert's subjectivity that the doctors considered medically problematic—"the feeling of being alienated, with one's entire inner being, from one's own sex," as Westphal memorably put it in a footnote to his 1869 article. Same-sex desire was not the essence but merely a further extension of that basic gender trouble, a more developed "stage of the pathological phenomenon."[8]

That clinical definition drew on the inverts' own testimony and experiences. Karl Heinrich Ulrichs, the first political activist for homosexual emancipation, who began writing in the early 1860s, had described himself in a notorious Latin phrase as having a woman's soul enclosed in a man's body ("anima muliebris virili corpore inclusa").[9] Westphal was familiar with his writings. Nineteenth-century sexologists strongly disapproved of same-sex sexual behavior, to be sure, but such behavior, though obviously deviant, did not represent in and of itself an infallible sign of sexual difference,[10] not even according to the great German authority on sexual perversion, Richard von Krafft-Ebing, who was careful to distinguish "perversion of the sexual instinct" from mere "perversity in the sexual act."[11] Homosexual sex might in some cases turn out to be bad without being sick: it could be a mere vicious indulgence, an extreme form of debauchery; it was not in every instance an indication of "moral insanity." Deviant sex could be saved from pathology by normative gender identity and gender style: the conventionally feminine woman who allowed herself to be pleasured by a butch, or the straight-identified hustler who played a masculine role when he prostituted himself to inverted, effeminate men, did not routinely come in for sustained medical attention until well into the twentieth century.[12]

As late as 1919, petty officers in the U.S. Navy could ask "normal" enlisted men to volunteer to have sex repeatedly with "fairies" in order to expose the immoral conditions in and around a naval base;[13] and in the dockside bars of New York in the same period, sailors seeking easy women for sexual gratification could be redirected to fairies as plausible substitutes for them.[14] In many parts of the male world today, even in the industrialized liberal democracies, what counts as sexually normal sometimes has more to do with gender style and sexual role than with sexual object-choice (that is, the sex of the desired sexual object).[15]

Nonetheless, it is clear and undeniable that something changed in the course of the twentieth century. Gender inversion had to make room for a novel category: "homosexuality." The distinctively modern, narrowly delimited yet ambitiously universalizing concept of homosexuality appeared when same-sex sexual object-choice came to be categorically distinguished from sex-role reversal and began to qualify, in and of itself, as a marker of sexual difference.

The pace of transformation picked up after the end of the Second World War. In the field of sexology, the decisive break occurred in 1948, with the publication of the first Kinsey Report. Alfred Kinsey maintained that "inversion and homosexuality are two distinct and not always correlated types of behavior."[16] Homosexuality, as Kinsey understood that concept, referred to the sameness of the sexes of the persons engaged in a sexual act. It did not admit any categorical difference between men who played insertive sexual roles and men who played receptive sexual roles in same-sex sexual contacts. It applied to all same-sex sexual actors alike. Kinsey rejected as mere "propaganda" the claim by some of the straight-identified men he interviewed that receiving oral sex from another man did not count as engaging in a homosexual act. According to Kinsey, the role you played didn't matter. The sex of your partner did. All "physical contacts with other males" that result in orgasm are "by any strict definition . . . homosexual," Kinsey insisted, no matter who does what to whom and no matter how tough or effete the men involved in sex with each other might happen to look.[17]

⚬⚬⚬

Kinsey and his categories of sexual behavior reflected the culmination of a long process of change in the systems of both sexual classification and sexual desire. That process had begun much earlier, and it had been under way for a considerable time, but it was not complete until the twentieth century. Heterosexuality had been slowly coming into existence among the middle classes in England, northwestern Europe, and their colonies ever since the late seventeenth century. As time went by, its definition gradually became more stringent, requiring stricter avoidance of any expression of same-sex affection.[18] In the United States, sexual, emotional, and romantic bonds between men, which had once been conventional, started to dissolve well before the end of the nineteenth century, and middle-class men began to avoid physical contact with other men for fear of being considered deviant.[19]

At the same time, a relatively new social type emerged: what we would now call "the straight-acting and -appearing gay man." This was a man differentiated from other men *only* by his same-sex sexual object-choice, by the direction of his erotic desire, by his attraction to males. His homosexual desire now defined him—it made him gay through and through—but it also left him completely indistinguishable *in every other respect* from normal men. His gayness was no longer a sign of gender inversion, of sex-role reversal. It was an expression of a single feature of his personality, what could henceforth be called his "sexuality." Since it had to do only with sex, and not with gender, this new gay sexuality was entirely compatible, at least in theory, with perfect, faultless, unimpeachable masculinity. The mere fact of desiring men no longer prevented a gay man from being "straight-acting and -appearing." You could look like a regular guy, even though you were totally gay. And you could be gay without being disfigured by any visible stigmata of gender deviance, or queerness—without appearing to be different in any way from normal folk.

To be gay, according to this emerging twentieth-century definition, was to have *a sexuality, not a culture.* For some men—at least, for some *modern* men—homosexuality was merely a kind of erotic automatism, an unreasoning reflex that was natural and involuntary: a *sexual instinct.* It was not rooted in consciousness; it was not the result of moral or aesthetic choice; it did not arise either from bad habits or from cultivated taste; and so it did not express itself in multiple aspects of the personality. It was, quite simply, an instinctual drive—in short, a sexuality—not an ethos or a way of being, let alone a distinctive, non-standard cultural practice. The best-known early portrait of the straight-acting and -appearing gay man, the most eloquent example of this new sexual type (though by no means the first instance of it), is the title character of E. M. Forster's 1913–1914 novel *Maurice.*[20]

As the twentieth century progressed, this emergent sexual type took more solid form and shape. He appeared in gay fiction with increasing frequency. Indeed, he became the preferred hero of gay romance, the normal gay man whose ideal sexual partner (which he seeks and inevitably finds) is another straight-acting and -appearing gay man just like himself. This romantic ideal was built on systematic contrasts with other, earlier, queerer types; in fact, it thrived on explicit put-downs of effeminate or gender-deviant men, from whom the hero or the author recoiled in horror. That is what we find especially in the explicit gay male fiction that emerged on both sides of the Atlantic in the wake of the Second World War: Gore Vidal's *The City and the Pillar* (1948), Rodney Garland's *The Heart in Exile* (1953), James Baldwin's *Giovanni's Room* (1956), and Mary Renault's *The Charioteer* (1953), not to mention all of her Greek romances. A similar phenomenon appeared in lesbian fiction in the postwar period with Patricia Highsmith's *The Price of Salt* (1952) and, most aggressively, Rita Mae Brown's *Rubyfruit Jungle* (1973), in which butch lesbians from earlier working-class lesbian bar culture are subjected to savage ridicule and intense sexual depreciation.

ᗡᘐ

Fiction was not the only place where homosexuality triumphed over inversion. Although the Stonewall rebellion may have been sparked by drag queens, gay liberation in at least some of its later manifestations encouraged lesbians and gay men to act out new, positive, non-deviant sex and gender roles in everyday life. To be sure, new styles of hypermasculinity had appeared among gay men much earlier, in the aftermath of the Second World War; they seem to have been popularized in that period via the nascent gay social networks inadvertently created by the mass mobilizations of the war and the gay bars in coastal cities that catered to military personnel. Already by the late 1940s, as the historian George Chauncey has demonstrated and as much anecdotal information attests, a new, distinctively American butch style began to be adopted by some gay men: a look defined by the wearing of a white T-shirt, blue jeans, and a leather jacket.[21] Whatever post-Stonewall mythology might claim, it was not only after 1969 that gay men learned how to be butch, or that butch styles began to compete with earlier "effete" modes of self-presentation among gay men.[22]

But if gay liberation, which tended in any case to promote forms of androgyny, was not directly responsible for the invention of gay masculinity, the 1970s did see the new gender-conformist styles become generalized and hegemonic in the gay male social worlds that were taking shape in the metropolitan centers of the United States. As a result, earlier, gender-deviant practices of homosexuality came to look increasingly archaic. The ideology of the post-Stonewall period positively encouraged the rejection of previous, abject, supposedly self-hating forms of lesbian and gay male behavior. It insistently championed new, enlightened, egalitarian, symmetrical practices of both sex and gender, elevating them to the status of trademarks of lesbian and gay liberation, and transforming them into privileged elements in new lesbian and gay male self-understandings.

The emerging gay-affirmative sciences of homosexuality contributed to this ideological makeover by helping to shatter the lingering stereotypes. In San Francisco, the new *Journal of Homosexuality* published article after article throughout the second half of the 1970s showing that, contrary to all the old myths, most gay men were actually *not* effeminate.[23] In Paris, Michel Foucault asserted in a 1978 interview that male homosexuality had no fundamental connection with femininity: drag was merely an outmoded strategy of resistance to earlier sexual regimes.[24] Soon, no doubt, it would wither away.

The irony of this updated brand of gay liberation is that it did not always liberate. In some cases, it also imposed new constraints. And it gave rise to its own brand of censorship. Archivist and memoirist Joan Nestle was told by her lesbian-feminist comrades that it might be okay for her to celebrate butch-femme roles in the lesbian bar culture of the 1950s. But if she dared to champion role-playing among lesbians in the present-day world of the 1970s, she would be herstory.

ᘒᕽᘐ

By the late 1970s, then, lesbian and gay male life in the gay urban ghettos of the United States and Western Europe came to be distinguished by the hegemony of lesbian feminism and the emphatically masculine culture of the so-called gay male "clone," both of which sought to banish gender polarities and asymmetrical role-playing from homosexuality. That move was not, to be sure, an effort to eliminate all gender identities or all roles. Certain privileged gender styles, such as gay male virility, and certain approved performances of sexuality, such as egalitarian sexual roles, were actively promoted and valorized. But they weren't promoted *as* styles or roles, *as* explicit performances of sex and gender. Instead, they were valorized as reflections of healthy, liberated gayness itself, as universal truths about homosexuality and signs of its natural, undistorted expression. And they contrasted proudly with older gay styles.

Those older styles went underground, but they did not disappear altogether. Rather, they coexisted with the new, emerging embodiments of lesbian and gay male identity and alternated with them, often within the same individual. But if the 1970s now stand out in retrospect as an unfortunate chapter in the long, grim history of transgender oppression, they were also, for many lesbians and gay men, a time of gender euphoria. A giddy sense of exhilaration accompanied the discovery, made and ceaselessly remade throughout lesbian and gay male urban communities in the period, that homosexuality was *not* irretrievably wedded to gender non-conformity, that lesbians and gay men were and could be "normal."

As if to demonstrate and to dramatize that stunning breakthrough, so incredible and yet so true, gay men threw themselves headlong into a collective project of normative gender performance. By 1975 or so, it suddenly started to seem that everyone in the gay male world (or maybe just in the gay cruise bars I went to in San Francisco) had completed a crash course in how to be butch. It was as if we'd all finally figured out how to impersonate straight men, or at least how to imitate our favorite straight-acting and -appearing heroes from the world of postwar gay romantic fiction.

An article in a 1975 issue of London's *Gay News* provided helpful hints about how to pull off that difficult trick and make a successful transition from archaic gay male forms of life to modern gay male identity. It afforded a satirical (if revealing) glimpse of the techniques gay men were employing behind the scenes to embody the newer, stricter standards of masculine self-presentation that the gay world now imposed: "I have found that practicing in front of a mirror is a good way of ridding oneself of these added afflictions [i.e., effeminacy]," explained the writer. "I was able to learn more normal movements and expressions that way. Of course it took years of practice, but now I can relax in public without the acute embarrassment of finding myself limp-wristed or adopting effeminate postures."[25] Further pointers about "being butch" and perfecting "butch movement," "butch noises," "the butch body," "butch dressing," and "butch drugs" were provided in 1982 by Clark Henley in a scathing and hilarious but genuinely instructive guide, *The Butch Manual*. According to Henley, the real motivation behind the transition from queen to butch was simply the desire to "get laid," which gay masculinity made possible to an extent previously undreamed of.[26]

In the gay society of the period, in short, the shift from deviant to normative gender styles, the rise of sex as both symbol and practice, and the euthanasia of traditional gay male culture were all strictly correlated. As queen was to butch, so culture was to sex. Now that gay men were living their homosexuality not as a cultural practice but as a sexual identity, they required a new gender style; and the masculine gender style that they adopted, by expanding their sexual opportunities, enabled them to consolidate a definition of gay existence and a model of gay identity that focused on sex at the expense of culture—and that excluded the feminine identifications that had informed and defined much of traditional gay male culture.

⚬⚬

And so in the rapidly expanding gay enclaves of the major cities in the United States and elsewhere during the 1970s, a new and supposedly modern style of gay masculinity acquired ever more solid form, achieving a spectacular visibility.[27] My straight friends in San Francisco would ask me why all the gay men in the city seemed to have among them only three or four different looks: construction worker, college athlete, lumberjack, motorcyclist. Frances Fitzgerald, visiting the

Castro district in San Francisco in the same period, described the side-walks as overflowing with "young men dressed as it were for a hiking expedition," all wearing denim jeans, flannel shirts, hiking boots, and down-filled nylon flight jackets.[28] "It would be easy enough to treat gay macho as nothing more than a matter of shifting fashions," concedes Alice Echols in a book on the culture of 1970s disco music. "But embedded in this macho turn were changes in gay men's identity and subjectivity. Gays not only presented themselves differently, they regarded themselves differently, searched out unfamiliar sorts of sexual partners, and expanded their sexual repertoire."[29]

Indeed, the new clone style was much more than a style of gender presentation. It was also a sexual style, which consisted in the down-playing of polarized roles.[30] Gone were the supposedly self-hating queens who lived only to service straight trade, who spent a lifetime on their knees. No longer were gay men alternately one another's sisters and one another's rivals for the favors of the young and the beautiful; now they were one another's preferred objects of desire. "We're the men we've been looking for" was the watchword of the 1970s, and as if to prove it, gay men held hands and kissed in public.[31] Mutuality and reciprocity were the expected sexual protocols, in gay life as well as in gay porn. "One-sided" homosexual relations, though they might still exist, were a vestige from the premodern past. Or so maintained Dr. Charles Silverstein and Edmund White, the authors of the first edition of *The Joy of Gay Sex,* published in 1977. "This sort of [active/passive] role-playing, held to as a strict division, seems increasingly on the wane," they added, assuring their readers that "most gay men would denounce" such role-playing nowadays "as 'old-fashioned' or 'unliberated.'"[32]

Just eight years earlier, in 1969, White had taken a very different line. He had admitted that "many gay men are constantly trying to reproduce with their lovers a facsimile of straight marriage. One gay man plays the 'butch' while the other plays the 'femme.'"[33] But by 1977, all that was already ancient history. From the freshly minted official perspective of the post-Stonewall gay male world—and from the personal insight that many gay men had gained through intense sexual experimentation in the wake of gay liberation—polarized sex-roles existed only in homophobic fantasy. Gay relationships were no longer "one-sided," no longer divided into active partners who played the butch and passive partners who played the femme. "Which of you wears the pants in the family? Which of you is the husband, and which is the wife?" Those were the kinds of questions that only a clueless straight person would ask.

Modern gay sex was not polarized or hierarchical. It was mutual, and its mutuality positioned the two partners identically in relation to each other. There were no tops; there were no bottoms. There was but a single homosexual identity—namely, gay. Hence, successful sexual relationships involved equal partners of the same age, the same wealth, and the same social standing, each of them doing everything with and to the other with perfect reciprocity. The typical modern gay male couple pictured by Silverstein and White consisted of "a 35-year-old lawyer in love with a 35-year-old doctor"; the two of them would "share expenses and household duties" and "take turns fucking each other."[34]

Robert Ferro went even further. The ideal love affair described in his 1985 novel *The Blue Star* is one in which erotic reciprocity gives rise to such a simple, hearty, natural fellowship among equal partners that sex takes on the jovial mateyness of the all-American sport of baseball. Addressing the reader with a wry, ingratiating charm, but not the slightest intended irony, the narrator recalls, "We made love to each other several times, taking turns as if at bat, as if still playing a game in which first he and then I stepped up and loved."[35]

The analogy from baseball was not a complete accident. The erotic model of equal affections it implies turns out to be just as dear to a leading character in Mark Merlis's 1998 novel *An Arrow's Flight*. This man, significantly, came to sexual maturity during the "age of heroes" immediately after Stonewall. His most stubborn, cherished image of gay love is chastely embodied by "a pair of boys playing catch. . . . Lazy and silent on a spring morning, in perfect communion."[36] The pornography produced by Falcon Studios in the 1970s provided the visual counterpart: it promoted a model of gay sex as a wholesome, easygoing masculine exchange among friendly, mutually respectful teammates, and it offered its bedazzled viewers tantalizing glimpses of a gay comradeship at once sexual and fraternal, inclusive and tender, virile but non-judgmental, happily free of roles, hierarchy, and sexual difference.

That classic, utopian vision—as old as Walt Whitman, as new as the latest circuit party or other gathering of the gay male "tribe"—did not long survive unscathed. For in 1990 came the "queer" moment, with its militant vindication of deviant sex and gender styles, its men in dresses and leather and pearls, its delight in butch display and high-femme theatrics, its reclamation of tops and bottoms, and its multiplication (or rediscovery) of queer sub-identities: twink, bear, emo. Ever since then, it's been a bit hard to take seriously the romance of gay male love as an undifferentiated brotherhood, an innocent manly pastime, the sexual equivalent of baseball. The closest gay sex comes to team sports nowadays is "Gag the Fag." I am referring to those compilations of semi-amateur porn videos, sold over the Internet and now past their fifth installment, that feature acts of oral intercourse so rough as to provoke vomiting. What kind of sex could be less fraternal, less egalitarian, less reciprocal, less symmetrical?[37] It is certainly a far cry from that game of catch among upright, amiable youths lazily tossing a ball back and forth in perfect masculine communion on a spring morning.

☙❧

Already by the early 1990s, the compulsory loyalty oaths to egalitarian sex and gender roles that gay men had been obliged to swear for more than a decade came in for gentle caricature from Pansy Division, the queer San Francisco rock band. Here is the opening verse of a song called "Versatile":

> There's a few straight guys I know
> They wanna know who plays the woman's role
> I shake my head and say it's not like that
> Some guys have the imagination of a doormat

> Our roles are not cast in stone
> We trade off getting boned
>   Cause we're *versatile*.[38]

In these lyrics, the typical protest at straight people's perennial, exasperating inability to appreciate the true meaning of gay male sex and gender roles is succeeded by the predictable, out-and-proud claim to have transcended old-fashioned, gendered paradigms ("Our roles are not cast in stone")—but that claim quickly turns out to be hollow. At least, it is undercut by the very terms in which it is articulated. These boys aren't *really* versatile, after all: they just "trade off getting boned."

"Versatility," in other words, is not an unambiguously virile boast, not at least as it is used here. It functions as a transparent cover for the continuing practice and enjoyment of "one-sided," "unliberated," *passive* role-playing. Contrary to what Robert Ferro had implied with his language of batting and hitting, being versatile consists in politely waiting to take one's turn at being a bottom. Roles did not disappear in 1969, or in 1975, then, despite the many obituaries that were written for them. They just went underground for a time, and a little dose of queerness was all it took to resuscitate them. Or so Pansy Division slyly implied.

The corrosive skepticism that emerged in the 1990s about the gender-normativity and egalitarianism of post-Stonewall, pre-queer gay styles made it hard to believe that anyone had ever taken gay male clone culture seriously. Recent converts to the cult of performativity in queer theory have tried, accordingly, to interpret the 1970s clone style, as well as butch-femme role-playing among lesbians, as a knowing parody of gender roles, as a send-up of normative sexual conventions.[39] But back in the 1970s, at least so far as gay male clones were concerned, nothing could have been further from the truth. The desire to carry off a gender presentation that did not appear to lag behind the historical curve was intense and genuine. Also, as Henley and Echols rightly emphasize, gay hypermasculinity was an *erotic* style, and that meant it was played very straight, at least when a gay man was looking for action, which was often. As Leo Bersani put it in 1987, "Parody is an erotic turn-off, and all gay men know this. Much campy talk is parodistic, and while that may be fun at a dinner party, if you're out to make someone you turn off the camp."[40]

An acquaintance of mine, a gay man of my own generation, still records the message on his answering machine thirty times over, until he's sure his voice reveals no traces of effeminacy. There's nothing tongue-in-cheek about such a performance: it couldn't be more earnest. And in fact it was quite wise, in that post-Stonewall era of butch one-upmanship, not to take too many chances. There was no higher compliment you could pay the trick of the moment than to say, "You know, when I saw you walk into the bar tonight, I thought to myself, 'There's gotta be some mistake. Does this guy know it's a gay bar? He *can't* be gay. Is he here for real? I can't believe he's not straight.'" To which this paragon of masculinity would invariably reply, if he was in a mood to be agreeable, "Well, you know, if I just happened to see you walking down the street, I would never think *you* were gay." Such compliments—for that is indeed what those remarks purported to be—were not only exchanged in all seriousness; they were uttered in a swoon of erotic delirium. In such circumstances, nothing was more scandalous, or more unforgivable, than for the guy one was dating to show up for a romantic dinner wearing an earring—which is not to say that such catastrophes never happened.

In short, post-Stonewall gay male life was defined by the emergence of a new masculine, non-role-specific practice of gender and sex, which gave rise to a new style and a new form of life, embodied by the gay clone or butch gay man. Those developments betokened the proud triumph of an undifferentiated *gay sexuality* over an earlier, discredited, effeminate *gay culture,* from which the new sex-centered model of gay male identity offered a long-overdue and welcome refuge.

෴

No wonder that in the heady atmosphere of those glory days in the late 1970s, before AIDS or the rise of the New Right, when sex was everywhere (if you were under thirty, urban, butch, and not too bad-looking), and when utopia seemed to be just around the corner—no wonder that young gay men like me had little use for Judy Garland. Traditional gay male culture—with its female icons, its flaming camp style, its division between queens and trade, its polarized gender roles, its sexual hierarchies, its balked romantic longings, its senti-mentality, its self-pity, and its profound despair about the possibility of lasting love—all that seemed not only archaic and outdated but re-pulsive. It was an insult to the newer, truer, and better definitions of gayness that gay men had recently invented, popularized, and labored to embody as well as to exploit. In such a context, gay male culture, as it had been traditionally constituted, appeared to be nothing more than a series of stereotypes—and homophobic stereotypes, at that—though all too often internalized, sadly, by gay men themselves.

So I had to move to Australia, settle down with a boyfriend half my age, and undergo my own gay initiation in order to see for the first time, in the 1990s, the movies from the 1930s and 1940s that I had studiously avoided seeing in the 1970s. (They turned out to be pretty good.) It was only then that I was introduced to the American gay cultural curriculum that gay American men who were twenty years older than me already knew by heart, but that I had resisted learning about from them. Since I underwent this gay initiation at the hands of a much younger lover, I am constitutionally immune to the claim that pre-Stonewall gay male culture is irrelevant to more recent gen-erations of gay men, or out of date—even if it is, undeniably, and en-dearingly, dated . . . and even if it cannot help *looking* archaic from our current, post-Stonewall perspective.

To study gay male subjectivity by studying traditional gay male culture seems like such an intriguing thing to do nowadays precisely because it feels so counter-intuitive, so shockingly retrograde, espe-cially in the light of the social, conceptual, generational developments I have just traced. It represents a reversal of previous, long-held con-victions, a complete betrayal of the most cherished notions that many of us thought we believed about the nature of male homosexuality and that we also tried to make other people believe. It violates, in particular, the official post-Stonewall creed that gay men are no different from anybody else, that sexual object-choice has nothing to do with gender style, that gay sexuality has no relation to femininity, and that homosexuality is a sexual orientation, not a culture or a subculture.

Which is no doubt why my class aroused so much hostility among so many gay men.

∞

For example, in the spring of 2000, before I had even taught "How To Be Gay" for the first time, a man named John in Annapolis, Maryland, sent an e-mail to the University of Michigan's English Department, protesting against the class. (John used his full name, but I am withholding it, to protect his privacy.) John's message was addressed not to me but to the director of undergraduate studies, who had issued a public statement defending the class. John disagreed with that statement and, appealing to the authority of my administrative superiors to resolve the matter, he urged them, in the strongest terms, to cancel the class and remove it from the English Department's curriculum.

So far, there was nothing unusual about John's message. It resembled countless others that had been sent by members of the Christian Right to various offices at the University of Michigan. But John was not a religious conservative. He identified himself as a gay man in his mid-thirties, who was no supporter of any of the right-wing evangelical organizations that had been lobbying against the class. Instead, he said he was deeply disturbed by a number of its features, which promoted what he considered to be stereotypes of gay people. Merely by offering such a course, he argued, I was implying that gay men as a group were characterized by "universalities" that could be discovered, enumerated, and presented to undergraduates as if such things were facts. But far from being facts, these sorts of generalizations about gay men were common misconceptions—for instance, that gay men were fashion-savvy, or design-savvy, or had a penchant for dressing like women.

John had been fighting those stereotypes his entire life, he said, and he didn't like seeing them propped up by institutions of higher education. Surely, every enlightened person understood that human individuals are all unique. There were lots of effeminate straight men and lots of masculine gay men. Everyone was different, and people didn't "fall into neat little boxes." John himself happened to belong to the latter category: he made it clear that he considered himself a masculine gay man. And as someone who didn't fit the usual gay stereotypes, he resented the assumption that just because he was gay, he was bound to like certain things, such as particular works of music and art. What would be next, he asked sarcastically—a course for African Americans that would teach them how to enjoy fried chicken, ribs, and watermelon?

In short, John admired any and all efforts to teach young people to be tolerant of others, especially those unlike themselves. But he objected to clichés and assumptions and stereotypes that would "give students a skewed impression of gay men in America." Being gay, he insisted, was a sexual orientation, *not* a subculture.

It would be altogether too easy to demean or to dismiss this complaint by highlighting the writer's defensiveness about his masculinity or by making fun of his evident panic at the prospect of being lumped together with a bunch of screaming queens. To be sure, as a self-described masculine gay man, John had everything to lose by being identified with men who were deviant not only in their sexual practices but also in their gender style, and who therefore ranked lower on the scale of social acceptability than he did.[41] If he objected to the promotion of stereotypes, that was not necessarily because he had problems with stereotypes in and of themselves—after all, the straight-acting and -appearing gay man that he claimed to be was nothing if not a stereotype. Rather, it was because the *particular* stereotypes he believed my class was promoting happened to be at odds with his own proud and "positive" image of himself as virile and dignified.

That's what John meant when he said that such stereotypes gave "a skewed impression of gay men in America": they failed to differentiate between sexuality and gender, to distinguish male homosexuality from effeminacy, to acknowledge the existence of straight-acting and -appearing gay men, to separate those men from their degraded, effeminate brethren, and to credit them with the social respectability to which their praiseworthy gender achievement entitled them.

Such recognition is in fact hard to come by. Claiming a normatively masculine gender identity is always a dicey act for a gay man to carry off in a society that routinely continues to associate male homosexuality with effeminacy. And since one of the demands that our society makes on homosexuality is that it be—if not visible—at least legible, that it always reveal itself to careful, expert scrutiny, any attempt to assert the entirely unmarked character of male homosexuality, to insist that it does not produce any decipherable signs of its difference, is bound to be met with skepticism and resistance.[42] So John faced an uphill battle in trying to establish his masculine credentials, and he needed all the help he could get, which my scandalous class did not exactly give him. (It may be worth noting in this connection that I never received any protests about my class from gay men who prided themselves on being flagrantly effeminate and who were alarmed that my reference to "muscle culture" in the course description might lead to their being mistaken for a bunch of buff military types or boring gym bunnies who wear track suits, like to watch team sports, and have no sense of verbal wit.)

The main reason it would be unwise to dismiss John's objections in some righteous or condescending way is that to do so would be to underrate their political force and to overlook their grounding in a particular set of social and historical developments, to which in fact they offer an important and useful clue. John was registering and expressing a pervasive, enduring belief among gay men of the post-Stonewall era, a belief I once held myself, a belief we were taught to consider politically necessary as well as politically progressive—

namely, that homosexuality is a sexual orientation, not a lifestyle or culture; that it is downright homophobic to represent gay men as marked by certain typical, or stereotypical, traits; that gay men are all individuals; that it is impossible to generalize about us as a group; that we are not any different from normal people. The official line of the post-Stonewall gay movement in the United States has gone something like this: "We are not freaks or monsters. We are the same as you: we are ordinary, decent people. In fact, we are just like hetero-sexuals except for what we do in bed (which is nobody's business but our own—and, anyway, the less said about it, the better)."

For a short time, around the birth of the "queer" movement at the turn of the 1990s, it became fashionable to claim the opposite. Those who embraced a queer identity (or non-identity) used to take a line that exactly reversed the official post-Stonewall one: "We queers are totally unlike anyone else; we do not resemble you at all. We are com-pletely different from heterosexuals—except for what we do in bed (which is more or less what everyone does in bed, with some minor, insignificant variations)."

But that queer fashion didn't last long, and a lot of lesbians and gay men in the United States, like John from Annapolis, have now gone back to claiming that gay people are defined, if at all, only by a non-standard sexual preference which in and of itself does not strictly cor-relate with any other feature of the personality. In all other aspects of their lives, gay people are the same as everyone else. (That tendency may actually reflect a recent development of international scope, what Rogers Brubaker has called "the return of assimilation.")[43] In American popular usage nowadays, to be sure, the word "gay" may mean "stereotypically gay" or "culturally gay," while men who are de-fined by their sexuality, by the sex they have with men, are more likely to be termed "homosexual." But in the official language of the gay movement, "gay" remains an identity marker attached to sexual pref-erence. To be gay, according to this latter outlook, is to have a sexual-ity, a sexual orientation; it is *not* to have a distinctive culture or psy-chology or social practice or inner life, or anything else that is different from the norm. Especially if—in the case of gay men—that difference implies any identification with women or femininity. Merely to question this doctrine is to risk conjuring up the dread specter of sexual inversion, opening the door to a return of Victorian psychiatry, with all its ancient prejudices about the congenital abnormality and psychopathology and gender deviance of gay men.

But so long as we cling to the notion that gayness is reducible to same-sex sexual object-choice, that it has nothing to do with how we live or what we like, that our homosexuality is completely formed prior to and independent of any exposure to gay culture—and so long as we hold to that belief as to a kind of dogma—then the persistence of gay culture will remain a perpetual embarrassment, as well as an insoluble analytic puzzle.

☙

Will Fellows makes a similar point at the beginning of his own book about male homosexuality as a cultural practice. In *A Passion to Preserve: Gay Men as Keepers of Culture,* Fellows inquires into the particular role gay men have played in historic preservation, architectural restoration, and various antiquarian pursuits. "At first, I was bothered by this strong, gender-atypical trend" in gay male behavior, he confesses. "I suppose I saw the apparently disproportionate presence of gay men in historic preservation as the stuff of stereotype. And so I failed to take it seriously." Fellows blames his initial, instinctive refusal to see anything significant in this pattern of cultural practice among gay men on

> the old saw about gay males being no different from straight males except for their sexual orientation. This notion developed as a central tenet of the gay rights movement since the 1970s. . . . If outside of our sex lives we gays are just like straights, then it must be only a stereotypical illusion that gay men are inordinately drawn to being house restorers and antiquarians—or interior designers, florists, hair stylists, fashion designers, and so forth. Now it's clear to me that gay men really are extraordinarily attracted to these kinds of work. Rather than

dismissing these realities as the stuff of stereotype, I see them as the stuff of archetype, significant truths worthy of exploration.[44]

In speaking of archetypes and essential gay differences, Fellows goes further than I would go; I try to distinguish my view from his in Chapter 15 of this book. But he is certainly right to note the perennial defensive reflex that is immediately triggered nowadays by any suggestion that "gender variance" or "gender-atypical" behavior might be a part of gay male identity—a transphobic reflex which our friend in Annapolis perfectly exemplifies. Fellows knows that routine by heart. He both anticipates it and reproduces it unerringly: "'I'm homosexual,' they will protest, 'but I'm *not* effeminate.'" More controversially, and more intriguingly, Fellows counters those claims by contending that the mere failure to *appear* effeminate does not support such a defensive assertion on the part of a gay man, since gender variance "may be manifested more internally in his interests, aptitudes, values, emotional constitution, and communication style."[45] We'll see some eloquent testimony to that effect in the following pages.

Unlike Fellows, I do not regard gender variance as the key to understanding gay male subjectivity. But the project of my class and of this book agrees with his insofar as it bucks the historical trends that are responsible for making gay male culture a permanent embarrassment to gay men—and that do so by constituting gay culture as inherently backward, archaic, unmasculine, unsexual, and therefore inassimilable to modern, normative gay identity. These are the same historical trends that have made the denial of any and all non-sexual differences between gay and non-gay people, including differences in culture or gender style, an article of faith in the ideology of the post-Stonewall gay movement. Such a denial lies behind the insistence that younger gay men, healthy and untouched by homophobia, have no need of gay male culture—and certainly no need of a gay male culture that implies some sort of female identification or effeminacy.

A similar denial persists, more surprisingly, throughout much writing in the academic field of "queer theory." There it assumes the protective coloration of an axiomatic opposition to "essentialism"—the stubborn but ultimately untenable belief that social identities are grounded in some inherent property or nature or quality common to all the members of an identity-based group. The rejection of essentialism did not prevent the original founders of queer theory from asking, "What do queers want?" or from exploring the particularities of gay culture.[46] But as queer theory has become institutionalized, the understandable reluctance to accept essentialist assumptions about lesbians and gay men has hardened into an automatic self-justifying dogmatism, a visceral impulse to preempt the merest acknowledgment or recognition of *any* cultural patterns or practices that might be distinctive to homosexuals.[47]

Barry Adam, a sociologist and one of the inventors of lesbian/gay/queer studies, has put the point as follows.

> We are now in a period when difference is the order of the day, and queer orthodoxy denies the search for, or assertion of, commonality now that the commonality posited by gay/lesbian identities has been exposed as never really having existed (which is why queer theory will never be able to account for why so many women and men defy the odds to affirm identity again and again). But a sense of mutual recognition, commonality, and—dare one say—identity endures despite the many fractures and assaults that try to undermine it.[48]

The very attention that queer theory has lavished on difference, intersectionality, and comparison has ended up screening out the question of how, for a large segment of homosexual American men during the past century or so, being gay has been experienced through highly patterned forms of embodied sensibility—even as those patterns tend routinely to be disavowed by gay men in their efforts to escape "stereotypes" and "labels." It is no accident that the studies of gay male culture that do focus most intensely on that question have tended to be undertaken by academics like Will Fellows and John Clum, who write at least in part for non-academic audiences, or by community-based intellectuals like Michael Bronski, Neil Bartlett, and David Nimmons—all of whose work falls outside the canon of queer theory.[49]

The general denial of any and all homosexual specificity, especially cultural specificity, is an eloquent symptom of our current predicament. It testifies to the emergence of a powerful taboo, what legal theorist Kenji Yoshino has called a "new form of discrimination" that "targets minority cultures rather than minority persons."[50] We may value diversity and difference, but we flinch at the very notion that minorities might be *culturally* different.[51] And anyway, gay culture in its manifold concrete manifestations often seems to be much too lowbrow a topic for serious intellectual inquiry, which may also explain why many academic queer theorists—even or especially some of the most prominent ones—tend to shy away from it.

☙❧

This book, nonetheless, champions queer politics over gay politics in a very particular way. While honoring the traditions of gay liberation and gay pride that emerged in the wake of the Stonewall riots, it explores and even celebrates certain non-standard practices of sex and gender. It also attempts to reclaim the culture of pre-Stonewall gay men by connecting it with such post-Stonewall developments as the queer and transgender movements. At the same time, it is deeply gay-positive. For it is unashamed of gay male culture, even gay culture's most unsettling or objectionable elements. At least, it is unashamed of gay shame—and therefore willing to linger over some features of gay culture that continue to make gay men nowadays ashamed of both gay culture and themselves.

Unlike the kinds of hostile stereotypes that are intended to demean and denigrate the members of a minority group, the stereotypes about gay male culture and identity that I am interested in here are stereotypes that have been elaborated and propounded by at least some gay men themselves. That alone makes them worthy of being treated with seriousness, respect, curiosity, and analytical rigor—even though certain proud gay men, like John from Annapolis, find them "skewed" or even self-hating.

If, for example, it actually were the case that African Americans largely defined themselves *to themselves* by their shared understanding that being Black implied a distinctive, unusual, or marked preference for fried chicken, ribs, and watermelon (to use John's example), I would not in fact be afraid to inquire into the cultural meanings that might be involved in the selective appropriation of those foods.[52] Being Black, after all, can also be understood as a set of peculiar and defining cultural practices, though it is a rare event when such a model of Black identity makes its way into respectable political discourse— even as a joke. On January 21, 2008, in the debate before the Democratic Party's electoral primary in South Carolina, Barack Obama was asked what he thought of Toni Morrison's remark that Bill Clinton was the first Black American president. He replied, "I would have to investigate more Bill's dancing abilities."[53] Black writers and critical race theorists have recently taken up the topic of "how to be Black" and have treated it as worthy of sustained investigation.[54]

In the case of gay men, it is not only (or even chiefly) homophobes who think that gay men like Judy Garland. Gay men themselves—or, at least, some gay men in the United States and Great Britain during the past sixty years—have thought the same thing.[55] We are not dealing with a hostile stereotype, then. We are dealing—at least, within certain historical, geographic, racial, and generational limits—with a collective self-recognition, though a self-recognition that admittedly continues to occasion a good deal of shame and therefore to produce a considerable amount of unease, and even outright denial.

In order to face down that shame and resist that impulse to denial, it is tempting to be shameless, to throw caution to the winds, to go all the way to the other extreme and to entertain, if only for a moment or two, the assumption—as our man in Annapolis said—that just because one is gay, one must like certain things, such as particular works of art and music. That assumption is plainly indefensible when it is put in those terms. But what if we tried to discover what was behind it? What if it were possible to connect the experience of gayness with particular cultural tastes, with the love of certain cultural objects? What if there actually were a certain logic to that connection? What if we could derive the characteristic themes and experiences of gay culture from the social conditions under which that culture arises and is reproduced? What if we went even further and considered the possibility that gay male tastes for certain cultural artifacts or social practices reflect, within their particular contexts, ways of being, ways of feeling, and ways of relating to the larger social world that are fundamental to male homosexuality and distinctive to gay men, despite gay men's many differences from one another? What if gay male subjecthood or subjectivity consisted precisely in those ways of being, feeling, and relating?

What if, in short, post-Stonewall gay male attitudes were *wrong,* and it turned out that male homosexuality was less about sex and more about culture, as well as the feelings, emotions, and complex combinations of affect (as epitomized by some gay men's love of Judy Garland) that cultural practices imply? What if those old queens at the Castro movie theater understood something about gayness— about *how to be gay*—that gay men of my generation, and the ones that came after it, completely missed, at least when we were young and new to the scene?

Which brings me back to my original, hazardous hypothesis. Perhaps there really is such a thing as gay male subjectivity. And perhaps gay men's cultural practices offer us a way of approaching it, getting hold of it, describing it, defining it, and understanding it.

That, at least, is the hypothesis on which this investigation will proceed.

PART TWO

American Falsettos

$\smash{\text{\LARGE }}$ 3 $\smash{\text{\LARGE }}$

GAY IDENTITY AND ITS DISCONTENTS

So what was it that those old queens at the Castro movie theater understood about how to be gay that many members of my own generation missed? If I had to convey in a few words what I think it was, I would say they knew that *gay male desire* cannot be reduced either to *sexual* desire or to gay *identity*.

Sexual desire is only one aspect of gay male desire. Sex is not the sum of queer pleasure. Gay desire seeks more than the achievement of gay identity. Gay identity does not answer to all the demands of gay desire. Gay identity is inadequate to the full expression of gay subjectivity. Gay identity may well register the fact of gay desire; it may even stand in for its wayward promptings, its unanticipated urges and satisfactions. But gay identity does not—it cannot—capture gay desire in all its subjective sweep and scope. *It cannot express it.*

Desire into identity will not go.

Gay identity cannot express gay desire or gay subjectivity because gay desire is not limited to desire for men. Gay desire does not consist only in desire for sex with men. Or desire for masculinity. Or desire for positive images of gay men. Or desire for a gay male world. All of those desires might, conceivably, be referred to gay identity, to some aspect of what defines a gay man. But gay male desire actually comprises a kaleidoscopic range of queer longings—of wishes and sensations and pleasures and emotions—that exceed the bounds of any

singular identity and extend beyond the specifics of gay male existence.

That is why a social movement grounded in a gay identity defined
by exclusive reference to gay people—with its LGBTQ community
centers and organizations, its lesbigay magazines and novels and
movies and popular music and TV shows and cable channels, its
neighborhoods, bars, clubs, vacation resorts, and churches, its political representatives and leaders and spokespeople and human-rights
lobby groups and street marches and demonstrations, its theoretical
and scholarly breakthroughs, historical discoveries, university classes,
and fields of research—that is why all this commercial and political and cultural infrastructure of gay identity remains a perennial letdown, leaving many members of its gay constituency perpetually
unsatisfied. Gay identity—gayness reduced to identity or understood
as identity—fails to realize male homosexual desire in its unpredict-
able, unsystematic ensemble. It answers to only a single dimension of
gay male subjectivity.

And yet, *identity* has become the preferred category for thinking
about homosexuality. Moreover, it has been promoted at the direct
expense of pleasure or feeling or *subjectivity.*[1]

⊗⊗

The lesbian and gay movement has long fought to win for queer people the status of a political minority. It has tried hard to persuade others to see us as defined by a political category—namely, gay identity—
because such a category is *morally neutral.* And so the lesbian and gay
movement has presented us as members of a social group that has
suffered and continues to suffer, through no fault of our own, from
both formal and informal discrimination—ranging from a lack of
equal rights to casual disrespect and denigration. To be gay, on this
view, is to be a member of a socially disadvantaged minority. That is
certainly a fair enough view of our situation. But there is also a quite
specific ideological payoff that comes from defining homosexuality as
a political and social condition, rather than a subjective one: such a
purely political definition of gayness helps to ensure that homosexu-

ality will never again be understood as a kind of mental illness—as a sickness for which gay people as individuals are to blame, instead of the homophobic society in which we live.

The lesbian and gay movement has had good reason, then, to downplay the subjective experience of homosexuality, to pass over what homosexuality *feels like* to us. It has been perfectly right to worry that any attention to our supposed mental or emotional peculiarities would simply reconfirm ancient prejudices about our psychological abnormality, prejudices that have served so often to justify discrimination against lesbians and gay men. So it has minimized our subjective and cultural differences, even denied them. It has waged a sustained, consistent, decades-long ideological struggle to portray homosexuality as a political category, or at most a social category, not an emotional or psychological particularity. As a result of all those efforts by lesbian and gay activists, writers, artists, and scholars, the only credible differences (beyond sexual differences) that can be assigned to gay people nowadays, at least by anyone who wishes to appear enlightened and politically mainstream, are purely *social* differences.

So the lesbian and gay movement's gambit has been largely successful. If anything, it has been rather *too* successful. For it has effectively closed off the entire topic of gay subjectivity to respectable inquiry, making it impossible for us to inquire into ourselves or to explore in any systematic or meaningful way our unique sensibilities and cultures—beyond matters of sexuality.[2] We have ended up imposing a sanitizing blackout on many distinctive aspects of queer life that might otherwise qualify as its most original and, possibly, its most praiseworthy features.

For all its undeniable benefits, gay pride is now preventing us from knowing ourselves.

ↀↀↀ

Indeed, the whole point of gay identity politics has been to stop people (ourselves included) from asking too many awkward or prying questions about what goes on in our inner lives. One of the overarching aims of identity politics in general has been to make the world safe for minority subjectivity by shifting the public's gaze away from the distinctive features of minority subcultures, especially from everything that might make people who don't belong to those subcultures feel uncomfortable with them, suspicious of them, or excluded from them. By focusing attention, instead, on specifically political (and therefore less viscerally upsetting) demands for equal treatment, social recognition, and procedural justice, progressive social movements have achieved significant gains for members of stigmatized groups. Accordingly, campaigns for minority rights have persistently championed identity (who we are) over subjectivity (how we feel) and emphasized such matters as social equality, the benefits of diversity, the pleasures of difference, the ethics of peaceful coexistence.

The ultimate effect has been to imply that the spectrum of minority identities is no more shocking or offensive than a banquet of ethnic cuisine at an international food festival: a smorgasbord of delectable but insignificant and meaningless variations, open to all; an invitation to broaden our cultural range, providing something for everyone to enjoy—without anyone feeling obligated to sample everything, especially anything that looks particularly gross or disgusting. Stepping back from the details of queer life, we take shelter in inoffensive generalities: promoting human rights, celebrating diversity, valuing difference, supporting multiculturalism, fighting for social justice.

The greatest beneficiaries of this vogue for representing cultural difference in terms of innocent and harmless diversity have been those marginalized groups that still bear a heavy burden of stigma and whose public behavior continues, for that reason, to arouse strong general aversion: African Americans using Black English in White society, gay men kissing on the street, butch women claiming leadership roles and asserting authority over men, or disabled people painfully and obtrusively negotiating a built environment not designed for them. Identity helps to "cover" the indiscreet and disruptive features of socially excluded groups, their most flagrantly visible mani-

festations—precisely those defining attributes of stigmatized minorities that caused them to be stigmatized in the first place.[3] Identity
provides a protective shield against the uneasiness that stigmatized
populations often occasion in "normal" people—that is, people who
don't suffer from the stigma in question and come comfortably close
to embodying the social norm.

Identity can perform this important practical and political function
because it allows and indeed encourages normal people to categorize
the members of a stigmatized population as a single group, not on
the basis of their offending behavior but, more neutrally, on the basis
of their "identity"—that is, their common membership in a "community." The category of "identity" offers plausible grounds on which to
support as a matter of principle the equal treatment of individuals
belonging to such a community by representing them as *a general
class of persons*—as a group like any other—and by downplaying their
shared, flamboyant differences, all those weird and disturbing shenan-
igans that at least partly define, distinguish, and constitute the group
in the first place. As Michael Warner puts it, with reference to sexual
minorities, "Identity . . . allows us to distance ourselves from any actual manifestation of queerness."[4] The politics of identity performs
in this way an important practical service. Despite springing from a
model of social difference, identity politics, insofar as it insists on
identity as a general—even universal—social category, contributes to
the transcendence of *particular* differences and thus to the identity-
blind project of assimilation.[5]

It is precisely because the goal of mainstream gay politics has been
to promote a benign attitude of acceptance toward sexual minorities,
represented not as subjects of a distinctive way of being and feeling
but as members of a generic identity-based group, that gay people
have been pressured to mask their queerness, rein in their sensibilities, and play down their differences from regular folks. "Progress in
gay rights," Daniel Harris argues, "is often won at the expense of our
indigenous, unacculturated idiosyncrasies as a minority which must
be toned down or erased altogether in order for us to achieve com-

plete social acceptance. Gay liberation and the gay sensibility are staunch antagonists."[6]

That antagonism has not led to the total exclusion of gay sensibility from the public scene, of course, nor have political imperatives succeeded in suppressing all undignified expressions of lesbian and gay desire, subjectivity, and cultural specificity. Gay pride celebrations in major urban centers still do have their uniquely queer, transgressive, carnivalesque contingents—from dykes on bikes to boy-lovers, from drag queens to porn stars. But such figures represent a distinct embarrassment to the official, public image of American gay identity, with its politics of respectability, social responsibility, and affirmation.[7] In the week following any gay pride parade, dozens of letters typically appear in the local newspapers (both mainstream and gay) complaining that gay pride has become a freak show and that the presence of all those flaming creatures at the march gives homosexuality a Bad Name and is Bad For The Cause.

Gay identity politics has certainly procured for us an undeniable and inestimable array of liberties and permissions. But now it is also starting to reveal the defects of its very virtues and to subject us to a surprising number of increasingly bothersome constraints. We may have become proud of our gay identity, and unabashed about our same-sex desires and relationships. Yet we remain hopelessly ashamed of how queerly we feel and act—ashamed of our instincts, our loves and hates, our attitudes, our non-standard values, our ways of being, our social and cultural practices.[8] Instead of celebrating our distinctive subjectivity, our unique pleasures, and our characteristic culture, we have achieved gay pride at their expense.

∽

When, for example, I say that I am gay—when I "identify" as gay or disclose my gay "identity"—I adopt an *identity-based strategy*, generated by gay identity politics itself, for dealing with the social difference that my sexual difference makes in a heteronormative world. In particular, I choose to represent my sexuality as a neutral feature of my social being, more or less as if I were declaring my ethnicity or gender. In so doing, I avail myself of a positive, non-phobic, non-pathological term provided for me by a multi-generational political movement for lesbian and gay liberation, pride, and dignity. By making the term "gay" available to me, the movement has given me a way of naming my sexuality without describing it and without making specific reference to my sexual desires, feelings, or practices. I can acknowledge my sexuality openly and unambiguously, even while I bracket the obnoxious details of my sexual behavior and cultural dissidence. The gay identity-label also enables me to present myself socially without recurring to pejorative or otherwise tainted psychological, theological, criminological, sociological, sexological, medical, or moral language ("pervert," "sodomite," "deviant," "sex fiend," "psychopath," "homosexual").

I wasn't always so keen on the term "gay" myself, I admit. For a while, back when I first encountered it in the early 1970s, it struck me as an ill-judged piece of political jargon—which, by its cheery insistence on how happy we were all supposed to be, merely invoked the specter it was all too obviously struggling to exorcize, the specter of a sad and pathetic homosexuality.

But that was then. This is now.

The advantage of "gay," nowadays, is that it no longer means anything in itself. It certainly doesn't imply that gay people are *gay* in the sense of upbeat or cheerful. The word has become a symbolic designation, not a descriptive or an expressive one. It functions entirely as a conventional term of reference. It simply refers to people who make a same-sex sexual object-choice, suggesting perhaps, as well, that they are not ashamed of their sexuality and do not seek to hide it.

As such, "gay" permits my sexuality to declare itself socially under the cover of a polite designation, almost a euphemism, and in terms of an *identity* rather than an erotic subjectivity or a sexual behavior. It allows me to present myself as a member of a people or nation or race, a human collectivity at any rate, instead of as a deviant individual—a monster, freak, criminal, sinner, or social outcast. (I may well *choose* to style myself as a deviant, as a social or sexual pariah, which is what I do when I label myself "queer," but at least that's my choice; it's no longer a life sentence.)

So the term "gay" *identifies* my sexuality without evoking its lived reality and without dwelling on my sexual feelings, fantasies, or practices. In that sense, it sounds relatively respectable, and it functions in the same way that "husband" or "wife" does for married people, referring to a sexual identity without foregrounding explicitly what is sexual about it.

That is a great convenience.

But that convenience comes at a certain cost. For one thing, the prospect of achieving social acceptance by promoting gay identity over gay sexuality makes it tempting to construct a kind of official, public gay identity totally divorced from sex. That is the temptation Michael Warner eloquently warns us against in *The Trouble with Normal,* urging us not to turn our backs on the sophisticated and adventurous queer culture we have created around sex, not to sell out those members of our communities who do not (or who cannot) bury their sexuality discreetly within the sphere of private life, and not to purchase respectability at the expense of sex.[9]

Similarly, John Howard, a prominent gay historian, complains that American lesbian and gay history "often glosses over the erotic interactions of queer historical subjects. Concerned with identity, culture, and politics, it sometimes politely overlooks the arguably defining feature of the enterprise, homo*sex*."[10] As gay men have gained entry into popular culture and media representation precisely by bracketing or downplaying the specifically sexual dimensions of their lives—witness the success of such movies and TV shows as *Philadelphia, Will and Grace, Queer Eye for the Straight Guy, Rent,* and *Brokeback Mountain*—a number of voices have been raised to support Warner's protest against this desexualizing of gay men. I have contributed to that critique myself, and I am not going to belabor those earlier arguments here.[11] The case, I believe, has been well made, even if the consensus in its favor is not as broad as I would like it to be.

Instead, I now have a different, almost an opposite point to make. I'm going to argue that the transformation of homosexuality from a sexual perversion into a social identity, and the political requirements of gay pride, have tended to militate against any serious gay inquiry into the inner life of homosexuality—especially those *non-sexual* dimensions of it that gay people are still unsure or nervous about. Gay subjectivity, and the distinctive cultural practices that manifest it, may now have become just as disreputable, just as taboo, as queer sex. One name for this strategic avoidance of gay subjectivity, for this refusal to explore it, is, quite simply, "gay identity." Or, at least, gay identity functions in that way when it is taken to be an elemental, primary term, a term with no component parts and no subjective dimensions, a term that has to be accepted at face value and admits of no further analysis. Gay people simply exist. Some people are gay. I have a gay identity. And that's that. (You got a problem with that?)

Well, yes, actually, I do have a problem with it. Not, obviously, with the fact that some people are gay. And not just with the way that gay identity often ends up closeting sexuality (though I do share Warner's concern and I fully endorse his critique). After all, gay identity does at least acknowledge gay sexuality to the extent that it insists on same-sex sexual attraction as the defining feature of gay identity, and it does provide a social basis on which we can assert pride in our sexual relationships and sexual subjectivities. My basic problem with the political functioning of gay identity nowadays is that in the course of claiming public recognition and acceptance of the fact of homosexual *desire* (sometimes at the expense of gay sex, to be sure), the official gay and lesbian movement has effectively foreclosed inquiry into queer sensibility, style, emotion, or any specific, non-sexual form of queer *subjectivity* or *affect* or *pleasure*.

That suppression once served a crucial political purpose: it was only by deemphasizing how queerly we felt, and by denying how culturally different we were from straight people, that we were able to expunge from homosexuality the taint of abnormality and to shrug off the heavy burden of psychopathology, of sickness. Now the imperative to deny our difference is less urgent than it once was. So why are we still so skittish? Our avoidance is all the more puzzling insofar as it perpetrates a grave slander against us: it implies that we are just like everybody else. And so it obscures the very things about gay life and gay culture that make them interesting and valuable. It denies the unique genius in being queer.

⚭

This habit of foregrounding identity and backgrounding subjectivity has not always felt like a constraint. The promotion of gay identities at the expense of gay subjectivities could be more easily tolerated during the 1980s and early 1990s, when that protective tendency seemed to reflect the urgent demands of a catastrophic political situation.

With the rise of the New Right, the increasing devastation of HIV/ AIDS, the newly fashionable homophobia unleashed by the moral panic surrounding the epidemic, and the failure of most governments to respond effectively to the medical disaster overtaking their own citizens, the understandable impulse of the gay movement was to insist on our survival as a people, to defend ourselves as *members of a group* that was at great *collective* risk. And so we strove to highlight our common belonging to various social and ethnic identity-categories and we sought to play down those subjective dimensions of homosexuality, as well as those distinctive features of gay male culture—to say nothing of the emotional and erotic specificities of queer existence—which in the minds of many people were responsible for the spread of HIV in the first place.

If gay men did not feel terribly constrained by that bracketing of emotion, sensibility, affect, and the felt difference of their lived experiences, if the overwhelmingly *political* representations of gayness as a collective social identity during this period did not strike them as particularly oppressive, that was due to a second, more subtle factor. Gay subjectivity, far from having been silenced, seemed everywhere to be triumphant. The public gay response to HIV/AIDS, after all, was positively drenched in affect. Or, rather, it was drenched in two specific affects—grief and anger—accompanied and amplified by their corollary public expressions: mourning and militancy.[12]

Grief and anger, however, though they were undeniably passionate emotions, were also politically righteous emotions. They expressed not individual sensibility but the personal experience of collective devastation. The more personal they were, the more exemplary they could come to seem—exemplary of gay men's suffering, loss, and victimization *as a group.*

So grief and anger, far from being discreditable affects, were politically imperative ones, affects we were politically committed to having. In that sense, grief and anger were not individualizing or personalizing, however individual or personal they might also be; they didn't reduce to matters of private subjecthood, if that was defined by a unique, unshareable interiority. Far from being limited to the personal, grief and anger propelled gay identity further into the public sphere. They increased its human dignity and they accelerated its transformation into a publicly claimable identity, deserving of recognition, acceptance, and protection. There was no political tension between the emotions of anger and grief and the demands of political visibility.

There were, however, some queer emotions that gay people were not supposed to have, and that were not politically respectable.[13] Leading gay writers and intellectuals, such as Larry Kramer and Paul Monette, made the distinction very clear.[14] Bad gay emotions included narcissism, shame, self-loathing, passivity, sentimentality, cowardice, and supposedly destructive (by which was often meant "promiscuous") forms of sexuality. Unlike grief and anger, these emotions were *merely* personal, in the sense that they expressed not group identity but individual failings. They even implied pathology: they symptomatized the lingering effects of the injuries we had suffered during the previous centuries of societal oppression, effects from which we had insufficiently liberated ourselves. HIV/AIDS no longer permitted us the luxury of incomplete political identification, the luxury of not struggling for psychic decolonization. The enemy was not only in the corridors of power, but also in our souls ("Hitler in my heart," as Antony Hegarty, the lead singer of the group Antony and the Johnsons, put it many years later). It was more than ever necessary to rid ourselves of whatever affects prevented us from coming together collectively in a newly militant and even militarized movement. This was not the moment to celebrate the anti-social, self-indulgent queer pleasures of narcissism and passivity.[15]

Part of what distinguished good gay emotion from bad gay emotion, then, was that the good kind was not personally or psychologically revealing. Anger and grief could be publicly claimed and acted out precisely because they did not express some peculiar, individual, personal, and possibly pathological inward condition afflicting gay men. Rather, they expressed our collective situation of political oppression and resistance, our collective victimization by an epidemic and by a society that smugly watched it happen. They also expressed our refusal to go quietly, to keep our suffering out of the public eye, to hide our sexuality, to closet our relationships, to let our oppressors off the hook.

As such, feelings of anger and grief did not need to be denied. After all, they originated not in our damaged psyches, but in our objective, beleaguered situation. They were psychological responses to an external threat, an external devastation—a reaction to a calamity that had been visited upon us from outside ourselves. They were a *healthy* response to loss.

HIV/AIDS was precisely *not* the inner truth of male homosexuality, not the outward and visible sign of an inward or spiritual illness, not the punishment of gay sin or gay crime, not what we had asked for. Hence the characteristic political tactic of turning our grief into anger, our mourning into militancy. The point was to express our personal and collective insistence that HIV/AIDS was a public-health catastrophe, exacerbated by indifference and homophobia, not the working-out of the inner logic of male homosexuality itself. It was a terrible historical accident, and it had nothing to do with us or with who we were—and so our emotional response to it also had nothing to do with us, or with who we were as gay men, except insofar as we were being collectively blamed for the very epidemic of which we were the victims.

In the long shadow of the HIV/AIDS epidemic, it has been possible for gay men to dodge the awareness of having imposed a blackout on the expression or investigation of queer affect. After all, gay life has long been saturated with affect, soaked in tears and suffused with rage. Now that HIV/AIDS activism, though not HIV/AIDS itself, has been receding from the forefront of gay male life, at least among White people in the developed world, now that the political requirements of HIV/AIDS activism are changing, now that grief and anger are starting to lose their monopoly on the range of queer affects that can be openly expressed, and now that queer culture is reinventing continuities between contemporary lesbian and gay existence and earlier, pre-Stonewall forms of sexual outlawry, it seems increasingly possible to inquire into aspects or dimensions of the inner life of homosexuality that not so long ago seemed politically dubious, not to say unpalatable—and, in any case, off limits to detailed exploration.[16]

HOMOSEXUALITY'S CLOSET

*C*ontemporary gay culture has been slow to seize its newfound opportunity to explore the inner life of homosexuality. When questions about the distinctive features of gay male subjectivity are raised, even inadvertently, the typical response is to silence them. Nevertheless, this censorship, though automatic, is usually not so quick or so total as to prevent us from getting a glimpse of the various queer affects that are hurriedly being shoved back into the closet. It is therefore possible to form an idea of the purpose behind the clampdown—and to figure out what in particular is being so actively and so anxiously defended against by means of it.

Consider a typical example, chosen almost at random. In the "Arts and Leisure" section of the *New York Times* on Sunday, October 29, 2000, Anthony Tommasini, the paper's main classical-music critic, who is an openly gay man, published a story about David Daniels, the celebrated countertenor, who at the time was still a young and up-and-coming performer.[1] Having just released a magnificent recording of Handel's *Rinaldo* with Cecilia Bartoli, Daniels was about to perform the title role in a new and much-anticipated production at the New York City Opera. As Tommasini noted, though in much more guarded terms, Daniels had once been a struggling tenor who occasionally delivered impromptu operatic performances at gay parties, where he sang female parts in a high falsetto voice. After undergoing psychotherapy—which appears to have worked only too well, as we shall see—Daniels decided in 1992 to come out . . . as a countertenor, and to pursue a serious musical career by means of the voice he had previously used only to provide his friends with camp entertainment.

Daniels quickly established himself by singing operatic roles originally written for the high, powerful voices of seventeenth- and eighteenth-century *castrati* (male singers who had been castrated as boys so as to preserve their soprano vocal register and to qualify them for life-long careers as performers in single-sex church choirs). For the past hundred and fifty years, right up until very recently, such roles have always been sung by women. But Daniels did not stop there. Retaining his love for vocal music of the later, Romantic period, and even the twentieth century, he daringly recorded a number of songs and arias written expressly for the female voice and customarily performed only by sopranos.[2]

Of course, Daniels is not the first gay man to take pleasure in singing, if only to himself, great works from the female vocal repertory, as any opera queen will tell you (and in the gay world nowadays, perhaps no one but an opera queen would be willing to make such an embarrassing admission). But he is exceptional in establishing an artistic reputation among the general concert-going public by singing works that are normally off-limits to male performers.

There are of course some countertenors who are straight. But they are relatively few and far between. Something about the particular quality of the sound one is required to produce, and about the social meanings ascribed to the kind of voice required to produce it, seems to attract gay male singers—or to bring out a male singer's queer potential. In any case, David Daniels is no exception. Despite being "a young, virile male," according to Tommasini, who is "sturdily built," "exudes a square-shouldered masculine confidence," loves to play basketball, and "can often be found in the park, elbowing fellow players in a pickup game," he turns out, sure enough, to be a fag. Or rather, as our newspaper of record and its out-of-the-closet music critic put it, "he is an openly gay male, who readily admits to keeping his beard short and scruffy not out of macho display but because it gives him 'some semblance of a jaw line' and because his 'other half' likes it." That description keeps the accent firmly on gay identity, on gayness as same-sex desire. Gay identity is expressed here by a light-hearted adherence to masculine gender norms, as well as by a proper if modest pride in one's appearance, while same-sex desire makes itself visible in the respectable form of a conjugal relationship (Daniels does in fact wear a wedding ring, at least when he is giving recitals).

☙❧

So why does he sing so funny? He seems virtually normal. Is there actually something wrong with him? Might there be any connection, of any sort, between being gay and "the gender-blurring ambiguity of the voice"—or the fact that, "when he starts to sing, his alto voice has a tender beauty that seems classically feminine"? Is Daniels just a big queen, a fairy, a gay cliché after all?

For all the trouble Tommasini takes to shatter those very stereotypes, by emphasizing so pointedly and heavy-handedly Daniels's virility, physical sturdiness, square shoulders, masculine confidence, and (did he really have to go that far?) passion for team sports, he still can't seem to help trafficking in all the usual signifiers of gayness, all those tired equations of homosexuality with gender deviance, effeminacy, and masculine lack, invoking everything from "ambiguity" to "gender-blurring" to androgyny to castration to femininity. We are clearly not so far removed from the ancient association of homosexuality with gender inversion and psychological deviance after all, even if Tommasini is careful in the end to drain those gay signifiers of all significance. "To Mr. Daniels, the way he sings feels perfectly natural," Tommasini insists, though by the time he makes that remark it is rather too late for a return to innocent naturalness—too late to put the queer cat back into the bag of gay normality.

Still, the purpose behind Tommasini's belated insistence on Daniels's sense of his own perfect naturalness (hard-won, admittedly, through years of therapy) is to conjure away all those ghoulish phantoms of gay psychopathology and gender deviance that Tommasini's own uneasy obsession with Daniels's queer musical persona had called up in the first place. Tommasini's point is that Daniels may be unusual, but please don't conclude that he is perverse. No, he was born that way, and—for him, at least—singing like a woman is normal. End of story. Although "Mr. Daniels knows that in his case [his gender-deviant singing] is given extra resonance" by the fact that he's gay, that resonance is quickly deprived by Tommasini of any possible, well, resonance. "While acknowledging that an androgynous quality is built into a countertenor voice, Mr. Daniels said he doesn't think about it."

And indeed he doesn't, at least to judge by what he is quoted as saying in Tommasini's article. Daniels admits that his practice of performing the female vocal repertory without resexing the pronouns in the texts of the songs he sings is something that a heterosexual performer would be less likely to do—but that just seems to mean that the only thing about gayness that counts for him is sexual object-choice, the directionality of erotic desire, its homosexual focus, the maleness of the male love-object. It is, apparently, *not* a question of sensibility, or affect, or identification, or pleasure, or subjective positioning, or gender dissonance, let alone a relation to femininity. It is not even a matter of cultural practice. The fact that Daniels was a gay performer before he was a professional countertenor, or that he claimed a public gay identity by becoming a countertenor, yields no information at all about any possible relations among his voice, his performance, and his gayness, and it throws no light on the connections between musicality and sexuality.[3]

Singing the female vocal repertory is no more indicative of Daniels's subjectivity, finally, than playing basketball: they're both just *fun activities* that ultimately tell us nothing about the individual who takes part in them. And, anyway, "reality in the theater . . . is never literal," Daniels says. No wonder, then, as Tommasini points out in the opening line of his article, that "David Daniels hates the term 'falsetto.'"

౸౨

I don't mean to sound like I have a personal gripe with David Daniels. I don't blame him one bit, in fact, for being cagey, if that's actually what he's up to. Tommasini's article alone provides all the justification anyone could ever want for such wariness: it indicates exactly why gay men would be well advised to think twice before using the *New York Times* as a vehicle for exploring the emotional or erotic meaning of their feminine identifications. Indeed, there is something representative about the way the *Times* article insistently constructs a connection between Daniels's gender-blurring, on the one hand, and his homosexuality, on the other, while following Daniels's lead in refusing to acknowledge any substantive relation between the two. In part, this is simply a classic instance of journalistic innuendo: the article's presumption that "we all know what *that* means" exempts it from having to claim that *that* means anything at all. Tommasini's rhetoric simply reflects and reveals the current conditions under which gay people typically gain admittance to the public sphere—and to the official discourse of the news in particular: our difference from normal folk is at once hyped and disavowed.

But we can get a better idea of the entity being closeted here by noticing what it is that the article refuses to name except by implication.

The target of the article's elaborate mobilization of suggestion, connotation, association, and sexual coding is no longer homosexuality, as it would have been back in the Bad Old Days.[4] At least it is no longer homosexuality *if by homosexuality we mean same-sex erotic desire and same-sex sexual object-choice.* After all, those are the very things that both the gay countertenor and his gay critic are happy to acknowledge openly and explicitly.

What remains unspoken, and what is therefore constantly, insistently *implied*, is the woman's soul supposedly enclosed in David Daniels's male body—the secret, inchoate transgendered condition evidenced by his high-pitched singing and by his paradoxical combination of masculine and feminine attributes, patterns of feeling, and personae. The closet operates here to conceal not *homosexuality as identity or desire* but *homosexuality as queer affect, sensibility, subjectivity, identification, pleasure, habitus, gender style.*

What remains literally unspeakable is no longer the love that dare not speak its name. Daniels and Tommasini are quite happy to talk about *that*. Instead, it is a less classifiable but still quite specific dimension of faggotry: whatever it is in particular that accounts for why so many countertenors are gay.

After all, no one—no gay man, anyway—who has heard David Daniels sing, or who has listened to his recording of Romantic art songs written for the soprano voice, could fail to discern *some* connection between his appropriation of the female vocal repertory and the queer form of emotional life that often seems to accompany homosexuality. What is the nature of that connection? Is there any meaningful relation that links the cultural practice of singing countertenor roles to a pattern of affect, to a particular way of feeling, and that links either or both to homosexuality?

Don't ask Daniels. Don't ask Tommasini. Don't ask the *Times*. And don't ask gay men.

No one is talking.

∽ 5 ∽

WHAT'S GAYER THAN GAY?

$\mathscr{T}$o be fair to Daniels and Tommasini, no one in queer studies is talking, either. At least, no one seems to be in much of a hurry to tackle these questions.

There has in fact been a tacit understanding on the part of many of us who work in the field of queer studies that matters of gay subjectivity are best left unexamined. Perhaps we worry that we wouldn't like what we would find. Perhaps we fear that whatever we did find would be used against us. (As it surely would be, so those fears are hardly groundless.) Speaking about how queer studies has treated material dating back to the Bad Old Days of pre-liberation lesbian and gay male life, Heather Love makes a similar point about the field's instinctive reflex of refusal and avoidance. "Although critics have been attentive, especially in the last couple of decades, to the importance of shame, violence, and stigma in the historical record, certain forms of [queer] experience still remain off limits for most. These are representations that offer too stark an image of the losses of queer history. What has resulted is a disavowal of crucial aspects of this history and of the conditions of queer existence in the present."[1]

In the case of queer subjectivity, this reflex of disavowal makes itself felt in a different form: the only kind of subjectivity that qualifies for "serious" lesbian and gay analysis is that which can be safely theorized in the register of psychoanalytic abstraction. Which is a procedure so conventional, so speculative, so detached from the daily practices of queer life, and so personally uninvolving, that it no longer has the capacity to unsettle anyone. In fact, psychoanalysis continues to be the privileged method within queer studies, as within cultural studies in general, for thinking about the workings of human subjectivity. But psychoanalysis—as I have argued at length in *What Do Gay Men Want?*—is not useful for understanding the collective subjectivity of specific social groups.

It is a psychoanalytic truism, of course, that desire exceeds identity, that identity does not and cannot capture the boundless play of desire. So psychoanalysis is hardly incompatible with the argument being put forward here. If I avoid couching this argument in psychoanalytic terms, that is first of all because I don't need to do it, since I have plenty of concrete evidence on which to base my conclusions. I much prefer to make my case by looking closely at the social phenomena themselves—by performing a close reading of cultural objects or undertaking a thick description of queer cultural practices—rather than by appealing to the authority of any preexisting theory or doctrine. And I am wary in general of replacing descriptions with interpretations, concrete objects and practices with "a shadow world of 'meanings,'" thereby refusing to see social phenomena for what they are in themselves, in all their particularity, and ignoring what is there to be observed.[2]

Second, when psychoanalytic thinkers advance their claim about desire exceeding identity, the main purpose, or outcome, is to destabilize heterosexual identity, *to free heterosexuality from identity*—a procedure whose effect is ultimately not to undermine but to promote and to universalize heterosexuality.[3] (Some queer theorists similarly invoke psychoanalysis to cast doubt on the reality of gay sexual orientation: the result, however, is not to reverse that heterosexist effect but to deepen it.) I choose to take a different route, and to dramatize the limits of gay male identity by attending to the cultural practices and life experiences of gay subjects themselves.

🙰

One of the few people in the world of queer studies who *is* talking is D. A. Miller. In an extraordinary 1998 book called *Place for Us,* Miller sets out to explore gay male subjectivity through an analysis of gay men's pleasures and cultural practices—specifically, their emotional investments in the Broadway musical. And he comes to the conclusion that I have taken as the starting point for this part of my argument—namely, that gay male desire cannot be reduced to gay identity, to gayness *as* identity. Gay identity is therefore not adequate to the expression of gay subjectivity. This insight, I now believe, not only constitutes a theoretical breakthrough; it also explains why so many cultural practices characteristic of male homosexuality extend beyond the realm of gay sex—be they singing in falsetto or flower-arranging, diva-worship or interior design.

Or, for that matter, the cult of Broadway musicals. That gay men love Broadway musicals is of course a cliché, a stereotype.[4] As John Clum says in his own book about the gayness of the Broadway musical, "It is a stereotype that gay men have been particularly invested in musical theater, indeed that love of musical theater is a sign of gayness" (29). But the mere fact that such a notion is a stereotype doesn't mean it's untrue. "Like all stereotypes, it is problematic," Clum allows, "at best partially accurate, and it may be generational, though if my [drama] students are any indicator, it continues to have some validity" (5).[5] To call it a stereotype, then, is neither to refute it nor to grasp its significance. And merely to expose it as a stereotype is not to disable its efficacy or to diminish its power. Just as straight men who like Broadway musicals have to expend quantities of effort in order to overcome the skepticism that naturally greets their claims to heterosexuality, as Miller points out, so, in the case of gay men, "though not all" or "even most . . . are in love with Broadway, those who aren't are hardly quit of the stereotype that insists they are."[6]

A stereotype doesn't have to be generally valid in order to contain some truth.[7] The problem is that whatever truth it does contain is made available to us, Miller observes, "only in the short-circuited form of a joke" (66). Whose effect is to foreclose, almost instantaneously, any potential insight or recognition that the stereotype fleetingly affords, thereby rendering the truth behind it inaccessible to serious thought. In this way, whatever truths may be reflected in stereotypes become impossible to specify and to analyze. Or so Miller laments. But he remains undeterred in his effort to locate those truths, and in particular to uncover the social and emotional logic that identifies gay men with Broadway in the popular mind, as well as in gay culture and the lived experience of many gay men.

The result has much to tell us about the relation of gay desire to aesthetic form, of sexuality to culture. So Miller's analysis merits our sustained attention.

☯

"In the psyche of post-Stonewall man," Miller begins, "the Broadway musical lies like a nervously watched pod that, having been preserved from a past geological epoch, may nonetheless—say, at any temperature above frigidity—split open to reveal a creature that, in comparison with the less primitive forms of life around it, even with those which must have evolved from it, will appear monstrous beyond recognition" (26). By "post-Stonewall man," Miller refers not only to those gay men who grew up after the Stonewall riots. He also refers to those men, like himself, who had come of age before Stonewall— when the Broadway musical was still a living cultural form,[8] and a public gay male culture did not yet exist—and who were so thoroughly and improbably transformed by their experience of gay liberation that it gradually came to seem "perfectly ordinary that I, of all people," as Miller remarks, "should frequent the company of men wearing weight belts, or nipple rings, and utterly strange not only that I should still be hearing music I have known since I was a child, but also that there should be others, many of these men among them, in the same strange situation as myself" (23–24). The changes in Miller's society, and in the conditions of his sexual and emotional life, have been so momentous that what stand out as bizarre, and cry out for explanation, are not the flamboyant contrasts with the past but the dogged continuities—the persistent power and appeal of the world of feeling he had known before he could even imagine the transformative possibility of gay pride, before he could succeed in claiming and inhabiting a gay identity.

The music that Miller had known since he was a child is not just any old music. It is music that belongs to "the only [gay genre] that mass culture ever produced" (16). The golden-age, definitive version of the Broadway musical was "entirely the conception of four gay men" and therefore the only "general cultural phenomenon" with a gay male following *at whose creation gay men were indisputably present—* unlike, in other words, grand opera or *All about Eve* (39). Yet in Miller's eyes, that gay presence is merely a sign of *the musical's intrinsic gayness as a form:* it may be a contributing cause of the musical's gayness, but it is not the complete explanation for it.

What is it, then, that explains the nature of the Broadway musical's gay appeal? And why does the inner life of male homosexuality that finds expression in gay men's notoriously passionate attachment to the Broadway musical now appear so strange, indeed so monstrous, in the eyes of contemporary gay men, whether they are survivors from the pre-Stonewall era, relatively recent products of the post-Stonewall era, or both? Miller suggests that it is the outmoded brands of sentimentality mobilized by the Broadway musical that have come to mark it as defining an immature and now-outgrown stage in the development of the gay male subject. In fact, it is precisely because the Broadway musical's appeal is rooted in the emotional vicissitudes of pre-Stonewall gay *childhood* that the affects connected with it occasion nowadays so much adult embarrassment. Those affects date back to a time before an achieved gay life or a mature sexual existence was conceivable, and their intrinsically archaic character expresses a retrograde state of feeling, even as their persistence in the inner life of the adult gay man signals his humiliating failure to evolve beyond it.

If the Broadway musical had a formative impact on the character, outlook, taste, and overall sentimental makeup of the proto-gay child growing up in the 1950s, that is because it afforded him a figurative language in which to give systematic and limpid expression to "those early *pre-sexual* realities of *gay* experience" that shaped his subjective existence in that hostile environment (26; I have added italics to bring out Miller's insistence that there can be gay experience before sex— that since "gay experience" includes many dimensions of subjective life beyond same-sex eroticism, it is possible to attribute a specifically gay experience to a child who has yet to form any clear idea of the eventual orientation of his sexual desire). The continuing appeal of the Broadway musical to gay men nowadays is therefore highly discreditable. Not only does it betoken gay men's refusal to transcend their abject origins; it also registers the continuing satisfaction they take in childish queer pleasures that don't come directly from gay sex—the sole source from which specifically *gay* pleasure, gay identity-based pleasure, ought to come, or so we now like to think.

Even worse, the particular queer pleasure that the Broadway musical still affords certain gay men is one that the sex they are now able to have does not provide. It is a pleasure that sexual fulfillment has not rendered obsolete. And, worst of all, this distressing state of affairs, archaic though it clearly is, continues to the present day. For it appears that the same "early pre-sexual realities of gay experience" persist in shaping the subjective existence of at least some proto-gay children now, even in the comparatively enlightened period following the world-historical event called Stonewall. That makes the gay male cult of the Broadway musical a perennial embarrassment to contemporary gay identity, which insists on being grounded entirely in a sexual orientation—not in a lifestyle, a subculture, a pattern of affect, or a subjectivity.[9]

What are those early presexual realities of gay experience that adult gay men today are supposed to have outgrown? Miller identifies three related queer affects that the gay cult of the Broadway musical once expressed, distilled, preserved, and now mercilessly exposes to view: (1) "the solitude, shame, secretiveness by which the impossibility of social integration was first internalized"; (2) "the excessive sentimentality that was the necessary condition of sentiments allowed no real object"; and (3) "the intense, senseless *joy* that, while not identical to these destitutions, is neither extricable from them" (26). Those queer affects constitute elements or aspects of gay male subjectivity that, at least for gay men of a certain background and generation, took abiding shape early in their subjective lives. The persistence and prominence of such queer affects in the inner lives of adult gay men help to explain why gay subjectivity cannot be reduced to homosexual desire or to gay identity.

What makes those queer affects look so grotesque nowadays is not just how pathetic, pitiable, dreary, or politically outdated they may be in themselves, but also how systematically they have been excluded from gay expression by the once-unimaginable gay identity and gay pride that have supplanted the very exclusions and social impossibilities that produced them. "Precisely against such [pre-sexual] realities [of gay experience]," Miller argues, "is post-Stonewall gay identity defined: a declarable, dignified thing, rooted in a community, and taking manifestly sexual pleasures on this affirmative basis" (26). Now that we have gay identity, now that we have gay sex, what on earth would we still want with the Broadway musical? Official, public, out-and-proud gay identity has no tolerance for shame, solitude, secretiveness, and no patience for those who choose to wallow either in an abject state of emotional isolation or in the compensatory, manic joys of a solitary queer fantasy life.

Nowadays, proud gay men do not ground their identity in their loneliness, lovelessness, hopelessness, isolation, and sentimentality. Quite the opposite. We fashion a gay self (to the extent that we do) by proudly affirming a common, collective gay identity, claiming this gay identity openly, visibly, unashamedly, and communally, constructing on that basis a shared culture and society—full of opportunities for emotional and erotic expression—and thereby attaining to a *healthy* gay sexuality, defined by our eroticization of other gay men *as* gay, and ultimately crowned by the successful achievement of a *relation-*

ship. And, by the way, we don't want to be reminded that 'twas not ever thus.

Miller is not nostalgic, of course. "No gay man could possibly regret the trade" of pre-Stonewall gay abjection for post-Stonewall gay pride, he acknowledges. No gay man "could do anything but be grateful for it—if, that is, *it actually were a trade*" (26; italics added). The problem, it turns out, is that instead of winding up in triumphant possession of a gay pride and freedom that we can wholeheartedly call our own, we have constructed a gay identity that actively *represses* both the pathos and the pleasure of those residual queer affects that we prefer to think we have liberated ourselves from and that we claim have simply vanished from our consciousness. Instead of transcending the secret shame and solitary pleasures of our sentimentality, as we would like to think, we have assiduously closeted them.

For example, back in the Bad Old Days, Miller observes, a gay man had to be careful to hide his physique magazines in the closet. What was acceptable to display in one's living room, by contrast, was one's collection of playbills and original-cast Broadway musical albums. Nowadays it is fashionable—or, at least, it was fashionable in the comparatively defiant gay male culture of the 1980s and 1990s, when Miller was writing—for a gay man to manifest his gay pride, his sexual liberation, by keeping his stash of gay porn visibly exposed next to his bed, along with various other erotic accessories. But that does not mean that his closet lost its previous function. On the contrary. That closet now serves to hide his old collection of original-cast albums— if their owner has not taken the further precaution of jettisoning them altogether (26–27). After all, no gay man acquires social or erotic credit by coming off as a show queen.

ଡ଼ଠ

Or so Miller discovered when he made the mistake of using an original-cast album of *South Pacific* as a courting-gift. It turns out that there's no quicker or surer way to put an end to a budding romance. The reasons for that are revealing. For they indicate the gulf that separates gay subjectivity from gay identity—and that correspondingly divides gay culture from gay sex, gay desire from the desire for an actual relationship with a man.

Miller recounts that he once gave a tape of *South Pacific* to a guy with whom he was secretly in love, a tape that reproduced the surface noise of the vinyl record he had possessed since he was a child—noise that became especially noticeable during "Some Enchanted Evening," the track he had evidently played most often and the one to which he wanted particularly to call his love-object's attention.

If that ploy was what Miller had supposed would work, or would constitute a romantic lure, he was swiftly disappointed. His strategy proved to be a disaster, in fact, precisely because it turned out to be a success.

> On the following day, as he thanked me for the music, with an even politeness that to my ear couldn't help diminishing the "great enjoyment" professed by his words, he added with a laugh, as between friends who shared exactly the same viewpoint on things: "How awful, though, to end up some old queen in a piano bar watering your drink every time they played 'Some Enchanted Evening'!" Would it have done me any good if I had known at the time—what I did not learn until several years later—that by his own account he had burst into "hysterical sobbing" as soon as, through my good offices, he heard the very first bars of the song for which, a day after, he would convey to me his thorough contempt? As strange as it seems, I had always had a presentiment that my gift, on which I set great hopes, would prove futile. For I was attempting to impart to him that *homosexuality of one* which—even had he accepted it, or were himself to return the favor—must have restrained either of us from ever joining the other across a crowded room. (22–23)[10]

Gay desire typically seeks fulfillment, and finds it, in solitary queer pleasure. That is why gay desire is often the enemy of gay sociality. The emotions that gay men invest in the Broadway musical, like the emotions released by it, are best savored all by oneself. They are at home in privacy, secrecy, isolation, loneliness, and fantasy. The soli-

tude in which they flourish is not a sign of their fragility, but a testimony to their stubborn autonomy. For that solitude is where they
have maintained themselves, and maintained their hold on the gay
subject, since childhood. No wonder, then, that the pleasures bound
up with these solitary transports remain entirely sufficient to themselves and require no supplementation from external sources, such as
other people. No wonder that they are positively refractory to sexual
exchange. They are not about being with anyone else. They are about
being all alone with your dreams.

Those dreams may take the form of longing for a boyfriend, but
they get in the way of having one. That continues to be true even in
our more enlightened age, despite the availability of gay identity, the
comparative acceptance of gay sexuality, and the visibility of gay relationships.

For example, it was the case for many years that gay men looking
for partners on the Internet would attach the poster from *Brokeback
Mountain* to their profiles. In so doing, they betrayed emotional instincts every bit as much at cross-purposes with their ostensible goals
as D. A. Miller's were when he thought he could acquire a boyfriend
by giving him that old recording of "Some Enchanted Evening." For
what is the point of such a gesture if not to impart to your prospective love-objects a "homosexuality of one"?

Far from inviting another person to join you in romantic bliss, far
from announcing to your suitors that you have learned the lesson of
the film, opened your soul to the possibility of gay love, and made
room in your life for someone to share it with, the invocation of
Brokeback Mountain indicates that you have no need or place in your
life for anyone else, because your inner world is fully occupied by the
gay romance you are already living out in it with utter and complete
sufficiency. You have so thoroughly anticipated your ideal relationship, along with the enchanted evening on which you will meet the
love of your life across a crowded room, bar, or webpage, that you are
in fact unable to accommodate the real thing. Which is just as well,
since no actual relationship could possibly equal the satisfactions of

the imaginary romance you have been fervently enjoying in the solitude of your own imagination, in the isolation of your singular homosexuality.

ೲ

Broadway, then, is not something that modern gay pride can be proud
of. Because this kind of gay culture, as we'll see in Chapter 10, is so
inimical to gay eroticism, so deflating of sexual intensity, so antagonistic to the displays of stolid virility that solicit gay male sexual desire, it produces widespread aversion on the part of gay men, at least
when they want to appear modern instead of archaic—that is, when
they wish to present themselves as sexual subjects and objects.

In fact, to judge from the evidence we have reviewed so far, gay
men nowadays have a tendency to treat the Broadway musical—or
Judy Garland, or Barbra Streisand, or grand opera, or any of the other
cultural artifacts that supposedly encode similar forms of archaic
gay male sentiment—with phobic rejection, avoidance, repudiation.[11]
Like D. A. Miller's polite but skittish love-object, gay men pride themselves on their easy and casual contempt for such artifacts, enjoying
the social and erotic credit they get by denouncing them, keeping
them at arm's length, and disclaiming all personal susceptibility to
them. What is more, gay men often dis-identify from such artifacts
even or especially when they are profoundly moved by them. Or pro-
fessionally involved in producing them.

For all his love of the Broadway musical, or indeed because of it,
Miller himself was hardly immune to that tendency. On discovering
that a man he was dating not only owned some recordings of Broadway musicals, but had actually amassed a *collection* of them, Miller
suddenly heard himself exclaim,

"My God, you really *are* gay." By which I must have been expressing,
not my amazement at the sexual orientation of my new friend, already established to my complete satisfaction, but my suddenly altered sense of his standing *within* the gay milieu, as in a strange sort of

swimming pool where such acts of grown-up sex as we had been intending to perform took place at the shallow end, with little danger
that, from whatever positions we came to assume, we couldn't at a
moment's notice recover our land legs, while the kid stuff like listening to Broadway albums . . . had required him to submit to a nearly
total immersion in what my first phobic ejaculation confirmed was
pretty deep water. (22)

Pointing as it does to a formative, isolating experience of unshareable
sentimentality, the queer appeal of the Broadway musical—which
takes the gay subject back to its presexual but ecstatic enjoyment of
"kid stuff" and to all the shameful, embarrassing emotional vicissitudes of its solitary childhood—is much harder, much hotter for gay
men to handle than the identity-affirming adult pleasures of gay sex.
To which pleasures, Miller implies, the Broadway musical, and the
delights of listening to it, would seem to be inexorably and implaca-
bly fatal.

In short, post-Stonewall gay man, Miller suggests, tends to treat
any cultural practice that may betray his archaic queer emotions, and
thus reveal the affective structure of his early subjective formation,
very much the same way as "the general culture around him perse-
cutes and tolerates . . . his own homosexuality" (27). According to
Miller, in other words, the Broadway musical and the discreditable
sentimentality it encodes have come to signify to gay men the sort of
shameful interiority that *homosexuality itself* once represented.

"Homosexuality" and "Broadway" have now traded places. As homosexuality has become increasingly public and dignified, the life
of queer affect and feeling has become more and more demonized,
more and more impossible to express openly, to explore, to celebrate.
It has become an embarrassment. And so, like those playbills and
original-cast Broadway musical albums, once proudly displayed and
now hidden away, it has been closeted. Not because we are ashamed
of our homosexuality, but because official post-Stonewall homosexuality is ashamed of our cultural practices and the distinctive pleasures
they afford. With the result that queer feeling and queer subjectivity

are what gay men nowadays routinely disavow, consigning them to a zone that effectively functions as *homosexuality's closet.*

Which is exactly what Anthony Tommasini and David Daniels demonstrated.

೧೦

Miller was determined to open homosexuality's closet door by at least a good crack or two. He proceeded to do so by means of literary and social analysis, demonstrating that it is possible to approach gay male subjectivity without recourse to ego psychology. If we return to examine the three instances of queer subjectivity that Miller ascribed to the proto-gay male child of the 1950s and that he identified as "early pre-sexual realities of gay experience," we find that they consist not in aspects of an originary pathological formation, but in psychic inscriptions upon the subject of the pathogenic consequences of living in a homophobic social world. The affects involved are not specific to the individual: they are collective and generic.

For example, "the excessive sentimentality that was the necessary condition of sentiments allowed no real object" points not to some typical or characteristic or distinctive identifying feature of gay male subjectivity *per se,* but to the particular effects on the psychic life of the Cold War–era gay male subject of his compulsory membership in a society that made the merest possibility of openly expressing same-sex desire or gender dissidence unimaginable and inconceivable, let alone the possibility of acting on it and making it a prominent, public part of daily life.

Similarly, since the Broadway musical flourished at a historical moment when nothing specifically gay could be allowed to enter the realm of mass public representation, and since the gay men who created it could do so only by engineering the systematic and absolute exclusion of their own sexual identity from visibility within it, the proto-gay response to the particular gayness of the Broadway musical necessarily involved an awareness of the systematic and absolute exclusion of gay male identity from overt recognition within the musi-

cal itself. That awareness was not simply a recognition of the absence
of gay men as such from the scene of cultural origination, but a realization of the hopelessness of their ever being acknowledged *under
that description* by the cultural forms that they themselves had created—and thus an awareness of the utter hopelessness of any social acknowledgment of gay identity (32–39). The Broadway musical
thereby taught its proto-gay adepts that their responsiveness to the
gayness of the genre could be expressed only on the condition of
their isolation and concealment.

> [No boy was] ever so overwhelmed by his passion [for the Broadway
> musical] that he forgot to manage the secrecy in which he indulged it,
> or if he did, if once . . . he was by some chance distracted enough to
> omit to draw the curtains on his performance [i.e., singing and danc-
> ing along with original-cast Broadway albums], so that other boys in
> the neighborhood had been able to catch him in the act of vibrating
> sympathetically to the numbers that neither he nor they had ever seen,
> he soon understood—that is to say, too late—that his sense of embar-
> rassment had been given to him, like the gag reflex in his throat, to
> warn against the social humiliation that must ensue if he were such a
> cockeyed optimist as not to heed it. (11)

The practice of listening to, and singing along with, recordings of
Broadway musicals taught those who enjoyed that activity a cautionary lesson in shame, imparting to them an awareness of the impossibility of ever translating gay desire and gay sentiment into public
expression or into a socially viable reality—as well as an acute consciousness of the danger involved in even trying. It is in that sense
that the Broadway musical itself has come to stand, as Miller puts it,
for "the solitude, shame, secretiveness by which the impossibility of
social integration was first internalized."

The very impossibility of expressing gay desire in a socially meaningful fashion served to magnify and intensify it, rendering all the
more precious and pleasurable the aesthetic form of the Broadway
musical through whose enjoyment alone that impossibility could be

suspended and the proto-gay subject's solitary, secret sentimentality could be given an exuberant, reality-defying expression. That is precisely what Miller means when he invokes "the intense, senseless *joy* that, while not identical to these destitutions, is neither extricable from them."

☯

The genius of Miller's approach to the Broadway musical is that it enables him to inquire into gay male subjectivity and its constitution, while side-stepping the psychic life of the individual by using a mass-cultural form popular with gay men to document and to recover the distinctive organization of subjectivity produced in gay men as a group by a specific set of historical and cultural conditions. That is an irreducibly *social* approach to the constitution of gay subjectivity.

Miller's emphasis on collective rather than individual subjective formation was not, however, a strategy for escaping the psychic altogether. Rather, its effect was to locate psychic life in the social rather than in the merely personal.

Miller made that point clear in the course of explaining why gay men's peculiar but shared investments in particular works of mainstream popular culture might be a good source of information about the distinctive features of gay male subjectivity.

> The stuff of mass culture (as our first culture) conducts psychic flows with an efficiency that the superior material of no second, later culture ever comes close to rivaling. It is by way of *Shane,* not Sophocles or Freud, that Oedipus stalks our dreams. . . . We do not begin to understand how fundamentally this stuff outfits our imagination of social space, and of our own (desired, represented, real) place in it, by refusing to acknowledge the stains that such psychic flows may have deposited in a given sample. On the contrary, our cathexes correspond to an objective structure of soliciting, shaping, and storing them that contributes far more to the significance of a work of mass culture than the hackneyed aesthetic design, or the see-through ideological proposition, that is all that remains when they are overlooked. (68–69)

This is in the first instance an argument for the significance of mass culture in "the sentimental history of social groups,"[12] and in the second instance an argument for bringing to the study of mass culture a brand of critique distinct from the purely ideological, a critique that focuses on the *content* of *form* itself. But it is also a manifesto for the project of using the documented appeal of mass culture as a point of entry into a non-individualizing, non-personalizing, and non-normalizing analysis of gay male subjectivity.

∽

Ultimately, what the gay male love of the Broadway musical taught Miller is the very lesson on which I have been insisting here—a lesson I originally learned from him—namely, that gay identity is inadequate to the expression of gay subjectivity. Gay identity does a very bad job of capturing what it feels like to be gay, because it fails to translate into expressive form the full extent and range of gay desire. Even gay sex, or its telltale signs, or the presence of gay men, or their public visibility and acceptance are insufficient to the tasks of representing *what it feels like* to be gay and expressing what gay men want. All those things may stand in for us; they may denote who we are. But they do not convey what we feel; they cannot by their mere presence embody our emotional world, our longings and aspirations, our sentimentality, our pleasures, the feelings that make us queer. The Broadway musical, for all its lack of specifically gay subject matter, comes a lot closer and does a better job. As an aesthetic form, and as a specifically gay genre, it gives expression to a kaleidoscopic range of queer emotions, pleasures, and desires.

That does not mean that the Broadway musical performs such a function for all gay men. Barry Adam, for example, claims to be completely unresponsive to the gay appeal of the Broadway musical. And yet he does not hesitate to accept Miller's claim that the musical offers a clue to the workings of gay male subjectivity. "I, for one, am not alone in being left cold by the Broadway musical / opera complex that is undeniably an important facet of culture for many gay men," Adam writes, "but I nevertheless recognize the subjective location Miller points to. Musical theater is one of a number of possibilities that speak to *the sense of difference, desire to escape, and will to imagine alternatives* that seems a widespread childhood experience of many pregay boys."[13]

What makes the Broadway musical so perfectly adapted to capturing and expressing that alternative outlook, that driving desire—the profound sense of difference that often reaches back into gay childhood—is, Miller argues, the musical's very *form*. For Miller, the most distinctive formal property of the Broadway musical is its alternation of drama and music, of speaking and singing, which not only brings about an unnaturally close juxtaposition of those two quite contrasting modes, but also involves abrupt and deliberately disorienting shifts from one to the other.

That practice of mode-shifting achieves its most characteristic realization, and produces its greatest impact on the spectator, when it is heightened, as it often is in the Broadway musical, by the very brusqueness of the transition from one mode to the other—for example, when performers who have been speaking ordinary dialogue suddenly, without preliminary orchestral accompaniment or any other warning, break into song. The immediate effect is to cut us loose from a familiar reality and to catapult us into a more lyrical, more vital, more vivid, and more wacky universe. In its exhilarating determination to stop the show, "to send the whole world packing,"[14] and in its shameless celebration of an alternate reality, of a magical Technicolor world somewhere over the rainbow, "theatrical rather than realistic,"[15] where normal people (even major-league baseball teams) unexpectedly burst into song and dance, the lyrical ethos of the Broadway musical—its interruptive, reality-suspending, mode-shifting form—expresses gay desire, and answers to what gay men want, far better than anyone who literally denotes or embodies gayness. At least, it once did. It could also speak eloquently to the sense of difference, the desire to escape, and the will to imagine alternatives that were all such prominent parts of the childhood experience of so many proto-gay boys in the pre-Stonewall era of the 1950s and 1960s, and that remain important parts of queer childhood experience to this day.

By virtue of its very form, then, whose function is to effect a break from the ordinary, to disrupt the normal order of things, to derealize the known world and banish its drab reality so as to open up a new and different realm—a realm with its own lyrical, harmonious, passionate, playful, vibrant, intense, manic, nonsensical ways of being and feeling—by virtue of its very form, *and what that form implies,* the classic Broadway musical actually succeeded and may still succeed in realizing homosexual desire. It constitutes a proper vehicle for the expression of queer feeling. It certainly corresponds to the structure of gay subjectivity, and to the requirements of gay existence, better than gay identity does. It may even convey better than gay sex what it means to have a gay sexuality. It doesn't disclose who we are—after all, we never appear in it, at least not as visible gay men. Instead, it projects what we want, what we aspire to, what we dream of. It translates into a concrete vision our sense of difference, our longing to escape, and our wish for an alternate reality. That is why the Broadway musical can serve as a figural representation as well as a powerful expression of gay desire. Everything depends on *the content of its form,* on *the meaning of its style.*

To establish that point, and to show in precisely what sense it is true, Miller undertakes a lengthy, detailed reading of the 1959 Arthur Laurents–Jule Styne–Stephen Sondheim musical *Gypsy* and tries to account for its emotional appeal to some gay men of the period (and to numbers of gay men ever since). His reading combines a critical description of the work itself with an original theory of gay male development and an attempt at autobiographical recovery and self-analysis. It is a performance of queer subjectivity in its own right. By adopting that strategy, Miller seeks to give substantive meaning to the proposition, often voiced by gay men in connection with the early impact on them of one or another work of popular culture, that such-and-such a work "made me gay" (66; that is another mark of Miller's bravery: most of us would instinctively flinch at any explanation of homosexuality that is couched in the terms of an aetiology, an origin story, fearing as we do that any developmental account of how someone became gay necessarily implies a pathological cause). Because Miller's analysis takes the form of a unique experiment in critical writing, it is unparaphraseable. Interested readers are warmly advised to consult his demonstration in full.

Miller's important conclusion, however, can be quickly summarized. Because the form of the Broadway musical itself functions as a vehicle of gay male desire, no enlightened effort to inject a thematic element of gay identity into the musical itself—to make its gayness more overt, to add gay subject matter to it—can actually make it more gay. Rather the contrary. When at last gay men do appear in their own right on the Broadway stage, and when the musical attempts to achieve gayness *through* its explicit representation of homosexual subjects, the musical ceases to provide much of what gay men want. That is why making the Broadway musical more explicitly gay-themed—for example, by including characters who are gay men or even creating an entire musical about gay life (as in the case of *La Cage aux Folles*)—does not succeed in making the musical itself more satisfactory as a vehicle of gay desire, whatever novel identity-affirming pleasures this new gay musical may nonetheless afford.

Instead, according to Miller, the explicitly gay-themed musical "works positively against the recognition of the homosexual desire that diffuses through 'other' subjects, objects, relations, all over the form" (132). By containing and confining homosexuality to the fixed, local habitation of a particular character or theme—to a materialization of *gay identity*—the new gay musical implies that such a habitation is the only place in the musical where homosexuality resides, where gay subjectivity is at home. But as Miller demonstrates, with a subtlety and attention to detail that defeat summary, it is in the form of the Broadway musical itself that homosexual desire once took up pervasive (if unverifiable and unlocalizable) residence. For homosexual desire is a volatile affect, an elusive way of feeling, a solitary, sentimental projection. Only an aesthetic form as sly, as tricky, and as queer as the Broadway musical could give it so powerful and moving an expression in an otherwise hostile world.

John Clum agrees.

> The uncloseted gay musical, however earnestly it attempts to recreate gay experience, is not as complex or captivating as earlier closeted musicals. . . . [W]e show queens found more cause for joy, more recognition, in our readings of shows of the past than in more recent, more ostensibly gay musicals. . . . The irony of theater . . . is that there is often more gayness to be read in ostensibly straight characters. . . . For the most part, openly gay musicals are less "gay," in all senses of the word, than their closeted Broadway predecessors. . . . . The magical moments in the musical theater I know and love are extravagant allegories of our experience. . . . Gay critics can lament the ostensible heterosexism of the classic musical, but these shows offered an opulent world in which desire could go in a number of directions and could be read simultaneously in seemingly opposite ways. (10, 47, 246, 282)

The Broadway musical is "the most illogical of art forms"—just as opera is the most electrifying (xii).[16] Musical theater is "the queerest of art forms, the one in which gender is most clearly a performance that can be exploded or radically altered, the form in which everything can be seen as drag. It is the most openly flamboyant of art forms, . . . less rarified than opera or ballet, but equally larger than life" (36, 28).[17] In fact, if D. A. Miller is correct, it is not only gender that gets exploded by the Broadway musical, but straight reality itself. The Broadway musical, as a queer art form, is therefore *more gay* than any gay man, than anyone with a gay identity, could ever be.

And so, even when the Broadway musical appears to treat what Miller calls "other" (that is, non-gay) subjects, it contrives to be more gay than any representation of gay men or gay identity. Although the classic Broadway musical of the 1940s and 1950s strictly banished from its scene anyone or anything that could register explicitly as homosexual in the minds of its audience, it "can now seem to have rendered a far richer account of [gay] desire" than any explicit representation of that desire on the Broadway stage today can do (132).

෧෮

The problem, or the paradox, is that the gay identity "to which we have entrusted our own politics, ethics, sex lives . . . stands in an essentially reductive relation to the desire on which it is based." Gay identity is but "a kind of homogenous precipitate that can never in itself suggest how variously such desire continues to determine the density, color, taste of the whole richly embroiled solution out of which, in so settled a state, only a small quantity of it has fallen" (132). Gay identity is therefore not up to the job of capturing or expressing gay desire, which exceeds in its transformative, world-altering aspirations and uncategorizable pleasures the comparatively humdrum persons or themes that "gay" merely denominates.

In the era when all gay denotation was banned from Broadway, the musical performed a much more gay-expressive "double operation: not only of 'hiding' homosexual desire, but also of manifesting, across all manner of landscapes, an extensive network of hiding places—call them latencies—apparently ready-made for the purpose." The Broadway musical created a world in which gay desire, though never visible, was everywhere at home.

What made the Broadway musical so gay, in the end, was not that it portrayed gay desire (it didn't), but that it realized it. By its wide-ranging hospitality to gay desire as well as by its very form, whose interruptive mode-shifting abolished normal, ordinary reality and replaced it with a lyrical, playful, wacky, ecstatic alternative, the musical conveyed to certain kinds of gay spectators, "even as it was being denied, *the homosexual disposition of the world*" (132–133). Without ever recognizing gay men, and in the very act of disavowing their existence, the Broadway musical permitted them to partake in queer ways of being and feeling. It put them in imaginative and emotional possession of a queer reality. *It denied their identity, but it offered them a world*. Nothing short of that "sublime vision," as Miller calls it (133), could adequately express—without reducing, simplifying, or betraying—the world-making force of gay desire.

THE QUEEN IS NOT DEAD

The inability of gay identity to capture the "sublime vision" that Miller speaks of is precisely what I discovered, at considerable personal cost, the first time I taught a course in gay male studies at the University of Michigan. Which I did the first semester I worked there, in the fall of 1999. It was, for once, a fairly conventional course—a survey of contemporary gay male literature.

In putting together that course, I had implicitly accepted the notion, derived from the premises of post-Stonewall gay liberation (to which I still uncritically subscribed), that gay identity was the key to gay studies. Accordingly, I assumed that what gay men wanted above all was the one thing that had always been denied them—namely, an opportunity to affirm their _identity_ as gay men by seeing themselves literally represented in (for example) gay male literature and by taking part in an open, dignified, explicit, and communal gay male culture. Which they could now do at long last by, among other things, enrolling in a college course that focused explicitly on gay men and gay male literature, a course taught by an openly gay man, a course dealing with fiction about gay men written by gay men that could give voice to gay male experience. Wasn't that the kind of educational experience that the gay movement had long been working to make possible? And to make available to interested college students, whether they were gay or not?

The response I got, however, was quite different from what I expected. My gay male students, who on the first day of class had indeed said gratifying and predictable things such as "I'm taking this course because I've waited my entire time in college to be able to take a course like this," soon acted as if they were having second thoughts. They certainly started looking very bored, and they ended up treating the course like just any other tedious English class with a lot of difficult reading to do and too many papers to write.

But that's not because they were completely insensible to the appeal of gay culture. There was at least one thing that held their interest.

As the semester wore on, the attendance sheet I circulated to keep track of student participation kept taking longer and longer to make its way around the classroom. By the time it finally reached me, it was lusciously decorated—more and more floridly as the term drew to a close. Some of the gay male students in the class, it turned out, were compensating for their evident lack of interest in the assigned readings and the class discussions by embellishing the back of the attendance list with amusing drawings of various members of the class, including myself on occasion, decked out in drag and embodying various female characters from *The Golden Girls* or *Steel Magnolias* (Figures 2 and 3).[1]

Those students may not have been fans of Judy Garland or the Broadway musical (though who knows?), but they knew what they liked.

In short, my students had no trouble responding to the queer charm of certain non-gay representations. They enjoyed appropriating and queering works of mainstream, heterosexual culture. In fact, they *preferred* doing that to reading gay novels. They got more of a charge out of non-gay sources than they got out of the explicitly gay texts we were supposed to be studying. At least, they discovered more queer possibilities in adapting and remaking non-gay material, and thus more uses for it, than they found in good gay writing.

The obvious conclusion was that the hard-won possibility of an

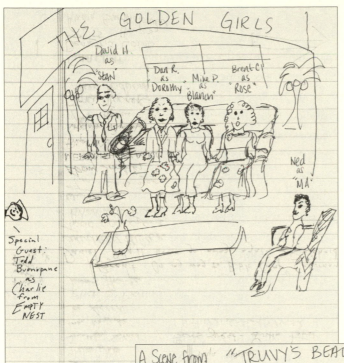

2 Attendance sheet for the course entitled "Contemporary Gay Male Fiction," University of Michigan, November 30, 1999. By kind permission of Brent Caburnay.

3 Attendance sheet for the course entitled "Contemporary Gay Male Fiction," University of Michigan, December 2, 1999. By kind permission of Brent Caburnay.

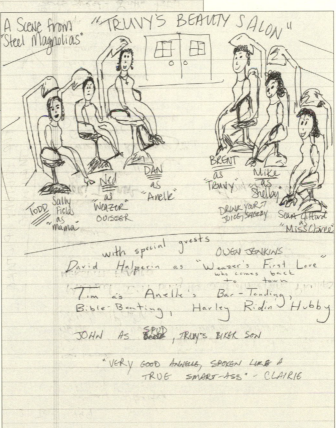

open, uncensored, explicit, and reflective gay male literature had not exactly extinguished the queer appeal of all that oblique, encrypted material so beloved of traditional gay male culture. It still hasn't. Coded, indirect, implicit, figural representations that somehow manage to convey "the homosexual disposition of the world" continue to exercise a powerful attraction that unencoded, direct, explicit, literal representations of gay men and gay life have trouble equaling. Such coded material, though not itself gay-themed (any more than the classic Broadway musical was), conforms to the requirements of gay desire more closely, and often succeeds in expressing such desire better, than gay identity or its tokens can do.[2]

Which is why gay men nowadays, who finally have the opportunity to watch TV shows about gay men and gay life and gay sex, like *Queer as Folk,* massively prefer *Sex and the City* or *Desperate Housewives*—just as D. A. Miller continued to prefer *South Pacific* or *Gypsy* to *La Cage aux Folles* or *Rent*. (Of course, the fact that *Queer as Folk* used to be the most moralistic show on television probably didn't help.)

☙☙

Gay men routinely cherish non-gay artifacts and cultural forms that realize gay desire instead of denoting it. They often prefer such works, along with the queer meanings those works express, to explicit, overt, thematically gay representations. There are in fact quantities of non-gay cultural forms, artworks, consumer products, celebrities, and performers that gay men invest with gay value. Cultural objects that contain no explicit gay themes, that do not represent gay men, that do not invoke same-sex desire, but that afford gay men opportunities for colonizing them and making them over into vehicles of queer affirmation exercise a perennial charm: they constantly get taken up by gay male culture and converted to queer uses. These objects serve a purpose that even "positive images" of gay men do not fulfill.

Like the Broadway musical, non-gay cultural forms offer gay men a way of escaping from their particular, personal queerness into total, global queerness. In the place of an identity, they promise a world. So long as it is the property of an individual, queerness always runs the risk of disfiguring the person: it marks the individual as weird, abnormal, disreputable, and subject to the demeaning judgment of the majority. It implicates the individual's identity and "spoils" that identity (to use Erving Goffman's apt term) by imparting to it a social taint of wrongness, repulsiveness, defectiveness.[3] But while being faggy may be a bad thing for a *person* to be, it ceases to be disabling as soon as it stops referring to a person and applies instead to an entire world, to a weird or wacky universe of someone's creation. When we participate in such a universe, we trade in our individual fagginess for a universal fagginess that is no longer our personal property and that does not register as a personal defect or blemish. A fagginess that comes to be shared, that gets transferred to a common landscape of the imagination, that constitutes an entire world, and that becomes universal is a fagginess that no longer defines us as individuals, taints our identity, and disfigures us both personally and socially.

No wonder that gay identity, for many gay men, is an identity well lost. Not only is it, like all stigmatized identities, an irreparably spoiled identity. It is also an obstacle to the world-making pleasures of nonidentity. The queer movement of the early 1990s, which elaborated that insight, merely rediscovered what earlier gay adepts of the Broadway musical had already known, and what my gay students had somehow figured out for themselves: certain non-gay cultural forms, such as the musical, or grand opera, or pop music, or women's daytime TV, provide a liberation far more complete than gay politics can offer, since the latter aspires only to improve the world and does not alter your situation in it or your subjection to it—not, at least, immediately. Instead of replacing your gay identity with a new and better one, participation in non-gay cultural forms exempts you from having to have an identity at all. You lose yourself and gain a world.

So when gay men appropriate non-gay cultural forms and bring out the queerness they find in them, they escape from their personal queerness into a larger, universal, non-stigmatizing queerness. From classical sculpture to techno music, from Saint Sebastian to Miss

Piggy, from Venice to Broadway, innumerable non-gay cultural forms and figures have succumbed to the cultural perversions of gay men. (What do perverts do, after all, if not pervert?) As a result of such queer world-making projects, in which gay men lose their individual homosexual identity through an appropriation of heterosexual culture as well as a deep immersion in *its* queerness rather than their own, many non-gay forms not only morph into gay forms but even turn into widely recognized symbols of gayness. Such once-straight but now-gayed items ultimately come to function for straight society as a kind of shorthand for gay male culture itself: witness the fate of "Broadway" or "techno music."

So it would be easy to take a leaf from Miller's book and to demonstrate his point (about non-gay cultural forms being gayer than gay ones) by looking at other instances besides Broadway. For example, Alice Echols points out that, with the exception of Sylvester,

> the biggest stars of gay disco were heterosexual African American women. Even though disco was powered in part by gay liberation, its deejays and dancers shied away from politically explicit music. Tellingly, Motown artist Carl Bean's 1977 gay anthem "I Was Born This Way" fell flat with gay men. By contrast, optimistic tracks such as Sister Sledge's "We Are Family," McFadden and Whitehead's "Ain't No Stoppin' Us Now," and Dan Hartman's "Relight My Fire," which invoked the righteousness of love, equality, and community but without reference to any specific group, were massively popular in gay discos.[4]

History loves to repeat itself—especially, Marx quipped, as farce. Echols's account of Carl Bean's failure to appeal to gay men with "I Was Born This Way" evokes a more recent fiasco of the same type, which illustrates the general point that non-gay forms are often gayer than gay-themed ones.

In 2011, Lady Gaga released a gay anthem of her own, "Born This Way," which she performed at the Grammy Awards and on *Saturday Night Live,* and which she selected as the title track of her second studio album. It was billed (according to Out.com) as "the queer anthem to end all queer anthems. Elton John went so far as to say it would erase 'I Will Survive' from our memories, our jukeboxes, and our pride parades."[5] Recognizing that she had been catapulted to pop stardom by her huge gay fan base, Gaga had been taking increasingly overt and explicit political positions in favor of gay and lesbian rights; in 2010 she had given political speeches and rallied her fans on behalf of the repeal of "Don't Ask, Don't Tell," the Congressional statute banning non-heterosexuals from serving openly in the U.S. military.[6] This political engagement culminated in her new single, "Born This Way," which insisted that "God makes no mistakes" and that all of "life's disabilities" (among which Gaga explicitly includes non-standard sexualities and genders, homophobically enough, along with non-White racial and ethnic identities) are therefore natural and right. The song was a defiant defense of individual differences, particularly of stigmatized ones which "left you outcast, bullied or teased," and an implicit rebuke to biblically based homophobia, especially of the evangelical Christian variety, which holds homosexuality to be a sinful choice rather than a natural, or innate, condition.[7]

Despite Elton John's prediction, Gloria Gaynor's 1978 disco classic "I Will Survive," which makes not the slightest reference to gay men, will in all likelihood survive "Born This Way." Gaga's queer anthem has left her gay fans grateful but underwhelmed. Commenting on the general disappointment, Mark Simpson wrote, "This is an atrocious, disastrous mistake on Gaga's part. . . . And it's because I'm a fan I'm so disappointed. . . . It's a catchy single, of course, and will make a lot of money, but everything about this song is backwards. . . . It's as if someone decided to remake *The Rocky Horror Picture Show* as a GLAAD public service announcement, with Harvey Fierstein or Dan Savage in the role of Frank-N-Furter."[8]

Gaga, in short, has simply mistaken the nature of her gay appeal. The latter has a lot to do with everything that is *not* explicitly gay-themed about her persona and her performance but that speaks to a queer sensibility and subjectivity—her outrageous look, her defiance of normality, her collaboration with Beyoncé, her reinvigoration of

pop music—and relatively little to do with her belated bisexual identification or political support for gay identity.[9]

Gaga has tried from the start to take control of her gay appeal.
Much like Bette Midler before her, she has played explicitly to her gay
audience, offering herself as a vehicle for gay male identification in
particular. "Gaga's music does not provide gay culture with straight
artifacts to recode," writes Logan Scherer, "but provides it with already recoded material—with a kind of ready-made gay culture. In
effect, Gaga does the cultural work for gay men. She takes straight
tropes of pop music and recodes them into consciously campy gay
anthems, admitting that her music, while universally popular, is
uniquely made for gay fans. Whereas someone like Beyoncé gives us,
generally, unironically straight music that we can recode into gay culture, Gaga does the work for us."[10]

Nonetheless, there is a difference, Scherer maintains, between
Gaga's earlier hits, like "Poker Face," and "Born This Way": the former is, "on the surface, a song about a flirty girl hiding her true emotions from the guy who's pursuing her and whom she's pursuing, but
the subtext of the song is the poker face of the closet that hides and
feigns sexuality, and this is what made the song such a hit with Gaga's
gay audience: the song incorporates the clichés of straight pop songs
while ingeniously smuggling in this queer subtext." With "Born This
Way," Gaga brings that queer subtext to the fore. As a consequence,
the gay appeal of her song now resides in the pop-musical form, its
rhythm and harmonies, rather than in the content of its painfully earnest lyrics.[11] It is the form of the song that saves it. Otherwise, by appealing openly, explicitly, thematically to her gay audience, Gaga—
paradoxically—has cut her connection to it. (Enter Adele, whose
apolitical sentimentality, combined with her extraordinary vocal talents, made her an instant hit with gay men, if not exactly a full replacement for Gaga.)

꒰ꉺ꒱

We keep being told that gay culture is dead. Traditional gay male culture, or so the story goes, was tied to homophobia, to the regime of

the closet, to the Bad Old Days of anti-gay oppression. That is why it is no longer relevant.[12] Now that we have (some) gay rights, and even gay marriage (in half a dozen states, at least, as well as in Canada, several European countries, South Africa, Argentina, and Nepal), the sense of exclusion, and of specialness, that gay men have long felt is out of date. Once upon a time, gay culture was rooted in "the aestheticism of maladjustment," as Daniel Harris calls it. With those roots in social rejection and marginalization now definitively severed, traditional gay culture is certain to wither away. In fact, it has already withered away. "The grain of sand, our oppression, that irritated the gay imagination to produce the pearl of camp, has been rinsed away," Harris explains, "and with it, there has been a profound dilution of the once concentrated gay sensibility."[13]

Similar arguments also used to be made about drag, highlighting its outdatedness and forecasting its imminent disappearance. But since drag continues all too obviously to live on, no doubt to the embarrassment of many, and since it continues to take new forms—from *RuPaul's Drag Race* on the Logo Channel to late-night appropriations of deserted Walmarts for drag displays by queer youth—the reports of its demise that continue to be issued seem increasingly to lack confidence and conviction.

In the case of gay culture in general, however, a death knell is continually sounded, often by forty-something gay men projecting their sense of generational difference, as well as their utopian hopes for the future, onto younger guys—or anyone who represents the latest generation of gay men to emerge onto the scene. These kids are said to live in a brave new world of acceptance and freedom, mercifully different from that prison house of oppression, that "cage of exclusion" (albeit "gilded . . . with magnificent ornaments"), which their elders knew.[14]

If you want to gauge just how well younger gay men nowadays are assimilated into American society at large, you only have to look —or so the advocates of this view insist—at how ignorant of gay culture these boys are, how indifferent to it they are, how little need they have of it. That, you are assured over and over again, is a particularly telling sign: it shows that gay kids nowadays are happy and healthy and well-adjusted. "For the first time," starting apparently in the 1990s, according to Andrew Sullivan, "a cohort of gay children and teens grew up in a world where homosexuality was no longer a taboo subject and where gay figures were regularly featured in the press." The result of that change in mass-media representation, Sullivan contends, was a complete merging of straight and gay worlds, as well as a new fusion between straight and gay culture, with the latter now losing its edge and distinctiveness:

> If the image of gay men for my generation was one gleaned from the movie *Cruising* or, subsequently, *Torch Song Trilogy*, the image for the next one was MTV's "Real World," Bravo's "Queer Eye," and Richard Hatch winning the first "Survivor." The new emphasis was on the interaction between gays and straights and on the diversity of gay life and lives. Movies featured and integrated gayness. Even more dramatically, gays went from having to find hidden meaning in mainstream films—somehow identifying with the aging, campy female lead in a way the rest of the culture missed—to everyone, gay and straight, recognizing and being in on the joke of a character like "Big Gay Al" from "South Park" or Jack from "Will & Grace."[15]

Too bad no one bothered to tell my students. Maybe they would have stopped identifying with *The Golden Girls* and immersed themselves instead in *The Swimming-Pool Library*. Then I could have taught a successful class on contemporary gay male fiction. And I wouldn't have had to write this book.

◌◯◌

In fact, the new generation of gay kids on whose behalf such declarations are ostensibly made often refrain from making those kinds of categorical assertions themselves. My lesbian and gay male students, including the ones who later enrolled in "How To Be Gay," may have been properly skeptical of claims that a lot of arcane material from obscure reaches of American popular culture in the distant past somehow constitutes *their* culture, but they did not insist that gay culture was absolutely dead. I would have been perfectly willing to believe them, if they had told me so, just as I am prepared to accept at face value the triumphal obituaries for gay culture that we are repeatedly proffered. Andrew Sullivan is quite right, in a sense: public culture *has* changed, and homosexuality now is much more fully integrated into it. That certainly makes a big difference, and it makes traditional gay male culture at least *look* a lot less relevant. Already in the 1970s, my own generation thought we were well beyond having to find gay meaning in mainstream films, Broadway musicals, or other mainstream cultural objects. Moreover, my interest in gay history makes me inclined to see a close, specific, and contingent connection between the particular contours and contents of traditional gay male culture and the singular social conditions in the past under which it was formed—conditions that may very well have produced it—such as homophobia, the closet, and political oppression, which D. A. Miller so eloquently evoked.

Those conditions have hardly vanished, of course, and that is one reason gay culture is not a mere relic of times gone by. Despite occasional optimistic claims to the contrary, homophobia is still around and is wonderfully adaptable, assuming new guises and finding new means of expression every day.

There is another reason for the stubborn persistence of gay culture. Although much, indisputably, *has* changed, gay or proto-gay children still grow up, for the most part, in heterosexual families and households. A few of them may have children's books which teach them about the existence of gay people, or about families with parents of the same sex. They may watch TV sitcoms or reality shows with gay or (more rarely) lesbian characters. All of that certainly contributes significantly to the destigmatization of homosexuality. But a culture that places less stigma on homosexuality is not the same thing as a gay culture. And adding gay characters to mainstream cultural forms does not make those forms themselves queer.

So gay kids still have to orient themselves somehow in relation to mainstream, heteronormative culture, which remains their first culture. They still have to achieve—painfully or joyously, gradually or almost instantly—a dissident, queer perspective on it. That process constitutes their earliest and most formative experience as cultural consumers and subjects. (We'll explore the implications of this further in Chapter 16.)

That is why I refuse to confine my account of gay male culture to some distant epoch, to some historical era well and truly over—if only minutes ago, depending on who is writing the obituary. It's not because I have some naive or dogmatic belief in gay culture's persistence, its eternal relevance, its unchanged and unchanging greatness. And it's not because I am living in the past. It's because just at the moment when I myself expected to find traditional gay male culture dead and buried, and when I thought modern gay identity had definitively triumphed over it, my own students told me different. Via that attendance sheet.

∽∞∾

What all this indicates to me is that gay identity—the concept on which the entire design of my class on contemporary gay male literature was implicitly and uncritically based—does not answer, even now, to what many gay men want when they look for gay representations. Gay culture may or may not be dead, but the politicized and sexualized gay identity that was supposed to replace it, that many of us were convinced actually *had* replaced it, has not exactly prevailed over it. And traditional gay culture itself refuses to disappear completely. Like homophobia, it is adept at taking new forms and finding new expression.

Gay people have been reluctant to recognize this. And they have been even slower to acknowledge it. Gay identity, or some "post-gay" version of it, remains what many gay people think they want. It is what they think they prefer to traditional gay culture. But only until, for instance, they encounter an identity-based politics, or movement, or literature—a literature, written by gay authors, that actually portrays gay people and gay life. Confronted by such an identity-based culture, by the world they thought they had wanted, many gay people become rapidly and radically disillusioned with it.

There is something familiar, even classic about that sort of disillu-sionment, something that should resonate with the experience of many gay men. The disappointment in literary representations re-flects and perhaps simply repeats a perennial erotic letdown. It echoes that old inability of gay sex to fulfill gay desire, the refusal of gay de-sire to find satisfaction in gay sociality—the persistence of what D. A. Miller called a "homosexuality of one." Like a boy home alone, look-ing for romance with the ideal boyfriend, who imagines what a good time he might be having if he could just manage to pull himself to-gether, get dressed, and go out . . . only to realize, on arriving at the place of his dreams, which is indeed populated by gay men, all of them similarly looking for romance, that those *real* gay men are all somehow the *wrong* gay men, not at all the ones he had been pictur-ing to himself when he had originally thought about going out—so the gay literature that gay men have written, in order to fulfill the demand for the kind of open, explicit representation of gay men, gay life, and gay male sexuality that gay men themselves had thought they wanted, often turns out to be the wrong gay literature, less grat-ifying to its gay readers than the non-gay culture that gay men had al-ready appropriated and resignified to express their longings and their dreams.[16]

The perennial conviction on the part of gay men that they have now moved beyond the sad necessity of traditional gay culture turns out, in short, to be an illusion—a constitutive misrecognition through which every gay generation symptomatically repeats the reductionist program of identity, only to act out its discontent with that program, and ultimately to reject it, without ever quite admitting to itself what it is doing or feeling. So that is another reason traditional gay male culture never dies.

☞☜

One implication of all this, and not the least surprising one, is that some young gay men today may well have more in common with gay men in the period before Stonewall than anyone of my generation has been prepared to believe or to admit. Perhaps, in some important respects, Stonewall did not make such a huge difference after all. Despite the vast historical and social changes in the conditions of gay male life that have taken place over the past fifty years, gay kids continue to grow up in a straight world, straight culture continues to matter deeply to them, and gay male culture still operates through—and indeed thrives on—a metaphorical or figural reading of straight culture: a reappropriation of it that is also a resistance to it.

Furthermore, what gay men have always sought out is not only direct or literal representations of themselves, but also figural or metaphorical or encoded or encrypted representations of gay desire. *There seems to be something about figurality itself that they like.* And it's not hard to figure out what that is. For by freeing the imagination from the confines of a particular, literal representation of gay male identity, figuration is more easily able to convey what D. A. Miller called "the homosexual disposition of the world." It is better able to capture the kaleidoscopic range and breadth of gay subjectivity. It therefore stands a better chance of answering to the needs of gay desire and queer pleasure.

Another way of putting this is to say that gay identity affirms itself not only through *identity,* an experience of sameness with other gay men like oneself, but also through *identification,* the feeling of closeness to, or affinity with, *other people*—with anything and everything that is not oneself. Identification, too, expresses desire: a desire to bring oneself into relation with someone or something that is different from oneself.

So if gay men of an earlier era knew how to attune themselves to gay aspects of the Judy Garland persona, maybe it wasn't only because they didn't have Barney Frank or Rufus Wainwright or Anderson Cooper to identify with instead. And maybe it wasn't just because they were oppressed or did not enjoy the right to marry. Perhaps they were seeking a wider range of expression. Perhaps they were looking for a way of imaginatively expanding their experience, going beyond themselves, escaping from the known world, and realizing their desires without being limited by who they were. That may well have been the whole point of identifying with Judy Garland: she wasn't a

gay man, but in certain respects she could somehow express gay desire, what gay men want, *better* than a gay man could. That is, she
could actually convey *something even gayer than gay identity itself.*[17]

Similarly, young gay men today evidently continue to find meaning and value in artifacts of heterosexual culture that were not created for them but that they can make their own and invest with a variety of queer significations. The kinds of relations they can create *with*
those objects serve to express a richer sense of what it means to them
to be gay than the more straightforward audience relations that they
can establish with images of gay men.

Which is the point that D. A. Miller made about the pre-Stonewall
Broadway musical: its queer figurality offered a more satisfactory answer to gay desire than any representation of gay men possibly
could.

So here is the lesson I took from my failure to interest my gay male
students in contemporary gay male fiction. Instead of asking what on
earth we would still want with the Broadway musical—or with torch
songs, divas, grand opera, old movies, or the perfect interior—now
that we have gay identity and gay sex, I concluded, rather against my
better instincts, that the more pressing question to ask was the opposite one: Why on earth would we want gay identity, when we have (as
we have always had) gay identification? Why would we want Edmund
White, when we still have *The Golden Girls?* Or rather, since there are
very good reasons for wanting to have gay identity, and gay men, at
least some of the time, we might wonder *what gay identification does
for us that gay identity cannot do.* And what it is exactly that Judy Garland or the Broadway musical or other congenial artifacts of mainstream culture offer us that an explicit, open, unencrypted gay male
culture does not provide. I actually didn't much like those questions;
they didn't make me very comfortable. But I wanted to find some answers to them. That's why I decided to teach "How To Be Gay."

ↂ

The only real reward for asking such difficult and unwelcome questions is the prospect that any successful answers to them we manage

to come up with will tell us something useful and enlightening about gay male subjectivity. At least, it seems likely that one possible approach to the non-pathologizing, non-homophobic understanding of gay male subjectivity lies in the study of gay men's cultural identifications, in gay men's emotional investments in non-gay social and artistic forms. The history of gay male cultural identifications reveals a virtually unlimited quantity of such investments, virtually all of them as yet untouched by gay critical analysis. And yet, gay critical analysis would not have very far to look for material.

Just for starters, a catalogue of supremely gripping moments from the history of classic Hollywood film, all of them consisting in notable dialogue spoken by one or another of the greatest female movie stars, has been provided by the gay Argentine novelist Manuel Puig. It takes the form of a series of quotations, each one appended to the beginning of a chapter in Puig's 1974 "detective story," *The Buenos Aires Affair.* No need to assemble a gay male canon of queer moments from Hollywood cinema: Puig has already done it for us.[18]

Another glimpse of this plenitude is afforded by Neil Bartlett, the gay English novelist, historian, playwright, and theatrical director, who speaks about finding his own sources of artistic inspiration in what passes for mainstream culture.

> By "mainstream" I mean those points of entry which the mainstream allows me, to its mechanics and economics, *by accident;* certain moments . . . It's not a tradition so much as a cluster of artistic flashpoints—points of aesthetic excess at which the mainstream becomes ripe for my evil purposes, for plucking. So my mainstream is very picky; one that most people wouldn't recognise. It is deeply queer, kinky, complicated, melodramatic, over-determined, disruptive and disrupted.[19]

All the more striking, then, that it has been so seldom examined. Queer studies of popular media abound, but nearly all of them focus on the cultural object, and perform an ideological critique of it, demonstrating how that object is shaped by and reproduces the regimes of heteronormativity (or race or class or nation) and/or how it resists them. Almost no one except Miller has performed a *formal* critique of a gay male cultural object or been interested in reading mass culture from the point of view of the gay male subject who is the consumer of it.[20] And very few queer theorists have attempted to derive an account of gay male subjectivity from an *inductive* study of the history of gay male cultural appropriations rather than from a *deductive* application to them of psychoanalytic theory or some other theoretical dogma.

Which is a pity, because the study of gay male cultural practices provides an opportunity to apply Virginia Woolf's dictum about the difference between the sexes to the difference between sexual cultures: "The two classes still differ enormously. And to prove this, we need not have recourse to the dangerous and uncertain theories of psychologists and biologists; we can appeal to facts."[21] If we are really interested in describing or accounting for the differences between gay and straight male subjectivity, then, we do not need to bother ourselves with such arcane matters as comparative hypothalamus size or perverse internalization of the Law of the Father. All we need to do is look at the highly distinctive uses gay men make of straight culture, beginning with the phenomena themselves, and focus on the details.

Which is what I will do now.

PART THREE

Why Are the Drag Queens Laughing?

CULTURE AND GENRE

*M*y point of departure for this admittedly hazardous project may come as something of a surprise. If, in order to identify the distinguishing features of gay male subjectivity, I need to describe gay male culture in all its specificity—and to define, in particular, its queer relation to mainstream culture, its non-standard use of mainstream cultural objects—I must begin by invoking the literary-critical concept of *genre*. So let me explain why I have to talk about genre, if I want to talk about gay male culture.

A culture is not the same thing as a collection of individuals. Almost any statement one can make about a culture will turn out to be false as soon as it is applied to individuals. For example, French culture is characterized by a very particular relation to the production and consumption of wine. But that doesn't mean every French individual necessarily embodies such a relation or exhibits it in personal practice. Nor does it imply that wine has the same meaning or value for all members of French society. Although the French in general may indeed care more about wine than Americans do, some people in the United States care a great deal more about wine than do many people in France. Just because you're French doesn't mean you have to like wine, and you can refuse to drink a drop of wine and still be French. It also takes more than liking wine to be French: liking wine, however passionately, will not in itself make you French. At the same time, certain social practices pertaining to wine *are* distinctive to French culture, and although not all or even most French people take part in those practices, to be French is to be alert to the cultural meanings of wine-drinking, to have at least *some kind of attitude* to the practice of wine consumption and appreciation, even if it is an attitude of total indifference or rejection.

The same sorts of things could be said about gay men and Broadway musicals. Or about gay men and any of the various cultural practices that are stereotyped as gay.

The lesson should be clear. The kind of coherence that a culture has will not necessarily be reflected in any uniformity of attitude or behavior on the part of a population. Conversely, the mere counting of individual preferences will not necessarily disclose the systematic, characteristic shape of a culture. A careful sociological survey of a population may produce detailed and accurate information about the tastes of individuals, and it may be able to tabulate variations in likes and dislikes among different demographic subgroups. But precisely because a culture is more than a mass of individuals, such statistical maps, though rich in implications, may still fail to identify leading cultural traits. Even worse, they may factor such traits out of the analysis altogether—by measuring empirical fluctuations (according to region, social class, race, gender, or sexuality) that have only a quantitative, descriptive value and remain culturally neutral instead of turning out to be qualitatively significant and culturally salient.

Yet culture is not an illusion. To stick with our previous example, there are real cultural differences between France and the United States. A few years ago I took some friends of mine from Paris, who were making their first trip to North America, directly from the Detroit airport to a local deli in Ann Arbor. From the effusive, familiar way the waitress greeted us and inquired about our feelings on various subjects, my French guests immediately assumed she was an old friend of mine. That was a mistake. But it was no accident. On the contrary, it was a misunderstanding that was also the logical outcome of a cultural difference.[1] Moreover, it reveals a basic truth about the form in which cultural differences appear and the medium in which they are most flagrantly manifested. It shows that cultural differences are expressed less tellingly by demographic variations in matters of preference or taste than by divergences in observable discursive practice—by the *pragmatics of discourse* (how people interact with one another in concrete social situations) and, more specifically, by the *pragmatics of genre.*

Cultural differences are reflected concretely and pragmatically by the conventions of speech and behavior that govern personal interactions in particular social contexts. Such conventions specify, for example, what a waitress can say to a new customer without causing shock, confusion, disorientation, or outrage. Or, rather, the pragmatic considerations that determine the difference, in a particular social context, between what counts as a normal interaction and what counts as a bizarre, disturbing, or offensive one give rise to structural regularities in discursive practice that constitute conventions—and ultimately entire *genres*—of speech.

Those genres vary from one culture to another. "It is helpful to describe any given local culture as a specific array of genres," Ross Chambers writes, "where genre is understood as a conventional habitus entailing understandings and agreements that don't need to be specifically negotiated concerning the 'kinds' of social interaction that are possible under the aegis of that culture. . . . What genres regulate, with varying degrees of rigidity and flexibility, is the social appropriateness of discursive behavior."[2] The regulatory work that genres perform produces the unique patterns of social and discursive practice that define specific cultures. So there is a mutually constitutive relation between culture and genre. Taken together, in combination or in different combinations, specific genres of speech and interaction help to endow each community, each subgroup within it, and each culture with its own distinctiveness. As the story about my French friends shows, the generic conventions governing what a server can say to a complete stranger in Ann Arbor without causing surprise differ from those governing similar interactions in Paris.

That is how I understand the pragmatics of genre.[3] Genres are usually understood as formal kinds of literary discourse, such as "epic" or "lyric." But in fact routine patterns of speech connected to common social interactions also display the regularity and dependability we associate with literary genres. Moreover, these genres of speech perform the same regulatory function in codifying discursive practices that literary genres do—only they perform their regulatory function not in the realm of literary composition and reception, but in the sphere of communication, social behavior, and personal interaction —defining appropriate subject matter, forms of interpersonal relationality, and styles of communication.[4] In that sense, genres are not only formal but also pragmatic: they provide people, *in their daily practices,* with concrete means of interacting with one another and negotiating specific social situations—and they instruct them in the right ways to do so.[5]

The systematic formal differences that distinguish conventional kinds of literary discourse from one another represent one example of the pragmatics of genre—indeed, the most familiar and obvious example of such a pragmatics—and much of what I have to say here will refer to those traditional generic divisions among kinds of literature. But, for the purposes of the present study, I have no interest in the formal properties of different kinds of literature in themselves and I will not be paying attention to genres as formal organizing principles of *literary* discourse. I am concerned with genres to the extent that they produce regularities in social behavior and discursive practice throughout a wide range of human interactions.[6] The traditional divisions among formal kinds of literary discourse represent instances of such regularities, but they are far from being the only instances of them. So when I invoke those divisions here, my purpose will not be to distinguish different branches of literature, different modes of representation, or different formal systems of discourse, as much as to describe different horizons of expectation for speech and behavior.

ҩѺҩ

Any number of considerations make the attempt to speak of "gay male culture" risky, problematic, even inadvisable. The foremost danger is that of *essentialism,* of seeming to imply that there is some defining feature or property of gayness that all gay men share—an untenable notion, which we should categorically reject. But we should likewise reject the accusation of essentialism that might be leveled against this undertaking. For to make such an objection, to condemn as "essentialist" any effort to describe the distinctive features of gay male culture, is to confuse a *culture,* and the practices that constitute it, with the indeterminate number of *individuals* who, at any one time and to varying degrees, may happen to compose it. There *is* such a thing as French culture, but it does not extend either universally or in its entirety to all the individuals who define themselves as French or who, at a given moment, find themselves residing within the borders of the French nation. And French culture, in some of its generic forms or features, may be shared by people who are not French but who live in France, or who admire French culture, or who identify with French culture, or who have adopted some of the standard practices that typify French culture.

In fact, "culture" seems a somewhat crude, imprecise, and downright culture-bound term to use in this context—a nineteenth-century, European, and occasionally chauvinist term, tainted by its implication in the rise of nationalism, the emergence of scientific racism, the development of Victorian social science, and the expansion of Western imperialism, for which the idea of cultural superiority sometimes provided a convenient justification. Nor is "culture" necessarily the best way to capture the distinctiveness of the activities, attitudes, feelings, responses, behaviors, and interactions that I am trying to describe. But "culture" remains our default term for covering the relation between *forms* and *social processes;* it is not an exact designation so much as a placeholder for a more general and more precise category articulating the formal with the social, for which there is no name—though "genre" comes close, at least at a molecular level.[7] If I continue to invoke "culture" here, that is because I understand it in this categorical way. I want to distance it from its old-fashioned, exclusionary, elitist meaning, and to use it in a descriptive, quasi-anthropological, and, above all, *pragmatic* sense—most immediately, as a designation for the totality of the generic practices that link social life with discursive forms and behavioral conventions,[8] and that thereby define, within different social contexts, particular horizons of expectation for speech and personal interaction.

As in the case of French culture, so in the case of what I have been calling, perhaps unwisely, "gay male culture," it is *practices,* not *people,* that are the proper objects of study. Gay cultural practices have a consistency and a regularity that gay people as a group do not have. Gay people are different from one another, whereas gay culture displays a number of persistent, repeated features.

Kinds of practice, to be sure, bear *some* relation to kinds of people. It is people, especially groups of people, who generate particular cultural practices. The origin of specific cultural practices can often be located in the histories and vicissitudes of specific groups of people. Otherwise, it would not be possible to speak of certain cultural practices as *French* practices or *gay* practices. Cultures do not exist independently of the people who produce them: they are shaped by the social life of human communities, and the forms they take reflect the local, particular, material situations that give rise to them. But cultural practices have their own unique constituencies, which are not exactly coextensive with any single demographic group, and their distribution in a population does not strictly follow the lines of demarcation—themselves extremely blurred—that mark the boundaries between different communities or different social collectivities. "Culture," in our media age, is no longer the unique property of a "people," as traditional anthropology would have it.

Hence, gay male cultural practices are not all, or even mostly, shared by all members of the gay male population in the United States, let alone the world, while at least some of those practices are shared by many people who are not gay themselves. Not every man who happens to be homosexual necessarily participates in gay male culture or displays a characteristically gay sensibility. (Sad, but true.) And plenty of non-gay people take part in gay male culture. Some, in fact, are quite brilliant at it.

Much contemporary youth culture draws freely on traditional forms of gay male irony, such as camp, to mock received cultural values.[9] (I'll have occasion to return to that point, with reference to the indie rock band Sonic Youth, in Chapter 18.) But not all straight people who embrace gay male culture are young radicals, hipsters, or counter-cultural types. Newt Gingrich chose ABBA's song "Dancing Queen" as the standard ringtone on his cell phone, while John McCain liked to play "Take a Chance on Me" at his campaign rallies during the 2008 presidential election cycle.[10] ABBA itself, of course, was not a gay band, being composed of two married heterosexual couples, but some of its songs were popularized in gay clubs and became gay anthems—before being reappropriated by straight culture . . . and taken up by professional homophobes like Gingrich and McCain.

Just as jazz and hip-hop were originally invented (as already composite forms) by African Americans, and just as they took shape, flourished, and developed in and through the life of that particular social group—only to be taken up later by others, who sometimes built them into new and hybrid forms, and sometimes diluted them almost beyond recognition—so camp was first elaborated by gay men as a collective, in-group practice before other social groups, seeing its subversive potential and its wide applicability, claimed it for their own purposes.

Being homosexual is therefore neither a necessary nor a sufficient condition for participating in gay culture. Culture is a practice, not a kind of person. The account of gay male culture I am about to offer here refers, accordingly, to *genres of discourse* and to *genres of social interaction,* not to individuals or populations.

☯

One advantage of focusing our inquiry on gay *culture,* instead of on gay *people,* is that it allows us effectively to side-step essentialist questions. We can avoid becoming entangled in debates about whether gay people are different from non-gay people, or whether "gay culture" applies only, or primarily, to some classes or races or generations or nationalities, but not to others. The point is not to evade the politics of class or race or nation, or to obscure the specific ways those variables may determine the social construction of homosexuality or gay subjectivity in certain contexts. It's simply that for the purposes of understanding gay male culture, we are concerned necessarily not with *kinds of people* but with *kinds of discourse* and *kinds of interaction,* irrespective of who happens to be the subject of them. It is gay culture, after all, which is our topic—not gay men, and not gay identity. The immediate goal is to bring to light some pragmatic features of gay male culture and to describe the forms of subjective experience, or the collective structures of feeling, that particular ways of interacting and communicating express or produce in those persons, gay or straight, who participate in the culture constituted by such generic practices.

It would surely be possible to apply this procedure to specific minority subforms or species of gay male culture—ethnic or racial or national or generational or sexual—and to identify, describe, and specify the generic features that define Latino gay cultures, or Jewish gay cultures, or working-class gay cultures, or deaf gay cultures, or S/M gay cultures, or gay drag cultures, or the gay cultures of urban American youth. Even those subspecies of gay male culture all designate multiple cultures, and one would need to differentiate each specific instance of gay male culture from the others, as well as to identify the genres or subgenres that set them off from one another, that generate their distinctive, characteristic features, and that thereby define them. Such a project would be extremely valuable; it would provide a total description of gay male cultures in the United States. But it far exceeds my ambition, and it would occupy many, many volumes.[11] It will be difficult and delicate enough simply to identify some of the generic or pragmatic elements that endow gay male culture with its specificity, determine its difference, and distinguish it from mainstream, heterosexual culture.

One obvious inference to draw from this limitation is that the gay male culture I will be describing is a culture of White, middle-class men. But it is not at all certain that middle-class men played a leading role in shaping traditional gay male culture or wielded a preponderant influence on it. And although the racial constituency of that culture was overwhelmingly White, the participants in it cannot be delimited so as to be made securely coextensive with any specific social group, as defined by race, ethnicity, nationality, age, ability, or even sexuality.

So, in what follows, I will not speak specifically of White American middle-class gay male culture, any more than I will assume that membership in gay male culture is restricted to gay men. That is not because I wish to give my statements a falsely universal application, let alone because I wish to promote White supremacism, but because it is impossible to determine with any precision the specific *population* that qualifies as the subject of a specific *culture*. I prefer to allow the exact ethnic or racial contours of the gay culture under consideration to shift as the particular points of reference change in the course of the analysis.

Inasmuch as that analysis takes gay culture to be defined by a set of generic practices, it necessarily looks for a systematic and coherent account of that culture's specificity not to sociology or anthropology, but to the most traditional method for describing genres—namely, *poetics*. It is poetics—the social and formal analysis of different kinds or conventions of discourse—that, ever since Aristotle, has given us a systematic anatomy of genres.

By specifying poetics as the category in terms of which I have chosen to frame and orient my analysis, I mean to emphasize that this study will focus above all on *social and cultural forms* in their positivity, as autonomous objects of description and interpretation, and will not reduce them to mere expressions or products of social process. My analysis, to be sure, will not ignore the social life of cultural forms. On the contrary, the social and political contexts of gay male culture will often provide the keys to understanding it, as well as an empirical basis for interpreting specific texts, objects, and practices. I will certainly be considering how particular social and political conditions give rise to particular social and cultural forms. But this project is not a historical or sociological investigation, and social processes in themselves do not constitute its chief concern. So the focus of the analysis will not be on the sociology of taste, the ethnography of specific sexual communities, the relations of particular audiences to popular culture, the operations of the mass media, social inequality, structural violence, or the play of power—which may seem surprising, given how much all those areas of study can contribute to understanding gay male culture. But in order to bring out the specificity and distinctiveness of gay male culture, to give a systematic account of gay male cultural difference, it is necessary to examine gay male culture's pragmatics, especially its genres of discourse and social interaction. And just like any exercise in poetics, a study of gay male cultural poetics must concentrate on the definition and articulation of *forms as things in their own right*.

If, despite everything, this inquiry into the poetics of gay male culture still risks coming off as essentialist, I am willing to take that risk—not only because, having spent much of my career trying to contest essentialist approaches to lesbian and gay male history,[12] I consider my own anti-essentialist credentials to be impeccable, and beyond reproach, but also because to be deterred by such a risk from exploring gay male culture would be to surrender any hope of identifying its distinguishing features and defining its particular genius.

_____

Let's begin with an observation made forty years ago by the anthropologist Esther Newton. In her 1972 book, *Mother Camp,* a pathbreaking ethnographic study of female impersonators and drag queens in Chicago and Kansas City, Newton remarks that "one of the most confounding aspects of my interaction with the impersonators was their tendency to laugh at situations that to me were horrifying or tragic."[13]

According to her own admission, Newton was "confounded" by a queer violation of the boundary between genres. Situations that are "horrifying or tragic" should not elicit laughter from those who

witness them. If or when they do, conventional bystanders are confounded, because their social and discursive expectations—far from
being met—have been turned upside down.

In fact, the drag queens' transgression of the pragmatic conventions of discursive behavior that govern human interaction in ordinary social life was so confounding to the lesbian anthropologist, and
so disturbing, that she allows (in the passage just quoted) for the possibility of error in her observation—the possibility that she might
have simply got it all wrong or that she might have been the victim,
like my Parisian friends in Ann Arbor, of some basic cultural misunderstanding. Making an effort to give the drag queens the benefit of
the doubt, Newton hedges, conceding that the situations laughed at
by the female impersonators were specifically horrifying or tragic
"to me."

That skeptical qualification provides a means of saving the day for
normative conventions of discourse and behavior, for standard genres
of social practice. It leaves open the possibility that the situations the
drag queens laugh at aren't *really* horrifying or tragic—or aren't horrifying or tragic *to them*. Maybe, from *their* perspective, those situations look absurd or comic in ways that Newton simply cannot
fathom. In which case, it would be completely normal (according to
the generic conventions that govern social interaction in Newton's
culture) to laugh at those situations. Laughter, after all, is a perfectly
conventional response to comedy. So perhaps that is why the drag
queens are laughing. Perhaps the problem lies not with them but with
Newton, who is unable to locate the comedy at the origin of all that
hilarity. In which case, Newton would be registering some sort of
misunderstanding on her part, but not something far more unsettling—such as a disruption of the conventional patterns of normal
human feeling, or a violation of those basic social expectations that
define the limits of the comprehensible within a given culture.

What laughter is *not* a conventional generic response to is . . . tragedy. And yet, despite her doubts, Newton suspects that in fact it *is*
tragic situations at which the drag queens are laughing. Whence her

confusion and perplexity. After all, she insists, those situations were horrifying or tragic "to me" in ways she could not apparently deny. Bizarre as it might seem, and reluctant as Newton was to believe it, laughing at tragedy is really what Newton's drag queens appeared to her to be doing. No wonder Newton was confounded. But, then, that's why anthropologists do ethnography in the first place. People who belong to other cultures do strange things, things that mystify anthropologists, and it is the business of anthropologists to inform us about them and, if possible, to explain them.

ⓧ

Gay male culture, it turns out, actually has a long history of laughing at situations that *to others* are horrifying or tragic. "One must have a heart of stone," Oscar Wilde said, "to read the death of Little Nell [in Charles Dickens's novel *The Old Curiosity Shop*] without laughing." Straight sentimentality—especially when its arm-twisting emotional power seems calculated to mobilize and to enforce a universal consensus, to impose a compulsory moral feeling—is just begging for an ironic response, and gay male culture readily provides it by treating such sentimentality as a laughable aesthetic failure, thereby resisting its moral and emotional blackmail.

Similarly, the scenes of sadistic cruelty and abuse in Robert Aldrich's gothic psycho-thriller, *What Ever Happened to Baby Jane?*—scenes that shocked American audiences with their brutality and horror when the film was released in 1962—elicit gales of laughter from gay male audiences, who delight in the melodramatic confrontations between Bette Davis and Joan Crawford, those ancient Hollywood rivals, both playing once-glamorous and now-fallen stars locked in a demented battle for supremacy: grotesque, extravagant images of a monstrous, abject femininity.

Tony Kushner's apocalyptic play *Angels in America* offers a more recent example of this gay male cultural tendency to violate the generic expectations proper to comedy and tragedy, and to do so once again by taking a degraded femininity as its comic target. At one particularly poignant moment in the play, the suffering Prior Walter, ravaged by AIDS and demoralized by his lover's abandonment of him amid the misery of his illness, encounters the dowdy Mormon mother of the clean-cut, square-jawed man his former boyfriend has run off with. This personage, newly arrived in New York from Utah, asks him curiously if he is a "typical" homosexual. "Me? Oh I'm *stereotypical,*" he replies grimly and defiantly, making an effort to overcome his pain and exhaustion. "Are you a hairdresser?" she pursues. At which point Prior, breaking down and bursting into tears, exclaims, "Well it would be *your* lucky day if I was because frankly . . ."[14]

Prior's inspired repartee wittily defuses a potentially hurtful encounter by at once embracing and refuting gay stereotypes, contesting their power to pigeonhole, reduce, trivialize, and exotify him. His biting mockery turns the tables on his clueless tormentor, even as he stereotypically asserts—in the midst of physical and emotional collapse—his undiminished critical capacity to adjudicate matters of taste and fashion. The jarring effect produced by such an incongruous, wrenching juxtaposition of the horrifying and the hilarious is what gives a particularly sharp edge to the emotional intensity of the scene. Here the audience is actually being provoked, propelled—and, in that sense, instructed—by the gay playwright to laugh at a situation that is both horrifying and tragic, and that remains so even as the audience's emotional involvement in it is punctured, though by no means halted or abolished, by the camp put-down of straight imperviousness to self-lacerating gay irony, to the doubleness of gay male speech.

This technique of pivoting from horror to humor and back again is in fact typical of gay male cultural production—and it is a prominent element in the broader gay male response to HIV/AIDS. The English playwright Neil Bartlett, in an interview given in the early 1990s, at about the same time that Kushner was finishing *Angels in America,* describes a similar moment in a different play that also deals with mortal illness. The play is by Charles Ludlam, whose Ridiculous Theatrical Company in New York specialized in pastiche, as well as in outlandish drag restagings of various classics from the history of world drama. Although Ludlam's *Camille* (an adaptation of George Cukor's 1936 film *Camille* starring Greta Garbo, based on Alexandre Dumas's novel *La Dame aux camélias* and Giuseppe Verdi's opera *La Traviata*) was first performed in 1973, nearly a decade before anyone had heard of HIV/AIDS, what Bartlett says about it is silently informed by an acute awareness of the surrounding epidemic, which claimed Ludlam himself in 1987.

> I think the blow-job gag in the final act of *Camille* is the funniest thing ever performed. It's this absolutely great moment where you're really crying—it's the final act of *Camille* and she's in bed [dying of consumption] and Armand [her lover] is there. . . . [I]t's very moving and you're going, "I am about to be terribly moved, this is really going to get to me." And she starts coughing, and he [the actor playing Camille] reproduces precisely Maria Callas's cough, and Armand is sitting by the side of the bed, and she starts coughing and coughs more and more, and eventually collapses into Armand's lap, and everyone thinks that she's coughing, and then the maid comes in and goes, "Oh! I'm sorry!" The leap from *Camille* to this terrible, terrible gag . . . And the maid communicates this delicious sense of, "Oh, they've got back together again, she can't be too bad, things are looking up." It's heaven! That is one of the great moments of world theatre.[15]

That wrenching switch from tragic pathos to obscene comedy leaves the horror of mortal agony intact, but it does not hesitate to interrupt the tearful sentimentality that such a tragic scene might seem to solicit or to demand from its audience. Bartlett even describes the "gag"—and never was that term more apt—as "the *funniest* thing ever performed," although by his own account it occurs at a moment of tragic poignancy "where you're really crying."

Once again, we are confronted with the incongruous eruption of laughter at a scene of horror. That was in fact a hallmark of Ludlam's theatrical technique, as one of his collaborators has recently emphasized:

What Charles Ludlam mastered, both as actor and director, was an ability to sustain the pathos of a tragic situation even as he dipped into moments of ridiculousness. Comedy and tragedy could exist simultaneously in his world because as an actor he identified with, experienced, and communicated the tragic dimension of whatever role he was playing. He could quickly pivot out from this tragic stance to a comic take, joke, or so-called "camp" signification and just as quickly pivot back into tragedy. He was skilled enough to take his audience along on a journey through many such twists and turns in the course of a play. As an audience member, you laughed your ass off and cried your eyes out at the same time.[16]

This deliberate crossing of tragic and comic genres is rooted, as Neil Bartlett observed in the interview just quoted, in long-standing traditions of gay male culture, including drag performance, which has served to canonize, preserve, and renew those traditions.

If you don't take such traditions into account, and if you don't recognize the systematic violation of the generic boundary between tragedy and comedy enshrined in them for what it actually is—namely, a gay male cultural habit, a deliberate *anti-social* aesthetic intervention—then you simply cannot comprehend the gay male cultural response to HIV/AIDS. For that response has often featured works of outrageous impertinence, even apparent heartlessness. Consider, for example, "AIDS Barbie's New Malibu Dream Hospice," a graphic on the back cover of the ninth issue of *Diseased Pariah News,* a zine created by Tom Shearer (who died in 1991) and Beowulf Thorne, a.k.a. Jack Henry Foster (who died in 1999). *DPN* was a "publication of, by, and for people with HIV disease" which encouraged "infected people to share their thoughts" and to hook up "in an atmosphere free of teddy bears, magic rocks, and seronegative guilt."[17] Accordingly, *DPN* no. 9 invented an imaginary accessory for a new version of the iconic Barbie doll, updated to reflect the grotesque reality of the epidemic (Figure 4).

Shearer justified the decision to approach "the plague of the cen-

4 Back cover of *Diseased Pariah News*, no. 9 (1994).

tury from the angle of *humor*" in an editorial in the opening issue: "So what we're hoping to do here is bring some much-needed levity to the experience of HIV infection. We should warn you that our editorial policy does not include the concept that AIDS is a Wonderful Learning Opportunity and a Spiritual Gift From Above. Or a punishment for our Previous Badness. Nor are we much interested in being icons of noble tragedy, brave and true, stiff upper lips gleaming under our oxygen hoses."[18]

Other instances of this refusal by gay men to treat HIV/AIDS as a "noble tragedy" range from Robert Patrick's play *Pouf Positive* (1987), with lines such as "It's my party and I'll die if I want to" (reappropriating the title and refrain of a classic 1963 pop song by Lesley Gore, "It's my party, and I'll cry if I want to"), to the Sodomy Players' *AIDS! The Musical!* (1991) by Wendell Jones and David Stanley, to John Greyson's musical comedy film about the epidemic, *Zero Patience* (1993). Gay male culture has produced so many "comic representations of AIDS," in fact, that the Canadian critic Scott Alan Rayter was able to devote an entire volume to the topic.[19]

The gay Australian activist artist David McDiarmid, who died of complications from HIV/AIDS in 1995, and whose late work attempted to promote acceptance for the sexuality of HIV-positive gay men in an era pervaded by anxiety and desperation, can serve as another exemplar of this gay male cultural habit of laughing at situations that are horrifying or tragic. For instance, in 1994 McDiarmid created a computer-generated laser print on craftwood, now in the collection of the National Gallery of Victoria in Melbourne, which similarly invokes Lesley Gore: it features against a rainbow-colored background a contrasting rainbow-colored text that reads, "IT'S MY PARTY, AND I'LL DIE IF I WANT TO, SUGAR."[20] (Compare the title of Randal Kleiser's 1996 film about an AIDS suicide, "It's My Party.") McDiarmid also produced a mock-up of a pornographic magazine for HIV-positive gay men, an equivalent of *Playboy,* called *Plagueboy,* which purported to feature such articles as "Half-Dead and Hot" and "Sex and the Single T-Cell." And in his spoof on the popular magazine

Vanity Fair, which he titled *Vanity Bear,* McDiarmid composed an obituary for a friend in the form of an "obitchery." He even went so far as to craft the following headline for the obituary of Peter Tully, his longtime collaborator and best friend of twenty years, in the *Sydney Star Observer:* "Moody Bitch Dies of AIDS."[21]

This determination to treat as funny what is undeniably heartbreaking is hardly a universal feature of gay male responses to HIV/AIDS. But it is also not untypical, and it expresses an attitude that may well be distinctive to gay male culture. Many stigmatized social minorities fashion a shared identity and a sense of in-group solidarity by extracting from the history of their persecution a number of defining tragic episodes and by transforming those episodes into sources of communal self-assertion and political activism. In most instances, that collective traumatic history is effectively sacrosanct, off-limits even to in-group parody. Think of the Holocaust, for example. Or slavery. There have been, admittedly, a few irreverent treatments of them—by Mel Brooks or Sarah Silverman, Kara Walker or Isaac Julien.[22] Indeed, there are always *some* exceptions to any generalizations of this sort. But those exceptions are the kinds that typically prove the rule. A Broadway musical comedy about the Third Reich is unimaginable—and when Mel Brooks does imagine such a thing in his 1968 film *The Producers,* complete with an opening number called "Springtime for Hitler," he represents it as calculated almost scientifically to flop, to elicit an ineluctably certain rejection from New York Jewish audiences. (The show's ultimate success is a perverse, unforeseeable, comic accident—and an unanticipated tribute to its camp aesthetic.)

Whereas the gay filmmaker Isaac Julien, in his brilliant short film *The Attendant* (1993), does not hesitate to examine the history of slavery, its representation, and its afterlife in contemporary Britain by staging gay interracial sadomasochistic scenes in the Wilberforce House Museum, an institution located in the city of Hull that celebrates the life and work of the anti-slavery abolitionist William Wilberforce and contains some of the most celebrated art objects produced by the nineteenth-century abolitionist movement. In Julien's eerie, witty exploration of this hushed institutional space, the characters in the paintings come to life; the unstable relations of authority, domination, submission, control, and surveillance that characterize the interaction among the staff and the visitors to the museum get theatricalized, played out, and reversed; and the mode of documentary realism, typically employed to expose historical atrocities, is shattered when the sequences shot in black and white are suddenly infiltrated by tiny, hunky Technicolor cupids or cross-cut with erotic tableaux in extravagant color. This is not, to be sure, a spoof in the style of Mel Brooks, but neither is it a standard approach to the legacy of slavery or the politics of racial inequality. It is not, despite all the supernatural elements, a devastating tragic vision on the order of Toni Morrison's *Beloved*. The Black gay artist attends to the erotics of both slavery and abolitionism, bringing out the sentimental pornography implicit in abolitionism's propagandistic anti-slavery art, and drawing on the aesthetics of gay male culture for his camp depiction of social, institutional, and racial domination.[23] In this remarkable and original queer film, as in many gay male responses to HIV / AIDS, nothing is sacred.[24]

☙❧

In order to specify the exact nature of the cultural work performed by this insistent, and persistent, violation of generic boundaries—a transgressive practice characteristic of gay male culture, which seems determined to teach us to laugh at situations that are horrifying or tragic—I am going to examine in detail the gay male reception, appropriation, and queering of one classic artifact of American popular culture. The analysis of that artifact will occupy the central portion of this book, spanning Parts Three and Four. By taking up this one example, I will try to describe how gay male culture generates and elaborates a distinctive way of feeling, and a unique way of relating to the world, through its practice of reappropriating bits of mainstream culture and remaking them into vehicles of gay or queer meaning. Instead of attempting a comprehensive survey of gay male culture and demonstrating how each and every instance of gay male cultural appropriation works—how it decodes a mainstream heterosexual cultural object and recodes it with queer values—I will focus on the queering of one particular item. I will have everything I can do simply to account for its gay male appeal and its queer uses and re-uses. For I will be dealing with the ethos of a genre—with the particular way a genre makes you feel—and, thus, with the content of form itself. What I'll have to specify, in particular, is not the meaning of a representation, but the *substance of a style.*

And I'll have to consider this single instance of gay male cultural subversion from a number of different angles in order to bring out all of its dimensions. Its challenge to heteronormative culture is wide-ranging; its implications are complex and vast.

At the same time, the logic behind gay male culture's selection and reutilization of this particular item appears more clearly when that choice can be examined in the light of the highly distinctive gay male cultural practice that Esther Newton described—namely, the practice of laughing at situations that are horrifying or tragic.

The reappropriation and queering of this one object, then, will not only confirm the typicality of that gay male cultural practice. More important, it will illustrate how gay male culture produces *through* that practice a set of crucial and profound transformations in a constellation of mainstream values—values that bear on sex and gender but that go far beyond them.

THE PASSION OF THE CRAWFORD

Mildred Pierce, the film directed by Michael Curtiz for which Joan Crawford won an Oscar in 1945, is a gay male cult classic. To be sure, it is only one of many old movies that hold a place of honor in traditional gay male culture, and it is hardly the most prominent among them. But it has never entirely lost its appeal. Along with such films as *The Women* (1939), *Johnny Guitar* (1954), *What Ever Happened to Baby Jane?* (1962), and *Strait-Jacket* (1964), *Mildred Pierce* helped Crawford achieve her status as a notorious gay icon.

Just how notorious is Joan Crawford's gay cult status? Well, check out Michael Lehmann's 1989 film *Heathers.* When in that movie Christian Slater and Winona Ryder kill two football jocks at their high school and disguise the murder as a gay double suicide, they establish the sexual identity of their victims beyond a shadow of a doubt by planting on them, along with a fake suicide note, a number of telltale "homosexual artifacts," as they call them—including mascara, a bottle of mineral water, and, most notably, a "Joan Crawford postcard."

That joke works because it appeals to homophobic clichés—the kind of homophobic clichés that dumb football jocks and their doltish parents are likely to accept as gospel. But the Joan Crawford cult is not just an outmoded stereotype. Gay boys are still collecting Joan Crawford postcards. Two decades after *Heathers,* the spring 2008 issue of a gay travel magazine called *The Out Traveler* (a spin-off from *Out* magazine) offered its presumably more enlightened readership a list of community-based destinations devoted to various gay cult figures, designed for out-and-proud tourists who want to make "the ultimate gay pilgrimage." Inviting them to "celebrate the lives and times of gay-popular icons old and new at these carefully (sometimes obsessively) curated private collections and diva museums," the magazine recommended seven different locales, among them "The Legendary Joan Crawford Collection" in San Francisco, assembled not by some aged movie queen but by a youthful Crawford enthusiast.

> The clippings, cigarette cards, rare vintage photos, letters, film reels, and scrapbooks of 32-year-old San Francisco resident and Crawford devotee Neil Maciejewski's expansive collection prove just why this classic Hollywood "mommie" truly was the dearest. Get a history lesson and a preview of the wares on his website, then e-mail for a private viewing at his Noe Valley home. *LegendaryJoanCrawford.com*[1]

Contrast all this with the response of straight film critic David Denby: "Must we hate Joan Crawford?"[2] Denby's presumptively inclusive "we" ignores, and excludes, a lot of gay men.

So what *is* it about Joan Crawford? And where do we locate the source of the apparent truth, universally acknowledged, that a young man in possession of a Joan Crawford postcard must necessarily be gay—or, at least, could not possibly be straight? What produced that bit of seemingly incontrovertible folk wisdom?

And what, to take another example, is the particular point of featuring Joan Crawford in the opening section of an elegy to the generations of men lost to AIDS by the Black gay poet Craig G. Harris?

> "Marc with a 'c'
> Steven with a 'v'
> and a hyphen in between,
> thank you,"
> he'd explain,
> and God help you

if you spelled either
incorrectly

couldn't cook to save his soul,
except for baked chicken
and steamed broccoli

couldn't match his clothes
and I never found him
particularly handsome
but he was my first true love
and a seminal thinker

he could interpret Kant,
Descartes, and Fanon
over breakfast or half asleep,
pump out a more than respectable
first draft of a one-act
in two hours or less,
and recall every line
Joan Crawford
ever spoke before a camera[3]

The full weight of Crawford's importance can be measured by her climactic position in this sequence and the way her name occupies an entire line of verse—coming right after the word "line" for extra emphasis, in case we missed it.

And similarly: What is the cultural or sexual logic that accounts for the presence of the following item, halfway down a widely circulated Internet list of "100 Best Things about Being a Gay Man"? "46. You understand, viscerally, Joan Crawford."[4] Where does that visceral gay understanding come from? What, in short, explains gay male culture's obsession with Joan Crawford and with her most famous and only Oscar-winning performance?

A complete answer to those large, over-determined questions would probably require many volumes of cultural history and social analysis. But we can narrow down the topic, and get a manageable grip on it, by concentrating our attention on *Mildred Pierce* and by making use of the framework set up in the previous chapter. To judge from that one movie, and a number of other Crawford vehicles as well, Joan Crawford excelled in the portrayal of strong women who nonetheless fall victim, at least for a while, to the potential *horror and tragedy* of normal family life. In the decades following *Mildred Pierce,* Crawford tried to capitalize on her success in that film, specializing in similar roles and making them her trademark, her own personal brand, defined by a signature combination of *glamour* and *abjection* (that is, extreme, degrading humiliation).[5]

Does gay male culture teach us to laugh at Joan Crawford, then? It would be inaccurate to reduce the gay male cultural response to Crawford, and to the horrifying or tragic domestic situations into which Hollywood loved to plunge her, to anything quite so simple as "laughter"—though laughter clearly does contribute to that response. At least, there is nothing simple or straightforward about the kind of laughter that emanates from those audiences whom gay male culture has trained to respond to horrifying or tragic situations with such incongruous, confounding hilarity. In this case, laughter itself, the mere fact of it, does not register other crucial aspects of the gay male cultural response—such as the intensity of the identification with the female star, or the depth of intoxication with her and her dramatic situation—although it may be a sign of them.

☙

So let's take a closer look at *Mildred Pierce* and examine a few details in it, one at a time. We can begin by considering a single line spoken by Crawford in a single memorable scene, the most notoriously shocking and celebrated scene in the entire movie.[6] Not coincidentally, the line solicits parody and reperformance from gay men—at least, if one of my former boyfriends is at all typical.

Here is the context. Mildred Pierce is a doting, dutiful, self-sacrificing, martyred mother, blindly devoted to her selfish, unfeeling, ungrateful, scheming, vicious, hateful, greedy, no-good daughter,

Veda (played by Ann Blyth). Separated from her unemployed, erratic husband, she has been forced to become a self-reliant, hard-working, hard-headed businesswoman, and she has managed to translate her humble domestic skills into the lucrative ownership of a successful restaurant chain. When the scene begins, Mildred and Veda have just come home from a formal meeting with a wealthy family. The family's sweet, good-looking, dopey son has secretly married Veda, and the boy's worldly, snobbish mother is determined to have the marriage annulled. But at the family conclave, Veda, on the advice of Mildred's sleazy business partner, Wally, claims that she is pregnant by the son, a claim that is at least sufficiently plausible for the family lawyer to recommend paying Veda off to the tune of $10,000. With that, the meeting concludes, and Mildred and Veda return to their modest bungalow. Veda has the check in hand.

In the format of this book, the best I can do is transcribe the scene and include a few stills from it (Figures 5–9).

Lighting, facial expression, vocal inflection, music, camera angles, and the visual rhetoric of classic Hollywood film noir cinematography contribute considerably more to the impact of the film on the spectator than mere text and editing. I will come back to some of these elements. In the meantime, readers are advised to have a look for themselves. The film is widely available on DVD.

> **SHOT** (1) *Fade up on* VEDA, *reclining on sofa. She takes the check in both hands and kisses it.*
>
> VEDA: Well, that's that.
>
> *VEDA rights herself. Pan out to reveal* MILDRED *standing nearby.*
>
> MILDRED: I'm sorry this had to happen. Sorry for the boy. He seemed very nice.
>
> VEDA: Oh, Ted's all right, really. [*laughs*] Did you see the look on his face when we told him he was going to be a father?
>
> MILDRED: I wish you wouldn't joke about it. [*crosses behind sofa*]
>
> VEDA: Mother, you're a scream, really you are. [*turns to face* MILDRED, *kneels on sofa*] The next thing I know, you'll be knitting little garments.
>
> MILDRED: I don't see anything so ridiculous about that.

5 Frame capture from *Mildred Pierce* (Michael Curtiz, 1945). Mildred and Veda struggle over the check.

6 Frame capture from *Mildred Pierce* (Michael Curtiz, 1945). Veda slaps Mildred.

7 Frame capture from *Mildred Pierce* (Michael Curtiz, 1945). Mildred collapses against the railing of the stairway.

8 Frame capture from *Mildred Pierce* (Michael Curtiz, 1945). "Get out before I kill you."

9 Frame capture from *Mildred Pierce* (Michael Curtiz, 1945). A parting glance.

VEDA: If I were you, I'd save myself the trouble. [*rises, crosses room*]

MILDRED [*realizing, crosses to* VEDA, *puts hands on her shoulders*]: You're not going to have a baby?

VEDA [*turning away*]: At this stage it's a matter of opinion, and in my opinion I'm going to have a baby. [*puts check into purse*] I can always be mistaken. [*closes purse, puts it on table*]

MILDRED: How could you do such a thing? How could you?

VEDA: I got the money, didn't I?

MILDRED: Oh, I see.

VEDA [*crosses to stairs*]: I'll have to give Wally part of it to keep him quiet, but there's enough left for me.

SHOT (2) *close up on* MILDRED

MILDRED: The money. That's what you live for, isn't it? You'd do anything for money, wouldn't you? Even blackmail.

SHOT (3) *return to* (1)

VEDA: Oh, grow up.

MILDRED: I've never denied you anything. Anything money could
buy I've given you. But that wasn't enough, was it? All right, Veda,
from now on things are going to be different.

VEDA [*turns, crosses to* MILDRED]: I'll say they're going to be different.
Why do you think I went to all this trouble? Why do you think I
want money so badly?

MILDRED: All right, why?

SHOT (4) *close up on* VEDA, *with* MILDRED *in foreground of frame*

VEDA: Are you sure you want to know?

MILDRED: Yes.

VEDA: Then I'll tell you. With this money I can get away from you.

SHOT (5) *reverse of* (4)

MILDRED [*with a slight gasp*]: Veda!

VEDA: From you and your chickens and your pies and your kitchens
and everything that smells of grease.

SHOT (6) *return to* (1)

VEDA: I can get away from this shack with its cheap furniture, and
this town and its dollar days, and its women that wear uniforms
and its men that wear overalls. [*turns back to table, picks up purse*]

MILDRED: Veda, I think I'm really seeing you for the first time in my
life, and you're cheap and horrible.

VEDA: You think just because you made a little money you can get a
new hairdo and some expensive clothes and turn yourself into a
lady.

SHOT (7) *return to* (4)

VEDA: But you can't. Because you'll never be anything but a common frump,

SHOT (8) *return to* (5)

VEDA: . . . whose father lived over a grocery store and whose mother took in washing.

SHOT (9) *return to* (4)

VEDA: With this money I can get away from every rotten stinking thing that makes me think of this place or you.

SHOT (10) *return to* (1). *VEDA turns and runs upstairs with purse.*

MILDRED [*raises her voice*]: Veda!
VEDA turns and stops. MILDRED crosses to stairs.

SHOT (11) *new establishing shot of VEDA and MILDRED on stairs*

MILDRED [*reaching for purse*]: Give me that check.
VEDA: Not on your life.
MILDRED [*taking purse*]: I said give it to me.
MILDRED opens purse, removes check, tears it up. VEDA slaps her very hard. MILDRED falls against stair railing with a look of horror, then pulls herself back up on her feet. Pull in close on her face.
MILDRED: Get out, Veda. Get your things out of this house right now before I throw them into the street and you with them. Get out before I kill you.

SHOT (12) *close on VEDA*

SHOT (13) *return to* (11). *VEDA turns and runs upstairs.*

SHOT (14) *close on MILDRED. We hear a door slam. Pull in, then fade out.*

I can still hear the note of pleasure in my ex-boyfriend's voice as he practiced saying, to no one in particular, in his best Joan Crawford accent (complete with palatalized *l*'s), "Get out. Get out before I kill you." My question is: What is so gratifying about this particular line, and what is so funny—or at least so delectable—about this horrific scene, with its physical and emotional violence? What accounts for the mesmeric fascination that this and other notorious highlights from Joan Crawford's performing career have exercised on gay male culture, and what can they tell us about male homosexuality as a queer—that is, anti-social—sensibility or subjectivity?

These are obvious questions, but they are almost never asked.[7] They are no doubt fiendishly difficult to answer, especially without recourse to some ready-made theory. So let's defer that daunting task for the moment, until we have assembled the empirical evidence we'll need—and until we have built up, on that basis, a framework sufficiently robust to guide our interpretation with some measure of security.

Ethan Mordden, the gay novelist and critic, gives us a few hints about how to think about the figure of Joan Crawford and her gay appeal. In his book-length cultural history of "the women who made Hollywood," he sketches with a few quick brush-strokes the situation in which Crawford found herself during the latter part of her career, and produces a picture rich in implications for the questions we are trying to answer. "Joan Crawford is one of stardom's tragic figures, because she was one of the few who knew exactly how it worked and what it meant, yet even she could not master it. . . . Even as convinced fans called her the greatest of movie stars, the definition of kind, even as writers told of her climb to the summit, even as drag queens did Mildred Pierce into their mirrors, in the opulent, pathetic homage of the loser to the winner . . . she was dying alone in despair."[8] This horrifying and piteous portrait of Crawford focuses on the contrast between her glamour and her abjection, a characteristic combination never displayed to more spectacular effect than in Mildred Pierce itself, and especially in the scene we have just witnessed, where her austere elegance and dignified bearing contrast with the abuse she suffers and the social and emotional mortification her face so eloquently registers. Also worth remarking is Mordden's casually knowing reference to the constant tribute paid to Crawford's most famous character by her homosexual fans, in the double register of adoring imitation and vengeful parody. Mordden implies that Crawford's performance of glamorous and abject femininity in *Mildred Pierce* was so potent, so intense, so perfect, and at the same time so extravagantly theatrical, that no drag queen could either resist it or equal it. But that, on Mordden's own account, does not seem to have kept drag queens from trying. . . .

So what exactly is the relation between feminine glamour and feminine abjection in the eyes of gay male culture? What is the logic that underlies their combination and makes it so gripping and so suggestive? How is that combination of glamour and abjection connected to gay male culture's distinctive violation of the generic boundaries between tragedy and comedy, specifically the practice of laughing at situations that are horrifying or tragic?

In order to arrive at an answer to those questions, let's consider another example, closely related to the previous one.

༺༺༻

In real life, Joan Crawford adopted five children, the eldest of which was a girl named Christina. In adulthood, Christina Crawford wrote a best-selling memoir about Life with Mother, called *Mommie Dearest,* in which she recounted Crawford's demented, alcoholic abuse of her adoptive children.[9] The autobiography was made into a film of the same title in 1981, with Faye Dunaway in the title role.

That movie is an even more notorious gay male cult classic than *Mildred Pierce.* It is famous in particular for the scene in which Crawford, in a drunkenly sentimental mood, enters her children's bedroom at night and, suddenly appalled at the sight of a wire hanger incongruously suspended amid the delicate, matching upholstered hangers carefully chosen for her daughter's wardrobe, violently beats Christina with it and trashes her room. In the same issue of *The Out Traveler* that encouraged its readers to visit "The Legendary Joan Crawford Collection" in San Francisco, so that they could discover "just why this classic Hollywood 'mommie' truly was the dearest," a separate article entitled "The Best Gay-Owned Spas in the U.S." noted that the "Mexican-born gay skin care guru Enrique Ramirez" was offering female clients at his Face to Face spa in New York "the Mommie Dearest Massage to relieve edema and back pain during pregnancy (don't worry, no wire hangers are used)."[10]

Mommie Dearest contains a number of other scenes that replay, in their own extravagant way, the mother-daughter conflict so memorably portrayed in *Mildred Pierce*. Here is one of them, along with the background you need to understand it. Christina has been caught making out with a boy at her boarding school; her mother has been called and—against both her daughter's wishes and the advice of the headmistress—has indignantly removed her daughter from the school. Mother and daughter (the one righteous, the other sullen) arrive home, where a reporter from a women's magazine has taken up residence in order to do an in-depth story about Joan Crawford's professional and domestic life (Figures 10–16).

> **SHOT** (1) *Night. Car pulls into driveway, stops.*
>
> **SHOT** (2) *Interior of car.* TINA *in foreground;* JOAN *in background, at the wheel.*
>
> JOAN [*turning to* TINA, *with quiet intensity*]: All right. Tina, look at me. Barbara Bennett is here from New York doing a cover story on me for *Redbook*. Tina, look at me when I'm talking to you.
>
> **SHOT** (3) *reverse of* (2). TINA *turns to face* JOAN.
>
> **SHOT** (4) *return to* (2).
>
> JOAN: This is very important to me.
>
> **SHOT** (5) *return to* (3)
>
> JOAN: I don't want any trouble from you.
>
> **SHOT** (6) *return to* (2). JOAN *exits car.*
>
> **SHOT** (7) *Interior of house.* BARBARA *in foreground at desk, back to camera, typing.* JOAN *enters from rear.*

10 Frame capture from *Mommie Dearest* (Frank Perry, 1981). Joan slaps Christina for the first time.

11 Frame capture from *Mommie Dearest* (Frank Perry, 1981). Joan checks out the damage.

12 Frame capture from *Mommie Dearest* (Frank Perry, 1981). "Why can't you give me the respect that I'm entitled to?"

13 Frame capture from *Mommie Dearest* (Frank Perry, 1981). Joan loses it.

14 Frame capture from *Mommie Dearest* (Frank Perry, 1981). Joan strangling Christina.

JOAN: We're back.

BARBARA: You're gonna love this.

SHOT (8) *reverse to* BARBARA*'s face.*

BARBARA: Movie star manages to have it all: career, home, and family. [*stretches out arms*]

SHOT (9) *return to* (7). JOAN *laughs, imitates* BARBARA*'s gesture.*

JOAN: Let me see that.

15 Frame capture from *Mommie Dearest* (Frank Perry, 1981). Joan and Christina, seen from above amid the wreckage.

16 Frame capture from *Mommie Dearest* (Frank Perry, 1981). Joan defiant.

JOAN *crosses to* BARBARA *at desk.* TINA *enters from rear.*

BARBARA: My God, Christina. It can't be.

SHOT (10) *return to* (8)

BARBARA: The last time I saw you, you were four.

SHOT (11) *close on* TINA.

TINA: How are you, Miss Bennett?

SHOT (12) *close on* JOAN.

BARBARA: God, call me Barbara. Teaching you some fancy manners at Chadwick.

JOAN: That's not *all* they're teaching her.

SHOT (13) *new close up on* BARBARA.

BARBARA [*slight pause, then trying to cover the tension*]: Well, how do you like school?

TINA: Very much, thank you.

SHOT (14) *return to* (12)

JOAN [*bitterly*]: She got expelled.

SHOT (15) *new close up on* TINA.

TINA: That's a lie.

SHOT (16) JOAN *from rear. Her head snaps around.*

SHOT (17) *return to* (15)

SHOT (18) *return to* (16). JOAN *rises.*

JOAN: Excuse me, Barbara.
JOAN *turns and crosses forward toward camera—i.e., toward* TINA.
JOAN: Tina, I want to talk to you.

SHOT (19) *return to* (15)

SHOT (20) *return to* (18)

JOAN [*meaningfully*]: In the other room.

SHOT (21) *return to* (8)

SHOT (22) *return to* (7). TINA *and* JOAN *exit.*

SHOT (23) TINA *and* JOAN *proceed through foyer to opposite side,* TINA *in lead. Pan along through to room opposite.* JOAN *slams purse on table, faces* TINA.

JOAN [*now raising her voice*]: Why do you deliberately defy me?

SHOT (24) *reverse to* TINA*'s face.*

TINA: Why did you tell her I got expelled?

SHOT (25) *return to* (23), *only tighter. JOAN crosses to TINA.*

JOAN: Because you did get expelled.

SHOT (26) *return to* (24)

TINA: That is a lie.

SHOT (27) *return to* (25). *JOAN slaps TINA.*

SHOT (28) *return to* (24)

SHOT (29) *return to* (25). *JOAN slaps TINA again.*

SHOT (30) *return to* (24)

SHOT (31) *return to* (25)

JOAN: You love it, don't you?

SHOT (32) *return to* (24)

JOAN: You *love* to make me hit you!

SHOT (33) *shot of BARBARA entering room.*

BARBARA: Joan.

SHOT (34) *return to* (25)

JOAN: Barbara, please! Please, Barbara!

SHOT (35) *return to* (33)

JOAN: Leave us alone, Barbara. If you need anything, ask Carol Ann. [BARBARA *turns and leaves*]

SHOT (36) *return to* (25)

JOAN: This is wonderful. This is WONDERFUL! [*pull out*] You, you deliberately embarrass me in front of a reporter. A reporter! I told you how important this is to me. I told you! [*turns her back to TINA*]

SHOT (37) *return to* (24)

TINA: Why did you adopt me?

SHOT (38) *return to* (36). *JOAN wheels around.*

JOAN: What?

SHOT (39) *return to* (24)

TINA [*with even intensity*]: Why did you adopt me?

SHOT (40) *return to* (36)

JOAN: Because I wanted a child. Because I wanted someone to love.

SHOT (41) *return to* (24)

TINA: Don't you act for me. I wanna know. Why did you adopt me?

SHOT (42) *return to* (36)

JOAN: Maybe I did it for a little extra publicity.

SHOT (43) *return to* (24)

SHOT (44) *return to* (36)

JOAN: That's not true. You know that's not true.

SHOT (45) *return to* (24)

TINA: Maybe just a little true.

SHOT (46) *return to* (36). *TINA crosses out of frame to right.*

SHOT (47) *new establishing shot. TINA in foreground, JOAN in back-ground on riser.*

JOAN: I don't know what to do with you.

SHOT (48) *tight close up on TINA's face as she turns.*

TINA [*loud*]: Why not?

SHOT (49) *close on JOAN, as she walks toward camera—i.e., toward TINA.*

JOAN: I don't ask much from you, girl. WHY CAN'T YOU GIVE ME THE RESPECT THAT I'M ENTITLED TO? WHY CAN'T YOU TREAT ME LIKE I WOULD BE TREATED BY ANY STRANGER ON THE STREET?

SHOT (50) *return to* (48)

TINA: BECAUSE I AM NOT ONE OF YOUR FANS!

SHOT (51) *new establishing shot.* TINA *in foreground,* JOAN *in background, facing each other.* JOAN *raises hands to* TINA*'s throat, falls forward, shrieks.*

SHOT (52) *shot of glass-topped end table with lamp.* TINA *falls backward onto it,* JOAN *on top of her, her hands around* TINA*'s throat. Table buckles, lamp crashes to floor.*

TINA [*choking*]: Mommie!
JOAN: Dammit, love me, you!

SHOT (53) *close on* TINA, *choking.*

TINA: Mommie!

SHOT (54) *close on* JOAN, *strangling.*

JOAN: Say it! Say it! Say it! You've hated me—

SHOT (55) TINA *and* JOAN *viewed from behind,* JOAN *on knees astride* TINA.

JOAN: You never loved me!

SHOT (56) *return to* (53)

JOAN: You never, you've always taken and taken—

SHOT (57) *return to* (54)

JOAN: You never wanted to be my daughter—

SHOT (58) TINA *and* JOAN *viewed in profile.*

JOAN: You've always hated everything! Everything, everything! Love me!

SHOT (59) *return to* (54). BARBARA *and* CAROL ANN *enter and pull* JOAN *off* TINA.

CAROL ANN: Joan, get off! Get off, you're gonna kill her!
JOAN *rises, screaming.*

> **SHOT** (60) *return to* (58). *TINA manages to kick JOAN off. JOAN rises to her knees, grabs her crotch. BARBARA and CAROL ANN on their knees in the background. TINA rolling around and choking in foreground.*
>
> JOAN: Get out! Get out!
>
> **SHOT** (61) *close up on TINA.*
>
> TINA [*crying*]: Mommie.

I once heard an entire movie theater full of gay men (or was it a video bar?) shout at the screen, in unison with the actress, and in a single voice, "I AM NOT ONE OF YOUR FANS!" The better-known line, however, which some of those gay men also declaimed, is the one immediately preceding it: "WHY CAN'T YOU GIVE ME THE RESPECT THAT I'M ENTITLED TO?"

Once again, the same questions arise. Why these lines? Why this scene? Why the delectation with which gay male culture affectionately rehearses these moments of horror and abuse? And how does the scene in *Mommie Dearest* repeat and reinterpret similar dramatic moments from *Mildred Pierce*?

Instead of trying to answer those questions right away—we *will* get to them, eventually—let us consider a third and final cinematic example.

෬෬

Half a century after the release of *Mildred Pierce,* John Epperson—a gay male drag performer, better known by his stage name, Lypsinka —restaged the foregoing scene from *Mommie Dearest.* In a performance at the New York drag festival called Wigstock, Epperson combined the scene from *Mommie Dearest* with other moments from the same movie, plus the rousing song "But Alive" from the Broadway musical *Applause!* (based on that other gay male cult classic, Joseph L. Mankiewicz's 1950 film *All about Eve*), where the song is set in a gay bar. (Epperson has since gone on to mount entire one-man/woman shows about Joan Crawford called *Lypsinka Is Harriet Craig!* and, more recently, *The Passion of the Crawford.*)[11] The performance was recorded

17 Frame capture from *Wigstock: The Movie* (Barry Shils, 1995). Lypsinka: "You, you deliberately embarrass me in front of a reporter."

18 Frame capture from *Wigstock: The Movie* (Barry Shils, 1995). Lypsinka being fierce.

in a 1995 film called *Wigstock: The Movie*, directed by Barry Shils, which includes both performance clips and interviews with the performers. No transcription can do justice to Epperson's routine (Figures 17–18). Here's the best one I can provide.

> **SHOT** (1) *shot from audience. Musical fanfare.* LYPSINKA *removes her black cloak to reveal a petite, cream-colored dress beneath.*
> LYPSINKA: Well, how do I look? [*laughs*]

SHOT (2) *shot from stage right.*

LYPSINKA: Barbara Bennett is here doing a cover story on me for *Red-book*. I don't want any trouble from *you!* [*Admonishing gesture to her entourage of male dancers, who fall away from her. Music begins. LYPSINKA has sudden look of horror as she casts her eyes downward.*]

SHOT (3) *shot from audience. LYPSINKA crouches down, runs her hand over back of a loudspeaker as though checking for dirt, then rises, examining her hand.*

SHOT (4) *shot from audience. LYPSINKA, standing, addresses audience.*

LYPSINKA: This is wonderful. This is wonderful!

SHOT (5) *shot from audience. LYPSINKA addresses entourage and audience alternately.*

LYPSINKA: You, you deliberately embarrass me in front of a reporter. A reporter! I told you how important this is to me. I told you!

SHOT (6) *shot from stage right. LYPSINKA turns from entourage in resignation.*

LYPSINKA: I don't know what to do with you.

SHOT (7) *shot from stage right. Entourage dancing.*

SHOT (8) *shot inside studio, as LYPSINKA and entourage rehearse this number out of costume. LYPSINKA crouches in front of room, examining hand as before, then rises to address entourage.*

LYPSINKA: How? How could this happen? How could you humiliate me this way? [*LYPSINKA mimes slapping member of entourage.*]
LYPSINKA: Look at me. Why can't you give—

SHOT (9) *return to shot of stage from audience.*

LYPSINKA: —me the respect that I'm entitled to? [*audience cheers*] Why? Why? [*LYPSINKA jumps up and down*] Answer me. This is appalling. [*dances*]

SHOT (10) *shot from stage right. LYPSINKA crosses stage right. Dancing* stops. *"BARBARA BENNETT"—a little person in drag—enters stage left with steno pad and pencil.*

BARBARA: *[sings]* I'm known—

SHOT (11) *shot of BARBARA from audience.*

BARBARA: —as Barbara.
LYPSINKA: Barbara—

SHOT (12) *shot of studio rehearsal.*

LYPSINKA: —please! Please, Barbara!
LYPSINKA shoos BARBARA away. BARBARA reclines on back of entourage member stage left; LYPSINKA sits on back of entourage member stage right.
LYPSINKA *[sings]*: I feel groggy and weary and tragic—

SHOT (13) *shot of stage from audience.*

LYPSINKA: Punchy and bleary and fresh out of magic,
  But alive! But alive! But alive!
LYPSINKA and BARBARA rise.
LYPSINKA: I feel twitchy and bitchy and manic—

SHOT (14) *shot of BARBARA from stage right. BARBARA mimes pulling something off of LYPSINKA's skirt and stomping on it.*

LYPSINKA: Calm and collected and choking with panic,
  But alive—

SHOT (15) *shot of LYPSINKA and BARBARA from audience. BARBARA taking notes.*

LYPSINKA: But alive! But alive!

SHOT (16) *cut to interview of LYPSINKA out of drag.*

LYPSINKA: The name "Lypsinka" tells you what you're going to see, but it also drips with irony, I think, this name, um, and I wanted the name to evoke also an exotic, one-name fashion model, i.e., Verushka, or Dovima, or Wilhelmina: Lypsinka.

SHOT (17) *cut back to stage, shot from audience.*

LYPSINKA [*sings*]: I'm a thousand different people—

SHOT (18) *shot from stage right.*

LYPSINKA: —every single one is real.

SHOT (19) *cut to audience view of* BARBARA, *who is pursuing* LYPSINKA *across stage to right and becoming entangled in her skirts.*

LYPSINKA: I've a million different feelings—[*LYPSINKA pushes BAR-BARA away to left.*]

SHOT (20) *audience view.* LYPSINKA *turns to address* BARBARA.

LYPSINKA: Okay, but at least I feel!

SHOT (21) *shot of* BARBARA, *taking notes.*

LYPSINKA: And I feel—

SHOT (22) *shot from audience.*

LYPSINKA: —rotten, yet covered with roses,
    Younger than springtime and older than Moses,
    But alive—

SHOT (23) *shot of* LYPSINKA *and* BARBARA *from upper stage right.*

LYPSINKA: But alive! But alive!

SHOT (24) *cut to interview.*

LYPSINKA: Sooner or later, um, it just sort of became real that, um, I was used as a female model, and in '91 Thierry Mugler actually had the nerve to put me on his runway in Paris. And I've done a lot of fashion stuff since then.

SHOT (25) *cut back to stage, shot from upper stage right.*

LYPSINKA [*sings*]: And I feel brilliant and brash and bombastic—

SHOT (26) *cut to shot of* LYPSINKA *and* BARBARA *from rear of stage.*

LYPSINKA: Limp as a puppet, and simply fantastic,
  But alive! But alive! But alive!

SHOT (27) *shot of* BARBARA *from audience.* BARBARA *crosses to center stage, where she is picked up, held aloft and spun around by entourage.*

ENTOURAGE [*sings*]: She's here, she's here, can you believe it?
  She's here, oh, god, I can't believe it!
  She's here, it's just too groovy to believe! Woooh!
Pan out to include LYPSINKA, *stage left.* LYPSINKA *rolls her eyes, sticks out tongue at audience.*

SHOT (28) *shot from upper stage right. Having put* BARBARA *down, entourage dances, arms upraised.*

SHOT (29) *shot of* BARBARA *dancing in unison with entourage downstage left, near* LYPSINKA.

LYPSINKA [*hands on hips*]: Barbara, please! [LYPSINKA *shoos* BARBARA *stage right.*] Please, Barbara! [LYPSINKA *kicks a foot in* BARBARA'*s direction.*]

SHOT (30) *shot from audience.* LYPSINKA *center stage. Dance.* LYPSINKA, *appearing to grow dizzy, staggers upstage.*

SHOT (31) *shot from upstage right.* LYPSINKA *crosses upstage to join entourage.*

SHOT (32) *shot from audience.*

ENTOURAGE [*sings*]: I admit I'm slightly cuckoo,
  But it's dull to be too sane.
As they sing they surround LYPSINKA, *screening her from the audience's view. On "sane," they jump away stage left and right. As they do so,* LYPSINKA *rips off her skirt to reveal her legs.*
LYPSINKA [*sings/speaks*]: And I feel brilliant! Bombastic! [*cheers from entourage*] Super! Fantastic! [BARBARA *enters stage right.*] Alive! [BARBARA *slaps* LYPSINKA *on now-exposed thigh.*]
LYPSINKA [*to* BARBARA]: Barbara, please! [*pan out*] Alive! [BARBARA *slaps* LYPSINKA *on thigh again. To* BARBARA]: Barbara, please! [*pan*

left] Alive! [*BARBARA grabs onto LYPSINKA's leg. LYPSINKA, walking, drags her across stage to left. LYPSINKA turns and shakes fist at BAR-BARA, who detaches herself and flees right to join entourage, pursued by LYPSINKA. Pan right.*]

LYPSINKA [*turning to audience*]: Don't fuck with me, fellas!

In reading the transcription of this film clip, you will have noticed how the crowd of mostly gay men watching Lypsinka's performance cheers wildly at her delivery of the line, "Why can't you give me the respect that I'm entitled to?" They know that line. They hear it coming. They love it. They respond to it. And they celebrate Lypsinka's delivery of it.

Not only, then, has Joan Crawford, along with her implication in these violent scenes of mother-daughter conflict, been taken up by gay male culture and made the focus of reperformance and parody. She has also elicited a characteristic response that is both distinctive and specific to gay male culture. Straight male culture does not reproduce itself by transmitting to each new generation of boys a detailed knowledge of these movies, nor does it teach its members to learn selected lines from *Mommie Dearest* by heart, nor does it stage festivals at which those lines are repeated in front of audiences who await them with anticipation and greet them with enthusiasm. Lesbian bars may occasionally show clips from *Mommie Dearest,* but the movie is not a staple of heterosexual female cultural institutions, nor does it enjoy the cult status among women of, say, *Thelma and Louise.*

To be sure, not all gay men know these movies, reperform these lines, or restage these scenes of horror in a comic mode. And the Joan Crawford cult, though still current, is undoubtedly showing its age. But the gay male world has created certain enduring social institutions that make it possible for these particular moments from straight, mainstream culture to be selected, decontextualized, replayed, and recoded with queer meanings. And the circulation and communal sharing of these queered cinematic moments appear to play a crucial role in the social process by which people, both gay and straight, are initiated into the culture of male homosexuality, come to recognize it as such, and gradually forge a sense of personal and cultural identity—if only to the extent of participating in festivals like Wigstock. This procedure is one crucial element of the cultural practice of male homosexuality, an important part of the initiatory process by which gay men as well as many others learn how to be gay.

✑✇

If there were any doubt that straight culture and gay culture, irrespective of the sexuality of the individuals who happen to participate in those cultures, understand the logic of genre differently, and therefore respond dissimilarly to the staging of horrifying or tragic situations—if there were any doubt about any of that, a glance at the next example would suffice to dispel it.

Consider a few of the 230 comments on the movie version of *Mommie Dearest* that have been posted to the Amazon.com retail website. Some of the writers see nothing humorous about the film or about Faye Dunaway's performance. They say things like this (I am quoting them directly):

> I find nothing funny about it. It has the usual jokes now and then, but truly I've never even cracked a smile while watching this movie, it was never meant to be funny. There is nothing funny about child abuse, alcoholism, or any of the other themes shown in this movie.

> I've always believed that this film has been misunderstood. Admittedly I can understand why people would laugh at scenes like the one where Faye Dunaway shouts to her daughter, "Tina, bring me the ax!" But is child abuse really funny? I don't think so. I must admit that the scenes of child abuse, perhaps exploitative, are chilling and realistic.

> This movie was downright brutal. How could anyone treat their kids that way? I mean, she got mad if her daughter used wire hangers. She only allowed her kid to have one toy for their birthday and Christmas. If she was my mom I would have to kill myself to be in peace!!!

I didn't laugh or smile at any of this the slightest bit. I guess you people are incredibly insensitive to child abuse or something. You just lowered my opinion of the human race by several notches. I'd like to move to another planet where people don't think this movie is funny.

Motives for wanting to be known as the parent of someone else's child should always be questioned—like Crawford's motive for publicity. Also, money does not guarantee a healthy, happy environment. For all her wealth, Crawford provided an extremely dysfunctional home for her adoptees. And the abuse an adoptee suffers is compounded by the emotional damage that comes with adoption itself, so please watch this movie with Christina in mind.

It would be careless to overlook the underlying message here—how Joan Crawford adopted the children for all the wrong reasons, and hence treated them in the manner that she did. And tormenting a child over wire hangers etc. is no laughing matter, even if it appeared like that in the movie to some. This other side of Joan Crawford was a manifestation of her addiction to ostentation, insecurities, fear, work stress, non-maternal instincts, power hungry, calculating ways. There was no real depth to her love for the children. She was self-centered, and so everything she did revolved around that.

Earnest, judgmental, sententious, moralistic, therapeutic, *literal:* How much straighter can you get? Could anyone doubt that these views, with their essentially documentary relation to the movie and its supposedly serious portrayal of important social and psychological problems, could spring from anything but a heterosexual culture, regardless of the sexuality of the individuals who penned those remarks?

Now consider some of the other reactions.

If you don't love this movie you're dead. It made me uneasy when I first saw it as a young teenager. Now it's so horrible that it soars on every level. It's a train wreck, and you'll love it.

I have to say that I'm baffled by the people who actually take this movie seriously and are seemingly offended by those of us who feel it has well deserved its claim to the title—campiest movie of all time!

My favorite line in this movie is not the over-used "No wire hangers!" but another line from later in the same scene. Joan has beaten the ungrateful brat Christina over the head with Dutch Cleanser, and seeing what she has done, Joan looks at the mess she has made and barks at Christina, "Clean up this mess." Christina stares up at her and asks, "How?" Joan responds, "You figure it out." Words to live by.

I sat in a movie theater watching in wide-eyed wonder at the image of Faye Dunaway as Joan Crawford, and I knew I was in for a treat! And boy, did Faye deliver! She was always a bit over the top with directors that didn't know how to handle her (much like Crawford herself) but I wasn't ready for the spectacle I was about to witness! And I howled with laughter and loved her for it! Yes, Crawford would not likely be voted "Mother of the Year," but the image of Faye, dressed in black and her face covered in cold cream and a slash of red lipstick, is nothing less than a camp nightmare as she stalks about, ripping clothes from the dreaded wire hangers, her face a Kabuki mask of torment! Faye took her place as a Camp Madonna with this performance and, if you dare, watch it more than once, even twice.

The most awesome movie of all time. It's incredible from beginning to end. I've seen it close to 100 times, and can lip synch absolutely every scene in my sleep. The planets and stars lined up on this one.

A trainwreck with eyebrows. Faye Dunaway chews, swallows, and spits out the scenery, the script, and the co-stars—subtlety and sensitivity take a back seat to glaring color, great thumping plot points, and a diva's performance that would make the best of Bette look rank. Miss D's performance is so over the top and so incredibly awful that the release of the DVD is a blessing—we can now control the Dunaway Dosage, and watch it a bit at a time.

Joan Crawford, with her impossibly-arched eyebrows and gargantuan shoulderpads, was a camp icon long before *Mommie Dearest* even went before the cameras. Thanks to Faye Dunaway's performance in the film, Joan Crawford rose to the position of camp's High Priestess, and fans wouldn't have it any other way.

Girl, this movie is too much! Miss Dunaway deserved an Oscar for playing the legendary Joan Crawford, who adopted two blonde brats who constantly interfered with her career. Tina got a ghetto beating for using wire hangers and not eating her rare meat for lunch. How DARE that blonde jezebel wench disrespect Miss Crawford?! I also liked the part when Joan choked Tina after she made that flip comment "I'm not one of your FANS!" That'll teach her! All in all, an excellent movie with fabulous costumes, makeup, set design, and whatnot. You go, Miss Crawford![12]

It would be hasty, I think, to conclude that the authors of the second set of comments endorse child abuse or approve of adopting children for the purposes of publicity or professional advancement. It would also be a mistake to believe that they are heartless or insensitive to the horrors depicted in the film. On the contrary, they admit that "it made me uneasy," that it is like a "trainwreck"; and they take it seriously enough to watch it repeatedly and to find in it "words to live by." So their enjoyment of it does not exclude an awareness of everything about the incidents depicted in the film that had horrified the first set of commentators. The second set of commentators laugh at what their straight (or straight-acting) comrades found *merely* tragic or horrifying.

Of course, we have no way of knowing whether the authors of the second batch of reviews are all gay men (some of the most enthusiastic commentators talk of seeing the movie with their husbands or wives), any more than we have any way of knowing whether the authors of the first batch of reviews are all straight (some of the most solemn commentators mention seeing the movie before or after coming out). But we don't need to know what their sexuality is; what we need to know is their cultural affiliation, the particular standpoint from which they view and interpret the movie. Whether or not they happen to be gay, the second set of reviewers subscribe to a mode of viewing and relating to the movie that they recognize as "camp." By invoking that category, they acknowledge their participation in gay male culture, as well as their personal identification with it. They may not be fully aware of doing that, for they may not all realize to what extent *camp* is a gay male genre. But their appeal to camp is nonetheless an admission of their engagement in a cultural and aesthetic practice characteristic of gay men, their willingness to enter into a specific relation to the film that has been devised for them by gay male culture, and their eagerness to assume an attitude that they understand at some level to be representative of a distinctively gay male style of cultural dissidence, a gay male style of resistance to received mainstream values.[13]

In what do that attitude and that style consist? Let us consider a particularly eloquent example.[14]

೧X

At the annual "Invasion of the Pines"—a drag event that takes place every Fourth of July in New York's gay vacation colony on Fire Island—a prominent presence for years was the contingent of "Italian widows." These were gay men of Mediterranean descent who dressed in the black frocks and veils donned by Italian peasant women upon the death of their husbands.[15]

In southern Italy and Sicily, the permanent wearing of black sets these women apart and makes them highly visible figures of mourning, authority, seniority, and autonomy in traditional village life. The Fire Island Italian widows *could* be seen as a mere spoof of that conventional female role and of the potent performative identity of Italian widowhood—an outright parody of straight society's high moral drama of family values, gender subordination, and sentimental seriousness—if it weren't for the fact that the Italian widows at the Pines were all men who had themselves lost lovers, friends, or members of their local community to AIDS.

The Fire Island Italian widows were not just performing a mockery of mourning, then. They were also performing the real thing. Their grief was at once parodic and real. Their annual appearance at the Fire Island festival constituted something of a ritual—a public, communal enactment of loss and pain—and in that way the widows came to serve as unofficial mourners on behalf of everyone in the local community.[16] Just as they made fun of their Mediterranean heritage while also proudly parading it, so they mocked their suffering even as they put it on prominent display. They insisted on expressing that suffering, and on representing it to the larger social world, without expecting the world to accord them the pious deference and the formal acknowledgment of their losses that real Italian widows demand and receive. By over-performing their grief as well as their ethnicity, they mocked the claims to high seriousness that heterosexual culture willingly grants both family tragedy and communal membership, and they made fun of an identity that was actually their own—even as they continued to clamor, *Mommie Dearest*-style, for the respect they were entitled to.

And they did it for a very particular reason. As gay men mourning their friends or partners in public, the Italian widows would have known that the emotions they felt and displayed were necessarily consigned by conventional cultural codes to the realm of the incongruous, the excessive, the melodramatic, the hysterical, the inauthentic—at any rate, the less than fully dignified. Their grief, however genuine, was disqualified from being taken seriously, partly because male widowhood can never claim the kind of hallowed public space that female widowhood routinely occupies (has any grieving man in American history achieved the iconic status of Jackie Kennedy?), and partly because gay love constitutes a public obscenity, and so the pain of gay lovers evokes smirks at least as often as it elicits tears.

Gay loss never quite rises to the level of tragedy. No would-be gay tragedy can escape a faint tinge of ridiculousness, as Charles Ludlam understood, and as the multiple online parodies of the trailer for *Brokeback Mountain* attest. It is no accident that the most effective public expression of gay mourning for the generations lost to AIDS, the NAMES Project Quilt, took the form of a homely, humble artifact—and of a feminine (that is, devalued) cultural production characteristic of the rural working class: the American equivalent of the peasant class to which black-clad Italian widows belong. The Quilt took care not to aspire to the dignity or grandeur of a conventional (heroic, masculine) funerary monument. Instead, it positively courted an appearance of unseriousness, even of laughable triviality (albeit on a vast scale), thereby both anticipating and preempting potential depreciation.

Public expressions of grief for the death of gay lovers tend to come off as a bad imitation, a spoof, or at most an appropriation of heterosexual pathos, and thus an unintended tribute to it. The Fire Island Italian widows, occupying as they already did the cultural space of parody—of the fake, the derivative, the out of place, the disallowed, the unserious—had only one way to impose their grief publicly, and that was by embracing the social devaluation of their feelings through a parodic, exaggerated, melodramatic, self-mocking, grotesque, explicitly role-playing, stylized performance.

Through drag, in short.

"Only by fully embracing the stigma itself can one neutralize the sting and make it laughable," concludes Esther Newton.[17]

☙☙

Here, then, is yet another instance in which gay men appear to express their distinctive subjectivity, and to perform acts of cultural resistance, by channeling flamboyant, hyperbolic, or ludicrous displays of female suffering. Which raises a disturbing question. It might seem that gay male culture incites us to laugh *not* at situations that are horrifying or tragic *in general,* but at certain situations that feature *women,* from Little Nell to Joan Crawford, in particularly horrifying or tragic circumstances—exposed, insulted, betrayed, humiliated, assaulted, hysterical, dying, mourning, out of control. Over and over again in the examples I have cited, it turns out to be a woman whose extravagant, histrionic style of emotional expression gets taken up by gay male culture, parodied, and appropriated as a vehicle for individual or collective gay male self-expression. It might also seem to be women, often lower-class women, whose feelings, and whose pain, gay male culture finds to be consistently funny.

I shall have much to say about the question of misogyny and gay male culture in Chapter 18. In the meantime, the Fire Island Italian widows shed a revealing light on this consistent pattern, which is indeed pervasive in gay male culture and defines a particular style of gay male cultural resistance. The Fire Island Italian widows suggest—contrary to the impression we might have gotten from the evident pleasure gay male culture takes in the delirious scenes of woman-on-woman abuse in *Mildred Pierce* and *Mommie Dearest*—that gay male culture does not teach us to laugh at the horrifying or tragic situations of *women only.* What the example of the Fire Island Italian widows demonstrates, and what the earlier examples of Tony Kushner, David McDiarmid, Tom Shearer, Beowulf Thorne, and Isaac Julien all implied as well, is that it is gay male subjects' *own* suffering which drives this characteristic form of self-lacerating irony and supplies the motive and the cue for laughter. It is not women alone whose suffering gay male culture represents as funny: gay male culture also and above all sees itself, *its own plight,* in the distorted mirror of a devalued femininity.

The appalled and anguished hilarity with which gay male culture views that spectacle indicates how clearly it perceives the cruel absurdity of its own situation reflected in it. The ridiculousness that attaches to undignified feminine pain in a society of male privilege would have resonated particularly with the experience of gay men during the first fifteen years of the AIDS crisis, from 1981 to 1996, before the introduction of anti-retroviral therapy, when AIDS was an invariably fatal condition and straight society routinely dismissed the reality of gay men's suffering, denying them the sympathy it grudgingly accorded the epidemic's "innocent victims."[18] In that context, the laughter with which gay male culture greeted its own horrifying and tragic situation expressed, as so often, a simultaneous identification with the values and perspectives of both the privileged and the abject. Inasmuch as gay men are empowered as men, but disempowered as gay, such a double identification is logical.[19] At the same time, the paradoxes and contradictions it generates account for some of the most distinctive and pervasive features of gay male culture. Gay male culture typically operates in two social registers at once, adopting the viewpoint of the upper and lower strata of society, of the noble and the ignoble, and relying on the irony fundamental to camp to hold aristocratic and egalitarian attitudes together in a delicate, dynamic equipoise. The brand of humor that results may be demeaning, but it is not just demeaning, or not demeaning of other people only. It is also highly self-reflexive and self-inclusive: it applies to gay subjects themselves.

What is so funny, in this context, about traditional Italian widows? It is not their feelings, emotions, or sufferings. It is the performative dimensions of their social identity, the deadly serious act they solemnly, unironically carry out. That is what the Fire Island Italian widows exaggerated, and poked fun at, through their incongruous reperformance of it. Far from displaying their indifference to the actual suffering of actual Italian widows, or laughing at the pain of grieving women, the Fire Island Italian widows put on a show that testified to their envy, admiration, and unrealizable desire for the prestige and social credit—for the *éclat*—of that undeniably dramatic but wholly conventional, time-honored feminine role. Their act was a kind of homage—rather like those drag queens doing Mildred Pierce into their mirrors (according to Ethan Mordden's formula), driven to endless longing and despair by the very power and perfection of women's feminine masquerade.

It is because the role of widow is a feminine role that it qualifies in men's eyes as performative, as having an *enacted* dimension, just as all feminine roles, all feminine forms of embodiment and self-presentation, necessarily come off in a male-dominated society as performative, at least to some degree. In this, feminine roles differ from masculine roles, which can assert straightforwardly their claims to naturalness and authenticity (even men in uniform look less costumed, less artificial, than do conventional women in evening dress:

that is what spells the difference between feminine *masquerade* and masculine *parade*). Hence, feminine roles are less serious than masculine ones, and that in turn makes them relatively more available for reappropriation and parody. The Fire Island Italian widows did not hesitate to exploit that vein of misogyny in the ambient sexism of the larger society for the purpose of staging their act of social defiance.

It was in fact a brilliant tactic on the part of the Fire Island Italian widows to seize and take up the hallowed, demonstrative role of widow, since it was the one role in their ethnic tradition that allowed —indeed, that positively required—bereaved individuals to make *a life-long public spectacle of private pain*. By transferring that role from a female to a male subject, and by performing it year after year, the Fire Island Italian widows exaggerated it, denaturalized it, and theatricalized it, which did have the effect of calling attention to its performative dimensions and making it even more laughable. But that was merely a consequence of their larger strategy.

For by bringing out the performativity of Italian widowhood, the Fire Island Italian widows made widowhood itself mobile, portable, transposable to others, and thus available to themselves. The effect of their masquerade was not to devalue the social performance of widowhood or to dismiss the reality of the pain it dramatizes—which would have completely defeated the point of reperforming it—but to reclaim it, figuratively and ironically, for themselves. The Fire Island Italian widows might be guilty of cultural theft, but not callous enjoyment of female suffering. They could well be accused of lacking proper respect for actual Italian widows. And indeed their act was disrespectful. But not because it expressed contempt for widows in particular, or for women in general, or for the pain of widowhood, but because it implied a principled disrespect for all socially constructed and asymmetrical gender polarities, for the cultural prestige that accrues to those who embody them, and for all social performances that demand to be taken straight—and that are the privileged domain of those with the authority to impose such demands on others. The ultimate thrust was to challenge the monopoly of dignity held by those whose mourning is endowed with authenticity and, to that extent, with immunity to devaluation and derision.[20]

In their quest to create a social space and an expressive language for representing their own experience of loss, the Fire Island Italian widows turned to the nearest available cultural resource, to a model of *permanent, inconsolable mourning* thematically appropriate to their emotional and ethnic situation but wildly at odds with their gender. The result was much less dignified and respectable than even the flamboyant feminine role they parodied. They sought to gain by that ridiculous means an admittedly tenuous access to an established social identity that—unlike their own identity—legitimated and authorized the ongoing public expression of grief. They must have known that their title to such an identity was dubious at best. In their social and cultural situation, their claim to the status of "widow" was in fact laughable. Insisting on their right to it nonetheless, they managed to acquire an absurd, and obviously fake, but—in practice—quite effective license to translate their personal and communal pain into a demonstrative, assertive social form and to stage an imposing performance of public mourning. *No real Italian widows were harmed during the making of this performance.* Instead, those real widows furnished a model, a metaphor, an image, a role, that could serve as a kind of *proxy* for a gay male Mediterranean widowhood under performative construction—a widowhood that was itself, necessarily and agonizingly, both outlandish and valid, facetious and all too real.

SUFFERING IN QUOTATION MARKS

𝒯he Fire Island Italian widows, like David McDiarmid, Tom Shearer, and Beowulf Thorne, make fun first and foremost of their own suffering. If they laugh at situations that are horrifying or tragic, that's not because they do not feel the horror or the tragedy of them, but because they do. They laugh in order not to cry, in order not to lapse into maudlin self-pity.[1] But that's not the whole story. For the pain does not cease when they laugh at it—it may, if anything, become sharper and more precise. But now it has an acknowledged place, a specific social and emotional location, which means it is no longer quite so incapacitating, or so isolating. The effect is not to evade the reality of pain, but to share it and, thus, to cope with it. Or, in the words of Joan Crawford, as played by Faye Dunaway and quoted by one of our Amazon reviewers, to "figure it out." Esther Newton puts it succinctly: "The humor does not cover up; it transforms."[2]

Whence this general truth: *camp works to drain suffering of the pain that it also does not deny.* This explains why horror can cohabit with hilarity in the poetics of gay male discourse, and human calamities like the HIV/AIDS epidemic can become vehicles of parody without the slightest implication of cruelty, distance, or disavowal—without that "momentary anaesthesia of the heart" which the philosopher Henri Bergson thought all comedy required.[3]

According to a heterosexual and heteronormative cultural standard, which measures the sincerity of public sentiments by how straight they are intended to be taken—by the vehemence of their categorical refusal to cop to their own performativity, by their solemn avoidance of any acknowledgment of theatricality or role-playing, of any winking complicity with their audience about the formal or conventional nature of their expression and about the prohibition against admitting to it—according to that standard, the Fire Island Italian widows would certainly seem to have been trivializing their feelings, not taking them fully seriously. Their purpose, after all, was to preempt the social disqualification of their suffering, and to escape being seen as merely pathetic, by withdrawing any claim to the serious consideration from which they were in any case debarred, while at the same time exposing the relentless earnestness of heterosexual theatrics which confuse compulsory social roles with essences and refuse to recognize personal authenticity as a cultural performance.

And, indeed, when viewed from a mainstream, heteronormative perspective, the tactic of presenting one's own suffering as *a performance of suffering* can only undercut both that suffering's authenticity and its dignity. But since the suffering in question was their own, neither David McDiarmid nor the Fire Island Italian widows could exactly be accused of breezy indifference to it or skepticism about its reality. If their brand of humor seemed to trivialize suffering, that is not because they were heartless, unfeeling, cavalier, or insensitive to pain and grief—whether their own or other people's. Unlike the kind of mockery that fortifies you in an illusory sense of immunity to what other people are going through, that insulates you from their suffering, the sort of trivialization that is involved in this kind of humor is not an exercise in denial. For despite its outrageous impertinence, it has an egalitarian, inclusive thrust: it implies that no tragedy, not even yours, can or should claim so much worth as to presume an unquestionable entitlement to be taken completely seriously—that is, to be taken straight—in a world where some people's suffering is routinely discounted.

To make your own suffering into a vehicle of parody, to refuse to exempt yourself from the irony with which you view all social identities, all performances of authorized social roles, is to level social distinctions. By disclaiming any pretense to be taken seriously and by forgoing all personal entitlement to sympathy, sentimentality, or deference, you throw a wrench into the machinery of social depreciation. When you make fun of your own pain, you anticipate and preempt the devaluation of it by others. You also invite others to share in your renunciation of any automatic claim to social standing, and you encourage them to join you amid the ranks of people whose suffering is always subject, at least potentially, to devalorization—and whose tragic situations are, thus, always susceptible of being laughed at. You thereby repudiate the hierarchies of social worth according to which modern individuals are routinely classed. You build a collective understanding and sense of solidarity with those who follow you in your simultaneous pursuit and defiance of social contempt. And in that way, you lay the foundation for a wider, more inclusive community.

⌾⌾

The distinction between the kind of humor that is socially inclusive and the kind of humor that is socially exclusive is part of a larger cultural poetics. For example, and not coincidentally, that distinction is also what defines the generic difference between *camp* and *kitsch* in the pragmatics of discourse, according to Eve Kosofsky Sedgwick. The application of the "kitsch" designation, Sedgwick argues, entails a superior, knowing dismissal of *someone else's* love of a cultural artifact, a judgment that the item is unworthy of love and that the person who loves it is the "unresistant dupe" of the "cynical manipulation" that produced it. When I label an object "kitsch," I treat the appreciation of it as a fault, as a lapse of taste, as evidence of a debased sentimentality that I myself have transcended and that I do not share. I thereby exempt myself "from the contagion of the kitsch object."

In keeping with the social logic that Sedgwick carefully traced and analyzed under the now-canonical description "epistemology of the closet," accusation here operates as a vehicle of individual self-exoneration. The very act of calling something "kitsch" is a way of demonstrating that the person who makes that "scapegoating attribution" is himself above loving such unworthy stuff—though the very vehemence attaching to the phobic dis-identification implicit in that denial inevitably casts doubt on its genuineness. "Kitsch," in short, is a word one never applies to objects of one's own liking, but employs only to disqualify the sentimental, uncritical, bad object-choices made by other people.[4]

Whereas a judgment that something is *camp,* Sedgwick contends, does not confer a similar exemption on the judge. Camp is not about *attribution,* but about *recognition.* It declares your delight and participation in the cultural subversions of camp. "Unlike kitsch-attribution, then, camp-recognition doesn't ask, 'What kind of debased creature could possibly be the right audience for this spectacle?' Instead, it asks *what if:* What if the right audience for this were exactly *me?*"[5] Camp ascription therefore produces an effect precisely opposite to that of kitsch labeling. It marks the person making the judgment as an insider, as someone who is in the know, who is in on the secret of camp, already initiated into the circuits of shared perception and appreciation that set apart those who are able to discern camp and that create among such people a network of mutual recognition and complicity. It takes one to know one, indeed—and that, camp implies, far from being shameful, is fabulous.

The ability to identify a particular object as camp, and to induce others to share that perception, thereby creates a basis for community. It inducts those who appreciate and who savor camp into a common fellowship of shared recognition and *anti-social aesthetic practice.* (By "anti-social," I do not mean *hostile to communal belonging,* then, but *contrary to social norms.*) Unlike kitsch, but like David McDiarmid and the Fire Island Italian widows, camp allows no possibility for distance, dis-identification, or self-exemption. On the contrary, the recognition of something as camp is itself an admission of one's own

susceptibility to the camp aesthetic and of one's willingness to participate in a community composed of those who share the same loving
relation to the ghastly object.

No wonder clips from *Mommie Dearest* are played in gay video bars.
No wonder they tend to be consumed in company, among friends,
rather than by oneself.

ೕೕ

David Caron makes a similar point about camp. In a brilliant, unpublished lecture (you had to be there, darling), he said, "Far from reproducing an exclusionary class structure, camp simultaneously produces
and is produced by a community of equals. In its most outrageous
manifestations it mocks social inequalities by enacting them to an absurd degree. Camp, then, is a mode of being-with-friends. I am talking of collective, group friendship here, not of a one-on-one relationship." And Caron adds, "Collective friendship, [like camp,] exists only
in and through its own enactment. It is decentered and unruly. It goes
nowhere and produces nothing other than itself. It is, therefore, a social critique at work, in that it flouts the supposedly mature models
of socialization—the couple, the production of children—and reclaims an evolutionary stage we were supposed to discard long ago,
along with sexual indeterminacy."[6] (It was for similar reasons that
D. A. Miller called the enjoyment of Broadway musicals, even on the
part of adults, "kid stuff.")

Caron's description of camp as "a social critique at work" is precise
and well judged. Camp is not criticism, but critique. It does not aim
to correct and improve, but to question, to undermine, and to destabilize. In this, it differs from satire, which would be an appropriate
way of responding to kitsch, since satire functions as a *criticism,* a put-
down of inferior objects and practices. Whereas camp makes fun of
things not from a position of moral or aesthetic superiority, but from
a position internal to the deplorable condition of having no serious
moral or aesthetic standards—a condition that it lovingly elaborates

and extends, generously or aggressively, so as to include everybody. Camp doesn't preach; it demeans. But it doesn't demean some people at other people's expense. It takes everyone down with it together.

That instinctive race to the bottom, that impulse to identify with the outrageously disreputable and the grotesque, may explain why, as feminists sometimes complain and as we have already seen, camp particularly delights in and systematically exploits the most abject, exaggerated, and undignified versions of femininity that a misogynistic culture can devise.[7] In such a culture, even glamorous women have something caricatural about them. "Divas—or at least the personae divas choose—are cartoon women," John Clum observes. "They express in an exaggerated way parts of women, which become separate from an entire personality."[8] Those caricatures of femininity constitute the epitome of what our culture regards as unserious, and they dramatize the full consequences of the social and symbolic violence which a male-dominated society directs against anyone who qualifies as "feminine." But for camp, the unserious is not just a disqualification. It is also a potential source of collective strength—hence, a strategic opportunity. By seizing that opportunity, camp endows its antisocial aesthetics with a political dimension.

Michael Warner accordingly discerns a democratic thrust, and ultimately an ethical vision, in the pragmatics of camp discourse. This egalitarian impulse, he argues, springs from an awareness and understanding of the irredeemable, ineradicable indignity of sex (especially, but not exclusively, queer sex).

> In those circles where queerness has been most cultivated, the ground rule is that one doesn't pretend to be *above* the indignity of sex. And although this usually isn't announced as an ethical vision, that's what it perversely is. In queer circles, you are likely to be teased and abused until you grasp the idea. . . . A relation to others, in these contexts, begins in an acknowledgment of all that is most abject and least reputable in oneself. Shame is bedrock. Queers can be abusive, insulting, and vile toward one another, but because abjection is understood to be the

shared condition, they also know how to communicate through such camaraderie a moving and unexpected form of generosity. No one is beneath its reach, not because it prides itself on generosity, but because it prides itself on nothing. The rule is: Get over yourself. Put a wig on before you judge. And the corollary is that you stand to learn most from the people you think are beneath you. At its best, this ethic cuts against every form of hierarchy you could bring into the room.[9]

Caron's and Warner's points about the anti-hierarchical, communitarian tendencies of gay male culture recall the views of the early French gay liberationist Guy Hocquenghem, who argued that male homosexuality implied the novel possibility of "horizontal" social relations, instead of the "vertical" ones promoted by heterosexual reproduction and filiation. According to this vision, homosexuality might lead to the multiplication and expansion of non-hierarchical structures of coexistence in place of the usual graduated social relations of parents and children, bosses and workers, superiors and inferiors.[10]

We can begin to make out here a series of logical and emotional connections among a number of the phenomena we have observed. What we may be dealing with, in fact, is *a constellation of related cultural values,* linked internally both by the way they seem to reinforce one another and by the shared anti-social vision that informs them. This network of ideas and values includes: the notion that the stigma of homosexuality can be overcome not by resisting it, but by embracing it; the surrender of any statutory claim to be taken seriously; an ironic perspective on all social identities; the habit of treating authenticity as a *performance* of authenticity; the refusal to accord dignity to the suffering of individuals who find themselves in horrifying or tragic situations, even or especially when you happen to be one of them; the simultaneous taking up of a socially superior and a socially inferior attitude, which entails a constant put-down of yourself; the frankly acknowledged indignity of sex and the democratizing impulse to spread that indignity around; the anti-hierarchical inclusiveness of camp humor, its lack of self-exemption, and its constitutive function in creating community.

ↀↀↀ

Implicit in everything we have seen so far is the assumption, basic to camp and drag culture, that *all identities are roles.* That is what Susan Sontag means when she remarks in her famous 1964 essay, "Notes on 'Camp,'" that "Camp sees everything in quotation marks. It's not a lamp, but a 'lamp'; not a woman, but a 'woman.' To perceive Camp in objects and persons is to understand Being-as-Playing-a-Role. It is the farthest extension, in sensibility, of the metaphor of life as theater."[11] In this passage, Sontag may be overplaying the insincerity of camp, its alienation and distance from the objects and practices it takes up, and underplaying its genuine love of them, its passionate belief in them.[12] But she is right to emphasize the fundamental perception of all identities as roles.

Sontag is wrong, however, to insist on that basis that "the Camp sensibility is disengaged, depoliticized—or at least apolitical." After all, the denaturalizing effect of all those quotation marks can be profound. Sontag derives the apolitical nature of camp from the axiom that camp emphasizes style and slights content; she speaks of camp as incarnating "a victory of 'style' over 'content,'" though it would be more accurate to say, as Sontag hastens to do, that camp introduces "an attitude which is neutral with respect to content."[13] In other writings of hers from the same period, Sontag inveighs against the kind of criticism that ignores or trivializes "style" and that gives primacy instead to the "interpretation" of "content"; she calls for putting the notion of content in its place.[14] When it comes to camp, however, the victory of style over content that gay male culture achieves makes Sontag nervous.

Sontag elsewhere tries to advance the cause of style, arguing that the denigration of style as purely "decorative" is ultimately political: it "serves to perpetuate certain intellectual aims and vested interests."[15] And in "Notes on 'Camp,'" Sontag recognizes that "the whole point of Camp is to dethrone the serious."[16] But all this makes her claim that camp is depoliticized, or at least apolitical, all the more bizarre. For though such a claim may represent a good description of the thematics of camp, its effect is to dismiss the possibility of an anti-social politics that would consist precisely in an undoing of the serious—or whatever succeeds in qualifying as such. This anti-social politics would deprivilege "content" in favor of the abjected, abominated, effete category of "style"; it would undermine the legitimacy of gender hierarchies that elevate masculinity to the rank of seriousness (concerned with reality and the true content of things), while downgrading femininity to the status of triviality (concerned with such frivolous matters as style and appearance); it would challenge the authenticity of naturalized identities and call into question the conventional scale of values that determines relative degrees of social dignity.

Such an anti-social politics would begin by reversing the conventional valences of style and content. And that is exactly what camp does. Camp, as Richard Dyer observes, is "a way of prising the form of something away from its content, of reveling in the style while dismissing the content as trivial." Dyer cites a number of instances in which gay male culture treats style as valuable, while bracketing content as neutral or irrelevant:

> Gay men have made certain "style professions" very much theirs (at any rate by association, even if not necessarily in terms of the numbers of gays actually employed in these professions): hairdressing, interior decoration, dress design, ballet, musicals, revue. These occupations . . . are clearly marked with the camp sensibility: they are style for style's sake, they don't have "serious" content (a hairstyle is not "about" anything), they don't have a practical use (they're just nice), and the actual forms taken accentuate artifice.[17]

For Sontag, this very tendency of camp to prise the form of something away from its content and thereby to convert "the serious into the trivial" is a "grave matter."[18] And, in a sense, she is quite right. For

that gravity is a sign of exactly how much is at stake when "the serious" is dethroned, when it stands to lose its preeminence over "the
trivial," when style manages to prevail over content. By taking an
ironic distance on the ethical-political value of seriousness to which
Sontag so earnestly clings, camp poses a fundamental political challenge to what normally passes for politics. And that is a political function camp can perform only by being apolitical.[19]

It is camp's alienated queer perspective on socially authorized values that reveals Being to be a performance of being ("Being-as-
Playing-a-Role") and that enables us to see identities as compelling
acts of social theater, instead of as essences. That alienated vision performs a vital, indeed a necessary function for stigmatized groups. By
refusing to accept social identities as natural kinds of being, as objective descriptions of who you are, and by exposing them, instead, as
performative roles, and thus as *inauthentic,* stigmatized groups achieve
some leverage against the disqualifications attached to those identities. By putting everything in quotation marks, especially everything
"serious"—and thereby opening a crucial gap between actor and role,
between identity and essence—camp irony makes it possible to get
some distance on "your" self, on the "self" that society has affixed
to you as your authentic nature, as your very being. Embracing the
stigma of homosexuality becomes possible as a tactic for overcoming
it only when those who embrace it also refuse to recognize it as the
truth of their being, when they decline to see themselves as totally,
definitively, irrievably described by it.[20] Forgoing your claim to dignity is a small price to pay for undoing the seriousness and authenticity of the naturalized identities and hierarchies of value that debase
you. Converting serious social meanings into trivial ones is not only
an anti-social aesthetic practice, then. It is also the foundation of a political strategy of social contestation and defiance.

ℚℐ

There are in fact many good reasons why the queer perspective on
identity should be alienated. In order to escape persecution in a ho-

mophobic world, queers have to do their best to conceal the appearance of queerness, to hide the visible stigmata of homosexuality, and
to pass as straight, at least some of the time. Which means that queers
who wish to remain covert must figure out how to impersonate normal people. They have to *act* straight. They have to get into straight
drag.[21]

Not only does this requirement explain the distinctive value that
gay male culture places on both *style* and *role-playing;* it also explains
the logic of the connection between them. Why are style and role-
playing so intimately associated? "Because," as Dyer says, "we've had
to be good at disguise, at appearing to be one of the crowd, the same
as everyone else. Because we had to hide what we really felt (gayness)
for so much of the time, we had to master the façade of whatever social set-up we found ourselves in—we couldn't afford to stand out in
any way, for it might give the game away about our gayness. So we
have developed an eye and an ear for surfaces, appearances, forms:
style."[22]

The stakes in manipulating appearances and social forms, in mastering style and passing for normal, are highest in the case of males
who happen to be gay, since the social rewards for success in performing masculinity are so lucrative. In order to reap those rewards, Esther Newton observes, "the covert homosexual must in fact impersonate a *man,* that is, he must *appear* to the 'straight' world to be
fulfilling (or not violating) all the requisites of the male role as defined by the 'straight' world."[23] And if he is to succeed in bringing off
that act, a gay man will first have to do some rigorous anthropological fieldwork of his own: he will have to take very careful note of how
the members of his own society behave. He will have to study, in particular, how straight men perform heterosexual masculinity.

Straight men, of course, also have to learn how to act like straight
men. But straight men do not routinely regard masculinity as a style,
nor do they consider their own impersonation of straight men to be a
performance. They do not have a *conscious* consciousness of embodying a social form. Part of what is involved in being straight is learning

to imitate straight men, to perform heterosexual masculinity, and then forgetting that you ever learned it, just as you must ignore the fact that you are performing it.[24]

Gay men, by contrast, are distinguished precisely by their conscious consciousness of acting like straight men whenever they perform normative masculinity. Gay men must represent to themselves the social form they seek to embody in order to embody it: they are necessarily aware of behaving according to a preexisting social model. In the course of remembering and reconstituting what straight men have forgotten, in the course of consciously reproducing the acts that straight men are no longer conscious of performing, gay men inevitably come to see what heterosexual culture considers to be a natural and authentic identity—a form of being, an essence, a *thing*—as a social form: a performance, an act, a *role*.

There are other factors that explain why gay men tend to perceive masculinity as a social form, rather than as a natural ontology. Gay men's study of straight men's performance of straight masculinity is not only self-protective; it is also erotic. Masculinity, in at least some of its incarnations, is typically a turn-on for gay men. So you have an erotic motive to try to identify the precise lineaments of the look or style that so arouses your desire whenever you encounter it in certain guys. And if you are to understand the social logic that renders that *particular* look or style so powerfully attractive to you, you are going to have to observe it very closely. You will have to define its exact composition, its distinctive features, and the stylistic system in which those features cohere. After all, even a slight deviation from that style, even a slight modification of that look could have momentous consequences: the minutest alteration could ruin the whole effect, puncture your excitement, and deflate your interest. So the details matter. You need to figure out what they are.

The very exigency of your desire forces you to specify, and to clarify (if only to yourself), what it is about the masculinity of the men who turn you on that so moves you, what precise erotic meaning is encoded in this or that embodied feature (as opposed to minor variations on it), and what about it so inspires you and causes you to find it so compelling. You have to do your best to identify the specific erotic value of each and every fine point of that masculine performance —to capture the exact meaning of *that* gesture, *that* walk, *that* way of speaking, *that* set of the shoulders, *that* shake of the head, *that* haircut's neckline, *that* hang of the sweatpants, *that* light-hearted way of flirting with other men or dismissing an idea considered to be foolish.

You have to determine (*pace* Richard Dyer) what a hairstyle is "about."

In short, *you have to grasp a social form in all its particularity.* In order to get to the bottom of the mystery of homosexual attraction, you have to focus your attention on the object of your desire in its most complete contextual realization, its full social concreteness, its specific social systematicity. You have to understand it not as an idea, or as a representation of something, or as a figure for something else, but as *the thing itself*—a thing that, in itself, is social to its very core. That is what Proust ultimately discovered, and that is what became the starting point for his grand literary experiment, *In Search of Lost Time:* in order to seize things in their essence, you have to seize them in their social being. Social forms are things in themselves, whose meaning lies in nothing other than their style and resides nowhere except in the formal qualities that define them.

Heterosexual desire is also a mystery, of course, and straight people could also engage in a similarly searching inquiry into the relation between their erotic desires and particular social forms. Some of them surely do: witness Nabokov's *Lolita.* But the tormented book-length quest that constitutes that novel—Humbert Humbert's "endeavor . . . to fix once and for all the perilous magic of nymphets"— stems precisely from the perverted nature of the narrator's attraction to prepubescent girls. To the degree that heterosexual desire approaches the social definition and ideal of normality, it ceases to force itself on the consciousness of heterosexuals as a mystery in need of elucidation. The very blatancy, ubiquity, prevalence, obviousness, even vulgarity of the canonical definitions of sexual attractiveness in heterosexual culture relieve straight people of the imperative to define the exact social forms that correspond to their desires. Which is why they tend not even to see those forms as *social* in the first place.

 exon

From a gay male perspective, forged precisely by a lack of exemption from that imperative, every *thing* in the social world is also a *performance*. Every thing is a "thing." The barest bones of social life acquire the look of a full-scale costume drama.

So it is easy to understand how the social vicissitudes of gay male subjectivity inexorably conduce to an expansion and generalization of the category of drag. For drag, in at least one of its manifestations, as Newton points out, "symbolizes that the visible, social, masculine clothing is a costume, which in turn symbolizes that the entire sex-role behavior is a role—an act."[25] The result is to universalize "the metaphor of life as theater." Every identity is a role or an act, and no act is completely authentic, if authenticity is understood to require the total collapse of any distinction between actor and role. Rather, every identity is performative: social being *is* social theater, and vice versa.

There is no relation of externality for gay male culture between *being* and *playing a role,* between actor and act. They may be distinct, but they are not separate; rather, they constitute each other.[26] That doubleness, that twofold aspect of social existence, is not an ontological split but a single composite nature, an intrinsic property of things.[27] Playing a role *is* the mode of existing in the social world. That is what social being is. (The *locus classicus* of this queer insight is Genet's play *The Maids.*) Which is also what heterosexual culture represses and cannot acknowledge, since to do so would be to forgo the privileges that attach to authenticity, to the social status of being a natural thing, whose existence is nothing but the truth of its essence.

Whereas for gay male culture—which understands being as playing a role, essence as an effect of performance—*taking something seri-*

ously does not preclude treating it as an act. There is no opposition between the two. Conversely, if seriousness is an act, a performance, and if seeing something as an act is not to take it seriously, then gay male culture is perfectly entitled to convert the serious into the trivial, to laugh at what passes for serious—at what achieves seriousness by the very excellence and solemnity of its performance.[28]

And indeed, what could possibly be more appropriate, more *realistic* to take unseriously, to laugh at, than the hostile and unalterable realities of the social world, even or especially when they are horrifying or tragic, when they are matters of life and death—and when they are happening to you? Camp, after all, is "a form of self-defence."[29] How else can those who are held captive by an inhospitable social world derealize it enough to prevent it from annihilating them? (That is one of the themes of Sartre's *Saint Genet.*) If that is what "trivializing" your own or someone else's feelings means, if it means not taking them literally or unironically, then to trivialize them is hardly to devalue or to cheapen them. On the contrary, it is the very mode of claiming them and, if you're lucky, surviving in spite of them.

This doubleness of a perspective that is also one, that operates by means of irony to hold multiple points of view in dynamic equipoise, is crucial to the effectiveness of camp. Camp undoes the solemnity with which heterosexual society regards tragedy, but camp doesn't evade the reality of the suffering that gives rise to tragedy. If anything, camp is a tribute to its intensity. Camp returns to the scene of trauma and replays that trauma on a ludicrously amplified scale—so as to drain it of its pain and, in so doing, to transform it. Without having to resort to piety, camp can register the enduring reality of hurt and make it culturally productive, thereby recognizing it without conceding to it the power to crush those whom it afflicts.[30] In this way, camp provides gay men with a cultural resource for dealing with personal and collective devastation: a social practice that does not devalue the suffering it also refuses to dignify.

≈ 10 ≈

THE BEAUTY AND THE CAMP

The literature on camp is vast. Theoretical debates have raged over what exactly camp is and how it should be defined. And the topic continues to attract academic critics.[1] But professors hardly hold a monopoly on efforts to describe the distinctive features of camp: those efforts began long ago among communities of gay men. As Richard Dyer wrote in 1977, "Arguments have lasted all night about what camp really is and what it means." Dyer mentions two varieties of camp, which describe two major instances of it: "camping about, mincing and screaming; and a certain taste in art and entertainment, a certain sensibility."[2] What those two instances share is the alienated, ironic perspective on socially authorized (or "serious") values that we have already observed.

There are good reasons to avoid becoming entangled in these larger debates over the meaning and definition of camp. Such debates have already gone very far; they have become highly specialized and sophisticated; in any case, they exceed the topic before us.[3] Camp is worth exploring here only insofar as it enables us to identify and to understand the peculiar features of gay male discourse, its unique pragmatics. The distinctive nature and operations of camp, it turns out, make particular sense when they are brought into relation with the long-standing gay male cultural habit of refusing to exempt oneself from social condemnation, as well as the practice of laughing at situations that are horrifying or tragic.

The connection between camp and that characteristic way of crossing the genres of tragedy and comedy emerges with particular clarity from some further observations by Esther Newton. She reminds us that before "camp" was the name of a sensibility, it was the designation of a kind of person. Her account of that figure also demonstrates that the function of camp can be more easily specified and explained when camp is situated in the context of the social environment from which it emerged. Gay male cultural practices are better and more systematically understood when they are restored to their original, concrete, pragmatic discursive and social situations than when they are abstracted from them and analyzed in terms of aesthetic theory, as Susan Sontag preferred to do, however brilliantly.

Commenting on "the fundamental split between glamour and humor" in both drag performance and gay male subculture as a whole, Newton made a series of ethnographic observations about gay male social life that remain of far-reaching significance.

> At any given homosexual party, there will be two competing, yet often complementary people around whom interest and activity swirl: the "most beautiful," most sexually desirable man there, and the "campiest," most dramatic, most verbally entertaining queen. The complementary nature of the two roles is made clearest when, as often happens, the queen is holding the attention of his audience by actually commenting (by no means always favorably) on the "beauty" and on the strategies employed by those who are trying to win the "beauty's" favors for the night. The good party and the good drag show both ideally will feature beautiful young men and campy queens. *In neither is it likely that the two virtues will be combined in the same person.* The camp, both on and off stage, tends to be a person who is, by group criteria, less sexually attractive, whether by virtue of advancing age or fewer physical charms or, frequently, both. Whatever the camp's "objective" physical appearance, his most successful joke is on himself.[4]

What characterizes the camp, according to this account, is his deliberate refusal of self-exemption from the mockery he directs at the
larger social world, as well as his tendency to make fun of his own
abjection—to laugh, like the Fire Island Italian widows, David McDiarmid, Tom Shearer, or Beowulf Thorne, at his own suffering. Camp
is not only a mode of cultural appropriation, a way of recycling bits
of mainstream culture; it is also productive, a creative impulse in its
own right, a strategy for dealing with social domination.

What explains the phenomenon observed by Newton? Why is it
that, in order for a party composed of gay men to be truly successful,
there has to be at least one each of two different species of gay man
present: the beauty and the camp? What makes each essential?

Well, if, on the one hand, no one beautiful is in attendance, the
gathering loses all erotic interest. It declines into a tea party, a meeting of the "sisterhood,"⁵ a merely congenial get-together of like-
minded individuals, with nothing to prove to each other and no one
to put on a butch act for. Under those conditions, the participants can
afford to let their hair down and abandon all pretense of being better
or sexier than they are. That may make for a fun and convivial evening, but it will be lacking in sexual excitement—and as a mixer, as an
occasion for romance, it will clearly be a dud. But if, on the other
hand, no camp is present, the party becomes a relentlessly competitive struggle for the most attractive available partners, an exercise in
mutual one-upmanship, an endless display of humorless butch theatrics, which takes place at everyone's expense and produces relentless
posturing and suffocating seriousness. So the camp and the beauty
are equally necessary, and both are indispensable to successful gay
male social life.

The opposition between the beauty and the camp that Newton describes appears in all its antagonistic splendor in a scene toward the
end of the first act of Mart Crowley's 1968 play *The Boys in the Band,*
the first breakthrough theatrical hit that explicitly and successfully
put gay male social life (as it was being lived in New York City) onto

the international stage. The Cowboy, a stunningly handsome male hustler who has been brought to a birthday party as a sexual gift for its guest of honor, happens to complain about and to seek sympathy for an athletic injury he lately sustained at the gym: "I lost my grip doing my chin-ups," he says—no one is much interested in the details, but he rattles on, with endearingly clueless self-absorption—"and I fell on my heels and twisted my back." Emory, the camp, rejoins, "You shouldn't *wear* heels when you do chin-ups."[6]

The joke does a lot of social and cultural work. It highlights the Cowboy's typically macho imperviousness to irony, his lack of any awareness of the possible doubleness of his own speech; it points up his glaring absence of wit (which is both a defect and, at least for the purposes of butch attractiveness, a cardinal virtue); it crosses, in classic camp fashion, the codes of masculinity and femininity[7] (compare the apocryphal quip by Tallulah Bankhead to a priest at High Mass swinging his censer: "Honey, I love your frock, but your purse is on fire"); it punctures the atmosphere of masculine seriousness surrounding straight male athletic performance and its erotic appeal to gay men; it testifies to the camp's inability even to imagine a male world inhabited exclusively by "normal" men; it shifts the tenor of the conversation from a tediously, unironically masculine one to an ironically effeminate one; it cuts the Cowboy down to size by pretending to mistake him for a practicing drag queen, hence several rungs lower on the scale of sexual prestige than the rank he actually occupies; and it implicitly rebukes the other men present for taking the Cowboy so seriously, while at the same time doing nothing to alter the attractiveness that continues to make him an object of their erotic interest.

☙❧

The categorical split in traditional gay male culture between beauty and camp, between glamour and humor, turns out to be isomorphic with a number of other symmetrical and polarized values, which correlate in turn with a basic opposition between masculine and feminine gender styles. (Camp, obviously, "is not masculine. By definition, camping about is not butch.")[8] This basic opposition between masculine and feminine shapes gay male subjectivity and produces many of the systematic contrasts that structure the gay male world and its values. One of those contrasts is between male homosexuality as a sexual practice and male homosexuality as a cultural practice. The ancient antagonism between beauty and camp helps us to understand why gay culture is so incompatible with gay sex.

We have been concerned with gay culture, not with gay sex, so we have been dwelling on the feminine side of this traditional gender polarity—where camp and drag are also located. But now it is time at least to notice the existence of the other half of the polarity, and to say something about gay masculinity, if only to explain why we have been, necessarily, neglecting it.

The traditional split between camp and beauty, or between humor and glamour, coincides, specifically, with the old sexual division between queens and trade: that is, between effeminate and virile styles of performing male sex and gender roles. On one side of the divide are gay-acting men—effeminate or, at least, not "real" men—who lack the virile credentials that would make them seriously desirable to other gay men. On the other side are straight or straight-acting men, who are able to carry off a butch performance without too much seeming effort but who are nonetheless willing, for whatever reason, to enter into sexual commerce with a queen.[9] Since effeminacy is a turn-off, whereas masculinity is exciting, queens are attracted to trade, but not to each other. So the division between queens and trade involves a whole system of polarized gender styles, gender identities, erotic object and subject positions, sex-roles, sexual practices, and sexual subjectivities.

The opposition between queens and trade was supposed to have disappeared with gay liberation, when gayness was fashioned into a singular, unified, homogeneous identity—and when, as many observers noted about the rise of "clone" culture, gay men all suddenly started to look and act like trade (and to sleep with each other).[10] But the hoary division between queens and trade continues to resurface within gay male sexual culture. The queer movement at the turn of the 1990s temporarily rehabilitated gender-deviant styles, and traces of them remain. Moreover, drag shows continue to be popular, and they continue to pair drag queens with muscle boys, just as the Broadway musical pairs divas with chorus boys.[11] Meanwhile, polarized sexual roles (top versus bottom) have not ended up on the garbage heap of history, as gay liberationists of the 1970s had predicted. Instead, they proliferate all over the online gay cruising sites that have sprouted up on the Internet.

Consistent with the ancient division between queens and trade is the split between ironic camp complicity and earnest butch posturing, between sisterhood and sex, between conviviality and eroticism. Those divisions, which structure all traditional gay male culture, are grounded in the opposition between the beauty and the camp and enforced by the law that prevents them from being the same person.

That opposition, for example, is what explains the gay male habit of tricking with strangers instead of with friends. It also explains the difficulty of making it to a second date, let alone a third one. For romantic interest depends on a certain mystery, or at least a degree of blankness, in the love-object. The love-object has to be able to accommodate the fantasy of butch desirability that the would-be lover projects onto it. Familiarity—and gay recognition, in particular—may spoil that accommodating blankness. They breed erotic disillusionment, even as they also enable friendliness, affection, congeniality, complicity, and solidarity.[12]

Thus, a man who arouses your desire initially appears to you as a pure archetype, as an embodiment of the masculine erotic value that makes him attractive. In your perception, he is *the* jock, *the* paratrooper, *the* boy next door. But as soon as you have him, he becomes an individual instead of an essence, an ordinary queen instead of a Platonic idea.[13] He ceases to be pure Beauty and starts to become camp. He becomes a sister. So you stop sleeping with him. He may continue to frequent the gym, but he might as well be working out in high heels, so far as you are now concerned.

Beauty, because it is the object of sexual desire—because it is *hot*—has nothing intrinsically ironic about it. Gay male culture takes it very seriously. Beauty evokes literal, witless, pathetically earnest longing, the sort of longing that has no distance on itself and no ability to step aside and look critically at itself from an alienated perspective.

That is what camp is for. The camp takes revenge on the beauty for beauty's power over gay men (which is why it is fitting that the camp be unattractive himself), and he does so on behalf of the community of gay men as a whole, with whom he shares a cozy if ambivalent complicity. The camp's role is to puncture the breathless, solemn, tediously monotonous worship of beauty, to allow the gay men who desire and who venerate beauty to step back ironically from their unironic devotion to it, to see it from the perspective of postcoital disillusionment instead of anticipatory excitement.

So that explains why camp is about cutting everyone down to size, especially anyone whose claim to glamour threatens to oppress his less fortunate comrades, such as the camp himself. Camp is about deflating pretension, dismantling hierarchy, and remembering that all queers are stigmatized and no one deserves the kind of dignity that comes at the expense of someone else's shame. That is also why camp, as we have seen, is inclusive and democratic, why it implies a world of horizontal rather than vertical social relations. And that is why it both presumes and produces community.

The function of the beauty, by contrast, is to promote a different and conflicting set of values, values that gay male culture cherishes no less than it cherishes the value of community. Beauty is aristocratic, not democratic. By its very nature it is above average, distinguished, extraordinary, precious, and rare; it therefore occupies an elite rank. The desire for beauty is not about making common cause with others, but about wanting to have—and, by having, to be—the best. Beauty holds out the possibility of transcending shame, escaping a community of the stigmatized, acceding to the rapt contemplation of pure physical and aesthetic perfection, leaving behind all those sad old queens, forsaking irony for romance, attaining dignity, and achieving true and serious worth, both in your own eyes and in other people's. Beauty is noble, heroic, masculine. Those are qualities we associate not with humor or comedy but with grandeur and dignity—the sorts of values that are at home in tragedy.

Camp and beauty are not just opposed, then: each is the other's competitor and antagonist. The camp's function is defined in opposition to the beauty's, and vice versa. In its original pre-Stonewall social and pragmatic context, as described by Esther Newton, camp emerged as a weapon that gay male culture fashioned in a hopeless if valiant effort to resist the power of beauty. Camp and beauty operate in strict relation to each other, and camp is best understood when it is seen in this *relational* context—as gay male culture's way of trying to disintoxicate itself from its own erotic and aesthetic passion for masculine beauty. Camp represents gay male culture's attempt to undo its romantic seriousness, to level the invidious distinctions between queens and trade that gay male culture has borrowed from the opposition between masculine and feminine in the dominant, heteronormative gender system and that it has made fundamental to its own vision of the world.

Now, the association of masculine beauty and glamour with social superiority, seriousness, sexiness, dignity, and romance may well strike you as sexist and politically retrograde—probably because that is exactly what it is. But it is unreasonable to expect gay male culture to dismantle the dominant social and symbolic system of which it is merely the lucid and faithful reflection. Gay male culture's virtue is to register—and then to resist—forms of social stratification that continue to structure our world, but that modern liberal societies routinely deny, and that a host of contemporary hypocrisies and pieties, including popular, sentimental varieties of feminism, typically work to obscure.

ʘχʘ

If gay male culture teaches us (whether we are gay men or not) to laugh at situations that are horrifying or tragic, that is because it strives to maintain a tension between *egalitarian ethics* and *hierarchical aesthetics.* It insists on keeping those mutually opposed values in permanent, antagonistic equipoise. For it is only by preserving that polarity, promoting that contradiction, and by making each set of values balance the other out that it can maintain the right and necessary doubling of perspective that keeps everybody sane.

The tension between egalitarian ethics and hierarchical aesthetics pervades gay male culture, spanning its democratic and aristocratic tendencies, its feminine and masculine identifications, its divisions between femme and butch, between queens and trade. That tension defines, produces, and perpetuates a distinctive brand of gay male subjectivity. It is a subjectivity formed in dichotomy. On the one hand, gay culture and queer sensibility; on the other hand, sexual desire.

Tony Kushner, distinguishing what he calls "Fabulousness" from eroticism, bears witness to this opposition between sensibility and desire, between culture and sex. "What are the salient features of Fabulousness? Irony. Tragic history. Defiance. Gender-fuck. Glitter Drama. It is not butch. It is not hot. The cathexis surrounding Fabulousness is not necessarily erotic. The Fabulous is not delimited by age or beauty."[14] The only item out of place in this list, it seems to me, is "tragic history." Its inclusion says a lot about Kushner, and his preoccupations with historical drama, or melodrama, but not much about the usual gay definition of fabulousness.[15] Nonetheless, what Kushner's statement reveals and emphasizes is the fundamental conflict in gay male subjectivity between culture and eroticism.

It is precisely because gay male cultural practices are inimical to gay male sexual practices, because they are so deflating of sexual excitement, that gay culture (falsetto singing, Broadway musicals, fashion and design) arouses such powerful aversion among gay men who like to think of themselves as sexual subjects—even when those gay men are themselves producers and consumers of gay culture. That is also why gay culture causes so much embarrassment and why its persistence elicits so much denial. Gay culture is something of a dirty secret to out-and-proud gay men, to any gay men in fact who wish to affirm their eroticism, their masculinity, their worth as sexual subjects and objects, who ground their identity in their sexuality and define themselves by their same-sex desire instead of by their queer sensibility. As D. A. Miller demonstrated, gay culture is at the opposite pole from the unironic pose of virile stolidness that apes normality, commands respect, and solicits gay men's sexual desire. And, conversely, sexual desire among gay men carefully avoids trafficking in the cultural subversions of camp, which after all would entail the subversion of that very desire: the deflation of its butch theatrics, the ruin of its masculine parade.

The polarity between camp and beauty, though strict, is not absolute. Cracks regularly do appear in the partition. Drag queens and muscle boys always perform together; each of them requires the presence of the other. And some gay men do desire feminine men; drag queens do not lack boyfriends. The opposition between the beauty and the camp may itself be an element internal to camp culture, a camp projection rather than a natural reality. In practice, the camp and the beauty often can—and do—coincide.

And that can make for some novel, unprecedented cultural effects. In a leather and backroom bar in Mexico City, called Tom's, which I visited in the summer of 2006, gay porn played soundlessly on the video screens while soprano arias from grand opera blared over the speaker system. The overall effect was surprisingly sweet—at once very apt, very funny, and even rather hot. Sophisticated gay male culture actually delights in playing with the opposition between the feminine and the masculine: between camp and beauty, culture and sex, queer subjectivity and gay male identity. Much contemporary gay male culture represents a sustained effort to recombine the beauty and the camp. Substantial skill and ingenuity are required to do so in the case of men, and the droll task of rising to that challenge affords gay male culture a multitude of incitements and opportunities to display its dynamism and inventiveness, as well as to manifest its perpetual capacity to startle and surprise.

The opposition between the beauty and the camp corresponds exactly to the contrast between glamour and abjection. But whereas glamour and abjection (or glamour and humor) take some ingenuity to combine in the case of masculinity—since they represent a fundamental, categorical split, a polarity between good and bad, noble and ignoble, virile and effeminate, serious and unserious men—glamour and abjection coincide easily in the case of femininity. Because even glamorous women, as John Clum observed, are cartoon women—who express only parts of women, aspects of femininity exaggerated to an outlandish degree—and because femininity always has something performative and artificial about it, exceptional feminine glamour is never far from caricature.

The more pronounced or elaborate femininity is, the more it lends itself to parody, and the more it leads to a loss of dignity, to a fall from seriousness. For that reason, representations of feminine abjection do not always feature—they do not need to feature—humble women, lower-status women, impoverished, sick, miserable, or struggling women. They can focus just as easily on wealthy, stylish, glamorous, or formerly glamorous women who are hysterical, extravagant, desperate, ridiculous, passionate, obscene, degraded, on the verge of a nervous breakdown, or simply unable to carry off successfully a high-quality feminine masquerade, who fail to sustain the dignity required to be taken even somewhat seriously as women.

That account reads like a description of drag. And now we are at last in a position to understand why gay male drag specializes in combined portrayals of glamorous and abject femininity. For it is through identification with femininity that gay men can manage to recombine the opposed values of beauty and camp that divide gay male culture. It is through identification with a femininity that is at once glamorous and abject that gay men are able to meld upwardly mobile aesthetic aspiration with the ethical leveling of social distinctions.

Femininity functions here, as it did in the case of the Fire Island Italian widows, as a kind of *proxy identity* for gay men. The combination of feminine glamour and abjection that gay men assume through feminine identification and appropriation—through drag, in other words, or through the cult of Joan Crawford—makes available to gay men a position that would otherwise be difficult for them to claim in their own persons, so long at least as they retained a masculine gender identity: namely, a position at once dignified and degraded, serious and unserious, tragic and laughable. For that is the only position that can hope to be, according to the terms of gay male culture's value system, unitary and complete.

๏

The two poles of gay male subjectivity are represented, aptly though oddly enough, by two classic American novellas, both of them published more than a hundred years ago. The generic difference that grounds this cultural binary, then, has been in existence for quite some time.

The title character of Willa Cather's "Paul's Case" (1905) encapsulates in his person the full range and breadth of gay male sensibility. Cather grotesquely lards her text with every sign and marker of gayness she can think of—except homosexual desire.[16] Her narrator describes Paul as follows.

> His clothes were a trifle out-grown and the tan velvet on the collar of his open overcoat was frayed and worn; but for all that there was something of the dandy about him, and he wore an opal pin in his neatly knotted black four-in-hand, and a red carnation in his buttonhole. . . . Paul was tall for his age and very thin, with high, cramped shoulders and a narrow chest. His eyes were remarkable for a certain hysterical brilliancy, and he continually used them in a conscious, theatrical sort of way, peculiarly offensive in a boy. The pupils were abnormally large . . . [and] there was a glassy glitter about them [etc., etc.].[17]

Like the classic invert of nineteenth-century medical discourse, according to Michel Foucault's famous, satirical portrait of him, Paul emerges from Cather's lugubrious description as "a personage—a past, a case history and a childhood, a character, a form of life; also a morphology, with an indiscreet anatomy and possibly a mysterious physiology" (this is Foucault speaking, not Cather).[18]

To be specific, Paul is an effete, hysterical dandy. He is addicted to theater and music, though he has no real understanding of the arts; nonetheless, he is given to a "peculiar intoxication" with middle-aged foreign sopranos, especially when they wear tiaras and are surrounded by an aura of fame (120). He is drawn to artificiality in all its forms—anticipating Sontag's assertion that "the essence of Camp is its love of the unnatural: of artifice and exaggeration"[19]—and he excels at playing roles. Paul is inauthentic and sterile, a constant liar and fantasist, with delusions of grandeur. He is happy to give up his life in exchange for the incomparable thrill of spending a week at the old Waldorf-Astoria Hotel in New York City, a deeply affirming experience which gives him "a feeling that he had made the best of it, that he had lived the sort of life he was meant to live" (135).

Paul is perhaps the gayest character in all of literature,[20] if only in the sense that large portions of Cather's narrative seem single-mindedly designed to affix to his every attribute and action an over-determined gay meaning.[21] But he is all queer sensibility and no homosexual desire. At no point in the story does Paul express the slightest sexual interest in anyone of his own sex (or in anyone else, for that matter). He feels no attraction to other people. In fact, with one exception, he spends the entire story in no one's intimate company but his own. "He was not in the least abashed or lonely," Cather's narrator tells us. "He had no especial desire to meet or to know any of these people" at the Waldorf (132).

The single exception, however, is telling. One afternoon in New York, Paul falls in with "a wild San Francisco boy, a freshman at Yale" (another heap of gay clichés—how did Cather know?), and the two of them spend a night out on the town, "not returning . . . until seven o'clock the next morning." Their after-hours escapade has not been a success, however. "They had started out in the confiding warmth of a champagne friendship, but their parting in the elevator was singularly cool" (132). Their disillusionment is quick indeed: they don't even have to bed down in the Waldorf in order to lose interest in each other.

Homosexuality in Paul's case is not about other people. It is cer-

tainly not about same-sex attraction; it is not even about sexual contact. In fact, it is not about erotic desire at all. Homosexuality is about
lounging around by yourself in a luxurious hotel room, wearing silk
underwear and elegant clothes, sprinkling your body with violet water, smoking cigarettes, drinking champagne, surrounding yourself
with fresh flowers, enjoying a sense of power, and being "exactly the
kind of boy [you] had always wanted to be" (130). It is about solitary
queer pleasure—what D. A. Miller called a "homosexuality of one."[22]

Neil Bartlett, writing about Oscar Wilde, says, "Whenever I imagine him posed, it is not naked or against a bare wall. It is not with
other people (other men) but, most characteristically, as a single man
in a room, in an interior."[23] Bartlett's image of the representative gay
man is not one of human relatedness or sexual communion but of *an
individual alone in a room with his things*. This is gayness not as perverted sexuality but as solitary queer sensibility, which is of an aristocratic rather than a communitarian kind. "Paul's Case" represents a
brilliant thought-experiment by means of which Cather tries to imagine how Oscar Wilde might have turned out if he had been born into
a lower-middle-class family in Pittsburgh.[24] Paul is Wilde's American
avatar, as Cather intended him to be. He isn't beautiful. He isn't sexy.
He isn't your idea of a hot date, the boyfriend you always wanted. He
is more queen than trade. His nervousness, hysteria, impulsiveness,
love of glamour, and "morbid desire for cool things and soft lights
and fresh flowers" (122) are all socially coded as unmanly traits, and
they inscribe his gay sensibility under the signs of neurosis and, specifically, femininity.

☙❧

Herman Melville, by contrast, banishes almost all trace of femininity from the human landscape of "Billy Budd" (1891). Something of
"the feminine in man," to be sure, may still linger dangerously in the
manly heart, but at least there are no fresh flowers in Melville's depiction of the British Navy.[25] Melville portrays a tough all-male world,
lacking even the faintest hint of queer sensibility, but at the same time

utterly besotted with male beauty—with its "comeliness and power, always attractive in masculine conjunction" (292)—and universally shot through with same-sex desire. His sailors are all in love with Billy, but nothing about them is gender-deviant, artificial, or abnormal. They may "do his washing, darn his old trousers for him," or even make him "a pretty little chest of drawers" (296), but if they ever aspire to wear silk underwear, they certainly don't let on about it. The contrast could not be starker: Paul represents a case of queer sensibility and pleasure without same-sex desire, whereas Billy occasions rampant same-sex desire without evincing or eliciting the slightest spark of queer sensibility.

Unlike Paul, Billy is hot. "A fine specimen of the *genus homo*," thinks Captain Vere—mentally undressing him under the cover of a hastily assembled set of biological, biblical, and artistic alibis—"who in the nude might have posed for a statue of a young Adam before the Fall" (345). Billy is in fact the ideal one-night stand, endowed with a physique worthy of idolatrous worship, but not exactly a lot of fun to have around at breakfast the next morning. (What on earth would you talk to him about?) Melville underscores the point by giving him a stutter. Billy's desirability is exactly commensurate with his inability to speak. Happily removed from verbal communication, let alone from any knowing, ironic complicity with others ("To deal in double meanings . . . was quite foreign to his nature"; 298), he has almost no subjectivity whatever. He's all good-natured, innocent physicality—it's rather as if he were a big, friendly pet. Melville's narrator does not shrink from the demeaning comparison. "Of self-consciousness he seemed to have little or none, or about as much as we may reasonably impute to a dog of Saint Bernard's breed" (301; the analogy recurs at 358–359). In short, Billy is the apotheosis of trade: a sublimely beautiful object, but only an object, with no interiority, no psychology, no wit, and no sensibility to spoil the dazzling surface effect of his perfect physical form.

Which is why, for all his romantic glamour, Billy has no staying power. Once you've had him, you can't wait to get rid of him. No wonder the main characters in the story, Vere and Claggart, are both in such a hurry to see him dead. Even the ship's chaplain exploits Billy's vulnerability the night before his execution in order to kiss his cheek, but it never so much as occurs to him to think of trying to save the hunky sailor from annihilation: "the worthy man lifted not a finger to avert the doom of such a martyr to martial discipline" (373). After all, the moral agony to which innocent Billy is subjected by his court-martial and ensuing condemnation only serves to add a new, titillating, and troubling dimension of inwardness to what had been his perfection as a physical object: "the rare personal beauty of the young sailor" is "spiritualized now through late experiences so poignantly profound" (375).

That nascent spiritualization of Billy's magnificent flesh offers his admirers a spectacle far too captivating to interrupt by putting an end to his suffering. If that weren't creepy enough, Billy is also made to love, forgive, bless, and even embrace those who murder him, a kind of medieval ordeal climaxing in a cunningly orchestrated, intensely charged, unseen emotional and physical exchange with Captain Vere—an ecstasy of sacrificial cruelty and mutual submission far more shattering than sex, but the closest thing to sex that this butch world has to offer. And once dead, Billy can attain immortality as an object of endless, elegiac desire. Melville both anticipates and reverses Wilde: each man may kill the thing he loves, but each man also loves the thing he kills. Let that be a warning to partisans of virility, to those who prefer gay eroticism to gay culture. Murder is precisely where a total absence of camp will lead you.

This point was made again by Rainer Maria Fassbinder, in his film adaptation of Jean Genet's *Querelle,* a novel which merely takes the extra step of transforming Melville's tale of moral pornography into gay pornography. And, speaking of gay pornography, the lesson I have derived from Melville has now been brilliantly if inadvertently illustrated by Chris Ward's 2008 foray into cowboy porn, *To the Last Man,* a "Western epic" in which the story line is dotted with a series of dramatic murders—something of a novelty in gay porn—as if nothing less could serve to guarantee the virility of the male characters who have sex with one another on-screen. (Ward has, however, released a non-violent version of the movie for squeamish or morally rigorous consumers, who like their gay sex manly but not to the point of being homicidal.)[26]

၁ၖၥ

The polarity of queer sensibility and sexual desire reminds those who participate in gay male culture of their inescapable implication in gendered values, erotic dichotomies, and other social meanings. Whether it is the epistemology of the closet and its multiple double binds, the pervasive regime of heteronormativity and homophobia, the supreme significance of gender, the unarguable allure of masculinity, the unquenchable desire for beauty, or the impossibility of experiencing homosexuality naively and innocently as something wholly natural, the world gay men inhabit constantly reminds them of their lack of exemption from the brute realities of sexual stratification, cultural signification, and social power. The Fire Island Italian widows do not have the possibility, the capability, of choosing whether or not to accede to a dignified public role that both acknowledges and honors their grief; they cannot determine whether or not their losses will ever be allowed to rise to the status of tragedy in the eyes of the world. Their drag performance, their simultaneous act of fake and real mourning, is a response to social conditions and cultural codes that they cannot alter, but can only resist.

The political function of camp appears clearly in this light. "Camp," as Esther Newton says (borrowing a phrase from Kenneth Burke), "is a 'strategy for a situation.'"[27] Camp works from a position of disempowerment to recode social codes whose cultural power and prestige prevent them from simply being dismantled or ignored. It is predicated on the fundamental gay male intuition that power is everywhere, that it is impossible to evade power, that no place is outside of power.[28] Camp is a form of resistance to power that is defined by an awareness of being situated within an inescapable network of relations of meaning and force, by the perception that the encompassing regime of heteronormative signification is unalterable, but that a certain freedom is nevertheless attainable in relation to it. Dominant social roles and meanings cannot be destroyed, any more than can the power of beauty, but they can be undercut and derealized: we can learn how not to take them straight. Their claim on our belief is weakened, their preeminence eroded, when they are parodied or punctured, just as sex and gender identities are subverted when they are theatricalized, shown up as roles instead of as essences, treated as social performances instead of as natural identities, and thus deprived of their claims to seriousness and authenticity, of their right to our moral, aesthetic, and erotic allegiance.

But to derealize dominant heterosexual or heteronormative social roles and meanings, to disrupt their unquestioning claims to seriousness and authenticity, is not to do away with them or to make their power disappear. It is to achieve a certain degree of leverage in relation to them, while also acknowledging their continuing ability to dictate the terms of our social existence.[29] That explains why gay male culture has evolved an elusive cultural practice and mode of perception, known as camp, which involves not taking seriously, literally, or unironically the very things that matter most and that cause the most pain. It also explains why gay male culture encourages us to laugh at situations—such as those portrayed in *Mildred Pierce* and *Mommie Dearest*—that are horrifying or tragic. Just as camp works to puncture the unironic worship of beauty whose power it cannot rival or displace, so gay male culture struggles to suspend the pain of losses that it does not cease to grieve.

∾

Perhaps that is another reason why gay male culture produces so much aversion in gay men, why it elicits so much denial, and why contemporary gay men tend to project it onto earlier generations of archaic, pathetic queens—onto anyone but themselves. Traditional gay male culture is a way of coping with powerlessness, of neutralizing pain, of transcending grief. And who nowadays wants to feel powerless, who wants to think of himself as a victim? Who even wants to admit to vulnerability? Liberalism is over, people! It's no longer fashionable to claim you are oppressed. Our society requires its neoliberal subjects to butch up, to maintain a cheerful stoicism in the face of socially arranged suffering. It teaches us not to blame society for our woes, but to take responsibility for ourselves—to find deep, personal meaning in our pain, and moral uplift in accepting it.

Gay pride itself is incompatible with an identity defined by failure, disappointment, or defeat. American manliness, and therefore American gay masculinity, mandate rugged independence, healthy self-confidence, high self-esteem: in short, the denial of need, pain, "resentment, self-pity, and various other unconsoled relations to want."[30]

So it is understandable that a set of cultural practices designed to cope with the reality of suffering, to defy powerlessness, and to carve out a space of freedom within a social world acknowledged to be hostile and oppressive would not only fail to appeal to many subordinated people nowadays, but would constitute precisely what most of us—including women, gay men, and other minorities—must reject in order to accede to a sense of ourselves as dignified, proud, independent, self-respecting, powerful, and happy in spite of everything.

And in the particular case of gay men, gay culture is what many of us must disavow in order to achieve gay pride—at least, a certain kind of gay pride. It's not that gay pride reflects a different and less agonizing social experience of homosexuality. In its own way, gay pride, too, is a response to continuing stigmatization and marginalization. As Lauren Berlant writes, "no population has ever erased the history of its social negativity from its ongoing social meaning."[31] Rather, gay pride offers a different solution to the same problem, by aspiring to a better future—better, that is, than the world as we know it.

That is a worthy aspiration. It helps to explain the continuing appeal of utopianism, both in queer theory and in the lesbian and gay movement as a whole.[32] But it indicates, as well, why traditional gay male culture—which reckons with the world as it is, with the way we lived and still live now, and which seeks less to change the world than to resist its inflictions (even at the cost of appearing reactionary, rather than progressive)—affords such an important emotional and political resource, not only to gay men but also to many different kinds of socially disqualified people, at least to those whose sense of irredeemable wrongness makes them willing to pay the achingly high price for it.

PART FOUR

Mommie Queerest

∽ II ∾

GAY FAMILY ROMANCE

*W*hat does culture have to do with sexuality? What is the relation between sexual preferences and cultural preferences? How can gay male culture's infatuation with *Mildred Pierce* and *Mommie Dearest* help us to understand that relation? And what is it about those two movies that explains the secret of their gay appeal?

For answers to those questions, we must look to the poetics of gay male culture and, in particular, to the meaning of social forms. But we need not ignore or exclude other styles of reasoning, other explanations that might recommend themselves to us. It would in fact be better to take advantage of the insights that different interpretations afford, so as to arrive at an understanding of gay male culture that is plausible, inclusive, wide-ranging, undogmatic, and hospitable to various points of view.

So let's return to those movies and consider some psychological and thematic hypotheses about their gay appeal, before moving on to a social, pragmatic, and, necessarily, formal analysis. This roundabout approach may seem digressive, but it is actually designed to be incremental and cumulative: it aims to construct, step by step, on the basis of a series of interconnected observations, a coherent and, ultimately, systematic description of male homosexuality as a cultural practice.

We can pick up where we left off at the end of Chapter 10, and interpret the gay appeal of those movies, and of the two previously highlighted scenes in them, in the light of our understanding of camp.

The spectacle of the angry mother would function, according to this interpretation, as a way of reperforming and working through one of the greatest terrors, or potential terrors, of queer childhood. If one of the functions of camp humor is to return to a scene of trauma and to replay that trauma on a ludicrously amplified scale, so as to drain it of the pain that camp does not deny, then the camp appropriation of these dramas of mother-daughter conflict might be thought to confront the fear that haunts many a gay boyhood and that leaves a traumatic residue in the inner lives of many gay adults: the fear that the adored mother might express—if only unawares, or despite herself—her unconquerable aversion to her offspring, her disgust at having begotten and raised a deviant child. Even the most loving mother would be hard-put never to betray to her queer son at least a modicum of disappointment in him. The possibility that your mother might turn against you, and reject you, doubtless remains a perennial nightmare scenario in the minds of many queer kids, a source of panic never entirely laid to rest, and often exacerbated by the volatility of the emotional relations between gay boys and their mothers. It is this volatility that is captured by the dual focus on *both* mother and daughter in the scenes from *Mildred Pierce* and *Mommie Dearest*.

The potency of those scenes can be attributed in part to the way they solicit the spectator's identification with each character, the way they invite a simultaneous emotional involvement with the rebellious child and the indignant parent. Each scene tempts its audience to take both sides in the quarrel it portrays. And that is only logical. For in its appeal to the emotions of the adult spectator, each scene replays the divided loyalty that originally characterized the gay child's (and perhaps every child's) struggle for love and recognition, his simultaneous efforts to be the spontaneous object of his mother's attention and to exercise sufficient power over her to command that attention. In that struggle, the child is bound to be self-divided, to feel a split allegiance, insofar as he is compelled to be both for and against his mother. (According to Proust, who understood this ambivalence so well and portrayed it so vividly in the first section of *Swann's Way*, the child's struggle for control of his mother's love inexorably sets the stage for subsequent, similarly foredoomed adult attempts to possess the subjectivity of other love-objects.) By inviting the spectator's double identification with the mother and the daughter, each of the two scenes provides a vehicle for staging and replaying the impossibly divided loyalties of the abject and power-hungry child.

It is not hard to discover how each scene solicits the gay male spectator's identification with the daughter, though the solicitations are different in the case of each scene. In *Mommie Dearest,* the daughter claims power through her moral triumph over the mother, and she invites the spectator to join her in taking a vengeful pride in her (temporary) assertion of personal autonomy. What begins as adolescent rebellion ends in heady moral victory as the parent is at last indicted, judged, and condemned out of her own mouth. The daughter finally sees through, and rejects, the mystifications of the parental contract, realizing that her mother's toxic declarations of love merely function as strategies for licensing endless emotional abuse. In this moment of triumphant vision and resistance, the daughter achieves her moral independence—though the mother's histrionic response, magnified by the character's alcoholic dementia and fueled by her giddy abandonment of all sense of social propriety, easily upstages the daughter's earnest, self-satisfied moralism.

In *Mildred Pierce,* by contrast, it is precisely the daughter's refusal of the moral upper hand in the argument, and of all family values, that makes her so perversely appealing. She voices a hatred of middle-class domesticity, of a feminine role defined by hard work, responsibility, and selfless devotion to family, opting instead for glamour, leisure, wealth, elegance, and freedom from compulsory social ties—the sort of freedom that only money can buy. In rejecting all claims of familial piety, and basking in a flagrant, unnatural ingratitude, she flaunts her sense of superiority to conventional bourgeois canons of morality, normality, and naturalness.

∞

Such a feeling of superiority to boring, normal people has long been a noted (celebrated or abominated) feature of gay male subjectivity. It reflects the elitist, aristocratic tendency in gay male culture, also evident in the gay male cult of beauty and aesthetics. The most striking and characteristic expression of that sense of superiority is the stubborn refusal to believe that you are in fact the offspring of the individuals who claim to be your parents. Four years before Freud observed and described the generic version of this "family romance" —the child's fantasy that his real parents are not the ones who are actually raising him and that his true people come from a nobler or more glamorous world than that of his ostensible family—Willa Cather had already diagnosed a gay case of it in Paul.[1]

Cather's narrator tells us that once Paul had gotten to New York, and ensconced himself in the Waldorf, he very quickly "doubted the reality of his past."

> Had he ever known a place called Cordelia Street, a place where fagged looking business men boarded the early car? Mere rivets in a machine they seemed to Paul,—sickening men, with combings of children's hair always hanging to their coats, and *the smell of cooking* in their clothes. Cordelia Street—Ah, that belonged to another time and country! Had he not always been thus, had he not sat here [in the dining-room of the Waldorf] night after night, from as far back as he could remember, looking pensively over just such shimmering textures, and slowly twirling the stem of a glass like this one between his thumb and middle finger? He rather thought he had. . . . He felt now that his surroundings explained him. . . . *These were his own people,* he told himself.[2]

Profoundly revolted by the drab lower-middle-class world into which he was born, Paul recoils especially, and repeatedly, from the "greasy odour" of cooking (122, 125, 131), which signifies to him everything about the unrefined dreariness, gross physicality, and suffocating daily rituals of reproductive heterosexuality—everything about the aesthetic wasteland of commonplace family life—against which his soul rebels.

Paul would have found a soul mate forty years later in Mildred Pierce's daughter Veda, who also longs to get away (as she emphasizes to her mother) from "your chickens and your pies and your kitchens and *everything that smells of grease,* . . . from this shack with its cheap furniture, and this town and its dollar days, and its women that wear uniforms and its men that wear overalls." Veda does not hesitate to assume a posture of disdainful hauteur in addressing her mother: "You've never spoken of your people, where you came from," she says, detaching herself rhetorically from her maternal lineage, as if Mildred's "people" were not in fact also her own. And she does everything she can to magnify the class differences that separate Mildred from the world to which Veda herself aspires and, in her own imagination, rightfully belongs. "You think just because you made a little money you can get a new hairdo and some expensive clothes and turn yourself into a lady. But you can't. Because you'll never be anything but a common frump, whose father lived over a grocery store and whose mother took in washing." (Joan Crawford's mother, Anna, did in fact take in washing at one point while Joan was growing up.)

Many gay men report having entertained just such a family romance when they were boys: the conviction that they were exceptional creatures completely unrelated to the stupid, thuggish, crass society around them. They felt as if they'd been born outside their natural element, as if they were secretly descended from royalty—little princes whom some malign fate had, for mysterious reasons, consigned at birth to be raised by a family of peasants and who were simply waiting for the day when their true identity would be revealed, when the spell would be lifted, and when they would finally be set free, free from the tedious routines of ordinary life among normal folk, and restored at last to their rightful place in the society of the

rich and famous, of the world's beautiful and sophisticated people.[3]
The longing for a life of aesthetic grace and harmony, of sensual luxury and pleasure, the drive to rise in the world and mingle with the
upper classes, the aspiration to acquire, collect, and consume—to surround oneself with beautiful, rare, expensive objects or, in Paul's case,
with "cool things and soft lights and fresh flowers"—all this has come
to symbolize the essence of a certain kind of gay male subjectivity,
ever since the time of Oscar Wilde.[4]

∽

In his inexhaustible study of Wilde and gay male culture, Neil Bartlett
devotes an entire chapter, called "Possessions," to gay men's relation
to their *things*.[5] Like "the excessive sentimentality that was the necessary condition of sentiments allowed no real object"—sentiments
which the Broadway musical cultivated in its proto-gay fans, according to D. A. Miller—gay men's insistent desire for precious possessions springs, according to Bartlett, from a permanent sense of fundamental frustration at the *particular* unavailability *to us* of the objects
we most want. "Material wealth and sensual pleasure have a very specific function for us," Bartlett explains; "they compensate for other
forms of poverty."[6] Bartlett carefully left those other forms of poverty
unspecified—he clearly had in mind a broad spectrum of social and
political deprivations—but he allowed for the possibility that there
might be a very specific "hunger that gapes beneath" our quest for
possessions (175).

   The true source of that hunger, Bartlett implied, is a lack of erotic
satisfaction of a very general and basic kind. Sexual deprivation is
fundamental, and crucial, to the subjective experiences of gay men,
not because we are all pathetic, sex-starved rejects who never succeed
in finding acceptable partners, but because adult satisfaction cannot
quite make up for a previous history of unfulfillment. (As George
Haggerty says, speaking of the gayness of the pastoral elegy, "A love
that is constituted in loss is a love that yields a longing that can never
be fulfilled.")[7]

Early on in our lives, at whatever point we become urgently aware of our desires, gay men discover that most of the human beings who attract us are not the least bit interested in having a sexual relationship with us, that they are not and cannot be attracted to us in return, and that some of them regard the mere fact of our desire for them as abhorrent. (To be sure, it is possible to generalize this phenomenon to people other than gay men, since everyone has at one time or another felt that many of the glamorous people they desired were beyond them, unavailable to them, and even possibly repelled by them; but at least heterosexuals do not experience their love-objects as being *categorically* off-limits to them, on account of their belonging to the wrong sex, which is what gay men experience.) Even as adults, we do not escape the awareness that, in the eyes of most men, we fail to qualify as possible candidates for either sex or love. So our desire for men, in many cases, is impossible from the start, *impossible as such*. It is therefore infinite, and necessarily confined in the first instance to *fantasizing* about them. We develop, early on, a habit of communing with imaginary lovers, and it is a habit we never quite abandon.

What may be in and of itself an easy desire to satisfy becomes, when it is denied and frustrated, an impossible dream. The protracted experience of erotic lack which all gay men who grow up in straight society necessarily and painfully undergo turns the ordinary fulfillment of ordinary homosexual desire into an unattainable fantasy— which it often remains even when, later in life, a small-town boy moves to a gay metropolis where the sexual fulfillment of his former erotic daydreams turns out at last to be child's play. For belated access to sexual objects, no matter how numerous or glamorous they may be, can do little to close the long-established gap between fantasy and reality in the demand for erotic gratification. (Which is why the myriad opportunities for sexual satisfaction and love that gay liberation offers us have led not to the withering away of the gay porn industry, but to its hypertrophic expansion.) Once the very prospect of "getting what you want" has been consigned to the realm of fantasy, erotic gratification ineluctably takes on hyperbolic proportions, exits the realm of the attainable, and becomes indissolubly associated with impossible rapture.

No wonder homosexual desire routinely verges on an obsession with absolute, unearthly perfection, with flawless archetypes or Platonic essences (the perfectly beautiful man: Dorian Gray; the technically flawless image of a beautiful man: Robert Mapplethorpe's "The Perfect Moment"; the perfect operatic diva: the Lisbon Traviata). Since they devote so much solitary time and effort, early on in their lives, to studying the specific attributes of their ideal love-objects, determining what combination of features—or what social form—corresponds most exactly to the requirements of their desire, gay men tend, while still quite young, to arrive at a detailed and rigorous mental picture of what it is precisely that they want. And they are not likely to settle for anything less. Also, if most of the men you grew up wanting were bound to reject you anyway, through no fault of your own, and if your prohibited desire for them was therefore destined to express itself only in dreams, in hopeless fantasies of sexual fulfillment and romantic bliss, then you had no reason to let the world constrain your daydreams or limit the scope of your fantasies to the narrow field of the possible. And so, when the time eventually comes to leave that dreamscape, you may find it difficult to make compromises with humdrum reality.

The commitment to perfection, and the refusal to settle for anything (or anyone) less, generate the peculiar merging of eroticism and aestheticism that is distinctive to gay male culture. For an impossible but perfect object excites a very particular kind of desire. The ecstatic practice of erotic worship, combined with a despair of sexual satisfaction, produces a specific attitude toward objects of longing that is characteristic of gay male culture: an attitude of passionate but detached contemplation, at once critical and idealistic. By mingling the rapt transports of sexual idolatry with a distant, almost clinical appreciation of beauty, gay men achieve a kind of disinterestedness in their relation to erotic objects that brings their experience of sexual desire very close to that of pure aesthetic contemplation.

At least since Kant, it has been conventionally assumed that physical beauty and artistic beauty awaken very different kinds of response in normal (heterosexual) human subjects. The alleged difference between our responses to beautiful bodies and to beautiful works of art is supposed to ground a fundamental distinction between interested and disinterested attraction, between instrumental, selfish, egoistic, excited interestedness and non-instrumental, selfless, altruistic, contemplative disinterestedness.[8] Aestheticism, moreover, is usually thought to express a quest for perfection, or a commitment to perfect beauty, that is largely irrelevant to the cruder, baser workings of sexual excitation. Gay male culture, by contrast, is notorious for its habit of fusing erotics and aesthetics.[9]

⊘⊘⊘

That may be why there is always something reactionary about the gay male cult of beauty. Gay male culture's distinctive brand of erotic aestheticism (or should that be aesthetic eroticism?), and its insistence on perfection in its erotico-aesthetic objects, tend to produce an absolute privileging of the beautiful. This takes a number of well-known forms: an elevation of style over content; a championing of the aesthetic at the expense of the political; and a consequent, stubborn indifference to the social meaning of glamour, to its often retrograde political content. Dubious as those tendencies may be, gay male aestheticism does not flinch from them. Instead, it demands to be recognized for what it is—namely, a radically uncompromising defense of beauty, a principled refusal to subordinate *beauty as a value* to any social or political consideration that claims, however plausibly, to be more serious or more worthy. Gay male culture does not pretend to be ambivalent about aesthetic perfection, nor can it claim in all seriousness or sincerity to be deeply critical of it.

The *locus classicus* for this opposition between the apolitical or even reactionary aesthetics of gay male culture and an earnest political engagement in struggles for social progress is Manuel Puig's 1976 novel, *Kiss of the Spider Woman*. Puig portrays two social outcasts: the first is a gay man besotted with a female movie star, whose glamorous and now-dated films, full of adoration for the upper classes, were originally designed to promote Nazi propaganda; the second is a straight, austere, ideologically correct Marxist revolutionary, whose political commitments no less than his heterosexuality initially rule out any sympathy with either faggotry or aestheticism (especially when the aestheticism in question is of such a reactionary kind). The two characters, who have both been arrested by the authorities for their menace to the social order, find themselves locked up in the same prison cell. Their dialectical interaction culminates in a series of exchanges and a partial blurring of identities, demonstrating that aesthetics and politics, fantasy and fortitude, faggotry and machismo, gay male culture and straight male culture actually have a lot to offer each other—at least, in Puig's conception.

What makes Puig interesting to us is his observation that the bits of mainstream culture selected by gay male culture for its own queer purposes often do *not* turn out to be the most politically progressive, experimental, or avant-garde items, but—to the surprise of outsiders, who somehow expect gay men to favor the sorts of artworks that either promote progressive social change or put into effect disruptive, subversive programs of formal aesthetic innovation—prove in fact to be the most dated, old-fashioned, reactionary artifacts, including flamboyantly sexist, racist, classist, and homophobic ones. *Mildred Pierce* is a good example.

◌✕◌

Adapted from James M. Cain's highly perverse 1941 novel of the same title, with its dark suggestions of a mother's latent, incestuous desire for her own daughter, *Mildred Pierce* was transformed into a comparatively moral tale by Hollywood producer Jerry Wald, screenwriter Ranald MacDougall, and director Michael Curtiz. Cain himself, despite several pressing invitations, refused to make the changes requested by Wald, and Catherine Turney, the screenwriter who produced the first and relatively faithful adaptations of the novel, eventually asked that her name be removed from the film's credits. The resulting movie is an edifying, cautionary fable about the evils of divorce and the mayhem caused by independent women.[10]

The problems begin when Mildred's husband loses his job in the Depression and ceases to be able to support his family, ultimately forcing Mildred to take over the role of breadwinner and to become— by dint of hard, selfless work—a successful, commanding, and ultimately very wealthy businesswoman. Mildred's increasing autonomy and her husband's economic emasculation lead to the breakdown of their marriage and to Mildred's affair with a dissolute, ethnically ambiguous scion of an aristocratic but impoverished family, Monte Beragon (played by Zachary Scott, fresh from his memorably sinister debut as an evil spy in the 1944 film *The Mask of Demetrios,* based on an Eric Ambler novel). The first time Mildred sleeps with Monte, her younger daughter dies of pneumonia—typical Hollywood retribution for adultery on the part of a mother. By the end of the movie, Mildred has repented of her independent ways and, having paid the price, returns to her husband, who in the meantime has found decent and manly employment "in a defense plant." As he escorts her from the court house, whose steps are being scrubbed by two self-abnegating women, the sun rises on their happy future. Whatever the movie's subversive pleasures, which are certainly many, no one could ever accuse it of being politically progressive.

As has often been remarked, *Mildred Pierce* is not only a classic Hollywood melodrama, a good example of a "woman's film," and a masterpiece of Warner Brothers film noir (at least in its framing episodes). It is also a story highly suited to the end of the Second World War, when the demobilization of millions of American men required the redomestication of women and their reassignment to the home from the workplace, to which they had been called to fill jobs temporarily vacated by the men who were now returning to claim them. Warner Brothers actually delayed the release of the film until October 20, 1945, more than two months after the Japanese capitulation, in order to enhance the story's relevance to the historical moment.[11]

The title character's rise, through hard work, self-sacrifice, and a love-less second marriage, to wealth, glamour, and high social position—along with her corresponding frustration, disappointment, corruption, and victimization—adds up to a highly conservative, moralistic tale, and the film's sexual politics are accordingly retrograde. Although *Mildred Pierce* titillates its audience with the transgressive spectacle of female strength, autonomy, feistiness, and power—even a certain female masculinity—it does so on the condition of Mildred's eventual surrender of her independence and her return to a state of domestic and sexual subordination. The film is also notable for Butterfly McQueen's uncredited portrayal of Mildred's Black ser-vant, Lottie, in some ways the most admirable character in the whole movie, but also the vehicle of persistent, vicious racial stereotyping. In short, the movie's politics of class, race, ethnicity, sex, and gender are pretty awful.

Those political blemishes do not, however, affect the film's aes-thetic success, especially when the film is viewed with the right dis-tance and irony. For gay male culture, at least, the movie's true poli-tics lie in its aesthetics: its style exceeds what its ostensible message conveys. Joan Crawford entirely dominates the visual field, and her every flicker of emotion—indelibly registered by her flawless acting, by the masterly lighting of her face with its superb complexion, and by the brilliant camera work and editing—is instantly and eloquently telegraphed to the spectator. In setting aside the explicit content of the film in favor of its melodramatic power and sumptuous film noir style, the camp enjoyment of it would seem to vindicate Susan Son-tag's claim about the apolitical character of camp, its preference for aesthetics over politics, its neutrality "with respect to content," and its "way of seeing the world as an aesthetic phenomenon."[12]

It is this elevation of beauty to a supreme value (not only the beauty of Joan Crawford but also the beauty of a flawless melodra-matic and cinematic style), and this comparative indifference to the political terms in which such aesthetic perfection is materialized, that have earned gay male culture its bad reputation—especially among feminists—for reactionary politics, hostility to women, acceptance of oppressive social conditions, promotion of a mythic rather than a critical attitude toward received values, and collaboration with the forces of social domination.

☙❧

But gay male culture is unfazed by its detractors and unashamed of its loves. It uncompromisingly defends the aesthetic autonomy of each and every cultural artifact it deems worthy of appropriation. It treats beauty as a fundamental organizing principle of the world. Accordingly, it insists on viewing each individual object within the object's own aesthetic frame, as an aesthetic ensemble, as the effect and expression of an integrated aesthetic system. It does not attempt to see through the style of the object to its content, to distinguish its successful aesthetic achievement from its odious political message or from its implication in a despicable social order. Rather, it discovers a different content, an alternate meaning—a counter-thematics—in an aesthetic object's very style.

Committed to style, and "neutral with respect to [overt, explicit] content," gay male aestheticism takes each item it values—be it a formica-and-vinyl kitchen table set from the 1950s or a collection of Fiesta ware from the 1930s, a Madonna video or an Yma Sumac song, a mid-century American ranch house or a French chateau—as a coherent, internally consistent stylistic whole, as a manifestation of a historically and culturally specific system of taste whose incarnation in the object is so total that this very completeness produces a pleasurable recognition in itself and affords a satisfaction of its own.[13] That willingness to subordinate aesthetic judgment of the individual object to an appreciation of the totality with which it embodies a single, integrated aesthetic or historical system is what led Sontag to conclude that "the way of Camp is not in terms of beauty, but in terms of the degree of artifice, of stylization."[14]

In fact, gay male aestheticism tends to blur the distinction between beauty and stylization, insofar as it locates meaning or content in

form itself, finding value in any object that exhibits perfect conformity to a specific aesthetic order, to a specific style. It rejoices in any
and all examples of complete stylistic coherence. It therefore takes
special delight in neglected artifacts from earlier periods that wholly
embody various outdated, obsolete styles.[15]

Consider, for example, the following entry, dated to 1945, from the
journal of the British writer Denton Welch, in which he records a
happy discovery he has just made in a junk shop.

> Then I walked down the last aisle and saw in the middle what looked
> at first like a not very remarkable early-to-mid-Victorian little couch—
> Récamier thickened and toughened and having developed turned
> stumpy legs instead of delicate out-sweeping Greek ones. But what
> really held my glance when I looked nearer was the covering of the
> couch, the flat loose cushion and the round tailored sausage one. They
> were all of tomato soup *red horsehair,* dirtied of course, but, remem-
> bering its life of eighty, ninety, perhaps nearly a hundred years, really
> in wonderful condition. And what a wonderful stuff too, this never
> before seen red horsehair, glistening like glass threads, rich and hard
> and heartless, built to wear people out, not be worn out by them. The
> cushions made so stiffly and truly, everything about the couch show-
> ing solid worthiness, as much as any Victorian piece I had seen; and its
> ugly, Gothic, sharp parrot smartness simply calling out to be used, sat
> upon and loved. Its appeal to me was so strong that excitement leaped
> up in me in a gulp.[16]

Welch bought it immediately. Did I mention he was gay?

This blurring of the distinction between beauty and stylization allows for the possibility of appreciating, even loving, objects that are
acknowledged to be ugly, like Denton Welch's little Victorian couch.
Which is what gives camp its democratic thrust, thereby attenuating
the elitist or aristocratic tendencies of gay male aestheticism. "Camp
taste turns its back on the good-bad axis of ordinary aesthetic judgment," Sontag says; it is "a mode . . . of appreciation—not judgment."[17] Setting aside any extrinsic criteria by which such an object
might be judged, camp aestheticism upholds form—the stylistic co-

herence of a fully achieved style—as a value in itself. Without exactly confusing that value with beauty, it nonetheless grants it significant aesthetic worth, resisting any mode of assessment that would insist on applying to the object a supposedly more rigorous, serious, or substantive set of external standards, either moral or aesthetic.

The camp sensibility thereby justifies "the world as an aesthetic phenomenon" (something Nietzsche thought that only Greek tragedy, or Wagner, could do). *It treats Style as a Utopia in its own right*—however awful any particular style may be or however appalling the social meanings it may encode in any specific context.[18] In this refusal to be distracted from an aesthetic apprehension by any alien or extrinsic order of values, even or especially by progressive political values, camp culture engages in its own kind of anti-social critique, its own uncompromising defense of fantasy and pleasure, and thus its own brand of political resistance (that is one of Puig's messages in *Kiss of the Spider Woman,* just as it is one of Sartre's messages in *Saint Genet*).[19]

ᥫᩢ

Good taste and bad taste both play important, if different, roles in gay male aestheticism. The cultivation of good taste is dialectically opposed to camp and its worship of bad taste, its love of aesthetic catastrophe—*dialectically* opposed, I say, because good taste and bad taste make necessary reference to each other, each implying the other and each of them constantly readjusting its own definition in relation to the other.

Taste itself, whether good or bad, is nonsensical without a scale and measure of value, without degrees of refinement and distinction.[20] A certain snobbery is built into aestheticism, with its panoply of standards, criteria, judgments, and perceptions, its efforts to discern the better from the worse, the fine from the gross, the original from the imitation, the rare from the vulgar. In short, aestheticism depends on a notion of hierarchy. However out of place such a notion may be in a democratic or egalitarian ethics, hierarchy does have a rightful place—an inevitable place—in the realm of aesthetics. No human being may deserve the kind of dignity that comes at the price of someone else's shame, but that doesn't mean everyone is entitled to sing "Casta Diva" (the great soprano aria in the first act of Bellini's *Norma*) or that every performance of it is as good as every other—any more than it means that every person you pass on the street is equally good-looking. "All God's children," Fran Lebowitz reminds us, "are not beautiful. Most of God's children are, in fact, barely presentable."[21]

Just as camp expresses an impulse to identify with the outrageously disreputable and the gorgeously grotesque—an instinctive race to the bottom whose social effect is fundamentally egalitarian—so good taste is a way of trading up, of social climbing. In gay male culture, good taste is allied with aristocratic pretensions, including the worship of beauty and an identification with the glamorous world of the upper classes, while the cultivation of taste itself expresses a general sense of superiority to those who lack the discernment necessary to appreciate either good taste or bad. Gay men, Sontag notes, "constitute themselves as aristocrats of taste."[22]

Neil Bartlett agrees, and he emphasizes the aristocratic dimensions of the gay male cult of taste. "The imagery of our rooms makes it clear that we have staked our survival on upward social mobility," he says (180). But that upward social mobility is not necessarily literal. As Bartlett quickly explains, upward social mobility is itself a metaphor. It may take the form of a longing for wealth and social privilege, but what it signifies is the aspiration to achieve a more gratifying way of life, a life of refinement, distinction, and pleasure; it does not aim at social superiority for its own sake.

If gay male aestheticism gives rise to an identification with the upper classes, that is because gay male culture values *pleasure* over *utility*. It takes as objects of aesthetic delectation what others have created for mere use—incidentally beautiful things originally produced and shaped for some specific, practical, ostensibly worthy purpose: beautiful bodies inadvertently formed by athletic competition or hard physical labor, grand buildings erected in the course of national or industrial rivalries, elegant clothing designed to gratify the demands of upper-class ostentation. Gay aestheticism annexes these by-products of other people's serious, single-minded striving to its own ironic, disaffiliated quest for pleasure.[23]

Gay male culture yearns above all for the freedom and power to gratify its taste for beauty or style. That is why gay male identification with the aristocracy does not entirely depend for its expression on spending-power (though disposable income helps). Glamour and luxury are all very nice, and no doubt highly welcome, but they are not required. Only people who don't take pleasure seriously make the mistake of believing it to be essentially expensive.

Taste, to be sure, implies a hierarchy of value. But a hierarchy of value does not entail social hierarchy or economic privilege. You don't need money to have taste, and you don't need a lot of money to gratify it (even if you do need some). Though an aristocracy of taste may represent an elite, it differs from traditional aristocracies insofar as it is constituted on the basis of neither social nor economic power. At least in principle, it is open to all.

"To be a connoisseur," Bartlett explains, "is to be a member of an elite—not necessarily an elite of the wealthy, though always close to it in inspiration at least. We may no longer pose as aristocrats; but the crucial point is that we still see ourselves as somehow above or apart from the world of production, licensed to play. There is a new 'aristocracy,' bigger and easier to enter than the old one (you can do it), one of sensibility, by which I mean one that understands how pleasure works and how it can be obtained" (181). So the kind of aristocracy to which some gay men aspire may turn out to involve a different kind of superiority altogether from what "aristocracy" normally implies, a superiority not incompatible with "the democratic *esprit* of Camp."[24]

The luxury prized by gay male culture can be achieved without literal extravagance. It consists in the ability to obtain pleasure and to live out fantasy. One way to do all that may be to insinuate yourself somehow into a world of glamour and exclusivity, but you need not acquire a fortune in order to accede to a more gratifying, more beautiful, more refined existence. You can do it in ways that are essentially or aspirationally middle class: singing along to recordings of Broadway musicals, arranging flowers, collecting things, clubbing, or *merely positioning the furniture just so.* (Whence the old joke: How can you tell if your cockroaches are gay? You come home and all your furniture is rearranged.) You can also attain a life of glamour by having sex, at least by enjoying untrammeled sexual pleasure with untold numbers of desirable people.

All these kinds of luxury make it possible for you to live in a better world, not necessarily a more expensive one. They represent potential points of entry into a way of being finally in tune with your vision of erotic and aesthetic perfection, instead of an existence that requires you to sacrifice your dreams to the service of reality—to the dreary, dutiful life of Cather's Cordelia Street in Pittsburgh (aptly named after King Lear's modest, unambitious, literal-minded daughter)—as straight society would prefer you to do.[25]

In that sense, Paul's struggle in Cather's story or Veda's struggle in *Mildred Pierce* is the struggle of gay male culture as a whole.[26]

ⓧ

Not only does Veda champion the cause of escape, by means of money (in her case), from the suffocating world of heterosexual family values; she also rebels against biological determinism itself. She treats her pregnancy as a revisable option, as if it were possible for her to choose whether or not to be pregnant at any given moment, whether or not to alter her reproductive situation simply by changing her mind: "It's a matter of opinion. At the moment, my opinion is I'm going to have a baby. I can always be mistaken."

So Veda's revolt against the family is a revolt not merely against its values, but against the very conditions and norms of heterosexual femininity. She stakes a claim to an explicitly perverse femininity, one defined by its exemption from filial duty, from honor, from reputation, from family, from material dependency, from heterosexual re-productivity, and finally from biology—or, at least, from the determi-nation that overtakes women because of the biological functioning of their bodies and its social symbolism. This is an eminently queer resistance, a revolt against heteronormative sociality. Veda offers a po-tent symbol to gay men.

But so does the outraged mother. Who could fail to sympathize with her hurt, her stunned disbelief at the cruelty and ingratitude of her daughter? And who could fail to admire the power of her moral indignation, the righteousness with which she rejects the daughter who has despised and rejected her sincere and long-suffering love? In any case, she is the main character, the star, and the chief focus of the spectator's interest. Veda's repugnant but powerfully charismatic character produces, then, a sense of divided loyalties on the part of the gay male viewer, a complex emotional involvement in this scene of double rejection.

Those divided loyalties are not just psychological. To be sure, that split allegiance might revive or rekindle the childhood memory of a mother imagined as both uniquely indulgent and signally severe, touched by her closeness to her son yet morally or aesthetically dis-gusted by his queerness. It might reflect the gay son's internalization of both the mother's heteronormative morality and her loving sus-pension of it in his favor, her double attitude of rejection and accep-tance. But it might also express his uncertain and ambivalent relation to the family form and to heteronormative culture itself: his simulta-neous contempt for the heterosexual family, its values, symbolism, and emotional claustrophobia, on the one hand, and, on the other, his lingering investment in the honorable and dignified form of life that the family represents and in the bonds of love that it institutes.

Such vicissitudes do not explain or exhaust by themselves the gay appeal of the two scenes in those movies, however. Let us pursue some other social considerations.

MEN ACT, WOMEN APPEAR

D. A. Miller has a different explanation for the peculiar terror that maternal rejection holds for at least some gay men. He gives that terror a central place in his effort to account for the gay appeal of *Gypsy,* a Broadway musical whose plot—significantly enough—revolves once again around a mother-daughter conflict. In the case of *Gypsy,* Miller argues, the figure of the mother acquires a specific meaning. For *Gypsy* is a musical explicitly about the musical, set in the context of vaudeville, and Miller connects the mother with access to the stage, with the permission accorded the queer male child to perform. When the mother suddenly turns on her daughter at the climax of the second-act finale, Miller contends, *Gypsy* administers a particularly nasty shock to the gay male spectator.

Theatrical or musical performance in Western society is not a male birthright. It is far from an inevitable destiny for a man. Men in our society are not routinely summoned to the stage for the purposes of self-display or the pleasure of being gazed at by mixed audiences. "Though male and female alike may and indeed must appear on the musical stage," Miller points out, "they are not equally welcome there: the female performer will always enjoy the advantage of also being thought to *represent* this stage, as its sign, its celebrant, its essence, and its glory; while the male tends to be suffered on condition that, by the inferiority or subjection of his own talents, he assist the enhancement of hers."[1] For a man to occupy the stage and to claim it for himself is to cast doubt on his masculine credentials, as Fred Astaire and Gene Kelly quickly discovered.[2] Far from consolidating masculine gender identity, the act of appearing on stage entails a certain amount of gender trouble for male performers—trouble which in turn gives rise to a number of complex strategies for containing it and managing it.

What is true for the Broadway stage holds true for the performing arts in general and for performance itself. (Though we should not ignore local variations: John Clum reminds us that "British musicals have historically focused on men, from Ivor Novello and Noël Coward to Jean Valjean and the Phantom. American musicals focus on women, from Ethel Merman to Bernadette Peters and Betty Buckley.")[3] As a rule, any activity that can be construed as "performing" will turn out to be risky business for a man. This is partly because to offer oneself as an object of display in our society is to step into the focus of a putatively male gaze and thereby to take the chance of being feminized. It is also because male performance runs up against a fundamental principle that for centuries has governed the gendered division of representational labor in Western culture. According to that law, that structure of meaning, *doing* is gendered as masculine and *performing* is gendered as feminine. As John Berger summed it up in a celebrated formula, *"men act* and *women appear."*[4]

Men do get to perform in public, of course, and sometimes they can perform without deferring to women or casting doubt on their masculine credentials. But they do so only under very special circumstances that produce a specifically masculine coding of their activity—such as when they perform as athletes, or as action heroes, or as politicians. Competitive sports, to pick only the first example, can enjoy a different gender status from that of theatrical performance, and acquire a different social meaning as a result, precisely because the men who are watched playing sports are supposed to be *doing* something, not merely *appearing*. That is especially true for team sports, where the players are watched not for themselves, not as objects of interest in their own right—as they are in gymnastics or diving, where athletic competition could more easily be accused of providing a diaphanous pretext for conspicuous self-display, and where the masculinity of the participants is therefore more readily impugned. Rather, when the members of a sports team play a match, they are watched as if incidentally, as the authors of an *event*, as the doers of a deed, with the game itself being the point of interest. It is the game that furnishes male spectators with the necessary alibi and cover for the pleasures of gazing at the players, just as it provides the players, in turn, with a proper justification for exhibiting themselves.[5]

Sports, especially (but not only) team sports, are understood to constitute *action*. That is what makes them socially appropriate for men, as well as affirmative and consolidating of masculine gender identity, according to the terms of Berger's analysis. It is also what makes them socially awkward for women—that is, normatively feminine women (lesbians don't feel the same constraints)—though such awkwardness may be diminishing in the United States, especially since congressional passage in 1972 of Title IX of the Education Amendments Act and the corresponding increase in female students' participation in high-school and college athletics.[6] In the case of men, since competitive team sports are thought to constitute action, male players in a sports match do not appear to be putting on a show for an audience. Instead, their tumultuous activity is imagined to attract an audience, which naturally gathers round them, drawn to the intrinsically gripping spectacle of men in combat. Male competition is usually an edifying sight, and it can be counted on to elicit a respectful gaze from onlookers, whereas the spectacle of female competition, of women in combat . . . well, in the eyes of male spectators at least, that has an unfortunate way of shading off into a display of something vaguely obscene, abject, or disreputable, something that comes uncomfortably close to female mud wrestling.

In a sports match, in any case, we consider that an actual contest is taking place. It is happening before our eyes: an action is occurring, and we are watching a real event, just as we watch other significant events that take place around us. A game, in other words, is *not* a performance—at least, it is not socially coded as such. When Vaslav Nijinsky imitated the mere *look* of tennis, as if it were a performance or a dance show instead of an athletic competition, and used the distinctive movements of tennis players as the basis for his notorious 1913 ballet *Jeux*, critics were outraged: they complained indignantly that he seemed to have no understanding of the actual rules of the game or the point of playing it.[7] It is no accident, then, that sports matches—with one or two rare exceptions—are never reenacted, restaged, or reperformed exactly as they originally transpired. They must be seen to occur only once, because their very definition demands that they appear to be *unscripted:* in order to qualify as an "event," they must consist in a single, spontaneous action that concludes once and for all when it is over and that cannot be repeated. Their masculine gender-coding both requires and results from the event's unique, historically specific status. That is what imparts to action its singular prestige.

Of course, in our postmodern society, male sports stars get to cultivate a flamboyant image which they embellish with performative antics of various sorts. That tendency, which began perhaps with the boxer Muhammad Ali, has come to be an expected, or at least a tolerated, feature of the mass-mediated sports world, just as it is now a feature of straight masculinity. We see it in the little dances that football players do in end zones as well as in the jewelry, tattoos, and hairstyles of professional basketball players like Dennis Rodman (though Rodman claimed he never "fit into the mold of the NBA man").[8] And that doesn't even begin to account for the meteoric career of David Beckham, who has devoted himself to *appearing* at least as much as he has to *doing.*[9] Professional sports are becoming more and more like theater, a vast and endless melodrama continually played out on cable channels like ESPN and in the sports pages of newspapers and magazines. Sporting events themselves, however, still retain a gender-coding distinct from that of staged performance.

By contrast with sports stars, those entertainers whose job it is not to win a contest but to perform a scenario on a stage—whether in serious theater, the Broadway musical, the opera, or the ballet—are feminized as a consequence. Even though such performers often do exceptionally strenuous things on stage, they are considered not to *do* but to *appear*. And for a simple reason: *their action is predetermined and dictated by the stipulations of a preexisting script.*[10] They aren't making their own decisions; they aren't acting on their own authority; they aren't putting into play a chosen strategy for dealing with a rapidly changing set of circumstances, in accordance with certain rules and their best, lightning-quick assessment of their total situation. No, they have been told how to behave, and their performance acknowledges their submission to the dictates of others, as well as to a specific series of formalized demands that they have undertaken to carry out. Instead of having a deed to do, *they have a role to play*.

That, significantly, entails no gender trouble for divas or ballerinas or actresses. But, given the standard opposition in heteronormative culture between roles and essences—which is isomorphic with other corresponding oppositions between artifice and nature, appearing and being, inauthenticity and authenticity, performance and identity, femininity and masculinity—it does pose a considerable problem for the gender identity of male singers or dancers or actors. Because such figures do not accomplish an action but perform an already defined and scripted role, they lack, despite all their virtuosity (and musculature, at least in the case of dancers), the masculine dignity of sports stars or politicians of either gender, who do not know at the start of the game what exactly they will be doing with their bodies or how they will conduct themselves in the course of the action that is to follow.

๑๐

It is in this context of gender panic surrounding "the forbidden fantasy of male theatrical exhibition," and the consequently dubious status of the male performer, that the mother, according to D. A. Miller, reveals her true significance—as both the source and validation of her son's desire to perform, as well as the site of a particularly precious social permission (75). The mother's approval exempts her son from the terroristic surveillance and enforcement of masculine sex-roles, while his identification with her gives him access to the space of performance itself.

> Yet why should he brave such stigma at all if he hadn't been enlisted under the power—more ancient and tenacious—of a *solicitation?* For if he now finds himself putting up with a theatre whose clientele throws fruit at him, it is because his desire to perform was first exercised elsewhere, through a so much more heartening modeling of theatrical identities and relations that, in effect, he still hasn't left this earlier stage, where, just as he had taken his first steps, or uttered his first words there, he would sing and dance for a woman who called him to performance, and acclaimed him with applause even before he was through, prompting him if he faltered with some song or dance of her own, almost as though she were coaching him to be her understudy in a role that either generosity, or timidity, or some other thing kept her from playing herself. In short, contending against the established musical-theatrical regime that feminizes access to the performing space, a Mother Stage has universalized the desire to play there. (80–81)

This punning statement is at once a reading of *Gypsy,* an allegory of gay male development (all that talk of "stages"), and an exercise in cultural theory. The mother figures here as stage, audience, coach, and star: the ground of the boy's identity and the portal through which he gains access to himself as a subject. She is a figure of the musical (86) and the person in whose name the musical genre is elaborated (83). Just as her encouragement accompanied her son's first words or first steps, so her indulgence provides a lasting warrant for his performance—which he executes at once *for her, with her, and as her* (86). It is in her shadow, under her auspices, and through an identification with her that the queer boy who happens to be her son is encouraged/prohibited to accede to his own social and subjective agency—that is, to perform—and is thereby enabled to secure, precariously and improbably, his own identity, his own uncertain and provisory place in a hostile social world.

In the context of *Gypsy*, Miller is able to argue that the mother's rejection of the daughter, and the mother's attempt to reclaim the stage for herself at the end of the musical, produce a particularly disempowering and devastating shock when viewed from the perspective of a boy whose own access to performance had originally been authorized by the figure of his mother—a mother who had once led him to believe that, through her, he might have a place. The mother's final turn against her offspring reanimates the dread that her love had always excited, the dread "of being exiled from her presence" (112). After all, it was his mother's permission that not only had managed to suspend, if only for a time, the prohibitive feminine gendering of the theatrical stage, but also had allowed the boy to pretend to the sort of social identity and subjective fullness that he could achieve only by imaginatively performing it. In the end, Miller concludes, *Gypsy* (especially its cataclysmic concluding number, "Rose's Turn") allows no possibility of either "reconciliation" or "choice . . . between the adored mother who keeps a place for us and the resented monster who keeps it from us" (120).

∾

It is tempting to make a corresponding argument about the gay appeal of the climactic confrontation between mother and daughter in *Mildred Pierce*. At the least, it is tempting to speculate that the camp value of that melodramatic episode may lie in its invitation to gay men to return harmlessly to the scene of a similar trauma (real or fantasized): the trauma of being exiled from the mother's presence and from the limelight of her indulgence, permission, and social validation. It is by appropriating *Mildred Pierce*'s hyperbolic reenactment of the scene of maternal rejection, and *Mommie Dearest*'s even more histrionic version of it, that gay male culture can, on this interpretation, restage in an exaggerated, ludic, and reparative mode the horror of the mother's savage withdrawal of the warrant she once gave her queer child to perform, the warrant that licensed his very existence as a subject.

And some such socio-symbolic dynamic may be operative in the gay male response to *Mildred Pierce* and *Mommie Dearest*. It may well explain the specificity of the emotional impact of those two scenes on a gay male audience. But we should note that what makes such a hypothesis compelling in the case of *Gypsy* is its strict connection with Miller's close reading of the musical itself, a reading that generates the hypothesis in the first place. Miller does not depend on vague psychological generalities of the sort I have been trafficking in throughout the preceding paragraph. His reading does not demand to be applied to other musicals, let alone to other cultural forms, and it loses its point when it is generalized. Miller is not articulating a general truth: he is describing the specific meaning of a specific social form. At this juncture in the development of queer cultural analysis, *each vehicle of gay male identification—each line, each scene, each movie or musical, each diva—needs to be studied in all its particularity,* so as to disclose the meaning of the unique formal structure that constitutes it.

In the present case, it is enough to observe that *Mildred Pierce* is indeed about performance, specifically about the performance of maternal abjection. But it is not about the stage, nor does it represent the mother as a figure who provides her child with a precious point of entry to the performance of a socially valorized identity. (On the contrary: Mildred marries Monte in order to offer Veda a chance to escape the degrading necessity of performing musical numbers before a male audience on a cabaret stage.) No doubt the scene of violent confrontation between mother and daughter in *Mildred Pierce* offers the gay spectator a camp opportunity to work through the traumatic possibility of maternal rejection and, hence, social deauthorization. Nonetheless, Miller's reading does not apply directly to *Mildred Pierce* with the same degree of plausibility or rigor as it does to *Gypsy*. Miller's usefulness to us is of a more general nature.

The virtue of Miller's analysis is to locate the meaning of maternal rejection in the social codes of performance and the sexual politics of spectacle. It thereby provides a model for how to situate the drama of mother-daughter conflict, and the spectacle of a generational struggle between women, in an analysis of the symbolic and subjective dimensions of the structures of social meaning, in an understanding of the social and political semantics of cultural form that does not depend on clichés of pop psychology or psychoanalysis. The same thing applies to Proust's portrayal of the child's attempt both to be loved by the mother and to control her. These approaches allow us to connect gay male subjectivity with a larger set of social dynamics and cultural meanings.

No doubt some gay men have found in the scene in *Mildred Pierce* a means of reworking the spectacle of maternal rage so as to defuse the hurtful trace-memories of maternal rejection, a rejection with highly specific emotional resonances for queer children. But there are other ways of using the structural elements of the scene to produce an analysis of its gay appeal.

☙❧

The spectacle that magnetizes the audience's attention in both scenes from *Mildred Pierce* and *Mommie Dearest* is the spectacle of women "losing it," of women who pass beyond the breaking point and go out of control. That spectacle of raw emotion, of free-flowing, unobstructed passion finally bursting through the decorum of social life, is one long associated with the female subject. From Ovid's *Metamorphoses* to *Madame Bovary*, women are the traditional vehicle in European culture for the expression of erotic subjectivity, and of emotional excess. At least until the time of Rousseau and Goethe, when men began to take the business of erotic subjectivity over from women, and to write about male sexual sensibilities in their own persons or in the persons of male characters, women were the preferred medium for the representation of passionate emotion. Female characters were useful to male authors. They allowed such authors to pen scenes of passion and to voice hyperbolic emotion without having to speak in their own persons. In this way, women became established sites for the extreme expression of human feeling.

Another reason emotional excess has been traditionally gendered as feminine is that it correlates with relative powerlessness. People in authority don't have to yell and scream to get what they want. They simply make their wishes known. Newcomers to power may exhibit a tendency to throw temper tantrums—executives may mistreat their subordinates, wealthy housewives may torment their servants—but histrionics are generally supposed to be incompatible with the dignity of command. And the more authority you have, the less likely you are to "lose it."

Joan Crawford, in *Mommie Dearest,* despite her tyrannizing of Christina and her many outbursts of hysterical abuse, cannot manage to wrest from her adoptive daughter the respect to which she considers herself entitled—and it is precisely for this reason that she has to bewail the absence of it and make impotently violent efforts to reclaim it. That is partly what motivates the histrionics. It is Joan Crawford's very powerlessness that intensifies her rage: she cannot do—she can only vent. So "losing it" signifies the complete opposite of social effectiveness. It reveals the outlines of *a politics of emotion* that gay men share with women and other subordinated persons whose desires are deauthorized and who cannot get the respect they seek: a politics of hysteria or emotional surplus.[11] Such hysteria is inflated further by the delegitimation of all public manifestation of homosexual feeling. The life of gay sentiment, socially disqualified from the start, can find expression only in what looks like histrionics, rage, maudlin self-pity, hyperbolic passion, and excess.

But it might also be possible to argue the opposite: that the spectacle of women "losing it" conveys not powerlessness but the frightening power of the downtrodden, when they finally snap under the burden of intolerable oppression. The two scenes from *Mildred Pierce* and *Mommie Dearest* display, according to this perspective, the uncanny terror of a womanliness that breaks through the norms of polite decorum and finally lets itself go.

Mildred Pierce's underwriting of what we might now call moments of feminist rage helps to explain the particular appeal of Joan Crawford to her legions of female fans: she's the good girl, tough but brave and loyal, hard-working and decent, destined to rise in the world, but faced with terrible odds, who—when pushed to the breaking point—is fully entitled to strike out and let the world have it, especially the people she loves who have let her down. Notorious not only for her combination of glamour and abjection, but also for her demented fury, both in a number of her film roles and in select stories about her personal life, Joan Crawford could symbolize resistance, feistiness, strength, determination, and invincible will—a (feminist) spirit encapsulated in her infamous rebuke to the board of directors of Pepsi-Cola, who, after her husband's death, had tried to sideline her in an unsuccessful effort to prevent her from succeeding him as chairman of the board: "Don't fuck with me, fellas!" As that very line indicates (recall Lypsinka's performance of it), Joan Crawford made a career out of asserting herself despite, and in the midst of, her evident vulnerability.

Divas may be cartoon women, but they are not without a certain power and authority of their own. After all, divas are superstars. They are not only caricatures of femininity and epitomes of what our society regards as unserious—not only extravagant, grotesque, and larger than life. They are also *fierce*. Femininity in them gathers force, intensity, authority, and prestige. Femininity may lack social seriousness, but it is not bereft of passion or fury or dominance. For all its unseriousness, it retains an element of danger. Without trying to claim male power or privilege and, thus, without seeming to take on masculine gender characteristics (unlike, in this respect, certain female politicians or lawyers or executives or other women in positions of authority), divas nonetheless manage to achieve a position of social mastery. Instead of contesting or subverting conventional femininity, they acquire power through an exaggerated, excessive, hyperbolic, over-the-top performance of it (that is precisely what makes some feminists suspicious of them).

Abjection, moreover, can be just as powerful as glamour. Those who are relegated to the ranks of the unserious have no reason to behave themselves. Unconstrained as they are by propriety, they can become completely unrestrained. *They have nothing to lose by "losing it."* They can afford to let themselves go, to be extravagant, to assert themselves through their undignified and indecent flamboyance. Divas are people for whom glamour represents a triumph, perhaps the only possible triumph—and for whom Style is a true Utopia. Aestheticism becomes a weapon in their hands. By wielding it, divas manage to be successful against the odds.

Divas disclose a form of power that gay men can claim as their own. In *Mildred Pierce*, Joan Crawford embodies precisely that kind of fierceness. Confronting her disdainful daughter with a sudden flash of fury in that notorious, climactic scene, she gives eloquent and glamorous expression to the ferocity already simmering within people who have long been marginalized and abused—a ferocity easily ignited under conditions of extreme stress. Call it the power of hysteria, or call it the insurrection of the abject; call it even feminist rage: perhaps these are all different names for the same thing. In any case, what we are dealing with in the scenes from both *Mildred Pierce* and *Mommie Dearest* is not the terroristic power of male intimidation and domination, but the power of the victim who isn't going to take it any more, and who returns in triumph, "wounded and dominant," to confront her persecutors with the full force of her pain.[12]

If only the teased and bullied queer child, when cornered on the playground, or if only the abused lover, when betrayed and mistreated by his boyfriend, could manage to summon and to channel that righteous, triumphant fury, the fierceness and glamour of Joan Crawford, he might find within himself the courage, the strength, and the conviction to bash back.

Such moments have in fact been possible. At least one of the stories about the Stonewall riots has it that what inspired the crowd outside the bar to resist, what set off its fury and caused the riots, was the sight of a drag queen who was being hustled into a police van and

who, in a sudden spasm of outrage, hit an officer with her purse.[13]
The entire history of gay liberation, contestation, and resistance may
owe a direct debt to *Mildred Pierce,* then—or, if not exactly to *Mildred
Pierce,* at least to the social form and emotional experience of which
it is both a classic instance and a definitive mass-cultural expression:
the drama of enraged female powerlessness suddenly and dazzlingly
transformed into momentary, headlong, careless, furious, resistless
power.

⌘

There are other possible interpretations of this moment when social
barriers fall before the onrush of unstoppable emotion. Something
about the exhilaration of an affect that triumphs over social inhibition
suggests the euphoria inchoate in any heroic refusal to live a lie. The
emotional keynote in these scenes, according to such a view, would
be not excess but honesty. If we read the two scenes straight as moments of truth, we may find in them an echo-effect of the experience
(actual or imagined) of coming out of the closet. On this account, the
appeal of these scenes to gay men derives from gay men's personal
recognition of the giddy, intense boldness of that vertiginous resolve
when you finally decide to say what you've been bottling up inside
for so long. On this (typically post-Stonewall) reading, the crucial
threshold is crossed when Veda says to Mildred, with mingled menace, provocation, aggression, insinuation, and seductiveness, "Are you
sure you want to know? [Mildred: "Yes."] Then I'll tell you." Veda's
subsequent avowal is met with an equal candor on Mildred's part,
in her wonderfully camp reply (suitable for repetition and reperformance on any number of occasions): "Veda, I think I'm really seeing
you for the first time in my life, and you're cheap and horrible."

⌘

All of the interpretations rehearsed in both this chapter and the previous one touch on important aspects of the scene from *Mildred Pierce.*
We will return to elements of them. But some of them depend too

obviously on a thematic or psychological or allegorical reading, which treats the mother-daughter conflict as a simple encoding of gay male experience (maternal rejection, disempowerment, defiance, coming out). Much gay male experience, of course, *is* encoded in that scene: it is surely the case that some gay men thrill to this cinematic moment because they find represented in it emotions that are familiar to them from their own lives, situations of which they already have abundant personal experience and considerable direct knowledge. Which may explain why gay male culture has seized on the scene, and on the movie as a whole.

But more needs to be said before we can fully understand how Joan Crawford has come to serve as proxy identity for some gay men. Too many of the interpretations I have just rehearsed share a common tendency to explain gay male culture's choice of its material over-literally, explaining it away instead of explaining it, and forgetting the important lesson that we have already learned: what gay men love about their non-gay cultural icons is those icons' very figurality. All those literalist interpretations imply, instead, that the gay men who respond to *Mildred Pierce* can do so only by translating the terms of that movie entirely into their own reality—by *gaying* Joan Crawford, and by reading the mother-daughter melodrama as a literal representation of gay male life—rather than by understanding it as a figure, or metaphor, and as a point of entry into a queer world. Such literalism makes this cinematic moment into a mere reflection of gay *identity* instead of a powerful vehicle of gay *identification* and an expression of gay desire. Just as, in the case of the Broadway musical, it is not by putting gay men or representations of gay male life on the stage that you realize gay desire, so in this case it is not by interpreting Mildred Pierce or Joan Crawford as a stand-in for a gay man that you are likely to unlock the secret of their gay appeal.

This literalizing tendency recurs in explanations that highlight Joan Crawford's masculinity—why, just look at those shoulder pads!—or that treat her and Faye Dunaway in *Mommie Dearest* as drag queens, as if those considerations alone explained gay male culture's fascination with her.[14] No one, of course, could miss the butch theatrics of Joan Crawford's performance in *Johnny Guitar,* or deny that *Mommie Dearest* is premised on the uncanny pleasures of female impersonation (if only Faye Dunaway's impersonation of Joan Crawford). But the problem with these literal interpretations is that by appearing to be so knowing, so certain about what is at stake for gay male culture in the iconic figure of Joan Crawford (whether that be butch display or hyperfeminine performance), such interpretations hasten to close down the interpretive issues before us, pretending to a more complete understanding of gay male culture's relation to femininity than they can deliver. Instead of identifying the specific elements that actually elicit the subjective involvement of gay male spectators, they offer a truism masquerading as the truth of gay identification. In this way, they presume the answer they should be looking for, and they effectively block further inquiry into the logic behind the gay male response—as if a passing glance at those shoulder pads were enough to settle the whole matter once and for all.

Also, the two interpretations tend to cancel each other out. It is hard to see how Joan Crawford can be both a butch woman and a drag queen at the same time, both lacking in femininity and hyperperforming femininity. Or, rather—and this is perhaps the point of each interpretation—it is hard to see how both claims could be true unless the point of each of them is that Joan Crawford isn't really a woman at all, that she represents gay male identity and is, appearances to the contrary notwithstanding, a gay man in drag.

But that conclusion is inaccurate. It denies Crawford's famous and formidable feminine glamour, which admittedly depends on a strategic mingling of masculine and feminine features, and it resists acknowledging what we have learned to call "female masculinity," the many sorts of masculinity that women, *as women,* can perform.[15] It is unfair to Crawford, insofar as it refuses to recognize or attend to her carefully cultivated—and shifting—style of female embodiment, as well as her complex negotiation of feminine identity. It is unflattering, in different ways, both to women and to gay men, because it ignores what makes them different from each other and it fails to credit them with their subjective specificities, which after all are what lay the basis for the possibility of cross-identification. And so it misunderstands how a proxy identity produced by such cross-identification actually works—that is, how exactly Joan Crawford functions as a proxy identity for some gay men.

⊙⊙

In any case, it is critically important not to reduce gay identification to gay identity. For such a reduction would remove the very problem it had set out to solve, erasing what it proposes to explain—namely, the meaning of gay male culture's feminine identifications. If Joan Crawford, or other feminine figures with whom gay men have identified, were not really women, if they were somehow disguised versions of gay men all along, then one could not properly speak of gay men's relations to them as *identifications*. Gay male culture's fixation on those figures would simply represent a reflection of gay male *identity* itself. There would be no process of decoding and recoding to study, and gay men's cultural practices would tell us nothing in particular about gay male subjectivity beyond some common and obvious psychological commonplaces. Instead of inquiring into the logic underlying gay male culture's refashioning of heterosexual culture, we would be observing gay culture's identity-consolidating recognition of gay meanings already present in heterosexual culture. That is not to interpret the phenomenon, but to abolish it—by collapsing identification into identity, by reducing desire to identity. It is to deny the very existence of gay culture—to abolish male homosexuality as a specifically cultural practice.

If *Mildred Pierce* and the Broadway musical were simply encoded representations of gay identity, we would expect that the open, explicitly gay, out-and-proud, identity-based culture of the post-Stonewall period would have put them out of business long ago, since nowadays gay men have access to the real thing, to uncensored and direct representations of themselves: they no longer have to settle for encrypted or figural versions, and they don't have to go to all the trouble of reappropriating them. Remember what Andrew Sullivan gleefully proclaimed when he announced "the end of gay culture": gay men nowadays no longer have "to find hidden meaning in main-stream films—somehow identifying with the aging, campy female lead in a way the rest of the culture missed."[16] And Sullivan is per-fectly right: gay men *don't have to do this* any more. But they still do it. They do it anyway. For lots of gay men, Joan Crawford, the Golden Girls, Lady Gaga, and many other camp icons continue to exercise a certain power and appeal, though mainstream gay commentators like Sullivan, who would prefer that they didn't, assert that they don't. That seemingly confident assertion, however, expresses not a fact but a wish—and one that is not likely to be fulfilled anytime soon.

It is not even clear that the term "identification," borrowed from ego psychology for the sake of mere convenience, gets at what is re-ally going on in gay male culture's investments in figures like Joan Crawford. Identification was classically defined by Freud as a desire to be, rather than a desire to have, but it is highly uncertain whether gay men (or other adepts of gay culture who thrill to *Mildred Pierce*) literally want to *be* Joan Crawford—however much they may enjoy the sensation of projecting themselves into her persona or imagining themselves in her role. In fact, it is very likely that most of Joan Craw-ford's queer fans do not seriously wish to be her and would certainly not choose to be her, if they could. The term "identification" seems to be yet another example of a crude, imprecise placeholder for a more accurate description or analysis or category that we cur-rently lack. "Identification" is a way of saying that gay male culture is, somehow, complexly engaged with the figure of Joan Crawford—that some gay men have been mesmerized by that figure, struck by its figural possibilities, emotionally involved with it, or trans-ported by the relations of proximity or correspondence or coinci-dence that they have been able to establish with it. "Identification," "dis-identification," and "cross-identification" all represent efforts to articulate the general, vague conviction that the engagement of gay male culture with Joan Crawford's image or persona accomplishes something important, something meaningful, something particularly valuable for those who participate in that culture.

What we may be dealing with, in the end, is a specific kind of engagement that somehow mobilizes complex relations of similarity and difference—but without constituting subjects or objects in the usual ways. Instead, that mobilization produces fields of practice and feeling that map out possibilities for contact or interrelation among cultural forms and their audiences, consumers, or publics, and that get transmitted from one generation to another. We simply have no good languages for that phenomenon—only a variety of critical vernaculars (such as "identification"), all of them misleading or harmful or inexact. The most we can hope to do, in this situation, is to remain open to the indeterminate character of those fields of practice and feeling, along with the metaphorical or figural nature of the social processes themselves.

13

THE SEXUAL POLITICS OF GENRE

*L*et us return to the two scenes from *Mildred Pierce* and *Mommie Dearest*. Now that we are able to situate their gay appeal in the larger context of the sexual politics of cultural form, we can begin to discern a central element in the gay response to those scenes that we have been neglecting. The key to understanding the logic behind gay culture's appropriation of the two scenes, it turns out, can be found in a single, simple, and basic—if paradoxical—fact: the entire drama of mother-daughter conflict is one from which, by definition, men are absent.[1]

The quickest and easiest way to grasp the full significance of that absence is to consider how different the effect of the two scenes, their meaning, and their reception would be if they featured not a mother and a daughter, but a father and a son.

Once you ask yourself that question, you don't need to reflect on it for very long. The differences are decisive, and their consequences apparent.

A story about a father who throws his son out of the house or disowns him, or about a father who plots against his son or plans his death; an incident in which a son strikes his father; a story about a son who tries to kill his father: the mere mention of such scenarios is sufficient to evoke the familiar masterplots of European literature and culture—to say nothing of Freudian psychoanalysis. We are immediately transported to the world of the Bible, to the story of Joseph and his brothers, or the tale of the prodigal son. We are reminded of the epic generational quarrel between Achilles and Agamemnon in Homer's *Iliad,* or the theater of dynastic/domestic turmoil that reaches all the way from the *Oedipus Rex* of Sophocles to the plays of Eugene O'Neill and Arthur Miller.

Such generational struggles between father and son are very serious business. Indeed, they are the stuff of high tragedy.

A generational conflict between women, by contrast, even at its most serious or passionate, cannot rise above the level of melodrama.

That is not, of course, a statement of my personal feelings about the matter. I am not endorsing this cultural attitude, or the social meaning of gender that it expresses; I'm simply reporting it. It is a cultural fact that in Western society a generational conflict between women cannot help appearing, at least in the eyes of a socially authorized (i.e., male) spectator, as vaguely disreputable—tending to the excessive, the hysterical, the hyperbolic, or the grotesque—and, in any case, less than fully serious.

Can you think of a single example of a generational conflict between women in Western literature that can claim the same tragic grandeur as the male generational struggles of the *Iliad* or *Oedipus Rex?* Conflicts between mothers and sons are genuine contenders for that lofty status (consider *Hamlet* or the *Oresteia,* just for starters), but struggles between women belonging to different generations are simply not the stuff of tragedy. Sophocles's *Electra* comes closest, but ultimately what gives that drama its seriousness is its proximate, ancillary relation to the dynastic preoccupations of male culture: paternal inheritance, royal succession, the transmission of property from father to son, and the continuation of the male line. Electra steps into a patriarchal function (and thus into a tragic dignity), because the male heroes are absent from the scene for most of the play and no one but Electra is willing to take the place of the male heir. Electra alone volunteers to fill that essential role and to oppose the ascendancy of her mother. Sophocles is careful, nonetheless, to stop the action cold, just as Electra, Joan Crawford–like, reaches for the axe. It is at that critical juncture that male heroes suddenly appear on the scene, take over from Electra, and complete the dramatic action, making sure it remains fully serious and dignified. Sophocles thereby preserves the sublime beauty of his tragedy from the melodramatic bathos of *Mommie Dearest*.

The reaction of a heterosexual male friend of mine to Jules Dassin's 1978 film *A Dream of Passion*—a brilliant interrogation of the possible contemporary uses of Euripides's *Medea* for feminist politics— exemplifies and enacts the cultural logic at work here. *A Dream of Passion* features Dassin's famous wife, Melina Mercouri, playing an iconic Greek actress, one rather like herself, who returns to Greece from political exile, after the fall of the military junta in 1973, to perform the role of Medea. Her male director, who in the plot of the movie is also her former husband, judging that her interpretation of the role is too political, too feminist, and not sufficiently passionate, arranges for her to meet a young American woman (played by Ellen Burstyn), who happens to be serving a life sentence in Athens for the crime of killing her children: knowing nothing of classical literature, or feminism, she seems to have unwittingly reincarnated the personage of Medea when her Greek husband, like Jason in the plot of the original story, abandoned his foreign spouse on his native soil for a Greek wife. The encounter between the two women changes the actress's understanding of herself, of her identity as a woman, of the history and politics of her relations with men; and ultimately it alters her interpretation of the dramatic role, though whether it does so for better or for worse is difficult to say. The result is a contemporary feminist (or perhaps a counter-feminist) version of Euripides's celebrated tragedy.

The movie is a determined attempt to revive a tragic mode of feeling, to reanimate the true spirit of tragedy in a modern context by drawing on an ancient source, and to figure out whether such a thing as feminist tragedy is possible. I found the film deeply moving, and I took it seriously, so I was startled—and deflated—when my friend, an accomplished dramatist himself, said to me gently but reprovingly as the lights came up, "David, it *was* a trifle overwrought."

My friend was not entirely wrong about the movie. Nonetheless, his urbane and effortless put-down indicates the kinds of barriers that any drama of passionate female feeling, of tension and conflict between older and younger women, has to surmount before being admitted by culturally privileged men to the protected, exclusive preserve of tragic seriousness (within which *Long Day's Journey into Night, Death of a Salesman,* and *All My Sons* manage to come off, by dint of some miraculous feat of cultural magic, and in utter defiance of all the evidence to the contrary, as *not* overwrought—not even "a trifle").

ᘓᕣᘒ

Mommie Dearest offers a particularly clear and instructive demonstration of the relations between gender and genre. It enables us to discern the sexual politics that electrify the protective cordon surrounding the privileged domain of tragedy. For *Mommie Dearest*'s solemn portrayal of emotional and physical violence is a stellar example of failed seriousness—the very quality that Susan Sontag correctly identified as a defining feature of camp.[2] But why does the movie's effort to represent a situation that is both tragic and horrifying fall through, or fall short of the requirements for true seriousness, and become laughable?

There are plenty of reasons you could cite: the two-dimensional, kabuki-like character portrayals; the overacting; the extended scenes of outrageous emotional excess; the earnestness and sententiousness of the story—"great thumping plot points," as one of our Amazon reviewers aptly put it, to which "subtlety and sensitivity take a back seat." The visual editing also contributes an important element, especially the alienating deployment of raised and distant camera angles at the end of the scene (see, for example, Figure 15), which encourages the spectator's emotional detachment from the characters and turns the confrontation between the two women into pure spectacle—a spectacle staged specifically for distant and bemused (male) consumption.

Particularly humiliating to the characters, and therefore flattering to the spectator, especially the male spectator, is the insistent glimpse of Tina's childish white underwear. Such an undignified, downright demeaning exposure of the character's pathetic vulnerability would be utterly unthinkable in *Mildred Pierce;* it would be as out of keeping with the suave style of the movie as those removed and alienating camera angles. The glimpse of Tina's underwear is at once pitiful, ridiculous, distancing, and titillating. Without exactly being pornographic, it combines the two characteristics of pornography that cultural feminists deplore—in fact, it may do so better than some works of actual pornography—namely, the prurient and the degrading.

But the centrality of the conflict between mother and daughter in the plot of the movie does a lot to compound the story's overall lack of dignity. In fact, by magnifying the histrionics of *Mildred Pierce* to a grotesque degree, *Mommie Dearest* brings out the implicit unseriousness of the earlier film, despite its relative earnestness, tastefulness, and verisimilitude. By pushing to an extreme the elements of overheated feeling, emotional excess, and passionate intensity already present in *Mildred Pierce, Mommie Dearest* teaches us to view the earlier movie's more realistic and (relatively) sober representation of the conflict between mother and daughter as already imbued with a deliriously over-the-top quality, already verging on the hysterical, already given over to a reductive, patronizing vision—at once glamorous and abject—of women and femininity: already disqualified, in short, as a candidate for serious consideration, for the honorific status of tragedy.

And once *Mildred Pierce,* too, begins to be viewed as excessive—as "overwrought"—which is to say, once it ceases to be taken straight and comes to be regarded instead with a modicum of detachment, condescension, and irony (as it was not by its original, working-class female audience), it forfeits its claim to tragic dignity, just as *Mommie Dearest* does, and sinks helplessly to the degraded status of melodrama, that despised and abject subgenre.

◯◯◯

Gay men, for all their cultural differences from straight men, are still men, and their relation to the melodramatic scene of maternal conflict is therefore bound to be different in at least one crucial respect from the emotional involvement of those female spectators who were the prime targets of classic Joan Crawford movies and who were, in any case, her biggest fans. However rapturously or deliriously gay male spectators may identify with the characters in the movie, their identification is mediated by their gender difference. It has to be more oblique than the identification of women, who could see themselves in Crawford on the basis of a shared social positioning, of common experiences, struggles, and aspirations—on the basis, that is, of some degree of identity.

Gay men can certainly identify with Mildred Pierce, but, being men, they cannot do it straightforwardly or unironically. Their identification, however headlong and intoxicated, requires a certain amount of imaginative work. It is *necessarily* accompanied by a significant degree of dis-identification and distance, and it is inevitably filtered by irony. But irony doesn't spell rejection, and "dis-identification" here is precisely *not* the opposite of "identification": it is not a refusal or a repudiation of identification. What we are dealing with, once again, is a complex play of identity and difference, an oscillating ironic doubleness—the very kind of ironic doubleness that is essential to camp sensibility. This simultaneous coincidence of passionate investment and alienated bemusement, so typical of gay male culture, is what structures the gay male response to the scene.

I do not mean to imply, of course, that women cannot also have an ironic or distanced perspective on *Mildred Pierce*. I do not suppose for a moment that their relation to the film is destined to be and to remain one of unqualified earnestness, of uncritical, literal identification and mirroring, as if they were incapable of bringing to the film a camp sensibility of their own.[3] My point is simply that their relation to the film is not necessarily, inevitably ironic; furthermore, their unironic identification is mightily encouraged by the film. It is only with a certain lapse of time and a corresponding change of taste or fashion that it becomes easier and nearly irresistible for many women not to take the movie straight, as gay men could never do. And, as time goes on, some women may even allow themselves to be schooled in the dynamics of spectatorial irony and in the play of identification/dis-identification by gay male viewing practices, which lately have become so pervasive and so widely appealing. Nonetheless, for female spectators an ironic response to the movie is not predestined or inescapable. Even today, those feminist film critics who are women continue to debate, in all earnestness, how seriously to take the film—in particular, how seriously to take the film's feminist implications—a question that gay male critics largely ignore, and that appears not to interest them.

෬ඥ

The gay male spectator, positioned eccentrically with respect to the canonical form of the nuclear family, is also more likely than either straight women or straight men to nourish an ironic perspective on the drama of familial conflict itself. Within the miniature world of the family, however, there is nothing ironic about performances of either love or hate. Family dramas are compulsively overacted, inflated out of all proportion to the apparent stakes in them, and thus ineluctably histrionic. What gets expressed in family conflicts tends almost inevitably to exceed what is actually felt. In fact, the only way that what is felt *can* be expressed seems to be through an insistently hyperbolic acting-out of it.

Do you feel that your daughter's, or your lover's, behavior to you implies a certain lack of deference to your sensibilities? Don't just say so. Scream at them. Ask them, in aggrieved, self-pitying, and grandiose tones, "Why can't you give me the respect that I'm entitled to?"

This apparently necessary and unavoidable overacting is also what endows the emotional excesses of personal interactions within the family with their intrinsic falseness. Are you taken aback by your daughter's, or your lover's, coldness to you? Don't just remonstrate with them. Make them feel how utterly shocked and disappointed you are in them, how nothing in your entire existence has prepared you for their lamentable, culpable ingratitude. Say, with haughty disdain, "[Veda,] I think I'm really seeing you for the first time in my life." That is certainly a grand, crushing pronouncement. It indicates the boundless extent of your hurt and disgust. But as a statement of fact, it is, obviously, less than completely honest. Considered in itself, it's perfectly untrue.

Finally, it is the very falseness of the sentiments expressed in family conflicts that, when combined with their extravagant expression, motivates their violence. For so much excessive and hollow emotion requires justification, and no rational explanation is available to justify its hyperbolic extremes. Since no adequate justification can be found, you will have to assert it by force. Violence is required. Slap your mother. Slap your daughter. Slap your lover.

The mingled violence, sentimentality, falseness, and histrionics of the emotions that are at the heart of family conflicts make the family into a permanent site of melodrama. For melodrama, as a degraded subgenre, is characterized by precisely such a combination of elements: a pitch of emotional intensity that appears to be excessive or extravagant; overacting; hence, falseness (if spectators judge a performance to be "melodramatic," what they mean is that they find it hokey and "untrue to reality"); and a plot adorned with violent climaxes.

It makes no difference whether the family in question is your family of origin, your family of choice, or your newly composed gay or lesbian family.

Being, as it is, a permanent site of melodrama, the family virtually demands that we bring an ironic perspective to bear on it. And in fact an ironic relation, which is to say the relation to drama of a spectator who is at once involved with it and disengaged from it—in this case, the specific relation to female melodrama of a gay male spectator—may be the best, perhaps the only possible defense against the suffocating emotional claustrophobia of family life. For what irony allows, in keeping with the pragmatics of camp, is the possibility of viewing the histrionics of family life as both horrifying and hilarious at the same time, without assimilating either dimension of those histrionics to the other. It offers an alienated outlook on intense emotion that—unlike the withering judgment of my straight friend on *A Dream of Passion*—is neither skeptical nor reductive.

Mildred Pierce and *Mommie Dearest,* when they are viewed from that alienated (though still emotionally engaged) perspective, teach gay men—and anyone else who subscribes to gay male culture—how to survive the woes of the family unit. For they teach them the practical uses of irony. Or perhaps the converse is true: the pleasure that gay male culture takes in appropriating those films reflects the ironic attitude gay men had long cultivated in order to distance and thereby to insulate themselves from the hurtful histrionics of family life—without, however, denying the deadly earnestness of those histrionics, their power to inflict real injury and pain. In any case, irony provides an effective and handy weapon against an inescapable social form whose ideological functioning requires, in order to prevail, both an uncritical belief in it and the violent assertion of its authenticity.

ᗧᗡ

Gay male culture's hard-won ironic vision of the falseness and performative character of family sentiments also registers something more general and more profound about emotional expression. It reflects the very structure of *the social life of feeling*. In particular, it testifies to the inevitable gap between what is *felt* and what in any specific context is capable of being *expressed*.

A certain effort of will is usually required in order to render the expression of a feeling adequate to the nature of the feeling itself—as the melodrama of everyday family life demonstrates. And such an effort may be strenuously necessary for gay men, who have no ready-made social forms available to them for expressing their feelings, and whose every expression of an emotion therefore has to orient itself in relation to a preexisting, heteronormative social form, or genre, of which it can be only an imitation or a parody. No wonder gay men have a reputation for being given to melodrama in their styles of emotional expression. But even for heterosexuals, even beyond the melodramatic world of the family, the task of conveying outwardly what is felt inwardly may have something awkward or histrionic or embarrassing about it. There is almost inevitably an element of excess, or inauthenticity, or even travesty in the expression of any grand passion. One might even say that what makes a passion grand, what inflates the emotions that constitute it, is this very consciousness of the impossibility of their transparent expression—and the consequent need to find a way of bodying them forth that will answer to the representational requirements of their grandeur.

Such a gap between feeling and its expression, when *not* acknowledged ironically, generates the tragic sublimity that attaches to the master narratives of male generational conflict in European culture. In Homer's *Iliad,* for example, when Agamemnon insults Achilles by taking away his war prize, it is Achilles's denial of any possibility of translating his own feeling of personal hurt and public injury into adequate social expression that leads to his tragic decision to reject Agamemnon's subsequent offer of compensation—and, along with it, the validity of all symbolic social forms.

The tragic necessity of accepting, instead of refusing, the inevitable gap between feeling and its expression provides the point of the rebuke that Ajax addresses to Achilles in Book 9 of the *Iliad.* It is here that Achilles announces his intention to refuse any and all material compensation for the social degradation and emotional damage he has suffered from Agamemnon. Complaining that Achilles is "pitiless," Ajax advances a radical argument that acknowledges the incommensurable distance in social life between what we feel and what we can do about it. That incommensurability, he implies, is at once a consequence of human mortality and a generative source of the symbolic social forms whose reparative functioning affords the sole means of bridging (but not closing) the gulf between human subjectivity and human sociality:

> And yet a man takes from his brother's slayer
> the blood price, or the price for a child who was killed, and the
>   guilty
> one, when he has largely repaid, stays still in the country,
> and the injured man's heart is curbed, and his pride, and his
>   anger
> when he has taken the price; but the gods put in your breast a
>   spirit
> not to be placated.
>
>   (Homer, *Iliad* 9.632–637; trans. Lattimore)

Ajax's little disquisition on the institution of the blood price emphasizes that human sociality depends on the viability of transactions that do not *express* the feelings of social actors, but that merely *represent, symbolize,* or otherwise *figure* them.

For if the family of a murdered man accepts a payment of money from the murderer and surrenders, in exchange for that sum, all hope and intention of revenge, that is not because the bereaved kinsmen are emotionally satisfied by the deal, or because the money compensates them for their loss, let alone because it restores the murdered relative to life. On the contrary, it is precisely because *nothing* will compensate them for their loss, because nothing in the world corresponds to what the grieving and angry family wants, because nothing they can do (including revenge) will serve to translate their feelings into an adequate form of personal or public expression, that they can agree—however grudgingly—to make do with a purely symbolic restitution (in the form of money). For such a symbolic restitution is the only kind of restitution that they can ever expect to obtain for what is, after all, an irreparable and irremediable loss.

That is also what Achilles eventually discovers for himself, once he kills Hector in a vain attempt to expiate his own fatal mistakes. It is only then that he comes to realize the emotional futility of that heroic deed—its inability to compensate him for the loss of Patroclus or to assuage his own sense of responsibility for the death of his beloved companion.[4]

According to the *Iliad*, human sociality depends on the viability of purely symbolic transactions. It requires surrendering all hope of ever finding in the world an adequate objective correlative of what we feel and a satisfactory means of expressing it.[5] Unless social mediations are understood from the start to be necessarily (and merely) *symbolic*, not *expressive*, they will be found to be grossly insufficient. In which case we are likely to reject them, as Achilles does. And so they will lose all efficacy and cease to function: they will no longer be able to do the job of knitting people together in a web of social exchange, both now and in the future. Then all human communication and sociality will break down and the fabric of human relationality will unravel—as it does for a while in the bleak latter portion of the *Iliad*.

Achilles reconciles himself to the incommensurable gap between feeling and its expression only in his final meeting with Priam, who sets him an example of *how to live by it*—how to occupy that very gap. Renouncing any attempt to express outwardly what he really feels about Achilles, Priam, in his selfless determination to ransom from Achilles the corpse of his son, Hector, kisses the hands of the man who has killed his children.

That celebrated and pathetic gesture does not translate Priam's grief and anger into a meaningful public form. Far from expressing what Priam feels, it expresses the utter impossibility of his ever expressing it.

And so it attests to the need for public, social gestures that do not express emotion but stand in for it—that represent it without aspiring to express it—and that convey it by means of a set of generic, agreed-

upon symbols and substitutions, thereby securing the smooth operation of conventional social relations.

෨෧

In this context, the gap between feeling and expression is tragic, because it is the manifestation of a basic existential catastrophe—a fatal,
irreparable, inescapable void in human meaning. The understandable
human impulse to close it, to find a way of *literally* expressing what
we truly feel, is not only foredoomed but destructive: it threatens the
symbolic mediations that hold the entire social world together. Not
only will our stubborn impulse to close that gap not succeed, but
it will damage our social existence even further, by discrediting the
symbolic forms through which we represent what we feel and by
means of which we maintain our social relations with one another.

To insist on expressing fully what we feel will result in endless,
pointless violence. It will also endanger the only channel by which we
can actually communicate. For language itself is a realm of symbols
to which we resort when, at the end of infancy, we discover that we
have no direct means of expressing our longings, and no hope of obtaining what we want on our own. Only by substituting words (that
is, symbols) for what they designate can we achieve a limited commerce with the world outside ourselves.

So the passionate human drive to find a proper form for the outward expression of our feelings—a form that would be adequate to
those feelings and fully commensurate with their magnitude or intensity—is ultimately misdirected, destructive, and doomed to failure. We have to learn to resist it. Tragic wisdom consists in renouncing it. Not because giving it up will make us happy, but because
refusing to compromise our desire for the real thing will accomplish
nothing and will make us even unhappier and more miserable: it will
lead to the loss of the few things of value in the world that we actually possess, and it will cause us to destroy the very beings whom
we most cherish.

That, at least, is the vision of classical tragedy, as it typically emerges from heroic clashes between men of different generations.

To treat the inauthenticity inherent in any social expression of feeling as anything *less* than tragic, to refuse to see in it anything less sublime than a chafing at the limits of mortality, is to fail to endow it with its full human significance and gravity and to refuse to recognize it for what tragedy claims it is: namely, a fatal sign of the profound and painful breach that the male quarrel with heaven, or with the father, opens in the very order of human meaning—the symptom of *an existential crisis that puts sociality itself at risk*. Unless the inauthenticity intrinsic to the social expression of feeling is understood to be tragic and not comic—serious instead of ridiculous or deflating—tragedy cannot get the respect it is culturally entitled to. Nor can it claim the prestige that accrues to it as the one aesthetic form that makes such an agonizing truth at once available to us and temporarily, spiritually bearable.

To fail to take seriously the inauthenticity inherent in the social expression of feelings is to refuse to take tragedy at its word. And it is to deprive masculinity, correspondingly, of its heroic grandeur and self-importance. For if that inauthenticity turns out *not* to be a tragic expression of mortal limitations that are built into the very structure of human existence—limitations that only heroic masculine striving, in its furious attempt to transcend them, can reveal to us and force us to confront—and if, instead, inauthenticity proves to be merely comical—an embarrassing, disqualifying, even hilarious effect of the everyday exposure of being-as-playing-a-role, and consequently of cultural meanings as acts of social theater—then tragedy is dethroned from its position of preeminence, its wisdom is devalued and its pathos cut down to size. And the same is true for the heroic brand of masculinity that underwrites tragedy: once its dignity is shown up as exaggerated and unnecessary, its status is irredeemably degraded, and it is reduced to a grandiose pose, an empty bluff, a flamboyant act, a song and dance.

The ultimate effect is to turn Homer's *Iliad* into a Broadway musi-cal—something that no one has yet attempted.[6] It is to queer tragedy. Or, more exactly, to turn tragedy into melodrama.

◎◎

For what tragedy cannot survive is the merest hint that it might, just possibly, be "a trifle overwrought." It cannot recover from the percep-tion, or suspicion, that its intense bursts of emotional expression may have been inflated beyond the strict requirements of the extreme situ-ations it depicts, of the mortal agonies which provided the motive and the cue for all that passion. Social and emotional inauthenticity may be at the core of tragedy's vision of the world, but it is fatal to tragedy as a form. Should tragic suffering ever be perceived as a mere performance or impersonation of suffering, should archetypal tragic destinies come off as histrionic roles, then tragedy will necessarily in-cur a loss of authentication, of social credit, and will forfeit its author-ity as a vehicle of existential truth. If the audience ever suspects that tragedy's dramatic extravagances are not wholly justified, that they are even the teeniest bit excessive, that the high pitch of emotion which distinguishes tragic feeling, which elevates it to the heights of sublimity, is less than fully motivated—in short, that passion is not be-ing *felt* so much as it is being faked or *performed*—then tragedy ceases to produce a properly tragic effect and lapses into melodrama.

Melodrama, for its part, is all about the staging of extreme feel-ing, and it places a premium on performance. Melodrama is tragedy's bourgeois inheritor. It was created to please and entertain the sorts of people—chiefly the middle classes, and especially women—who did not enjoy the benefits of an elite classical education, who could not read Greek or Latin, and who therefore had little access (before the heyday of cheap and plentiful classical translations) to the refined aes-thetic experience of ancient tragedy, just as they did not possess the cultivated sensibilities necessary either to appreciate the classical Eu-ropean drama that claimed to be its modern successor or to savor the stiff formality of the verse in which it was composed.

For the members of the bourgeoisie, who did not see their own lives, their own world, and their own values reflected in classical tragedy, ancient or modern, a new and more popular genre had to be invented: a genre of middle-class family drama, spoken in prose, closer in its subject matter to their daily experience and better attuned in its sentimental register to their emotional needs—but, despite all those concessions, not reducible to comedy. For if middle-class family drama, or melodrama, *had* been reducible to comedy, if it had treated bourgeois family misfortunes as trivial or laughable, it would simply have been demeaning and cheapening bourgeois life. And so it would not have fit the purposes for which it was designed.

That—at the risk of a gross oversimplification—is the genealogy of melodrama. Melodrama transplanted the heroics, the strife, and the pathos of classical tragedy to the comparatively humdrum world of bourgeois existence. Classical tragedy had often taken place within a family—a royal family, to be sure, but still a family—and melodrama could preserve its focus on the family and its setting within the household, thereby endowing the social and emotional situations of bourgeois domestic life with a new sense of grandeur, urgency, and intensity. Melodrama gave the middle classes an experience of high drama that they could call their own, that they could understand in their own terms and in their own language. Melodrama took their social, financial, and matrimonial preoccupations as a point of departure for the staging of emotions as extreme as those of classical tragedy. It was tragedy for the middle classes.

But that democratization came at a certain social cost. For women are obviously less serious than men, and the middle classes are less dignified than the elite. The kind of tragedy to which melodrama gave new form and life was therefore a degraded, second-class brand of tragedy, suitable for depicting the lives of those who were ineligible for the authentic tragic stage because, as housewives or as bankers or as clergymen, they didn't exactly qualify as classical heroes. In its very striving to elevate the bourgeoisie, melodrama risked debasing the tragic genre itself. It could not, despite all its extravagant efforts, make bourgeois existence come off as fully serious—except, of course, from the deluded perspective of the bourgeoisie itself.

For the concerns of the middle classes, being the concerns of ordinary people, can never achieve the dignity required for total seriousness. They are certainly laughable when compared to the troubles of Iphigenia or Phèdre or Hamlet (though Shakespearean tragedy is always closer in its themes and domestic preoccupations to the concerns of the bourgeoisie, which makes it easier to adapt to the needs of a modern popular audience).[7] Eloping with the wrong man may indeed turn out to be fatal for Samuel Richardson's Clarissa, but the consequences are not exactly cosmic: they are not quite so world-shattering as those that flow from Paris's seduction of Helen—viz., "the broken wall, the burning roof and tower / And Agamemnon dead." When viewed from the elevated position of the social elite, middle-class tragedy is *mere* melodrama.

ᥫᩣ

If "melodrama" now becomes a pejorative term, that is because the evident sympathy that melodrama brings to the fate of ordinary people appears, at least from a privileged perspective, to be misplaced and unjustified, to be a form of pandering, to be motivated exclusively by an unworthy, groundless, partisan, *sentimental* attachment to otherwise unexceptional characters. In fact, the "sentimentality" with which melodrama is often taxed, and which is considered one of its hallmarks, is ultimately nothing more than the tendency to lavish tenderness, dignity, and esteem on the sorts of low-ranking people who do not deserve (in the eyes of the elite) such a large dose of serious consideration, and who get it from melodrama only because melodrama reflects its audience's close identification with such folks and the intensity of that audience's emotional involvement in their lives.

The high pitch of emotional intensity that melodrama brings to the vicissitudes of ordinary people, which would be appropriate for the elite subjects of tragedy but becomes ludicrous when it is worked up in order to invest undeserving lives with urgent meaning, cannot fail to bring a smile to the face of the socially entitled. *Aristocrats laugh at situations that are horrifying or tragic to the bourgeoisie.* One must have a heart of stone, as Oscar Wilde said, to read the death of Little Nell without laughing.

Now we can see how gay male culture's notoriously snooty attitude, its sporadic identification with the aristocracy, and its consequent practice of laughing at situations that the middle classes find horrifying or tragic, serve a clear and important strategic function. By such means, gay male culture achieves a certain social and critical leverage against the sort of heterosexual sentimentality whose claims to seriousness depend on the importance of being earnest. To see through such claims, to reveal that seriousness as a pose, is to exercise the sort of lofty condescension to which only a superior social position—or, failing that, an aristocracy of taste—gives you rightful access.

If gay men seem to have staked their survival on upward social mobility, as Neil Bartlett suggested—or if gay male culture often expresses an identification with the upper classes, or with glamour, beauty, and elite cultural practices or forms (such as grand opera) that might seem to exclude the masses—that is not because gay culture reflects the interests of a lofty social caste, of men who enjoy the privileges of racial or class superiority and who come from the upper classes themselves. Rather the opposite. Gay male culture's identification with aristocratic values or attitudes is a strategy of resistance to specific forms of disempowerment that stem from social inferiority. It is a means by which you can claim the elevated position proper to a social elite, and the critical posture toward normal folk that such a position allows, without necessarily belonging to the upper classes yourself.

Aristocratic identification, after all, has long provided a vehicle for members of the bourgeoisie, or for anyone who lacks elite status and authority, to contest the social power of serious people—that is, people whose social position requires others to treat them seriously, and whose earnestness is a way of enforcing that requirement. Aristocratic identification asserts a kind of aesthetic or imaginary superiority over such people.

Aristocracy thereby provides the disempowered with a proxy identity: it represents a symbol, a figure, a pose (or counter-pose) whose function is to exempt those who adopt it from the abjection to which they would otherwise be liable. It is a way for the middle classes to aggrandize themselves, rather like Veda in *Mildred Pierce,* by despising everything that is middle-class (Veda is never more middle-class than when she is looking down on her father's mistress for being "distinctly middle-class"). The hatred, the contempt, the scathing derision with which the more socially ambitious members of the middle class regard middle-class culture, and thereby affirm their own superiority and exceptionalism, are unknown outside the middle class. No one has ever attacked the values of the bourgeoisie with as much ferocity as the bourgeoisie itself has done (just think of Flaubert, or indeed the entire genre of the nineteenth-century bourgeois novel).

⟳

By its very definition, then, melodrama is failed tragedy. It may be earnest, but it is not serious. And yet melodrama stubbornly refuses to admit it. Although when measured against the aristocratic standard of classical tragedy, melodrama cannot help falling short of the dignity that tragedy enjoys, it does not recognize its failure. That's what makes melodrama—when it is viewed from a condescending perspective, as if from a position of social privilege or superiority— come off as camp. At least, melodrama would seem a perfect fit for Sontag's definition of camp as "a seriousness that fails." ("Of course, not all seriousness that fails can be redeemed as Camp," Sontag hastens to add. "Only that which has the proper mixture of the exaggerated, the fantastic, the passionate, and the naïve.")[8]

To appreciate and to savor melodrama as camp is to save it from total abjection. Camp, as we have seen, is not criticism but critique. It does not take melodrama literally or unironically, but it does not criticize it either. To treat melodrama as camp is therefore to reverse, though hardly to erase, the superior, condescending attitude toward it. If we refer to the results of our earlier exploration of the pragmatics of camp, we will realize that a full appreciation of melodrama as camp implies not only a devaluation of melodrama, but also a recognition of one's own sentimental implication in melodrama. It necessarily involves a willing, socially inclusive participation in the unworthy pleasures of melodramatic performance—pleasures that arise from both its gripping emotional intensities and its self-canceling histrionics, from its seriousness as well as its failure. Melodrama is camp only when the term "melodrama" is not used exclusively as a criticism, only when its pejorative force is spread around and shared— when, in other words, the tawdry label of "melodramatic," abject and glamorous at once, is embraced and applied to oneself.[9]

Otherwise, when the term "melodrama" is conventionally used as a scapegoating attribution, it functions as a put-down. When the genre is cited pejoratively and made to function as a disqualification, as the name of a debased aesthetic category, melodrama no longer registers as camp. Instead it operates according to the social logic of the "kitsch" designation—as a means of disparagement. That is why "melodrama," understood as a degraded, unworthy literary form, is typically invoked to characterize, and to devalue, the sentimental lives of *other people*. To call someone or something "melodramatic" is to refuse to accord to *their* suffering the dignity proper to tragedy, which socially privileged people, or those who aspire to occupy a position of social privilege, tend to want to reserve for themselves.

Suffering that cannot claim to be *tragic* must come off as *pathetic*. This is the term that describes the undignified alternative to tragic suffering. And if, in our perversity, or our love of melodrama, we insist on taking seriously what should be regarded as merely pathetic, if we insist on treating untragic suffering not as pathetic but as dignified, we convict ourselves of sentimentality. Which is to say, we commit a fault of taste. We thereby invite those who would dignify themselves at our expense to accuse us of finding pleasure in kitsch.

If melodrama incurs the label of "kitsch," that is because it *willingly* traffics in sentimentality. It refuses to dismiss as unserious the pathetic kinds of suffering—exaggerated, fantastic, passionate, or naive, to adopt Sontag's vocabulary—that cannot rise to the level of tragedy. And because the pathetic suffering in which it glories is destined from the start to register in the eyes of a privileged or disengaged spectator as "overwrought," as excessive or histrionic, *melodrama has nothing to fear from the perception that the emotions it stages are not totally authentic, that they are not being felt so much as they are being performed.*

Unlike tragedy, melodrama does not have to justify its extravagances. It does not have to discipline itself in order to guard against the calamitous possibility that its characters may express more than they really feel. It does not need to limit itself to staging emotions that are never excessive, that are strictly and completely motivated, that do not betray the faintest hint of sentimentality. Melodrama can claim the privilege ordinarily reserved for divas: it can be as fiercely histrionic as it likes. It can make an overt appeal to the emotions of its audiences, and its actors can pull out all the stops in order to produce the desired sentimental effect. Melodrama can therefore afford to privilege performance, to place a premium on the staging of intense emotion. Unlike tragedy, it can make the dramatic performance of passion a value, and a source of pleasure, in itself.

☙❦

That, of course, is what we find displayed so prominently in *Mildred Pierce* (to say nothing of *Mommie Dearest*). It was her performance, after all, that earned Joan Crawford the Oscar. And it is her performance, as Ethan Mordden noted, that has been both the envy and the despair of gay men. Joan Crawford's performance in *Mildred Pierce* is apparently a performance that anyone with a taste for melodrama— that is to say, anyone who cannot claim, who does not desire, or who cannot aspire to the grandeur and prestige of tragic sublimity—cannot resist imitating, or *reperforming.*

Certainly Crawford's matchless impersonation of maternal martyrdom and abjection has not dissuaded less talented performers from "doing" her. Nor has it diminished our pleasure in these second-rate renditions, as *Mommie Dearest* (and its gay cult) shows. If it proves nothing else, *Mommie Dearest* at least testifies to the defining role of the performative element in producing the distinctive pleasure of melodrama.

Not only does the scene of generational conflict in *Mommie Dearest* push to an extreme of histrionic extravagance and delirious excess *Mildred Pierce*'s spectacle of the mother-out-of-control, offering us the camp pleasure of an over-the-top performance performed for performance's sake. It also shows up Joan Crawford's portrayal of Mildred Pierce *as a performance,* in the sense that it reveals that Crawford herself, far from being martyred by her helpless, self-sacrificing devotion to her daughter, was sublimely faking it in *Mildred Pierce.*[10] Once the cameras stopped rolling, it was Crawford—not her daughter—who was really calling the shots.

For Joan Crawford, it turns out, long-suffering motherhood was not about abject selflessness, as *Mildred Pierce* implies. On the contrary, it was . . . the role of a lifetime.

In this way, *Mommie Dearest* imparts retrospectively to *Mildred Pierce* an element of inauthenticity already implicit in the dramatic staging, in the acting-out, in the social expression and public performance of any passionate emotion.

14

TRAGEDY INTO MELODRAMA

Emotional inauthenticity may be fatal to tragedy, but it is not damaging to melodrama, and it is not ruinous to the self-image or the culture of gay men. Gay men, after all, are debarred from the high seriousness of tragedy.[1] We have no place in its existential anguish—although we do have to deal with the fallout from the cultural supremacy of the genre, which means that we have inevitably to forge a (dissident) relation to its pragmatics, including the social and emotional conventions, the hierarchies of value, and the structures of feeling that the tragic genre both mobilizes and reinforces. It is that entire cultural system of gender, power, and genre, the politics of emotion produced and maintained by it, and the distinctions of rank, class, and status grounded in it, that I have tried to describe in the preceding chapter.

Gay male culture, as typified by the appropriation of female melodramas such as *Mildred Pierce,* can be understood as an instinctive response to that system and as a strategy for resisting the values enshrined in it.[2] *That is the meaning of melodrama as a gay style.* Gay male culture opts—well, it doesn't really have a lot of choice, but it makes the best of a bad situation—to position its adherents in a social and emotional location that a complex set of interlocking cultural codes and aesthetic practices marks out as the place of melodrama. And then it tries to turn that position to its advantage.

For gay men have relatively little to fear, in the first place, from the disqualifications that attach to melodrama. Our dignity, such as it is, cannot aspire to be wrapped in grandeur and pathos, to be surrounded by the official pageantry of masculine heroics. And it doesn't depend on all that cultural stage machinery. It is only by *not* taking ourselves seriously, even in the midst of tragedy and horror, that we can most effectively assert our claims to a suffering that, though it may never rise to the level of tragic sublimity, need not therefore sink to the depths of the merely pathetic.

That is why gay male culture eschews tragedy and deliberately embraces melodrama as a pragmatic genre. In a typically democratizing camp gesture, it applies the label "melodramatic" to itself and to everyone else. As the Fire Island Italian widows demonstrated, for gay male culture the serious is nothing more (but also nothing less) than a performance of seriousness, an impersonation of it. It is only by exulting in our inauthenticity, as the widows did, by representing our feelings in the guise of a melodramatic camp performance, that we can endow them with a modicum of truth.[3]

For those who pretend to the dignity of seriousness, of course, any acknowledgment of the performativity of seriousness represents *a failure of authentication* and therefore *a loss of authorization,* hence a lack of seriousness itself. But for gay men—at least, when we are not trying to lay claim to a straight male dignity—such revelations cannot inflict much further damage. And so they count not as failures but simply as further illustrations, elaborations, and confirmations of being-as-playing-a-role. Gay male culture positively glories in inauthenticity because inauthenticity has the potential to level differential scales and degrees of seriousness, to dismantle social hierarchies based on them, and to promote a more egalitarian social order—at least, one more favorable to stigmatized or marginalized groups. That is why melodrama, and not tragedy, is the aesthetic form most congenial to gay male culture.

૭⟨૦⟩

The uphill path gay men must climb to attain acceptance and equality is steepest where it passes through the terrain of erotic feeling and romantic love. For in a homophobic society, any expression of a senti-

ment inspired by gay sexual desire or love will register as inappropriate, extravagant, obscene, grotesque, excessive, histrionic—and, thus,
as performative rather than authentic. For gay men, then, the task of
translating feeling into social expression faces a set of more than usually rigorous challenges when the feeling in question is erotic. Such a
feeling inevitably risks coming off as willful, enacted, shoved in people's faces, inauthentic, or (in a word) staged. For all of those reasons,
but especially because of its shameless performativity, the expression
of gay male erotic feeling is necessarily consigned to the realm of
melodrama.

But it is not merely the case that gay male feeling is *forced* to assume a posture of emotional inauthenticity because it is relegated
to the abject generic realm of the melodramatic. Gay men also have
reason to be alienated from the deadly narcissism of masculine self-
importance, from its histrionics unredeemed by irony. (If the motives for such alienation were not already abundantly evident and self-
explanatory, the large and highly lethal dose of unironized masculine
histrionics that the world has had to absorb since September 11, 2001,
would more than justify that alienated gay perspective.) Gay men
have equal reason to see through the involuntary melodrama of family life, with its compulsory overacting, its emotional violence. In
short, gay men know—at least, we certainly ought to know—the
costs of high seriousness, the tyranny of social roles that cannot afford to acknowledge their own performativity.

Those personal costs are highest in the case of romantic love. For
much of the emotional destructiveness in love-relationships derives
precisely from the lover's failure to see his feelings or his behavior as
optional, as shaped (at least in part) by a contingent social role, as the
effect of performing a cultural script and inhabiting a romantic identity. The *human cost of love* results from mistaking the social institution of love for the natural, spontaneous, helpless expression of a
powerful emotion. By blocking the lover's perception that his behavior in love is in fact a performance—rather than the involuntary result
of some omnipotent impulse—romanticism turns love into an ines-

capable destiny. *Plus fort que moi* ("Stronger than I am," or "I can't help it"): that is romantic love's motto. Its effect is to deprive the lover of any sense of being in control of his emotions or his actions, and thereby to exempt him from any responsibility for his feelings.

Gay men may be particularly susceptible to the myth of romance, and therefore particularly in need of the ironic perspective on love that gay male culture supplies. Like gay identity, romantic love—especially when it presents itself as the truth of our deepest feelings, as a kind of emotional bedrock—provides an alibi and a cover for the shameful details of gay sexuality. It offers us a way to represent our desires in public without displaying too much queerness, and it repackages gay eroticism in an honorable, dignified, socially accredited form. Instead of saying, "Please sit down—there's something I've been meaning to tell you," we get to say, "Mom, Dad, I'd like you to meet Lance." Romance redeems homosexuality. It transcends the sickness of perversion and dissipates the pathological taint of gayness in the glory of the happy couple.

But there are other reasons gay men may be especially susceptible to romance. Romance allows us to escape any awareness of the social oddness and incongruity of homosexuality; it returns us to the innocent spontaneity of the natural. It allows us to feel profoundly right. When we're in love, we aren't perverts—we're just doing what comes naturally. We are yielding to the laws of our nature, expressing our real selves, testifying to the profound truth of our feelings, achieving and manifesting our authenticity. Natural instinct is deeper, stronger, and truer than any social arrangement or moral prejudice; it trumps any judgment on gay love that reason can make. It defeats all criticism. Romantic love grants us an imaginary exemption from social hostility, it allows us to celebrate ourselves and our feelings without viewing them through the lens of other people's disapproval. It makes us newly indifferent to how we are regarded. And it gives us access to a source of personal meaning with which to make sense of our lives.

That is exactly what's so dangerous about romantic love. It incites us to make the personal into the real. Since we lack any social incentive to fall in love, and since we also lack any standard, outward, public form *of our own* by which to define and represent our conjugal relations, we have to personalize existing social forms in order to make them ours. We borrow heterosexual models of relationality and adapt them to our purposes, while looking to the realm of the personal and the private in order to endow them with special, distinctive significance—to generate the meanings and the rituals that give shape, consistency, and validity to our feelings.[4] The more personal or private such modes of valorization and legitimation are, the less distance we have on them, the less ironic is our perspective on them, and the more mythic those social forms and rituals become.

℘෨

Such self-authorized, self-generated, self-validated forms and rituals may be particularly tyrannical toward those who produce them. They have nothing of the conventional or the artificial about them that generally attaches to accepted or enforced social roles, and that allows the social actor some distance from them, hence some leverage in relation to them.[5] When you generate a role yourself, you don't have an easily detached perspective on it. It becomes *your* role. Which is to say, it becomes *who you are.*

And once it becomes who you are, you're stuck with it. You can't get out of it—at least, not very easily. How, after all, can you get rid of your authentic self?

When you have stripped a social form of its formulaic, symbolic, conventional, widely accepted meaning, and endowed it with a deeply or purely personal, private significance, you have effectively rendered it authentic. (That's another way of saying it becomes who you are.) Which also means that you have deprived yourself of a ready-made procedure for escaping from it—for dismantling, designifying, desacralizing, and jettisoning it. You become the prisoner of your own authenticity. Contemporary gay identity—serious, official, oppressive, inescapable—offers a dire lesson in the consequences of too much authenticity. No wonder so many gay people can't bear it.

Think of the difference, say, between a heterosexual wedding and a gay commitment ceremony. Married people nowadays can always get divorced. Divorce is one of the many privileges of marriage, one of the many benefits that accrue to those who are permitted to marry. But how do you end what, when you first entered into it, you had chosen to call—in a private ritual of affirmation that you staged in front of all your friends and solemnly commanded them to witness— "a life partnership"? And after it is over, what do you call your next lover? Do you say, "I'd like you to meet my *second* life partner"? How many lives do you think you have?

∽

Conventional romantic love already has a defiant, antinomian character, as Michael Warner has pointed out. The social function of romantic love is to be anti-social, to represent a private, spontaneous, anarchic rebellion against the order of society. Love is the one socially conventional emotion that is conventionally defined as being opposed to social conventions. Falling in love is thus the most conformist method of being an individual. Conversely, falling in love is the most original and spontaneous way to conform, perhaps the only way of conforming to social demands that will never make you look like a conformist. It is the one way that you can behave like everyone else and still claim, at the same time, that you did it your way.[6]

Gay romantic love may feel even more like something socially rebellious rather than like something socially scripted, and gay people may therefore tend to ascribe to their love affairs a dangerous and excessive degree of emotional truth, of personal authenticity.[7] Which risks imparting to those relationships an intensity and an inelasticity that can be suffocating, while you are in them, and that later makes them very difficult to escape. Similarly, the social opprobrium attached to such relationships may make gay people feel particular pressure to champion their *naturalness*, which is to say their involuntariness. And that may make gay love relations seem even more inescapable.

Gay male culture has therefore had to devise a number of reme-
dies against the romantic ills to which it is vulnerable. That, after all,
is what camp is for. Camp is designed to puncture the romantic appeal of beauty, to mock the seriousness with which you might be
tempted to endow your own emotions, especially your feelings of
love and desire, and to deconstruct the kind of authenticity with
which you might be tempted to invest them. Camp, as we have seen,
is a practice internal to a dialectic in gay male culture that revolves
around a series of oppositions between romance and disillusion, seriousness and unseriousness, authenticity and inauthenticity—between
the unironic intensity of gay men's desire for masculine beauty and
the ironic deflation of that intensity.

Camp belongs to one side of that polarity. It is the antidote to romanticism. It breaks into the self-contained world of passionate desire and interrupts its unironic single-mindedness—its systematic exclusion of competing values, its obliviousness to its larger social
context, its obsessive focus on the desired object, and its refusal of alternate perspectives. Camp is a reminder of the artificiality of emotion, of authenticity as a performance. At the same time, camp is not
the whole story. For it represents a challenge to the power of a feeling
for which it knows itself to be no match. It does not seek or hope to
conquer love, or to end our breathless, religious veneration of beauty.
It merely strives to render their effects less toxic—by making the value
and prestige of romantic love less axiomatic.

Gay male culture's reappropriation and recirculation of the figure
of Joan Crawford in general, and its fascination with that one scene in
Mildred Pierce in particular, may make specific sense when they are
seen in this light. A thorough appreciation of the costs of taking love
seriously, of the tyranny of unironized or tragic romantic roles, may
be what informs and explains gay male culture's intoxication with
Joan Crawford's melodramatic performance of maternal abjection
and defiance. It may also be what fortifies the gay tendency to identify with her demented character. The enraged mother who, pushed

to an extremity of feeling by her ungrateful child, "loses it" serves to dramatize—to melodramatize—the breaking-point in any love-relation that had appeared, until that point, to be inescapable, unconditional, involuntary.

The maternal bond is at once the most involuntary *and* the most conventional of social relations. When that bond snaps under the pressure of supreme stress, the effect is to open a space of contingency and freedom within any emotional and social relation—such as erotic passion—whose very strength *as* a bond, and whose very identity as a passion, had seemed to take it forever out of the realm of the optional.

In this context, the scene of mother-daughter conflict administers a salutary dose of reality; it underwrites a sharper understanding of the politics of romanticism. For it punctures romanticism's cult of the involuntary, its promotion of compulsory romantic ties, its idealization of emotional unfreedom. When Mildred Pierce tells her daughter, "Get out before I kill you," she indicates that, contrary to what romanticism would have us believe, love is not our destiny. There is in fact a way out.

Gay male culture's investment in the scene of mother-daughter conflict may well have to do, in other words, with the unfavorable social and discursive conditions under which gay men accede to the possibility of emotional expression, and of erotic expression most of all. It may have to do, specifically, both with the powerful, sinister lure of romanticism to gay men and with the cure for romanticism that the gay celebration of inauthenticity affords. It does not refer literally to the maternal itself, but alludes to the emotional situation which the maternal figures—namely, the abject situation of one who believes she has no choice but to love unconditionally . . . until she is pushed to the brink.

Indeed, if one function of camp is to return to the scene of trauma and to replay that trauma on a ludicrously amplified scale, so as to neutralize its pain without denying it, then the particular trauma that the camp enjoyment of the melodramatic scene of mother-daughter conflict in *Mildred Pierce* replays is not the trauma of maternal rejection, but the trauma of unconditional, unalterable, endless love.

ᏋᎤ

What started out looking like a particular obsession on the part of gay men with the figure of the mother turns out to have more to do with gay men's fraught relation to the dangerously seductive, oppressive, inescapable, helpless, would-be tragic role of the romantic lover. To say this is not to turn Mildred Pierce into a gay man or to reduce gay men's identification with her to mere identity—to a mirroring, a self-recognition, a consolidation of the gay ego. It is to understand her, rather, as offering a *proxy identity* to gay men. Joan Crawford as Mildred Pierce figures and makes available to gay men an emotional situation that they can explore, so as to gain a perspective on aspects of their own predicament. She enables them to try on, to try out, to compare, and to criticize certain ways of being and feeling.

For the mother is both a literal and a figurative character. In her, those two orders of meaning are not separate or independent. The mother is at once a person and a function. She is simultaneously real and symbolic. She is always both herself and a representation, a mother and an emblem or expression of motherhood, a symbol of the maternal—a figure, that is, for a particular social and emotional situation.

As such, the mother has long functioned as a camp alter ego for gay men. Witness the old habit among gay men of referring to themselves in the first person not as "I" but as "Your mother." Thus, "Your mother is very tired today—you will have to be nice to her." Or, "Your mother can't help herself—she loves you too much." W. H. Auden managed to demolish forever the most celebrated line of poetry Stephen Spender wrote by means of precisely such a camp subversion. "I think continually of those who were truly great" becomes impossible to take seriously, once the line's first-person pronoun is robbed of its grandeur and pathos by being turned into a domestic diva. "Your mother thinks continually of those who were truly great" exposes once and for all Spender's poetic "I" as a posture, as a melodramatic performance.[8]

✂

Melodrama, we know, is a category that normally applies to the suffering of *other people*. It disqualifies other people's suffering as being unworthy of our full sympathy, and it demeans their emotional lives as lacking in high seriousness. If the term "melodramatic" is disparaging of other people's feelings, if it subverts the authenticity of their feelings and denies those people the standing necessary for social accreditation and, thus, for serious consideration, that is because it refuses to accord their sufferings the aristocratic and masculine dignity of tragedy. Instead, the label "melodramatic" identifies their sufferings as merely pathetic. And once qualified by that label, their sufferings become as unserious—and, ultimately, as potentially laughable—as the women and the middle-class folks whose sufferings the debased genre of melodrama, in its misplaced sentimentality, takes seriously. But when gay men speak of themselves in the first person as "Your mother," or when they represent their grief through the deliberate theatrics and histrionics of a drag performance—through an ironic impersonation of Italian widows, say—they embrace that very *déclassement* and situate *their own feelings* in the category of melodrama.

The application of the "melodrama" label, then, does not always produce an effect of social exclusion and symbolic violence. It does not always participate in the kitsch logic of denigration. It is not always a put-down of *other people*. When the label is applied to yourself, it can also exemplify the camp practice of inclusiveness—a communal practice that consists in refusing to exempt yourself from the universal deflation of other people's pretensions to authenticity and seriousness, yet without forgoing all claims to be treated decently yourself.

Many years ago I asked a friend of mine in Boston, who had been living with the same boyfriend for a very long time, if it had ever occurred to them to want to get married. "Oh, no," he said with a laugh, "we'd have terrible fights over who got to wear the wedding dress." That witticism, if it had been directed against someone other than oneself, or against someone other than the person one loved, would have registered as *merely* demeaning in its implicit demotion of a man from the noble rank of male dignity to the lower rank of female triviality. And it would be doubly demeaning in the context of gay male love: since male homosexuality sees in masculinity an essential erotic value, to portray oneself or one's partner as characterized by a feminine identification, and to expose that feminine identification to public mockery, would be to depreciate oneself or one's boyfriend as a sexual object and as a vehicle of sexual fantasy.

Hence, Proust thought that the only way gay men could ever get beyond desiring straight men, and could succeed in desiring one another, would be to fool each other, to impersonate the real men they had so catastrophically failed to be themselves, and to maintain the charade for the longest time possible (though they could never succeed at keeping up the pretense for very long).[9]

That was in the Bad Old Days, of course, before gay liberation, when the gay world was still polarized by the division between queens and trade. But even (or especially) after Stonewall, the foredoomed tactic of butching up in order to be desirable did not exactly die out. Leo Bersani conveys powerfully the sense of gay chagrin at the ineluctable failure of gay masculinity by citing "the classic put-down: the butch number swaggering into a bar in a leather get-up opens his mouth and sounds like a pansy, takes you home where the first thing you notice is the complete works of Jane Austen, gets you into bed, and—well, you know the rest."[10]

Or in the unlikely event that, even after getting you into bed, he still managed to keep up butch appearances, all your remaining illusions would be shattered—according to the lead character in Armistead Maupin's *Tales of the City* (1978)—when you eventually excused yourself to use his bathroom and discovered his supply of personal cosmetics.

> I meet some person . . . male-type . . . at a bar or the baths, and he
> seems really . . . what I want. A nice mustache, Levi's, a starched khaki
> army shirt . . . strong . . . Somebody you could take back to Orlando
> and they'd never know the difference. Then you go home with him to
> his house on Upper Market, and you try like hell not to go to the bath-
> room, because the bathroom is the giveaway, the fantasy-killer. . . . It's
> the bathroom cabinet. . . . Face creams and shampoos for *days.* And on
> the top of the toilet tank they've all always got one of those goddamn
> little gold pedestals full of colored soap balls![11]

Who knew colored soap balls could be so fatal to true love?

It is in this context that my friend's remark about his boyfriend and
himself both coveting the wedding dress reveals its true significance.
To utter it is to know oneself and one's love-object as unworthy of
the serious consideration that is masculine dignity's due. It is to disclaim all pretense to masculine authenticity, and the erotic credit that
accrues to it, and to refuse in camp fashion to dignify oneself at the
expense of someone else's shame. At the same time, it insists that
such inauthenticity is not incompatible with gay love. It refuses to
make gay love contingent on the successful impersonation of masculinity, either one's own or one's boyfriend's, and it refuses the current
tendency in gay male culture to keep upping the standards of acceptable gay masculinity, requiring gay desirability to depend on increasingly desperate performances of stolid, brutal, unironic virility. On
the contrary, it demonstrates that inauthenticity is not fatal to love,
that seriousness does not have to prevail over irony in order for love
to thrive and to endure.

To see through one's own erotic illusions without withdrawing
from one's love-object its worthiness to be loved, to disclaim one's entitlement to respect while continuing to assert it, to love and be loved
without endowing one's love with dignity: this is the possibility that
traditional gay male culture holds out to its adherents. The supreme
wisdom consists in living one's love life *knowingly* as melodrama—understanding full well (if not necessarily explicitly) that melodrama
signifies both a degraded genre of literary discourse and a debased

pragmatic genre of emotional expression: a despised, feminized, laughable, trivial *style* of expressing one's feelings.[12]

No wonder my friends in Boston could build a lasting life together, while the gay baths and backrooms and sex clubs and online cruising sites thrive on the business of gay romantics, who prefer their own illusions, their fantasies of love, to actual people—people who, after all, cannot sustain those illusions, not at least for very long. That last remark is hardly intended as a put-down of those of us who frequent the baths and backrooms and sex clubs, by the way; it's just a reminder of what those unique gay male institutions are for. Which is not to help us live happily ever after, but to enable us to crowd as many antisocial thrills as possible into the moment and to provide us with a structured communal space in which to heighten, express, and discharge our romantic fantasies—without doing ourselves or our partners any lasting emotional harm.

ලා

To live one's love life as melodrama, to do so knowingly and deliberately, is not of course to refuse to take it seriously—as any gay Joan Crawford fan, and certainly any opera queen, can tell you. But it is to accept the inauthenticity at the core of romantic love, to understand romantic love as a social institution, an ideology, a role, a performance, and a social genre, while still, self-consciously and undeceivedly, succumbing to it.

In short, it is to do what is otherwise culturally impossible—impossible for normal folks, that is: to combine passion with irony.[13]

Gay male culture has in fact elaborated a distinctive, dissident perspective on romantic love, a camp perspective, which straight people often regard as cynical, precisely because its irony—which emphasizes the performativity of romantic roles—seems to them to undermine the seriousness and sincerity of love, and thereby to demean it. But to demean love is also to desublimate it, to break the romantic monopoly on it, to make it more widely available, to put it to a variety of social uses, and to end the antagonism between love and society, between love and friendship, between the happy couple and the community. Gay male culture's vision of love is not a cynical one. Rather, just as a camp perspective on family conflicts provides for an attitude toward intense emotion that is alienated without being either skeptical or reductive, so the effect of living one's love life knowingly as melodrama is to cultivate an outlook on love that is *disabused, but not disenchanted*.

Far from being fatal to love, a camp sensibility is the result and expression of love's self-knowledge. It indicates that the fusion of gay desire and gay sisterhood, of the beauty and the camp, though never easy, is possible, and can happen.

There is, in sum, an erotics of melodrama. At their wisest, gay men's love relationships exemplify and embody it. And one of gay male culture's jobs is to enshrine that erotics, to preserve it, to communicate it, and to transmit it.

ᗉᕱᗡ

But if melodrama has an erotics, it also has a politics. If you wanted any additional confirmation of that, look no further than the stories about the drag queen who started the Stonewall rebellion by hitting that police officer with her handbag, as if to say—like Faye Dunaway playing Joan Crawford playing an outraged, martyred mother—"Why can't you give me the respect that I'm entitled to?"

Or consider the following story about the funeral of Vito Russo, gay militant, leading member of ACT UP New York, and author of *The Celluloid Closet* (a study of the portrayal of gay men in Hollywood movies). The first speaker at the funeral, in December 1990, was David Dinkins, then mayor of New York; he quoted, without apparent irony, a remark that Vito Russo had made to him a few days before, when Dinkins had visited the dying man's bedside: "In 1776, Edmund Burke of the British Parliament said about the slavery clause, 'A politician owes the people not only his industry but his judgment, and if he sacrifices his judgment to their opinions, he betrays them.'" Although Dinkins may not have realized it at the time, Russo was hardly prais-

ing him. He was upbraiding Dinkins for betraying his gay constitu-
ents by appointing a homophobic health commissioner, by canceling
New York's pilot needle-exchange program, and by failing to defend
homeless people with HIV or to combat the rising tide of anti-gay violence. When the mayor left, the following speaker at Russo's funeral
pointed out that Russo's dying reproach to Dinkins did not derive
from Russo's encyclopedic knowledge of eighteenth-century political
oratory. It was cribbed from a movie—specifically, the movie version
of a Broadway musical about the American Revolution, 1776.[14]

Douglas Crimp, who recounts this incident and provides the background I have just summarized, does so in the course of making a
passionate and powerful plea for basing a progressive politics not on
identity but on identification. Such an emphasis, he argues, will be
able to avoid producing the sorts of misunderstandings and tensions
that led to political conflicts among the various groups affected by
HIV/AIDS in the United States in the early 1990s. Crimp's model for
an identificatory, coalition-based queer politics—a politics that can
reach across the divides of gender, race, class, sexuality, and other social differences—is summed up in the title of his essay: "Right On,
Girlfriend!" That melodramatic exhortation does not express a serious vision of solidarity between gay men and their lesbian and feminist allies so much as it evokes a form of camp solidarity among gay
men themselves, a form of solidarity that can acknowledge—and can
mobilize the political energies of—gay men's feminine identifications,
including the feminine identifications of movie queens and Judy Garland fans like Vito Russo. "Right on, girlfriend!" is exactly how Vito
Russo's friends might have responded to him when, with virtually his
dying breath, he somehow summoned the strength to rebuke Mayor
Dinkins.

It is precisely because such identifications depend on the queerness
of the gay men who make them, *not* on the actual gender or sexual
identity of the women with whom those gay men identify—and it is
precisely because such queer *identifications* do *not* therefore presume
a relation of *identity* with the lesbians and feminists with whom some

gay men may wish to forge coalitions—that such queer identifications can become the starting-point for renegotiating political collaborations among differently situated groups, and can thereby conduce, according to Crimp, to "a broadening of alliances rather than an exacerbation of antagonisms."[15] In this way, it may be possible to move beyond the mere presumption or "fantasy of coalition . . . [which] sidesteps the processes and practices that would make such coalition possible."[16]

◯╳◯

That is the point I would like to make about the political uses of Joan Crawford, and of women's melodrama more generally, by gay men. The work of all gay male cultural politics can be summed up in a single, simple formula: *to turn tragedy into melodrama.* The historical function of gay male culture has been—and its ongoing political task remains—to forge an ironic perspective on scenes of compulsory, socially validated and enforced performance, to decommission supposedly authentic social identities and return them to their status as willfully or witlessly iterated roles.

Hegel once said, in a parenthetical remark, that womankind *(die Weiblichkeit)* is the eternal irony of the community *(die ewige Ironie des Gemeinwesens).*[17] Coming from him, that was not exactly a compliment. But he was making an important political point.

Hegel was talking not about melodrama but about tragedy—about Sophocles's *Antigone.* He was highlighting Antigone's ironic relation to the world of masculine power, a relation typical of women who, Hegel said, pervert the universal purpose of government to private purpose through intrigue. It was just such an ironic relation to masculine authority, Hegel implied, that informed Antigone's resistance to the law and enabled her to justify, *without needing to invoke any general principle,* her defiance of the state.

Judy Garland is not Antigone. But if, on the night of Judy Garland's funeral on Friday, June 27, 1969, Hegel had been among the queens who gathered outside the Stonewall Inn during the police raid on it, he might have whistled a different tune—assuming, that is, he could whistle at all. At least, he might have realized that the politics of irony is not limited to women, or to biological women, and that it is best embodied not in tragedy but in the dissident audience relations of melodrama, specifically in the audience relations of gay men to female melodrama, and thus in gay male culture's queer, inclusive, loving identification with it.[18]

In any case, if it is an ironic position that gay men share with women, and if it is our ironic identification with women that enables us to extract lessons in political defiance from Joan Crawford's glamorous performance of maternal martyrdom and abjection, then perhaps those feminine identifications of ours are identifications that, far from attempting to closet, we should be eager to claim for our own—to understand, to appreciate, and to cherish.

PART FIVE

❧ ❧ ❧

Bitch Baskets

⚲ 15 ⚲

GAY FEMININITY

The explanation for the specific forms that the cultural practice of male homosexuality has taken in recent Anglo-American societies would seem to be obvious. A quick review of some basic facts might suffice to settle the whole question. For a man to sing in a high-pitched falsetto voice is to sound like a woman. Flower-arranging, interior decorating, and hairdressing are feminine professions. *Mildred Pierce* is a "woman's picture," and Joan Crawford's largest and most devoted fan base was composed of working-class women ("She was always a bigger hit with women than with men," David Denby observes).[1] Aesthetics and style are traditionally feminine concerns, just as politics, business, and sports are traditionally masculine ones. And if gay male automobile drivers have shown a preference for the VW Golf and the Ford Probe, as has been claimed, that is because—as a particularly talented straight male student of mine once put it, appealing to one of those popular formulas in which our culture's sex and gender norms find their most highly condensed and trenchant, if repellent, expression—that is because those cars are "bitch baskets."

So why make such a mystery about the logic behind gay male culture? And why spend an entire book working up gingerly and laboriously to the simple and stunningly obvious conclusion that should have been evident right from the start? Isn't the explanation for the characteristic practices favored by gay male culture blindingly clear?

If gay men have gravitated to drag, Hollywood melodramas, grand opera, camp, or fashion and design, it's surely because they are all feminine forms, or at least because they are traditionally coded as such.

In short, it looks like those Victorian doctors were right all along. What defines gay male subjectivity is its reversal of sex roles, its cross-gendering, its inverted, transgendered psychology. Despite their male bodies, gay men have the souls, the nature, the tastes, the attitudes, the feelings, the subjectivity of women. Period.

⊘✗⊙

That gay men have "qualities or characteristics generally possessed by girls and women" is also the conclusion drawn by Will Fellows from his own study of gay men's cultural practices.[2] In particular, he finds that "gay men are a prominent and highly talented presence," even an "apparently disproportionate presence," in many "female-dominated fields that revolve around creating, restoring, and preserving beauty, order, and continuity" (x)—specifically, those activities whose purpose is to conserve material cultures from the past. Such activities include historic preservation, antiquarianism, architectural restoration, interior design, fashion and style. Fellows devotes a lengthy, eloquent, richly documented book, *A Passion to Preserve* (2004), to "gay men as keepers of culture."

Like me, Fellows wants to explore the various ways in which gay men differ from straight men, ways that—like the love of Broadway musicals—go well beyond sexual behavior and often manifest themselves in early childhood, years before sexual orientation finds expression in the specific form of sexual activity. In the course of doing research for an earlier book, *Farm Boys,* about gay men from rural backgrounds,[3] Fellows noted that "gender-role nonconformity was prominent" in many of the life stories he collected, especially in the early chapters of them.[4]

> As boys, most of the men I spoke with had been especially drawn to doing things that lay outside the range of activities approved for males.

> Instead of working in the fields or repairing farm machinery, they pre-
> ferred doing things in and around the house, and were often very good
> at them: gardening, cooking, food-canning, flower-arranging, deco-
> rating, sewing and other needlework. At first, I was bothered by this
> strong gender-atypical trend. . . . There must be plenty of gay men out
> there who were regular, gender-typical farm boys, I thought. . . . Then,
> as it eventually occurred to me that what I was seeing was perhaps
> characteristic of gay childhood, this trend toward gender-atypicality
> began to intrigue me. . . . All of this led me to wonder: If we differ
> from straight men only in terms of sexual orientation, not in any other
> essential ways, why was I discovering this preponderance of gay men
> who had been manifestly queer since childhood, usually years before
> their sex lives got going? (ix–x)

This train of thought leads Fellows to the conclusion that "gayness
comprises much more than sexual partners and practices" (262). He
approvingly quotes a remark that John Clum makes at the start of his
own book about musical theater and gay male culture—"For me, being gay has as much to do with an investment in certain kinds of culture as it has with my sexual proclivities" (x)—apparently endorsing
the faintly dismissive, lightly depreciative attitude toward sex implied
by Clum's use of the quaint term "proclivities" to refer to homosexual object-choice.[5] For Fellows, "gay" is not synonymous with, and
should certainly not be reduced to, "homosexual" (13).[6]

Interested as he is in "some of the distinctive dimensions of gay
male lives beyond sexuality per se" (x), in the "non-sexual dimensions
of gay men's natures" (243), Fellows consistently downplays sexuality,
regarding it as one of the *least* "essential ways" that gay men differ
from straight men—or, rather, he considers it merely a sign of a more
profound difference, which has to do with the distinctiveness of "gay
sensibility," understood as "an essential facet of human nature" (262).
Although he initially defines "gay" as encompassing "both gender
identity and sexual orientation," and as referring to "a male who is
[both] gender atypical (psychologically and perhaps physically androgynous or effeminate) and decidedly homosexual in orientation if
not in practice" (13), and although his final verdict defines gay men as

"being uncommonly constituted in both gender identity and sexuality" (263), he concludes that his "inquiry into gay men's natures *is really about gender orientation,* not about sexual orientation per se" (262; my italics).

In foregrounding issues of gender orientation, specifically "gender-role nonconformity" and "gender atypicality," as clues to "gay men's natures" (at least the natures of those gay men who are "preservation-oriented"; 243), and in scanting issues of sexuality, Fellows does not hesitate to appeal for authoritative support to earlier theories of homosexuality, dating back to the Victorian period, that defined gay men as having a woman's soul in a man's body, as belonging to a third sex or an intermediate sex. In particular, he repeatedly invokes the celebrated socialist philosopher and early gay activist Edward Carpenter (1844–1929), who in 1908 published a book called *The Intermediate Sex: A Study of Some Transitional Types of Men and Women.* According to Fellows, Carpenter "understood gay men as 'intermediate men' —'men with much of the psychologic character of women'" (14).[7] Fellows also quotes Freud's disciple and rival Carl Jung, specifically Jung's 1954 essay "Psychological Aspects of the Mother Complex," to the effect that a gay man "may have good taste and an aesthetic sense which are fostered by the presence of a feminine streak. He may be supremely gifted as a teacher because of his almost feminine insight and tact" (243).[8]

Although furiously opposed by the political culture of the post-Stonewall gay movement, this venerable tradition of defining homosexuality in terms of gender inversion or sex-role reversal, rather than in terms of sexuality, is hardly extinct. As Fellows notes, it was upheld by Harry Hay, the founder of the modern gay movement in the United States and a chief source of inspiration for the Radical Faeries.[9] And it continues to flourish within several important schools of contemporary gay male spirituality, which see gay men as modern shamans, as the descendants of traditional healers, prophets, and wizards who in many societies draw their insight, power, and religious authority from a perceived combination of the two spirits of male and female (254, 262, 244–246, 281n17). The notion that lesbians and

© 2014 INTUIT INC. # 1225 1-800-433-8810

10533

Jewish Reconstructionist Camping
Corporation Operating Account
1299 Church Road
Wyncote, PA 19095-1824
(833) 226-7428

HUDSON VALLEY BANK, NA
50-930/219

08/02/2019

PAY TO THE
ORDER OF

Cam Barker

$ **32.90

Thirty-two and 90/100*** DOLLARS

Cam Barker
7105 Fairways Drive
Longmont, CO 80503

MEMO

Void After 90 Days

PROTECTED AGAINST FRAUD

CASH ONLY IF ALL CheckLock™ SECURITY FEATURES LISTED ON BACK INDICATE NO TAMPERING OR COPYING

⑈010533⑈ ⑆021909300⑆ 1800934⑈407⑈

Intuit® CheckLock™ Secure Check   Details on Back

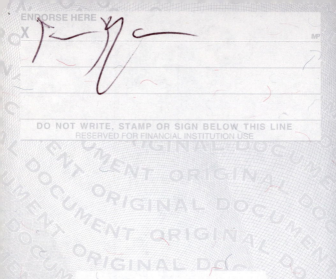

As the issuer, this *CheckLock™*
Secure Plus check may help reduce
your risk of fraud and liability.

To learn how to protect your business,
call our check fraud experts at
1-800-548-0289 or visit:
www.intuitmarket.com/fraudcenter

gay men nowadays should be understood as belonging to a third or fourth sex or gender is undergoing something of a revival in many fields of recent queer and transgender scholarship.[10]

☙❧

One can easily imagine the shock and outrage of the Stonewall generation at this return of the repressed in the field of gay male self-definition. "Could it be that all those horrible pundits have been right, and homosexuals are indeed the 'third sex'?" Edmund White asked incredulously, as early as 1969.[11] Many gay men today may have similar reactions.

Indeed, we have witnessed a number of them. A sense of outrage was already palpable in the protest against my class by John from Annapolis: no, he had insisted, gay men are not fashion-savvy or design-savvy, as some would have us believe, nor do they have a penchant for dressing like women. We have seen examples of similar defensiveness and disavowal in David Daniels and Anthony Tommasini, not to mention D. A. Miller's scandalized love-object, who hastily dried the tears sent coursing down his cheeks by "Some Enchanted Evening." And we are used to hearing the constant, insistent assertion—repeated endlessly for decades now, and in the teeth of all the evidence to the contrary—that gay male effeminacy is a thing of the past, that polarized sex roles are antiquated, homophobic notions, that "the queen is dead," that there is no difference between gay people and straight people, that there is no such thing as gay male culture beyond a series of hostile stereotypes. Gay men who want to style themselves as virile, non-queer, post-gay, or simply as ordinary, regular guys whose sexual preference does not mark them as different from normal folk, recoil instinctively from any aspect of male homosexuality that might seem to express or signify effeminacy. That is why they tend to disclaim any participation in gay culture or even any knowledge of its existence, despite their active involvement at times in the life of gay communities.

What exactly are all these people afraid of? That the carefully erected façade of gay masculinity, hard won through individual and collective effort, will come tumbling down like a house of cards to disclose the outlines of that abominated Other, the fairy or queen? That the long-awaited historical and personal achievement of dignified—that is to say, virile—gay identity will have been for nothing and that gay men will once again be overtaken by shades of pathology, by demeaning stereotypes, and by inescapable gender-deviant queerness? That every gay man is at risk of embodying the abject, despised figure he secretly both fears and believes himself to be?

No one wants to be a cliché, of course, but gay male effeminacy is not just a stereotype: it is a damaging one with a long history. The association of gay men with femininity is a cause for particular anxiety because it represents a throwback, a symbol of age-old homophobic prejudice. It resuscitates a host of ancient bogeymen that have been used in the past to harm us—to turn us into figures of fun, objects of abuse, creatures of satire, victims of hatred, moral condemnation, and violence—and it reminds us uncomfortably of those hoary medical understandings of sexual deviance that Edmund White shuddered to recall, according to which same-sex desire was a symptom of sex-role reversal and homosexual men were congenital inverts embodying the sexual nature of women. For all that we may deplore the flagrant misogyny behind the degrading force of those stereotypes, their power to humiliate us is no less effective, no less real. The enlightened ideology of the post-Stonewall gay movement has exhorted us to reject, refute, and transcend such demeaning clichés—to prove them wrong, to become virtually normal ourselves, and to accede on that basis to an erotic community of equals.

Masculinity represents not only a central cultural value—associated with seriousness and worth, as opposed to feminine triviality—but also a key erotic value for gay men. Gay men's sexual dignity depends on it, as well as our erotic prestige and desirability. So it is pretty clear why no gay man—at least, no gay man who has not been transformed by the practice of camp and by its radical perspective on gender and social hierarchy—would be particularly eager to associate himself with the highly feminized pursuits of traditional gay male culture. To participate openly and avowedly in cultural practices that seem to express a transgendered subjectivity, or that are marked as feminine—whether because queer sensibility itself is aligned with the feminine side of the traditional division between queens and trade, or simply because the worship of divas or other female icons would seem to reflect a profound identification with women on the part of gay men—is socially, and erotically, risky for gay men, no matter how proud or self-accepting they may be.

Witness the scene in Norman René's 1990 film *Longtime Companion*, where the usually virile Fuzzy is caught by his boyfriend in the act of deliriously lip-synching a jazzy female vocal number from *Dreamgirls*. Fuzzy had the volume turned up so high that he didn't hear his boyfriend opening the door to their apartment until it was too late. The look of mortification that flits across Fuzzy's face when he realizes what has happened eloquently registers the magnitude of his gaffe and the depth of his embarrassment—though as soon as his face is out of his lover's field of vision, he follows up that mortified look with an insouciant shrug of resignation and a defiant smirk of guilty pleasure. Fuzzy has had a close call, and the joke is not likely to be lost on either the gay or the straight members of the audience. Any gay man who forsakes the ranks of the privileged gender and the desired gender style, who lowers himself to the undignified, abject status of the effeminate, the fairy, the poof, the bitch, the sissy, the flaming queen, incurs the easy ridicule and cheap contempt of both the straight world and the gay world—and even, for all he knows (or fears), the disdain of his own lover.[12]

If homophobia sometimes functions less to oppress homosexuals than to police the behavior of heterosexuals and to strong-arm them into keeping one another strictly in line with the requirements of proper sex and gender norms, for fear of appearing to be queer, it may be that one of the social functions of transphobia is to police the behavior of lesbians and gay men and to terrorize them into conforming to the gender style deemed appropriate to their respective sexes.

And there are certainly plenty of other bad reasons, in addition to transphobia, for gay men nowadays to reject Fellows's argument out of hand: sexism, misogyny, effeminophobia, and/or a willingness to pander to them; machismo, snobbery, shame, denial; knee-jerk anti-essentialism and various other sorts of post-Stonewall gay liberation dogmatism. Gay scholars and critics are no less exempt from those tendencies than other gay men. As a child of the Stonewall era myself, I want instinctively to find political or social explanations for the way gay men are, not biological or psychological or congenital causes, and I also want to assert the centrality in male homosexuality of same-sex eroticism, not just queer or transgendered sensibility.

∞

Fellows poses a useful challenge to the standard post-Stonewall view. If I have decided to begin this chapter by discussing his account of gay men's cultural practices and outlining my disagreements with it, that is because I admire his work and I take his challenge seriously. The notion that "gayness comprises much more than sexual partners and practices," that "some of the distinctive dimensions of gay male lives [extend] beyond sexuality per se," that what makes gay men different from straight people lies in the "non-sexual dimensions of gay men's natures," and that male homosexuality can therefore be understood as a specifically cultural practice, not just a sexual one, represents a key insight. It is the basis on which I have built this entire book. And there is no denying that many of the cultural practices associated with male homosexuality comprise activities that are coded by our society as feminine. Each of those two points is important; instead of being evaded, they merit serious and sustained reflection. Gay men should not flinch from them. The challenge for queer studies is to account for them through social analysis, instead of ascribing them to the natural order of things.

For cultural practices are not likely to be rooted in nature, and any attempt to locate their origins in gay men's natures will only put them off-limits to further critical inquiry, by implying that there is nothing to explain beyond the natural facts of the matter, beyond the way things just naturally are. That tendency is being ominously reinforced these days by the current vogue for locating sexuality and gender identity in genetics, genomics, the workings of the brain, neural path-ways, and cognitive development—a tendency often hotly contested by psychologists and psychiatrists, who see in cognitive science a threat to their professional authority as well as to their share of a lu-crative market.[13] My own approach to gay male culture is designed to counter both of those approaches: its methodological purpose is to argue against biological as well as psychological reductionism.

For Fellows, gay male cultural practices are natural expressions of sexual intermediacy and reveal the natural essence of gay men. He speaks of the "essential ways" in which gay men differ from straight men, of "gay men's natures," of "gay sensibility" as "an essential facet of human nature." In his final wrapping-up, he deliberately refuses to hedge the matter, rejecting mealy-mouthed qualifications and speak-ing grandly, sweepingly, inclusively, and in universalizing terms of "our two-spiritedness" and "our intermediate natures" (259). Gay men, in his view, do indeed partake of a natural condition: we share the common property of belonging to a third or intermediate sex, halfway between male and female (but tending to the latter).

That explicitly essentialist or essentializing vision of gay men's na-tures brings with it the usual, well-known drawbacks, the problems that typically plague all essentialist models of social identity. So let me rehearse a couple of them. Without wishing to be dogmatic about it, I think it is fair to say that the effect of Fellows's approach is to *over-generalize* the phenomenon he so richly and empirically describes, while also *homogenizing* it into a single "rather consistent pattern," al-beit an admittedly "intricate" and "complex" one (25). Furthermore, by treating that pattern, whose most prominent feature is "gender atypicality," as representative of "preservation-minded gay men" (25), and ultimately of gay men in general, Fellows ends up imposing it on us as a truth about ourselves that we are obligated to recognize—or else find ourselves accused of being in denial (it is because of such strong-arming tactics that opponents of essentialist models of homo-sexual difference often highlight the implicitly coercive, disciplining, or "legislative" operation of essentialist theories).[14]

Beyond all those problems, which are typical of any attempt to represent social identities in essentialist terms, there is another weakness of an interpretive or critical sort in this argument. The *particular* essentialist model of gay male identity that Fellows promotes, his vision of gay men as natural antiquarians, architectural restorers, lovers of old houses, and "keepers of culture," has trouble accounting for those gay men—and we know there are some of them out there, even fairly significant numbers of them—who are passionate and committed modernists, who instinctively hate ornament, Victorian fussiness, and period detail, who long for clean lines and abstract forms, spaces of Zen purity and Japanese abstraction, and who would never be caught dead within a hundred yards of a doily. Some of those guys could be in the grips of a reaction formation, of course—victims of internalized homophobia or gender panic, desperately repressing and denying their deep, instinctual desires for chintz or plush or gilt—but that's probably not true of every one of them.

Fellows's model also fails to account for aesthetically unaligned gay men who really don't care about history, old houses, design or style, preserving the past, or living in the perfect interior, and whose taste is embarrassingly subject to frequent, egregious lapses. "All the gay men I know are terrible slobs, including you," John Weir's mother told the novelist and critic over the telephone, when she called him up to discuss *Queer Eye for the Straight Guy* and the exploits of the Fab Five: "Do you think you could get them to clean up your apartment?"[15] Even the Fab Five were hardly immune to gross errors of judgment, while the merest peek into any shop or clothing catalogue catering to gay men is enough to shatter forever the notion that gay men necessarily, essentially have good taste. Of course, gay men may find themselves pressured by gay culture to get with the program and to acquire good taste . . . sooner or later.

☙❧

When it comes to gender orientation, to gay men's allegedly female characteristics, or (as Fellows emphasizes, somewhat more cautiously) gay men's combination of masculine and feminine attributes, there is substantial disagreement about the matter on the part of the subjects themselves. Gay men do not all see themselves as sexual intermediates. Some of them even take strong exception to the view that they have "qualities or characteristics generally possessed by girls and women." Fellows's antithesis can be found in Jack Malebranche, author of *Androphilia—A Manifesto: Rejecting the Gay Identity, Reclaiming Masculinity* (2007), who denies gay men's essential, innate femininity and has little use for the female-dominated fields in which gay men, according to Fellows, excel.[16]

Malebranche willingly admits that gayness is about more than sexuality. That, in his opinion, is exactly what is wrong with it.

> The word gay has never described mere homosexuality. Gay is a subculture, a slur, a set of gestures, a slang, a look, a posture, a parade, a rainbow flag, a film genre, a taste in music, a hairstyle, a marketing demographic, a bumper sticker, a political agenda and philosophical viewpoint. Gay is a pre-packaged, superficial persona—a lifestyle. It's a sexual identity that has almost nothing to do with sexuality. . . . The gay sensibility is a near-oblivious embrace of a castrating slur, the nonstop celebration of an age-old, emasculating stigma applied to men who engaged in homosexual acts. Gays and radical queers imagine that they challenge the status quo, but in appropriating the stigma of effeminacy, they merely conform to and confirm long-established expectations.[17]

Malebranche (that, of course, is not his real name) seems to have his finger on the pulse of the times.[18] His book has received accolades from online reviewers, and his fellow travelers are legion.

Or so we can gather from the following statement. "Masculinity is a trait to be honored, respected & treated with dignity. Such a view is[,] sadly, a far cry from the moral turpitude that has swallowed the gay male-community & now stands as its spokesperson." No, that is not a homophobic jeremiad from the Christian Right: it is an online promotion for the "g0y" identity, "A New Identity in Male Sexuality." And no, "g0y" is not Yiddish for "Gentile": it's "gay," or "guy," with a zero in place of the middle letter.

"G0y" refers to masculine guys who like other masculine guys, who value masculinity and cherish intimacy with other men, who reject effeminacy, and who consider anal intercourse "completely degrading & repulsive to masculinity."[19] Here is how their homepage puts it:

> So, you're a normal guy who happens to like other guys—probably lots. But you don't relate to "GAY" for lots of reasons. You may even find the term to be offensive to your sense of masculinity or personal ethics; at least the way the term is often used in public & often by the press! "Guys should never play a 'female role' sexually." Right? "Anal-Sex is degrading, dirty & disrespectful." Right again? "Manhood is about respect." Agreed? Well, you're not alone! Actually, +63% of ALL MEN deal with some degree of same sex attraction. Yup! . . . But, unlike the press & "gay media" who call all things like this as "gay"— we're part of a big movement of guys—men who reject the notions that "Men who love men are automatically part of 'gay' anything!" Find out why![20]

It would be as easy as it would be pointless to make fun of these folks—by observing, for example, that their hearty masculine disregard for the niceties of punctuation is queerly at odds with their suspiciously unrestrained, rather emotional, downright feminine overuse of the exclamation mark. But there's no real ethical or intellectual advantage to be gained by pulling masculine rank, acting superior, or aggrandizing ourselves at their expense—that's just a little bonus, a bitchy pleasure, which is hard to resist. Luckily, it's quite unnecessary. After all, these guys, or g0ys, freely acknowledge that their signature movie, the work of art emblematic of their whole movement, is *Brokeback Mountain*.[21] So why bother being needlessly cruel? No doubt Fellows would be just as pleased to leave such folks out of his imagined community of gay men as they would be relieved to escape from it.

The problem for Fellows and his essentialist, third-sex model of gayness is that the men who claim to recognize themselves in this masculinist definition of homosexuality hardly represent some tiny fringe group. "Gay rodeos are extremely popular events all over America," John Clum observes, adding, "I wish I heard more irony from the folks who attend them."[22] Irony, however, is the last thing you can expect from the *Brokeback Mountain* crowd. What remains so awkward for Fellows, in any case, is that the virile, gender-normative style taken up and promoted by advocates of the "g0y identity" clearly strikes a chord with a considerable number of guys who, like it or not, fall into the category of gay, even according to Fellows's own definition of it, but who disavow any and all gender-atypicality. When I last accessed the g0y website, on June 23, 2011, it had had nearly 700,000 hits.

ⓧ

This little skirmish over essentialism and its critical liabilities was undoubtedly predictable, if not a bit stale, and in any case the issues are well known and familiar by now. Still, the main reason for dispatching the whole topic as quickly and economically as possible is that it doesn't address the most important and interesting questions raised by the femininity of gay male cultural practices—namely, *what is femininity,* and *whose femininity are we talking about anyway?* Third-sex theories do not, unfortunately, provide adequate answers to those questions. Instead, they tend to evade them by naturalizing the social. That is, they accept at face value the standard social definitions of gender and go on to treat them, unaltered, as transparent reflections of natural facts. They take various practices that are conventionally marked as feminine or masculine—but that may have nothing to do with maleness or femaleness—and affirm their gender codings, with the result that anyone of the other sex who takes up those practices appears to reveal by that "gender-atypical" choice a natural, underlying condition of sexual intermediacy. In this way, third-sex theories collapse the distinction between sex and gender, and rewrite the social as the natural.

The gender dispensation under which most of us live is a radically polarized one, and it tends to enforce a dichotomous model of male and female as "opposite" sexes. Social practices that are not coded as conventionally masculine—such as flower-arranging or dancing—are quickly and unreflectively coded by our societies and by ourselves as feminine (although the details may vary from one society to another: for example, baking is coded as feminine in the United States and as masculine in France). But not everything that fails to qualify as properly masculine, according to the stringent social criteria designed to safeguard the purity of that rare and precious essence, is necessarily feminine. The ecstatic worship of divas from the world of opera or popular music may not be terribly butch, but that doesn't mean it is feminine—in the sense that women as a group consume Maria Callas or Judy Garland tracks at the same pace that Rufus Wainwright does, or flock to the opera as they do to makeup counters, or collect Cher or Madonna videos for fear of being thought unwomanly.

When a man's passionate interest in historic preservation or period restoration is taken to mean that he has the "psychologic character of women" (to borrow Edward Carpenter's phrase), the social language of gender is hastily translated into the natural reality of sex. I completely agree with Fellows that there is often some truth in stereotypes—"However trite they may seem," Fellows says, "gay stereotypes are useful in examining gay men's natures" (246)—but in converting such stereotypes into archetypes (x, 247), and into the truths of our nature, Fellows places too much faith in clichés, in social fantasies about masculinity and femininity that seem obvious and right to us only because they conform to widespread, generally accepted notions about sex and gender, notions that start to look thoroughly incoherent as soon as we examine them up close.

The reason it's a good idea to resist falling into conventional ways of thinking about gender, ways that the gender ideology of our society constantly promotes, is that otherwise we will be inclined to accept, without considering them properly, a lot of bogus ideas about women and men that we would find utterly implausible if they didn't happen to agree with the polarized concepts of gender that gender-stereotyping reinforces by representing them as mere common sense.

In particular, we would rush, without thinking too carefully about it, to consider any habit or practice or attitude or interest that our culture defines as unmasculine, or as out of keeping with conventional norms of masculinity, as "feminine," whether or not it had anything to do with the habits or practices or attitudes or interests of any women we actually know. Such a credulous belief in the truthfulness of conventional notions is entirely understandable, especially when it is grounded in such deeply rooted and seemingly unarguable ideologies as those pertaining to sex and gender, but it is also misplaced and entirely unnecessary.

For example, Fellows assembles a number of personal narratives that testify powerfully to the extent of gay men's passion for aesthetic perfection, for ideal beauty—a phenomenon that we have already observed. In particular, he calls attention to the obsessiveness with which some gay men value, enjoy, and fixate on what many other people regard as trivial, minor, or virtually imperceptible fine points of architectural or interior design.

> Preservation-minded gays have a penchant for meticulous attention to design detail. . . . While on a house tour in Savannah, a Georgia preservationist remarked with a hint of scorn, "It seems like new buildings that are built to look like old buildings never have *quite* the right pitch to the roof. *Those little details.*" Chicago preservationist and Louis Sullivan devotee Richard Nickel remarked, "People say rightly of me that I'm too fussy, but if you're not analytic over everything, then soon enough you're a slob and anything goes." Believing that "all existence is rehearsal for a final performance of perfection," Georgia's Jim Sullivan was clearly of the same fastidious breed. (31)

I would be prepared, with Fellows, to accept such aesthetic fastidiousness as characteristic of gay male culture. The maniacal obsession with getting that shade of paint, the angle of that roof, the texture of that surface exactly right is one that may well be a salient, distinctive gay male *cultural* trait. We have noted the importance gay male culture places on *style*—its characteristic tendency to accord value to any coherent expression of a historically specific system of taste, and the pleasure it takes in recognizing how that system completely determines the formal composition of a particular object. Outmoded but totally consistent and methodical styles, abandoned by fashion and socially devalued, typically spark camp appreciation. In the same way, old buildings that no one else cares about, but that exhibit the features of a complete stylistic system, may evoke passionate enthusiasm—the very kind of enthusiasm, in fact, that gay male culture typically bestows on all outmoded aesthetic forms that one can love without having to take seriously, like Baroque opera or the "woman's pictures" that constitute a large component of Hollywood melodrama.

I would happily concede that a passionate emotional investment in specific elements of style, a meticulous concern for the niceties of architectural or interior design, for fine points of aesthetic detail, is not usually considered a particularly masculine characteristic. But is it feminine? Are women generally thought to be that fanatical, as a sex, about precise matters of aesthetic form? Some fashionable ladies are, of course, highly fastidious about their appearance, and about matters of style in general. But do women generally have a reputation for feeling as if something catastrophic has happened, as if the world has come undone, as if humanity has failed to live up to its full and glorious potential, whenever a single minor but unnecessary aesthetic fault has been committed?

No, not if we believe Chaz, or Chastity, a sometimes transgendered hairdresser in Hickory, North Carolina, who was interviewed in 2004 by E. Patrick Johnson for a book on Black gay men of the American South. When asked how members of the local community reacted to seeing Chastity (Chaz's female alter ego) in church or the mall or a doctor's office, Chaz indicated that they knew she was not exactly what she seemed: "No natural woman . . . pays that particular amount of attention to detail."[23]

The same logic applies to some of the other gay male cultural practices mentioned here. Though the Broadway musical may be congenial to straight women in ways it is not to straight men, though it may create less gender trouble for its heterosexual female audience than for its heterosexual male audience,[24] there does not seem to be a straight female equivalent to the intensely solitary, wildly ecstatic, excessively sentimental childhood experience of the musical that D. A. Miller describes.[25] The Fire Island Italian widows put on drag, but they do not resemble women, nor do they intend to do so. Some female figures that are gay male icons are quite repellent to straight women (starting with Joan Crawford and Bette Davis in Robert Aldrich's 1962 movie, *What Ever Happened to Baby Jane?*). Many gay male cultural practices are therefore not masculine or feminine or "two-spirited," nor do they exactly demonstrate a combination of masculine and feminine characteristics or a condition halfway between male and female. Rather, they imply something else, something unique, or at least a particular formation of gender and sexuality that is specific to some gay men and that has yet to be fully defined.

❧

So how can we describe gay male culture's particular, non-standard formation of gender and sexuality? What is the cultural logic behind it? What kind of social and emotional work do gay men's so-called "feminine" identifications do? What, in fact, *is* the gay male relation to femininity?

In order to begin to answer that question, we need to understand gay male "femininity," or what passes for "femininity" in gay male culture, as *its own phenomenon, or range of phenomena*—as something quite distinct from the various kinds of femininity exhibited or performed by women. Which is precisely why some writers prefer terms like "gender-role non-conformity" and "gender atypicality" to describe gay male practices of gender: those terms indicate, by their very neutrality, a certain suspension of judgment about what the exact meaning of gay male gender dissidence really is, a refusal to define any and all departures from canonical masculinity automatically, unreflectively, and uncritically as "feminine." So much the better. But then the trick is to *keep* those terms in suspense, to prevent "gender-role non-conformity" and "gender atypicality" from getting equated straightforwardly and simplistically with "femininity."

It is useful in this context to recall our earlier conclusion that "femininity" in gay male culture is, typically, a *proxy identity*: it is an identity that stands in or substitutes for a form of existence that gay men cannot claim—or, at least, that they cannot claim so easily—in their own persons. Which is why they borrow it from others, in this case from women (or, in other cases, from aristocrats). "Femininity" is a means by which gay men can assert a particular, non-standard, anti-social way of being, feeling, and behaving. It represents, more particularly, an ethos at odds with specific forms or manifestations of traditional heterosexual masculinity. As a proxy identity, "femininity" is a clear expression of gay male gender dissidence, a rejection of standard, canonical, established forms of heterosexual masculinity. But that doesn't mean that gay "femininity" necessarily signifies an actual identification with *women*. However much it may *refer* to women, which it obviously does, it is not always or essentially *about* women. It is its own form of gender atypicality, and it has to do specifically with gay men themselves.

One of the methods by which gay male culture elaborates and consolidates its distinctive attitude of social and cultural resistance is to claim, appropriate, and translate into gay male terms certain values or ideals that are profoundly alien to traditional heterosexual masculine culture. Some of those values or ideals are associated with women and are marked as feminine. For example, gay male culture valorizes performance and role-playing; it cherishes melodrama; it exhibits a fascination with a particular style or way of being defined by a distinctive blend of glamour and abjection. All of those cultural forms or genres are more closely aligned in our world with femininity than with masculinity. And in a social and symbolic system where gender differences are systematically polarized, dichotomized, and turned into binary oppositions, any gesture that implies a refusal of conventional masculinity is certain to be read as feminine.

So it is understandable that gay male cultural practices—which promote and disseminate non-standard ways of being and feeling for men, which recode bits of mainstream heterosexual culture with dissident or atypical gender meanings, and which instruct others in that socially deviant and oppositional ethos—it is indeed understandable that such practices might make it look like gay men have qualities or characteristics generally possessed by girls and women. And that's also what gay male culture may *feel like* to many of the gay men, and to many of the straight people as well, who participate in that culture. (So Fellows is not exactly wrong to interpret gay male cultural practices as feminine.) But that need not indicate that gay men belong to a third or intermediate sex, that they have a different biology or psychology from straight men, or that they are possessed of a separate, essential, archetypical nature.

ᗢᗡ

One of my reasons for selecting the figure of Joan Crawford in the first place and for choosing to study the mesmerizing spectacle she offers of mingled glamour and abjection, both in *Mildred Pierce* and in its descendants, is that her gay appeal forces us to confront two notorious aspects of gay male subjectivity that make gay men nowadays particularly squeamish—and therefore particularly loath to explore them: namely, identification with women and attachment to the mother.[26]

Those two themes are both central and taboo in contemporary gay male culture. They are very far from being extinct—as anyone can testify who has been to a drag show or seen Pedro Almodóvar's 1999 film *All about My Mother,* which condenses an entire tradition of cultural reflection on the part of gay men about their relations to femininity and to the figure of the mother.[27] But no self-respecting gay man wants to address those topics nowadays, except in the form of a joke or a put-down. Once upon a time, gay men had a reputation for being able to talk about nothing but their mothers. Now they refuse to go near the subject.

And no wonder: "feminine" identification and mother-fixation recall the hoariest clichés of pop-psychoanalytic homophobia. If what
the cultural practice of male homosexuality ultimately reveals about
the nature of gay male subjectivity is how closely it turns out to resemble that stock of popular and pseudo-scientific caricatures, it's
hardly surprising that so many gay men would want to have nothing
to do with gay culture. That is why it is so important to deal with
those unfortunate and embarrassing issues in an open and positive
way. They haven't disappeared, after all; they're just not spoken about.
And yet it is perfectly possible to free them from their phobic associations and give them a gay-affirmative interpretation.

In the previous two chapters, accordingly, I described the significant erotic and political stakes in gay male culture's "feminine" identifications and maternal investments, at least as the cult of Joan Crawford and her avatars illuminates them. And I set out a number of
reasons why gay men ought not to be afraid of them—why, instead of closeting them, we should not hesitate to embrace them. I
was also determined to take the battle deep into enemy territory—
onto terrain long occupied by psychoanalytic thinking and homophobic commonplaces about gay male interiority. I wanted to show
that it is possible to rescue from the grip of pathology even such
demonized aspects of gay male subjectivity as mother-fixation and
so-called "femininity." And I wanted to indicate how an analysis of
gay male cultural practices could produce a non-normalizing, nonpsychological or non-psychoanalytic account of gay male subjectivity.

Now it is time to extend this exploration of gay male femininity
further (I'll stop putting those annoying quotation marks around *femininity*, but I will continue to understand by *femininity*, as the term
applies to gay men, not the qualities and characteristics of women
but the non-standard formation of gender and sexuality that is distinctive to gay male culture). We need to look more closely at how
that proxy identity, femininity, functions in gay male culture—to
deepen our understanding of *what gay male femininity is* and *what it is*

for. Instead of running from the specter of gay male gender deviance, being ashamed of it, greeting it with stubborn and stolid silence or denial, and consigning it to homosexuality's newly built closet, we need to continue—in a spirit of unprejudiced and panic-free inquiry —to inquire into the meaning of gay male femininity, without fearing that any investigation of it will necessarily return us to homophobic clichés about our abnormal psychology.

Most of all, we shouldn't be so sure before we start that we already know what gay femininity is, how it functions, or what it means.

GENDER AND GENRE

*T*wo fundamental premises will guide the inquiry that follows. First, the phenomena under consideration should be analyzed with reference to social factors, not biological ones. Second, gender orientation and sexual orientation should not be radically separated from each other or systematically distinguished in any account of male homosexuality. Both of those premises reflect personal and intellectual preferences of mine, not scientific axioms, but let me attempt to justify them—or, at least, to explain why I prefer to think about gay male cultural practices in this way—since my approach has in fact broad methodological implications.

Modern Americans have fallen into the bad habit of locating the source of all non-standard behavior in either nature or the individual. Which side of that dichotomy they come down on may depend on their politics or their religion, but they all seem to agree that those are in any case the only two options. Homosexuality, criminality, addiction, even the preference for certain consumer products (in the case of identical twins separated at birth) are currently considered either the result of inborn traits, no doubt located in our genes or genomes—the current shorthand for "nature" (it used to be hormones, and blood before that)—or the expression of an idiosyncratic quirk, a personal choice, a sin, a defect, or some other individual characteristic. What is missing from all this speculation is the notion of *the social* as a mode of being which is constitutive of both individual and collective experience. The social refers to a form of existence that arises from the shared life of human communities and does not result directly from either natural determinations or individual variations.

As a cultural practice and an identity, being gay is a social experience in the same way that being American, or middle class, or Chicano is a social experience. It's neither a natural condition nor an individual peculiarity, but a collective phenomenon, a consequence of social belonging. But that doesn't mean it's a choice. I could even say it's the way you're born—in the sense that if you're born and raised in America, you inevitably become an American, of one sort or another, whether you want to become an American or not. And your subjective life, your instincts and intuitions, will necessarily be shaped by your being an American, by your connectedness to American culture. But this doesn't mean there's a gene that causes you to have an American subjectivity, or a gland in your brain that makes you American.

Nonetheless, being American, like being gay or being straight, is deeply personal, deeply defining of you as an individual, deeply shaping of your sensibility, your way of seeing the world, your responses to other people. Even if you are African American or Asian American, being American still gives you a subjectivity that is distinct from the subjectivity of those who aren't American.

In the same way, gay male culture and gay male subjectivity are constituted socially. In that very limited respect, being gay is like being American. By insisting that homosexuality is a social form of being, I do not mean to imply that homosexuality is something learned, or that people acquire a homosexual orientation because they are taught to be gay by others—"recruited," as it were, into the "gay lifestyle." I am not talking here about what causes either homosexuality or heterosexuality, any more than I am talking about the European discovery and colonization of America—the process that eventually produced an American national identity. I'm speaking about the way males who *already are homosexual,* like people who are already born and raised in America, come to acquire a particular social identity, with a distinctive consciousness, a set of cultural practices, and a resulting subjectivity. The process by which people become American is pretty well known, even if the details merit further study. The process by which people become gay is less well known, which is why it's worth investigating.

Becoming gay is mysterious, because—unlike becoming American—it does not happen through primary socialization. Parents and schools don't teach kids how to be gay in the same way they teach kids how to be American. (Though they sometimes do teach kids how to be straight in ways that backfire so badly you could almost say they really *do* teach kids how to be gay.) Most other social groups—whether minority groups like African Americans or majority groups like unhyphenated Americans—are initiated into their cultures at home and at school, as well as through TV and the movies. But they tend to misrecognize or deny the kinds of cultural practices that they engage in and the effects that those cultural practices produce.[1] Heterosexuals don't usually tell themselves that, by watching a film like *Titanic,* they are undertaking an initiation into the culture of heterosexuality, into a very specific ideology of romantic love as a source of salvation, and into a literally catastrophic model of feminine gender identity as a calamitous condition requiring rescue ("he saved me, in every way that a person can be saved"). But that is in fact what they are doing.[2]

It is precisely because the social reproduction of gay male culture does *not* get carried out by mainstream social institutions—whose very functioning as vehicles of cultural initiation remains invisible and unremarked because it is so obvious—that gay male acculturation remains a mysterious affair, especially when it seems to be largely complete, or at least well under way, by some point in early childhood. That is why it will be necessary to devote a lot of attention to it, as I plan to do in a moment. Nor does the social reproduction of gay male culture get carried out by gay male social institutions either—not initially, at least: it takes place in a heteronormative (family) context.

That is why it inevitably involves the appropriation and queering of *mainstream* cultural objects. After all, mainstream cultural objects (like the Broadway musical) are the *only* cultural objects that hetero-normative social institutions readily make available to a proto-gay child. What is not at all clear is how cultural resistance, or queer counter-acculturation, happens *within* a heteronormative context. Our social model of gay male subjectivity will have to provide some account of that.

In any case, it will be important not to begin from a falsely stark opposition between an insufficiently robust model of the social, un-derstood as a mere surface effect of haphazard interactions among people (instead of as a systematic ensemble that is thoroughly consti-tutive of their subjectivity), and an overly positivistic model of the natural, understood as the deep, formative structure that determines our being. It will also be crucial not to be distracted by psychology, pop- or other, from this fundamentally social process of subject-formation, not only because psychology tends to medicalize and pathologize social dissidence, especially sexual dissidence, but also because our concern here is not with individual mental life but with collective structures of feeling.

ℭℨ

Social life reaches down very deep into the subjectivity of the indi-vidual. It shapes what appear to us to be our profound, abiding intu-itions about the world and about ourselves. We have already surveyed some instances of basic intuitions or subjective truths that, though deeply felt, reflect not our biological natures or our psychological vi-cissitudes but the social order of our world and the values associated with it. For example, people in our society perceive generational struggles between men as tragic, at least potentially, whereas they feel that generational struggles between women do not qualify for equally serious, or completely serious, consideration. Conflicts be-tween women are excessive, histrionic, overwrought—in any case, they are less than fully dignified. Authority is masculine, since it issues in command; hysteria is feminine, since it expresses powerlessness. Masculinity is more dignified than femininity, just as the upper classes are more dignified than the lower ones (even if the latter sometimes qualify as more virtuous than the former). Dignified suffering is tragic; undignified suffering is pathetic. Laughter is not an appropriate response to tragedy and horror, but to take pathetic suffering seriously is to fall prey to sentimentality, to succumb to the vulgar appeal of melodrama, to make an emotional investment in kitsch, all of which is a fault when judged according to standards of good taste.

Femininity is trivial, unserious (the same judgment applies to anyone whom we consider less worthy than ourselves), no doubt because it is highly performative. Role-playing is at odds with the manifestation of an essential identity—of one's true being—and so performance necessarily implies inauthenticity, and a lack of real seriousness. Any mode of being or feeling that can be disqualified as unserious—such as the performative or the melodramatic—is not truly masculine and displays instead an affinity with the feminine. The distinction between style and content, or style and substance, is a crucial one for separating appearance from reality: style counts as feminine and substance as masculine, since masculinity is fundamentally concerned with the true content of things, whereas femininity is concerned with frivolous matters such as appearance. Men act; women appear.

It is all very well to denounce such repugnant notions as idiotic, as being nothing more than outlandish social prejudices—outdated, quaint, threadbare, cartoonish. Indeed, when they are stated baldly in the form of propositions, as I have just done, no one in their right mind would assent to them. But because they mostly do not present themselves to us as propositions, but as perceptions of the world or gut feelings or deeply personal and original insights, they continue to command a certain allegiance at an intuitive level on the part of many people. That is why cultural commentators like Camille Paglia and Harvey Mansfield, who traffic in such prejudices or who mobilize them in order to endow their views with a specious plausibility, never fail to find a receptive audience—an audience more than willing to jettison its supposedly "politically correct" beliefs (which it had evidently never embraced very eagerly or sincerely to begin with) in favor of what gets lightly but effectively passed off as sheer natural reality and as obvious common sense.

What this indicates is just how much of what we take to be reality is socially constituted without ceasing to appear to us as real. Social constructions are not false, in other words, and it is mistaken to regard social analysis as implying that our fundamental intuitions about the world are erroneous or groundless. On the contrary, they are very well grounded—it's just that they are grounded in our social existence, not in the nature of things. To search for the social grounds of subjectivity is therefore not to invalidate people's deepest feelings and intuitions or to reduce them to the status of mere illusions or delusions.[3] It is, quite simply, to explain them.

⊙⋈⊙

My second premise is that working models of gay male subjectivity should not attempt to cordon off gender orientation from sexuality. Because gay male cultural practices often manifest themselves in childhood, long before the start of sexual activity, and because they seem largely unrelated to sexual activity of any kind, it is tempting to see them as representing a phenomenon entirely independent from erotic life. Furthermore, because many of those practices take the form of certain pursuits that are associated with girls and women, they can be interpreted as expressing a deep, underlying, congenital, originary, non-standard (feminine) gender orientation instead of a (gay) sexual orientation. That general outlook does have a certain appeal. And it may be an entirely appropriate way to understand some transgender individuals as well as transgender culture. In the case of gay men, however, the trick is not only to distinguish gay male cultural practices from gay male sexual practices, but, having done so, to figure out how they are related. What is the logical or emotional connection between a liking for Judy Garland and a liking for sex with men? Is it possible to identify any conceivable relation between the gay male desire for sexual contact with men and a taste for grand opera, or the Broadway musical, or period design?

Historically, there has been a tendency to conceptualize the sexual practices and gender identities of gay men separately from each other, to give one priority and to treat the other—if at all—only as a mere consequence of the first. The result has been either to promote sexuality at the expense of gender or to privilege gender over sexuality. The post-Stonewall gay movement tried to do the former; third-sex theories generally do the latter.

Since homosexuality had for so long been treated as a psychological abnormality or pathology consisting in sex-role reversal or gender inversion, a prominent strain in post-Stonewall gay male political thought and culture attempted to sever homosexuality from gender and to present it as a purely sexual orientation, having to do entirely with sexual object-choice and thereby proving to be fully consistent with normative masculinity. It also discouraged traditional forms of queeniness in men, considering them both unsexy and retrograde—unfortunate survivals from a bygone era of sexual oppression and internalized homophobia. What made a man gay was not his non-standard gender style or his feminine subjectivity, but the directionality of his sexual desire, his erotic attraction to men, his social membership in a gay male world of equals, the quantity and virility of his sexual partners. That is what gay liberation meant, at least in part: the liberation of sexuality from gender, the freedom to be masculine, and the multiplication of sexual opportunities that the new butch styles of homosexuality afforded—precisely by enabling gay men to eroticize other gay men *as* gay men.

Nowadays, in the light of the queer and transgender movements, that post-Stonewall model of gay male virility, though it still has plenty of fans (as we just witnessed in the preceding chapter), is starting to seem "quaint."[4] The Stonewall rebellion no longer looks like the beginning of the world-historical defeat of homophobic gender stereotyping, the definitive release of gay people from centuries of bondage to degrading gender identities, but rather like the hollow and short-lived triumph of the misguided fantasy of a gender-free homosexuality. In particular, the post-Stonewall victory of gay identity over the dykes and queens of an earlier era now appears less like the dawn of liberation than like just another strategy of domination—the final chapter in the long history of transgender oppression from which, only now, are we starting thankfully to emerge.

But it is also possible that the pendulum may have swung too far in the opposite direction. Although it is surely true, as Fellows says, that "gayness comprises much more than sexual partners and practices," we need not necessarily conclude that gay culture derives largely from feminine gender orientation and from the otherwise "non-sexual dimensions of gay men's natures," as he also insists. And since, in our homophobic and sex-phobic society, gay sex is always easy to denounce and very hard to defend, it seems unworthy to purchase respectability for gay male culture by saving it from a discreditable implication in gay male sexuality, as Larry Kramer (twice quoted by Fellows) labors to do: "Surely gay culture is more than cocks," Kramer says. "The only way we'll have real pride is when we demand recognition of a culture that isn't just sexual" (as if a culture that *was* just sexual would be completely shameful—or, at least, as if it would be something no decent human being would take pride in).[5]

The real problem, however, is not that gay culture is likely to be reduced to nothing more than cocks. The challenge for critics and interpreters is the opposite: it is to figure out what most of gay male culture—historic preservation, to take only the handiest example, or the cult of Joan Crawford—could possibly have to do with cocks. It's less a question of saving gay male culture from being reduced to sex than of preserving some conceptual and emotional connection between gay male cultural practices and the same-sex sexual practices that make homosexuality a *sexual* orientation.

Fellows manages to capture quite brilliantly the sexlessness of much gay male culture, the breathless absorption in a world of fascinating and precious objects, the maniacal preoccupation with sconces and silver and cut glass and woodwork and all those aesthetic satisfactions that seem to have nothing to do with sexual pleasure. And, indeed, much of gay male culture delights in activities that—unlike gay sex, which is socially condemned as abnormal and unnatural—inspire widespread admiration on the part of straight society, insofar as they involve making the world beautiful. It is understandable that what some gay men would prize and cherish in those activities is precisely their merciful exemption from sexuality and, thus, from punitive judgment, whether other people's or gay men's own. Instead of a physical, animal act that can be experienced as undignified, filthy, shameful, and perverse (at least, if you're doing it right), architectural restoration or musical performance or art-collecting is not only socially respectable, public-spirited, and praiseworthy; it also, just like modernist abstraction in this one respect, affords a redemptive opportunity to transcend the body and its functions—to escape from the tainted identity of being a (homo)sexual subject and from all the stigma that attaches to it. Just think of Liberace (who was also a house restorer on the side): only by constructing for himself an elaborately artificial identity as a classy and glamorous artist, as a purveyor of high musical culture, could he neutralize the contempt he otherwise would have incurred for being such a queen.[6]

No doubt a certain part of the appeal of queer cultural practices to gay men lies precisely in their remove from overt sexuality: they make available to gay men *forms of queer expression other than the strictly sexual.* Furthermore, cultural practices offer gay men outlets for their passions that belong to a supposedly higher order than sexual activity and that may even partake of the ascetic, the spiritual, or the selfless. Fellows captures beautifully the kind of unironic, religious devotion characteristic of certain gay male cultural practices—a devotion that is neither explicitly campy nor implicitly sexual, that makes no reference to gayness, and that has rather to do with a total, serious, *spiritual* absorption in the aesthetic object, which is venerated both as an absolute value in itself and as an escape from one's own self, including one's sexual subjectivity. In complete, selfless immersion in eighteenth-century row houses or musical theater or Joan Crawford memorabilia—all those "clippings, cigarette cards, rare vintage photos, letters, film reels, and scrapbooks" in Neil Maciejewski's collection (as described in *The Out Traveler*)—some gay men may find possibilities for an experience of intense rapture that sexuality itself, for whatever reason, does not or cannot offer them.

As a child of the Stonewall era, I want to resist the unsexing of gay male culture, even if one result of my bias will be that I fail to do justice to the passionate, sexless, *unironic,* worshipful intensity that accompanies some gay men's near-religious devotion to objects of non-sexual beauty and that imparts to such devotion an aura of self-lessness, asceticism, and spirituality.[7] The literal, earnest, non-camp, and de-eroticizing effort to lose the self in the aesthetic object and to transcend one's own gayness in the process is clearly an important dimension of some gay men's cultural practices. (Other gay men may feel that such experiences of rapturous absorption in non-sexual objects actually makes them *more* queer.) In any case, this sort of sexless aestheticism is not something I have emphasized, since it seems to me to imply a certain repudiation of gayness, a refusal of homosexual specificity, a flight from both gay identity and gay sexuality.[8] I prefer to examine those gay cultural practices that make willing reference to homosexuality, just as I also prefer to explore those gay male expressions of passionate devotion to a cultural object and those experiences of delirious bedazzlement with it that betray some ironic self-awareness and that fail to take themselves completely straight. Throughout the whole course of this book, I have kept my observations about gay male culture tied to various themes in gay male eroticism and to the conditions under which gay men accede to the subjective experiences of desire and love. That is what I will also try to do now.

☙❧

Let us consider a very simple and obvious fact. In a heterosexual and heteronormative society—that is, in the sort of society in which most readers of this book happen to live—to desire a man is to take up a feminine position. Not necessarily a feminine identity, but a position in the field of discourses and practices that is socially marked as feminine. That is because women are the only people who are thought to be naturally, normally susceptible of feeling sexual attraction to men. Hence, for anyone who inhabits a world of heteronorms, to experience sexual desire for a man is to occupy a subject position that is considered proper to women, in the sense of rightly belonging to women—and, thus, a subject position that is culturally identified and inflected as feminine.

Although sexual desire itself may be independent of gender orientation, and is certainly distinguishable from it, sexual desire in a heteronormative social world is bound to be closely associated with gender orientation, because each is coded with reference to the other. That is, the experience of feeling sexual desire for members of one particular sex signifies, both to other people and to the person (gay or straight) who experiences it, a relation of similitude, resemblance, identity, or some other kind of structural correspondence with the customary gender role of those who belong to the other sex. To be attracted to one sex is to feel like you belong to the other. That may be less true for the (rare) kind of male same-sex desire that takes an exclusively phallic, aggressive, and sexually dominant form; if, however, all the objects of such a desire remain male, even that traditionally masculine style of homosexual desire is not likely to escape some association with female subjectivity or a feminine gender role. And the less male homosexual desire expresses itself in such aggressive, phallic ways, the more closely bound to a feminine gender role it will seem to be.

What this means is that gender and sexuality are strictly related. Sexual desire for a sexually specific kind of object is both the expression of a *sexual subjectivity* and the marker of a *gender identity*. A man who feels homosexual desire is necessarily placed in the sexual subject position and in the social role of a woman, certainly according to other people's perceptions of him and also—at least at some level or to some extent—according to his own perception of himself. At the same time, most such men retain the social status and the sense of subjective empowerment that belong to fully entitled males. To be recognized and treated as male is inevitably to be socially and subjectively constituted as male. The result of that gender-constitutive process appears in many aspects of masculine subject formation that are taken for granted and are therefore instinctive: they range from a sense of entitlement to one's feelings and opinions to a sense of owning public space or at least of being at home in it, to enjoying the right to speak and the ability to impose oneself and one's views on a group, to claiming an erotic autonomy and a sexual subjectivity of one's own.

Gay men, then, are both like and unlike straight men, just as they are both like and unlike straight women. They are like straight men in that they are men and most of them are accorded, at least initially, the dignity and sense of subjective empowerment that generally attach to men in a system of male dominance. They are not like straight men insofar as they desire men and do not desire women; also, unlike straight men, they find themselves assimilated to a feminine gender role by virtue of the directionality of their erotic desire, even if that desire expresses itself in a sexually aggressive way.

Gay men are unlike straight women insofar as they are men, but they are like them in occupying a desiring relation to the male sex and in being considered unmasculine partly on that basis.

A male subject of same-sex desire is therefore gendered in complex and often contradictory ways. That complexity is nothing more than the consequence—ineluctable, though not, of course, total or all-determining—of the social semiotics of gender and sexuality in a heteronormative world. The unique, transverse social situation of men who desire men produces a gendering of gay male subjectivity that is specific and irreducible to the gendering of any other subject position.

So gay male subjectivity is assimilable neither to the subjectivity of heterosexual women, as some third-sex theories would imply, nor to the subjectivity of straight men, as some advocates of gay virility might prefer. It needs to be understood independently, on its own terms.[9]

Given all those considerations, it would be unwise to try to conceptualize gay male femininity, or those gay male cultural practices that might appear to manifest it, in isolation from same-sex sexual desire, which is correlative with it. Gay femininity is very much a homosexual phenomenon, insofar as same-sex desire cannot be dissociated from its conditions of formation; it is not just an expression of sexual intermediacy or effeminacy, with no erotic component. Although a queer child may not translate his erotic feelings into sexual activity before he grows up and comes out, which can sometimes take many years, that does not mean he does not experience erotic attraction while still a child—including erotic attraction of a homosexual kind. It is not clear which comes first, same-sex desire or gender dissonance, and neither should be presumed to be the source or origin of the other.

It would be equally unwise to cordon off gay male cultural practices from all implication in gender inversion, gender deviance, or gender atypicality—the way some critics, who approach them from a post-Stonewall understanding of male homosexuality as a purely sexual and masculine identity, attempt to do.[10] Most gay male cultural practices, after all, from diva-worship to interior decorating, turn out to be strongly inflected by feminine meanings, and there is no point in obfuscating that fact.

⚭

It might seem misguided, in any approach to gay male subjectivity, to ignore psychic factors and to place so much emphasis on social semiotics, on the codes of sex and gender, treating them as determinative of the vicissitudes of gay male subject-formation. It might seem as if I were limiting my conceptual model to superficial phenomena, to labels or signs or categories or ideologies, avoiding the deep, internal processes by which the individual subject is formed and oriented. But social meanings, like gender and nationality, are not superficial: they are constitutive of human subjectivity. And I'm not trying to offer a genetic account of sexuality, or to explain what causes individuals to be gay or straight—*either* sexually *or* culturally; rather, I'm inquiring into the origins of the cultural practices adopted by those who, for whatever reason, turn out to be gay or straight in either sense.

Moreover, I don't take social codes to be *ideas,* to which individuals may or may not assent; I don't regard them as thoughts about sex and gender which individual people are free to accept or reject—although, like many feelings, they do contain a certain propositional content. Rather, I consider semiotic codes to be constitutive of the meanings out of which individual subjectivity is born. They define the social and symbolic context within which subjectivity takes shape and are therefore basic to the social formation of gendered and sexual identities.

Under heteronormative conditions, it is only natural for a male subject to experience his desiring relation to men, quite unreflectively, as feminine and to identify with a feminine role on that basis. This is not some logical, deliberative, conscious process—as if an initially masculine man were suddenly to be flooded with insight and say to himself, "Oh dear, I really like guys, so that must mean I am like a woman—I guess I had better start identifying with girls." The association is instinctive or intuitive, not reflective. The basic heteronormative coordinates of gender and sexuality map out the constitutive conditions under which each subject of heteronormative culture accedes to subjective agency and intelligibility. It is an originary, formative process, which is thoroughly social from the start.

A certain gender orientation at odds with heteronormative masculinity is therefore bound to be built into gay male sexual subjectivity. It should not be surprising, then, if many gay men display gender-atypical characteristics or if many gay male cultural practices seem to express feminine identifications—identifications marked as feminine not by reference to women, necessarily, but by forms of dissent from heteronormative masculinity. That is why femininity hardly exhausts the meaning or content of gay male cultural practices.

℗℗

Gender identity is formed very early in the life of the individual. And how is it formed, after all, if not in relation to preexisting social models of gender and sexuality, embodied both by a child's earliest caregivers and by the gender values belonging to the cultural forms that those caregivers make available to the child—and that have shaped their own styles of conduct and emotional expression? The differential gender-mapping of cultural forms produces the (heteronormative) social-semiotic system in which a child's caregivers participate, a system that has already contributed to forming their own subjectivities and determining their personal styles of feeling and behavior. Gay (or proto-gay) subjects may well find those styles of expression, along with the entire conventional social-semiotic system of gender and sexuality that subtends them, to be uncongenial, if not downright alien. Under those conditions, it is hardly surprising that many gay (or proto-gay) subjects resist interpellation by traditional codes of masculinity and femininity, or that they find scant personal meaning in the cultural forms and activities that such codes inflect as traditionally masculine or feminine. In which case, they may adopt certain evasive strategies that enable them to dodge the social summons to experience the world in heterosexual and heteronormative ways.

Those standard, straight ways of experiencing the world include ways of feeling as well as ways of responding to cultural objects and activities already coded for gender and sexuality, ways of orienting oneself in relation to all the constellations of interconnected values responsible for inflecting persons, behaviors, and genres of discourse with the dense social meanings that they bear, meanings that also refer—however obliquely—to gender and sexuality. The central portion of this book has been dedicated to tracing the logical connections among a few of the interrelated values that form those constellations, and to showing how they impart gendered and sexual meanings to many elements of the cultural field—how they structure a larger poetics of culture in terms of gender and sexuality.

Gay femininity is a cultural formation, then, not just a psychosexual one. Gender orientation is an orientation to cultural practices, cultural forms, and their meanings; it is not simply a sexed and gendered subjectivity removed from a cultural context. We should therefore not construe the feminine position of the gay male subject in narrowly sexual and gendered terms, as if it were a mere psychosexual condition, the inevitable consequence of some mechanical working-out of a rigid sexual geometry, of a shifting oedipal configuration of predetermined anatomical and psychological variables. The feminine position that gay male subjects take up is not exclusively defined by the directionality of erotic desire and a corresponding gender role, nor is its meaning exhausted by them. For that feminine position both reflects and expresses a distinctive situatedness within an entire field of discourses and social practices.

Once again, the generic codes of the Broadway musical may be illuminating. "In traditional musical comedies," John Clum observes, "gender assignments of songs are quite specific. The women got the sensitive songs, the torch songs or songs of unrequited love. The men usually move from songs of philandering to love duets. The women's songs allowed the lyricist space for more private expression."[11] There is a tight fit, in other words, between gender and genre.

Which implies that feminine identification on the part of gay men is more than the determinate result of the playing-out of the heteronormative logic that coordinates gender and sexual object-choice. It reflects a larger cultural logic by which generic practices connect femininity with particular forms of expression and an extensive set of cultural values. "Feminine identification" is the term which the language of psychology uses to describe what is actually a concrete social process of positioning oneself within a set of cultural codes that define a multitude of emotional and affective roles, attitudes, and practices of personal life. As Stuart Hall reminded us some time ago, "ideology as a *social practice* consists of the 'subject' positioning himself in the specific complex, the objectivated field of discourses and codes which are available to him in language and culture at a particular historical conjuncture."[12]

So when male subjects who desire males take up a feminine position, they may not so much be yielding to the inexorable force of a rigid set of social norms—to the social logic of heteronormativity—as they may be gravitating toward certain affective and discursive possibilities that are already present in the larger culture. Such possibilities are coded for gender, and associated with gender, but they are not specifically about gender. Rather, they acquire a specific gender association through the differential gendering of the genres that produce them. So a gay subject who is drawn to those affective or discursive possibilities may be expressing not an identification with women so much as an attraction to the cultural values associated with certain practices that happen to be coded as feminine by generic conventions. He may, to invoke Clum's Broadway example, have a particular predilection for sensitivity, or emotional intensity, or private forms of expression—the sorts of values that are at home in the songs conventionally assigned by the pragmatics of the musical genre to the subgenre of songs sung by women.

In other words, the differential gender-mapping of everything from men's and women's songs in Broadway musicals to the genres and styles of expression that we call tragedy and melodrama produces a cultural landscape in which many emotional and discursive practices are coded for masculinity or femininity. Gay femininity may turn out to consist in a *cultural* identification with or attraction to particular gendered modes of feeling and expression, as well as a repulsion to others. Once dislodged from their obligatory, conventional masculine positioning by the fact of their same-sex desire, gay male subjects develop atypical gender identities by working out various kinds of dissident relations to the standard gender values attached to cultural forms.

ⓄⓍⓄ

Let us consider a representative, indeed a notorious example. It displays one gay subject's dissident relations to the mainstream gender coding of standard cultural values. I am referring to a poem by Frank O'Hara, a gay poet who played a central role in the formation of the so-called New York School of poets, painters, and musicians. The poem appeared in his 1964 collection *Lunch Poems*.[13]

> Lana Turner has collapsed!
> I was trotting along and suddenly
> it started raining and snowing
> and you said it was hailing
> but hailing hits you on the head
> hard so it was really snowing and
> raining and I was in such a hurry
> to meet you but the traffic
> was acting exactly like the sky
> and suddenly I see a headline
> LANA TURNER HAS COLLAPSED!
> there is no snow in Hollywood
> there is no rain in California
> I have been to lots of parties
> and acted perfectly disgraceful
> but I never actually collapsed
> oh Lana Turner we love you get up

O'Hara appropriates here the ambient melodrama of conventional journalistic discourse—with its emotionally overwrought, attention-getting headlines, its breathless fascination with the lives of public figures and celebrities, and the keyed-up sense of drama it brings to the portrayal of current events in the news—in order to stage his own dissident relation to the mainstream genres, discourses, and cultural forms that define conventional heterosexual masculinity. It is from those dominant cultural forms, discourses, and genres that he manages to carve out for himself a flagrantly non-standard position within the field of gender and sexuality.

O'Hara represents his attitude to the banner headline as one of mingled credulity and skepticism. He portrays himself as both a dupe and a disillusioned critic of the inflated journalistic discourse he ventriloquizes. Far from exempting himself from the hysterical excitement that the blaring headline strives to impart to the mass audience targeted by its address, he happily assimilates himself to that audience, appropriating the headline's melodramatic rhetoric, citing it, and reproducing it with mock seriousness. By opening the poem with the words of the headline and enunciating them in his own voice, he actively (which is to say, passively—that is, with *active passivity*) occupies the subject position that the trashy headline stakes out for the unresisting reader. At the same time, O'Hara's citation exposes the overheated rhetoric of journalistic discourse, making fun of the headline for its melodramatic excess, for its strenuous effort to get us to invest so much urgent and misplaced meaning in the minor details of the life of a celebrity we don't actually know—though we might be induced by the tabloid press to feel that we do know her—especially when our own lives do not qualify for the same kind of impassioned consideration or sympathy.

O'Hara joins in the headline's exclamation, repeating it as if it expressed his own shock and dismay, and claims the utterance for himself before the reader of the poem even realizes that O'Hara is simply quoting the tabloids. To speak in one's own voice, if one is the sort of cultural dupe that O'Hara at first presents himself as being, is to adopt the trite language and the tendency to melodramatic overstatement that characterize conventional journalistic discourse. By the end of the poem, however, O'Hara has differentiated the movie star's plight from his own. Though he makes no virtue of "never actually collaps[ing]" (after all, he has "been to lots of parties / and acted perfectly disgraceful"), his comparatively stalwart behavior presents a contrast to the privileged antics of the star, whose celebrity entitles her to benefit from a special indulgence and deference that he cannot claim. Challenging her to pull herself together and get back on her feet, he finally evinces a certain impatience: far from being able to count on any outpourings of sympathy for his own lapses, he has had to fend for himself without them, and that is surely why his concluding exhortation conveys both tenderness and toughness before the spectacle of feminine glamour and abjection.

O'Hara's knowing combination of alarmed concern and bemused detachment registers his recognition that he is not qualified to be a subject of such flamboyant and melodramatic celebrity discourse, even as it testifies to his admiration and envy of those who are.[14] His ironic voicing of the headline ultimately discloses its discourse to be ungrounded except in the trope of celebrity melodrama itself. By sharing in its groundless excitement, O'Hara projects his own lack of seriousness, especially when judged according to the criteria of heterosexual masculinity. That impression is compounded by the lack of punctuation, as well as by the deliberate ditziness and irrelevance of his dispute with his friend over the correct description of the weather. Further undermining O'Hara's masculinity is his breathless response to the news of a trivial event in the life of a female movie star and his assumption of an attitude of schoolgirl excitability and prurience before the spectacle of scandal, as well as a more solemn attitude of veneration proper to Lana Turner's female fans. Finally, there is his telling use of the phrase "trotting along," to describe his own movement through the streets of New York, which completes this self-portrait of masculine gender dissonance. Real men don't trot.

O'Hara's ironic reuse of melodrama does not contest elite society's punitive judgments against that disreputable subgenre, but knowingly embraces them. He flamboyantly displays a set of affects understood to be silly or pathetic, at once inviting and defying social contempt. He uses melodrama and the social values associated with it to mark out for himself a specific subject position that is clearly at

odds with heterosexual masculinity, that implies a non-standard formation of gender and sexuality—and that in those respects is identifiable as feminine. Ultimately, though, what O'Hara's appropriation of
the melodrama of journalistic discourse expresses is a larger, more
comprehensive resistance to conventional forms of sexual and gendered discourse and embodiment. That resistance does not involve
the explicit assumption of a feminine identity. At no point in the poem
does the speaker use a feminine pronoun or attribute to characterize
himself. Instead, O'Hara discreetly constructs for himself a persona
that is neither conventionally masculine nor conventionally feminine.
Nor is it a persona that is divorced from sexual desire ("I was in such a
hurry to meet you," he says). Rather, his poem stages a subjectivity
that is—inexplicitly but recognizably, unmistakably—gay.

That subjectivity is not individual but collective. "Oh Lana Turner
we love you," O'Hara writes. This first-person plural invokes, to begin with, the virtual community of Lana Turner's fans, whoever they
are. But it also slyly smuggles in the possibility of a different and more
specific collectivity, an audience of movie queens and gay men in general, a community forged by the shared worship of this feminine icon.
In fact, the poem opens up a space for many *we*'s, many inhabitants
of that plural pronoun: it imagines fandom as the site of multiple col-
lectives produced by love and identification, not limited to any one
gender or sexuality, all of them queerly connected through their
transverse relations to the movie star and her mass-mediated image.
It ultimately promotes the vision of a love supported by every mediation that such a love can find in cinema (whether as art or as commodity), in friendship, and in melodrama as an emotional and pragmatic genre—though it does not insist that such a vision is realizable.
The queer world of belonging it imagines, rather, is a projection of
gay desire.

☙❧

"Melodrama" and "tragedy" refer not only to different genres of
drama, then, but also to different pragmatic genres of discourse, dif-

ferent modes of feeling, and different styles of emotional expression, as well as to differential degrees of social worth and differently valorized social performances—all of which are correlated in turn with the difference between femininity and masculinity. Since the systematic interconnection and hierarchical distribution of the social values that contribute to defining those generic differences are formative of human subjectivity as it takes shape within specific cultural contexts, it is not surprising that even quite young children orient themselves, both inwardly and outwardly, with reference to that basic cultural poetics—the conventions of discourse, feeling, and expression that such genres represent.

Long before they ever have sex, in other words, young people have genre.

Which may be all they need in order to forge certain non-standard relations to normative sexual and gender identities. For by making non-standard emotional connections to cultural forms, they effectively refuse the pressing social invitation to assume a conventional, heteronormative positioning and they effectively acquire non-standard sexual and gender identities, identifications, and orientations.

Children, in other words, may not yet be conscious of making a sexual object-choice (though some of them may be quite aware of it, especially when that object-choice is a non-standard and disapproved one), but they are very alert to the standard gendered and sexual coding of specific conventions of emotional expression—conventions which obey in turn the laws of genre and which correspond with pragmatic generic distinctions, like the distinction between tragedy and melodrama. Such distinctions differentiate not only *kinds of discourse,* but also *kinds of feeling, styles of emotional expression,* and *conventions of behavior and social interaction.* Children are exposed to genres of discourse, behavior, and emotional expression from an early age.

It is partly *through* such genres, after all, that children find their own voices and personalities, that they gain access to subjective expression, that they acquire character. So the strict correlation between genres of discourse, feeling, expression, and behavior, on the one hand, and forms of gender and sexuality, on the other, is likely to be clear and palpable to children at an instinctive, intuitive, visceral level, even to very young children, and it is likely to be formative of their subjectivities, although—like most adults, in this respect—they remain largely unaware of that correlation and lack any conscious or explicit terms in which to articulate the inchoate perceptions and intuitions that it generates.

It was therefore in vain that the writer Samuel Delany—trying to raise his three-year-old daughter in a non-sexist environment in the United States in 1977, and despairing of being able to find a sufficient quantity of children's picture books that featured female subjects in leading roles—set about "with white-out and felt-tip pen" to re-sex the pronouns attached to the animal hero in the somewhat androgynous picture book that he had finally selected to read to the little girl. "I began the story," he recounts, "and at the first pronoun, Iva twisted around in my lap to declare: 'But Daddy, it's a *boy* bear!'" Delany, taken by surprise, was nonetheless prepared for that objection.

> "I don't think so," I said. "The book says 'she' right there."
> "But it's *not!*" she insisted.
> I was sure of my argument. "How do you know it's a boy bear?"
> "Because he's got pants on!"
> Surely she had fallen into my trap. "But *you're* wearing pants," I explained. "In fact, you're wearing the *same* kind of Oshkosh overalls that Corduroy [the bear] is wearing. And you're a little girl, aren't you?"
> "But Daddy," declared my three-year-old in a voice of utmost disdain at my failure to recognize the self-evident, "that's a *book!*"

As Delany himself acknowledges, his daughter was right. Already at the age of three, she was more attuned than he was to the pragmatics of genre—particularly to the unspoken narrative and gender conventions governing the stories in animated children's books and shaping narrative discourse in our society more generally. Delany had thought his daughter was still innocent of those conventions—still a *tabula rasa,* a blank slate. But she was thoroughly versed in their complex protocols, even at her tender age. Indeed, those protocols are so "sedimented," as Delany puts it, "that a single instance of rhetorical variation, in 1977, registered not as a new and welcome variant but, rather, as a mistake self-evident to a three-year-old."[15]

☙❧

Genre shapes the sensibilities of young people from their very first encounters with others, from their initial experiences of sociality, and so it forms their subjectivities. Most children grow up in heterosexual environments, where they are introduced to standard genres of discourse, feeling, expression, and behavior—including the conventions of emotional expression that their parents' spontaneous manifestations of feeling often mirror and reproduce. Even children raised by lesbian or gay male parents are initially exposed, at least to some degree, to mainstream cultural genres and styles of expression.

The fact that popular culture nowadays routinely includes gay and (considerably less often) lesbian characters in the diegetic register of their stories does not change the generic design of those stories themselves (that is, it doesn't change whether or not they are comedies or melodramas), nor does it alter the modes of feeling that are codified by traditional generic conventions and that adults take up in their interactions with others. *Will and Grace* is still a situation comedy; *La Cage aux Folles* and *Rent* are still Broadway musicals; *All about My Mother* and *Bad Education* are still melodramas—and none of them is likely to be part of early childhood education anyway. Whereas books about queer families that *are* designed specifically for elementary-school-age children, like *Heather Has Two Mommies, Jenny Lives with Eric and Martin,* or *And Tango Makes Three,* though they may well contribute to the destigmatization of homosexuality and conduce to greater social tolerance, hardly break down the heteronormative monopoly on forms of expression held by the major popular genres.

In any case, mainstream cultural forms provide the only genres most children know. So those children who acquire a non-standard or dissident gender or sexual identity necessarily forge that identity in relation to mainstream cultural forms. Either they have to *invent* perverse relations to such forms, or they have to *find* in such forms opportunities or occasions or permissions for particular non-standard ways of feeling. In either case, they express queer ways of feeling by devising their own (dissident, deviant) ways of relating to the mainstream cultural objects to which they are exposed, and by identifying with peculiar aspects of those objects that are either non-heteronormative or that lend themselves to non-heteronormative feeling.[16]

Which may explain why some gay or proto-gay male subjects gravitate, early on, to specific genres of discourse or feeling, along with their related cultural forms (such as Hollywood melodramas or Broadway musicals). A certain gay student of mine remembered that once, at a much younger age (probably around seven), he held his astonished family captive one summer day, while they cooled their heels in the parking lot of a supermarket, by performing for them all the roles from *The Sound of Music,* or at least all the songs from it. Another gay friend of mine, while still in middle school, rewrote Christina Crawford's autobiography *Mommie Dearest* and made it into a play—only he turned the Christina character into a boy, in the hope that when the play was staged he could play that part himself; the change of sex provided him with a dramatic role that could mediate between his masculine identity and his emotional identification with an abject but powerful, melodramatic feminine role model.

Although "not a single twelve-year-old boy was ever brought before a psychiatrist, or prayed to Jesus for help, on account of his collection of original cast albums," D. A. Miller writes, the Broadway musical has proved to be "not one whit less indicative [of homosexual development] than those [other, more recognizable 'signs' of it] that were horrifically transparent from the moment they appeared."[17] I have tried to explain why, to suggest what relation the poetics of

American culture might have constructed between genres of discourse—or styles of expression, or kinds of social performance—and forms of sexuality.

☙❧

The formative, subjectivating effects of genre provide the solution to a persistent puzzle about how kids can get initiated so early into the *cultural* practice of homosexuality. Gay male identity, after all, seems to be a relatively late formation, reaching back no further than adolescence. And gay male culture, as it is collectively practiced and transmitted, is largely an artifact of gay male urban communities, which are composed of grown-ups. Membership in gay male culture—both for gay men and for those women and straight men who enroll in it—is something acquired in the course of later life, through a process of adult socialization. So how can such a process of adult socialization account for what clearly look, at least in retrospect, to have been the gay cultural practices precociously embraced early in their lives by many boys who later turn out to be gay? How do we explain why gay or proto-gay subjects take up the cultural practice of male homosexuality while they are still children, and why certain heterosexual subjects, who will later discover in themselves a deep affinity with gay male culture, sometimes experience a strong and unerring attraction to its cultural forms from an early age, without being aware of such an attraction, at least not under that description?

Furthermore, what sense does it make to speak of culture without reference to processes of socialization or acculturation? Or, rather, how can there be a culture of male homosexuality if there is no evidence of or even possibility for the existence of a process of *primary socialization,* the kind of socialization that takes place in infancy?

The very notion of *culture,* especially in its classic, nineteenth-century, anthropological formulation, presumes a central, even a foundational role for *language.* Cultural groups are conventionally identified by reference to linguistic communities. Language-use defines the boundaries of a culture: a culture, at the very least, is composed of individuals who all speak the same language. To learn a human language is the beginning of acculturation and socialization. Language provides a point of entry into culture.

But gay men, despite some distinctive and characteristic uses of language that differentiate them from other language-users, do not form a separate linguistic group.[18] So if they are to qualify as members of a culture, gay men would need to be constituted as a group through some primary process of socialization akin to language acquisition. Watching Joan Crawford movies with a bunch of your gay friends, at the age of thirty-five, hardly fills the bill.

Language is just one example, albeit a privileged one, of what defines a culture. In fact, culture is usually assumed to consist in various arbitrary but systematic patterns of thought and behavior that have been deeply ingrained in the perception and habits of those who belong to specific human living-groups. Like language, which serves as a model for other processes of acculturation, those patterns of thought and behavior are impressed on children from an early age, whether they are deliberately taught to them or whether they are simply absorbed by children from the people who raise them.

In any case, acculturation refers to a routine process of socialization that takes place identically, or nearly so, throughout a particular group or population. It goes on within all the families that constitute a single society or cultural unit, such that all the members of a particular human living-group spontaneously end up being, for example, native speakers of a single language—even though they learned it in different settings and in slightly different versions.

Real cultural patterns, according to this standard notion of culture, are like linguistic structures. They shape human subjects in specific, profound ways. Because they are impressed on the individual so early, at such a formative age, they are stubborn, enduring, and constitutive of the self. Culture is preserved by regular, long-standing processes of social reproduction that transmit particular patterns of thought and behavior from one generation to the next and consolidate the collective identity of the group. By reproducing itself with each new generation, culture maintains the identity of the community from the past into the future. Any "culture" that is not acquired through primary socialization would have to be comparatively superficial, a shifting fashion or habit or outlook, rather than an ingrained way of being and behaving; it would not be very deeply rooted in the subjective life of the individual or the group, and so it would be easy to alter and vulnerable to change.

Gay men do not seem to belong to a "culture" in any robust sense of that term. Unlike, say, Americans, they do not constitute a social group that continually renews itself across the generations by means of sexual reproduction and primary socialization. According to those criteria, the kind of gay male culture that is acquired only in later life would hardly seem to qualify as a culture at all.

That is exactly why John Clum is so skeptical: "Is there an indigenous gay culture?" he asks. "Literally, the answer is no. Gayness is not like ethnicity. We do not share a language, a race, or religion."[19]

But that's not quite the whole story either. For gay male culture, as we have seen, *does* exhibit precisely the stubborn intransigence we associate with language-based cultures. Despite the widely held conviction that gay male culture is constantly going out of date, it turns out to have changed a lot less over time than we like to claim. Gay liberation has actually not been all that successful in its efforts to remake the subjective lives of gay men. It has not managed to install gay politicians or sports figures in the place of female divas, nor has it ended the gay male cultural valorization of taste or style—even if gay fashions have evolved since the 1950s. Gay men have not stopped finding gay meaning in female icons, from *The Golden Girls* to *Desperate Housewives* to Lady Gaga.[20]

Like the gay students and friends of mine mentioned earlier, many people (both homosexual and heterosexual) who grew up after Stonewall still report having forged queer relations with objects of mainstream culture in their childhood. They seem to have engaged in the cultural practices of male homosexuality well before they engaged in the sexual ones—before they reached sexual maturity, came to think of themselves as gay (or straight), and came into contact with any of the formal or informal institutions of gay sociability. And those who make gay male cultural identifications often describe those identifications as instinctive, natural, unshaped by social attitudes or prejudices, and as a persistent, enduring aspect of their personhood, deeply anchored in their subjectivity.

Will Fellows assembles a multitude of eloquent personal testimonials to that effect, documenting both the strength and the ubiquity of such perceptions, with specific reference to historic preservation and architectural restoration: "Even as a child growing up in a nondescript farmhouse, I had an eye for the more interesting and attractive buildings" (29); "Gay men are very sensitive to beauty. It's perhaps a hackneyed stereotype, but I believe in it—I simply *know* it" (30); "I've been in love with old buildings and the stories of the people behind them since I was a kid" (51); "As a child I had a great interest in buildings and architecture" (61); "I think I'm genetically predisposed to be a collector" (70); "Mother said I brought home my first treasure when I was seven" (99); "Even as a kid I was always wanting to fix things up" (111); "From my earliest memories I was always fascinated with houses and what happened inside them" (118); "From the time I was three years old, I knew that I was going to be an artist" (131); "Is it a compulsion or an obsession? I don't know" (210).

Recall, in this connection, Barry Adam's explanation for the visceral appeal of opera and the Broadway musical to some gay boys: "Musical theater is one of a number of possibilities that speak to the sense of difference, desire to escape, and will to imagine alternatives that seems a widespread childhood experience of many pregay boys." The very same thing could also be said about historic preservation. Adam concedes that "there may be no single universal pregay experience," but he suggests that all these cultural activities, and the powerful draw they exert, "nevertheless indicate a range of core experiences with broad resonance among gay and potentially gay men that exceed the notion of 'gay' as 'just' a social construction or discursive effect."[21]

Where do those core experiences come from? Or, more specifically, how do gay or proto-gay children learn to engage in such canonical gay male cultural practices—how is it that they come to speak
the language of gay male culture so fluently, as if it were their mother
tongue—at such a tender age, without having been nurtured from
the cradle by gay men? How is it possible that the process of socialization into the cultural practice of homosexuality can begin long before
the subjects of acculturation are mature enough to enter gay male
communities and take part in the social exchanges of gay male life?
What explains how proto-gay subjects acquire gay culture almost as
if it *were* their native language, as if it truly were for them an indigenous culture? How is gay culture transmitted and acquired, not just in
adult life, but in childhood? Is there, in short, a gay male equivalent of
a process of primary socialization?

Those are precisely the sorts of questions to which our model of
cultural poetics provides answers, at least in a general and hypothetical way.

For we have already established the three conditions whose conjunction is both necessary and sufficient to explain the social reproduction of gay male culture. (1) If even conventional, heteronormative genres of discourse are also genres of feeling and styles of
personal expression; (2) if mainstream genres of discourse, genres of
feeling, and styles of personal expression are coded for gender and
sexuality according to a standard cultural poetics—by being inflected
with specific sets of social values that are differentially associated with
specific gendered and sexual roles; and (3) if such genres of discourse
and styles of feeling or expression are formative of individual subjects
from an early point in their lives—then something like primary socialization into gay male culture is indeed possible, insofar as a dissident
relation to those genres of discourse and expression constitutes a dissident formation of gender and sexuality. Children may have limited
exposure to the highly developed cultural forms that contain and perpetuate genres of discourse and expression—and even if they are exposed at an early age to musicals, say, or melodramas, they might not

get a lot out of them—but they are thoroughly exposed to the styles of personal expression defined by those forms, since such styles of expression shape ordinary emotional life and construct the various *pragmatic* ways that children's caregivers speak, express themselves, and relate to children.

In other words, a process of socialization into gay male cultural practices can begin at an early age, long before the start of an active sex life or the beginning of adult participation in a gay community, because already at that age proto-gay subjects begin forging, or perhaps merely finding, a non-standard relation to the sexed and gendered values attached both to mainstream genres of discourse, feeling, behavior, and personal expression and to the cultural forms (musicals, tragedies, melodramas, historic preservation, various aesthetic practices and pursuits), and their correlate emotional forms in individual behavior, that embody, disseminate, routinize, reinforce, and consolidate those genres. And proto-gay subjects respond to the queer solicitation of certain features or elements in those mainstream forms that speak to these kids' sense of difference, desire to escape, and will to imagine alternatives, as Barry Adam puts it.

☯

What I have just proposed here is not, obviously, a theory of what causes male homosexuality. Instead, I have offered an admittedly speculative account of how some individuals (both gay and straight) acquire a gay male cultural orientation, whose coordinates extend to the fields of both sexuality and gender. My account has been abstract, highly schematic, and undoubtedly simplistic, but at least it is supported by a certain amount of empirical evidence—namely, the evidence provided by a critical analysis of gay male cultural practices and the larger cultural poetics on which they are based. Such an analysis has occupied the major portion of this book. So I can claim to have put forward a conceptual model for understanding the social process of acculturation by which a gay male cultural sensibility is formed.

The acquisition of a gay cultural sensibility takes place within a larger social system that produces both homosexuals and heterosexuals, as well as others who fail to fit neatly into those two categories. Why is it that some of the boys whose sexual subjectivities are formed by this system grow up to become gay, while others do not? Despite a number of claims to the contrary, there is actually no one today—including me—who is able to offer a clue, let alone a complete answer, to that riddle. Nor should we search for answers by focusing narrowly on the constitution of individual subjects, as psychoanalysts do, even if larger social processes necessarily unfold through cumulative small-scale processes, such as those that take place at the level of individual development. For we are dealing not with an individual case but with a collective phenomenon: the mass formation of gay and straight sexualities and subjectivities. That is a feature of our society as a whole, and it is to be accounted for by social factors as well as by individual ones.

The reasons some boys become homosexual, whatever they are, must be more or less the same as the reasons some boys become heterosexual, given that it is only in the last three hundred years or so that boys have started becoming either one or the other. Both homosexuality and heterosexuality are artifacts of the same socio-sexual system, a system largely coincident with Western modernity, though one that has evolved differently for women and for men.[22]

It would be nice to know in detail how that system operates and how it mass-produces and distributes these relatively new brands of sexual subjectivity—but, until we do, it is pointless to speculate about the process. Psychologists and psychoanalysts have no more wisdom to offer on this topic than anyone else, which is why third-sex theories are suddenly popular once again: if homosexuality and heterosexuality are actually hard-wired into our bodies, we no longer need to figure out where they come from, nor do we have to come up with causal explanations for why some individuals end up straight while others turn out to be gay. Cognitive science, which also locates the causes of sexual and gender identity in our brains rather than in our societies, makes a similar appeal by offering physiological answers to complicated social questions.

What I have tried to explain is not why some male subjects become gay, but how gay (and some straight) subjects might come to acquire a gay culture, in the sense of relating to cultural objects and forms— to Broadway musicals, old houses, melodrama, Joan Crawford, the performing arts, or aesthetic perfection, among many other things— in specific ways that implicate both their sexual subjectivity and their gender orientation.

The aim has not been to explain the logic behind each and every gay male cultural practice in all its specificity. It was difficult enough to elucidate the gay appeal of one scene in one Joan Crawford movie. The point was rather to indicate where one might set out to look for explanations—namely, in the ways that interlocking constellations of social values attached to cultural forms are socially coded for gender and sexuality, and in the ways that human subjectivity, including sexual subjectivity, is constituted in relation to those pre-existing constellations of sexually inflected values.

What I have tried to do, in short, is to offer a conceptual model for understanding the complex interrelation among sexual orientation, gender identity, and cultural practices, and for reconstituting the social logic underlying it.

⟨ **17** ⟩

THE MEANING OF STYLE

It is hardly surprising that genres of discourse and feeling, as well as styles of personal expression, should turn out to be coded for gender and sexuality, when nearly all cultural objects are inflected with similar kinds of meaning. We have already seen one instance: there is nothing neutral (or neuter), apparently, about "little gold pedestals full of colored soap balls." They are evidently so saturated with feminine significations and so redolent of sexual passivity that merely putting one in your bathroom is sufficient to shatter any and all pretense to true manliness.

There may be nothing very mysterious about the process by which such an object comes to be associated with a specific sexual and gender style. In the case of this example from *Tales of the City,* the item in question seems to express a certain feminine touch in home decorating, a fussy impulse to prettify even the empty space "on the top of the toilet tank." A quick social-semiotic analysis would probably suffice to explain why a man who owned such an item could not possibly be "somebody you could take back to Orlando and they'd never know the difference."

Other gender codes are more subtle and more elusive, however.

I once had occasion to go shopping in a design showroom for bathroom fixtures with a certain boyfriend, in anticipation of a home renovation that we had fantasized about but that we never managed to afford. At the store we were confronted by a display of something like fifty or a hundred model faucets. There was a great variety of shapes, sizes, and styles. Many, we could instantly agree, were dreadful, and they could be easily and quickly eliminated from consideration. A few of them struck us as possibilities. But there were other cases—painful cases—in which disagreements between us seemed to reveal not relatively innocuous divergences of taste but profound, embarrassing, personally disfiguring lapses of character, culpable failures to sustain an attitude expressive of the right sort of gender or sexual identity (mostly on my part, of course).

My boyfriend would pause, aghast, while I pointed to a candidate and indicated that I considered it a possible or at least a conceivable choice for our bathroom sink. Looking at me in disbelief and (mock?) horror, he would exclaim, "Oh no. No, please. Say it ain't so! Don't tell me I am married to a man who thinks *that* is an attractive fixture." Properly shamed and disgraced, as well as feeling exposed and discomfited, I would try to recover from my gaffe, withdraw my suggestion, and assure him that I hadn't been thinking or seeing clearly when I praised that particular object—though I'm not sure it was possible to recover from such an egregiously revealing mistake, once it had been made. For I had not only committed an error of taste; I had also disclosed something shameful about my whole personality, including my sexual subjectivity—something until then unsuspected even by the man I had been living and sleeping with for quite some time. (Well, maybe he really *had* secretly suspected it all along, but now he had the irrefutable, sickening confirmation.)

If the liking for individual cultural objects and artifacts can seem to be revealing not just of our tastes but also of our *identities,* it is because their aesthetic style is pervaded by an entire symbolism, extending to gender and sexuality—a symbolism that is both palpable and very difficult to describe. The fact that you like a particular knob for a faucet says a lot about what you consider classy, elegant, stylish, or cool, and that means it says a lot about your social aspirations as well as the social class you come from.[1] But that's not all it says. It also expresses aspects of your gender and sexual identity, because, within the society in which we live, the exact arrangement and design of shapes, thicknesses, curves, colors, and other stylistic features, however abstract and non-representational they may be, participate in a specific and highly loaded cultural semantics. They have a particular social and cultural history, and as a consequence they become bearers of a complex cultural symbolism in which gender and sexuality are implicated. Style is saturated with meaning, including sexual and gendered meaning, and so your liking for a particular style reveals a lot about your own sexual and gender identity, about the way you position yourself with respect to already established fields of social and sexual meaning.

We don't ordinarily think about cultural objects in such terms; that's not how they immediately present themselves to us. But when we are confronted with a choice among them—especially the sort of choice that, we imagine, will say something about ourselves, about our tastes and personalities, that will indicate not only what we like but also who we are—in those circumstances we react instinctively to the way such artifacts might reflect on us, which includes an awareness of their coding for gender and sexuality. We recoil from one design, which we would never, *never* have in our home—or wear, or drive—not only because it is ugly, but also because it is, say, cute, or fussy, or showy, or melodramatic. Which is to say, it would betray us: it would express, and thereby reveal, something disgraceful or disreputable or at least potentially discreditable about us, something undesirable or pathetic or pretentious or unattractive, something damaging to our identity. We respond so strongly to these encoded meanings that there can be little doubt that they are really there, or that we know what they are, but—except in a few instances, which are either very obvious or extravagantly repulsive—we would be very hard-pressed to say what they are, to name them, to specify what exactly those meanings consist in, what in particular those meanings actually *mean*.

And even in those obvious or repulsive cases, it may be more difficult to explain the logic behind our tastes than we would expect. What is it, exactly, that I abhor in a certain style of interior decoration, a certain model of car, the color or pattern of a tie? Why do I shudder at the very thought of acquiring a little gold pedestal full of colored soap balls, or a garden gnome?

This mysterious state of affairs is itself mysterious. It's not just that those questions are perplexing in themselves. What's more perplexing is our inability to answer them or even to understand the grounds of our difficulty in answering them. There's already something mildly odd about the fact that cultural objects and activities and artifacts have meanings that implicate gender and sexuality. But given that such artifacts are, transparently, obviously, undeniably coded for gender and sexuality—and given that their sexual and gendered meanings are clear enough to us that we have no difficulty acting on our recognition of them, expressing our visceral responses, our attractions and repulsions—it's even odder that we have such a hard time specifying those meanings. Why can't we do it?

In most cases, we have no concepts and no language adequate to the task of describing the sexual and gendered meanings which such objects encode, which means we can't fully explain, in a sequential and logical way, our immediate, often vehement reactioïns to particular objects on the basis of their sexual and gender coding. But the problem is not just one of finding the right category or the right vocabulary to articulate our perceptions. It is a matter of representation and representability. We don't have a ready way to specify the sort of meaning that is expressed not by a representation of something but by the thing itself.

This inability is baffling. We are not dealing with the mysteries of the universe or the wonders of nature, after all; we are dealing with human cultural productions and their significations, with our own social world. Each object or activity has been manufactured and designed with careful intent and laborious deliberation by people like ourselves. It has been specifically intended to produce the specific effect on us that it does in fact produce. So why can't we specify what that effect is? Why can't we describe coherently and systematically what the object means to us, along with the precise stakes in our response to it? Why can't we identify the values that are at issue in our likes and dislikes, which seem to play such a crucial role in defining who we are?

In some cases a contextual study of design styles and their history might be enough to clear up the mystery behind our instinctive responses to individual objects by indicating the cultural traditions to which those objects allude, the genealogy of representations from which they descend, and the network of associations on which they draw to generate their meanings and acquire the specific social values they express. In other cases, the relations among style, taste, class, gender, sexuality, and identity remain bafflingly elusive, at least given the current array of available instruments of critical, social, and semiotic analysis. It takes a vast effort to unpack those meanings.

That is what makes the task of accounting for gay male culture, for gay male taste, so complicated, at least when you get down to details. Any truly satisfying explanation of the gay male appeal of Joan Crawford, say, would have to be based on a comprehensive understanding of the social-semiotic workings of her cinematic image and their implication in specific orders of sexual and gendered signification.

For example, there is a fleeting but utterly heart-stopping moment toward the end of *Mildred Pierce*. Mildred is setting out from her darkened office to confront Monte, who, she now realizes, has betrayed and bankrupted her. For just an instant, as Mildred dashes across the room to the telephone, the shadow cast by some outside light through the Venetian blinds in the French doors of her office falls, twice, in thin parallel slats over the curves of Joan Crawford's suited, sinuously sheathed, voluptuous body and across her stricken, majestic, knowing, indignant, but resolutely composed face.

All this happens within a *single second* of the film's playing time. The entire sequence of images, though very brief, is filled with potent, eloquent cinematic meaning which substantially enhances the power that Joan Crawford's persona exercises over her audience and

19 Frame capture from *Mildred Pierce* (Michael Curtiz, 1945). Mildred, having pulled herself together and made a decision, sets out to make a telephone call.

20 Frame capture from *Mildred Pierce* (Michael Curtiz, 1945). Mildred in shadow.

contributes to defining the particular brand of femininity that she incarnates.

But what meaning? What does this perfectly standard film noir device convey? Film noir criticism, for all its sophistication, elaboration, and accomplishment, cannot help us out here; it has nothing to say about the specific meaning of *this* stylistic element in the context of *this* movie.[2]

21 Frame capture from *Mildred Pierce* (Michael Curtiz, 1945). Mildred approaches the telephone.

22 Frame capture from *Mildred Pierce* (Michael Curtiz, 1945). Mildred at the telephone.

The exact effect that the shot, the lighting of the face, and the face itself all produce exceeds what the technical analysis of visual rhetoric in cinema allows us to capture, because visual analysis cannot get at the contextual, social dimension of the image. It can get at the form, but not at the content of the form. It can describe the style, but not the meaning of that style.

Style does have content. It has to have content, in fact, to *be* style. It must mean *something*. Otherwise it would not even constitute a for-

mal arrangement—not, at least, in the perception of masses of human subjects. It would be disorder, a mere disarrangement, at once
formless and meaningless. Only when style has meaning, only when
it is about something, does it register as style, which is to say as a *particular* style. A hairstyle *is* about something. It *has* to be about something. If it is not about anything, it's not a hairstyle—it's just hair. (Or
perhaps it's bad hair: if style is never just style without content, so
content is never just content without style, and content that *looks* as if
it is just content is probably the result of an inept, deplorable style.)

But what is style about? Describing the content of a form or the
meaning of a style is a very different sort of undertaking from explaining the content of a statement. The brief obscuring and then revealing of Joan Crawford's face by the shadows of the Venetian blinds
is not a proposition in an assertion, but an element of a style. The
meaning it has derives from its function within an entire aesthetic system, which itself is non-representational, in the sense that it is not
about anything else besides itself.

In short, a stylistic element is not empty of meaning, or lacking in
signification—it is about something, it refers to something. But what
it is about, the thing it refers to, is nothing other than itself, nothing
other than its value within an internally consistent, formal system of
meaning. *It is the thing itself.* Which is why, as D. A. Miller says, "style"
is a "spectacle" that is "hard to talk about . . . hard even to *see.*"[3] Or as
Oscar Wilde put it, "The true mystery of the world is the visible."[4]

The central part of this book was devoted to seeing, to understanding, and to talking about *the meaning of melodrama as a gay style*—and
to talking about it in its own terms as its own kind of thing.

Hard though it may be to specify the meaning of a style, then, it is
not completely impossible. It can be understood, so long as it is described in its own terms.

Let us consider once more that fleeting sequence of images from
Mildred Pierce. The overall effect—of the lighting, the composition of
the shot, and the movement of the actress—is to intensify the mood
of the moment, to deepen the seriousness of the new and dire turn in

the plot. The passing shadow of the blinds on Crawford's face and body contributes to the drama of the scene. It conveys a sense of dark foreboding. It builds a palpable tension, suggesting that a climax is not far off and that the spectator should be prepared for an accelerating pace and an impending action. It is both tender and scary, implying that Mildred is being forced to act within the limits of certain narrowing constraints—and, possibly, rising dangers—of which the spectator is now suddenly aware, more aware than Mildred herself appears to be. The shot also communicates a heightened determination on Mildred's part, a new resolve, as well as a gathering of Joan Crawford's dramatic powers. It says to the spectator something like, "Get ready for Joan. She's a-coming. She's on her way. Watch out— here we go!"[5]

So style can be analyzed: it can be made to speak, to say something in its own terms—it can be made not to refer to something else, but to say what it itself means. In the case of this sequence from *Mildred Pierce,* what we would need in order to complete the analysis, to specify the exact value of each particular stylistic element within the context of its system, is a deep technical knowledge of the production values and working principles of the individuals who composed the shot. Its value was understood clearly enough at the time the film was made; after all, someone designed the shot and set it up with great care and deliberateness—presumably for the purpose of conveying the particular effect that it still so powerfully and heart-stoppingly conveys. They knew what they were doing. They might not have had a critical language, or meta-language, in which to describe what they were doing; nor in all likelihood would they have formulated their rationale in the terms formalist critics would understand: they were artists and were operating according to a thoroughly internalized aesthetic logic. They may not even have had a conscious consciousness of the meaning they were making. But if they had been asked at the time what they were doing, why they were making those choices, and what effect they were trying to achieve, they surely could have said *something,* if only within the language of the style in which they were working. Unfortunately, we no longer have access to what they knew.[6] And it is not even clear how much access they had to it themselves. They may simply have been immersed in the material vocabulary of the style they were so deftly and ably elaborating.

ᴏᴏᴏ

The project of attempting to specify the meaning of style is not new. Art historians have been writing about the history and function of style for centuries. In 1979 Dick Hebdige wrote a celebrated book concerned entirely with "the meaning of style," which he took to be the key to understanding the identity of a minority subculture.[7]

And already in 1964, Susan Sontag inveighed "against interpretation," against the kind of art criticism that preferred content to style, that seemed addicted to *meaning* and consistently determined to find more of it, always more meaning. Interpretation, according to her polemical critique, reduced "the work of art to its content" and then *interpreted* that content in order to extract meaning from it.[8] Sontag vehemently opposed psychology, as well as the hegemony in liberal circles of psychological humanism. Instead of a hermeneutics of interpretation, a quest to discover what a work of art deeply, truly means, she urged us to take up an erotics of art, an appreciation of surfaces, a description of aesthetic values, of style and its effects. She promoted the "pure, untranslatable, sensuous immediacy" of art and our experience of it.[9]

In making such a stark opposition between the hermeneutics of depths and the erotics of surfaces, however, Sontag missed what exactly it is about surfaces that makes their sensuous immediacy so appealing: their incarnate meaning. And so she missed, or dismissed, something that is integral to aesthetics and the study of aesthetics, something that is identical to neither content nor style, that is neither deep meaning nor superficial beauty—and therefore neither masculine nor feminine—namely, *style as its own thematics, or counterthematics*. Although Sontag did call for the description and analysis

of form, she preferred to invert that critical protocol and to emphasize instead the need "to examine in detail the *formal* function of
subject-matter."[10] But her attachment to form and to style should
have compelled her to see the necessity of a different undertaking, of
a *hermeneutics of style*—a hermeneutics of "surfaces" that would be
not suspicious but descriptive—and to recognize the potential importance of an inquiry into the content of form that would highlight the
thematics, or the queer counter-thematics, of style itself.

At her best, that is exactly what Sontag managed to accomplish,
though she tended to obfuscate it. For example, she presents her
"Notes on 'Camp'" as a description of a "sensibility or taste."[11] But
what she was really describing in that essay was a *style of relation* to
various cultural objects. And what she was trying to specify was the
precise *meaning* of that style. In fact, the original title, or at least the
initial designation, of her essay was "Camp as Style."[12] Camp, after
all, is not the formal property of an object; it is not a particular, inherent artifactual style—that is, an aesthetics. Nor is it a psychology, a
specific subjective condition. Nor is it a behavior—an ethics or a politics. Camp does involve aesthetics, affect, ethics, and politics. But it is
best understood as a style of relating to things, a genre of practice, a
pragmatics.

Sontag's preoccupation with the meaning of camp as a style is
what makes her essay on camp still worth reading today. Even though
she does not present her analysis in those terms, her understanding
of style easily allows the notion of style to be extended and applied
to the pragmatics of camp. As Sontag wrote in "On Style" the following year:

> Style is a notion that applies to any experience (whenever we talk
> about its form or qualities). And just as many works of art which have
> a potent claim on our interest are impure or mixed with respect to
> the standard I have been proposing, so many items in our experience
> which could not be classed as works of art possess some of the quali-

ties of art objects. *Whenever speech or movement or behavior or objects exhibit a certain deviation from the most direct, useful, insensible mode of expression or being in the world, we may look at them as having a "style," and being both autonomous and exemplary.*[13]

It is precisely because style is a deviation from the norm and a mode of autonomous existence, because it is both strange in itself and exemplary of itself—because it is its own queer thing—that its meaning is laborious to describe. And that is also why the objects of cultural studies are maddeningly difficult to analyze. The simplest of them condense a long history as well as a vast and complex range of interconnected meanings, meanings embodied in and inseparable from their very form or style—the shape of that faucet, the abrupt transition from speaking to singing characteristic of the Broadway musical, the lighting of Joan Crawford's face and her delivery of a line that conveys the glamorous extremity of maternal abjection.

To account satisfactorily for the gay appeal of *Mildred Pierce,* we would have to perform a stylistic analysis of nearly every shot in the film, a more complete version of the kind of analysis I just tried to sketch out for one sequence of images. We would have to specify the exact meaning of each of those shots. And then we would have to tie the value of that meaning directly to the specific social situation of gay men.

But in fact it would be wrong to reduce the visual style of *Mildred Pierce* to mere camerawork. The visual style of the film is not limited to camera angles or editing. It also resides in the acting and the conventions of acting. And any serious account of the movie's visual style would have to include all the pro-filmic elements, such as the stage set, the lighting, the production design, and especially the clothes worn by the actresses: the costumes and the underlying fashion system. We would have to include the music as well. All those elements are part of *Mildred Pierce*'s style; together they manage to impart to the film a particular style of its own that seems perfect and yet somehow also extravagant. And it is that very excess that makes the film's style stand out, that makes it so memorable and so gripping. Without taking all those stylistic elements into consideration, and without specifying their meaning—or affect—and its relation to the vicissitudes of gay male existence, we will never be able to account fully for the gay appeal of specific cultural objects, such as *Mildred Pierce,* or for the cultural object-choices of gay men.

Such an analysis would be possible—there are models for it, starting with Roland Barthes's *S/Z* and D. A. Miller's Proustian reading of *Gypsy*—and it would be desirable. But the exercise required, though necessary and unavoidable, would be almost endless. What I have been able to offer in this book is only a small down-payment on that immense project.

Thankfully, not all cultural objects or activities that have been taken up by gay men require such an extended stylistic analysis. So let us return to our exploration of gay male femininity, and consider some cultural practices and genres of discourse that are less complex than an entire Hollywood movie, but whose style likewise encodes a particular set of gendered and sexual meanings.

✄

I have already contrasted the different gendered positions in which sports and the performing arts, respectively, place male performers. Insofar as sports and the performing arts both qualify as mass leisure occupations and as public spectacles, they might seem to solicit largely identical responses from their audiences. Both of them consist of activities that showcase the talents of ordinary people, people like ourselves, who nonetheless do extraordinary things—things that almost everyone can do to some degree, like catching a ball or singing, and that everyone can therefore understand, but that very few people can do with such exceptional skill and virtuosity. Both sports and the performing arts produce spectacles for the pleasure of large audiences, live as well as remote. Both kinds of spectacle involve displays of considerable daring. And they are both highly dramatic.

The player who receives a pass when he is in a position to score, the batter who faces a decisive pitch, the singer who at a moment of total scenic and auditory exposure takes a breath before hitting the long-awaited high note: all of them in their way are action heroes, who have to perform under pressure, for high stakes, visibly, in public, on once-and-only occasions, at great risk of personal disgrace. The cultural organization of play in our society arranges for such performers what might be thought of as lyrical moments—very brief, transient moments of crucial intensity, a fraction of a second in which everything hangs in the balance. It is to occasions like these that the players are summoned to rise, to exhibit all their dexterity, and to magnetize the spectators with dazzling displays of quick thinking, agility, technical and tactical prowess. The dramatic spectacle provided by the public performance of rare and difficult feats, carried out in the instant with maximum exposure and under immense pressure, constitutes the main source of the thrills for which the audiences of both sports and the performing arts willingly pay great sums of money.[14]

And yet, the two activities have radically different class and gender codings. The class implications are less difficult to figure out than the gendered ones. Any kid can kick an object around—it doesn't even have to be a ball—and practice his athletic skills anywhere in the world. He doesn't need money, connections, encouragement by sports figures, or a privileged cultural background, although all of those things come in handy, especially if he wants to rise in the profession of sports or become an Olympic athlete. But at the outset, at least, all he needs is talent, good health, and good luck—things that are not limited to the upper classes, even if the material living conditions of the upper classes favor the cultivation of all three. So it is easy to see why sports should have a democratic dimension and why they should seem to represent a form of excellence to which anyone can aspire—a form of excellence that is open to, and that can be appreciated by, the common man. Opera, which requires complex collaborations among singers, musicians, writers, composers, stage designers, directors, choreographers, and language coaches, would seem to be closed, with respect to both its audience and its performers, to all but members of the social elite.

But is this actually the case? During the 1980s, I used to work out at a mostly gay gym in my mostly gay neighborhood in Boston. The gym had various organized activities in which I did not participate, such as team sports, including volleyball. I remember opening my locker one day to see a notice that had been taped to the inside of the metal door by the staff, announcing that a team composed of the best volleyball players from the gym would be competing against rival teams in a volleyball tournament in another city. Wishing them luck and success, the announcement ended, "Ritorna vincitor!"

That's Italian for "Come back a conqueror!" or "Return victorious!" And just in case you didn't get it, the reference is to the great soprano aria in the first act of Verdi's 1871 opera, *Aida*. Indeed, in order to get that reference, you would need to have come from a highly privileged background, or to have grown up in an Italian or artistic household, listening and going to the opera—*or* you would have had to undergo an initiation into gay male culture which, though it may present itself as an aristocracy of taste and though it may identify with a social elite, with the sort of people who go to the opera, is hardly limited in its participants to members of the upper classes. Membership in my gym was expensive, in other words, but it wasn't *that* expensive.

Such an initiation into gay male culture would have had to be performed not only on the person who wrote the notice that I found on the inside of my locker door, but also on those who, like me, opened their lockers and read it. If that allusion to *Aida* was to be meaningful to its intended audience, in its social context, a significant amount of preliminary cultural work would already have had to be carried out by many participants in the local gay community. The members of my former gym could not exactly be described, on the whole, as exceptionally cultivated people—people who could necessarily be expected to be familiar with the arts in general and classical music in particular, let alone with the complete libretti of Verdi operas in the

original Italian. The poster's target readership would have had to be
introduced, no doubt one by one, to selected aspects of grand opera,
to have had the meanings of particular words explained to them, and
to have been initiated into a distinct universe of feeling linked to a
specific way of living their homosexuality. The social operations of
gay male culture, specifically its practices of initiation, would have
had to compensate for the arcane, elitist features of the operatic form
that would otherwise have limited an appreciation of it to cultural
sophisticates.

಄ಁ

What is the gay male appeal of "Ritorna vincitor!"? The answer takes
us away from the class associations of opera and a step closer to appreciating how the style of the utterance is coded for gender and sexuality. We already know why sports are socially marked as masculine
whereas the performing arts are socially marked as feminine: it all
has to do with the specific social coding of doing versus appearing,
combat versus performance, unscripted versus scripted activity, action versus role-playing—and, in particular, with the conventional,
polarized gender values and meanings assigned to those dichotomies
according to a strict, binary opposition between masculinity and femininity. In the case of this soprano aria, there's a bit more to add, a few
extra considerations that may help to explain why heads of state do
not typically appeal to "Ritorna vincitor!" in order to send off their
national teams to the Olympics or to cheer for them in sports stadi-
ums (even if the triumphal military march from *Aida* does get played
and even sung at European soccer matches).

In fact, the social pragmatics of genre make it socially and culturally impossible for a national leader to wish an athlete representing
his country success by exclaiming "Ritorna vincitor!" The tacit generic conventions of public heterosexual culture prohibit it, and vio-
lations of those conventions get social actors into real trouble. When
one of the American soldiers in Iraq who arrested Saddam Hussein
borrowed a line from Tosca, the eponymous heroine of Giacomo
Puccini's opera, and remarked, "E avanti a lui tremava tutta Baghdad"

("And, before him, all Baghdad used to tremble"), he was thought to have violated the policy of "Don't Ask, Don't Tell," which banned non-heterosexuals from serving openly in the U.S. military.[15]

Why? *What is the meaning of that gay style of utterance?* At first, it would hardly seem that anything could be less queer than *Aida,* created for the formal celebrations of the opening of the Suez Canal. Could we cite a better instance of the pomp and circumstance of official, heterosexual culture than this nineteenth-century pageant of imperialism, nationalism, militarism, colonialism, and European chauvinism? Of course, that was then, and this is now. Fashions have changed, and nowadays it would be hard to find a better example of unintentional camp than this outlandish, extravagant, absurd, demented costume drama, with its histrionic overstatement, its emotional excess, and its demonstration of the power of erotic passion to overturn the norms of family, nation, race, and social hierarchy.

In order to explain further the gay meaning encoded in the notice I found inside my locker, I need to say something about the identity of Aida herself and about the dramatic situation in which she finds herself when she sings the aria, "Ritorna vincitor!" It is surely significant for the gender coding of opera that, like the Broadway musical, opera accords pride of place to female performers and organizes its plots as well as its music around them, so as to put them constantly in the spotlight. Accordingly, the title role of Verdi's opera is sung by a woman. And not only is Aida a woman—she is also both a princess and a slave. Specifically, she is an Ethiopian slave, captive in Egypt, who is actually the daughter of the Ethiopian king, and who has just joined a mob of frenzied, bellicose Egyptians in wishing their military leader—in reality, her secret lover—success in his impending battle against the Ethiopians, led by her own father. A chorus of Egyptians, egging their hero on to victory, cry "Ritorna vincitor!" and Aida echoes them. In the famous aria that follows, she recoils in horror and confusion from the sentiment she has just uttered, repeating, in anguish and amazement, the treasonous send-off she has given her lover, commenting on her implicit betrayal of her homeland and her father, reflecting on the conflict between erotic love and patriotic

love, between family and husband, between duty and desire, and calling on the gods to pity her in her perilous and abject (if undeniably
glamorous) condition.

So the phrase "Ritorna vincitor!" already bears a heavy burden of
dramatic irony in the text of Verdi's opera, and the ironies multiply
when the phrase is cited and reused by gay men more than a century
later in the context of a local sporting event. The citation implies,
first, a cross-gender identification on the part of gay men, a cultural
relation to femininity—this much is suggested both by the feminine
coding of the operatic form itself and by the female subject of the utterance that the author of the notice inside the locker, as well as its
reader, quote and ventriloquize. But that is not all. The gay usage also
interpellates the speaker of the utterance (in this case, both the man
who wrote the notice and the man who is intended to read it) as a
royal woman, as a Black woman, as a slave woman, and as a woman
who is destined to be destroyed by love. Once again, we witness the
multiplication of glamorous and abject roles, as well as an acknowledged delight in the melodramatic form itself.

But if what we rediscover here is the homosexual love of melodrama,
we also cannot fail to notice the valorization of melodrama as a vehicle for the expression of homosexual love, for the adoration of a male
love-object. The gay male appropriation of "Ritorna vincitor!" implies not only cross-gender identification but also same-sex erotic desire, not only a feminine subject position but a homosexual and melodramatic one as well—a posture of desperate, forbidden desire for a
heroic warrior. And so, in the context of the volleyball tournament,
the gay appropriation of that line injects an implicitly sexual element
into the relation between the team and the club that supports it.
Evoking the standard division between queens and trade, it teases
the members of the gym, inviting them to identify with the female
speaker of the line, and thus to position themselves as queens, while
aligning the sporting heroes who make up the volleyball team with
her butch military love-object, and so representing them as trade. By

claiming for the collective subject of the utterance the persona of a captive, doomed princess tragically in love with a martial hero, and by recapitulating the heterosexual theatrics of the love story, the citation ironically constructs for the team's fans a feminine subject position of passionate, delirious, despairing, and transgressive sexual desire, combining feminine gender role, homosexual desire, melodramatic histrionics, racial difference, and subversive wit.

In particular, the operatic citation points to the possibility of an erotic connection between the fans, who voice the send-off, and the team members, who represent the gym at the tournament not only as its protagonists, but also as the sexual partners (or perhaps as the desired sexual partners) of (some of) its members. Which is a reminder that we're dealing with an openly *gay* gym here, in which the team members qualify not only as figures of local pride, but also as figures of implicit erotic admiration and even explicit sexual appreciation. The allusion to *Aida* imparts a specifically erotic dimension to the ordinary practices and pleasures of athletic hero-worship, at once literalizing and sexually allegorizing the heroic qualities of the sporting hero. The success of this gay male cultural appropriation of opera depends, then, not only on its coding for gender, but also—at least once the gay subject is positioned in the subject position of a desiring straight woman—on its coding for gay sexuality.

Furthermore, it is worth emphasizing the melodramatic thematics of secret, illicit, forbidden, foredoomed love, which contributes to making the love of Aida a possible basis for homosexual identification. Yet another part of the effect of the citation derives from its deliberate, knowing incongruity, from the consciousness of the comic inappropriateness of citing grand opera in the context of a competitive sporting event—especially given the former's feminine gender coding and the latter's masculine one, as well as the former's highbrow coding as an elite art form requiring only cool, disengaged spectatorship and the latter's lowbrow coding as a participatory activity proper to mass culture that calls for sweaty exertion on the part of anyone and everyone who claims to be a real man.

Finally, the multiple intended ironies of this incongruous citation underwrite a sense of in-group distinctiveness, solidarity, and unity of sentiment among the members of the gym—that is, a sense of collective *identity* (something that is proper to locally based sports clubs supporting individual teams). The fact that the supporters of *this* team can cheer their athletes on by using *this* reference to *Aida* implies that they share, or that they can be presumed to share (I'm sure there must have been some guys who didn't get it), a common set of social practices and cultural understandings distinctive to gay men. The allusion to *Aida* thereby serves to consolidate the identity of the members of the gym as belonging to a particular social group—a group composed of gay men—which subscribes to a particular, typical, or stereotypical, culture.

In short, the multiple ironies produced by invoking opera in the context of a sporting event impart to the members of the gym a shared consciousness of being part of a specifically gay collectivity. Those ironies also undermine the chauvinism that typically attaches to team sports: it is impossible to take the valediction "Ritorna vincitor!" straight. So the overall effect of the operatic reference is to transform and transvalue the nature and definition of team spirit in order to make an altered, ironic version of it available to the gay members of this gym. Which becomes possible once athletic competition is rid of its conventional function in heterosexual culture—that is, once it no longer operates as an instrument of terror typically used to intimidate boys into masculine conformity—and is transformed into a counterpublic vehicle of communal gay male knowingness, of conscious erotic and cultural solidarity.

☙❧

This instance of gay male feminine identification, then, actually expresses neither an underlying female nature nor a masculine one, nor something in between. Rather, it expresses something else—something specifically gay. It actually helps to constitute a gay identity that does not equate straightforwardly with any existing gender position, but that is defined instead by its dissonance, by its departure from the conventional gender map of masculinity and femininity.

Gay male culture uses a female subject position and a feminine identification to contest the normal coding of cultural objects and activities in accordance with a strict gender polarity, masculine versus feminine, while also taking up a female subject position in order to make possible a sexualizing—in fact, a homosexualizing—of cultural activities (sports, opera) that are normally coded as heterosexual. The result is to refuse the dominant sexual- and gender-coding of cultural values and to forge a non-standard, dissident relation to cultural practices, a relation more in tune with gay desire.

Gay male culture does not exactly position its subjects at some intermediary point—halfway, say—between masculinity and femininity. It affords an alternative, a new set of possibilities. Just as the counter-thematics of style can be reduced neither to content nor to form, which means such counter-thematics can be pegged neither to masculinity nor to femininity, and should not therefore be confused either with depths of hidden meaning or the meaningless, purely sensuous sheen of surfaces, so gay male culture's melodramatic style allows no calamity, and no emotion that calamity awakens, to be perceived as purely tragic or purely pathetic. Hence, gay male culture's melodramatic style treats love not as pure passion or as pure irony, but always as something else that, rather than existing somewhere in between the two, incorporates elements of both while departing from them.

Gay male culture's investment in style as a thematics of its own implies a uniquely gay male form of reading. The only way to analyze gay male culture is to use this uniquely gay male form of reading to read the styles that gay male culture forges. This is not to say that only gay men can understand gay male culture. Rather, gay male culture itself is a form of understanding, a way of seeing men, women, and the world.

18

IRONY AND MISOGYNY

*G*ay male subjectivity may be socially constituted, but social constructions are not irreversible fatalities: they are not inescapable determinations.[1] They may not be alterable at will, susceptible of being rebuilt at any moment from the ground up according to a totally new design, but they do allow some room for improvisation, resistance, negotiation, and resignification. It may not be possible to undo your social positioning, but it is possible to own it, to take advantage of it, to reorient it, to turn it to perverse reuses. Gay male cultural practices and identifications (such as the camp citation of "Ritorna vincitor!") illustrate that point.

Gay male cultural practices, then, are comprehensible in the context of the larger system of interrelated cultural values that collectively define both personal and social identity within contemporary American society. But that context alone does not determine how gay cultural practices work or what effects they achieve. The cultural practice of male homosexuality often aims to forge a particular, dissident relation to heteronormative cultural values, a necessary and determined resistance to the dominant sexist and heterosexist coding of them, and a distinctive, perverse recoding of them—which is to say, a queering of them. Let us summarize how that queering operates in the case of gay femininity.

The homosexual desire that gay men feel places them in the subject position of women, and marks them symbolically as feminine, but it also allows them to retain at least some features of traditionally masculine gender roles. Many gay male cultural practices accentuate the feminine positioning of gay men, actively encouraging their participants (of either sex) to take up the socially devalued and marginalized position of women, and even to exaggerate its marginality and degradation.

Gay male cultural practices therefore tend to place their subjects, whether those subjects be gay or straight, in the position of the excluded, the disqualified, the performative, the inauthentic, the unserious, the pathetic, the melodramatic, the excessive, the artificial, the hysterical, the feminized. In this, gay culture simply acknowledges its location—the larger social situation in which gay men find themselves in straight society—as well as its unique relation to the constellation of social values attached to that society's dominant cultural forms. Given how both social and psychic life, both the social world and human subjectivity, are structured in a heteronormative society, and given heteronormative society's hostile judgment against both homosexuality and effeminacy, gay men have little choice but to occupy that abject, feminized realm.

But we can still resist our social positioning. And the most immediate way for gay men to defy social humiliation, and to assert our own subjective agency, is not to deny our abjection, or strive to overcome it, but actively to claim it—by taking on the hated social identity that has been affixed to us. That identity, after all, is the only identity we have. Resistance to it requires us to engage with it, to find value in it, and to invent opportunities for self-affirmation in the limited but very real possibilities that it makes available to us, which include possibilities of manipulating, redeploying, renegotiating, resignifying, and perverting it. Whence gay male culture's tendency to carve out for its participants an absurdly exaggerated, excessive, degraded feminine identity, which is also a highly ironic one, clearly designed to support a larger strategy of political defiance.

Gay male culture typically assumes an abject position only to redefine it, to invert the values associated with it, to take an ironic distance from them, to challenge them, and to turn them against themselves. For example, gay male culture applies the label "melodramatic" to itself, not just to those it laughs at, thereby throwing a wrench into the machinery of social depreciation. For to forgo any claim to social dignity is also to preempt others' efforts to demean you, and it is to strike an ironic attitude toward your own suffering. It is to refuse the cultural dichotomy that treats the suffering of others as *either* tragic *or* (merely) pathetic, according to their degree of social prestige. It is to know one's own hurt to be laughable, without ceasing to feel it—and to embrace inauthenticity as an ironic means of contesting other people's claims to seriousness, thereby challenging the underlying logic of social devaluation that trivializes the pain of unserious people.

Such ironic reuses of melodrama do not contest elite society's punitive judgments against that disreputable subgenre, but knowingly embrace them, calling down on the necessarily flamboyant performance of feelings judged to be pathetic the social contempt that such performances also defy. Gay male culture's self-consciously melodramatic ethos explains the high value it sets on artificiality, performance, inauthenticity, camp humor, and a disabused (but not disenchanted) perspective on love.

By taking up, while ironically redefining, the social roles and meanings traditionally assigned to women, gay male culture performs a unique, immanent social critique and effects a characteristic but recognizable form of political resistance.

ᖬᖬ

Gay male culture's simultaneous embrace and ironic reversal of the abject social positioning of women may help to explain certain perennial misunderstandings between gay men and feminists, as well as the reputation for misogyny that gay male culture has acquired. Far from attempting to elevate the position of women, to re-present them as dignified, serious, heroic, authoritative, capable, talented, loving, pro-

tective, and generally better than men—far from attempting to promote a *positive image* of women, in other words—traditional gay male
culture consistently delights in excessive, grotesque, artificial, undignified, revolting, abject portrayals of femininity, and it seeks its own
reflection in them. It can afford to do so, because gay men, being
men, are—unlike women—never in danger of being completely reduced to their social marking or positioning as feminine.

Women themselves, however, may not always find the experience of being women terribly ironic, let alone downright hilarious,
although they may well want or need, on occasion, to step back from
it and to distance themselves from its social meanings. To women,
therefore, gay male culture may appear to collaborate with straight
male culture in denigrating women; it may seem to reinforce the depreciation and devalorization of women, implicit or explicit, that is
typical of patriarchal societies and of the cultural attitudes upheld
by them. Despite its loving celebration of various divas, stars, and
feminine-identified activities, gay male culture's investments in femininity may well seem entirely consistent with a pronounced hostility to real women.[2] Hence, the eternal feminist reproach: that's *not*
funny.

I believe the tension between traditional gay male culture and feminism is based at least in part on a misunderstanding of the political
design of gay male culture. The gay male cult of Joan Crawford, as
I have interpreted it, allows me to clear up some of that misunderstanding, if not all of it.

Gay male culture's embrace of degrading representations of the
feminine is not an endorsement of them. Those representations, after
all, are ridiculous—at least, they appear to be ridiculous as soon as
one is no longer either the chief beneficiary of them or the immediate, personal target of them (as gay men are not). Gay male culture's
appropriation of those representations is not approving but strategic.
Its acceptance of a position of disempowerment, which gay men
partly share with women, is merely provisory, merely the first stage in

a strategy of resistance. To be sure, it does express a sense of the futility of attempting to escape wholly, once and for all, from a position of social disempowerment—the futility of trying to seal yourself off from the damaging impact of degrading representations. But there is a certain wisdom in the acceptance of disempowerment.

After all, you can't overcome social denigration merely by inverting its terms, by attempting to substitute positive images for negative ones. As anyone who has lived through the second wave of feminism has now had ample opportunity to observe, every supposedly positive image of women that feminists attempt to promote quickly gets reconfigured by our society into an offensive and oppressive stereotype. For example, once the upstanding, dignified, capable figure of the "strong" woman, so dear to feminism, migrates to Hollywood, she quickly turns into either an impossible, unattainable paragon (*Charlie's Angels: Full Throttle,* from 2003) or a power-hungry, castrating, love-starved, unfeminine monster (*Fatal Attraction,* from 1987). So there is no safety in so-called positive representations—*especially when you don't have the social power to make them stick.* Other strategies of resistance are necessary.

Gay male culture's active passivity, its delight and pride in submission, its willingness to identify with the terms in which women and gay men are caricatured or demeaned, should be seen not as a ratification of those terms, but as another expression of the camp intuition that there is no outside to power, that minorities and stigmatized groups cannot choose how we are regarded and what value our society sets on our lives. We are subject, like it or not, to social conditions and cultural codes that we do not have the power to alter (not in the short run, anyway), only the power to resist. Taking up a position in which we are inexorably situated is not to consolidate it, nor is it to accept the adverse conditions under which we accede to representation. It is the beginning of a process of reversal and resignification: it is a way of claiming ownership of our situation with the specific purpose of turning it around, or at least trying to turn it to our account.[3] As we have already observed, dominant social roles and meanings cannot be destroyed, but they can be undercut and derealized: it is possible to learn how not to take them straight.

ۼ

If gay male culture embraces the disqualification of femininity, then, it does so in order to challenge and to interrupt some of the most noxious consequences of that disqualification, for gay men if not for women. Its strategy is to reappropriate an already degraded femininity and to redefine that degraded status ironically, so as to contest the nexus of values responsible for its degradation, to dismantle others' claims to dignity, and thus to level the social playing field. Feminists recognize this, of course, but many of them tend to be unpersuaded by it, unconvinced of the wisdom of the camp strategy of accepting, appropriating, citing, and recoding hateful representations. With the notable exceptions of Esther Newton, Judith Butler, and their followers, many feminists—especially straight feminists—tend to regard irony as a poor alibi for the recirculation and perpetuation of demeaning stereotypes. Irony, on their view, cannot excuse the sin of compounding the original social insult.

But gay male culture's strategic, ironic reappropriation of a devalorized *femininity* neither implies nor produces a continued insult to *women*. For gay femininity, though it necessarily *refers to* women, is not necessarily *about* women, as we have seen. Just as gay femininity often consists in cultural practices (diva-worship or architectural restoration) that are socially marked as feminine but have nothing to do with femininity as it is embodied by women themselves, so gay male culture's delight in grotesque versions of femininity does not imply a contempt for or a hostility to actual women. Many gay male cultural practices that feature female figures, that refer to women or that mobilize aspects of femininity, have in fact *nothing at all to do with women*.

In most versions of camp humor, for example, it is not actual women who are objects of mirth (or envy, or admiration) but contemporary cultural constructions of the feminine—femininity in its performative dimension, femininity as social theater. The target is the already anti-feminist model of femininity produced by the heteronormative order and promoted by its gender ideology.

Gay male culture's knowing embrace of degraded models of femininity does not in fact constitute a gay male insult to women, in other words, because it is *femininity*—not *women*—that is being insulted. Nor are gay men the ones who are doing the insulting. It is the larger cultural symbolism of femininity itself, and the social semantics of gender in which that symbolism is inscribed, that constitute an insult to women. But gay men are not responsible for *that*. On the contrary, gay men are themselves the victims of the cultural symbolism of femininity—though they suffer from it differently from women. Gay male culture's anti-social brand of aesthetics adopts that symbolism precisely in order to challenge it.

If gay male culture borrows the demeaning cultural symbolism attached to femininity, and if it even takes pleasure in doing so, that is because it sees a strategic opportunity, which it gleefully exploits, in feminine identification—an opportunity to undo the seriousness with which our society treats its own gender constructions. In the course of claiming femininity as a proxy identity for gay men, gay male culture exposes and denaturalizes it. It combats the cultural symbolism of femininity by magnifying its absurdities. The effect, which may not always be deliberate or intended, is to explode that cultural symbolism—to undermine its power and authority, to puncture its solemn respectability, and to erode its plausibility. By treating feminine identities as roles instead of essences, as social performances instead of natural conditions, gay culture threatens their dignity as well as their legitimacy and thereby weakens their claims on our belief. But it also goes further and shows up the mad extravagance of our cultural constructions of the feminine. *For femininity, as our society imagines it, reveals its utter incoherence, excessiveness, and absurdity more clearly when it is embodied and enacted by men than when it is embodied and enacted by women.*

Women, too, have had to struggle against the social category of the feminine. Femininity as we know it is a sexist construction, and women are the ones who are most affected by it. It is they who suffer from it the most. Women therefore have to figure out how to take advantage, if they can, of the prestige and social rewards that conventional femininity makes available to them, without purchasing respectability at the price of their own devalorization, of their own trivialization and abjection. That is no easy trick. At the very least, feminist politics requires the partial desymbolization and derealization of femininity as it is currently defined, practiced, and enforced; it demands the disaggregation of femininity from womanhood and femaleness. Which means that feminist politics depends on the possibility of seeing gender as a role, as a performance, as something other than natural or authentic.[4] Gay male culture, as I have tried to describe it, is entirely consistent with that project and offers powerful support for it.

This doesn't mean that gay male culture is exempt from misogyny or that its feminist credentials are spotless.[5] Gay men can be misogynistic: Why, after all, should they be so different from anyone else—including both straight men and many women—in that unfortunate respect? Many drag shows are plainly divorced from any feminist consciousness; they are often blithely, casually misogynistic, and so are many other instances of gay male culture. The practices I have tended to focus on here may not be typical. They may not be representative of gay male culture as a whole.

But they do make an important point. The kind of gay male culture that tends most to misogyny is likely to be the masculinist variety promoted by Jack Malebranche and the g0y brotherhood; they are the ones, after all, who dream of inhabiting a world without women (of any sex). Gay femininity may have its misogynist streak, but its misogyny tends to be less pronounced than the misogyny generated by gay masculinity in its panicked determination to eradicate any hint of the feminine in man.

If traditional gay male culture's ironic send-up of femininity does not necessarily express hostility to women, however, that still does not tell us what effects it has on actual women or how positive those effects are.

Furthermore, even though gay culture's parodies of femininity may denaturalize that conventional and socially devalued gender role, undercut its status as a natural essence, and treat it instead as a social performance—and even though gay culture's grotesque caricatures of femininity may sometimes be designed to achieve that very end— many women may feel that the target of all this gender parody is not *femininity* alone, but *femaleness* as such. They may feel that gay male aggression is being directed against the very condition of being a woman.

Convenient as it would be to maintain—for the purposes of framing a political apology for gay male culture—an absolutely airtight distinction between femininity as a gender role or performance and femaleness as a sexed or biological condition, the boundary between them often turns out to be less sharp or hermetic than one might wish, especially since some gay male cultural practices themselves tend to fudge it. And the distinction I have tried to draw between femininity and femaleness may be a distinction without a difference for many women, who often find the two categories difficult, if not impossible, to separate in their daily experiences of gender and gender identity. They may not be wrong to feel personally targeted, to feel attacked in their very being as women, by gay male culture's exuberant portrayals of extravagant, flamboyant, hysterical, suffering, debased, or abject femininity.

Let us reconsider the Fire Island Italian widows from this perspective. Their act, I argued, is not misogynist: it does not express hatred for women, so much as envy of some women's ability to carry off a public spectacle of private pain. By putting on Italian-widow drag, they attempted to appropriate for themselves, however ironically, a feminine role that they would ordinarily be denied. Their demonstration of the performativity of Italian widowhood aimed to make the status of widow transferable to themselves, so they could claim the social privileges that go with that status—namely, the entitlement to grieve for lost loved ones before the eyes of the world.

But the very appropriation of that honorable female role can also be seen as a male theft of female privilege, as a familiar instance of masculine cultural imperialism. It typifies the male insistence on claiming the status of a universal subject—the status of one to whom no experience, and no social role, is ever definitively closed. Moreover, since being a widow is one of the few gender-specific, conventional feminine roles that is held in wide esteem, and that commands a certain social power and prestige, when gay men claim it, they deprive women of their monopoly on it, and of the social dignity that accrues to them via their unique ownership of it.

It is of course entirely consistent with the logic and implicit politics of gay male cultural practices to hold that no one is naturally or automatically entitled to that kind of dignity, and that it is dishonorable to claim a social privilege at the expense of others in a world in which some people are disqualified from serious consideration because of their social marking. But there are many people, some women among them, who do not share that view. Those who feel that the grounds of their own social dignity are being trespassed, or even pulled out from under them, may not welcome that undeniable political encroachment—especially when the social privileges attaching to their conventional gender identity are already so few, so far between, so provisional, and so easily forfeited. Women do have something to lose in this situation, even if it is not something that gay male culture considers worth retaining. So they would be entirely justified in objecting to losing it.

The Fire Island Italian widows could claim that they do not address themselves to women—that straight women, at least, are not the direct, intended, immediate audience of their performance. The same is true of many gay male cultural practices. To the extent that the politics of gay male culture may require defending or salvaging, that task is easier to accomplish when we consider that much of gay culture takes place within a largely tribal context: it is undertaken and carried out among the members of a specific social group, and it is destined for in-group consumption. It is not specifically targeted at heterosexual women or designed for a straight social world where it could well produce obnoxious effects for all women, where it might lower them in the eyes of straight men and encourage or comfort the latter in their misogyny. Context and reception make a big difference. Within the confines of its own tribal universe, the political effect of gay male culture's caricatures of femininity may actually turn out to be comparatively harmless to women.

Nonetheless, it is worth asking what the cumulative effect or impact of gay male culture on women ultimately is. What does gay femininity do for women, not just for gay men? Straight women and lesbians, butch women and femme women, and women variously positioned along a transgender spectrum have all responded differently to gay male cultural reappropriations of femininity. It is certainly legitimate to inquire where such reappropriations leave all these actual women, and whether gay femininity contributes to the improvement or impairment of women's symbolic, discursive, and material situations. Those interesting, complex questions demand to be addressed on a case-by-case basis. Although a full-scale treatment of them would exceed the scope of this study, and should be reserved for a separate, detailed analysis, it may be possible to shed some light on those questions by examining one test case that brings out the distinctiveness of gay male culture's relation to femininity and helps to define more precisely the specific political thrust of its irony.[6]

ള☙

In 1990 Sonic Youth, the classic punk / grunge / indie rock band, creators of *Confusion Is Sex* (their first album, issued in 1983), included a song, or scream—in any case, a track—called "Mildred Pierce" on their cross-over *Goo* CD, their first release for Geffen Records. The song is actually one of Sonic Youth's earliest compositions. Its initial title was "Blowjob." The original nine-minute demo tape of that track can be heard on the 2005 deluxe reissue of *Goo*.[7]

The nature of the connection between oral sex and Joan Crawford's cinematic alter ego may not be immediately evident. The evil genius responsible for the association turns out to be Raymond Pettibon, a graphic artist much beloved of Sonic Youth's bass player Kim Gordon and widely popular in the Los Angeles punk scene (Pettibon's older brother founded the legendary band Black Flag).[8] According to Stevie Chick, "The title [of the track] . . . was taken from a T-shirt owned by Thurston [Moore, the group's lead singer and guitarist], featuring a Raymond Pettibon illustration of Hollywood diva Joan Crawford in her role as the titular heroine of classic noir *Mildred Pierce*, with the word 'Blowjob?' scrawled underneath."[9] "Blowjob" was initially intended to be the title of both the track and the entire Geffen Records CD, with Pettibon's image of Crawford reproduced on its sleeve, but when David Geffen overruled that idea, the song was edited down to two minutes and retitled "Mildred Pierce," the CD was renamed *Goo*, and a different Pettibon image was chosen for the cover.[10]

Sonic Youth are perfectly queer-friendly. Their cultural references include many gay artists and works. And in 1994 the band achieved gay immortality with "Androgynous Mind" (on *Experimental Jet Set, Trash and No Star*) which—perhaps by way of tribute to their newly deceased protégé and fan Kurt Cobain—reclaimed God for gay identity:

> Hey sad angel walks, and he talks like a girl
> Out trying to think why it stinks, he's not a girl
> Now he's kicked in the gut, they fucked him up, just enough
> They got me down on my knees, I kiss his ring, God is love
>
> Androgynous mind, androgynous mind
> Androgynous mind, androgynous mind
> Androgynous mind, androgynous mind

Hey hey are you gay? are you God?
My brain's a bomb, to turn you on
Everything is all right
God is gay, and you were right[11]

God may be gay, but Sonic Youth are not. Thurston Moore and Kim
Gordon got married in 1984 and stayed married, to each other, for
twenty-seven years.

Sonic Youth's take on Joan Crawford is not easy to gauge from
"Mildred Pierce." The track itself is largely instrumental, and the lyrics are pretty rudimentary:

Mildred Pierce
MILDRED!!!!!!
MILDRED PIERCE!!!!!
MILDRED PIERCE!!!!!
NOOOOOOOOOOOOOOOOOOOOOOOOOOOH!!!!!!!!!!
MILDRED PIERCE!!!!!
MILDRED PIERCE!!!!!
WHYYYYYYYYYYYYYYYYYYYYYYY!!!?!!!!
MILDRED PIERCE!!!!!
WHAAAAAAAAAAAAAAHHHH!!!!!!!!!!!![12]

What does Mildred Pierce do for Sonic Youth? The question is
worth asking, because straight hipster irony is probably the dominant
mode nowadays of detaching and appropriating bits of mainstream
culture and refashioning them into vehicles of cultural dissidence, according to a process analogous to the gay male cultural practice we
have been examining.

If we want to figure out straight hipster culture's attitude to Joan
Crawford and her Oscar-winning role, we will learn more by examining Dave Markey's 1990 music video of Sonic Youth's "Mildred Pierce"
than by poring over the lyrics of the band's track on *Goo*. The video
includes performance clips and shots of the band members playing their instruments (including a shirtless Moore with "MILDRED

PIERCE" written on his hairless, adorably scrawny chest in what purports to be lipstick), alternating with pans of movie marquees, of Joan Crawford's star on Hollywood Boulevard, and of other locations in and around Hollywood. But the most interesting feature of the video is a flamboyant impersonation of Joan Crawford by Markey's friend Sophia Coppola, who appears briefly but repeatedly throughout the video in a series of very rapid cameos.[13]

The exact tenor and tone of Coppola's performance, as well as the particular impression it leaves, are hard to describe in mere words. You have to watch the video (it's available on YouTube and on Sonic Youth's 2004 DVD *Corporate Ghost: The Videos, 1990–2002*).[14] In the context of a printed book, the best I can do to convey the video's general flavor is to include a few stills from it.

An online commentator on the video, a fan of Sonic Youth, tries to capture "what SY are trying to convey" by remarking, "Sometimes I imagine that they're channeling Ms. Crawford's inner turmoil and pain."[15]

That may be true of Moore's singing, or screaming, though the track's original title, "Blowjob," implies a less sentimental and more satirical attitude. Kim Gordon, however, describing her fascination with the spectacle of onstage "vulnerability," especially after a performer has experienced a "breakdown," provides some justification for the fan's compassionate reading of the video. Here she is speaking about Mariah Carey and Karen Carpenter, but her remark could apply just as easily to Joan Crawford: "I'm sure they're similar A-type personalities—driven perfectionists who just want to please people so much."[16] Gordon seems drawn to vulnerable female performers who hurt themselves in their drive to provide their audiences with a display of perfection.

Whether or not Sonic Youth actually felt Joan Crawford's pain, Coppola's portrayal of Crawford in Markey's video does not come off as especially empathetic. Coppola certainly delivers a brilliant, exaggerated, highly theatrical rendition of conventional femininity run amok—"if you can call that acting," she is reported to have said.[17]

23 Frame capture from the music video "Mildred Pierce" (Dave Markey, 1990). Sophia Coppola as Faye Dunaway as Joan Crawford, complete with wire hanger.

24 Frame capture from the music video "Mildred Pierce" (Dave Markey, 1990). The ordeal of lipstick.

With her pouting, bloated, painted lips (to which she applies lipstick in one sequence; see Figure 24), her thick, darkened eyebrows, her bulging eyes lined with black mascara, and her 1960s outfit, Coppola could just as easily be doing a Maria Callas imitation. She tilts her head back, so as to display the whites of her eyes; she looks wildly about, her mouth held in a wide grimace; she impulsively raises her hands to smooth her hair, thrusts them pleadingly and defensively in

25 Frame capture from the music video "Mildred Pierce" (Dave Markey, 1990). Gasping for breath.

26 Frame capture from the music video "Mildred Pierce" (Dave Markey, 1990). The scream.

front of her, or runs them down either side of her neck, as if gasping for breath. The ultimate effect is one of hysterical excess, rather in keeping with Moore's screaming.

The image of Joan Crawford that Coppola projects is grotesque, even mildly censorious. Her Crawford is narcissistic, maniacally obsessed with her appearance, though unable to restrain her movements or to control the seething anxieties that burst through her elegant, well-coiffed, carefully put-together persona. Coppola's performance

is an absolutely classic enactment of a woman visibly "losing it"—
what Gordon, perhaps, would describe as breakdown and vulnerability—and it pays tribute to Faye Dunaway's precedent-setting star turn
in *Mommie Dearest,* which taught us to treat Crawford herself as a
kind of visual shorthand for feminine glamour and abjection combined, for delirious extravagance and dramatic, hysterical, helpless
disintegration. It's as if Coppola were imitating a drag queen imitating Faye Dunaway imitating Joan Crawford.

For that reason alone, the relation to femininity staged by Markey
in the music video makes gay male culture's relation to femininity
look comparatively simple and straightforward by comparison. The
band members present themselves as deliriously passionate Joan
Crawford devotees, but the attitude to Crawford implied by Coppola's knowingly over-the-top portrayal tells a dizzyingly complex story.

∾

The SY video seeks to acquire a certain hip credibility by impressing
its audience with its suave deployment of some obscure, wacky, dated
cultural references. It uses the disturbing twistedness of the arcane
material it has unearthed to consolidate a group identity around that
bit of dark insider knowledge, thereby setting its social world and its
audience apart from the unhip, the normals. Joan Crawford, or her
commodified image, provides a means of registering difference and
dissent from mainstream American culture.

Hence, Coppola's performance is *intended* to be camp.[18] She can't
afford to be taken straight. She *tries* to look like a drag queen, and her
act directly appeals to the precedent of drag performance, already understood to be at one remove from the involuntary impersonation
of authorized gender models—from the everyday normative performance of gender—that is femininity itself.[19] She delivers an imitation
of an imitation of an imitation, and our hip understanding of that—
if, indeed, we *are* hip enough to get it—is registered by the irony and
knowingness with which we view Coppola's performance. The video
encourages us to take up a stance of mingled detachment and superi-

ority, as we enjoy our shared sense of being in on a joke. There is, in other words, nothing ironic about this irony: it is, as irony goes, perfectly serious.

Faye Dunaway, by contrast, is not a drag queen. Nor was she trying to imitate one when she portrayed Crawford, even if her kabuki-like makeup often made her face look like a mask and her volcanic outbursts of rage, self-pity, despair, and emotional need typically achieved a physical expression so outlandish and so undignified as to be at odds with conventional female embodiment. It was left to gay male culture to appropriate her performance and to claim for ourselves her spectacular failure to sustain a serious, moralistic portrayal of a deeply disturbed and dysfunctional woman. Gay male culture's embrace of *Mommie Dearest* encourages gay men to occupy that abject position, making it ironically our own, identifying with such demented femininity while also refusing to take it literally—thereby resisting the film's tendency to treat women as the locus of some awesome, frightening, demonic Otherness, as the vehicles of a dangerous and destructive emotional excess that is, supposedly, wholly unique to them.

The SY video also refuses to take Joan Crawford's demented femininity seriously, and it similarly delights in Coppola's failure to project a tragic, authentic image of a glamorous woman on the verge of a nervous breakdown. So its gender politics could be described in analogous terms. But where camp is inclusive, straight hipster irony is exclusive. It invites us to enjoy, not to share, Coppola's/Crawford's insane histrionics. The figure of Joan Crawford serves as a ready-made symbol of out-of-control, female freakishness and camp extravagance, but the video encourages no real participation in the extravagance and not much sympathy with the freakishness. Sonic Youth do not genuinely aspire to make such freakishness their own.

Instead, Coppola's caricature of Crawford expresses Sonic Youth's distinctive, dissident slant on mainstream American entertainment. It signals the band's alienation from a consumer culture that already commodifies feminine emotion, that markets it and repackages samples of it for mass enjoyment. The ultimate purpose of Coppola's impersonation of a female impersonation of Joan Crawford is to grant Sonic Youth access to a subcultural style of queer cultural resistance, directly opposed to such commodification, which they can invoke, appropriate for themselves, and proffer to their audience as a hip alternative to it.

ᘉᘁᘉ

Straight hipster culture actually thrives on the "artificial appropriation of different styles from different eras," according to a scathing cover story about hipsters in the hipster magazine *Adbusters;* it loves to play with "symbols and icons" of marginalized or oppressed groups, once those symbols and icons "have been appropriated by hipsterdom and drained of meaning."[20] In another, now-notorious attack on hipsters, Christian Lorentzen goes even further. "Under the guise of 'irony,'" he complains, "hipsterism fetishizes the authentic and regurgitates it with a winking inauthenticity."[21]

Lorentzen was anticipated by queer playwright Charles Ludlam, founder and director of the Ridiculous Theatrical Company in New York. Ludlam did not live long enough to know and to despise hipsters, but he had already come across what he termed "heterosexual camp," for which he had very little esteem: "The thing that's really horrible is heterosexual camp, a kind of winking at you saying, 'I don't really mean it.'"[22] By contrast, the kind of irony that defines gay male camp does not express distance or disavowal. As we have seen, it is fully compatible with passion, pain, and belief.[23]

Although hipsterism's habit of ironic citation—fetishizing the authentic and regurgitating it with a winking inauthenticity, as Lorentzen puts it—certainly resembles camp, and although the SY video engages in a subcultural practice that is arguably analogous to camp, there is in fact a clear distinction to be drawn between the two. The SY video fetishizes camp itself and grounds its own cultural identity, or anti-identity, by looking to camp for authenticity, by invoking it as an authentic counter-cultural aesthetic practice, which hipsters can then ironize and thereby deauthenticate in their turn.

That procedure is the exact opposite of the gay male cultural practice we have been studying. Instead of appropriating, and queering, mainstream cultural objects, straight hipsterism delights in reappropriating minority cultural forms, seizing authentically queer or dissident "symbols and icons," and using them to consolidate its own identity, while exempting itself—through its heterosexual privilege and its hip knowingness—from the social disqualifications that gave rise to those anti-social forms in the first place.

By treating camp as its straight man, as fodder for its irony—by trying to produce a camp version of camp, through reappropriating gay male culture's appropriation of *Mildred Pierce*—straight hipster culture turns a gay cultural practice into a vehicle for the affirmation of its own identity, or anti-identity. It makes that practice into a means of asserting its alienated perspective and consolidating its anti-social credentials. But it does so without maintaining any further affiliation or identification with gay male culture. The video appropriates gay symbols and icons, just as the *Adbusters* article says, while draining them of specifically homosexual meaning.[24]

Gay male culture does the same thing with symbols and icons of femininity, of course—but in draining them of their sexist meaning, it performs a specific act of civil disobedience, of political resistance. The effect of the SY video is rather different. And here, it seems to me, is where we can measure the divergence between the queer performance styles on which Coppola draws for her impersonation of Joan Crawford and the kind of straight hipster irony her antics authorize—the kind of irony that permeates this video.

Hipsters have to be ironic about identity. Because they would never seriously identify themselves as hipsters, they need their own identity as hipsters to be an anti-identity. Which is what every contemporary identity aspires to be. Every social identity nowadays disclaims its own identity; at least it wants the option, some of the time, to refuse identity "labels"—to be "post-[your identity here]." Contemporary, mainstream gay identity also likes to deny its difference, to play down its social salience, to soft-pedal its queerness, as we have seen. But camp does just the opposite: it is nothing if not flamboyant. Once you use "Ritorna vincitor!" to send off your local volleyball team, you really have no place left to hide.

Unlike camp, which allows no possibility for distance or dis-identi-fication, straight hipster irony is at once satirical and apathetic; it signals both detachment from and a certain sense of superiority to the "authentic" cultural forms and aesthetic practices that hipsterism fetishizes—even if it is quite fond of them, in its way. By acknowledging straight hipsters' affection for such quaint cultural forms and practices, while refusing to express that affection except in a grotesque, exaggerated fashion, in case someone should get the wrong idea, straight hipster irony maintains and consolidates (though it's much too cool to flaunt it) a distant and disengaged position for hipsters—that is, a position of relative social privilege.[25]

∞

The point is effectively underscored and exemplified by a line in an ironic article on irony, dated February 3, 2008, posted to the website called "Stuff White People Like," and now published in a best-selling book of the same title. Written by "clander" (Christian Lander), the founder of the site, the article expresses a hipsterish take on White hipsters—meaning, actually, straight, upper-middle-class White hipsters. Lander, a Canadian and a self-described "PhD dropout" who now lives in Los Angeles, has a number of interesting and amusing things to say about irony's appeal to such people, about why irony figures so prominently among the stuff White people like. His most telling and self-aware observation seems to be the following: "But the reason that white people love irony is that it lets them have some fun and feel better about themselves."[26]

That kind of irony allows cool straight prosperous White people, including Lander, to deal with the shame of being privileged and

White by distancing themselves from the culture to which they already belong, comforting them with the possibility of being less than fully implicated in it, positioning themselves above it and outside of it through a critical perspective on it, as well as through an identification with marginalized people, thereby allowing them to continue to participate in it with a clearer conscience. I doubt many of us would accept that as a good description of camp irony, which—at least as I have described it—leaves its practitioners little opportunity for self-exemption.

๑ฒ

Despite its frank delight in absurd and outlandish sexist representations, gay male culture's ironic appropriation of femininity does not express a lack of personal implication in those representations or a sense of invulnerability to the symbolic violence of reductive stereotypes. On the contrary, it indicates a willingness to see oneself reflected in such sexist representations. It demonstrates an exhilaration in identifying with the lowest of the low, and it signals a resistance to the cultural technology by which social exclusion is brought about. It therefore implies a greater degree of solidarity with women, or at least a greater investment in struggles against sexism, than does the straight exploitation of camp style, which distances itself from the female figures whose demented flamboyance it takes such pleasure in staging.

"Camp means a lot at a gathering of queers," wrote Richard Dyer in 1977, especially when it is "used defiantly by queers against straightness: but it is very easily taken up by straight society and used against us." The straight media "appreciate the wit, but they don't see why it is necessary. They pick up the undertow of self-oppression without ever latching on to the elements of criticism and defiance of straightness." Which is to say, "The context of camp is important too. . . . So much depends on what you feel about men and women, about sex, about being gay."[27]

PART SIX

What Is Gay Culture?

JUDY GARLAND VERSUS IDENTITY ART

In the run-up to New York's Gay Pride celebration, in June of 2008, *Time Out New York (TONY)* published a feature called "What Is Gay Culture?"[1] The staffers of the magazine acknowledged that the answer to that question eluded them. They tried to compensate for their inability to meet the challenge they had set themselves by making a classic defensive gesture, combining humility with defiance: "We realize that we don't have all the answers," they admitted, "but we do know that it's the questions themselves that really matter" (16). Although I shall have some unkind things to say about their effort, I can only sympathize with their feelings of inadequacy, with their embarrassment at failing to meet the expectations they had gone out of their way to raise. Unlike them, however, I'm in no position to be defiant.

It is an awful thing to have an idea that is bigger than you are. Many are the times I regretted ever setting out to understand the relation between male homosexuality and cultural form or to explain the logic behind gay male culture's fascination with particular artifacts of mainstream culture. I'm not an expert on popular culture, and I have no background in any style profession, so I wasn't well equipped to take this project on. I have stuck with it, even though I knew I would never be able to come up with all the answers, or even very many of them, precisely because the questions matter more than any answers

I could produce. But that has not made me less determined to find at least some answers.

If my course "How To Be Gay" had not caused a scandal, and if it had not done so repeatedly, I probably would not have made myself write this book. I simply would have taught the course, using the class discussions to explore the central questions about gay male subjectivity that puzzled me, coming up with various ideas, hypotheses, and solutions, working through them with a generation of students, and publishing occasional essays on the topic, as moments of enlightenment offered themselves to me. But once the course became notorious, it was clear that I would need to do more to justify the entire project—to address the topic in some sustained, if partial, fashion, and to arrive at some real answers.

As I tried to answer the unanswerable questions I had set myself, I came to have a lot of admiration for earlier writers on the topic who did manage to produce distinguished answers, convincing interpretations of male homosexuality as a cultural practice. I see my own efforts as supplementing theirs, not superseding them. From Jean-Paul Sartre to Susan Sontag, from Esther Newton to Neil Bartlett, from D. A. Miller to Richard Dyer, a number of previous thinkers and researchers have puzzled over the issues, and I have tried to take advantage of their insights and to pay tribute to their achievements. But I have not attempted to summarize their ideas, to synthesize them, or to systematize them and consolidate them into a kind of *summa*.

When I started out on this adventure, I was more ambitious. I wanted to explain all of gay culture. I intended to integrate everything into a single, comprehensive theory. I even had my own hypotheses about the reasons for the gay male appeal of Judy Garland. (But because Richard Dyer had already accounted for it so well, I did not feel the need to add further speculations of my own, even though I think that Dyer did miss a few things here and there and that more remains to be said.) I ultimately realized, however, that even if I could lay everything out, explain and justify my methods, anticipate and preempt all conceivable objections to my project, review and criticize the work of my predecessors, and build a single, coherent, cumulative argument, no one would put up with such an elaborate, ponderous exercise or want to read to the end the massive volume that would result.

And so I changed course, lightened my project and my prose, published certain parts of the overall argument separately,[2] and omitted a number of intuitions that could not be supported by the relatively limited analysis that I settled for undertaking in its stead—though I have tried to include a few of those intuitions here and there, sometimes by means of suggestion or insinuation, even if that meant making claims in passing that I didn't know how to defend.

I found that by concentrating my attention on a single figure, Joan Crawford, and on a single scene in a single movie, not only did I have more than enough material to go on, but the material I had was so rich in implications that it touched on many aspects of gay male culture which would have been impossible to treat fully, directly, and independently of one another in a single volume. So I confined myself to one cultural object, and to one instance of the pragmatics of genre, and I tried to draw out the wider implications of my limited material. The result, I hope, has been to shed light on an elusive topic—a topic that has been relatively neglected even within feminist studies and queer theory—namely, *the sexual politics of form.*

I am aware of the limitations of my approach. I would have liked to extend it further, to cover many facets of gay male culture and to write additional chapters about them. Any decent account of gay culture would have to survey and to examine a great number of its characteristic practices, genres, social and aesthetic forms. Opera, pop music, fashion and style, architecture and design, printing, painting and the fine arts; the gay lure of British culture, French culture, Arabic culture, Japanese culture; divas and their defining features in different national contexts (Mexico, Argentina, France, Turkey, Israel, Egypt, Lebanon, Japan); dishing, bitching, and camping; urbanity, suavity, and wit; even pet-ownership, especially the predilection for certain kinds of dogs and cats: all of that needs to be included in any general description of how to be gay.

And sex, what about sex? Cruising, body modification, open relationships, circuit parties, clubbing, pornography, intergenerational romance, friendship, and the distinctive combination of promiscuity and solitude, of erotic intensity and austerity, aestheticism and asceticism—how on earth could I have left out everything that makes gay male erotic life so distinctive and unique?

Well, you've got to start somewhere. You can't cover everything. No book can do it all. I also admit that there's something pleasingly perverse about devoting so much time nowadays to thinking about the gay appeal of an archaic figure like Joan Crawford and of a largely forgotten cult movie like *Mildred Pierce*. Of course, I needed to pick an established and uncontroversial example of gay men's cultural practices. I had to appeal to a well-documented case of gay men's emotional investments in selected bits of mainstream culture, even if that meant picking something old-fashioned and not terribly current.

In any case, there are particular advantages to studying a classic—a canonical work that is *not* of our time. Precisely because Joan Crawford does not loom large in our own culture, however we define it, we can attempt to inquire into her gay appeal without feeling personally implicated by the result—or, at least, without feeling quite so personally implicated as we might feel if we picked an object in which we are currently invested (like Lady Gaga). Our own identities are not immediately on the line. And even if we lack an instinctive understanding of what Joan Crawford meant to gay men of earlier eras, we at least have the privilege of being able to step back from the gravitational field of her powerful attraction and consider the nature of her appeal in a relatively detached, unimpassioned way—calmly, curiously, and from a number of possible perspectives—which means we are more easily able to forge a critical meta-language in which to talk about it.

෴

We also have the necessary distance at this point to ask a number of other questions. How would my account of gay male culture have had to change if it had revolved around a different figure? Some answers to *that* question have already been provided by Richard Dyer's study of gay men and Judy Garland, Neil Bartlett's study of gay men and Oscar Wilde, even D. A. Miller's study of gay men and the Broadway musical, all of which offer quite distinct visions of gay male culture and gay male subjectivity—though ones that are not incompatible with the picture I have sketched here.

For example, Richard Dyer's classic essay "Judy Garland and Gay Men" highlights her "combination of strength and suffering," identifying it as a source of her gay appeal.[3] That gripping combination would seem to correspond in certain ways to the combination of glamour and abjection that distinguishes Joan Crawford's screen persona and that accounts, at least in part, for the power she exercises over her gay male fans. Both strength/suffering and glamour/abjection could be reduced to a more basic formula, a general equation, an underlying structure defined by the binary of *power* and *vulnerability*. But the two sets of contrasting values are not at all the same, and the differences between them point in interestingly divergent directions. So it is not a good idea to abstract them, despecify them, generalize them, homogenize them, and reduce them to a universal grammar of gay male culture.

An interpretation of gay male culture based on a study of the gay appeal of Maria Callas or Tammy Faye Bakker or Tonya Harding or Oprah Winfrey or Princess Diana might well lead to some very different conclusions. It might not challenge the entire analysis I have laid out, since all of those gay icons exhibit some of the features displayed by Joan Crawford: a tendency to "lose it" in public, a talent for melodrama as well as for pathos, a volatile mix of glamour and abjection, and larger-than-life performances of conventional (if excessive) femininity. But the details of their embodiment and their star quality (or monstrosity) are all different, and those differences count. All of those figures need to be studied in their specificity in order to disclose the secret of their gay appeal. It is not useful at this point to amalgamate their features into a simple, imprecise diagram, a few general truths, a universal cultural grammar.

In any case, the constellation of genres, practices, and values that I have described—the whole camp-diva-abjection-aesthetics-roleplaying-inauthenticity-melodrama nexus—represents only one dimension of gay male culture and subjectivity. It is certainly not to be taken for the whole of gay culture, nor does it reflect the full scope of gay men's subjectivity. Even a slight modification in the design of my project would have had far-reaching consequences for the resulting picture of gay male existence offered here. Simply switching from one female Hollywood icon to another could be decisive. What if, instead of Crawford, my exploration of gay male culture had taken as its paradigm example her rival and sometime antagonist Bette Davis? What if, in the place of *Mildred Pierce,* I had chosen to focus on such gay cult classics from among Davis's films as *Jezebel, Dark Victory, The Letter, The Little Foxes, Deception, Now, Voyager,* or *All about Eve?* How would my model of gay male subjectivity have to change? What different picture of gay culture would result?

Conventional wisdom has it that Bette Davis was the great screen sadist, just as Joan Crawford was the great screen masochist. That wisdom reflects the character types both actresses excelled at playing, especially during the second halves of their careers, and it depends in part on their spectacular division of roles in the one movie in which they played opposite each other, *What Ever Happened to Baby Jane?* (1962), where Bette Davis ultimately takes Joan Crawford prisoner, keeping her literally bound and gagged. But although that conventional understanding of the two actresses as embodying opposite identities and personality types is probably exaggerated and too schematic, it seems undeniable that Bette Davis's distinctive ethos and style produce a visual, emotional, moral, and sensual impact very different from Joan Crawford's. In particular, Davis's glamour, which is every bit as dazzling as Crawford's, seems to be much less bound up with abjection. Even if Davis is not necessarily a sadist in many of her screen roles, her characters often do take an unmixed pleasure in coming out on top, wielding power or authority, defying social conventions, and getting their way even or especially at the cost of other people's suffering.

That is why a friend of mine tries to find out whether the latest guy he's dating has a liking for Bette Davis or Joan Crawford. Such preferences do not simply reflect different tastes in movies, or matters of aesthetic partisanship in general. They tell my friend a lot about the kind of guy he's dating, the nature of the relation he is destined to have with him—in particular, what the sex is going to be like . . . in the long run.

A model of gay male subjectivity based on an understanding of the peculiar gay appeal of Bette Davis might well differ, then, from the limited and partial model of gay male subjectivity that I have sketched out here and that I extracted from one line of Joan Crawford's. The two models would not be totally dissimilar, to be sure: I imagine—and I am not about to anticipate the outcome of a separate research project that I hope someone will undertake, so I don't want to presume—but I imagine that both models of gay subjectivity would likely make *some* reference to melodrama, camp, diva-worship, and gay male femininity, for example. The differences between them might well be significant, however. And the resulting picture of gay male culture and subjectivity might be even more different if it took as its starting point a practice like gardening or window-dressing or home decoration, not to mention diving or heavy-metal music or religious mysticism.[4]

Those differences would confirm us, nonetheless, in our basic approach to the topic. Far from returning us to a psychological model of gay male subjectivity, they would highlight the sexual politics of cultural form, the meaning of style, the far-reaching aesthetic, gendered, and sexual consequences of formal or stylistic differences, the constitutive effects of the pragmatics of genre—the cultural poetics, in short, of human subjectivity.

☙❧

Though gay male culture may no longer be preoccupied with either Joan Crawford or Bette Davis, it continues to reserve a large share of its attention for Hollywood stars, divas, pop icons, and various contemporary feminine figures incarnating different combinations of strength and suffering, glamour and abjection, power and vulnerability. It continues to make passionate investments in aestheticism and to display an ironic taste for melodrama, both as an artistic form and as a mode of feeling or personal expression. It continues to be divided between aristocratic and democratic impulses, between elitist aspirations and identifications with the lowest of the low. But it doesn't understand its persistent attachment to these traditional sources of queer pleasure, and it doesn't know how to make sense of its own obsessions.

The feature article on gay culture in *Time Out New York* is striking in this connection, not only because it freely confesses its own incapacity to deal with its chosen topic, but because it registers so clearly and symptomatically a larger confusion about what "gay culture" could possibly mean, refer to, or consist in. Indeed, the "Gay & Lesbian editor" of *TONY,* Beth Greenfield, herself admits that gay culture "may be a difficult concept to pin down" (though "it sure is an exciting one to ponder"). The examples of gay culture that she lists reveal, accordingly, a number of slippages among different conceptions or definitions of it.

> When *Time Out New York*'s queer staffers sat down to figure out what would go into a feature about "gay culture," we quickly realized it would be no easy task. Did we want to tackle it in the classic, universal sense—as in Judy Garland, campy drag shows and *Stone Butch Blues?* Did we want to talk about new queer indie films, and why they are often low-budget and unimpressive? Or about the hottest, freshest talents around, and how they're shaking up media ranging from music and downtown theater to edgy lit and trans burlesque? (16)

A lot is being compressed into a small space here, so it's no wonder that some weird amalgams get made. For instance, it's not clear how Judy Garland exemplifies gay culture "in the universal sense" that drag does. Drag is an international queer phenomenon, which does indeed make it almost universal, whereas the gay male appeal of Judy Garland tends to be limited to the English-speaking world—or to some restricted portions of it.

Similarly, it's hard to see how *Stone Butch Blues,* Leslie Feinberg's powerful transgender working-class novel published in 1993, nearly a quarter-century after the Stonewall riots, could qualify as "classic" in quite the same way as Judy Garland. The problem is not one of relative merit or importance. Feinberg's novel *is* a classic, and it has had a major impact on readers all over the world. But it's a classic in part because of how clearly and explicitly it articulates an experience of queer *identity* that had rarely been described before in such lucid, moving language. (Perhaps Beth Greenfield wanted to replace that classic *cri de coeur* of lesbian/transgender misery, Radclyffe Hall's 1928 novel *The Well of Loneliness,* with a less politically obnoxious, more up-to-date version.) Judy Garland, by contrast, became the focus of a gay male cult in the years before Stonewall because, far from finding new words to describe queer experience, she somehow gave voice to gay men's unspeakable longings *without* ever enunciating them. She thereby served as an effective vehicle of gay male *identification.* She was a figure gay men could identify with, not—like Feinberg's novel—a champion of queer identity itself.

Some of these confusions may be generational. John Clum, growing up in the 1950s, did not suffer from any such confusion. "For many of us," he writes, "there was something called 'gay culture' and it involved camp as a discourse and musical theater as an object of adoration."[5] But that was a long time ago. *TONY*'s queer staffers themselves point out that much uncertainty about what gay culture is today may arise from what they call "the ever-present generation gap," which "can seem particularly wide in our community." That gap, in their understanding of it, divides, predictably, "folks over thirty"—who are likely to be found "catching the latest Paul Rudnick play or ducking into a lively piano bar for the evening"—from "queers in their twenties and younger [who] may have less of a need to belong to anything other than society at large. They came out in their teens, after all, and find themselves more or less accepted everywhere they go" (16).

It is always hard to tell whether assertions like this—which are by now so familiar to us, and which insist that gay culture is out of date, a thing of the past, irrelevant to the younger generation, and no longer necessary in a world where lesbians and gay men can now get married or be elected heads of state (at least in Iceland)—it is always hard to tell whether such assertions are statements of fact or expressions of desire, startled discoveries of unanticipated good news or articulations of a wish that gay culture would simply disappear. In any case, we have already had occasion to take stock of many similar claims. Young queers fit easily into youth culture, we are told; they don't like to be labeled, they don't feel the need for a separate, distinct social world, and they don't identify with gay culture.[6]

And a good thing, too, I might add, because the social costs of insisting on your differences from normal people are exorbitant *when you have no choice but to integrate yourself into heterosexual society*—because substantive gay alternatives to the straight world no longer exist, now that the urban infrastructures of gay life have been largely dismantled. And if you want your straight friends to accept you as one of them, despite your being queer, you would be wise to deny that you wish "to belong to anything other than society at large." What, after all, does such a denial indicate, if not that straight society at large is actually a good deal less accommodating of queer kids, especially queer kids who want to proclaim their difference from straight kids, than we are sometimes led to believe?

Witness John Clum, to take only the example nearest to hand. Clum reported in the late 1990s that "gay fraternity boys" on a lesbigay e-mail list at Duke University "spoke of how it was all right to be openly gay in a fraternity as long as you played by the rules of gender appropriate behavior. No sissies or queens, please."[7] Reacting sharply to this trend, gay legal scholar Kenji Yoshino has issued an eloquent critique of "covering," the tendency on the part of stigmatized groups to acknowledge their differences but to minimize the significance and the visibility of those differences, so as to be acceptable to society at large. Gay people may now come out of the closet, but they get ahead in the world only if they make sure that their non-standard identities do not obtrude flamboyantly on the consciousness of straight people. In order to resist that pressure, Yoshino wants to call our attention to "the dark side of assimilation." He argues that when women and minorities defensively downplay their differences, they cave in to "covering demands" that simply reflect the ongoing realities of racism, sexism, and homophobia. "Covering is a hidden assault on our civil rights," he argues.[8]

Sometimes those assaults do not stay hidden. It is all very well to celebrate the fact that "queers in their twenties and younger . . . find themselves more or less accepted everywhere they go," at least in New York, and the last thing I want to do is to minimize that good news. But I'd also rather not try telling it to Kevin Aviance—the brilliant African American performance artist who led two workshops for my "How To Be Gay" class in 2000 and 2001—even if he was no longer in his twenties in 2006 when his jaw was broken in front of a gay bar in the East Village by half a dozen guys who attacked him while shouting anti-gay insults.

The notion that traditional gay male culture is completely meaningless and irrelevant to the younger generation, or the new and upcoming generation, is one I espoused fervently when I considered myself a member of such a generation, back in the 1970s. Now that I've gotten older and changed my mind, I wonder what makes *teenagers* our leading authorities on gay culture and its ongoing relevance, or why we should necessarily measure the continuing meaningfulness of gay culture by gauging how well it plays to the youngest gay men, those who are least likely to have been exposed to it or initiated into it, and who in any case know next to nothing about it. Even I knew virtually nothing about Judy Garland when I was younger. I got to know her only when I had to do my homework in order to teach "How To Be Gay" for the first time. Judy Garland, after all, was not exactly an icon for *my* generation.

Ever since the 1970s, as we've already seen, gay men have been drawing self-serving generational comparisons between well-adjusted gay people in their teens and twenties, who have no need of gay culture, and all those older queens who are fanatically attached to it. A particularly witty and trenchant, but otherwise quite typical, instance of this contrast can be found in the central, programmatic conversation between Nick (played by Steve Buscemi) and Peter (Adam Nathan) in Bill Sherwood's 1986 film of contemporary gay life in New York, *Parting Glances*—one of those low-budget, independent queer films that *TONY*'s staffers would probably find "unimpressive," but that I happen to think highly of. In that scene, the cute gay twentysomething club kid with patriotic sentiments, romantic longings, and Republican politics boasts of his normality to a thirtysomething punk rocker with AIDS, only to end up begging his older acquaintance, nostalgically, "Show me the Village." And that was already almost three decades ago; the cute Reaganite club kid, if he survived, would be past fifty by now. Which is old for a teenager.

If all these perennial claims of generational difference turned out to be accurate, and still current, then it would seem that the folks over thirty who haunt the piano bars today were, just a short time ago, the new generation who came out in their teens and felt no personal connection with gay identity, gay culture, or gay community. Between feeling no need to belong to anything and feeling an irresistible urge to walk through the beckoning doorway of your local piano bar, there is not some unbridgeable chasm between the generations, it turns out, but merely a slender border zone no wider than a decade.

๑๐

The persistent denial that gay culture exists or that it is relevant to the younger generation is part of a larger pattern. Gay people seem to be constantly discovering, and then rediscovering—always with the same shock of surprise, the same unanticipated astonishment—what a trivial thing their gayness is, how little it matters to them, how insignificant it is in the larger scheme of things, how little they identify with it, how little they need to belong to a culture built around it. They continually assert, with the same hollow insistence, that being gay does not define them. And perhaps it doesn't. But being gay still seems to be the only thing they ever talk about. They talk about it endlessly. The more they talk about it, the more they feel an obligation to proclaim how unimportant it is. On a list of the ten most significant things about me, they always say, being gay comes in at number ten.

Even the folks who are actually in charge of the gay media, whose job it is to produce and maintain a public gay culture, feel duty-bound to take the same loyalty oaths to the insignificance and irrelevance of being gay. "Oscar Raymundo, twenty-five, could be considered a professional gay," aptly observes Scott James in the annual Gay Pride state-of-the-gay report for the *New York Times*. "He writes a gay blog, and edits for the Web site Queerty. But he said being gay is not as important as other aspects of his life—he has faced more discrimination for being Latino, he said."[9] When the topic of what it means to you to be gay comes up, the thing to do is to shift it to some more politically respectable identity, even though being gay is how you make your living.

The fact that you have to say, over and over again, how unimportant to you being gay is, in order to retain some kind of social or cultural credibility, is an eloquent sign of the times we live in. For it actually indicates just how important being gay truly is—if only to the extent that it dramatizes how much pressure you evidently feel to proclaim that being gay is unimportant. If it were really so unimportant, why would you have to keep saying so?

"I, for one, can say I'm really not proud to be gay," proudly writes Bre DeGrant in Salon.com, penning the compulsory gay-disavowal article for the annual Gay Pride issue. "I'm not proud to be in a gay community. I'm more proud that I survived abuse as a child, that I'm on the Dean's List, and that I'm on track for my nursing degree after years of indecision. Basically, I'm proud of the things I've accomplished. I don't want to be known as the gay girl. I want to be known for all of the things I am instead of just one of the things I happen to be. My entire personality doesn't revolve around being a lesbian." Except, that is, when writing an article for the Gay Pride issue of Salon, an article that revolves around nothing else but being a lesbian.

"I understand that oppressed minorities need a community to feel acceptance until they become integrated into the rest of society," De-Grant concedes. "But as we grow more and more accepted, as we evolve from a psychiatric case to just another person, do we still need to actively disassociate ourselves from mainstream society and our straight counterparts? Will we still need gathering places when the rest of our peers accept us in nongay bars, nongay community centers, and nongay houses of worship?"[10] Well, unless we truly relish the dismal prospect of spending the rest of our lives hanging out in nongay houses of worship, the answer to that question is surely going to be a resounding yes.

Corresponding to the perennial disavowal of the importance of gay identity is the constant denial, especially on the part of gay men, of the importance of gay sex. Scott James fastens upon a twenty-three-year-old Stanford graduate with a Master's degree in computer science, who lived in a gay dorm at Stanford and moved to the Castro neighborhood in San Francisco immediately upon graduating; the more his social life revolves around being gay, the more he insists on the unimportance of being gay, just as coming out at the age of sixteen was a complete "non-event." "Socially, he is seeking a relationship, not casual liaisons, meeting men mostly through 'friends of friends.' . . . 'I'm inspired by the gay couples I know who want to get married,' he said." And James goes on to remark, with apparent satisfaction, "Others in [his] generation also appear to have less of an obsession with sex, which is reflected in some social media. Grindr, a smartphone application that connects gay men by GPS proximity, has more than 25,000 San Francisco users. Though some exploit the technology for pursuing sex, 67 percent in a recent customer survey said they use the app primarily to make friends."[11]

What amazing news! Gay men are no longer interested in sex. They're interested in relationships. They want to get married. Have you ever heard anything like that before? Well, perhaps you've heard something rather like it every year during Gay Pride for the past thirty years, or at any moment when some incident produces a passing curiosity in the straight media about the current state of gay life in the United States. And no doubt you're always astounded by the news, which is why people keep telling it to us. We are regaled non-stop with reports about "the new gay teenager," the divisions in the gay community, the generational conflicts, the changing modes of gay life, the disappearance of gay politics, of gay dance parties, of gay sex, of gay culture. Gay kids these days don't feel a political urge to manifest their sexuality. They feel comfortable in their sexuality. They find themselves more or less accepted everywhere they go.

So why do they keep killing themselves when they get outed?

The report by Scott James is actually quite informative. To be sure, it doesn't tell you much about what it is that more than 25,000 gay boys in San Francisco are actually doing on Grindr. (If, as one Grindr user told another reporter, you're using Grindr primarily to make friends, if you're simply networking, "if you're just there to meet people in a nonsexual context, why aren't you wearing a shirt in your picture?")[12] But it does say a lot about the social pressure that two-thirds of those boys feel to deny that they're using Grindr for sexual hook-ups. So it's not especially surprising that the young man interviewed by James says he is looking for a relationship. Everyone is looking for a relationship. Why, even I am looking for a relation-ship—I just have to have sex with thousands of men to find the one I really want.

☙❧

To be sure, the social and political conditions of gay life have been changing very rapidly over the past fifty years, and gay culture has been changing along with them. Even practices that appear to be continuous over the course of many years may be less stable than they look. The irony with which we regard Joan Crawford movies now is surely very different from the irony with which gay men watched *Mildred Pierce* in the '50s and '60s, when the melodrama, social setting, and gender styles seemed less far-fetched and therefore less emotionally alien than they do today (which is why no universalizing, psychoanalytically phrased theory of gay spectatorship can account for gay viewing practices in all their specificity). Gay men's identification with the female stars in classic Hollywood movies would have been more immediate and intense in the old days, when ironic distance from the characters they played took more of an effort to achieve. It is entirely to be expected that every half-generation of gay men would feel disconnected from the cultural objects and the ways of relating to them that had been so meaningful to the half-generation before them. And the volatile interactions between gay male culture and its heteronormative context have constantly evolved. That in turn has altered the nature, the methods, and the goals of gay cultural borrowing, appropriation, and reuse.

When Todd Haynes, once an architect of the "new queer cinema" of the early 1990s, remade *Mildred Pierce* for HBO in 2011, his slow-paced, six-hour, comparatively faithful adaptation of the James M. Cain novel never lost an opportunity to remind its viewers, by means of its rich social realism and insistent period detail, how far away in world and time they were from the family drama Cain had depicted. Haynes made distance and irony into the very conditions of spectatorship, effectively alienating his audience from the spectacle and depriving it of the need to balance passionate absorption with a countervailing irony in order to bring itself into a meaningful relation with the scenario. Which is one reason his version is so much less gripping than the original movie, despite the visual beauty of the cinematography and the enhanced plausibility of the story. No wonder it did not evoke an equivalent response from gay male viewers. Kate Winslet's earnest portrayal of the title character—inexperienced, ordinary, downtrodden, pitiable, and often pathetic, more victim than independent woman—has nothing of the fierceness, elegance, and authority with which Joan Crawford embodied an aristocratic model of middle-class femininity.

So I don't want to imply that the *TONY* writers are simply in denial when they attempt to describe the generational differences between succeeding versions of gay male culture. But those differences provide no excuse for refusing to acknowledge the remarkable continuities across the generations. Or for dating gay culture irrevocably to the past.

ༀ

It is altogether too easy to be snide at the expense of *TONY,* I admit, and my goal is certainly not to be snide—that's just a catty, self-indulgent detour on the way to my main point. Which is a simple one. The fundamental hesitation about what gay culture is that the writers responsible for this feature article seem to feel arises from a basic and characteristic uncertainty: Does gay culture refer to queer artifacts produced by queers themselves or to works of mainstream culture produced by heterosexuals, which queers then appropriate for their own uses, queering them in the process?

The *TONY* feature foregrounds this dilemma by including a poll, addressed to its readers, called "Which Is Gayer?" It pairs instances of explicit, identity-based, out-and-proud, post-Stonewall gay culture with bits of the surrounding culture that lend themselves to queer appropriation. In that way, direct, unencrypted representations of gayness are opposed to coded, figural representations of gayness, and readers are asked to choose the ones they prefer, to vote for the representations that answer more satisfyingly to their ideas of gay culture or to their desires for what they would like it to be. As the *TONY* lead-in puts it, "You don't have to be openly gay to be really queer." So which is gayer, the magazine asks, *Brokeback Mountain* or *Sex and the City?* Truman Capote or Herman Melville?[13]

In other words, do you prefer the kind of gay culture that is rooted in gay identity or the kind that is rooted in gay identification? Would you rather listen to Rufus Wainwright or Judy Garland? *TONY* solves *that* problem by giving first place in its list of "Top ten moments in NYC gay culture" not to the Stonewall riots—they come in at number two—but to "Rufus Does Judy," the 2006 performance at Carnegie Hall in which Rufus reperformed Judy's legendary 1961 concert, singing all the same songs in the same order and in the same venue.[14] Nonetheless, TONY poses the choice to its readers in fairly stark terms. Do you still feel "a need to connect with some sort of LGBT culture"? If not, "Why cling to old-fashioned notions of barroom communities and identity art?" (16).

The problem is that what is *really* old-fashioned is not gay bars and baths, or the communities they produce, or David Hockney paintings of boys diving into swimming pools, or novels of gay male life by Andrew Holleran and Edmund White—old-fashioned though they all may be. Long before there was an open, explicit gay male culture, with its own "identity art," there was already a gay male cultural practice that consisted in appropriating, decoding, recoding, and queering figures like Judy Garland and Joan Crawford, finding homosexual meaning in the novels of Herman Melville, and embracing all-female melodramas like *The Women* or *Sex and the City*. These are precisely the sorts of mass-media cultural objects that can still serve as vehicles of queer feeling (Lady Gaga, anyone?). As it turns out, they are also the objects that the TONY staffers particularly adore, much preferring them to those unimpressive, low-budget movies by new queer filmmakers which they tend to despise (Ariel Schrag, a contributor to the TONY forum and a former writer for *The L Word*, expresses particular disdain for the MIX queer experimental film festival in New York).

In lobbying for an understanding of how "really queer" certain cultural icons or objects can be that do not register as "openly gay," the TONY staffers demonstrate—unwittingly, and despite their conviction of being trend-setters—just how archaic their model of gay culture is. For their delight in finding queer meaning in cultural items that do not depict homosexuality explicitly, and that were not produced by an openly gay culture, recapitulates a pre-Stonewall gay practice of queering straight culture—that is, it recalls and reproduces gay culture "in the classic, universal sense." Far from dying out, that practice lives on, and the TONY editors bear witness in their cultural preferences to its continuing vitality, even as they claim that tradi-tional gay culture is no longer relevant to their own generation.

There is, however, a kind of contemporary gay culture that the *TONY* staffers do champion. Even while they lampoon "identity art" as old-fashioned, at least when it consists of items they don't happen to like, they are eager to celebrate gay culture when it is produced by "the hottest, freshest talents around" with a reputation for "shaking up media ranging from music and downtown theater to edgy lit and trans burlesque." But those instances of gay culture, which they hold up to us for admiration, seem to consist precisely of new work that bears on queer life, or at least that expresses a queer sensibility, and is produced in any case by the current crop of queer artists. And what is that if not "identity art"?

It is only because that new work is supposedly so sharp and smart and trendy that it doesn't come in for that derogatory label . . . yet. You can just imagine what tomorrow's queer teenagers will be saying about "downtown theater" and "trans burlesque," as well as the folks over thirty who love them, ten years from now.

☙❧

The point of this analysis is not to ridicule the *TONY* staffers, but to bring out the kinds of conflicts and denials around gay culture that gay people constantly display. The contributors to *TONY* provide a typical example. They represent a symptom of our larger malaise.

In the end, Beth Greenfield's answer to the question "What is gay culture?" is a generous one. It includes images of gay people as well as straight icons with whom they identify, a culture of gay identity as well as a culture of gay identification, youth as well as age, gay people as well as straight people. Her evocation of the scene at the first of the Gay Pride parades in the New York summer season, the one in Jackson Heights on June 1, is intended to span all those oppositions: "Queens Pride '08 remains one of the city's most vibrant, least com-mercialized and most ethnically diverse festivals. Check it out and you could find yourself thinking—amid Colombian drag queens, gay cops, queer-youth groups and flocks of Indian families applauding on the sidelines—that you've just stepped into the very heart of the elusive gay culture." That is entirely as it should be.

But it still leaves us with some questions to consider.

CRE 20 ERD

CULTURE VERSUS SUBCULTURE

Gay culture can refer to new works of literature, film, music, art, drama, dance, and performance that are produced by queer people and that reflect on queer experience. Gay culture can also refer to mainstream works created mostly by heterosexual artists, plus some (closeted) queer ones, that queer people have selectively appropriated and reused for anti-heteronormative purposes.

The distinction is of course neither airtight nor absolute. Even the most original contemporary gay writers frame their work in relation to mainstream society and history or initiate a dialogue with received cultural forms. Neil Bartlett's novels *Ready to Catch Him Should He Fall* (1991) and *Mr Clive and Mr Page* (1996) imagine what the gay equivalent of heterosexual courtship, romance, marriage, conjugality, family, property accumulation and transmission, inheritance, and reproduction might look like; those novels refer back, for their central terms and preoccupations, to preexisting heterosexual social and cultural institutions. The later novel even cites and reworks a number of actual historical documents in order to adapt them to a gay male theme. And yet it is a wholly original work of contemporary gay literature, whose goal is to give form to a specifically gay way of life.

Similarly, in *An Arrow's Flight* (1998), Mark Merlis offers a gay retelling of the Fall of Troy and the story of the Greek hero Philoctetes—though he could also be understood as creating a Homeric myth of the Vietnam War, gay liberation, and the onset of the HIV/AIDS epidemic. Jamie O'Neill reclaims Irish Republican history for gay liberation and for gay male love in his novel *At Swim, Two Boys* (2001), whose very title invokes an earlier, classic, non-gay novel by Flann O'Brien.[1] And Michael Cunningham's most successful work, *The Hours* (1998), seems gayest not when it tries to represent gay male characters but when its author tries to write like—or, indeed, to *be*—Virginia Woolf, rather like Rufus channeling Judy.

The list of original works by gay men that take straight society or mainstream culture as their point of departure could be almost infinitely extended. Nonetheless, there is a distinction to be drawn between the kind of gay culture that consists in new work by (in this case) gay men who for the first time in history reflect directly and openly and explicitly on gay male experience as it is being lived, or as it might be lived (or might have been lived), and the kind of gay culture that is parasitic on mainstream culture. The latter finds in the non-gay world queer representations that can be made to express gay male subjectivity or feeling—with a little tweaking, if necessary—and that afford gay men an imaginative point of entry into a queer utopia, somewhere over the rainbow, which is not entirely of their own making.

The difference between these two versions of gay male culture can be understood in terms of a broader distinction (though, once again, not an airtight one) between culture and subculture. Gay writers, artists, performers, and musicians have been creating an original culture for well over a century now, even if many of them have had to operate under the cover of heterosexual subject matter and only a few, such as Walt Whitman, André Gide, Thomas Mann, Marcel Proust, Radclyffe Hall, Jean Genet, and James Baldwin, were able to treat gay themes explicitly. By contrast, drag, camp, and various cultural appropriations and identifications are all, properly speaking, *subcultural* practices, insofar as they are in a dependent, secondary relation to the preexisting non-gay cultural forms to which they respond and to which they owe their very existence—such as social norms of masculinity and femininity; the serious business of politics; authentic identities and emotions; mainstream figures like Judy Garland or Joan Crawford; and mainstream aesthetic or social practices, from opera, Broadway musicals, torch songs, and popular music to architecture, historic preservation, flower-arranging, fashion and style.

The most eminent examples of gay male cultural production before the era of gay liberation lie somewhere in between. They are dependent on preexisting cultural forms, which provide them with social authority and protective camouflage, and they are easily claimed by mainstream culture, but they also constitute significant achievements of queer expression and vital resources for the formation and elaboration of gay identity—virtual bibles of gay existence. I am thinking, for example, of Oscar Wilde's dramatic and non-dramatic works, Marcel Proust's *A la recherche du temps perdu,* Virginia Woolf's novels and essays, W. H. Auden's poetry, and Noël Coward's songs.

A subculture is not the same thing as a culture. The dynamics of its formation, its aims and purposes, and its politics are all necessarily different. A subculture is in an oppositional (if not adversarial) relationship to an already existing set of authoritative cultural values, and it refers, explicitly or implicitly, to a world that is not its own independent creation. It is an expression of resistance to a dominant culture and a defiance of a social order. If I have spoken consistently throughout this book of gay male culture rather than subculture, that's not because I've been trying to dodge the implication that the gay male cultural practices with which I've been most concerned are secondary, subcultural ones, but only because I have wanted to avoid littering my text with that unlovely, compound term. The endless repetition of "culture" and "cultural" has been bad enough.

In any case, this book has had little to say about gay male culture of the original kind, the sort of gay cultural production that is predicated on the existence of gay identity and on the ability of representational practices to convey it; it has been preoccupied almost exclusively with gay male culture of the subcultural variety. In fact, it has largely taken for granted the notion that male homosexuality as a cultural practice consists in a series of subcultural responses to mainstream culture—namely, the appropriation and resignification of heterosexual forms and artifacts.

But I hardly wish to deny the existence of a gay-authored gay culture or to undervalue it. Much original gay male culture is grounded not in identification with non-gay figures or with non-gay social and cultural forms, but in gay male identity itself and in the effort to explore it. Gay men still look for representations of themselves and reflections of their existence in cultural productions, and they are interested in finding out about other gay men past and present, how gay men have managed their lives, their loves, their struggles for freedom and dignity. To those ends, gay men have created a vibrant, wide-ranging, explicit body of writing, film, and music, a distinguished accumulation of scholarship and criticism, as well as institutional spaces for further study and reflection and discovery.

Moreover, there is a vast popular literature devoted to disseminating useful knowledge about gay men to gay men, from grooming advice to gay history to what to expect from a gay love-affair.[2] The original edition of *The Joy of Gay Sex,* published in 1977, contains not only illustrated articles describing different sexual positions, but also explanations of what discos are, why gay men go to them, and how one should behave in them, as well as entries about the particular importance of friendships in the lives of gay men or about how to cope with jealousy and still have a happy relationship that is not sexually exclusive. Although the title of that manual promises that it will be about gay sex, the book was actually designed to be an all-purpose user's guide to gay male life.

Some gay men do venerate their historical forebears, as Bartlett's book on Wilde testifies. They make lists of gay male heroes and role models.[3] And they keep an eye out for traces of their own history. There has long existed a clandestine knowledge that circulates among gay men about the submerged life and work of earlier gay figures— whose homosexuality, though well known, is usually relegated to the unspoken margins of official histories, where it stays concealed from the uninitiated. ("Did you know that Cole Porter / Maurice Sendak / Richard Chamberlain . . . ?") Similarly, gay men have often exchanged bits of information about where in straight public culture one can locate little gems of gay wit, secret double meanings with a gay significance, or sly winks and nods that gay male artists have somehow managed to slip into mainstream movies or music where they remain protectively hidden and usually go unnoticed—except by those who know where to look for them.[4] Nothing I say here is intended to question the value of all that.

On the contrary. If, as I confessed at the outset, I was the wrong person to teach a class on "how to be gay," just as I am the wrong person to write a book on the topic, that is because I have always been grateful for and deeply invested in explicit, non-encrypted, identity-based gay male culture, especially literary fiction. The emergence of such fiction in the past several decades provided me with an exhilarating, instructive, necessary experience—with a kind of epistemic breakthrough—insofar as it enabled me to read, at long last, about people like myself and to understand my larger situation. I no longer had to insert myself, somehow, into those visions of life produced by non-gay writers, no matter how humane, profound, or inclusive they aspired to be. Just as straight readers have always done with mainstream literature, I could finally read fictional works to see my own life reflected, explored, analyzed, and reimagined. Through gay literature I could come to understand my place in the world.

My sense of myself as a gay man has evolved at least partly through that experience. If I could, I would want to honor the achievements of the gay men who, since Stonewall, have written, in English, novels, stories, and plays about gay male life and whose work has meant so much to me. I think particularly of Neil Bartlett, Alan Hollinghurst, Mark Merlis, Jamie O'Neill, Christos Tsiolkas, John Weir, Dale Peck, Melvin Dixon, Joe Keenan, and Adam Mars-Jones; also Robert Ferro, Tony Kushner, Albert Innaurato, Robert Glück, Dennis Cooper, John Rechy, James Purdy, Samuel Delany, Ethan Mordden, Essex Hemphill, Allan Gurganus, Stephen McCauley, David Feinberg, James

Robert Baker, Gary Indiana, Randall Kenan, David Leavitt, and many
others.

By contrast, I have been slow to appreciate and to enjoy the divas
and the camp perspectives that the subcultural practice of male homosexuality held out to me, and I have retained an ambivalent attitude toward them. Which is why writing this book has gone against
the grain of my own instincts some of the time—though it has also
taught me a lot about how to be gay, and it has made me gayer as a
result.

If for the purposes of this study I have wanted to turn my back on
gay male culture proper, and to investigate the nature and the workings of gay male subculture instead, that is because the latter is mysterious in ways that the former is not. It is abundantly obvious why
gay men produce and consume a culture that consists in representations of gay men and of gay male experience. And it would even be
easy to understand why, in an era before such an open, explicit gay
male culture was possible, gay men's cultural expression took the
form of the subcultural practice of appropriating and resignifying select items from the surrounding heterosexual culture. What is less
expected is that the emergence of an open, explicit gay male culture
should not have put an end to those subcultural practices or extinguished the appeal of reading heteronormative artifacts queerly
against the grain. Gay men still engage in the reappropriation and recoding of straight culture.

Even the panel of "local LGBT culture makers," assembled by
Time Out New York in order to answer the what-is-gay-culture? question, acknowledge that much, however grudgingly. Here is what they
say in response to the query, "Have you seen *Gypsy?*"

ARIEL SCHRAG: What is *Gypsy?*

STACEYANN CHIN: I've never seen it.

CHRISTIAN SIRIANO: I haven't. Wait, I think I've seen the movie, but
    I can't remember. What's it about?

ARIEL SCHRAG: Isn't there a mother and a daughter in it? It's kind of
    coming back to me . . .

CHRISTIAN SIRIANO: Sounds fabulous!

DOUGLAS CARTER BEANE: I haven't seen it for a while. I like to see it every seventy-two months—I love that overture. I even put a joke in *Xanadu* about *Gypsy!*

KAI WRIGHT: I haven't seen it, but for gay Broadway, give me *Xanadu*. That was fucking brilliant! I urge you to go.

DOUGLAS CARTER BEANE: Working on *Xanadu* made it pretty clear that the word "camp" is still used to dismiss something. People are still saying the show is too gay, even though it appeals to a wide audience. They would never think of calling *Fiddler on the Roof* "too Jewish," or *The Wiz* "too black," or *Camelot* "too long"—oh wait, they do say that.

GLENN MARIA: I actually saw *Gypsy*. And I'm the weird, fat trannie— the one who's supposed to be into weird and freaky shit. People always come up to me and talk about obscure avant-garde artists that I "should" know. But the reality is, I love *Gypsy*. When I perform, I jump out of spandex sacks and tap-dance to show tunes.[5]

It is clear that traditional gay male culture—that is, subculture—continues to provide queers of all sorts with emotional, aesthetic, even political resources that turn out to be potent, necessary, and irreplaceable. The open and explicit gay male culture produced by gay liberation has not been able to supplant a gay male subculture, grounded in gay identification with non-gay forms, or to substitute for it an original gay male culture grounded in the vicissitudes of gay identity. The impetus driving much gay cultural production still springs less from gay existence than from gay desire.

☯

So, then, have I written a reactionary book? Have I, by insisting on the continuing relevance, power, and indeed wisdom of much traditional gay male subculture, betrayed the revolutionary achievements of gay liberation, rejected the new gay identity it produced, and turned my back on its goals of social and individual transformation, along with its original cultural creations?

If I have often cast a withering glance on post-Stonewall gay identity, and on the politics, literature, music, and sexuality that derive from it, I have done so less out of personal conviction than out of an experimental attitude, one that consists in testing what initially seemed to me to be a counter-intuitive hypothesis: that the Golden Girls might still matter to us a lot more than Edmund White, that *Desperate Housewives* might prove queerer than *Queer as Folk*.

But I have also been motivated by the shock and disappointment of seeing a revolutionary movement of sexual liberation and political insurgency settle down into a complacent, essentially conservative form of identity politics that seeks less to change the world than to claim a bigger piece of it. Many gay people nowadays seem determined to imitate and to reproduce the most trite, regressive social values of heteronormative culture: family, religion, patriotism, normative gender roles—that venerable trinity of *Kinder, Küche, Kirche*. They have also taken up the heterosexual ethic of erotic impoverishment, which lobbies for the benefits of renouncing sexual pleasure. The less sex you have, so this ethic goes, the more meaningful it will be, and what you should want above all in your sexual life is not pleasure but meaning, meaning at the expense of pleasure, or meaning to the exclusion of pleasure. That is the ethic against which gay liberation once led a world-historical rebellion.

Much of the openly gay-themed culture that has emerged since Stonewall continues to share the revolutionary goals of gay liberation. Its originality, artistic experimentation, and sheer brilliance are very far removed from the standard gay identity politics of the mainstream gay movement. But that genuinely inventive gay culture has suffered the same fate as the identity-based culture that emerged in the same period, insofar as both seem to arouse in gay audiences a similar sense of tedium. It is as if contemporary gay people have a hard time distinguishing truly original, innovative queer work from the comparatively trite, politically earnest, in-group cultural productions that you find on the Logo Channel.

My intention has been not to depreciate post-Stonewall gay culture but to champion the forms of social resistance to heteronormativity that much of pre-Stonewall gay culture represented and continues to represent, while exploring the reasons why so many gay men seem to find the official, parochial, rainbow-flag-draped gay identity-based culture that has replaced it so unsatisfying and deficient. I have wanted to discover the source of so much gay discontent.

എ

That discontent is real, and sometimes the political complaint I have just articulated merely serves as an alibi for gay homophobia. Gay men are highly critical, if not contemptuous, of their artists, writers, and filmmakers, just as they are disdainful of their political leaders. That is why gay male cultural production (to say nothing of gay male politics) is such a thankless affair. Gay men may claim they want to see representations of themselves and their lives, but they often don't like the representations of gay men that gay men produce, or they fail to stay interested in them.

And you can understand their lack of enthusiasm. Gay men don't excite gay men. Gay men have female icons—divas, fashion models, Hollywood stars, and nowadays even female politicians—to identify with. And they have straight male icons—sports heroes, photospread models, stars of the big and small screens, men in uniform—to desire. Either way, they don't need gay men. And they don't need to read novels, watch movies, take classes, see exhibitions, or go to cultural festivals that focus on gay men.

In 1978 the Canadian sociologist Barry D. Adam, whom I have already had occasion to cite, published his doctoral dissertation (which became the first of his many books), called *The Survival of Domination: Inferiorization and Everyday Life*. A comparative study of Blacks, Jews, lesbians, gay men, concentration camp prisoners, children, and other inmates of "total institutions," it was an early classic of lesbian / gay / queer studies, and it remains worth reading today. Among the coping mechanisms for dealing with social domination that Adam found to be common to the various oppressed groups he studied were what he called the "flight from identity" and "in-group hostility."[6]

Those phrases referred to social and individual strategies by which members of oppressed groups sought to lessen the personal cost and psychological pain of social rejection. They tried, for example, to escape the social marking responsible for their inferior status by refusing to identify with the group to which they belonged, by showing dislike or contempt for other members of that group—especially for those individuals more indelibly marked than themselves by the stigmatizing signs that identified them as belonging to it—and by shunning contact with people from their own communities.

Adam's account of social domination and its consequences continues to have a lot of explanatory power. Still, as Adam himself would be the first to admit, and as his subsequent work suggests, the vicissitudes of inferiorization and abjection do not entirely explain or exhaust the meaning of the phenomena I have been trying to explore. The contemporary gay repudiation of contemporary gay culture, and the ongoing popularity of suitably queered items appropriated from mainstream, heterosexual culture, cannot be reduced to a mere symptom of internalized homophobia. Nor does the perennial gay preference for camp rereadings of heterosexual culture merely reflect a failure to achieve gay pride or the incurable effects of social domination. On the contrary, the strategic appropriation of straight culture continues to serve vital purposes for gay men, and others, and to provide an important, if implicit, vehicle of social critique and political resistance.

The persistence and popularity of traditional gay male cultural practices more than forty years after Stonewall may indeed reflect the continuation of adverse political conditions, of ongoing experiences of anti-gay oppression, exclusion, social domination, and stigma—but not in the sense that they are simply pathological consequences of social hostility. Rather, as we have seen, they represent both a recognition of the difficult situation of gay male life and a determined response to it, including a categorical rejection of the mainstream social values which demean and devalue gay men.

Nonetheless, I think we need to inquire more closely into the reasons why the open and explicit and gay-themed gay male culture that gay liberation made possible continues to have such a difficult time finding a gay male constituency. Why do so many gay men continue to worship and to identify with non-gay figures, to prefer cultural representations from which gay men are absent? It would be good to know whether *society is to blame* for the fact that so many gay men seek non-gay alternatives to the vibrant, ambitious, artistically accomplished, diverse, highly energized, and uncompromisingly "out" gay culture that is now available to them . . . just as they sometimes still have trouble desiring other gay men *as* gay men instead of as facsimiles of straight men or specious embodiments of straight masculinity.

Gay liberation, in other words, may still have a lot of work to do.

QUEER FOREVER

*A*nd when gay liberation has done its work, what then? Will gay male culture, of the subcultural variety I have described here, wither away? Will it lose its appeal? Will gay men of the future be unable to understand, except in a kind of pitying, embarrassed way, why their forebears who lived in the twentieth and twenty-first centuries found so much meaning, so much delight in heterosexual cultural forms that excluded them, at least insofar as such forms contained no explicit representations of gay men or gay male life?

Is the gay male culture, or subculture, that I have described here the product of homophobia? If it is not itself necessarily homophobic, is it nonetheless the result of oppressive social conditions? Is it rooted in social hostility and rejection? And so when homophobia is finally overcome, when it is a thing of the past, when gay liberation triumphs, when gay people achieve equal rights, social recognition, and acceptance, when we are fully integrated into straight society, when the difference between homosexuality and heterosexuality has no greater social significance than the difference between righthandedness and lefthandedness does now—when all that comes to pass, will it spell the end of gay culture, or gay subculture, as we know it?

That is indeed what Daniel Harris and Andrew Sullivan have claimed. I have disputed their assertions that gay male culture, or subculture, is a thing of the past, that it is obsolete and out of date. But perhaps their prognostications were not wrong, only premature. Perhaps the day is coming when more favorable social conditions will vindicate their claims. What was a defective analysis of our present may turn out to be an accurate prediction of our future. Time may yet prove them right.

There is good precedent for such an outlook.

People have wondered, for example, whether Ralph Ellison's *Invisible Man,* James Baldwin's *Another Country,* or Harper Lee's *To Kill a Mockingbird* would become incomprehensible or meaningless if there ever came a time when race ceased to be socially marked in American society (the presidency of Barack Obama, admittedly, makes such a prospect seem harder rather than easier to imagine at the moment). Similarly, would the humor of Lenny Bruce or Woody Allen lose its ability to make us laugh when or if Jews become thoroughly assimilated? Isn't that humor already starting to look a bit archaic?

Any serious attempt to answer those questions would take us well beyond the scope of the present study. But it may be possible to explore them in greater depth with reference to gay culture. For the future of gay culture really does seem to be clouded, and many voices have already heralded its imminent demise. What have yet to be considered are the specific social factors that are putting the survival of gay culture in doubt.

❦

Gay culture's apparent decline actually stems from structural causes that have little to do with the growing social acceptance of homosexuality. There has been a massive transformation in the material base of gay life in the United States, and other metropolitan centers, during the past three decades. That transformation has had a profound impact on the shape of gay life and gay culture. It is the result of three large-scale developments: the recapitalization of the inner city and the resulting gentrification of urban neighborhoods; the epidemic of HIV/AIDS; and the invention of the Internet.

In order to appreciate the nature of the change and its decisive, far-reaching effects, we need to recall the conditions under which gay culture emerged in the years immediately preceding those three large-scale developments. To begin with, gay liberation in the 1960s produced a wave of gay migration that by the 1970s had brought hundreds of thousands of gay men from all regions of the country to New York, San Francisco, Los Angeles, Chicago, Boston, Houston, Miami, and half a dozen other big cities. In particular, gay men moved from the comparative isolation of small towns or rural areas to specific urban districts, the so-called gay ghettos that were taking shape in major metropolitan centers.

The concentration of large numbers of gay people in particular urban neighborhoods had decisive political, economic, and cultural consequences. It provided a power base for a gay political movement. It supported a large commercial infrastructure, including not only bars, bathhouses, and other unique sexual institutions, but also a local, community-based press and other forms of communication,[1] along with bookstores and coffeehouses. It created the kind of mass public that is essential to underwrite a flourishing cultural scene and to inspire constant political ferment. Finally, it produced queer communities freed from the surveillance of straight folks, where new kinds of collective reflection, consciousness-raising, cultural effervescence, and self-constitution could take place. The gay ghettos gave rise, in short, to new forms of life.

The people who established those ghettos were not chiefly middle-class folks. The Castro, the Folsom, and the Polk Street enclaves in San Francisco were not populated by guys who had waited for a job to open up at a downtown law firm or the University of California at Berkeley (though there were plenty of lawyers and academics). The new urban migrants were mostly people from modest backgrounds who, in the relative prosperity that marked the late '60s and early '70s, could find the same menial jobs in California that they had held in Iowa or Alabama. They saved up their money for months or years and eventually moved to a big city, where reasonable rents in the gay neighborhoods that were forming in former ethnic, working-class, or postindustrial areas made it possible for people of limited means to support themselves working as waiters or nurses while still inhabiting a gay urban center—though they might have to share an apartment with several roommates in order to split the rent. Even so, they could make gay life, gay sex, and gay culture the center of their existence, and they could build a life around those new possibilities. Many people did: it was the gay equivalent of the Exodus.

And if you wanted to get laid, in those days, you had to leave the house. The Internet was a decade or two in the future, and cell phones were not even on the horizon. In order to find sexual partners, you had to attach yourself to one of the institutions of gay male social life: bars, bathhouses, the Metropolitan Community Church, the local gay business association, the gay biker club, the gay chorus, one of the gay political organizations or pressure groups. In many of those social contexts, especially in sexual institutions such as the bars and the baths, you were bound to meet all sorts of people you would never have encountered in your own social circles, along with numbers of people you would never have chosen to meet on your own, including a whole bunch you wouldn't have wanted to be caught dead with, if it had been up to you.

But it wasn't up to you. You had to take the crowds that congregated in gay venues as you found them. You couldn't select the folks you were going to associate with according to your own criteria for the kind of men you approved of or thought you wanted as buddies. You had to deal with a wide range of people of different social backgrounds, physical types, appearances, gender styles, social classes, sexual tastes and practices, and sometimes (in the case of White folks) different races. Which meant that you were exposed to many different ideas about what it meant to be gay and to many different styles of gay life. You might not have wanted to be exposed to them, but you didn't have much choice.

"I still remember the terrifying, giddy excitement of my first forays into gay pubs and clubs," writes June Thomas in an extraordinary tribute to the role of the gay bar in gay history and community, "the thrill of discovering other lesbians and gay men in all their beautiful, dreary, fabulous, sleazy variety."[2] As if that were not enough, the new gay public culture virtually guaranteed that people who moved to a gay enclave would encounter a lot of old-timers who were more experienced at being gay and more sophisticated about it than they were.

Moreover, those veterans of urban gay life often held shockingly militant, uncompromising, anti-homophobic, anti-heterosexist, anti-mainstream political views. People who had already been living in gay ghettos for years had had time and opportunity to be "liberated": to be deprogrammed, to get rid of their stupid, heterosexual prejudices, to achieve a politicized consciousness as well as a *pride* in their gay identity. By encountering those people, with their greater daring and sophistication and confidence, the new arrivals from the provinces often found their assumptions, values, and pictures of the right way to live, of how to be gay, seriously challenged. Their old attitudes were liable to be shaken up.

The sheer mix of people in the new gay social worlds favored a radicalization of gay male life. It lent weight and authority to the more evolved, sophisticated, experienced, and radical members of the local community. And so it tended to align the coming-out process with a gradual detachment from traditional, heterosexual, conservative, mainstream notions about the proper way to live. Although guys who looked like regular guys, who displayed an old-fashioned, standard masculinity, were often prized as erotic objects, many of the new recruits to the gay ghettos found themselves gradually argued out of their old-fashioned, rustic, parochial, unenlightened views—their "hang-ups" and their "unliberated" attitudes—including their adherence to rigid gender styles, inappropriate romantic fantasies, restrictive sexual morality, political conservatism, prudery, and other small-town values. Psychic decolonization was the order of the day: gay men needed to identify, and to jettison, the alien, unsuitable notions that the ambient culture of heterosexuality had implanted in their minds.

Many gay men rejected the radical ideology of gay male life, to be sure, and many people formed their own subgroups within gay communities according to their sexual tastes, gender styles, identifications with a particular social class, political sympathies, morals, values, interests, and habits. There was a great variety of outlooks and ways of life. But most of the new inhabitants of the gay ghettos shared the experience of taking part in a new, exhilarating, and unprecedented social experiment: the formation of a community around homosexual desire, gay sex, and gay identity.[3]

ᏣᏲᏈ

That social experiment proved to be short-lived. For during the same period, the recapitalization of American cities, along with its necessary basis in urban planning and renewal, was already starting to change the urban landscape of the United States. A massive inflow of capital drove vast urban redevelopment schemes, gradually removing the cheap, fringe urban zones on the border of former industrial or mixed-use areas where gay businesses, residences, and sex clubs had flourished, and replacing them with highways, high-rises, sports complexes, convention centers, and warehouse stores. In San Francisco, the planning process began in the 1950s. By the 1960s, it was well under way, though its implementation was delayed by a decade of political conflict during the 1970s.

The AIDS epidemic facilitated the ultimate triumph of urban redevelopment by removing or weakening a number of social actors—both individuals and communities—opposed to the developers' plans to rezone, reconfigure, raze, and rebuild entire neighborhoods. In the end, the malign coincidence of the HIV/AIDS epidemic with a surge of urbanism, property development, gentrification, and a corresponding rise in real estate prices in the 1980s destroyed the gay ghettos that had formerly been centers of gay life and gay culture in the late 1960s, 1970s, and early 1980s. That destruction has had vast consequences for gay communities, especially for radical sexual subcultures. Ultimately, it has come to affect how all gay people live.[4]

AIDS decimated a couple of generations of gay men. By the end of 2005, there had been over 550,000 deaths from AIDS in the United States. More than 300,000 of those deaths were among men who have sex with men.[5] In the San Francisco Bay Area alone, tens of thousands of gay men died, including some 17,000 in the city of San Francisco itself.[6] At the same time, the waves of gentrification that contributed to the transformation of gay neighborhoods resulted in an economic boom in inner-city real estate, as suburbanites began to return to the newly gentrified inner cities, with the result that property values in U.S. urban centers skyrocketed.

The gay men of modest incomes who had populated the gay ghettos and who later died of AIDS were often not property owners. And those who did own their own homes often had no living heirs or surviving lovers to pass them on to. As real estate prices climbed, the vacancies left by AIDS were not filled by new waves of working-class gay migrants. The former gay ghettos, now that they had been transformed from modest, ethnic, or working-class neighborhoods into stylish urban enclaves, attracted people with serious money who didn't object to the dwindling presence of gay people and who could afford the rapidly rising rents—or who could spend the considerable sums now required to purchase residential property.[7] So the gay population was slowly diluted and dispersed—as data from the 2010 Census has confirmed.[8] As a result, the entire social infrastructure of gay male life gradually deteriorated.

That has had a devastating effect on gay culture. Without significant gay populations concentrated in local neighborhoods, the power base of the gay movement in specific municipalities was significantly weakened.[9] The economic base of the gay media was also much reduced: in one city after another, local gay newspapers went out of business. Those papers had provided a forum for political discussions. They had facilitated the exchange of views about the needs of communities, the implementation of local policies, the politics of sex, the threat of AIDS and what to do about it. And they encouraged the mobilization of gay people around various issues affecting them where they lived. The gay press had also provided a focus for cultural life, for the promotion of new plays, musicals, art shows, and performances targeted at small-scale gay audiences. Similarly, gay newspapers and bookstores had publicized emerging work in gay history and queer theory, interpreting its breakthroughs to the community in a language that interested readers could understand.

The dispersal of gay populations and the decline of gay neighborhoods meant the disappearance of the material and economic base of the gay press. Local gay newspapers were now replaced by national, highly capitalized glossy magazines aimed at a niche market defined by a delocalized gay identity. The new gay glossies were not about to cover political debates of purely local interest, much less critique the market category of gay identity on which their business depended. In an effort to appeal to everyone, to a national public of prosperous gay individuals who could afford the products advertised in their pages (which paid the costs of staff salaries, printing, and distribution), these publications became increasingly uncontroversial, commercial, and lightweight, eventually turning into the gay equivalent of in-flight magazines.

☯

This loss of a queer public sphere was redeemed by the rise of the Internet and the production of virtual communities. Face-to-face contact in gay neighborhoods, which had already been on the wane, now became increasingly dispensable.[10] You could find gay people online. You didn't have to live in a gay neighborhood, which was no longer very gay and which you couldn't afford anyway. In fact, you didn't even have to move to a big city. You didn't have to live among gay people at all. You never had to leave your bedroom. Gay life became a paradise for agoraphobes.

The Internet has completed the destruction of the non-virtual gay commercial infrastructure. "In 2007, *Entrepreneur* magazine put gay bars on its list of businesses facing extinction, along with record stores and pay phones," June Thomas observes. "And it's not just that gays are hanging out in straight bars; some are eschewing bars altogether and finding partners online or via location-based smartphone apps like Grindr, Qrushr, and Scruff. Between 2005 and 2011, the number of gay and lesbian bars and clubs in gay-travel-guide publisher Damron's database decreased by 12.5 percent, from 1,605 to 1,405."[11] The decline was even steeper before 2005. Thomas estimates that "the number of gay bars [in major cities] has declined from peaks in the 1970s. . . . In 1973, Gayellow Pages placed 118 gay bars in San Francisco; now there are 33. Manhattan's peak came in 1978, with 86; the current tally is 44."[12] Meanwhile, "Grindr launched in March 2009 and currently has more than two million users, one-half of them in the United States. Eight thousand guys sign up for the service every day."[13] No wonder Thomas asks, in dismay, "Could the double whammy of mainstreaming and technology mean that gay bars are doomed?"[14]

The replacement of gay bars by online social-networking sites means that you can now select the gay people you want to associate with before you meet them or come to know them. You can pick your contacts from among the kinds of people you already approve of, according to your unreflective, unreconstructed criteria. You don't have to expose yourself to folks who might have more experience of gay life than you do or who might challenge your unexamined ideas about politics. You can hang on to your unliberated, heterosexist, macho prejudices, your denial, your fear, and you can find other people who share them with you. You can continue to subscribe to your ideal model of a good homosexual: someone virtuous, virile, self-respecting, dignified, "non-scene," non-promiscuous, with a conventional outlook and a solid attachment to traditional values—a proper citizen and an upstanding member of (straight) society.

In short, the emergence of a dispersed, virtual community and the disappearance of a queer public sphere, along with the loss of a couple of generations of gay men to AIDS, has removed many of the conditions necessary for the maintenance and advancement of gay liberation—for consciousness-raising, cultural and political ferment, and the cross-generational transmission of queer values. The lack of a critical mass of gay people physically present in a single location makes it difficult for the pace of gay cultural sophistication to accelerate. It stymies the diffusion of gay culture. It also eliminates the material preconditions for a community-based, politically and socially progressive media culture, and it favors instead the growth of glossy lifestyle magazines and cable channels, targeted at a national niche market, grounded in a canonical, official, mainstreamed gay identity, and hostile to progressive intellectual, political, and aesthetic expression, especially to forms of reflection and critique.

Under these conditions, the agenda of gay politics and gay life is captured by the concerns of people who live dispersed and relatively isolated, stranded among heterosexuals in small towns and rural areas, instead of bunched together in metropolitan centers. And what are the concerns of gay people who find themselves in such locations? Access to mainstream social forms: military service, church membership, and marriage.

That explains a lot about the character and preoccupations of contemporary gay politics. When gay people are deprived of a common, communal existence, of a social world of their own, the keynote of gay politics ceases to be resistance to heterosexual oppression and becomes, instead, assimilation—that is, accommodation to the mainstream, the drive to social acceptance and integration into society as a whole. It's all about the need to fit in, to adapt yourself to the locality in which you already happen to be living and working. Issues like gay military service or marriage equality, which had formerly been about access to benefits, distributive justice, and the removal of discriminatory barriers, now become struggles over the symbolism of social belonging. They are reframed to center around social recognition, the definition of citizenship, the meaning of patriotism, the practice of religious worship, the idea of family. There are still important material demands behind such struggles for inclusion, but they tend to be subordinated, at least in the rhetoric of the movement, to the goals of assimilation and conformity.

In such a context, gay culture seems an increasingly bizarre, insub-

stantial, intangible, nebulous, irrelevant notion. It is the sign of a failure (or refusal) to assimilate. What would gay people want nowadays
with a separate culture anyway? Such a thing might have made sense
in the Bad Old Days of social oppression and exclusion. Now it is simply a barrier to progress. It impedes the achievement of assimilation.
No wonder we keep asking, with barely suppressed impatience, why
gay culture doesn't simply disappear. Surely social acceptance and integration will spell the end of gay culture. Since gay people are no
longer so oppressed, there is little reason for them to band together in
separate social groups, let alone to form distinct cultural communities. The assimilation of gay people into straight society has put an
end to all that. Gay culture is a vestige from an earlier time. It is archaic, obsolete. Gay culture has no future.

ᏬᎳᏬ

These predictions, I believe, overlook a crucial consideration. Social
acceptance, the decriminalization of gay sex, the legalization of homosexual social and sexual institutions, the removal of barriers to
same-sex marriage, to military service, to the priesthood and psychoanalysis, along with other previously off-limits professions, should
not be confused with the end of sexual normativity, let alone the collapse of heterosexual dominance.

Some gay people, to be sure, may see social equality as tacitly implying an affirmation of the essential normality of lesbigay folks.
That is indeed what it signifies to many people, straight as well as gay,
for better or for worse. And of course the release of gay people from
social oppression, as well as the breakdown of the once-universal consensus about the fundamental pathology of homosexuality, which
served to justify that oppression, represent absolutely momentous developments, of wide scope and astonishing rapidity, whose significance cannot be overstated. In fact, the gay movement (as David Alderson argues) may be the only progressive social movement from
the 1960s to have prevailed, to have consolidated its successes, and
to have realized some of its most far-fetched aims (such as gay

marriage)—despite the rise and eventual triumph of the New Right during the past thirty-five years. Nonetheless, gay liberation and, more recently, the gay rights movement have not undone the social and ideological dominance of heterosexuality, even if they have made its hegemony a bit less secure and less total.

Instead, what seems to be happening is the reverse. Gay people, in their determination to integrate themselves into the larger society, and to demonstrate their essential normality, are rushing to embrace heterosexual forms of life, including heterosexual norms. In so doing, they are accepting the terms in which heterosexual dominance is articulated, and they are positively promoting them. Not only have gay versions of radical politics, radical sex, and radical styles of life fallen out of fashion among us; gay people seem to be rediscovering and championing the superiority of heterosexual social forms, including astonishingly archaic forms (like wedding announcements in the society pages of local newspapers) that heterosexuals themselves are abandoning.[15] We are trying to beat heterosexuals at their own game.

Mere normality no longer seems to satisfy assimilationist-minded gay people. Normality itself is no longer *normal enough* to underwrite gay people's sense of self-worth. We are witnessing the rise of a new and vehement cult of gay ordinariness. In an apparent effort to surpass straight people in the normality sweepstakes and to escape the lingering taint of stigma, gay people lately have begun preening themselves on their dullness, commonness, averageness. A noticeable aggressiveness has started to inform their insistence on how boring they are, how conventional, how completely indistinguishable from everyone else.

In a recent op-ed piece in the *New York Times* about the possibility of Americans electing an openly gay president, Maureen Dowd quoted Fred Sainz of the Human Rights Campaign, a gay Washington-based political lobbying organization, who "fretted to his husband that a gay president would be anticlimactic. 'People expect this bizarro and outlandish behavior,' he told me. 'We're always the funny neighbor wearing colorful, avant-garde clothing. We would let down people with our boringness and banality when they learn that we go to grocery stores Saturday afternoon, take our kids to school plays and go see movies.'"[16] Electing a gay president would change nothing, apparently: nobody would be able to tell the difference. It would be a "non-event." (In which case, why bother?)

A particularly striking example of this attitude was provided by Patrick Califia-Rice in a cover story for the Queer Issue of *The Village Voice* on June 27, 2000. In an article pointedly entitled "Family Values," Califia-Rice (the former lesbian writer Pat Califia) gave an account of queer parenthood that emphasized its lack of queerness. The article's header succinctly summarizes what makes Califia-Rice's family so queer: "Two Dads with a Difference: Neither of Us Was Born Male." But the opening line insists that this difference makes no difference. "Our mornings follow a set routine," Califia-Rice begins, "that any parent with a high-needs baby would recognize."[17]

The *Voice* announces its Queer Issue with a programmatic banner headline on the cover: "Don't Call Us Gay." But Califia-Rice's article could just as easily have been subtitled "Don't Call Us Queer."

As Califia-Rice takes care to indicate, both he and his male partner are "transgendered men (female-to-male or FTM), and my boyfriend is the mother of my child" (48). According to the article, Califia-Rice met his partner, Matt, when they were both still women and lesbians. They began a "torrid affair," but Califia-Rice was in another relationship at the time and broke off the affair with Matt; when they got back together, three years later, "Matt had been on testosterone for several years, had chest surgery and a beard. . . . Our relationship was a scandal. We were generally perceived as a fag/dyke couple rather than two gay/bi men in a daddy/boy relationship, which was how we saw ourselves" (48). Soon Califia-Rice began the process of transitioning from female to male.

Meanwhile, Matt Califia-Rice, who wanted a child and didn't think he would be allowed to adopt one, "had been unable to take testosterone for a couple of years because of side effects like blinding migraines." Doctors informed him that it was still "biologically possi-

27 Cover of *The Village Voice*, 45, no. 25, June 27, 2000:
"Trans Dads Patrick and Matt Califia-Rice with their son, Blake."

ble" for him to conceive a child and give birth to one, and the couple "found three men who loved us but didn't love children" to donate their sperm. Patrick and Matt's son was born a year and a half later (48).

It would be hard to imagine a queerer family: two same-sex parents of different generations, who form a paederastic couple; both of them men, but neither of them born male; one of whom gave birth to a child *after* transitioning from female to male; and a son with three possible biological fathers and no positively identifiable one. It is quite understandable that Patrick Califia-Rice, who is painfully aware of the hostility and intolerance that a non-standard family such as his provokes, should want to play down its queerness and champion its ordinariness. He may have been fortified in that impulse by the support he received from his and his partner's "birth families and straight neighbors," in shocking contrast to the outrage expressed by "a handful of straight-identified homophobic FTMs online who started calling Matt by his girl name, because real men don't get pregnant. One of these bigots even said it would be better for our baby to be born dead than be raised by two people who are 'confused about their gender'" (48).

Nonetheless, what is striking about this testimony is its insistence on, precisely, "family values." The cover of the *Voice* announces that its special issue will contain "Portraits of Radical Lives," and indeed it is difficult to picture a life more radical than the one described by Califia-Rice. "Our family configuration is bound to be controversial," he acknowledges, "even among lesbians and gay men, especially those who believe mainstreaming is the best strategy for securing our civil rights." But Califia-Rice's article engages in its own kind of mainstreaming. Not only does it celebrate the possibility of "enjoy[ing] a place at the table" (48), evoking the title of a notorious book by right-wing gay polemicist Bruce Bawer.[18] It also contains lyrical evocations of the banality of coupled domesticity, adorned with sentimental commonplaces that most heterosexual journalists nowadays might well be embarrassed to publish:

Since the baby arrived, there are precious few moments when Matt and I can meet each other alone. The occasions when lust can break through the fence are even more rare. We are oddly shy during these adult-only interludes, as if becoming parents has made us strange to one another. The house is sticky. Piles of clean laundry that we can't find time to put away topple over and get mixed up with the dirty clothes. Yet we continue to be loving and kind with each other and with Blake. Matt especially is a monument of patience. I am often struck dumb by his profound and consistently deep love for our son. (46)

Move over, John Updike!

Patrick Califia-Rice had good reason to defend the ordinariness, the basic humanity of his existence, surrounded as he was by enemies gay, straight, and trans. His over-compensatory rhetoric is entirely understandable. What makes it significant is that it represents an unusually revealing instance of a far more general tendency—a tendency on the part of many gay people today to insist on being not just "virtually normal," as Andrew Sullivan used to claim, but utterly banal.[19] The effect of this insistence is to erase the specificity and distinctiveness of queer life, thereby denying its ability to contribute anything of value to the world we live in.

When on June 24, 2011, the State of New York enacted a law permitting people of the same sex to marry, the Associated Press requested a response to that historic development from openly gay New York City Council Speaker Christine Quinn, who had broken the news of the state legislature's suspenseful final vote during a press conference by New York mayor Michael Bloomberg. Quinn declared, according to the AP, that "the decision [would] change everything for her and her partner."

What did Quinn mean by "everything"? The changes she went on to enumerate had nothing to do with increased material benefits, equality before the law, the progress of human rights, the rewards of distributive justice, the defeat of homophobia, the breaking-up of the heterosexual monopoly on conjugality and private life, or the removal of legal barriers to the formation and preservation of intimate relationships. Any of those changes might well have qualified as momentous. Quinn, however, described the impact that the legalization of gay marriage would have on herself and her partner in these words: "Tomorrow, my family will gather for my niece's college graduation party, and that'll be a totally different day because we'll get to talk about when our wedding will be and what it'll look like, and what dress Jordan, our grand-niece, will wear as the flower girl. And that's a moment I really thought would never come."[20]

Is the moment Quinn describes really the one we have all been so urgently waiting for? Is *this* the glorious culmination of a century and a half of political struggle for gay freedom and gay pride? And how is this new and "totally different day," which sounds a lot like heterosexual business-as-usual, actually all that different from the day that went before it? Is the whole purpose of gay politics, or gay culture, to return gay people to the fold of normal middle-class heterosexual family life, with all its obligatory rites and rituals—to enable us to reproduce the worst social features, the most ghastly clichés of heterosexuality?

⌾

Sometimes I think homosexuality is wasted on gay people.

⌾

What Quinn's testimony plainly indicates is that the end of discrimination, the rectification of social injustice, and the leveling of all differential treatment of sexual minorities—even should it occur—would not be the same thing as the end of the *cultural dominance* of heterosexuality, the disappearance of heterosexuality as a set of cultural norms. Social equality for gay people will not in and of itself make the world gay. It will not enable us to attain a queerer world more in line with our desires, our wishes, and our fantasies. It should therefore not be confused with, nor will it lead to, the erasure of gay subjective specificity or cultural difference.

Gayness would still be a deviation with respect to the cultural norm, the ways in which the majority of people live or expect to live, and the socio-cultural forms which their lives take or aspire to take.

What makes gay people different from others is not just that we are discriminated against, mistreated, regarded as sick or perverted. That alone is not what shapes gay culture. (That indeed could end.) It's that we live in a social world in which heterosexuality retains the force of a norm. In fact, heterosexuality is the name for a system of norms that goes far beyond the relatively harmless sexual practice of intercourse between men and women.

"The received wisdom, in straight culture," as Michael Warner describes it,

> is that all of its different norms line up, that one is synonymous with the others. If you are born with male genitalia, the logic goes, you will behave in masculine ways, desire women, desire feminine women, desire them exclusively, have sex in what are thought to be normally active and insertive ways and within officially sanctioned contexts, think of yourself as heterosexual, identify with other heterosexuals, trust in the superiority of heterosexuality no matter how tolerant you might wish to be, and never change any part of this package from childhood to senescence. Heterosexuality is often a name for this entire package, even though attachment to the other sex is only one element.[21]

This system of norms may not describe how people actually behave. It's a system of *norms,* after all, not an empirical description of social existence. But it does define the expectations that many people have for the way they and other people live. It implies that "gender norms, [erotic] object-orientation norms, norms of sexual practice, and norms of subjective identification" are congruent and stable.[22] "If you deviate at any point from this program," Warner adds, "you do so at your own cost. And one of the things straight culture hates most is any sign that the different parts of the package might be recombined in an infinite number of ways. But experience shows that this is just what tends to happen. . . . No wonder [heterosexuality] needs so much terror to induce compliance."[23]

Because, as Warner emphasizes, sexual desire for a person of a different sex is "only one element" of this larger package, heterosexuality can cease to be an all-powerful *sexual* norm and still exert normative power. In fact, as a specifically sexual norm, heterosexuality seems to be loosening up a bit. It is gradually becoming less unbending and inflexible. It may even be losing its monopoly on acceptable sexual behavior. But for the survival of gay culture, what matters is not the normativity of heterosexuality as a sexual practice. What matters is the larger package—the fact that heterosexuality remains a social and cultural norm, that heterosexuality retains the power of *heteronormativity*.[24]

Heteronormativity is a system of norms connected with a particular form of life, a form of life that comprises a number of interrelated elements, all of them fused into a single style of social existence. That system of norms does not so much describe how people live or ought to live as it defines a horizon of expectations for human life, a set of ideals to which people aspire and against which they measure the value of their own and other people's lives.

According to those norms, the dignity and value of human life find expression in a particular form of intimate, coupled existence. Such an existence, in order to be brought into being, requires a stable domestic life indivisibly shared with one other person of more or less the same age, but of a different gender and a different sex (the one that person was born with, subject to no modifications), in an exclusive, dyadic, loving, non-commercial arrangement that is conducted in a jointly inhabited home space, established and consolidated by the ownership of property and other kinds of wealth that can be transmitted to future generations. Intimacy, love, friendship, solidarity, sex, reproduction, child-raising, generational succession, caretaking, mutual support, shared living space, shared finances, property ownership, and private life go together and should not be parceled out among different relationships or otherwise dispersed. They should all take place under one roof. They combine to constitute a single, uniquely valuable, and more or less compulsory social form. Ideally, you should have all of those components together—or not at all. (This is what Michael Warner calls the "totalizing tendency" of heteronormativity.)[25]

Linked to this single form of life are models of appropriate community membership, of public speech and self-representation, political participation, freedom, family life, class identity, education, consumption and desire, social display, public culture, racial and national fantasy, health and bodily bearing, trust and truth.[26] All are associated with heterosexuality as a sexual practice and preference. But this heteronormative system can accommodate some minor variations in sexual preference without undergoing any significant alteration in its basic structure—and without imperiling the social dominance of the single form of life in which heteronormativity finds its most powerful and imposing expression.

Heteronormativity can therefore survive the end of the monopoly of heterosexuality on sexual life. Just as you can participate in gay culture without being homosexual, so you can participate in heteronormativity without being straight. Gay people nowadays often do participate in heteronormativity in this sense—either because they dearly want to or because they find themselves pressured to conform to the single model of dignified human intimacy that heteronormativity upholds. In neither case is it a matter of sex; in both cases it is a matter of cultural norms. For what heteronormativity involves is not only the normativity of a specific sexual practice, but also the obviousness and self-evidence of a style of social existence which carries with it an unquestioned prestige and normative power.

Heteronormativity represents the privileging of a normative horizon of expectation for human flourishing. It generates an ethics of personal and collective reproduction, implying an orientation toward a future. It yields an aesthetics of social being, which attaches to the shape of a proper life and gives it beauty and value. It embodies an imaginative structure that imparts meaning to the form of individual existence. There is also the dimension of heteronormativity that Warner calls "reprosexuality—the interweaving of heterosexuality, biological reproduction, cultural reproduction, and personal identity" into a style of life that produces "a relation to self that finds its proper temporality and fulfillment in generational transmission" and gives rise to an ethos of "self-transcendence" as the basis of human dignity.[27]

The dominance of heteronormativity depends on the pervasiveness and inescapability of that ethos—much more than it does on compulsory heterosexuality as a sexual practice. Just as gay culture is more taboo nowadays than gay sex, so it is the culture of heterosexuality—what we call heteronormativity—that currently provides the strongest guarantee of heterosexuality's social legitimacy. Social equality for gay men and other sexual outlaws, should we ever achieve it, will not in itself overthrow heterosexuality's cultural and normative dominance, or the single form of intimacy it produces and imposes. So gay equality alone will not spell the end of heteronormativity and its social ramifications. Heteronormativity may well be qualified, restricted, limited, and possibly undermined or weakened to some extent that is now hard to predict. But the model of human life that it represents, and that it promotes as a horizon of aspiration for every proper human subject, will not disappear with the legalization of gay marriage or the ability of non-heterosexuals to serve openly in the U.S. military.

That is why queer politics is so much more far-reaching, so much more transformative than the politics of gay rights. "Because the logic of the sexual order is so deeply embedded by now in an indescribably wide range of social institutions, and is embedded in the most standard accounts of the world," Warner observes, "queer struggles aim not just at toleration or equal status but at challenging those institutions and accounts."[28] Queer politics takes aim at the very heart of our modernity.

೧೦

Gay men, like all queers, are necessarily detached or alienated, at least to some degree, from heteronormative culture, as well as from the received forms of personal and social life that heteronormativity fashions, elevates, and normalizes, rendering them "mainstream." Gay life does not easily accord with the basic premises of heteronormativity. And to the extent that the social protocols of normal or heteronormal life continue to be alien to gay men, gay men cannot take their world for granted in the same way that straight people can.

In that sense, gay men are also alienated from "nature," which is to say from social definitions of the natural. They remain at a certain distance from what passes for innocent, spontaneous, natural feeling, from the kind of feeling that seems natural—insofar as it is completely at home within heteronormative social conventions, and insofar as it fits those conventions and does not challenge or violate them. Unlike heterosexuals with normal desires—who (in the words of gay poet Frank Bidart) "live as if, though what they / desire is entirely what they are / expected to desire, it is they who desire"—gay men cannot mistake their desire for a confirmation and ratification of their subjective sovereignty. They do not experience their desire as proof of their human agency, as a vindication of the naturalness of their human nature, as an expression of their spontaneous alignment with the natural, given world.[29] They cannot perceive their instincts, their emotions, their longings and lusts as the default settings of a universal human nature, as obvious, self-evident, and completely in harmony with the way that things just naturally are—with human nature *tout court*.

Many heterosexuals are also alienated from heterosexual culture, from the culture of heterosexuality. Much of what I have written here about male homosexuality—its status as a particular social form, its performativity, its inauthenticity, the inability of a social identity to capture the desire that defines it—could also be said about heterosexuality. The difference is not one of social vicissitudes or actual degrees of "naturalness," but one of consciousness. Straight men have to learn to perform one or another version of heterosexual masculinity, and they may well have a consciousness of the inauthenticity of the form—they may well find it a constraining imposition on their spontaneous instincts. But they do not often have a *conscious* conscious-

ness of their social being as a performance. Why not? Because the
culture of heterosexuality, which insists on its own naturalness, encourages straight people to endow their desires and their ways of living with a self-evident taken-for-grantedness. The ideological weight
of normality both impedes an active awareness of the social specificity of heterosexual forms of life—it prevents heterosexuals from
thinking of heterosexuality as a profound enigma that calls for pains-
taking investigation—and warns heterosexuals against inquiring too
deeply into heterosexuality as a specific social form. Indeed, it dis-
courages them from inquiring into social forms in general.

Queers, however, are forced to engage in at least a modicum of
critical reflection on the world as it is given. As Michael Warner says,
"Queers do a kind of practical social reflection just in finding ways of
being queer."[30] That practical social reflection gives rise to a second-
order processing and reprocessing of immediate experience. Queer
people's distance on the social world (as defined and naturalized by
heteronorms), and the acutely *conscious* consciousness they have of
the different forms in which life presents itself to different people, issue inevitably in an irreducible critical attitude.

The queer reprocessing of personal and social experience turns
out, in other words, to be productive. It is in fact essential to the arts—
to literature, to creative and critical thought, to cultural production in
general. The kind of practical social reflection and second-order processing that queers do instinctively, necessarily, is of course available
to anyone, and it is characteristic of every artist, every stylist, every
cook, and every theologian, whether gay or straight. But it is an activity to which gay men are particularly given because of the particularity of their social situation.[31]

Which may be why there are so many gay men in the arts and in
various cultural professions. No doubt "the great majority of gays,"
as Edmund White wrote in 1980, "are as reassuringly philistine as the
bulk of straights" (one of the benefits of gay liberation, he argued,
would be to liberate "many talentless souls" from the compulsion to
produce bad art and free them to become plumbers and electrical en-
gineers).[32] But the point is not that gay men themselves are innately

"artistic," even if all of them are alienated, to some extent, from unprocessed experience (which might account for why those gay men who are *not* innately artistic nonetheless feel a queer compulsion to produce art, as White complained). The point is that homosexuality, in addition to representing a departure from nature, or a resistance to what passes for the natural, also demonstrates a consistent affinity with culture. Homosexuality has a particular, special relation to culture. Its very existence dramatizes the workings of the cultural, rather than the natural, order. It is innately, necessarily on the side of culture.

For what is culture if not a turning aside from nature, from the givenness of the world, especially from the givenness of the social world, from the self-evidence of human existence and everything about it that we unreflectively take for granted? The conscious consciousness of (some) gay men is itself the essence of that *clinamen,* that swerve away from the gravitational pull of the obvious, of the way things just are. Sexual difference or dissidence is likely to be the starting point for a more categorical, more conscious, more programmatic deviation from nature and from everything in the social world that passes for natural.

"Whenever speech or movement or behavior or objects exhibit a certain deviation from the most direct, useful, insensible mode of expression or being in the world," Susan Sontag wrote nearly fifty years ago, "we may look at them as having a 'style.'"[33] Without style, or form, there is no such thing as culture. Sontag's "deviation" is the very ground of culture, then—its origin and its definition. Only a departure from the given can bring culture into existence, and can yield the distance and detached reflection necessary to cultural activity.

In a certain sense, homosexuality *is* culture.

Which is why society needs us.

ꙮ

Where would we be without the insights, the impertinence, the unfazed critical intelligence provided by gay subculture? And where would we be without its conscious consciousness, its awareness of so

much about the way we live our lives that is particular to specific
social forms? Without that alienated perspective, those social forms
would pass for obvious, or natural—which is to say, they would remain invisible, and the shape of our existence would escape us.

And what kind of spiritual freedom would heterosexuals achieve
without the benefit of the detached, alienated perspective on their
world, and its socially naturalized values, that gay male subculture—
now that it is no longer secret—affords them? How otherwise would
they stay honest? Without the benefit of various queer cultures—of
the queerness of culture itself, of the queerness that *is* culture—how
would heterosexuals acquire an understanding of the protocols and
priorities of the heteronormative world in which they remain immersed?

Which points to a final paradox. It may be heterosexuals, nowadays, who appreciate, and who need, gay male culture more than gay
men do themselves.

෨෬

We will be queer forever.

Gay kids still grow up, for the most part, in heterosexual families
and in heteronormative culture. That is not going to change to any
great extent. And even kids who do not grow up in straight families are still exposed, to an overwhelming degree, to heterosexual cultural forms. Heterosexual culture remains the first culture we experience, and our subjectivities, our modes of feeling and expression, our
sense of difference are all bound to take shape within the context and
framework of heterosexual culture.

Gay men, as Sartre wrote sixty years ago, avail themselves simultaneously of two different systems of reference.[34] That is because of the
typical social situation in which gay male subjectivity originates and
in which gay male cultural practices assume their initial form: the situation of growing up and being raised by heterosexual parents in
a normatively and notionally, if not actually, heterosexual environment. From our earliest years, many of us are asked to act in ways

that are at odds with the way we feel and the way we instinctively respond to the established social order. We are called to subjectivity by a demand to be inauthentic. We are required by the social vicissitudes of our very existence to *play a role* that involves faking our own subjectivity.

Those social conditions have great explanatory power for the phenomena we have been studying here. The formation of gay male subjectivity in an originary experience of inauthenticity defines for many gay men what it is to be gay. It accounts for the doubleness of gay consciousness, for that hypersensitivity to the artificial nature of semiotic systems—a hypersensitivity which expresses itself so distinctively in camp and which generates the specific battery of hermeneutic techniques that gay men have evolved for exposing the artifice of social meaning and for spinning its codes and signifiers in ironic, sophisticated, defiant, inherently theatrical ways.[35] And so it conduces to the production of the gay cultural forms and styles with which we have become familiar.

So long as queer kids continue to be born into heterosexual families and into a society that is normatively, notionally heterosexual, and so long as they remain alienated from heteronormative social forms, they will have to devise their own non-standard relation to heterosexual culture. And they will have to find ways of understanding, receiving, and relating to heterosexual culture that express or condense their lack of subjective fit with its protocols. Straight culture will always be our first culture, and what we do with it will always establish a certain template for later, queer relations to standard cultural forms. Gay subjectivity will always be shaped by the primeval need on the part of gay subjects to queer heteronormative culture.

That is not going to change. Not at least for a *very* long time. And we'd better hope it doesn't. For what is at stake is not just gay culture. It is culture as a whole.

1. Diary of a Scandal

1. Matthew S. Schwartz, "Gay Course Penetrates U-M Curriculum," *Michigan Review,* April 12–30, 2000. Matt later requested, and obtained, my permission to audit the course; his commitment to the Men's Glee Club ultimately took priority over it, queerly enough.

2. Those looking for pointers about how to effect such conversions should consult the not entirely tongue-in-cheek advice offered by [John] Mitzel, "How to Proselytize," *Fag Rag* 6 (Fall 1973): 11.

3. See Raymond Williams, "Structures of Feeling," *Marxism and Literature* (Oxford: Oxford University Press, 1977), 128–135, who formulates the concept of "a structure of feeling" in order to describe a dynamic mode of social formation that mediates between the subject and culture, thereby blending "psychology" and "aesthetics." Williams presents his concept, tellingly, as a social analogue of the literary term "style" and associates it with minority formation.

4. See June Thomas, "The Gay Bar: Is It Dying?" Slate.com, June 27, 2011, www.slate.com/id/2297604/ (accessed July 11, 2011): "Unlike other minorities, queers don't learn about our heritage from our birth families. Bars are our Hebrew school, our CCD, our cotillion. As activist pioneer Dick Leitsch wrote in *Gay* magazine in September 1970: 'Gay bars . . . teach and enforce the ethics and rules of gay life and pass on traditions and gay culture.'"

5. For a comprehensive example, see Stephen Colbert's segment on "How to Ruin Same-Sex Marriages," www.colbertnation.com/the-colbert-report-videos/343140/august-05-2010/how-to-ruin-same-sex-marriages (accessed August 11, 2010).

6. "Armstrong Successfully Turns Student Body Gay," *Every Three Weekly* 12.4 (October 2010): 1, 11.

7. Isabelle Loynes, "Having a Stroke Made Me Gay," *Daily Mirror,* September 22, 2011, www.mirror.co.uk/news/top-stories/2011/09/22/having-a-stroke-made-me-gay-115875-23436853/ (accessed September 24, 2011). The "before" and "after" photos alone make this article worth consulting.

8. For humorous testimony to the widespread, taken-for-granted belief in male homosexuality as a cultural orientation, see Freeman Hall, *Stuff that Makes a Gay Heart Weep: A Definitive Guide to the Loud and Proud Dislikes of Millions* (Avon, MA: Adams Media, 2010).

9. C. G. Jung, "Psychological Aspects of the Mother Complex," *The Archetypes and the Collective Unconscious,* vol. 9, pt. 1, of Jung, *Collected Works* (Princeton: Princeton University Press, 1968), 86–87, para. 164, as quoted and cited by Will Fellows, *A Passion to Preserve: Gay Men as Keepers of Culture* (Madison: University of Wisconsin Press, 2004), 243. James J. Gifford observes that "artistic temperament . . . is frequently seen as a homosexual signal" in the pioneering work of Edward Irenaeus Stevenson, both in his 1906 novel *Imre* and in his monumental *summa* of 1908, *The Intersexes;* see Gifford's Introduction to Edward Prime-Stevenson, *Imre,* ed. James J. Gifford (Peterborough, ON: Broadview Press, 2003), 20.

10. Esther Newton, *Mother Camp: Female Impersonators in America,* 2nd ed. (Chicago: University of Chicago Press, 1979; first publ. 1972), 29 (my emphasis).

11. Richard Florida, *The Rise of the Creative Class, and How It's Transforming Work, Leisure, Community and Everyday Life* (New York: Basic Books, 2002, 2004), xvii, 257. Florida often writes as if it is the presence of gay people in a city that correlates with the potential for economic growth, but in fact his claim is based on data gathered from the 1990 U.S. Census, which revealed only the existence of households composed of "unmarried partners" of the same sex, as he acknowledges (pp. 255, 333). So it is actually not the presence of *gay people* but of *gay couples,* which may mean lesbian couples, that is a good sign for future economic development, though Florida never says this. To be fair, Florida went on to supplement that 1990 Census data with figures from the 2000 Census, which did collect information about the sexual orientation of individuals.

12. Ibid., 256–260, xvii–xviii, 294, 296.

13. John M. Clum, *Something for the Boys: Musical Theater and Gay Culture* (New York: Palgrave / St. Martin's, 2001), 8.

14. See the exhibition catalogue, which features both gay and non-gay figures venerated by gay men: *Gay Icons* (London: National Portrait Gallery Publications, 2009).

15. I'm not making up that bit about gay cars. For a list of models supposedly favored by gay people, see the notorious article by Alex Williams, "Gay by Design, or a Lifestyle Choice?" *New York Times,* Automotive Section, April 12, 2007.

16. For a fuller version of this plea for an impersonal, non-individualizing, non-psychologizing approach to the study of the human subject, see David M. Hal-

perin, *What Do Gay Men Want? An Essay on Sex, Risk, and Subjectivity,* rev. ed. (Ann Arbor: University of Michigan Press, 2009).

17. On lesbian cinematic spectatorship, see Patricia White, *Uninvited: Classical Hollywood Cinema and Lesbian Representability* (Bloomington: Indiana University Press, 1999); also Valerie Traub, "The Ambiguities of 'Lesbian' Viewing Pleasure: The (Dis)articulations of *Black Widow,*" in *Body Guards: The Politics of Gender Ambiguity,* ed. Julia Epstein and Kristina Straub (New York: Routledge, 1991), 305–328; Judith Mayne, "Lesbian Looks: Dorothy Arzner and Female Authorship," *How Do I Look? Queer Film and Video,* ed. Bad Object-Choices (Seattle: Bay Press, 1991), 103–135; Ann Pellegrini, "Unnatural Affinities: Me and Judy at the Lesbian Bar," *Camera Obscura: Feminism, Culture, and Media Studies* 65 = 22.2 (2007): 127–133; Lisa Henderson, "Love and Fit," *Camera Obscura: Feminism, Culture, and Media Studies* 67 = 23.1 (2008): 172–177; and Amy Villarejo, *Lesbian Rule: Cultural Criticism and the Value of Desire* (Durham, NC: Duke University Press, 2003). See, further, Terry Castle, "In Praise of Brigitte Fassbaender (A Musical Emanation)," *The Apparitional Lesbian: Female Homosexuality and Modern Culture* (New York: Columbia University Press, 1993), 200–238, 268–273. On the relations between gay male and female, feminist, and lesbian spectatorship, see Pamela Robertson, *Guilty Pleasures: Feminist Camp from Mae West to Madonna* (Durham, NC: Duke University Press, 1996).

18. I refer here to the brilliant, though as yet unpublished, work by my former student Emma Crandall. Publish it, Emma!

19. Compare Brian Larkin, "Indian Films and Nigerian Lovers: Media and the Creation of Parallel Modernities," in *The Anthropology of Globalization: A Reader,* ed. Jonathan Xavier Inda and Renato Rosaldo (Oxford: Blackwell, 2002), 350–378, who does not discuss gay audiences in particular; Gayatri Gopinath, "Bollywood/Hollywood: Queer Cinematic Representation and the Politics of Translation," *Impossible Desires: Queer Diasporas and South Asian Public Cultures* (Durham, NC: Duke University Press, 2005), 93–130, 208–213.

20. See, for example, Richard Parker, *Beneath the Equator: Cultures of Desire, Male Homosexuality, and Emerging Gay Communities in Brazil* (New York: Routledge, 1999); Niko Besnier, "Transgenderism, Locality, and the Miss Galaxy Beauty Pageant in Tonga," *American Ethnologist* 29.3 (2002): 534–566; Martin F. Manalansan, *Global Divas: Filipino Gay Men in the Diaspora* (Durham, NC: Duke University Press, 2003); William L. Leap and Tom Boellstorff, eds., *Speaking in Queer Tongues: Globalization and Gay Language* (Urbana: University of Illinois Press, 2003); Juana Maria Rodriguez, *Queer Latinidad: Identity Practices, Discursive Spaces* (New York: New York University Press, 2003); Gopinath, *Impossible Desires;* Tom Boellstorff, *The Gay Archipelago: Sexuality and Nation in Indonesia* (Princeton, NJ: Princeton University Press, 2005); Mark McLelland, *Queer Japan from the Pacific War to the Internet Age* (Lanham, MD: Rowman and Littlefield, 2005); William J. Spurlin,

Notes to Pages 19–20
462

Imperialism within the Margins: Queer Representation and the Politics of Culture in Southern Africa (New York: Palgrave Macmillan, 2006); Lisa Rofel, *Desiring China: Experiments in Neoliberalism, Sexuality, and Public Culture* (Durham, NC: Duke University Press, 2007); Ricardo L. Ortiz, *Cultural Erotics in Cuban America* (Minneapolis: University of Minnesota Press, 2007); Fran Martin, Peter A. Jackson, Mark McLelland, and Audrey Yue, eds., *AsiaPacifiQueer: Rethinking Genders and Sexualities* (Urbana: University of Illinois Press, 2008); Lawrence La Fountain–Stokes, *Queer Ricans: Cultures and Sexualities in the Diaspora* (Minneapolis: University of Minnesota Press, 2009).

21. George Archibald, "'How To Be Gay' Course Draws Fire at Michigan," *Washington Times*, August 18, 2003, A1.

22. I have speculated at length about the reasons for the panic that perennially surrounds the male instruction of boys. See my essay "Deviant Teaching," *Michigan Feminist Studies* 16 (2002): 1–29; reprinted, with revisions, in *A Companion to Lesbian, Gay, Bisexual, Transgender, and Queer Studies*, ed. George E. Haggerty and Molly McGarry (Malden, MA: Blackwell, 2007), 144–165.

23. Here, for the record, is the complete text of the press release.

AFA-MICHIGAN URGES CANCELLATION OF U of M CLASS "HOW TO BE GAY"

LANSING—The American Family Association of Michigan Wednesday urged Gov. John Engler, the Legislature, and the University of Michigan Board of Regents to push for cancellation of a class scheduled for the University of Michigan's fall semester entitled, "How To Be Gay: Male Homosexuality and Initiation."

UM's Fall 2000 catalogue says the course—offered by Professor David Halperin—"will examine the general topic of the role that initiation plays in the formation of gay identity . . . [and] . . . the course itself will constitute an experiment in the very process of initiation that it hopes to understand."

AFA-Michigan President Gary Glenn, Midland—in a written statement e-mailed Wednesday to the governor, members of the House and Senate appropriations committees, U.M. President Lee C. Bollinger, and the U.M. Board of Regents—said "the proposed course, which openly admits its purpose is to recruit and 'initiate' teenagers into the homosexual lifestyle, is already national news and a source of embarrassment to Michigan, its citizens, and our university system."

"UM actually wants to force Michigan taxpayers to pay for a class to openly recruit and teach teenagers how to engage in a lifestyle of high-risk behavior that is not only illegal but many believe immoral, behavior that further increases the burden on taxpayers to pay for its public health consequences," Glenn wrote.

"Rather than 'experiment' in recruiting and 'initiating' our teenagers into the homosexual lifestyle, Professor Halperin should tell students the truth, that homosexual behavior will make them 8.6 times more likely to catch a venereal disease, with a 1-in-10 chance of acquiring the potentially fatal HIV virus," he said. "UM may as well force taxpayers to pay for teaching students how to play Russian Roulette." (See Center for Disease Control study at: <http://www.cdc.gov/epo/mmwr/preview/mmwrhtml/mm4835a1.htm> www.cdc.gov/epo/mmwr/preview/mmwrhtml/mm4835a1.htm.)

"On behalf of Michigan families whose tax dollars and children are at stake, AFA-Michigan urges you to do everything in your power to stop this outrage before it becomes a reality this fall," Glenn wrote.

He said, however, that just the proposal of a class on "How To Be Gay," and especially Professor Halperin's description of it in the course catalogue, makes an important concession in the ongoing debate over homosexual behavior.

"If such a renowned expert says you need a course from the University of Michigan to learn 'how to be gay,' then it's obvious that high-risk homosexual behavior is a 'learned' lifestyle that is a matter of choice, not genetics," he said.

Halperin wrote in UM's Fall 2000 course catalogue: "Just because you happen to be a gay man doesn't mean that you don't have to learn how to become one. Gay men do some of that learning on their own, but often we learn how to be gay from others, either because we look to them for instruction or because they simply tell us what they think we need to know, whether we ask for their advice or not."

24. "B+ Could Try Harder," *Sydney Star Observer,* March 23, 2000, 10. Many thanks to Jason Prior for clipping this article and sending it to me.

25. Edward Albee, *Who's Afraid of Virginia Woolf? A Play* (New York: Athenaeum, 1962), 3–6.

26. See, generally, Martin Meeker, *Contacts Desired: Gay and Lesbian Communications and Community, 1940s–1970s* (Chicago: University of Chicago Press, 2006). For the notion of a queer public sphere, or "queer counterpublic," see Lauren Berlant and Michael Warner, "Sex in Public," *Critical Inquiry* 24.2 (Winter 1998): 547–566.

Compare Daniel Harris, *The Rise and Fall of Gay Culture* (New York: Hyperion, 1997), 21: "Over the decades gay men have become so adept at communicating their forbidden desires through camp allusions that a sort of collective amnesia has descended over the whole process, and we have lost sight of the fact that our love for performers like Judy Garland was actually a learned behavior, part of our socialization as homosexuals."

27. "Skool Daze," *San Francisco Bay Times,* March 30, 2000, 9–10.

28. For my information and quotations in this paragraph, I rely on Hanna LoPatin,

"'How To Be Gay' Course under Fire from House," *Michigan Daily,* ca. May 24, 2003. See also Beth Berlo, "Michigan Legislators Debate Gay Studies," *Bay Windows* (Boston), June 8–14, 2000; Antonio Planas, "Gay Course at U-M Scrutinized by Group," *State News* (Michigan State University), August 6, 2003.

29. At the request of a local newspaper, I attempted to intervene in the debate, but my response did not appear until two days after the primary. See "U of M Course Has No Intentions of Recruiting Gays" (Letter to the Editor), *Hastings Banner,* 147.32, August 10, 2000, 4.

30. Geoff Larcom, "'Outrage' over Gay Identity Class Prompts Run for U-M Regent Seat," *Ann Arbor News,* August 22, 2000; Charlie Cain, "Divisive Issues Top U-M Race: GOP Considers Quotas, Gays in Picking Candidates," *Detroit News,* August 25, 2000, 1.

31. Jen Fish, "U of Michigan Regents Hear 'How To Be Gay' Class Complaints," *Michigan Daily,* October 20, 2000.

32. Geoff Larcom, "U-M Gay Studies Class Leads Lawmakers to Seek Controls: Bill Would Give State Legislators the Power to Prohibit Courses," *Ann Arbor News,* Thursday, August 21, 2003.

33. For the information in this paragraph, I am indebted to Kim Kozlowski, "Man on a Mission," *Detroit News,* February 4, 2001. See also Jay McNally, "Modern-Day Gideon: Gary Glenn Wages War for Family Values," *Credo,* March 5, 2001.

34. Kozlowski, "Man on a Mission."

35. Dustin Lee, "Gay Courses and the First Amendment," *Michigan Review,* April 12–30, 2000.

2. History of an Error

1. John M. Clum, *Something for the Boys: Musical Theater and Gay Culture* (New York: Palgrave / St. Martin's, 2001), 2, makes precisely this complaint about Ethan Mordden's writing about the Broadway musical. Some prominent exceptions to the general pattern include Clum himself; Michael Bronski, "Judy Garland and Others: Notes on Idolization and Derision," in *Lavender Culture,* ed. Karla Jay and Allen Young (New York: Jove, 1979), 201–212; Al LaValley, "The Great Escape," *American Film* (April 1985): 28–34, 70–71; Wayne Koestenbaum, *The Queen's Throat: Opera, Homosexuality, and the Mystery of Desire* (New York: Poseidon Press, 1993); Sam Abel, "Opera and Homoerotic Desire," *Opera in the Flesh: Sexuality in Operatic Performance* (Boulder, CO: Westview, 1996), 58–75; Kevin Kopelson, *Beethoven's Kiss: Pianism, Perversion, and the Mastery of Desire* (Stanford: Stanford University Press, 1996); D. A. Miller, *Place for Us: Essay on the Broadway Musical* (Cambridge, MA: Harvard University Press, 1998); Mitchell Morris, "It's Raining Men: The Weather Girls, Gay Subjectivity, and the Erotics of Insatiability," in *Audible Traces: Gender, Identity, and Music,* ed. Elaine Barkin and Lydia Hamessley (Zurich: Carciofoli Verlagshaus, 1999), 213–229; Richard Dyer, "Judy

Garland and Gay Men," *Heavenly Bodies: Film Stars and Society* (New York: St. Martin's, 1986), 141–194, and *The Culture of Queers* (London: Routledge, 2002); Ellis Hanson, ed., *Out Takes: Essays on Queer Theory and Film* (Durham, NC: Duke University Press, 1999); Patrick E. Horrigan, *Widescreen Dreams: Growing Up Gay at the Movies* (Madison: University of Wisconsin Press, 1999); Brett Farmer, *Spectacular Passions: Cinema, Fantasy, Gay Male Spectatorships* (Durham, NC: Duke University Press, 2000); Michael DeAngelis, *Gay Fandom and Crossover Stardom: James Dean, Mel Gibson, and Keanu Reeves* (Durham, NC: Duke University Press, 2001); Roger Hallas, "AIDS and Gay Cinephilia," *Camera Obscura* 52 = 18.1 (2003): 84–127; Steven Cohan, *Incongruous Entertainment: Camp, Cultural Value, and the MGM Musical* (Durham, NC: Duke University Press, 2005); the double issue of *Camera Obscura* entitled "Fabulous! Divas," *Camera Obscura: Feminism, Culture, and Media Studies,* 65 and 67 = 22.2 (2007) and 23.1 (2008); and, most recently, Marc Howard Siegel, "A Gossip of Images: Hollywood Star Images and Queer Counterpublics" (Ph.D. diss., University of California, Los Angeles, 2010). For a brilliant analysis of gay male musical culture by someone who is not a gay man, see Nadine Hubbs, *The Queer Composition of America's Sound: Gay Modernists, American Music, and National Identity* (Berkeley: University of California Press, 2004).

2. For the notion, underlying the argument of this book as a whole, that style has a meaning, and that form has a content, I am directly indebted to Myra Jehlen, *Five Fictions in Search of Truth* (Princeton, NJ: Princeton University Press, 2008), and to my many conversations with the author.

3. Already in the 1970s, mutual accusations of self-hatred and internalized homophobia were being exchanged between gay activists critical of gay male effeminacy who favored a virile style of gay deportment and others critical of the vogue for gay masculinity who defended effeminacy: see Alice Echols, "The Homo Superiors: Disco and the Rise of Gay Macho," *Hot Stuff: Disco and the Remaking of American Culture* (New York: Norton, 2010), 121–157, esp. 124–134.

4. Compare Echols, "Homo Superiors," 128, who attributes "gays' . . . identification with tragic, doomed women like Garland" during the pre-disco period to the notion—widely accepted by gay men at the time—that "gayness . . . signaled failed masculinity."

5. Clum, *Something for the Boys*, 23, quips that this "new, far more sexual gay culture" was "a form of musical theater in which everyone could be a performer." Spoken like a true show queen! (Clum proudly identifies himself as such throughout his book.)

6. For the quotation, see Andrew Holleran, *Dancer from the Dance: A Novel* (New York: Morrow, 1978), 15, and rpt. (New York: Bantam, 1979), 7, as cited by Echols, "Homo Superiors," 130.

7. C. Westphal, "Die conträre Sexualempfindung: Symptom eines neuropathischen (psychopathischen) Zustandes," *Archiv für Psychiatrie und Nerven-*

krankheiten 2 (1870): 73–108 (the fascicle of the journal in which Westphal's article was published actually appeared in 1869); Arrigo Tamassia, "Sull' inversione dell' istinto sessuale," *Rivista sperimentale di freniatria e di medicina legale* 4 (1878): 97–117. The latter was the earliest published use of "inversion" that Havelock Ellis, at least, was able to discover; see Ellis, *Sexual Inversion = Studies in the Psychology of Sex,* 3rd ed., vol. 2 (Philadelphia: F. A. Davis, 1922), 3.

See, generally, the fundamental study by George Chauncey, Jr., "From Sexual Inversion to Homosexuality: The Changing Medical Conceptualization of Female Deviance," in *Homosexuality: Sacrilege, Vision, Politics,* ed. Robert Boyers and George Steiner = *Salmagundi* 58–59 (1982–1983): 114–146, revised in *Passion and Power: Sexuality in History,* ed. Kathy Peiss and Christina Simmons (Philadelphia: Temple University Press, 1989), 87–117.

8. Westphal, "Conträre Sexualempfindung," 107n, explaining his choice of "contrary sexual feeling" as a clinical designation for the mental condition he had identified: "Es soll darin ausgedrückt sein, dass es sich nicht immer gleichzeitig um den Geschlechtstrieb als solchen handle, sondern auch bloss um die Empfindung, dem ganzen inneren Wesen nach dem eigenen Geschlechte entfremdet zu sein, gleichsam eine unentwickeltere Stufe des pathologischen Phänomens." See, further, David M. Halperin, "How To Do the History of Male Homosexuality," in Halperin, *How To Do the History of Homosexuality* (Chicago: University of Chicago Press, 2002), 104–137 and 185–195, esp. 127–130.

9. See Hubert C. Kennedy, "The 'Third Sex' Theory of Karl Heinrich Ulrichs," in *Historical Perspectives on Homosexuality,* ed. Salvatore J. Licata and Robert P. Petersen = *Journal of Homosexuality* 6.1–2 (1980/1981): 103–111; as well as Hubert C. Kennedy, *Ulrichs: The Life and Works of Karl Heinrich Ulrichs, Pioneer of the Modern Gay Movement* (Boston: Alyson, 1988), 43–53.

10. This formulation is highly deliberate. I do not want to deny that same-sex sexual contact could qualify as deviant in the period, and I don't want to make a falsely stark and simplistic historical division between an era of inversion followed by an era of homosexuality, as if the two never occurred together, coincided, or were conflated. Nonetheless, I continue to believe it is useful to distinguish between them, as I have done, most recently, in "How To Do the History of Male Homosexuality," where I emphasize the temporal overlaps between inversion and homosexuality. Henning Bech, *When Men Meet: Homosexuality and Modernity,* trans. Teresa Mesquit and Tim Davies (Cambridge: Polity Press, 1997), 85ff. and 239–242, argues powerfully that historians have overplayed the distinction between inversion and homosexuality, and perhaps he is right. Bech cites evidence that same-sex sexual contact in itself was targeted as both criminal and pathological in the nineteenth century even without an element of gender deviance. But his examples tend to occur quite late in the nineteenth century, and his claim that *"before* the modern homosexual, men's same-sex attraction was

not inescapably . . . conceptualized in terms of femininity" (242), while accurate, is misleading, because at no time was men's same-sex sexual attraction *inescapably* conceptualized in terms of gender deviance. What Bech's sociological model of male homosexuality as a concept and form of existence gains in inclusiveness and systematicity it loses in historical precision.

11. Richard von Krafft-Ebing, *Psychopathia Sexualis,* quoted in Arnold I. Davidson, "Closing Up the Corpses: Diseases of Sexuality and the Emergence of the Psychiatric Style of Reasoning," in Davidson, *The Emergence of Sexuality: Historical Epistemology and the Formation of Concepts* (Cambridge, MA: Harvard University Press, 2001), 1–29, 217–224 (quotation on p. 23): *"Perversion* of the sexual instinct . . . is not to be confounded with *perversity* in the sexual act; since the latter may be induced by conditions other than psychopathological. The concrete perverse act, monstrous as it may be, is clinically not decisive. In order to differentiate between disease (perversion) and vice (perversity), one must investigate the whole personality of the individual and the original motive leading to the perverse act. Therein will be found the key to the diagnosis."

12. See Chauncey, "From Sexual Inversion to Homosexuality."

13. See Lawrence R. Murphy, *Perverts by Official Order: The Campaign against Homosexuals by the United States Navy* (New York: Harrington Park Press, 1988); George Chauncey, Jr., "Christian Brotherhood or Sexual Perversion? Homosexual Identities and the Construction of Sexual Boundaries in the World War One Era," *Journal of Social History* 19 (1985/1986): 189–211, rpt. in *Hidden from History: Reclaiming the Gay and Lesbian Past,* ed. Martin Bauml Duberman, Martha Vicinus, and George Chauncey, Jr. (New York: New American Library, 1989), 294–317, 541–546.

14. See George Chauncey, *Gay New York: Gender, Urban Culture, and the Making of the Gay Male World, 1890–1940* (New York: Basic Books, 1994), 81–83. Also, Matt Houlbrook, "'London's Bad Boys': Homosex, Manliness, and Money in Working-Class Culture," in Houlbrook, *Queer London: Perils and Pleasures in the Sexual Metropolis, 1918–1957* (Chicago: University of Chicago Press, 2005), 167–194.

15. See the extraordinary research done by Australia's National Centre in HIV Social Research: for example, Michael Bartos, John McLeod, and Phil Nott, *Meanings of Sex between Men* (Canberra: Australian Government Publishing Service, 1993). See also Jane Ward, "Straight Dude Seeks Same: Mapping the Relationship between Sexual Identities, Practices, and Cultures," in *Sex Matters: The Sexuality and Society Reader,* ed. Mindy Stombler, Dawn M. Baunauch, Elisabeth O. Burgess, and Denise Donnelly, 2nd ed. (New York: Allyn and Bacon, 2007), 31–37; Jane Ward, "Dude-Sex: White Masculinities and 'Authentic' Heterosexuality among Dudes Who Have Sex with Dudes," *Sexualities* 11.4 (2008): 414–434; Eric Anderson, "'Being Masculine Is Not about Who You Sleep with . . . ': Heterosexual Athletes Contesting Masculinity and the One-time Rule of Homosexual-

ity," *Sex Roles* 58.2 (2008): 104–115; and Amanda Lynn Hoffman, "'I'm Gay, For Jamie': Heterosexual / Straight-Identified Men Express Desire to Have Sex with Men" (M.A. thesis, San Francisco State University, 2010).

16. Alfred C. Kinsey, Wardell B. Pomeroy, and Clyde E. Martin, *Sexual Behavior in the Human Male* (Philadelphia: W. B. Saunders, 1948), 615. The point was considerably expanded by a subsequent writer in the Kinsey tradition, C. A. Tripp, *The Homosexual Matrix* (New York: McGraw-Hill, 1975), 22–35, who devotes an entire chapter to it.

    Kinsey was anticipated by Havelock Ellis and Sigmund Freud, who distinguished sexual object-choice from gender role, but who did not limit their definitions of "homosexuality" to same-sex sexual behavior as consistently or as categorically as Kinsey did.

17. Kinsey et al., *Sexual Behavior in the Human Male,* 616, 623.

18. See Louis-Georges Tin, *L'invention de la culture hétérosexuelle* (Paris: Editions Autrement, 2008), who traces the earliest stages of this evolution back to the literary culture of the Middle Ages.

19. Chauncey, *Gay New York,* 111–121; E. Anthony Rotundo, *American Manhood: Transformations in Masculinity from the Revolution to the Modern Era* (New York: Basic, 1993), 274–279; Axel Nissen, *Manly Love: Romantic Friendship in American Fiction* (Chicago: University of Chicago Press, 2009).

20. Nils Axel Nissen correctly observes to me that the eponymous hero of *Imre,* a short novel by "Xavier Mayne" (Edward Irenaeus Stevenson), privately printed in 1906, has the best claim to be the first representation of a straight-acting gay man. See now the superb scholarly edition of *Imre* by James J. Gifford (Peterborough, ON: Broadview Press, 2003).

21. I derive this information from a public lecture by George Chauncey at a conference in Oslo, "Homosexuality 2000," in August 2000; a Norwegian translation appears in *Kvinneforskning* 3–4 (2000): 56–71. Here is John Richardson speaking about the impression made on him by the poet James Schuyler in the summer of 1949: "With his short haircut, tight blue jeans, and white T-shirt, he epitomized the fresh American sailor-boy look that would soon become mandatory for young men everywhere": John Richardson, *The Sorcerer's Apprentice: Picasso, Provence, and Douglas Cooper* (New York: Knopf, 1999), 62. See also the opening photospread of a San Francisco leather bar in Paul Welch and Ernest Havemann, "Homosexuality in America," *Life* Magazine, 56.26 (June 26, 1964): 66–80. For additional background, see Gayle S. Rubin, "The Valley of the Kings: Leathermen in San Francisco, 1960–1990" (Ph.D. diss., University of Michigan, 1994).

22. The term "effete" is featured in Robert K. Martin's unpublished memoir of gay life at Wesleyan University in the early 1960s, "Scenes of Gay Life at Wesleyan before Stonewall," delivered as a lecture at the conference "Homosexuality 2000" in Oslo; a Norwegian translation appears in *Kvinneforskning* 3–4 (2000): 27–39.

This tension between feminine and masculine models of male homosexuality replicates the ideological and political conflicts that took place in Germany at the turn of the twentieth century between Magnus Hirschfeld's Scientific-Humanitarian Committee, which viewed homosexuality as a natural abnormality according to the transgender model formulated originally by Karl Heinrich Ulrichs, and the Gemeinschaft der Eigenen ("Community of the Special") founded by Adolf Brand and Benedikt Friedländer, which promoted male homosexuality as an intensified form of manliness. The two sects were influential and were both allied with broader social movements, but they did not give rise to popular, subcultural styles of gay male deportment.

23. Brenda D. Townes, William D. Ferguson, and Sandra Gillam, "Differences in Psychological Sex, Adjustment, and Familial Influences among Homosexual and Nonhomosexual Populations," *Journal of Homosexuality* 1.3 (1976): 261–272; Joseph Harry, "On the Validity of Typologies of Gay Males," *Journal of Homosexuality* 2.2 (Winter 1976–1977): 143–152; Michael W. Ross, Lesley J. Rogers, and Helen McCulloch, "Stigma, Sex, and Society: A New Look at Gender Differentiation and Sexual Variation," *Journal of Homosexuality* 3.4 (Summer 1978): 315–330; Gary J. McDonald and Robert J. Moore, "Sex-Role Self-Concepts of Homosexual Men and Their Attitudes toward Both Women and Male Homosexuality," *Journal of Homosexuality* 4.1 (Fall 1978): 3–14; Michael W. Ross, "Femininity, Masculinity, and Sexual Orientation: Some Cross-Cultural Comparisons," *Journal of Homosexuality* 9.1 (1983): 27–36.

24. See Foucault's interview with Jean Le Bitoux, "Le gay savoir," in *Entretiens sur la question gay* (Béziers: H&O, 2005), 45–72, esp. 58–63; in English as "The Gay Science," trans. Nicolae Morar and Daniel W. Smith, *Critical Inquiry* 37.3 (Spring 2011): 385–403.

25. Paul Myers, "Façade," *Gay News: Europe's Largest Circulation Newspaper for Homosexuals* 66 (March 13–16, 1975): 16. I should point out that the author is instructing the reader not about how to be butch but about how to pass for straight. It is tempting to construe the entire article as ironic, and thus as a protest *against* gay masculinity, but that would not diminish its historical value as a witness to changing gay male gender styles. (I am deeply grateful to Jason Prior for uncovering this article in the course of his own research, for sharing it with me, and for allowing me to cite it.)

26. Clark Henley, *The Butch Manual: The Current Drag and How To Do It* (New York: New American Library, 1984; orig. publ. New York: Sea Horse Press, 1982), 13. An updated version of this guide, containing a similar mixture of satire and how-to advice for the ACT UP generation, was provided in 1990 by Michelangelo Signorile and photographer Michael Wakefield in a cover story entitled "The New Clone vs. the Old Clone," for New York's *Outweek* magazine. See Michelangelo Signorile, "Clone Wars," *Outweek* 74 (November 28, 1990): 39–45; to which should be added a couple of important corrections and supplements

by Richard Hunter, Michael Tresser, James Lynch, and John Maresca in the Letters section of *Outweek* 76 (December 12, 1990): 5.

27. For those who know French, a brilliant satirical perspective on this transformation is provided by the song "Viril," by P. Philippe and M. Cywie, performed in 1981 by Jean Guidoni, of which a video is available at www.dailymotion.com/video/xt37x_guidoni-81-viril_music (accessed January 11, 2009). Thanks to Rostom Mesli for directing my attention to this performance.

28. Frances Fitzgerald, *Cities on the Hill* (New York: Simon and Schuster, 1986), 34; also 54: "Now 'the Castroids,' as they sometimes called themselves, were dressing with the care of Edwardian dandies—only the look was cowboy or bush pilot: tight blue jeans, preferably Levi's with button flies, plaid shirts, leather vests or bomber jackets, and boots"; 62–63: "There was the clone style proper: short hair, clipped mustache, blue jeans, and bomber jacket." For more details, see Martin P. Levine, *Gay Macho: The Life and Death of the Homosexual Clone,* ed. Michael S. Kimmel (New York: New York University Press, 1998), esp. 60, for an anatomy of the canonical butch types: "Western, Leather, Military, Laborer, Hood, Athlete, Woodsman, Sleaze, Uniforms." For a contemporary appreciation of the "Castro Street Clone," see Edmund White, *States of Desire: Travels in Gay America* (New York: Dutton, 1980), 45–46.

29. Echols, "Homo Superiors," 123.

30. See Dr. Charles Silverstein and Edmund White, *The Joy of Gay Sex: An Intimate Guide for Gay Men to the Pleasures of a Gay Lifestyle* (New York: Crown, 1977), 185: "Since the advent of feminism and gay liberation, 'role-playing' has taken on a decidedly negative aura. . . . To the gay liberationist role-playing conjures up a picture of two men living out a grotesque parody of heterosexual married life"; 186: "The disadvantages of role-playing are manifold and increasingly obvious"; 187: "In the late sixties, the birth of modern feminism and gay liberation called for the abolition of all role-playing."

31. See Echols, "Homo Superiors," 121 and 127, quoting the protagonist of Edmund White's 1997 novel *The Farewell Symphony,* which is set in the 1970s.

32. Silverstein and White, *Joy of Gay Sex,* 10–11.

33. Edmund White, "The Gay Philosopher" (1969), *The Burning Library: Essays,* ed. David Bergman (New York: Knopf, 1994), 3–19 (quotation on p. 18).

34. Silverstein and White, *Joy of Gay Sex,* 10–11.

35. Robert Ferro, *The Blue Star* (New York: Dutton, 1985), 64; cf. 121: "we did everything equally to each other."

36. Mark Merlis, *An Arrow's Flight* (New York: St. Martin's, 1998), 14.

37. See Damon Ross Young, "Pain Porn," in *Porn Archives,* ed. Tim Dean, Steven Ruszczycky, and David Squires (Durham, NC: Duke University Press, forthcoming).

38. Pansy Division, *Undressed* (Lookout! Records, 1993), track 1.

39. "The clone's performance of butch as a kind of self-conscious dress-up, even a

form of drag, distinguishes his brand of machismo from its more earnest and tyrannical straight counterpart. . . . Even as the gay clone mimed heterosexual masculinity, he helped to reveal that 'so-called original' as 'illusory' and contingent, as its own brand of (humorless) performance": Richard Meyer, "Warhol's Clones," in *Negotiating Lesbian and Gay Subjects,* ed. Monica Dorenkamp and Richard Henke (New York: Routledge, 1995), 92–122 (quotation on p. 112), quoting Judith Butler's classic essay, "Imitation and Gender Insubordination," in *Inside/Out: Lesbian Theories, Gay Theories,* ed. Diana Fuss (New York: Routledge, 1991), 13–31, rpt. in *The Lesbian and Gay Studies Reader,* ed. Henry Abelove, Michèle Aina Barale, and David M. Halperin (New York: Routledge, 1993), 307–320. See also Sue-Ellen Case, "Towards a Butch-Femme Aesthetic," *Discourse* 11 (Winter 1988–1989): 55–73, rpt. in *The Lesbian and Gay Studies Reader,* 294–306. For opposing views, see Esther Newton, "Dick(less) Tracy and the Homecoming Queen: Lesbian Power and Representation in Gay Male Cherry Grove," in Newton, *Margaret Mead Made Me Gay: Personal Essays, Public Ideas* (Durham, NC: Duke University Press, 2000), 63–89, 270–276; and Biddy Martin, "Sexualities without Genders, and Other Queer Utopias," *diacritics,* 24.2–3 (Summer/Fall 1994): 104–121, rpt. in Biddy Martin, *Femininity Played Straight: The Significance of Being Lesbian* (New York: Routledge, 1996), 71–94.

40. Leo Bersani, "Is the Rectum a Grave?" in *AIDS: Cultural Analysis / Cultural Activism,* ed. Douglas Crimp, *October* 43 (Winter 1987): 197–222 (quotation on p. 208).

41. On this point, see the detailed discussion in Esther Newton, *Mother Camp: Female Impersonators in America,* 2nd ed. (Chicago: University of Chicago Press, 1979; first publ. 1972), 23–25, 31–33, and, especially, 103–104.

42. On the requirement that male homosexuality be legible, and on the contradictions and paradoxes to which that requirement gives rise, see the classic study by Lee Edelman, *Homographesis: Essays in Gay Literary and Cultural Theory* (New York: Routledge, 1994).

43. Rogers Brubaker, "The Return of Assimilation? Changing Perspectives on Immigration and Its Sequels in France, Germany, and the United States," *Ethnic and Racial Studies* 24 (July 2001): 531–548, cited and discussed in Kenji Yoshino, *Covering: The Hidden Assault on Our Civil Rights* (New York: Random House, 2006), x–xi. Yoshino goes on to offer a judicious critique of the politics of assimilation and its implicit refusal to address continuing practices of discrimination.

44. Will Fellows, *A Passion to Preserve: Gay Men as Keepers of Culture* (Madison: University of Wisconsin Press, 2004), ix–x.

45. Ibid., 14. Compare Clum, *Something for the Boys,* 30: "'I'm gay, but I'm no sissy' . . . is the watchword of the majority of gay men these days."

46. I quote the opening sentence of a classic essay by Michael Warner, "Introduction," in *Fear of a Queer Planet: Queer Politics and Social Theory,* ed. Warner (Minneapolis: University of Minnesota Press, 1993), vii–xxxi (quotation on p. vii); an

earlier version of this essay, minus the opening sentence, had appeared as "Introduction: Fear of a Queer Planet," *Social Text* 29 (1991): 3–17. See also Eve Kosofsky Sedgwick, *Epistemology of the Closet* (Berkeley: University of California Press, 1990); and Sedgwick, *Tendencies* (Durham, NC: Duke University Press, 1993).

47. It is an eloquent sign of the times that Brett Farmer, introducing his brave and original study of gay men's distinctive relation to the movies, has to spend pages justifying his project against the anticipated objection on the part of queer theorists that it is illegitimately essentialist. See Farmer, *Spectacular Passions*, 6–15.

48. Barry D. Adam, "How Might We Create a Collectivity That We Would Want To Belong To?" in *Gay Shame*, ed. David M. Halperin and Valerie Traub (Chicago: University of Chicago Press, 2009), 301–311 (quotation on p. 306). By way of support, Adam cites an earlier essay of his: "Love and Sex in Constructing Identity among Men Who Have Sex with Men," *International Journal of Sexuality and Gender Studies* 5.4 (2000): 325–339.

49. Fellows, *Passion to Preserve;* Clum, *Something for the Boys;* Neil Bartlett, *Who Was That Man? A Present for Mr Oscar Wilde* (London: Serpent's Tail, 1988); David Nimmons, *The Soul beneath the Skin: The Unseen Hearts and Habits of Gay Men* (New York: St. Martin's, 2002).

50. Yoshino, *Covering*, 22.

51. In an op-ed piece in the *New York Times* on March 26, 2006, Orlando Patterson inveighed against "a deep-seated dogma that has prevailed in social science and policy circles since the mid-1960s: the rejection of any explanation that invokes a group's cultural attributes—its distinctive attitudes, values and predispositions, and the resulting behavior of its members." He went on to welcome recent historical, political, intellectual developments that "have made it impossible to ignore the effects of culture" on the shape of Black life in the United States, though by this he meant only the factors internal to Black society that might account for underachievement and poverty. This appeal to the "effects of culture" might well explain why so many people remain wary of "any explanation that invokes a group's cultural attributes."

52. In capitalizing the terms "Black" and "White," I'm following an orthographic practice in cultural studies intended to signal that these color terms are not descriptors, but designations of ethnic identities.

53. Ten months later, in an appearance on the *Ellen DeGeneres Show* on October 22, 2008, Obama said, "Michelle may be a better dancer than me, but I'm convinced I'm a better dancer than John McCain." See youtube.com/watch?v=88ogl_jJcGo (accessed October 27, 2008).

54. Baratunde Thurston, a Black comedian and blogger, has announced a new book called *How To Be Black* as forthcoming from HarperCollins in February 2012; see his website, baratunde.com (accessed August 9, 2011). Compare Michelle M. Wright, *Becoming Black: Creating Identity in the African Diaspora* (Durham, NC:

Duke University Press, 2004), who takes a rather different approach to the question from my own, though I believe we share some of the same concerns.

55. See Dyer, "Judy Garland and Gay Men."

3. Gay Identity and Its Discontents

1. The following paragraphs summarize a more detailed argument which I laid out in an earlier book, *What Do Gay Men Want? An Essay on Sex, Risk, and Subjectivity* (Ann Arbor: University of Michigan Press, 2007; rev. ed., 2009), esp. 1–10.

2. The one exception, the one kind of inquiry into gay male subjectivity that has reclaimed a certain legitimacy, is research into gay men's motives for engaging in risky sex in the context of HIV/AIDS; see Halperin, *What Do Gay Men Want?*

3. "Covering" is the word that Kenji Yoshino borrows from Erving Goffman in order to refer to a self-protective practice on the part of members of devalued social groups that consists in downplaying or deemphasizing their cultural particularities, especially particularities that are obtrusive and likely to provoke hostility or discomfort in "normal" people. "Covering," as Yoshino defines it, is therefore distinct from "passing," insofar as it does not involve deception, denial, or a refusal to identify; on the contrary, "covering" occurs when an individual openly avows and acknowledges her stigmatized identity but then chooses not to insist on it and plays down any stereotypical trait that symbolizes it, veiling that trait discreetly instead of "flaunting it" or "shoving it in our faces." See Kenji Yoshino, *Covering: The Hidden Assault on Our Civil Rights* (New York: Random House, 2006), esp. 17–19.

    "Covering" in this sense is continuous with "closeting," as that term is commonly employed in queer studies; see, generally, Eve Kosofsky Sedgwick, *Epistemology of the Closet* (Berkeley: University of California Press, 1990). Yoshino considers the closet to be operative only in the case of "passing," even though he freely admits that passing and covering can shade into each other. Following Sedgwick, I give the concept of the closet greater scope in the analysis that follows (in this chapter and the next two).

4. Michael Warner, *The Trouble with Normal: Sex, Politics, and the Ethics of Queer Life* (New York: Free Press, 1999), 31.

5. Yoshino, *Covering*, offers a powerful critique of the politics of assimilation, one that is in many respects congenial to the argument I am trying to make here and that provides additional support for it. At the same time, Yoshino retreats from the implications of that critique and, dramatizing the very phenomenon of "covering" that he claims to expose and to denounce, embraces a politics of assimilation himself by endorsing what he calls a "universal" quest for authenticity (27, 184–196). He says, for example, "It may be the explosion of diversity in [the United States] that will finally make us realize what we have in common" (192); and "Told carefully, the gay story becomes a story about us all" (27). But

what if it didn't become such a story? What if it turned out to be a story about gay people—a story *just* about gay people? Would that make it less interesting, less valuable, less worth telling? Yoshino's own example shows how a universalist model of identity politics paradoxically functions to erase difference and promote assimilation.

For another typical instance of sexual despecification as a universalizing strategy whose effect is to erase gayness, see John Lahr's review of Matthew Bourne's all-male version of *Swan Lake* in the *New Yorker* (October 19, 1998): the male duets, Lahr wrote, are "not really about gay sex but about sexuality itself." The review is cited, quoted, and aptly criticized in John M. Clum, *Something for the Boys: Musical Theater and Gay Culture* (New York: Palgrave / St. Martin's, 2001), 208–209, on precisely these grounds.

6. Daniel Harris, *The Rise and Fall of Gay Culture* (New York: Hyperion, 1997), 84.

7. For a critique of "homonormativity," see Lisa Duggan, *The Twilight of Equality? Neoliberalism, Cultural Politics, and the Attack on Democracy* (Boston: Beacon Press, 2003).

8. See, now, Heather Love, *Feeling Backward: Loss and the Politics of Queer History* (Cambridge, MA: Harvard University Press, 2007).

9. Warner, *The Trouble with Normal*. See also Gayle Rubin, "Thinking Sex: Notes for a Radical Theory of the Politics of Sexuality," in *Pleasure and Danger: Exploring Female Sexuality*, ed. Carole S. Vance (Boston: Routledge and Kegan Paul, 1984), 267–319, revised and updated in *The Lesbian and Gay Studies Reader*, ed. Henry Abelove, Michèle Aina Barale, and David M. Halperin (New York: Routledge, 1993), 3–44.

10. John Howard, *Men Like That: A Southern Queer History* (Chicago: University of Chicago Press, 1999), 15.

11. See David M. Halperin, "Gay Identity and Its Discontents," *Photofile* 61 (December 2000): 31–36, somewhat expanded as Halperin, "Identité et désenchantement," trans. Paul Lagneau-Ymonet, in *L'infréquentable Michel Foucault: Renouveaux de la pensée critique*, ed. Didier Eribon (Paris: EPEL, 2001), 73–87; Spanish translation by Graciela Graham in *El infrecuentable Michel Foucault: Renovación del pensamiento crítico*, ed. Eribon (Buenos Aires: Letra Viva / EDELP, 2004), 105–120.

12. I am invoking the celebrated formula that Douglas Crimp proposed in "Mourning and Militancy," *October* 51 (Winter 1989): 3–18. Crimp, even at the time, argued that the AIDS activist movement was in danger of repressing its own emotional needs in its drive to political action. See, now, the detailed exploration of AIDS activist feeling in Deborah B. Gould, *Moving Politics: Emotion and ACT UP's Fight against AIDS* (Chicago: University of Chicago Press, 2009).

13. On the difference between emotions that are politically good and those that are politically bad, see Sianne Ngai, *Ugly Feelings* (Cambridge, MA: Harvard University Press, 2004); and Anne Anlin Cheng, *The Melancholy of Race: Psychoanalysis,*

Assimilation, and Hidden Grief (New York: Oxford University Press, 2002), both discussed in Love, *Feeling Backward,* 12–14, with considerable pertinence to the issues reviewed here.

14. For an early brilliant critique of this gay tendency to distinguish between good and bad emotions, see Lee Edelman, "The Mirror and the Tank: 'AIDS,' Subjectivity, and the Rhetoric of Activism," *Homographesis: Essays in Gay Literary and Cultural Theory* (New York: Routledge, 1994), 93–117, 256–260. See also Paul Morrison, "End Pleasure," *The Explanation for Everything: Essays on Sexual Subjectivity* (New York: New York University Press, 2001), 54–81, 181–184.

15. In this context, some writers stand out for their bravery. See Leo Bersani's praise of sex in general, and of gay men's sexual culture in particular, for being "anticommunal, antiegalitarian, antinurturing, antiloving": "Is the Rectum a Grave?" in *AIDS: Cultural Analysis / Cultural Activism,* ed. Douglas Crimp = *October* 43 (Winter 1987): 197–222 (quotation on p. 215). See also Lee Edelman's praise of gay male narcissism and passivity in "The Mirror and the Tank."

16. See, for example, Douglas Crimp, "Mario Montez, For Shame," in *Regarding Sedgwick: Essays on Queer Culture and Critical Theory,* ed. Stephen M. Barber and David L. Clark (New York: Routledge, 2002), 57–70. Crimp calls his project "Queer before Gay." It was anticipated in certain respects, as Crimp himself acknowledges, by Eve Kosofsky Sedgwick, "Queer Performativity: Henry James's *The Art of the Novel*," *GLQ: A Journal of Lesbian and Gay Studies* 1.1 (1993): 1–16. The work of Crimp and of Sedgwick has been reprinted in *Gay Shame,* ed. David M. Halperin and Valerie Traub (Chicago: University of Chicago Press, 2009), 49–75, which is a compendium of some recent attempts to move queer politics and queer theory beyond gay pride.

4. Homosexuality's Closet

1. Only after drafting an early version of the following paragraphs in 2001 (see David M. Halperin, "Homosexuality's Closet," *Michigan Quarterly Review* 41.1 [Winter 2002]: 21–54, esp. 26–29) did I come across a similar analysis by John Clum of a different interview with David Daniels in a 1998 issue of the *New Yorker:* see John M. Clum, *Something for the Boys: Musical Theater and Gay Culture* (New York: Palgrave / St. Martin's, 2001), 34–35. While Clum and I are both interested in the way Daniels publicly presents his sexual and gender identity, and while we are both critical of how the liberal print media normalize him, we derive rather different lessons from the interviews we examine.

For Tommasini's openness as a gay man, see his biography of Virgil Thomson, starting with the Acknowledgments. Anthony Tommasini, *Virgil Thomson: Composer on the Aisle* (New York: Norton, 1997), xii: "Many thanks to my partner, Ben McCommon, for helping me get through the rough times." (By contrast, Tommasini does not identify himself as a gay man in his *New York Times* article.)

I am indebted to Nadine Hubbs for this reference, for her incisive criticism of this section of my book, and for opening up to me the world of queer musicology, whose impact is easy to discern in much of what follows.

2. David Daniels, with Martin Katz (piano), *Serenade,* Virgin Classics, no. 5454002 (1999). An earlier recording of European countertenors presents itself in a much more explicitly camp style; see Pascal Bertin, Andreas Scholl, Dominique Visse, *Les Trois Contre-ténors,* Harmonia Mundi, no. 901552 (April 1995).

3. For some pioneering efforts to open up the musicality/sexuality nexus as a topic for future research in a queer mode, see Philip Brett, "Musicality, Essentialism, and the Closet," and Suzanne G. Cusick, "On a Lesbian Relationship with Music: A Serious Effort Not to Think Straight," both in *Queering the Pitch: The New Gay and Lesbian Musicology,* ed. Philip Brett, Elizabeth Wood, and Gary C. Thomas (New York: Routledge, 1994), 9–26 and 67–84.

4. See D. A. Miller, "Anal *Rope,*" *Representations* 32 (Fall 1990): 114–133, reprinted in *Inside/Out: Lesbian Theories, Gay Theories,* ed. Diana Fuss (New York: Routledge, 1991), 119–141, for a classic account of the operations of homosexual implication in discourses governed by the regime of the closet. Miller clearly establishes that such operations originate in the shadow kingdom of *connotation,* whose mode of signification is particularly characteristic of the closet. For a brilliant analysis of some journalistic instances, provided by the *New York Times* and *Life* magazine in the early 1960s, see Lee Edelman, "Tearooms and Sympathy; or, The Epistemology of the Water Closet," *Homographesis: Essays in Gay Literary and Cultural Theory* (New York: Routledge, 1994), 148–170, 263–267.

5. What's Gayer Than Gay?

1. Heather Love, *Feeling Backward: Loss and the Politics of Queer History* (Cambridge, MA: Harvard University Press, 2007), 17.

2. Susan Sontag, "Against Interpretation," *Against Interpretation and Other Essays* (New York: Farrar, Straus and Giroux, 1966; orig. publ. 1964), 3–14, esp. 6–10 (quotation on p. 7).

3. For a compelling demonstration of how the psychoanalytic destabilization of heterosexual identity conduces, paradoxically but ineluctably, to the consolidation of heterosexual privilege, see Paul Morrison, *The Explanation for Everything: Essays on Sexual Subjectivity* (New York: New York University Press, 2001).

4. For a couple of eloquent examples, see Christopher Guest's film *Waiting for Guffman* (1996), and Neil Patrick Harris's opening number at the 2011 Tony Awards "Broadway: It's Not Just for Gays Any More," www.youtube.com/watch?v=-6S5caRGpK4 (accessed June 17, 2011). The Broadway musical still functions so ubiquitously as a signifier of male homosexuality in popular culture—for instance, in TV shows such as *Will and Grace, Queer Eye for the Straight Guy, Desperate Housewives,* and *Glee*—that it would be impossible to cite all the occurrences of what has now become an obvious commonplace, a truth univer-

sally acknowledged. John M. Clum catalogues a number of examples throughout the course of his richly detailed survey, *Something for the Boys: Musical Theater and Gay Culture* (New York: Palgrave / St. Martin's, 2001), esp. 28, 36–38; all further page references to this book will be incorporated in the text.

5. Clum, *Something for the Boys*, 36–37, cites the example of two students who spontaneously perform "a perfect imitation of Ethel Merman doing 'You Can't Get a Man with a Gun.'" He goes on to comment, "This, too, is gay culture, the maintaining of a flamboyant tradition of musical theater and musical divas these kids have never experienced first hand, but somehow know."

6. D. A. Miller, *Place for Us: Essay on the Broadway Musical* (Cambridge, MA: Harvard University Press, 1998), 16. All further page references to this book will be incorporated in the text. Unless otherwise noted, all italics that appear in quoted extracts from this book are Miller's own.

7. Compare Daniel Harris, *The Rise and Fall of Gay Culture* (New York: Hyperion, 1997), 34: "Stereotypes often contain a grain of truth even though we are forbidden to say so in polite society."

8. On the limited temporality of the Broadway musical, see Frank Rich's cover story on Stephen Sondheim, "Conversations with Sondheim," *New York Times Magazine*, March 12, 2000, 38–43, 60–61, 88–89, which appeared under the headline, "'You Can't Bring It Back. It's Gone.'" Clum, *Something for the Boys*, does a good job of describing the historical specificity of different varieties of musical theater and the reasons for its decline as a cultural form.

9. The embarrassing emotional consequences for the post-Stonewall gay subject of these enduring realities of pre-Stonewall experience are well brought out by Love, *Feeling Backward*, 20, in the course of her own commentary on Miller: "There is something uncanny, of course, about the appearance of such [adolescent] feelings [in the adult, post-Stonewall man] after the fact and out of context. . . . The appearance of such feelings outside of their proper historical context, in subjects whose only experience of gay identity is of the post-Stonewall variety, is still more disturbing. The circulation of pre-Stonewall forms of life and structures of feeling throughout the post-Stonewall world suggests a historical continuity even more complex, incorrigible, and fatal than that of individual character. The evidence is written in the subjectivities of queer men and women who grew up after Stonewall who are as intimately familiar with the structures of feeling Miller describes as with the rhetoric of pride that was meant to displace it. Such continuities suggest that direct experience of the pre-Stonewall moment is not solely responsible for a range of feelings that we today designate as pre-Stonewall, feelings that are all the more shameful given the 'tolerance' of the contemporary moment."

10. Compare the similar account of the solitary, sentimental appeal of opera provided by Wayne Koestenbaum, *The Queen's Throat: Opera, Homosexuality, and the Mystery of Desire* (New York: Poseidon Press, 1993), 46–83, esp. 76–80.

11. For a typical instance of such phobic disavowal combined with an effort at dis-

engaged tolerance (in regard to Judy Garland), see Michael Joseph Gross, "The Queen Is Dead," *Atlantic Monthly,* August 2000, 62–70. For a similar impulse by a gay male critic to disavow the queeniness of grand opera and to rescue it for a dignified gay identity and a "healthy" gay sexuality, see Sam Abel, "Opera and Homoerotic Desire," *Opera in the Flesh: Sexuality in Operatic Performance* (Boulder, CO: Westview, 1996), 58–75.

12. I refer here to the passage from Proust which Miller has selected as his book's epigraph: "That bad music is played, is sung more often and more passionately than good, is why it has also gradually become more infused with men's dreams and tears. Treat it therefore with respect. Its place, insignificant in the history of art, is immense in the sentimental history of social groups." Miller is quoting, somewhat freely, the following passage: Marcel Proust, "Eloge de la mauvaise musique," *Les Plaisirs et les jours,* ed. Thierry Laget (Paris: Gallimard, 1993), 183.

13. Barry D. Adam, "How Might We Create a Collectivity That We Would Want to Belong To?" in *Gay Shame,* ed. David M. Halperin and Valerie Traub (Chicago: University of Chicago Press, 2009), 301–311 (quotation on p. 305; italics added). Compare Al LaValley, "The Great Escape," *American Film* (April 1985): 28–34, 70–71; LaValley speaks of the "utopian and alternate world" that gay men find in Hollywood movies and in aesthetic experience in general (29).

14. See Miller, *Place for Us,* 3: the Broadway musical's "frankly interruptive mode-shifting" between book and lyrics "had the same miraculous effect on [proto-gay boys in the 1950s] as on every character, no matter how frustrated in ambition or devastated by a broken heart, who felt a song coming on: that of sending the whole world packing." Compare Clum, *Something for the Boys,* 5–6.

15. Clum, *Something for the Boys,* 13, speaking specifically of old-time, unmiked female singers in Broadway musicals, "belters" like Ethel Merman, and "the grand gesture that went with the big noise."

16. Clum, *Something for the Boys,* 5–7, goes on to make an interesting argument that the queer pleasure of opera consists in the transcending of the body through music, whereas Broadway musicals feature glamorous performers with lithe bodies flamboyantly decked out in gorgeous clothes: in musical theater, Clum says, the musical triumphs over mortality.

17. On Clum's view, the Broadway musical therefore confirms the truth that "every gay man learns by puberty—everything involved with gender and sex is role-playing one way or another. That's what unites gay men" (23).

6. The Queen Is Not Dead

1. On the enduring gay appeal of *The Golden Girls,* see Charles Grandee, "House of Dames," *New York Times Magazine, Part Two: Home Design, Spring 2002,* April 14, 2002, 52ff.

2. "One might have expected Stonewall to make [Hollywood] star cults outmoded

among gays," wrote Al LaValley as long ago as 1985, "yet neither gay openness nor the new machismo has completely abolished the cults." Al LaValley, "The Great Escape," *American Film* (April 1985), 71.

3. I allude to the classic work by Erving Goffman, *Stigma: Notes on the Management of Spoiled Identity* (Englewood Cliffs, NJ: Prentice-Hall, 1963).

4. Alice Echols, *Hot Stuff: Disco and the Remaking of American Culture* (New York: Norton, 2010), 147.

5. See www.out.com/slideshows/?slideshow_title=Lady-Gagas-Born-This-Way -Love-It-or-Leave-It&theID=1#Top (accessed June 6, 2011).

6. Katie Zezima, "Lady Gaga Goes Political in Maine," *New York Times,* September 20, 2010.

7. Lyrics available online at www.metrolyrics.com/born-this-way-lyrics-lady-gaga .html (accessed June 6, 2011).

8. Mark Simpson, "Bored This Way: Gaga Lays a Giant Egg," www.out.com/ slideshows/?slideshow_title=Lady-Gagas-Born-This-Way-Love-It-or-Leave-It& theID=3#Top (accessed June 6, 2011).

9. Compare Mark Simpson, "That Lady Gaga Backlash Is So Tired Already," *Out Magazine,* September 24, 2010: "When was the last time pop music mattered? When was the last time you cared? Until Lady Gaga came along, just a couple years ago, pop seemed thoroughly pooped. Some nice tunes and haircuts here and there and some really excellent financial institution ad soundtracks, but really, who thought pop could ever trouble us again as a total art form? Gaga has single-handedly resurrected pop. Or at least she's made it seem like it's alive. Maybe it's a kind of galvanic motion—those pop promos sometimes look like Helmut Newton zombie flicks—but boy, this is shocking fun."

10. Logan Scherer, personal communication, June 5, 2011.

11. Ibid.

12. Clum, in *Something for the Boys: Musical Theater and Gay Culture* (New York: Palgrave / St. Martin's, 2001), suggests that "show queens predominated at a moment in gay history when the closet was still an operative principle for gay men" (27; and passim).

13. Daniel Harris, *The Rise and Fall of Gay Culture* (New York: Hyperion, 1997), 37, 34, as quoted and cited by Clum, *Something for the Boys,* 22, 34.

14. This is Andrew Sullivan, "The End of Gay Culture," *New Republic,* October 24, 2005, www.tnr.com/politics/story.html?id=cac6ca08-7df8-4cdd-93cc-1d2 0cd8b7a70 (accessed July 13, 2009), quoting Michael Walzer.

15. Sullivan, "End of Gay Culture."

16. For a canonical representation of the classic gay male night out, see Howard Cruse, "Billy Goes Out" (1979?), in Cruse, *Dancin' Nekkid with the Angels: Comic Strips and Stories for Grownups* (New York: St. Martin's, 1987), 66–72. For an example of the dissatisfactions with official gay culture, see the remarks by the transgender performance artist Glenn Maria to Smith Galtney, "Let the Gays

Begin: Six City Culture Makers Attempt to Answer Our Burning—Possibly Flaming—Questions," *Time Out New York* 661 (May 29–June 4, 2008): 18–21: "I don't have Logo, but I once got a gift bag filled with movies from Here! TV. They were so bad! I thought the idea of putting us on TV was to see something you might relate to" (20).

17. See David Caron, "Shame on Me, or the Naked Truth about Me and Marlene Dietrich," in *Gay Shame*, ed. David M. Halperin and Valerie Traub (Chicago: University of Chicago Press, 2009), 117–131.

18. On Puig and Hollywood cinema, see Marc Howard Siegel, "A Gossip of Images: Hollywood Star Images and Queer Counterpublics" (Ph.D. diss., University of California, Los Angeles, 2010), esp. 55–57. Siegel also discusses gay filmmaker Matthias Müller's 1990 short film *Home Stories*, which similarly assembles a collage of diva moments from classic Hollywood cinema: see "Gossip of Images," 64–69, recapitulating Siegel's earlier analysis in "That Warm Night in the Park," *The Memo Book: Films, Videos and Installations by Matthias Müller,* ed. Stefanie Schulte Strathaus (Berlin: Vorwerk 8, 2005), 208–217.

19. Alan Sinfield, "'The Moment of Submission': Neil Bartlett in Conversation," *Modern Drama* 39 (1996): 211–221 (quotation on p. 218).

20. Another notable exception is Richard Dyer, especially "Judy Garland and Gay Men," *Heavenly Bodies: Film Stars and Society* (New York: St. Martin's, 1986), 141–194; and Dyer, *The Culture of Queers* (London: Routledge, 2002). See also Alexander Doty, *Making Things Perfectly Queer: Interpreting Mass Culture* (Minneapolis: University of Minnesota Press, 1993); Doty, *Flaming Classics: Queering the Film Canon* (New York: Routledge, 2000); and the essays collected in Ellis Hanson, ed., *Out Takes: Essays on Queer Theory and Film* (Durham, NC: Duke University Press, 1999).

21. Virginia Woolf, *Three Guineas* (San Diego: Harcourt Brace, 1938), 17.

7. Culture and Genre

1. Compare Raymonde Carroll, *Evidences invisibles: Américains et français au quotidien* (Paris: Seuil, 1987); in English as *Cultural Misunderstandings: The French-American Experience,* trans. Carol Volk (Chicago: University of Chicago Press, 1988).

2. Ross Chambers, *Untimely Interventions: AIDS Writing, Testimonial, and the Rhetoric of Haunting* (Ann Arbor: University of Michigan Press, 2004), 24–25. My understanding of genre has been decisively shaped by Chambers, though it is far less precise, consistent, and systematic than his.

3. For a review of critical-theoretical writing on the pragmatics of genre, see Ross Chambers, "Describing Genre," *Paragraph* 16.3 (1993): 293–306. The understanding of the pragmatics of genre contained in this body of work derives from the thought of the sociolinguist M. A. K. Halliday (see, especially, *Language as Social*

Semiotic: The Social Interpretation of Language and Meaning [Baltimore: University Park Press, 1978]); it is distinct from the influential views of Carolyn R. Miller, "Genre as Social Action," *Quarterly Journal of Speech* 70 (1984): 151–167, who also lobbies for a pragmatic and ethnomethodological approach to genre, but whose treatment of genre is largely confined to the sphere of rhetoric, and to rhetorical action, and rarely extends to social interaction, even though she does refer to Halliday and accords prominence in her definition of genre to "situation" and "social context."

In *The Female Complaint: The Unfinished Business of Sentimentality in American Culture* (Durham, NC: Duke University Press, 2008), 4, Lauren Berlant proposes to treat femininity as a genre *"like* an aesthetic one," insofar as femininity can be seen as "a structure of conventional expectation that people rely on to provide certain kinds of affective intensities and assurances." That is a similarly social but somewhat less pragmatic understanding of genre from mine.

4. Chambers, *Untimely Interventions*, 25, explaining Halliday's notions of *"field, tenor,* and *register* as the areas of appropriateness that genres regulate."

5. Chambers, "Describing Genre," 296, summarizing the work of Anne Freadman, speaks of genre as embedded in "ceremonial or ritual, regulatory 'settings,' which control the regularities of practice that make social interactions possible."

6. Hence, according to John Frow, genres are not principally "a matter of the categorization of texts" but "a matter of the textual categorization and mobilization of information about the world"; see Frow, "'Reproducibles, Rubrics, and Everything You Need': Genre Theory Today," *PMLA* 122.5 (October 2007): 1626–1634 (quotation on pp. 1632–1633). This formulation, however, still privileges textuality over pragmatics, insofar as it continues to treat genres as forms of discourse rather than as forms of (discursively mediated) action or interaction.

7. Compare June Howard's account of sentimentality as a genre in "What Is Sentimentality?" *Publishing the Family* (Durham, NC: Duke University Press, 2001), esp. 213–245, 298–302. Ross Chambers goes further and, drawing on Anne Freadman's work, speaks of genre as "the phenomenon whereby the discursive construction of *subject* positions is articulated with the historical and social production of *collective* discursive practices" ("Describing Genre," 294; italics in original). That formulation opens up new possibilities for describing how gay subjectivity is actually constituted, and it points the way to a discursive, nonpsychological science of gay male subjectivity. That is not the project I am attempting here—I am neither so ambitious nor so rigorous—but I hope that my formal and discursive analysis of gay male cultural practices might at least contribute to it.

8. Compare Chambers, "Describing Genre," 304: "But the first task for cultural studies, then, if it is to draw inspiration from Freadman's analytic practice, would be to examine the constitution of generic 'fields' and the nature of the

field they themselves constitute—a field that might well prove to be synonymous with, but considerably more precise, than whatever it is that is designated
by that obscure 'mana'-word, *culture,* itself."

9. For some striking examples, see Nicholas Graham, "U.S. Soldiers in Afghani-
stan Remake Lady Gaga's 'Telephone' Music Video" and "U.S. Soldiers Remake
Kesha's 'Blah Blah Blah' Video into 'Don't Ask, Don't Tell' Spoof," *Huffington
Post* (April 29–30, 2010; and May 12, 2010), www.huffingtonpost.com/2010/04/29/
telephone---the-afghanist_n_557123.html and www.huffingtonpost.com/2010/
05/12/us-soldiers-remake-keshas_n_573831.html (accessed May 14, 2010). See
also the commentary by Mark Simpson, "Why Straight Soldiers Can't Stop Acting Gay on Video," posted on marksimpson.com (accessed May 14, 2010).

10. Maeve Reston, "Newt Gingrich, 'Dancing Queen,'" *Los Angeles Times,* May 19,
2011, available online at articles.latimes.com/2011/may/19/news/la-pn-newt
-gingrich-dancing-queen-20110519 (accessed June 4, 2011).

11. For an early effort in one of these directions, see Charles I. Nero, "Toward
a Black Gay Aesthetic: Signifying in Contemporary Black Gay Literature," in
Brother to Brother: New Writings by Black Gay Men, ed. Essex Hemphill (Boston:
Alyson, 1991), 229–252. Compare José Esteban Muñoz, *Disidentifications: Queers
of Color and the Performance of Politics* (Minneapolis: University of Minnesota
Press, 1999).

12. For some examples, see David M. Halperin, *How To Do the History of Homosexuality* (Chicago: University of Chicago Press, 2002); Halperin, *One Hundred Years
of Homosexuality, and Other Essays on Greek Love* (New York: Routledge, 1990);
and Halperin "Is There a History of Sexuality?" *History and Theory* 28.3 (October
1989): 257–274.

13. Esther Newton, *Mother Camp: Female Impersonators in America,* 2nd ed. (Chicago:
University of Chicago Press, 1979; first publ. 1972), 109.

14. Tony Kushner, *Angels in America: A Gay Fantasia on National Themes,* Part 2: *Pere-
stroika* (New York: Theatre Communications Group, 1996), 97.

15. Adrian Kiernander, "'Theatre without the Stink of Art': An Interview with Neil
Bartlett," *GLQ: A Journal of Lesbian and Gay Studies* 1.2 (1994): 221–236 (quotation
on p. 234).

16. Kestutis Nakas, e-mail message to Chad Allen Thomas (September 3, 2008),
quoted by Thomas in "Performing Queer Shakespeare" (Ph.D. diss., University
of Michigan, 2009), ch. 1.

17. Editorial statement, *Diseased Pariah News* 1 (1990): 1.

18. T.S. [Tom Shearer], "Welcome to Our Brave New World!" *Diseased Pariah News*
1 (1990): 2. Italics and ellipsis in original.

19. Scott Alan Rayter, "He Who Laughs Last: Comic Representations of AIDS"
(Ph.D. diss., University of Toronto, 2002). Rayter argues that gay male writers
and artists, such as Tony Kushner and John Greyson, reject the customary "reliance on a tragic model" in framing their responses to HIV/AIDS (18), refusing

to take for granted the normal assumption, apparent in a film like *Philadelphia,* that tragedy is the most "appropriate and suitable" vehicle for representing AIDS (58–66). Instead, "gay playwrights often use comic styles and modes . . . to denaturalize these conventions of the 'realistic problem play'" (56–57). This rejection of the tragic, according to Rayter, is designed to frustrate the audience's desire for closure, by "heightening anxiety, through humour and laughter, while rejecting any easy catharsis" (150). But the result is not a complete embrace of the comic; rather, the writers and filmmakers Rayter examines self-consciously question the use of the comic even as they exploit it, remaining ambivalent about their use of the comic form and incorporating that ambivalence into the work itself. "If humour has a place in AIDS representation . . . it will always be a contested site—one where competing factions use, take up, and respond to that humour in a plethora of ways" (52).

Rayter is careful to distinguish among camp, "black humour" (which he claims works by encouraging the audience not to laugh, but to "recoil" [74]), and sarcasm (39). David Román, *Acts of Intervention: Performance, Gay Culture, and AIDS* (Bloomington: Indiana University Press, 1998), 88–115, is particularly critical of camp for the purposes of AIDS activist interventions, though he makes a partial exception for *AIDS! The Musical!* On the latter, see also the account by John M. Clum, *Something for the Boys: Musical Theater and Gay Culture* (New York: Palgrave / St. Martin's, 2001), 267–268; Clum provides a good discussion of *Zero Patience,* as well (274–276).

20. A reproduction of David McDiarmid's artwork can be viewed on the National Gallery of Victoria's website: www.ngv.vic.gov.au / ngvart / 20080828 / index.html (accessed September 19, 2008).

21. On David McDiarmid's activist art, see C. Moore Hardy, "Lesbian Erotica and Impossible Images," and Ted Gott, "Sex and the Single T-Cell: The Taboo of HIV-Positive Sexuality in Australian Art and Culture," *Sex in Public: Australian Sexual Cultures,* ed. Jill Julius Matthews (St. Leonards, NSW: Allen and Unwin, 1997), 127–138 and 139–156. It should be noted that McDiarmid's title, "Moody Bitch Dies of AIDS," invokes the words of a sign that Peter Tully himself would carry when he dressed up as his alter ego, "Judy Free": "Moody Bitch seeks a kind considerate guy for Love Hate relationship." See the film by Tony Ayres, *Sadness: A Monologue by William Yang* (1999).

22. On the last two artists, see Christina Sharpe, *Monstrous Intimacies: Making Post-Slavery Subjects* (Durham, NC: Duke University Press, 2010), 111–187, 212–221. On Kara Walker, see Arlene R. Keizer, "Gone Astray in the Flesh: Kara Walker, Black Women Writers, and African American Postmemory," *PMLA* 123.5 (October 2008): 1649–1672, esp. 1670: "Though Walker is not gay, her work is profoundly queer, and queer-of-color theory has produced a conceptual matrix that illuminates her artistic formation and practice."

23. See Isaac Julien, "Confessions of a Snow Queen: Notes on the Making of *The*

Attendant," in *Critically Queer,* ed. Isaac Julien and Jon Savage = *Critical Quarterly* 36.1 (Spring 1994): 120–126. My interpretation of the film is much indebted to the excellent study by Christina Sharpe, "Isaac Julien's *The Attendant* and the Sado-masochism of Everyday Black Life," *Monstrous Intimacies,* 111–152, 212–214.

24. "One reveler [in the annual Sydney Gay and Lesbian Mardi Gras Parade] dressed as Osama bin Laden led a group of dancing 'Binlettes,' who sported pink se-quins and improvised 'miniburkas,' which only covered the head. Osama's right-hand man, who identified himself as 'Greenie,' said the bearded leader was here to terrorize the intolerant. 'It's about bringing back the gayness for Osama: Ex-press the flesh!' Greenie said. 'He's been in a cave for a long time. Bill Clinton couldn't do it, George Bush couldn't do it, Barack Obama doesn't want to do it . . . but he's come out today for the Gay and Lesbian Mardi Gras here in Syd-ney.'" Quoted from an unsigned article, "Bin Laden Parodied in Sydney Gay Mardi Gras," *Japan Times,* March 1, 2010, 3.

8. The Passion of the Crawford

1. Justin Ocean, "Viva la Diva!" *The Out Traveler* (Spring 2008): 26.

2. David Denby, "Escape Artist: The Case for Joan Crawford," *New Yorker,* January 3, 2011, 65–69 (quotation on p. 65).

3. Craig G. Harris, "Hope against Hope," in *Brother to Brother: New Writings by Black Gay Men,* ed. Essex Hemphill (Boston: Alyson, 1991), 148–154 (quotation on pp. 148–149).

4. See, for example, www.commonplacebook.com/jokes/gay_jokes/100_best _things.shtm (accessed October 20, 2008).

5. This combination of glamour and abjection may recall the similar "combina-tion of strength and suffering" that Richard Dyer identified as a source of Judy Garland's gay appeal; see Dyer, "Judy Garland and Gay Men," *Heavenly Bodies: Film Stars and Society* (New York: St. Martin's, 1986), 141–194, esp. 149.

6. The distinguished gay critic, novelist, and cultural historian Ethan Mordden goes out of his way to mention this line and to highlight its particularly horrify-ing violence. See Ethan Mordden, *Movie Star: A Look at the Women Who Made Hollywood* (New York: St. Martin's, 1983), 88.

7. One exception is Sam Staggs, who in his dazzling book-length commentary on *All about Eve,* makes an effort to explain its gay appeal; see Sam Staggs, *All about "All about Eve": The Complete Behind-the-Scenes Story of the Bitchiest Film Ever Made* (New York: St. Martin's Griffin, 2001; first publ. 2000), 241–246, though the entire book can be taken as an effort at explanation. See also Sam Staggs, *Close-Up on Sunset Boulevard: Billy Wilder, Norma Desmond, and the Dark Hollywood Dream* (New York: St. Martin's, 2002). Another exception, and a most distinguished one, is Richard Dyer, "Judy Garland and Gay Men," as well as Dyer, *The Culture of Queers* (London: Routledge, 2002). And see Brett Farmer, *Spectacular Passions: Cinema, Fantasy, Gay Male Spectatorships* (Durham, NC: Duke University Press,

2000); Farmer deserves a lot of credit for taking on this topic and for giving it his best shot, but he is inevitably hampered by his psychoanalytic method, which leads him to substitute theoretical commonplaces and deductive applications of Lacanian dogma for what should have been detailed, original readings of the films he analyzes.

8. Mordden, *Movie Star,* 84.

9. Christina Crawford, *Mommie Dearest: A True Story* (New York: William Morrow, 1978).

10. Adam H. Graham, Matthew Link, and Benjamin Ryan, "The Best Gay-Owned Spas in the U.S.," *The Out Traveler* (Spring 2008): 22–23 (quotation on p. 22).

11. The first of Epperson's shows was reviewed by Ben Brantley in the *New York Times* on February 10, 1998; the second, by Charles Isherwood in the *New York Times* on May 7, 2005. See John M. Clum, *Something for the Boys: Musical Theater and Gay Culture* (New York: Palgrave / St. Martin's, 2001), 138–139.

12. I have consulted the Amazon website a number of times, most recently on September 23, 2008.

13. Compare Esther Newton, *Mother Camp: Female Impersonators in America,* 2nd ed. (Chicago: University of Chicago Press, 1979; first publ. 1972), 56: "Camp style represents all that is most unique in the homosexual subculture." For some attempts at a systematic, pragmatic account of "camp style" and its relation to "subculture," see Keith Harvey, "Describing Camp Talk: Language / Pragmatics / Politics," *Language and Literature* 9.3 (2000): 240–260; also, Harvey, "Camp Talk and Citationality: A Queer Take on 'Authentic' and 'Represented' Utterance," *Journal of Pragmatics* 34 (2002): 1145–1165; and Ross Chambers, "'Isn't There a Poem about This, Mr. de Mille?' On Quotation, Camp and Colonial Distancing," *Australian Literary Studies* 23.4 (October 2008): 377–391. Chambers defines camp as a "genre-quoting genre" of a type that often offers "convenient rallying points for affiliations of an unofficial, *non*-national, *non*-familial, *non*-state-sanctioned kind, such as define friendship and communitarian groups" (p. 381). That is why, in Chambers's view, camp is not a cultural practice, properly speaking, but a subcultural one: it has to be understood in a secondary relation to the existing genres it cites.

14. With this example, we say good-bye for the moment to Joan Crawford, without having completed the close reading of the scenes of mother-daughter conflict in *Mildred Pierce* and *Mommie Dearest* with which we began. But this detour, though necessary, is only temporary: we'll return to those scenes in Part Four, when we'll be in a better position to understand their gay male appeal.

15. The tradition began not on July 4, in fact, but on July 12, 1976—date of the first "Invasion" of the Pines by lesbians and gay men, wearing drag, from the neighboring community of Cherry Grove. According to local legend, that colorful eruption aimed to protest the refusal by the owner of the Botel at the Pines to serve a popular Italian American drag queen from Cherry Grove. For the historical background, see Esther Newton, *Cherry Grove, Fire Island: Sixty Years in*

America's First Gay and Lesbian Town (Boston: Beacon Press, 1993), 268–271, 344–346. The rest of my information about the Italian widows also comes from Esther Newton, specifically from a lecture and slide show entitled, "Dick(less) Tracy and the Homecoming Queen: Lesbian Power and Representation in Gay Male Cherry Grove," delivered on February 7, 2000, at the University of Michigan in Ann Arbor. An extended version of that talk, which unfortunately does not include the slides showing the Italian widows, has been published in Esther Newton, *Margaret Mead Made Me Gay: Personal Essays, Public Ideas* (Durham, NC: Duke University Press, 2000), 63–89, 270–276.

16. Esther Newton, personal communication, February 4, 2009.

17. Newton, *Mother Camp*, 111. Newton adds: "By accepting his homosexuality and flaunting it, the camp undercuts all homosexuals who won't accept the stigmatized identity." Compare Edmund White, who in "The Gay Philosopher" (1969) speaks of "the famous mordant gay humor, which always attempts to cancel the sting of any jibe by making it funny"; White, *The Burning Library: Essays*, ed. David Bergman (New York: Knopf, 1994), 3–19 (quotation on p. 8).

18. Those needing to refresh their memories of AIDS discourse in the 1980s may consult Douglas Crimp, ed., *AIDS: Cultural Analysis / Cultural Activism* = *October* 43 (Winter 1987).

19. For the definitive study of gay men's combined social empowerment and disempowerment and its consequences for gay male subjectivity and culture, see Earl Jackson, Jr., *Strategies of Deviance: Studies in Gay Male Representation* (Bloomington: Indiana University Press, 1995).

20. This analysis of the meaning of the Italian widows' drag is not intended to obscure the reality of male privilege or to deny the power imbalances between gay men and lesbians in the society of Cherry Grove and the Pines on Fire Island; for the details, see Newton, "Dick(less) Tracy." Those material realities underlie the drag performance and generate its conditions of possibility, but they do not constitute or determine its meaning, which is the interpretive point at issue here.

9. Suffering in Quotation Marks

1. See Esther Newton, *Mother Camp: Female Impersonators in America*, 2nd ed. (Chicago: University of Chicago Press, 1979; first publ. 1972), 109: "Camp humor is a system of laughing at one's incongruous position instead of crying. . . . When the camp cannot laugh, he dissolves into a maudlin bundle of self-pity."

2. Ibid., 109.

3. I follow here the brilliant observations in Scott Alan Rayter, "He Who Laughs Last: Comic Representations of AIDS" (Ph.D. diss., University of Toronto, 2002), 7–9. Rayter argues that AIDS humor contradicts Bergson's eloquent and influential description of comedy.

4. Eve Kosofsky Sedgwick, *Epistemology of the Closet* (Berkeley: University of California Press, 1990), 150–157, esp. 154–156.

5. Ibid., 156.

6. An expansion of this argument can now be found in David Caron, "The Queerness of Group Friendship," in Caron, *My Father and I: The Marais and the Queerness of Community* (Ithaca: Cornell University Press, 2009), ch. 5, esp. 198–206. See also Heather Love, *Feeling Backward: Loss and the Politics of Queer History* (Cambridge, MA: Harvard University Press, 2007), 7, who similarly speaks of camp's "refusal to get over childhood pleasures." Compare Susan Sontag's claim: "The Camp insistence on not being 'serious,' on playing, also connects with the homosexual's desire to remain youthful"; Sontag, "Notes on 'Camp,'" *Against Interpretation, and Other Essays* (New York: Farrar, Straus and Giroux, 1966; first publ. 1964), 275–292 (quotation on pp. 290–291).

7. For a different point of view, emphasizing the potential power and glamour to be found in abjection, see Eve Kosofsky Sedgwick, "Divinity: A Dossier, a Performance Piece, a Little-Understood Emotion (written with Michael Moon)," *Tendencies* (Durham, NC: Duke University Press, 1993), 215–251.

8. John M. Clum, *Something for the Boys: Musical Theater and Gay Culture* (New York: Palgrave / St. Martin's, 2001), 175.

9. Michael Warner, *The Trouble with Normal: Sex, Politics, and the Ethics of Queer Life* (New York: Free Press, 1999), 35; see, generally, 33–38 for Warner's full argument. Richard Dyer, *The Culture of Queers* (London: Routledge, 2002), 50, sounds a sensible, cautionary note: "A bunch of queens screaming together can be very exclusive for someone who isn't a queen or feels unable to camp. The very tight togetherness that makes it so good to be one of the queens is just the thing that makes a lot of other gay men feel left out."

10. See Guy Hocquenghem, *Le Désir homosexuel* (Paris: Fayard, 2000; first publ. 1972), 117. Hocquenghem, unfortunately, was making not a social observation but a theoretical deduction from the challenge posed by male homosexual relations to the oedipal structuring of both the heterosexual family and heterosexual society. For more on Hocquenghem's thinking, see the special issue of the journal *Chimères* devoted to his work and influence: *Désir Hocquenghem* = *Chimères* 69 (April 2009).

   For a survey of the possibilities for horizontal social relations in a non-gay-specific context, see Michel Maffesoli, *L'Ombre de Dionysos: Contribution à une sociologie de l'orgie* (Paris: LGF / Livre de Poche, 1991; first publ. 1982). And for a somewhat extravagant application of Maffesoli's thought to gay male life, see Frédéric Vincent, "La Socialité dionysiaque au coeur de la tribu homosexuelle: Une intuition de Michel Maffesoli," in *L'objet homosexuel: Etudes, constructions, critiques,* ed. Jean-Philippe Cazier (Mons, Belgium: Editions Sils Maria, 2009), 161–168.

11. Sontag, "Notes on 'Camp,'" 280. For Sontag's elaboration of this point about camp as the "theatricalization of experience," see pp. 286–287. Sontag's phrase,

"to perceive Camp in objects and persons," is somewhat unfortunate. As Dyer, *Culture of Queers,* 52, rightly points out, "Camp is far more a question of how you respond to things rather than qualities actually inherent in those things."

12. See Marc Howard Siegel, "A Gossip of Images: Hollywood Star Images and Queer Counterpublics" (Ph.D. diss., University of California, Los Angeles, 2010), 165–167. Siegel criticizes Sontag for her reductive view of the way gay men appropriate mainstream culture; he interprets her claim that "Camp sees everything in quotation marks" as implying too great an ironic distance between gay male audiences and the objects of their predilection—as if camp signified, "I don't really mean it." Siegel wants to argue, instead, "that such ironic quotation is not what is most interesting and productive—or even queer—about [gay men's] reevaluation of popular culture" (166). Quotation, in Siegel's view, is simply an acknowledgment that the cultural object in question comes from outside gay male culture itself.

I agree that irony and camp do not exhaust the meaning or content of gay men's often passionate investment in heterosexual culture, but I also don't interpret camp's tendency to see everything in quotation marks as a refusal, a denial, an evasion, or a disavowal of how much gay men mean it when they take up a (despised) artifact of popular culture for queer veneration. Sontag's emphasis on quotation, role-playing, and theatricalization may not succeed in doing justice to gay male culture's delirious intoxication with particular objects (and the same could be said about my own analysis), but the practice of camp citationality which she invokes actually constitutes, in my view, a means of combining identification and dis-identification, belief and disbelief, proximity and distance, love and irony.

13. Ibid., 277, 287. Prominent among those who have taken up the task of refuting Sontag's claim about the apolitical nature of camp are Jack Babuscio, "Camp and the Gay Sensibility," in *Gays and Film,* ed. Richard Dyer (London: British Film Institute, 1977), 40–57; Moe Meyer, "Introduction: Reclaiming the Discourse of Camp," in *The Politics and Poetics of Camp,* ed. Meyer (London: Routledge, 1994), 1–22; and Keith Harvey, "Describing Camp Talk: Language/Pragmatics/Politics," *Language and Literature* 9.3 (2000): 240–260.

14. Susan Sontag, "Against Interpretation" (first publ. 1964), *Against Interpretation,* 3–14; Sontag, "On Style," (first publ. 1965), *Against Interpretation,* 15–36, esp. 20.

15. Susan Sontag, "On Style," 15. See, further, Pier Dominguez, "Susan Sontag, Superstar; or, How To Be a Modernist Genius in Post-Modern Culture: Gender, Celebrity and the Public Intellectual" (M.A. thesis, Columbia University, 2008).

16. Sontag, "Notes on 'Camp,'" 288, adding, "Camp is playful, anti-serious." That is why, for Sontag, "Camp and tragedy are antitheses" (287).

17. Dyer, *Culture of Queers,* 52.

18. Sontag, "Notes on 'Camp,'" 276.

19. Compare Hocquenghem, who remarks in a different context, "Le caractère

apolitique, au sens d'inexistant dans la sphère de la politique révolutionnaire traditionnelle, de la question homosexuelle, est peut-être aussi sa chance" (*Le Désir homosexuel,* 158; "The apolitical character of the gay cause, by which I mean its absence from the sphere of traditional revolutionary politics, is also perhaps its advantage").

20. On the politics of gay description, see David M. Halperin, "The Describable Life of Michel Foucault," in Halperin, *Saint Foucault: Towards a Gay Hagiography* (New York: Oxford University Press, 1995), 126–185. On "escape from identity" as a strategy for coping with social domination more generally, see Barry D. Adam, *The Survival of Domination: Inferiorization and Everyday Life* (New York: Elsevier, 1978), 89–93; also, Denise Riley, *"Am I That Name?" Feminism and the Category of "Women" in History* (Minneapolis: University of Minnesota Press, 1988).

21. See Newton, *Mother Camp,* 108: "The homosexual is stigmatized, but his stigma can be hidden. . . . Therefore, of crucial importance to homosexuals themselves and to non-homosexuals is whether the stigma is displayed so that one is immediately recognizable or is hidden so that he can pass to the world at large as a respectable citizen. The covert half (conceptually, but not necessarily numerically) of the homosexual community is engaged in 'impersonating' respectable citizenry, at least some of the time."

22. Dyer, *Culture of Queers,* 59. See also Babuscio, "Camp and the Gay Sensibility."

23. Newton, *Mother Camp,* 108.

24. For a brilliant and perceptive investigation of the fine points, see Mark Simpson, *Male Impersonators: Men Performing Masculinity* (London: Cassell, 1994). For an analysis of a specific aspect, see Scott F. Kiesling, "Playing the Straight Man: Displaying and Maintaining Male Heterosexuality in Discourse," in *Language and Sexuality: Contesting Meaning in Theory and Practice,* ed. Kathryn Campbell-Kibler, Robert J. Podesva, Sarah J. Roberts, and Andrew Wong (Stanford, CA: CSLI Publications, 2002), 249–266, rpt. in *The Language and Sexuality Reader,* ed. Deborah Cameron and Don Kulick (New York: Routledge, 2005), 118–131. For the notion of *habitus,* which accounts powerfully and precisely for the embodiment and reproduction of normative heterosexual masculinities, see Pierre Bourdieu, *Outline of a Theory of Practice,* trans. Richard Nice (Cambridge: Cambridge University Press, 1977), 72–95, 214–218.

25. Newton, *Mother Camp,* 101. Newton's insight has since been elaborated with subtlety and philosophical rigor in Judith Butler, *Gender Trouble: Feminism and the Subversion of Identity,* 2nd ed. (New York: Routledge, 2006; first publ. 1990); and Butler, *Bodies That Matter: On the Discursive Limits of "Sex"* (New York: Routledge, 1993).

26. On this topic, see the typically prescient observations by Jean-Paul Sartre, *Saint Genet: Comédien et martyr* (Paris: Gallimard, 1952), 156. Richard Dyer, "Judy Garland and Gay Men," *Heavenly Bodies: Film Stars and Society* (New York: St. Martin's, 1986), 141–194, speaks similarly of "the way that the gay sensibility holds

together qualities that are elsewhere felt as antithetical: theatricality and authenticity" (p. 154).

27. Sontag, "On Style," 18, makes a version of this point by saying, "Our manner of appearing *is* our manner of being. The mask is the face." The problem with this admittedly striking claim is that its contrasting terms are dichotomous from the start: Sontag's statement is not so much a description of social life as a deliberate paradox. It depends on a play of antitheses which Sontag treats as opposites, thereby effectively *impeding* the possibility of bringing them together. (Compare Dyer's observation in the previous note about "the way that the gay sensibility holds together qualities that are *elsewhere felt* as antithetical.") Sontag's dichotomy is misleading in this context for the very reason that it takes the difference between being and appearing to be *simply* antithetical and thus to be more polarized than it actually is. After all, if in fact a mask really is also a face, then it is no longer just a mask, and our manner of being is not exactly the same as our manner of appearing: our manner of being is rather a manner of constituting our identity by performing it.

   It is necessary to rearticulate the issue in these revised terms precisely in order to bridge the polarity between being and appearing, which Sontag wants to do but cannot do because she overstates the differences between them, turning them into metaphysical oppositions. Sontag's paradox consequently makes it *more* difficult to understand how being and appearing could actually turn out to coincide in the concrete practices of social life.

28. Qualifying her claim that camp is "anti-serious," Sontag says, "More precisely, Camp involves a new, more complex relation to 'the serious.' One can be serious about the frivolous, frivolous about the serious" ("Notes on 'Camp,'" 288). Sontag even allows at one point that "there is seriousness in camp" (287). Compare Patrick Paul Garlinger, "All about Agrado; or, The Sincerity of Camp in Almodóvar's *Todo sobre mi madre*," *Journal of Spanish Cultural Studies* 5.1 (February 2004): 97–111. Garlinger argues that camp is in fact compatible with sincerity.

29. Dyer, *Culture of Queers*, 49, goes on to say: "Particularly in the past, the fact that gay men could so sharply and brightly make fun of themselves meant that the real awfulness of their situation could be kept at bay—they need not take things too seriously, need not let it get them down."

30. Dyer, "Judy Garland and Gay Men," 180, speaks of "the knife edge between camp and hurt, a key register of gay culture."

10. The Beauty and the Camp

1. For the latest and most distinguished contribution to this debate, see Ross Chambers, "'Isn't There a Poem about This, Mr. de Mille?' On Quotation,

Camp and Colonial Distancing," *Australian Literary Studies* 23.4 (October 2008): 377–391. Chambers describes camp as queer but not necessarily gay—a "performance genre" which involves "a collective interaction of performance and audience, somewhat akin to acting," and offers a "rallying point" for "affiliations of an unofficial, *non*-national, *non*-familial, *non*-state-sanctioned kind" (381); understood in this way, camp becomes an appropriate vehicle for expressing various sorts of cultural and political dissidence beyond the merely (homo)sexual.

2. Richard Dyer, *The Culture of Queers* (London: Routledge, 2002), 49. Dyer's essay was originally published in the *Body Politic* 36 (September 1977).

3. For an excellent survey of critical writing on camp, see Fabio Cleto, ed., *Camp: Queer Aesthetics and the Performing Subject: A Reader* (Ann Arbor: University of Michigan Press, 1999). For two very different analyses that indicate the range of possible approaches to camp, see Kim Michasiw, "Camp, Masculinity, Masquerade," *differences* 6.2–3 (1994): 146–173; and Chambers, "'Isn't There a Poem about This?'"

4. Esther Newton, *Mother Camp: Female Impersonators in America,* 2nd ed. (Chicago: University of Chicago Press, 1979; first publ. 1972), 56 (emphasis added).

5. Ibid., 111.

6. Matt Crowley, *The Boys in the Band* (1968), in Stanley Richards, ed., *Best Plays of the Sixties* (Garden City, NY: Doubleday, 1970), 801–900, esp. 844–845.

7. Compare Esther Newton, *Mother Camp,* 107: "Masculine-feminine juxtapositions are, of course, the most characteristic kind of camp"; and Dyer, *Culture of Queers,* 61: camp "does undercut sex roles."

8. Dyer, *Culture of Queers,* 49.

9. "In traditional gay male culture, 'trade' designates the straight-identified man who, although willing to have sex with gay men (usually in the inserter role), refuses gay identifications and give-away behaviors such as kissing"; Thomas Waugh, *Hard to Imagine: Gay Male Eroticism in Photography and Film, from Their Beginnings to Stonewall* (New York: Columbia University Press, 1996), 423, n. 27. For a more detailed semantic and historical analysis of the term "trade," see Gayle S. Rubin, "The Valley of the Kings: Leathermen in San Francisco, 1960–1990" (Ph.D. diss., University of Michigan, 1994), 81–89. For the study of "trade" in a particular context, see Barry Reay, *New York Hustlers: Masculinity and Sex in Modern America* (Manchester, UK: Manchester University Press, 2010).

10. See, for example, Esther Newton's 1978 preface to the second edition of *Mother Camp,* esp. p. xiii, where she notes that on the streets of Greenwich Village the "limp wrists and eye makeup" have been replaced by "an interchangeable parade of young men with cropped hair, leather jackets, and well-trimmed moustaches . . . a proliferation of ersatz cowboys, phony lumberjacks, and . . . imitation Hell's Angels," adding, "This is playing with shadows, not substance." For a similar sentiment, see Ethan Mordden, "Interview with the Drag Queen," *I've a*

Feeling We're Not in Kansas Anymore (New York: New American Library, 1987), 1–9. See, further, Richard Dyer, "Dressing the Part," *Culture of Queers*, 63–69, on the commerce between straight and gay male styles.

11. See John M. Clum, *Something for the Boys: Musical Theater and Gay Culture* (New York: Palgrave / St. Martin's, 2001), 8–9.

12. As one gay man told Martin Levine, "Familiarity for me kills desire. Knowing someone is a turn-off because their personality ruins the fantasy I have of them." Martin P. Levine, *Gay Macho: The Life and Death of the Homosexual Clone*, ed. Michael S. Kimmel (New York: New York University Press, 1998), 93; quoted in Jeffrey Escoffier, *Bigger Than Life: The History of Gay Porn Cinema, from Beefcake to Hardcore* (Philadelphia: Running Press, 2009), 138.

13. I am paraphrasing a brilliant passage from Sartre's commentary on Genet (no translation can do it justice): "La 'méchanceté' bien connue des pédérastes vient en partie de ce qu'ils disposent simultanément de deux systèmes de références: l'enchantement sexuel les transporte dans un climat platonicien; chacun des hommes qu'ils recherchent est l'incarnation passagère d'une Idée; c'est le Marin, le Parachutiste qu'ils veulent saisir à travers le petit gars qui se prête à leur désir. Mais, dès que leur désir est comblé, ils rentrent en eux-mêmes et considèrent leurs amants merveilleux sous l'angle d'un nominalisme cynique. Finies les essences, adieu les archétypes: restent des individus quelconques et interchangeables. 'Mais je ne savais pas,' me dit un jour un pédéraste en me désignant une petite frappe de Montparnasse, 'que ce jeune homme était un *assassin!*' Et le lendemain: 'Adrien? Une lope sans intérêt.'" Jean-Paul Sartre, *Saint Genet: Comédien et martyr* (Paris: Gallimard, 1952), 146–147; compare 349ff.

14. Tony Kushner, "Notes toward a Theater of the Fabulous," in *Staging Gay Lives*, ed. John Clum (Boulder, CO: Westview, 1996), vii, as quoted and cited by Clum, *Something for the Boys*, 5.

15. Summarizing Kushner's career, a *New York Times* critic recently remarked, "Perhaps alone among American playwrights of his generation [Kushner] uses history as a character, letting its power fall on his protagonists as they stumble through their own and others' lives." Andrea Stevens, "Cosmos of Kushner, Spinning Forward," *New York Times*, June 10, 2009.

16. Compare the discussion in Scott Herring, *Queering the Underworld: Slumming, Literature, and the Undoing of Lesbian and Gay History* (Chicago: University of Chicago Press, 2007), 69–71. Herring goes on to argue, however, that Cather's story ultimately "refuse[s] sexual identifications of any kind" (74)—a reading which owes more to Leo Bersani's theory of self-loss than it does to Cather. Jane Nardin, by contrast, probably goes too far in the direction of literalness in her identification of Paul as a fairy or invert: see Nardin, "Homosexual Identities in Willa Cather's 'Paul's Case,'" *Literature and History*, 3rd series, 17.2 (Autumn 2008): 31–46.

17. Willa Cather, "Paul's Case: A Study in Temperament," *Coming, Aphrodite! and Other Stories*, ed. Margaret Anne O'Connor (New York: Penguin, 1999), 116–136

(quotation on p. 116). All further page references to this work will be incorporated in the text. As to Paul's carnation, it is worth remarking that Cather had reviewed Robert Hichens's thinly disguised satire of Oscar Wilde entitled *The Green Carnation* when that book appeared in 1894; see Claude J. Summers, "'A Losing Game in the End': Aestheticism and Homosexuality in Cather's 'Paul's Case,'" *Modern Fiction Studies* 36.1 (Spring 1990): 103–119; rpt. with slight alterations as "'A Losing Game in the End': Willa Cather's 'Paul's Case,'" in Summers, *Gay Fictions: Wilde to Stonewall, Studies in a Male Homosexual Literary Tradition* (New York: Continuum, 1990), 62–77, 224–226.

18. Michel Foucault, *The History of Sexuality*, vol. 1: *An Introduction*, trans. Robert Hurley (New York: Vintage, 1980), 43 (translation modified); for the original text, see Michel Foucault, *La Volonté de savoir*, Histoire de la sexualité, 1 (Paris: Gallimard, 1984; first publ. 1976), 59.

19. Susan Sontag, "Notes on 'Camp'" in Sontag, *Against Interpretation, and Other Essays* (New York: Farrar, Straus and Giroux, 1966; first publ. 1964), 275.

20. Thanks to Brandon Clements for this hyperbolic but justified remark. For corroboration, see Larry Rubin, "The Homosexual Motif in Willa Cather's 'Paul's Case,'" *Studies in Short Fiction* 12.2 (Spring 1975): 127–131, apparently the first critical article to deal with this obvious but hitherto unmentioned fact. See also Summers, "Losing Game"; and Nardin, "Homosexual Identities."

21. "What, then, are the clues with which Cather has been so lavish? These are so numerous that one despairs of setting them all down in a short paper" (Rubin, "Homosexual Motif," 129). For an opposing view, see Loretta Wasserman, "Is Cather's Paul a Case?" *Modern Fiction Studies* 36.1 (Spring 1990): 121–129. Wasserman reads Cather's story without reference to homosexuality, though her powerful interpretation does not invalidate Nardin's historical arguments for seeing an implicit homosexuality in Cather's portrait of Paul (Nardin, "Homosexual Identities").

22. D. A. Miller, *Place for Us: Essay on the Broadway Musical* (Cambridge, MA: Harvard University Press, 1998), 23; the entire passage was quoted in Chapter 5. See Heather Love, *Feeling Backward: Loss and the Politics of Queer History* (Cambridge, MA: Harvard University Press, 2007), 180, n. 21, who rightly insists, against Scott Herring's interpretation of "Paul's Case" in *Queering the Underground*, on Paul's "intense loneliness and isolation." Rubin, "Homosexual Motif," 130, takes the Yale boy to be "a foil to Paul . . . a red-blooded American youth who is in town over the weekend to relieve his sexual drive" and whose incompatibility with Paul stems from not sharing Paul's sexual and aesthetic interests; that is certainly a plausible reading, but it need not rule out other ones. Compare, for example, the following passage by Denton Welch, an English novelist and painter of the 1940s, who noted in his journal, apropos of a likable soldier who had offered to help him repair a punctured bicycle tire, "I can never be true friends with anyone except distant women—far away. For I wish for communion with the inarticulate and can only fray and fritter with the quick. I

would tinsel, tinsel all the day if I were so placed. Yet I love myself and my company so much that I would not even ask the soldier to come in for fear of his becoming a regular visitor. I even feel that people pollute my house who come into it"; Michael De-la-Noy, ed., *The Journals of Denton Welch* (New York: Dutton, 1986), 11.

23. Neil Bartlett, *Who Was That Man? A Present for Mr Oscar Wilde* (London: Serpent's Tail, 1988), 173.

24. See Summers, "Losing Game"; also, Eve Kosofsky Sedgwick, "Willa Cather and Others," *Tendencies* (Durham, NC: Duke University Press, 1993), 167–176. Herring (*Queering the Underground,* 81) draws an interesting parallel between Paul and his namesake, the French poet Paul Verlaine, a favorite of Cather's and another sexual outlaw.

25. Herman Melville, "Billy Budd, Sailor (An Inside Narrative)," *Billy Budd, Sailor, and Other Stories* (New York: Penguin, 1986), 287–385 (quotation on p. 362). All further page references to this work will be included in the text. This edition of Melville's story reproduces the Reading Text established by Harrison Hayford and Merton M. Sealts, Jr., and published by the University of Chicago Press in 1962.

26. On his blog, in an entry dated October 23, 2008, the director Chris Ward justified his gambit as follows: "It is true that *To the Last Man* is a very violent movie. It is a Western epic, as true to a Hollywood blockbuster as gay porn will ever be. Ben Leon, Tony Dimarco, and I decided that we wanted to make a real Western movie—not some cheesy porno rip-off as has been made in the past. We shot on location in Arizona, used real horses, real guns, hired some real cowboys to be in the cast—in short, we spent lots of time, money, and energy to be as authentic as possible. In this spirit we made the decision to stay true to the Western genre—which requires violence. The Old West was a very violent place— on the ranch where the movie was filmed, there was a graveyard with a memorial to everyone who had died on the property. The monument listed how each person was killed: one man was killed by Indians up at the river; another person had been shot in a drunken fight at a saloon; still another died of injuries from a fist fight; the best one was the guy who died in a 'horse wreck.' No one in the graveyard lived past about 40 years of age. Today Hollywood films are rife with violence—it is part of modern entertainment. *To the Last Man* looks to the examples of the Coen Brothers and Tarantino. It's not a porn movie from the 1990s nor is it *Little Miss Sunshine.* It's a film for the 21st century and it reflects the entertainment values of 2008." See www. chriswardpornblog.com/ (accessed November 13, 2008).

27. Newton, *Mother Camp,* 105.

28. On this point, and on Foucault's famous statement that "power is everywhere," see David M. Halperin, *Saint Foucault: Towards a Gay Hagiography* (New York: Oxford University Press, 1995), 29–30.

29. That is precisely Leo Bersani's objection to camp; see Leo Bersani, "Is the

Rectum a Grave?" in *AIDS: Cultural Analysis / Cultural Activism,* ed. Douglas Crimp = *October* 43 (Winter 1987): 197–222, esp. 208. See also Leo Bersani, *Homos* (Cambridge, MA: Harvard University Press, 1995), esp. 45–53.

30. Miller, *Place for Us,* 6. Compare his statement on p. 13: "The only socially credible subject is the stoic who, whatever his gender, obeys the gag rule incumbent on being a man."

31. Laurent Berlant, *The Female Complaint: The Unfinished Business of Sentimentality in American Culture* (Durham, NC: Duke University Press, 2008), 9.

32. See José Esteban Muñoz, *Cruising Utopia: The Then and There of Queer Futurity* (New York: New York University Press, 2009).

11. Gay Family Romance

1. Sigmund Freud, "Family Romances" (1909; first publ. 1908), trans. James Strachey, in *The Standard Edition of the Complete Psychological Works of Sigmund Freud,* vol. 9: 1906–1908, ed. James Strachey (London: Hogarth Press, 1959), 235–242. For a wonderful exploration of this topic with reference to gay men, art collecting, and William Beckford in particular, see Whitney Davis, "Queer Family Romance in Collecting Visual Culture," in *Queer Bonds,* ed. Damon Young and Joshua J. Weiner = *GLQ: A Journal of Lesbian and Gay Studies* 17.2–3 (2011): 309–329.

2. Willa Cather, "Paul's Case: A Study in Temperament," *Coming, Aphrodite! and Other Stories,* ed. Margaret Anne O'Connor (New York: Penguin, 1999), 116–136 (quotation on pp. 131–132; italics added). All further page references to this work will be incorporated in the text.

3. See Jean-Paul Sartre, *Saint Genet: Comédien et martyr* (Paris: Gallimard, 1952), 398–399; David Sedaris, "Chipped Beef," in Sedaris, *Naked* (Boston: Little, Brown, 1997), 1–6. The sentiment is not unique to gay men; for a lesbian equivalent, see Laurie Essig, "Harry Potter's Secret," *New York Blade News,* January 7, 2000, 13: "Certainly many of us felt the same rush of excitement when we came out as Harry Potter did when he figured out that he was not the same as his ridiculously ordinary family."

4. Compare the gay English writer Denton Welch, who, in his journal entry for August 22, 1942, recalls in similar terms his feelings as an eleven-year-old schoolboy: "And now I see myself as I was then, running up to the cold dormitory, hiding myself in the bedclothes, imagining my cubicle transformed with precious stones and woods. Praying, always praying for freedom and loveliness." See Michael De-la-Noy, ed., *The Journals of Denton Welch* (New York: Dutton, 1986), 6.

5. Denton Welch expresses astonishment at a visitor to his house who "seemed surprised that anyone should love things enough to seek them out and prize them" (*Journals of Denton Welch,* 200).

6. Neil Bartlett, *Who Was That Man? A Present for Mr Oscar Wilde* (London: Ser-

pent's Tail, 1988), 181. All further page references to this work will be incorporated in the text. Unless otherwise noted, all italics that appear in quoted extracts from this book are Bartlett's own.

7. George Haggerty, "Desire and Mourning: The Ideology of the Elegy," in *Ideology and Form in Eighteenth-Century Literature,* ed. David H. Richter (Lubbock:
Texas University Press, 1999), 203; quoted by Heather Love, "Compulsory Happiness and Queer Existence," *New Formations* 63 (Spring 2008): 52–64 (quotation
on p. 52).

8. For additional arguments in favor of this distinction, see Susan Sontag, "On
Style," in Sontag, *Against Interpretation, and Other Essays* (New York: Farrar,
Straus and Giroux, 1966; first publ. 1964), 15–36, esp. 26–27.

9. For a brilliant demonstration, see Dennis Cooper, "Square One," in Cooper,
Wrong: Stories (New York: Grove Weidenfeld, 1992), 81–92. For an example, see
an undated entry in Denton Welch's journal for the year 1943 (*Journals of Denton
Welch,* 63–64):

> "Today I have been to Ightham Moat. It was less spoilt than I remember it. I
> wanted so much to own it and undo all that was done in 1889. The drawing-
> room could be lovely, with its Chinese wallpaper, if the two blocked windows
> could be opened, if some of the garish paint could be taken off the Jacobean
> mantelpiece, if the 'exposed' beams could be covered in again and if the appall-
> ing little 1889 fireplace could be swept away. How lovely to have elegant nostal-
> gic tea out of a Georgian silver teapot and urn-shaped milk jug in such a room
> properly restored and furnished!
>
> "The great hall too needs stripping of its dreary panelling and the old medi-
> eval windows opened to air again. Then the courtyard, squalid with weeds and
> a huge dog kennel, large and elaborate as a Gothic chapel. What a waste!
>
> "I biked out on to the main road where I rode a little way with a dark, wide-
> shouldered, football-bottomed youth. I could see where his pants stopped, the
> flannel of his trousers were so thin and meagre. He took off his coat, rolled up
> his sleeves, bent only on getting to the top of the hill. Dark, sulky, good-looking.
> I guessed that he was probably a little simple minded. Sulky looking people
> nearly always are."

10. On the differences between the novel and the film, see the informative and as-
tute reading by Robert J. Corber, "Joan Crawford's Padded Shoulders: Female
Masculinity in *Mildred Pierce,*" *Camera Obscura* 62 = 21.2 (2006): 1–31; expanded
in Corber, *Cold War Femme: Lesbianism, National Identity, and Hollywood Cinema*
(Durham, NC: Duke University Press, 2011), 97–126, 203–206. On the production
history of the film, see Albert J. LaValley's introduction to the published screen-
play, *Mildred Pierce* (Madison: University of Wisconsin Press, 1980), 9–53, esp. 21–
30, as reported and cited by Linda Williams, "Feminist Film Theory: *Mildred
Pierce* and the Second World War," in *Female Spectators: Looking at Film and Television,* ed. E. Deidre Pribram (New York: Routledge, 1988), 12–30, esp. 13.

11. Corber, "Crawford's Padded Shoulders," 104, citing James C. Robertson, *The Casablanca Man: The Cinema of Michael Curtiz* (New York: Routledge, 1993), 91. Williams, "Feminist Film Theory," which provides the exact date of the film's release (p. 14), also usefully complicates and qualifies the standard reading of the film as an allegory of women's removal from the workplace to the home in the aftermath of the war (esp. 21–28).

12. Susan Sontag, "Notes on 'Camp'" (first publ. 1964), in Sontag, *Against Interpretation*, 275–292 (quotation on p. 277); also, Sontag, "On Style," 27–28.

13. Perhaps that is what explains, at least in part, the antiquarianism of gay male culture, or of a certain version of it: "I am not concerned with dead stones or lifeless furniture," declared Charlotte von Mahlsdorf, the German collector and author of the celebrated transgender memoir, *Ich bin meine eigene Frau:* "They are embodiments that mirror the history of the men who built them, who lived in them." See Charlotte von Mahlsdorf, *I Am My Own Woman: The Outlaw Life of Charlotte von Mahlsdorf, Berlin's Most Distinguished Transvestite,* trans. Jean Hollander (Pittsburgh: Cleis Press, 1995), 124–125, as quoted by Will Fellows, *A Passion to Preserve: Gay Men as Keepers of Culture* (Madison: University of Wisconsin Press, 2004), 11. The memoir originally appeared in the same year, 1992, as a remarkable documentary film of the same title by the pioneering gay German director Rosa von Praunheim.

    Similarly, in his journal Denton Welch remarks, "Yet how I loathe nature lovers! My thoughts are never on nature though I go out to roam for hours in the fields every day. My thoughts always go to history, to what has happened century after century on each spot of earth" (*Journals of Denton Welch,* 5). Later, Welch records a sense of wonder at nature, but he notes that "this feeling, so bandied about, seldom visits me in a form that is not mingled with history" (206).

14. Sontag, "Notes on 'Camp,'" 277. See also Sartre, *Saint Genet,* 422.

15. It may be worth quoting Sontag at length on this point. The passage of time, she says, can bring out the element of enjoyable and outlandish fantasy in a cultural object: "Time may enhance what seems simply dogged or lacking in fantasy now because we are too close to it, because it resembles too closely our own everyday realities, the fantastic nature of which we don't perceive. We are better able to enjoy a fantasy as fantasy when it is not our own. This is why so many of the objects prized by Camp taste are old-fashioned, out-of-date, démodé. It's not a love of the old as such. It's simply that the process of aging or deterioration provides the necessary detachment—or arouses a necessary sympathy. When the theme is important, and contemporary, the failure of a work of art can make us indignant. Time can change that" ("Notes on 'Camp,'" 285). *Mildred Pierce* is surely more enjoyable now than it was in 1945. For a lengthy set of reflections on gay men's loving relation to outdated artifacts, see Fellows, *Passion to Preserve.*

16. *Journals of Denton Welch,* 240.

17. Ibid., 286, 291. Sontag also says that "Camp is a solvent of morality" (290).

18. On aesthetics as a gay male utopia, see Al LaValley, "The Great Escape," *American Film* (April 1985): 28–34, 70–71. On Style as a refuge from the Person, and thus a means of queer escape from a stigmatized identity and a tainted psychology, see D. A. Miller, *Jane Austen; or, The Secret of Style* (Princeton: Princeton University Press, 2003); also D. A. Miller, *8½ [Otto e mezzo],* British Film Institute (Basingstoke: Palgrave Macmillan, 2008), 88: "In style, substance loses any such power of pressure, dissolving into a play of movement and light; marks of dishonour, feelings of shame, behaviours of abashment—these suddenly have no more pertinence than the rules of a schoolmarm in the Wild West, or the laws of a nation in a foreign embassy. . . . Style is personality without 'person.'" On aestheticism as an alternative to psychology and psychoanalysis, see Ellis Hanson, "Wilde's Exquisite Pain," in *Wilde Writings: Contextual Conditions,* ed. Joseph Bristow (Toronto: University of Toronto Press, 2002), 101–123; and Hanson, "Confession as Seduction: The Queer Performativity of the Cure in Sacher-Masoch's *Venus im Pelz,*" in *Performance and Performativity in German Cultural Studies,* ed. Andrew Webber (London: Peter Lang, 2003), 41–66.

19. Compare Daniel Harris, *The Rise and Fall of Gay Culture* (New York: Hyperion, 1997), 34–35: "In the case of gay men, our seemingly hereditary predisposition for tastefulness and the arts, for belting out show tunes in piano bars and swooning over *La Traviata,* is not an innate character trait but a pragmatic response to the conditions of a hostile environment. We are aesthetes by need, not by nature."

20. See Joseph Litvak, *Strange Gourmets: Sophistication, Theory, and the Novel* (Durham, NC: Duke University Press, 1997).

21. Fran Lebowitz, *Metropolitan Life* (New York: Dutton, 1978), 6; quoted and discussed by Denise Riley, *Impersonal Passion: Language as Affect* (Durham, NC: Duke University Press, 2005), 34–35.

22. Sontag, "Notes on 'Camp,'" 290.

23. For a contrary view, see John M. Clum, *Something for the Boys: Musical Theater and Gay Culture* (New York: Palgrave / St. Martin's, 2001), who opposes aestheticism to the pleasure principle and who asserts that among "many affluent folks, gay and straight," in recent years, "aestheticism" has been "replaced by hedonism," a hedonism that has taken the specific form of consumerism. "The most displayed gay cultural product is not a play, musical, painting, ballet, or symphony, but underwear" (25). See also Mark Simpson, "Gay Dream Believer: Inside the Gay Underwear Cult," in *Anti-Gay,* ed. Simpson (London: Freedom Editions, 1996), 1–12; Simpson would probably agree with Clum, and so would Harris (*Rise and Fall of Gay Culture*). It's a claim worth considering, but it implies a surer distinction between aestheticism and hedonism than I would be prepared to make in the context of gay male culture.

24. Sontag, "Notes on 'Camp,'" 289. On pp. 288–291, Sontag argues that camp trans-

lates an aristocracy of taste into a democratic form: it is "dandyism in the age of mass culture" (289).

25. See Fellows, *Passion to Preserve,* 5–6, for an autobiographical account of his engagement with an old children's book, *Hans and Peter,* about two boys who "live in unpleasant rooms with disagreeable views" and who "plan their dream house, which they will build when they have grown up," but who in the meantime discover and fix up "a deserted shack in a wooded field" with a "lovely, verdant view from its window," to which they invite their parents and other adults. Fellows quotes a number of "preservation-minded gays" who testify to their "penchant for meticulous attention to design detail," their passionate investment in specific, precise aesthetic elements to which others attach little importance—an attitude neatly summed up by one of them who insists that "all existence is rehearsal for a final performance of perfection" (31).

26. Although I admire Dianne Chisholm for raising important political questions in her critique of Bartlett's account of gay men's relation to their possessions, it will be clear from what I say about Bartlett here that I also have reservations about her reading of him. See Chisholm, "The City of Collective Memory," *Queer Constellations: Subcultural Space in the Wake of the City* (Minneapolis: University of Minnesota Press, 2005), 101–144, esp. 129–131.

12. Men Act, Women Appear

1. D. A. Miller, *Place for Us: Essay on the Broadway Musical* (Cambridge, MA: Harvard University Press, 1998), 71. All further page references to this work will be incorporated in the text. John M. Clum, *Something for the Boys: Musical Theater and Gay Culture* (New York: Palgrave / St. Martin's, 2001), 8, makes the point succinctly: "The musical doesn't give us much to identify with among the men onstage."

2. See Steven Cohan, "'Feminizing' the Song-and-Dance Man: Fred Astaire and the Spectacle of Masculinity in the Hollywood Musical," in *Screening the Male: Exploring Masculinities in Hollywood Cinema,* ed. Steven Cohan and Ina Rae Hark (London: Routledge, 1993), 46–69. See also a later chapter by Cohan, "Dancing with Balls: Sissies, Sailors, and the Camp Masculinity of Gene Kelly," in Cohan, *Incongruous Entertainment: Camp, Cultural Value, and the MGM Musical* (Durham, NC: Duke University Press, 2005), 149–199, 348–349; and Jeffrey Masten, "Behind Gene Kelly," unpublished manuscript.

3. Clum, *Something for the Boys,* 7.

4. John Berger, Sven Blomberg, Chris Fox, Michael Dibb, and Richard Hollis, *Ways of Seeing* (London: British Broadcasting Corporation and Penguin Books, 1972), 47 (italics in original). The whole passage (pp. 45–47) is worth quoting in full, but a few excerpts provide a sense of the basic line of reasoning: "A man's presence is dependent upon the promise of power which he embodies . . . a woman's presence expresses her own attitude to herself. . . . If a woman throws a glass on

the floor, this is an example of how she treats her own emotion of anger and so of how she would wish it to be treated by others. If a man does the same, his action is only read as an expression of his anger. . . . One might simplify this by saying: *men act* and *women appear.* Men look at women. Women watch themselves being looked at. . . . The surveyor of woman in herself is male: the surveyed, female. Thus she turns herself into an object—and most particularly an object of vision: a sight." This represents an elaboration, for the art historian, of the final sections of Freud's essay on narcissism. Paul Morrison, in turn, has taken Berger's insight in a queer direction; see "Muscles," in Morrison, *The Explanation for Everything: Essays on Sexual Subjectivity* (New York: New York University Press, 2001), 113–139, 187–191. I have been deeply influenced by his formulations.

5. That is why sports provide a cover and an alibi for men who would otherwise risk emasculation by dancing in front of an audience; see Maura Keefe, "Men Dancing Athletically," *Gay and Lesbian Review Worldwide* 13.6 (Nov.–Dec. 2006): 15–16.

6. According to the Women's Sports Foundation, "Since the passage of Title IX, increases in athletic participation for both males and females have occurred at both the high school and collegiate levels. In 1970, only 1 out of every 27 high school girls played varsity sports. Today, that figure is one in 2.5. Female high school participation increased from 294,015 in 1971 to 2,472,043 in 1997. College participation has more than tripled, from 31,000 to 128,208. Both male and female athletic participation made steep increases immediately after the passage of Title IX at the high school level. Men's and women's rises in participation have also followed a similar pattern at the collegiate levels. However, male athletes still receive twice the participation opportunities afforded female athletes." See Women's Sports Foundation, www.womenssportsfoundation.org/Content/Articles/Issues/Title-IX/T/Title-IX-Q--A.aspx (accessed June 29, 2010).

7. See Keefe, "Men Dancing Athletically." See, for additional details, Kevin Kopelson, *The Queer Afterlife of Vaslav Nijinsky* (Stanford, CA: Stanford University Press, 1997), 181–185.

8. See www.brainyquote.com/quotes/authors/d/dennis_rodman.html (accessed February 5, 2009).

9. On David Beckham, see the now-classic analyses by Mark Simpson, "Meet the Metrosexual" (Salon.com, July 22, 2002); "Beckham, the Virus" (Salon.com, June 28, 2003); and "Sporno" (*Out Magazine,* May 2006, and the V&A Fashion and Sport catalogue 2008). All are now collected in Simpson, *Metrosexy: A 21st-Century Self-Love Story* (Marksimpsonist Publications, 2011), 20–29, 84–89. See, generally, David Coad, *The Metrosexual: Gender, Sexuality, and Sport* (Albany: SUNY Press, 2008).

10. I owe this insight to KT Lowe, whom I wish to thank for giving me this entire line of reasoning.

11. Compare the brilliant feminist analysis by Rosemary Pringle, "Bitching: Relations between Women in the Office," *Secretaries Talk: Sexuality, Power and Work* (Sydney: Allen and Unwin, 1988), 231–249.

12. I quote the evocative phrase of Louise Glück, the final words of her poem "Messengers," in Glück, *The House on Marshland* (New York: Ecco Press, 1975), 10.

13. The incident is recounted in a letter by Edmund White, written two weeks after the event and quoted in Jonathan Ned Katz, "The Stonewall Rebellion: Edmund White Witnesses the Revolution," *The Advocate* 527 (June 20, 1989): 40. Lee Edelman cites this document in his essay "The Mirror and the Tank: 'AIDS,' Subjectivity, and the Rhetoric of Activism," in Edelman, *Homographesis: Essays in Gay Literary and Cultural Theory* (New York: Routledge, 1994), 93–117, 256–260; he offers the following commentary: "The drag queen striking the cop with her purse to defend the dignity of her narcissism before the punitive gaze of the law remains a potent image of the unexpected ways in which 'activism' can find embodiment when the dominant notions of subjectivity are challenged rather than appropriated" (113).

    For more details, see David Carter, *Stonewall: The Riots That Sparked the Gay Revolution* (New York: St. Martin's, 2004), 148: "The first hostile act outside the club occurred when a police officer shoved one of the transvestites, who turned and smacked the officer over the head with her purse. The cop clubbed her, and a wave of anger passed through the crowd, which immediately showered the police with boos and catcalls, followed by a cry to turn the paddy wagon over" (see also 261). Compare Lucian K. Truscott IV, "The Real Mob at Stonewall," *New York Times*, June 25, 2009: "The young arrestees paused at the back of the waiting paddy wagon and struck vampy poses, smiling and waving to the crowd."

14. In fact, Joan Crawford's gender coding is subtle and subject to both variation and manipulation. For a very useful and careful analysis, see Robert J. Corber, "Joan Crawford's Padded Shoulders: Female Masculinity in *Mildred Pierce*," in Corber, *Cold War Femme: Lesbianism, National Identity, and Hollywood Cinema* (Durham, NC: Duke University Press, 2011), 97–126, 203–206.

15. See Judith Halberstam, *Female Masculinity* (Durham, NC: Duke University Press, 1998).

16. Andrew Sullivan, "The End of Gay Culture," *New Republic* (October 24, 2005), available online at www.tnr.com/politics/story.html?id=cac6ca08-7df8-4cdd-93cc-1d20cd8b7a70 (accessed July 13, 2009).

13. The Sexual Politics of Genre

1. Sam Staggs, *All about "All about Eve": The Complete Behind-the-Scenes Story of the Bitchiest Film Ever Made* (New York: St. Martin's Griffin, 2001; first publ. 2000), 241, understands the gay male response to *All about Eve* in a similar way: "But more than anything, [the movie] is about women in conflict, and gays cheer for

this theme (cf. Scarlett versus Melanie, Baby Jane versus Blanche, Veda and Mildred Pierce, Mommie Dearest and Christina)." He does not expand further on this observation and leaves us to wonder about how to explain the general phenomenon.

2. Susan Sontag, "Notes on 'Camp,'" *Against Interpretation, and Other Essays* (New York: Farrar, Straus and Giroux, 1966; first publ. 1964), 283. Also 282: "It seems unlikely that much of the traditional opera repertoire could be such satisfying Camp if the melodramatic absurdities of most opera plots had not been taken seriously by their composers."

3. See, generally, Pamela Robertson, *Guilty Pleasures: Feminist Camp from Mae West to Madonna* (Durham, NC: Duke University Press, 1996).

4. See the famous opening of Book 24 (lines 3–22) of Homer's *Iliad,* in Richmond Lattimore's translation:

>   only Achilleus
> wept still as he remembered his beloved companion, nor did sleep
> who subdues all come over him, but he tossed from one side to the other
> in longing for Patroklos, for his manhood and his great strength
> and all the actions he had seen to the end with him, and the hardships
> he had suffered; the wars of men; hard crossing of the big waters.
> Remembering all these things he let fall the swelling tears, lying
> sometimes along his side, sometimes on his back, and now again
> prone on his face; then he would stand upright, and pace turning
> in distraction along the beach of the sea, nor did dawn rising
> escape him as she brightened across the sea and the beaches.
> Then, when he had yoked running horses under the chariot
> he would fasten Hektor behind the chariot, so as to drag him,
> and draw him three times around the tomb of Menoitios' fallen
> son [Patroklos], then rest again in his shelter, and throw down the dead man
> and leave him to lie sprawled on his face in the dust. But Apollo
> had pity on him, though he was only a dead man, and guarded
> the body from all ugliness, and hid all of it under the golden
> aegis, so that it might not be torn when Achilleus dragged it.
> So Achilleus in his standing fury outraged great Hektor.

5. On this point, see James M. Redfield, *Nature and Culture in the* Iliad: *The Tragedy of Hector* (Chicago: University of Chicago Press, 1975), 104. Redfield's reading of the *Iliad* has decisively shaped my understanding of the issues.

6. The closest Broadway has gotten to the *Iliad* is *The Golden Apple* (1954), a musical-comedy fantasia based on the Troy saga but set in the state of Washington at the beginning of the twentieth century. It was the work of John Latouche (book, lyrics) and Jerome Moross (music), and it won the New York Drama Critics Circle Award for Best Musical. For details see Ken Mandelbaum, *Not since Carrie: Forty Years of Broadway Musical Flops* (New York: St. Martin's, 1991), 341–

345. The *Odyssey*, however, *was* made into a musical of the same title, with book and lyrics by Erich Segal, and with Yul Brynner in the starring role. After touring for a year, it was renamed *Home Sweet Homer* and lasted exactly one Sunday matinee on Broadway (Mandelbaum, 31–32).

Compare, generally, Sontag, "Notes on 'Camp,'" 286–287, which presents camp as antagonistic to the high seriousness of great art, such as the *Iliad*. Camp represents, according to Sontag, an alternate aesthetic sensibility.

7. See Paul Morrison, "'Noble Deeds and the Secret Singularity': Hamlet and Phèdre," *Canadian Review of Comparative Literature / Revue Canadienne de Littérature Comparée* 18.2 (June and September 1991): 263–288; rpt. in *Reading the Renaissance,* ed. Jonathan Hart (New York: Garland, 1996), 179–202. See also Michael D. Bristol, *Shakespeare's America, America's Shakespeare* (London: Routledge, 1990).

8. Sontag, "Notes on 'Camp,'" 283.

9. The genius of Pedro Almodóvar's queer cinema lies in its simultaneous belief and disbelief in melodrama, in its passionate embrace of the form and its critical disengagement from it. Almodóvar fuses melodrama's emotional intensities with its self-canceling histrionics, its seriousness with its failures. He thereby conveys the impression of taking melodramatic plots completely literally, while at the same time maintaining an ironic, bemused perspective on them. That combination of headlong devotion and ironic distance, of a loving identification with melodrama and a cool distance from it, both as an artistic form and an emotional posture, is what Daniel Mendelsohn misses, when, in analyzing the work of gay directors such as Almodóvar and Todd Haynes, he posits two kinds of melodrama, and contrasts "camp" or "parodic" with "straight" or "deadly earnest" versions of it, as if they represented alternate and mutually exclusive approaches to the genre; see Mendelsohn, "The Melodramatic Moment," *New York Times Magazine,* March 23, 2003, 40–43. For a sharp corrective, see Kathryn Bond Stockton, *Beautiful Bottom, Beautiful Shame: Where "Black" Meets "Queer"* (Durham, NC: Duke University Press, 2006), 212–216; and, more generally, Alejandro Herrero-Olaizola's forthcoming book on camp, melodrama, and Latin America in Almodóvar's films.

10. Compare Neil Bartlett, *Who Was That Man? A Present for Mr Oscar Wilde* (London: Serpent's Tail, 1988), 169: "a fake . . . , when detected, alarmingly reveals that a fake has just as much life, as much validity as the real thing—until detected. It is then revealed as something that has no right to exist. It puts into question authenticity. It even has the power to damage, specifically and effectively, certain specific forms of authentication."

14. Tragedy into Melodrama

1. Ang Lee's 2005 film *Brokeback Mountain* is often put forward as an exception to this rule and is presented as an example of a gay tragedy. The film itself surely

aspires to that status. But even Heather Love, who tries hard to make a plausible case for the movie as a tragedy, blurs her own focus on questions of genre, first by calling its "tragic view of gayness . . . melodramatic," and then by shifting her preferred generic designation for the film to pastoral elegy. That indeed seems to be a more apt category than tragedy for the film, and certainly for the short story by Annie Proulx on which the film is based. See Heather Love, "Compulsory Happiness and Queer Existence," *New Formations* 63 (Spring 2008): 52–64, esp. 55 and 58ff.

2. Susan Sontag, observing that camp "converts the serious into the frivolous," argues that camp incarnates the "victory of . . . irony over tragedy" and insists that "Camp and tragedy are antitheses." See Sontag, "Notes on 'Camp,'" *Against Interpretation, and Other Essays* (New York: Farrar, Straus and Giroux, 1966; first publ. 1964), 276, 287.

3. Neil Bartlett, *Who Was That Man? A Present for Mr Oscar Wilde* (London: Serpent's Tail, 1988), 167: "On 16 November 1897 he wrote: 'My existence is a scandal.' . . . The characteristic name for the heroic life of things or people which have no right to exist was invented, along with so many other features of our lives, during the life and times of Mr Oscar Wilde. . . . If you can't be authentic (and you can't), if this doesn't feel like real life (and it doesn't), then you can be *camp.*"

4. For a brilliant attempt to imagine what a public, but queer, ritual of love might look like, and how it might be founded in the existing social institutions of gay male life, see Neil Bartlett, *Ready To Catch Him Should He Fall* (New York: Dutton, 1991; first publ. 1990). For a survey of the actual rituals that real, nonfictional gay people adopt to celebrate their love, compare Ellen Lewin, *Recognizing Ourselves: Ceremonies of Lesbian and Gay Commitment* (New York: Columbia University Press, 1998).

5. This may be one of the characteristic woes of modernity more generally; see Richard Sennett, *The Fall of Public Man* (New York: Knopf, 1977).

6. Michael Warner, *The Trouble with Normal: Sex, Politics, and the Ethics of Queer Life* (New York: Free Press, 1999), 100–104.

7. For some testimony to this effect, see Lewin, *Recognizing Ourselves,* esp. 191–192.

8. See Charles Osborne, *W. H. Auden: The Life of a Poet* (New York: Harcourt Brace Jovanovich, 1979), 273, reporting the reminiscence of Auden's New York friend John Button, published in September 1974, a year after Auden's death, in the Boston magazine *Fag Rag.*

9. For example, Proust says that gay men's "desire would be permanently unsatisfiable if their money did not procure them real men, and if their imagination did not end up having them take for real men the inverts to whom they prostitute themselves" ("leur désir serait à jamais inassouvissable si l'argent ne leur livrait de vrais hommes, et si l'imagination ne finissait par leur faire prendre pour de vrais hommes les invertis à qui ils se sont prostitués"). Marcel Proust,

A la recherche du temps perdu, vol. 3: *Sodome et Gomorrhe* and *La Prisonnière,* ed. Jean-Yves Tadié, Antoine Compagnon, and Pierre-Edmond Robert, Bibliothèque de la Pléiade (Paris: Gallimard, 1988), 17.

10. Leo Bersani, "Is the Rectum a Grave?" in *AIDS: Cultural Analysis / Cultural Activism,* ed. Douglas Crimp = *October* 43 (Winter 1987): 197–222 (quotation on p. 208).

11. Armistead Maupin, *Tales of the City* (New York: Harper and Row, 1978), 219. All ellipses are in the original, except for the one after "bathroom cabinet," where I have omitted a bit of the narrative. For further details about the practice of masculinity on the part of gay men of that time and place, see pp. 71–72, where Mona, in order to console her friend Michael for breaking up with Robert the Marine recruiter, remarks: "Christ! You and your Rustic Innocent trip! I'll bet that asshole had a closetful of lumberjack shirts, didn't he? . . . He's down at Toad Hall [a long-extinct cruise bar in the Castro] right now, stomping around in his blue nylon flight jacket, with a thumb hooked in his Levi's and a bottle of Acme beer in his fist."

12. This is not a piece of wisdom that is limited to gay men, though some of its canonical expressions retain a certain kinship with gay culture. On Plato, see David M. Halperin, "Love's Irony: Six Remarks on Platonic Eros," in *Erotikon: Essays on Eros, Ancient and Modern,* ed. Shadi Bartsch and Thomas Bartscherer (Chicago: University of Chicago Press, 2005), 48–58. On Shakespeare, see Edward A. Snow, "Loves of Comfort and Despair: A Reading of Shakespeare's Sonnet 138," *English Literary History* 47.3 (Autumn 1980): 462–483.

13. In his wonderful essay on gay men's relation to Judy Garland, which serves as one of the chief inspirations for my own project, Richard Dyer has some trenchant and eloquent things to say about gay men's ability to combine passion with irony: see Dyer, "Judy Garland and Gay Men," *Heavenly Bodies: Film Stars and Society* (New York: St. Martin's, 1986), 141–194, esp. 154–155.

14. See Douglas Crimp, "Right On, Girlfriend!" in *Fear of a Queer Planet: Queer Politics and Social Theory,* ed. Michael Warner (Minneapolis: University of Minnesota Press, 1993), 300–320, esp. 300ff., from whom I have lifted this entire account.

15. Ibid., 313–318 (quotation on p. 317).

16. Lisa Maria Hogeland, "*Invisible Man* and Invisible Women: The Sex/Race Analogy of the 1970s," *Women's History Review* 5.1 (1996): 31–53 (quotation on p. 46); cited in Ellen Samuels, "My Body, My Closet: Invisible Disability and the Limits of Coming-Out Discourse," in *Desiring Disability: Queer Theory Meets Disability Studies,* ed. Robert McRuer and Abby L. Wilkerson = *GLQ: A Journal of Lesbian and Gay Studies* 9.1–2 (2003): 233–255 (quotation on p. 234). Hogeland is summarizing here the argument of Tina Grillo and Stephanie M. Wildman, "Obscuring the Importance of Race: The Implications of Making Comparisons between Racism and Sexism (or Other Issues)," in *Critical White Studies: Looking behind*

the Mirror, ed. Richard Delgado and Jean Stefancic (Philadelphia: Temple University Press, 1997), 619–626.

17. Hegel, *Phenomenology of Spirit*, Chapter VI.A.b.38–475.

18. Just how much the Stonewall Riots had to do with the death and funeral of Judy Garland has been a matter of dispute. A lot is made of the coincidence by Stephen Maddison, who reviews some of the controversy: see Maddison, *Fags, Hags and Queer Sisters: Gender Dissent and Heterosocial Bonds in Gay Culture* (New York: St. Martin's, 2000), 1–12. Compare, however, John Loughery, *The Other Side of Silence: Men's Lives and Gay Identities: A Twentieth-Century History* (New York: Henry Holt, 1998), 316; and now David Carter, *Stonewall: The Riots That Sparked the Gay Revolution* (New York: St. Martin's, 2004), 260–261. Carter makes a very powerful, careful, and convincing historical argument that the rioters at the Stonewall Inn were not in fact spurred to militancy by mourning for Judy Garland.

15. Gay Femininity

1. David Denby, "Escape Artist: The Case for Joan Crawford," *New Yorker*, January 3, 2011, 65–69 (quotation on p. 65).

2. Will Fellows, *A Passion to Preserve: Gay Men as Keepers of Culture* (Madison: University of Wisconsin Press, 2004), 14. Further page references to this work will be incorporated in the text.

3. Will Fellows, *Farm Boys: Lives of Gay Men from the Rural Midwest* (Madison: University of Wisconsin Press, 1996).

4. For a detailed exploration of the ways that gender and sexuality mutually construct each other in male childhood, see David Plummer, *One of the Boys: Masculinity, Homophobia, and Modern Manhood* (Binghamton, NY: Harrington Park Press, 1999).

5. The reference is to John M. Clum, *Something for the Boys: Musical Theater and Gay Culture* (New York: Palgrave / St. Martin's, 2001), 19.

6. In support of this position, Fellows cites Rictor Norton, *The Myth of the Modern Homosexual* (London: Cassell, 1997), 132, which makes an eloquent appeal of a similar kind to students of gay history: "Queer historians need to widen the definition of 'homosexuality' so as to encompass queer culture rather than just queer sex and the laws against it. . . . Queer history is still too much a part of the 'history of sexuality' and needs to be resituated within the history of non-sexual culture and ethnic customs" (Fellows, *Passion to Preserve*, 267–268n).

7. Fellows, *Passion to Preserve*, 268, n. 3, gives as his source for this quotation the following reference: Edward Carpenter, *Selected Writings*, vol. 1: *Sex* (London: GMP Publishers, 1984), 278. Fellows quotes Carpenter again, approvingly, on pp. 247, 253–254, and 257.

8. Fellows, *Passion to Preserve*, 275, n. 1, gives as his source for this quotation the fol-

lowing reference: C. G. Jung, *The Archetypes and the Collective Unconscious,* vol. 9, pt. 1 of *Collected Works* (Princeton, NJ: Princeton University Press, 1968), 86–87, para. 164.

9. For an account of the Radical Faeries, see Scott Lauria Morgensen, "Arrival at Home: Radical Faerie Configurations of Sexuality and Place," *GLQ* 15.1 (2008): 67–96. Morgensen provides a useful overview of the movement and a multitude of references to earlier writings related to it.

10. The best introduction to this revival, which has gained considerable momentum since, is provided by Gilbert Herdt, ed., *Third Sex, Third Gender: Beyond Sexual Dimorphism in Culture and History* (New York: Zone Books, 1994).

11. Edmund White, "The Gay Philosopher," in White, *The Burning Library: Essays,* ed. David Bergman (New York: Knopf, 1994), 3–19 (quotation on p. 5). White indicates that the essay was written and circulated in 1969 but never published until it was collected by Bergman for this anthology. Fellows (*Passion to Preserve,* 260), who quotes and cites this sentence, implies that White *accepted* the third-sex model after "a lifetime of pondering similar phenomena" (in fact, White was no more than twenty-nine when he wrote the essay). White does indeed refute various objections to the idea that homosexuals constitute a "third sex," but his discussion of this point is subordinated to a larger argument against all theories, or myths, of homosexuality. ("Was it nature or nurture?" he asks skeptically on p. 5.) He concludes: "None of the metaphors I've suggested quite fits the homosexual. . . . It's about time homosexuals evolved metaphors that fit the actual content of their lives" (pp. 18–19).

12. Fellows, *Passion to Preserve,* 260–263, vigorously denounces such "effeminophobia," as he calls it, surveying some of the scholarly literature on it and providing an eloquent account of self-censorship on the part of the gay men he interviewed, some of whom systematically suppressed evidence of their feminine identifications when they came to edit the written transcripts of their earlier conversations with Fellows (261).

13. For a moving and intelligent popular account of these controversies as they bear on transgender children, see Hanna Rosin, "A Boy's Life," *Atlantic* (November 2008), www.theatlantic.com/doc/200811/transgender-children (accessed July 29, 2009). A gay psychoanalyst has since entered the fray, pleading humanely for a less pathologizing treatment of gender-variant boys; see Ken Corbett, *Boyhoods: Rethinking Masculinities* (New Haven, CT: Yale University Press, 2009).

14. See Judith Butler, "Imitation and Gender Insubordination," in *Inside/Out: Lesbian Theories, Gay Theories,* ed. Diana Fuss (New York: Routledge, 1991), 13–31; rpt. in *The Lesbian and Gay Studies Reader,* ed. Henry Abelove, Michèle Aina Barale, and David M. Halperin (New York: Routledge, 1993), 307–320.

15. John Weir, "Queer Guy with a Slob's Eye," *New York Times,* August 10, 2003. On the stereotype that gay men "all have impeccable taste," see Clum, *Something for the Boys,* 21.

16. Jack Malebranche, *Androphilia—A Manifesto: Rejecting the Gay Identity, Reclaiming Masculinity* (Gardena, CA: Scapegoat Publishing, 2007). The book's original title, judging from the publisher's website, was, perhaps more fittingly, *Androphilia: A Homosexual Fetishist's Manifesto*. A follow-up by the same author appeared a couple of years later; see Nathan F. Miller and Jack Donovan (a.k.a. Malebranche), *Blood-Brotherhood and Other Rites of Male Alliance* (Portland, OR: Jack Donovan, 2009); the book proposes blood-brotherhood as an alternative to gay marriage.

17. I am quoting from Malebranche's website: www.jack-donovan.com/androphilia/?page_id=10 (accessed January 4, 2009).

18. See, once more, www.jack-donovan.com/androphilia/ (accessed January 5, 2009): "Jack Donovan is my 'real life' name, and the name I'll be using for my artwork in the future. I always regretted using the Malebranche pseudonym for *Androphilia*—it should have remained an online handle."

19. The notion that anal intercourse, or any kind of bodily "penetration," is incompatible with masculinity and therefore out of keeping with any dignified form of sexual intimacy among men seems to have provided the basis for a number of online gay male communities. See, for example, heroichomosex.org/ (accessed January 4, 2009). The website's motto is "HEROIC HOMOSEX: TO LOVE ANOTHER MAN AS AN EQUAL AND A MAN WITH TOTAL FIDELITY."

20. See g0ys.org/ (accessed January 4, 2009).

21. See www.goys.eu/ (apparently the British version; accessed January 4, 2009), where we find the following commentary.

A personal note

Before, of the many thousands of films I have seen from silent classics to new releases, I could not say I had one clear favorite. *Brokeback* changed that; it is the best film I have ever seen. On getting home after seeing this film for the first time, I searched the Internet, unsettled, looking for I knew not what. I discovered the goy movement. I feel this way despite the fact that the sex acts implied are not what I would do as a gay man.

I do not expect to ever have the privilege of being so totally shaken by a work of art again in my lifetime. You would not be reading this now if it were not for *Brokeback Mountain*.

Tips on watching this film on DVD

·   Try not to read the short story or anything on message boards before watching the film for the first time.
·   Do not talk to people who may spoil the story, even by joking.
·   Do not read the insert of the DVD as the titles of the chapters will spoil the story.

- · Treat the DVD as if you were at the cinema; prepare yourself to sit and watch for two hours at a stretch.
- · Watch with other people who are really interested and will not talk during the performance, or otherwise view on your own.
- · Make sure you are not disturbed. Put the phone on voicemail and the bell out. Turn off your mobile. Unplug the doorbell. Tell people you live with who are not watching that you want two hours for yourself. (Some people watch on laptops while parked in the car to get away from their family for two hours).
- · Sit fairly near the screen directly in front of the TV. Turn the lights low or out altogether.
- · Have tissues to hand if you know you cry when watching old Hollywood films.
- · Use the bathroom before you press play.
- · If you are disturbed while watching, rewind a couple of minutes to get back into the story.
- · Do not ask questions, just watch it with your heart and let yourself flow with the scenes.
- · At the end of the film—you will know when the end is approaching— Ennis makes a phone call to the wife of Jack (played by Michelle Williams). Watch carefully during this scene, because the inset flashbacks explain what "really" happened.
- · Pay attention to the shirts.
- · Sit through the end credits to listen to the music.
- · If you feel you need support after watching this film, go to www.ennisjack .com.

That final website is indeed worth a visit.

22. Clum, *Something for the Boys*, 30.
23. E. Patrick Johnson, *Sweet Tea: Black Gay Men of the South* (Chapel Hill: University of North Carolina Press, 2008), 352.
24. On this point, see D. A. Miller, *Place for Us: Essay on the Broadway Musical* (Cambridge, MA: Harvard University Press, 1998), 9–10.
25. There may be an exception, however, in the case of *Wicked;* see Stacy Wolf, *Changed for Good: A Feminist History of the Broadway Musical* (New York: Oxford University Press, 2011), esp. 219–235.
26. I find it interesting, in this connection, that Richard Dyer, in the course of an otherwise superb analysis of Judy Garland's appeal to gay men, avoids the maternal aspects of her persona: when he comes to what he himself acknowledges is her gayest film, *I Could Go On Singing* (1962), he interprets her character's relation to her adolescent son as an erotic allegory rather than as a maternal melodrama, thereby missing much of the movie's gay appeal. See Richard Dyer,

"Judy Garland and Gay Men," *Heavenly Bodies: Film Stars and Society* (New York: St. Martin's, 1986), 141–194.

27. See Stephen Maddison, "All about Women: Pedro Almodóvar and the Heterosocial Dynamic," *Textual Practice,* 14.2 (2000), 265–284; Leo Bersani and Ulysse Dutoit, "'Almodóvar's Girls' *(All about My Mother),*" *Forms of Being: Cinema, Aesthetics, Subjectivity* (London: British Film Institute, 2004), 74–123.

16. Gender and Genre

1. Joe Kort reports that a local news show about my class "How To Be Gay" featured an African American woman who remarked, by way of expressing her opposition to the class, "No one had to teach me how to be black." He goes on quite properly to retort, "How untrue. Her family and culture taught her from the day she was born." See Joe Kort, *10 Smart Things Gay Men Can Do To Find Real Love* (New York: Alyson, 2006), 5–6.

2. For a few hints about this, see Michael Warner, *The Trouble with Normal: Sex, Politics, and the Ethics of Queer Life* (New York: Free Press, 1999), 102. See, generally, Lauren Berlant, *The Female Complaint: The Unfinished Business of Sentimentality in American Culture* (Durham, NC: Duke University Press, 2008), especially 169–205, on *Now, Voyager.* Compare David M. Halperin, "Deviant Teaching," in *A Companion to Lesbian, Gay, Bisexual, Transgender, and Queer Studies,* ed. George E. Haggerty and Molly McGarry (Malden, MA: Blackwell, 2007), 146–167.

3. Will Fellows, *A Passion to Preserve: Gay Men as Keepers of Culture* (Madison: University of Wisconsin Press, 2004), is consistently hostile to social-constructionist approaches to sexuality and subjectivity, which he regards as entailing an "assimilationist-minded" denial of the existence of gay male culture and of the two-spiritedness of gay male subjectivity; he looks to Camille Paglia for authoritative confirmation of his view (esp. 260–262). Although it is certainly the case that a social-constructionist approach is opposed to the notion that there are "essential differences between gay males and straight males," as Fellows correctly states (261), it need not carry with it all the unfortunate consequences that Fellows rightly laments. In fact, if the "essential differences" between gay and straight men with which Fellows is concerned are understood to be effects of social processes, it might even be possible to reconcile his views with those of social constructionists, such as myself.

4. "Quaint" is the word Fellows uses to characterize the near-extinct "tradition" of post-Stonewall gay masculinity (*Passion to Preserve,* 280, n. 11), which he describes as follows: "Gay men in the 1970s and 1980s affected a hyperbutch look (denim, leather, flannel, facial hair, stiff wrists) and began to proffer themselves as thoroughly regular guys" (262).

5. For the first quotation, see Fellows, *Passion to Preserve,* 267, note 2, citing Larry Kramer, "Sex and Sensibility," *The Advocate* (May 27, 1997), 59, 64–65, 67–69. The

second quotation (Fellows, *Passion to Preserve,* 262) is from Kramer's 1985 play, *The Normal Heart,* where it is part of a rant by a character who serves as Kramer's mouthpiece in the drama; Fellows cites the Penguin edition of the play (New York, 1985), 114. For a similar complaint that practitioners of lesbian and gay studies reduce homosexuality to sex, see Lee J. Siegel, "The Gay Science: Queer Theory, Literature, and the Sexualization of Everything," *New Republic,* November 9, 1998, 30–42; rpt. in Lee Siegel, *Falling Upwards: Essays in Defense of the Imagination* (New York: Basic Books, 2006), 182–214.

6. On Liberace's activity as a restorer of neglected houses, see Fellows, *Passion to Preserve,* 31–32, 133–134.

7. These are aspects of gay men's cultural practices that Fellows, *Passion to Preserve,* brings out very well (esp. 244–246, 249–254).

8. For the specification of "escape from identity" (or "flight from identity") as a tactic that stigmatized or captive populations typically use to cope with social domination—in this case, homophobia—see Barry D. Adam, *The Survival of Domination: Inferiorization and Everyday Life* (New York: Elsevier, 1978), 89–93.

9. For the most systematic, rigorous, and sophisticated theoretical elaboration of the social, psychic, and erotic consequences of the simple fact that gay men are like straight men insofar as they are men, but different from them insofar as they are gay, see Earl Jackson, Jr., *Strategies of Deviance: Studies in Gay Male Representation* (Bloomington: Indiana University Press, 1995), especially the first chapter, "Calling the Questions: Gay Male Subjectivity, Representation, and Agency" (pp. 1–52, 267–274). For a brilliant, subtle, and thoroughgoing study of the unique subjectivity and gender positioning of gay men, see Jean-Paul Sartre, *Saint Genet: Comédien et martyr* (Paris: Gallimard, 1952).

10. See, for example, Sam Abel, "Opera and Homoerotic Desire," in *Opera in the Flesh: Sexuality in Operatic Performance* (Boulder, CO: Westview, 1996), 58–75.

11. John M. Clum, *Something for the Boys: Musical Theater and Gay Culture* (New York: Palgrave / St. Martin's, 2001), 61.

12. Stuart Hall, "Culture, the Media and the 'Ideological Effect,'" in *Mass Communication and Society,* ed. James Curran, Michael Gurevitch, Janet Woollacott, et al. (London: Edward Arnold, 1977), 315–348 (quotation on p. 330), as cited by Ken Tucker and Andrew Treno, "The Culture of Narcissism and the Critical Tradition: An Interpretive Essay," *Berkeley Journal of Sociology* 25 (1980): 341–355 (quotation on p. 351). See, generally, Hall's discussion of the constitutive role of ideology in "Deviance, Politics, and the Media," in *Deviance and Social Control,* ed. Paul Rock and Mary McIntosh (London: Tavistock, 1974), 261–305; reprinted in *The Lesbian and Gay Studies Reader,* ed. Henry Abelove, Michèle Aina Barale, and David M. Halperin (New York: Routledge, 1993), 62–90.

13. See *The Collected Poems of Frank O'Hara,* ed. Donald Allen (Berkeley, CA: University of California Press, 1995), 449.

14. Compare the remark of German filmmaker Matthias Müller, speaking about

his love of Lana Turner in reference to this poem: "As a homosexual, I have a special relationship to the suffering of his [Douglas Sirk's] female protagonists in a restrictive, normative society, but I also envy these female characters their privilege of being able to live out their emotions uninhibitedly on the domestic stage, through their large, expansive gestures. In this sense, even though their fates are distant from my own reality, these figures still invite me to identify with them." Scott MacDonald / Matthias Müller, "A Conversation," *The Memo Book: Films, Videos, and Installations by Matthias Müller,* ed. Stefanie Schulte Strathaus (Berlin: Vorwerk 8, 2005), 233, as quoted and cited by Marc Howard Siegel, "A Gossip of Images: Hollywood Star Images and Queer Counterpublics" (Ph.D. diss., University of California, Los Angeles, 2010), 67.

15. Samuel R. Delany, "The Rhetoric of Sex, the Discourse of Desire," in *Heterotopia: Postmodern Utopia and the Body Politic,* ed. Tobin Siebers (Ann Arbor: University of Michigan Press, 1994), 229–272 (quotation on p. 234).

16. See, for example, Jeffery P. Dennis, "The Boy Who Would Be Queen: Hints and Closets on Children's Television," *Journal of Homosexuality* 56.6 (August–September 2009): 738–756.

17. D. A. Miller, *Place for Us: Essay on the Broadway Musical* (Cambridge, MA: Harvard University Press, 1998), 17. Wayne Koestenbaum, however, claims that his early fondness for show tunes did in fact cause him anxiety. "Predictive sign: a fondness for musical comedy. I worried, listening to records of *Darling Lili, Oklahoma!, The Music Man, Company,* and *No, No, Nanette,* that I would end up gay." See Wayne Koestenbaum, *The Queen's Throat: Opera, Homosexuality, and the Mystery of Desire* (New York: Poseidon Press, 1993), 11.

18. The fundamental work on gay men's language is by William L. Leap, *Word's Out: Gay Men's English* (Minneapolis: University of Minnesota Press, 1996). The project it outlines is a fascinating and important one, but the book itself does not succeed in living up to its promise. See also the important collection by William L. Leap, ed., *Beyond the Lavender Lexicon: Authenticity, Imagination, and Appropriation in Lesbian and Gay Languages* (Amsterdam: Gordon and Breach, 1995). A brilliant meditation on gay men's relation to language is provided by Neil Bartlett, *Who Was That Man? A Present for Mr Oscar Wilde* (London: Serpent's Tail, 1988), 77–91. See, as well, Edmund White, "The Political Vocabulary of Homosexuality," in *The State of the Language,* ed. Leonard Michaels and Christopher Ricks (Berkeley, CA: University of California Press, 1980), 235–246; Bruce Rodgers, *The Queen's Vernacular: A Gay Lexicon* (San Francisco: Straight Arrow Books, 1972); James W. Chesebro, ed., *Gayspeak: Gay Male and Lesbian Communication* (New York: Pilgrim Press, 1981); Kira Hall and Mary Bucholtz, *Gender Articulated: Language and the Socially Constructed Self* (New York: Routledge, 1995); Anna Livia and Kira Hall, ed., *Queerly Phrased: Language, Gender, and Sexuality* (New York: Oxford University Press, 1997); Paul Baker, *Fantabulosa: A Dictionary of Polari and Gay Slang* (London: Continuum, 2002); Kathryn Campbell-Kibler,

Robert J. Podesva, Sarah J. Roberts, and Andrew Wong, ed., *Language and Sexuality: Contesting Meaning in Theory and Practice* (Stanford, CA: CSLI Publications, 2002); Don Kulick, "Transgender and Language: A Review of the Literature and Suggestions for the Future," *GLQ* 5.4 (1999): 605–622; Deborah Cameron and Don Kulick, *Language and Sexuality* (Cambridge: Cambridge University Press, 2003); and, for an overview, Deborah Cameron and Don Kulick, ed., *The Language and Sexuality Reader* (New York: Routledge, 2005).

19. Clum, *Something for the Boys,* 19.

20. On the continuing gay appeal of divas, see the double issue of *Camera Obscura* entitled "Fabulous! Divas," *Camera Obscura: Feminism, Culture, and Media Studies* 65 and 67 = 22.2 (2007) and 23.1 (2008); also, the collection by Michael Montlack, ed., *My Diva: 65 Gay Men on the Women Who Inspire Them* (Madison: University of Wisconsin Press, 2009).

21. Barry D. Adam, "How Might We Create a Collectivity That We Would Want To Belong To?" in *Gay Shame,* ed. David M. Halperin and Valerie Traub (Chicago: University of Chicago Press, 2009), 301–311 (quotation on pp. 305–306).

22. On the different historical temporalities of lesbian and gay male sexualities, see David M. Halperin, "The First Homosexuality?" *How To Do the History of Homosexuality* (Chicago: University of Chicago Press, 2002), 48–80, esp. 78–80, and Valerie Traub, "The Present Future of Lesbian Historiography," in *A Companion to Lesbian, Gay, Bisexual, Transgender, and Queer Studies,* 124–143.

17. The Meaning of Style

1. The basic and pioneering study of this phenomenon is Pierre Bourdieu, *Distinction: A Social Critique of the Judgement of Taste,* trans. Richard Nice (Cambridge, MA: Harvard University Press, 1984; first publ. 1979). Bourdieu examines how taste cultures are created and distributed within social collectivities, such as families, social classes, local communities, ethnic groups, and other social formations that reproduce themselves and their aesthetic standards across the generations through biological reproduction, inheritance, primary socialization, and similar sorts of mainstream social mechanisms—in other words, that reproduce themselves heterosexually. His analysis pertains to tastes that are linked to social class, but it does not apply specifically to the acquisition and transmission of gay taste, or to the kinds of counter-acculturation that are at issue here.

2. Film noir criticism does attempt to capture the meaning of film noir style *in general.* It is perfectly able to describe how a standard element, like the use of the shadow cast by Venetian blinds, condenses the play with light and shadow that is fundamental to film noir style. Thus, as Damon Young explains, "Whereas traditional cinematography starts with white space and fills it with shapes, film noir starts with black space and lights some parts of it. Objects and people are always disappearing into shadow space. One never knows what is going to

emerge into the realm of visibility—which is never fully available, but always striated by zones of obscurity. The shadows from a Venetian blind perfect this effect of striation, this play with light and shadows (and all the metaphorical meanings that shadows have accrued)." Damon Young, personal communication, June 17, 2011.

Other critics try to go further and offer greater specificity. James Naremore, for example, commenting on a color film, *The Glass Shield* (1994), says it uses "venetian blind shadows" to create "a sense of isolation and fear," in keeping with the chiaroscuro effects of black-and-white lighting in conventional film noir: see Naremore, *More Than Night: Film Noir in Its Contexts* (Berkeley: University of California Press, 1998), 248–249, 189. Robert E. Smith notes that in Anthony Mann's black-and-white *Raw Deal* (1948), "the moonlight which shines through the Venetian blinds of Marsha Hunt's bedroom" constitutes an "artful and often poetic approximation of natural light"; see Smith, "Mann in the Dark: The *Films Noir* of Anthony Mann," in *Film Noir Reader,* ed. Alain Silver and James Ursini (Pompton Plains, NJ: Limelight Editions, 2006), 189–202 (quotation on p. 191). Most interesting of all is Tom Conley, who associates Venetian blinds with the immobility of the present in film noir: "The present is confining, artificial, cast under dim three-point lighting fragmenting the figure of the characters. The outside is seen across orders of Venetian *blinds.* Actors stare through their slits, as if disheartened avatars of the nineteenth-century novel and painting, figures whose search for bliss leads to gazes into the absolute nothing of the world outside. They are striated by the shadows of light cutting their bodies into lines." About *Mildred Pierce,* Conley has this to say: "The lush Californian coast of *Mildred Pierce* (Warner, 1945) is shot in the past tense, in flashbacks that lead forward to the stale odor of acrid coffee and cigarettes in a police station in the early hours of the morning. Outside space or light tends to be evoked but closed *off* or set apart by narrative immobilized in no-exit situations." See Conley, "Stages of 'Film Noir,'" *Theatre Journal* 39.3 (October 1987): 347–363 (quotations on p. 350).

All three writers, in short, imply *something* about the meaning of Venetian blinds in film noir style: the blinds convey isolation and fear (Naremore), artificiality and distance from the natural world (Smith), or the separation of interior space from an outside space imagined as the space of the past, plenitude, sunlight, and nature, with the interior space represented as a space of stasis, of the immobility of "no-exit" situations (Conley). None of these critics, however, attempts to identify the meaning of the fleeting shadow of Venetian blinds as an element of visual style in the specific context of this specific moment in this specific scene in *Mildred Pierce.* Much less do they try to get at what that stylistic element might mean *to* a specific segment of the audience of the movie, belonging to a specific sexual subculture.

3. D. A. Miller, *8½ [Otto e mezzo]*, British Film Institute (Basingstoke: Palgrave Mac-

millan, 2008), 74–75; also 86–88. Despite valiant efforts to describe the meaning of Fellini's visual style, Miller's account is less satisfying than his elucidation of the meaning of Jane Austen's literary style: see, for example, his brilliant and sure description of the content of a formal element in the narrative of *Emma* in *Jane Austen; or, The Secret of Style* (Princeton, NJ: Princeton University Press, 2003), 61–68. For a systematic argument to the effect that style is its own thing, see Myra Jehlen, *Five Fictions in Search of Truth* (Princeton, NJ: Princeton University Press, 2008), especially the remarks on Flaubert's style (13–46, 133–143), to which I am deeply indebted.

4. Oscar Wilde, *The Picture of Dorian Gray*, ch. 2. The passage was complete in the earliest version of the novel: see Oscar Wilde, *The Picture of Dorian Gray: An Annotated, Uncensored Edition*, ed. Nicholas Frankel (Cambridge, MA: Harvard University Press, 2011), 99. Susan Sontag quotes a slightly different formulation, which she attributes to a different source, in the second epigraph to her essay "Against Interpretation," in Sontag, *Against Interpretation, and Other Essays* (New York: Farrar, Straus and Giroux, 1966; first publ. 1964), 3–14 (see p. 3).

5. My affectionate thanks to Michael Forrey for working out with me the meaning of this shot.

6. For some testimony by the creators of film noir that indicates how they understood the meaning of their aesthetic, see Robert Porfirio, Alain Silver, and James Ursini, eds., *Film Noir Reader 3: Interviews with Filmmakers of the Classic Noir Period* (New York: Limelight Editions, 2002), esp. 42, 125, and 230–231. These statements do indicate how careful and deliberate the filmmakers were in setting up shots and establishing a style, but they are couched in a language so close to the film noir aesthetic itself that they do not yield much information about what the elements of film noir style actually mean.

7. Dick Hebdige, *Subculture: The Meaning of Style* (London: Routledge, 1979).

8. Sontag, "Against Interpretation," 8.

9. Ibid., 9.

10. Susan Sontag, "On Style" (first publ. 1965), in *Against Interpretation*, 15–36 (quotation on p. 20).

11. Susan Sontag, "Notes on 'Camp'" (first publ. 1964), in *Against Interpretation*, 275–292, esp. 275–276 (quotation on p. 276).

12. Pier Dominguez, "Susan Sontag, Superstar; or, How To Be a Modernist Genius in Post-Modern Culture: Gender, Celebrity and the Public Intellectual" (M.A. thesis, Columbia University, 2008), 16. Dominguez discovered that one of the issues of *Partisan Review* that preceded the issue in which Sontag's famous essay on camp appeared contained an announcement of her forthcoming contribution under the rubric "Camp as Style." Whether that was actually a preliminary title or merely a description of the topic of the essay remains unclear, but in either case it is telling.

13. Sontag, "On Style," 36 (emphasis added).

14. See John M. Clum, *Something for the Boys: Musical Theater and Gay Culture* (New York: Palgrave / St. Martin's, 2001), xii. Clum compares and contrasts the Broadway musical with baseball in gay/straight terms: "Some of us also love the arcana of musical theater the way other men love baseball statistics" (see also pp. 23, 137).

15. On the camp form of this sort of utterance, see Keith Harvey, "Camp Talk and Citationality: A Queer Take on 'Authentic' and 'Represented' Utterance," *Journal of Pragmatics* 34 (2002): 1145–1165, esp. 1151–1152.

18. Irony and Misogyny

1. For a very clear and patient elaboration of the distinction, see Judith Butler, *Bodies That Matter: On the Discursive Limits of "Sex"* (New York: Routledge, 1993), 4–12.

2. Compare John M. Clum, *Something for the Boys: Musical Theater and Gay Culture* (New York: Palgrave / St. Martin's, 2001), 48: "Our enthusiasms may reveal that for all our interest in femininity, we're often not really interested in women."

3. Compare Moe Meyer, "Introduction: Reclaiming the Discourse of Camp," in *The Politics and Poetics of Camp*, ed. Meyer (London: Routledge, 1994), 1–22, esp. 11: "Parody becomes the process whereby the marginalized and disenfranchised advance their own interests by entering alternative signifying codes into discourse by attaching them to existing structures of signification. Without the process of parody, the marginalized agent has no access to representation, the apparatus of which is controlled by the dominant order. . . . Camp, as specifically queer parody, becomes, then, the only process by which the queer is able to enter representation and to produce social visibility. This piggy-backing upon the dominant order's monopoly on the authority of signification explains why Camp appears, on the one hand, to offer a transgressive vehicle yet, on the other, simultaneously invokes the specter of dominant ideology within its practice, appearing, in many instances, to actually reinforce the dominant order."

4. See the influential arguments in Judith Butler, "Imitation and Gender Insubordination," in *Inside/Out: Lesbian Theories, Gay Theories*, ed. Diana Fuss (New York: Routledge, 1991), 13–31; rpt. in *The Lesbian and Gay Studies Reader*, ed. Henry Abelove, Michèle Aina Barale, and David M. Halperin (New York: Routledge, 1993), 307–320.

5. On the general question of gay male misogyny, see Richard Dyer's sensible remarks in "Gay Misogyny," in Dyer, *The Culture of Queers* (London: Routledge, 2002), 46–48.

6. I want to express my particular gratitude to D. Nathaniel Smith for urging me to think through this issue and for patiently working it out with me.

7. See www.sonicyouth.com/mustang/sy/song92a.html (accessed January 15, 2009).

8. See David Browne, *Goodbye 20th Century: A Biography of Sonic Youth* (New York: Da Capo, 2008), 202, 210: "Pettibon specialized in black-ink drawings that felt like cells taken randomly from comic strips, yet worked on their own. In an article for *Artforum* in 1985, Gordon praised Pettibon's work as 'statements unto themselves' that 'feed off the simplistic morals of made-for-TV movies, which center around "contemporary" questions.'"

9. Stevie Chick, *Psychic Confusion: The Sonic Youth Story* (London: Omnibus, 2008), 170. See, further, Browne, *Goodbye 20th Century*, 210–211.

10. Chick, *Psychic Confusion*, 173–174.

11. Quoted from LyricsMode.com: www.lyricsmode.com/lyrics/s/sonic_youth/androgynous_ mind.html (accessed January 15, 2009). Cobain had already asserted that "God is gay" in the closing line of "Stay Away" on *Nevermind* (1991). Another possible source could be the Nirvana song "All Apologies" from the 1993 *In Utero* CD:

What else should I be
All apologies
What else could I say
Everyone is gay
What else could I write
I don't have the right
What else should I be
All apologies

I quote again from LyricsMode.com: www.lyricsmode.com/lyrics/n/nirvana/all_ apologies.html (accessed on January 16, 2009).

12. Quoted from LyricsMode.com: www.lyricsmode.com/lyrics/s/sonic_youth/mildred_ pierce.html (accessed January 15, 2009). I have checked it for accuracy. There is now a Dutch punk band called Mildred Pierce—inspired, I presume, by the classic SY track.

13. For the background, see Browne, *Goodbye 20th Century*, 220.

14. The YouTube address is www.youtube.com/watch?v=IMgY_x4TigA (accessed August 1, 2009).

15. The comment was posted on the YouTube site for the SY video (see previous note). It is worth quoting in full: "This song has always provoked many theories as to what SY are trying to convey. Sometimes I imagine that they're channeling Ms. Crawford's inner turmoil and pain (from beyond the grave, perhaps?) that she so brilliantly used in her portrayal of Mildred Pierce. This tune is equal parts haunting and headbanging, a rare feat that can only be accomplished by the genius of bands like Sonic Youth."

16. See the May 12, 2004, VH1 interview by C. Bottomley, "Sonic Youth: Medicine for Your Ear," www.vh1.com/news/articles/1486965/05122004/sonic _youth.jhtml, accessed January 22, 2009. Gordon's reflections are worth quoting

in full: "I saw her [Mariah Carey] doing a cover of the '70s disco song, 'Last Night a DJ Saved My Life.' I just couldn't get it out of my head. She was bouncing through this set of gangsta rappers. It was right after her breakdown and she seemed so vulnerable. And she was barely singing! It stuck with me. She and Karen Carpenter [the anorexic subject of Sonic Youth's "Tunic"] are both about the body. Karen was trying to get rid of hers. Aesthetics have changed a lot since Karen. I'm sure they're similar A-type personalities—driven perfectionists who just want to please people so much. Karen's voice showed a lot of vulnerability—more so than Mariah. She made the words she was singing her own. That's a scary thing to do when you're standing in a media spotlight. You lose a sense of your identity. It's a narcissist thing." Those comments may hint at how Gordon and Coppola related to Joan Crawford's performance as Mildred Pierce.

17. Browne, *Goodbye 20th Century,* 220.

18. Susan Sontag's warnings against "deliberate camp" are pertinent in this context. See "Notes on 'Camp,'" in Sontag, *Against Interpretation, and Other Essays* (New York: Farrar, Straus and Giroux, 1966; first publ. 1964), 282: "Camp which knows itself to be Camp ('camping') is usually less satisfying. The pure examples of Camp are unintentional; they are dead serious. . . . Genuine Camp . . . does not mean to be funny. . . . It seems unlikely that much of the traditional opera repertoire could be such satisfying Camp if the melodramatic absurdities of most opera plots had not been taken seriously by their composers. . . . Probably, intending to be campy is always harmful."

19. See Butler, "Imitation and Gender Insubordination," esp. 312–316.

20. Douglas Haddow, "Hipster: The Dead End of Western Civilization," *Adbusters,* 79 (July 29, 2008), www.adbusters.org/magazine/79/hipster.html (accessed August 1, 2009, at which point 4,167 online comments had been posted to it; they are worth consulting every bit as much as the article itself). Thanks to D. Nathaniel Smith for referring me to this essay.

21. Christian Lorentzen, "Kill the Hipster: Why the Hipster Must Die—A Modest Proposal to Save New York Cool," *Time Out New York* (May 30–June 5, 2007), available online at newyork.timeout.com/articles/features/4840/why-the-hipster-must-die (accessed August 1, 2009). Lorentzen goes on to write, "Those 18-to-34-year-olds called hipsters have defanged, skinned and consumed the fringe movements of the postwar era—Beat, hippie, punk, even grunge. Hungry for more, and sick with the anxiety of influence, they feed as well from the trough of the uncool, turning white trash chic, and gouging the husks of long-expired subcultures—vaudeville, burlesque, cowboys and pirates." He accuses them of transforming "gay style" into "metrosexuality."

22. Charles Ludlam, "Camp," *Ridiculous Theatre, Scourge of Human Folly: The Essays and Opinions of Charles Ludlam,* ed. Steven Samuels (New York: Theater Communications Group, 1992), 227, as quoted and discussed in Marc Howard Siegel,

"A Gossip of Images: Hollywood Star Images and Queer Counterpublics" (Ph.D. diss., University of California, Los Angeles, 2010), 165.

23. Siegel, "Gossip of Images," 163–167 and passim, emphasizes the importance of "belief" for understanding gay male investments in Hollywood cinema; I am indebted to his argument.

24. Compare Matt Siegel, "Are Hipsters Stealing Gay Style? Or Something Else?" *Queerty,* May 4, 2009, www.queerty.com/are-hipsters-stealing-gay-style-or-some thing-else-20090504/ (accessed June 27, 2011): "Hipsters are emulating *queer* style, not *gay* style. To me, 'queer' implies a resistance to assimilation which is ironically (and you know how much the hipsters love irony!) the very thing hipsters are doing: assimilating. . . . There is a major difference between hipsters and gays." Siegel's column elicited 102 responses at last count, some of which are worth consulting.

25. Such a privileged position is perfectly appropriate to "a class of individuals that seek to escape their own wealth and privilege by immersing themselves in the aesthetic of the working class" and of other oppressed social groups, according to the unsparing judgment of Haddow ("Hipster").

26. See stuffwhitepeoplelike.com/2008/02/03/50-irony/ (accessed January 6, 2009); Christian Lander, *Stuff White People Like: The Definitive Guide to the Unique Taste of Millions* (New York: Random House, 2008), 63. My information about Lander comes from his author's note, as well as from an interview he did with Gregory Rodriguez, "White Like Us: A Blogger Explores the Attitudes and Foibles of a New Minority Group," *Los Angeles Times,* February 25, 2008 (www.latimes.com/news/opinion/la-oe-rodriguez25feb25,0,1952462.column, accessed January 14, 2009). Many thanks to D. Nathaniel Smith for putting me on to Lander's article and the interview with him.

27. Dyer, *Culture of Queers,* 51. Compare Meyer, "Reclaiming the Discourse of Camp," 1: "Because un-queer appropriations interpret Camp within the context of compulsory reproductive heterosexuality, they no longer qualify as Camp. . . . In other words, the un-queer do not have access to the discourse of Camp, only to derivatives constructed through the act of appropriation."

19. Judy Garland versus Identity Art

1. *Time Out New York* 661, May 29–June 4, 2008, 16–21. Further page references to this article will be incorporated in the text.

2. David M. Halperin, *What Do Gay Men Want? An Essay on Sex, Risk, and Subjectivity* (Ann Arbor: University of Michigan Press, 2007; rev. ed. 2009); Halperin, "Small Town Boy: Neil Bartlett Learns How To Be Gay," *"Identities": Journal for Politics, Gender and Culture* 13 (2007–2008): 117–155, reprinted, with revisions, in *Tiresias: Culture, Politics and Critical Theory* 3 (April 2009): 3–35; Halperin, "Be-

yond Gay Pride" (with Valerie Traub), in *Gay Shame,* ed. David M. Halperin and Valerie Traub (Chicago: University of Chicago Press, 2009), 3–40; Halperin, "Introduction: Among Men—History, Sexuality, and the Return of Affect," in *Love, Sex, Intimacy, and Friendship Between Men, 1550–1800,* ed. Katherine O'Donnell and Michael O'Rourke (Basingstoke: Palgrave, 2003), 1–11; Halperin, "Deviant Teaching," in *A Companion to Lesbian, Gay, Bisexual, Transgender, and Queer Studies,* ed. George E. Haggerty and Molly McGarry (Malden, MA: Blackwell, 2007), 146–167; Halperin, "Homosexuality's Closet," *Michigan Quarterly Review* 41.1 (Winter 2002): 21–54; Halperin, "Gay Identity and Its Discontents," *Photofile* (Sydney) 61 (December 2000): 31–36; Halperin, "Des lits d'initiés," *L'Unebévue* (Paris) 16 (Autumn 2000): 23–39.

3. Richard Dyer, "Judy Garland and Gay Men," in Dyer, *Heavenly Bodies: Film Stars and Society* (New York: St. Martin's, 1986), 141–194 (quotation on p. 149).

4. See, for example, Derek Jarman, *Derek Jarman's Garden,* with photographs by Howard Sooley (London: Thames and Hudson, 1995); Simon Doonan, *Confessions of a Window Dresser: Tales from the Life of Fashion* (New York: Penguin Studio, 1998); Andrew Gorman-Murray, "Homeboys: Uses of Home by Gay Australian Men," *Social and Cultural Geography* 7.1 (February 2006): 53–69; Gorman-Murray, "Gay and Lesbian Couples at Home: Identity Work in Domestic Space," *Home Cultures* 3.2 (2006): 145–168; Greg Louganis, with Eric Marcus, *Breaking the Surface* (New York: Random House, 1995).

5. John M. Clum, *Something for the Boys: Musical Theater and Gay Culture* (New York: Palgrave / St. Martin's, 2001), 23.

6. This generational ideology has been recorded, elaborated, amplified, accepted as true, and provided with academic credibility by Ritch C. Savin-Williams, *The New Gay Teenager* (Cambridge, MA: Harvard University Press, 2005). Savin-Williams projects "that the gay adolescent will eventually disappear. Teens who have same-gendered sex and desires won't vanish. But they will not need to identify as gay" (21).

7. Clum, *Something for the Boys,* 28.

8. Kenji Yoshino, *Covering: The Hidden Assault on Our Civil Rights* (New York: Random House, 2006), xi, 17–19.

9. Scott James, "Celebration of Gay Pride Masks Community in Transition," *New York Times,* June 26, 2011, A27A.

10. Bre DeGrant, "Why I Don't Celebrate Gay Pride," Salon.com, June 27, 2011, www.salon.com/life/feature/2011/06/27/out_not_proud_open2011/index.html (accessed June 27, 2011).

11. James, "Celebration of Gay Pride."

12. Quoted in June Thomas, "The Gay Bar: Its New Competition," Slate.com, June 30, 2011, www.slate.com/id/2297608 (accessed July 12, 2011).

13. I am quoting from the web-based version of *Time Out New York* (*TONY*): newyork.timeout.com / things-to-do / this-week-in-new-york / 22619 / poll-which

-is-gayer?package=80456 (accessed July 1, 2011). The print version contains a boiled-down equivalent by Erin McHugh called "Queer Factor" (21), whose two columns make *TONY*'s preferences clear: "Gay" (*Brokeback Mountain*, Truman Capote) and "Gayer" (*Sex and the City*, Herman Melville).

14. Available only on the web-based version of *TONY*: newyork.timeout.com/things-to-do/this-week-in-new-york/22683/top-ten-moments-in-nyc-gay-culture?package=80456 (accessed July 1, 2011).

20. Culture versus Subculture

1. For discussions of Jamie O'Neill's homosexualizing of Irish identity and Irishing of gay male love, see my review of his novel in the *London Review of Books* 25.10 (May 22, 2003): 32–33; as well as Jodie Medd, "'Patterns of the Possible': National Imaginings and Queer Historical (Meta)Fictions in Jamie O'Neill's *At Swim, Two Boys*," *GLQ* 13.1 (2006): 1–31, which offers several useful and welcome correctives to the somewhat over-hasty critique of O'Neill in my review.

2. For an extraordinary example of an early effort to create a new, alternative, identitarian, "counterpublic" gay discourse of love, see Michael Denneny, *Lovers: A Story of Two Men* (New York: Avon, 1979).

3. Consider British pop singer Holly Johnson's 1994 dance hit "Legendary Children (All of Them Queer)." I reproduce the lyrics below.

Michelangelo . . . Leonardo da Vinci
William Shakespeare . . . Nijinsky
Alexander the Great . . . Tchaikovsky
Bernstein . . . Mahler . . . Liberace

Oh come let us adore them
Those legendary children
You know you can't ignore them
Those legendary children

Add your name to this hall of fame
The answer is clear
They're All Of Them Queer
Add your name to this hall of fame
Stand up and cheer
They're All of Them Queer

Andy Warhol . . . Johnny Ray
William Burroughs . . . Jean Genet
Isherwood . . . Wilde . . . Capote . . . Auden
Jean Cocteau . . . Joe Orton

You know you can't ignore them
Those legendary children
Oh come let us adore them
Those legendary children

Add your name to this hall of fame
The answer is clear
They're All of Them Queer
Add your name to this hall of fame
Stand up and cheer
They're All of Them Queer

Be careful not to bore them
Those legendary children
You know you can't ignore them
Those legendary children

Mapplethorpe . . . Crisp . . . Keith Haring
Derek Jarman . . . Candy Darling
Hartman . . . Sommerville . . . in the house
Diaghilev . . . Nureyev . . . Michael Mouse

Little Richard . . . George O'Dowd.
Divine . . . Cole Porter . . . Say it loud!
Holly . . . Wolfgang . . . Plenty Handbag
Brenda Yardley . . . What a fag!

(If only being gay guaranteed that you would be a genius. And how did Mahler and Mozart get onto the list, anyway?)

Compare the following claim by Ned Weeks, the hero of Larry Kramer's play *The Normal Heart* (1985) and fictional alter ego of the playwright himself: "I belong to a culture that includes Proust, Henry James, Tchaikovsky, Cole Porter, Plato, Socrates, Aristotle, Alexander the Great, Michelangelo, Leonardo da Vinci, Christopher Marlowe, Walt Whitman, Herman Melville, Tennessee Williams, Byron, E. M. Forster, Lorca, Auden, Francis Bacon, James Baldwin, Harry Stack Sullivan, John Maynard Keynes, Dag Hammarskjöld . . ." See Larry Kramer, *"The Normal Heart" and "The Destiny of Me": Two Plays by Larry Kramer* (New York: Grove Press, 2000), 109.

4. See Matthew Tinkcom, *Working Like a Homosexual: Camp, Capital, Cinema* (Durham, NC: Duke University Press, 2002).

5. Smith Galtney, "Let the Gays Begin: Six City Culture Makers Attempt to Answer Our Burning—Possibly Flaming—Questions," *Time Out New York* 661 (May 29–June 4, 2008): 18–21 (quotation on pp. 20–21).

6. Barry D. Adam, *The Survival of Domination: Inferiorization and Everyday Life* (New

York: Elsevier, 1978), 92 (on the "flight from identity," more generally termed "escape from identity," 89–93) and 106–114 (on "in-group hostility").

21. Queer Forever

1. For the origins of these developments, see Martin Meeker, *Contacts Desired: Gay and Lesbian Communications and Community, 1940s–1970s* (Chicago: University of Chicago Press, 2006).

2. June Thomas, "The Gay Bar: Is It Dying?" Slate.com, June 27, 2011, www.slate.com/id/2297604/ (accessed July 12, 2011).

3. Compare, for a later period, the testimony of Guillaume Dustan, *Dans ma chambre* (Paris: P.O.L., 1996), 75.

4. I am summarizing a history that has been partially documented for San Francisco in great detail by Gayle S. Rubin, "Elegy for the Valley of Kings: AIDS and the Leather Community in San Francisco, 1981–1996," in *In Changing Times: Gay Men and Lesbians Encounter HIV/AIDS,* ed. Martin P. Levine, Peter M. Nardi, and John H. Gagnon (Chicago: University of Chicago Press, 1997), 101–144, esp. 107–123; also, Rubin, "The Miracle Mile: South of Market and Gay Male Leather, 1962–1997," in *Reclaiming San Francisco: History, Politics, Culture,* ed. James Brook, Chris Carlsson, and Nancy J. Peters (San Francisco: City Lights, 1998), 247–272, esp. 259–267.

5. Patrick S. Sullivan and Richard J. Wolitski, "HIV Infection among Gay and Bisexual Men," in *Unequal Opportunity: Health Disparities Affecting Gay and Bisexual Men in the United States,* ed. Richard J. Wolitski, Ron Stall, and Ronald O. Valdiserri (Oxford: Oxford University Press, 2008), 220–247.

6. "As of December 31, 2010, a total of 19,341 deaths have occurred among San Francisco AIDS cases since the beginning of the epidemic," of whom 17,444 are estimated to be among men who had sex with men. See San Francisco Department of Public Health, *HIV/AIDS Epidemiology Annual Report,* 2010, p. 23, Table 5.1.

7. On Boston's South End, see Sylvie Tissot, *De bons voisins: Enquête dans un quartier de la bourgeoisie progressiste* (Paris: Raisons d'agir, 2011).

8. For an analysis, see Gary J. Gates, *Same-Sex Couples: U.S. Census and the American Community Survey* (Los Angeles: Williams Institute, n.d.), services.law.ucla.edu/williamsinstitute/pdf/CensusPresentation_LGBT.pdf (accessed August 30, 2011); Sabrina Tavernise, "New Numbers, and Geography, for Gay Couples," *New York Times,* August 25, 2011, A1.

9. For an early account of this process, describing how Dianne Feinstein and wealthy developers managed to break the stranglehold of gay power over City Hall in San Francisco after the assassination of Harvey Milk and Mayor George Moscone in 1978, see Frances Fitzgerald, "The Castro," in Fitzgerald, *Cities on the Hill* (New York: Simon and Schuster, 1986), 25–119.

10. As June Thomas also points out, it is not only the Internet that has undermined the traditional commercial gay infrastructure. A number of new face-to-face forms of gay socializing have also emerged. "When it comes to nightlife, gay revelers have more options than ever. Gay men have the circuit party scene—lavish multiday, multivenue annual events, such as the Palm Springs and Miami white parties—where the emphasis is on grand spectacle and production values that exceed anything that would be possible at a neighborhood bar. In some cities, groups use the Web to organize 'guerrilla gay bars,' a sort of flaming flash mob in which homosexuals descend unannounced on a straight bar and turn it gay for one night only. And in most cities, freelance promoters produce regular 'parties' at straight venues as an alternative to the 'gay every day' bar scene. The trend took off in the 1980s, when the community's desire for variety outpaced the supply of gay venues, and accelerated after 2000, when it became easier to publicize events via email." Thomas, "The Gay Bar: Its New Competition," June 30, 2011, www.slate.com/id/2297608 (accessed July 12, 2011).

11. Thomas, "Gay Bar: Is It Dying?"

12. June Thomas, "The Gay Bar: Can It Survive?" Slate.com, July 1, 2011, www.slate.com/id/2297609 (accessed July 12, 2011).

13. Thomas, "Gay Bar: Its New Competition."

14. Thomas, "Gay Bar: Is It Dying?"

15. There are, of course, many exceptions to this trend; see, for example, Amanda Sommers, "Not Playing House the Way Mom and Dad Do: Same-Sex Commitment without Marriage" (M.A. thesis, Smith School for Social Work, 2010).

16. Maureen Dowd, "A Gay Commander in Chief: Ready or Not?" *New York Times,* December 18, 2010, WK9.

17. Patrick Califia-Rice, "Family Values," *Village Voice,* 45.25 (June 27, 2000): 46–48 (quotation on p. 45). All further references to this article will be included in the text.

18. Bruce Bawer, *A Place at the Table: The Gay Individual in American Society* (New York: Poseidon Press, 1993).

19. Andrew Sullivan, *Virtually Normal: An Argument about Homosexuality* (New York: Knopf, 1995).

20. Associated Press, "NY Legalizes Gay Marriage 42 Years after Stonewall," June 25, 2011, www.bostonherald.com/news/national/northeast/view.bg?articleid=1347820&format=&page=2&listingType=natne#articleFull (accessed July 8, 2011).

21. Michael Warner, *The Trouble with Normal: Sex, Politics, and the Ethics of Queer Life* (New York: Free Press, 1999), 37–38.

22. Ibid., 39.

23. Ibid., 38.

24. For the original formulation of "heteronormativity," see Michael Warner, "Introduction: Fear of a Queer Planet," *Social Text* 29 (1991): 3–17.

25. Ibid., 8.

26. Ibid., 6. I have directly borrowed a number of Warner's formulations.

27. Ibid., 9. See, further, Damon Young's forthcoming essay, *"The Living End,* or Love without a Future."

28. Warner, "Introduction: Fear of a Queer Planet," 6.

29. Frank Bidart, "The Second Hour of the Night," in Bidart, *Desire* (New York: Farrar, Straus and Giroux, 1997), 27–59 (quotation on p. 53).

30. Warner, "Introduction: Fear of a Queer Planet," 6.

31. See, generally, Christopher Reed, *Art and Homosexuality: A History of Ideas* (New York: Oxford University Press, 2011).

32. Edmund White, "The Political Vocabulary of Homosexuality," in *The State of the Language,* ed. Leonard Michaels and Christopher Ricks (Berkeley: University of California Press, 1980), 235–246 (quotation on p. 246).

33. Susan Sontag, "On Style," *Against Interpretation, and Other Essays* (New York: Farrar, Straus and Giroux, 1966; first publ. 1965), 15–36 (quotation on p. 36).

34. Jean-Paul Sartre, *Saint Genet: Comédien et martyr* (Paris: Gallimard, 1952), 146: "Ils disposent simultanément de deux systèmes de références." I am taking Sartre's statement in a different and more general direction from the one he intended; for the context, see Chapter 10, where the entire quotation appears in note 13.

35. Many thanks to Edward Baron Turk for helping me to articulate this formulation.

ACKNOWLEDGMENTS

I have been thinking about the topic of this book for a dozen years, and I have been dining out on it extensively. Many people have contributed ideas and insights to it, and I have freely helped myself to their observations and suggestions. So I have a lot of acknowledging to do.

My earliest and many of my best interlocutors have been at the University of Michigan in Ann Arbor, which gave me a number of occasions, both formal and informal, to present my work. I am deeply, proudly, happily indebted to my friends and colleagues—and to the university as a whole.

Let me highlight in particular the early, formative influence of discussions I had with Ross Chambers, Valerie Traub, Suzanne Raitt, Brenda Marshall, Patsy Yaeger, Jill and Tobin Siebers, Nadine Hubbs, Aric Knuth, Zachary Sifuentes, Brent Armendinger, Jennifer Moon, Sherri Joyner, LaMont Egle, and Jack Tocco.

Other early, decisive influences on the conceptualization of this project were Michael Warner, Myra Jehlen, Gay Hawkins, and Jean Allouch. This book also reflects a number of inspiring discussions I have had over the years with Lee Monk, David Caron, Didier Eribon, Mark Simpson, Mandy Merck, Amalia Ziv, Daniel Boyarin, Lauren Berlant, Linda Williams, Whitney Davis, Candace Vogler, Jill Casid, Rostom Mesli, Isabelle Châtelet, Sasho Lambevski, Matthieu Dupas,

Kirk Ormand, David Alderson, Neil Bartlett, Dee Michel, Anne Curzan, Emma Crandall, Zachary Manning, Marie Ymonet, Stephen Orgel, Randy Mackie, Kane Race, Susana Bercovich, Michael Forrey, Damon Young, Marc Siegel, and Martha Nussbaum.

Myra Jehlen was a constant companion and spiritual guide throughout the entire, extended process of conceptualizing and composing the manuscript; she read and discussed in detail with me many drafts and many versions from its very inception. The result bears the imprint of her ideas. I cannot begin to thank her enough.

A great number of other friends and colleagues read versions of the manuscript, in whole or in part (some of them more than once) and gave me invaluable advice, help, courage, cautions, strenuous, rigorous criticism, and indispensable insight. I am grateful and indebted to them in equal measure. For their heroic efforts, I offer eternal thanks to Alison MacKeen, Damon Young, Valerie Traub, Paul Morrison, Pier Dominguez, Michael Warner, and Marie Ymonet. I have also been considerably helped and inspired by the readings and critiques of Peter Gosik, D. Nathaniel Smith, Matthew Chess, Logan Scherer, Gregg Crane, Mark Simpson, Marc Siegel, Esther Newton, Nadine Hubbs, Martha Nussbaum, Gayle Rubin, Aaron Boalick, June Howard, and Jill Casid.

☯

It is conventional in the acknowledgments section of academic books for professors to thank their students for stimulating their thinking, or some such thing. My situation is rather different. This book emerges directly from a series of five workshops that took the form of college classes and that provided me with an opportunity to test out the ideas in this book as they evolved over an extended period of time. I have worked out my thinking in close, intense, and often contentious collaboration with dozens of students. Some of those students will, I hope, have recognized the words, thoughts, or ideas of theirs that I have not hesitated to appropriate for my own purposes: I can bring to mind specific instances in which this book has quoted, exploited, and incorporated the remarks, arguments, suggestions, stories, and reactions of Chris Chubb, Brandon Clements, Claude Coltea, Aric Knuth, Rohin Guha, KT Lowe, Joseph Keckler, D. Nathaniel Smith, Libby Kanouse, Sarah Ray, and Nick Falzone. Let me thank as well, for their challenges, suggestions, and criticisms, Sabrina Spiher, Nava EtShalom, Martin Halprin, Mike Radakovich, Jesse Kropf, Patrick Franklin, Gina Chopp, Erin Markey, Sarah Szymanski, Emily Bate, Suraj Patel, Molly Bain Frounfelter, Katie Nitka, Alice Mishkin, Chris Tobin, Caitlin Cullen, Paul Farber, Naomi Gordon-Loebl, Adam Lewis, Caspar van Helden, Chris Glinski, Matthew Rindfleisch, John Trummer, Brian Hull, Jeff Souva, Esther Lindstrom, Celeste Brecht, and Preston Gaspar. I apologize to any others whose names do not figure in that list but who may have discerned their influence on the preceding pages.

A number of my students have read all or part of the manuscript of this book in a number of different versions, or have heard portions of it in lecture form, and have discussed it with me in detail: I am enormously grateful to Alex Bacon, Andy Kravis, Jesse Kropf, Peter Gosik, Suraj Patel, Jack Tocco, and D. Nathaniel Smith for their criticisms, suggestions, encouragement, and invaluable help.

☙❧

My thinking has been tried out on, and much altered by, the audiences who responded to lectures I gave on various topics related to this book, in such different venues as the Ecole Lacanienne de Psychanalyse in Paris; the Ecole Lacanienne de Psychanalyse in Strasbourg; the Centre National d'Art et de Culture Georges Pompidou in Paris; the Maison de l'Homosocialité in Bordeaux; the conference "Homosexuality 2000" in Oslo; the annual convention of the National Council of Teachers of English, which met that year in Milwaukee; the annual convention of the American Anthropological Association, which met that year in New Orleans; the annual conference on Gender Studies of the Programa Universitario de Estudios de Género at the Universidad Nacional Autónoma de México; the 2nd Annual

Global iPrEx ("Iniciativa Pre-exposición") Investigators Meeting in San Francisco; the Ecole des Hautes Etudes en Sciences Sociales in Paris; Pioneer High School in Ann Arbor, courtesy of the Ann Arbor / Ypsilanti Gay Lesbian Straight Education Network; the London Legal and Social Theory Seminar at the London School of Economics; the conference on "les corps sans organes" at the Musée du Louvre in Paris; the conference on "Queer Zagreb" in Zagreb; the conference on "Living Remains" at the Center for 21st-Century Studies at the University of Wisconsin–Milwaukee; the conference on "Manhood in American Law and Literature" at the University of Chicago; Oberlin College (my alma mater); Queen Mary College, University of London; University College, University of Toronto; Sussex University; Tel Aviv University; the University of Vienna; Cornell University; the University of Iowa; the University of California in Los Angeles; the University of California in Berkeley; the University of California in Irvine; the University of Texas in San Antonio; Boğaziçi University in Istanbul; Arizona State University; New York University; Northwestern University; the University of Pennsylvania; Yale University; Central Michigan University; the University of Chicago; the University of Victoria in British Columbia; the University of Washington in Seattle; Tufts University; the University of Maine at Farmington; the University of North Carolina in Chapel Hill; the Columbia University Law School; and the University of Manchester in the United Kingdom (twice!). I wish to thank the many friends and colleagues who made it possible for me to present my work to audiences in those locations.

I must single out for special thanks three audiences for their substantive help with particular problems of interpretation that I could not solve on my own. These were the audiences at the National Centre in HIV Social Research at the University of New South Wales in Sydney; at a conference entitled "'Il n'y a pas de rapport sexuel': Centenaire Jacques Lacan," at La Villette in Paris; and at the Centro Cultural Rector Ricardo Rojas at the Universidad de Buenos Aires, all of whom contributed significantly to the formulation of some of the basic hypotheses on which I later built the speculations presented here.

ᘒᘓ

In order to help me complete this book, the Institute for the Humanities at the University of Michigan awarded me a John Rich Professorship and Michigan Faculty Fellowship. The John Simon Guggenheim Memorial Foundation also gave me a fellowship. The College of Literature, Science, and the Arts at the University of Michigan gave me two leaves from teaching (including a Michigan Humanities Award) as well as a sabbatical, plus salary support to supplement the Guggenheim Fellowship, so as to enable me to spend an entire year completing the manuscript. I am deeply grateful for all this financial assistance, and particularly to the late John Rich. I wish to express heartfelt thanks to the Institute for the Humanities, to the Guggenheim Foundation, to the Department of English Language and Literature, and to the College of LSA at the University of Michigan. I feel extraordinarily fortunate to have had colleagues and patrons who believed from the beginning in this wacky project of mine and who generously supported it. Every academic should be so lucky.

ᘒᘓ

I would like to thank the editors of *Michigan Feminist Studies, Michigan Quarterly Review, Photofile* (Sydney), and *L'Unebévue* (Paris) for giving me the chance to explore my ideas in earlier articles. In addition, John J. Cleary, George E. Haggerty, Molly McGarry, Katherine O'Donnell, Michael O'Rourke, and Daniel C. Shartin were kind enough to include some of my previous writings on related topics in various collected volumes. Valerie Traub and I collaborated on an essay which anticipated some of the thinking presented here, while Leo Bersani and Michael Lucey participated in a co-authored volume in which I speculated about the gay appeal of Joan Crawford. And Mathieu

Trachman provided a forum for my thoughts in an online interview about the evolution of gay culture.

I have occasionally needed to quote some postings from bulletin boards on the Web in order to support my arguments. I made every effort to contact the authors of such material, but I did not succeed, and in many cases the individuals who wrote the texts I have cited were not identifiable—either because their real names and addresses were withheld or because their postings were anonymous. I would have liked to thank them. So let me express my gratitude here to everyone whose material I have used and who contributed significantly, in this way, to the argument of my book.

❧

Matt Johnson, Chad Thomas, Mira Bellwether, Matthew Chess, and Logan Scherer helped me in various ways, as well as giving me prompt and crucial assistance in locating hard-to-access materials, and Jim Leija saved me from a couple of embarrassing errors.

Maria Ascher copy-edited the manuscript with sympathy, insight, kindness, flexibility, acuity, skill, and tact. Shanshan Wang shepherded it through publication. Lisa Roberts deserves credit for the typeface and the brilliant design, both inside and out. Kathryn Blatt proofread the first print version and gave me the benefit of eyes sharper than mine. Andrew Rubenfeld also scrutinized the page proofs, and I am greatly indebted to him for the comprehensive index. Lindsay Waters encouraged me, welcomed the book proposal, and entered into the spirit of the project. I am grateful to all of them, and to everyone at Harvard University Press, for an easy, enjoyable, and efficient collaboration.

❧

The epigraph to the book comes from Albert T. Mollegen, *Christianity and Modern Man: The Crisis of Secularism* (Indianapolis, IN: Bobbs-Merrill, 1961), 30. The quotation purports to be a paraphrase of Saint Augustine, though nothing in the writings of Augustine exactly corresponds to it. I am grateful to the late Bill Clebsch for citing the phrase to me and to Mark Jordan for identifying its source.

ⓧ

Finally, I want to express my deep appreciation to Wouter Vandenbrink. As soon as I saw his brilliant photographic series "gayboy walking (after Eadweard Muybridge)," in an open-air installation in Amsterdam, I knew I wanted it for the cover of my book. Wouter generously, graciously, and immediately gave me his permission to reproduce it. (I should point out that the series is linear in the original—one long set of horizontal panels.) I am also grateful to Wouter's model, Roy Seerden, for agreeing to allow me to use his image to illustrate the argument at the core of this book—namely, that social forms are things in themselves.

What I particularly love about this photographic series is its camp essentialism—its invocation of time-lapse photography to fix the motion of a gay male body in its social and formal particularity, defying the spectator's anxieties (or certainties) about stereotypes. I also love its daring, ironic, if somewhat more distant citation of the ghastly genre of Victorian medical photography, which documented the physical symptoms of masturbators, hysterics, and other perverted personalities, so that psychiatric experts could diagnose their conditions by recognizing, inscribed on their very bodies, the signs of pathology. Here the artist—and, by the way, I have no idea if Wouter Vandenbrink would agree with this interpretation—has taken up that visual technology, with its characteristic blend of clinical objectivity and pornographic curiosity, both to extend it and to defy its pathologizing effects, to celebrate the loving irony with which gay men recognize gayness in one another and scrutinize the appearance of every man they know to be gay for corroborating signs of gayness. The result is to offer us a lyrical and tender vision of a gay male body and of some of the markers that might enable viewers to identify it as gay, without reducing it to that marking or implying that the gestures in which we might read the subject's gayness necessarily define either it or him. All this is condensed in the artist's witty homage to Eadweard Muybridge and to the origins of time-lapse photography itself.

My last reason for choosing this image was to see if reviewers of this book would be able to get beyond it, to do anything more than read the body of the boy on its cover for its most obvious features— its nudity; its gender style; its Whiteness, youthfulness, slenderness, and relative hairlessness—and then go on to make the standard complaints about its lack of representativity, its privileges, defects, and exclusions, its irresponsible projection of a falsely universal gayness. As if any single body could possibly represent all gay men, any more than any one book could describe all of gay male culture; as if such a complaint were the only thing or the chief thing to say about such an image; as if the entire critical enterprise necessarily ended with such observations, instead of beginning from them. As always, I want most of all to discover what gay male studies, what queer theory, what queer cultural studies, what sexuality studies, what gender studies, and what queer social critique have to tell us now.

INDEX

THIRD EDITION

Classroom Assessment

Principles and Practice
for Effective Instruction

James H. McMillan

Virginia Commonwealth University

PEARSON

Boston ■ New York ■ San Francisco
Mexico City ■ Montreal ■ Toronto ■ London ■ Madrid ■ Munich ■ Paris
Hong Kong ■ Singapore ■ Tokyo ■ Cape Town ■ Sydney

Senior Editor: *Arnis E. Burvikovs*
Editorial Assistant: *Christine Lyons*
Marketing Manager: *Tara Whorf*
Composition and Prepress Buyer: *Linda Cox*
Manufacturing Buyer: *Andrew Turso*
Cover Administrator: *Kristina Mose-Libon*
Editorial-Production Service: *Matrix Productions Inc.*
Electronic Composition: *Omegatype Typography, Inc.*

For related titles and support materials, visit our online catalog at www.ablongman.com.

Between the time Website information is gathered and then published, it is not unusual for some sites to have closed. Also, the transcription of URLs can result in unintended typographical errors. The publishers would appreciate notification where these errors occur so that they may be corrected in subsequent editions.

Library of Congress Cataloging-in-Publication Data

McMillan, James H.
   Classroom assessment : principles and practice for effective instruction / James H. McMillan. — 3rd ed.
      p.   cm.
   Includes bibliographical references and index.
   ISBN 0-205-38090-5
   1. Educational tests and measurements.   2. Examinations.   3. Examinations—Validity.
4. Examinations—Interpretation.   I. Title.

LB3051.M462499   2004
371.26—dc21   2003051828

Printed in the United States of America

10   9   8   7   6   5   4   3   2   1   08   07   06   05   04   03

CONTENTS

7   **Selected-Response, Short-Answer, and Essay Items: Assessing
Deep Understanding and Reasoning   168**

PREFACE

It wasn't too many years ago that I took my first tests and measurements course. I remember it well because I was fairly apprehensive—what would this have to do with teaching? Would I have to use complex mathematics and learn about the technical aspects of testing that really had little to do with what I wanted to do day in and day out in the classroom? Well, the course met my negative expectations! It was interesting, but not really very helpful when applied to teaching.

If you are getting ready to take a testing, pupil evaluation, or assessment course or part of a course, or if you are about to participate in a classroom assessment in-service program, you may have some similar thoughts, and I can empathize. But the instruction that this book offers is quite different from my initial experience and, I believe, will meet your needs as a teacher. Over the past few years, the assessment field has changed so that much more emphasis is placed on how *student evaluation is an integral part of teaching*, not something that's done after instruction to measure only what students have learned.

This book, then, is designed to provide *prospective and practicing teachers* with (1) a *concise presentation* of assessment principles that clearly and specifically relate to instruction, (2) *current research and new directions* in the assessment field, and (3) *practical and realistic* examples, suggestions, and case studies. Furthermore, the style of writing is *nontechnical, easy to understand, and interesting*.

The approach I have taken to meet these criteria is to build assessment into the instructional process, focusing on assessment concepts and principles that are essential for effective *teacher decision making*. The emphasis throughout is on helping teachers to understand the importance of *establishing credible performance standards* (learning targets), *communicating these standards* to students, and *providing feedback* to students on their progress. There is much less emphasis on technical measurement concepts that teachers rarely find useful, though there is extensive discussion of aspects of assessment that result in *high quality and credibility*, such as fairness, matching assessment to clearly and publicly stated learning targets, positive consequences, and practicality.

The book is organized by what teachers do before, during, and after an instructional segment, rather than by type of assessment technique. Thus, the chapter sequence reflects the steps teachers take in using assessment as part of instruction. Chapters 1 through 3 present the fundamental principles of assessment and instruction, with an emphasis on the importance of the teacher's *professional judgment and decision making* as integral to making useful and credible assessments. Chapter 4 summarizes assessment activities that occur before instruction begins, and Chapter 5 examines assessment that occurs during instruction. Chapters 6 through 10 discuss various types of assessments for different types of learning outcomes that are measured at the end of an instructional segment. Chapter 11 reviews the assessment of students who have disabilities and are included in the regular classroom. Chapter 12 examines what teachers do with assessment information in the form of grading and reporting the results. Finally, Chapter 13 summarizes important information concerning the administration, interpretation, and use of standardized tests.

Several instructional aids have been included to facilitate understanding and applying the material. These include *cognitive maps* at the beginning of each chapter to provide graphic overviews; *boldface key terms*; *quotes from teachers* throughout to illustrate practical applications; *chapter summaries* to review essential ideas; *self-instructional review exercises*, with answers, to provide opportunities for practice and application; *suggestions for conducting action research*; extensive use of *examples, diagrams, charts, and tables; case studies for reflection*; and a *glossary* of key terms. Several additional enhancements have been made to improve the third edition:

- More emphasis is placed on assessment *for* learning and the importance of newer theories of learning and motivation.
- The newly released *Student Evaluation Standards* have been incorporated.
- The newly released revision to Bloom's *Taxonomy of Educational Objectives* has been incorporated.
- More emphasis is placed on standards-based education and implications for assessment.
- The treatment of reliability and factors affecting reliability has been expanded.
- More emphasis is placed on student self-assessment and student-led conferences for grading.
- New material on curriculum/teaching and assessment alignment has been added.
- New examples are used throughout the text.
- Presentation of many assessment principles and procedures is more concise.
- The book's Companion Website (www.ablongman.com/mcmillan_assessment3e) has been revised, with enhanced capabilities to use the World Wide Web.

Acknowledgments

Throughout the development and writing of this book, I have been fortunate to have the support and assistance of a group of classroom teachers who have provided quotations, practical examples, and suggestions. I am very grateful for their willingness to help, for their patience in working with me, and, most of all, for keeping me grounded in the realities of teaching. They include Steve Eliasek, Daphne Patterson, Craig Nunemaker, Judy Bowman, Jeremy Lloyd, Marc Bacon, Mary Carlson, Michelle Barrow, Margie Tully, Rixey Wilcher, Judith Jindrich, and Dan Geary. I am grateful that Steve Myran and Suzanne Nash were able to contribute to the case studies from their experience in the classroom. I am very thankful that Susan McKelvey has assisted me in several ways for this third edition—editing, doing research, and monitoring permissions.

I would also like to express my appreciation to the following college and university professors who offered insightful and helpful comments and suggestions: For the first edition, Cheri Magill, Virginia Commonwealth University; H. D. Hoover, University of Iowa; Kathryn A. Alvestad, Calvert County Public Schools; John R. Bing, Salisbury State University; John Criswell, Edinboro University of Pennsylvania; George A. Johanson, Ohio University; Catherine McCartney, Bemidji State University; and Anthony Truog, University of Wisconsin, Whitewater; for the second edition, Lyle C. Jensen, Baldwin-Wallace College; Cathleen D. Rafferty, Indiana State University; Gerald Dillashaw, Elon College; Daniel L. Kain, North Arizona University; Charles Eiszler, Central Michigan University; Betty Jo Simmons, Longwood College; and for the third edition, Gyu-Pan Cho, University of Alabama; Saramma T. Mathew, Troy State University; E. Michael Nussbaum, University of Nevada; and Kit Juniewicz, University of New England.

Finally, I am very grateful for the encouragement and direction of my editor, Arnis Burvikovs, as well as the support of others at Allyn and Bacon.

1 The Role of Assessment in Teaching

This book is about how classroom assessments can be used by teachers to improve student learning. Over the past twenty years or so, research on teacher decision making, cognitive learning, student motivation, and other topics has changed what we know about the importance of assessment for effective teaching. For example, one finding is that good teachers continually assess their students relative to learning goals and adjust their instruction on the basis of this information. Another important finding is that assessment of students not only documents what students know and can do but also influences learning. Assessment that enhances learning is as important as assessment that documents learning. As a result of this

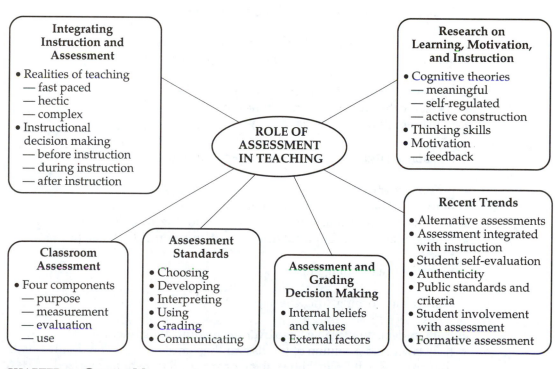

Integrating Instruction and Assessment

- Realities of teaching
  — fast paced
  — hectic
  — complex
- Instructional decision making
  — before instruction
  — during instruction
  — after instruction

Research on Learning, Motivation, and Instruction

- Cognitive theories
  — meaningful
  — self-regulated
  — active construction
- Thinking skills
- Motivation
  — feedback

ROLE OF ASSESSMENT IN TEACHING

Classroom Assessment

- Four components
  — purpose
  — measurement
  — evaluation
  — use

Assessment Standards

- Choosing
- Developing
- Interpreting
- Using
- Grading
- Communicating

Assessment and Grading Decision Making

- Internal beliefs and values
- External factors

Recent Trends

- Alternative assessments
- Assessment integrated with instruction
- Student self-evaluation
- Authenticity
- Public standards and criteria
- Student involvement with assessment
- Formative assessment

CHAPTER 1   Concept Map

1

research, new purposes, methods, and approaches to student assessment are being developed. These changes underscore a new understanding of the important role that assessment plays in instruction and learning. This chapter summarizes the research on teacher decision making to show how assessment is integrated with instruction and how teachers make decisions about their assessment and grading practices. The major components of assessment are reviewed, with an emphasis on current conceptualizations that are consistent with recent research related to learning and motivation. Finally, assessment competencies for teachers are summarized to lay the foundation for what is covered in subsequent chapters.

Integrating Instruction and Assessment

The Realities of Teaching

Classroom life is fast paced, hectic, and complex. To illustrate this reality, I have summarized some of what Michelle Barrow does during a typical day in her first-grade classroom. She has ten boys and eleven girls in her class, four of whom are from racial minority groups and six of whom are from single-parent families. As many as four of her students will participate in the gifted/talented program, and four students were retained. See how easy it is for you to get through this list of disparate tasks.

Before school begins in the morning, Michelle:

- reviews what was learned/taught the previous day
- goes over student papers to see who did or did not grasp concepts
- prepares a rough agenda for the day
- has instructional materials ready
- speaks with aide about plans for the day
- puts journals on student desks

As soon as students enter the classroom, Michelle:

- greets students at the door
- reminds students to put away homework
- speaks with Brent about his expected behavior for the day
- reminds Anthony about what he is to do if he becomes bothered or frustrated by others
- gives Colin a morning hug

During the morning, Michelle:

- calls students to the table to go over the reading assignment
- has Dawn read a column of words and then goes back and randomly points to words to see if Dawn knows them or simply has them memorized
- comments to Lucy that she has really improved since the first day of school

- discusses with Kevin the importance of doing homework every night
- listens as Tim attempts to sound out each word and gradually blends them together
- reminds Maggie that she is to be working in her journal rather than visiting and talking with others
- gives Jason, Kory, and Kristen a vocabulary sheet to do since they have completed their journals
- reviews with all students work to be done in centers, how many students should be in each center, and how to complete the contract
- observes students in learning centers before calling reading groups to tables
- helps Catherine decide which center to go to
- warns Alex and Colin to get to centers rather than playing around
- calls up middle reading level group, asks what an action word is, and has each student give an example of an action word
- verbally reinforces correct answers, gives each student a copy of the week's story, goes through the book and points out action words
- notices that Jenna is not giving answers or pointing out action words but is instead looking at other students
- calls up the low reading group and focuses on letters *m* and *f*
- asks students to write an *m* on their chalkboards
- notices that Kevin has poor fine-motor skills and makes a mental note to send a message to his parents telling them that he should practice his handwriting
- checks on Anthony to see how many centers he has completed
- reminds students about rewinding the tape player and filmstrip
- notices that students in the writing center are not doing as they were instructed
- gives students a five-minute warning to get ready to go to physical education
- walks beside Anthony down the hall, verbally praising him for following directions
- taps Brent on his shoulder, looks at Maggie
- calls up high reading group, reviews action words
- does gifted/talented curriculum with high group
- notices that Sarah has some difficulty answering higher-level thinking questions
- makes a mental note to split gifted group up into two smaller groups

After lunch, Michelle's day continues as she:

- begins math lesson on beginning addition with hippo counter
- walks behind Scott and gives the next problem to the class
- walks to orange table and observes students as they solve a problem
- punches cards of students who have followed directions
- notices that another table immediately stops talking and starts paying attention
- collects hippo counters and has students line up for recess
- sends Jackie to the nurse for a sore throat
- once outside, reminds students of boundaries
- plays "red light green light" with a group of students
- calls Colin and Maggie to sit out for five minutes

- notices Kristen is playing by herself, not with Andrea
- back in classroom, calls students by tables to get a drink and wash hands
- tells students to rewrite sloppy copies
- reminds Kevin and Brent to use guide lines on the paper
- praises and gives punches on cards to Sarah and a few other students for good handwriting and concentration
- assists Dawn with what she is to do
- reaffirms Catherine's question that she is doing the right thing
- notices that Tim is watching others, asks him if he needs help
- gives five-minute warning for music time, notices students working more intensely
- has students line up for music once papers have been collected
- while students are in music, looks over their writing, arranges the papers into groups
- checks in nurse's office for any mail or messages

After students leave for the day, Michelle continues to teach by:

- grading student papers
- making sure materials are ready for the next day
- making notes in her gradebook about notes sent home and how the day went
- checking portfolios to see progress
- calling some parents

Was it difficult to get through the list? If so, you have some empathy for the hectic nature of classrooms and the need to make many decisions quickly about students and instructional activities. What is represented here is just a small sample of Michelle's actions, all of which are based on decisions that in turn depend on how well she has assessed her students. How did she decide to discuss with Kevin the importance of homework? What made her decide to warn Alex and Colin? What evidence did she use to decide that Jenna was not paying attention to the lesson? In each of these cases, Michelle had to conduct some kind of assessment of the student before making her decisions. The role of an effective teacher is to reach these decisions reflectively, based on evidence gathered through assessment, reasoning, and experience.

Each decision is based on information that Michelle has gathered through a multitude of student interactions and behavior. Research indicates that a teacher may have as many as 1,000 or even 1,500 interactions with students *each day* (Billups & Rauth, 1987; Jackson, 1990). Often these interactions and decisions occur with incomplete or inaccurate information, making the job of teaching even more difficult.

Consider how the following aspects of Michelle's and other teachers' classrooms affect decision making (Doyle, 1986).

1. Multidimensionality: Teachers' choices are rarely simple. Many different tasks and events occur continuously, and students with different preferences and abilities must receive limited resources for different objectives. Waiting for

one student to answer a question may negatively influence the motivation of another student. How can the teacher best assess these multiple demands and student responses to make appropriate decisions?

2. Simultaneity: Many things happen at once in classrooms. Good teachers monitor several activities at the same time. What does the teacher look for and listen for so that the monitoring and responses to students are appropriate?

3. Immediacy: Because the pace of classrooms is rapid, there is little time for reflection. Decisions are made quickly. What should teachers focus on so that these quick decisions are the right ones that will help students learn?

4. Unpredictability: Classroom events often take unanticipated turns, and distractions are frequent. How do teachers evaluate and respond to these unexpected events?

5. History: After a few weeks, routines and norms are established for behavior. What expectations for assessment does the teacher communicate to students?

It is in these complex environments that teachers must make some of their most important decisions—about what and how much students have learned. Action is based on these decisions. Accurate and appropriate student assessment provides the information to help teachers make better decisions. In the classroom context, then, **assessment** is the gathering, interpretation, and use of information to aid teacher decision making. Assessment is an umbrella concept that encompasses different techniques, strategies, and uses.

Instructional Decision Making and Assessment

It is helpful to conceptualize teacher decision making by *when* decisions are made—before, during, or after instruction—and then examine how assessment affects choices at each time. Preinstructional decisions are needed to set learning goals, select appropriate teaching activities, and prepare learning materials. As instructional activities are implemented, decisions are made about the delivery and pace in presenting information, keeping the students' attention, controlling students' behavior, and making adjustments in lesson plans. At the end of instruction, teachers evaluate student learning, instructional activities, and themselves to know what to teach next, to grade students, and to improve instruction. Figure 1.1 presents examples of the types of questions teachers ask at these different points in the instructional process. The figure also offers examples of the type of assessment information needed to make these decisions.

Figure 1.2 illustrates further how assessment is involved in each stage of the instructional process. This figure shows how preinstructional assessment is used to provide information to transform general learning goals and objectives into specific learning targets. You will usually be provided with general state, district, or school learning goals for a particular grade level or subject. These goals are used as a starting point to develop more specific learning targets that take into account the characteristics and needs of the students and your style and beliefs. Preinstructional assessment is an absolutely essential step for effective instruction. If you can't identify what specific knowledge, skills, attitudes, and other learning targets are

FIGURE 1.1   Examples of Questions for Decision Making and Assessment Information

When Decisions Are Made	Questions	Assessment Information
Before Instruction	How much do my students know?	Previous student achievement; test scores; observations of student performance
	Are my students motivated to learn?	Observations of student involvement and willingness to ask questions
	Are there any exceptional students? If so, what should I plan for them?	Student records; conference with a special education teacher
	What instructional activities should I plan? Are these activities realistic for these students?	Overall strengths and needs of students; comments from previous teachers; evaluations of previous teaching
	What homework assignments should I prepare?	Student progress and level of understanding
	What is acceptable evidence that students have attained desired proficiences?	Determine which assessment methods will provide needed evidence
During Instruction	What type of feedback should I give to students?	Quality of student work; type of student
	What question should I ask?	Observation of student understanding
	How should a student response to a question be answered?	Potential for this student to know the answer
	Which students need my individual attention?	Performance on homework; observations of work in class
	What response is best to student inattention or disruption?	Effect of the student on others
	When should I stop this lecture?	Observation of student attention
After Instruction	How well have my students mastered the material?	Achievement test results in relation to a specified level
	Are students ready for the next unit?	Analysis of demonstrated knowledge
	What grades should the students receive?	Tests; quizzes; homework; class participation
	What comments should I make to parents?	Improvement; observations of behavior
	How should I change my instruction?	Diagnosis of demonstrated learning; student evaluations

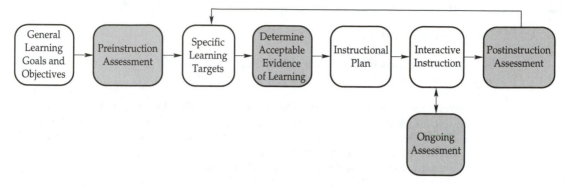

FIGURE 1.2   Relationship between Instruction and Assessment

important, it is unlikely that students, parents, or the teacher will know when they have been successful. In other words, you must determine what it is that students should know, understand, and be able to do at the end of an instructional unit.

The next step in instructional decision making is to specify the evidence that is needed to document student learning. This evidence is identified up front, *before* determining instructional plans, because it should influence the nature of instruction. This approach to planning is known as "backward design" (Wiggins, 1998; Wiggins & McTighe, 1998). It is called "backward" because conventional instructional planning typically considers assessment an activity that is done after instruction. But it is very helpful to think like an assessor before planning learning activities. This helps accomplish a true integration of assessment and instruction.

Once acceptable evidence is identified, the teacher selects instructional strategies and activities to meet the targets. This is often operationalized as a lesson plan or instructional plan. It consists of what teachers will do and what they will have their students do for a specific period of time. During instruction, there is interaction between the teacher and students that constantly involves making assessments about how to respond to students appropriately and keep them on task. During this time, assessment information is used to monitor learning, check for progress, and diagnose learning problems.

After instruction, more formal assessment of learning targets is conducted, which loops back to inform subsequent learning targets, instructional plans, and interactive instruction. Assessment at the end of an instructional unit also provides information for grading students, evaluating teaching, and evaluating curriculum and school programs.

Classroom assessments define what is really important in schooling. Regardless of publicly stated objectives, outcomes, or standards, the nature of classroom assessments defines what is valued and what students are learning. In other words, classroom assessment, which is clearly a major function of teaching, is essential in defining the nature of what students learn in school. Clearly, what is assessed and how it is assessed, in the classroom, deliver strong messages about what is valued.

Case Study for Reflection

In a recent study, teachers were asked whether assessment drives instruction or instruction drives assessment. Here is what a few of them said:

"I would say my plan determines my assessments. What I teach is what I assess."
"I guess a little bit of both but I guess assessment comes from your lesson plans. You can't have the test made up if you have some unforeseen circumstance you don't get to teach something during the week. It wouldn't be fair to have that on the test."
"In the remedial class, assessment somewhat dictated lesson plans."
"Assessments absolutely drive lesson plans. I'll introduce it, assess what students know, and how fast they pick it up and then adjust my plans or write my plans accordingly."
"What we teach determines the assessment."
"It's both, really. For instance, the writing rubric sometimes comes first because I know a certain skill that I want to teach them. So I'll design whatever final product I want them to come up with. Then I'll do my lesson plan to lead up to that."

The point is that assessment is not only an *add-on* activity that occurs after instruction is completed. Rather, assessment is integrally related to all aspects of teacher decision making and instruction. Michelle Barrow did assessment *before* instruction by reviewing the performance of students on the previous day's work to see who did and who did not grasp the concepts. She used this information to plan subsequent instruction. *During* instruction Michelle constantly observed student work and responded to provide appropriate feedback and to keep students on task. *After* instruction she graded papers, checked student progress, and made decisions about the focus of instruction for the next day.

In the first of the case studies that will appear in each of the chapters, teacher comments are made about whether assessment drives instruction or instruction drives assessment (McMillan & Workman, 1999). From what the teachers said, is it apparent that assessment should drive instruction? How would you respond to this question?

With this introduction, we will now consider more specifically what is meant by such terms as *test* and *assessment* and how current conceptualizations enhance older definitions of *measurement* and *evaluation* to improve teaching and learning.

What Is Classroom Assessment?

Classroom assessment can be defined as the collection, evaluation, and use of information to help teachers make better decisions. Conceptualized in this way, assessment is more than *testing* or *measurement,* which are familiar terms that have been used extensively in discussing how students are evaluated.

The four essential components to implementing classroom assessment are purpose, measurement, evaluation, and use. These components are illustrated in

Figure 1.3, with questions to ask yourself at each step. The figure shows the sequence of the components, beginning with identification of purpose.

Purpose

Whether done before, during, or after instruction, the first step in any assessment is to clarify the specific purpose or purposes of gathering the information. A clear vision is needed of what the assessment will accomplish. That is, why are you doing the assessment? What will be gained by it? What teacher decision making is enhanced by the information gathered through the assessment process? Perhaps most important, how will student learning be enhanced by the assessment? We have traditionally thought about assessment as a way to measure what students have learned and to grade them. But other reasons for doing assessment need to be considered. For example, will your assessment be designed deliberately to improve student performance and not simply to provide an audit of it? Is the nature of the assessment such that it will provide user-friendly feedback to students? Do the results of the assessment make it possible to track student progress in learning, not just current status? Has the assessment motivated students to learn? Do the assessments accurately communicate your expectations to students and what is most valued? Do the assessments provide a realistic estimation of what students are able to do outside the classroom? Is the purpose to assess breadth or depth of student learning? You will need to consider these questions to fully integrate assessment with instruction.

Measurement

The term *measurement* has traditionally been defined as a systematic process of assigning numbers to performance. It is used to determine how much of a trait, attribute, or characteristic an individual possesses. Thus, **measurement** is the process by which traits, characteristics, or behavior are *differentiated*. The process of differentiation can be very formal and quantitative, such as using a thermometer to measure temperature, or can consist of less formal processes, such as observation ("It's very hot today!"). Typically, measurement is used to assign numbers to describe attributes or characteristics of a person, object, or event. A variety of techniques can be used to measure a defined trait or learning target, such as tests, ratings, observations, and interviews.

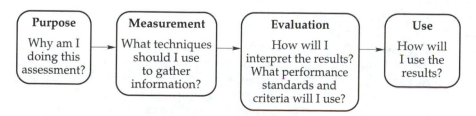

FIGURE 1.3   Components of Classroom Assessment

Evaluation

Once measurement is used to gather information you will need to place some degree of value on different numbers and observations. This process is identified in Figure 1.3 as *evaluation,* the making of judgments about quality—how good the behavior or performance is. **Evaluation** involves an *interpretation* of what has been gathered through measurement, in which value judgments are made about performance. For example, measurement often results in a percentage of items answered correctly. Evaluation is a judgment about what each percentage correct score means. That is, is 75 percent correct good, average, or poor? Does 75 percent indicate "mastery" or "proficiency"?

Teachers' professional judgments play a large role in evaluation. What is a "good" student paper to one teacher may be only an "adequate" paper to another teacher. Thus, assessment is more than *correctness;* it is also about value.

An important determinant of how you evaluate a performance is the nature of the performance standards you employ. **Performance standards** are used to determine whether a performance is "good" or "bad." Increasingly, such standards refer to high, specific, and valued measurable results that indicate a specific level of performance.

Criteria also play an important part in the evaluation process. **Criteria** are the specific behaviors or dimensions that are evidenced to successfully attain the standard. These criteria may be the most important influences on evaluation. They may be called *scoring criteria, scoring guidelines,* or *rubrics.* For example, take as a standard that students know all state capitals in the United States. The criteria are what the teacher uses to conclude that the student does, indeed, know the capitals. For one teacher this may mean giving the students a map and having them write in the capital for each state; for another teacher it may mean answering twenty multiple-choice questions correctly. Often teachers use criteria for scoring tests and papers without a clear standard. In fact, if only informally, teachers must have some type of criteria in mind to make assessment evaluations.

Both standards and criteria communicate to students the teacher's expectations of them. The nature of questions and feedback, the difficulty of assignments, and the rigor of the criteria tell students what the teacher believes they are capable of achieving. These expectations are important in motivating students and in setting an academic achievement climate in the classroom.

As you can see, setting standards and criteria is a critical component of assessment, one that we will consider in much greater detail in Chapter 2.

Use

The final stage of implementing assessment is how the evaluations are used. The use of test scores and other information is closely tied to the decisions teachers must make to provide effective instruction, to the purposes of assessment, and to the needs of students and parents. As indicated in Figure 1.2, these decisions depend on *when* they are made; they can also be categorized into three major uses: diagnosis, grading, and instruction.

Diagnosis.   Diagnostic decisions are made about individual students as well as group strengths, weaknesses, and needs. Typically, information is gathered that will allow the teacher to diagnose the specific area that needs further attention or where progress is being made. The diagnosis includes an assessment of *why* a student may be having difficulty so that appropriate instructional activities can be prescribed. For example, teachers use homework diagnostically to determine the extent of student understanding and to identify students who do not understand the assignment. A pretest may be used to diagnose specific gaps in student knowledge that need to be targeted. Students are closely monitored to check motivation, understanding, and progress. Standardized test scores may be used before instruction diagnostically to plan instructional activities. Such *sizing-up* assessments are done in the beginning of the year to obtain an idea of the abilities and interests of the students.

Grading.   Grading decisions are clearly based on measurement-driven information. While most teachers must adhere to grading scales and definitions, there is a great amount of variability in what teachers use to determine grades, how they use the process of grading to motivate students, and the standards they use to judge the quality of student work. Some teachers, for example, use grading to *control* and *motivate* (e.g., "This assignment will be graded"), and often teachers use completed work as a basis for giving privileges and otherwise rewarding students (e.g., "good" papers are posted). Grades and associated written comments also provide *feedback* to students and parents.

Instruction.   Teachers constantly make instructional decisions, and good teachers are aware that they must continuously assess how students are doing in order to adjust their instruction appropriately. One type of decision, termed a *process* instructional decision, is made almost instantaneously, such as deciding to end a lecture or ask a different type of question. *Planning* instructional decisions are made with more reflection; they might include changing student seating arrangement or grouping patterns, spending an extra day on a particular topic, or preparing additional worksheets for homework. It is hoped that teachers will use credible measurement information with clear standards to evaluate student behavior accurately.

An important aspect of teaching is *communicating expectations* to students, and assessments are used continuously during instruction to indicate what is expected of students. The teacher's expectations are communicated to students by the nature of the questions the teacher asks (e.g., are the questions easy or hard?), by how the teacher acknowledges student answers, by the type of feedback teachers give to students as they are completing assignments, and in many more subtle ways of responding to students. The nature of the tests teachers give and how they evaluate student answers communicate standards that students are expected to meet.

Finally, assessment processes can be used *as* instruction. Recently developed performance and authentic assessments are long term and provide opportunities for student learning. As we will see in later chapters, such assessments are useful as teaching tools as well as methods to document student learning. As such, they educate and improve student performance, not merely audit it (Wiggins, 1998).

Research on Learning, Motivation, Instruction, and Curriculum: Implications for Assessment

As summarized in Figure 1.4, recent research on learning, motivation, and instruction has important implications for the nature and use of classroom assessments. It is becoming increasingly clear that effective instruction usually does much more than present information to students. Rather, good instruction provides an environment that engages the student in active learning that connects new information with existing knowledge. Contemporary cognitive theories have shown that learning is *meaningful* and *self-regulated.* Learning is an ongoing process in which students actively receive, interpret, and relate information to what they already know, understand, and have experienced. Effective assessment, in turn, promotes this process (Phye, 1997a).

There is a growing awareness that it is essential for students to develop thinking skills (e.g., skills in problem solving and decision making). Students need to be able to apply what they learn to real-world demands and challenges, work with others to solve problems, and be self-regulated learners who have an awareness and willingness to explore new ideas and develop new skills. Instruction and curriculum as well as assessment need to be designed and delivered to enhance these skills.

Recent research on motivation suggests that teachers must constantly assess students and provide feedback that is informative. By providing specific and meaningful feedback to students and encouraging them to regulate their own learning, teachers encourage students to enhance their sense of self-efficacy and self-confidence, important determinants of motivation (Brookhart, 1997). Meaningful learning is intrinsically motivating because the content has relevance. The implication here is that assessment does not end with scoring and recording the results. Motivation is highly dependent on the nature of the feedback from the assessment. Thus, in keeping with the integration of assessment with instruction, feedback is an essential component of the assessment process.

There have also been significant recent changes in curriculum theory that have clear implications for classroom assessment. Due in part to the standards-based movement, curriculum is now based on the premise that all students can learn, that standards for learning need to be high for all students, and that equal opportunity is essential. Curriculum needs to show students how learning is connected to the world outside of school.

Shepard (2000) has nicely illustrated the shared principles of contemporary curriculum theories, cognitive and constructivist learning theory, and recent trends in classroom assessment (Figure 1.5). Her overlapping circles signify that the changes we have seen from older behavioristic theories of learning and motivation, curriculum designed for social efficiency, and principles derived from scientific measurement overlap to provide a new set of ideas to guide classroom assessment. Although the changes in principles of curriculum, learning, and motivation are now fairly well established, classroom assessment practices are only beginning to change. Furthermore, recent high-stakes testing at the state level has nudged many educators back toward behavioristic and scientific (e.g., objective) measurement theories.

FIGURE 1.4   Linking Instruction and Assessment: Implications from Cognitive Learning Theory

Theory	Implications for Instruction/Assessment
Knowledge is constructed. Learning is a process of creating personal meaning from new information and prior knowledge.	• Encourage discussion of new ideas. • Encourage divergent thinking, multiple links and solutions, not just one right answer. • Encourage multiple modes of expression, for example, role play, simulations, debates, and explanations to others. • Emphasize critical thinking skills: analyze, compare, generalize, predict, hypothesize. • Relate new information to personal experience, prior knowledge. • Apply information to a new situation.
All ages/abilities can think and solve problems. Learning isn't necessarily a linear progression of discrete skills.	• Engage all students in problem solving. • Don't make problem solving, critical thinking, or discussion of concepts contingent on mastery of routine basic skills.
There is great variety in learning styles, attention spans, memory, developmental paces, and intelligences.	• Provide choices in tasks (not all reading and writing). • Provide choices in how to show mastery/competence. • Provide time to think about and do assignments. • Don't overuse timed tests. • Provide opportunity to revise, rethink. • Include concrete experiences (manipulatives, links to prior personal experience).
People perform better when they know the goal, see models, know how their performance compares to the standard.	• Discuss goals; let students help define them (personal and class). • Provide a range of examples of student work; discuss characteristics. • Provide students with opportunities for self-evaluation and peer review. • Discuss criteria for judging performance. • Allow students to have input into standards.
It's important to know when to use knowledge, how to adapt it, how to manage one's own learning.	• Give real-world opportunities (or simulations) to apply/adapt new knowledge. • Have students self-evaluate: think about how they learn well/poorly; set new goals, why they like certain work.
Motivation, effort, and self-esteem affect learning and performance.	• Motivate students with real-life tasks and connections to personal experiences. • Encourage students to see connection between effort and results.
Learning has social components. Group work is valuable.	• Provide group work. • Incorporate heterogeneous groups. • Enable students to take on a variety of roles. • Consider group products and group processes.

Source: Herman, J. L., Aschbacher, P. R., & Winters, L. The National Center for Research on Evaluation, Standards and Student Testing (CRESST). *A Practical Guide to Alternative Assessment.* Alexandria, VA: Association for Supervision and Curriculum Development, pp. 19–20. Copyright © 1992 by The Regents of the University of California.

Reformed Vision of Curriculum

- All students can learn.
- Challenging subject matter aimed at higher-order thinking and problem solving
- Equal opportunity for diverse learners
- Socialization into the discourse and practices of academic disciplines
- Authenticity in the relationship between learning in and out of school
- Fostering of important dispositions and habits of mind
- Enactment of democratic practices in a caring community

Cognitive and Constructivist Learning Theories

- Intellectual abilities are socially and culturally developed.
- Learners construct knowledge and understandings within a social context.
- New learning is shaped by prior knowledge and cultural perspectives.
- Intelligent thought involves "metacognition" or self-monitoring of learning and thinking.
- Deep understanding is principled and supports transfer.
- Cognitive performance depends on dispositions and personal identity.

Classroom Assessment

- Challenging tasks to elicit higher-order thinking
- Addresses learning processes as well as learning outcomes
- An ongoing process, integrated with instruction
- Used formatively in support of student learning
- Expectations visible to students
- Students active in evaluating their own work
- Used to evaluate teaching as well as student learning

FIGURE 1.5   Shared Principles of Curriculum Theories, Psychological Theories and Assessment Theory Characterizing an Emergent, Constructivist Paradigm

Source: Shepard, L. A. (2000). The role of assessment in a learning culture. *Educational Researcher* 29(10), 4–14.

The research from cognitive learning and curriculum theories has laid the foundation for significant changes in classroom assessment. As we discover more about how students learn, we realize that assessment practices, as well as instructional practices, need to change to keep pace with this research.

Recent Trends in Classroom Assessment

In the past decade, some clear trends have emerged in classroom assessment. More established traditions of focusing assessment on "objective" testing at the *end* of instruction are being supplemented with, or in some cases replaced by, assessments *during* instruction—to help teachers make moment-by-moment decisions—and with what are called "alternative" assessments. **Alternative assessments** include authentic assessment, performance assessment, portfolios, exhibitions, demonstrations, journals, and other forms of assessment that require the active construction of meaning rather than the passive regurgitation of isolated facts. These assessments engage students in learning and require thinking skills, and thus they are consistent with cognitive theories of learning and motivation as well as societal needs to prepare students for an increasingly complex workplace.

Another trend is the recognition that knowledge and skills should not be assessed in isolation. Rather, it is necessary to assess the application and the use of knowledge and skills together. More emphasis is now placed on assessing thinking skills and collaborative skills that are needed to work cooperatively with others. Newer forms of assessment provide opportunities for many "correct" answers, rather than a single right answer, and rely on multiple sources of information.

One of the most important advances in both instruction and assessment is the emphasis on **authenticity** (Wiggins, 1993, 1998). Authentic instruction and assessment focus on knowledge, thinking, and skills exhibited in real-life settings outside school that produce the student's best, rather than typical, performance. To accomplish this, students need multiple "authentic" opportunities to demonstrate the knowledge and skills and continuous feedback. This kind of emphasis results in greater student motivation and improved achievement. In this way authenticity effectively integrates instruction, assessment, and motivation. Consider the following characteristics of authentic instruction and assessment in light of what occurs in traditional classrooms (Tombari & Borich, 1999).

Authentic instruction and assessment emphasize the following:

- Students are assessed on what was taught and practiced in ways that are consistent with assessment methods.
- The focus is on solving problems and accomplishing tasks like those done by professionals in the field.
- Standards or criteria for success are public, shared with the students.
- Assessment occurs over time to provide meaningful feedback so students can improve.
- Learning and assessment contexts are similar to "real life."

Another important trend is to involve students in all aspects of assessment, from designing tasks and questions to evaluating their own and others' work. Engaging students in developing assessment exercises, creating scoring criteria, applying criteria to student products, and self-assessment all help students understand how their own performance is evaluated. This understanding, in turn, facilitates student motivation and achievement. Students learn to confidently evaluate their performance as well as the performance of other students. For example, if students are taught to internalize the key elements of what should be included in comprehending a short story, they are better able to monitor their progress toward achieving learning targets. Likewise, when students generate lists of the ways good essay answers differ from weak ones, they learn the criteria that determines high student performance. Thus, there is a change of emphasis from the teacher providing all assessment tasks and feedback to promoting student engagement in the assessment process. This is best accomplished when there is "a continuous flow of information about student achievement . . . to advance, not merely check on, student learning" (Stiggins, 2002, p. 761). That is, assessment *for* learning becomes as important as assessment *of* learning. Stiggins (2002, p. 761–762) identifies eight ways that assessment *for* learning can be facilitated:

1. Understanding and articulating in advance of teaching/learning targets
2. Informing students about learning goals in terms that students understand, from the very beginning of the teaching and learning process
3. Becoming assessment literate and able to transform expectations into assessment exercises and scoring procedures that accurately reflect student achievement
4. Using classroom assessment to build students' confidence in themselves as learners and help them take responsibility for their own learning
5. Translating classroom assessment results into frequent descriptive feedback, providing students with specific insights as to how to improve
6. Continuously adjusting instruction based on the results of classroom assessment
7. Engaging students in regular self-assessment, with standards held constant so that students can watch themselves grow over time
8. Actively involving students in communicating with their teacher and parents about their achievement status and improvement

Student engagement in assessment is closely related to another recent trend: a greater emphasis on what is termed "formative" assessment. **Formative assessment** is information that is provided to students during instruction to help them learn. It is often contrasted with **summative assessment,** which documents student performance at the end of a unit of study. Recent research has found that effective formative assessment enhances student learning (Black, & Wiliam, 1998; Brookhart, 2001). By receiving specific feedback about their progress, students are better able to compare actual with targeted performance and make adjustments. As we will see in Chapter 5, formative assessment is the central component of assessments that are made as students are learning from instruction.

These and other recent trends in classroom assessment are summarized in Figure 1.6. In presenting these trends, I do not want to suggest that what teachers have been doing for years is inappropriate or should necessarily be changed. Much of what we have learned about evaluating students from previous decades is very important and useful. For example, properly constructed multiple-choice tests are excellent for efficiently and objectively assessing knowledge of a large content domain. What is needed is a *balanced* approach to assessment, in which appropriate techniques are administered and used in a credible way for decision making. Just because the assessment focuses on complex thinking skills or uses portfolios does not mean it is better or more credible. Assessment technique must be matched to purpose and must be conducted according to established quality standards. Some of the

FIGURE 1.6 Recent Trends in Classroom Assessment

From	To
Sole emphasis on outcomes	Assessing of process
Isolated skills	Integrated skills
Isolated facts	Application of knowledge
Paper-and-pencil tasks	Authentic tasks
Decontextualized tasks	Contextualized tasks
A single correct answer	Many correct answers
Secret standards	Public standards
Secret criteria	Public criteria
Individuals	Groups
After instruction	During instruction
Little feedback	Considerable feedback
"Objective" tests	Performance-based tests
Standardized tests	Informal tests
External evaluation	Student self-evaluation
Single assessments	Multiple assessments
Sporadic	Continual
Conclusive	Recursive
Assessment *of* learning	Assessment *for* learning
Summative	Formative

recent trends, such as making standards and criteria public, are helpful procedures regardless of the assessment employed, and they will improve traditional as well as newer types of measurement by engaging students in the entire assessment process.

Teachers' Classroom Assessment and Grading Practices Decision Making

Every teacher makes many decisions about the types of assessments that will be used, when these assessments are used, and grading. Consistent with previous research, a recent survey of over 1,000 teachers showed that these decisions result in highly individualized and idiosyncratic practices (McMillan, Workman, & Myran, 1998). Each teacher creates his or her own practices. This suggests that you, too, will develop your own assessment and grading practices.

To better understand the decision-making process teachers use, I participated in a study in which in-depth, individual interviews were conducted with twenty-eight teachers to investigate the reasons teachers gave for the assessment decisions they made (McMillan & Workman, 1999). The results have interesting implications because of the strong connection between this decision-making process and instruction.

We found that two major sources of influence affect assessment and grading practices decision making. One source lies within the teacher and consists of beliefs and values about teaching, and learning more generally, that provide a basis for explaining how and why specific assessment and grading practices are used. A second source lies external to the teacher, consisting of pressures that need to be considered. We found that these two sources of influence are in constant tension. Although internal beliefs and values that reflect a desire to enhance student learning are most influential, external pressures cause teachers to engage in certain practices that may not be in the best interests of student learning.

These influences are depicted in Figure 1.7 to show the nature of the internal and external factors and how these factors are in tension. Internal beliefs and values include a philosophy of teaching and learning, and assessment practices are consistent with that philosophy. For example, if teachers believe that all students can succeed and that individual differences among students should be accommodated, then the teacher uses multiple types of assessment to allow sufficient opportunities to show success. If teachers believe it is important to get students involved, engaged, and motivated, they may use performance assessments and give points for student participation and effort. To better understand how much students know and can do, most teachers rely on assessments in which students show their work.

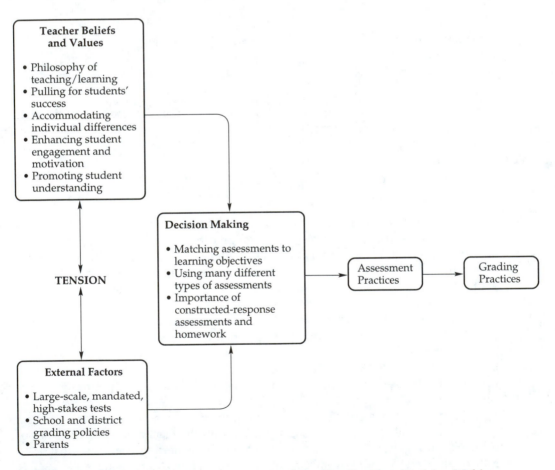

FIGURE 1.7   A Model of Teacher Assessment and Grading Practices Decision Making

External pressures include school or school division assessment and grading policies that must be followed, parental demands, and large-scale, high-stakes testing. Teachers want to collect assessment information that will show parents why specific grades were given. Externally mandated large-scale testing of students can be very influential, as well as in direct contradiction to teachers' internal beliefs and values. For example, if statewide testing consists of multiple-choice items covering a great amount of material and student performance will have important consequences, teachers feel pressure to use the same kinds of tests for classroom assessments. This may be in direct conflict with wanting to use performance assessments that are more engaging and informative about what students really understand.

Think about the model in Figure 1.7 in relation to your own beliefs and values and in relation to external pressures you may need to consider. Your decision making should consider these sources of influence so that the assessment and grading practices you implement reflect the relative importance of each. The most important question is this: To what extent are your assessment and grading practices consistent with principles of good instruction, and to what extent will the right kinds of student learning be enhanced?

Assessment Standards for Teachers

Before closing this chapter, I want to familiarize you with important sets of assessment standards for teachers. In 1990, the American Federation of Teachers, the National Council on Measurement in Education, and the National Education Association published a set of standards for teacher competence in educational assessment.

The standards organize the teacher's professional role and responsibilities into activities occurring before, during, and after the appropriate instructional segment. The standards also include responsibilities of the teacher for involvement in school and district decision making and involvement in the wider professional roles of teachers. These roles and responsibilities, which emphasize teacher activities that are directly related to assessment, are outlined in Appendix A. Throughout these roles and responsibilities, instruction is integrated with assessment. This is consistent with newer trends in assessment, and it forms the basis for the assessment content that is presented in this book.

The standards also indicate seven specific areas of assessment knowledge or skills that a teacher should possess to perform assessment roles and responsibilities. Specifically, teachers should be skilled in:

1. choosing assessment methods appropriate for instructional decisions
2. developing assessment methods appropriate for instructional decisions
3. administering, scoring, and interpreting the results of both externally produced and teacher-produced assessment methods
4. using assessment results when making decisions about individual students, planning teaching, developing curriculum, and making recommendations for school improvement
5. developing valid pupil grading procedures

6. communicating assessment results to students, parents, other lay audiences, and other educators
7. recognizing unethical, illegal, and otherwise inappropriate assessment methods and uses of assessment information

Three additional documents summarize important assessment knowledge and skills for teachers: the *Code for Professional Responsibilities in Educational Measurement* (National Council on Measurement in Education, 1995, http://assessment.iupui.edu/ncme/code1), *Principles and Indicators for Student Assessment Systems* (National Forum on Assessment, 1995, www.fairtest.org), and the *Student Evaluation Standards* (Gullickson, 2003). Appendix B summarizes the most recent standards, which were developed with the assistance of sixteen major educational organizations and reflect an international consensus about assessment skills needed by teachers.

Summary

This chapter introduced assessment as an integral part of teacher decision making and instruction. As a systematic method of collecting, interpreting, and using information, good assessment improves student learning. Major points in the chapter are the following:

- Assessment includes four major components: purpose, measurement, evaluation, and use.
- Measurement consists of differentiating behavior and performance.
- Evaluation involves professional judgment of the value or worth of the measured performance.
- Recent research on learning, motivation, and instruction suggests the need to use more alternative forms of measurement, such as performance assessments, portfolios, and authentic assessments.
- Teacher assessment and grading decision making is influenced by internal beliefs and values and external factors.
- Professional standards have been developed to provide a framework for what teachers need to know about classroom assessment.

WHAT'S COMING

You have now been introduced to classroom assessment and some of the directions such assessment is taking. I want to give you an overview of the rest of this book—how it is organized, what you can expect, and how you can make the most of the application exercises at the end of each chapter.

The sequence of topics followed in the book reflects the steps teachers take in using assessment as part of instruction. The next two chapters present fundamental principles of any type of assessment. In Chapter 2 we consider how purpose is clarified through the development of appropriate learning targets. Chapter 3 reviews criteria that enhance the quality and credibility of assessments. With this background, methods of assessment are presented in the sequence teachers use when planning and delivering instruction. Single chapters are devoted to assessment before and during instruction. Chapters 6–10 then present major methods of assessment, based on the different types of learning targets being assessed. These assessments are conducted at the end of a unit of instruction. In this book, the method of assessment follows from what needs to be assessed to emphasize that teachers first determine purpose and learning targets and then select and implement appropriate assessments. Chapter 11 focuses on issues concerning the assessment of students with special needs in inclusive settings. Chapter 12 examines what teachers do with assessment information in the form of grading and reporting information. The last chapter summarizes important information concerning the administration, interpretation, and use of standardized tests.

SELF-INSTRUCTIONAL REVIEW EXERCISES

Each chapter contains self-instructional exercises. They are intended to check your understanding of the content of the chapter. An answer key is provided to give you immediate feedback. Remember that you will learn most if you don't look at the key before you answer the question.

1. What is the relationship between teacher decision making, complex classroom environments, and assessment?

2. What does it mean when we say that assessment is not an add-on activity?

3. What is the difference between a *test* and an *assessment*?

4. Refer to Figure 1.1. Identify each of the following examples as preinstructional assessment (pre), ongoing assessment (og), or postinstructional assessment (post).

   a. giving a pop quiz
   b. giving a cumulative final exam
   c. giving students praise for correct answers
   d. using homework to judge student knowledge
   e. reviewing student scores on last year's standardized test
   f. changing the lesson plan because of student inattention
   g. reviewing student files to understand the cultural backgrounds of students

5. Identify each of the following quotes as referring to one of the four components of classroom assessment: purpose (P), measurement (M), evaluation (E), and use (U).

   a. "Last week I determined that my students did not know very much about the Civil War."
   b. "This year I want to see if I can assess student attitudes."
   c. "The test helped me to identify where students were weak."
   d. "I like the idea of using performance-based assessments."
   e. "I intend to combine several different assessments to determine the grade."

6. How do assessments communicate expectations for student learning?

7. Why, according to recent research on learning, is performance assessment well suited to effective instruction?

ANSWERS TO SELF-INSTRUCTIONAL REVIEW EXERCISES

1. Complex classroom environments influence the nature of teacher decision making, and assessment is needed to make good decisions.

2. "Add-on" means assessment that occurs at the end of an instructional unit, for example, the midterm or final exam. However, the teacher also assesses students before and during instruction. Assessment should not be thought of as only testing at the end of instruction.

3. A test is only one part of assessment. Assessment refers to measuring something, evaluating what is measured, and then using the information for decision making. A test is one way to measure.

4. a. og, b. post, c. og, d. og, e. pre, f. og, g. pre.

5. a. E, b. P, c. E, d. M, e. U.

6. Expectations are set by the nature of the standards and criteria used in the assessments and the way teachers provide feedback and otherwise respond to students.

7. Recent learning research has shown the importance of connecting new to existing information, of applying knowledge, and of thinking skills. Performance assessments foster these behaviors by relating content and processes to problem solving in meaningful contexts.

SUGGESTIONS FOR ACTION RESEARCH

At the end of each chapter are suggestions for action research. The intent of these suggestions is to help you apply what you are learning from the book to practical situations. By conducting this type of informal research, the principles and ideas presented will have greater relevance and meaning to you.

1. Investigate the time that is taken for assessment in the classroom by observing some classes. Compare your results to how much time the teacher believes is devoted to assessment. Also note in your observations the nature of teacher decision making. What kinds of decisions are made? How, specifically, does information from assessment contribute to this decision making?

2. Conduct an interview with a teacher or two and ask them some questions about assessment. For example, you could take Figure 1.6 and ask the teachers if they believe the so-called recent trends are actually evident. You could ask about the relationship between assessment and teaching/learning to see the extent to which assessment and teaching are integrated. Use Figure 1.7 to ask about "internal" and "external" factors that affect their assessment, grading practices, and decision making.

3. Interview a school administrator about what teachers need to know about assessment. Ask about the assessment standards to get a perspective on the reasonableness of the standards.

2 Establishing Learning Targets

Good classroom assessment begins with establishing appropriate *learning targets*. How else will you know what to teach and what to assess? In recent years there has been much controversy about what the learning targets should be and who should set them, evidenced most visibly by standards-based school reform. In this chapter we review the complex nature of learning targets and present a framework that will help you to determine them for your students. Establishing clear, specific, and valued learning targets is an essential first step toward improved classroom assessment.

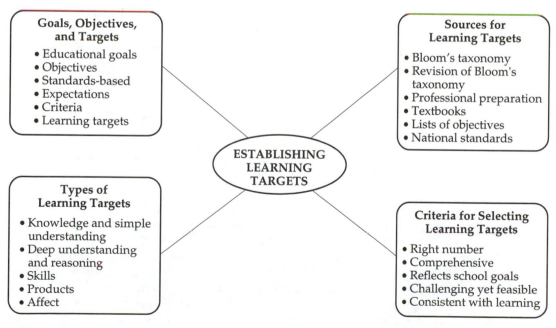

Goals, Objectives, and Targets

- Educational goals
- Objectives
- Standards-based
- Expectations
- Criteria
- Learning targets

Sources for Learning Targets

- Bloom's taxonomy
- Revision of Bloom's taxonomy
- Professional preparation
- Textbooks
- Lists of objectives
- National standards

ESTABLISHING LEARNING TARGETS

Types of Learning Targets

- Knowledge and simple understanding
- Deep understanding and reasoning
- Skills
- Products
- Affect

Criteria for Selecting Learning Targets

- Right number
- Comprehensive
- Reflects school goals
- Challenging yet feasible
- Consistent with learning

CHAPTER 2   Concept Map

What are Learning Targets?

The answer to this question is not as obvious as it may seem. Your first reaction may be that a learning target is simply a clear description of what students should know and be able to do. You may think of a *target* as a goal, objective, competency, outcome, standard, or expectation. Yet each of these terms has come to mean something different, and it is important to review these differences to enable you to understand better just what you need to do to establish learning targets that will facilitate credible assessments.

Educational Goals

An **educational goal** is a very general statement of what students will know and be able to do. Goals are written to cover large blocks of instructional time, such as a unit, semester, or year, and indicate in broad terms what will be emphasized during that time period. Some examples of educational goals require that students will be able to:

> know how to think critically and solve problems
> work collaboratively with others
> understand the scientific method
> appreciate cultural differences
> develop an appreciation for fine arts
> learn to think independently
> become good citizens

Goals provide a starting point for more specific learning objectives. By beginning with goals, you will have a general outline that can be validated by parents, teachers, and other school officials. In most school systems, educational goals are listed as defining the mission of the system, but these are usually too broad to be of much practical help in your classroom. Goals will also be found in district curriculum guides, textbooks, and teaching materials.

Objectives

Educational objectives are usually relatively specific statements of student performance that should be demonstrated at the end of an instructional unit. However, over the years, the term **objective** has been used in many different ways, depending on words that specify the type of objective and the intent of the user. The term *global objective* means essentially the same thing as *educational goal*. Gronlund (1995) uses the term *instructional objective* to mean "intended learning outcomes" (p. 3). Gronlund emphasizes that instructional objectives should be stated in terms of specific, observable, and measurable student responses. This type of emphasis is based on a behavioral philosophy of teaching and learning. Instructional objectives are therefore sometimes referred to as *behavioral, performance,* or *terminal* objectives. These types of objectives are characterized by the use of action verbs such as *add, state, define, list, contract, design, categorize, count,* and *lift.* Action verbs are important because they indicate what the students actually do at the end of the unit. Here are some examples of instructional objectives.

The student will:

summarize the main idea of the reading passage
underline the verb and subject of each sentence
write a title for the reading passage
list five causes of the Civil War
identify on a map the location of each continent
explain the process of photosynthesis

The degree of specificity used for instructional objectives can vary. Some are very specific while others are more general. For example, highly precise behavioral objectives may include the following:

1. *Behavior:* specific behavior as indicated by action verbs
2. *Audience:* description of the students who are expected to demonstrate the behavior (e.g., grade level or group)
3. *Criterion:* description of the criteria used to indicate whether the behavior has been demonstrated (e.g., answering eight of ten questions correctly, or judgment of writing based on grammar, spelling, sentence construction, and organization)
4. *Condition:* circumstances, equipment, or materials used when demonstrating the behavior (e.g., with or without class notes, open book, using graph paper, given a calculator)

When objectives are written to include these rules, they are highly specific, as in the following examples:

From a standing still position on a level, hard surface (condition), male students (audience) will jump (behavior) at least two feet (criterion).

Given two hours in the library without notes (condition), students in the high reading group (audience) will identify (behavior) five sources on the topic "national health insurance" (criterion).

Although these rules for writing objectives are helpful in indicating what students will demonstrate, including all of them is usually too time-consuming to write and too confining for teachers. Proponents of instructional objectives emphasize that teachers should learn to write them at an appropriate level of generality—not so narrow that it takes much too long to write and keep track of the objectives, and not so general that the objectives provide little guidance for instruction. Ideally, objectives should be stated in terms that are specific enough to inform teaching and assessment but not limit the flexibility of the teacher to modify instruction as needed. Also, it is best to focus on *unit* rather than daily lesson plan instructional objectives. These intermediate-level objectives help keep the focus of student learning on the main understandings, learning processes, attitudes, and other learning outcomes of the unit as a whole. Writing objectives that are too specific results in long lists of minutia that are time-consuming to monitor and manage. Some examples of instructional objectives that are too specific, too broad, and about the right level of specificity (intermediate) are shown in Figure 2.1.

Another approach is to state a goal or more general objective and then state *examples* of specific objectives that indicate the various types of student performances required. For example:

General Objective	Understands the structure of U.S. government
Specific Objectives	Lists five functions of the presidency
	Describes the purpose of each major branch of the federal government
	Explains what the concept of checks and balances means
	Distinguishes between the Senate and the House of Representatives
General Objective	Knows the meaning of spelling words
Specific Objectives	Writes correct definitions for 80 percent of the words
	Identifies correct antonyms for 50 percent of the words
	Identifies correct synonyms for 70 percent of the words
	Draws pictures that correctly illustrate 80 percent of the words
	Writes sentences that include correct usage of 80 percent of the words

Whether you focus on general or specific objectives, the main point is to describe what students will know and be able to do and what constitutes sufficient evidence that students have learned, and not what you will do as a teacher to help students obtain the knowledge and skills identified. What you plan to do as a teacher may be called a **teaching objective** or *learning activity* and may include such things as lecturing for a certain amount of time, asking questions, putting students in groups, giving feedback to students individually, conducting experiments, using a map to show where certain countries are located, asking students to solve math problems on the board, having students read orally, and so on. These teaching objectives describe the activities students will be engaged in and what you need to do to be sure that the activities occur as planned. Regardless of the specific labels, as a teacher you will need to develop lesson plans that will include general learning targets, more specific learning targets, teaching objectives, activities, materials needed, and plans for assessment of student learning. Figure 2.2 illustrates a typical lesson plan.

Standards-Based Education

It is likely that you have heard or read about national and state **"standards"** that have been developed in most subject areas. The standards movement in education has been ubiquitous and powerful, fueled by concerns about the low performance of students. The intent of the standards has been to "clarify and raise expectations,

FIGURE 2.1 Specificity of Instructional Objectives

Too Specific	About Right	Too Broad
Given a two-paragraph article from the newspaper, the student will correctly identify ten statements that are facts and five statements that are opinions in less than ten minutes without the aid of any resource materials.	Students will state the difference between facts and opinions.	Students will learn how to think critically.
Based on reading the content of Lincoln's and Douglas's debates over one week, the student will, without any aids, write four paragraphs in one hour that summarize, with at least 80 percent accuracy, their areas of agreement and disagreement.	Students will identify areas of agreement and disagreement in the debates between Lincoln and Douglas.	Compare and contrast the Lincoln/Douglas debates.
The student, given grid paper, will analyze data on the frequency of student birthdays in each month and construct a bar graph in one hour in teams of two of the results that show the two most frequent and two least frequent months.	Given frequency data and grid paper, students will construct bar graphs of selected variables.	Students will construct bar graphs.

and . . . provide a common set of expectations" (Kendall & Marzano, 1997, p. 5). Consequently, the term *standards* usually means higher levels of student achievement, especially as contrasted with "minimum competency."

Two types of educational standards often are addressed: content standards and performance standards. **Content standards** (not to be confused with *curriculum* standards) are statements about what students should know, understand, and be able to do. Content standards describe "the knowledge and skills that students should attain" (Kendall & Marzano, 1997, p. 20). The way in which content standards are presented differs depending on the source. One format, for example, may describe content as information:

The constitution sets forth the organization of the government and describes powers of different branches of national government, states, and the people.

More typically, a content standard includes a description of the nature of the knowledge:

Students will demonstrate an understanding of the purposes of the constitution.

FIGURE 2.2   Example of a Lesson Plan

Learning Target   Students will differentiate between vertebrate and invertebrate animals by correctly recalling the difference and naming examples of animals in each category.

Materials Needed   Textbook, eight copies of pictures and sketches of the anatomies of vertebrate and invertebrate animals, colored pencils, paper.

Instructional Activities   Set up groups of three or four students.
Give each group a set of animal pictures and ask them to classify the pictures into two major groups.
Monitor student work for fifteen minutes.
Ask students to indicate how the animals in each category are the same and how they are different.
Emphasize the presence of a backbone as the major differentiating feature.
Ask students to further classify vertebrate and invertebrate animals into further categories.
Ask students to draw concept maps of different types of animals, using different colored pencils.

Assessment   Without notes, students will be asked to recall the difference between invertebrate and vertebrate animals and give four examples of different types of animals in each category. Give the students a new set of animal pictures and have them apply their rules for group membership to sort the pictures.

Content standards can also vary greatly in specificity. Note the generality of the following content standard:

> Students will understand how immigration has influenced American society.

A more specific content standard would be:

> Students will compare the contributions of Socrates, Plato, and Aristotle to Greek life.

Content standards may also differ with respect to the nature of the learning or performance. Some standards use the term "knows" to describe student attainment, and others emphasize "understanding" or reasoning skills. As we will see, these important differences influence how students are assessed. Finally, standards are often organized by grade level. The term **benchmark** may be used to identify content standards for a particular grade or developmental level.

Keep in mind that content standards are similar to what have been called general objectives. In both, the emphasis is on what students can demonstrate after instruction. The value of the standards movement is that the extensive amount of work that has been done to identify standards enables you to draw on the work of others to identify what outcomes are best for your students. Figure 2.3 includes examples of content standards and benchmarks based on work by subject-matter organizations.

A **performance standard** indicates the level of proficiency that must be demonstrated to indicate the degree to which content standards have been attained. Performance standards address issues of attainment and quality. By indicating *degree* of attainment, performance standards are able to distinguish different levels of accomplishment. This is quite different from a behavioral objective, which typically has a single level. In other words, a performance standard describes what students must *do* and how different levels of proficiency on the content standards result. As described by McTighe and Ferrara (1998), performance standards "set expectations about how much students should know and how well students should perform" (p. 34).

Ideally, the performance standard indicates what students must do as well as different levels of performance. In reality, however, you will probably find that what are called "performance standards" contain a description of what students must do but do not include levels of attainment. For example, consider the following content standard:

> The student will understand the right of free speech.

A performance standard that contains a description of what the student must do to demonstrate this competency might be the following (Glatthorn, 1998):

> Examines issue of right to free speech, explaining importance of that right in a democracy and noting limitations established by the courts (p. 23).

Another example is found in standards that first indicate what students should know and understand (content standards) and then indicates what students should be able to do (performance standard) (National Standards for United States History: Exploring the American Experience, Grades 5–12, 1994):

> **What students should know:** The causes of the American Revolution, ideas and interest involved in forging the revolutionary movement, and the reasons for the American victory.
>
> **What students should be able to do:** Demonstrate understanding of the causes of the American Revolution by:
> - Explaining the consequences of the Seven Years War and the overhaul of English imperial policy following the Treaty of Paris in 1763, demonstrating the connections between the antecedent and consequent events.
> - Comparing the arguments advanced by defenders and opponents of the new imperial policy on the traditional rights of English people and the legitimacy of asking the colonies to pay a share of the costs of empire.
> - Reconstructing the chronology of the critical events leading to the outbreak of armed conflict between the American colonies and England. (p. 72)

What is not indicated with this performance standard is any degree of attainment. To do this, it is necessary to establish *criteria* and then use descriptors of different levels with these criteria (e.g., not proficient, proficient, advanced, or complete, partial, or none).

FIGURE 2.3   Examples of Content Standards

Science

Standard: Understands the basic concepts of the evolution of species

Benchmarks:

Level I (Grades K–2)

- Knows that some kinds of organisms that once lived on Earth have completely disappeared (e.g., dinosaurs, trilobites, mammoths, giant tree ferns, horsetail trees)

Level II (Grades 3–5)

- Knows that fossils of past life can be compared to one another and to living organisms to observe their similarities and differences

Level III (Grades 6–8)

- Knows that the fossil record, through geologic evidence, documents the appearance, diversification, and extinction of many life forms
- Knows basic ideas related to biological evolution
- Understands the concept of extinction and its importance in biological evolution

Language Arts

Standard: Uses grammatical and mechanical conventions in written expression.

Benchmarks:

Level I (Grades K–2)

- Forms letters in print and spaces words and sentences
- Uses complete sentences in written compositions
- Uses declarative and interrogative sentences in written compositions
- Uses nouns, verbs, adjectives, and adverbs in written compositions
- Uses conventions of spelling in written compositions
- Uses conventions of capitalization in written compositions
- Uses conventions of punctuation in written compositions

Level II (Grades 3–5)

- Writes in cursive
- Uses exclamatory and imperative sentences in written compositions
- Uses nouns, verbs, adjectives, and adverbs in written compositions
- Uses coordinating conjunctions in written compositions
- Uses negatives in written compositions
- Uses conventions of spelling, capitalization, and punctuation in written compositions

Level III (Grades 6–8)

- Uses simple and compound sentences in written compositions
- Uses pronouns, nouns, verbs, adjectives, and adverbs in written compositions
- Uses prepositions and coordinating conjunctions in written compositions
- Uses interjections in written compositions
- Uses conventions of spelling, capitalization, and punctuation in written compositions
- Uses standard format in written compositions

FIGURE 2.3   Continued

Civics

Standard: Understands the roles of political parties, campaigns, elections, and associations and groups in American politics

Benchmarks:

Level I and II

- Not appropriate for these levels

Level III (Grades 6–8)

- Understands the role of political parties
- Knows the various kinds of elections
- Understands the ways in which individuals can participate in political parties, campaigns, and elections
- Understands the historical and contemporary roles of prominent associations and groups in local, state, and national politics
- Knows how and why Americans become members of associations and groups, and understands how membership in these associations provides individuals with opportunities to participate in the political process.

Level IV (Grades 9–12)

- Knows the origins and development of the two-party system in the United States, and understands the role of third parties
- Understands how and why American political parties differ from ideological parties in other countries
- Knows the major characteristics of American political parties, how they vary by locality, how they reflect the dispersion of power, and how they provide citizens with numerous opportunities for participation
- Understands how political parties are involved in channeling public opinion, allowing people to act jointly, nominating candidates, conducting campaigns, and training future leaders, and understands why political parties in the United States are weaker today then they have been at times in the past
- Knows the characteristics of initiatives and referendums
- Understands the significance of campaigns and elections in the American political system, and knows current criticisms of campaigns and proposals for their reform
- Knows historical and contemporary examples of associations and groups performing functions otherwise performed by the government such as social welfare and education
- Understands the extent to which associations and groups enhance citizen participation in American political life

Source: Adapted from Kendall, J. S., & Marzano, R. J. (1997). *Content knowledge: A compendium of standards and benchmarks for K–12 education.* Aurora, CO: Mid-continent Regional Educational Laboratory, pp. 86, 326–329, 451–452. Adapted by permission of McREL.

Criteria

One of the most frustrating experiences for students is not knowing "what the teacher wants" or "how the teacher grades." Perhaps you can recall being in a class in which you did an assignment with little guidance from the teacher about how he or she would grade it. Once your assignment was returned with comments, your reaction might well have been, "If I had only known what the teacher was looking for I could have provided it!" Essentially, this issue is concerned with the criteria the teacher uses for evaluating student work and whether students know, *in advance*, what those criteria are. Here is a poignant illustration of how a lack of clear criteria can be unfair. The following actually happened a few years ago to a sixth grader:

> [The student] was given the following problem to solve: "Three buses bring students to school. The first bus brings 9 students, the second bus brings 7 students, and the third bus brings 5 students. How many students in all do the buses bring? The student answered "21 kids," and the answer was marked wrong. After encouragement by my colleague the student asked the teacher "Why?" The reason was that the student said "kids" instead of "students." (Arter, 1996, p. VI-1: 1)

Criteria, then, are clearly articulated and public descriptions of facets or dimensions of student performance that are used for judging the level of achievement. As pointed out in Chapter 1, criteria may be called *scoring criteria, rubrics, scoring rubrics,* or *scoring guidelines.* (The term *performance criteria* may also be used.) Although criteria have been promoted most for more recent alternative and performance assessments, the issue of how student responses will be evaluated lies at the heart of any type of assessment. The key component of criteria is making your professional judgments about student performance clear to others. All methods of assessment involve your professional judgment. If you use multiple-choice testing, judgment is used to prepare the items and decide which alternative is correct. In an essay test, judgment is involved in preparing the question and in reading and scoring answers. Clearly articulated criteria will help you in many ways, including:

- defining what you mean by "excellent," "good," or "average" work
- communicating instructional goals to parents
- communicating to parents, students, and others what constitutes excellence
- providing guidelines for making unbiased and consistent judgments
- documenting how judgments are made
- helping students evaluate their own work

When specifying criteria, it is necessary to summarize the dimensions of performance that are used to assign student work to a given level. The dimensions are what you consider to be essential qualities of the performance. They can be identified by asking yourself some questions: What are the attributes of good performance? How do I know when students have reached different levels of performance? What examples do I have of each level? What do I look for when evaluating student work? Criteria are best developed by being clear on what constitutes excellence as well as proficiency in the performance area of interest. By identifying and prioritizing key elements, the most important aspects of the performance will be utilized.

Once the dimensions have been identified, you can develop a quantitative or qualitative scale to indicate different levels of performance. Label each level as "good," "excellent," "poor," and so on. Examples of criteria for different types of performance are shown in Figure 2.4. Many more examples are presented in Chapters 8 and 9.

Although it is very helpful for students to know the criteria as communicated in a scoring rubric, it is even more helpful if students can see an example of a finished student product or performance and your evaluation of it. These examples are called **exemplars** or **anchors**. For example, if you have established four levels of performance, an exemplar of work at each level will make the criteria more clear. To emphasize once again, you should share the exemplars with students *before* they begin their work. This will help students internalize the standards that you use and know what constitutes excellence. The exemplars could be as simple as giving students examples of the type of math word problems that will be on a test and how their answers will be graded. Of course you don't want to give students something that they will memorize or copy, but you do need to give them a sense of the difficulty of the task.

Expectations

It is important to distinguish expectations from standards and learning targets. An **expectation** is what you communicate to your students about the level of performance that you think they will be able to demonstrate. This is different from the learning target because it is based on students' previous achievement, aptitude, motivation, and other factors. It may be reasonable to think that most, if not all, of your students will not be able to attain the standard or the highest level of performance. For example, we set a high standard for what constitutes a good play in football, but our expectations for middle school students differ from what we expect of professionals. In school you may have a high standard for a research paper, but your expectations of the students, because of their lack of previous learning, may not meet this high standard. If your expectations are the same as your standards, it is likely that either your standards will drop to accommodate most students or your expectations will not be consistent with the reality of how students can perform. In either case, you are not doing what is in the best interests of the students. If your standards are lowered, students may attain a false sense of competency; if your expectations are too high, students may be frustrated at what they see as impossible demands. What you need to do is make high standards clear and then teach in a way that is consistent with realistic, yet challenging expectations. You want students to go the extra step, so be explicit with them about why the standards are high.

FIGURE 2.4 Examples of Performance Criteria

Making an Oral Presentation[1]

Excellent	Pupil consistently faces audience, stands straight, and maintains eye contact; voice projects well and clearly; pacing and tone variation appropriate; well organized, points logically and completely presented; brief summary at end
Good	Pupil usually faces audience, stands straight, and makes eye contact; voice projection good, but pace and clarity vary during talk; well organized but repetitive; occasional poor choice of words and incomplete summary
Fair	Pupil fidgety; some eye contact and facial expression change; uneven voice projection, not heard by all in room, some words slurred; loosely organized, repetitive, contains many incomplete thoughts; little summarization.
Poor	Pupil body movements distracting, little eye contact or voice change; words slurred, speaks in monotone, does not project voice beyond first few rows, no consistent or logical pacing; rambling presentation, little organization with no differentiation between major and minor points; no summary

Knows the Difference between Statements and Questions

More Than Adequate	Successfully identifies twenty of twenty-five sentences as statements or questions, lists three characteristics of statements and questions, generates four original examples of statements and questions
Adequate	Successfully identifies eighteen of twenty-five sentences as statements or questions, lists two characteristics of statements and questions, generates two examples of statements and questions
Less Than Adequate	Successfully identifies fewer than eighteen of twenty-five sentences as statements or questions, lists one or no characteristics of statements and questions, generates no examples of statements or questions

Estimation[2]

Not Understanding	Makes unrealistic guesses, does not use strategies to refine estimates, cannot model or explain the specified strategy, cannot apply strategy even with prompts
Developing Understanding	Refines guesser estimates by partitioning/comparing, etc., can model, explain, and apply a strategy when asked, has some strategies, others are not yet in place, uses estimation when appropriate
Understanding/ Applying	Makes realistic guesses or estimates, refines estimates to suggest a more exact estimate, uses estimation when appropriate, recognizes and readily uses a variety of strategies

[1]*Source:* Airasian, P. W. (2001). *Classroom assessment* (4th ed.). New York: McGraw-Hill, pp. 231–232. Reproduced with permission of the McGraw-Hill Companies.

[2]*Source:* Beyer, A., & others (1993). *Alternative assessment: Evaluating student performance in elementary mathematics.* Ann Arbor Public Schools. Palo Alto, CA: Dale Seymour Publications, p. 7. Used by permission of Pearson Education, Inc.

Case Study for Reflection

Ms. Beckner decided to try a new way to assess her third-grade students' science projects. She used a rubric with specific criteria, which both she and her students created. She wanted students to be aware of the different components that need to be a part of their final presentation. She prepared the first two areas for the rubric:

Blast off for an "A"

1. Students' science projects will result in an appropriate demonstration product, including an attractive visual display and a two-page report. (Examples of last years' projects in hallway.)
2. Students' two-page report with their project will clearly describe the scientific concept their project represents. (Examples on back table.)

Three other levels (Mission Control, Ground Crew, and Delayed Flight) were also identified, with two criteria for each. After the exemplars were prepared and on display, Ms. Beckner discussed plans for science projects and asked her students to help her decide what a great science project might look like. Students' ideas were all put on the board, and from these, Ms. Beckner guided them through a selection process for two more criteria for an "A" science project. Through the use of good examples of previous student work, these students had a clearer idea of what the words "appropriate demonstration product" and "attractive visual display" in criterion 1 and "clearly describe" in criterion 2 actually meant. They also had internalized the assessment criteria by participating in the creation of some of them. After the projects were completed, Ms. Beckner found that her students not only scored better on their projects than in previous years, but they enjoyed the process much more because they understood what was expected of them.

Does all this planning for assessment take away too much time from actual teaching of the content?

What are some problems that might arise when using student suggestions for determining criteria?

What did Ms. Beckner do right in coming up with the criteria?

What would be some additional examples of criteria that could be used in this assignment?

Learning Targets

What, then, is a learning target? In this book **learning target** is defined as a statement of student performance that includes *both* a description of what students should know, understand, and be able to do at the end of a unit of instruction *and* as much as possible and feasible about the criteria for judging the level of performance demonstrated (see Figure 2.5).

The word *learning* is used to convey that targets emphasize the importance of how students will *change*. Learning implies a focus on the demonstrated competence of students, not on what you do as a teacher. Change reflects the need to know more than what they know or do at the end of instruction. Change requires

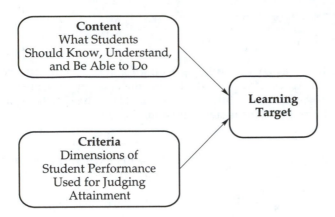

FIGURE 2.5 Components of Learning Targets

knowledge of where students are in relation to the target before instruction as well as at the end of instruction.

It is essential to include something about the criteria for judging levels of performance in the target. Think for a moment about a target at which one would shoot an arrow. The performance might be stated as "the student will hit the target with an arrow." But you need to communicate more than simply "hit the target." How far away is the target? How large is the target? Does it matter where the arrow hits the target? In other words, you need to indicate something about the dimensions of the performance that translate into qualitatively different levels of performance. Two teachers can state the same learning objective, but if different criteria are used to evaluate the performance, then in reality students in each class are learning something different.

A similar case can be made for learning subjects in school. The target "students will know state capitals in the United States" means something different if the student has to recall all fifty capitals from memory rather than if the student can correctly match half of the names of capitals with states. You must be able to articulate, as part of the target, the criteria you will use to judge performance, and remember, students should know these criteria *before* instruction. This does not need to be done in a single sentence. It is easier, in fact, to think about targets as a description of what will be assessed and how it will be judged. These two aspects of the target can be separated into different sentences. For example, this describes what students need to know:

> Students will demonstrate an understanding of the effect of the sun on seasons, length of day, weather, and climate.

Information about criteria could be added with another sentence:

> Students will demonstrate their understanding by correctly answering short-answer questions about each relationship.

If a matching test is used, try this description:

> Students will demonstrate their understanding by correctly matching all effects with the four elements discussed.

In practice, you would not be so wordy in describing the target. It is understood that "students will demonstrate" so you can simply say "understand effect of sun on seasons, length of day, weather, and climate." The information about criteria can be shortened by simply referring to "matching" or "short answer."

Learning targets for units of instruction in Figure 2.6 include both what students should know or be able to do and some aspects of the criteria. Note that some are written as one sentence and some are more detailed than others in aspects of criteria. The intent is not to worry about including specific aspects of criteria. Rather, the hope is that you will be aware of the effect of the criteria on the nature of the learning that occurs and your evaluation of it.

FIGURE 2.6   Examples of Unit Learning Targets

Students will be able to explain how various cultures are different and how cultures influence people's beliefs and lives by answering orally a comprehensive set of questions about cultural differences and their effects.

Students will demonstrate their knowledge of the parts of a plant by filling in words on a diagram for all parts studied.

Students will demonstrate their understanding of citizenship by correctly identifying whether previously unread statements about citizenship are true or false. A large number of items is used to sample most of the content learned.

Students will be able to explain why the American Constitution is important by writing an essay that indicates what would happen if we abolished our Constitution. The papers will be graded holistically, looking for evidence of reasons, knowledge of the constitution, and organization.

Students will know the difference between components of sentences by correctly identifying verbs, adverbs, adjectives, nouns, and pronouns in seven of eight long, complex sentences.

Students will be able to multiply fractions by correctly computing eight of ten fraction problems. The problems are new to the students; some are similar to "challenge" questions in the book.

Students will be able to use their knowledge of addition, subtraction, division, and multiplication to correctly solve word problems that are similar to those used in the sixth-grade standardized test.

Students will demonstrate their understanding of how visual art conveys ideas and feelings by correctly indicating, orally, how examples of art communicate ideas and feelings. Grades will be based on equal weighing of ideas and feelings.

Types of Learning Targets

How do you identify appropriate learning targets for your students? It is helpful to begin by realizing that many different kinds of targets are appropriate, because in most classrooms a variety of outcomes are stressed. The challenge is to organize and prioritize your targets to reflect what is most important. To do this, you need to think about a few categories that encompass typical types of learning targets. In this book, categories described by Stiggins and Conklin (1992) are used because these categories are viewed by teachers as important and because each type of target is clearly related to different approaches to assessment. The major categories of targets (see Figure 2.7) are introduced in this chapter and then expanded on and linked with specific kinds of assessment in subsequent chapters. Note that the categories are not presented as a hierarchy or in order. None of the categories is more important than any other. Each simply represents types of targets that can be identified and used for assessment.

Knowledge and Simple Understanding Learning Targets

Knowledge of subject matter is the foundation on which all other learning is based. As such, it represents what students need to *know* to solve problems and perform skills. This knowledge may be as simple as mastery of facts and information demonstrated through recall (e.g., remembering dates, events, places, definitions, and principles), or it may involve simple understanding (e.g., summarizing a paragraph, explaining charts, concept learning, or giving examples). *Knowing* usually refers to more than simple rote memory, even though some rote memorization may be needed. A student can *know* how to pronounce certain words by memorizing the links between letters and sounds, but it is also necessary to *understand* the meanings of the words.

FIGURE 2.7   Types of Learning Targets

Knowledge and Simple Understanding	Student mastery of substantive subject matter and procedures
Deep Understanding and Reasoning	Student ability to use knowledge to reason and solve problems
Skills	Student ability to demonstrate achievement-related skills, such as reading aloud, interpersonal interaction, speaking in a second language, operating equipment correctly and safely, conducting experiments, operating computers, and performing psychomotor behaviors
Products	Student ability to create achievement-related products such as written reports, oral presentations, and art products
Affective	Student attainment of affective states such as attitudes, values, interests, and self-efficacy

Deep Understanding and Reasoning Learning Targets

Recent advances in cognitive psychology and computer accessibility to information have resulted in increased attention to more sophisticated understanding and thinking skills. Such capabilities may be described with a number of different terms, including *problem solving, critical thinking, analysis, synthesis, comparing, intellectual skills, intellectual abilities, higher-order thinking skills,* and *judgment.* Research in cognitive psychology has shown that our ability to use knowledge to think about things is dependent on how we construct the knowledge and the demands that are placed on using the knowledge to reason and solve problems. This research has helped us to classify and understand what is termed "deep" understanding and the different reasoning processes that are used. Several reasoning frameworks are presented in Chapter 7. The challenge with these targets is defining precisely what is meant by *reasoning, critical thinking, problem solving,* and so on. The frameworks will help you to formulate definitions that meet your needs.

Skill Learning Targets

A skill is something that the student demonstrates, something that is done. Although, in one sense, recalling information and showing reasoning skills by answering questions is *doing* something, skill learning targets involve a behavior in which the knowledge, understanding, and reasoning are used overtly. For example, at one level students can demonstrate their knowledge of how a microscope works by recalling correct procedural steps, but skill is needed when the students show the teacher how to do the steps with a microscope. It is like the difference between knowing how to manage classrooms by listing seven principles of classroom management, even analyzing case studies of classroom management, and actually being able to manage students in a classroom. Thus, in elementary school, students are expected to demonstrate reading skills and how to hold pencils to write; older students may be required to demonstrate oral presentation skills or speak in a foreign language. Most skills require procedural knowledge and reasoning to use the knowledge in an actual performance.

Product Learning Targets

Products, like skills, are dependent on prior attainment of knowledge and reasoning targets. Products are samples of student work that demonstrate the ability to use knowledge and reasoning in the creation of a tangible product such as a term paper, report, artwork, or other project. Thus, products are used to demonstrate knowledge, understanding, reasoning, and skills. Performance-based assessments are examples of how product learning targets are measured.

Affective Learning Targets

This final category is broad, complex, and, to a certain extent, controversial. The term **affective** includes emotions, feelings, and beliefs, which are different from

cognitive learning such as knowledge, reasoning, and skills. Affect can be described as being positive or negative, and most teachers hope that students will develop positive attitudes toward school subjects and learning, themselves as learners, other students, and school. Affect can also refer to motivational dispositions, values, and morals. Although most teachers believe that positive affect is an important outcome as well as a determinant of cognitive learning, many believe that schools should be concerned only with cognitive learning targets. Because affective learning targets are complex, they are difficult—but not impossible—to assess.

Sources of Learning Targets

The categories of learning targets just presented provide a start to identifying the focus of instruction and assessment (and provide the organizational structure of this book), but you will find other sources that are more specific about learning targets. Several of these sources are identified in the following sections.

Bloom's Taxonomy of Objectives

Perhaps the best-known source for conceptualizing learning targets is the *Taxonomy of Educational Objectives I: Cognitive Domain* (Bloom, 1956). As implied in the title, this initial taxonomy covered cognitive learning objectives. Later publications of the taxonomy focused on the affective and psychomotor areas. Thus, "Bloom's taxonomy," as it has become known, consists of three domains—cognitive, affective, and psychomotor.

Bloom's taxonomy of the cognitive domain has received considerable attention and has been used to specify action verbs to accompany different types of cognitive learning (see Figure 2.8; other domains are presented in later chapters). The cognitive domain contains six levels. Each level represents an increasingly complex type of cognition. Although the cognitive domain is often characterized as having "lower" and "higher" levels, only the knowledge level is considered by authors of the taxonomy to be lower; all other levels are higher. The first level, knowledge, describes several different types of knowledge. The remaining five levels are referred to as "intellectual abilities and skills."

Bloom's taxonomy can be very helpful when formulating specific learning targets, even though this categorization of cognitive tasks was created more than forty years ago, and since that time there have been significant changes in the educational and psychological theories that formed the basis for the taxonomy. Current theories emphasize thinking processes, characterize the learner as an active information processor, and stress domain-specific thinking and learning. The taxonomy, in comparison, was based on a focus on outcomes or objectives, learners as an object and as a reactor in the learning situation, and broad, single organizing principles that cut across different domains (Tittle, Hecht, & Moore, 1993). The taxonomies are still valuable, however, in providing a comprehensive list of possible learning objectives with clear action verbs that operationalize the targets.

FIGURE 2.8   Bloom's Taxonomy of Educational Objectives: Cognitive Domain

Level	Illustrative Verbs
Knowledge: Recalling and remembering previously learned material, including specific facts, events, persons, dates, methods, procedures, concepts, principles, and theories	Names, matches, lists, recalls, selects, retells, states, defines, describes, labels, reproduces
Comprehension: Understanding and grasping the meaning of something; includes translation from one symbolic form to another (e.g., percent into fractions), interpretation, explanation, prediction, inferences, restating, estimation, generalization, and other uses that demonstrate understanding	Explains, converts, interprets, paraphrases, predicts, estimates, rearranges, rephrases, summarizes
Application: Use of abstract ideas, rules, or generalized methods in novel, concrete situations	Changes, demonstrates, modifies, produces, solves, constructs, applies, uses, shows
Analysis: Breaking down a communication into constituent parts or elements and understanding the relationship among different elements	Distinguishes, compares, subdivides, diagrams, differentiates, relates, classifies, categorizes
Synthesis: Arranging and combining elements and parts into novel patterns or structures	Generates, combines, constructs, assembles, formulates, forecasts, projects, proposes, integrates
Evaluation: Judging the quality, worth, or value of something according to established criteria (e.g., determining the adequacy of evidence to support a conclusion)	Justifies, criticizes, decides, judges, argues, concludes, supports, defends, evaluates, verifies, confirms

Bloom's Revised Taxonomy of Objectives

Recently, a revision to Bloom's original taxonomy was proposed "to refocus educators' attention on the value of the original *Handbook* . . . and to incorporate new knowledge and thought into the framework" (Anderson & Krathwohl, 2001, p. xxi–xxii). The revised taxonomy uses a two-dimensional model as a framework for identifying and writing learning objectives. The knowledge dimension, summarized in Figure 2.9, includes four levels that describe different types of knowledge with a number of subcategories. The cognitive process dimension includes six major categories and numerous subcategories that describe increasingly complex thinking (Figure 2.10). The reason for dividing the original single list into two dimensions is to create a matrix in which educators can identify the specific nature of the learning that is targeted.

FIGURE 2.9   Knowledge Dimension of Revised Taxonomy

Major Types	Definition
Factual Knowledge	The basic elements students must know to be acquainted with a discipline or solve problems in it
Conceptual Knowledge	The interrelationships among the basic elements within a larger structure that enable them to function together
Procedural Knowledge	How to do something, methods of inquiry, and criteria for using skills, algorithms, techniques, and methods
Metacognitive Knowledge	Knowledge of cognition in general as well as awareness and knowledge of one's own cognition

Source: Adapted from Lorin W. Anderson & David R. Krathwohl, *A taxonomy for learning, teaching, and assessing: A revision of Bloom's taxonomy of educational obejctives.* Published by Allyn and Bacon, Boston, MA. Copyright © 2001 by Pearson Education. Reprinted by permission of the publisher.

FIGURE 2.10   Cognitive Process Dimension of New Taxonomy

Major Types	Definition
Remember	Retrieve relevant knowledge from long-term memory
Understand	Construct meaning from instructional messages, including oral, written, and graphic communication
Apply	Carry out or use a procedure in a given situation
Analyze	Break material into its constituent parts and determine how the parts relate to one another and to an overall structure or pattern
Evaluate	Make judgments based on criteria and standards
Create	Put elements together to form a coherent or functional whole; reorganize elements into a new pattern or structure

Source: Adapted from Lorin W. Anderson & David R. Krathwohl, *A taxonomy for learning, teaching, and assessing: A revision of Bloom's taxonomy of educational obejctives.* Published by Allyn and Bacon, Boston, MA. Copyright © 2001 by Pearson Education. Reprinted by permission of the publisher.

For each learning objective, there would be a noun that describes the type of knowledge and a verb that indicates the level of cognitive processing that is needed. The advantage of this, according to the authors, is that teachers and administrators will be able to be more precise than they could be with the older taxonomy. Figure 2.11 shows how an educational objective could be classified according to the two dimensions.

Only time will tell if the new two-dimensional taxonomy will take hold. It is clear that a revised taxonomy was needed, but this version may be more complicated for teachers to work with and thus less practical. Further delineation of each of the dimensions will be incorporated in Chapters 6 and 7.

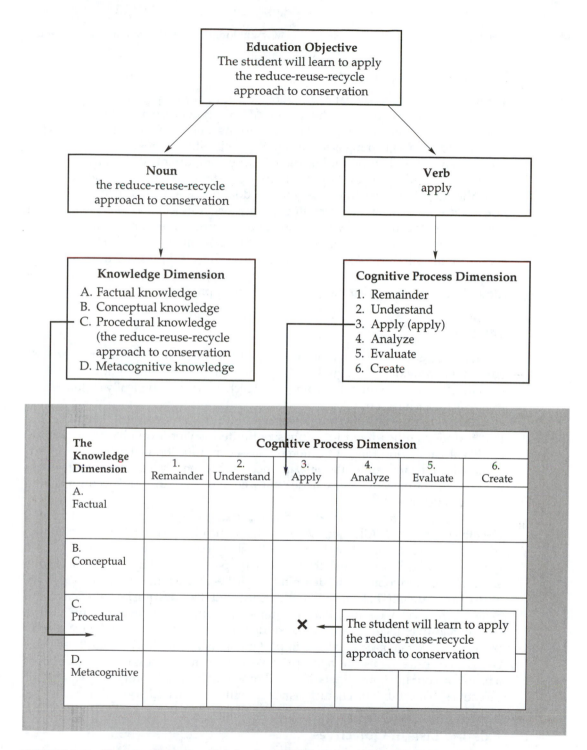

FIGURE 2.11   How an Objective (the Student Will Learn to Apply the Reduce-Reuse-Recycle Approach to Conservation) Is Classified in the Taxonomy Table

Source: Adapted from Lorin W. Anderson & David R. Krathwohl, *A taxonomy for learning, teaching, and assessing: A revision of Bloom's taxonomy of educational objectives.* Published by Allyn and Bacon, Boston, MA. Copyright © 2001 by Pearson Education. Reprinted by permission of the publisher.

Professional Preparation

Throughout your professional preparation you have been exposed to essential principles and methods of different disciplines. As you master each discipline you will be able to identify what is most important for learning. Perhaps you have heard that the best way to learn something is to teach it. Put yourself in the role of teacher even as you take courses. What specific knowledge is most important? What do you need to be able to do with the knowledge? What are *you* doing as a student? Do you *really know* the subject, inside and out, so you can do more as a teacher than simply read notes or do exactly what the curriculum guide says? You will find that the quality of your assessments will follow from the depth of your understanding of what you teach. The more you understand, the better the assessments. It is also important to keep current with the professional literature in both the subjects you teach and education in general. This literature will keep you up-to-date and will give you many ideas about the kinds of learning targets that are appropriate.

Textbooks

Most textbooks for students are accompanied by an instructor's guide or a teacher's edition that provides information to help you plan lessons, deliver appropriate instruction, and assess student learning. The teacher's edition typically includes "objectives" for each lesson.

Although the objectives in a teacher's edition can be useful, keep in mind that textbook authors tend to emphasize limited, lower-level objectives that are applicable to a wide range of different classes and locations. Furthermore, textbook objectives are neither the *only,* nor necessarily the *best,* source for your learning targets. The objectives need to be reviewed in relation to your specific teaching situation and approach.

Three major criteria can be used to evaluate the appropriateness of textbook objectives (Brophy & Alleman, 1991). First, are the objectives stated with clear descriptions of what students will know or be able to do following instruction? Even if the behavior is clearly stated, the textbook probably will not indicate what criteria should be used to complete the learning target. Second, are the objectives appropriate for your students? Have your students learned the prerequisite knowledge and skills? Is the level of learning that is required appropriate for your students? Third, do the objectives include most of the student outcomes? How complete and comprehensive are the objectives? Are important areas overlooked? Using these three criteria, you can appraise the appropriateness and completeness of the objectives as a basis for your learning targets. You will probably need to modify and expand the objectives to meet unique characteristics of both yourself and your students.

Existing Lists of Objectives

You will find it helpful to locate and review lists of objectives that have already been developed. A number of sources can be used to locate these lists. Most methods of teaching textbooks, particularly those in each subject area, contain illustrative objectives as well as references that can be consulted. Yearbooks and handbooks in different disciplines sometimes contain objectives. Special reports issued by professional groups, such as the National Council of Teachers of Mathematics, the National Council of Teachers of English, the National Council for the Social Studies, and the National Science Teachers Association, contain extensive lists of objectives that emphasize thinking skills and applications to real-life problems. For example, the report *Science for All Americans: Project 2061,* prepared by the American Association for the Advancement of Science, recommends four goals for science education: understanding scientific endeavors, developing scientific perspectives about the world, developing historical and social views on science, and developing scientific "habits of mind."

An excellent source is state- or local-level curriculum guides. Although these guides may present objectives at different levels of specificity, they are very helpful in their comprehensive nature of critical objectives. In whatever state you are teaching, it would be worthwhile to contact your state department of education and inquire about existing curriculum guides or frameworks. If you are in a large school or school district, there will probably be a list of instructional objectives for you that you should consult as a starting point. In addition, most states will be responding to the national standards movement by developing a set of state-level core standards for all students.

National and State Standards

I have already pointed out that national content and performance standards have been developed in several areas. These standards will be excellent sources for your learning targets because they are being developed with criteria that result in high-quality, complex learning. The national Technical Planning Group (Wurtz, 1993) suggests that standards should be:

- *World class:* at least as challenging as current standards in other leading industrial countries, though not necessarily the same
- *Important and focused:* parsimonious, while including those elements that represent the most important knowledge and skills within a discipline
- *Useful:* developing what is needed for citizenship, employment, and lifelong learning
- *Reflective of broad consensus building:* resulting from a process of comment, feedback, and revision, including educators and the lay public
- *Balanced:* between the competing requirements for depth and breadth, being definite or specific, and being flexible or adaptable; also balanced between theory or principles and facts or information, formal knowledge and applications, and being forward-looking and traditional
- *Accurate and sound:* reflecting the best scholarship within the discipline
- *Clear and usable:* sufficiently clear so that parents, teachers, and students can understand what the standards mean and what the standards require of them

- *Assessable:* sufficiently specific so their attainment can be measured in terms that are meaningful to teachers, students, parents, test makers and users, the public, and others
- *Adaptable:* permitting flexibility in implementation needed for local control, state and regional variation, and differing individual interests and cultural traditions
- *Developmentally appropriate:* challenging but, with sustained effort, attainable by all students at elementary, middle, and high school levels (pp. iii–iv)

As you can see, this is a most ambitious set of criteria! Most of the groups working on the standards have completed their work The mail and Internet addresses and phone numbers of the councils and associations working on different subject areas are contained in Appendix C.

The strengths and limitations of these six sources of objectives for establishing learning targets are summarized in Figure 2.12. Initially you may find that textbooks and existing lists of objectives contain ideas that will be most easily translated into practice.

FIGURE 2.12　Strengths and Limitations of Different Sources for Establishing Learning Targets

Source	Strengths	Limitations
Bloom's Taxonomy	Established; well known; comprehensive; contains action verbs; hierarchical design	Dated; based on behavioristic learning theories; not consistent with recent cognitive theories of learning
Revision of Bloom's Taxonomy	Consistent with recent learning theory; contains action verbs	New; untested; may be overly complex
Professional Preparation	Focus on essentials of a discipline; personal experience	Difficult to translate into targets and keep up-to-date; may be confined to a specific type of target
Textbooks	Directly related to instruction; easily adapted	Tend to emphasize lower-level targets; lacks criteria; need to be modified
Existing Lists of Objectives	Comprehensive; good ideas for targets	May not relate well to a local situation; need to be modified
National and State Standards	High standards; comprehensive; reflects national expertise; reflects current research on learning; discipline specific	May not relate well to local situation; need to be modified; may not be politically acceptable

Criteria for Selecting Learning Targets

After you have consulted existing sources of objectives and begun the task of selecting your learning targets, you will need to make some choices about which ones to keep, which need revision, and which are not feasible. The following criteria will help you judge the adequacy of your learning targets. They are summarized in Figure 2.13 in the form of a checklist.

1. *Establish the right number of learning targets.* The number of different learning targets will vary, depending on the length of the instructional segment and the complexity of the target. Obviously, the longer the instructional period, the more targets are needed. Also, more complex targets, such as those requiring reasoning, take more time. I have found the following general rules of thumb appropriate: 40–60 targets for a year; 8–12 for a unit; 1–3 for a single lesson. Hundreds of targets for a year are clearly too many.

2. *Establish comprehensive learning targets.* It is essential that the targets represent all types of important learning from the instructional unit. Be careful not to overemphasize knowledge targets. Try to maintain a balance among the five areas (knowledge and simple understanding, deep understanding and reasoning, skills, products, and affect). Higher priority may be given to targets that integrate several of these areas. Do not rely too heavily on textbook objectives or teacher's guides.

3. *Establish learning targets that reflect school goals.* Your targets should be clearly related to more general school, district, and state learning goals. Priority may be given to targets that focus on school improvement plans or restructuring efforts.

4. *Establish learning targets that are challenging yet feasible.* It is important to challenge students and seek the highest level of accomplishment for them. You will need to develop targets that are not too easy or too hard. It is also important to assess the readiness of your students to establish these challenging targets. Do they have necessary perquisite skills and knowledge? Are they developmentally ready for the challenge? Do they have needed motivation and attitudes? Will students see the targets as too easy? As we will see in the next chapter, these questions need to be answered through proper assessment before your final selection of learning targets, instructional activities, and your assessment of student learning.

FIGURE 2.13 Checklist for Selecting Learning Targets

✓ Are there too many or too few targets?
✓ Are all important types of learning included?
✓ Do the targets reflect school goals?
✓ Will the targets challenge students to do their best work?
✓ Are the targets consistent with research on learning and motivation?
✓ Are the targets established before instruction?

5. *Establish learning targets that are consistent with current principles of learning and motivation.* Because learning targets are the basis for learning and instruction, it is important that what you set as a target will promote learning that is consistent with what we know about how learning occurs and what motivates students. For example, will the targets promote long-term retention in a meaningful way? Do the targets reflect students' intrinsic interests and needs? Do the targets represent learning that will be applicable to life outside the classroom? Will the targets encourage a variety of instructional approaches and activities?

After you identify the targets, it is best to write them out before teaching. This will allow a ready reference throughout the lesson and free you to concentrate on the fast-paced and complex activities in the classroom. From year to year you will find it necessary to revisit your targets and make appropriate modifications depending on changes in your students, curriculum, textbooks, and state requirements.

Summary

Learning targets—what students should know and be able to do and the criteria for judging student performance—are contrasted in this chapter with more traditional terms such as *goals, objectives,* and *expectations.* The major points include the following:

- Goals are broad statements about student learning.
- Instructional or behavioral objectives are specific statements that indicate what students should know and be able to do at the end of an instructional unit.
- Expectations are the teacher's beliefs about what students are capable of achieving.
- Goals, objectives, and expectations focus on what students do rather than on what the teacher does in instruction.
- Experience has demonstrated that it is not practical to write very specific behavioral objectives that include all aspects of the criteria and testing conditions.
- Learning targets need to contain as much about criteria as possible and feasible, because criteria are critical in establishing the standards on which performance toward the learning target is judged.
- Criteria are clearly stated dimensions of student performance that the teacher examines in making judgments about student proficiency. These criteria should be public and explained to students before each instructional unit.
- Exemplars and anchors are important examples that help students understand how teacher evaluations are made.
- Five types of learning targets are introduced: knowledge and simple understanding, deep understanding and reasoning, skill, product, and affect.
- Sources for constructing learning targets include Bloom's taxonomy, the revision of Bloom's taxonomy, your professional preparation, textbooks, existing lists of objectives, and national and state standards.
- Criteria to be used in selecting targets were indicated. You should strive for the right number of comprehensive, challenging targets that will reflect school goals and will be consistent with current principles of learning and motivation.

SELF-INSTRUCTIONAL REVIEW EXERCISES

1. Identify each of the following as a goal (G), behavioral objective (BO), or expectation (E).

   a. My students will pass all their exams.
   b. Students will be familiar with global geography.
   c. It is unlikely that Tom will finish his test.
   d. Students will answer ten of twelve questions about ancient Egypt in fifteen minutes without use of notes.

2. What does the term *criteria* have in common with behavioral objectives? How is it different from what is contained in objectives?

3. Suppose a teacher pulls out a graded paper that was handed in by a student from a previous year's class and distributes it to the class. What would the paper be called in relation to assessment?

   a. Rubric
   b. Anchor
   c. Scoring criteria
   d. Performance criteria

4. Give at least three reasons why using public criteria that are shared with students before instruction is an effective teaching/learning tool for evaluating student work.

5. Why is it important to include criteria in learning targets?

6. Identify each of the following as a knowledge or simple understanding (K), deep understanding or reasoning (R), skill (S), product (P), or affect (A) target.

   a. shooting free throws
   b. recalling historical facts from the Revolutionary War
   c. comparing vertebrates to invertebrates
   d. identifying the organs in a dissected frog
   e. working cooperatively with others
   f. building a three-dimensional structure from sticks and glue

7. Why may Bloom's original taxonomy of educational objectives not be the best source for identifying classroom learning targets?

8. What are some examples of at least one learning target in each of the five areas that could be stated for you concerning the content of this book?

ANSWERS TO SELF-INSTRUCTIONAL REVIEW EXERCISES

1. a. E, b. G, c. E., d. BO.

2. Criteria are part of what would be included in a behavioral objective. Criteria, in contrast to objectives, contain descriptions of different levels of performance.

3. b.

4. Could have selected from communicating goals and different levels of work to parents, documenting judgments, helping students evaluate their own work, motivating students.

5. Criteria are needed to completely understand the nature of the target and what it takes to achieve different levels of performance. Without criteria, targets are statements similar to simple behavioral objectives (without conditions, criteria, and audience).

6. a. S, b. K, c. R, d. K, e. A, f. P.

7. Bloom's taxonomy is not aligned very well with more recent research on learning and motivation.

8. For example,

Knowledge and Simple Understanding: Students are able to recall and write accurately 80 percent of the definitions of key terms in the chapter.

Deep Understanding and Reasoning: Students are able to analyze five examples of learning targets and modify them in writing so that they correspond better to the criteria in the chapter.

Skill: Students will use the library computer system to locate critiques of three published tests.

Product: Students can construct learning targets after receiving an instructional unit on teaching fractions. The targets are judged by the extent to which criteria are included. Or students can construct a multiple-choice test that corresponds to the criteria in the book.

Affect: Students increase the importance they give to constructing criteria for learning targets.

SUGGESTIONS FOR ACTION RESEARCH

1. Obtain some examples of student work from teachers that demonstrate different levels of performance on the same assessment. How easy is it to see how the examples are different? See if the criteria you use to differentiate the examples are the same as the criteria the teacher used.

2. In small groups, generate some examples of student performance on the same learning target that would demonstrate qualitatively different levels of achievement concerning the content of this chapter or Chapter 1.

3. Examine textbook objectives and national standards in your area of expertise. How are they similar, and how are they different?

4. Interview a teacher and ask about using textbook objectives. How useful are these objectives? What determines whether or not the teacher will use them?

5. In a group of three or four other students, develop a scoring rubric that could be used for judging the performance of a student on an assignment, project, or test that was used in a school setting. Find or generate examples of student work that illustrate different levels of performance.

CHAPTER

3

Establishing High-Quality Classroom Assessments

Classroom assessment consists of determining purpose and learning targets, systematically obtaining information from students, interpreting the information collected, and using the information. In Chapter 2, establishing learning targets was identified as the first step in conducting assessments. Once you have determined *what* to assess, you will probably be concerned with *how* to assess it. That is, what methods of data collection will you use to gather the information? At this point it is important to keep in mind several criteria that determine the quality and credibility of the assessment methods you choose. In this chapter, we review these criteria and

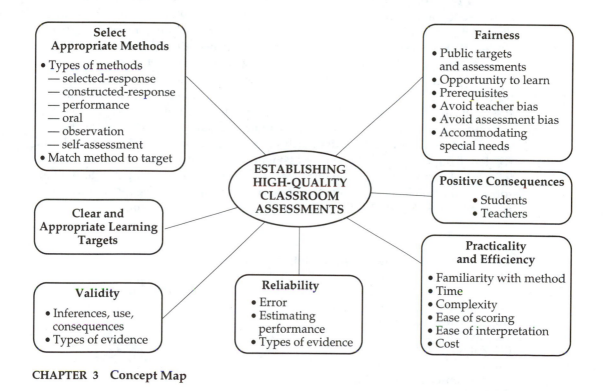

Select Appropriate Methods

- Types of methods
  — selected-response
  — constructed-response
  — performance
  — oral
  — observation
  — self-assessment
- Match method to target

Clear and Appropriate Learning Targets

Validity

- Inferences, use, consequences
- Types of evidence

ESTABLISHING HIGH-QUALITY CLASSROOM ASSESSMENTS

Reliability

- Error
- Estimating performance
- Types of evidence

Fairness

- Public targets and assessments
- Opportunity to learn
- Prerequisites
- Avoid teacher bias
- Avoid assessment bias
- Accommodating special needs

Positive Consequences

- Students
- Teachers

Practicality and Efficiency

- Familiarity with method
- Time
- Complexity
- Ease of scoring
- Ease of interpretation
- Cost

CHAPTER 3   Concept Map

provide suggestions for practical steps you can take to keep the quality of your assessments high.

What Is High-Quality Classroom Assessment?

Until recently, the quality of classroom assessment was determined by the extent to which specific psychometric standards of validity, reliability, and efficiency were met. These standards were originally derived for large-scale, published, standardized objective tests and are still very important, at least conceptually, for most types of assessments. However, for published tests the emphasis is on highly technical, statistically sophisticated standards. Thus, complex statistical procedures, such as correlation, are used to provide estimates of validity, reliability, and measurement error. Different types of validity and reliability are stressed, along with sampling error to estimate efficiency. To interpret standardized tests properly, it is necessary to have a basic understanding of these properties.

But in most classrooms such technical qualities have little relevance because the purpose of the assessment is different. This is not to say that the *ideas* of validity and reliability are not important criteria for classroom assessment. High-quality classroom assessment involves many other criteria as well, substituting technically pleasing types of validity and reliability with concerns about how the assessments influence learning and provide fair and credible reporting of student achievement. For teachers the primary determinant of quality is how the information influences students. Thus, the focus is on the use and consequences of the results and what the assessments get students to do, rather than on a detailed inspection of the test itself.

High-quality classroom assessments, then, are technically sound and provide results that demonstrate and improve targeted student learning. High-quality assessments also inform instructional decision making. As pointed out in Chapter 1, our understanding of learning and motivation, and our realization that much more is demanded of students than demonstrating simple knowledge, has changed how we define high-quality classroom assessments, and because assessment is an essential part of instruction, high-quality teaching and learning is impossible without sound and credible assessment. The criteria of high-quality classroom assessment are presented in Figure 3.1. Each will be summarized in some detail.

FIGURE 3.1   Criteria for Ensuring High-Quality Classroom Assessments

Clear and appropriate learning targets
Appropriateness of assessment methods
Validity
Reliability
Fairness
Positive consequences
Practicality and efficiency

Clear and Appropriate Learning Targets

As discussed in Chapter 1, sound assessment begins with clear and appropriate learning targets. Remember that the learning target includes both what students know and can do and the criteria for judging student performance. Are the targets at the right level of difficulty to motivate students? Is there adequate balance among different types of targets? Are the targets consistent with your overall goals and the goals of the school and district? Are the targets comprehensive, covering all major dimensions that you hope to change and need feedback about? Are the criteria for judging student performance clear?

Appropriateness of Assessment Methods

As you are well aware, a number of different types of assessment methods can be used in the classroom. Some of these methods were introduced in Chapter 1. Although your ultimate choice of an assessment method will depend on how well all of the criteria in Figure 3.1 are met, the match between type of target and method is very important. Even though most targets may be measured by several methods, the reality of teaching is that certain methods measure some types of targets better than other methods do. That is, particular methods are more likely to provide quality assessments for certain types of targets. Thus, one of your first tasks, once you have identified the targets, is to match them with methods.

Types of Assessment Methods

Many different approaches or methods are used to assess students. I have categorized them in Figure 3.2 according to the nature and characteristics of each method. A brief description of the methods is presented to facilitate an understanding of how the methods should be matched to targets. The methods are covered in much more detail in later chapters.

Figure 3.2 divides different methods of assessment into four major categories: selected-response, constructed-response, teacher observation, and self-assessment. The major distinguishing characteristic of most classroom assessments is whether the items use selected-response or constructed-response formats. In the **selected-response** format students are presented with a question that has two or more possible responses. Students then select an answer from the possible choices. Common selected-response items include multiple-choice, true/false, and matching. These kinds of items may also be called *objective*, referring to the way the answers are scored. A single correct or best answer is identified for each item, and scoring is simply a matter of checking to determine if the correct choice was made. This feature makes it easy to score a large number of items efficiently by using scantron sheets and machines to read the answers (hence the term *machine-scorable* tests).

A **constructed-response** format requires students to create or produce their own answer in response to a question or task. Brief constructed-response items are those in which students provide a very short, clearly delineated answer, such as filling in a blank at the end of a sentence, writing a few words or a sentence or two,

FIGURE 3.2 Different Assessment Methods

Selected-Response	Constructed-Response				Teacher Observation	Student Self-Assessment
	Brief Constructed-Response Items	*Performance Tasks*	*Essay Items*	*Oral Questioning*		*Self-Report*
• Multiple-choice • Binary-choice (e.g., true/false) • Matching • Interpretive	• Short answer • Completion • Label a diagram • "Show your work"	*Products* • Paper • Project • Poem • Portfolio • Video/audio-tape • Spreadsheet • Web page • Exhibition • Reflection • Journal • Graph • Table • Illustration *Skills* • Speech • Demonstration • Dramatic reading • Debate • Recital • Enactment • Athletics • Keyboarding	• Restricted-response • Extended-response	• Informal questioning • Examinations • Conferences • Interviews	• Formal • Informal	• Attitude survey • Sociometric devices • Questionnaires • Inventories *Self-Evaluation* • Ratings • Portfolios • Conferences • Self-reflection • Evaluate others' performances

or answering a mathematics problem by showing how they arrived at the answer. Although many constructed-response assessments require considerable subjectivity in judging an answer, brief constructed-response items are objectively scored in one sense because there is typically a single correct answer that is easily identified.

Performance assessments require students to construct a more extensive and elaborate answer or response. A well-defined task is identified and students are asked to create, produce, or do something, often in settings that involve real-world application of knowledge and skills. Proficiency is demonstrated by providing an extended response. Performance formats are further differentiated into products and performances. The performance may result in a product, such as a painting, portfolio, paper, or exhibition, or it may consist of a performance, such as a speech, athletic skill, musical recital, or reading. (Be aware that many use the term "performance assessment" to refer to both performances and products, and others use "performance-based.")

Essay items allow students to construct a response that would be several sentences (restricted response) to many paragraphs or pages in length (extended response). Restricted-response essay items include limits to the content and nature of the answer, whereas extended-response items allow greater freedom in response.

Oral questioning is used continuously in an informal way during instruction to monitor student understanding. In a more formalized format, oral questions can be used as a way to test or as a way to determine student understanding through interviews or conferences.

Teacher observations, like oral questions, are so common that we often don't think of them as a form of student assessment. But teachers *constantly* observe students informally to assess student understanding and progress. Teachers watch students as they respond to questions and study, and teachers listen to students as they speak and discuss with others. Often nonverbal communication, such as squinting, inattention, looks of frustration, and other cues, is more helpful than verbal feedback. Observation is used extensively as well in performance assessments, and other formal observational techniques are used to assess classroom climate, teacher effectiveness, and other dimensions of the classroom.

Self-assessment refers to students' reporting on or evaluating themselves. In *self-evaluation of academic achievement*, students rate their own performance in relation to established standards and criteria. In *self-report inventories*, students are asked to complete a form or answer questions that reveal their attitudes and beliefs about themselves or other students. Examples of self-report instruments include attitude surveys, sociometric devices, self-concept questionnaires, interest inventories, and personality measures.

Matching Targets with Methods

Figure 3.3 presents the Matching Targets with Methods Scorecard. This figure summarizes the relative strengths of different methods in measuring different targets. Notice that several methods may be used for some targets. This is good in that it provides more flexibility in the assessments you use, but it also means there is no simple formula or one correct method.

FIGURE 3.3   Matching Targets with Methods Scorecard

| | Assessment Methods | | | | | |
Targets	Selected-Response and Brief Constructed-Response	Essay	Performance	Oral Question	Observation	Self-Assessment
Knowledge and Simple Understanding	5	4	3	4	3	3
Deep Understanding and Reasoning	2	5	4	4	2	3
Skills	1	3	5	2	5	3
Products	1	1	5	2	4	4
Affect	1	2	4	4	4	5

Note: Higher numbers indicate better matches (e.g., 5 = excellent, 1 = poor).

The scorecard has been prepared to give you *general* guidelines about how well particular assessment methods measure each type of target. Remember that the numbers (1 = poor, 5 = excellent) represent the relative strength of the method to provide a high-quality assessment. Variations to what is presented in the figure should be expected. For example, good selected-response items *can* provide a high-quality measure of reasoning, but such items are difficult and time-consuming to prepare. What I have considered in assigning the numbers is both technical strengths and practical limitations. When each method is described in greater detail in later chapters, the variations will become more obvious. For now, however, the scorecard will give you a good overview and provide some preliminary information to use in selecting methods that are appropriate.

Knowledge and Simple Understanding.   Well-constructed selected-response and brief constructed-response items do a good job of assessing subject matter and procedural knowledge and simple understanding, particularly when students must recognize or remember isolated facts, definitions, spellings, concepts, and principles. The questions can be answered and scored quickly, so it is efficient for teachers. These formats also allow you to adequately sample from a large amount of knowledge. Asking students questions orally about what they know is also an effective way to assess knowledge, but this takes much more time and the results are difficult to record. It also takes advance planning to prepare the questions and a method to record student responses. Thus, assessment by oral questioning is best in situations when you are checking for mastery or understanding of a limited number of important facts or when you are doing informal diagnostic assessment. This is usually done during instruction to provide feedback about student progress.

Essays can be used effectively to assess knowledge and understanding when your objective is for students to learn large chunks or structures of knowledge that are related. For example, essays are effective in measuring whether students know the causes of World War II or the life cycles of different types of animals.

Using performance assessments presents some difficulties for determining what students know. Because performance assessments are time intensive for teachers and students, they are usually not the best choice for assessing vast amounts of knowledge. Much of the preparation for the performance often takes place out of class, and the final paper or product typically does not provide opportunities for demonstrating that the student has mastered specific facts. When the performance involves a demonstration of a process or series of steps, knowledge of the process or steps can be assumed when they are demonstrated. However, performance assessments are very good for measuring student understanding that reflects more than surface knowledge.

Deep Understanding and Reasoning.   Deep understanding and reasoning skills are demonstrated most efficiently in essays. Usually essays focus directly on specific reasoning skills by asking students to compare, evaluate, critique, provide justification for, organize, integrate, defend, and solve problems. Time is provided to allow students to use reasoning before answering the question. When oral questions require deep understanding and reasoning for an answer, they are excellent, but also inefficient, for systematic assessment of all students at the end of a unit.

Performance assessments are also effective in measuring deep understanding and reasoning skills as long as the product or demonstration clearly illustrates procedures that reveal reasoning or a performance from which we can infer reasoning. For example, by observing students demonstrate how to go about planning a budget for a family of four, you can draw inferences about how the student used all the information provided and balanced different priorities. Science projects illustrate the ability to interpret results and make conclusions.

Selected-response and brief constructed-response questions *can* be an excellent method for assessing certain aspects of deep understanding and reasoning. When the item demands more than simply recalling or recognizing a fact, reasoning may be needed. For example, if an item requires the student to interpret a chart, analyze a poem, or apply knowledge to solve a problem, thinking skills can be measured. However constructing selected-response items that assess deep understanding and reasoning is very time-consuming.

Student self-evaluations of the reasoning they used in answering a question or solving a problem can help you diagnose learning difficulties. Students can be given sample graded answers and then asked to compare these to their responses. Students can also be involved in scoring teams to actually provide evaluations of student answers.

Skills.   Performance assessments are clearly the preferred method to determine systematically whether or not a student has mastered a skill. Whether the student is demonstrating how to shoot a basketball, give a persuasive speech, sing a song, speak in a foreign language, or use a microscope, the skill is best assessed by observing the student perform the task. On a more informal basis, teachers use observation extensively to assess progress in demonstrating skills.

Selected-response and brief constructed-response tests and oral questioning can be used to assess student knowledge of the skills, such as knowing the proper sequence of actions or recognizing the important dimensions of the skill. But this represents prerequisite knowledge and is not the same as measuring the extent to which the student can actually *do* it.

As with essays, student self-evaluations can be used to focus students on how well their demonstration of skill meets stated criteria. Student evaluations of others' demonstrations are also useful.

Products.   It is not difficult to see that the best way to assess student products is to have students complete one through a performance assessment. The best test of being able to write persuasively is to write a letter that argues for something; if you want students to be able to act, have them participate in a play.

Like skills, you can use objectively scored items, essay items, and oral questions to determine whether students know the components of the product or to evaluate different products. But there is no substitute for actually creating the product.

Student self-evaluations are very effective with performance assessment because students need to focus on the performance criteria and make judgments about their own performance in relation to the criteria. It is also effective to have students judge each others' performances.

Affect.   Affective outcomes are best assessed by either observing students or using student self-reports. Remember that *affect* refers to attitudes, values, feelings, self-concept, interests, and other feelings and beliefs. Because these traits are complex, it is especially important to have clear learning targets.

The most direct and efficient way to assess affect is to ask the students directly through self-report surveys and questionnaires. This method has limitations, but it is still superior to trying to infer affect from behavior. Also, direct oral questioning can be revealing if the right relationship exists between teacher and student and if the atmosphere is conducive to honest sharing of feelings.

Observation can be effective in determining, informally, many affective traits (e.g., motivation and attitudes toward subjects and student self-concept are often apparent when the student shows negative feelings through body posture, a reluctance to interact with others, and withdrawal). Some performance assessments provide ample opportunities for teachers to observe affect, though like other observations, this is usually nonsystematic and inferences are required. Because you are both the observer and the one making the inference, you need to be careful to avoid bias. Having clear targets helps to prevent personal opinion or biases from clouding the assessments.

You must make many choices to ensure that you match targets to methods. As you learn about what it takes to do high-quality assessments with each of the methods, your matches will be better. The next two criteria, validity and reliability, are essential to determining this quality.

Validity

What Is a Valid Assessment?

Classroom assessment is a process that includes gathering, interpreting, and using information. This conceptualization has important implications for how we define a familiar concept that is at the heart of any type of high-quality assessment—validity. **Validity** is a characteristic that refers to the appropriateness of the inferences, uses, and consequences that result from the assessment. Validity is concerned with the soundness, trustworthiness, or legitimacy of the claims or inferences that are made on the basis of obtained scores. In other words, is the interpretation made from test results reasonable? Is the information that I have gathered the right kind of evidence for the decision I need to make or the intended use? How sound is the interpretation of the information? Validity has to do with the consequences of the inferences, not the test itself. Thus, it is an inference or use that is valid or invalid, not the test, instrument, or procedure that is used to gather information. Often we use the phrase "validity of the test," but it is more accurate to say "the validity of the interpretation, inference, or use of the results."

You probably have or will come across a somewhat different definition of validity, something like "the extent to which a test measures what it is supposed to measure." Although this notion is important to many decisions and uses, it tends to focus validity on the instrument, as if it were a characteristic that the instrument always possesses. In reality, the same test or instrument can be valid for one purpose and invalid for another. Actually, validity is always a matter of degree, depending on the situation. For example, a social science test may have high validity for inferring that students know the sequence of events leading up to the American Revolution, less validity for inferring that students can reason, even less validity for inferring that students can communicate effectively in writing, and virtually no validity for indicating a student's mathematical ability. An assessment is not simply valid or invalid, it is valid to some degree in reference to specific inferences or uses.

How Is Validity Determined?

Validity is always determined by professional judgment. This judgment is made by the user of the information (the teacher for classroom assessment). An analysis is done by accumulating evidence that would suggest that an inference or use is appropriate and whether the consequences of the interpretations and uses are reasonable and fair.

The process of determing validity is illustrated in Figure 3.4. Traditionally, the validity of the inference has come from one of three types of evidence: content-related, criterion-related, and construct-related evidence. However, these categories do not adequately address the consequences and uses of the results. Thus, we will consider how classroom teachers can use these three types of evidence, as well as

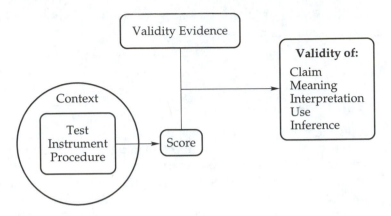

FIGURE 3.4   Determining Validity

consideration of consequences and uses, to make an overall judgment about the degree of validity of the assessment. Figure 3.5 summarizes the major sources of information (evidence) that can be used to establish validity.

Content-Related Evidence.   One feature of teaching that has important implications for assessment is that often a teacher is unable to assess everything that is taught or every instructional objective. Suppose you wanted to test for everything sixth-grade students learn in a four-week unit about insects. Can you imagine how long the test would be and how much time students would take to complete the test? What you do in these situations is select a *sample* of what has been taught to assess, and then you use student achievement on this sample to make inferences about knowledge of the entire universe or domain of content, reasoning, and other objectives. That is, if a student correctly answers 85 percent of the items on your test of a sample of the unit on insects, then you infer that the student knows 85 percent of the content in the entire unit. If your sample is judged to be representative of the universe or domain, then you have **content-related evidence** for validity. The inference from the test is that the student demonstrates knowledge about the unit.

Adequate sampling of content is determined by *your* professional judgment. This judgment process can be haphazard or very systematic. In a superficial review

FIGURE 3.5   Sources of Information for Validity

Content-Related Evidence	The extent to which the assessment is representative of the domain of interest
Criterion-Related Evidence	The relationship between an assessment and another measure of the same trait
Construct-Related Evidence	The extent to which the assessment is a meaningful measure of an unobservable trait or characteristic

of the target, objectives, and test, validity is based only on *appearance*. This is sometimes referred to as face validity. *Face validity* is whether, based on a superficial examination of the test, there seems to be a reasonable measure of the objectives and domain. Does the test, on the face of it, look like an adequate measure? Although it is important to avoid face *in*validity, it is better if the evidence is more structured and systematic.

Once the complete domain of content and objectives is specified, the items on the test can be reviewed to be certain that there is a match between the intended inferences and what is on the test. This process begins with clear learning targets. Based on the targets, a **test blueprint** or **table of specifications** is sometimes prepared to further delineate what objectives you intend to assess and what is important from the content domain. The table of specifications is a two-way grid that shows the content and types of learning targets represented in your assessment (Figure 3.6). Constructing this type of **blueprint** may seem like an imposing task, and in practice teachers find that the amount of work needed to construct one usually outweighs the benefits. An alternative to the table of specifications is a complete, detailed list of learning objectives. Essentially, this list includes all of the cells that would be checked or completed in the table of specifications. At the very least, keep a picture of the table in your mind as a way to check what is being assessed.

I want to emphasize that the goal of a blueprint is to systematize your professional judgment so that you can improve the validity of the assessment. As illustrated

FIGURE 3.6 Format for a Table of Specifications[1]

	Learning Target					
Major Content Areas	*Knowledge/ Simple Understanding*	*Deep Understanding and Reasoning*	*Skills*	*Products*	*Affect*	*Totals*
1. (Topic)	No./%	No./%	No./%	No./%	No./%	No./%
2. (Topic)	No./%	No./%	No./%	No./%	No./%	No./%
3. (Topic)	No./%	No./%	No./%	No./%	No./%	No./%
4. (Topic)	No./%	No./%	No./%	No./%	No./%	No./%
.	.	.	.	.	.	.
.	.	.	.	.	.	.
.	.	.	.	.	.	.
N (Topic)	.	.	.	.	.	.
Total no. of items/% of test	No./%	No./%	No./%	No./%	No./%	*Total no. of items/100%*

[1]The table is completed by indicating the number of test items (No.) and the percentage of items from each type of learning target for each topic. For example, if the topic were assessment, you might have reliability as one topic. If there were four knowledge items for reliability and this was 8 percent of the test, then 4/8% would be included in that table under knowledge.

in Figure 3.7, your judgment is used to determine what types of learning targets will be assessed (knowledge and simple understanding, deep understanding and reasoning, skills, products, or affect), what areas of the content will be sampled, and how the assessment measures both content and type of learning. At this point, you are making decisions about the importance of different types of targets, the content assessed, and how much of the assessment is measuring each target and area of content. If the assessment does, in fact, reflect an actual or modified table of specifications, then there is content-related evidence of validity.

Another consideration related to this type of evidence is the extent to which an assessment can be said to have *instructional* validity. **Instructional validity** is concerned with the match between what is taught and what is assessed. How closely does the test correspond to what has been covered in class and in assignments? Have students had the opportunity to learn what has been assessed? This type of evidence for validity is important for making reasonable inferences about student performance. Again, your professional judgment is needed to ensure that, in fact, what is assessed is consistent with what was taught. One way to check this is to examine the table of specifications after teaching a unit to determine whether the emphasis in different areas or on different targets is consistent with what was emphasized in class. For example, if you emphasized knowledge in teaching a unit (e.g., basic facts, definitions of terms, places, dates, names), it would not be logical to test for reasoning and then make inferences about the knowledge students learned in the class.

Criterion-Related Evidence.   Another way to ensure appropriate inferences from assessments is to have evidence that a particular assessment is providing the same result as another assessment of the same thing. **Criterion-related evidence** provides such validity by relating an assessment to some other valued measure (criterion) that either provides an estimate of current performance (concurrent criterion-related evidence) or predicts future performance (predictive criterion-related evidence). Test developers and researchers use this approach to establish evidence that a test or other instrument is measuring the same trait, knowledge, or attitude by calculating a correlation coefficient to measure the relationship between the assessment and the criterion.

FIGURE 3.7 Professional Judgments in Establishing Content-Related Evidence for Validity

Learning Targets	Content	Instruction	Assessment
What learning targets will be assessed? How much of the assessment will be done on each target area?	What content is most important? What topics will be assessed? How much of the assessment will be done in each topic?	What content and learning targets have been emphasized in instruction?	Are assessments adequate samples of students' performance in each topic area and each target?

Classroom teachers do not conduct formal studies to obtain correlation coefficients that will provide evidence of validity, but the principle *is* very important for teachers to employ. The principle is that when you have two or more measures of the same thing, and these measures provide similar results, then you have established, albeit informally, criterion-related evidence. For example, if your assessment of a student's skill in using a microscope through observation coincides with the student's score on a quiz that tests steps in using microscopes, then you have criterion-related evidence that your inference about the skill of this student is valid. Similarly, if you are interested in the extent to which preparation by your students, as indicated by scores on a final exam in mathematics, predicts how well they will do next year, you can examine the grades of previous students and determine informally if students who scored high on your final exam are getting high grades and students who scored low on your final are obtaining low grades. If a correlation is found, then an inference about predicting how your students will perform, based on their final exam, is valid. Based on this logic, an important principle is to conduct several assessments of the learning targets; try not to rely on a single assessment.

Construct-Related Evidence.   Psychologists refer to a *construct* as an unobservable trait or characteristic that a person possesses, such as intelligence, reading comprehension, honesty, self-concept, attitude, reasoning ability, learning style, and anxiety. These characteristics are not measured directly, in contrast to performance such as spelling or how many push-ups a person successfully completes. Rather, the characteristic is *constructed* to account for behavior that can be observed. Whenever constructs are assessed, the validity of our interpretations depends on the extent of the **construct-related evidence** that is presented. This evidence can take many forms, any one of which is probably insufficient by itself.

The three types of construct-related evidence are theoretical, logical, and statistical. One important type of evidence derives from a clear theoretical explanation or definition of the characteristic so that its meaning is clear and not confused with any other construct. This is particularly important whenever you emphasize reasoning and affect targets. For example, suppose you want to assess students' attitudes toward reading. What is your definition of *attitude*? Do you mean how much students *enjoy* reading, *value* reading, or *read* in their spare time? Are you interested in their *desire* to read or their perception of *ability* to read? None of these traits is necessarily correct as a measure of attitude, but you need to provide a clear definition that separates your construct from other similar, but different constructs.

Logical analyses can be one or more of several types. For some reasoning constructs, you can ask students to comment on what they were thinking when they answered the questions. Ideally their thinking reveals an intended reasoning process. Another logical type of evidence comes from comparing the scores of groups who, as determined by other criteria, should respond differently. These groups can be taught students compared to untaught students, before being taught and after being taught groups, age groups, or groups that have been identified by other means to be different on the construct.

Statistical procedures can be used to correlate scores from measures of the construct with scores from other measures of the same construct and measures of similar, but different constructs. For example, self-concept of academic ability scores from one survey should be related to another measure of the same thing but less related to measures of self-concept of physical ability. These statistical approaches are used for many standardized, published surveys and questionnaires. For a teacher, however, it will be most practical to use clear definitions and logical analyses as construct-related evidence.

Figure 3.8 summarizes suggestions for enhancing the validity of classroom assessments.

FIGURE 3.8   Suggestions for Enhancing Validity

- Ask others to judge the clarity of what you are assessing.
- Check to see if different ways of assessing the same thing give the same result.
- Sample a sufficient number of examples of what is being assessed.
- Prepare a detailed table of specifications.
- Ask others to judge the match between the assessment items and the objective of the assessment.
- Compare groups known to differ on what is being assessed.
- Compare scores taken before to those taken after instruction.
- Compare predicted consequences to actual consequences.
- Compare scores on similar, but different traits.
- Provide adequate time to complete the assessment.
- Ensure appropriate vocabulary, sentence structure, and item difficulty.
- Ask easy questions first.
- Use different methods to assess the same thing.
- Use *only* for intended purposes.

Case Study for Reflection

Ms. Pollard teaches middle school mathematics. In a typical week she gives several mini-quizzes for quick assessments of student understanding and an end-of-week test. She also has a weekly problem-solving question. Homework is checked, and she also collects a great deal of anecdotal evidence focused on student effort and achievement in their daily work. Although Ms. Pollard is an experienced teacher, she wasn't sure how she should respond to her principal when asked about the "validity" of her classroom assessments.

Questions for Consideration
1. From the information she collects, what kind of validity evidence should she say she has obtained?
2. How should Ms. Pollard respond to the principal's query?
3. What possible pitfalls should she avoid so that her inferences about student learning will be valid?

Reliability

What Is a Reliable Score?

Like validity, the term *reliability* has been used for many years to describe an essential characteristic of sound assessment. **Reliability** is concerned with the consistency, stability, and dependability of the scores. In other words, a reliable result is one that shows similar performance at different times. Suppose Mrs. Hambrick is assessing her students' addition and subtraction skills. She decides to give the students a twenty-point quiz to determine their skills. Mrs. Hambrick examines the results but wants to be sure about the level of performance before designing appropriate instruction. So she gives another quiz two days later on the same addition and subtraction skills. The results for some of her students are as follows:

Student	Addition		Subtraction	
	Quiz 1	Quiz 2	Quiz 1	Quiz 2
Rob	18	16	13	20
Carrie	10	12	18	10
Ryann	9	8	8	14
Felix	16	15	17	12

The addition quiz scores are fairly consistent. All four students scored within one or two points on the quizzes; students who scored high on the first quiz also scored high on the second quiz, and students who scored low did so on both quizzes. Consequently, the results for addition are reliable. For subtraction, on the other hand, there is considerable change in performance from the first to the second quiz. Students scoring high on the first quiz score low on the second one, and students scoring low on the first quiz score high on the second. For subtraction, then, the results are unreliable because they are not consistent. The scores contradict one another.

So what does Mrs. Hambrick make of the mathematics scores? Her goal is to use the quiz to accurately determine the defined skill. She cannot know the *exact* level of the skills, but, as in the case of addition, she can get a fairly accurate picture with an assessment that is reliable. For subtraction, on the other hand, she cannot use these results alone to estimate the students' real or actual skill. More assessments are needed before she can be confident that the scores are reliable and thus provide a dependable result. But even the scores in addition are not without some degree of error. In fact, *all* assessments have error; they are never perfect measures of the trait or skill. Let's look at another example to illustrate this point.

Think about the difference between a measure of attitude toward science and time required to run a mile. The measure of attitude will have a relatively high degree of error, but the measure of time will be precise, with little error (highly reliable). This is because there are many more influences on how students answer questions about their attitudes (such as the student's mood that day, the heat in the room, poorly worded items, and fatigue) than there are on a timekeeper's ability to press the stopwatch and read the time elapsed. This is not to say that the measure of time is without any error. It's just that measuring time will have much less error than measuring attitudes.

Assessment Error

The concept of error in assessment is critical to our understanding of reliability. Conceptually, whenever we assess something, we get an *observed* score or result. This observed score is a product of what the *true* or *real* ability or skill is *plus* some degree of *error:*

Observed Score = True Score + Error

Reliability is directly related to error. It is not a matter of all or none, as if some results are reliable and others unreliable. Rather, for each assessment there is some *degree* of error. Thus, we think in terms of low, moderate, or high reliability. It is important to remember that the error can be positive or negative. That is, the observed score can be higher or lower than the true score, depending on the nature of the error. Sometimes you will know when a student's score is lower than it should be based on the behavior of the student at the time of the assessment. For example, if the student was sick, tired, in a bad mood, or distracted, the score may have negative error and underestimate the true score. This is obviously a subjective judgment, which is fine for many types of classroom assessment.

Figure 3.9 shows how different sources of error influence assessment results. Notice how reliability is influenced by factors within the student (internal sources of error), such as mood and physical condition, as well as external factors, such as the quality of the test, scoring errors, and test directions. The actual or true knowledge, reasoning, skill, or affect is captured to some extent by the assessment, but the internal and external sources of error also contribute to the score. In the end, you get an observed score that is made up of the actual or true performance plus some degree of error.

An important practical implication of knowing about error in testing is that small differences between scores of different students should be treated as if they were the same. Typically, your interpretation of a score of 75 should be the same as your interpretation of a score of 77. These observed scores are so close that, when we consider error that can be positive or negative, the true scores of the students should be considered equal (e.g., 75, plus or minus 3, or 77, plus or minus 3).

How Is Reliability Determined?

Reliability is determined by estimating the influence of various sources of error. If there is little error, then the reliability is high or strong. If there is much error, the reliability is low or weak. How, then, is this "amount of error" estimated? In large-scale and standardized testing, estimating error is done statistically with correlation procedures that produce reliability coefficients. These coefficients are then used to estimate the precise amount of error that should be used in interpreting the results. This index is called the **standard error of measurement (SEM).** It will be discussed in fur-

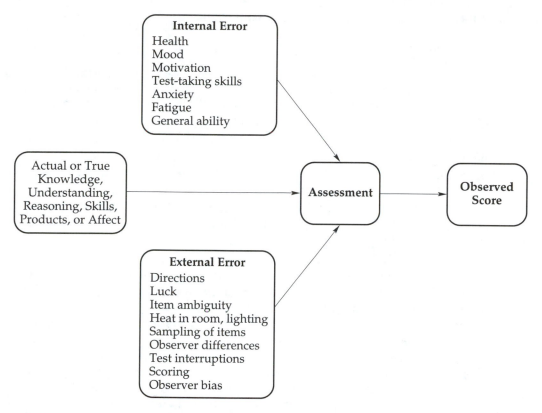

FIGURE 3.9   Sources of Error in Assessment

ther detail in Chapter 13. In classroom assessment, there is rarely any statistical estimate of reliability (although software programs make this very easy for objective
tests). Rather, in the classroom, reliability is determined by noting some sources of
error, such as those in Figure 3.9, by using logic associated with different measures of
the same thing, and by observing the consistency with which students answer questions on the same topic. For example, if Ms. Lopez knows that Susan is distracted by a
family problem and has difficulty concentrating, a reasonable conclusion is that a low
score is being influenced by this problem. In other words, there is considerable error
in Susan's observed performance. If it seems like different students score highest on
different measures of the same skill, this lack of consistency points to low reliability. If
one subgroup of students always score well each time a quiz in given, while another
subgroup always score low, this consistency is logical evidence of good reliability.

Sources of Reliability Evidence

Like validity, making good judgments about reliability is based on using one or
more sources of evidence to justify score interpretations. We will consider the five
most common types of reliability evidence (summarized in Figure 3.10).

FIGURE 3.10   Sources of Evidence in Estimating Reliability

Source of Evidence	Description
Stability	Scores from two administrations of the same assessment to the same group of individuals with a time interval between the assessments
Equivalence	Two forms of the same assessment given at about the same time
Internal Consistency	A single administration of the assessment
Scorer or Rater Consistency	Agreement between two or more scorers or raters on the same performances
Decision Consistency	Percentage of decisions that are the same

Evidence Based on Stability.   A stability estimate of reliability refers to consistency over time. It is produced by administering an assessment to a group of individuals, waiting for a specified amount of time (typically a week or more), and then readministering the same assessment to the same group of individuals. A correlation between the two sets of scores is calculated as an indicator or reliability. This type of estimate is also called **test-retest** reliability. Stability estimates constitute good evidence when the trait being measured is not expected to change during the time span between the assessments (e.g., with readiness tests that assume little change between the time of the assessment and entrance into the group or program). Stability estimates are not good for traits that easily change, such as some attitudes and other affective characteristics.

Evidence Based on Equivalent Forms.   An estimate of equivalence is obtained by administering two forms of the same assessment to a group of students and correlating the scores. The approach is to generate two forms of an assessment that are equal in what is being measured. If the two forms are given at approximately the same time, as with our earlier example of Mrs. Hambrick's students, then an estimate of only equivalence is obtained. If there is a significant time delay between the administrations, then a stability feature is added, providing what is called an *equivalence and stability estimate.*

   In classroom assessment, teachers rarely use equivalence evidence because it would be too time-consuming to make and administer two similar assessments of the same thing. But, again from a logical standpoint, the *idea* of equivalence is relevant if students are offered makeup tests or if teachers want to use a pretest-posttest design to conduct some action research. Logic is also used to determine whether different assessments of the same trait show similar results (e.g., test scores being consistent with homework and quizzes). When students who score high with one assessment also score high with the others, while students who score low on one assessment score low on the others, there is overall consistency and good reliability.

Equivalent forms evidence is used extensively in standardized testing and high-stakes testing because several forms of the same test are needed to allow retakes and makeup testing. These estimates are statistical, reported as reliability coefficients.

Evidence Based on Internal Consistency. Internal consistency evidence is based on the degree of homogeneity of the scores on items measuring the same trait. Only a single form of the assessment is needed for this kind of evidence. This approach assumes that the scores of items measuring the same trait should give consistent results. Suppose a teacher has a twenty-item test on the parts of a flower. If students who truly master this knowledge get all or almost all the items correct, while students who knew nothing about flowers got all or almost all of the items wrong, then there would be internal consistency. In other words, are the items functioning together in a consistent manner?

There are three common types of internal consistency estimates: split-half, Kuder-Richardson, and Coefficient Alpha. In the split-half method, the test items are divided into "equal" halves and each half is scored as a separate test. The two tests are then correlated. The Kuder-Richardson formulas (KR20 and KR21) are used for tests in which each item is scored dichotomously (e.g., right or wrong). You can think of KR approaches as the average of correlating the totals from all possible halves. This is the type of reliability that is calculated for teachers on most scoring software. The Coefficient Alpha is used when a scale has more than two possible responses, such as attitude surveys.

From a practical standpoint, internal consistency evidence is relatively easy to obtain. There is no need to develop a second form, nor is it necessary to give the assessment more than once. There are some limitations, however. First, there needs to be a sufficient number of items. One rule of thumb is that five items are needed to measure a single trait or skill. Second, internal consistency is not appropriate for tests with a time limit (called "speeded" tests), though usually in classroom assessments there is sufficient time to complete the assessments. Third, it is somewhat limiting if all you know is that students answer consistently *at one time.* Typically, teachers need to make inferences about student knowledge over time. After all, we want students to remember what they have learned, and we want them to retain skills over time. That is a more complete and accurate indication of student learning than what can be demonstrated within only a short time frame. This is consistent with using quizzes during a unit and then a larger, more comprehensive assessment at the end of the unit.

Evidence Based on Scorer or Rater Consistency. Whenever student responses need to be judged, rated, or scored, such as when teachers grade essays, writing samples, performance assessments, and portfolios, error can be contributed because of characteristics of the person doing the evaluation (e.g., halo effect, biases, fatigue, expectations, other idiosyncrasies). To take account of this kind of error, evidence can be gathered concerning the extent to which two or more raters agree in their evaluations. For example, if two teachers score twenty student essays and give fifteen of them the same score, then the percentage of agreement, 75 percent, indicates rater consistency. It is also possible to use correlations between two raters. Scorer or rater evidence is best when there is good variation of products to be judged, when the criteria for scoring are clear, and when there is training for the scorers or raters.

Evidence Based on Decision Consistency.   A final kind of evidence is particularly important in making judgments about whether students are "proficient" or whether they "pass." These kinds of decisions or classifications are used as the basis for reliability, rather than the scores themselves. Consistency is estimated as the percentage of same classifications on two or more administrations of the same test. For example, suppose a group of 20 students takes the same "minimum competency" test twice. On the first testing, 10 students were judged "competent" and 10 students were judged to be "not competent." On the second testing all "competent" students were again classified as "competent," but only 8 of 10 "not competent" students were judged that way. Thus, of the 20 classifications, 18 matched, which can be converted to a percentage—90 percent in this example. This approach can also be used in conjunction with rater consistency. Of the total number of decisions made, what percentage were the same?

Factors Influencing Reliability Estimates

While a number of different sources of error will contribute to estimates of reliability, a few factors that affect results should be kept in mind. One factor is the spread of scores. Calculated reliability coefficients are directly related to the degree of dispersion of the scores. Other things being equal, if there is a large range of scores, the reliability will be higher. Another important factor is the number of items in the assessment. The greater the number of items, the greater the reliability. The number of students also makes a difference—the higher the number of students, the stronger the reliability. Difficulty of items also affects reliability. The best reliability coefficients are obtained when items are not too easy or too hard. Items that are carefully constructed will improve reliability. Poorly worded or unclear items lead to poor reliability. The more objective the scoring, the greater the reliability. Typically, multiple-choice tests obtain better estimates of reliability than do constructed-response, performance, or portfolio assessments. Finally, traditional estimates of reliability are a function of the homogeneity of the students. If students are homogeneous on the trait being measured, there will be little variability in scores, which lowers the correlation. Strong reliability is obtained when students are generally heterogeneous on what is being assessed.

Figure 3.11 summarizes suggestions for developing and implementing highly reliable classroom assessments. The degree of reliability needed is dependent on the type of decision that will be made on the basis of the results. Higher reliability is needed when the decision has important, lasting consequences for individual students (e.g., placement to receive special education services). When the decision is about groups and is less important, the reliability does not need to be as high (e.g., whether to repeat a part of a unit of instruction).

FIGURE 3.11   **Suggestions for Enhancing Reliability**

- Use a sufficient number of items or tasks. (Other things being equal, longer tests are more reliable.)
- Use independent raters or observers who provide similar scores to the same performances.
- Construct items and tasks that clearly differentiate students on what is being assessed.
- Make sure the assessment procedures and scoring are as objective as possible.
- Continue assessment until results are consistent.
- Eliminate or reduce the influence of extraneous events or factors.
- Use shorter assessments more frequently than fewer long assessments.

Fairness

A *fair* assessment is one that provides all students an equal opportunity to demonstrate achievement and yields scores that are comparably valid from one person or group to another (Heubert & Hauser, 1999). We want to allow students to show us what they have learned from instruction. If some students have an advantage over others because of factors unrelated to what is being taught, then the assessment is not fair. Fair assessments are *unbiased* and *nondiscriminatory*, uninfluenced by irrelevant or subjective factors. That is, neither the assessment task nor scoring is differentially affected by race, gender, ethnic background, handicapping condition, or other factors unrelated to what is being assessed. Fairness is also evident in what students are told about the assessment and whether students have had the opportunity to learn what is being assessed. The following criteria, summarized in Figure 3.12, represent potential influences that determine whether or not an assessment is fair.

Student Knowledge of Learning Targets and Assessments

How often have you taken a test and thought, "Had I only known the teacher was going to test *this* content, I would have studied it"? A fair assessment is one in which it is clear what will and will not be tested. Your objective is not to fool or trick students or to outguess them on the assessment. Rather, you need to be very clear and specific about the learning target—what is to be assessed and how it will be scored.

FIGURE 3.12   **Key Components of Fairness**

- Student knowledge of learning targets and assessments
- Opportunity to learn
- Prerequisite knowledge and skills
- Avoiding teacher stereotypes
- Avoiding bias in assessment tasks and procedures

And this is very important: Both the content of the assessment and the scoring criteria should be *public*. Being public means that students know the content and scoring criteria before the assessment and often before instruction. When students know what will be assessed, they know what to study and focus on. By knowing the scoring criteria, students understand much better the qualitative differences the teacher is looking for in student performance. One way to help students understand the assessment is to give them the assessment blueprint, sample questions, and examples of work completed by previous students and graded by the teacher.

When students know the learning targets and scoring criteria in advance, it is likely that they will be more intrinsically motivated and involved to obtain true mastery, rather than mere performance. It helps to establish a *learning* goal orientation for students, where the focus is on mastering a task, developing new skills, and improving competence and understanding. In contrast, when a *performance* goal orientation is established, in which students perform to get a grade, recognition, or reward, motivation is extrinsic and less intense, and students are not as engaged or involved. With specific learning targets and criteria, based on your determination of the nature of evidence needed (remember Figure 1.2), students are more likely to establish a learning goal orientation and put forth more effort.

Opportunity to Learn

Opportunity to learn is concerned with sufficiency or quality of the time, resources, and conditions needed by students to demonstrate their achievement. It concerns the adequacy of instructional approaches and materials that are aligned with the assessment. Fair assessments are aligned with instruction that provides adequate time and opportunities for all students to learn. This is more than simply telling students, for example, that a test will cover certain chapters. Ample instructional time and resources are needed so that students are not penalized because of a lack of opportunity.

Prerequisite Knowledge and Skills

It is unfair to assess students on things that require prerequisite knowledge or skills that they do not possess. This means that you need to have a good understanding of prerequisites that your students demonstrate. It also means that you need to examine your assessments carefully to know what prerequisites are required. For example, suppose you want to test math reasoning skills. Your questions are based on short paragraphs that provide needed information. In this situation, math reasoning skills can be demonstrated only if students can read and understand the paragraphs. Thus, reading skills are prerequisites. If students do poorly on the assessment, their performance may have more to do with a lack of reading skills than with math reasoning.

Another type of prerequisite skill is concerned with test taking. Some students bring better test-taking skills to an assessment than other students do, such as knowing to read directions carefully, pacing, initially bypassing difficult items, checking answers, and eliminating wrong answers to multiple-choice items rather than looking for the right answer. These skills are not difficult for students to learn, and it is advisable to make sure all students are familiar with them before an assessment is administered.

Avoiding Stereotypes

Stereotypes interfere with your objectivity. It is your responsibility to judge each student on his or her performance on assessment tasks, not on how others who share characteristics of the student perform. Although you should not exclude personal feelings and intuitions about a student, it is important to separate these feelings from performance. Stereotypes are judgments about how groups of people will behave based on characteristics such as gender, race, socioeconomic status, physical appearance, and other characteristics. It is impossible to avoid stereotypes completely because of our values, beliefs, preferences, and experiences with different kinds of people. However, we *can* control the influence of these prejudices.

Stereotypes can be based on groups of people, such as "jocks have less motivation to do well," "boys do better in math," "students from a particular neighborhood are more likely to be discipline problems," and "children with a single parent need extra help with homework." You can also *label* students with words such as *shy, gifted, smart, poor, learning disabled, leader,* and *at-risk*. These labels can affect your interactions and evaluations by establishing inappropriate expectations. The nature of teacher expectations is discussed in greater detail in the next chapter.

Avoiding Bias in Assessment Tasks and Procedures

Another source of bias can be found in the nature of the actual assessment task—the contents and process of the test, project, problem, or other task. Bias is present if the assessment distorts performance because of the student's ethnicity, gender, race, religious background, and so on. Popham (2002) has identified two major forms of assessment bias: offensiveness and unfair penalization.

Offensiveness occurs if the content of the assessment offends, upsets, distresses, angers, or otherwise creates negative affect for particular students or a subgroup of students. This negative affect makes it less likely that the students will perform as well as they otherwise might, lowering the validity of the inferences. Offensiveness occurs most often when stereotypes of particular groups are present in the assessment. Suppose a test question portrayed a minority group in low-paying, low-status jobs and white groups in high-paying, high-status jobs. Students who are members of the minority group may understandably be offended by the question, mitigating their performance. Here is an example of a biased mathematics test question that may result in offensiveness:

> Juan Mendez gathers lettuce for his income. He receives fifteen cents for every head of lettuce he picks. Juan picked 270 heads of lettuce on Tuesday. How much money did he make?

Unfair penalization is bias that disadvantages a student because of content that makes it more difficult for students from some groups to perform as compared to students from other groups. That is, bias is evident when an unfair advantage or disadvantage is given to one group because of gender, socioeconomic status, race, language, or other characteristic. Suppose you take an aptitude test that uses rural, farm-oriented examples. The questions deal with types of cows and pigs, winter wheat, and farm equipment. If you grew up in a suburban community, do you think you will score as well as students who grew up on a farm? Similarly, will a student whose primary language is Spanish have an equal opportunity to demonstrate oral reading skills in English as students whose primary language is English? Do test items containing sports content unfairly advantage boys? Here is a reading comprehension test question that is biased with unfair penalization:

> Write a persuasive essay about the advantages of sailing as recreation. Include in your essay comparisons of sailing with other types of recreation such as hiking, swimming, and bowling.

Teachers don't *deliberately* produce biased assessments. It is most often unconscious and unintended. For these reasons, bias can be minimized by having others review your assessments, looking specifically for the types of bias presented here and, of course, by your own sensitivity to bias when creating the assessments. It should be noted that assessment tasks are not necessarily biased solely on the basis of differential performance by minority groups or other groups students may be members of. For example, just because Asian Americans score higher on the SAT than Native or African Americans does not mean that the SAT is biased to give an unfair advantage to Asian Americans.

Cultural differences that are reflected in vocabulary, prior experiences, skills, and values may influence the assessment. These differences are especially important in our increasingly diverse society and classrooms. Consider the following examples of how cultural background influences assessment:

- Knowledge from the immediate environment of the student (e.g., large city, ethnic neighborhood, rural, coastal) provides a vocabulary and an indication of the importance or relevance of assessment tasks.
- Depending on the culture, rules for sharing beliefs, discussion, taking turns, and expressing opinions differ.
- Respect and politeness may be expressed differently by students from different backgrounds (e.g., not looking into another's eyes, silence, squinting as a way to say no, looking up or down when asked a question).
- Learning style differences—which are exhibited in preferences for learning alone or in a group, for learning by listening or reading, for reflective or impulsive responses, and in the ability to think analytically or globally—influences a student's confidence and motivation to complete assessment tasks.

The influence of these differences will be minimized to the extent that you first understand them and then utilize multiple assessments that will allow all students to demonstrate their progress toward the learning target. If an assessment technique or approach advantages one type of student, another technique may be a disadvantage to that type of student. By using different types of assessments, one provides a balance to the other. Students who are unable to respond well to one type of assessment will respond well to another type. This points out an important principle of high-quality assessment—*never rely solely on one method of assessment*. This does not mean, however, that you should arbitrarily pick different methods.

You need to select your assessments on the basis of what will provide the fairest indication of student achievement for *all* your students.

Accommodating Special Needs

Another type of assessment task bias that has received a lot of attention recently is the need to accommodate the special abilities of exceptional children. An assessment is biased if performance is affected by a disability or other limiting characteristic when the student actually possesses the knowledge or skill being measured. In other words, when assessing exceptional students, you need to modify the assessment task so that the disabling trait is not a factor in the performance. For example, students with hearing loss may need written directions to complete an assessment that you give orally to other students. Chapter 11 deals with assessing students with special needs in some detail.

Positive Consequences

The nature of classroom assessments has important consequences for teaching and learning. Ask yourself these questions: How will the assessment affect student motivation? Will students be more or less likely to be meaningfully involved? Will their motivation be intrinsic or extrinsic? How will the assessment affect how and what students study? How will the assessment affect my teaching? How much time will the assessment take away from instruction? Will the results allow me to provide students with individualized feedback? What will the parents think about my assessments? High-quality assessments have consequences that will be positive, for both students and yourself.

Positive Consequences on Students

The most direct consequence of assessment is that students learn and study in a way that is consistent with your assessment task. If the assessment is a multiple-choice test to determine the students' knowledge of specific facts, then students will tend to memorize information. If the assessment calls for extended essays, students tend to learn the material in larger, related chunks, and they practice recall rather than recognition when studying. Assessments that require problem solving, such as performance-based assessments, encourage students to think and apply what they learn. A positive consequence, in this sense, is the appropriate match between the learning target and the assessment task.

Assessments also have clear consequences on student motivation. If students know what will be assessed and how it will be scored, and if they believe that the assessment will be fair, they are likely to be more motivated to learn. Is the assessment structured so that students will be able to show their best performance?

Motivation also increases when the assessment tasks are relevant to the students' backgrounds and goals, challenging but possible, and structured to give students individualized feedback about their performance. What good is a high score on an easy test? Authentic assessments provide more active learning, which increases motivation. Giving students multiple assessments, rather than a single assessment, lessens fear and anxiety. When students are less apprehensive, risk taking, exploration, creativity, and questioning are enhanced.

Finally, the student–teacher relationship is influenced by the nature of assessment. When teachers construct assessments carefully and provide feedback to students, the relationship is strengthened. Conversely, if students have the impression that the assessment is sloppy, not matched with course objectives, designed to trick them (like some true/false questions we have all answered!), and provides little feedback, the relationship is weakened. How quickly do you return papers or tests to students? What types of comments do you write on papers or projects? Assessment affects the way students perceive the teacher and gives them an indication of how much the teacher cares about them and what they learn.

Positive Consequences on Teachers

Like students, teachers are affected by the nature of the assessments they give their students. Just as students learn depending on the assessment, teachers tend to teach to the test. Thus, if the assessment calls for memorization of facts, the teacher tends to teach lots of facts; if the assessment requires reasoning, then the teacher structures exercises and experiences that get students to think. The question, then, is how well your assessments promote and encourage the teaching you want and what you want your students to learn.

There is often a trade-off between instructional time and the time needed for assessment. If your assessments require considerable time for preparation, administration, and scoring, then there is less time for instruction.

A goal of high-quality assessments is that they will lead to better information and decision making about students. Will the assessment help you make more valid judgments, or will it tend to make judgments about students more difficult? As a result of assessment, are you likely to label students inappropriately?

Finally, assessments may influence how you are perceived by others. Are you comfortable with school administrators and parents reviewing and critiquing your assessments? What about the views of other teachers? How do your assessments fit with what you want to be as a professional?

Practicality and Efficiency

High-quality assessments are practical and efficient. It is important to balance these aspects of assessment with previously mentioned criteria. As I have already pointed out, time is a limited commodity for teachers. It may be best to use extensive performance assessments; but if these assessments take away too much from instruction or energy needed for other professional activities, it may be better to think about less time-consuming assessments. Essentially, ask yourself this question: Is the information obtained worth the resources and time required to obtain it? Other factors to consider include your familiarity with the method of assessment, the time required of students to complete the assessments, the complexity of administering the assessment, the ease of scoring, the ease of interpretation, and cost. We'll consider each briefly.

Teacher Familiarity with the Method

Teachers need to know about the assessment methods they select. This includes knowledge of the strengths and limitations of the method, how to administer the assessment, how to score and properly interpret student responses, and the appropriateness of the method for given learning targets. Teachers who use assessment methods with which they are not familiar risk time and resources for questionable results.

Time Required

Other things being equal, it is desirable to use the shortest assessment possible that provides credible results. In other words, gather only as much information as you need for the decision or other use of the results. The time required should include how long it takes to construct the assessment, how much time is needed for students to provide answers, and how long it takes to score the results. The time needed for each of these aspects of assessment is different for each method of assessment. Multiple-choice tests take a long time to prepare but a relatively short time for students to complete and for teachers to score. Thus, if you plan to use this format over and over for different groups of students, it is efficient to put in considerable time preparing the assessment as long as you can use many of the same test items each semester or year (keep objective tests secure so you don't have to construct an entirely new test each time). Essay tests, on the other hand, take less time to prepare but take a long time to score. Performance assessments are probably most time intensive (in preparation, student response time, and scoring). For all types of assessments, reuse questions and tasks whenever possible.

Another consideration in deciding about time for assessment is reliability. The reliability of a test or other assessment is directly related to its length—the longer the test, the greater is its reliability. In general, assessments that take thirty or forty minutes provide reliable results for a single score on a short unit. If separate scores are needed for subskills, more time may be needed. A general rule of thumb is that six to ten objective items are needed to provide a reliable assessment of a concept or specific skill.

Complexity of Administration

Practical and efficient assessments are easy to administer. This means that the directions and procedures for administration are clear. Assessments that require long, complicated directions and setup, like some performance assessments, are less efficient and may, because of student misunderstanding, have adverse effects on reliability and validity.

Ease of Scoring

It is obvious that some methods of assessment, such as objective tests, are much easier to score than other methods, such as essays, papers, and oral presentations. Like other traits, scoring needs to match your method and purpose. In general, use the easiest method of scoring appropriate to the method and purpose of the assessment. Objective tests are easiest to score and contribute less scoring error to reliability. Scoring performance assessments, essays, papers, and the like is more difficult because more time is needed to ensure reliability. For these assessments, it is more practical to use rating scales and checklists rather than writing extended individualized evaluations.

Ease of Interpretation

Objective tests that report a single score are usually easiest to interpret, and individualized written comments are more difficult to interpret. Many subjectively evaluated products are given a score or grade to enhance ease of interpretation. It is necessary to provide sufficient information so that whatever interpretation is made is accurate. Often grades or scores are applied too quickly without enough thought and detailed feedback to students. This can be partially remedied by sharing a key with students and others that provides meaning to different scores or grades. Interpretation is easier if you are able to plan, before the assessment, how to use the results.

Cost

Because most classroom assessments are inexpensive, cost is relatively unimportant. It would certainly be unwise to use a more unreliable or invalid assessment just because it costs less. Some performance assessments are exceptions, because the cost of materials can be an important factor. Like other practical aspects, it is best to use the most economical assessment, other things being equal. But economy should be thought of in the long run, and unreliable, less expensive tests may eventually cost more in further assessment.

Summary

High-quality classroom assessments provide reliable, valid, fair, and useful measures of student performance. Quality is enhanced when the assessments meet these important criteria:

- It is best to match the method of assessment to learning targets. Knowledge and simple understanding targets are matched best with selected-response and brief constructed-response items, deep understanding and reasoning targets with essays, and affective targets with observation and student self-reports. Performance assessments are best for measuring deep understanding skills and products.
- Validity is the degree to which a score-based inference is appropriate, reasonable, and useful. Inferences are valid or invalid—not tests.

- Different types of evidence are used to establish the validity of classroom tests, the most important of which is content-related evidence.
- Whether face validity, a test blueprint, or instructional validity, the teacher's professional judgment is needed to ensure that there is adequate content-related evidence.
- Construct-related evidence is provided by theoretical, logical, and statistical analyses.
- Reliability is used to estimate the error in testing. It measures the degree of consistency when several items measure the same thing and stability when the same measures are given across time.
- Different sources of error should be taken into consideration when interpreting test results.
- Sources of evidence for obtaining reliable scores include stability, equivalence, internal consistency, scorer or rater consistency, and decision consistency.
- Reliability is improved with increases in the spread of scores, number of items, number and heterogeneity of students, and with items that are clear and have medium difficulties.
- Assessment is fair if it is unbiased and provides students with a reasonable opportunity to demonstrate what they have learned.
- Fairness is enhanced by student knowledge of learning targets before instruction, the opportunity to learn, the attainment of prerequisite knowledge and skills, unbiased assessment tasks and procedures, teachers who avoid stereotypes, and accommodating special needs.
- Positive consequences for both teachers and students enhance the overall quality of assessment, particularly the effect of the assessments on student motivation and study habits. Assessments need to take into consideration the teacher's familiarity with the method, the time required, the complexity of administration, the ease of scoring and interpretation, and cost to determine the assessment's practicality and efficiency.

SELF-INSTRUCTIONAL REVIEW EXERCISES

1. Should teachers be concerned about relatively technical features of assessments such as validity and reliability? Why or why not?

2. Match the description with the type of assessment.

   _____ **(1)** Based on verbal instructions   **a.** Selected response
   _____ **(2)** Made up of questionnaires and surveys   **b.** Essay
   _____ **(3)** Selection or supply type   **c.** Performance
   _____ **(4)** Constructs unique response to   **d.** Oral question
               demonstrate skill   **e.** Observation
   _____ **(5)** Either restricted or extended   **f.** Self-assessment
               constructed response
   _____ **(6)** Used constantly by teachers informally

3. For each of the following situations or questions, indicate which assessment method provides the best match (selected response, S; essay, E; performance, P; oral question, OR; observation, OB; and self-report, SR).

   a. Mrs. Keen needs to check students to see if they are able to draw graphs correctly like the example just demonstrated in class.
   b. Mr. Garcia wants to see if his students are comprehending the story before moving to the next set of instructional activities.
   c. Ms. Powell wants to find out how many spelling words her students know.
   d. Ms. Tanner wants to see how well her students can compare and contrast the Vietnam War with World War II.
   e. Mr. Johnson's objective is to enhance his students' self-efficacy and attitudes toward school.
   f. Mr. Greene wants to know if his sailing clinic students can identify different parts of a sailboat.

4. Which of the following statements is correct, and why?

   a. Validity is impossible without strong reliability.
   b. A test can be reliable without validity.
   c. A valid test is reliable.

5. Mr. Nelson asks the other math teachers in his high school to review his midterm to see if the test items represent his learning targets. Which type of evidence for validity is being used?

   a. Content-related
   b. Criterion-related
   c. Instructional
   d. Construct-related

6. The students in the following lists are rank ordered, based on their performance on two tests of the same content (highest score at the top, next highest score second, etc.) Do the results suggest a reliable assessment? Why or why not?

Test A	Test B
Germaine	Ryann
Cynthia	Robert
Ryann	Steve
Steve	Germaine
Robert	Cynthia

7. Which aspect of fairness is illustrated in each of the following assessment situations?

   a. Students complained because they were not told what to study for the test.
   b. Students studied the wrong way for the test (e.g., they memorized content).
   c. The teacher was unable to cover the last unit that was on the test.
   d. The story students read, the one they would be tested on, was about life in the northeast during winter. Students who had been to that part of the country in winter showed better comprehension scores than students who had rarely even seen snow.

8. Is the following test item biased? Why or why not?

   Ramon has decided to develop a family budget. He has $2,000 to work with and decides to put $1,000 into the mortgage, $300 into food, $200 into transportation, $300 into entertainment, $150 into utilities, and $50 into savings. What percent of Ramon's budget is being spent in each of the categories?

9. Why is it important for teachers to consider practicality and efficiency in selecting their assessments, as well as more technical aspects such as validity and reliability?

ANSWERS TO SELF-INSTRUCTIONAL REVIEW EXERCISES

1. Yes, but not in the way psychometricians do with published, standardized tests. Validity and reliability are essential to fairness, proper interpretation of assessments, and teacher decision making. Both validity and reliability are best estimated by teacher judgment and logical analysis and not statistically, unless the statistics are easily provided.

2. (1) d, (2) f, (3) a, (4) c, (5) b, (6) e.

3. a. OB, b. OR, c. S, d. E, e. SR, f. S.

4. a. Yes, if the score is not consistent or stable, the inference will likewise not be consistent or stable and hence inaccurate and invalid. b. Yes, a measure of the circumference of your big toe is very reliable but not very valid for measuring your ability to read. c. No, tests are not valid or invalid, only inferences are.

5. a.

6. Not very reliable. Germaine scored highest on Test A but near the bottom on Test B; Robert scored at the bottom on Test A but near the top on Test B. A reliable assessment would result in nearly the same rank ordering for both tests.

7. a. Student knowledge of assessment. b. Student knowledge of assessment. c. Opportunity to learn. d. Biased content.

8. Probably not. For bias to exist, it needs to be fairly obvious. In this example, a minority group name is used, but it would be unlikely to elicit negative affect from Hispanic members of the class. There is no content that is clearly biased.

9. Because the time you have is limited, and priorities need to be set so that you balance instruction with assessment.

SUGGESTIONS FOR ACTION RESEARCH

1. Interview a teacher and ask about the types of assessments he or she uses. See if there is a match between the assessment methods and targets consistent with Figure 3.2. Also ask about validity and reliability. How does the teacher define these concepts, and how are they determined informally, if at all, by the teacher? How does the teacher account for error in testing? Finally, ask about additional criteria for making assessments fair and unbiased. Does the teacher make it clear to students what they will be tested on? Do all students have the same opportunity to do well?

2. Prepare a table of specifications for a test of this chapter. Include all the major target areas. Compare your table with those of other students to see how similar you are with respect to what you believe is most important to assess. Also include examples of test items.

3. Ask a group of high, middle, or elementary school students, depending on your interest in teaching, about what they see as fair, high-quality assessment. Ask them to generate some qualities that they believe contribute to good assessments, and then ask them specifically about each of the criteria in the chapter. Also, ask them how different kinds of assessments affect them; for example, do they study differently for essay and multiple-choice tests?

Assessment before Instruction: Learning about Your Students

A hallmark of an effective teacher is being able to match instructional activities with the knowledge, skills, and affect students bring to the classroom. Consequently, an important assessment process takes place before formal instruction. This occurs before the school year begins, continues for the first week or two of school, and occurs again whenever needed throughout the school year as new topics are introduced. You have set your general learning targets. High-quality initial assessments are needed before more specific learning targets, instructional activities, and subsequent assessments are finalized.

Important planning decisions are made before formal instruction. These decisions can be made thoughtfully and with reflection because there is less sense of im-

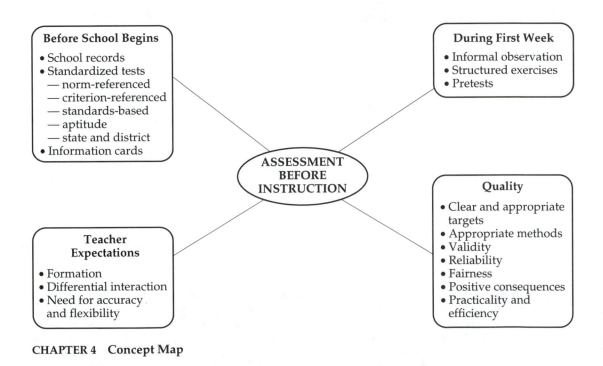

Before School Begins

- School records
- Standardized tests
  — norm-referenced
  — criterion-referenced
  — standards-based
  — aptitude
  — state and district
- Information cards

During First Week

- Informal observation
- Structured exercises
- Pretests

ASSESSMENT BEFORE INSTRUCTION

Quality

- Clear and appropriate targets
- Appropriate methods
- Validity
- Reliability
- Fairness
- Positive consequences
- Practicality and efficiency

Teacher Expectations

- Formation
- Differential interaction
- Need for accuracy and flexibility

CHAPTER 4   Concept Map

mediacy. During this time, then, you will be able to gather and process assessment information that will help you to make decisions concerning questions such as:

Do students have the content knowledge and intellectual skills to handle the material?

Are students likely to be interested in this content?

How can I plan for instruction that will motivate these particular students?

What are the implications of individual differences among the students?

Are some students likely to be far behind others? If so, how can this be accommodated?

Answers to these questions will allow you to base planning decisions concerning grouping, activities, content, and other instructional elements on current abilities, interests, and potential for learning. It is difficult to be responsive to students' strengths, weaknesses, and needs with appropriate individualization unless you *know* what those strengths, weaknesses, and needs are. Airasian (2001) uses the phrase "sizing-up assessment" to describe the kinds of information that teachers need to know about their students. He stresses the need to gather information about the knowledge, skills, dispositions, and more general characteristics of students so that the teacher can adequately plan instruction. This requires getting to know not only the entire class but individuals as well. Given the current emphasis on helping every child be successful, it is important to spend enough time sizing up each student. Effective instruction is not only targeted to the group; it is also structured to be tailored to each individual. This is a challenge for middle and high school teachers who have 150 or more students each semester, especially if this kind of assessment needs to be done in the first week or so of school. In the end, knowing the academic strengths and weaknesses of your students, as well as their interests, attitudes, and backgrounds will provide foundation for designing effective instruction. Assessments made for planning purposes occur before the start of school, during the first few days or week, and throughout the year when you are beginning new instructional units. We consider each of these planning periods in this chapter.

Before School Begins: What Do You Know about Your Students?

Before school starts, it is likely that you will have some knowledge of the students you will be teaching. There certainly is no lack of available information. School records, test scores, comments from other teachers, sibling performance, and other sources of information are readily available. The teachers' lounge may be the source of much discussion about students. Although there is disagreement about *how much* teachers should know about their students before they have them in class, it is probable that you will know *something*. Not only will the teacher use this information to plan instruction, it may also influence the teacher's initial expectations about what students are capable of achieving and may, in turn, determine how the teacher interacts with the students. We will consider four major sources of information gathered before school begins—school records, standardized test scores, state and district test scores, and information cards—and we will examine how expectations may be formed from each source.

School Records

The major preclass systematic source of information about students is school records. These records, often contained in a student's cumulative file, include report cards, written comments from other teachers, information about or from parents, inventories, results of standardized testing, attendance, health records, special placements, portfolios of student work, and other information. The specific types of information contained in school records depends on school policies and procedures.

Some teachers choose to examine information in these records before school begins with the thought that it is best to know as much as possible about the backgrounds of their students. Most teachers, on the other hand, do not want to know too much about their students from other sources. These teachers prefer to use their own interactions with the students as the primary preinstruction source of information. They are wary of forming inappropriate expectations on the basis of other information.

This is how Betty, an elementary teacher, expresses it (Davis, 1995):

> I usually look at the report cards at the beginning of the year . . . but I guess I like to form my own judgments of kids . . . and not really go by exactly what it says in here. . . . I would rather see for myself. (p. 187)

As indicated in Figure 4.1, using information in school records before meeting the students has both advantages and disadvantages. On the positive side, reviewing student records will help you get to know and understand your students more quickly. You can reinforce previous accomplishments and avoid repeating unnecessary material in class. School records can identify areas in which you need to gather further information to more fully understand the students. Perhaps most important, school records can help you establish accurate and realistic expectations.

On the negative side, information in school records can be outdated or inaccurate, and recent changes in students may be overlooked. Such records may lead to inappropriate expectations, and teachers may have preconceived ideas that prevent students from changing old patterns of performances.

The advantages far outweigh the disadvantages as long as certain precautions are taken. Most of the disadvantages arise from inappropriate interpretations of the information. Because teachers need to know as much as possible about their students, information from a variety of sources provides a more complete picture than the teacher is able to form on his or her own. For example, when grades, standardized test scores, and teacher comments point to the same conclusion, the inference you make about the student is more valid. It is also wise to look for patterns

FIGURE 4.1   **Advantages and Disadvantages of Using School Records**

Advantages	Disadvantages
Provides additional information to help understand students	Information can be outdated
	Student changes may be overlooked
Helps teachers know students more quickly	Standardized test results may be misinterpreted
Previous accomplishments are not forgotten	May prevent teachers from making an objective assessment
Provides long-range perspectives on the students	First impressions may be inaccurate
Prevents needless repetition of some assessments	May lead to inappropriate teacher expectations
Enhances grade level and school-to-school transitions	Teachers are unable to view students with a "clean slate"
Identifies specific areas in which teachers need to look or gather additional evidence	Previous information may be biased, invalid, or unreliable
Helps prevent inaccurate teacher expectations	
Allows instruction to begin more quickly	

of achievement that may occur over several years. Particularly in elementary school, prior knowledge of students will help provide smooth transitions from one grade to the next, especially when students move from one school to another. Here is how one elementary teacher puts it (Davis, 1995):

> I always look at the parent's occupation to see if their parents are working outside the home . . . which gives me an idea of perhaps how hectic their schedules might be. . . . I look to see how much education the parents have . . . so that I might weigh the experiences the child will get outside of school. . . . I look at the report card. . . . I many times look for behavioral problems with that child . . . to check to see how the child did socially. . . . I try to glance at them . . . from the cumulative folder at the beginning of the school year. . . . I glance at the report card and see overall how that child did. (pp. 157–158)

An effective teacher should regard preclass information tentatively, combining it with his or her own observations and initial assessments of the students. Initial impressions should be treated as hypotheses that may be confirmed or disproved with subsequent assessments. Others' insights and previous student performance can augment your evaluations during the first few days of school so that instruction can begin as soon as possible. This is helpful as long as you are able to resist forming rigid expectations.

Most teachers want to know about special characteristics of students that will require instructional accommodations. It is important to know about physical or serious emotional difficulties. For example, if a student is on medication for hy-peractivity, teachers need to know what the side effects are and what to do if the medication is not taken as prescribed. Some physical challenges of students will re-quire certain room arrangements. You will also want to know if a student is receiv-ing special services for a learning disability. Often it is helpful to know of any difficult home situations that could affect student performance. At the very least, elementary teachers need to know whom to contact at home and who may be pick-ing up or dropping off students.

Standardized Test Scores

Standardized tests have been much criticized as having few positive implications for teaching. The argument is made that because of broad coverage and infrequent test-ing, heavy reliance on selected-response formats, encouragement to "teach to the test," cultural bias, and inappropriate ranking and comparing students, the informa-tion from these tests is not very helpful. Despite these criticisms, however, it is likely that standardized testing will continue, if for no other reason than it has traditionally been used to provide the public with information for accountability. Parents expect to see such test scores and have learned to rely on them as measures of achievement.

Standardized test results, when used appropriately, can provide helpful in-formation for instructional planning. The key is being able to understand the scores that are reported as well as the limitations on how scores should be inter-preted. As long as results from these tests are not used as the *sole* criterion, scores can be used to form conclusions about the ability or prior achievement of students.

In this chapter, we consider standardized tests briefly in the context of in-structional planning. Chapter 13 presents a more complete discussion of the nature of these tests and includes examples of the types of reports you are likely to see. Five different types of standardized tests may be used for classroom planning: norm-referenced achievement test batteries, criterion-referenced achievement test batteries, aptitude tests, readiness tests, and state or district achievement tests.

Norm-Referenced Achievement Test Batteries.   Norm-referenced achievement test batteries are the most common type of standardized test. They are character-ized by qualities shared by other types of large-scale standardized tests, including high technical quality, precise directions for administration, uniform scoring pro-cedures, equivalent or comparable forms, and test manuals for interpretation of the scores. When standardized tests are **norm-referenced,** national samples of stu-dents have been used as the *norming* group for interpreting relative standing. Be-cause these tests are designed to be used in different schools throughout the country, they tend to provide broad coverage of each content area to maximize po-tential usefulness in as many schools as possible. Thus, close inspection of the ob-jectives and types of test items is needed to determine how well the test matches the emphasis in the local curriculum.

For a **test battery** several individual tests are normed on the same national sample. This allows us to compare the scores of the different tests to determine stu-dents' strengths and weaknesses. Such comparisons are possible only when the tests have used the same national sample and cannot be done with different standardized tests that have different norming groups.

The results of test batteries are reported by objective or skill area. Some tests, such as the *Metropolitan Achievement Tests,* the *Stanford Achievement Tests,* and the *California Achievement Tests,* have *diagnostic* batteries. These batteries have more items in each area than the survey forms of the tests, which allow for greater confidence when comparing achievement levels. Each battery is identified with a descriptive title, such as *spelling, punctuation, letter recognition, fraction computations, graphs,* and so on, but the best way to be sure about the match between what the battery says it is testing and your instructional planning is to examine the objectives and the type of test items that are used. (You won't be able to review items from the actual tests because they are secured.) With knowledge of the objectives and the nature of the items, particularly difficulty level, your interpretations of the scores are more accurate.

Two types of scores are reported for each student for standardized achievement tests. One type of score indicates how the student's performance compares to that of the norming group. The scores to indicate this relative standing are typically percentile rank, grade equivalent, or a type of standard score. We will consider the first two types in this chapter and standard scores in Chapter 13.

Percentile Rank. The **percentile rank,** or *percentile score,* indicates the percentage of the *norm group* that is at or below the same raw score. In other words, the percentile score tells us the percentage of the norm group that the student outscored. The percentile score is based on the number of items answered correctly, but it does not indicate the *percentage* of items answered correctly. Thus, a student scoring at the 70th percentile did better on the test than 70 percent of the norming group (70 percent of the norming group scored below this student).

Because the percentile rank is calculated by comparison to the norming group, the nature and characteristics of this group determine the score. Thus, if the norming group is representative of the entire nation, a percentile score using this group will not be the same as a score determined by local norms. If the local community and school are stronger academically than the rest of the nation, the local norm percentile rank scores will be lower, even though the student answered the same number of items correctly. All of this shows how an accurate interpretation of percentiles on standardized tests depends on the norm group, and the norm group for many tests can be national, local, regional, suburban, or urban. If the norm group is local, it is important to remember that, by definition, half the students will be above the 50th percentile and half will be below it.

Percentile scores are very useful in indicating relative strengths and weaknesses. If a student scores consistently higher in mathematics than in language arts, then it can be concluded that the student is stronger in mathematics than language arts (at least as defined by the tests). However, this relative strength does not indicate, in a more diagnostic way, specific skills that should be addressed or remediated. This interpretation is dependent on the *number* of *relevant* items answered correctly. This is determined by the percentage correct and an inspection of the nature of the objectives measured by the test items.

Grade Equivalent.   A grade equivalent score is commonly reported and commonly misinterpreted. There is a practical quality to expressing performance in relation to grade level, but this is easily misleading. **Grade equivalent (GE)** scores are expressed in terms of a year and month in school, assuming a ten-month school year. Thus, a 5.2 GE refers to fifth grade, second month (some tests delete the decimal and report the score as 52). This means that the student's raw score on the test is the same as the median score that would be obtained by the norming group of students who are in the fifth grade, second month. As with other norm-referenced measures, then, GEs indicate a student's standing in relation to the norming group. Consider Jack, a third grader who has obtained a GE of 5.7 on his mathematics achievement test. Does this mean that Jack is achieving above grade level? Does it suggest that Jack could do as well as most other fifth graders? Should he be promoted to the fifth grade? The answer to each of these questions is no. What we *can* say is that Jack has achieved about the same as students in the norming group who are in the seventh month of the fifth grade, if such students actually took the test. Compared to the other third graders in the norming group, Jack is above average, but this does not tell us much about how he could do with fifth-grade material or whether he should be in a different grade. If Jack had taken a test designed for the fifth grade, he may not have achieved a score as high as 5.7. Grade equivalent scores are useful for measuring growth or progress, and, like standard scores, they can be averaged for making group comparisons.

Criterion-Referenced and Standards-Based Achievement Tests.   In recent years, testing companies have made **criterion-referenced,** or more recently **standards-based,** tests available. The procedures for developing these tests are very similar to what teachers do for classroom tests. General goals and more specific learning targets, standards, or objectives are identified, and then items are constructed to measure these targets, standards, or objectives. The items are reviewed and field-tested to ensure technical quality. The prerequisite skills for each grade or topic are often identified. This is especially helpful information for determining whether students have the needed skills to move ahead.

Many testing companies offer tailor-made criterion-referenced tests for individual states or districts. The state or district selects the objectives it wants measured from a large bank of objectives provided by the publisher. Once the objectives are identified, appropriate items are pulled from a large bank of items. These tests are especially helpful because they can be matched so well with local learning goals.

The scores from criterion-referenced and standards-based tests are reported as the percentage of items answered correctly or mastery/nonmastery. It is important to know who has set the standard for mastery/nonmastery, particularly for tests that are not customized for the district. Other guidelines for interpreting these test scores for instructional planning are summarized in Figure 4.2. The suggestions emphasize using your own professional judgment about the adequacy of the definition of skill or area assessed and the items that measure it.

It is becoming increasingly common for teachers to have access to student scores from state-mandated accountability programs. These scores may be from students the teacher had the previous year or from students currently enrolled in the

FIGURE 4.2   Suggestions for Interpreting Criterion-Referenced and Standards-Based Standardized Tests

1. Check the specificity and clarity of the definitions of the achievement domains and skills that are assessed. They should be delimited, clearly specified, and match well with your instructional plans.

2. Are there a sufficient number of items to measure each separate skill or objective? If there are fewer than six items, interpret with caution or combine with other items into larger clusters. With a small number of objective items, the influence of guessing increases, which decreases reliability.

3. How difficult are the test items? You will need to inspect sample items to gauge difficulty. Answering fewer items that are more difficult may mean the same thing as answering all easy items correctly.

4. Base your interpretation on what is measured by reviewing sample items, as well as on what the publisher says the items measure.

Source: Adapted from Linn, R. L. & Gronlund, N. E., *Measurement and assessment in teaching,* 8th edition. Copyright © 2000, p. 479. Reprinted by permission of Pearson Education, Inc., Upper Saddle River, New Jersey.

class. Analyzing scores of students from last year is helpful in confirming their progress and determining weaknesses in curriculum or teaching that should be addressed in the current year. Scores of current students, indicating their performance at the end of the previous school year, are helpful as long as the interpretation takes into account several factors. First, these scores are usually reported in categories or subscales as well as for the total test, and these groupings of items refer to student performance in the corresponding domains of knowledge and skills. It is not what the individual items measure but what is represented by the items that is important. The tests sample from the larger domains. Thus, it is important to generalize from the group of items to the targets, objectives, or subscales they represent. Second, these scores should be disaggregated, if possible, by groups of students. This allows for more specific probing of certain students to confirm what is suggested by the test scores. In doing this, be careful of using the average score, since this value is distorted by a few high or low scores. Third, consider possible sources of error or student motivation issues that could effect student performance. Fourth, be wary of comparing the percentage of items answered correctly for different subscales or domains. Because items differ in difficulty, such comparisons are usually not warranted. Fifth, keep interpretations at the level of groups of students rather than individual student, unless there are unusually high or low scores. Finally, as with other types of assessments, consider these as barometers of student performance that could be quite different with changes over the summer; always verify with other information.

Aptitude Tests.   Standardized **aptitude tests** measure a student's cognitive ability, potential, or capacity to learn. This ability is determined by both in-school and out-of-school experiences. Thus, aptitude tests are less specifically tied to what is taught in school than are achievement tests.

Aptitude tests are developed to enable you to predict future achievement. They provide a measure of current developed ability, not innate capacity that cannot change. This level of ability is helpful in planning instruction in two ways: knowing the general capabilities students bring to the class in different areas and knowing the discrepancies between aptitude and achievement.

An understanding of the general ability levels of your students will help you design instructional experiences and group students appropriately. Suppose one class has an average aptitude score of 83 (below average) and another a score of 120 (above average). Would you use the same teaching materials and approaches in each of these classes? Similarly, would you give the same assignments to individual students who differ widely in ability? Research in aptitude-treatment interactions suggests that student achievement is maximized when the method of instruction or learning activity matches the aptitude. For example, low-ability students may need remediation, and high-ability students would benefit most from enrichment activities. For cooperative learning, it is best to form groups that have mixed levels of aptitude.

Aptitude tests are also used for determining *expected* learning by examining any discrepancy between ability and achievement. If there is a large discrepancy and if other information is consistent, a student may be an underachiever. Many standardized test services provide a report that includes both aptitude and achievement test score results and presents predicted scores. This makes the determination of discrepancy easier.

Readiness Tests.   **Readiness tests** are actually a specialized type of aptitude test. However, readiness tests, because of the high number of items from specific skill areas, can also be used diagnostically to determine the skills students need to improve if they are to be successful in school. Thus, readiness tests both predict achievement and diagnose weaknesses.

Most readiness tests are used in early elementary grades and for reading. The tests are helpful in identifying particular skills and knowledge to plan instruction and in designing remedial exercises. For example, the *Boehm Test of Basic Concepts—Revised* assesses student comprehension of the basic verbal concepts that are needed for comprehension of verbal communication (e.g., concepts such as many, smallest, nearest). Reading readiness tests are helpful in identifying skills that need to be mastered, such as visual discrimination of letters, auditory discrimination, recognition of letters and numbers, and following instructions. Readiness tests should *never* be used as the sole criterion for determining whether a child has the skills and knowledge to begin kindergarten or first grade. Scores from these tests should always be used with other information to provide a more comprehensive evaluation of readiness.

Uses of Standardized Tests.   I have mentioned throughout this discussion of different types of standardized and other large-scale tests some uses for planning instruction before the beginning of the year and during the first week. These suggestions, and some others, are included in Figure 4.3. Remember that results from this type of testing should *never be used as the only source of information to make deci-*

FIGURE 4.3   Suggestions for Using Standardized Tests for Instructional Planning

1. **Use results for identifying the level and range of student ability.** In conjunction with other information, these tests can provide objective evidence of the students' learning ability and achievement.

2. **Use differences between different subjects or skills to identify the students' relative strengths and weaknesses.** Focus instruction on improving weak areas, especially if the weak areas are consistent for a group of students. Use aptitude tests for ability, norm-referenced achievement tests to identify general strengths and weaknesses, criterion-referenced tests to identify specific strengths and weaknesses, and readiness tests to identify learning errors or deficiencies.

3. **Use results to provide an initial perspective of overall ability and achievement.** In conjunction with other information, use the results to establish realistic expectations. Do not form fatalistic expectations from low test scores, nor unrealistically high expectations from high test scores.

4. **Use test results to identify specific weaknesses in students that may be hindering progress.**

5. **Use results to identify discrepancies between ability and achievement.** Interpret with caution; verify with other evidence.

6. **Use results for modifying learning targets.** Initial learning targets can be modified by test results. If students are weak in an important area, new targets can be established. Targets that students have already attained can be changed to the right level.

7. **Use results, with other evidence, for initial student grouping.**

8. **Use results to identify areas that need further investigation.** Standardized tests are like car temperature gauges—the scores can indicate that something is wrong, but further investigation is needed to confirm the nature of the problem. This may be accomplished by checking other records of a student's performance, talking with other teachers who have taught the student, closely observing the student's in-class performance, and asking the student to perform specific tasks that can confirm difficulties.

sions about instruction. Rather, it is important to use several sources of information to provide an accurate portrait of your students.

Information Cards

At the elementary level, it is common to complete some kind of information card or sheet that provides the students' new teachers with a summary of important information. These cards are especially helpful if they are targeted to placements in groups. For example, the last reading or mathematics unit completed by a student can be indicated to give the teacher a sense of where to begin instruction. It is a convenient way to communicate any special problems or to note special circumstances that may be difficult to clarify in a cumulative folder. Often these cards are for teachers' eyes only and are not part of the cumulative folder. It is not uncommon for teachers to review the cards and destroy them. Figure 4.4 shows a sample information card.

Name _____	Grouping/Placement Information Card	Placement for Year 20 _____ /_____
Grade _____ Sex _____ DOB_____		
Student # _____ Tel _____		Grade _____

Reading Placement

GRP   Open Court   (Circle One)

Beginning Level: _____ Unit: _____

Grade Avg. for Year: E S M N   (Circle One)
                        A B C D U

Comments: _____

_____

Math Placement

Basic Math Facts at Grade Level:
    Mastery/Nonmastery   (Circle One)
CSMP: Successful/Unsuccessful   (Circle One)

Grade Avg. for Year: E S M N   (Circle One)
                        A B C D U

Comments: _____

_____

Pertinent Information:

General Behavior: ☐ Excellent   ☐ Good   ☐ Average   ☐ Poor
General Work Habits: ☐ Excellent   ☐ Good   ☐ Average   ☐ Poor
Special Services Rec'd: ☐ Reading   ☐ Chapter 1 ☐ LD   ☐ Gifted   ☐ Speech   ☐ Other
Confidential Folder: ☐ Yes   ☐ No

Health Problems: _____

Retained in Grade _____ Year _____

Moved to New Classroom: _____ Grade _____ Month/Year

Comments: _____

Current Teacher _____ Form # 1085-1989

FIGURE 4.4   **Example of an Information Card**

After the First Week: Now What Do You Know about Your Students?

Once school has started, you will make more targeted preinstructional assessments to learn about your students. The nature of these assessments varies considerably by grade level and general learning goals. At the elementary level, teachers are usually concerned about both academic and social dimensions, and at the secondary level, teachers tend to focus on academic preparation, ability, and student interest in the subject. Teachers tend to view this information as much more important than information gleaned from previously taken tests. The information comes mainly from two sources—informal observation and structured exercises—and is usually gathered during the first week of the year or semester.

Informal Observation

Most preinstructional assessment consists of informal observation. During the first few days of school, teachers are constantly looking for any clues about the nature of their students. These observations are made from spontaneous student behavior. The typical four steps involved are collecting information, interpreting the information, synthesizing the information, and naming the characteristic of the student the observation describes (Gordon, 1987).

During the first step, the teacher observes student appearance and behavior. What type of clothes does the student wear? Is the student clean? Does the student talk with other students? What nonverbal cues are present? What kind of vocabulary does the student use? How well does the student speak? How does the student's face look? Is the student courteous? Does the student volunteer to answer questions? It is not so much a matter of looking for certain types of appearance or behavior as it is a careful mental recording of student actions, reactions, and interactions with other students. Stiggins (2001) uses the term **personal communication** to describe forms of teacher–student interactions that provide preinstructional information as well as information throughout the year. Like a good physician, with experience effective teachers know what to attend to.

The second step is interpreting what has been observed. At this point, teachers make judgments about what the appearance or behavior means. For example, a teacher may form the following tentative explanations:

> "Tom is always late to school and unprepared. I wonder if there is a situation at home that I need to know about."

> "Anne is eager to answer almost every question with a smile. She is listening and motivated to learn and participate."

> "Tim doesn't participate much and rarely looks directly at me when I speak to him. This may mean he has low self-esteem."

> "Jane does not interact much with the other students. Perhaps she is not well liked by them."

In each case, an interpretation is made from the observation. It is this interpretation that provides meaning.

Naturally, different teachers can observe the same behavior and come up with different interpretations. In this sense, informal observations are *subjective*. That is, meaning is derived only by professional judgment of what is observed. Of course, it is possible for an observation to be *biased*, or heavily influenced by what the teacher wants to see or wants to believe. Your own perspectives, preferences, and attitudes influence how you interpret your observations. Because each of us views the world differently, differences in interpretation can be expected. It is important to understand how your background may influence your interpretations, and it is best to obtain corroborating interpretations provided by different sources of information (e.g., another teacher or more structured assessment).

In the third step, interpretations are synthesized into meaningful traits or characterizations of the students. This involves inductive thinking whereby several separate interpretations are pulled together to form a tentative conclusion about the trait or characteristic (e.g., "Tom is motivated," "Erin is from a dysfunctional home," "Jose is way behind on social skills"). At this point it is important to be aware of the need to have a sufficient number of interpretations so that the synthesis provides an accurate description. It is also helpful to use others' interpretations to validate your own.

The fourth step is naming the trait or characteristic. This step is idiosyncratic in that your definitions of terms such as *motivated, behind, uncooperative, easily distracted, talkative, able,* and so on, are not necessarily the same as others' definitions. Thus, how you characterize a student or class has meaning according to your definition of the trait. Furthermore, the more general name of the trait is likely to be remembered and influence subsequent interactions. That is, you are less likely to remember the specific behaviors and more likely to recall that the student was self-confident, lazy, shy, capable, and the like.

As shown in Figure 4.5, it is important to emphasize the cyclical nature of these informal observations. As you begin to make observations and interpretations, you will arrive at tentative syntheses. Then you will make further observations and interpretations to confirm or change these tentative conclusions.

Structured Exercises

A good approach to evaluating current student knowledge and skills is to design informal, structured exercises that will provide you with an opportunity to observe students in the context of specific performance situations. These exercises are not like a formal pretest, but they are more structured than informal observation.

One approach is to design a class activity in which all the students participate. This could be a writing assignment, an oral presentation, or group work. For example, asking students to write about their summer vacation, in class, can help to identify language arts skills. Students can interview each other about their summer vacations and make short presentations to the class. Games can be used to observe students' math skills. Students can be asked to read aloud. A common technique is to ask students to write information about themselves on cards, such as names of family members, hobbies, and interests. Any one of these demonstrations of knowledge or skills would not be sufficient for instructional planning, but as you build a portrait of your students from many such observations—and combine this information with previous test scores, student records, and comments from other teachers—by the end of the first week of school you will have a pretty accurate idea of the strengths and weaknesses of your students.

One aspect of successful structured exercises is to keep them *nonthreatening.* This is important because you want to minimize student anxiety, which may be

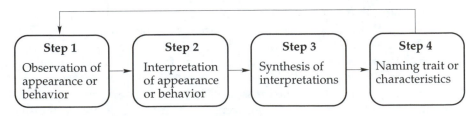

FIGURE 4.5   Steps in Informal Observation

Case Study for Reflection

Mr. James has been a seventh-grade teacher for five years and always feels overwhelmed for the first few weeks of each school term. He has often wondered how to better acquaint himself with his students' abilities and personality traits, which might positively affect his teaching and assessment practices. Mrs. Smith, in the classroom next door, has said that she often uses anecdotal records to help her with this identification process. Mr. James wants to try this approach also. He has decided to keep notepads handy to jot down student behaviors, abilities, and insights throughout the day.

1. What are some foreseeable problems with this project, which Mr. James has not yet considered?
2. Should Mr. James consider alternative ways to achieve this goal?

high anyway at the beginning of the year. Obviously, it is best not to grade the exercise. In addition, you will want to arrange the conditions to be as comfortable as possible. Having a student read orally to a small group or only to you is probably less threatening than reading to the entire class. If students are able to work at their own pace, without strict time constraints, they are more likely to feel less threatened. Avoid comparisons of students.

Pretests

During the first few days of school, some teachers ask students to complete a formal pretest of the content that will be covered. The pretest would supposedly indicate what students know and don't know or what they can or cannot do. For several reasons, however, it is doubtful that the information from a pretest will be very helpful in planning instruction. First, at least in the fall, students have returned from vacation and have probably not thought too much about world history, algebra, or other school subjects. Their actual or true knowledge may not be reflected on a surprise test. With some review, the knowledge would be much better. Second, it is hard to motivate students to do their best on such tests. What do they have to gain by trying hard to answer the questions? This is especially true for older students. Third, to be helpful diagnostically, the pretest would need to be fairly long and detailed, which would be difficult to find time for during the first week. Finally, presenting students with a pretest may not be the best way to start a class. Asking students what they know about something they will learn may be intimidating and create anxiety about the class (on the other hand, a pretest can communicate to students that the teacher is serious about learning). For these reasons, formal pretests are not used very often. The validity of the information is questionable, and the effect on the classroom environment and teacher–student relationships may be negative. If you use a pretest, do not grade it or average it into final grades.

If a pretest is to be used successfully, it needs to be short and targeted to specific knowledge and skills. Students need to be motivated to do their best work, and the teacher needs to make clear to students that the purpose of a pretest is to help them learn more and help the teacher plan more effective instruction. The results may suggest the need for further diagnostic assessment. Cheri Magill, a German teacher, puts it this way:

> Preassessment was a very important part of my diagnosing the content knowledge of students taking German. When planning my first lessons for them I incorporated short diagnostic tests designed to let me know their degree of skill in manipulating specific sentence patterns, verb tenses, article forms, and declinations of nouns. This information, once analyzed, helped me identify what content to emphasize and what content I could safely ignore. Knowing that students could not, for example, correctly form the past tense of certain verbs was not enough. Further assessment was needed to determine exactly what stood in the way. Was it the meaning of the verb? Was it how to correctly form the participle? Was choosing and/or conjugating the correct helping verb the problem? Was word order an issue? Getting the data from student performance on these short diagnostic tests helped me assess their needs and better plan instruction at the appropriate level of difficulty for them.

Notice that the pretests helped Cheri Magill assess student needs. The information was used with other assessments to plan instruction.

Teacher Expectations

Some teachers may not want to review student records or test scores because they want to avoid forming inappropriate expectations. This is a valid concern, but the real issue is not whether expectations will be acquired, but forming *realistic, accurate* expectations that are flexible. **Teacher expectations** are beliefs about what students are capable of knowing or doing, and preinstructional assessments are important in forming these beliefs. You will have expectations. They cannot be avoided. What you want to do is make sure they are as unbiased as possible, relevant to the subject matter to be taught.

Expectations are based on a number of different student attributes, including socioeconomic status, test scores, classroom performance, appearance, knowledge of siblings, name, gender, and race. The expectations may affect the nature of the interactions the teacher has with the students, which can, in turn, affect subsequent student performance. This cycle of influences is illustrated in Figure 4.6.

In their worst form, teacher expectations can be self-fulfilling and detrimental. Students become what is expected of them. According to Good and Brophy (2003), the process looks like this:

1. Early in the year, the teacher forms expectations.
2. The teacher interacts differently with the students, consistent with these expectations.
3. This treatment informs students about what they may achieve or what behavior is appropriate for them.
4. If the teacher's treatment is consistent over time and students do not resist, it will affect the self-concept and classroom conduct of the students.

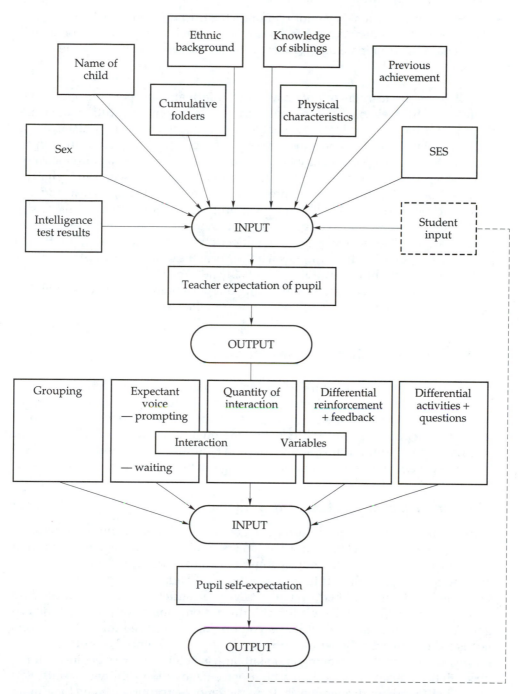

FIGURE 4.6   The Behavioral Cycle between Teacher Input and Learner Output

Source: Braun, C., Teacher expectation: Sociopsychological dynamics. *Review of Educational Research, 46,* 206. Copyright © 1976 by the American Educational Research Association. Reprinted by permission of the publisher.

5. Subsequent student behavior reinforces the teacher's initial expectations.
6. Eventually, student achievement is affected: high-expectation students will achieve at their potential, low-expectation students will achieve less than their potential.

It is best for teachers to obtain as much information as possible about their students so that their expectations are accurate. Classroom observation and classroom performance of students are what teachers use most to form initial expectations. Standardized tests and other external sources of information are helpful because they are independent of what are sometimes a teacher's unconsciously biased perceptions. If anything, teachers tend to dismiss low test scores in their evaluations of students. This is a safe approach; if you are going to err, err toward more positive expectations. It is better, however, to have realistic expectations of students. This will allow you to target instruction more accurately, and it will help to provide appropriate evaluations of student performance. For example, is it best to give similar feedback to two students who perform the same when one student has high ability and the other low ability? Probably not. Your feedback will depend on how the performance is related to ability. If your perception of the student's ability is not accurate, your feedback will be less helpful than it could be.

High-Quality Preinstructional Assessment

Teacher assessments of students before instruction form the foundation for many instructional decisions and influence the nature of subsequent interactions between the teacher and students. So it is very important to employ certain procedures and approaches that will enhance the quality of these assessments. Not surprisingly, these procedures, summarized in Figure 4.7, can be organized around the more general points made in Chapter 3 regarding high-quality assessments.

Clear and Appropriate Learning Targets

Before you begin to examine information about your students, you need to establish clear learning targets that are not too specific. These targets should include some idea of the criteria that you will use to evaluate student learning. My suggestion is to begin with unit targets. Consider different types of targets as well. Once the targets are identified, you can design preinstructional assessments to give you information that will have a direct influence on your modification of the targets. You may find that the emphasis you originally intended for certain targets needs to be changed to better meet the needs of your students. For example, suppose you have mostly reasoning and skill targets before the class begins. If it appears that your class will contain a high percentage of low-ability students, you may need to rethink this emphasis. It may be more appropriate to include more knowledge targets to provide students with the prerequisite skills they need.

FIGURE 4.7   Criteria for Ensuring High-Quality Preinstructional Assessments

Clear and Appropriate Learning Targets. Base preinstructional assessments on initial unit learning targets.

Appropriateness of Assessment Methods. Match the method of assessment with the learning targets.

Validity. Strengthen the validity of your inferences by using multiple methods over time and looking for discrepancies.

Reliability. Reduce error in preinstructional assessment by using multiple methods and giving students the benefit of the doubt.

Fairness. Avoid inappropriate expectations by using procedures to reduce bias.

Positive Consequences. Consider the effect of the preinstructional assessments. Will they promote student learning?

Practicality and Efficiency. Use assessments that are familiar and not too time-consuming.

Clarity in learning targets also focuses your attention on right areas. Otherwise, it is easy to form more general opinions that may be stereotypes. Initial impressions are strong and influence subsequent observations and decisions.

Appropriateness of Assessment Methods

Your methods of preinstruction assessment need to match the type of information you need. Generally, the strengths of preinstructional assessment methods are similar to those in Chapter 3. For knowledge and simple understanding targets, it is best to examine test scores from previous years and ask knowledge questions during the first week. Deep understanding, reasoning, and skill targets are assessed by aptitude test scores, informal observation, and performance on structured exercises. Product targets can be assessed by looking at student work from the previous year (portfolios are good for this type of assessment). Affect targets will depend on your informal observations of the students and their interactions with each other.

Validity

Preinstruction assessments are valid if the inferences you make about your students are accurate. To enhance validity, you need to use multiple assessment methods for each learning target and look for consistency with these results. I cannot stress enough how important it is to *never rely on a single source of information.* Be careful not to allow inferences about some targets to influence inferences about other targets. For example, you may infer that a particular student has weak writing skills. Before you conclude that the student also has weak reading skills and a poor vocabulary, you need to gather information about each of these areas. It would be invalid to conclude that the student had poor reading skills by examining only his or her writing skills.

It is helpful to look for consistency across time. Once you have formulated an initial impression, examine further student behavior for evidence that is inconsistent with this impression. Give the student opportunities to demonstrate behavior that is inconsistent with your impression. Given such opportunities, consistent behavior would provide evidence for valid inferences.

The validity of your impressions and expectations will also be influenced by your general beliefs and philosophy of education, which form a lens through which your observations are filtered. For example, interpretations of knowledge and skill may be affected by whether you believe all students can succeed, or whether you believe in maximizing the learning of each student.

Reliability

Remember that reliability is concerned with how much error is present in the assessment. Multiple assessments reduce the overall error, as do those that are longer. That is, standardized test scores are more reliable than your informal observations over a day or two. Keep a proper perspective about error. Realize that any single assessment may be determined more by error than anything else, and give students the benefit of preinstructional assessments that are borderline. Schedule a sufficient number of observations to establish a pattern of behavior or response. Treat initial evaluations as tentative judgments that are confirmed with additional information. When in doubt, ask other teachers for their judgments.

Fairness

A fair preinstructional assessment is one that provides an equal opportunity to all students. This means that your interpretation of the information is not influenced by race, gender, ethnic background, handicapping condition, or other factors unrelated to what is being assessed. It is important to remain unbiased. Sometimes teachers will interpret cultural differences as deficits, forming lower expectations because of race or ethnicity. It is also difficult not to form expectations based on student socioeconomic status. Students from poor families are often expected to know less and be less capable than students from affluent homes. Keep the focus on student performance and behavior and suspend judgments made on the basis of cultural or economic differences.

Positive Consequences

You will want to conduct preinstructional assessment so that the results will have positive consequences for you and your students. If the information is viewed as helpful, this attitude will facilitate positive consequences. You should feel more confident about your teaching as you plan instruction on an assessment foundation. If you use the information to form realistic expectations, your behavior toward the students will communicate positive, realistic messages about what they will achieve.

Practicality and Efficiency

Like all assessments, those done before instruction need to be practical and efficient. It is most productive to use information that you are familiar with and that will not take too much time. For example, you may find that the specific skills listed on standardized test reports for your students are too numerous to consider individually. You may find it helpful to look for specific grades or teacher comments in cumulative files, making note of unusual or conflicting information that will need further investigation. During the first week, your assessments need to be simple and direct, providing sufficient information but not more than you need for planning. Whatever methods and approaches you use, try to be as clear as possible about how you will use the information *before* you collect it. It is easy to assess with the thought that the results may be of use, but often, without carefully considering its specific use, information is collected but never used.

Summary

Assessment occurs before instruction to facilitate instructional planning. Some information is available before school begins, though the most relevant information is gathered by the classroom teacher after school begins. Major points in the chapter for effective use of preinstructional assessment include the following:

- Before school begins, information is contained in school records, standardized tests, and information cards. School records contain grades, teacher comments, and other data. Teachers should carefully review this information to learn as much as possible about their students in order to form accurate yet flexible expectations.
- Combine information in school records with teacher observations and other direct assessments.
- Different types of standardized tests provide important information.
- Proper interpretation of scores from norm-referenced standardized tests depends on the nature of the norm group and on understanding relative standing as indicated by percentile rank and grade equivalent.
- Test batteries can indicate strengths and weaknesses.
- Criterion-referenced and standards-based tests measure performance on clearly defined skills or areas.
- Aptitude and readiness tests measure capacity to learn.
- During the first week of school, teachers use informal observation, structured exercises, and pretests to supplement existing information.
- Pretests should be short and should not interfere with establishing a positive classroom climate.
- Informal observation consists of observing student behavior, interpreting it, synthesizing, and naming the trait or characteristic. Nonthreatening, informal exercises are used to assess specific skills.

■ Teacher expectations are teacher beliefs about what students are capable of achieving.

■ Expectations are formed from many sources of information before instruction. These expectations should be realistic and avoid negative self-fulfilling prophecies.

■ Criteria for high-quality preinstructional assessment were presented.

SELF-INSTRUCTIONAL REVIEW EXERCISES

1. Summarize the advantages and disadvantages of using information in school records to learn about students before school starts. Do you agree that it is best to know as much as possible about your students? Why or why not?

2. What kind of information would lead one to conclude that a student has clear weaknesses in a particular skill?

3. How is it possible for all school districts in a state to be above the 50th percentile on a standardized norm-referenced test?

4. Indicate whether each of the following characteristics refers to a norm-referenced (NR), criterion-referenced (CR), aptitude (A), or state (S) standardized test. More than one may apply to each characteristic.

   a. Reports scores as percentage of items correct
   b. Shows capacity to learn
   c. Reports grade equivalents
   d. Reports percentile scores
   e. Readiness test

5. Using Figure 4.6 as a general guide, draw a diagram that illustrates a teacher expectation that has applied to you or one that you have observed. Label each part of the diagram so you can identify each step of the expectation process.

ANSWERS TO SELF-INSTRUCTIONAL REVIEW EXERCISES

1. Refer to Figure 4.1 for the advantages and disadvantages of using school records. The major issue related to knowing as much as possible about the students before you meet them is your confidence about forming appropriate expectations. As long as you keep in mind the need to be flexible in your expectations, more information is better than less.

2. When the information from several different sources suggests the same conclusion, when there is a pattern of performance for several years, and when your own informal assessment coincides with what is in school records.

3. Because norms are established in one year (e.g., 1995) and then used for several more years, and current scores (1999) are compared to the 1995 norms. Before new norms are established, all the school districts may target skills assessed on the test.

4. a. clearly CR, some NR and S, not A; b. A; c. NR; d. NR, A, maybe S; e. A.

5. The answer to this question will vary depending on the individual student, but it should correspond to the figure. Remember that expectations do not influence students unless there is differential teacher behavior. In other words, fully operational expectations include both the teacher's belief about students and the teacher's behavior toward the students.

SUGGESTIONS FOR ACTION RESEARCH

1. Ask for access to school records to review the contents. For several students, determine if the information is consistent. For example, are standardized test scores and grades consistent? Compare the composite picture of some students as determined from a review of their records with observations of them in the classroom and teachers' comments.

2. Interview several teachers about how they use information about their students before instruction. Ask them what data they use and why and how they gain access to it. If they do not use specific sources of information, such as pretests, ask them why they do not. Ask them if they like to have special information about all their students and on what they base their expectations of their students.

3. Observe some students informally in a classroom and make some judgments about their academic strengths and weaknesses. Then compare your judgments with those of the teacher or school records. Ask the teacher what you could do to make more accurate judgments.

4. Locate a standardized test manual to determine the definition of some of the knowledge and skills that are assessed. Through a review of the objectives and sample items, compare what the test is assessing with what is taught in a local school curriculum.

CHAPTER 5

Assessing Student Progress during Instruction

Based on assessments done before school and during the first week, you have set your learning targets and planned your lessons. Now is the time for instruction. As we have seen, teaching is fast paced and hectic. Many different tasks and events occur simultaneously, and decisions must be made quickly. Research has shown that in this complex environment, effective teachers employ a process of beginning instruction, assessing student progress, making decisions about what to do next, responding to students, and revising planned instruction as appropriate. During the process of instruction, then, assessment takes place simultaneously to inform teacher decision making. It is as if instruction and assessment are woven seamlessly together, where assessment is essentially indistinguishable from instruction. All of this happens very

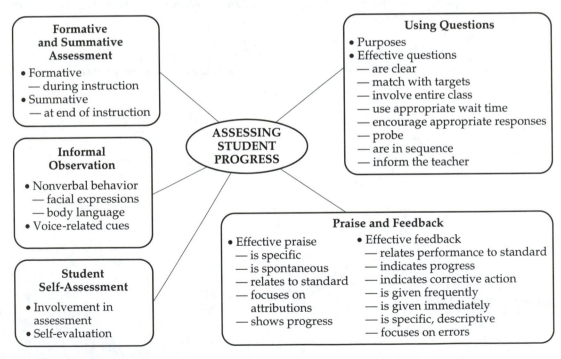

CHAPTER 5   Concept Map

quickly. Jeremy Lloyd is a high school mathematics teacher. This is how he characterizes the importance of integrating instructional decision making with assessment:

> Teachers need to create a warm and trusting classroom. Students need to trust their
> teachers not to make unrealistic demands, move too quickly through new material,
> or lead them too far, too soon, from the comfort zone of knowledge they have al-
> ready mastered. Teachers moving too quickly will "lose" their students. Teachers
> will gain their students' trust when they move forward cautiously, stopping often to
> review progress with students, and providing them with opportunities to ask ques-
> tions. This is especially important when students are being challenged to be creative
> and engage in different kinds of problem solving. The teacher must be able to gauge
> when "enough is enough" for a while, and then bring the class together again for
> some reassurance and confidence-building through some "lower level" learning.
> Then the class can go back to working on riskier learning targets. When the class is
> engaged in this kind of work, the teacher, more than ever, needs honest and straight-
> forward feedback from students. They must feel comfortable about letting their
> teacher know exactly what they are thinking and feeling; at the same time the
> teacher is constantly conducting checks for understanding.

A key element in this process is continuous monitoring by teachers to ascer-
tain their students' reactions to instruction and students' progress toward understanding the content or accomplishing the skill. How is the flow of activities?
How are students responding to the activities? Are they interested and attentive?
Should I speed up or slow down? Should I give more examples? Here is where
good assessment is essential to effective teaching and where assessment drives instruction. You need to know what to look for in your students while you deliver
instruction, how to interpret what you see and hear, how to respond to the students, and then how to adjust your teaching. Strickland and Strickland (1998)
point out that effective teachers are "always searching for patterns, supporting
students as they take risks and move forward, and watching in order to better facilitate student learning . . . and try to understand how each student is progressing" (p. 31). In this chapter, we look at the two primary methods you use to assess
students while teaching—observation and asking questions—as well as how you
provide helpful feedback and effective praise, and how student self-assessment facilitates students' ongoing involvement in assessment.

The importance of integrating assessment into teacher decision making
is emphasized in the Assessment Standards for School Mathematics (NCTM, 1995):
"The quality of teachers' instructional decisions depends, in part, on the quality of
their assessment and their purposeful sampling of evidence during instruction"
(p. 45). Such teaching blurs the lines between instruction and assessment, seeing assessment as an opportunity for learning rather than an interruption in learning.

Formative and Summative Assessment

As pointed out in Chapter 1, formative assessment occurs during instruction: formative and summative assessment. Formative, or *informal*, assessment occurs as
you proceed with a lesson or unit to provide ongoing feedback to the teacher and

FIGURE 5.1   Characteristics of Formative and Summative Assessments

	Formative	Summative
Purpose	To monitor and improve instruction and student learning	To document student performance on a learning unit
Time of Assessment	During instruction	After instruction is completed
Assessment Techniques	Informal observation, listening to student questions and responses to teacher questions	Chapter tests, final exams, reports, term papers, projects
Use of Information	To improve a process while it is ongoing	To judge its success in student learning and instruction, and to identify systematic student errors
Structure	Flexible, informal	Fixed, formal, standard-ized for all students

Source: Adapted from Airasian, P. W. (2001). *Classroom assessment* (4th ed.). New York: McGraw-Hill, p. 145. Reproduced with permission of the McGraw-Hill Companies.

student (Airasian, 2001; Phye, 1997a). The purpose of formative assessment is to provide corrective actions as instruction occurs to enhance student learning. It consists of informal observation, questioning, student responses to questions, homework, worksheets, and teacher feedback to the student. Formative assessment is integrated with instruction on a daily basis. It is flexible and idiosyncratic.

In contrast, summative, or *formal,* assessment takes place at the end of a unit of study. Its primary purpose is to document student performance after instruction is completed. We are all familiar with this type of assessment in the form of term papers, chapter achievement tests, final exams, and research projects. Summative assessments are also used to identify patterns in the errors that students make. This is accomplished by examining wrong answers to discern systematic mistakes. Such an analysis is often helpful in making decisions about the type of instruction a student needs.

We will examine several types of summative assessment methods in the next few chapters. This chapter focuses on formative assessments. Figure 5.1 summarizes the characteristics of both types of assessment.

Informal Observation

No assessment activity is more pervasive for most teachers than the informal observation of student behavior. Teachers constantly look at students and listen to what is occurring in the class. These observations are made to determine such factors as:

- the nature of student participation in class discussion
- the kinds of questions asked
- the interpersonal skills used in cooperative groups
- the correctness of student responses to questions
- the nature of student responses to examples
- how students react to an assignment
- how students react to grades on a test
- the verbal skills demonstrated in expressing thoughts
- the pacing of a lesson
- whether more examples are needed
- which students to call on
- the interest level of the students
- the degree of understanding demonstrated in student answers

This list could go on and on. Informal observation is unstructured in the sense that there is no set format or procedure, but it is not random. For example, effective teachers learn to observe key students in each class who show their reactions more clearly than others. Some of these students are vocal and stand out, and others are quiet leaders.

We first consider the observation of nonverbal behavior, and then we will look at vocal cues such as pauses and tone of voice.

Assessing Nonverbal Behavior

Teachers rely greatly on students' body language, facial expressions, and eye contact to accurately observe and interpret student behavior. These actions are called *nonverbal* because the message is communicated by something about the student other than the content of what he or she says. These nonverbal cues are often more important than what is said. According to Mehrabian (1981), as much as 93 percent of a message is communicated by nonverbal factors. Some of this is through general appearance and behavior such as body language, gestures, and facial expressions, and some is communicated by vocal cues that accompany what is said, such as tone of voice, inflection, pauses, and emphasis.

Nonverbal behaviors help you to assess both meaning and emotion. For instance, we rely on facial and bodily expressions to determine the intent of the message. Nonverbal cues punctuate verbal messages in much the same way that exclamation points, question marks, boldface, and italics focus the meaning of written language. Knapp (1996) suggests that this punctuation occurs in the following ways:

- *Confirming or Repeating.* When nonverbal behavior is consistent with what is said verbally, the message is confirmed or repeated. For instance, when Sally gave the correct answer to a question, her eyes lit up (facial expression), she sat up straight in her chair and her hand was stretched up toward the ceiling (body motion), and her answer was animated and loud (voice quality). She indicated nonverbally as well as verbally that she knew the answer.

- *Denying or Confusing.* Nonverbal and verbal messages are often contradictory, suggesting denial or confusion. For example, Ms. Thomas has just asked her class if they are prepared to begin their small group work. The students say yes, but at the same time look down with confused expressions on their faces. The real message is that they are not ready, despite what they have said.
- *Strengthening or Emphasizing.* Nonverbal behavior can punctuate what is said by adding emotional color, feelings, and intensity. These emotions strengthen or emphasize the verbal message. Suppose Mr. Terrell suggested to Teresa that she take the lead in the next school play. Teresa responds by saying, "No, I wouldn't want to do that," while she shakes her head, avoids eye contact, and becomes rigid. Teresa doesn't just mean no, she means NO! If she really wanted to take the lead, her nonverbal behavior would deny her verbal response.
- *Controlling or Regulating.* Nonverbal behavior can be used to control others and regulate the nature of the interaction. In a cooperative learning group, you may observe that when Tom goes to ask David for some help, David controls the conversation by looking away.

You will find that emotions and feelings are often communicated more clearly and accurately by nonverbal than by verbal cues. Not only are nonverbal cues the richest source of information on affect, they are the most stable and consistent. Because most nonverbal behavior is not consciously controlled, the messages are relatively free of distortion and deception. It is not difficult, when you consciously attend to appropriate nonverbal behavior, to determine mood, mental state, attitude, self-assurance, responsiveness, confidence, interest, anger, fear, and other affective and emotional dispositions. This is especially helpful when the nonverbal message conflicts with the verbal one. That is, *how* students say something, through their nonverbal behavior, is as important, if not more so, than *what* they say. Think about a student who answers a question but does so with a slow, low voice, looking away. Even if the answer is correct, these nonverbal cues are telling you something important about the student's level of confidence. Your interpretation would be different for a student who looked directly at you, spoke with authority, and whose face displayed excitement. In this section we look at how specific nonverbal behaviors communicate different meanings and emotions and how teachers respond to these cues.

Facial Expressions.   The face is the most important source of nonverbal information because it is the primary outlet for emotions and it rarely distorts meaning. The face projects a great variety of messages, in part because of the complex and flexible set of muscles. To know what to look for it is best to focus on three areas: the brows and forehead; the eyes, lids, and nose; and the lower face. The upper portion of the face is more likely to indicate feelings of concern and anger (e.g., the brows are lowered and drawn together in anger). The lower area, particularly the mouth, will communicate happiness and amusement. Smiles, frowns, twisted lips, a raised chin, a clenched mouth, and other expressions are also fairly clear in what they communicate.

Let's see how you do with a short test of facial meaning (The Facial Meaning Sensitivity Test, Leathers, 1997). Figure 5.2 shows ten photographs of different facial expressions. Match the following states with the pictures:

Facial Meaning	Photograph # (from Figure 5.2)	Facial Meaning	Photograph # (from Figure 5.2)
Disgust	_____	Contempt	_____
Happiness	_____	Surprise	_____
Interest	_____	Anger	_____
Sadness	_____	Determination	_____
Bewilderment	_____	Fear	_____

The correct choices are disgust = 1, happiness = 3, interest = 8, sadness = 10, bewilderment = 2, contempt = 9, surprise = 7, anger = 6, determination = 4, and fear = 5.

For the purposes of teaching, you need to be especially careful to attend to facial expressions of bewilderment and interest. Teachers use these emotions extensively to gauge student understanding and motivation. Emotions similar to bewilderment are confusion, doubt, frustration, and puzzlement. Obviously these cues suggest that the student is not understanding or is not progressing. Interest conveys anticipation, excitement, and attention. These emotions are important as an indication of attention.

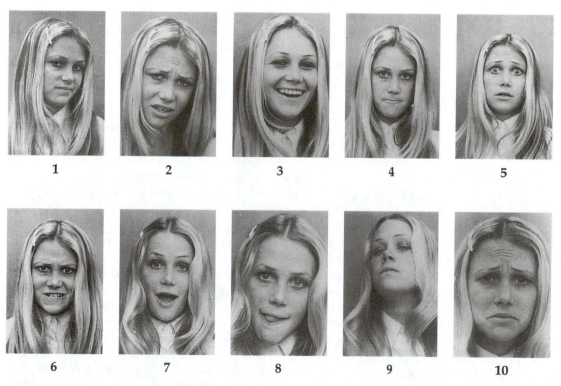

FIGURE 5.2   The Facial Meaning Sensitivity Test

Source: Leathers, D. G., *Successful nonverbal communication: Principles and applications*, 3rd edition. Copyright © 1997, p. 36. All rights reserved. Reprinted by permission of Allyn & Bacon.

The most informative aspect of the face is the eye and the nature of eye contact. Eye contact indicates a readiness to communicate, and continued direct eye contact signifies confidence and competence. Students who use positive eye contact, who look directly at you and watch your movements, are probably attentive and interested.

Averted eyes often suggest an unwillingness to respond, a lack of confidence, or a general sense of apathy. For example, if a student looks down before responding, looks away from teachers when interacting with them, keeps eyes downcast, or looks at the ceiling, a reasonable interpretation is that the student may lack confidence, knowledge, or skills and may have other negative emotions. When most of the students in a class start looking around the room, at each other, and out the window, they have lost interest and are not involved. This may mean that students do not understand well enough, or it may mean they are bored (in some cultures the lack of eye contact may indicate respect for an authority figure or older person, and not a lack of self-confidence or other negative feeling).

The pupils of the eyes convey the intensity of emotion shown more generally in the face. They tend to enlarge as we become more interested in something, more emotionally aroused, and happier with positive anticipation. Pupils contract as we become less interested and have more negative emotions such as sadness, sorrow, and indifference.

Body Language.   Like facial expressions and voice, body language, movement, and posture communicate messages. The meaning associated with different bodily cues is best understood by considering five categories of nonverbal behavior, each of which is based on a different function or purpose: emblems, illustrators, affect displays, regulators, and adapters (Ekman & Friesen, 1969).

An *emblem* is a body cue that has a direct one- or two-word verbal translation. Emblems are used to consciously communicate a particular message, such as holding up your hand with your palm facing the other person (which means "wait"), putting your finger to your puckered lips ("quiet"), and waving toward yourself ("come over"). Most of these emblems are substitutes for words.

Although not much research has been done on emblems in schools, you should be aware of possible cross-cultural differences. For example, nodding your head in the United States means that you agree, but in Japan it acknowledges only that you have received the other person's message.

An *illustrator* is used to increase clarity and awareness and to augment what is being said. It reinforces the strength of the emotional message. For example, holding your fingers close together augments "small," and pointing to an object clarifies what you intend to communicate about. If a student's fist is clenched, it may indicate anger in association with what the student has verbalized.

The third type of bodily communication is the *affect display.* These cues show emotion through the position and posture of the body and certain gestures. If the student has a rigid, tense, slumped body with arms and legs crossed, the affect is negative and defensive. Students with open, relaxed bodies who lean toward the teacher and do not fidget or tap something communicate positive affect, attention, and confidence. Suppose you notice that a student is slumped in her chair and has one hand to her mouth and the other arm clenched to her body. How would you interpret this body language? It is likely that the student is not very confident about the lesson or assignment and generally has negative emotions that will probably interfere with learning.

Regulators are used to indicate the initiation, length, and termination of verbal messages. Students use these cues to inform the teacher about whether they want to initiate a response, are finished with a comment or thought, or want to continue speaking. An obvious initiation regulator is to raise the hand or index finger. Other initiation regulators include eye contact, head nodding, smiles, and raised eyebrows. When students do not want to make a comment, they may use such "turn-denying" behaviors as staring at something (especially looking down at the desk) and slumping in the chair. Students who want to continue speaking may lean toward you, use gestures to punctuate their thoughts, and display an enthusiastic, expectant face.

The final category to describe different functions is the *adapter*. Adapters are a rich source of information about attitudes, levels of confidence, and anxiety. They include behaviors such as picking at oneself, chewing nails, and fidgeting (these indicate nervousness, anxiety, and concern). Covering the face with one's hands indicates that a message is undesirable, painful, or unpleasant.

Gestures.   Gestures are hand and arm movements that individuals use to communicate, either supplementing verbal messages or acting as the sole means through which meaning is conveyed. Gestures play an important role in child development and learning. For example, young children often point to answers or use some kind of gesture to indicate understanding. Students often use gestures as part of an explanation of something or as an answer. Gesturing allows students to express learning in a simple and direct way, often demonstrating understanding that is not apparent through language.

By paying attention to gestures, teachers are able to confirm whether students have a complete or partial understanding of something. Understanding is partial when there is discord between gestures and speech. It is more complete when gestures and speech are in concurrence. Some research suggests that gesture–speech mismatches indicate a readiness for learning (Roth, 2001).

Assessing Voice-Related Cues

Voice-related cues include tone of voice, loudness, intensity, pauses, silences, voice level, inflection, word spacing, emphases, and other aspects of voice that add color to the content of what is said. The potential of vocal cues to provide information about a student's level of understanding, confidence, and emotional state is exceeded only by facial expressions.

A summary of recent research on the relationship between vocal cues and messages is presented in Figure 5.3 (Leathers, 1997). Although this research has not been conducted with teacher/student dyads or groups, the findings do have important implications. For example, on the basis of vocal cues you would expect students who are confident in their knowledge or skill to be relatively loud rather than quiet, to have a rather rapid speaking rate, to speak in a high pitch, and to speak fluently with few

FIGURE 5.3   Vocal Cues and Messages

Vocal Cue	Message
Loudness	*Loud*—competent, enthusiastic, forceful, self-assured, excited *Quiet*—anxious, unsure, shy, indifferent
Pitch (musical note voice produces)	*High*—excited, explosively angry, emotional *Low*—calm, sad, stunned, quietly angry, indifferent *Variety*—dynamic, extroverted
Rate	*Fast*—interested, self-assured, angry, happy, proud, confident, excited, impulsive, emotional *Slow*—uninterested, unsure, unexcited, unemotional
Quality (combination of attributes)	*Flat*—sluggish, cold, withdrawn *Nasal*—unattractive, lethargic, foolish

pauses, "ahs," sentence changes, throat clearings, word repetitions, and incomplete sentences. Students who are unsure of their knowledge or ability to perform a skill are likely to speak quietly, in a low pitch with little variety, and to speak slowly with many pauses and frequent throat clearings. The student who lacks confidence will speak nonfluently, the voice will be flat, more like a monotone rather than showing variety in pitch and rate. Research has also determined that persons who demonstrate little variation in pitch and rate tend to be viewed as introverts, lacking assertiveness and dynamism. Voices that are clear, articulate, and confident are viewed as positive.

You will need to be careful not to infer lack of knowledge, confidence, anxiety, or motivation *solely* on the basis of vocal cues. Like nonverbal behavior, voice is one of many pieces of evidence that you need to consider to make an accurate assessment.

The challenge of being a teacher is being able to observe these nonverbal and verbal cues, make appropriate interpretations, and then take corrective action when needed. To help you with this I have prepared a table that combines different types of nonverbal behaviors and vocal cues in relation to particular messages students send (Figure 5.4).

I also asked some teachers to summarize the nonverbal behavior and vocal cues they attend to, how they interpret what they see and hear, and the action they take following their observation and interpretation. Examples of the teachers' responses include the following:

Nonverbal Behavior	Interpretation	Action
Students start to look around the room and at each other.	Some students are not understanding; some may be bored.	Refocus students; review previous lesson; reteach lesson; regroup students.
Room quiets; students are writing in their notebooks.	Students are motivated and on-task.	Keep going—it may not last long!

FIGURE 5.4   Messages Students Convey through Nonverbal Behavior and Vocal Cues

Message	Facial Expressions	Body Language	Vocal Cues
Confident	Relaxed, direct eye contact; pupils enlarged	Erect posture; arms and legs open; chin up; hands waving; forward position in seat	Fluent; few pauses; variety in tone; loud
Nervous	Tense; brows lowered; pupils contracted	Rigid; tense; tapping; picking	Pauses; "ah" sounds; repetition; shaky; soft; fast; quiet
Angry	Brows lowered and drawn together; teeth clenched	Fidgety; hands clenched; head down	Loud or quiet; animated
Defensive	Downcast eyes; pupils contracted; eyes squinted	Arms and legs crossed; leaning away; leaning head on hands	Loud; animated
Bored	Looking around; relaxed; pupils contracted	Slumped posture; hands to face	Soft; monotone; flat
Frustrated	Brows together; eyes downcast; squinting	Tense; tapping; picking; placing fingers or hands on each side of head	Pauses; low pitch
Happy	Smiling, smirking; relaxed; brows natural; pupils enlarged	Relaxed; head nodding; leaning forward	Animated; loud; fast
Interested	Direct eye contact; brows uplifted	Leaning forward; relaxed; opening arms and legs; nodding; raising hand or finger	Higher pitch; fast
Not Understanding	Frowning; biting lower lip; squinting eyes; looking away	Leaning back; arms crossed; head tilted back; hand on forehead; fidgeting; scratching chin; leaning head on hands	Slow; pauses; "ah," "um," "well" expressions; low pitch; monotone; quiet; soft

Nonverbal Behavior	Interpretation	Action
Students pull materials from desk quickly.	Students understand the assignment.	Begin monitoring individuals.
Many students wave hands eagerly.	Students are confident of answer.	Ask students to write answers so most will participate or call on lower-ability students.
Students slump in chairs, look down, and avoid eye contact when questions are asked.	Students seem to be losing contact or no longer understand.	Use a "mind capture" to refocus student attention. Cautiously, encourage students to ask questions.
Some students are sleeping in class.	May be boredom or fatigue.	Check to see which students have jobs and how much they work.

Nonverbal Behavior	Interpretation	Action
Students squint and adjust the focus of their eyes.	Indicates a lack of under-standing, frustration, or boredom.	Rephrase the question or ask the students what it is that they do not understand.

Sources of Error in Informal Observation

In a busy classroom, it's difficult to make continuous informal observations that are accurate, whether of individual students or of groups. Some of the more common errors that teachers make in their informal observations and interpretations are presented in Figure 5.5. To make accurate, reliable observations, it is best to first learn what to look for and listen to. Next, you need to be aware of the types of errors that are possible and consciously monitor yourself so that these errors are not made. Finally, it is helpful if you are able to use a few simple procedures:

- Ask yourself, is the verbal message consistent with the nonverbal behavior? Is this behavior normal or unusual?
- Plan time to do informal observation while not actively teaching a lesson to the entire class (e.g., during seat work, small group work, and individual interactions).
- Keep a list of possible errors from Figure 5.5 in a place that is easily referred to, such as in your desk. Make a habit of referring to the list frequently.
- When possible during the school day, write down informal observations, your interpretations, and the action you took. Be sure to keep the interpretations separate from the observations. The brief, written descriptions of behavior are essentially **anecdotal observations** or *notes.* These notes will provide accurate records of what transpired and will help make observations more accurate. In addition, anecdotal records can be used to document personal insights and student reactions that otherwise are easily forgotten or distorted (see Hill, Ruptic, & Norwick, 1998, for a more extensive discussion of anecdotal notes).
- At the end of the day, set aside a few minutes to record, briefly, important informal observations. Refer to your notes each week to look for patterns and trouble spots that need attention.
- If you are unsure about what a nonverbal behavior may mean, and the implications are serious, check them out with the student during an individual conference. For example, if you are picking up from nonverbal behavior that a student does not understand a procedure, even though the student's answers are correct on worksheets, ask the student directly about how he or she felt about the procedure and inquire about his or her confidence. You may discover that the student was concerned with other things at the time, and this affect was being displayed.
- Consciously think about informal observations of behavior in relation to student understanding and performance of learning targets. Those that directly relate to the targets are most important.
- Don't be fooled by students who appear to be on-task and interested but aren't.

FIGURE 5.5   Sources of Error in Informal Observation

1. Leniency or generosity	Teachers as observers tend to be lenient or generous.
2. Primacy effects	Teacher's initial impressions have a distorting effect on later observations.
3. Recency effect	Teacher's interpretations are unduly influenced by his or her most recent observation.
4. Logical generalization errors	Teacher makes assumptions that some nonverbal behavior generalizes to other areas (e.g., lack of confidence in math means lack of confidence in English).
5. Failure to acknowledge self	Teacher fails to take into account his or her influence on the students.
6. Unrepresentative sampling	Teacher erroneously interprets behaviors that do not accurately reflect the student or do not occur frequently enough to provide a reliable measure.
7. Observer bias	Teacher's preconceived biases and stereotypes distort the meaning of what is observed.
8. Failure to consider student perspective	Teacher fails to obtain student interpretations that would clarify the teacher's impressions.
9. Student reactions to being observed	Some students get nervous or uneasy when observed by teachers (e.g., students would behave differently if the teacher were not present).
10. Lack of consideration for the rapid speed of relevant action	Teacher may miss critical behaviors because of the speed of what occurs in the classroom.
11. Lack of consideration for the simultaneity of relevant action	Teacher may fail to account for more than one message being sent at the same time.
12. Student faking	Teacher may fail to realize that students are faking (e.g., eye contact and nodding does not always indicate engagement); as students become more sophisticated they develop strategies to make themselves appear to be on-task.

Source: Adapted from Evertson, G., & Green, J. (1986). Observation as inquiry and method, p. 183. In M. C. Wittrock (Ed.), *Handbook of research on teaching* (3rd ed., pp. 162–213). New York: Gale Group. Reprinted by permisson of The Gale Group.

Remember, do not base an interpretation solely on the basis of a single nonverbal behavior or vocal cue.

Using Questions to Assess Student Progress

Good instruction involves much more than simply presenting information and giving students assignments to work on. Effective teaching requires constantly monitoring your students' understanding during instruction. Along with observing nonverbal behavior, teachers rely heavily on how students answer questions during instruction to know if the students understand what is presented or can perform skills. Thus, the questions teachers ask in the classroom and subsequent teacher–student interaction are essential components of effective instruction. Oral questioning, therefore, is the predominant method of assessing student progress during instruction. Most teachers ask hundreds of questions each day (Morgan & Saxton, 1991). Except for lecturing, some type of questioning in student–teacher interactions is the most frequently used instructional strategy.

Questioning typically occurs in four formats: teacher-led reviews of content, discussions, recitations, and interactions with individual students. The review may be a fast-paced drill that is designed to cover specific knowledge. Discussions are used to promote student questioning and exchange ideas and opinions to clarify issues, promote thinking, generate ideas, or solve a problem. Recitations, the most common format for questioning, take place between reviews and discussions. In a recitation, the teacher asks questions as part of the presentation of material to engage students in what they are learning. Teachers question students individually in order to obtain information that is specific to the student. This allows teachers to individualize assessment and target suggested next steps.

Purposes of Questioning

Teachers use questions for five major purposes: to involve students in the lesson, to promote students' thinking and comprehension, to review important content, to control students, and to assess student progress. We will review the first four purposes briefly, then discuss in greater depth the use of questioning for formative assessment.

Questions can conveniently and efficiently grab students' attention and engage them in the lesson. Questions can challenge beliefs, provoke students, and get them to think about the topic under discussion by creating a sense of cognitive dissonance, imbalance, or disequilibrium. Second, questions can promote student reasoning and comprehension by helping them think through and verbalize their ideas. By actively thinking through answers to questions, student understanding is enhanced. Learning is also enhanced by listening to the answers of other students, because these answers may represent a way of expressing ideas that makes more sense to the student than the way the teacher explains things.

Third, questions signal to students important content to be learned and provide an opportunity for students to assess their own level of understanding in these areas. The types of questions asked also indicate how the students should prepare to demonstrate their understanding. For instance, asking questions that compare and contrast (e.g., How were presidents Carter and Clinton similar?) will cue students that they need to learn about how these presidents were similar and different, not just characteristics of each one. If you ask simple recall questions (e.g., What three major legislative initiatives occurred during the Clinton presidency?), you will tell your students that they need to memorize the names of these initiatives.

Fourth, questions are used to control student behavior and manage the class. Questions asked at random of different students—and that require brief, correct answers—maintain student attention. Teachers often ask a specific question of a student who is not paying attention to stop inappropriate behavior. Conversely, questions can be used to reinforce good behavior. Questions are also used to refocus students and to remind them of the classroom rules and procedures. Through the use of good questions students will keep actively involved in learning, preventing opportunities for student misbehavior.

The final purpose of questioning is to obtain information about student understanding and progress. This is accomplished if the questions are effective and elicit information that will help you. We will review characteristics of good questions and questioning skills in relation to this purpose.

Characteristics of Effective Questioning to Assess Student Progress

Your goal is to ask questions during instruction that will provide you with accurate information about what students know, understand, and can do. With this goal in mind, the following suggestions and strategies will help you:

1. **State Questions Clearly and Succinctly so That the Intent of the Question Is Understood.**   Students understand the question if they know how they are to respond. Questions are vague to students if there are too many possible responses or if the question is too general. With such a question, students wonder, "What does he mean?" Because they are unsure of what is intended, they are less willing to answer the question, and you are less likely to find out what they know. This occurs for a single vague question and for run-on questions (those in which two or more questions are asked together). For example, if a fourth-grade teacher wants to determine current student understanding of noun–verb agreement in sentences, an inappropriately vague question might be:

> What is wrong with the sentences on the board?

It would be better to ask:

> Read each of the three sentences on the board. In which sentence or sentences is there agreement between the noun and the verb? In which one or ones is there disagreement? How would you correct the sentence(s) in which the verb and noun do not agree?

Other questions that are too vague:

> What did you think about this demonstration?
> What about the early explorers of America?
> Can you tell me something about what you learned?
> What do you know about the solar system?

2. **Match Questions with Learning Targets.**   The questions you ask should reflect your learning targets, the degree of emphasis of different topics that will be assessed more formally in a unit test, and the difficulty of learning targets. Ask more questions and spend more time questioning with difficult learning targets. This will give you sufficient information to make sure students understand. Try to ask questions in rough proportion to how you will eventually test for student learning.

We have all been in classes where much class time was spent discussing something that was covered only lightly on the test. Try to avoid this.

Matching questions to learning targets requires that the questions be phrased to elicit student responses that are required in the learning target. For this purpose, most oral questions will correspond to either knowledge or reasoning targets. Knowledge targets focus on remembering and understanding. Questions that assess knowledge targets often begin with *what, who, where,* and *when.* For example, "What is the definition of *exacerbate*?" "What is the sum of 234 and 849?" "When did Columbus discover America?" "Who is Martin Luther King?" These are examples of knowledge questions that generally require factual recall or rote memorization of dates, names, places, and definitions.

Other knowledge questions go beyond simple factual recall and assess student understanding and comprehension. Students are required to show that they grasp the meaning of something by answering questions that require more than rote memory, for example, "What is the major theme of this article?" "What is an example of a metaphor?" and "Explain what is meant by the phrase 'opposites attract.'" "How do you find the area of a parallelogram?" More thinking is required than simple rote memory. These types of questions are effective when you want to assess more than one student in whole group instruction since each student uses his or her own words for the answer. If there is only one way to state the correct answer, only one student can answer it correctly.

More time is needed to respond to reasoning questions. These questions are generally *divergent* in that more than one answer can be correct or satisfactory. In a reasoning question, the teacher asks students to mentally manipulate what they know to analyze, synthesize, problem-solve, create, and evaluate. Reasoning questions will include words or intents like *distinguish, contrast, generalize, judge, solve, compare, interpret, relate,* and *predict,* such as "Relate the causes of the Civil War to the causes of World War I. How are they the same and how are they different?" "What was the implication of the story for how we live our lives today?" "What would happen if these two liquids were mixed?" As you might imagine, reasoning questions are excellent for promoting student thinking and discussion, but they are relatively inefficient for assessing student progress.

It is generally recommended that teachers balance knowledge with reasoning questions to keep student attention and enhance a broad range of student abilities.

3. Involve the Entire Class.   You will want to ask questions to a range of different types of students in your class, rather than allowing a few students to answer most questions. Balance is needed between students who volunteer and those who don't, high- and low-ability students, males and females, and students near and far from you. It is easy to call on the same students most of the time, so it's best to be aware of who has and who has not participated. If you are judging the progress of the class as a whole, it is especially important to obtain information from different students, although normally if your better students are confused or having difficulty, chances are good that this is true for the rest of the class as well. If slower students respond correctly, then most students are ready to move on.

Involvement will be enhanced if everyone's responses are supported. One technique for engaging most students is to address the question to the class as a whole, allow students time to think about a response, and then call on specific students. This encourages all the students to be responsible for an answer, not just a single student if you call the name first. Teachers who restrict their questioning to a small group of students are likely to communicate inappropriate expectations. Also, it is most fair if all students have the opportunity to benefit from the practice of answering questions.

4. Allow Sufficient Wait Time for Student Responses. A more accurate assessment of what students know will occur if students have sufficient time to think about and then respond to each question. Students need this time to process their thoughts and formulate their answers. Research shows that some teachers have difficulty waiting more than a single second before cuing a response, calling on another student, or rephrasing a question. It has been shown that when teachers can wait three to five seconds, the quality and quantity of student responses are enhanced. This includes an increase in the length of responses, unsolicited but appropriate responses, speculative responses, and the number of responses to reasoning questions and a decrease in failures to respond (Good & Brophy, 2003). It follows from these findings that longer wait time will result in better assessment. Answers are better and more representative for the class as a whole.

It may be difficult for you to wait more than a couple of seconds because the silence may seem much longer. It's helpful to tell students directly that such wait time is not only expected, but required, so that immediate responses do not take opportunities away from students who need a little more time. This will help alleviate your own insecurity about having so much silence during a lesson. Reasoning questions will naturally require more wait time than knowledge questions.

5. Give Appropriate Responses to Student Answers. Your responses to student answers will be very important for gathering valid information about student progress, because your style and approach—the climate and pattern of interaction that is established—will affect how and if students are likely to answer your questions. Each student's response should be acknowledged with some kind of meaningful, honest feedback. Feedback is part of ongoing assessment because it lets students know, and confirms for you, how much progress has been made. In the course of a class recitation or discussion, this feedback is usually a short, simple phrase indicating correctness, such as answering, for example, "right," "correct," "no," or maybe by doing something as simple as nodding your head. We will consider more about feedback later in this chapter.

6. Avoid Questions Answered by a Yes or No. There are two reasons to avoid yes/no questions or other questions that involve a choice between stated alternatives. First, if there are two alternatives, such as those available when answering a yes/no or true/false question, students can guess the correct answer 50 percent of the time. After a while, students tend to key into teacher behaviors or the way such a question is phrased to guess correctly. In any event, you will need to ask a lot of such questions to assess student progress accurately.

Second, these types of questions do not reveal much about a student's understanding of the content. They are not very diagnostic in nature. If you want to use such questions, do so sparingly and as a warm-up to questions that are better able to assess student learning. Adding a simple *why* after an answer to a yes/no question will increase its diagnostic power considerably. It is better to use these types of questions with students individually rather than in groups.

7. Probe Initial Responses When Appropriate. Probes are specific follow-up questions. Use them to better understand how students arrived at an answer, their reasoning, and the logic of their response. Examples of probes include phrases such as "Why?" "How?" "Explain how you arrived at that solution," and "Please give me another example."

8. Avoid Tugging, Guessing, and Leading Questions. Asking these types of questions makes it difficult to obtain an accurate picture of student knowledge and reasoning. Tugging questions ask a student to answer more without indicating what the student should focus on. They are usually vague questions or statements that follow what the teacher judges to be an incomplete answer. For example, "Well? . . ." "And? . . ." and "So? . . ." are tugging questions. It is better to use a specific probe. For example, if the question is "Why were cities built near water?" and a student answered "So the people could come and go more easily," a tugging question would be "And what else?" A better probe would be "How did coming and going affect the travel of products and food?"

Guessing questions obviously elicit guessed answers from students, for example, "How many small computer businesses are there in this country?" This type of question is useful in getting students' attention and getting students to think about a problem or area, but it is not helpful in assessing progress.

Leading questions, like rhetorical questions, are more for the teacher to pace a lesson than for obtaining information about student knowledge. Therefore, these types of questions ("That's right, isn't it?" or "Let's go on to the next chapter, okay?") should be avoided.

9. Avoid Asking Students What They Think They Know. It is not usually helpful to ask students directly if they know or understand something. The question might be, "Do you know how to divide fractions?" or "What do you know about the War of 1812?" or "Is everyone with me?" Students may be reluctant to answer such questions in class because of possible embarrassment, and if they do answer, the tendency is to say they know and understand when the reality is that they don't. If your relationship with your students is good, asking them if they understand or know something may work well.

Another approach, with older students, is to distribute a sheet at the beginning of class that lists all the subject areas you plan to teach. Ask the students to check off the subjects they know about or to indicate the degree to which they are confident of knowing a specific content area. Assure them that their answers will remain anonymous. Like oral questions, however, this strategy is generally not as good as asking direct questions that require the student to demonstrate understanding, knowledge, or skills.

FIGURE 5.6 Do's and Don'ts of Effective Questioning

Do	Don't
State questions clearly and succinctly.	Ask yes/no questions.
Match questions with learning targets.	Ask tugging questions.
Involve the entire class.	Ask guessing questions.
Allow sufficient wait time for students to respond.	Ask leading questions.
Give appropriate responses to student answers.	Ask students what they know.
Probe when appropriate.	
Sequence questions appropriately.	
Ask questions of all students, not just those you know will answer correctly.	

10. Ask Questions in an Appropriate Sequence. Asking questions in a planned sequence will enhance the information you receive to assess student understanding. Good sequences generally begin with knowledge questions to determine if students know enough about the content to consider reasoning questions. For example, consider the following situation. After having her students read an article about the United States military involvement in Haiti in 1994, Mrs. Headly asks the question, "Should the United States stay in Haiti and enforce the local laws until a new government is formed?" Students give some brief opinions, but it's clear that this reasoning question is premature. She then asks some knowledge questions to determine whether students understand enough from the article to ask other reasoning questions, such as "What was the condition of Haiti before the United States involvement?" "Historically, what has happened in Haiti the last two times a new government has taken control?" "How did the people of Haiti receive the American soldiers?" Such questions also serve as a review for students to remind them about important aspects of the article. Once students show that they understand the conditions and history, then divergent questions that require reasoning would be appropriate.

Figure 5.6 summarizes the do's and don'ts of using effective questioning to assess student progress toward meeting learning targets.

Providing Feedback and Praise

As already noted, an essential component of assessment is use of the information gathered. One way teachers use assessment information is to know how to respond to students after they demonstrate their knowledge, reasoning, skill, or performance. The teacher's response is called *feedback*—the transfer of information from the teacher to the student following an assessment. Thus, one purpose of assessment while teaching is instructional; another purpose is to provide information to make decisions about the frequency and nature of feedback to students. Of course in one sense feedback is also provided in the form of grades on unit tests and report cards, though normally grades offer very limited feedback. Our discussion will focus on the characteristics of effective feedback that is provided both during and after instruction. In Chapter 12 feedback as grades is discussed in greater detail.

Research literature, as well as commonsense experiences, has confirmed that the right kind of feedback is essential for effective teaching and learning. Corrective feedback is needed for learning and motivation, and assessment is needed to provide the feedback. The key is that the feedback must be *useful* and *helpful*. A simple definition of **feedback** is confirming the correctness of an answer or action, that is, whether it is right or wrong. This is what we do with most tests—tell students what they got right and what they missed; it is also the extent of the feedback many teachers give to a students' answers to oral questions—"Good," "That's right," "Close," and so on. Feedback of this nature is only part of what students need to improve their learning. Students also need to know *why* their performance was graded as it was and what *corrective procedures* are needed to improve their performance. When feedback is presented as information that can guide the student's meaningful construction of knowledge and understanding, learning and intrinsic motivation are enhanced (Mayer, 2002).

To further illustrate the importance of effective feedback, consider these two examples. First, good coaching requires effective feedback. Ryann, a gymnast, has a goal to earn a score of 10. After she has completed a routine, the judges give her a score of, say, 8.5 or 9.2. This is analogous to a teacher giving a student a score or grade. But simply knowing the score doesn't help Ryann know what she needs to do to improve her score. When the judge immediately indicates, specifically, why certain points were deducted, then Ryann knows what to work on. Furthermore, if the judge or coach tells Ryann how she can correct the skill, she has the corrective procedures needed. Similarly, a student who receives a 70 percent on a test knows that he or she has not done well, but unless otherwise indicated, this information alone does not tell the student what to do next. Or suppose you just started to learn golf. You miss the ball. Your skill level is obviously low. But knowing that is not enough. You need to get feedback about *why* you missed it. Is it because of your stance, your hand grip, the position of your head, your backswing, or some other aspect of your swing? When the teacher tells you precisely what you did wrong, what you need to correct, and how you can correct it, effective feedback has been provided.

Characteristics of Effective Feedback

Feedback is helpful when it has the following six characteristics (Elawar & Corno, 1985; Kindsvatter, Wilen, & Ishler, 1996; Mayer, 2002; Wiggins, 1993, 1998):

1. relates performance to standards
2. indicates progress
3. indicates corrective procedures
4. is given frequently and immediately
5. is specific and descriptive
6. focuses on key errors

1. *Relate Performance to Standard.* The first of these essential components is that feedback shows how the performance compares to a standard, exemplar, or goal. As emphasized previously, it is important for students to know the standards they will be judged against before learning and assessment. This information makes it much easier for you to show students how their performance compares to this standard and for students to self-assess their work. You can write standards on the board, show exemplars of student work, and reinforce the meaning of scores and grades to make this process more efficient. Word your feedback to refer to these standards; for example, "John, your paper did not include an introductory paragraph, as shown here on our exemplar" or "Your answer is partially correct but, as I said in my question, I am looking for an example of a sentence with both adjectives and adverbs." Student self-assessment can be promoted by asking students to critique their work according to the examples that you provide.

2. *Indicate the Progress Students Have Made.* Progress is indicated by placing the feedback in the context of previous and expected performance. This encourages the student and helps to define what needs to be done next; for example, "Maria, your division has improved by showing each step you have used in your work. Now you need to be more careful about subtraction."

3. *Indicate Corrective Action That Students Can Take.* Corrective action is pragmatic and possible. It gives students specific actions in which they can engage to improve. As an example, "You have made seven errors in the use of commas in your paper. Please refer to chapter three in your text and review the rules for using commas" or "Your understanding of how to use adverbs can be enhanced if you work through a computer program that is available." Such feedback explains how to correct the performance.

4. *Give Feedback Frequently and Immediately if Possible.* The best kind of feedback is given continually as we perform. This goal is not usually possible in classrooms, except with the help of recent computer programs, but feedback in a frequent and timely fashion is much better than getting it only after the performance is completed. When Ryann does gymnastics, her coach gives her feedback on how well she is performing as she does her routine, not just after she has finished ("straighten your legs, point your toes, lift your chin, smile"). It is more difficult for students to change what was learned than it is for them to adjust their current behavior or when learning something for the first time. Consequently, you will not want to have long periods of teaching and learning time without feedback. This is one reason that frequent testing is recommended, even though testing by itself does not ensure adequate feedback. Of course, this assumes that tests are returned promptly, which they certainly should be if you want to use the results as feedback to improve learning.

You provide more frequent, immediate feedback when you (1) develop or select activities with built-in opportunities for feedback; (2) circulate to monitor individual work, making comments to students; (3) provide exemplars and directions to students so they can self-assess; (4) use examples of ongoing student work to show all students mistakes and corrections; and (5) use techniques during recitation to monitor the progress of all students. The last suggestion can be achieved by having students complete practice exercises individually, then give the answer, and ask for a show of hands of those answering correctly. At the elementary level, you can ask students to close their eyes and raise their hands if they got the answer correct or if a particular choice was correct; for example, "Close your eyes. If you think A was correct, raise your hand."

5. *Give Specific and Descriptive Feedback.*   It is important to be as specific and descriptive as possible when giving feedback. If the feedback is vague or general it will not be helpful to the student; it will only communicate a sense of goodness or badness of the performance. If feedback is comparative rather than descriptive, there is little to gain by it. For example, saying to a student "you did better than most students in the class" is comparative, and as feedback it indicates nothing about what was correct or incorrect or how the student can improve. A descriptive statement specifies in exact terms the nature of the performance; for example, "Your speech was delivered too quickly. It will help you to pronounce each word more slowly and to pause between each sentence" or "I really liked the way you read your story this morning. You pronounced the words very clearly and spoke enthusiastically." How often have you received feedback like "good work," "nice job," "excellent," "awkward," and "OK"? What did these vague messages mean? Feedback like this, if you can call these phrases feedback, provides very little that is helpful.

Research shows that middle and high school students find written teacher comments on assignments and papers most helpful when the comments provide constructive criticism. This suggests that you should make specific, descriptive comments on errors or incorrect strategies, and that you should balance this criticism with comments about progress and positive aspects of the student's work.

6. *Focus Feedback on Key Errors.*   It is not practical to provide detailed and specific feedback to every student on homework and other assignments. You will need to make some choices about what to focus on, and it is best to determine what the most significant error is or what changes will be most helpful to the student. For example, it is relatively easy to comment on misspellings and grammatical errors on student papers, but is this the most important aspect of the paper the student needs feedback about? A study of sixth-grade teachers demonstrated that feedback can be improved dramatically when teachers use four questions as a guide (Elawar & Corno, 1985). The first question helps the teacher focus on significant errors; the remaining questions summarize, in a different way, the other characteristics of effective feedback:

    a. What is the key error?
    b. What is the probable reason the student made this error?
    c. How can I guide the student to avoid this error in the future?
    d. What did the student do well that I could note?

Characteristics of Effective Praise

Most teachers use praise ubiquitously in the classroom. It can be thought of as a type of feedback to the student, but it is also used frequently to control student behavior and for classroom management. In general, research shows that teachers use too much praise and use it inappropriately as positive reinforcement (Good & Brophy, 2003).

Like effective feedback, praise can be helpful to students if it draws attention to student progress and performance in relation to standards. It is also a good type of message to accompany other types of feedback. This is especially true when the praise focuses on student effort and other internal attributions so that students know that their efforts are recognized, appreciated, and connected to their performance.

Praise is most effective when it is delivered as a spontaneous but accurate message, giving the teacher's genuine reaction to student performance, and when it includes a specific description of the skill or behavior that is commended. You should praise students simply and directly, in natural language, without gushy or dramatic words. A straightforward, declarative sentence is best. For example, say: "Good; you did a wonderful job of drawing the vase; your lines are clear and the perspective is correct," not "Incredible!" or "Wow!" Try to be specific about what you are praising, and include your recognition of the student's effort. For example, say "This is an excellent job of paraphrasing the story. It is well organized and you have captured each of the major elements of the story. I like the way you kept at this assignment and worked hard to provide the detail you did." Call attention to progress and evidence of new skills. For instance, say, "I notice that you have learned to move sentences around with the blocking feature on your computer. Keep learning new ways to improve your computer and writing skills."

Try to use as many different phrases as you can when praising. If you say the same thing over and over it may be perceived as insincere with little serious

Case Study for Reflection

Ms. Watson, a tenth-grade algebra teacher at Eastbrook High School, recently attended a professional development workshop. The presenter addressed the characteristics of appropriate feedback for high school students. He said that it should, among other things, be given frequently and immediately. Ms. Watson argued that her students were old enough to wait for feedback from the teacher. She said that high school student tests could be quite lengthy and that sometimes it could take her a couple of weeks to get them all graded and returned to the students. She assured the presenter that her tenth-grade students never complained about her assessment practices.

Questions for Consideration
1. What advice could you give Ms. Watson to convince her that this assessment practice is not in the best interest of her students?
2. Do younger, elementary students need more feedback than older students?

attention to the performance. This is especially true if the phrase is a vague generality like "good" or "nice job." It is also best to keep your verbal praise consistent with your nonverbal behavior. Students quickly and accurately pick up teachers' nonverbal messages. So if the performance really is good, and progress is demonstrated, say your praise with a smile, using a voice tone and inflection that communicates warmth and sincerity.

Additional useful guidelines for effective praise are given in Figure 5.7.

FIGURE 5.7   Guidelines for Effective Praise

Effective Praise	Ineffective Praise
1. Is delivered contingently	1. Is delivered randomly or unsystematically
2. Specifies the particulars of the accomplishment	2. Is confined to global reactions
3. Shows spontaneity, variety, and other signs of credibility; suggests clear attention to the student's accomplishment	3. Shows a bland uniformity that suggests a conditioned response made with minimal attention
4. Rewards attainment of specified performance criteria (which can include effort criteria, however)	4. Rewards mere participation, without consideration of performance processes or outcomes
5. Provides information to students about their competence or the value of their accomplishments	5. Provides no information at all or gives students little information about their status
6. Orients students toward better appreciation of their own task-related behavior and thinking about problem solving	6. Orients students toward comparing themselves with others and thinking about competing
7. Uses student's own prior accomplishments	7. Uses the accomplishments of peers as the context for describing a student's present accomplishment
8. Is given in recognition of noteworthy effort or success at difficult (for this student) tasks	8. Is given without regard to the effort expended or the meaning of the accomplishment
9. Attributes success to effort and ability, implying that similar success can be expected in the future	9. Attributes success to ability alone or to external factors such as luck or task difficulty (easy)
10. Fosters endogenous attributions (students believe that they expend effort on the task because they enjoy the task or want to develop task-relevant skills)	10. Fosters exogenous attributions (students believe that they expend effort on the task for external reasons, e.g., to please the teacher, win a competition or reward)
11. Focuses students' attention on their own task-relevant behavior	11. Focuses students' attention on the teacher as an external authority figure who is manipulating them
12. Fosters appreciation of, and desirable attributions about task-relevant behavior after the process is completed	12. Intrudes into the ongoing process, distracting attention from task-relevant behavior

Student Self-Assessment

One of the most effective ways teachers can integrate assessment with instruction in a formative manner is to use student self-assessment continually, on a day-to-day basis. The purpose of self-assessment is to involve students deeply in the evaluation of their work so that immediate feedback can be incorporated and used to improve learning. The emphasis is on progress and mastery of knowledge and understanding, which increases confidence and motivation. Students learn to use assessment information to set performance goals, to make decisions about how to improve, to describe quality work, and to communicate their progress toward meeting learning targets (Chappuis & Stiggins, 2002).

Here are some examples of what students can do when they are involved in self-assessment (Chappuis & Stiggins, 2002; Stiggins, 2001):

- Examine samples of student performance to understand criteria by listing what it is about the samples that makes them examples of student work that meet the learning target.
- Analyze examples of student work according to scoring criteria. This helps students understand the criteria, which in turn helps them to self-assess their own work. Students can also suggest how the work can be improved.
- Develop a table of specifications for an objective test.
- Analyze their own work according to established scoring criteria. Rather than simply checking which answers are right or wrong, students can focus on why they missed items. With performance assessment and constructed-response assessments, students apply scoring criteria to understand the strengths and weaknesses of their work. As students get practice in identifying characteristics of good work, they become skilled at knowing what needs to be done to improve.
- Design practice tests. Students can work together to determine the most important learning targets and how the targets can be assessed. Developing and evaluating test items reinforces learning.
- Maintain learning portfolios. Self-reflections and examples of work to show improvement can be used to show students how their own involvement in assessment enhances their performance.
- Maintain records that allow students to monitor improvements.
- Participate in peer tutoring. To help others learn, students practice self-assessment to have confidence in evaluating the work of others.
- Participate in student-led teacher–parent conferences.

The goal of student self-assessment is to empower students so that they can guide their own learning. From a formative perspective, this takes place when students are able to evaluate their progress toward specific learning targets *as they learn* and use this information to know what further learning is needed to reach the targets. This approach allows students to give themselves meaningful formative feedback during instruction. Self-assessment and evaluation is individualized, allowing students to obtain meaningful information rather than relying on general evaluative feedback for the class as a whole. Assessment is not only integrated with instruction; it is also integrated with learning.

Student self-assessment is not without limitations. Perhaps the biggest challenge is to get students used to doing self-assessment. This will take time because most students are accustomed to receive only teacher feedback and appraisal. Some students will self-assess better than others, which will require some individual attention by the teacher. It may also be so time-consuming to have students involved in self-assessment that valuable instructional time is lost. Finally, you may need to develop a strong rationale for using student self-assessment if this is new for your school or department. With the current trend toward standardization of both assessment and instruction, your use of student self-assessment may not fit well with what is required or encouraged.

Summary

This chapter focused on what you can do to improve instruction by obtaining appropriate information from students as they learn. Key points in the chapter include the following:

- Assessing student progress consists of a teacher monitoring students and their academic performances to inform instructional decision making and the nature of feedback given to students.
- Formative assessment provides ongoing feedback from students to teachers and from teachers to students; summative assessment measures student learning at the end of a unit of instruction.
- Informal observation includes the teacher "reading" nonverbal behavior such as facial expressions, eye contact, body language, and vocal cues. These behaviors indicate student emotions, dispositions, and attitudes.
- Emotion is communicated best through facial expression. Eye contact is key to assessing attentiveness, confidence, and interest.
- Body language includes gestures, emblems, illustrators, affect displays, regulators, adapters, body movement, and posture.
- Voice-related cues such as pitch, loudness, rate, and pauses indicate confidence and emotions.
- Errors in informal observation are often associated with when the observations are made, sampling of student behavior, and teacher bias.
- Teachers use questions to involve students, promote thinking, review, control students, and assess student progress. Effective questions are clear, matched with learning targets, and involve the entire class, and allow sufficient wait time. Avoid yes/no, tugging, guessing, and leading questions, and keep questions in the proper sequence.
- Effective feedback relates performance to standards, progress, and corrective procedures. It is given frequently and immediately, and it focuses specifically and descriptively on key errors.

- Effective praise is sincere, spontaneous, natural, accurate, varied, and straight-forward. It focuses on progress, internal attributions, specific behaviors, and corrective actions.
- Student self-assessment can be used to help students understand learning targets, evaluate their own work, monitor progress, and know what needs to be done to improve their learning.

SELF-INSTRUCTIONAL REVIEW EXERCISES

1. To sharpen your interpretation of facial expressions, match the following pictures to the ten emotions listed in the chapter from Figure 5.2.

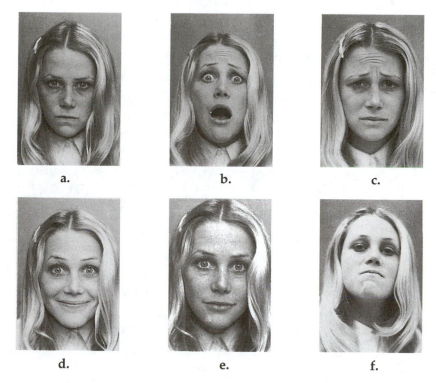

Source: Leathers, D. G. (1997). *Successful nonverbal communication: Principles and applications* (3rd ed.). New York: Macmillan, pp. 38–39.

2. Identify each of the following examples of body language as an emblem (E), illus-trator (I), affect display (AD), regulator (R), or adapter (A).

   a. Student leans toward you and raises both hands immediately after you ask a question.
   b. Student points to the pencil sharpener as if to ask, "May I sharpen my pencil?"

c. It seems that Johnny is always chewing on the end of his pencil.

d. You notice that Ken is picking at his cuticles.

e. Mary is sitting upright in her chair, arms on desk, chin up, with an expectant expression on her face.

f. Sam uses his hands to show how large the fish was.

3. Match the messages most likely to be conveyed with the descriptions provided. Each message may be used once, not at all, or more than once.

_____ (1) Pauses when speaking; eyes downcast	**A.** Confident	
_____ (2) Eyebrows uplifted; speaks fast; raises hand	**B.** Nervous	
_____ (3) Looks around room; slumped in chair with head resting in one hand	**C.** Angry	
_____ (4) Direct eye contact; speaks clearly with few pauses; uses variety in tone	**D.** Defensive	
	E. Bored	
_____ (5) Enlarged pupils; chin up; arms open	**F.** Frustrated	
_____ (6) Taps pencil; rigid body; pupils contracted	**G.** Happy	
_____ (7) Loud; eyebrows lowered; hands make fists	**H.** Interested	
_____ (8) Arms and legs crossed; leans away		

4. Mr. Bush had observed Trent carefully over the past few days because he was concerned that Trent would revert to his old pattern of cheating by looking at others' papers. What observation error is Mr. Bush most susceptible to, and why?

5. Mrs. Greene saw Renee staring out the window, obviously not concentrating on her work. Since Renee is a good student and this is not very typical of her, Mrs. Greene ignores the behavior. What type of observation error was Mrs. Greene careful *not* to make in this situation? What error is possible in her interpretation?

6. Why is it important to match the type of question you ask students in class with your learning targets?

7. How would a teacher preface a question to make sure students took sufficient time to think about the answer before responding?

8. What type of question—convergent or divergent—would be best to determine if students knew how to find the area of a rectangle?

9. Evaluate each of the following forms of feedback on the basis of the six characteristics in the chapter and the guidelines given in Figure 5.7.

a. "Lanette, that was a great job you did yesterday!"

b. "Jeff, your writing is improving. Your *b*s are much better because you are making a straighter line and not a loop."

c. "Robert, you have a good report. Your grammar is excellent, although you have some problems with sentence structure. The conclusion is incomplete. Work harder on providing more detail."

10. Indicate whether each of the following is characteristic of effective praise (EP) or ineffective praise (IP). If ineffective, indicate why.

a. "Sally, you did the best in the class!"

b. "Jon, I can see by your work that you are really good in math."

c. "This shows that you did the report well because you worked hard and because you are a good writer."

d. "Good work. This time you doubled the length and width before adding them to find the perimeter of the rectangle."

e. "You typed thirty-five words a minute with seven mistakes. This was among the best in the class."

11. What are some strengths and limitations of using student self-assessment as a means to provide formative information?

ANSWERS TO SELF-INSTRUCTIONAL REVIEW EXERCISES

1. a. anger, b. fear, c. sadness, d. interest, e. interest, f. determination.

2. a. R, b. E, c. A, d. A, e. AD, f. I.

3. (1) F, (2) H, (3) E, (4) A, (5) A, (6) B, (7) C, (8) D.

4. Mr. Bush is using previous behavior to motivate his informal observations, so his initial impressions may distort what he finds (primacy effect). He may also have a preconceived idea about what Trent would do (observer bias).

5. At least Mrs. Greene did not commit the error of unrepresentative sampling, since this was not a common occurrence. However, her interpretation that Renee was not thinking about her lesson may not be accurate. If this type of behavior became frequent and extensive, Mrs. Greene would want to ask Renee to get her perspective.

6. Matching questions with targets (1) helps to clarify to students what is important, (2) allows you to check student understanding of targets, (3) reinforces learning, and (4) balances emphasis given to each target.

7. The easiest way is the most direct—simply tell the students to wait a certain number of seconds before answering (e.g., fifteen or thirty seconds). You can also ask them to write their answer, then think about it, before responding orally.

8. Convergent; only one or two possible ways are correct.

9. **a.** Poor in almost all respects. Feedback is not specific or descriptive, it is not related to standards, nor does it focus on key errors. It is not given immediately, and no corrective actions are suggested.

   b. This is pretty good feedback as praise. It is specific, descriptive, and focuses on improvement. However, it might be better to include areas to improve as well.

   c. This feedback seems okay at first; you may well have received something like this many times. But when you look closely at what is said, the feedback is weak. The teacher does not indicate how Robert can improve nor does the teacher identify Robert's specific mistakes or problems in sentence structure, conclusion, or providing detail. The teacher has indicated there is "improvement," but this is not a clear indication of progress. The teacher also does not say how Robert can improve his difficulties, only that he has them.

10. **a.** IE; too general, compares performance only to others.
   b. IP; too general, and attributes success only to ability.
   c. EP; although general, still attributes success to both effort and ability (internal factors).
   d. EP; specific, shows progress.
   e. Both EP and IP; on the one hand the praise is specific, but on the other hand success is indicated by comparison to others.
11. Strengths: promotes better student understanding of targets and scoring criteria; promotes student self-reflection and self-evaluation; provides immediate, specific, and individualized feedback; leads to an awareness of progress; increases motivation. Limitations: self-assessment skills need to be taught; time needed for self-evaluation; differences between students requires individualized instruction; may not be supported because of other initiatives or alignment requirements; instructional time may be lost.

SUGGESTIONS FOR ACTION RESEARCH

1. While in a classroom, informally observe students' nonverbal behavior. It would be best if another observer could also observe in the class so that you could compare notes. Take a sheet of paper and draw a line down the middle. On the left-hand side, record a description of the nonverbal behavior—such as a facial expression, body language, or vocal cue—and on the right side, summarize your interpretation of each one. It would be interesting to check these out with the teacher for accuracy.

2. Ask a teacher about the kinds of questions he or she asks and what kinds of student responses are typical. Compare the teacher's comments to the suggestions for effective questioning presented in Figure 5.6. If possible, observe the teacher and record examples of effective and ineffective questioning.

3. Ask a group of students about the kind of feedback they get from teachers. Ask questions about how the feedback affects them.

4. Observe how teachers in two or three different classrooms use praise. What kind of praise is given by each teacher? What is the effect of the praise on the students? How could the praise you observe be improved?

5. Ask a group of students about self-assessment. What do they think about the idea? Do they think it would motivate them? Give them some specific examples of student self-assessment. Would they be interested in doing them? What do the students see as strengths and weaknesses? Do they think they have the skills to do self-assessment?

CHAPTER

6

Completion, Short-Answer, and Selected-Response Items:

Assessing Knowledge and Simple Understanding

You have taught your students, using assessment to inform your instructional decision making. Now you need to see how much your students have really learned and whether there are patterns of errors that require additional instruction. It's time for the weekly, unit, chapter, or semester test or quiz. These are **summative assessments,**

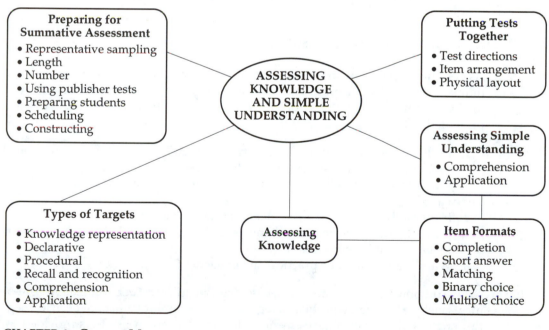

Preparing for Summative Assessment
- Representative sampling
- Length
- Number
- Using publisher tests
- Preparing students
- Scheduling
- Constructing

ASSESSING KNOWLEDGE AND SIMPLE UNDERSTANDING

Putting Tests Together
- Test directions
- Item arrangement
- Physical layout

Assessing Simple Understanding
- Comprehension
- Application

Types of Targets
- Knowledge representation
- Declarative
- Procedural
- Recall and recognition
- Comprehension
- Application

Assessing Knowledge

Item Formats
- Completion
- Short answer
- Matching
- Binary choice
- Multiple choice

CHAPTER 6   Concept Map

133

formal ones, that all of us have had to take to demonstrate how much we knew about specified subject matter or other information, or to exhibit what skills we have acquired. You will use these assessments to decide how much students have learned. Thus, results of these assessments have important consequences for students because they affect grades, placement in special classes or groups, and conferring of honors.

In this chapter and the next three, we will see how different learning targets can be conceptualized and how appropriate assessment methods can be used to measure each type of learning. The logic here is that *the nature of the learning target is what should influence which assessment method is used.* That is why chapter titles refer to type of target as well as type of assessment. As was pointed out in Chapter 3 (Figure 3.2), some assessment methods measure certain targets better than others. Your job is to first refine your learning targets, select the most appropriate type of assessment, prepare the assessment so that it will meet the criteria of high quality, administer it, and then score and interpret the results.

Knowledge and understanding learning targets are the ones most commonly assessed in summative tests. As you can probably confirm from your own experience, most tests require students to remember facts, definitions, concepts, places, and so on, usually by either recall or recognition. Some tests go beyond simple memorization and assess understanding. In this chapter, we examine different types of knowledge and simple understanding targets and the assessment methods that do the best job of measuring them. The following chapters will examine reasoning, skills and products, and affect targets, which for the most part are best measured with different assessment methods. We will begin, though, with some important considerations for preparing for any type of summative assessment of any type of target.

Preparing for Summative Assessment

As you think about how to construct the summative assessment, a number of preliminary steps will be helpful. The first step is to review what you think you want to do in light of the criteria for ensuring high-quality assessments that were presented in Chapter 3:

1. Do I have clear and appropriate learning targets?
2. What method of assessment will match best with the targets?
3. Will I have good evidence that the inferences from the assessments will be valid?
4. How can I construct an assessment that will minimize error?
5. Will my assessment be fair and unbiased? Have students had the opportunity to learn what is being assessed?
6. Will the assessment be practical and efficient?

Additional considerations when setting out to construct summative assessments include how you will obtain a representative sample of what has been learned, the length and number of assessments, whether you should use tests provided by publishers, how students should be prepared for the assessment, when the assessment should be scheduled, and when you should construct the assessment.

Representative Sampling

Most assessments *sample* what students have learned. It is rare, except for quizzes over short lessons, that you will assess everything that is included in your learning targets. There simply is not enough time to assess each fact or skill. Rather, you will select a sample of what students should know and then assume that the way they respond to assessments of this sample is typical of how they would respond to additional assessments of the entire unit.

As pointed out in Chapter 3, an important step in representative sampling is preparing a test blueprint or outline. This set of specifications is helpful because it indicates what students are responsible for learning. When assessment items are based on this outline, there is a greater likelihood that the sampling will be reasonable. You will literally be able to look at the blueprint to see how the sampling came out. Without a test blueprint or some type of outline of content there is a tendency to oversample areas that you particularly like and to overload the assessment with a disproportionately large number of questions about simple facts (mainly because these questions are much easier to write).

Another consideration when preparing a representative sample is to construct or select the appropriate number of items for the assessment. Suppose you are preparing a test for a six-week social studies unit on early civilizations, and you want to assess how much knowledge the students retained. How many items will be needed? Thirty? Sixty? Eighty? In the absence of any hard-and-fast rules, a couple rules of thumb will help determine how many items are sufficient. First, a minimum of ten items is needed to assess each knowledge learning target that encompasses the unit. Thus, if one learning target is that "students will identify the location of twenty-five ancient cities on a map," preparing a test that asks them to identify ten of the twenty-five would be reasonable. Which ten, you may be thinking? You can select randomly if all the cities are equally difficult to locate. Normally, however, your sampling will be purposeful so that a good cross section of difficulty is selected (in this case, different types of cities).

With more specific learning targets, as few as five items can provide a good assessment. For example, you can get a pretty good idea if a student knows how to multiply three-digit numbers by requiring students to supply answers to five problems. When reasoning, performance, and other skills are being assessed, we are usually confined to one or just a few items because they take so much time.

Number and Length of Assessments

Knowing how many items or questions are needed, you must then decide how many separate assessments will be given and the length of each one. This decision will depend on several factors, including the age of the students, the length of classes, and the types of questions. One rule of thumb, though, is that the time allocated for assessment is sufficient for all students to answer all the questions. We generally do not want to use *speeded* tests in school when it is important to obtain a fair assessment of what students know and can do. This is because **speeded tests,** which require students to answer as quickly as possible to obtain a high score, increase the probability that other factors, such as anxiety and test-taking skills, will influence the result.

There is an obvious relationship between the number and length of assessments. Many short assessments can provide the same, if not better, information than a single long assessment. It will help you to focus on length first without regard to the number of assessments. This will indicate what is needed to obtain a representative sample. Then you can decide whether what is needed is best given in one large block of time, three smaller tests, weekly assessments, or whatever other combination is best. If you wait until the end of a unit to begin constructing your assessment, you may find that there is insufficient time to administer the test so that other high-quality criteria are met.

The age of students and the length of their classes are other important considerations. Kindergarten and first-grade students have relatively short attention spans, so summative assessments usually last only five to ten minutes. Attention spans and stamina increase with age, but it is still best to use many short assessments rather than one or two long ones for elementary students. Thus, in later elementary grades, summative assessments typically should last between fifteen and thirty minutes.

Ironically, when students are old enough to have longer attention spans they are in middle or high schools where the length of the class usually determines the maximum length of the assessment. Consequently, most teachers plan unit and other summative assessments to last one class period, or approximately forty-five minutes in many schools. In this situation, you need to provide time for directions and student questions so you have to be careful not to end up with a speeded test. With block scheduling and other innovations more time is available for assessment.

Another important influence on the length of time it takes students to complete an assessment is the type of item used. Obviously, essay items require much more time to complete than objective items. It also takes students longer to complete short-answer items than multiple-choice or true/false questions. The nature of the subject is also important. For example, in a test of simple knowledge in a content area, students can generally answer as many as two to four items per minute. For more difficult items, one per minute is a general rule of thumb. In math, students may need as long as three or four minutes for each item. Experience will be your best guide. Initially, try some assessments that are short so you can get an idea of how long it takes students to complete each item. Using practice questions will also give you an idea about the number of items that would be reasonable in a unit test. The best practice is to give your students too much time rather than too little time to complete the assessment.

Use of Assessments Provided by Textbook Publishers

You will receive ready-made tests from textbook and instructional packages that can be used for summative assessments. These tests are prepared by the publisher for chapters and units. Some of these tests are adequate and may be useful if you remember a few key points. First, you can't assume that just because a test is provided that the results will be reliable or valid. You need to review the test carefully to make sure that fundamental principles of good assessment are followed. Second, a decision to use *any* type of assessment—whether provided in instructor's materials, by other teachers, or by yourself—is always made *after* you have identified the learning targets that you will assess. The prepared test may be technically sound, but if there is not a good match between what it tests and what you need tested, it should not be used in its entirety. Also, because these tests are often prepared by someone other than the textbook author(s), some sections may be stressed much more than others. Third, check the test carefully to make sure the language and terminology are appropriate for your students. The author of the test may use language that is not consistent with the text or the way you have taught the material. The vocabulary and sentence complexity may not be at the right level for your students. Fourth, the number of items for each target needs to be sufficient to provide a reliable measure.

The obvious advantage of using these "prepared" tests is that they can save you a great deal of time, especially when the test is provided in a format that can be simply copied. Feel free, however, to use only part of the test and to modify individual questions. Often the best use of the textbook test is to get ideas that provide a good starting point for you to prepare your own test.

Preparing Students for Summative Assessments

Your objective in summative assessment is to obtain a fair and accurate indication of student learning. This means that you need to take some simple, yet often neglected, steps to prepare your students so that they will be able to demonstrate what they know, understand, and can do (see Figure 6.1).

The first step is to make sure that all your students have adequate test-taking skills, such as paying attention to directions, reading each item in its entirety before answering it, planning and outlining responses to essay questions, and pacing themselves while answering the questions. (As one teacher told me, "When I first gave math tests students would include the item number with the problem; for example, if item 2 was 3 + 4, they would answer 9—incorrect answer but they knew how to add!") Students should be directed to answer all questions (guessing is rarely penalized in classroom tests, though you don't want to encourage mindless guessing). If there is a separate sheet for recording responses, teach students to check the accuracy of their answers.

A second step is to make sure students are familiar with the format and type of question and response that will be needed on the test. This is accomplished by giving students practice test items. If time is available, it is very instructive to have students practice writing test items themselves. This is good for review sessions. Familiarity with the type of question lessens test anxiety. Of course, you don't want to teach the test—that is, use examples in class that are identical to the test items—or

FIGURE 6.1   **Preparing Students for Summative Assessments**

- Teach test-taking skills.
- Familiarize students with test length, format, and types of questions.
- Teach to the test (do not teach *the* test).
- Review before the test.
- Tell students when the test is scheduled.

give students practice on the test items before they take the test. It's fine to teach *to* the test, in the sense that you want to instruct students about what they will eventually be tested on. It's also helpful to students if they know the length of the test and how much the test will count in their grade.

A review of the unit or chapter learning targets is both fair and helpful. There are several purposes for the review: to reacquaint students with material taught early in the unit, to allow students an opportunity to ask questions for clarification, to reemphasize the important knowledge and skills that students should focus on, and to provide an opportunity for students to check their understanding of what will be tested.

Finally, you will want to tell students, as soon as possible after beginning the unit, when the test is scheduled. This gives students an adequate period of time to prepare for the test. The lack of time to prepare and review for the test contributes to student anxiety and lessens the validity of the results.

Scheduling the Summative Assessment

To give students the best opportunity to show what they have learned you need to be careful when scheduling the test. Try to avoid giving a test on days that make it difficult for students to perform to their capability (e.g., prom day, right after spring vacation, after a pep rally). Also, try to schedule the test when you know you will be present and not when the class has a substitute.

When Summative Assessments Should Be Constructed

Summative assessments need to be planned well in advance of the scheduled testing date. A good procedure is to construct a general outline of the test before instruction, based on your learning targets and a table of specifications. At least identify the nature of the evidence needed to provide a fair indication of student learning. This does not include the development or selection of specific items, but it provides enough information to guide you in instruction. As the unit proceeds, you can make decisions about the format of the test and begin to construct individual items. The final form of the test should be determined no later than the review session. But don't try to finalize the test too soon. You will find that as you teach, your learning targets will most likely change somewhat or that the emphasis you place on certain topics is not as you planned. These expected instructional variations should be reflected in the test. Consequently, you want to allow the test and instruction to influence each other while teaching the content or skills.

With this summary of considerations for preparing any type of summative assessment, we now turn to knowledge and simple understanding targets.

Types of Knowledge and Simple Understanding Targets

The simple phrase "what students should know" is used frequently as a concept for inclusion of important learning outcomes and standards. But this phrase is also pretty vague. We need to be much more specific about what is meant by "know" and "knowledge." Once this is accomplished, appropriate assessment methods can be selected to foster as well as measure the type of learning that is desired.

Knowledge Representation

Until recently, Bloom's taxonomy provided a definition of *knowledge* for many educators. In this scheme, knowledge is the first, and "lowest," level of categories in the cognitive domain, in which knowledge is defined as remembering something. All that is required is that the student recall or recognize facts, definitions, terms, concepts, procedures, principles, or other information.

In the revision of Bloom's taxonomy (Anderson & Krathwohl, 2001), the original knowledge category is divided into two categories: a knowledge dimension and remembering as a cognitive process. There is a distinction between "factual knowledge" that is remembered and other types of knowledge (conceptual, procedural, and metacognitive). Factual knowledge encompasses basic elements about a discipline, including knowledge of terminology (specific verbal and nonverbal labels and symbols such as words, numerals, pictures and signs) and knowledge of specific details and elements (events, locations, sources of information, dates and other information pertaining to a subject). Further details with examples of factual knowledge remembering are shown in Figures 6.2 and 6.3. These correspond to the nature of learning that is the focus of this chapter. Regardless of the classification scheme, though, the important point is that when students are required to remember something, whether facts, concepts, or procedures, this represents the most basic and elementary form of learning. For our purposes here, *knowledge* will be used the same way it was defined in the original taxonomy to refer to the process of simply remembering something.

The contemporary view of knowledge is that remembering is only part of what occurs when students learn. You also need to think about how the knowledge is represented in the mind of the student. *Knowledge representation* is how information is constructed and stored in long-term and working memory (Gagne, Yekovich, & Yekovich, 1993). We will examine two types of knowledge representation that have direct application to assessment: declarative and procedural. These are major types of knowledge in the revision to Bloom's taxonomy (Figure 6.2).

Declarative Knowledge and Understanding

Declarative knowledge is information that is retained about something, knowing that it exists. The nature of the information learned can be ordered hierarchically, depending on the level of generality and degree of understanding that is demonstrated (Marzano, Pickering, & McTighe, 1993; Marzano, 1996) and the way the knowledge is represented. At the "lowest" level, declarative knowledge is similar to Bloom's first level—remembering or recognizing specific facts about persons, places, events, or content in a subject area. The knowledge is represented by simple association or discrimination, such as rote memory. At a higher level, declarative knowledge consists of concepts, ideas, and generalizations that are more fully

FIGURE 6.2   **Part of Knowledge Dimension of New Taxonomy.**

Major Types	Definition	Subtypes	Examples
Factual Knowledge	Basic elements of a discipline	Knowledge of terminology	Vocabulary; symbols
		Knowledge of specific details and elements	Major facts important to good health
Conceptual Knowledge	Interrelationships among basic elements that enable them to function together	Knowledge of classifications and categories	Forms of business ownership
		Knowledge of principles and generalizations	Law of supply and demand
		Knowledge of theories, models, and structures	Theory of evolution
Procedural Knowledge	How to do something, methods of inquiry, and skills, algorithms, and methods	Knowledge of subject-specific skills and algorithms	Painting skills; division algorithm
		Knowledge of subject-specific techniques and methods	Scientific method
		Knowledge of criteria for determining when to use appropriate procedures	Knowing when to apply Newton's second law

Source: Adapted from Lorin W. Anderson & David R. Krathwohl, *A taxonomy for learning, teaching, and assessing: A revision of Bloom's taxonomy of educational objectives.* Published by Allyn and Bacon, Boston, MA. Copyright © 2001 by Pearson Education. Reprinted by permission of the publisher.

understood and applied. This type of knowledge involves *understanding* in the form of comprehension or application, the next two levels in Bloom's original taxonomy.

In the revision of Bloom's taxonomy, understanding and application are cognitive process categories that are differentiated from remembering (Figure 6.3). I believe it is best to use the term *understand* as different from *remember,* and that understanding involves either comprehension or application. Comprehension understanding would be similar to what is called "understand" in the revised taxonomy and "comprehension" in the original taxonomy. Application understanding is the same as "application" in Bloom's original taxonomy and "apply" in the revision. Thus, for our purposes here, declarative knowledge can exist as recall, recognition, or understanding, depending on the intent of the instruction and how the information is learned. Assessments of procedural knowledge likewise measure recall, recognition, or understanding.

A further distinction of different levels or degrees of understanding is needed. Tombari and Borich (1999) point out that when we initially learn about something, our understanding is simple, undeveloped, and not very sophisticated. As we learn more and have more experience, our understanding deepens. For example, you may have had a surface or simple understanding of what the term *performance assessment* means before reading this book, but it is hoped that your understanding

FIGURE 6.3   Part of Cognitive Process Dimension of New Taxonomy

Major Types	Definition	Subtypes	Illustrative Verbs	Examples
Remember	Retrieval of knowledge from long-term memory	Recognizing	Identifying	Recognize dates of important events
		Recalling	Retrieving	Recall dates of important events
Understand	Construct meaning from oral, written, and graphic communication	Interpreting	Representing, translating	Paraphrase meaning in important speeches
		Exemplifying	Illustrating	Give examples of painting styles
		Classifying	Categorizing, subsuming	Classify different types of rocks
		Summarizing	Abstracting, generalizing	Write a summary of a story
		Inferring	Concluding, predicting	Draw a conclusion from data presented
		Comparing	Contrasting, mapping	Compare historical events to contemporary events
		Explaining	Constructing models	Show cause-and-effect of pollution affected by industry
Apply	Carry out a procedure	Executing	Carrying out	Divide whole numbers
		Implementing	Using	Apply procedure to an unfamiliar task

Source: Adapted from Lorin W. Anderson & David R. Krathwohl, *A taxonomy for learning, teaching, and assessing: A revision of Bloom's taxonomy of educational objectives.* Published by Allyn and Bacon, Boston, MA. Copyright © 2001 by Pearson Education. Reprinted by permission of the publisher.

will be richer and much more developed after you read the book and try some out on students. Thus, it is helpful to differentiate *simple* understanding from *deep* understanding. This distinction is important from an assessment perspective because the types of items that are best for assessing simple understanding are different from those that should be used to assess deep understanding.

The nature of the representation moves from rote memorization and association of facts to generalized understanding and usage. This is a critical distinction for both learning and assessment. As pointed out in Chapter 1, constructivist views contend that students learn most effectively when they connect new information meaningfully to an existing network of knowledge. Constructivists believe that new knowledge is acquired through a process of seeing how something relates, makes sense, and can be used in reasoning. This notion is quite different from memorized learning that can be demonstrated for a test. Although I don't want to suggest that some rote memorization is not appropriate for students, I do want to point out that your learning targets can focus on recall or understanding types of declarative knowledge and that your choice of assessment method and test items will be different for each of these.

According to Grant Wiggins (1998), who has focused extensively on the nature of understanding and its importance in assessment, it is critical for teachers to distinguish between surface recall and recognition knowledge and deeper understanding. Wiggins suggests that understanding, as contrasted to simply remembering, involves grasping the significance of an idea or fact, connecting it to other ideas, and being able to justify, use, and explain it. He uses words like "rethinking," "reflecting upon," "revising," and "reconsidering" to describe what students need to do to "reveal whether students can make newer, clearer, and better sense of complex data, facts, and experience" (p. 85). Wiggins contends that there are six facets to understanding: explanation, interpretation, application, perspective, empathy, and self-knowledge (Wiggins & McTighe, 1998). His work shows how assessment can be designed around these six facets. Some of what Wiggins advocates is covered in this chapter as *simple* understanding, and other aspects of his perspective, deep understanding, are covered in Chapters 7 and 8, which stress thinking skills and the use of student performances.

Let's look at an example of different types of declarative knowledge. One important type of information students learn about is geometric shapes. Each shape is a concept (mental structures that use physical characteristics or definitions to classify objects, events, or other things into categories). If students learn the concept of "rectangle" at the level of *recall* or *recognition*, then they simply memorize a definition or identify rectangles from a set of different shapes that look like the ones they studied in class. If students *understand* the concept of rectangle, however, they will be able to give original examples and identify rectangles of different sizes, shapes, and colors they have never seen before. Each of these levels of learning is "knowing something," but the latter is much closer to true student mastery and what constructivists advocate. Also, because these levels are hierarchical, understanding requires recall. Thus, it may be better to state learning targets that require understanding but teach and test for recall as well because one is a prerequisite to the other.

Procedural Knowledge and Understanding

Procedural knowledge is knowing how to do something. It is knowledge that is needed to carry out an action or solve a problem. What is demonstrated is knowledge of the strategies, procedures, and skills students must engage in; for example, how to tie shoes, how to divide fractions, or how to check out library books. Like declarative knowledge, procedural knowledge can be demonstrated at different levels. At the level of recall, students simply identify or repeat the needed steps. Understanding is indicated as students explain in their own words (comprehension) and actually use the steps in executing a solution (application).

Definitions of the two major types of knowledge are presented in Figure 6.4; examples are provided in Figure 6.5. These learning target categories will be used to

FIGURE 6.4   Definitions of the Levels of Declarative and Procedural Knowledge and Simple Understanding

Level	Declarative	Procedural
Knowledge	Remembers, restates, defines, identifies, recognizes, names, reproduces, or selects *specific facts, concepts, principles, rules, or theories.*	Remembers, restates, defines, identifies, recognizes, names, reproduces, or selects *correct procedure, steps, skills, or strategies.*
Simple Understanding: Comprehension	Converts, translates, distinguishes, explains, provides examples, summarizes, interprets, infers, or predicts, in own words, *essential meanings of concepts and principles.*	Converts, translates, distinguishes, explains, provides examples, summarizes, interprets, infers, or predicts, in own words, *correct procedure, steps, skills, or strategies.*
Simple Understanding: Application	Uses existing knowledge of concepts, principles, and theories, in new situations, to solve problems, interpret information, and construct responses.	Uses existing knowledge of correct procedures, steps, skills, or strategies, in new situations, to solve problems, interpret information, and construct responses.

FIGURE 6.5   Examples of Declarative and Procedural Knowledge and Simple Understanding

Declarative

Knowledge	Is able to define the word *democracy.*
Simple Understanding (comprehension)	Is able to give three examples of countries that are democracies.
Simple Understanding (application)	Is able to determine by its description whether a new country is a democracy.

Procedural

Knowledge	Is able to identify, in correct order, steps in the scientific method.
Simple Understanding (comprehension)	Is able to explain whether a set of procedures follows the scientific method.
Simple Understanding (application)	Is able to demonstrate in writing the correct use of the scientific method to solve a novel problem.

present examples of test items throughout the remainder of this chapter. The most effective methods for assessing knowledge are conveniently grouped into measuring recall or understanding. We now consider how different types of objective items can be used to assess the various knowledge targets, beginning with knowledge.

Assessing Knowledge

Knowledge is best assessed with completion, short-answer, and selected-response items. This section presents suggestions for using these types of items and tests, along with examples. You will determine which of these methods to use, based on their strengths and weaknesses in relation to your teaching situation and personal likes and dislikes. You need to be comfortable with whatever method you use, and this consideration is probably more important than other factors such as ease of construction and scoring. The suggestions for writing each type of item are applicable to assessing both understanding and reasoning.

Completion and Short-Answer Items

The most common and effective way to assess knowledge is simply to ask a question and require the students to answer it from memory. Items for which the student responds to an incomplete statement are *completion items;* a brief response to a question is a *short-answer item.*

Completion Items. The completion item offers the least freedom of student response, calling for one answer at the end of a sentence. Responses may be in the form of words, numbers, or symbols. If properly constructed, completion items are excellent for measuring how well students can recall facts because of these strengths: (1) they are easy to construct, (2) their short response time allows a good sampling of different facts, (3) guessing contributes little to error, (4) scorer reliability is high, (5) they can be scored more quickly than short-answer or essay items, and (6) they provide more valid results than a test with an equal number of selected-response items (e.g., multiple-choice). There are only two limitations of using completion items to measure knowledge. The first is in the scoring. It takes a little more time to score completion items than selected-response items. Second, if the sentence is not well written, more than one answer may be possible.

The following suggestions for constructing completion items use examples that measure either declarative or procedural knowledge. The suggestions are summarized in the form of a checklist in Figure 6.6.

1. Paraphrase Sentences from Textbooks and Other Instructional Materials. It is tempting to lift a sentence verbatim from materials the students have studied,

---

FIGURE 6.6   Checklist for Writing Completion Items

✓ Is verbatim language from instructional materials avoided?
✓ Is knowledge being assessed?
✓ Is a single, brief answer required?
✓ Is the blank at the end of the sentence?
✓ Is the length of each blank the same?
✓ Is the precision of a numerical answer specified?
✓ Is it worded to avoid verbal clues to the right answer?

and replace a word or two with blanks. However, statements in textbooks, when taken out of context, are often too vague or general to be good completion items. Also, you don't want to encourage students to memorize phraseology in the text. Consistent with constructivistic principles, you want students to connect what they learn with what they already know, even when it is recall. Thus, you want to paraphrase or restate facts in words that are different from those the students have read.

Examples

The textbook statement is "James Buchanan, elected president in 1856, personally opposed slavery."

Poor: James Buchanan, elected president in 1856, personally opposed _____ .

Improved: The name of the president who was elected in 1856, and who thought slavery was not proper, was _____ .

2. Word the Sentence so That Only One Brief Answer Is Correct.   The single greatest error in writing completion items is to use sentences that can be legitimately completed with more than one response. This occurs if the sentence is too vague or open-ended.

Examples

Poor: Columbus first landed on "America" _____ .

Improved: Columbus first landed on "America" in _____ .

Better: Columbus first landed on "America" in the year _____ .

In the first example, students could logically provide correct answers having nothing to do with the year. In the improved version an answer like "a boat" would be correct.

3. Place One or Two Blanks at the End of the Sentence.   If blanks are placed at the beginning or in the middle of the sentence, it may be more difficult for students to understand what response is called for. It is easier and more direct to first read the sentence and then determine what will complete it correctly. (That's why it's called a *completion* item.)

Examples

Poor: In 1945, _____ decided to have the atomic bomb dropped on Japan.

Improved: The name of the president who decided to have the atomic bomb dropped on Japan in 1945 was _____ .

You also will not want to use several blanks in a single sentence. This will confuse students and measure reasoning skills as much, if not more, than knowledge.

Example

> *Poor:* The name of the _____ who decided to have the _____
> _____ dropped on _____ in 1945 was _____ .

4. If Answered in Numerical Units, Specify the Unit Required. For completion items that require numerical answers, the specific units or the degree of precision should be indicated.

Examples

> *Poor:* The distance between the moon and the earth is _____ .

> *Improved:* The distance between the moon and the earth is _____ miles.

5. Do Not Include Clues to the Correct Answer. Test-wise students will look for clues in the way sentences are worded and the length of blanks that may indicate a correct answer. The most common wording errors are using single or plural verbs and wording the sentence so that the blank is preceded by "a" or "an." These clues can be eliminated by avoiding verb agreement with the answer, by using "a(an)," and by making all blanks the same length.

Examples

> *Poor:* The two legislative branches of the United States federal government
> are the _____ and the _____ _____ _____ .

> *Improved:* The two legislative branches of the United States federal government are the _____ and the _____ .

Short-Answer Items. Short-answer items, in which the student supplies an answer consisting of one word, a few words, or a sentence or two, are generally preferred to completion items for assessing knowledge targets. First, this type of item is similar to how teachers phrase questions and direct student behavior during instruction. This means that the item is more natural for students. Students are familiar with answering questions and providing responses to commands that require knowledge (e.g., "Write the definition of each of the words on the board"). Second, it is easier for teachers to write these items to more accurately measure knowledge.

Short-answer items are usually stated in the form of a question (e.g., "Which state is surrounded by three large bodies of fresh water?"). They can also be stated in general directions (e.g., "Define each of the following terms"), and they can require responses to visual stimulus materials (e.g, "Name each of the countries identified with arrows A–D").

Like completion items, short-answer items are good for measuring knowledge because students can respond to many items quickly, a good sample of knowledge is obtained, guessing is avoided, scoring is fairly objective, and results are generally more valid than those obtained from selected-response formats. The main disadvantage of short-answer items is that scoring takes longer and is more subjective than completion or selected-response items. Figure 6.7 summarizes the following suggestions in a checklist format.

FIGURE 6.7   **Checklist for Writing Short-Answer Items**

✓ Is only one answer correct?
✓ Are questions from textbooks avoided?
✓ Is it clear to students that the answer is brief?
✓ Is the precision of a numerical answer specified?
✓ Is the item written as succinctly as possible?
✓ Is the space designated for answers consistent with the length required?
✓ Are words used in the item too difficult for any students?

1. State the Item So That Only One Answer Is Correct.   Be sure that the question or directions are stated so that what is required in the answer is clear to students. If more than one answer is correct, the item is vague and the result is invalid. If you are expecting a one-word answer, use a single short blank.

Examples

Poor: Where is the Eiffel Tower located?

Improved: In what country is the Eiffel Tower located? *or* Name the country in which the Eiffel Tower is located.

Obviously, in the first item students could give several responses—Europe, Paris, France—each of which would be technically correct.

2. State the Item So That the Required Answer Is Brief.   Remember that short-answer items have answers that are short! Keep student responses to a word or two, or a short sentence or two if necessary, by properly wording the item, offering clear directions, and providing space or blanks that indicate the length of the response. In the directions, state clearly that students should not repeat the question in their answer.

Examples

Poor: What does the term *reptile* mean? _____

_____

Improved: Name three characteristics of reptiles.

1. _____
2. _____
3. _____

3. Do Not Use Questions Verbatim from Textbooks or Other Instructional Materials.   Most textbooks include review questions and questions for study. You don't want to use these same questions on tests because it encourages rote memorization of answers.

4. Designate Units Required for the Answer.   Students need to know the specific units and the degree of precision that should be used in their answer.

This will avoid the time students may take to try to figure out what is wanted—such as asking a question for clarification during the test—and it will mitigate scoring difficulties.

Examples

> *Poor:* When was President John F. Kennedy killed?
>
> *Improved:* In what year was President John F. Kennedy killed?

5. State the Item Succinctly with Words Students Understand.   It is best to state questions or sentences as concisely as possible and to avoid using words or phrases that may be difficult for some students to understand.

Examples

> *Poor:* What was the name of the extraordinary president of the United States who earlier had used his extensive military skills in a protracted war with exemplary soldiers from another country?
>
> *Improved:* What United States general defeated the British and later became president?

Matching Items

Matching items effectively and efficiently measure the extent to which students know related facts, associations, and relationships. Some examples of such associations include terms with definitions, persons with descriptions, dates with events, and symbols with names.

The major advantage of matching is that the teacher can obtain a very good sampling of knowledge. It is beneficial therefore to use matching when there is a great amount of factual information within a single topic. Matching is easily and objectively scored. Constructing good matching items is more difficult than creating completion or short-answer items, but it is not as difficult as preparing multiple-choice items. However, it is relatively easy to construct matching items that are weak measures. This usually occurs when there is insufficient material to include in the item and irrelevant information is added that is unrelated to the major topic that has been targeted for assessment.

In a matching item, the items on the left are called the *premises*. In the right-hand column are the *responses*. The student's task is to match the correct response with each of the premises. As long as the suggestions below are followed, matching items are excellent for measuring knowledge that includes associations.

1. Make Sure Directions Are Clear to Students.   Even though matching items are familiar to students, it is helpful to indicate in writing (or orally for young students) the basis for the matching and where and how student responses should be recorded. Generally, letters are used for each response in the right-hand column, and students are asked to write the selected letter next to each premise. Younger students can be asked to draw lines to connect the premises to the responses. It is important in the directions to indicate that *each response may be used once, more than once, or not at all*. This lessens the probability that, through a process of elimination, guessing will be a factor in the results.

2. Include Homogeneous Premises and Responses.   Avoid putting information from different lessons in the same matching item. You wouldn't want to include recent scientists, early U.S. presidents, and sports figures in the same item. Even though what is homogeneous varies from one person to another, this principle is the one most violated. For example, it makes good sense to use matching to test student knowledge of important dates during the Civil War. It would not be a good idea to contain both dates and men's names as responses. Testing homogeneous material with matching is effective for fairly fine discriminations among facts. For example, matching dates with events in one of the Civil War battles provides greater discrimination than matching dates with major battles.

3. Use Four to Eight Premises.   You do not want to have too long a list of premises. A relatively short list will probably be more homogeneous and will be perceived by students as more fair.

4. Keep Responses Short and Logically Ordered.   Usually the responses include a list of one- or two-word names, dates, or other terms. Definitions, events, and descriptions are in the premise column. Students will be more accurate in their answers if the responses are in logical order. Thus, if responses are dates they should be rank ordered by year; words or names should be alphabetized. Like premises, keep the number of responses to eight; ten at the most. Longer lists waste students' time and contribute to error by including reasoning abilities as part of what is needed to answer the item correctly.

5. Avoid Grammatical Clues to Correct Answers.   As with completion items, you need to be careful that none of your matches are likely because of grammatical clues, such as verb tense agreement.

6. Put premises and responses on the same page.   You don't want students to have to flip back and forth between two pages to answer the items. This is distracting and only contributes to error.

7. Use more responses than premises.   Using more responses than premises provides greater coverage of information and is a better indicator of knowledge by reducing guessing of some correct answers that occurs if the same number of premises and responses are used and each response is used only once.

Example

The following is an example of a good matching set. Notice the complete directions, responses on the right in logical order, and homogeneous content (achievements of early presidents).

> *Directions:* Match the achievements in column A with the names of presidents in column B. Write the letter of the president who had the achievement

on the line next to each number. Each name in column B may be used once, more than once, or not at all.

Column A

_____	**1** Second president
_____	**2** President when there were no severe external threats to the country
_____	**3** Declined to run for a third term
_____	**4** Wrote the Declaration of Independence
_____	**5** Last of the presidents from Virginia

Column B

A. John Adams
B. John Quincy Adams
C. Andrew Jackson
D. Thomas Jefferson
E. James Madison
F. James Monroe
G. George Washington

Suggestions for writing matching items are summarized in Figure 6.8.

True/False and Other Binary-Choice Items

When students select an answer from only two response categories, they are completing a **binary-choice item.** This type of item may also be called *alternative response, alternate response,* or *alternate choice.* The most popular binary-choice item is the true/false question; other types of options can be right/wrong, correct/incorrect, yes/no, fact/opinion, agree/disagree, and so on. In each case, the student selects one of two options.

Binary-choice items are constructed from propositional statements about the knowledge. A *proposition* is a declarative sentence that makes a claim about content or relationships among content. Simple recall propositions include the following:

Lansing is the capital of Michigan.
Peru is in the southern hemisphere.
The area of a square is found by squaring the length of one side.
Petosky is the name of a type of rock.

These propositions provide the basis for good test items because they capture an important thought or idea. Once the proposition is constructed, it is relatively

---

FIGURE 6.8   Checklist for Writing Matching Items

✓ Is it clear how and where students place their answers?
✓ Is it clear that each response may be used once, more than once, or not at all?
✓ Is the information included homogeneous?
✓ Are there more responses than premises?
✓ Are the responses logically ordered?
✓ Are grammatical clues avoided?
✓ Is there only one feasible answer for each premise?
✓ Is the set of premises or responses too long?
✓ Are premises and responses on the same page?

easy to keep it as is, rephrase and keep the same meaning, or change one aspect of the statement and then use it for a binary-choice test item. As such, the items provide a simple and direct measure of one's knowledge of facts, definitions, and the like, as long as there is no exception or qualification to the statement. That is, one of the two choices must be *absolutely* true or false, correct or incorrect, and so on. Some subjects, like science and history, lend themselves to this type of absolute proposition better than others.

Using binary-choice items has several advantages. First, the format of such questions is similar to what is asked in class, so students are familiar with the thinking process involved in making binary choices. Second, short binary items provide for an extensive sampling of knowledge because students are able to answer many items in a short time (two to five items per minute). Third, these items can be written in short, easy-to-understand sentences. Compared to multiple-choice items, binary-choice questions are relatively easy to construct. Finally, scoring is objective and quick.

The major disadvantage of binary-choice items is that they are susceptible to guessing, particularly if the items are poorly constructed, and often test-wise students can find clues to the correct answer. Thus, a combination of some knowledge, guessing, and poorly constructed items that give clues to the correct answer will allow some students to score well even though their level of knowledge is weak.

Writing good binary-choice items begins with propositions about major knowledge targets. In converting the propositions to test items, you will need to keep the items short, simple, direct, and easy to understand. This is best accomplished by avoiding ambiguity and clues. The following suggestions, summarized in Figure 6.9, will help accomplish this.

1. Write the Item So That the Answer Options Are Consistent with the Logic in the Sentence.   The way the item is written will suggest a certain logic for what type of response is most appropriate. For example, if you want to test spelling knowledge, it doesn't make much sense to use true/false questions; it would be better to use correct/incorrect as options.

FIGURE 6.9   Checklist for Writing Binary-Choice Items

✓ Does the item contain a single proposition or idea?
✓ Is the type of answer logically consistent with the statement?
✓ Are the statements succinct?
✓ Is the item stated positively?
✓ Is the length of both statements in an item about the same?
✓ Do the correct responses have a pattern?
✓ Are unequivocal terms used?
✓ Does the item try to trick students?
✓ Is trivial knowledge being tested?
✓ Are about half the items answered correctly with same response?

2. Include a Single Fact or Idea in the Item.   For assessing recall knowledge, avoid two or more facts, ideas, or propositions in a single item. This is because one idea or fact may be true and the other false, which introduces ambiguity and error.

Example

> *Poor:*   T   F   California is susceptible to earthquakes because of the collision between oceanic and continental plates.
>
> *Improved:*   T   F   Earthquakes in California are caused by the collision between oceanic and continental plates.

3. Avoid Long Sentences.   Try to keep the sentences as concise as possible. This allows you to include more test items and reduces ambiguity. Longer sentences tend to favor students who have stronger reading comprehension skills.

Example

> *Poor:*   T   F   A cup with hot water that has a spoon in it will cool more quickly than a similar cup with the same amount of hot water that does not have a spoon in it.
>
> *Improved:*   T   F   Hot water in a cup will cool more quickly if a spoon is placed in the cup.

4. Avoid Insignificant or Trivial Facts and Words.   It is relatively easy to write "tough" binary-choice items that measure trivial knowledge. Avoid this by beginning with what you believe are significant learning targets.

Examples

> *Poor:* Charles Darwin was twenty-two years old when he began his voyage of the world.
>
> *Poor:* An elephant spends about fifteen hours a day eating and foraging.

5. Avoid Negative Statements.   Statements that include the words *not* or *no* are confusing to students and make items and answers more difficult to understand. Careful reading and sound logic become prerequisites for answering correctly. If the knowledge can be tested only with a negatively worded statement, be sure to highlight the negative word with boldface type, underlining, or all caps.

Example

> *Poor:* United States senators are not elected to six-year terms.
>
> *Improved:* United States senators are elected to six-year terms.

6. Avoid Clues to the Answer.   Test-wise students will look for specific words that suggest that the item is false. When adjectives and adverbs such as *never, all, every, always,* and *absolutely* are used, the answer is usually false. Also, avoid any kind of pattern in the items that provides clues to the answer, such as all true items being longer, alternating true and false answers, tending to use one type of answer more than the other, or all the items being either true or false. It is best to write questions so that about 50 percent of the answers are true.

7. Do Not Try to Trick Students.   Items that are written to "trick" students by including a word that changes the meaning of an idea or by inserting some trivial fact should be avoided. Trick items undermine your credibility, frustrate students, and provide less valid measures of knowledge.

8. Avoid Using Vague Adjectives and Adverbs.   Adjectives and adverbs such as *frequent, sometimes, occasionally, typically,* and *usually* are interpreted differently by each student. It is best to avoid these types of words because the meaning of the statement is not equivocal.

Multiple-Choice Items

Multiple-choice items are used widely in schools, even though they may *not* be the best method for assessing recall knowledge (see Figure 3.2). Multiple-choice items have a **stem,** in the form of a question or incomplete statement, and three or more **alternatives.** The alternatives contain one correct or best answer and two or more **distractors.** For measuring knowledge, it is usually best to use a question as the stem and to provide one correct answer. A direct question is preferred for several reasons: It is easier to write, it forces you to state the complete problem more clearly in the stem, its format is familiar to students, it avoids the problem of grammatically tailoring each alternative to the stem, and questions place less demand on reading skills to understand the problem. Questions are clearly better for younger students. Items that assess the "best" answer allow for greater discrimination and are very effective for measuring understanding. In this type of item, each alternative may have some correct aspect, but one answer is better than the others.

Multiple-choice questions offer several advantages. Like other select-response items, they can provide a broad sampling of knowledge. Scoring is easy and objective, and it's good to give students practice on the type of items they are likely to encounter on standardized tests. Compared with binary-choice items, multiple-choice are typically more reliable. There is much less of a guessing factor, and they are free from response set. Multiple-choice items also usually have more diagnostic power because selection of certain distractors can pinpoint an error in knowledge.

However, there are also disadvantages. Multiple-choice questions take longer to answer than other types of objective items, and consequently they do not sample as well. Also, it is relatively difficult to write multiple-choice items, especially good distractors. Many teachers find that it isn't too hard to come up with one or two good distractors, but the third or fourth ones are often giveaways to students. This increases the probability that students will guess the right answer. Students learn that the way to study for multiple-choice items is to read and reread the material to focus on recognition. Much less energy is spent to recall information. Thus, like other selected-response items, the type of mental preparation prompted by knowledge multiple-choice items is not consistent with more contemporary theories of learning and information processing.

Suggestions for writing multiple-choice items are summarized in the following points and in Figure 6.10 in the form of questions. When you need to write the items, begin with the stem, then the correct response, and finally the distractors.

FIGURE 6.10   Checklist for Writing Multiple-Choice Items

✓ Is the stem stated as clearly, directly, and simply as possible?
✓ Is the problem self-contained in the stem?
✓ Is the stem stated positively?
✓ Is there only one correct answer?
✓ Are all the alternatives parallel with respect to grammatical structure, length, and complexity?
✓ Are irrelevant clues avoided?
✓ Are the options short?
✓ Are complex options avoided?
✓ Are options placed in logical order?
✓ Are the distractors plausible to students who do not know the correct answer?
✓ Are correct answers spread equally among all the choices?

1. Write the Stem as a Clearly Described Question or Task.   You want the stem to be meaningful by itself. It should clearly and succinctly communicate what is expected. If the stem makes sense only by reading the responses, it is poorly constructed. It is best, then, to put as much information as possible in the stem and not the responses, as long as the stem does not become too wordy. The general rule is this: Use complete stems and short responses. This reduces the time students need to read the items and reduces redundant words. Of course, you do not want to include words in the stem that are not needed; the stem is longer than the alternatives but is still as succinct as possible. In the end, a good indicator of an effective stem is if students have a tentative answer in mind quickly, before reading the options.

Examples

   Poor: Validity refers to
       a. the consistency of test scores.
       b. the inference made on the basis of test scores.
       c. measurement error as determined by standard deviation.
       d. the stability of test scores.

   Improved: The inference made on the basis of test scores refers to
       a. reliability.
       b. stability.
       c. validity.
       d. measurement error.

   Poor: What is the length of the table?
       a. 1 foot
       b. 3 feet
       c. 15 inches
       d. 24 inches

Improved: What is the length of the table in feet?

    a. 1
    b. 2
    c. 3
    d. 4

2. Avoid the Use of Negatives in the Stem.   Using words like *not* and *except* will confuse students and create anxiety and frustration. Often students simply overlook the negative, which leads to invalid results. It also takes longer to respond to such items. So try to word the stem positively. In cases where knowing what not to do is important, as in knowing rules of the road for driving, the negative stem is fine as long as the negative word is emphasized by boldface or underlining.

Examples

    Poor: Which of the following is not a mammal?

        a. Bird
        b. Dog
        c. Horse
        d. Whale
        e. Cat

    Improved: Which of the following is a mammal?

        a. Bird
        b. Frog
        c. Whale
        d. Fish
        e. Lizard

3. Write the Correct Response with No Irrelevant Clues.   There should not be any difference between the correct answer and distractors that would clue the student to respond on some basis other than the knowledge being tested. Common mistakes include making the correct response longer, more elaborate or detailed, more general, or more technical. Qualifiers such as *usually, some,* and *generally* are clues to the correct answer.

4. Write the Distractors to Be Plausible Yet Clearly Wrong.   The distractors are useless if they are so obviously wrong that students do not even consider them as possible answers. The intent of a multiple-choice item is to have students *discriminate* among what they see as *plausible* answers. Distractors should appear to be possibly correct to poorly prepared students. Distractors are intended to appeal to the uniformed and should not result in tricking students. A good approach to determining good distracters is to identify common misunderstandings or errors by students and then write distractors that appeal to students who have the misunderstandings. Other ways to write good distractors include the use of words that have verbal associations with the stem, important words (e.g., enduring, major, noteworthy), length and complexity that matches the stem, and the use of qualifiers such as *generally* or *usually*. Poor distractors contain content that is plainly wrong, grammatical inconsistencies, or qualifiers such as *always* or *never*, or they state the opposite of the correct answer.

The number of distractors depends on several factors. Most multiple-choice items have two, three, or four distractors. Other things being equal, an item with four distractors is best if the goal is to measure more depth of knowledge. More questions are possible with only two distractors, which may provide better coverage or breadth. Questions for young children often have only two distractors. One thing is sure: Don't add obviously wrong distractors just to get to three or four. Once you have had some experience with writing distractors, you can do an **item analysis** to determine whether the distractors are being used with equal frequency. If a particular distractor is rarely selected, then it should be modified to be more plausible. (Item analysis is also done to see if the item *discriminates* between high and low performers on the test, i.e., whether most high performers answered it correctly and most low performers missed it, and to determine item difficulty). A good rule of thumb is two or three distractors for each item.

Examples

> *Poor:* Which of the following is the largest city in the United States?
>
> **a.** Michigan
> **b.** London
> **c.** New York
> **d.** Berlin

> *Improved:* Which of the following is the largest city in the United States?
>
> **a.** Los Angeles
> **b.** Chicago
> **c.** New York
> **d.** Miami

> *Poor:* The first step in writing is to
>
> **a.** always rewrite.
> **b.** outline.
> **c.** grammatically correct.

5. Avoid Using "All of the Above," "None of the Above," or Other Special Distractors.   These phrases are undesirable for a number of reasons. "All of the above" is the right answer if only two of the options are correct, and some students may select the first item that is correct without reading the others. Only when students need to know what *not* to do would "none of the above" be appropriate. Be sure to avoid options like "A and C but not D" or other combinations. Items with this type of response tend to measure reasoning ability as much as knowledge, and, especially for measuring knowledge, the items take far too long to answer.

6. Use Each Alternative as the Correct Answer about the Same Number of Times.   If you have four possible choices, about 25 percent of the items should have the same letter as the correct response (20 percent if there are five choices). This avoids a pattern that can increase the chance that students will guess the correct answer. Perhaps you have heard the old admonition from test-wise students, "when in doubt, pick C." There is some truth to this for test writers who are not careful to use all the responses equally as the correct one.

Assessing Simple Understanding: Comprehension and Application

As stated earlier, comprehension and application are two types of knowing through which students demonstrate their understanding of something. We will consider each with some examples, using the aforementioned objective test methods. Other methods of assessment, such as essays, interpretive items, and performance assessments, are also good for measuring simple understanding but are even better for assessing deep understanding. We will consider these methods in Chapters 7 and 8.

Assessing Comprehension

Comprehension is demonstrated when students understand, in their own words, the essential meaning of a concept, principle, or procedure. They show this by providing explanations and examples, by converting and translating, and by interpreting and predicting.

Test items that assess knowledge can be changed easily to assess comprehension. For instance, to tap into translation, simply change the words used to describe or define something so that it is not verbatim from the instructional materials. Higher levels of comprehension require more work. Suppose that as a student you have learned that "photosynthesis is the process by which plants use light to make glucose." The following examples show how to measure this as knowledge or comprehension.

Examples

Knowledge (short-answer): Define photosynthesis: _____
_____

Comprehension (completion): Sunlight is used by plants to make energy in a process called _____ .

Comprehension (short-answer): Explain how plants get energy from the sun.
_____

_____

Comprehension (short-answer): What would happen to plants if they did not receive any sunlight for a long time?

Comprehension (binary-choice):   T   F   Plants that receive 50 hours of light will produce more glucose than plants that receive 10 hours of light.

Knowledge (multiple-choice): Which of the following is the process by which plants use light to make glucose?

   a. respiration
   b. photosynthesis
   c. energizing
   d. growing

Comprehension (multiple-choice): In plants, sugar is made by energy from the sun from which of the following?

   a. respiration
   b. photosynthesis
   c. energizing
   d. growing

Comprehension (multiple-choice): Which of the following is most consistent with the process of photosynthesis?

   a. Plants that get light do not need to make glucose.
   b. Plants that get less light make less glucose.
   c. Glucose is produced from plants before photosynthesis.
   d. Energy is stored in plants as glucose.

Other examples of items that assess comprehension are illustrated in Figure 6.11.

FIGURE 6.11   Examples of Items Assessing Comprehension

Learning Target: **Students understand the nature of food chains.**

Items

Completion:	Toxic chemicals can get in our bodies from what farmers spray on plants because of the _____ _____.
Short Answer:	Explain how a plant, a mouse, a snake, and a human can be part of a food chain.
Binary Choice:	T F Farmers rotate their crops to make sure each crop gets the same amount of sun.
Multiple Choice:	Which of the following would make fish travel through the ocean as if they were in a stream ?

   a. Current
   b. Waves
   c. Tide
   d. Wind

Assessing Application

Understanding is demonstrated through application when students are able to *use* what they know to solve problems in a *new* situation. This is a more sophisticated type of understanding than comprehension, and it includes the ability to interpret new information with what is known and to apply rules, principles, and strategies to new problems and situations. Obviously this is a very important type of learning target, since we want students to apply what they learn in school to new situations outside of school. Knowing something well enough to apply it successfully to new situations is called learning for *transfer*. The goal is to have sufficient understanding to transfer what is known to different situations.

Perhaps the best example of learning for application is mathematics. At one level, students can memorize the steps for solving certain kinds of math problems—that is, what to do first, second, and so forth. They may even show some comprehension by being able to explain the steps in their own words. But if they cannot apply the steps to new problems and get the right answer, we conclude that they really don't *understand* the process. That's why we give math tests with new problems. Students learn procedural knowledge in math, it is hoped at the application level. In many ways, understanding mathematics is demonstrated by successful application. Likewise, much of what we do in language arts instruction is focused on understanding at the application level. Students learn rules for grammar, sentence structure, to write drafts before final copy, and reading skills. We conclude that they actually understand how to read and write by demonstrating their skill with new material.

Your goal in assessing application is to construct items that contain new data or information that the student must work with to obtain the answer and to create new problems or applications in which students must extend what they know in a novel way. The extent of newness determines, to some extent, item difficulty and degree of understanding demonstrated. Items that contain completely new or unfamiliar material are generally more difficult than items in which there are only small differences between what was learned and the content of the question. This is why students may be able to solve new mathematics computational problems well but have trouble applying the same procedures to word problems that put the question in a new context.

The key feature of application items, then, is presenting situations that the students have not previously encountered. There are several strategies for constructing such items. One approach is to present a fictional problem that can be solved by applying appropriate procedural knowledge. For example, if students have learned about electricity and resistance, the following objective questions would test at the application level.

Examples

Application

1. Shaunda has decided to make two magnets by wrapping wire around a nail and attaching the wires to a battery so that the electric current can create a

magnetic force. One magnet (A) uses thin wire and one magnet (B) uses thick wire. Which magnet will be the strongest?

   a. A
   b. B
   c. A and B will be the same
   d. Cannot be determined from the information provided

2. T   F   Other things being equal, an electric stove with greater resistance will be hotter than a stove with less resistance.

3. To increase the heat produced from his electric iron, Mr. Jones would _____ the resistance.

Other examples of objective application items include the following:

Examples

1. What happens to water pollution when farmers use *less* fertilizer?

    _____

2. A researcher investigated whether a new type of fertilizer would result in greater growth of corn plants. What is the independent variable?

   a. Growth of corn plants
   b. The researcher
   c. Type of fertilizer
   d. Amount of sunlight

3. William is given a $2.00 allowance each week. He wants to save enough money to go to the movie, which costs $4.00, and buy some candy and a soft

Case Study for Reflection

Mr. Marshall, a fifth-grade teacher, has been teaching a multidisciplinary unit on the life cycle of a pond. This unit covered science content, mathematics, geography, reading, writing, research skills, and computer skills. He has decided that part of his unit assessment needs to consist of "objective" items. He is considering completion, short-answer, and selected-response items.

Questions for Consideration
1. What are some examples of learning targets that would be appropriate for the kinds of items Mr. Marshall wants to use?
2. Which unit topics and skills would be best assessed with each type of item? Why?
3. Which unit topics and skills would be better assessed using different kinds of items? Why?

drink at the movie. The candy will cost $1.50 and the drink will cost $2.50. How many weeks will William have to wait before he can go to the movie and buy the candy and soft drink?

a. 2
b. 3
c. 4
d. 5

Putting Tests Together

Once you have developed test items, they need to be put together in the form of a test. The following guidelines, which include suggestions for directions, arranging items, and the physical layout of the test, should be followed.

Preparing Test Directions

According to Gronlund (1993), test directions should include the following:

1. Purpose
2. Time allowed for completing the test
3. Basis for responding
4. Procedures for recording answers
5. What to do about guessing
6. How constructed-response items will be scored

The purpose of the test should be made clear to students well in advance of the testing date. This is usually done when the test is announced. Students need to know why they are taking the test and how the results will be used. A written statement of purpose will clarify the purpose for both students and parents, though usually the purpose is given to students orally.

Students need to know *exactly* how much time they will have to complete the test, even if the test is not speeded. It is helpful to indicate to students how they should distribute their time among various parts of the test. It is best to allow plenty of time for students so that they do not feel rushed. As indicated earlier, students can be expected to complete at least one multiple-choice and two binary-choice items per minute, but the actual time will depend on the difficulty of the items and student preparation. Obviously, elementary students will need more time than high school students. Your judgments about how many items to include will improve with experience. In the beginning, err on the side of allowing too much time.

The basis for responding simply refers to what students are to do to answer the question, that is, how to respond. This should be a simple and direct statement (e.g., "Select the correct answer," or "Select the best answer"). The procedure for responding indicates how students show their answers, whether they circle the answer, write the answer next to the item, write the word in the blank, and so on. If computations are to be shown, tell the students where they should write them.

In a test where all the items are of the selection type, students may ask about whether there is a penalty for guessing. In classroom tests it is very rare to find a correction for guessing. The best practice is to be very clear to students that they should try to answer each item (e.g., "Your score is the total number of correct answers, so answer every item").

The final suggestion for directions concerns the scoring criteria for constructed-response items. For these items it is important to clearly indicate the basis on which you will grade the students' answers. We will explore this in Chapter 7.

Arranging Items

Arranging items by level of difficulty (e.g., easy items first, then difficult ones) has little effect on the results. If you think your students gain confidence by answering the easiest items first, it's fine to order the items by increasing difficulty. The most important consideration in arranging items is item type. Keep all the items that use the same format together. Thus, keep all the multiple-choice items in one section, all the matching items in another, and so on. This reduces the number of times students need to shift their response mode. It also minimizes directions and makes scoring easier. Generally it is best to order items, in sections determined by type, based on how quickly students can answer. Items answered more quickly, such as completion and binary-choice, would generally come first, followed by multiple-choice and short-answer items. If possible, it is best to group the items according to learning targets and keep assessments of the same target or content together.

Physical Layout of the Test

Objective test items need to be formatted so that they are easy to read and answer. A few commonsense suggestions help to achieve this goal. First, all the information needed to answer an item should be on the same page. Avoid having part of an item on one page and the rest of the item on another page. Second, do not crowd too many items onto a page. Although we all need to be careful about wasting paper, a test that is crowded is likely to contain more errors than one that has reasonable spacing and white space. This means that multiple-choice options should not be listed horizontally on the same line. Rather, it is best if the options are listed vertically below the item.

Examples

> *Poor Format:* What is the movement of animals from one environment to another between summer and winter called? (a) conditioning (b) hibernation (c) territorial reflex (d) migration.

> *Improved Format:* What is the movement of animals from one environment to another between summer and winter called?

a. conditioning
b. hibernation
c. territorial reflex
d. migration

Finally, the format of the test should enhance scoring accuracy and efficiency. For older students, it is best to use a separate answer sheet that can be designed for scoring ease. This can be accomplished by simply repeating the directions and listing the items by number. Students circle or write in their answers. If you have students answer on the same piece of paper that contains the questions, leave blanks to the left of each binary-choice, multiple-choice, or matching item and blanks on the right-hand side of the page for completion items. For younger students, it is best to minimize transfer of answers by having them circle or underline the correct answer or write the answer in the space provided in the item.

Summary

This chapter examined the nature of knowledge and simple understanding learning targets and selected-response and brief constructed-response test items that can be used to assess students on these targets. Suggestions for preparing summative assessments and assembling a test were also presented. Major points include the following:

- Preparation for summative assessment includes appropriately sampling what students are responsible for knowing, having the appropriate length and number of assessments, carefully using the tests provided by publishers, preparing students, properly scheduling the assessment, and allowing instruction to influence the final makeup of the test.
- Knowledge can be classified as declarative or procedural.
- Declarative knowledge often emphasizes memorization of facts, concepts, and principles.
- Declarative understanding involves greater generalization and connection with existing knowledge.
- Procedural knowledge emphasizes memorization of skills, steps, and procedures.
- Procedural understanding emphasizes the application of process skills to new problems and situations.
- Understanding varies in degree, from simple to deep.
- Simple understanding is defined by comprehension and application.
- Completion and short-answer items are effective if memorization is avoided, a single brief answer is correct, wording is understood by all students, and the specific nature and length of the answer is clearly implied.
- Matching items are effective for assessing simple understanding of related facts or concepts as long as responses are short, premises and responses are

homogeneous, lists are logically ordered, no grammatical clues are given, and no more than ten premises are in one matching item.

■ Binary-choice items, such as true/false items, are effective if they are clearly, succinctly, and positively stated as single propositions or statements.

■ Multiple-choice items are effective if they are clearly and directly stated with one correct answer, include plausible distractors, and do not provide clues to the correct answer.

■ Simple understanding for application is assessed with objective items for application when previously learned facts or skills are used to solve problems in novel situations.

■ Objective tests are put together by considering the directions, proper arrangement of the items, and correct formatting of the contents of the test.

SELF-INSTRUCTIONAL REVIEW EXERCISES

1. Match the descriptions in column A with the criteria for constructing summative assessments in column B. Each criterion may be used once, more than once, or not at all.

   Column A   *Column B*

   _____ **(1)** Revision of a test provided in   a. Representative sampling
                    instructional materials   b. Length of assessment
   _____ **(2)** Use of test blueprint   c. Number of assessments
   _____ **(3)** Teaching test-taking skills   d. Use of publisher's test
   _____ **(4)** Using an adequate number of   e. Preparing students
                    items for each area   f. Scheduling assessments
   _____ **(5)** Providing time for student questions
   _____ **(6)** Chapter review

2. Identify each of the following descriptions as declarative (D) or procedural (P) and as knowledge (K) or simple understanding (SU).

   a. Define procedural knowledge.
   b. What is the sequence of steps in preparing an objective test?
   c. Give an example of a multiple-choice item that measures application.
   d. List three suggestions for constructing matching items.
   e. Predict whether students will have questions about how to answer the items in the test.
   f. Review the strategy a teacher has used to construct binary-choice test items to determine if they can be improved.

3. Match the suggestions or descriptions from column A with the type(s) of objective items in column B. Each type of item may be used once, more than once, or not at all; each suggestion or description may have more than one correct match.

   Column A   *Column B*

   _____ **(1)** Generally more time-consuming   a. Completion
                    to construct   b. Short answer
   _____ **(2)** Scoring may be a problem   c. Matching

_____ **(3)** Effectively measures relations

_____ **(4)** Conveniently constructed from instructional materials

_____ **(5)** Responses ordered logically

_____ **(6)** Correct answers spread equally among all possible choices

_____ **(7)** Verbatim language from textbooks is avoided

_____ **(8)** Uses clear, concise statements

_____ **(9)** Uses blanks of equal length

d. Binary choice

e. Multiple choice

4. Using the checklists for writing objective items, evaluate each of the following items and revise it so that it will be improved.

(1) _____ _____ are sloping ledges that are formed underwater next to most continents such as Australia and North America.

(2) How does energy from the sun affect the earth?

(3) Match the states with the characteristics.

_____ Florida

_____ New York

_____ Michigan

_____ Colorado

_____ Iowa

_____ Texas

_____ Utah

_____ Illinois

_____ Virginia

_____ North Carolina

a. St. Augustine

b. Bordered by Missouri and Minnesota

c. Alamo

d. Jamestown

e. Outer Banks

f. Lincoln

g. Largest city

h. Great Lake State

i. Great Salt Lake

j. Denver

(4) T F Students do not construct their own answers to every type of item except multiple choice.

(5) Circle the best answer.

Michigan is a (a) Great Lake State, (b) state in which the Rocky Mountains are located, (c) example of a state that is west of the Mississippi, (d) none of the above.

(6) Circle the correct answer.

Biodegradable substances are

a. nonrenewable resources.

b. materials that can be broken down into substances that are simpler and do not result in environmental pollution.

c. becoming less popular.

d. like fossil fuels.

ANSWERS TO SELF-INSTRUCTIONAL REVIEW EXERCISES

1. 1. d; 2. a; 3. e; 4. a; 5. b; 6. e.

2. a. DK, b. PK, c. DSU, d. DK, e. DSU, f. PSU.

3. 1. e; 2. a, b; 3. c; 4. a, d; 5. c, e; 6. d, e; 7. a, b, c, d, e; 8. a, b, c, d, e; 9. a.

4. (1) This may be lifted verbatim from the instructional material requiring memorization of a definition. The blanks are not at the end of the sentence. The length of the blanks gives a clue to the correct answer. It is not a concise statement, including only what is needed to answer the item.

Revision: The sloping ledge formed underwater next to most continents is the

_____ _____.

(2) This is poorly worded because many answers could be correct. There is no indication of how long the answer should be, and it is possible that a "correct" answer could be several sentences long—hardly short-answer!

Revision: Name two sources of energy from the sun that affect the earth. _____

_____.

(3) There are probably too many items in one list. Additional responses should be included as distractors. Better to have states listed on the right. Directions are inadequate. Format is difficult to score. Premises are not homogeneous and are on the wrong side. Do not mix cities with historical figures, geographic descriptions, and state mottos.

Revision: On the line next to each number in column A, write the letter of the state from column B that matches the geographic descriptions. Each state may be used once, more than once, or not at all.

Column A

_____ **(1)**	Is bordered by three Great Lakes
_____ **(2)**	Contains part of the Rocky Mountains
_____ **(3)**	Has an upper and lower peninsula
_____ **(4)**	Is bordered by the Ohio and Mississippi rivers
_____ **(5)**	Contains the Blue Ridge Mountains

Column B

a. New York
b. Virginia
c. Ohio
d. Michigan
e. Texas
f. Colorado
g. Illinois
h. Maryland
i. North Carolina

(4) The negatives in this item make it very hard to understand. State more directly the proposition to be tested. Directions need to be included.

Revision: If the statement is true, circle T; if it is false, circle F.

T   F   Students construct answers to multiple-choice items.

(5) The directions should indicate "correct" answer, not "best" answer. The alternatives should be listed vertically under the stem. The stem should be long, the alternatives short. Option (c) does not fit grammatically and is not concise. "None of the above" should be avoided. It would be better to use a question.

Revision: Circle the correct answer.

Which of the following is a characteristic of Michigan?

a. It is surrounded by the Great Lakes.
b. It contains the Rocky Mountains.

c. It is a single peninsula.
d. It borders the Atlantic Ocean.

(6) The correct answer, **b,** is obvious because of the complexity of the sentence in relation to the others. Fossil fuels are also biodegradable, so more than one correct answer is possible. The stem is short and the correct alternative long. It is more clearly stated as a question.

Revision: Circle the correct answer.

What type of material is broken down by decomposers into simpler substances that do not pollute the environment?

a. Nonrenewable
b. Biodegradable
c. Fossil fuel
d. Decomposition

SUGGESTIONS FOR ACTION RESEARCH

1. Collect some examples of test items. Analyze the items and the format of the test in relation to the suggestions provided in the chapter. Show how you would improve the items and format of the test.

2. Find ten examples of items that measure different types of knowledge targets (e.g., declarative, procedural, simple understanding). Change items that measure knowledge to ones that measure simple understanding.

3. Conduct an interview with two teachers and ask them about how they construct test items. Ask them if they use each of the test preparation guidelines (sampling, using publisher's tests, and so on). Ask them to give you some advice about putting together a test, and see if their advice is consistent with the suggestions in the chapter.

4. With another student, make up a knowledge test of the content of this chapter that could be taken in one hour. Begin with a table of specifications or outline and indicate the learning targets. Include knowledge and simple understanding items. Give the test to four other students for their critique, and then revise the test as needed. Show the original test and the revised one to your supervisor or teacher for his or her critique and further suggestions. Keep a journal of your progress in making up the test. What was difficult? How much time did it take? What would have made the process more efficient?

7 Selected-Response, Short-Answer, and Essay Items:

Assessing Deep Understanding and Reasoning

In this chapter, we examine the assessment of deep understanding and reasoning—how students use their knowledge for more complex thinking. As we will see, there are different ways to conceptualize cognitive skills such as thinking and reasoning. Two methods, the interpretive exercise and the essay question, are emphasized as the preferred approaches if using a paper-and-pencil test to assess these skills and accompanying deep understanding. In Chapter 8, we will see how

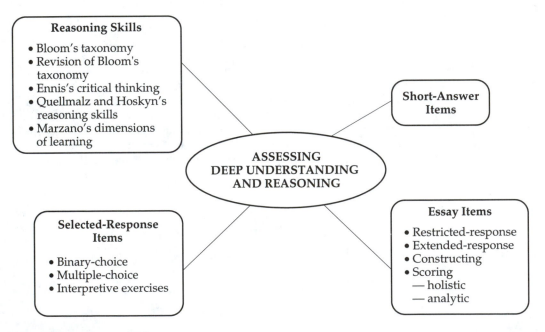

Reasoning Skills

- Bloom's taxonomy
- Revision of Bloom's taxonomy
- Ennis's critical thinking
- Quellmalz and Hoskyn's reasoning skills
- Marzano's dimensions of learning

Short-Answer Items

ASSESSING DEEP UNDERSTANDING AND REASONING

Selected-Response Items

- Binary-choice
- Multiple-choice
- Interpretive exercises

Essay Items

- Restricted-response
- Extended-response
- Constructing
- Scoring
  — holistic
  — analytic

CHAPTER 7   Concept Map

performance assessments also provide an excellent way to assess deep under-standing and reasoning.

What Are Reasoning Skills?

In Chapter 2, reasoning targets were defined as the use of knowledge for reasoning and problem solving. This suggests that reasoning is something students do with their knowledge, a kind of cognitive or mental operation that employs their un-derstanding to some end. Reasoning is more than knowledge, comprehension, or simple application. Of course, knowledge and simple understanding, like reason-ing, involve some type of thinking skill. Thinking occurs in the most fundamental process of remembering something, just as it does in demonstrating understand-ing and reasoning. It is in the nature of the thinking, however, that knowledge is distinguished from reasoning.

   Reasoning, as I have conceptualized here, involves some kind of mental ma-nipulation of knowledge. The task is to *employ* knowledge to interpret and draw in-ferences, solve a problem, make a judgment or decision, or engage in creative or critical thinking. Thinking is not normally content-free. Thus, I find it helpful to iden-tify three ingredients to reasoning. One is the mental skill needed to perform the task; a second is the declarative or procedural knowledge or simple understanding needed; and the third is the task itself. These ingredients differentiate cognitive skills such as analysis, comparison, and discrimination from the problem-solving or inter-pretation task (see Figure 7.1). The mental skills are used in conjunction with knowl-edge to perform the task. Even though we are sometimes interested in teaching and assessing students on their ability to perform certain types of mental operations,

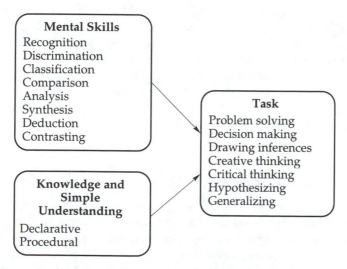

FIGURE 7.1   Major Components of Reasoning

such as analysis or deductive logic, we don't normally test these skills directly. Rather, we are usually interested in the *use* of these skills to demonstrate deep understanding or to perform a problem-solving task in subject-matter domains.

Assessing reasoning skills is challenging because the target is difficult to define. It is one thing to note the importance of teaching and testing *higher-order thinking* skills or *reasoning* skills, but operationalizing these general ideas into specific assessment targets is far from straightforward. The literature on thinking and reasoning identifies three distinct conceptualizations, each based in a different academic discipline. Educators have emphasized mental skills, as illustrated by Bloom's taxonomy. Psychologists have focused on the application of problem-solving strategies and processes. Philosophers have contributed to our understanding of deductive and inductive logic and to what is called "critical thinking." Each of these disciplines has had a different focus, but all could be labeled as thinking skills or reasoning in a broad sense. I will briefly present four thinking skill/reasoning frameworks that have been developed on the basis of these perspectives. Each represents a different way to organize, label, and define thinking skills.

I want to emphasize that selecting a way to operationalize thinking skills is up to you—there is no single right or best way. But assessing reasoning or thinking skills, no matter how one defines them in general, requires close attention to the nature of the specific mental operation involved. The following five frameworks are presented to give you suggestions and examples for developing reasoning targets.

Bloom's Taxonomy of the Cognitive Domain

Bloom's taxonomy has been described and, as previously noted, it is both the most used and the most dated conceptualization of thinking. This taxonomy has popularized the term *higher-order thinking skills* because the six levels are interpreted by most to be hierarchical (hence some are considered higher than others). However, conceptualizing the taxonomy as hierarchical does not make much practical sense. The third level, application, is considered lower than analysis, whereas comprehension, as measured by making an inference, is at the second level. Is the ability to make an inference a prerequisite for analysis? My experience is that trying to teach and test as though the taxonomy is a hierarchy is unrealistic. For me, it makes more sense to first identify the task, then examine the cognitive skills needed to complete the task, rather than to delay evaluation until skills in other levels are demonstrated. Furthermore, Bloom's taxonomy has now been incorporated into more contemporary conceptualizations.

Revision of Bloom's Taxonomy

In the revision of Bloom's taxonomy (Anderson & Krathwohl, 2001), three cognitive processes apply to deep understanding and reasoning: analyze, evaluate, and create. Analyze is essentially the same as *analysis* in other frameworks, while evaluate is similar to critical thinking and problem solving. The create process is similar to *inquiry* and emphasizes synthesis of information and problem solving. The three cognitive processes, with definitions and examples, are summarized in Figure 7.2.

FIGURE 7.2   Deep Understanding and Reasoning Parts of the Revision to Bloom's Taxonomy

Cognitive Process	Definition	Subtypes	Illustrative Verbs	Examples
Analyze	Break material into its constituent parts and determine how the parts relate.	Differentiating	Discriminating, distinguishing, focusing, selecting	Distinguish between relevant and irrelevant numbers in a math word problem.
		Organizing	Finding coherence, integrating, outlining	Structure historical evidence for and against a particular historical explanation.
		Attributing	Deconstructing	Determine the point of view of an author based on his or her political perspective.
Evaluate	Make judgments based on criteria and standards	Checking	Coordinating, detecting, monitoring, testing	Determine if conclusions follow from observed data.
		Critiquing	Judging	Judge which of two methods is the best way to solve a problem.
Create	Pull elements together to form a whole; reorganize elements into a new structure or pattern.	Generating	Hypothesizing	Generate hypothesis to account for observed phenomenon.
		Planning	Designing	Plan a research paper.
		Producing	Constructing	Build habitats for a specific purpose.

Source: Adapted from Lorin W. Anderson & David R. Krathwohl, *A taxonomy for learning, teaching, and assessing: A revision of Bloom's taxonomy of educational objectives.* Published by Allyn and Bacon, Boston, MA. Copyright © 2001 by Pearson Education. Reprinted by permission of the publisher.

Ennis's Taxonomy of Critical Thinking Dispositions and Abilities

Critical thinking is defined by Ennis (1987) as "reasonable reflective thinking that is focused on deciding what to believe or do" (p. 10). Ennis notes that critical thinking *involves* higher-order thinking skills, but the act of thinking critically must include a decision or judgment about a belief, action, or answer. Critical thinking is being able to carefully analyze a knowledge claim or information to judge its merit and worth in relation to the action or belief that results. It is the ability to evaluate and weigh information and evidence to make an informed judgment. These descriptions are similar to how Wiggins (1998) defines deep understanding. In the end, some judgments are better than others.

To promote "reasonable" thinking in making judgments, Ennis lists several abilities that should be employed. The "best" judgment results from being able to successfully apply these abilities. From a practical standpoint, the abilities are organized in a series of steps that are employed in the process of critical thinking. By following the steps and using the abilities, students are able to reason effectively.

Figure 7.3 presents the steps involved in critical thinking, along with the critical thinking abilities required and practical examples. Assessment of critical thinking as reasoning begins with identifying the task—the judgment that the student needs to make. Information is presented to the student, which is formulated to assess specific critical thinking abilities. Thus, you may purposefully include some illogical arguments or unreliable sources of information to see if students are able to recognize these and use them appropriately in defending their judgments. As we will see, essay-type test questions are best for this type of assessment because students can be asked to defend their judgments or answers.

Quellmalz and Hoskyn's Framework for Reasoning Strategies

Quellmalz (1987) and Quellmalz and Hoskyn (1997) conducted an analysis of the different ways of conceptualizing thinking and reasoning skills that had been presented in the literature. They concluded that the various frameworks contained four common elements that make sense for teaching and assessment: analysis, comparison, inference and interpretation, and evaluation.

Analysis is used in essentially the same way as it is in Bloom's taxonomy. In this operation, students divide a whole into component parts. This includes identification of the parts, the relationships among different parts, and the relation of parts to the whole. With this skill, students are able to break down, differentiate, categorize, sort, or subdivide.

The second element, comparison, is concerned with reasoning about similarities and differences. This skill is one in which the student compares, contrasts, and relates. Simple comparisons are done by pointing out one or a few similarities and differences, for example, by asking "How are two sentences the same or how are they different?" More complex comparisons require reasoning with many attributes or components.

Inference and interpretation requires deductive or inductive thinking. In a deductive task, students are asked whether one thing follows from another. Often, students are given a generalization or principles and are asked to identify or construct a correct conclusion. For example, giving students a fact like "Jane is taller than Shuanda, and Shuanda is taller than Frank," then asking "Is Jane taller or shorter than Frank?" is a task that requires deductive thinking. Inductive reasoning involves reaching a reasonable conclusion or generalization from information provided. Other thinking skills that require inference include hypothesizing, predicting, and synthesizing.

FIGURE 7.3 **Critical Thinking Steps and Abilities**

Steps	Abilities	Examples
Clarify problem	Identify or formulate a question; put the problem in context; ask questions or seek information to clarify the problem.	Which medication should Troy choose? What background factors would affect Troy's choice? Does Troy have any other options?
Gather information	Distinguish verifiable facts from value claims; determine the credibility of a source; distinguish relevant from irrelevant information, claims, or reasons; detect bias.	What information is based on opinion about the medications and what is based on objective evidence? Should the information from drug companies be used? Is it important to know that a medication tastes good? Would a company representative be biased about the company's medication?
Make inferences	Recognize logical inconsistencies in deductive reasoning; recognize unwarranted claims or generalizations from inductive reasoning.	The medication worked well with adults, but will it work as well with children? If the medication should not be used with adults, does this mean it shouldn't be used with children?
Conduct advanced clarification	Identify unstated assumptions; identify ambiguous or illogical arguments; determine the strength of an argument; detect fallacy labels such as *straw person, name-calling,* and *non sequitur*; detect inconsistencies; detect stereotypes; consider alternative judgments; distinguish cause and effect from relationships.	How good is the evidence that a particular medication will be effective? Is a particular argument for a medication reasonable? Is calling one of the medications silly and insignificant important? What are the advantages and disadvantages of each medication?
Make a judgment	Decide on an answer, solution, or course of action.	Selecting a medication and providing reasons for the decision.

Source: Adapted from: Ennis, R. H. (1987). A taxonomy of critical thinking dispositions and abilities. From *Teaching thinking skills: Theory and practice* by Joan Boykoff Baron and Robert J. Sternberg © 1987 by W. H. Freeman and Company. Used with permission; Norris, S. P., & Ennis, R. H. (1989). *Evaluating critical thinking*. Pacific Grove, CA: Midwest Publications; and Beyer, B. K. (1985). Critical thinking: What is it? *Social Education, 22,* 270–276.

In the final kind of reasoning, evaluation, students express or defend an opinion, judgment, or point of view. This is essentially the same as critical thinking. Students justify, explain, argue, and criticize.

The appeal of Quellmalz and Hoskyn's work is that the types of reasoning are easily applied to different subjects. Figure 7.4 presents examples of what are labeled reasoning strategies.

FIGURE 7.4   Applications of Quellmalz and Hoskyn's Framework of Reasoning Strategies

Cognitive Strategy	Domain		
	Literacy	*Social Science*	*Science*

Analyze	Narrative
	   Story, plot, and
	   character elements;
	   setting; style
	
	 Persuasive issue
	   Position, reasons,
	   evidence, conclusion
	
	 Expository
	   Main idea, support
	   and elaboration,
	   organization and
	   coherence, style
		Elements of an event, features of a culture, features of a historical period	Components of a process, features of animate and inanimate objects, evolution of species

Compare	Narrative elements, themes, points of view, evidence, accuracy, organization	Leaders, cultures, political systems, ideologies, time periods, accounts of an event	Regions, climates, scientific processes, energy sources, habitats, ecosystems
Infer and Interpret	Themes, motivation, mood, bias, predict cause and effect	Causes and influences, predict future effects, infer consequences	Test hypotheses, draw conclusions, infer consequences, link cause and effect, interdependencies
Evaluate	Significance, coherence, clarity, style, believability	Significance of contributions, practicality, credibility of arguments, alternative interpretations	Soundness of scientific procedures, credibility of conclusions, significance of findings, feasibility, impact

Source: Adapted from Quellmalz, E. S., & Hoskyn, J. (1997). Classroom assessment of reasoning strategies. From *Handbook of classroom assessment: Learning, adjustment, and achievement,* edited by Gary Phye, p. 108. Reprinted with permission from Elsevier Science.

Marzano's Dimensions of Learning

Marzano and his colleagues (Marzano, 1992, 1996; Marzano, Pickering, & McTighe, 1993) offer an instructional framework for organizing learning outcomes into five major categories (see Figure 7.5). Each of the categories represents a type of thinking that is important for successful learning. The dimensions of learning framework was

FIGURE 7.5   Dimensions of Learning

Dimension 1	Positive Attitudes and Perceptions about Learning
Dimension 2	Acquiring and Integrating Knowledge <ul><li>Declarative knowledge</li><li>Procedural knowledge</li></ul>
Dimension 3	Extending and Refining Knowledge <ul><li>Comparing</li><li>Classifying</li><li>Making inductions</li><li>Making deductions</li><li>Analyzing errors</li><li>Creating and analyzing support</li><li>Analyzing perspectives</li><li>Abstracting</li></ul>
Dimension 4	Using Knowledge Meaningfully <ul><li>Decision making</li><li>Investigation</li><li>Experimental inquiry</li><li>Problem solving</li><li>Invention</li></ul>
Dimension 5	Productive Habits of Mind <ul><li>Being clear and seeking clarity</li><li>Being open-minded</li><li>Restraining impulsivity</li><li>Being aware of your own thinking</li><li>Evaluating the effectiveness of your actions</li><li>Pushing the limits of your knowledge and abilities</li><li>Engaging intensely in tasks even when answers or solutions are not immediately apparent</li></ul>

Source: Adapted from Marzano, R. J. (1992). *A different kind of classroom: Teaching with dimensional learning.* Alexandria, VA: Association for Supervision and Curriculum Development; and Marzano, R. J., Pickering, D., & McTighe, J. (1993). *Assessing student outcomes: Performance assessment using the dimensions of learning model.* Alexandria, VA: Association for Supervision and Curriculum Development.

initially developed to show teachers how to use recent research and theory on learning, particularly constructivist ideas, to organize, plan, and execute instruction.

The instructional emphasis of the framework makes it ideal for identifying learning targets that are practical. The first dimension, positive attitudes and perceptions about learning, and the fifth one, productive habits of mind, are concerned with what I have called affect and are reviewed in Chapter 10. The second learning dimension, acquiring and integrating knowledge, is conceptually the same as what was covered in Chapter 6, including the distinction between declarative and procedural knowledge. Dimensions 3 and 4 (referred to as "complex" thinking or "reasoning strategies") are concerned with reasoning as I have defined it in this chapter. Dimension 3, extending and refining knowledge, emphasizes how students use thinking skills to extend and refine their knowledge to demonstrate understanding. This includes inductive and deductive thinking, analysis, and making comparisons. Dimension 4, using knowledge meaningfully, includes students' use of their knowledge to make decisions, conduct an investigation or experiment, solve a problem, and develop something unique.

Problem solving involves finding a solution that overcomes some kind of obstacle. This involves identifying the problem and obstacle, developing possible solutions, testing solutions, and finally evaluating the solutions. The steps in this process, then, include the following:

1. Identify the general problem.
2. Clarify the problem.
3. Identify and describe relevant constraints or obstacles.
4. Identify the most important obstacles.
5. Identify possible solutions.
6. Choose the best solutions.
7. Apply or test the best solutions.
8. Monitor effect of each solution.
9. Select the best solution.

To assess problem solving, you need to construct a task that lends itself to these steps and then ask questions that address the ability of the student to apply the steps successfully to arrive at a best solution.

Decision making is similar to problem solving, but it may or may not involve obstacles or constraints. The critical characteristic is that there are alternative, competing choices. In decision making, students need to understand the desired goal or result, evaluate the alternatives to be considered by identified criteria related to the situation, and select a course of action, plan, choice, or task on the basis of their evaluations. Like problem solving, then, to assess decision making you must clearly specify the steps and criteria for your evaluations.

The kind of thinking that is needed for each dimension is translated easily into questions that are applicable for all disciplines. In Figure 7.6, each of the complex reasoning skills in dimensions 3 and 4 is defined, along with examples.

It should be noted that Marzano (2001) has also created a new taxonomy of educational objectives. He suggests six levels: retrieval, comprehension, analysis, knowledge utilization, metacognition, and self-system thinking. The levels are

FIGURE 7.6   Definitions and Examples of Thinking Processes in Dimensions 3 and 4

Thinking Process	Definition	Example
Comparison	Describes similarities and differences between two or more items	Your task is to identify similarities and differences among different sizes of government.
Classification	Organizes items based on specific characteristics	Classify various waste materials on the basis of smell, toxicity, bulk, and any other attributes.
Induction	Creates a generalization from information	Observe the behavior of six people and synthesize your observations into three or four general ways people tend to behave.
Deduction	Describes logical consequences of generalizations or principles	Observe the following news clip and indicate whether the clip is an example of biased reporting.
Error Analysis	Identifies and describes specific errors in information or processes	Review recent news reports and give examples of inaccurate information.
Constructing Support	Develops well-articulated argument for or against a specific claim or assertion	Residents of a rural community object to a proposal to build a landfill on their farmland because it will pollute their water. Do you agree with their argument? Why or why not?
Abstracting	Identifies underlying theme or pattern from situations or information	Describe the major events people experience when going to the doctor. Is the process the same for going to the dentist?
Analyzing Perspectives	Considers opposing positions and the reasoning that supports each position	Write two letters to the editor, one in support of and one against allowing prayer in the schools.
Decision Making	Makes a selection among apparently equal alternatives	If you were Harry Truman, would you have decided to drop an atomic bomb on Hiroshima? What factors would be important in your decision?
Investigation	Examines and systematically inquires about something	What were the important determining events that led to the U.S. military involvement in Vietnam?
Problem Solving	Develops and tests a method or product for overcoming obstacles or constraints to reach a desired outcome	How can the United States reduce the high number of violent crimes?
Experimental Inquiry	Tests hypotheses that have been generated to explain a phenomenon	Observe what happens when the population of mice increases in this area. How can you explain what happened? What would happen if the population of mice decreased?
Invention	Develops something unique or makes unique improvements to a product or process	How would you change the way bills are passed in Congress to improve our system of government?

Source: Adapted from Marzano, R. J., Pickering, D., & McTighe, J. (1993). *Assessing student outcomes: Performance assessment using the dimensions of learning model.* Alexandria, VA: Association for Supervision and Curriculum Development. Adapted by permission of McREL.

integrated with three knowledge domains—information, mental processes, and psychomotor processes—creating a two-dimensional model similar in approach to Anderson and Krathwohl's revision of Bloom's taxonomy.

The various frameworks that have been presented provide different ways to think about deep understanding and reasoning. Through the verbs they use and examples, you can determine which framework is most closely related to the deep understanding and reasoning targets in your discipline or classroom. You should also feel free to adapt one or more frameworks to your teaching. It's fine to pick and choose, mix and match, and modify as appropriate.

Assessing Deep Understanding and Reasoning

Before we consider several methods that do a good job of assessing deep understanding and reasoning skills, two points should be emphasized. First, remember that each of the assessment methods we discuss in this book can be used to measure any learning target. Reasoning can be measured by selected-response items, and knowledge can be evaluated in student essays or performance products. However, some methods are better than others for assessing particular types of targets. Second, normally when we assess reasoning we are also measuring how much students understand. This is clearly illustrated in the scoring criteria for many essay items, in which students are graded for demonstrating an understanding of certain concepts or principles. But there is an important trade-off. Items that assess reasoning and deep understanding well cannot begin to sample the *amount* of knowledge and simple understanding that can be tested with simple objective items.

We will look at how the selected-response and short-answer items discussed in Chapter 6 work for assessing deep understanding reasoning, and then we will review two paper-and-pencil test methods that are better suited for assessing reasoning but that aren't as good for assessing knowledge—interpretive exercises and essays. In Chapter 8, we will examine performance assessing and its potential for measuring knowledge, reasoning, and skills.

Short-Answer and Selected-Response Items

We will consider some examples of how short-answer and selected-response items can be used to measure the isolated thinking skills required for reasoning tasks, but there are far too many thinking skills to cover all of them with each type of item. The suggestions in Chapter 6 for writing items are also applicable here.

Short Answer.   Short-answer items can assess thinking skills when students are required to supply a brief response to a question or situation that can be understood only by the use of the targeted thinking skills. Reasoning tasks, like decision making and critical thinking, are not assessed very well with short-answer items.

Examples

(Comparing) List three ways the recession of the 1980s was like the depression of the 1920s.

(Comparing) How does a pine tree differ from an oak tree?

(Comparing) Name one difference between vertebrate and invertebrate animals.

(Deductive reasoning) Coach Greene substitutes his basketball players by height, so that the first substitute is the tallest player on the bench, the next substitute is the next tallest, and so forth. Reginald is taller than Sam, and Juan is taller than Reginald. Which of these three players should Coach Greene play first?

(Credibility of a source) The principal needs to decide if the new block schedule allows teachers to go into topics in greater detail. He can ask a parent, teacher, or a principal from another school. Who should he ask to get the most objective answer?

(Analysis/prediction) People want health insurance, but they don't want to be forced to buy it from a company in their community. The law says that a person must buy health insurance from a company in his or her community. What action by the people is most likely?

(Investigating) Several paper towel companies claim that their product absorbs more liquid than the other brands. Design an experiment to test the absorbency of each brand of paper towel.

(Analysis) List the anatomical structures of the kidney, explain the function of each part, and describe how they all work together.

Binary-Choice.   Binary-choice items can be used to assess reasoning skills in several different ways. Students can be asked to indicate whether a statement is a fact or an opinion:

Examples

If the statement is a fact, circle F; if it is an opinion, circle O.

F   O   Literature is ancient Rome's most important legacy.
F   O   The word *Mississippi* has eleven letters.
F   O   The best way to wash a car is with a sponge.

Additional reasoning skills can be assessed using the same approach by developing some statements that are examples of the skill and some statements that are not examples. This can be done with many of the critical thinking skills (e.g., identifying stereotypes, biased statements, emotional language, relevant data, and verifiable data).

Examples

If the statement is an example of a stereotype, circle S; if it is not a stereotype, circle N.

S   N   Mexican Americans are good musicians.
S   N   Women live longer than men.

If emotional language is used in the statement, circle E; if no emotional language is used, circle N.

    E N   Health insurance reform is needed so that poor people with serious
            injuries will be able to lead productive lives.
    E N   Health insurance is going to cost a lot of money.

Logic can be assessed by asking if one statement follows logically from another:

Examples

If the second part of the sentence explains why the first part is true, circle T for true;
if it does not explain why the first part is true, circle F for false.

    T F   Food is essential *because* it tastes good.
    T F   Plants are essential *because* they provide oxygen.
    T F   Reggie is tall *because* he has blue eyes.

Multiple-Choice.   Simple multiple-choice items can be used to assess reasoning
in two ways. One way is to focus on a particular skill, like the binary-choice items,
to determine if students are able to recognize and use that skill. A second use is to
assess the extent to which students can use their knowledge and skills in performing a problem-solving, decision-making, or other reasoning task. The first use is illustrated with the following examples:

Examples

(Distinguishing fact from opinion) Which of the following statements about our
solar system is a fact rather than an opinion?

   a. The moon is made of attractive white soil.
   b. Stars can be grouped into important clusters.
   c. A star is formed from a white dwarf.
   d. Optical telescopes provide the best way to study the stars.

(Identifying assumptions) When Patrick Henry said "give me liberty or give me
death," his assumption was that:

   a. everyone would agree with him
   b. Thomas Jefferson would be impressed by the speech
   c. if he couldn't have freedom he might as well die
   d. his words would be taught to students for years

(Recognizing bias) Peter told the group that "the ill-prepared, ridiculous senator has
no business being involved in this important debate." Which words make Peter's
statement biased?

   a. important, senator
   b. important, business
   c. ill-prepared, ridiculous
   d. debate, involved

(Comparison) One way in which insects are different from centipedes is that:

    a. they are different colors
    b. one is an arthropod
    c. centipedes have more legs
    d. insects have two body parts

(Analysis) Reginald decided to go sailing with a friend. He took supplies with him so he could eat, repair anything that might be broken, and find where on the lake he could sail. Which of the following supplies would best meet his needs?

    a. bread, hammer, map
    b. milk, bread, screwdriver
    c. map, hammer, pliers, screwdriver
    d. screwdriver, hammer, pliers

(Synthesis) What is the main idea in the following paragraph?

Julie picked a pretty blue boat for her first sail. It took her about an hour to understand all the parts of the boat and another hour to get the sail on. Her first sail was on a beautiful summer day. She tried to go fast but couldn't. After several lessons she was able to make her boat go fast.

    a. sailing is fun
    b. Julie's first sail
    c. sailing is difficult
    d. going fast on a sailboat

The next few examples show how multiple-choice items can be used to assess the students' ability to perform a reasoning task.

Examples

(Hypothesizing) If there were a significant increase in the number of hawks in a given area,

    a. the number of plants would increase
    b. the number of mice would increase
    c. there would be fewer hawk nests
    d. the number of mice would decrease

(Problem solving) Farmers want to be able to make more money for the crops they grow, but too many farmers are growing too many crops. What can the farmers do to make more money?

    a. try to convince the public to pay higher prices
    b. agree to produce fewer crops
    c. reduce the number of farmers
    d. work on legislation to turn farmland into parks

(Critical thinking) Peter is deciding which car to buy. He is impressed with the sales representative for the Ford, and he likes the color of the Buick. The Ford is smaller and gets more miles to the gallon. The Buick takes larger tires and has a smaller trunk. More people can ride in the Ford. Which car should Peter purchase if he wants to do everything he can to ensure that his favorite lake does not become polluted?

   a. Ford
   b. Buick
   c. either car
   d. can't decide from the information provided

(Predicting) Suppose that the midwest United States, which grows most of the country's corn, suffered a drought for several years and produced much less corn than usual. What would happen to the price of corn?

   a. The price would rise.
   b. The price would fall.
   c. The price would stay the same.
   d. People would eat less corn.

Interpretive Exercises.   The best type of short-answer or selected-response item for assessing reasoning skills is usually the interpretive exercise. This type of item consists of some information or data, followed by several questions. The questions are based on the information or data, which can take the form of maps, paragraphs, charts, figures, a story, a table of data, or pictures. The form of the question makes it possible to ask questions that require interpretation, analysis, application, critical thinking, and other reasoning skills.

Interpretive exercises have four major advantages over other types of items. First, because there are several questions about the same information, it is possible to measure more reasoning skills in greater depth. Second, because information is provided, it is possible to separate the assessment of the reasoning skills from content knowledge of the subject. If content is not provided in the question, as is the case with most multiple-choice items, then a failure to provide a good answer could be attributed to either the student's lack of knowledge or lack of reasoning skill. In the interpretive exercise, students have all or most of the information needed as part of the question, so successful performance provides a more direct measure of reasoning skill. Clearly, the intent of the exercise is to assess how students use the information provided to answer questions. If students know ahead of time that the information will be provided, then they can concentrate their study on application and other uses of the information.

A third advantage of the interpretive exercise is that it is relatively easy to use material that students will encounter in everyday living, such as maps, newspaper articles, and graphs. Consistent with constructivist learning theory, this connects the material better with the student, increasing meaningfulness and relevance. Finally, because interpretive exercises provide a standard structure for all students and are scored objectively, the results tend to be more reliable. Students are unable to select a reasoning skill they are most proficient with, as they can do with essay questions.

They must use the one called for in each question. Like all objective items, the scoring is efficient, especially if the answers are not of the short-answer type. This is an important consideration in comparing interpretive exercises with essays and performance products, which are also used extensively for assessing reasoning skills.

Interpretive exercises have three limitations. First, they are time-consuming and difficult to write. Not only do you need to locate or develop the information or data that will be new for the students and at the right difficulty level, which could take considerable time, but you also need to construct the objective questions (multiple-choice ones will take longest). The information you first identify may need to be modified, and most teachers are not accustomed to writing several objective items for a single passage or example.

A second limitation is that you are unable to assess how students organize their thoughts and ideas or to know whether students can produce their own answers without being cued. Third, many interpretive exercises rely heavily on reading comprehension. This puts poor readers at a distinct disadvantage. It takes them longer to read the material for understanding, let alone reason with it. This disadvantage holds for other types of items that require extensive reading as well, but it is especially troublesome for interpretive exercises.

Whether you develop your own interpretive exercises or use ones that have already been prepared, the following suggestions will help ensure high quality (see Figure 7.7 for a checklist summary).

1. Identify the Reasoning Skills to Be Assessed before Selection or Development of the Interpretive Exercise. The sequence you use is important because you want the exercise to fit your learning targets, not have learning targets determined by the interpretive exercise. This is especially important given the number of different conceptualizations of thinking and reasoning skills. What may be called "critical thinking" or "analysis" in a teacher's manual may not coincide with what you think the target is. You need to have a clear idea of the skill to be assessed and then select or develop the material that best fits your definition.

2. Keep Introductory Material as Brief as Possible. Keeping the introductory material brief minimizes the influence of general reading ability. There should be just enough material so that the students can complete the reasoning task.

3. Select Similar but New Introductory Material. Reasoning skills are best measured with material that is new to the students. If the material is the same as that covered in class, you will measure rote memory or simple understanding rather

---

FIGURE 7.7 Checklist for Writing Interpretive Exercises

✓ Are reasoning targets clearly defined before writing the exercise?
✓ Is introductory material brief?
✓ Is introductory material new to the students?
✓ Are there several questions for each exercise?
✓ Does the exercise test reasoning (and not just simple understanding)?

than reasoning. The goal is to find or develop examples that are similar to what students have already studied. The material should vary slightly in form or content, but it should not be completely new. A good strategy to use to accomplish this is to take passages, examples, and data students have been exposed to and alter them sufficiently so that correct answers cannot be given by memory.

4. Construct Several Test Items for Each Exercise.   The test items can be short answer, multiple-choice, or binary-choice. Asking more than one question for each exercise obtains a better sample of the proficiency of students' reasoning skills. It would be particularly inefficient to have a very long introductory passage and a single question. One common approach for asking questions is to give the students a key of possible answers and have them apply the key to selected aspects of the introductory material (key-type item). For example, if after reading a passage students are asked to judge the relevance of different parts of the passage, the key could simply be:

Key: A   if the statement is relevant
        B   if the statement is irrelevant

Or if you are testing student ability to distinguish facts from opinions:

Key: A   if the statement is a fact
        B   if the statement is an opinion

If you use a key, do not mix different types of reasoning tasks in the same key (e.g., you wouldn't want to put relevant, irrelevant, fact, and opinion in the same key). Like a matching item, the choices should be homogeneous.

5. Construct Items So That the Answers Are Not Found in the Question. You do not want to use questions that can be answered without even reading the introductory material. This happens when students' general knowledge is such that they can determine the correct answer from the question alone.

Interpretive exercises are illustrated in the following four examples. Note that many different formats can be used for the items. The reasoning skills that are assessed are indicated in parentheses next to name of each example.

Example 1. Interpretive exercise[1] (drawing inferences, analyzing perspectives)
Two citizens spoke at the city council meeting. Here are their statements. Use the information to help you answer questions 10–13.

> CITIZEN A: The Bower House should be restored and used as a museum. A museum would help the people of the community learn about their heritage and would attract tourists to Grenville. We should not sell the property to the Opti Company. Grenville has grown too quickly, and a factory would bring even more people into the area. In addition, a factory's industrial waste would threaten the quality of our water.

> CITIZEN B: Grenville needs the Opti factory. The factory would provide needed jobs. The tax money it would bring into the community would help

improve our streets, schools, and other city services. A museum, on the other hand, would hurt our local economy. Taxes would have to be raised to pay for the restoration of the Bower House. A museum would not create enough jobs to solve our unemployment problem.

Key: Write the letter A next to each statement that Citizen A would most likely agree with.

Write the letter B next to each statement that Citizen B would most likely agree with.

_____ **(10)** Jobs are the foundation of a community.
_____ **(11)** Pollution problems will multiply.
_____ **(12)** We are in danger of losing the history of our community.
_____ **(13)** Hanging on to the past hurts the future.

Example 2. Interpretive exercise (recognizing the relevance of information)

Sally lost her pencil on her way to school. It was red and given to her by her grandmother. She wanted the teacher to ask the class if anyone found the pencil.

Key: Circle *yes* if the information in the sentence will help the class find the pencil.
Circle *no* if the information in the sentence will not help the class find the pencil.

yes   no   **1.** The pencil was new.
yes   no   **2.** Sally rides the bus to school.
yes   no   **3.** The pencil is red.
yes   no   **4.** The pencil was a present from Sally's grandmother.
yes   no   **5.** The pencil had a new eraser.
yes   no   **6.** The teacher knows Sally's grandmother.

Example 3. Interpretive exercise (analysis, inference, error analysis)

Based on Figure 7.8, circle T if the statement is true and F if the statement is false.

T   F   In 1990, more female than male students graduated from high school.
T   F   From 1980 to 1990, the percentage of female students graduating from high school increased gradually.
T   F   Overall, the best year for graduating students was 1987.
T   F   From 1980 to 1990, more female than male students graduated from high school.

Answer each of the following questions:

In what years did more male students than female students graduate?
_____

In what year was there the greatest difference between the percentage of male and female graduates? _____

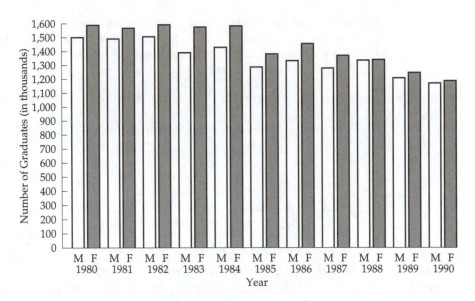

FIGURE 7.8 **Number of Male and Female Students Graduating from High School in the United States**

Source: U.S. Department of Education, Office of Educational Research and Improvement. (1994). *Digest of education statistics,* p. 188.

Essay Items

Essays can tap complex thinking by requiring students to organize and integrate information, interpret information, give arguments, give explanations, evaluate the merit of ideas, and conduct other types of reasoning. Although more objective formats are clearly superior for measuring knowledge, the essay is an excellent way to measure deep understanding and mastery of complex information, such as how students explain procedures or put together many discrete facts into a meaningful whole. Research on student learning habits shows that when students know they will face an essay test they tend to study by looking for themes, patterns, relationships, and how information can be organized and sequenced. In contrast, when studying for objective tests students tend to fragment information and memorize each piece.

Usually, essay items that assess knowledge and simple understanding require relatively brief answers. These may be called *short essay* or *restricted-response essay* to distinguish them from short-answer items, even though the length of the answer does not necessarily indicate the type of target being measured. We will focus here on both *extended-response* and *restricted-response* essay items. The extended-response format is the best one for assessing deep understanding and reasoning targets.

Examples: Restricted-Response Essay Questions

Why are hurricanes more likely to strike Florida than California?
Why are tomatoes better for your health than potato chips?
What is the effect on inflation of raising the prime interest rate?

Examples: Extended-Response Essay Questions

> Explain how the fertilizer farmers use to grow crops may pollute our lakes and streams.

> Describe the major events that led to the beginning of the Civil War, showing how the events are related.

> Give an example, new to me and not one from class, of how the law of supply and demand would make prices of some products increase.

Advantages and Disadvantages.   The major advantage of using essay questions is that deep understanding, complex thinking, and reasoning skills can be assessed. Essays motivate better study habits and provide students with flexibility in how they wish to respond. Written responses allow you to evaluate the ability of students to communicate their reasoning. Compared to developing selected-response items that measure reasoning, essay items are less time-consuming to construct. However, constructing a *good* essay question still takes considerable time.

The major disadvantages of essay items are related to scoring student responses. Reading and scoring answers is very time-consuming, especially if done conscientiously so that meaningful feedback is given to students. From a practical standpoint, most teachers find that they can give only a few essay items. Scoring essays is also notoriously unreliable.

In most classrooms, only a single individual, the teacher, judges the answers, and variations in mood, halo effects, expectations, the order in which students are evaluated, and other factors, affect the professional judgments that are made. This is not meant to imply that it is inappropriate to use subjective judgments in scoring. You *want* to be able to make judgments; that's one reason for using the essay format. When done appropriately, these judgments are professional, not intuitive. We will review guidelines for ensuring high-quality scoring shortly.

A final shortcoming of essay items is that they do not provide for very good sampling of content knowledge. The essay cannot sample well because relatively few questions are asked. Sampling is also limited to the reasoning skills that are assessed. For example, a single extended-response essay item that asks students to make a decision based on information provided may give you a good indication of one or two reasoning skills, but several shorter items could sample different types of skills.

Constructing Essay Items.   Essay items are strengthened by adhering to the following suggestions, summarized in Figure 7.9. In the next section we will review important principles for scoring student answers.

FIGURE 7.9   Checklist for Writing Essay Items

✓ Is the targeted reasoning skill measured?
✓ Is the task clearly specified?
✓ Is there enough time to answer the questions?
✓ Are choices among several questions avoided?

1. Construct the Item to Elicit Skills Identified in the Learning Target.   Once the reasoning skill is identified, the wording in the question needs to be such that the specific skill(s) will need to be used to answer the question. This is easier with restricted-response items that focus on a single reasoning skill. With extended-response items, the scoring criteria can be matched to the skills assessed. A good way to begin writing the item to match the target is to start with a standard stem, then modify it as needed for the subject and level of student ability. Some examples of such items are illustrated in Figure 7.10.

2. Write the Item so That Students Clearly Understand the Specific Task.   After reading an essay item, students ask, "What does the teacher want in my answer?" If the assessment task is described ambiguously, so that students interpret what is called for in the answer differently, many responses will be off target. Such responses lead to flawed interpretations by teachers. When students misinterpret the task, you don't know if they have the targeted skill or not, leading to invalid conclusions.

To clearly set forth the nature of the task, try to make the essay question as specific as possible. Don't be hesitant about stating the desired response explicitly.

Examples

Poor: Why do Haitian farmers have trouble making a living?

Improved: Describe how the weather, soil, and poverty in Haiti contribute to the plight of farmers. Indicate which of these three factors contributes most to the difficulties farmers experience, and give reasons for your selection.

Poor: How was World War I different from World War II?

Improved: How were the social and political factors leading up to World War I in Germany different from those leading up to World War II? Focus your answer on the ten-year period that preceded the beginning of each war.

You can see that each of the "poorly" worded items gives students too much freedom to write about any of a number of aspects of either Haiti or differences between the wars.

Another way to clarify to students the nature of the task is to indicate the criteria for scoring their answer in the question. This can be labeled a *scoring plan, scoring criteria,* or *attributes to be scored.* It essentially tells the students what you will be looking for when grading their answers. This is particularly important if the organization of the response or writing skills are included as criteria.

Examples of Scoring Criteria

(For Scoring Writing Skills)

- Organization
- Clarity
- Appropriateness to audience
- Mechanics

FIGURE 7.10   Sample Item Stems for Assessing Reasoning Skills

Skill	Stem
Comparing	Describe the similarities and differences between . . . Compare the following two methods for . . .
Relating Cause and Effect	What are major causes of . . . ? What would be the most likely effects of . . . ?
Justifying	Which of the following alternatives do you favor and why? Explain why you agree or disagree with the following statement.
Summarizing	State the main points included in . . . Briefly summarize the contents of . . .
Generalizing	Formulate several valid generalizations from the following data. State a set of principles that can explain the following events.
Inferring	In light of the facts presented, what is most likely to happen when . . . ? How would Senator X be likely to react to the following issue?
Classifying	Group the following items according to . . . What do the following items have in common?
Creating	List as many ways as you can think of for . . . Make up a story describing what would happen if . . .
Applying	Using the principle of . . . as a guide, describe how you would solve the following problem. Describe a situation that illustrates the principle of . . .
Analyzing	Describe the reasoning errors in the following paragraph. List and describe the main characteristics of . . .
Synthesizing	Describe a plan for proving that . . . Write a well-organized report that shows . . .
Evaluating	Describe the strengths and weaknesses of . . . Using the given criteria, write an evaluation of . . .

Source: Linn, R. L., & Gronlund, N. E. (2000). *Measurement and assessment in teaching,* 8th edition. Adapted by permission of Prentice-Hall, Upper Saddle River, New Jersey.

(For Scoring an Argument)

- Distinguishing between facts and opinions
- Judging credibility of a source
- Identifying relevant material
- Recognizing inconsistencies
- Using logic

(For Scoring Decision Making)

- Identifying goals or purpose
- Identifying obstacles
- Identifying and evaluating alternatives
- Justifying the choice of one alternative

3. Indicate Approximately How Much Time Students Should Spend on Each Essay Item.   You should have some idea of how much time students will need to answer each item. For restricted-response questions, the amount of time needed is relatively short and easy to estimate. For extended-response items, the estimate is more difficult. You can get some idea by writing draft answers, and as you gain more experience the responses of previous students to similar questions will be helpful. Take into consideration the writing abilities of your students, and be sure that even your slowest writers can complete their answers satisfactorily in the time available. (You want to assess reasoning, not writing speed!) If you are unsure about the time needed, err by providing more time than is needed rather than less time.

4. Avoid Giving Students Options as to Which Essay Questions They Will Answer.   Many teachers offer students a choice of questions to answer. For example, if there are seven questions, the teacher may tell students to answer their choice of three. Students love such questions because they can answer the items they are best prepared for. They will especially like this approach if they know before taking the test that they will have a choice. Then they can restrict their study to part of the material, rather than to all of it (you can avoid this by telling students *you* will select the items they will write on).

   Giving students a choice of questions, however, means that each student may be taking a different test. Differences in the difficulty of each question are probably unknown. This makes scoring more problematic, and your inferences of student ability less valid. It is true that you can't measure every important target, and giving students a choice does provide them an opportunity to do their best work. However, this advantage is outweighed by difficulties in scoring and making sound inferences.

Scoring Essays.   Scoring essay question responses is difficult because each student writes a unique answer and because many distractions affect scoring reliability. Obviously scoring is subjective, so it is important to practice a few procedures to ensure that the professional judgments are accurate.

   The following guidelines will help (see Figure 7.11).

1. Outline What Constitutes a Good or Acceptable Answer as a Scoring Key. This should be completed before administering or scoring student responses. If done before the test is finalized, an outline provides you with an opportunity to revise the stem or question on the basis of what you learn by delineating the response. It's important to have the points specified before reading student answers so that you are not unduly influenced by the initial papers you read. These papers can set the standard for what follows. The scoring key provides a common basis for evaluating each answer. An outline lessens the influence of other extraneous factors, such as vocabulary or neatness.

FIGURE 7.11   Checklist for Scoring Essays

✓ Is the answer outlined before testing students?
✓ Is the scoring method—holistic or analytic—appropriate?
✓ Is the role of writing mechanics clarified?
✓ Are items scored one at a time?
✓ Is the order in which the papers are graded changed?
✓ Is the identity of the student anonymous?

2. Select an Appropriate Scoring Method. Essays are scored in two ways: holistically or analytically. In **holistic** scoring, the teacher makes an overall judgment about the answer, giving it a single score or grade. The score can be based on a general impression or on attending to several specific scoring criteria to come up with a single score for each essay. This is often accomplished by placing essays in designated piles that represent different degrees of quality. The holistic method is most appropriate for extended-response essays (in which the responses are not limited and are generally long).

Analytic scoring is achieved by giving each of the identified criteria separate points. Thus, there would be several scores for each essay, and probably a total score that results from adding all the component scores. Analytic scoring is preferred for restricted-response questions (for which there is a limit to the amount of response the student provides). The advantage of analytic scoring is that it provides students with more specific feedback (though this should not replace individualized teacher comments). However, analytic scoring can be very time-consuming, and sometimes adding scored parts does not do justice to the overall student response. To avoid excessive attention to specific factors, keep the number of features to be scored analytically to three or four.

3. Clarify the Role of Writing Mechanics. Suppose you are a biology teacher and you use essay questions. Does it matter if students spell poorly or use bad sentence structure? Such writing mechanics can certainly influence your overall impression of an answer, so it is important to decide early about whether, and to what extent, these factors are included as scoring criteria. Regardless of how you decide to incorporate writing mechanics, it is generally best to give students a separate score for these skills (as long as it was one of your targets) and not add this score into the total.

4. Use a Systematic Process in Scoring Many Essays at the Same Time. When faced with a pile of papers to grade, it's tempting to simply start with the first paper, grade all the questions for that student, and then go on to the next student. To lessen the influence of order and your own fatigue, however, it is best to score one item at a time for all students, and to change the order of the papers for each question. Reliability will increase if you read all responses to question 1 in one order, all responses to question 2 in a different order, and so on. This avoids the tendency to allow the answer a student gives to the first question to influence subsequent evaluations of the remaining questions. It is also best to score all answers to each item in one sitting, if possible. This helps you to be consistent in applying criteria to the answers.

5. If Possible, Keep the Identity of the Student Anonymous.   It is best not to know whose answer you are grading. This avoids the tendency to be influenced by impressions of the student from class discussion or other tests. This source of error, which is probably the most serious one that influences results, is difficult to control because most teachers get to know the writing of their students. You can have students put their names on the back of the papers, but the best guard is to be consciously aware of the potential bias to keep it minimized.

Summary

This chapter focused on the assessment of deep understanding and reasoning skills. The following points summarize the chapter:

- Reasoning is mental manipulation of knowledge for some purpose. Many different thinking skills are involved.
- Bloom's taxonomy represents a popular, though dated framework for identifying reasoning skills. New categories are suggested in the revision of Bloom's taxonomy.
- Critical thinking involves the application of evaluative thinking skills, such as identifying irrelevant information, analyzing an argument, detecting bias, and using deductive logic, to decide what to do or believe.
- Quellmalz and Hoskyn's framework combines other conceptualizations to result in five major types of reasoning: recall, analysis, comparison, inference, and evaluation.
- Marzano's dimensions of learning has five levels: positive attitudes about learning, acquiring and integrating knowledge, extending and refining knowledge, using knowledge meaningfully, and productive habits of mind. Using knowledge includes decision making, problem solving, investigation, experimental inquiry, and invention. Each of these processes has steps that can be identified and assessed.
- Deep understanding and reasoning targets are best assessed by interpretive exercises and essay items, though selected-response and brief constructed-response questions can be used effectively to measure specific thinking skills.
- Binary-choice items are good for assessing a student's ability to discriminate among differences such as fact or opinion, relevant or irrelevant, and biased or unbiased.
- Multiple-choice items can be used to assess deep understanding and reasoning skills, but they are difficult to write.
- Interpretive exercises include information or data followed by objective questions that require students to reason about what was presented, providing a good measure of understanding and reasoning.
- Good interpretive items are difficult to write and may penalize students who are not good readers.
- Each interpretive item should have relatively short, familiar, but new introductory material and several questions that do not measure recognition from the introductory material.

- Essay items allow students to show their understanding reasoning skills by constructing an answer.
- Extended-response essays are best for assessing complex reasoning skills such as decision making and problem solving, and restricted-response items are better for assessing specific thinking skills, comprehension and application.
- The major disadvantage of essays is in the scoring, which is time-consuming and fraught with many potential sources of error.
- Good essays clearly define the task to students, specifically in terms of the skills that will be assessed. Students should know about how much time to spend on each essay item, and the option to choose items should be avoided.
- The scoring of essays is enhanced when an outline of an acceptable answer is made before testing students; when the correct method of scoring is used (holistic or analytical); when the scoring is done by question, not by student; when the order of papers is changed; and when students are anonymous.

SELF-INSTRUCTIONAL REVIEW EXERCISES

1. Identify the thinking or reasoning skill illustrated by each of the following examples, using this key:

A	analysis	P	problem solving
S	synthesis	I	inference
C	critical thinking	E	evaluation
D	decision making		

   a. Suppose you were President Johnson and had to decide whether to send more troops to Vietnam. What would you do? Why would you do it?
   b. State your reasons for agreeing or disagreeing with the following statement: Religious people are more likely to help others.
   c. Given what you know about sailing, what would most likely occur if a novice sailor tried to sail directly into the wind?
   d. Examine three different human cultures. What is common in all three cultures, and what principle about being human does this suggest?
   e. Examine four recent presidential speeches. Is any part of the speeches the same?
   f. How can the United States reduce the rate of teenage pregnancies?
   g. Suppose you had to choose between increasing taxes to reduce the U.S. budget deficit or decreasing federal spending to reduce the deficit. Which would you choose? Why? How would your choice affect retired persons?
   h. Examine the data on birth rates. What is likely to happen to the birth rate by the year 2010? Why?

2. Indicate whether each of the following would be best measured by an objective item (O), an interpretive exercise (I), or an essay question (E).

   a. Discerning the meaning of a series of pictures
   b. Asking students about the validity of an argument used in a debate tournament
   c. Analyzing a passage to identify irrelevant information and opinions
   d. Being able to construct a logical argument
   e. Knowing the sequence of steps involved in problem solving
   f. Giving examples of the principle of tropism

g. Being able to distinguish critical thinking from decision making

h. Determining whether Michelangelo would be regarded as a great artist if he lived today and, if so, why

i. Identifying several valid generalizations from the data presented

3. Evaluate the following interpretive exercise based on the weather map in Figure 7.12. What are its strengths and how could it be improved? What reasoning skills does it assess?

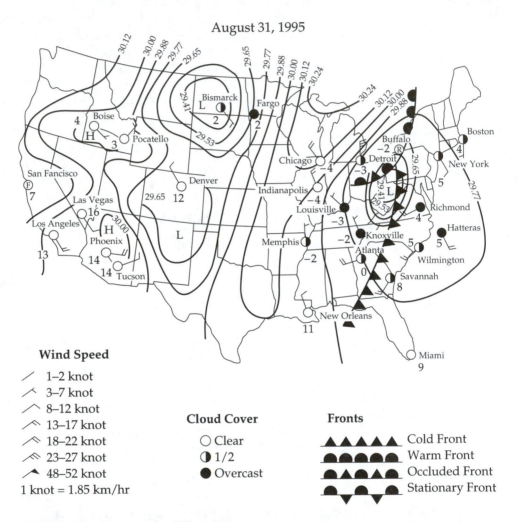

FIGURE 7.12   Forecasts and Temperatures

Source: Weather map: from *Earth Science: A Cambridge Work-A-Text* (weather map) by Otho E. Perkins © 1987 by Globe Fearon, an imprint of Pearson Learning Group, a division of Pearson Education, Inc. Used by permission. Key: from *Globe Earth Science* (weather map key) by Bryan Bunch and Barbara A. Branca © 1986 by Globe Fearon, an imprint of Pearson Learning Group, a division of Pearson Education, Inc. Used by permission.

Directions. Pretend you are a weather forecaster. Read the weather information and then answer the questions.

a. What four cities can expect rain?
b. What will the weather be like in Chicago and Los Angeles?
c. Which cities will have the highest temperatures?
d. Which city will have a partly cloudy day?
e. In what part of the United States will there be a high pressure area?
f. In what direction will the warm front be moving?
g. Would you go to the beach in Miami on August 31 to get a suntan? Why or why not?

4. Evaluate the following essay question. What learning targets does it appear to assess? How could it be improved?

Do you think freedom of the press should extend to the irresponsible sensationalism of Hearst during the era of the Spanish-American War? Justify your answer.

ANSWERS TO SELF-INSTRUCTIONAL REVIEW ITEMS

1. a. D; b. C; c. I; d. S; e. A; f. P; g. C; h. I.

2. a. I; b. I or E; c. I; d. E; e. O; f. E; g. O; h. E; i. I.

3. The general format of the question is appropriate, and it is good to have several questions about the material presented. Introductory information is kept to a minimum. Presumably students have been studying weather maps; this one should be new. Clearly the questions cannot be answered correctly unless the student can understand the map. The format of the questions could be improved so that students check or circle correct answers rather than taking time to write their answers (e.g., What will the weather be like in Chicago and Los Angeles? a. fair b. cloudy c. rainy d. windy). This would reduce the time students need to answer the questions and the time needed for scoring. The reasoning target assessed by the question is primarily inference. Question 7 assesses deductive reasoning. Application and understanding targets are also assessed. The assessment could be improved by asking additional questions about wind speed and direction and barometric pressure.

4. This essay question assesses evaluation and critical thinking skills. A decision must be made with reasonable justification. It also assesses constructing support and deductive reasoning. The item could be improved by indicating how much time students should take in answering it, by indicating scoring criteria, and by providing more specific information about what is expected. Including the word *irresponsible* gives students a clear tip to what the teacher is looking for. Phrases like *justify your answer* give students some direction but are vague. What level of detail is expected? How many reasons are adequate? What is meant by *justify?* There should also be an indication of the total points for the item.

SUGGESTIONS FOR ACTION RESEARCH

1. Devise some reasoning learning targets for this chapter or one of the previous chapters. Then construct four objective and two essay items to assess these targets.

2. Provide examples of five of Marzano's or Quellmalz and Hoskyn's reasoning skills from the discipline you teach. Share your examples with two other students for their critique.

3. Write an essay question with criteria for scoring and examples of responses that would be graded A, B, and C. Give the question, scoring criteria, and examples of responses with grades deleted to four other students for them to grade. Compare their judgments with the grades you assigned.

4. Examine two or three textbooks written for the area in which you wish to teach, either teacher's editions or the ones students use, and identify examples of the reasoning or thinking skills that are assessed. Then match the skills in the textbooks with the frameworks presented in the chapter.

5. Ask a teacher how he or she conceptualizes reasoning skills and how these skills are measured in the classroom. Compare the teacher's responses to the checklists presented in the chapter.

6. Observe some students as they take a test that assesses reasoning skills. How long does it take them to formulate an answer? How much time does it take to write an answer? If possible, examine their responses. How would you evaluate their work?

ENDNOTE

1. Adapted from California Achievement Test 5 Performance Assessment Component, CTB/Macmillan/McGraw-Hill, 1993, p. 39.

Performance Assessments

Assessing Deep Understanding, Reasoning, and Skills

In Chapters 6 and 7, we examined what are often called conventional *paper-and-pencil* methods of assessment. These techniques have been used effectively for many years to assess knowledge and understanding targets and, to a lesser extent, to assess reasoning targets. With greater emphasis on reasoning and being able to apply learning to situations and problems that are more like real life, there has been extensive

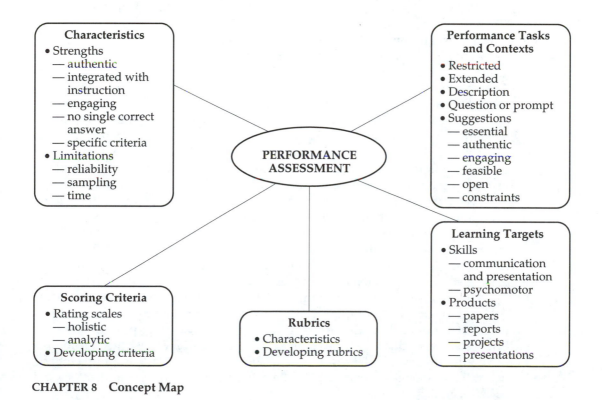

Characteristics
- Strengths
  — authentic
  — integrated with instruction
  — engaging
  — no single correct answer
  — specific criteria
- Limitations
  — reliability
  — sampling
  — time

Performance Tasks and Contexts
- Restricted
- Extended
- Description
- Question or prompt
- Suggestions
  — essential
  — authentic
  — engaging
  — feasible
  — open
  — constraints

PERFORMANCE ASSESSMENT

Learning Targets
- Skills
  — communication and presentation
  — psychomotor
- Products
  — papers
  — reports
  — projects
  — presentations

Scoring Criteria
- Rating scales
  — holistic
  — analytic
- Developing criteria

Rubrics
- Characteristics
- Developing rubrics

CHAPTER 8   Concept Map

interest in assessments that require students to *do* something, not simply know it or know how to do it. That is, it is one thing to demonstrate written knowledge about how to give a speech, but actually giving the speech represents a different kind of learning target. Students are required to show what they can do, not simply tell what they know or would do. This chapter focuses on these "new" assessments.

What Is Performance Assessment?

Simply put, a **performance assessment** is one in which the teacher observes and makes a judgment about the student's demonstration of a skill or competency in creating a product, constructing a response, or making a presentation. The term *performance* is shorthand for performance-based or *performance-and-product*. The emphasis is on the students' ability to perform tasks by producing their own work with their knowledge and skills. In some cases this is a presentation, such as singing, playing the piano, or performing gymnastics. In other cases, this ability is expressed through a product, such as a completed paper, project, or solution. Over the past decade, educators have taken what is best about performance-and-product assessment and used these principles to assess targets that previously were measured mostly by conventional objective tests. In doing this, however, the field has been deluged by confusing terms and definitions. Other terms, such as *authentic assessment* and *alternative assessment* are sometimes used interchangeably with performance assessment, but they actually mean something different. An **alternative assessment** is any method that differs from conventional paper-and-pencil tests, most particularly objective tests. Examples of alternative assessments include observations, exhibitions, oral presentations, experiments, portfolios, interviews, and projects. Some think of essays as a type of alternative assessment because they require students to construct responses.

Authentic assessment involves the direct examination of a student's ability to use knowledge to perform a task that is like what is encountered in real life or in the real world. Authenticity is judged in the nature of the task completed and in the context of the task (e.g., in the options available, constraints, and access to resources). Like any performance assessment, students plan, construct, and deliver an original response, and explain or justify their answers. The students are aware of the criteria and standards by which the work will be judged before beginning their work.

Performance assessment may or may not be authentic. In fact, we find that authenticity in terms of the real-world use of knowledge is one of several characteristics of performance assessment that is a matter of degree. Some performance assessments are more authentic than others.

Figure 8.1 summarizes the characteristics of performance assessments. Most of these characteristics are typically present to some extent in a performance assessment. But be careful. Because the term *performance assessment* is so popular, test publishers and some educators have come to use it as a label for constructed response, interpretive exercises, and essay items. All of this may seem confusing, but it reflects reality. It's as though there is an ideal for what a performance assessment should look like, and many variations are in practice.

FIGURE 8.1   **Characteristics of Performance Assessments**

- Students perform, create, construct, produce, or do something.
- Deep understanding and/or reasoning skills are needed and assessed.
- Involves sustained work, often days and weeks.
- Calls on students to explain, justify, and defend.
- Performance is directly observable.
- Involves engaging ideas of importance and substance.
- Relies on trained assessor's judgments for scoring.
- Multiple criteria and standards are prespecified and public.
- There is no single "correct" answer.
- If authentic, the performance is grounded in real-world contexts and constraints.

Strengths and Limitations
of Performance Assessments

The major benefits of performance assessments are tied closely to instruction. This explains much of the appeal of the approach. The intent is to integrate instruction and assessment, so that what is taught in the classroom is reflected in measures of student performance, and what is tested drives appropriate instruction. Learning occurs while students complete the assessment. Teachers interact with students as they do the task, providing feedback and prompts that help students learn through multiple opportunities to demonstrate what they have learned. Opportunities are provided for teachers to assess the reasoning processes students use in their work. Because the assessments are usually tied to real-world challenges and situations, students are better prepared for such thinking and performance once out of school. Also as real life, students justify their thinking and learn that often no single answer is correct. In this way, the assessments influence the instruction to be more meaningful and practical. Students value the task more because they view it as rich rather than superficial, engaging rather than uninteresting, and active rather than passive.

As pointed out in Chapter 1, much instruction is now based on constructivistic principles of learning, with an emphasis on applied reasoning skills and integrated subject matter. Performance assessments are better suited to measure these kinds of targets than are selected-response tests. Students are more engaged in active learning as a part of the assessment because that is what they need to perform successfully (as contrasted with memorizing information). Because the emphasis is on what students *do*, skills are more directly assessed and there are more opportunities to observe the process students use to arrive at answers or responses. Students who traditionally do not perform well on paper-and-pencil tests have an opportunity to demonstrate their learning in a different way.

Another advantage of performance assessments is that they force teachers to identify multiple, specific criteria for judging success. Teachers share these criteria with students before the assessment so that the students can use them as they learn. In this way, students learn how to evaluate their own performance through self-assessment. They learn how to ask questions and, in many assessments, how to work effectively with others.

Wiggins (1993) makes the point that performance assessment is simply applying the teaching/learning methods used successfully for years in the adult world. Musicians, artists, athletes, architects, and doctors all learn by getting feedback on what they do, and the important goal is not what they know but how what they know is demonstrated in practice. Thus, an important advantage of performance assessment is that this same approach can be applied to learning all content areas. It helps instruction target more important outcomes.

Finally, performance assessment motivates educators to explore the purposes and processes of schooling (Jamentz, 1994; Wiggins, 1998). Because of the nature of the assessments, teachers revisit their learning goals, instructional practices, and standards. They explore how students will use their classroom time differently and whether there are adequate resources for all students.

Bill Hadley, a high school mathematics teacher, illustrates how performance assessment can transform the classroom (Stenmark, 1991):

> In my general math classes this past year I decided not to give separate stand-alone tests but to assess my students' growth and understanding of mathematics through the use of performance assessments. . . . I assigned groups or pairs of students certain tasks to perform. Then by coaching, observing, and interviewing the students as they worked on these tasks, I was able to assess their knowledge and growth. The information I received was much more comprehensive and complete, and I found that I was able to give the students grades that I thought very accurately reflected their progress. . . . This positive experience with alternative assessment forms and with integrating assessment and instruction will enable me to employ similar methods more often in my other classes. I have discovered that tests do not have to be a primary or necessary type of assessment . . . traditionally structured tests seem to be an impediment to effective instruction. (p. 12)

The limitations of using performance assessment lie in three areas: reliability, sampling, and time. Unfortunately, performance assessments are subject to considerable measurement error, which lowers reliability. Like essay items, the major source of measurement error with performance assessments lies in the scoring. Because scoring requires professional judgment, there will be variations and error due to bias and other factors, similar to what affects evaluating essay answers. Although procedures exist that can minimize scoring error—such as carefully constructed criteria, tasks, and scoring rubrics; systematic scoring procedures; and using more than one rater—rating reliability is likely to be lower than what is achieved with other types of assessment. Inconsistent student performance also contributes to error. That is, student performance at one time may differ noticeably from what the student would demonstrate at another time (this might occur, for example, if on the day of the performance the student is ill).

Because it takes a lot of time for students to do performance assessments, you will have relatively few samples of student achievement and ability. Furthermore, we know that performance on one task may not provide a very good estimate of student proficiency on other tasks. This means that if you intend to use the results of performance assessment to form conclusions about capability in a larger domain of learning targets, you need to accumulate information from multiple tasks. This usually takes several months. Although the lack of generalization to a larger domain of targets is offset by greater depth and richness of information, you need to be careful in making properly constrained inferences (validity). In situations where a great amount of knowledge and simple understanding is to be demonstrated, such as in content areas, performance assessments do not provide a very good measure of the targets because of the lack of generalization.

The third major limitation of performance assessment concerns time. First, it is very time-consuming to construct good tasks, develop scoring criteria and rubrics, administer the task, observe students, and then apply the rubrics to student performance. For performances that cannot be scored later, adequate time needs to be taken with each student as he or she performs the task. Second, it is difficult, in a timely fashion, to interact with all students and give them meaningful feedback as they learn and make decisions. Finally, it is difficult to estimate the amount of time students will need to complete performance assessments, especially if the task is a new one and if students are unaccustomed to the format and expectations.

The strengths and weaknesses of performance assessments are summarized in Figure 8.2. The weaknesses are usually outweighed by the strengths, but that is only the case if the teacher's approach is thoughtful, reflective, and rigorous. Performance assessment is complex and demanding. Time, energy, and resources must be invested to meet goals identified in the strengths listed in Figure 8.2.

FIGURE 8.2   Strengths and Weaknesses of Performance Assessments

Strengths	Weaknesses
Integrates assessment with instruction.	Reliability may be difficult to establish.
Learning occurs during assessment.	Measurement error due to subjective nature of the scoring may be significant.
Provides opportunities for formative assessment.	Inconsistent student performance across time may result in inaccurate conclusions.
Tends to be more authentic than other types of assessments.	Few samples of student achievement.
More engaging; active involvement of students.	Requires considerable teacher time to prepare and student time to complete.
Provides additional way for students to show what they know and can do.	Difficult to plan for amount of time needed.
Emphasis on reasoning skills.	Limited ability to generalize to a larger domain of knowledge.
Forces teachers to establish specific criteria to identify successful performance.	
Encourages student self-assessment.	
Emphasis on application of knowledge.	
Encourages reexamination of instructional goals and the purpose of schooling.	

Learning Targets for Performance Assessments

Teachers in some fields have been using performance assessment for years because their learning targets require students to demonstrate skills or to generate a product (e.g., in subjects such as art, music, typing, athletics, writing, reading). Skills include the student's accomplishment of reasoning, communication, and psychomotor proficiencies. Products are completed works, such as term papers, reports, projects, and other assignments in which students use their skills and knowledge. What is new about performance assessment is that it is now being advocated for assessing understanding and for formal statewide testing in all content areas. Because the method of assessment for both of these uses in the content areas has mainly been selected-response paper-and-pencil tests, the popularity of performance assessment has represented a major change in what and how we assess students. Our experience to date indicates that substantial difficulties arise when using performance assessments for statewide accountability testing. In fact, some states, most notably Maryland, have recently curtailed use of performance assessments. However, for the right targets in the classroom, performance assessments can be very effective and enhance student learning. We'll turn now to these types of appropriate learning targets.

Skills

The reasoning skill targets delineated in Chapter 7 are often cited in describing performance assessment outcomes. Typically, students are given a problem to solve or are asked to make a decision based on information provided. The types of targets are essentially the same as those identified in Chapter 7. The difference lies in the nature of the task and the scoring criteria used to judge student answers. If the characteristics in Figure 8.1 are evident, the assessment can be called "performance," although sometimes it's neither easy nor necessary to know for sure if this label is accurate. If a student is asked to explain to the class how he or she arrived at a particular answer to a problem, is this a performance assessment because the student is performing a reasoning skill? From the standpoint of the learning target, a performance assessment is appropriate, but it may be that the nature of the task and the *scoring* of the result do not contain enough characteristics from Figure 8.1 to be an example of a performance assessment. In other words, we can call just about anything students do "performances," but that's not the same as implementing a systematic performance assessment as discussed here.

Communication and Presentation Skills.   Learning targets focused on communication skills involve student performance of reading, writing, speaking, and listening. For reading, targets can be divided into process—what students do before, during, and after reading—and product—what students get from the reading. Reading targets for elementary students progress from process skills such as being able to handle a book appropriately (e.g., right side up, turning pages), to products such as phonemic awareness skills (e.g., decoding, phonological awareness, blending), to product skills needed for comprehension and understanding (such as discrimination, contextual cues, inference, blending, sequencing, and identifying main ideas). For effective performance assessment, each of these areas needs to be delineated as a specific target. For instance, a word identification target may include naming and matching uppercase and lowercase letters, recognizing words by sight, recognizing sounds and symbols for consonants at the beginnings and ends of words, and sounding out three-letter words. For older students, reading targets focus on comprehension products and strategies and on reading efficiency, including stating main ideas; identifying the setting, characters, and events in stories; drawing inferences from context; and reading speed. More advanced reading skills include sensitivity to word meanings related to origins, nuances, or figurative meanings; identifying contradictions; and identifying possible multiple inferences. All reading targets should include the ability to perform a specific skill for novel reading materials. A variety of formats should also be represented.

Writing skill targets are also determined by a student's grade level. The emphasis for young students is on their ability to construct letters and copy words and simple sentences legibly. For writing complete essays or papers, elaborate delineations of skills have been developed. Typically, important dimensions of writing are used as categories, as illustrated in the following writing targets:

Purpose	Clarity of purpose; awareness of audience and task; clarity of ideas
Organization	Unity and coherence
Details	Appropriateness of details to purpose and support for main point(s) of writers response
Voice/tone	Personal investment and expression
Usage, Mechanics, and Grammar	Correct usage (tense formation, agreement, word choice), mechanics (spelling, capitalization, punctuation), grammar, and sentence construction

Other dimensions can be used when the writing skill being measured is more specific, such as writing a persuasive letter, a research paper, or an editorial. Writing targets, like those in reading, should include the ability to perform the skill in a variety of situations or contexts. That is, if students have been taught persuasive writing by developing letters to editors, the student may write a persuasive advertisement or speech to demonstrate that he or she has obtained the skill. Because writing is so easily collected and stored, it is also easy to provide students with examples of writing that illustrate the target before they demonstrate their competence. Writing is also used extensively for portfolios, which are discussed in greater detail in Chapter 9.

Oral communication skill targets can be generalized to many situations or focused on a specific type of presentation, such as giving a speech, singing a song, speaking a foreign language, or competing in a debate. When the emphasis is on general oral communication skills, the targets typically center on the following three general categories (Airasian, 2001):

Physical expression	Eye contact, posture, facial expressions, gestures, and body movement
Vocal expression	Articulation, clarity, vocal variation, loudness, pace, and rate
Verbal expression	Repetition, organization, summarizations, reasoning, completeness of ideas and thoughts, selection of appropriate words to convey precise meanings

A more specific set of oral communication skill targets is illustrated in the following guidelines for high school students:[1]

A. Speaking clearly, expressively, and audibly
   1. Using voice expressively
   2. Speaking articulately and pronouncing words correctly
   3. Using appropriate vocal volume

B. Presenting ideas with appropriate introduction, development, and conclusion
   1. Presenting ideas in an effective order
   2. Providing a clear focus on the central idea
   3. Providing signal words, internal summaries, and transitions

C. Developing ideas using appropriate support materials
   1. Being clear and using reasoning processes
   2. Clarifying, illustrating, exemplifying, and documenting ideas

D. Using nonverbal cues
   1. Using eye contact
   2. Using appropriate facial expressions, gestures, and body movement

E. Selecting language to a specific purpose
   1. Using language and conventions appropriate for the audience

For specific purposes, the skills are more targeted. For example, if a presentation involves a demonstration of how to use a microscope, the target could include such criteria as clarity of explanations, understanding of appropriate steps, appropriateness of examples when adjustments are necessary, dependency on notes, and whether attention is maintained, as well as more general features such as posture, enunciation, and eye contact.

Psychomotor Skills.   There are two steps in identifying psychomotor skill learning targets. The first step is to describe clearly the physical actions that are required. These may be developmentally appropriate skills or skills that are needed for specific tasks. I have divided the psychomotor area into five categories in Figure 8.3 to

FIGURE 8.3   **Examples of Psychomotor Skills**

Fine Motor	Gross Motor	Complex	Visual	Verbal and Auditory
Cutting paper with scissors	Walking	Perform a golf swing	Copying	Identify and discriminate sounds
Drawing a line	Jumping	Operate a computer	Finding letters	Imitate sounds
Tracing	Balancing	Drive a car	Finding embedded figures	Pronounce carefully
Eye–hand coordination	Throwing	Dissect a frog	Identifying shapes	Articulate
Penmanship	Skipping	Perform back walkover on balance beam	Discriminating on the basis of attributes such as size, shape, and color	Blend vowels
Coloring	Pull-ups	Operate a microscope		Use proper lip and tongue placement to produce sounds
Drawing shapes	Hopping	Sail a boat		
Connecting dots	Kicking	Operate a press drill		
Pointing				
Buttoning				
Zippering				

help you describe the behavior: fine motor skills (such as holding a pencil, focusing a microscope, and using scissors), gross motor actions (such as jumping and lifting), more complex athletic skills (such as shooting a basketball or playing golf), some visual skills, and verbal/auditory skills for young children.

The second step is to identify the level at which the skill is to be performed. One effective way to do this is to use an existing classification of the psychomotor domain (Simpson, 1972). This system is hierarchical. At the most basic level is *perception*, the ability to use sight, smell, hearing, and touch to be aware of a stimulus. The second level is *set*, which is a state of readiness to take action. The next level is *guided response*, which involves imitating a behavior or following directions. The fourth level is reached when an action becomes habitual and is done correctly with confidence. This is called *mechanism. Complex overt response* is the fifth level and involves correct actions comprising complex skills. The sixth level is *adaptation*, through which students can make adjustments to suit their needs. The final and highest level is *origination*, which refers to creating new actions to solve a problem. You can use the levels to determine the nature of the target for the skills identified from step 1. For instance, suppose you are interested in assessing your students' abilities to write capital letters correctly. At one level students need to be able to identify the letter, perhaps by locating an example of it on the wall (the perception level). Then they need to be physically prepared to write correctly (the set level—pencil sharpened, paper in the correct position), followed by being able to copy letters from the board (guided response). Then they can demonstrate their skill when drafting paragraphs (mechanism) and alter the shapes to accommodate different widths between lines (adaptation).

Products

Performance assessment products are completed works that include most of the characteristics in Figure 8.1 to some degree. For years, students have done papers, reports, and projects. What makes these products different when used for performance assessment is that they are more engaging and more authentic, and are scored more systematically with public criteria and standards. For example, rather than having sixth graders report on a foreign country by summarizing the history, politics, and economics of the country, students write promotional materials for the country that would help others decide if it would be an interesting place to visit. In chemistry, students are asked to identify an unknown substance. Why not have them identify the substances from a local landfill, river, or body of water? In music, students can demonstrate their proficiency and knowledge by creating and playing a new song. Figure 8.4 presents some other examples, varying in how authentic they are.

As a learning target, each product needs to be clearly described in some detail so that there is no misunderstanding about what students are required to do. It is not sufficient to simply say, for example, "Write a report on one of the planets and present it to the class." Students need to know about the specific elements of the product (e.g., length, types of information needed, nature of the audience, context, materials that can be used, what can be shown to the audience) and how they will be evaluated. One effective way to do this is to show examples of completed projects to students. These are not meant to be copied, but they can be used to com-

FIGURE 8.4   Performance Products and Skills Varying in Authenticity

Relatively Unauthentic	Somewhat Authentic	Authentic
Indicate which parts of a garden design are accurate.	Design a garden.	Create a garden.
Write a paper on zoning.	Write a proposal to change fictitious zoning laws.	Write a proposal to present to city council to change zoning laws.
Answer a series of questions about what materials are needed for a trip.	Defend the selection of supplies needed for a hypothetical trip.	Plan a trip with your family, indicating needed supplies.
Explain what you would teach to students learning to play basketball.	Show how to perform basketball skills in practice.	Play a basketball game.
Listen to a tape and interpret a foreign language.	Hold a conversation with a teacher in a foreign language.	Hold a conversation with a person from a foreign country in his or her native language.

municate standards and expectations. In other words, show examples of the target to the students. If the examples can demonstrate different levels of proficiency, so much the better. A good way to generate products is to think about what people in different occupations do. What does a city planner do? What would an expert witness produce for a trial? How does a mapmaker create a map that is easy to understand? What kinds of stories does a newspaper columnist write? How would an advertising agent represent state parks to attract tourists?

Constructing Performance Tasks

Once learning targets have been identified and you have decided that a performance assessment is the method you want to use, three steps remain to construct the task. The first is to identify the performance task in which students will be engaged; the second is to develop descriptions of the task and the context in which the performance is to be conducted; the third is to write the specific question, prompt, or problem the students will receive (Figure 8.5).

The performance task is what students are required to do in the performance assessment, either individually or in groups. The tasks can vary by subject and by level of complexity. Some performance tasks are specific to a content area, and others integrate several subjects and skills. With regard to level of complexity, it is useful to distinguish two types: restricted and extended.

Restricted- and Extended-Type
Performance Tasks

Restricted-type tasks target a narrowly defined skill and require relatively brief responses. The task is structured and specific. These tasks may look similar to short essay questions and interpretive exercises that have open-ended items. The difference is in the relative emphasis on characteristics listed in Figure 8.1. Often the performance task is structured to elicit student explanations of their answer. Students may be asked to defend an answer; indicate why a different answer is not correct; tell how they did something; draw a diagram; construct a visual map, graph, or flow chart; or show some other aspect of their reasoning. In contrast, short essay questions and interpretive exercises are designed to infer reasoning from correct answers. Although restricted-type tasks require relatively little time for administration and scoring in comparison with extended-type tasks (providing greater reliability

FIGURE 8.5   Steps in Constructing Performance Tasks

and sampling), it is likely that fewer of the important characteristics of authentic performance assessments are included.

Here are some restricted-type performance tasks:

Construct a bar graph from data provided.

Demonstrate a short conversation in French about what is on a menu.

Read an article from the newspaper and answer questions.

Review a zoning map of a city and indicate changes that would encourage more commercial development.

Flip a coin ten times. Predict what the next ten flips of the coin will be, and explain why.

Listen to the evening news on television and explain if you believe the stories are biased.

From the information given on three bar graphs showing the amount of carbohydrates, fats, and protein in two new food bars, select the one that would be most healthful. Justify your answer.

Using your own words and illustrations, construct a poster that explains the parts of flowers.

Sing a song.

Type at least thirty-five words per minute with fewer than six mistakes.

Show how to adjust the display of a computer screen.

Construct a circle, square, and triangle from provided materials that have the same circumference.

Write a term paper about the importance of protecting forests from being converted to farmland.

Using scissors, cut outlined figures from a page.

Recite a poem.

Many publishers provide performance assessments in a standardized format, and most of them contain restricted-type tasks.

Extended-type tasks are more complex, elaborate, and time-consuming. Extended-type tasks often include collaborative work with small groups of students. The assignment usually requires that students use a variety of sources of information (e.g., observations, library, interviews). Judgments will need to be made about which information is most relevant. Products are typically developed over several days or even weeks, with opportunities for revision. This allows students to apply a variety of skills and makes it easier to integrate different content areas and reasoning skills.

It is not too difficult to come up with ideas for what would be an engaging extended-type task. As previously indicated, one effective approach is to think about what people do in different occupations. Another way to generate ideas is to check curriculum guides and teacher's editions of textbooks, because most will have activities and assignments that tap student application and reasoning skills.

Perhaps the best way to generate ideas is by brainstorming with others, especially members of the community. They can be particularly helpful in thinking about authentic tasks that involve reasoning and communication skills. Here are a few ideas that could be transformed into extended-type tasks:

> Design a playhouse and estimate cost of materials and labor.
>
> Plan a trip to another country. Include the budget and itinerary, and justify why you plan to visit certain places.
>
> Conduct a historical reenactment (e.g., the Boston Tea Party, the Lincoln–Douglas debates, a Civil War battle).
>
> Diagnose and repair a car problem.
>
> Design an advertising campaign for a new or existing product.
>
> Publish a newspaper.
>
> Design a park.
>
> Create a commercial.
>
> Write and perform a song.
>
> Prepare a plan for dealing with waste materials.
>
> Design and carry out a study to determine which grocery store has the lowest prices.

Once you have a general idea for the task, you need to develop it into a more detailed set of specifications.

Performance Task Descriptions and Contexts

The performance task needs to be specified so that it meets the criteria for good performance assessment and is clear to students. This is accomplished by preparing a *task description.* The purpose of the task description is to provide a blueprint or listing of specifications to ensure that essential criteria are met, that the task is reasonable, and that it will elicit desired student performance. The task description is not the same as the actual format and wording of the question or prompt that is given to students; it is more like a lesson plan. The task description should include the following:

> Content and skill targets to be assessed
> Description of student activities
>> Group or individual
>> Help allowed
> Resources needed
> Teacher role
> Administrative process
> Scoring procedures

It is essential to clearly describe the specific content or skill targets to be assessed to make certain that the activities and scoring are well matched to ensure both valid and practical assessments. Think about what students will actually do to respond to the question or solve the problem by specifying the context in which they will work. Will they consult other experts, use library resources, do experiments? Are they allowed to work together, or is it an individual assignment? What types of help from others are allowed? Is there sufficient time to complete the activities? Once the activities are described, the resources needed to accomplish them can be identified. Are needed materials and resources available for all students? What needs to be obtained before the assessment? It will be helpful to describe your role in the exercise. Will you consult your students or give them ideas? Are you comfortable with and adequately prepared for what you will do? What administrative procedures are required? Finally, what scoring procedures will you use? Will scoring match the learning targets? Is adequate time available for scoring? Do you have the expertise needed to do the scoring? Is it practical?

One effective way to begin to design the task is to think about what has been done instructionally (Smith, Smith, & De Lisi, 2001). The assessment task should be structured to mirror the nature of classroom instruction so that what you are asking students to do is something that they are already at least somewhat familiar with.

Once the task description is completed and you are satisfied that the assessment will be valid and practical, you are ready to prepare the specific performance task question or prompt.

Performance Task Question or Prompt

The actual question, problem, or prompt that you give to students will be based on the task description. It needs to be stated so that it clearly identifies what the final outcome or product is, outlines what students are allowed and encouraged to do, and explains the criteria that will be used to judge the product. A good question or prompt also provides a context that helps students understand the meaningfulness and relevance of the task. A good performance task is illustrated in Figure 8.6.

Because considerable time is required to construct good performance tasks, you will want to use or adapt ones that have already been developed. Several professional organizations have organized networks and other resources for developing performance tasks, including the Association of Supervision and Curriculum Development (ASCD), the National Center for Research on Evaluation, Standards, and Students Testing (CRESST), the Mid-continent Regional Educational Laboratory (McREL), the Northwest Regional Educational Laboratory (NWRL), and the Council of Chief State School Officers (CCSSO). Also, many subject-oriented professional organizations, such as the National Council of Teachers of Mathematics, have good resources for identifying performance tasks.

Whether you develop your own tasks or use intact or modified existing ones, you will want to evaluate the task on the basis of the following suggestions (summarized in Figure 8.7) and characteristics summarized in Figure 8.8.

1. The Performance Task Should Integrate the Most Essential Aspects of the Content Being Assessed with the Most Essential Skills.   Performance assessment is ideal for focusing student attention and learning on the big ideas of a subject, the major concepts, principles, and processes that are important to a discipline. If the

FIGURE 8.6   Performance Task Prompt

Comparison Task

Grade-level range: Upper Elementary–Middle

Working in pairs, list as many insects as possible. Come up
with a classification system that focuses on key characteristics
of the insects and place the insects from your list in the appropriate categories. Do the same classification procedure two
more times, but from the following perspectives:

- An exterminator (sample categories: insects found in homes,
  flying insects, crawling insects, insects commonly found in
  kitchens, insects that prefer dark basements).
- A frog (sample categories: insects that fly above water,
  insects that can swim, insects that would make a big meal,
  insects that would make a little meal).

} Nature of Final Product

You will have to consult various resources (materials in the
classroom, peers, adults, and so on) to obtain the information
necessary to classify the insects accurately. When you turn in
your three classification systems, include a list of the resources
you used and explain in a short paragraph which were most
and least useful. Be ready to share with the class some interesting
things you discovered as a result of doing these classifications.
You will be assessed on and provided rubrics for the following:

} What Students Are Required to Do

1. Your understanding of the characteristics of insects.
2. Your ability to specify important defining characteristics
   of the categories.
3. Your ability to accurately sort the identified elements into
   the categories.
4. Your ability to effectively use a variety of information-
   gathering techniques and information resources.

} Criteria Used to Judge the Product

Source: Adapted from Marzano, R. J., Pickering, D., & McTighe, J. (1993). *Assessing student outcomes: Per-*
formance assessment using the dimensions of learning model. Alexandria, VA: Association for Supervision
and Curriculum Development, p. 51. Adapted by permission of McREL. © 1993.

FIGURE 8.7   Checklist for Writing Performance Tasks

✓ Are essential content and skills targets integrated?
✓ Are multiple targets included?
✓ Is the task authentic?
✓ Is the task teachable?
✓ Is the task feasible?
✓ Are multiple solutions and paths possible?
✓ Is the nature of the task clear?
✓ Is the task challenging and stimulating?
✓ Are criteria for scoring included?
✓ Are constraints for completing the task included?

FIGURE 8.8   Criteria for Performance Tasks

Essential	• The task fits into the core of the curriculum. • It represents a "big idea."	vs. Tangential
Authentic	• The task uses processes appropriate to the discipline. • Students value the outcome of the task.	vs. Contrived
Rich	• The task leads to other problems. • It raises other questions. • It has many possibilities.	vs. Superficial
Engaging	• The task is thought provoking. • It fosters persistence.	vs. Uninteresting
Active	• The student is the worker and decision maker. • Students interact with other students. • Students are constructing meaning and deepening understanding.	vs. Passive
Feasible	• The task can be done within school and homework time. • It is developmentally appropriate for students. • It is safe.	vs. Infeasible
Equitable	• The task develops thinking in a variety of styles. • It contributes to positive attitudes.	vs. Inequitable
Open	• The task has more than one right answer. • It has multiple avenues of approach, making it accessible to all students.	vs. Closed

Source: Reprinted with permission from *Mathematics assessment: Myths, models, good questions, and practical suggestions,* by Jean Kerr Stenmark. Copyright © 1991 by the National Council of Teachers of Mathematics. All rights reserved.

task encourages learning of peripheral or tangential topics or specific details, it is not well suited to the goal of performance assessment. Tasks should be broad in scope. Similarly, reasoning and other skills essential to the task should represent essential processes. The task should be written to integrate content with skills. For example, it would be better to debate important content or contemporary issues rather than something relatively unimportant. A good test for whether the task meets these criteria is to decide if what is assessed could be done as well with more objective, less time-consuming measures.

Example

Poor: Estimate the answers to the following three addition problems. Explain in your own words the strategy used to give your answer.

Improved: Sam and Tyron were planning a trip to a nearby state. They wanted to visit as many different major cities as possible. Using the map, estimate the number of major cities they will be able to visit on a single tank of gas (fourteen gallons) if their car gets twenty-five miles to the gallon.

2. The Task Should Be Authentic. This suggestion lies at the heart of authentic performance assessment. Grant Wiggins has developed a set of six standards for judging the degree of authenticity in an assessment task (Wiggins, 1998). He suggests that a task is authentic if it:

A. *Is realistic.* The task replicates the ways in which a person's knowledge and abilities are "tested" in real-world situations.
B. *Requires judgment and innovation.* The student has to use knowledge and skills wisely and effectively to solve unstructured problems, and the solution involves more than following a set routine or procedure or plugging in knowledge.
C. *Asks the student to "do" the subject.* The student has to carry out exploration and work within the discipline of the subject area, rather than restating what is already known or what was taught.
D. *Replicates or simulates* the contexts *in which adults are "tested" in the workplace, in civic life, and in personal life.* Contexts involve specific situations that have particular constraints, purposes, and audiences. Students need to experience what it is like to do tasks in workplace and other real-life contexts.
E. *Assesses the student's ability to efficiently and effectively use a repertoire of knowledge and skill to negotiate a complex task.* Students should be required to integrate all knowledge and skills needed, rather than to demonstrate competence of isolated knowledge and skills.
F. *Allows appropriate opportunities to rehearse, practice, consult resources, and get feedback on and refine performances and products.* Rather than rely on secure tests as an audit of performance, learning should be focused through cycles of performance-feedback-revision-performance, on the production of *known* high-quality products and standards, and learning in context. (p. 22, 24)

A similar set of standards has been developed by Fred Newmann (Newmann, 1997). In his view, authentic tasks require the following:

Construction of meaning (use of reasoning and higher-order thinking skills to produce meaning or knowledge)
   1. Organization of information
   2. Consideration of alternatives

Disciplined inquiry (thinking like "experts" searching for in-depth understanding)
   3. Disciplinary content
   4. Disciplinary process
   5. Elaborated written communication

Value beyond school (aesthetic, utilitarian, or personal value apart from documenting the competence of the learner)
   6. Problem connected to the world
   7. Audience beyond the school

Newmann summarizes these standards by saying that authentic tasks "demand construction of knowledge through disciplined inquiry and result in discourse, products, and performance that have value or meaning beyond success in school" (p. 366).

Example

Poor: Compare and contrast different kinds of literature.

Improved:[2] You have volunteered to help your local library with its literacy program. Once a week after school, you help people learn how to read. To encourage your students to learn, you tell them about the different kinds of literature you have read, including poems, biographies, mysteries, tall tales, fables, and historical novels. Select three types of literature and compare them, using general characteristics of literature and the specific characteristics of each genre that you think will help your students see the similarities and differences among the types of literature. Create a table or chart to visually depict the comparison.

Notice also how the improved version integrates content and language arts with two skills, comparison and communication.

3. Structure the Task to Assess Multiple Learning Targets. As pointed out in the first suggestion, it is best if the task assesses both content and skill targets. Within each of these areas there may be different types of targets. For instance, assessing content may include both knowledge and understanding and, as in the example above, both reasoning and communication skills. It is also common to include different types of communication and reasoning skills in the same task (e.g., students provide both a written and an oral report or need to think critically and synthesize to arrive at an answer).

4. Structure the Task so That You Can Help Students Succeed. Good performance assessment involves the interaction of instruction with assessment. The task needs to be something that students learn from, which is most likely when there are opportunities for you to increase student proficiency by asking questions, providing resources, and giving feedback. In this kind of active teaching, you are intervening as students learn, rather than simply providing information. Part of teachability is being certain that students have the needed prerequisite knowledge and skills to succeed.

5. Think through What Students Will Do to Be Sure That the Task Is Feasible. Imagine what you would do if given the task. What resources would you need? How much time would you need? What steps would you take? It should be realistic for students to implement the task. This depends both on your own expertise and willingness and on the costs and availability of equipment, materials, and other resources so that every student has the same opportunity to be successful.

6. The Task Should Allow for Multiple Solutions. If a performance task is properly structured, more than one correct response is not only possible but desirable. The task should not encourage drill or practice for which there is a single solution. The possibility of multiple solutions encourages students to personalize the process and makes it easier for you to demand that students justify and explain their assumptions, planning, predictions, and other responses. Different students may take different paths in responding to the task.

7. The Task Should Be Clear.   An unambiguous set of directions that explicitly indicates the nature of the task is essential. If the directions are too vague, students may not focus on the learning targets or may waste time trying to figure out what they should be doing. A task such as "Give an oral report on a foreign country" is too general. Students need to know the reason for the task, and the directions should provide sufficient detail so that students know how to proceed. Do they work alone or with others? What resources are available? How much time do they have? What is the role of the teacher? Here is an example of a clearly defined task (Marzano, Pickering, & McTighe, 1993):

> We will be reading George Orwell's 1984, which could be described as a work of projective investigation. We will also be studying what was happening in the world around the time this book was written, the decade of the 1940s.
>
> First, working in small groups, your task is to select specific events, ideas, or trends from the 1940s and show how Orwell projected them into the future. You'll be given a chart on which you can graphically depict these connections.
>
> Second, each person is to select a field of study that interests you (economics, science and technology, health care, fashion, sports, literature, the arts, politics, sociology) and select current events, ideas, and trends in that field, with an emphasis on areas where there is some controversy or disagreement.
>
> Finally, using your knowledge of the field, construct a scenario for the future that makes sense and is a plausible extension of the present. Present your scenario in any way you wish (written prose or poetry, art form, oral or video presentation, etc.). In your presentation, clearly communicate your predictions and how they plausibly extend the present. (p. 61)

8. The Task Should Be Challenging and Stimulating to Students.   One of the things you hope for is that students will be motivated to use their skills and knowledge to be involved and engaged, sometimes for days or weeks. You also want students to monitor themselves and think about their progress. This is more likely to occur when the task is something students can get excited about or can see some relevance for, and when the task is not too easy or too difficult. Persistence is fostered if the task is interesting and thought provoking. This is easier if you know your students' strengths and limitations and are familiar with what kinds of topics would motivate them. One approach is to blend what is familiar with novelty. Tasks that are authentic are not necessarily stimulating and challenging.

9. Include Explicitly Stated Scoring Criteria as Part of the Task.   By now you are familiar with this admonition. Specifying criteria helps students understand what they need to do and communicates learning priorities and your expectations. Students need to know about the criteria *before* beginning work on the task. Sometimes criteria are individually tailored to each task; others are more generic for several different kinds of tasks. What is shared with students as part of the task, however, may not be the same instrument or scale you use when evaluating their work. For example, for the task in suggestion 7, the following contains part of what you might share with students (Marzano, Pickering, & McTighe, 1993):

> You will be assessed on and provided rubrics for the following:
>
> A. Your understanding of the extent to which the present can inform the future
> B. Your depth of understanding of major events, ideas, and trends from a field of study
> C. Your ability to accurately identify what is already known or agreed upon about the future event
> D. Your ability to construct a scenario for some future event or hypothetical past event for which a scenario is not readily available or accepted
> E. Your ability to express ideas clearly
> F. Your ability to communicate effectively in a variety of ways (p. 61)

The identification of scoring criteria, and how you translate those criteria into a scale for evaluation, is discussed in the next section. From a practical perspective, the development of the task and scoring criteria is iterative: one influences the other as both are developed.

Another list of desirable criteria of performance tasks is illustrated in Figure 8.8. This figure shows how the characteristics are defined and contrasted with what often occurs during more traditional forms of assessment.

10. Include Constraints for Completing the Task. One of the hallmarks of authentic thinking and decision making is that such performance is done under constraints that are defined by context, rules, and regulations that are similar to conditions outside the classroom. According to Tombari and Borich (1999), these constraints include:

> *Time.* How much time would be allowed to complete the performance or product?
>
> *Reference material.* What other resources or information would typically be available?
>
> *Other people.* What kind of support would be provided by peers, experts, and others?
>
> *Equipment.* What kind of equipment would be available?
>
> *Prior knowledge of the task.* How much information would be provided in advance?
>
> *Scoring criteria.* What are the scoring criteria by which the performance or product will be judged? (p. 160)

The intent of considering such constraints is to define in a more realistic way the nature of the situation in which the performance or product is demonstrated. It allows students to more closely associate what they are doing with real-life contexts.

Scoring Criteria, Rubrics, and Procedures

After students have completed the task, you must evaluate their performance. Because responses are constructed by students, this is always a matter of reviewing their work and making a professional judgment about the skill or product. Rather than relying on unstated rules for making these judgments, performance assessments include *performance criteria,* what you call on or use to determine student proficiency.

Performance Criteria

Performance criteria (or *scoring criteria* or simply *criteria*) are what you look for in student responses to evaluate their progress toward meeting the learning target. In other words, performance criteria are the dimensions or traits in products or performance that are used to illustrate and define understanding, reasoning, and proficiency. Explicitly defined performance criteria help to make what is a subjective process clear, consistent, and defensible (Arter & McTighe, 2001).

Determining defensible criteria begins with identification of the most important dimensions or traits of the performance. This is a summary of the essential qualities of student proficiency. These dimensions should reflect your instructional goals as well as teachable and observable aspects of the performance. Ask yourself this question: "What distinguishes an adequate from an inadequate demonstration of the target?" Herman, Aschbacher, and Winters (1992) make these suggestions for identifying important dimensions:[3]

- What are the attributes of good writing, of good scientific thinking, of good collaborative group process, of effective oral presentation? More generally, by what qualities or features will I know whether students have produced an excellent response to my assessment task?
- What do I expect to see if this task is done excellently, acceptably, poorly?
- Do I have samples or models of student work, from my class or other sources, that exemplify some of the criteria I might use in judging this task?
- What criteria for this or similar tasks exist in my state curriculum frameworks, my state assessment program, my district curriculum guides, my school assessment program?
- What dimensions might I adapt from work done by national curriculum councils, by other teachers?

One of the best approaches is to work backward from examples of student work. These exemplars can be analyzed to determine what descriptors distinguish them. The examples can also be used as **anchor** papers for making judgments, and they can be given to students to illustrate the dimensions. The dimension is the trait you are looking for. For a speech, that dimension might be content, organization, and delivery. Delivery may be divided further into posture, gestures, facial expressions, and eye contact. For a singing performance, you could include pitch, rhythm, diction, and tone quality, and each of these can be further delineated. As you might imagine, you can go into great detail describing dimensions. But to be practical, you need to balance specificity with what is manageable (the next section includes some examples of what is reasonable).

The following is an example of criteria for a specific learning target.

Learning target: Students will be able to write a persuasive paper to encourage the reader to accept a specific course of action or point of view.

Criteria: Appropriateness of language for the audience.
Plausibility and relevance of supporting arguments.
Level of detail presented.
Evidence of creative, innovative thinking.
Clarity of expression.
Organization of ideas.

Once all the criteria have been identified, a rating scale is used to show qualitatively different levels of performance.

Rating Scales

A rating scale is used to indicate the degree to which a particular dimension is present. It provides a way to record and communicate qualitatively different levels of performance. Several types of rating scales are available; we will consider three: numerical, qualitative, and numerical/quantitative combined.

The numerical scale uses numbers on a continuum to indicate different levels of proficiency in terms of frequency or quality. The number of points on the scale can vary, from as few as three to ten, twenty, or more. The number of points is determined on the basis of the decision that will be made. If you are going to use the scale to indicate low, medium, and high, then three points are sufficient. More points on the scale permit greater discrimination, provide more diagnostic information, and permit more specific feedback to students.

Here are some examples of numerical scales:

Complete Understanding   5 4 3 2 1   No Understanding
of the Problem   of the Problem

Little or No Organization 1 2 3 4 5 6 7   Clear and Complete Organization

Emergent Reader   1 2 3   Fluent Reader

A qualitative scale uses verbal descriptions to indicate student performance. There are two types of qualitative descriptors. One type indicates the different gradations of the dimension. The simplest form is the checklist. This lists different dimensions and provides a way to check whether each dimension was evidenced (Figure 8.9). More complex scales summarize different levels of the dimensions.

FIGURE 8.9 **Checklist for Evaluating a Presentation**

Japan Presentation Criteria

Content

Yes	No	
_____	_____	**1.** Two or more aspects of Japanese society mentioned
_____	_____	**2.** The similarity between the United States and Japan presented
_____	_____	**3.** Explained the difference between the United States and Japan

Presentation

Yes	No	
_____	_____	**4.** Proper grammar used
_____	_____	**5.** Appropriate eye contact made
_____	_____	**6.** Varies tone and loudness
_____	_____	**7.** Enunciates words
_____	_____	**8.** Speaks clearly
_____	_____	**9.** Changes facial expressions
_____	_____	**10.** Faces audience

Source: Adapted from Bacon, M. (1993). *Restructuring curriculum, instruction, and assessment in the Littleton Public Schools.* Littleton, CO: Littleton Public Schools.

There is no indication of or reference to a standard in any of these scales. The idea is to describe the performance accurately, without indicating whether any particular point on any of the scales is considered passing or failing, or without indicating some other type of judgment about what the description means or how it is used. Typically, language provides the basis for the scale, including words such as:

> *minimal, partial, complete*
> *never, seldom, occasionally, frequently, always*
> *consistently, sporadically, rarely*
> *none, some, complete*

Some examples of more descriptive qualitative scales include the following:

Complete Understanding	Nearly Complete Understanding	Some Understanding	Limited Understanding
Uses capital letters appropriately most or all of the time	Uses capital letters appropriately some of the time	Rarely uses capital letters appropriately	
Always speaks clearly	Speaks clearly most of the time	Speaks clearly some of the time	Rarely speaks clearly

A second type of qualitative scale includes gradations of the criteria and some indication of the worth of the performance. That is, the evaluative component is incorporated in the rating. This is the most frequently used type of rating scale for performance assessments. Descriptors such as the following are associated with different points on the scale:

novice, intermediate, advanced, superior
inadequate, needs improvement, good, excellent
excellent, proficient, needs improvement
absent, developing, adequate, fully developed
limited, partial, thorough
emerging, developing, achieving
not there yet, shows growth, proficient
excellent, good, fair, poor

Regardless of whether a numerical or qualitative scale is used, an important decision is whether the scale and/or scoring will be *analytic* or *holistic*. A **holistic scale** is one in which each category of the scale contains several criteria, yielding a single score that gives an overall impression or rating. Advantages of using a holistic scale are its simplicity and the ability to provide a reasonable summary rating. All the traits are efficiently combined, the work is scored quickly, and only one score results. For example, in gymnastics, a single holistic score between 1 and 10 is awarded, in which separate judgments for various dimensions (flexibility, balance, position, etc.) are combined. The disadvantage of a holistic score is that it reveals little about what needs to be improved. Thus, for feedback purposes, holistic scores provide little specific information unless time is provided to break down the reasons for the overall score.

When the purpose of the assessment is summative, at the end of a unit or course, a holistic scale is appropriate. But even when used summatively, holistic scales can vary greatly in the specificity of what is used in the judgments. For example, the following holistic scale for reading is rather skimpy; very little is indicated about what went into the judgment.

Level 4: Sophisticated understanding of text indicated with constructed meaning.

Level 3: Solid understanding of text indicated with some constructed meaning.

Level 2: Partial understanding of text indicated with tenuous constructed meaning.

Level 1: Superficial understanding of text with little or no constructed meaning.

Contrast this scale with the one in Figure 8.10, which is also concerned with reading. It is obvious that this more developed and specific rubric provides a more detailed explanation of how the reading was judged and why each level was assigned. Even

FIGURE 8.10   Example of Holistic Rating Scale and Rubric

Reading Rubric	
Rating Scale	*Evaluative Criteria*
4	Reader displays a sophisticated understanding of the text with substantial evidence of constructing meaning. Multiple connections are made between the text and the reader's ideas/experiences. Interpretations are sophisticated and directly supported by appropriate text references. Reader explicitly takes a critical stance (e.g., analyzes the author's style, questions the text, provides alternative interpretations, views the text from multiple perspectives).
3	Reader displays a solid understanding of the text with clear evidence of constructing meaning. Connections are made between the text and the reader's ideas/experiences. Interpretations are made and generally supported by appropriate text references. Reader may reveal a critical stance toward the text.
2	Reader displays a partial understanding of the text with some evidence of constructing meaning. A connection may be made between the text and the reader's ideas/expressions, but it is not developed. Interpretations are not made and/or not supported by appropriate text references. Reader shows no evidence of critical stance toward the text.
1	Reader displays a superficial understanding of the text with limited evidence of constructing meaning. No connections are made between the text and the reader's ideas/experiences. Reader provides no interpretations or evidence of a critical stance.

Source: McTighe, J., & Ferrara, S. (1998). *Assessing learning in the classroom.* Washington, DC: National Education Association, p. 23.

with this more specific scale, however, how do you judge a student who showed multiple connections between the text and the reader's ideas/experiences but had interpretations that were not directly supported by appropriate text references? This kind of problem, in which the traits being assessed do not all conform within a single category, is almost certain to exist with holistic scales for some students.

An **analytic scale** (or *analytic-trait scale*) is one in which each criterion receives a separate score. If analytic scoring were used in gymnastics, each criterion such as flexibility, balance, and position would be scored separately. This kind of scale provides much better diagnostic information and feedback for the learner and is more useful for formative evaluation during instruction. Students are able to see their strengths and weaknesses more clearly. They are able to connect their preparation and effort with each evaluation. However, analytic scales take longer to create and score.

In general, to the extent possible based on practical constraints, it is best to use analytic rating scales. Like other good assessment techniques, once established, good analytic scales will serve you well for many years. For that reason, and the instructional advantages, it makes good sense to invest time in developing them. Two analytic scales and rubrics are illustrated in Figure 8.11. Actually, an

FIGURE 8.11   Examples of Analytic Scales and Rubrics

Rubric for a Fifth Grade Research Paper[1]

Rating Scale	Criteria		
	The learner will use multiple sources.	The learner will take adequate notes.	The written report will be well organized and contain sufficient information.
4	Information came from four or more sources.	Many details were apparent in notes in all categories (appearance, reproduction/offspring, habitat, diet, and unique characteristics)	The report was well organized and contained thorough and accurate information.
3	Information came from three sources.	Many details were evident in most, but not all, of the categories.	The report was well organized. Many details were evident, but some important information was missing in one or two categories.
2	Information came from two sources.	Notes were evident in all categories, but details were lacking.	The report was sometimes difficult to understand. Important information was missing in three or more categories
1	Information came from one source or no sources.	Few or no notes were taken.	The report was difficult to understand. Important information was missing in all categories.

The written report will have correct capitalization, usage, punctuation, and spelling.	The presentation will give sufficient and pertinent information to the audience.	The presentation will be easy to hear.
Accurate capitalization, punctuation, usage, and spelling were used throughout the written report.	The presentation was well organized and contained thorough and accurate information. The student did not read his or her report.	All of the presentation was easy to hear from the back of the classroom.
Several errors were evident, but the errors did not interfere with a reader's comprehension.	The presentation was well organized, but some important information was missing. The student did not read his or her report.	Most of the presentation was easy to hear from the back of the classroom.
Errors were evident, and several of the errors made it difficult for a listener to understand parts of the report.	The presentation was easy to understand, but details were missing *or* the student read his or her report.	Some of the presentation was easy to hear from the back of the room.
Many errors were evident throughout the written report that made it difficult for a listener to understand.	The presentation was difficult to understand and incomplete. Important information was missing.	Little of the presentation was easy to hear from the back of the room.

Oral Presentation Rubric[2]

Rating Scale	Evaluative Criteria		
	Organization	Delivery	Language Conventions
4	Coherent organization throughout; logical sequence; smooth transitions; effective introduction and conclusion.	Excellent volume; fluent delivery with varied intonation; effective body language and eye contact.	Highly effective use of language enhances the message; few, if any, grammatical mistakes.
3	Good organization generally but with some break in the logical flow of ideas; identifiable introduction and conclusion.	Adequate volume and intonation; generally fluent; generally effective body language and eye contact.	Generally effective use of language supports the message; minor grammatical errors do not interfere with message.
2	Flawed organization; ideas not developed; weak transitions; ineffective conclusion.	Volume is too low or too loud; delivery is not fluent; body language and eye contact do not enhance message.	Use of language not always aligned with the message; grammatical errors may interfere with message.
1	Lack of organization; flow of ideas difficult to follow; no evidence of transitions; no introduction or conclusion.	Message cannot be understood due to low volume; strained delivery; ineffective body language; lack of eye contact.	Major grammatical errors make the message very difficult or impossible to follow.

[1]*Source:* Adapted from Rickards, D. & Cheek, E. (1999). *Designing rubrics for K–6 classroom assessment.* Norwood, MA: Christopher-Gordon, p. 20.

[2]*Source:* McTighe, J., & Ferrara, S. (1998). *Assessing learning in the classroom.* Washington, DC: National Education Association, p. 24.

analytic scale can be as simple as a numerical scale that follows each criterion, such as the following, which could be used to evaluate creative writing:

	Outstanding		Competent		Marginal
Criterion	5	4	3	2	1
Creative ideas					
Logical organization					
Relevance of detail					
Variety in words and sentences					
Vivid images					

However, such scales still do not indicate much about why ideas were "competent" and not "outstanding" or why vivid images were rated "marginal." Analytic scales use language that is as descriptive as possible about the nature of the criterion that differentiates it from one level to the next. It will be much more helpful, for example, for students to know "that eye contact with the audience was direct and sustained for most of the presentation," rather than receiving feedback such as "excellent" or "completely." The difference between holistic and analytic scales is illustrated in Figure 8.12.

Rubrics

When scoring criteria are combined with a rating scale, we have the foundation for a complete *scoring guideline,* or what has come to be called a *rubric.* A **rubric,** or *scoring rubric,* is a scoring guide that uses criteria to differentiate between levels of student proficiency. Rubrics are worded in ways that communicate how teachers evaluate the essence of what is being assessed. According to Wiggins (1998), rubrics answer the following questions:

By what criteria should performance be judged?

Where should we look and what should we look for to judge performance success?

What does the range in the quality of performance look like?

How do we determine validly, reliably, and fairly what score should be given and what that score means?

How should the different levels of quality be described and distinguished from one another?

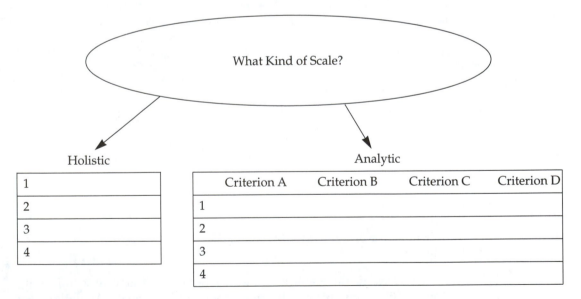

FIGURE 8.12   Differences between Holistic and Analytic Scales

Source: Adapted from Arter, J., & McTighe, J. (2001). *Scoring rubrics in the classroom: Using performance criteria for assessing and improving student performance.* Thousand Oaks, CA: Corwin Press. Reprinted by permission of Corwin Press, Inc.

A rubric uses descriptions of different levels of quality on each of the criteria, such as those found in Figures 8.10 and 8.11. For example, one of the criteria in judging the persuasiveness of a paper in the earlier example is plausibility and relevance of supporting arguments. Different levels of quality for those criteria could be expressed as follows:

> No supporting arguments
> Few supporting arguments that have weak plausibility and relevance
> Some supporting arguments that have acceptable plausibility and relevance
> Many supporting arguments that are clearly plausible and relevant

In addition, many rubrics label each category with evaluative language, using gradations of descriptors (e.g., inadequate, minimal, adequate, superior; novice, developing, developed).

Whether numbers, levels, or evaluative language is used with a rubric, the goal is to make criterion-referenced interpretations so that students are informed about specific deficiencies and strengths and so that teachers are clearer about what they use in making their judgments. An example of an excellent rubric is shown in Figure 8.13.

Developing Rubrics.   Rubrics are best developed by combining several different procedures. It is helpful to begin by clarifying how the discipline defines different levels of performance. This will give you an idea of the nature and number of gradations that should be used. It is also helpful to obtain samples of how others have described and scored performance in the area to be assessed. This can be done through the same sources that have developed performance criteria, such as national associations, state departments of education, and research organizations such as CRESST.

Another approach is to gather performance samples and determine the characteristics of the works that distinguish effective from ineffective ones. The samples could be from students as well as so-called experts in the area. You could start by putting a group of student samples into three qualitatively different piles to indicate three levels of performance. Then examine the samples to see what distinguishes them. The identified characteristics provide the basis for the dimensions of the rating scale. At this point, you can review your initial thinking about the scale with others to see if they agree with you. With feedback from others, you can write the first draft of the descriptors at each point of the rating scale.

Use the first draft of the rubric with additional samples of student work to verify that it works as intended. Revise as needed, and try it again with more samples of student work until you are satisfied that it provides a valid, reliable, and fair way to judge student performance. Don't forget to use student feedback as part of the process. As you might realize, this entire process is repeated over and over to improve the rubric.

Four suggestions for developing criteria for rubrics are illustrated graphically in Figure 8.14. Note how they combine your own understanding of what is being assessed with what others think and actual student performances. See Arter

FIGURE 8.13   Exemplary Example of a Rubric: Assessing a High School Senior Essay on Substance Abuse

9–8   The upper-range responses satisfy the following criteria:

    a. *Summary.* The summary should identify the main idea [of the reading].

    b. *Focus of agreement.* Agreement or disagreement may be complete or partial but writer must make clear what he or she is agreeing/disagreeing with. Specifically, 9–8 papers must address author's thesis, not substance abuse in general.

    c. *Support for agreement/disagreement.* Support should provide an analysis of argument and/or relevant and concrete examples.

    d. *Style and coherence.* These papers demonstrate clear style, overall organization, and sequence of thought. They contain few repeated errors in usage, grammar, or mechanics.

7   This grade is used for papers that fulfill basic requirements for the 9–8 grade but have less development, support, or analysis.

6–5   Middle range papers omit or are deficient in one of these four criteria:

    a. *Summary.* Summary is absent or incomplete, listing only author's thesis.

    b. *Focus of agreement/disagreement.* What the writer is agreeing or disagreeing with is not clear or is unrelated to author's proposals. Example: writer doesn't use enough phrasing like "on the one hand . . . on the other hand. . . ."

    c. *Support.* Writer only counterasserts; examples are highly generalized or not distinguishable from examples in the article. Analysis may be specious, irrelevant, or thin.

    d. *Style and coherence.* These papers are loosely organized or contain noticeable errors in usage, grammar, or mechanics.

4   This grade is used for papers that are slightly weaker than the 6–5 papers. Also, a student who writes his or her own parallel essay in a competent style should receive a 4.

3–2   These papers are deficient in two or more criteria. Typically they weakly paraphrase the article, or they have serious organization or coherence problems. Papers with serious, repeated errors in usage, grammar, or mechanics must be placed in this range.

Source: Adapted from Wiggins, G. P. (1998). *Educative assessment: Designing assessments to inform and improve student performance.* San Francisco: Jossey-Bass, p. 155. Reprinted by permission of John Wiley & Sons, Inc.

and McTighe (2001) for a compendium of excellent examples of many different rubrics in different subjects.

The following suggestions, summarized in Figure 8.15, will provide further help as you develop rubrics.

1. Be Sure the Criteria Focus on Important Aspects of the Performance.   There are many ways to distinguish between different examples of student work. You want to use those criteria that are essential in relation to the learning targets you are assessing. Because it is not feasible to include every possible way in which per-

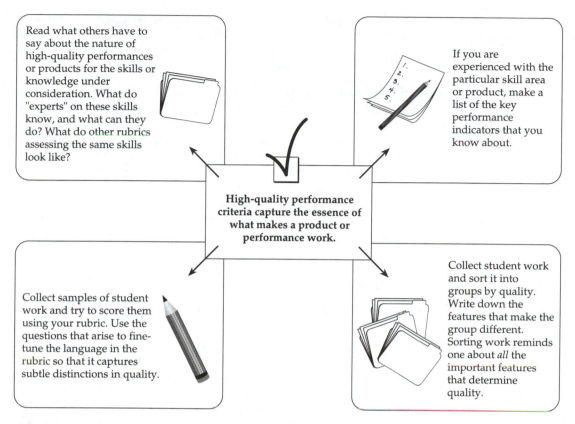

FIGURE 8.14   How to Identify Performance Criteria for Rubrics

Source: Arter, J., & McTighe, J. (2001). *Scoring rubrics in the classroom: Using performance criteria for assessing and improving student performance.* Thousand Oaks, CA: Corwin Press, p. 34. Reprinted by permission of Corwin-Press, Inc.

FIGURE 8.15   Checklist for Writing and Implementing Rubrics

✓ Do criteria focus on important aspects of the performance?
✓ Is the type of rating matched with purpose?
✓ Are the traits directly observable?
✓ Are the criteria understandable?
✓ Are the traits clearly defined?
✓ Is scoring error minimized?
✓ Is the scoring system feasible?

formances may differ, you need to identify those that are most important. For example, if you are making judgments about writing and use mechanics as one of the criteria, it would not be practical to include every grammatical rule in characterizing the descriptions. Rather, you need to select the few most important aspects, such as tense formation, agreement, and punctuation.

2. Match the Type of Rating with the Purpose of the Assessment. If your purpose is more global and you need an overall judgment, a holistic scale should be used. If the major reason for the assessment is to provide feedback about different aspects of the performance, an analytical approach would be best.

3. The Descriptions of the Criteria Should Be Directly Observable. Try to keep the descriptions focused on behaviors or aspects of products that you can observe directly. You want to use clearly visible, overt behaviors for which relatively little inference is required. Behaviors such as loudness, eye contact, and enunciation are easily and reliably observed. It is best to avoid high-inference criteria that are judged on the basis of behavior, such as attitudes, interests, and effort, because the behaviors are easily faked and are more susceptible to rater error and bias. This means that when the target is affective, the focus needs to be on behaviors that can be directly observed. Avoid the use of adverbs that communicate standards, such as *adequately, correctly,* and *poorly.* These evaluative words should be kept separate from what is observed.

Example

Poor: Demonstrates a positive attitude toward learning keyboarding skills.

Improved: Voluntarily gives to the teacher or other students two reasons why it is important to learn keyboarding skills.

4. The Criteria Should Be Written so That Students, Parents, and Others Understand Them. Recall that the criteria should be shared with students before instruction. The purpose of this procedure is to encourage students to incorporate the descriptions as standards in doing their work. Obviously, if the descriptions are unclear, students cannot apply them to their work and the meaningfulness of your feedback is lessened. Consequently, pay attention to wording and phrases; write so that students easily comprehend the criteria. A helpful approach to ensure understanding is simple but often overlooked—ask the students! It is also helpful to provide examples of student work that illustrate different descriptions.

5. The Characteristics and Traits Used in the Scale Should Be Clearly and Specifically Defined. You need to have sufficient detail in your descriptions so that the criteria are not vague. If a few general terms are used, observed behaviors are open to different interpretations. The wording needs to be clear and unambiguous.

Example (wood shop assignment to build a letter holder)

Poor: Construction is sound.

Improved: Pieces fit firmly together; sanded to a smooth surface; glue does not show; varnish is even.

6. Take Appropriate Steps to Minimize Scoring Error. The goal of any scoring system is to be objective and consistent. Because performance assessment involves professional judgment, some types of errors in particular should be avoided to achieve objectivity and consistency. The most common errors are associated with the *personal bias* and *halo effects* of the person who is making the judgment.

Personal bias results in three kinds of errors. **Generosity error** occurs when the teacher tends to give higher scores; **severity error** results when teachers use the low end of the scale and underrate students' performances. A third type of personal bias is **central tendency error,** in which students are rated in the middle.

The **halo effect** occurs when the teacher's general impression of the student affects scores given on individual traits or performances. If the teacher has an overall favorable impression, he or she may tend to give ratings that are higher than what is warranted; a negative impression results in the opposite. The halo effect is mitigated if the identity of the student is concealed (though this is not possible with most performance assessments), by using clearly and sufficiently described criteria, and by periodically asking others to review your judgments. Halo effects can also occur if the nature of a response to one dimension, or the general appearance of the student, affects your subsequent judgments of other dimensions. That is, if the student does extremely well on the first dimension, there may be a tendency to rate the next dimensions higher, and students who look and act nice may be rated higher. Perhaps the best way to avoid the halo effect is to be aware of its potential for affecting your judgment and monitoring yourself so that it doesn't occur. Other sources of scoring error, such as order effects and rater exhaustion, should also be avoided.

Case Study for Reflection

Here is how a high school teacher recently described the use of student suggestions in the development of a rubric for grading an action-research essay (Strickland and Strickland, 1998):

"So, we did the assessment brainstorming, and put all of the students' suggestions on the blackboard. Then, I asked them to lump the individual points into larger categories, and we arrived at these four: style, structure, quality of argument, and presentation. And then, I told them that they had 100 points to distribute among the four categories. We argued about that for a while, and eventually reached consensus (more or less) on this arrangement: 20, 20, 50, and 10, respectively. It's always interesting listening to the students' arguments about how to do this: The reasoning here was that the essay was content driven, according to the kids, so most of the marks should be for content. I didn't really agree with that: I wanted the reflection, and therefore possibly the structure, to be worth more, but I lost. The whole exercise was quite democratic, especially for a school setting, and I didn't want to impose my values on their opinions. As well, this was not the first time that we had done this kind of negotiated assessment thing during the semester, and so the students knew how to play the game." (p. 86)

Questions for Consideration
1. From this example, what would you say are the advantages and disadvantages of using student suggestions to develop a scoring rubric?
2. Did the issue of grading seem to interfere in any way with the establishment of the criteria?
3. How does the teacher modify the suggestions to incorporate more criteria that he or she believes are important and should be included?

To be consistent in the way you apply the criteria, rescore some of the first products scored after finishing all of the students, and score one criterion for all students at the same time. This helps avoid order and halo effects that occur because of performance on previous dimensions. Scoring each product several times, each time on a different criterion, allows you to keep the overall purpose of the rubric in mind.

7. The Scoring System Needs to Be Feasible.   There are several reasons to limit the number and complexity of criteria that are judged. First, you need to be practical with respect to the amount of time it takes to develop the scoring criteria and do the scoring. Generally, five to eight different criteria for a single product are sufficient and manageable. Second, students will be able to focus only on a limited number of aspects of the performance. Third, if holistic descriptions are too complex, it is difficult and time-consuming to keep all the facets in mind. Finally, it may be difficult to summarize and synthesize too many separate dimensions into a brief report or evaluation.

Summary

This chapter introduced performance assessment as a method to measure skill and product learning targets, as well as knowledge and reasoning targets. Important points made in the chapter include:

- In contrast to paper-and-pencil tests, performance assessment requires students to construct an original response to a task that is scored with teacher judgment.
- Authentic assessment involves a performance task that approximates what students are likely to have to do in real-world settings.
- Performance assessment integrates instruction with evaluation of student achievement and is based on constructivist learning theory. Multiple criteria for judging successful performance are developed, and students learn to self-assess.
- Major limitations of performance assessments include the resources and time needed to conduct them, bias and unreliability in scoring, and a lack of generalization.
- Performance assessment is used most frequently with deep understanding, reasoning, skill, and product learning targets.
- Communication skill targets include reading, writing, and speaking.
- Psychomotor skill targets consist of physical actions (fine motor, gross motor, complex athletic, and visual, and verbal/auditory) and the level to which the action is demonstrated (perception, set, guided response, mechanism, complex overt response, adaptation, and origination).
- Product targets are completed student works, such as papers, written reports, and projects.
- Presentation targets include oral presentations and reports.
- The performance task defines what students are required to do.
- Restricted-type tasks target a narrowly defined skill and have a brief response.

■ Extended-type tasks target complex tasks and have extensive responses. These may take several days or even weeks to complete.

■ The task description needs to clearly indicate the target, student activities, resources needed, teacher role, administrative procedures, and scoring procedures.

■ Effective tasks have multiple targets that integrate essential content and skills, are grounded in real-world contexts, rely on teacher help, are feasible, allow for multiple solutions, are clear, are challenging and stimulating, and include scoring criteria.

■ Scoring criteria are used to evaluate student performances.

■ Criteria are narrative descriptions of the dimensions used to evaluate the students.

■ Rating scales are used to indicate different levels of performance. Holistic scales contain several dimensions together; analytic scales provide a separate score for each dimension.

■ Qualitative rating scales verbally describe different gradations of the dimension. Complete scoring rubrics include both descriptions and evaluative labels for different levels of the dimension.

■ Scoring criteria are based on clear definitions of different levels of proficiency and samples of student work.

■ High-quality scoring criteria focus on important aspects of the performance, match the type of rating (holistic or analytical) with the purpose of the assessment, are directly observable, are understandable, are clearly and specifically defined, minimize error, and are feasible.

SELF-INSTRUCTIONAL REVIEW EXERCISES

1. How does authentic assessment differ from performance assessment?

2. Explain how each of the following words is important in describing the nature of performance assessment: *explain, reasoning, observable, criteria, standards, engaging,* and *prespecified*.

3. Identify each of the following as an advantage (A) or disadvantage (D) of performance assessment.

   a. resource intensive
   b. integrates instruction with assessment
   c. student self-assessment
   d. scoring
   e. reasoning skills
   f. active learning
   g. use of criteria
   h. length

4. Identify each of the following skills as fine motor (FM), gross motor (GM), or complex (C), and use the hierarchy in Figure 8.3 to identify the level of the skill.

   a. making up new dives
   b. tracing a picture of a lion just as the teacher did

   c. making cursive capital letters easily
   d. changing running stride to accommodate an uneven surface

5. Classify each of the following as a restricted (R) or extended (E) performance task.

   a. tie shoes
   b. prepare a plan for a new city park
   c. construct a building from toothpicks
   d. interpret a weather map
   e. enact the Boston Tea Party
   f. read a tide table

6. Evaluate the following performance task description. What is missing?

You have been asked to organize a camping trip in North Dakota. There are seven campers. Indicate what you believe you will need for a three-day trip, and provide reasons for your answer. Also include a detailed itinerary of where you will go while camping. You may use any library resources that you believe are helpful, and you may interview others who have had camping experience. As your teacher, I will answer questions about how you gather information, but I will not evaluate your answer until you have something to turn in.

7. Create a scoring rubric for the task presented in question 6. Show how each of the elements of writing and implementing scoring criteria presented in Figure 8.15 is followed in your answer. Include reasoning skills in your rubric.

ANSWERS TO SELF-INSTRUCTIONAL REVIEW EXERCISES

1. Authentic assessment refers to the nature of the task that approximates what is done in the real world. Performance assessment involves the construction of responses by students—it may or may not be authentic.

2. Students are required to *explain* their responses as well as to produce them; *reasoning* targets are usually assessed, students use *reasoning* skills to demonstrate their proficiency; student performance is judged by what is directly *observable*; *criteria* are used to judge the adequacy of the performance on the basis of *prespecified standards* that relate a description of the performance to a statement of worth; good performance tasks are those that are *engaging* for students.

3. a. D; b. A; c. A; d. D; e. A; f. A; g. A; h. D.

4. a. C, origination; b. FM, guided response; c. FM, mechanism; d. GM, adaptation.

5. a. R; b. E; c. E; d. R; e. E; f. R.

6. As a performance prompt, this isn't too bad, but as a performance task description it could be improved considerably. There is no indication of the targets, whether this is an individual or group project, the administrative process, and most important, no indication of the scoring criteria. It is a fairly authentic task and integrates different subjects. It does say something about the role of the teacher and resources, but more detail on both of these aspects could be provided.

7. There will be individual answers to this question, so you'll need to review each other's work by applying the questions in Figure 8.15. I would begin with an analysis of the essential understandings and skills needed to plan the trip. This would comprise the dimensions that are evaluated (e.g., the ability to use maps, the ability

to understand the impact of terrain and time of year on what will be needed, the extent to which plans follow from assumptions, the logic and soundness of reasons stated). I would then employ a scale to indicate the extent to which each of these dimensions is present (e.g., inadequate, adequate, more than adequate, or absent; developing, proficient, advanced). For example, for the extent to which plans follow from assumptions, you might note the following:

Absent There is no indication of assumptions or how plans are based on assumptions.

Developing Assumptions are not clearly stated but implied; plans are not explicitly related to assumptions but are implied.

Proficient Some assumptions are clearly stated and plans are explicitly related to the assumptions.

Advanced A comprehensive and well-thought-out list of assumptions is used; assumptions are explicitly related to plans.

SUGGESTIONS FOR ACTION RESEARCH

1. Identify a teacher who is using performance assessments and observe students during the assessment. Are they actively involved and on-task? Do they seem motivated, even eager to get feedback on their performance? How "authentic" is the task? Can there be more than one correct answer? Is instruction integrated with the assessment? If possible, interview some students and ask them how they react to performance assessments. What do they like and dislike about them? How do they compare to more traditional types of assessment? How could they be more effective?

2. Devise a performance assessment for some aspect of this chapter. Include the performance task and scoring rubric, using the criteria in Figure 8.8. Critique the assessments through class discussion.

3. Try out some scoring rubrics with teachers. You will need to formulate learning targets and the performance task. Construct exemplars of student work that illustrate different scores. Ask the teachers to give you some feedback about the scoring rubric. Is it reasonable? Does it allow for meaningful differentiation between important dimensions of the task? Is it practical? Would students understand the rubric? How could the scoring rubric be improved?

4. In a small group with other students, do some research on three examples of performance tasks in your field. Do they appear to meet the criteria in Figure 8.8? How could they be improved? Be prepared to present your findings to the class for discussion.

ENDNOTES

1. From "District 214's speech assessment rating guide." (n.d.) Township High School District 214, Arlington Heights, IL.

2. A comparison task from Marzano, Pickering, & McTighe, 1993, p. 50. *Assessing Student Outcomes: Performance assessment using the dimensions of learning model.* Alexandria, VA: ACSD.

3. Herman, J. L., Aschbacher, P. R., & Winters, L. The National Center for Research in Evaluation, Standards and Student Testing (CRESST). *A Practical Guide to Alternative Assessment.* Alexandria, VA: ASCD, p. 58. Copyright © 1992 by The Regents of the University of California.

Portfolios: Assessing Understanding, Reasoning, Skills, and Products

Portfolios are emerging as a prominent type of alternative assessment. Although the term *portfolio assessment* is an evolving concept, some professional standards have been established. It is becoming increasingly clear that this method of collecting and evaluating student work over time has significant advantages over more conventional approaches to assessment. Portfolios are much more than large student folders, however, and using them requires some changes in how students are involved in assessment. In this chapter, we review essential characteristics of effective portfolios, show how they can be integrated with instruction, and illustrate, with examples, how portfolios are designed and implemented.

Characteristics
- Clear purpose
- Systematic and organized sample of work
- Preestablished guidelines
- Student selection of some content
- Student self-reflection
- Documented progress
- Clear scoring criteria
- Conferences
- Advantages/disadvantages

Implementing
- Review nature of portfolios with students
- Supply content
- Include right number of entries
- Include table of contents
- Include student self-evaluation guidelines

PORTFOLIO ASSESSMENT

Teacher Evaluation
- Checklist of contents
- Portfolio structure
- Individual entries
- Entire contents
- Written comments
- Student–teacher conference

Planning
- Identify learning targets
- Identify use
- Identify physical structure
- Determine sources of content
- Determine self-reflection guidelines
- Determine scoring criteria

CHAPTER 9   Concept Map

What Are Portfolios?

In many professions, *portfolio* is a familiar term. Portfolios have constituted the primary method of evaluation in fields such as art, architecture, modeling, photography, and journalism. These professions have realized the value of documenting proficiency, skill, style, and talent with examples of actual work. In education, a **portfolio** can be defined as a purposeful, systematic process of collecting and evaluating student products to document progress toward the attainment of learning targets or show evidence that a learning target has been achieved. Arter and Spandel (1992) point out that portfolios involve student participation in the selection of what is included in the portfolio, specific and predetermined guidelines for the selection of materials and criteria for scoring, and evidence of student self-reflection on what has been accomplished. By including student participation in selection and student self-reflection, there is a clear emphasis on how portfolios are integrated with instruction. This is illustrated nicely by how two secondary teachers define *portfolio* (Porter & Cleland, 1995):

> A collection of artifacts accompanied by a reflective narrative that not only helps the learner to understand and extend learning, but invites the reader of the portfolio to gain insight about learning and the learner. (p. 154)

Defined in this way, then, a portfolio has several essential characteristics (Figure 9.1). First, a portfolio is *purposeful*. There is a clear reason why certain works would be included and how the portfolio is to be used. Second, rather than reflecting a haphazard collection of examples, the portfolio represents a *systematic* and *well-organized* collection of materials that make up a *sample*, not a comprehensive or exhaustive collection, of student work. Third, *preestablished guidelines* are set up so that it is clear what materials should be included. Fourth, students are engaged in the process by *selecting some of the materials* and by continually evaluating and *reflecting* on their work. Fifth, based on clear and well-specified *scoring criteria*, *progress* is documented with the evaluations. Finally, *conferences* are held between teacher and student to review progress, identify areas that need further improvement, and facilitate student reflection.

FIGURE 9.1   Characteristics of Portfolio Assessment

- Clearly defined purpose and learning targets
- Systematic and organized collection of student products
- Preestablished guidelines for what will be included
- Student selection of some of what is included
- Student self-reflection and self-evaluation
- Progress documented with specific products and/or evaluations
- Clear and appropriate criteria for evaluating student products
- Portfolio conferences between students and teachers

Source: Adapted from Arter, J., & Spandel, V. (1992). Using portfolios of student work in instruction and assessment. *Educational Measurement: Issues and Practice, II,* 36–44.

Although the precise nature of what is called *portfolio assessment* will be unique to a particular setting, three models have developed (Valencia & Calfee, 1991). That is, different teachers and school systems use different types of portfolios, depending on their needs and how portfolios fit with other assessments and instruction. The *show-case* portfolio includes a student selection of his or her best work. Because the student chooses the work, each profile of accomplishment is unique and individual profiles emerge. This encourages self-reflection and self-evaluation, but makes scoring more difficult and time-consuming because of the unique structure and content of each port-folio. The *documentation* portfolio is like a scrapbook of information and examples. It may include observations, tests, checklists, and rating scales, in addition to selections by both teachers and students. There is student self-reflection and also external eval-uation. The *evaluation* portfolio is more standardized. The purpose is more to asssess student learning than to enhance instruction, although student self-reflection may be included. Most of the examples are selected by teachers or are predetermined.

Burke (1999) lists the following as more specific types of portfolios.

- Writing—dated writing samples to show progress
- Process Folios—first and second drafts of assignments along with final prod-uct to show growth
- Literacy—combination of reading, writing, speaking, and listening pieces
- Best-Work—student and teacher selections of the student's best work
- Unit—one unit of study
- Integrated—a thematic study that brings in different disciplines
- Yearlong—key artifacts from entire year to show growth
- Career—important artifacts collected to showcase employability
- Standards—evidence to document meeting standards
- Working—collection of all student work before selections are made

Regardless of the specific type or label, portfolios have advantages and dis-advantages that determine whether you will find them useful in your own teach-ing. Portfolios combine the strengths of performance assessments with the ability to provide a continuous record of progress and improvement. The advantages that result serve as compelling reasons to use portfolios if needed resources are pro-vided. Basically, you will want to use portfolios if your instructional goals include improving student self-evaluation and showing concrete evidence of student products that demonstrate improvement. Like any method of assessment, there are limitations and trade-offs, so the choice depends on your overall goals and phi-losophy of instruction and learning.

Advantages

Perhaps the most important advantage of using portfolios, if you want to focus on improving learning rather than simply documenting performance, is that students are actively involved in self-evaluation and self-reflection (Hebert, 1998; Tombari & Borich, 1999; Wolf, 1989). Students become part of the assessment process. They re-flect on their performance and accomplishments, critique themselves, and evaluate their progress. This leads to setting goals for further learning. Students learn that self-evaluation is an important part of self-improvement; portfolios encourage and support critical thinking through student self-reflection. Students also apply decision-making skills in selecting certain works to be included and providing justifications for inclusion. In this sense, portfolios are open and always accessible to the student. This is quite different from teachers maintaining a private record of student accomplishments.

Closely related to self-assessment is the notion that portfolios involve *collaborative assessment.* Students learn that assessment is most effective when it is done with others. In addition to self-reflections, students learn from peer reviews and teacher feedback. They may evaluate the work of others and interact with teachers to come to a better understanding of the quality of their performance.

Another important advantage of portfolios is that they promote an ongoing process wherein students demonstrate performance, evaluate, and revise to learn and produce quality work. Assessment is continuous and integrally related to learning. Rather than being only summative, with scores or grades given at the end of an instructional unit, formal and systematic formative evaluation is conducted. This is different from the type of informal feedback teachers give to students, as summarized in Chapter 5. With portfolios, well-developed criteria are used to continually evaluate student progress.

Because portfolios contain samples of student work over time, they focus on self-improvement rather than comparison with others. The samples clearly document how students have progressed. This reinforces the idea that what is most important is how each student, as an individual, improves. This helps to focus the assessment on what is done correctly and on strengths, rather than on weaknesses or what is wrong. Because each student has a unique set of materials in his or her portfolio, assessment and learning are individualized. Thus, portfolios easily accommodate individual differences among students, even though the overall learning targets are the same, and can show unique capabilities and accomplishments. From the standpoint of constructivist learning theory, this kind of individualization is needed. As we will see, however, this is also a disadvantage when it comes to scoring.

Motivation is enhanced as students see the link between their efforts and accomplishments and as they exert greater control over their learning. They become more engaged in learning because both instruction and assessment shift from being completely externally controlled by the teacher to a mix of external and internal control. A sixth-grade teacher relates this kind of impact on students (Martin-Kniep, 1998): "With this portfolio, I saw better work than I had in the past. Students were more excited than they had ever been in my class. They were thrilled about what they had accomplished" (p. 60). As pointed out by Tombari and Borich (1999), this enables teachers to focus on students' persistence, effort, and willingness to change.

A hallmark of portfolios is that they contain examples of student products. This emphasis on products is helpful in several ways. First, products reinforce the importance of performance assessment to students and parents. Products provide excellent evidence to help teachers diagnose learning difficulties, meet with students, and provide individualized feedback. The concrete examples provided by the products are very helpful in explaining student progress to parents. It is much easier to clarify reasons for your evaluations when you have a set of examples in a parent conference. The emphasis on products also reminds teachers that there is a need to focus on performance activities.

Finally, portfolios are flexible. They can be adapted to different ages, types of products, abilities, interests, and learning styles. There is no single set of procedures, products, or grading criteria that must be used. You have the opportunity to customize your portfolio requirements to your needs and capabilities, to different learning targets, to available resources, and, most important, to differences among the students.

Here is how one mathematics teacher describes student reactions to what was obviously a positive experience (Stenmark, 1991):

> The students liked the portfolio. They felt it allowed them to "mess up" and not be penalized. They liked being able to choose the quality of the work. A test is only one grade and is not always your best effort. They felt a combination of the two, test and portfolio, was a good measure of what they had learned. The portfolio really was a cumulation of everything I had been trying. It reflected a wide variety of assignments and assessments. It forced me to use and acknowledge the principles of learning that are being uncovered by researchers. The students liked it, and I did too! (p. 35)

Disadvantages

There are some limitations to using portfolios. Like other performance assessments, scoring is the major drawback. Not only is scoring time-consuming, research on the reliability of scoring portfolios has shown that it is also difficult to obtain high inter-rater reliability. Inconsistent scoring results from criteria that are too general and can be interpreted differently, from such detailed criteria that raters are overwhelmed, or from the inadequate training of raters. Usually, criteria are too general, and raters have not received much training.

A second disadvantage is that portfolio assessment takes considerable time and other resources to do correctly. Many hours are needed to design the portfolios and scoring criteria, and many more hours will be spent reviewing, scoring, and conferencing with students and parents. Additional time may be needed to obtain the training to feel confident and to implement the portfolios properly. You need to decide if this amount of time is worth the effort. Let me emphasize that time and resources are needed to do portfolio assessment *correctly*. It's not the same as producing a folder of student work. Portfolio assessment, when done correctly, is very demanding; it requires time, expertise, and commitment.

A final limitation to consider is the potential for limited generalizability. With portfolios, you generalize from the examples and demonstrated performance according to the criteria to broader learning targets. In doing this, we need to be careful that the generalization is justified and that what is in the portfolio provides each student with a fair opportunity to demonstrate his or her level of competency on the general learning target. For example, if you are making judgments about the ability of a student to communicate by writing and the only types of writing in the portfolio are creative and expository, then the validity of the conclusion about writing more generally is weak. Figure 9.2 summarizes the advantages and disadvantages of portfolio assessment.

FIGURE 9.2   Advantages and Disadvantages of Portfolio Assessment

Advantages	Disadvantages
• Promotes student self-assessment • Promotes collaborative assessment • Enhances student motivation • Systematic assessment is ongoing • Focus is on improvement, not comparisons with others • Focus is on students' strengths—what they can do • Assessment process is individualized • Allows demonstration of unique accomplishments • Provides concrete examples for parent conferences • Products can be used for individualized teacher diagnosis • Flexibility and adaptability	• Scoring difficulties may lead to low reliability • Teacher training needed • Time-consuming to develop criteria, score, and meet with students • Students may not make good selections of which materials to include • Sampling of student products may lead to weak generalization • Parents may find portfolios difficult to understand

Planning for Portfolio Assessment

The process of planning and implementing portfolio assessment is illustrated in Figure 9.3. In this section of the chapter, we examine the planning phase of the process, which is represented in the first four steps. These steps are completed before implementation. Suggestions for planning are presented in the form of a checklist in Figure 9.4.

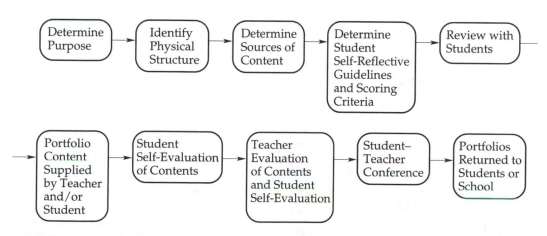

FIGURE 9.3   Steps for Planning and Implementing Portfolio Assessment

FIGURE 9.4   Checklist for Planning Portfolio Assessment

✓ Are learning targets clear?
✓ Are uses of the portfolio clear?
✓ Is the physical structure for holding materials adequate and easily accessed?
✓ Are procedures for selecting the content clear?
✓ Does the nature of the content match the purpose?
✓ Are student self-reflective guidelines and questions clear?
✓ Are scoring criteria established?

Purpose

Designing a portfolio begins with a clear idea about the purpose of the assessment. This involves both the specific learning targets and the use of the portfolio.

Learning Targets.   As suggested by the title of this chapter, portfolios may be used to assess understanding but are ideal for assessing product, skill, and reasoning targets. This is especially true for multidimensional skills such as writing, reading, and problem solving that are continually improved and demonstrated through products. With extensive self-reflection, critical thinking is an important target. Students also develop metacognitive and decision-making skills. As with other performance assessments, portfolios generally are not very efficient for assessing knowledge targets.

It is important to distinguish between learning targets for individual work samples and for the contents of the portfolio as a whole. The targets that reflect all contents tend to be broader and more general, such as "development as a reader," "adapts writing to audience," "speaks clearly," and "adapts writing style to different purposes." Further examples of learning targets for the portfolio as a whole are illustrated in Figure 9.14. Notice that the scoring is holistic, which matches the more general nature of the targets.

Uses.   I have already mentioned three primary uses for portfolios: documentation, showcasing, and evaluation. You need to indicate the degree to which each one is important because this will influence the contents of the portfolio and the criteria used for evaluation. For example, if the primary purpose is to document typical student work and progress, the portfolio will be highly individualized. It will tend to be a relatively loosely organized collection of samples selected by both the teacher and the student, accompanied by both student and teacher evaluations. There are many entries, representing different levels of performance, because the goal is to show what is typical, not necessarily the student's best work.

If the primary purpose is to illustrate what students are capable of doing, then the orientation is more toward a showcase type of portfolio. Only the student's best work is included. The emphasis is on student selection, self-reflection, and self-assessment, rather than on standardization for evaluation. This approach uses the portfolio to celebrate and showcase what each individual has achieved. Teachers often display the results in a book or folder. There may or may not be much indication of progress, but the emphasis is clearly on what has been accomplished rather than on improvement.

If the portfolios are used primarily for evaluation, there will be greater standardization about what to include and how the portfolios are reviewed. Most samples are selected by the teacher, and scoring is emphasized.

Some portfolios are used to show parents and others what students have achieved. If this is the primary purpose, more attention needs to be given to what will make sense to parents, with somewhat less attention to student self-reflection. In contrast, if portfolios are used primarily diagnostically and with students to help them progress, then more time is spent with student–teacher conferences during the school day. If the purpose is to help students self-reflect or peer review, then structure and support for these activities needs to be provided.

Most teachers implement portfolios for multiple purposes. Because your time and energy are limited, try to identify a *primary* purpose and design the portfolio based on that purpose. Wiggins (1998) points out that portfolio assessment is often implemented without sufficient attention to purpose and corresponding implications. He indicates, for example, that portfolios can primarily serve as instruction or assessment tools, focus on documentation or evaluation, be controlled by the teacher or student, and contain a sample of best work or show change over time. The specific nature of portfolio assessment differs depending on the importance of these various purposes. As a consequence, determining primary purpose, with clarity, is critical.

Identify Physical Structure

Once your purpose has been clarified, you need to think about some practical aspects of the portfolio. What will it look like? Most portfolios are contained in envelopes or folders. How large do the folders need to be? Where are they stored so that students can have easy access to them? Do you have boxes to put them in? Commonly used containers include cardboard boxes, file folders, file cabinets, cereal boxes, and accordion files. Putting folders on shelves where they are visible and accessible tells students they are important and should be used continuously. Your choices for these physical demands will influence to some extent what will be put in the portfolios. In addition, you will need to think about the actual arrangement of the documents in the portfolio. Is it done chronologically, by subject area, or by type of document? What materials will be needed to separate the documents?

Determine Sources of Content

The content of a portfolio consists of work samples and student and teacher evaluations. Work samples are usually derived directly from instructional activities, so that products that result from instruction are included. The range of work samples is extensive, determined to some extent by the subject. For example, in language arts you could use entries from student journals, book reports, audiotapes of oral presentations, workbook assignments, and poetry. In science, you might include lab reports, questions posed by students for further investigation, drawings, solutions to problems, and pictures of projects.

Select categories of samples that will allow you to meet the purpose of the portfolio. If you need to show progress, select tasks and samples that are able to show improvement. If you need to provide feedback to students on the procedures they use in putting together a report, be sure to include a summary of that process as part of the portfolio. Use work samples that capitalize on the advantages of portfolios, such as flexibility, individuality, and authenticity. The categories should allow for sufficient variation so that students can show individual work. This often means giving students choices about what they can include.

In some school systems, certain *core* items are required to be collected for all students. This is sometimes referred to as an *indicator* system. For example, in language arts the district may require each student to include at least three writing samples, two oral reading passages, reading logs, and four independent reading reports.

To give you a better idea of the types of work samples to include, refer to the examples in Figures 9.5 and 9.6. It is also helpful to consult other sources that include different kinds of portfolios. A number of books on portfolio assessment contain examples,[1] and examples are included in the performance assessment database referenced in Chapter 8.

Determine Student Self-Reflective Guidelines and Scoring Criteria

Before implementing a portfolio assessment, you need to establish guidelines for student self-reflection and the scoring criteria you will use when evaluating student performance. This needs to be done so that both the guidelines and criteria can be explained to students *before* they begin their work. In many cases, students can be involved in the development of self-reflective guidelines and scoring criteria. By working on these together, students will develop greater ownership of the process and will have experience in working collaboratively with you. However, keep in mind that, as the teacher, you have ultimate responsibility to control the process to ensure integrity and high quality. You will also need to be prepared to tell them how their portfolios will be evaluated.

Implementing Portfolio Assessment

Planning is complete. Now you begin the process of actually using the portfolios with your students. This begins with explaining to students what portfolios are and how they will be used. The checklist in Figure 9.7 summarizes the suggestions for effective implementation and use.

FIGURE 9.5   Examples of Portfolio Work Samples

Language Arts[1]	Mathematics[2]
• Projects, surveys, reports, and units from reading and writing	• A solution to an open-ended question done as homework
• Favorite poems, songs, letters, and comments	• A mathematical autobiography
• Interesting thoughts to remember	• Papers that show the student's correction of errors or misconceptions
• Finished samples that illustrate wide writing: persuasive, letters, poetry, information, stories	• A photo or sketch made by the student of a student's work with manipulatives or with mathematical models of multidimensional figures
• Examples of writing across the curriculum: reports, journals, literature logs	
• Literature extensions: scripts for drama, visual arts, written forms, webs, charts, time lines, murals	• A letter from the student to the reader of the portfolio, explaining each item
• Student record of books read and attempted	• A report of a group project, with comments about the individual's contribution
• Audiotape of reading	• Work from another subject area that relates to mathematics, such as an analysis of data collected and presented in a graph for social studies
• Writing responses to literacy components: plot, setting, point of view, character development, links to life, theme, literary links and criticism	
• Writing that illustrates critical thinking about reading	• A problem made up by the student
• Notes from individual reading and writing conference	• Artwork done by the student, such as string designs, coordinate pictures, and scale drawings or maps
• Items that are evidence of development of style: organization, voice, sense of audience, choice of words, clarity	• Draft, revised, and final versions of student work on a complex mathematical problem, including writing, diagrams, graphs, charts
• Writing that shows growth in usage of traits—growing ability in self-correction, punctuation, spelling, grammar, appropriate form, and legibility	• A description by the teacher of a student activity that displayed understanding of a mathematical concept or relation
• Samples in which ideas are modified from first draft to final product	
• Unedited first drafts	
• Revised first drafts	
• Evidence of effort—improvement noted on pieces, completed assignments	

[1]*Source:* Tierney, R. J., Carter, M. A., & Desai, L. E. (1991). *Portfolio assessment in the reading-writing classroom*, Norwood, MA: Christopher-Gordon Publishers, pp. 72–74. Used with the permission of the publisher.

[2]*Source:* Reprinted with permission from *Mathematics assessment: Myths, models, good questions, and practical suggestions*, by Jean Kerr Stenmark, p. 37. Copyright © 1991 by the National Council of Teachers of Mathematics. All rights reserved.

LANGUAGE ARTS PORTFOLIO

Integrated Unit on Spiders

Table of Contents

1. Letter to parents about what students have learned
2. Book review of *Charlotte's Web*
3. Web of characteristics of spiders
4. Water-color picture of spiders
5. Tape of student reading story, about spiders
6. Original short story (first and final drafts) about a spider
7. Science report on "arachnids"
8. Spider rap song
9. Pictures of group project on spiders
10. Self-assessment using a criteria checklist

GEOMETRY PORTFOLIO

Table of Contents

1. My "Math Phobia" Journal
2. Two geometry tests—corrections included
3. Glossary of geometry terms
4. Drawings of geometric shapes
5. Three problem-solving logs
6. String geometric design
7. Video of group project on angles
8. Essay on video, "Why Math?"
9. Research on math-related careers
10. Self-evaluation of portfolio using rubrics
11. Goal-setting for next quarter

BIOLOGY PORTFOLIO

Table of Contents

1. Reports on careers related to the field of biology
2. One lab report
3. One problem-solving log
4. Pamphlet on diabetes (group project)
5. Video of group presentation on the circulatory system.
6. Essay on germ warfare
7. Research paper on AIDS
8. Tape-recorded interview with college biology professor about AIDS
9. Self-evaluation of portfolio: using rubric
10. Goal-setting web

AMERICAN HISTORY PORTFOLIO

Table of Contents

1. Annotated bibliographies of five books written about the Civil War
2. Reading list of fifty books and articles related to the Civil War
3. One abstract of a research article
4. Tape of interview with local historian
5. Journal entries of trip to Gettysburg
6. Map of the Battle of Gettysburg
7. Video of oral presentation on Pickett's charge
8. Research paper on military tactics used at the Battle of Gettysburg
9. Venn diagram comparing Battle of Gettysburg and Battle of Chancellorsville
10. Critique of TV miniseries *The Civil War*
11. Peer evaluation of portfolio using rubric

FIGURE 9.6   Examples of Portfolio Contents

Source: From *The mindful school: How to assess authentic learning,* 3rd edition, by Kay Burke © 1999, 1994, 1993 Skylight Training and Publishing Inc. Reprinted by permission of Skylight Professional Development, www.skylightedu.com or (800) 348-4474.

FIGURE 9.7   **Checklist for Implementing and Using Portfolios**

- ✓ Are students knowledgeable about what a portfolio is and how it will be used?
- ✓ Do students know why portfolios are important?
- ✓ Are students responsible for or involved in selecting the content?
- ✓ Is there a sufficient number of work samples but not too many?
- ✓ Is a table of contents included?
- ✓ Are specific self-evaluation questions provided?
- ✓ Is the checklist of contents complete?
- ✓ Are scoring criteria for individual items and entire contents clear?
- ✓ Are individualized teacher-written comments provided?
- ✓ Are student–teacher conferences included?

Review with Students

Because many students will not be familiar with portfolios, you will need to explain carefully what is involved and what they will be doing. Begin with your learning targets, show examples, and give students opportunities to ask questions. Try to provide just enough structure so students can get started without telling them exactly what to do. Put yourself in the student's place—if you had to do this new thing, what would be your response and what would you like to know?

Consider some examples of ninth-grade student responses to learning that they will be doing portfolios in their English class (Gold, 1992). The teacher reports the following:

> To introduce the portfolios, I explained that, in addition to completing the reading and essays assigned in the standard syllabus, students would be composing a portfolio of outside writing. Each week they were to find something that sparked their imagination, sympathy, or indignation and then write about it . . . they would continue to file their pieces until June, when they would choose several for grading. (p. 22)

Some students responded:

> I hate the idea of doing a portfolio.
>
> I don't want to do all these writings because (1) I never was a good writer, (2) I have always felt writing is a waste of time, (3) I'm afraid I'll be behind the other students.
>
> [It is] just something else to worry about.
>
> Why am I doing this? It will be so boring. (p. 22)

Obviously these students were skeptical, and this type of reaction may be typical for students who have had little experience with portfolios. You will need to be prepared to help students understand why the process is important. If ungraded, portfolios may be viewed as busywork and not taken very seriously.

Supplying Portfolio Content

Who selects the content of the portfolio—the student, teacher, or both? If both the student and teacher supply samples, what should the proportions be? Are the entries prescribed? Answers to these questions depend on the age and previous experience of students and the purpose of the portfolio. It is not advisable to have preschool and primary students assume sole responsibility for selecting all the samples for their portfolios, although they certainly can be consulted and play an active role in selection. Older students should assume more responsibility for selection, although even older students who are inexperienced with portfolios will initially need considerable structure. Even if students are primarily responsible for selecting the contents, it will be helpful to provide guidelines about the nature of the works to be included. When the portfolios are used primarily for evaluation, it is best for teachers to make the selections or specifically prescribe what to include.

When deciding who will select the content, you need to consider somewhat conflicting goals. On the one hand, you want to foster student ownership and involvement, which is enhanced when students have input into what to include. On the other hand, you will probably need some degree of standardization so that equitable evidence of student performance and improvement is provided. This is best accomplished with greater teacher control. One effective compromise is for students and teachers to decide together what to include with nonrestrictive guidelines. For example, students can select, in consultation with the teacher, three pieces they believe demonstrate their writing ability and progress for a semester. Another approach is to give students some restrictions and include student explanations of the choices. The teacher might prescribe the categories of writing samples, such as poem, persuasive essay, and technical report, and students would select within each of these categories (Arter & Spandel, 1992). Regardless of who makes the selections, however, there need to be clear guidelines for what is included, when it should be submitted, and how it should be labeled.

Questions about the number of samples also need to be answered. You will find that too many indiscriminate samples become overwhelming and difficult to organize, but too few items will not provide enough information to be useful. A portfolio with more complex products that take a longer time to create will have fewer samples than one that illustrates the growth of a number of relatively simple skills. A general rule of thumb for a documentation portfolio is to add one sample every week or two, for a total of ten to fifteen different items. For showcase portfolios, as few as three samples may be sufficient. Some teachers differentiate between a *working* portfolio, in which students keep most of their work, and a *display* or *final* portfolio, in which selections are made from the working portfolio. Haertel (1990) suggests a value-added approach, in which students include only those samples that contribute to understanding how the student has improved or progressed. That is, the student or teacher might ask, "What value is added by each piece of evidence?" If a piece doesn't contribute something new, it's not included. The fewest number of samples will be contained in an evaluation portfolio, in which only samples that illustrate final performance are included.

To organize the portfolio, it is best to include a table of contents that can be expanded with each new entry. The table, which should be located at the beginning (some are pasted to the back of the front page of the folder), should include a brief description, date produced, date submitted, and date evaluated. A sample table can be provided, but ownership is enhanced if students have some flexibility to develop their own table or overview. Directions to students could be something like, "Suppose someone who doesn't know you is looking at your portfolio and you are not there to tell them important things. What would you need to tell them so that they could follow and understand your portfolio?" (Collins & Dana, 1993, p. 17).

Here is what Vicki Walker, a middle school mathematics teacher, says about the importance of using a table of contents (Lambdin & Walker, 1994):

> Since I've required a table of contents, I get far fewer portfolios that are just piles of papers with fragmented thoughts attached. Students seem to be more thorough regarding the layout of their work and the overall appearance of their portfolios, perhaps because they have more of a sense of a completed project. Each portfolio now has a definite beginning and end and a clearer vision-at-a-glance of what it contains and what message it is meant to convey. Furthermore, the table of contents allows for easier perusal on my part and has saved me a great deal of time during my evaluation process. (p. 321)

Student Self-Evaluations

One of the most challenging aspects of using portfolios is getting students to the point where they are comfortable, confident, and accurate in analyzing and criticizing their own work. These *reflective* or *self-evaluation* activities need to be taught. Most students have had little experience with reflection, so one of the first steps in using a portfolio is getting students comfortable with simple and nonthreatening forms of self-evaluation. One useful strategy to accomplish this is to begin with teacher modeling and critiques. Once students understand what is involved by seeing examples (e.g., using an overhead of work from previous, unnamed students), they can begin to engage in their own reflections orally with each other. After they have engaged in these elementary forms of reflection, are they prepared to proceed to more complex self-evaluations? This can take several weeks.

A good way to introduce students to self-evaluation is to have them label various pieces as "Best Work," "Most Creative," "Most Difficult," "Most Effort," "Most Fun," "Most Improved," and so on.

Students are used to sentence completion exercises in which they are given a stem, so the next step could be the use of such items to structure student evaluations. For example:

> This piece shows that I've met the standard because . . .
>
> This piece shows that I really understand the process because . . .
>
> If I could show this piece to anyone, I would pick _____ because . . .
>
> The piece that was my biggest challenge was _____ because . . .
>
> One thing that I have learned from doing this piece is that I . . .

Finally, questions can be asked to give students less structure in how to respond:

What did you learn from writing this piece?

What would you have done differently if you had more time?

What are your greatest strengths and weaknesses in this sample?

What would you do differently if you did this over?

What problems or obstacles did you experience when doing this? How would you overcome these problems or obstacles next time?

Is this your best work? Why or why not?

What will you do for your next work?

If you could work more on this piece of writing, what would you do?

Which sample would you say is most unsatisfying? Give specific reasons for your evaluation. How would you revise it so that it was more satisfying?

How did your selection change from rough draft to final copy?

Such reflection is completed for each individual work sample, for groups of pieces, and then for the portfolio as a whole. Student responses are insights into how involved students have been in reaching the learning target, what the students perceive to be their strengths, and how instruction can be tailored to meet needs (sometimes a student's perceived strengths are inaccurate and need to be corrected). Figures 9.8 and 9.9 present examples of student responses to self-reflective prompts. In Figure 9.8, students were asked to select a piece of writing that "is important to them," and explain why they made the selection. In this example, the responses from the same three students are indicated, appearing in the same order. The answers, although varied, illustrate what students think about themselves and what they believe they need to work on in the future. Figure 9.9 shows how younger students, in this case third graders, can be involved in self-reflection.

Students often are asked to engage in peer evaluations. These can be very helpful, especially when students are beginning to get used to the idea of self-reflection and the teacher is trying to establish a trusting environment. The focus of peer evaluations is on analysis and the constructive, supportive criticism of strategies, styles, and other concrete aspects of the product. Here are three examples of the type of feedback that you can provide to students. In this situation, students were asked to give advice to one another and to comment on "standout" selections (Lambdin & Walker, 1994):

> When I looked at the portfolio selections with Shawn, I noticed a lot of things I could have done better on. For instance, on my problem-solving section I did not do so good because it was the beginning of the year and I had not really gotten into school yet.
>
> I worked with Jeff today. He helped me see many things about my papers but most of all he helped me pick my best work. This is "How many books are in the library?" This work shows reasoning, estimation, observations, and many other things. This is why this work stands out so well. It shows what my work was. This was also challenging and exciting to me. Even though my estimation was 5,600 and

**FIGURE 9.8   Middle and High School Student Responses
to Self-Reflection Questions**

Why did you select this particular piece of writing?

"I believe it's my best piece all year. I think it's a very strong piece."
"It's the most thoughtful piece I have written all year."
"I had to use more references to do this writing, and you can see this by how much more details [*sic*] are in it."

What do you see as the special strengths of this paper?

"It shows that I can write a unique piece, different from the rest of the crowd."
"The wording and the form."
"I sense a strong ability to spot details from the text."

What was especially important when you were writing this piece?

"I wanted to write something that would stand out, that people would notice. And it was."
"What I thought friendship was all about."
"My main goal was to defend a thesis with as much information as possible."

What have you learned about writing from your work on this piece?

"I can begin to write something, and end up with something totally different."
"Writing a poem wasn't as hard as it seems."
"I have learned that when you are writing you must always stick to the topic."

If you could go on working on this piece, what would you do?

"I would make it longer, taking off the end, making many more levels of anticipation."
"Be more descriptive."
"I would go into the different ways each of the boys handled their tribes."

What kind of writing would you like to do in the future?

"Short stories, POEMS!"
"Narrative."
"I have always wanted to write a murder mystery."

Source: Camp, R. (1992). Portfolio reflections in middle and secondary school classrooms. In K. B. Yancy (Ed.), *Portfolios in the writing classroom*. Urbana, IL: National Council of Teachers of English. Copyright © 1992 by the National Council of Teachers of English. Reprinted with permission.

the actual was 19,000 I still think my reasoning and attitude towards this project was very good [*sic*].

Today I worked with Andrew. Helped me see the things I was doing wrong. I had a codecracker which didn't show a lot but he helped me see how to make it work. He told me to add an explanation about it for it to fit. I think a standout piece is my million's project. It shows everything I need. It has the original problem plus it shows all my work. It has an explanation about the problem and what we did. (p. 322)

More comprehensive reflection is done on all the contents of the portfolio, at the end of the semester or year. This evaluation focuses much more on the overall

REFLECTION

NAME _Allyza_   DATE _____

I selected this piece because _I thought it had very good hand writing and it was about me and my best friend Saron._

This piece's strengths are _It's hand-writing._

One thing I learned from completing this piece is _even when you pick out of a hat you can get what you want!_

One thing I would like to change or improve about this piece is _I think I should have wrote a bit more._

FIGURE 9.9 Elementary Student Self-Reflection

Source: An ASCD professional inquiry kit promoting learning through student data by Marian Leibowitz, ASCD, 1999, Folder 5 Activity 3, p. 10. Reprinted by permission. All rights reserved.

learning target. Notice how the following questions are different from what is asked about a single piece or sample in the portfolio (Camp, 1992):

What do you notice about your earlier work?

Do you think your writing has changed?

What do you know now that you did not know before?

At what points did you discover something new about writing?

How do the changes you see in your writing affect the way you see yourself as a writer?

Are there pieces you have changed your mind about—that you liked before, but don't like now, or didn't like before but do like now? If so, which ones? What made you change your mind?

In what ways do you think your reading has influenced your writing? (p. 76)

Here is how one twelfth-grade student answered these questions (Camp, 1992):

When I look back at my writing from the beginning of the year I realize that I have changed tremendously as a writer. My earlier work is not as explicit and does not seem like anything I would write now. . . . I know now that revising your work adds a great deal to the quality of the piece. If I may quote [my teacher], "Nothing is ever perfect the first time." Each piece of writing we did made me realize more and more things that could make my writing better. After these changes have been made I find that I look upon myself as a better and more sophisticated writer. At the beginning of this year I thought my "Lady and the Tiger" piece was the best I could ever do. When I look at it now I see a lot of places in which I could change it to make it 100% better. (pp. 77–78)

A more structured kind of self-reflection is illustrated in Figure 9.10 for a middle school social studies class.

Student self-reflection can also include comments or a review by parents. One of the advantages of using portfolios is that they are well-suited to parent involvement. At the beginning of the year, you will need to inform parents about what portfolios are and how they as parents can actively participate to be helpful. Students can consult their parents when selecting work samples, and parents can help students reflect on their work. Informally, parents can continuously provide advice and encouragement. More formally, parents can complete a form or answer a specific set of questions. A good example of this type of review is illustrated in Figure 9.11. Students can then incorporate parent comments and suggestions into their own reflection.

Teacher Evaluation

Teachers evaluate the contents of a portfolio in several different ways. These include checklists of contents, evaluations of the overall quality of how well the portfolio has been put together, evaluations of individual entries, and evaluations of learning targets as demonstrated by all the contents. We'll consider each of these types.

Checklists of Contents.   A summary to ensure that the contents of the portfolio are complete is often provided in the form of a simple checklist. The checklist can vary according to the level of specificity desired and by the audience. Some checklists are relatively brief, and others are long and detailed. A student checklist is illustrated in Figure 9.12. Others can be designed for teachers, administrators, or parents. Student checklists tend to be brief, but those for teachers and schools are typically more comprehensive.

Portfolio Structure Evaluation.   Portfolios can be evaluated according to how well students have demonstrated skill in completing the structural requirements, such as

FIGURE 9.10   Structured Student Assessment of Portfolio

Personal Assessment of Portfolio

Dear Student: Your portfolio consists of all the writing assignments you have completed in social studies thus far. This form will assist you in monitoring your portfolio and determining the strengths and weaknesses of your writing.

Part I: Read the statements below. Write the number that most honestly reflects your self-assessment. (Scale 1–5: 5=strong, 4=moderately strong, 3=average, 2=moderately weak, 1=weak)

_____ **1.** My portfolio contains all of the items required by my teacher.

_____ **2.** My portfolio provides strong evidence of my improvement over the course of the unit.

_____ **3.** My portfolio provides strong evidence of my ability to report factual information.

_____ **4.** My portfolio provides strong evidence of my ability to write effectively.

_____ **5.** My portfolio provides strong evidence of my ability to think and write creatively.

Part II: On the lines below, write the topic of each assignment. Rate your *effort* for each piece. (5=strong effort, 1=weak effort) In the space below write one suggestion for improving that piece.

_____ **1.** _____
_____

_____ **2.** _____
_____

_____ **3.** _____
_____

_____ **4.** _____
_____

_____ **5.** _____
_____

Part III: In assessing my overall portfolio, I find it to be (check one)

Very satisfactory   _____   Satisfactory   _____
Somewhat satisfactory   _____   Unsatisfactory   _____

Part IV: In the space below list your goal for the next marking period and three strategies you plan to use to achieve it.

Goal:

Strategies: 1.

2.

3.

Source: Goerss, D. V. (1993). Portfolio assessment: A work in process. *Middle School Journal, 25*(2), 20–24. Reprinted with permission from National Middle School Association.

FIGURE 9.11   Example of Parent Review and Evaluation Form

Parent Folder Review and Reflection

Student _____

Reader _____

Date _____

Please read everything in your child's writing folder, including drafts and commentary. Each piece is set up in back-to-front order, from rough draft to final copy. Further, each piece is accompanied by both student and teacher comments on the piece and writing process. Finally, the folders also include written questionnaires where students write about their strengths and weaknesses as writers.

We believe that the best assessment of student writing begins with the students themselves but must be broadened to include the widest possible audience. We encourage you to become part of the audience.

When you have read the folder, please talk to your children about their writing. In addition, please take a few minutes to respond to these questions.

- Which piece of writing in the folder tells you most about your child's writing?
- What does it tell you?
- What do you see as the strengths in your child's writing?
- What do you see that needs to be addressed in your child's growth and development as a writer?
- What suggestions do you have that might aid the class's growth as writers?
- Other comments, suggestions?

Thank you so much for investing this time in your child's writing.

Source: Writing portfolio: Current working model (1992). Used with permission of the Pittsburgh Public Schools, Pittsburgh, PA. (Note: Used during 1990s).

FIGURE 9.12   Example of Student Portfolio Checklist

Portfolio Checklist
(For Language Arts Class Only)

Name _____   Date _____

By the end of the year, your portfolio must contain the original copies of the following items:

_____ Student Assessment Letter(s)

_____ Reading Log and Book Reviews

_____ Reading Attitude Survey

_____ Writing Samples

Source: From *Portfolio assessment: Getting started*, by Alan A. De Fina. Copyright © 1992 by Alan A. De Fina. Published by Scholastic Professional Books, New York, p. 79. Reprinted by permission of Scholastic.

the selection of samples, thoroughness, appearance, self-reflection, and organization. These aspects can be evaluated by assigning points to each aspect according to a scale (e.g., 5 = excellent, 1 = poor), by making written comments, or both. When evaluating selections, consider the diversity of the samples, the time periods represented, and overall appropriateness. The quality of student reflection can be judged by the clarity and depth of thought, the level of analysis, and the clarity of communication. Organization can be evaluated by using a checklist to indicate whether required components are included, properly sequenced, and clearly labeled.

Evaluations of Individual Entries. The evaluation of each individual entry in the portfolio can be accomplished with the scoring criteria and rubrics that were discussed in Chapter 8, although often much less standardization is used with portfolios. Many teachers find that more individualized, informal feedback on work samples is effective and efficient, particularly when many items are included in the portfolio. Furthermore, it is likely that not every entry will be evaluated in the same way. However, it is important to provide sufficient feedback so that students know what has been done well and what needs to be improved.

Evaluation of Entire Contents. The learning targets for the portfolio as a whole are not the same as those for individual entries. Likewise, the criteria for judging progress toward meeting learning targets of all the contents together is different from what is used for each entry. The language of the evaluation reflects the more general nature of the target. The words used also emphasize the developmental nature of learning because the purpose is to focus on student improvement and progress. Thus phrases such as "students demonstrate the ability to understand increasingly complex software programs," "a greater number of self-evaluative criteria applied," "increased understanding of," or "increased ability to" are used. The scoring tends to be holistic because a number of different pieces of evidence are used to arrive at an overall judgment. Here is how one teacher describes holistic scoring for a mathematics portfolio (Stenmark, 1991):

> When it came to grading, I used a holistic method. I sorted portfolios into three main piles and then subdivided within those piles. I found myself basing my decisions on the kinds of assignments selected, tending to value those with writing more than those that showed straight computation, and on the quality of assignments, tending to value those that showed more mathematical understanding. (p. 37)

Three examples of scoring criteria for overall judgments are illustrated in Figures 9.13 and 9.14. You will also want to be sure to include individualized written comments for each student. This descriptive summary of performance and progress should highlight changes that have occurred, strengths, and areas that need improvement. It's usually best to point out the strengths and improvements first and then use language to address weaknesses that tells clearly what needs improvement but will not discourage students or lead them to a sense of futility. Words such as *improving, developing, partial,* or even *novice* are better than *unacceptable* or *inadequate*.

KENTUCKY MATHEMATICS PORTFOLIO
HOLISTIC SCORING GUIDE

Scoring Year: Spring _____

An individual portfolio is likely to be characterized by some, but not all, of the descriptors for a particular level. Therefore, the overall score should be the level at which the appropriate descriptors for the portfolio are clustered.

	NOVICE	APPRENTICE	PROFICIENT	DISTINGUISHED
PROBLEM SOLVING — Understanding/Strategies, Execution/Extensions	• Indicates a basic understanding of problems and uses strategies • Implements strategies with minor mathematical errors in the solution without observations or extensions	• Indicates an understanding of problems and selects appropriate strategies • Accurately implements strategies with solutions, with limited observations or extensions	• Indicates a broad understanding of problems with alternate strategies • Accurately and efficiently implements and analyzes strategies with correct solutions, with extensions	• Indicates a comprehensive understanding of problems with efficient, sophisticated strategies • Accurately and efficiently implements and evaluates sophisticated strategies with correct solutions and includes analysis, justifications, and extensions
REASONING	• Uses mathematical reasoning	• Uses appropriate mathematical reasoning	• Uses perceptive mathematical reasoning	• Uses perceptive, creative, and complex mathematical reasoning
MATHEMATICAL COMMUNICATION — Language, Representations	• Uses appropriate mathematical language some of the time • Uses few mathematical representations	• Uses appropriate mathematical language • Uses a variety of mathematical representations accurately and appropriately	• Uses precise and appropriate mathematical language most of the time • Uses a wide variety of mathematical representations accurately and appropriately; uses multiple representations with some entries	• Uses sophisticated, precise and appropriate mathematical language throughout • Uses a wide variety of mathematical representations accurately and appropriately; uses multiple representations within entries and states their connections
UNDERSTANDING/CONNECTING CORE CONCEPTS	• Indicates a basic understanding of core concepts	• Indicates an understanding of core concepts with limited connections	• Indicates a broad understanding of some core concepts with connections	• Indicates a comprehensive understanding of core concepts with connections throughout
TYPES AND TOOLS	• Includes few types; uses few tools	• Includes a variety of types; uses tools appropriately	• Includes a wide variety of types; uses a wide variety of tools appropriately	• Includes all types; uses a wide variety of tools appropriately and insightfully

PERFORMANCE DESCRIPTORS

PROBLEM SOLVING
• Understands the features of a problem (understands the question, restates the problem in own words)
• Explores (draws a diagram, constructs a model and/or chart, records data, looks for patterns)
• Selects an appropriate strategy (guesses and checks, makes an exhaustive list, solves a simpler but similar problem, works backward, estimates a solution)
• Solves (implements a strategy with an accurate solution)
• Reviews, revises, and extends (verifies, explores, analyzes, evaluates strategies / solutions; formulates a rule)

REASONING
• Observes data, records and recognizes patterns, makes mathematical conjectures (inductive reasoning)
• Validates mathematical conjectures through logical arguments or counter-examples; constructs valid arguments (deductive reasoning)

MATHEMATICAL COMMUNICATION
• Provides quality explanations and expresses concepts, ideas, and reflections clearly
• Uses appropriate mathematical notation and terminology
• Provides various mathematical representations (models, graphs, charts, diagrams, words, pictures, numerals, symbols, equations)

UNDERSTANDING/CONNECTING CORE CONCEPTS
• Demonstrates an understanding of core concepts
• Recognizes, makes, or applies the connections among the mathematical core concepts to other disciplines, and to the real world

WORKSPACE/ANNOTATIONS

Place an X on each continuum to indicate the degree of understanding demonstrated for each core concept.

DEGREE OF UNDERSTANDING OF CORE CONCEPTS				
	BASIC	BROAD	COMPREHENSIVE WITH CONNECTIONS	
	NONE	UNDERSTANDING		
NUMBER				
MATHEMATICAL PROCEDURES				
SPACE & DIMENSIONALITY				
MEASUREMENT				
CHANGE				
MATHEMATICAL STRUCTURE				
DATA				

PORTFOLIO CONTENTS
• Table of Contents
• Student Signature Sheet
• Letter to Reviewer
• 5–7 Best Entries

BREADTH OF ENTRIES

TYPES
○ INVESTIGATIONS/DISCOVERY
○ APPLICATIONS
○ NON-ROUTINE PROBLEMS
○ PROJECTS
○ INTERDISCIPLINARY
○ WRITING

TOOLS
○ CALCULATORS
○ COMPUTER AND OTHER TECHNOLOGY
○ MODELS/MANIPULATIVES
○ MEASUREMENT INSTRUMENTS
○ OTHERS

○ GROUP ENTRY

revised 8/95

FIGURE 9.13 Mathematics Holistic Scoring Guide

Source: Kentucky Department of Education (Office of Curriculum, Assessment, and Accountability), 1995. Used with permission.

FIGURE 9.14 Scoring Criteria for Writing Portfolio

Portfolio Exit Assessment

Student writer # _____   Grade _____

Teacher _____   School _____

Please circle the appropriate numerical ratings for the contents of this portfolio.

Accomplishment in Writing

- meeting worthwhile challenges
- establishing and maintaining purpose
- use of the techniques and choices of the genre
- control of conventions, vocabulary, sentence structure
- awareness of the needs of the audience (organization, development, use of detail)
- use of language, sound, images, tone, voice
- humor, metaphor, playfulness

Performance Rating

No Evidence Present NE	Inadequate Performance 1	2	3	4	5	Outstanding Performance 6

Use of Processes and Resources for Writing

- effective use of prewriting strategies
- use of drafts to discover and shape ideas
- use of conferencing opportunities to refine writing (peers, adult readers)
- effective use of revision (reshaping, refocusing, refining)

Performance Rating

No Evidence Present NE	Inadequate Performance 1	2	3	4	5	Outstanding Performance 6

Development as a Writer

- evidence of investment in writing tasks
- increased engagement with writing
- development of sense of self as a writer
- evolution of personal criteria and standards for writing
- ability to see the strengths and needs in one's writing
- demonstration of risk-taking and innovation in interpreting writing tasks
- use of writing for various purposes, genres, and audiences
- progress from early to late pieces; growth, development

Performance Rating

No Evidence Present NE	Inadequate Performance 1	2	3	4	5	Outstanding Performance 6

Source: Used with permission of the Pittsburgh Public Schools, Pittsburgh, PA. (Note: Used during 1990s).

256

Case Study for Reflection

Ms. Watson is really frustrated with the progress of her ninth-grade English classes. It's already March and state testing is coming up soon. What if her students aren't ready? It seems as though all she has worked on this year has been the writing portfolios. Last year, when her school district required every student to have one, it sounded like a good idea. Who could have known how much time it would take? Teacher conferencing with students, students' conferencing with each other, and students self-evaluating their own progress has taken time away from teaching. She promises herself that next year she will develop some strategies to help the whole process run more smoothly.

Questions for Consideration
1. What mistakes with writing portfolios did Ms. Watson make this school year?
2. Could you help her formulate a list of strategies to try next year so that the process will run more smoothly?

Overall evaluations can also address effort and the student's willingness to learn. A simple scale can be used (e.g., very willing to learn, somewhat willing to learn, resistant to learning) or individual comments can be written.

Student–Teacher Conferences

The final step in implementing portfolios, before returning them to the student or school file, is conducting a conference with each student to review the contents, student reflections, and your evaluations of individual items and all of the work together as related to learning targets. Conferences with students should be scheduled throughout the year; some suggest having one conference each month at the elementary level. Especially early in the year the conferences can be used to clarify purposes and procedures, answer questions, and establish trust. Although scheduling and conducting these conferences takes time, the sessions provide an important link between students and teachers.

It is best if students are given some guidelines to prepare for each conference. During the conference, allow the student to do most of the talking. Have students compare their reflections with your evaluations and make plans for subsequent work. Although weaknesses and areas for improvement need to be covered, show students what is possible and their progress, rather than what is wrong. Make sure that at the end of the conference there is a plan of action for the future. Limit the conference to no more than ten or fifteen minutes. You may want to have students take notes about what was discussed in the conference and make your own brief notes. Focus on one or two major topics or areas at each conference. This helps ensure a full and thoughtful discussion, rather than a superficial treatment of several areas.

FIGURE 9.15   Portfolio Implementation Timelines

Unit	Semester	Yearlong
1. Collect items for three or four weeks.	5. Collect items the entire semester.	10. Collect one to two items each week.
2. Select and reflect on items two weeks prior to the end of the unit.	6. Select seven to ten final items four weeks before the end of the semester.	11. Review all items at the end of each quarter and select three or four items. Date all items.
3. Conduct conferences in the last week.	7. Allow one week for students to select, organize, and reflect on contents.	12. Repeat each quarter. Students write reflections at the end of each quarter.
4. Grade the last week.	8. Allow one week for conferences.	13. Select the final ten to twelve items four weeks before the end of school.
	9. Allow one week for grading.	14. Allow two to three weeks for reflection, organization, and conferencing.
		15. Allow one to two weeks for grading.

Source: Adapted from *The mindful school: How to assess authentic learning,* 3rd edition, by Kay Burke. © 1999, 1994, 1993 Skylight Training and Publishing Inc. Reprinted by permission of Skylight Professional Development, www.skylightedu.com or (800) 348-4474.

Figure 9.15 summarizes steps in the implementation of portfolio assessment with an emphasis on when certain activities take place and the time needed to complete them. Specific timelines will depend on the type of portfolio and the degree of student involvement.

Summary

Portfolios are quickly becoming an important technique for both assessment and instruction. The essence of portfolios is to gather and evaluate, on a continual basis, student products that demonstrate progress toward specified learning targets. By combining principles of performance assessment with student self-reflection, portfolios can be powerful tools to improve student learning. With the flexibility inherent in portfolios, it is possible to individualize assessment so that you can maximize meaningful feedback to each student. Other major points in the chapter include:

- Portfolio assessment is systematic and purposeful.
- Portfolio assessment includes student selection of contents and student self-reflection.

- Different types of portfolios include showcase, documentation, and evaluation.
- Portfolios integrate assessment with instruction by focusing on improvement and progress.
- Portfolios are adaptable to individual students.
- Reliability of scoring is a limitation of portfolios.
- Portfolios require considerable teacher time for preparation and implementation.
- Portfolios may result in limited generalizability.
- Planning for portfolio assessment includes the identification of learning targets and uses, physical structures, sources of content, guidelines for student self-reflection, and scoring criteria.
- Implementing portfolio assessment includes reviewing with students, supplying content, student self-evaluations, teacher evaluations, and student–teacher conferences.
- Students should be meaningfully involved in the selection of work samples.
- Just enough work samples need to be included to meet the purpose of the portfolio.
- A table of contents should be included in the portfolio.
- Student self-evaluation needs to be taught. Students progress to eventually become skilled at analyzing and critiquing their own and others' works.
- The teacher evaluates checklists of contents, the student's ability to put together the portfolio, individual items, and the content as a whole, among other things, which may include scores from rubrics and written comments.
- Student–teacher conferences should be held throughout the year to review progress and establish plans.

SELF-INSTRUCTIONAL REVIEW EXERCISES

1. Indicate whether each of the following is an advantage (A) or disadvantage (D) of using portfolio assessment:

   a. collaboration between student and teacher
   b. student selection of contents
   c. scoring
   d. continuous monitoring of student progress
   e. training teacher to do portfolios
   f. generalizability
   g. student self-evaluation

2. Indicate whether it would be best to use a showcase (S), documentation (D), or evaluation (E) portfolio for each of the following purposes:

   a. to show examples of all of a student's work
   b. for the student to demonstrate his or her best work
   c. to show what students in a class are capable of doing
   d. to indicate the progress of the class on an important target
   e. for grading
   f. to show a student's progress

3. Evaluate the planning that is illustrated by the teacher in the following example. Is what she has planned consistent with what a portfolio is all about? Why or why not? Is her planning adequate? What else does she need to do?

Ms. Taylor has decided to implement a mathematics portfolio in her sixth-grade classroom. She believes the portfolios will increase student learning. She provides manila folders for the students and tells them that they will keep all their math worksheets and tests in it. She tells the students that they will be talking to her periodically about what is in the folder.

4. Match the description or example with the appropriate step in implementing portfolio assessment. Each step can be used more than once or may not be used at all:

    _____ **a.** rubric used to evaluate the sixth writing sample

    _____ **b.** Mr. Lind meets with students once a week

    _____ **c.** students ask questions about how to self-reflect

    _____ **d.** teacher prepares an overhead that outlines the basics of portfolio assessment

    _____ **e.** table of contents is prepared

    _____ **f.** students select three work samples

    _____ **g.** a checklist includes outline and self-reflection categories

    A. review with students
    B. supply content
    C. student self-reflection
    D. teacher evaluation
    E. student–teacher conference

5. The following scenario describes how a middle school social science teacher goes about implementing portfolio assessment in his class. After reading the scenario, review the checklist in Figure 9.7. Use this checklist as criteria to evaluate how well Mr. Trent does in using portfolios.

Gary Trent has read a lot lately about portfolios and decides to use them with his seventh-grade social studies classes. He spends the last week before school fine-tuning what he hopes his students can learn from doing the portfolios. Although he thinks he must give grades to ensure student motivation, he plans to use the portfolios to demonstrate to other teachers what his students are capable of achieving.

Gary decides to ask his students to bring something to class to hold the materials that will go in the portfolio. He explains to his students that they will be selecting one example each week from their work in his class that shows their best effort. Every month students meet with each other to critique what was included, and after the meeting students complete a self-evaluation worksheet. Throughout the semester Gary plans to talk with each student at least once about his or her portfolio.

Near the end of the semester, Gary collects all the portfolios, grades them, and returns them to his students. He makes sure that each student receives individualized comments with the grade.

ANSWERS TO SELF-INSTRUCTIONAL REVIEW EXERCISES

1. a. A; b. A or D (a disadvantage if students are not provided sufficient direction and supervision); c. D; d. A; e. D; f. D; g. A.

2. a. D; b. S; c. S; d. E; e. E; f. D.

3. This is not really portfolio assessment, at least not in the way portfolios have been discussed in this chapter. Neither the teacher nor the students select anything (everything is included), and there is no indication that any performance products are included. There is a lack of specification about the purpose of the portfolio. Folders will be used, but we don't know where they will be placed. There is no indication that student self-reflection guidelines and scoring criteria have been developed.

4. a. D; b. E; c. C; d. A; e. B; f. B; g. D.

5. Gary does something right in using portfolios but needs to be more specific and systematic in a number of areas. It's good that he takes time to plan what he wants to do. However, the stated purpose is not one of the major reasons that portfolios should be used. There is only a brief reference to learning targets and no indication that he has prepared specific scoring criteria or student self-reflection guidelines. Simply asking students to select one example of their work per week is probably too vague. Gary needs to be more specific about what kinds of work should be included and about the physical structure of the portfolio. Because he has several classes, it may not be feasible to store each portfolio in the room. It's not clear that students know enough about portfolios for the procedure to work. It's good that students select the content, and Gary is on target in emphasizing student self-reflection. One problem may be that there will be too many work samples by the end of the semester, making Gary's grading process difficult. It might be better to have students select one work example per week and then at the end of the semester choose a few items from these to demonstrate achievement. Gary's plan to meet with students at least once informally is okay, but there is no provision for a more formal conference near the end of the semester. It's good that he includes individualized written comments.

SUGGESTIONS FOR ACTION RESEARCH

1. Locate two or three examples of portfolios from different teachers. Review the contents of the portfolios carefully, looking for characteristics that have been discussed in this chapter. How are the portfolios alike, and how are they different? Are they being used for different purposes? Is the structure and content appropriate for the intended use?

2. Interview students who have had some experience with portfolios. Ask them what they like and don't like about doing portfolios, how much time it takes them to complete their work, and what the teacher does to help them. Focus on student self-reflection. Ask the students how they have self-evaluated themselves and what they think they have learned from the process.

3. Visit two or three classrooms and see how portfolios are organized and stored. If possible, talk with the teachers to get their views about how to organize portfolios so that they are practical.

4. Devise a student portfolio assignment for students. Include each of the steps in Figure 9.3, and include examples where possible. Then ask two or three teachers to review your assignment and give you feedback on how it could be improved, how much time it would take to implement, how realistic it would be, and what students would probably get out of it.

ENDNOTE

1. For example, *Authentic assessment in practice: A collection of portfolios, performances tasks, exhibitions, and documentation,* by Linda Darling-Hammond, Lynne Einbender, Fred Frelow, & Janine Ley-King, New York: NCREST, 1993; Lambdin & Walker; *Portfolio assessment: A handbook for educators,* by James Barton and Angelo Collins (Eds.), Menlo Park, CA: Innovative Learning Publications, 1997; *An introduction to using portfolios in the classroom,* by Charlotte Danielson and Leslye Abrutyn, Alexandria, VA: Association for Supervision and Curriculum Development, 1997; *The portfolio organizer: Succeeding with portfolios in your classroom,* by Carol Rohleiser, Barbara Bower, and Laurie Stevahn, Alexandria, VA: Association of Supervision and Curriculum Development, 2000; *The portfolio guidebook: Implementing quality in an age of standards,* by Richard Koch and Jean Schwartz, Norwood, MA: Christopher-Gordon, 2000; *The portfolio connection: Student work linked to standards* (2nd ed.), by Kay Burke, Robin Fogarty, and Susan Belgrad, Arlington Heights, IL: SkyLight Professional Development, 2001.

10 Assessing Affective Traits and Dispositions

Chapters 6 to 9 focused on what have traditionally been called *cognitive* learning targets and skills. We now turn to a set of student dispositions and traits that many educators regard as equally important, what have become known as *affective* outcomes. We'll look at how to define affective learning traits and targets and how, practically speaking, to assess these traits and targets in the classroom in a way that improves instruction and student cognitive learning. These targets, if well-conceptualized and assessed, are essential for providing students with the life skills they need.

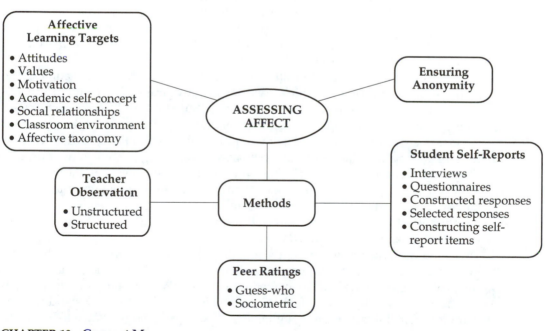

CHAPTER 10 Concept Map

Are Affective Targets Important?

Research has established clear linkages between affect and learning (Ormrod, 1999). Students are more proficient at problem solving when they enjoy what they are doing. Students who are in a good mood and emotionally involved are more likely to pay attention to information, remember it, rehearse it meaningfully, and apply it. Too much anxiety interferes with learning, and an optimum level of arousal is needed for maximum performance. Classrooms with more positive "climates" foster student engagement and learning much more than classrooms with negative climates (Fraser, 1994).

What is interesting about student affect is that despite this research, there is very little, if any, systematic assessment of affect in the classroom (McMillan, Workman, & Myran, 1998; Stiggins & Conklin, 1992). Teachers know that students who are confident about their ability to learn, who like the school subjects they study, who have a positive attitude toward learning, who respect others, and who show a concern for others are much more likely to be motivated and involved in learning. At the same time, though, most teachers do not rely on any kind of formal affective assessment procedures, nor do they state specific affective learning targets for their students. Why? Three reasons seem plausible. First, especially in the higher grades, schooling is organized and graded by subject matter. Cognitive subject matter targets are relatively agreed on as desirable for all students. There is a legitimate need to assess and report student attainment of cognitive targets completely apart from affect. This puts affect in the position of being important but still secondary to cognitive learning. It also makes coming to an agreement about which affective targets are appropriate for all students difficult. That is, it isn't easy to define attitudes, values, and interests, especially because these traits are more private and idiosyncratic.

Second, the assessment of affective targets is fraught with difficulties. The many potential sources of error in measuring affective traits often result in low reliability. Student motivation is a primary concern. Students need to take such assessments seriously to provide accurate results, yet many may be inhibited if their responses are not anonymous. They would find it easy to fake responses on self-report instruments if the results are to be used for grading or some other purpose. They may want to please the teacher with positive responses. Another source of error is that some affective traits are easily influenced by momentary or temporary moods. This is especially true for younger students, who may report much more negative affect after a bad day or session. Teacher bias can also have a significant influence on what may be recorded or perceived.

Finally, particularly in recent years, there has been a public outcry by some groups against teaching anything other than traditional academic content. These political and religious groups contend that schools have no right to emphasize attitudes, values, or beliefs that may be contrary to what they stand for and want for their children, even though many affect-related targets seem to have universal appeal (e.g., citizenship, positive attitudes toward subjects and learning, and respect for others). Nevertheless, teachers are wary of controversy, so it's easier to avoid affect altogether than to fight parents and special-interest groups.

What are the advantages, then, to systematically setting and assessing affective targets? Positive affective traits and skills are essential for:

- effective learning
- being an involved and productive member of our society
- preparing for occupational and vocational satisfaction and productivity (e.g., work habits, a willingness to learn, interpersonal skills)
- maximizing the motivation to learn now and in the future
- preventing students from dropping out of school

Most current school and school district mission statements include affective outcomes, and teachers constantly assess affect informally during instruction. The following sections discuss suggestions and techniques for taking affect to a more serious level. What better way can teachers signal to students that clearly defined positive affect is important than by systematically assessing it? This begins with identifying appropriate affect targets, which we consider next.

What Are Affective Traits and Learning Targets?

The term **affective** has come to refer to a wide variety of traits and dispositions that are different from knowledge, reasoning, and skills (Hohn, 1995). The term **affect** has a technical meaning that is rather restrictive: the emotions or feelings we have toward someone or something. However, attitudes, values, self-concept, citizenship, and other traits usually considered to be noncognitive involve more than emotion or feelings. In fact, most kinds of student affect involve both emotion and cognitive beliefs. Nevertheless, the literature refers to a range of possible outcomes as affective. I have summarized many of these in Figure 10.1. Although there isn't space to consider each of these affective traits in detail, I do want to look at a few of the more commonly used ones. Because of the general nature of the term *affect*, it is best to use these more specific dispositions when developing your learning targets.

Attitude Targets

Attitudes are internal states that influence what students are likely to do. The internal state is some degree of positive/negative or favorable/unfavorable reaction toward an object, situation, person, group of objects, general environment, or group of persons (McMillan, 1980). Attitudes do not refer to behaviors, what a student knows, right or wrong in a moral or ethical sense, or characteristics such as the student's race, age, or socioeconomic status. Thus, we always think about attitudes *toward* something. In schools, that may be learning, subjects, teachers, other

FIGURE 10.1   Affective Traits

Trait	Definition
Attitudes	Predisposition to respond favorably or unfavorably to specified situations, concepts, objects, institutions, or persons
Interests	Personal preference for certain kinds of activities
Values	Importance, worth, or usefulness of modes or conduct and end states of existence
Opinions	Beliefs about specific occurrences and situations
Preferences	Desire or propensity to select one object over another
Motivation	Desire and willingness to be engaged in behavior and intensity of involvement
Academic Self-Concept	Self-perceptions of competence in school and learning
Self-Esteem	Attitudes toward oneself; degree of self-respect, worthiness, or desirability of self-concept
Locus of Control	Self-perception of whether success and failure is controlled by the student or by external influences
Emotional Development	Growth, change, and awareness of emotions and ability to regulate emotional expression
Social Relationships	Nature of interpersonal interactions and functioning in group settings
Altruism	Willingness and propensity to help others
Moral Development	Attainment of ethical principals that guide decision making and behavior
Classroom Environment	Nature of feeling tones and interpersonal relationships in a class

students, homework, and other objects or persons. Usually, then, you can identify the positive or negative attitudes that you want to foster or at least monitor because they are related to current and future behavior. Some examples are:

> *A* **Positive** *Attitude Toward*
> learning
> school
> math, science, English, and other subjects
> homework
> classroom rules
> teachers
> working with others

staying on-task
taking responsibility for one's acts

A **Negative** *Attitude Toward*
cheating
drug use
fighting
skipping school
dropping out

Another characteristic about attitudes, one that distinguishes them from preferences and opinions, is that they are relatively stable. This means that attitudes are usually consistent over time in situations that are similar. Thus, when a student develops a negative attitude toward math, we think of that internal state as remaining relatively constant for months or even years. In contrast, a student may have a negative opinion about some math homework or may feel bad about a math test, but that is not the same as a more stable attitude.

Social psychologists, through extensive research, have found that attitudes consist of three elements or contributing factors (Forsyth, 1999):

1. an *affective* component of positive or negative feelings
2. a *cognitive* component describing worth or value
3. a *behavioral* component indicating a willingness or desire to engage in specific actions

The *affective* component consists of the emotion or feeling associated with an object or a person (e.g., good or bad feelings, enjoyment, likes, comfort, anxiety). When we describe a student as liking math or enjoying art, we are focusing on the affective component. The *cognitive* component is an evaluative belief (such as thinking something is valuable, useful, worthless, etc.). In school, students can think history is useless and mathematics is valuable. The *behavioral* component is actually responding in a positive way. A strong and stable attitude is evidenced when all three components are consistent. That is, when Sam likes science, thinks it's important, and reads *National Geographic* at home, he has a very strong positive attitude. But it's likely that for many students these components will contradict one another. Louise may not like English very much but think that it's important. What would her attitude be, in a general sense, toward English? That would depend on what components of the attitude you measure. If you measured only the affective component, the attitude would be negative; a measure of the cognitive component would reveal a positive attitude.

This tripartite conceptualization has important implications for identifying attitude targets. Are you interested in feelings, thoughts, or behaviors? If you want to have a learning target such as "students will have a positive attitude toward school," you need to include all three components in your assessment, because the general nature of the target would need to be consistent with the assessment. However, if your target is "students will like coming to school," then the assessment should focus on the affective component.

Value Targets

Values generally refer either to end states of existence or to modes of conduct that are desirable or sought (Rokeach, 1973). End states of existence are conditions and aspects of ourselves and our world that we want, such as a safe life, world peace, freedom, happiness, social acceptance, and wisdom. Modes of conduct are reflected in what we believe is appropriate and needed in our everyday existence, such as being, honest, cheerful, ambitious, loving, responsible, and helpful. Each of these values can be placed into categories consistent with different areas of our lives. Thus, you can think about moral, political, social, aesthetic, economic, technological, and religious values.

In school, we are usually restricted to values that are clearly related to academics and what is needed for effective functioning as a citizen and worker. Recently a great deal of debate has arisen about developing "character" and the role of schools in moral development. Citizenship is routinely identified as a valuable goal, as are work ethic and developing aesthetic appreciations. Consider how one national report has made the argument in relation to citizenship (*National standards for civics and government*, 1994):

> American constitutional democracy cannot accomplish its purposes, however, unless its citizens are inclined to participate thoughtfully in public affairs. Traits of public character such as public spiritedness, civility, respect for law, critical mindedness, and a willingness to negotiate and compromise are indispensable for its vitality. (p. 117)

But values can be a volatile area. I recommend that you stick with values that are relatively noncontroversial and that are clearly related to academic learning and school and district goals. Popham (2002) has suggested some values as being sufficiently meritorious and noncontroversial:

- *Honesty.*   Students should learn to value honesty in their dealings with others.
- *Integrity.*   Students should firmly adhere to their own code of values (for example, moral or artistic beliefs).
- *Justice.*   Students should subscribe to the view that all citizens should be the recipients of equal justice from governmental law enforcement agencies.
- *Freedom.*   Students should believe that democratic nations must provide the maximum level of freedom to their citizens.

Other relatively noncontroversial values include kindness, generosity, perseverance, loyalty, respect, courage, compassion, and tolerance. Popham also suggests, and I agree, that you should limit the number of affective traits targeted and assessed. It is better to do a sound job of assessing a few important traits than to try to assess many traits superficially.

Motivation Targets

In the context of schooling, motivation can be defined as the extent to which students are involved in trying to learn. This includes the students' initiation of learning, their intensity of effort, their commitment, and their persistence. In other words, *motivation* is the purposeful engagement in learning to master knowledge or skills; students take learning seriously and value opportunities to learn (Ames, 1990; McMillan & Forsyth, 1991). Most of the current research on motivation can be organized according to what is called the *expectancy × value* framework (Brophy, 1998; Feather, 1982). This model suggests that motivation is determined by students' expectations—their beliefs about whether they are likely to be successful—and the value of the outcome. Expectations refer to the *self-efficacy* of the student, which is the student's self-perception of his or her capability to perform successfully. Values are self-perceptions of the importance of the performance. That is, does the student see any value in the activity? Is it intrinsically enjoyable or satisfying? Will it meet some social or psychological need, such as self-worth, competence, or belonging, or will it help the student to attain an important goal? Students who believe that they are capable of achieving success, and that the activity holds value for them, will be highly motivated to learn. If they value the outcome but believe that no matter how hard they try they probably won't be successful, their motivation will be weak. Similarly, we see many very capable students who are unmotivated because the activity holds no importance for them.

I believe your motivation targets should follow from the expectancy × value theory (McMillan, Simonetta, & Singh, 1994). Like attitudes, it is too vague to use the general definition as an outcome, because you are unable to pinpoint the source of the lack of effort and involvement. Thus, I suggest that you focus motivation targets on self-efficacy and value, differentiated by academic subject and type of learning (e.g., knowledge, understanding, reasoning). Here are some examples:

- Students will believe that they are capable of learning how to multiply fractions. (self-efficacy)
- Students will believe that it is important to know how to multiply fractions. (value)
- Students will believe that they are able to learn how bills are passed in the U.S. Senate. (self-efficacy)
- Students will believe that it is important to know how bills are passed in the U.S. Senate. (value)

Another important consideration in assessing motivation is why students are learning, the reasons they give for their actions. When students do something because it is inherently interesting, enjoyable, or challenging, they are *intrinsically motivated.* In contrast, *extrinsic* motivation is doing something because it leads to a separate outcome (e.g., reward or punishment) (Ryan & Deci, 2000). Similarly, it has been shown that students who are motivated by a need to understand and master the task (mastery orientation) demonstrate more positive behavior and thinking than students who are doing something for the result or outcome (performance orientiation). Mastery orientation students are more engaged, have a natural inclination to generate solutions to difficulties, and generate more positive attributions to success and failure (success attributed to ability and moderate effort; failure to lack of effort).

Academic Self-Concept Targets

There is an extensive literature on self-concept and its cousin, self-esteem. Many educators refer to these characteristics when discussing students who have problems with school and learning (e.g., "Sam has a low self-concept," "Adrianne has a low opinion of herself"). There is no question about the importance of these beliefs, even with the controversy over whether self-concept and self-esteem proceed or result from academic learning. According to my definition of motivation, some level of positive self-efficacy is needed for achievement. It's also likely that this aspect of self-concept is formed, at least in part, when children experience meaningful success with moderate effort.

For setting targets, it is helpful to remember that self-concept and self-esteem are multidimensional (Marsh & Craven, 1997). There is a bodily self, an athletic self, a mathematics self, a social self, and so forth. Each of us has a self-description in each area, which is our self-concept or self-image. In addition, we also have a sense of self-regard, self-affirmation, and self-worth in each area (self-esteem). Thus, a student can have a self-concept that he is tall and thin, but feel very comfortable with that and accept this description. Another student can have the same self-concept but feel inferior or inadequate or have a low self-esteem.

I suggest staying away from global self-concept and self-esteem targets, as well as those that do not differentiate between a self-description and an evaluation of that description. Like attitudes and motivation, measuring general self-concept is simply not that helpful. This is because much of what makes up general self-concept comes from areas not directly related to academic learning. By specifying *academic* self-concept, or self-concept of academic ability, you will obtain a more valid indication of what students think about themselves as learners. If you set targets that are specific to subject areas, the resulting information will be more useful. Also, it's helpful to know where students draw the line between descriptions of themselves and whether they like those descriptions. From the standpoint of more serious mental or emotional problems, a general measure may be needed, but it's best to leave that to a school psychologist or counselor.

Social Relationship Targets

Social relationships involve a complex set of interaction skills, including the identification of and appropriate responses to social cues. Peer relations, friendship, functioning in groups, assertiveness, cooperation, collaboration, prosocial behavior, empathy, taking perspective, and conflict resolution are examples of the nature of social relationships that can be specified as targets. Many of these are important at the elementary level as needed skills for academic achievement. At the secondary level, interpersonal abilities are becoming more and more important as schools work with the business community to identify and promote the skills needed to be successful in the workplace. Furthermore, social interaction is a key element of knowledge construction, active learning, and deep understanding (Tombari & Borich, 1999). As interaction occurs, students are forced to adjust their thinking to accommodate alternative viewpoints, to defend their ideas, and to debate their opinions. These processes encourage a deep, rather than superficial, understanding and keep students engaged. Also, interaction can promote good reasoning and problem-solving strategies through observation and the give-and-take that ensues.

For each of these broad social relationship areas, specific targets need to be identified. For example, a target concerned with peer relationships might include showing interest in others, listening to peers, sharing, and contributing to group activities. Cooperative skills could include sharing, listening, volunteering ideas and suggestions, supporting and accepting others' ideas, taking turns, and criticizing constructively. The *National Standards for Civics and Government* (1994) suggests the following interpersonal targets:

- *Civility.* Treating other persons respectfully, regardless of whether or not one agrees with their viewpoints; being willing to listen to other points of view; avoiding hostile, abusive, emotional, and illogical argument.
- *Negotiation and Compromise.* Making an effort to come to agreement with those with whom one may differ, when it is reasonable and morally justifiable to do so. (p. 119)

Collaborative skills needed to work in small groups could include four components: (1) basic interaction, (2) getting along, (3) coaching, and (4) fulfilling particular roles (Hoy & Greg, 1994; Tombari & Borich, 1999). Skills for each of the components are summarized in Figure 10.2.

My recommendation is similar to suggestions about identifying attitude, motivational, and self-concept targets—that it is necessary to be very specific about the target. A general target about "improved social relationships" or "improved collaboration skills" simply does not provide the level of specificity needed to focus your instruction and assessment. Here are some examples of possible social relationship targets:

- Students will contribute to small group discussions.
- Students will change their point of view or attitude.
- Students will have sustained friendships with two or more other students.
- Students will demonstrate skills in helping other students solve a problem.
- Students will demonstrate that they are able to negotiate with others and compromise.

FIGURE 10.2   A Taxonomy of Collaborative Skills

Component	Definition	Skills
Basic Interaction	Students like and respect each other.	Listening Making eye contact Answering questions Using the right voice Making sense Apologizing
Getting Along	Students sustain their respect and liking for one another.	Taking turns Sharing Following rules Assisting Asking for help or a favor Using polite words
Coaching	Students both give and receive corrective feedback and encouragement.	Suggesting an action or activity Giving and receiving compliments or praise Being specific Giving advice Correcting and being corrected
Role-Fulfilling	Fulfilling specific roles creates positive interdependency and individual accountability.	Summarizer Checker Researcher Runner Recorder Supporter Troubleshooter

Source: Authentic assessment in the classroom: Applications and practice by Tombari/Borich © 1999. Reprinted by permission of Pearson Education, Inc., Upper Saddle River, NJ.

Classroom Environment Targets

If you have been in many classrooms, you will understand when to say that each classroom has a unique climate and feel to it; it's as though you can sense the degree to which a class is comfortable, relaxed, and productive, and whether students seem happy, content, and serious. Some classes are warm and supportive, and others seem very cold and rejecting, even hostile. Together, such characteristics make up what is called **classroom environment** or **classroom climate** (Raviv, Raviv, & Reisel, 1990). Obviously, a positive climate promotes learning, so a reasonable affective target would be to establish student feelings, relationships, and beliefs that promote this kind of environment.

Classroom environment is made up of a number of characteristics that can be used as affective targets. These include:

affiliation—the extent to which students like and accept each other

involvement—the extent to which students are interested in and engaged in learning

task orientation—the extent to which classroom activities are focused on the completion of academic tasks

cohesiveness—the extent to which students share norms and expectations

competition—the emphasis on competition between students

favoritism—whether each student enjoys the same privileges

influence—the extent to which each student influences classroom decisions

friction—the extent to which students bicker with one another

formality—the emphasis on enforcing rules

communication—the extent to which communication among students and with teacher is genuine and honest

warmth—the extent to which students care about each other and show empathy

Fraser (1999) suggests that is useful to compare students' perspectives on classroom environment with those of teachers. For example, it has been demonstrated in many settings that students prefer a more positive classroom environment than they perceive is present and that teachers thought that the environment was more positive than did students. Such a pattern of results helps inform teachers about what needs to be changed to enhance student learning.

Affective Domain of the Taxonomy of Educational Objectives

One of the earliest treatments of affective objectives was called the *Taxonomy of Educational Objectives, Handbook II: Affective Domain* (Krathwohl, Bloom, & Masia, 1964). It was a companion to Bloom's *Taxonomy* of the cognitive domain. Although the taxonomy was developed more than thirty years ago, it was constructed for conceptualizing attitudes, values, and other affective traits in a hierarchy, which is appealing from the standpoint of assessment.

The affective taxonomy arranges affective targets along a five-stage continuum. These stages, with definitions and examples, are summarized in Figure 10.3. Let's look at an example that refers to attitudes toward science. At the most basic level, *receiving,* students are merely aware of and perceive science. At the next level, students are able to pay attention to the science (*responding*). Next, the students indicate through their voluntary behavior that science has *value.* Once science is valued, it can be organized with other subjects and other values (*organization*). The highest stage is *characterization,* in which science is so highly valued that it becomes a determining tendency and influence on other aspects of the student's life.

The contribution of the affective taxonomy for classroom assessment of affect is that it helps you determine the standard or level of affect that is part of your target. It also provides good suggestions for using student behaviors as indicators of

FIGURE 10.3   Affective Taxonomy of Educational Objectives

Category (Level)	Definition	Examples
Receiving (*Attending*)	Develops an awareness, shows a willingness to receive, shows controlled or selected attention	Student considers reading books for extra credit Student pays attention to teacher lecture about smoking
Responding	Shows a willingness to respond and finds some initial level of satisfaction in responding	Student asks questions about different books Takes pleasure in playing sports
Valuing	Shows that the object, person, or situation has worth Something is perceived as holding a positive value, a commitment is made	Student reads continually, asks for more books Asks for further help in improving writing skills Practices sports all the time
Organization	Brings together a complex set of values and organizes them in an ordered relationship that is harmonious and internally consistent	Student develops a plan for integrating reading and sports Weighs concerns for social justice with governmental size
Characterization	Organized system of values becomes a person's life outlook and the basis for a philosophy of life	Student develops a consistent philosophy of life Reading forms the basis for most everything in the student's life

Source: Adapted from David R. Krathwohl, Benjamin S. Bloom, & Bertram B. Masia. *Taxonomy of educational objectives, handbook II: Affective domain.* Published by Allyn and Bacon, Boston, MA. Copyright © 1964 by Pearson Education. Reprinted by permission of the publisher.

affect at each of the levels. For example, suppose you want your students to develop an appreciation for classical music. At what level do you want your target? Will students simply be aware of what classical music is and what it sounds like (receiving)? Or do you want them to really *like* classical music (valuing)?

Methods of Assessing Affective Targets

There are really only three feasible methods of assessing affective traits and dispositions in the classroom: teacher observation, student self-report, and peer ratings. Because affective traits are not directly observable, they must be inferred from behavior or what students say about themselves and others. Some very sophisticated psychological measures can assess many affective traits, but these are rarely used by classroom teachers. As we will see, you need to rely on your own observation and some student self-reports.

Keep three considerations in mind whenever you assess affect. First, emotions and feelings (not more stable attitudes) can change quickly, especially for young children and during early adolescence. This suggests that to obtain a valid indication of an individual student's emotion or feeling, it is necessary to conduct several assessments over a substantial length of time. What you want to know is what the dominant or prevalent affect is, and if you rely on a single assessment there is a good chance that what you measure is not a good indication of the trait. Measure repeatedly over several weeks.

Second, try to use as many different approaches to measuring the affective trait as possible. Reliance on a single method is problematic because of limitations inherent in that method. For example, if you use only student self-reports, which are subject to social desirability and faking, these limitations may significantly affect the results. However, if student self-reports are consistent with your observations, then a stronger case can be made.

Finally, decide if you need individual student or group results. This is related to purpose and will influence the method that you should use. If your purpose is to use assessment for making reports to parents, then obviously you need information on each student. In this case, you should use multiple methods of collecting data over time, and keep records to verify your judgments. If the assessments will be used to improve instruction, then you need results for the group as a whole. This is the more common and advisable use of affective assessment, primarily because you can rely more on anonymous student self-reports (Popham, 2002).

Teacher Observation

In Chapter 5, teacher observation was discussed as an essential tool for formative assessment. Here the emphasis is on how teachers can make more systematic observations to record student behavior that indicates the presence of targeted affective traits.

The first step in using observation is to determine in advance how specific behaviors relate to the target. This begins with a clear definition of the trait, followed by lists of student behaviors and actions that correspond to positive and negative dimensions of the trait. Let's consider attitudes. We can identify the behaviors and actions initially by considering what students with positive and negative attitudes do and say. If we have two columns, one listing behaviors for positive attitudes and one listing behaviors for negative attitudes, we define what will be observed. Suppose you are interested in attitudes toward learning. What is it that students with a positive attitude toward learning do and say? What are the actions of those with a negative attitude? Figure 10.4 lists some possibilities. These behaviors provide a foundation for developing guidelines, checklists, or rating scales. The ones in the positive column are referred to as *approach* behaviors; those in the negative column *avoidance* behaviors. Approach behaviors result in more direct, frequent, and

FIGURE 10.4   Student Behaviors Indicating Positive and Negative Attitudes toward Learning

Positive	Negative
rarely misses class	is frequently absent
rarely late to class	is frequently tardy
asks lots of questions	rarely asks questions
helps other students	rarely helps other students
works well independently without supervision	needs constant supervision
laughs	is not involved in extracurricular activities
is involved in extracurricular activities	says he or she doesn't like school
says he or she likes school	rarely comes to class early
comes to class early	rarely stays after school
stays after school	doesn't volunteer
volunteers to help	often does not complete homework
completes homework	doesn't care about bad grades
tries hard to do well	never does extra credit work
completes extra credit work	never completes assignments before the due date
completes assignments before they are due	complains
rarely complains	sleeps in class
is rarely off-task	bothers other students
rarely bothers other students	stares out window

intense contact; avoidance behaviors are just the opposite, resulting in less direct, less frequent, or less intense contact. These dimensions—directness, frequency, and intensity—are helpful in describing the behaviors that indicate positive and negative attitudes.

How do you develop these lists of positive and negative behaviors? I have found that the best approach is to find time to brainstorm with other teachers. Published instruments are available that may give you some ideas, but these won't consider the unique characteristics of your school and students. The following characteristics were brainstormed by teachers to indicate a positive student attitude toward school subjects (e.g., mathematics, science, English):

> seeks corrective feedback
> asks questions
> helps other students
> prepares for tests
> reads about the subject outside of class
> asks about careers in the subject
> asks about colleges strong in the subject
> asks other students to be quiet in class
> is concerned with poor performance
> joins clubs

initiates activities
stays alert in class and on-task

Some behaviors that can be observed for working cooperatively with others in a group include the following:

stays with the group
gets physically close to others or keeps a distance
volunteers ideas
responds to questions
asks questions
supports and accepts others' suggestions
reacts positively to criticism
encourages others to participate
seeks clarification from others
encourages others to do well

Once a fairly complete list of behaviors is developed you will need to decide if you want to use an informal, unstructured observation or one that is more formal and structured. These types differ in preparation and what is recorded.

Unstructured Observation.   Unstructured observation is much like what was discussed in Chapter 5. In this case, however, your purpose is to make summative judgments.

An unstructured observation is open-ended; there is no checklist or rating scale for recording what is observed. However, you do know what affective trait you are focused on, and you have at least generated some guidelines and examples of behaviors that indicate the affective trait. In that sense, you have determined in advance what to look for, but you also need to be open to other actions that may reflect on the trait.

You begin by planning the time, date, and place of the observation. During the observation period, or just after it, record behaviors that reflect the affective trait. Some of what you record may correspond to the guidelines or a list of possible behaviors, but record other actions also—anything that may have relevance to the target. Keep your interpretations separate from descriptions of the behaviors. Usually the teacher takes brief anecdotal notes and then makes some sense of them at a later time. Actually, this is what teachers do regularly in their heads in a way that is even less systemic than these unstructured observations. The difference is in whether or not there is any predetermined list of behaviors, and whether the teachers record their observations.

Avoid making conclusions or inferences in what you record. You want to describe what you saw or heard, but not what that may mean. Words such as *unhappy, frustrated, sad, motivated,* and *positive* are your interpretations of observed behaviors. It is better to stick to simple descriptions, such as *frowned, asked question, stared out window,* or *kept writing the entire time.* Look for both positive and negative actions. The tendency is to be more influenced by bad or negative behavior, especially if it interferes with other students. Once descriptions from several different times are recorded, then you can look over all of them and come to conclusions about the affective trait. Don't rely on a single observation.

The advantage of the unstructured observation is that it is more naturalistic and you are not constrained by what is in a checklist or rating scale. There is no problem if specific behaviors aren't displayed, and behaviors that were not previously listed can be included. A disadvantage is that it is not practical to record much about student behavior on a regular basis. It's hard to find even fifteen or twenty minutes at the end of the day, and it is virtually impossible to find any time during the school day.

Structured Observation.   A structured observation differs from an unstructured one in the amount of preparation needed and the way you record what is observed. In structured observation, more time is needed to prepare a checklist or rating form that is to be used for recording purposes. This form is generated from the list of positive and negative behaviors to make it easy and convenient for you to make checks quickly and easily.

The format of the checklist is simple and straightforward. The behaviors are listed, and you make a single check next to each behavior to indicate frequency. Frequency can be indicated by answering yes or no, observed or not observed; by the number of times a behavior occurred; or by some kind of **rating scale** (always, often, sometimes, rarely, never; occasionally, consistently). Rating scales are used to describe behavior over an extended period of time. Two examples are illustrated in Figure 10.5 for assessing attitude toward reading. The first, labeled *frequency,* would be used to record the number of times each behavior was observed. The second type is a *rating* in which the teacher estimates how often each behavior occurs as defined by a set scale. Another example is shown in Figure 10.6. In this example the targeted affective trait is participation. A holistic rating scale is used to describe qualitatively different levels of participation. Notice that several behaviors are included in scores 2–5. This type of rating scale is helpful in providing a general overview of the trait being measured. It is important that the descriptive criteria match well with what is intended to be observed. Another type of rating scale, similar to the one in Figure 10.5, provides for a separate recording of how often the student shares information, listens to others, and so forth. Your choice of checklist or rating scale depends on the time frame (ratings are better for longer periods of time) and the nature of the behavior. Some behaviors are better suited to a simple checklist, like "follows instructions" and "completes homework." My experience is that a simple scale, with only three descriptors to indicate frequency (e.g., *usually, sometimes, rarely*) is usually sufficient. Additional rating scales are illustrated in Figure 10.8.

Figure 10.7 shows a sample holistic rating scale for assessing collaborative skills. Note that in this example several students are included on each page. Assessing students in groups can facilitate your understanding of group dynamics and effectiveness.

FIGURE 10.5   Checklists for Structured Observation of Attitudes toward Reading

Checklist 1 (Frequency Approach)

Name _____   Date _____   Time _____

Behaviors	*Frequency*
1. Looks at books on table	_____
2. Picks up books on table	_____
3. Reads books	_____
4. Tells others about books read	_____
5. Moves away from books on table	_____
6. Makes faces when looking at books	_____
7. Tells others not to read	_____
8. Expresses dislike for reading	_____

Checklist 2 (Rating Approach)

Name _____   Date _____   Time _____

Behaviors	*Always*	*Often*	*Sometimes*	*Seldom*	*Never*
1. Looks at books on table					
2. Picks up books on table					
3. Reads books					
4. Tells others about books read					
5. Moves away from books on table					
6. Makes faces when looking at books					
7. Tells others not to read					
8. Expresses dislike for reading					

Source: Testing and Educational Measurement. 4th edition, by Tom Kubiszyn & Gary Borich. Copyright © 1996 by Longman Publishers. Reprinted by permission of John Wiley & Sons, Inc.

With structured observation, it is best to state descriptions in the positive to avoid confusion. If there is a large number of behaviors, organize them into major categories. This will make it easier to record and draw inferences from the results. Other suggestions are summarized in Figure 10.9.

Student Self-Report

There are several ways in which students tell us about their affect as a self-report. The most direct way is in the context of a personal conversation or interview. Students

FIGURE 10.6   Scoring Criteria for Participation

Criteria	Mark
Listens attentively to instructions. Readily shares information. Always listens to others. Considers other points of view. Gets involved quickly and stays involved. Approaches the activity in an organized manner. Active participant who leads others.	5
Listens to instructions. Generally shares information and listens to others. Needs a start, but stays involved. Active participant.	4
Listens to instructions but may be distracted. Shares information sometimes and listens to others sometimes. Needs a start and reminders to stay on-task. Relies on others for clues for direction. Does not consider other points of view. In general, a passive participant in the activity.	3
Is distracted or disruptive during instructions. Needs a start and constant reminders to stay on task. Does not share information. Does not listen well to others. No consideration of other points of view. A very passive participant.	2
Is continually off-task and a nonparticipant in the activity. Does not get started. Relies completely on others.	1
Did not participate at all.	0

Source: Testing and educational measurement. 4th edition, by Tom Kubiszyn & Gary Borich. Copyright © 1996 by Longman Publishers. Reprinted by permission of John Wiley & Sons, Inc.

can also respond to a written questionnaire or survey about themselves or other students. First, we consider interviews.

Student Interview.   Teachers can effectively use different types of personal communication with students, such as individual and group interviews, discussions, and casual conversations, to assess affect. In some ways this is like an observation, but because you have an opportunity to be directly involved with the students it is possible to probe and respond to better understand. An important prerequisite for getting students to reveal their true feelings and beliefs is establishing trust. Without a sense of trust, students may not be comfortable expressing their feelings. They will tend to say what they think their teachers want to hear, say what is socially acceptable or desirable, or say very little, if anything. Younger students are usually pretty candid about themselves; older students may be more reserved. You enhance trust by communicating warmth, caring, and respect and by listening attentively to what the students communicate.

An advantage of interviewing is that you can clarify questions, probe where appropriate to clarify responses, and note nonverbal behavior. Students have an opportunity to qualify or expand on previous answers. These procedures help avoid ambiguity and vagueness, problems often associated with measuring affect.

Holistic Rating of Collaborative Skills

Setting: _____   Date: _____

Total time observed: _____

Directions: Rate the extent to which each group member demonstrated the listed categories of skill. Use the following scale:

5 = Highly competent at these skills
4 = Pretty good in using these skills
3 = Moderately good at these skills
2 = Awkward in using these skills
1 = Lacks these skills

1. *Basic interaction skills.* Student shows that he/she likes and respects other members of the group.

2. *Getting-along skills.* Student shows that he/she can make and keep friends in a group.

3. *Coaching.* Student shows that he/she can help and explain things to other group members.

4. *Role fulfilling.* Student carries out his/her assigned responsibilities.

FIGURE 10.7   Holistic Rating Scale for Collaborative Skills

Source: Authentic assessment in the classroom: Applications and practice by Tombari/Borich © 1998. Reprinted by permission of Pearson Education, Inc., Upper Saddle River, NJ.

It is difficult for some students, even when there is a trusting relationship, to articulate their feelings in a one-on-one interview. They may simply be unaccustomed to answering questions about attitudes and values. A group discussion or group interview is a good alternative for these students. People generally open up more in a group setting, as long as peer pressure and cliques don't interfere. Another advantage of using groups is that it is much more efficient than individual interviews. Also, feelings and beliefs can become clearer as students hear others talk. You can use students as leaders of group interviews. They may be able to probe better because they are familiar with the language and lifestyles of their classmates. Respected student leaders will be highly credible.

Be prepared to record student responses and your interpretations. During an interview it is difficult to write very much, and it's not practical to tape record, transcribe, and analyze the transcription. I suggest that you prepare a brief outline of the major areas that will be covered, leaving space to make brief notes as you interview. As soon as possible after the interview, go back over your notes and fill in enough

PRIMARY

SOCIAL SKILLS CHECKLIST

ASSESSMENT OF SOCIAL SKILLS

Dates: _10/21_
Class: _3rd Grade_
Teacher: _Forbes_

Rating:
+ = Frequently
✓ = Sometimes
O = Not Yet

Who	Listening (Skill 1)	Using First Name (Skill 2)	Taking Turns (Skill 3)	Encouraging (Skill 4)	Sharing (Skill 5)	Comments
1. Lois	✓	✓	O	✓	✓	
2. Connie	+	+	O	✓	+	Dropped in 2 areas
3. James	✓	✓	✓	✓	✓	
4. Juan	+	+	✓	+	+	
5. Beth	O	O	+	✓	✓	Improved in 2 areas
6. Michele	✓	✓	O	✓	✓	
7. John	✓	✓	O	✓	✓	
8. Charles	+	+	O	✓	+	
9. Mike	✓	✓	✓	✓	✓	Went from 5.0s to this in 2 months
10. Lana	+	+	✓	+	+	

Notes: Work with Lois on a regular basis.
Change her seat and group.

MIDDLE SCHOOL

OBSERVATION CHECKLIST

Student: _Denise_   Class: _Science_   Date: _12/5_
Type of Assignment: _Work Habits_

☐ Teacher   Date _____   Signed _____
☐ Peer   Date _____   Signed _____
☒ Self   Date _12/5_   Signed _Denise Smith_

	Not Yet	Sometimes	Frequently
WORK HABITS:			
• Gets work done on time	____	____	X
• Asks for help when needed	____	X	____
• Takes initiative	____	X	____
STUDY HABITS:			
• Organize work	____	____	X
• Takes good notes	____	____	X
• Uses time well	____	____	X
PERSISTENCE:			
• Shows patience	____	X	____
• Checks own work	X	____	____
• Revises work	____	X	____
• Does quality work	____	____	X
SOCIAL SKILLS:			
• Works well with others	____	X	____
• Listens to others	____	X	____
• Helps others	____	X	____

COMMENTS: _I always get my work done on time, and I am really organized. I just need to check my own work and help my group work._

FUTURE GOALS: _I need to be more patient with my group and try to work with them more. I worry about my own grades, but I don't do enough to help group members achieve their goals._

FIGURE 10.8   Examples of Rating Scales

Source: From *The mindful school: How to assess authentic learning,* 3rd edition, by Kay Burke. © 1999, 1994, 1993 Skylight Training and Publishing Inc. Reprinted by permission of Skylight Professional Development, www. skylightedu.com or (800) 348-4474.

FIGURE 10.9   Checklist for Using Teacher Observation to Assess Affect

✓ Determine behaviors to be observed in advance.
✓ Record student, time, date, and place.
✓ If unstructured, record brief descriptions of relevant behavior.
✓ Keep inferences separate from descriptions.
✓ Record both positive and negative behaviors.
✓ Make several observations of each student.
✓ Avoid personal bias.
✓ Record as soon as possible following the observation.
✓ Use a simple and efficient system.

detail so that what the student said and communicated are clearly indicated. Like observation, be careful to keep your descriptions separate from your interpretations.

Questionnaires and Surveys.   You have probably completed many commercial or standardized self-report attitude questionnaires or surveys, so you have a general idea what they are like. However, teachers rarely use such instruments in the classroom (Stiggins & Conklin, 1992). Why is this true when there are literally hundreds of instruments to choose from? I believe that there are several contributing factors. First, most published instruments are not designed to be used by teachers. They are intended more for research than instruction, and usually the affective trait is conceptualized as a general construct that is hard for teachers to use in planning or delivering instruction.

Second, affect is generally not afforded the status of achievement—it just isn't as important by comparison—so less than systematic measures are tolerated. Third, as mentioned previously, measuring affect is risky. Finally, most teachers have not had much training in how to use these instruments, or to develop their own, so they lack confidence. Whatever the reasons, I hope to show you that these instruments can be very helpful in providing one source of evidence on affect.

According to Stiggins (2001), one key to the successful use of student self-reports is to get students to take the questionnaires seriously. This will happen if students see that what you are asking about is relevant to them and that actions are taken as a result of the findings. You want to help students understand that they have nothing to lose and something to gain by being cooperative. In Stiggins's words, enlist "the support of the respondent as an ally, a partner" (Stiggins, 2001, p. 355).

Another key is using questions to which students are willing and able to provide thoughtful responses. This is accomplished if the wording of the questions is precise, if the format is easy to understand and respond to, and if the response options make sense. These and other suggestions are discussed in reviewing the major types of attitude, value, and self-concept self-report instruments.

Constructed-Response Formats.   A straightforward approach to asking students about their affect is to have them respond to a simple statement or question. Often, incomplete sentences can be used.

Examples

> I think mathematics is . . .
> When I have free time I like to . . .
> The subject I like most is . . .
> What I like most about school is . . .
> What I like least about school is . . .
> Science is . . .
> I think I am . . .

Essay items can be used with older students. These items provide a more extensive, in-depth response than incomplete sentences. You can ask students for reasons for their attitudes, values, or beliefs.

Examples

> Write a paragraph on the subject you like most in school. Tell me why. Comment on what it is about the subject and your experience with it that leads you to like it the most. Describe yourself as a student. Are you a good student? What are you good at? How hard do you try to get good grades? Does learning come easy or hard for you?

An advantage of the incomplete sentence format is that it taps whatever comes to mind from each student. You are not cuing students about what to think or suggesting how they should respond, so what you get is what is foremost and most salient in the student's mind. Of course, students need to be able to read and write and take the task seriously. If you use this method, be sure to give students enough time to think and write and encourage them to write as much as they can think about for each item.

There are two disadvantages to constructed-response formats. One is that even if you tell students that their answers are anonymous, they may think you'll recognize their handwriting; hence, faking is a concern. Second, scoring the responses takes time and is more subjective than more traditional objective formats. But this approach offers an excellent way to get a general overview of student perspectives, feelings, and thoughts.

Selected-Response Formats.   There are many different types of selected-response formats to choose from when assessing affective targets. We will look at a few commonly used scales. When you decide to create your own instrument and wonder which of these response formats would be best, try to match the format with the trait. There is no single best response format. Some work better with some traits, and some work better with others, depending on the wording and the nature of the trait. Your job will be to make the best match.

Most selected-response formats create a scale that is used with statements concerning the trait. A widely used format to assess attitudes, for example, is the **Likert scale.** This scale can be adapted to almost any type of affective trait, so it is very versatile. Students read statements and then record their agreement or disagreement with them according to a five-point scale (*strongly agree, agree, undecided, disagree, strongly disagree*). The statements are generated from your list of positive and negative behaviors or beliefs and are put in a form that makes sense for the response scale. The statements contain some indication of the direction of the attitude, as illustrated in the following examples. The response scale indicates intensity.

Examples

> Mathematics is boring.
> It is important to get good grades in school.
> It is important to complete homework on time.
> Class discussion is better than lectures.
> School is fun.
> I enjoy reading.

Science is challenging.
Science is difficult.

An advantage of this format is that many such statements can be presented on a page or two to assess a number of different attitudes efficiently (see Figure 10.10). Note that some negatively worded statements are included in the example. These should be used sparingly with younger children, with words like *not, don't,* or *no* appropriately highlighted or underlined.

The responses to the Likert scale are scored by assigning weights from 1 to 5 for each position on the scale so that 5 reflects the most positive attitude and 1 the most negative attitude (SA = 5, A = 4, NS = 3, D = 2, SD = 1). The scores from all the items assessing the same attitude trait are then totaled, though the percentage of responses to each position is probably more important than summary statistics. In other words, you wouldn't add the scores from items 1, 7, and 8 in Figure 10.9 because they address different traits, though you could add items 3, 9, and 10, which deal with attitudes toward school. When adding items and obtaining average scores of statements that are worded so that a "disagree" response refers to a more positive attitude or belief, the scoring needs to be reversed. Thus, the scoring for items 1, 5, 7, and 8 in Figure 10.10 should be reversed (SD = 5, D = 4, A = 2, SA = 1).

The reliability of overall scores is higher if several items assessing the same trait can be added together. This needs to be balanced with the practical limitation on the total number of items in the questionnaire and with the response of students

FIGURE 10.10   Likert Scale for School Attitudes

Student Opinion Survey

Directions: Read each statement carefully and indicate how much you agree or disagree with it by circling the appropriate letter(s) to the right.

Key: SA – Strongly Agree
       A – Agree
      NS – Not Sure
       D – Disagree
      SD – Strongly Disagree

1. Science class is challenging.	SA	A	NS	D	SD
2. Reading is important.	SA	A	NS	D	SD
3. I like coming to school.	SA	A	NS	D	SD
4. I like doing science experiments.	SA	A	NS	D	SD
5. Homework is hard for me.	SA	A	NS	D	SD
6. Cheating is very bad.	SA	A	NS	D	SD
7. Learning about circles and triangles is useless.	SA	A	NS	D	SD
8. I do *not* like to work in small groups.	SA	A	NS	D	SD
9. Doing well in school is important.	SA	A	NS	D	SD
10. I believe that what I learn in school is important.	SA	A	NS	D	SD

who feel that they don't need to be answering questions that are just about the same as items they have already responded to.

You can use the principle of the Likert scale to construct any number of different response formats. For younger children, for example, the five-point scale is usually truncated to three responses (agree, unsure, disagree), or even two (such as agree or disagree, yes or no, true or not true). Many self-report instruments use a Likert-type scale that asks students to indicate *how often* they have engaged in specific behaviors or had particular thoughts. These scales are easier to respond to because they are less abstract. They are best for behaviors and cognitive components of attitudes.

Examples

How often do you believe that most of what you learn in school is important?

a. always
b. frequently
c. sometimes
d. rarely
e. never

How frequently do you *dislike* coming to this class?

a. all the time
b. most of the time
c. sometimes
d. rarely
e. never

How often do you find the classroom activities interesting?

a. almost always
b. often
c. occasionally
d. rarely if ever

Another frequently used variation of the Likert scale is to ask students whether something is true for them. This can be a simple dichotomous item, such as a true/false statement, or you can use a scale.

Examples

How true is each statement for you?

If I want I can get good grades in science.

a. very true
b. somewhat true
c. not at all true

When I really try hard I can do well in school.

a. true
b. untrue

Students try hard to do better than each other in this class.

a. true
b. false

I am a good student.

a. yes
b. no

Scales are mixed in some questionnaires so that there are different scales for different items. In these types of items, the response formats are dependent on the terminology and intent of each item. Sometimes the nature of the trait is named in the item; then the scale gives students choices. For other items, the scale defines the trait being measured.

Examples

How important is it for you to be a good reader?

a. extremely important   **c.** somewhat important
b. very important   **d.** not important

Science is:

a. interesting
b. dull
c. difficult

Indicate how you feel about your performance on the test.

| _____ | _____ | _____ | _____ |
| immense pride | some pride | some failure | immense failure |

| _____ | _____ | _____ | _____ |
| very happy | somewhat happy | somewhat sad | very sad |

Indicate the extent to which you believe your performance on the project was a success or failure.

a. extreme success
b. somewhat successful
c. failure
d. extreme failure

Circle the statement that best describes your interest in learning *most of the time*.

a. I am pretty interested in what we learn.
b. This class is somewhat interesting, but I find my mind wandering sometimes.
c. I often find this class pretty boring.

For young students, the response format is often in the form of faces rather than words.

Examples

Learning about science

Reading books

For classroom climate and value targets, self-report questionnaires often ask students to select from several options. The options refer to different traits or values, rather than showing a range of the same trait.

Examples

I did well on this test because I:

a. studied hard.
b. got lucky.

Select one of the following:

a. Students in this class like to help each other out.
b. There is a lot of bickering between students in this class.

Select the statement that you agree with the most.

a. People should be required to volunteer to help those less fortunate.
b. People who find a wallet should give it to the police.

Interests are efficiently measured with checklists, ranking, or simple dichotomous choices.

Examples

Indicate whether you are interested (I) or uninterested (U) in learning about each of the historical topics listed.

_____ **a.** Vietnam War
_____ **b.** World War II
_____ **c.** holocaust
_____ **d.** depression
_____ **e.** stock market crash

Rank the following from most liked (1) to least liked (5).

_____ history
_____ sports
_____ science
_____ music
_____ art

Another common approach to measuring affective traits is to use variations of the **semantic differential.** These scales use adjective pairs that provide anchors for feelings or beliefs that are opposite in direction and intensity. The student would place a check between each pair of adjectives that describes positive or negative aspects of the trait. In the following examples, the traits are attitudes toward a test and a subject.

Examples

Science Test

| fair | ____ | ____ | ____ | ____ | ____ | unfair |
| hard | ____ | ____ | ____ | ____ | ____ | easy |

History

boring	____	____	____	____	____	interesting
important	____	____	____	____	____	useless
like	____	____	____	____	____	hate

An advantage of selected-response formats is that they make it easy to assure anonymity. Anonymity is important when the traits are more personal, such as values and self-concept. It is also a more efficient way of collecting information. However, you don't want to ask too many questions just because it is efficient. It's best to keep self-report questionnaires short. Although you need more than a single item to reliably assess an affective trait, if you have too many items students may lose concentration and motivation. Select only those traits that you will take action on; don't use items simply because it would be interesting to know what students think. It's also not a good idea to include open-ended items such as "Comments" or "Suggestions" at the end of a selected-response questionnaire.

Constructing Self-Report Items.   If you need to develop your own self-report items to assess affect targets, begin by listing the behaviors, thoughts, and feelings that correspond to each affective trait, similar to what I suggested earlier for observations. Once you select a response format, write sentences that are clear and succinct, and write direct statements that students will easily understand. You are not trying to assess knowledge, intelligence, reading ability, or vocabulary, so keep items simple and short. You may find that published instruments will give you some good ideas for how to word items, set up response formats, and in general lay out a questionnaire. Volumes 5 and 6 of the Educational Testing Service Test Collection are an excellent source to identify existing instruments. (The ETS Test Collection can be accessed through the Internet and other online data retrieval services.) I recommend Ruth Wylie's book for self-concept measures (1989) and Anderson (1981) for more information in general on measuring affect. In fact, you may find an existing instrument that meets your purpose very well. Now we move to some specific suggestions, with examples, for those who will be constructing items.

In wording the items, avoid the use of negatives, especially double negatives.

Example

> *Poor:* There isn't a student in this class who does not like to work with others.
>
> *Improved:* Students in this class like to work with each other.

If you are interested in present self-perceptions, which is usually the case, avoid writing in the past tense.

Example

> *Poor:* I have always liked science.
>
> *Improved:* I like science.

Avoid absolutes such as *always, never, all,* and *every* in the item stem. These terms, because they represent an all-or-none judgment, may cause you to miss the more accurate self-perception.

Example

> *Poor:* I never like science.
>
> *Improved:* I rarely like science.

Avoid items that ask about more than one thing or thought. Double-barreled items are difficult to interpret because you don't know which of the two thoughts or ideas the student has responded to.

Example

> *Poor:* I like science and mathematics.
>
> *Improved:* I like science.

These and other suggestions presented in this section are summarized in Figure 10.11. I should point out, however, that classroom teachers rarely have an opportunity to develop sophisticated instruments with strong and well-documented technical qualities. Thus, locally developed items and instruments should be used cautiously and in conjunction with other evidence.

Peer Ratings

Peer appraisal is the least common method of assessing affect. This is due to the relatively inefficient nature of conducting, scoring, and interpreting peer ratings.

FIGURE 10.11 Checklist for Using Student Self-Reports to Assess Affect

✓ Keep measures focused on specific affective traits.
✓ Establish trust with students.
✓ Match response format to the trait being assessed.
✓ Ensure anonymity if possible.
✓ Keep questionnaires brief.
✓ Keep items short and simple.
✓ Avoid negatives and absolutes.
✓ Write items in present tense.
✓ Avoid double-barreled items.

Also, teachers who are tuned in very much at all in a class can accurately observe what is assessed in peer ratings. However, two primary methods for obtaining peer ratings—the guess-who and sociometric techniques—represent approaches that can be used in conjunction with observation and self-reports to strengthen assessment of interpersonal and classroom environment targets.

Guess-Who Approach.   In this method, students are asked to list the students they believe best correspond to behavior descriptions. The descriptions may be positive or negative, though usually they are positive to avoid highlighting undesirable behaviors or traits. Typically there are only a few items in this approach so that students can complete it quickly, and scoring is done by simply tallying the number of times each student is listed. One disadvantage is that some shy and withdrawn students may be overlooked, resulting in a lack of information about them. Figure 10.12 illustrates a guess-who form for assessing concern for others.

Sociometric Approach.   Sociometric techniques are used to assess the social structure of the class and the interaction patterns among the students. This allows you to learn about the social acceptance and liking patterns of the students. The results can be used for forming small groups of students, targeting interventions with individual students, and identifying cliques, popular students, and social isolates.

Students are asked, in a form similar to what is shown in Figure 10.12, to nominate students they would like to work or play with. Although this is technically a self-report, the results are used as a way for students to rate each other. The questions would be like the following:

I choose these students to work with.
I would like to sit next to _____ .
I would like to have the following students on my team.

It is best to ask about general activities, such as who to work with or sit next to, rather than specific ones (e.g., walking to school or doing a report). It is also advisable to avoid asking negative items (e.g., I would not like to sit next to . . .").

FIGURE 10.12   Guess-Who Form for Assessing Students' Concern for Others

Directions

Listed below are descriptions of what some students in this room are like. Read the descriptions and write the names of the students who *best fit* each description. You may write the names of anyone in this room, including those who are absent. Your choices will not be seen by anyone else. Give the student's first name and the initial of the student's last name.

Remember

1. Write the names of students in this room who best fit each description.
2. Write as many names as you wish for each description.
3. The same person may fit more than one description.
4. Write the first name and initial of the last name.
5. Your choices will *not be seen* by anyone except you and me (teacher's name).

Write the names below each description

1. Here is someone who enjoys working and playing with others.
2. Here is someone who is willing to share materials with others.
3. Here is someone who is willing to help others with their homework.
4. Here is someone who makes sure others are not left out of games.
5. Here is someone who encourages others to do well in school.
6. Here is someone who is kind to others who have a problem.

Source: Linn, R. L., & Gronlund, N. E., *Measurement and assessment in teaching*, 8th edition, p. 325. Copyright © 2000. Adapted by permission of Pearson Education, Inc., Upper Saddle River, New Jersey.

Once the students have made their choices, you need to tabulate the results listing all the students and indicating the number of times each student was selected. This provides a measure of general social acceptance. Second, create a matrix to identify students who have selected each other. Finally, as illustrated in Figure 10.13, construct a **sociogram.** This is a diagram that shows the social structure of the group. In this example, the number of times any student was selected is depicted by the concentric circles (students with more than nine choices in the middle, six to nine choices in the second circle, etc.). Not all choices are shown; lines are used for mutual choices and rejections.

Although this is a very interesting and informative technique, constructing the sociogram takes considerable time. However, often teachers are surprised by the results, so if you intend to assess social adjustment and other interpersonal affect targets in depth, a sociogram would be very beneficial.

Which Method or Combination of Methods Should I Use?

We have covered three approaches to measuring affect—observation, student self-report, and peer ratings—and each method has advantages and disadvantages (see

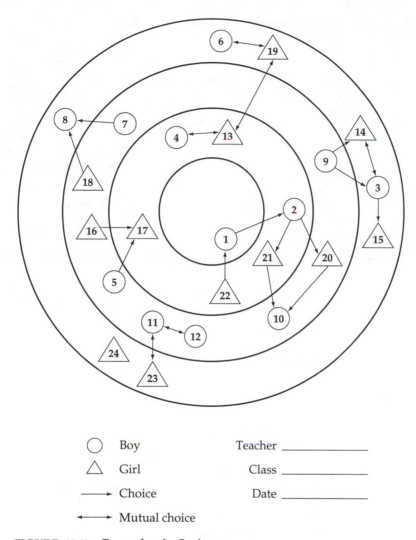

○	Boy
△	Girl
⟶	Choice
⟷	Mutual choice

Teacher _____

Class _____

Date _____

FIGURE 10.13   Example of a Sociogram

Figure 10.14). Your choice of which of these to use depends on a number of factors. Consider the type of affect you want to assess. You can get a pretty good idea of a student's general reaction to something or someone through observation, but to diagnose attitude components you'll need a self-report of some kind. Observation can be followed by peer ratings to get at socially oriented affect.

If you are interested in group responses and tendencies, which is generally recommended, then a selected-response self-report is probably best because you can assure anonymity and it is easily scored. Finally, you need to take into consideration

FIGURE 10.14   Advantages and Disadvantages of Methods to Assess Affect

	Strengths	Weaknesses

Observation	Can observe unobtrusively
	Can observe nonverbal
	  behavior
	Can observe natural behavior
		Observer bias
		Not usually anonymous
		Students unable to explain
		  reasons for behavior
		Can be time-consuming
		Absence of behavior doesn't
		  mean absence of affect

*Constructed-Response
Self-Report*
	Easy to develop
	Easy to administer
	Can be anonymous
	Elicits uncued responses
	Reasons for affect can be given
	Easy to focus on specific
	  affective traits
		Time-consuming to score
		Teacher bias
		Writing proficiency needed
		Unable to follow up
		Students may not understand
		  or follow directions

*Selected-Response
Self-Report*
	Easy to administer
	Easy to score
	Can be anonymous
	Easier to compare students
	Easy to focus on specific
	  affective traits
	Offers many examples of
	  existing instruments
		Reading proficiency
		  needed
		Reasons for affect not indicated
		Faking
		Response set
		Social desirability

Peer Rating	Easy to administer
	Focuses on interpersonal targets
	Students may find it easier to
	  think about others than
	  themselves
	Provides check on teacher
	  inferences
	Students perceive that
	  their input is important
		Difficult to score and interpret
		Faking
		Social desirability
		Teacher may not follow
		  through on choices

Source: Stiggins, R. J., *Student centered-classroom assessment* (3rd ed.). Copyright © 2001, p. 353. Adapted by permission of Prentice-Hall, Upper Saddle River, New Jersey.

the use of the information. If you intend to use the results for grading (which I do not recommend), then multiple approaches may be needed, and you'll need to be especially careful about faking on self-reports and even peer judgments. In the end, the choice of method depends most on your context, targets, and level of comfort in using any particular approach.

Case Study for Reflection

Mrs. Williams is a second-grade teacher at James Elementary School who has had difficulty in her classroom this semester. She has had to spend ever-increasing amounts of time and energy to keep students from verbally or physically abusing each other. She has noticed that many of these students also make disparaging remarks about themselves and call themselves "dumb" or "stupid." She has used anecdotal records and feedback from talking with the school counselor about the situation to help her assess the situation in her classroom. She has decided to take a fifteen-minute block of time every day next semester to teach appropriate social skills and to allow time for students to air their complaints in a nonviolent atmosphere. The counselor has assured her that these students have low self-esteem and that through classroom discussion and role-play they can learn to appreciate themselves and others. Mrs. Williams also plans to introduce a behavior modification plan for students, which will help her track student progress with improved social behavior. Mrs. Williams is concerned that the principal and parents of her students will not understand her attempts to assess student affective traits to improve the classroom environment.

Questions for Consideration
1. What should Mrs. Williams do before classes start next semester?
2. What strategies could she use to appropriately assess students to provide data that will be reassuring to the principal and parents?

Ensuring Anonymity

Anonymity has been mentioned several times as a desirable feature when assessing affect. Popham (2002) makes the argument that anonymity is not only desirable, but essential to obtaining valid results. He has pointed out that several techniques can be used to enhance perceived anonymity when you are interested in results for the class as a whole:

1. Direct students not to write their names or in any way identify themselves on their self-reports.
2. Inform students that their responses will be anonymous.
3. Position yourself in the class so that students know you cannot see their answers on self-reports.
4. Direct students not to write anything other than checking or circling to avoid your recognizing handwriting.
5. Provide a procedure for collecting self-reports so that you won't be able to identify responses (e.g., in a container in the back of the room, not on your desk).
6. Tell students why anonymity is important.
7. Use a response format that minimizes the likelihood that responses can be seen by other students.

Summary

This chapter considered student affect, an important but often neglected area. Sound assessment of affect begins with clear and specific affective targets. Suggestions were made for conceptualizing affective traits that most would consider essential for successful learning. Two methods are used most frequently for measuring affect in the classroom: teacher observation and student self-reports. Observation can be structured or unstructured, and there are many different formats for self-reports. In the end, you'll need to customize the assessment of affect for your students, school, and curriculum. Pick a few most important traits, do a good job of assessing them, and then use the results to improve instruction. Other essential points made in the chapter include:

- Positive affective traits influence motivation, involvement, and cognitive learning.
- Although the term *affect* refers to emotions and feelings, affective targets include cognitive and behavioral traits.
- Attitudes are predispositions to respond favorably or unfavorably. They include cognitive, affective, and behavioral components.
- Values are end states of existence or desired modes of conduct.
- Motivation is the purposeful engagement to learn. It is determined by self-efficacy (the student's beliefs about his or her capability to learn) and the value of learning.
- Academic self-concept is the way students describe themselves as learners. Self-esteem is how students feel about themselves. Both are multidimensional; it's best to avoid general measures of self-concept or self-esteem.
- Social relationship targets involve interpersonal interaction and competence.
- Classroom environment is the climate established through factors such as affiliation, involvement, cohesiveness, formality, friction, and warmth.
- The affective domain of Bloom's taxonomy defines different levels of affect in a hierarchical fashion, from attending to something to using something as a determining factor in one's life.
- Three methods are used to assess student affect: teacher observation, student self-report, and peer ratings.
- Teacher observation can be structured or unstructured. Several observations should be made; recording of behavior should occur as soon as possible after the observation. Inferences are made from what was observed.
- Student self-reports include interviews, questionnaires, and surveys. Trust between the students and the teacher is essential.
- Interviews allow teachers to probe and clarify in order to avoid ambiguity, though they cannot be anonymous and are time-consuming.
- Questionnaires are time-efficient and can be anonymous. Proper student motivation to take the questions seriously is essential.
- Constructed-response questionnaires tap traits without cuing students, which indicates what is most salient to students.
- Selected-response formats, such as the Likert scale, are efficient to score and can be anonymous when assessing groups.

- In constructing questionnaires, keep them brief, write in the present tense, and avoid negative and double-barreled items.
- Peer ratings can be used to assess interpersonal traits. Frequencies of nominations and sociograms are used to analyze the results.
- Use appropriate techniques for ensuring anonymity.

SELF-INSTRUCTIONAL REVIEW EXERCISES

1. What are some reasons that most teachers don't systematically assess affective targets?

2. Match the nature of the learning with the affective target. Each target may be used more than once or not at all.

_____ **(1)** cooperation and conflict resolution	**a.** attitude
_____ **(2)** student expectations and need to do well	**b.** value
	c. motivation
_____ **(3)** honesty and integrity	**d.** academic self-concept
_____ **(4)** character education	**e.** social relationships/
_____ **(5)** cognitive and affective components	collaboration
_____ **(6)** responding and organization	**f.** classroom environment
_____ **(7)** warmth in the classroom	**g.** affective taxonomy
_____ **(8)** thinking math is important but not liking it	
_____ **(9)** engagement and involvement	
_____ **(10)** kindness, respect, tolerance	

3. Critique the efforts of the teachers in the following two scenarios to assess affect. What have they done well and how could they improve?

Scenario 1: Mr. Talbot

Mr. Talbot decided that he wanted to assess his fifth graders on their attitudes toward social studies. He asks students to complete the sentence, "Social studies is . . ." Also, at the end of each week he summarizes how much students have liked the social studies units. He writes a brief description for each student, then gives each a rating of 1 to 5.

Scenario 2: Ms. Headly

Ms. Headly teaches art to middle school students. Because all the students in the school come through her class, she wants to be sure that students leave the class with a positive attitude toward art and strong aesthetic values. She decides to develop and administer a survey of art attitudes and values at the beginning and end of each semester. She consults other teachers to generate a list of thoughts and behaviors that are positive and negative. She uses a response format of "like me" and "not like me" with the fifty items. Ms. Headley instructs the students not to put their names on the surveys.

4. Identify each of the following as a characteristic of observation (O), constructed-response self-report (CRSR), selected-response self-report (SRSR), or peer rating (PR).

   a. can take into account nonverbal behaviors
   b. relatively easy to administer but difficult to score

  c. subject to teacher bias
  d. can be anonymous
  e. very time-consuming to gather data
  f. student explanations for answers can be provided
  g. the method of choice for checking which students are leaders
  h. can be done without students' knowledge or awareness

ANSWERS TO SELF-INSTRUCTIONAL REVIEW EXERCISES

1. Three reasons were given in the chapter: affect takes second seat to cognitive outcomes; assessing affect is difficult to do well; and teachers do not want to put up with controversy.

2. (1) e, (2) c, (3) b, (4) b, (5) a, (6) g, (7) f, (8) a, (9) c, (10) b or c.

3. *Scenario 1.* On the positive side, Mr. Talbot has used more than one method to assess attitudes, and he has a fairly narrow trait in mind. It's good that he isolates the affective component of attitudes (likes) and that his observation notes are brief. On the negative, though, his sentence is too broad and may not give him much information about attitudes. There is no indication that he has generated examples of approach and avoidance behaviors. Students could easily respond with answers like "short" or "in the morning," which wouldn't be much help. He should try to summarize more frequently than once a week, even though trying to write descriptions for each student will take a lot of time. He records his interpretations rather than student behavior.

   Scenario 2. For the most part, this is an example of good affective assessment. Ms. Headly took the time to first list behaviors, then establish a response format that would work, then develop the items. She ensured anonymity, and she looked at attitudes and values before and after her course. However, the survey is pretty long, and she is dependent on a single assessment method. It is possible that her bias would be perceived by students, and it might encourage them to provide positive answers at the end of the semester.

4. a. O and CRSR (interview); b. PR; c. O and CRSR; d. SRSR; e. O and CRSR; f. CRSR; g. PR; h. O.

SUGGESTIONS FOR ACTION RESEARCH

1. Identify some affective targets for students and construct a short questionnaire to assess the targets. If possible, find a group of students who could respond to the questionnaire. After they answer all the questions, ask them about their feelings toward the questions and the clarity of the wording. What do the results look like? Would the teacher agree with the results? How difficult was it to develop the questionnaire?

2. Interview several teachers about affective targets in the classroom. Ask them how they arrived at their targets and whether there is any systematic approach to assessing them. Ask what the advantages and disadvantages would be to using different kinds of assessment techniques, such as observation and student self-reports, and see if their answers match Figure 10.14.

Assessing Students with Special Needs in Inclusive Settings

One of most significant changes for teachers in the last two decades has been accommodating students with special needs who have been placed into regular classrooms. Students with mild disabilities are now routinely included with other students in the same class, and the regular classroom teacher is responsible for both instructing and evaluating these students. Teachers are also responsible for using assessment information to identify those students who may be eligible for special education services. In this chapter, we review the role of the regular teacher in identifying and adapting assessment practices so that they are fair and unbiased for students with special needs. First, we look briefly at the implications of the legal mandates in this area.

Legal Mandates
- PL 94-142
- PL 101-476 (IDEA)
- 1997 IDEA revision
- Nondiscriminatory assessment
- IEP
- Due process

Assessment Difficulties
- Comprehension lapses
- Auditory difficulties
- Visual difficulties
- Time constraints
- Anxiety
- Embarrassment
- Variability of behavior

ASSESSING STUDENTS WITH SPECIAL NEEDS

Identification
- Teacher observation
- Instructional interventions
- Prereferral
- Referral
- Identified
  — mental retardation
  — sensory impairment
  — physical impairment
  — learning disability
  — emotional disturbance
  — ESL students

Assessment Accommodations
- Test directions and construction
- Test administration
- Testing site
- Grading
- Reporting

CHAPTER 11   Concept Map

Legal Mandates

In 1975, the Education for All Handicapped Children Act, Public Law 94-142, was passed to provide free appropriate public education for school-aged individuals with special needs in the least restrictive environment. The act, which was updated in 1997 as the Individuals with Disabilities Education Act (IDEA), requires states to establish procedures to ensure that students with special needs are educated, to the maximum extent possible, with students who are not disabled, that is, in the least restrictive environment. The most common procedure for meeting this mandate has been to mainstream students with special needs by placing them in regular education classes with appropriate instructional support. The placing of these students is now known as **inclusion.** In fact, students can be removed from regular classes only when the severity of the disability prevents satisfactory instruction and learning progress. As a result, most classroom teachers must now be familiar with how students are identified as having "special needs" and how assessment procedures used in the course of regular classroom instruction need to be modified to ensure that these students are evaluated fairly.

Another important law was passed in 1986 to extend all rights and protections of PL 94-142 to preschoolers aged three to five (Public law PL 99-457). The effect of this law has been to encourage states to provide services for individuals from birth through kindergarten, with required services for three- to five-year-olds. The Americans with Disabilities Act of 1992 indicates further assurances for persons with disabilities, although these are not focused on schooling. In 1997 IDEA was amended, with final regulations published in 1999. The purpose of the 1997 amendments was to promote the following (Overton, 2003):

- Increased parental participation and involvement
- Ensuring student access to the general curriculum (mainstreaming)
- Preventing inappropriate identification and mislabeling
- Using mediation to resolve disputes and disagreements between parents and educators
- Ensuring the rights of students and their parents through due process
- Enhancement of student learning as determined through accountability mechanisms
- Providing for fair assessment of limited-English-proficiency students
- Using many and varied assessments
- Enhancement of individualized planning in the IEP

Thus, the trend is toward increasing governmental involvement in protecting the rights of individuals with disabilities, and you will be responsible for adhering to these regulations with students in inclusive settings.

According to PL 94-142 and IDEA, classroom teachers are responsible for gathering and providing the information used to identify students who may become eligible for special education services and for developing and implementing an **individualized education program (IEP).** The IEP is a written plan, developed by a team of individuals, that specifies the present level of knowledge and skills, annual goals, short-term learning objectives, the initiation and duration of special services, evaluation procedures, and the educational program (Spinelli, 2002). The teacher provides a major role in both determining and implementing the IEP, and monitors progress toward mastery of the goals and objectives. Assessments used by teachers provide the information necessary to determine if students are making satisfactory progress toward meeting learning targets as specified in the IEP. For both of these responsibilities, the act specifies that all testing and evaluation must be **nondiscriminatory.** For identification purposes, the law requires that the selection and administration of materials and procedures used for evaluation and placement must not be racially or culturally discriminatory. At a minimum, the law requires that (Wood, 2002):

1. Trained personnel administer validated tests and other evaluation materials and provide and administer such materials in the child's native language or other mode of communication.
2. Tests and other evaluation materials include those tailored to assess specific areas of educational need and not merely those designed to provide a single general intelligence quotient.
3. Trained personnel select and administer tests to reflect accurately the child's aptitude or achievement level without discriminating against the child's disability.
4. Trained personnel use no single procedure as the sole criterion for determining an appropriate educational program for a child.
5. A multidisciplinary team assess the child in all areas related to the suspected disability. (p. 11)

Essentially, these provisions mean that assessment must be planned and conducted so that the disability does not contribute to the score or result. That is, it would be unfair to use a test written in English to determine that a student whose primary language is Spanish has mental retardation, just as it would be unfair to conclude that a student with a fine motor disability did not know the answer to an essay question because there was insufficient time to write the answer.

With respect to writing and implementing the IEP, teachers have several responsibilities. As a member of a selected committee that writes the IEP, the regular classroom teacher provides important information, because the plan must be based on a clear and accurate documentation of the present level of educational functioning. This includes identification of a student's deficits and weaknesses, as well as the student's strengths. Although standardized test scores are used to establish levels of functioning, these scores need to be supplemented and corroborated by teacher observation and the student's classroom performance.

Another teacher responsibility is setting short- and long-term learning targets and specifying the criteria and evaluation procedures that will be used to monitor progress toward meeting the targets. Here, it is important to set truly *individualized* targets. Every student needs a customized set of realistic targets that takes into account identified strengths and weaknesses and preferred learning modes and styles. Appropriately delineated evaluation criteria and procedures need to reflect the degree of difficulty in the tasks, the variety of methods that should be employed, and a reasonable timetable.

Finally, teachers are responsible for ensuring that the student will participate in regular classroom activities to the maximum extent possible. This includes both formal and informal classroom assessments. Here, your understanding of what is required with each type of assessment and your knowledge of the specific disabilities of the students are used to ensure that, whenever possible, assessment procedures are not modified.

Assessing Students for Identification

The steps leading to identifying a student as having one or more of the disabilities that qualifies him or her to receive special education services are summarized in Figure 11.1. Identification must adhere to legal requirements and include a multidisciplinary evaluation (MDA) conducted by a multidisciplinary team (MTD) (Salvia & Ysseldyke, 2001). To examine your role in this process, as related to assessment, we consider two major categories of steps: those done before identification and the actual identification of various disabilities.

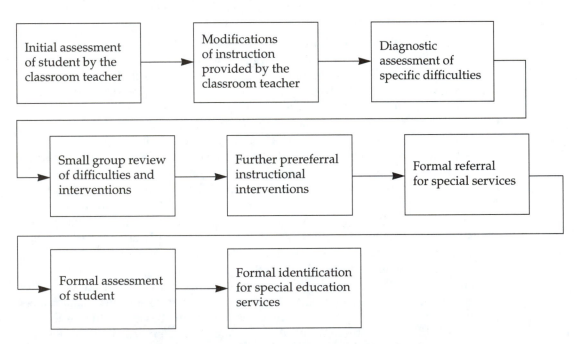

FIGURE 11.1   Steps for Identifying Students for Special Education Services

Steps before Identification

Initially, students are observed and evaluated by the classroom teacher, who then tries intervention strategies to see if these changes are sufficient for improving student performance. In effect, you need to be certain that relatively simple changes in teaching methods or materials are not sufficient to improve the student's performance.

If the student continues to have difficulties after you make these instructional interventions, the next step is to more closely analyze the student's ability to perform as expected. This usually includes the diagnostic assessment of specific learning difficulties or deficits using routine, teacher-made assessments. An analysis of errors may pinpoint these difficulties and suggest specific remediation strategies.

Some schools have a formal process of prereferral review for students with continuing difficulties. This may be called the prereferral committee or the child study team. In other schools, you will need to form your own small committee. Either way, the purpose of this group is to provide an external review of your tentative diagnosis and feedback concerning instructional interventions that have been tried. The group usually includes other teachers, school administrators, the school counselor, and special education teachers. Sometimes members of the committee may observe the student in class or conduct individual assessments. Often the committee will recommend additional interventions that may effectively address the problem, or a specific plan will be developed. In the event that the student still struggles, a comprehensive educational assessment is completed.

Formal referral is a serious step, because it suggests that the student may be eligible for special education services. Consequently, you will need to have specific documentation of the learning or behavior difficulties, interventions that have been tried, and the results of these interventions. It would be inadequate to simply say, for example, "Derek is always causing trouble in class. He likes to bother other students by poking and provoking them. We have tried several different approaches with Derek, each with limited success. He has a lot of trouble with mathematics." Rather, the information needs to be specific. For example:

> Derek physically touched, hit, or poked other students an average of fifteen times per day in a way that disturbed or bothered the students. He talks without raising his hand in class discussions 75 percent of the time. Time out, individual contracts, and sessions with the counselor have been used with limited success that soon dissipates. Derek has turned in homework only 20 percent of the time. In class, he is unable to complete mathematics assignments that deal with the addition and subtraction of complex fractions. He is off-task with mathematics assignments 50 percent of the time.

A screening committee will review the written referral, and the student's parents will be contacted. Suggestions for additional instructional interventions may be made. If the committee concludes that a formal assessment is needed, parental permission is secured and a comprehensive evaluation begins. This process includes the assessment of all areas of suspected disability, which is administered and interpreted by specialists in different areas (e.g., a school psychologist to administer intelligence, personality, and projective tests; a physical therapist to evaluate gross motor skills; and an audiologist to evaluate hearing acuity). Students are tested by a variety of methods, which may include additional informal observation by the regular classroom teacher. In any event, identification is confirmed when classroom teacher evaluations and those of the specialists coincide.

Identification

Following formal assessment, the student may be identified as having one or more specific educational disabilities. Each of the disabling conditions is confirmed by applying specific criteria. We will review the assessment criteria and implications of several common mild learning deficits, because students with these deficits are the ones most likely to be included in regular classes.

Mental Retardation.   Students are identified as having **mental retardation** on the basis of low scores on a standardized intelligence test and consistent deficits of what are termed *adaptive behaviors* that adversely affect educational performance. **Adaptive behaviors** are those that are needed for normal functioning in daily living situations, for example, expressive and receptive communication, daily living skills such as personal hygiene and eating habits, coping skills, and motor skills. The severity of the retardation is indicated in degrees: severe, moderate, and mild.

Although school psychologists will take care of the IQ testing, it may be up to you to provide much of the information regarding adaptive behaviors. Often, you accomplish this with the help of established adaptive behavior scales, such as the Vineland Adaptive Behavior Scale, the Adaptive Behavior Scale, and the Adaptive Behavior Inventory for Children. Teachers, as well as primary caregivers, are interviewed with these types of instruments to document the student's behavioral competence. In addition, it is important for you to confirm findings from these instruments with more informal observations.

You need to keep two cautions in mind when assessing adaptive behavior. First, no single adaptive behavior instrument covers all areas of behavior, and the data for these instruments are gathered from third-party observers. Thus, it is important to select the instrument that will provide the most valid inferences for the situation and to keep in mind that third parties may be biased. Second, you need to be careful that a student's cultural or linguistic background does not cause the student to be inappropriately labeled as having inadequate adaptive behavior. Some students who are perfectly capable of functioning in their day-to-day living environments may have difficulty functioning in the classroom because of the cultural or language differences. Thus, adaptive behavior is best evaluated relative to the context in which it occurs (Witt, Elliot, Daly, Gresham, & Kramer, 1998).

Sensory Impairment.   Students who have vision, hearing, or speech deficits may be identified as sensory impaired. This could include a communication disorder, such as stuttering or impaired articulation; visual difficulties, even with correction, including eye-hand coordination; or a hearing problem that interferes with educational performance. One of the first things you should do with students experiencing difficulty in learning is to check for visual and hearing acuity. Obviously, students who have trouble seeing or hearing will have trouble academically. Your close and careful observation of students will provide clues to these types of impairments.

Physical Impairment.   Other physical disabilities are not sensory, such as an orthopedic impairment (cerebral palsy, amputations) or a physical illness like epilepsy, diabetes, or muscular dystrophy. Generally, these conditions will be obvious, and resources will be provided to make appropriate accommodations.

Learning Disability.   A **learning disability** is identified when a processing deficit manifests itself in a severe discrepancy between performance and ability. This includes perceptual handicaps such as dyslexia, but not sensory or physical impairment, mental retardation, or environmental, cultural, or economic disadvantage. These students have average or above average intelligence, but function at low levels because of physiological, psychological, or cognitive processes involved in understanding and using language or mathematical reasoning. You may be asked to administer a standardized test to document the discrepancy, and you will surely be needed to comment on data from the student's cumulative folder and classroom performance and behavior. As before, the process is dependent on your careful observation and evaluation of the student.

It is important to be able to distinguish between a learning disability and slow learning. A slow learner may also have a discrepancy between ability and achievement and may need remedial education, but the reason for the low performance is not an impairment in intellectual functioning. It may well be due to emotional problems or economic disadvantage, but these types of deficiencies are not sufficient to identify a student as learning disabled.

Emotional Disturbance.   Also called an emotional disability, a behavioral disorder, or serious emotional disturbance, a student identified as **emotionally disturbed** consistently exhibits one or more of the following characteristics to a marked degree that clearly interferes with learning: poor academic performance not due to other disabilities; poor interpersonal relationships; inappropriate behaviors or feelings in normal circumstances; unhappiness, melancholy, or depression; or unfounded physical symptoms or fears associated with school or personal problems. Students who are emotionally disturbed often will become withdrawn.

You will need to make systematic observations of a student who may be classified under the category of emotional disturbed. This could include, for example, noting each time the student displays inappropriate behavior, such as crying or yelling, in normal circumstances for no apparent reason. When the inappropriate behavior continues for an extended time, under different conditions, a serious emotional problem may be found. However, final diagnosis will require consultation with a specialist, such as a counselor or school psychologist.

Figures 11.2 and 11.3 summarize the teacher's role in the assessment and identification processes. Figure 11.2 summarizes responsibilities for different steps

FIGURE 11.2   Classroom Teacher's Role in the Assessment Process

Steps in the Assessment Process	Regular Classroom Teacher's Role
Before referral	Use informal assessment methods to monitor daily progress, curriculum-based assessment, and behavioral observations; consult with committee members
	Implement educational interventions
Diagnosis of specific disability	Recognize behaviors and characteristics of specific disabilities so that students can be identified, evaluated, and served if appropriate
	Recognize behaviors and characteristics that indicate cultural or linguistic differences and that do not warrant special education services
Referral	Document through data collection of student work samples, behavioral observations, teacher-made tests, and other informal measures to identify educational strengths and weaknesses
	Consult with committee members
	Consult with parents
	Complete necessary referral forms
	Attend child study committee meeting and present appropriate data collected on student progress and behaviors
	Participate during development and implementation of identification and IEP for students in the regular class setting

Source: Adapted from Wood, J., *Adapting instruction to accommodate students in inclusive settings,* 4th edition, copyright © 2002, p. 36. Adapted by permission of Pearson Education, Inc., Upper Saddle River, New Jersey.

in the assessment process, and Figure 11.3 shows a teacher's responsibilities for identification in major categories. Generally, your observations of the student will be used to corroborate the specialists' findings.

Limited-English-Proficient Students

In the last ten years there has been a dramatic increase in the number of students who are classified as limited-English-proficient (LEP), English as a second language (ESL), English language learner (ELL), or bilingual. These students, while not being classified into one or more identified groups of students who receive special services, nonetheless have special needs. Often these students are included in regular classrooms, and teachers must deal with them in ways that are similar to how English-language students with special needs are taught and assessed.

Many of the steps used to identify these students are the same as those used to identify students with special needs. Teachers will need to depend on ESL teachers or language experts who are able to diagnose the student and suggest appropriate interventions. Although there is no formal referral for identification, there

FIGURE 11.3   Classroom Teacher's Role in the Identification Process

Disability	Teacher's Role	Questions
Mental retardation	Document adaptive behaviors; meet with child study committee	How well does the student function with daily life skills? Do deficits in daily living skills affect academic performance? Does cultural or linguistic background contribute to deficits in daily living skills?
Sensory impairment	Document visual, auditory, or speech impairments; meet with child study committee	Can the student see well enough? Is there adequate eye/hand coordination? Is there a problem with the student's hearing? Is there a speech problem of some kind?
Physical disability	Observe effect of disability on academic performance; meet with the child study committee	Does the disability adversely affect academic performance?
Learning disability	Document learning problems and achievement; interpret information in the cumulative folder; meet with the child study committee	Is there a large discrepancy between ability and achievement? Are sensory, physical, and mental disabilities ruled out?
Emotional disturbance	Document inappropriate behaviors and feelings; meet with child study committee	Does the student have average or above-average intelligence? Is the behavior extreme for the circumstances? Is the behavior fleeting or consistent? Are any other disabilities responsible for the poor performance? How well does the student interact with others? Is the student unhappy, depressed, or withdrawn much of the time?

are accommodations that should be implemented to assure fair and nondiscriminatory assessment.

Assessment Problems Encountered by Students with Special Needs

Your goal in assessing student learning is to obtain a fair and accurate indication of performance. Because disabilities may affect test-taking ability, you will need to make accommodations, or changes, in assessments when needed to ensure valid inferences and consequences. There are many justifiable ways to alter assessments for students with special needs. Before we consider these, it will be helpful to review the problems encountered by students with disabilities in testing situations. These difficulties are summarized in Figure 11.4.

Comprehension Difficulties

Many students with mild disabilities have difficulty with comprehension. This means that they may not understand verbal or written directions very well. If there is a sequence of steps in the directions, they may not be able to remember the sequence or all the steps, particularly if the directions are verbal. Lengthy written directions may be too complicated, and the reading level may be too high. There may be words or phrases that the student does not understand. If the directions include several different operations, the student may be confused about what to do. Obviously, without a clear understanding of how to proceed it will be difficult for these students to demonstrate their knowledge or skills.

Students with mild disabilities have even more difficulty understanding directions or test items that require reasoning skills. These students may respond well to knowledge and understanding questions and deal well with concrete ideas, but they may not respond very well to abstractions. For example, it would be relatively easy for such students to respond to a straightforward short-answer question such as "What are the characteristics of a democratic government?" but much harder to respond to a more abstract question such as "How is the government of the United States different from a socialistic government?"

FIGURE 11.4   Problems Encountered by Students with Special Needs That Impact Classroom Assessment

Problem	Impact on Assessment
Comprehension difficulties	Understanding directions; completing assessments requiring reasoning skills
Auditory difficulties	Understanding oral directions and test items; distracted by noises
Visual difficulties	Understanding written directions and test items; decoding symbols and letters; visual distractions
Time constraint difficulties	Completing assessments
Anxiety	Completing assessments; providing correct information
Embarrassment	Understanding directions; completing assessments
Variability of behavior	Completing assessments; demonstrating best work

Auditory Difficulties

Students with auditory disabilities have trouble processing information they hear quickly and accurately. Although they can hear, they will have difficulty processing the information easily. This makes it especially hard for these students to follow and understand verbal directions. Thus, their responses to oral tests and quizzes may be minimal, not because they haven't mastered the content, but because they don't fully understand the question. It is easy for teachers simply to read or talk too fast, but this does not allow sufficient time for students with auditory disabilities to process the information.

These students may also be sensitive to auditory distractions in the classroom. Such distractions are common in most classrooms, and it is easy to become accustomed to some background noise. This could include sound from the hallway or an adjoining classroom, talking among students, outside noise, desk movement, pencil sharpening, questions asked by students, teacher reprimands, school announcements, and so on. Although these sounds may seem "normal" and do not bother most students, those with auditory disabilities will be distracted and their attention will be diverted from the task at hand. This is a particular problem if the noise accompanies oral directions from the teacher, because the student will find it difficult to focus on the directions. It's not that these students are not paying attention or need to concentrate more. They have a disability that makes it difficult to discriminate sounds and keep focused.

Visual Difficulties

Students with visual disabilities have difficulty processing what they see. These students may copy homework assignments or test questions from the board incorrectly by transposing numbers or interchanging letters. Often the student has difficulty transferring information to paper. A cluttered board that requires visual discrimination may also cause problems. Visual disabilities also become a handicap on some handwritten tests if the test is not legible and clearly organized. The printing and cursive writing of most teachers is fine, but the handwriting of some teachers is not very legible for students with visual disabilities. Some students with a visual disability have difficulty decoding certain symbols, letters, and abbreviations, such as +, −, b and d, < and >, and n and m. One symbol may be confused with another, and test problems with many symbols may take a long time for these students to understand.

Some types of objective test items are a problem because of visual perceptual difficulties. For example, lengthy matching items pose particular problems because the student may take a long time to peruse the columns, searching for answers and identifying the correct letters to use. Multiple-choice items that run responses together on the same line make it hard to discriminate among the possible answers.

Visual distractions can also interfere with test taking. For some students, a single visual cue—such as students moving in the classroom when getting up to turn in papers, student gestures, teacher motions, or something or someone outside—disrupts their present visual focus and makes it difficult to keep their concentration.

Time Constraint Difficulties

Time can pose a major problem for many students with disabilities. Frequently visual, auditory, motor coordination, and reading difficulties make it hard for some students to complete tests in the same time frame as other students. It's not that the students are lazy or intentionally slow. It simply takes them longer because of their disability. Thus, students should not be penalized for being unable to complete a test, especially timed tests that are constructed to reward speed in decoding and understanding questions and writing answers.

Anxiety

Although most students experience some degree of anxiety when completing tests, students with disabilities may be especially affected by feelings of anxiety because of fear that their disability will make it difficult to complete the test. Some students are simply unable to function very well in a traditional test setting because the length or format of the test overwhelms them. It is not because they don't have the knowledge; they may think their disability will affect their work.

One general strategy to reduce unhealthy anxiety is to make sure that students have learned appropriate test-taking skills. They need to know what to do if they do not fully understand the directions and how to proceed in answering different types of items (e.g., looking for clue words in multiple-choice, true/false, and completion items; crossing out incorrect alternatives in multiple-choice items; crossing out answers used in matching items). They also need to know to skip difficult items and come back to them when they have answered all other questions.

Embarrassment

Students with disabilities may be more sensitive than other students to feelings of embarrassment. They often want to hide or disguise their problems so that they are not singled out or labeled by their peers. As a result, they may want to appear to be "normal" when taking a test by not asking questions about directions and handing in the test at the same time as other students do, whether or not they are finished. They don't want to risk embarrassment by being the only one to have a question or by being the last one to complete their work. Students with special needs may also be embarrassed if they take a different test than others.

Variability of Behavior

The behavior of students with disabilities varies greatly. This means that their disabilities may affect their behavior one day and not the next, and it may be impossible to predict this variability. This is especially true for students with emotional disturbances. For example, a student with a conduct disorder may be very disruptive one day and seem normal the next. Consequently, you will need to be tolerant and flexible in your assessments, realizing that on a particular day the disability may pose extreme difficulties for the student.

Assessment Accommodations

Once you understand how disabilities can interfere with valid assessment, you can take steps to adapt the test or other assessment to accommodate the disability. These accommodations can be grouped into three major categories: adaptations in test construction, test administration, and testing site (Wood, 2002).

Adaptations in Test Directions and Construction

The first component to adapt is the test directions. You can do this for all students, or you can provide a separate set of directions for students with disabilities. Here are some ways to modify test directions:

1. Read written directions aloud, slowly, and give students ample opportunity to ask questions about the directions. Reread directions for each page of questions.
2. Keep directions short and simple.
3. Give examples of how to answer questions.
4. Focus attention by underlining verbs.
5. Provide separate directions for each section of the test.
6. Provide one direction for each sentence (list sentences vertically).
7. Check the students' understanding of the directions.
8. During the test, check student answers to be sure that the students understand the directions.

The general format of the test should be designed to simplify the amount of information that is processed at one time. Accomplish this by leaving plenty of white space on each page so that students are not overwhelmed. The printing should be large, with adequate space between items; this results in a smaller number of items per page. The test should be separated into clearly distinguished short sections, and only one type of question should be on each page. The printing should be dark and clear. If bubble sheets are used for objective items, use larger bubbles. Be sure multiple-choice items list the alternatives vertically, and do not run questions or answers across two pages. Number each page of the test. Some students may be aided by a large sheet of construction paper that they can place below the question or cut out to allow a greater focus on a particular section of the test. If possible, design the format of an adapted test to look as much like the test for other students as possible.

Other accommodations to the format of the test depend on the type of item, as illustrated in the following examples.

Short-Answer and Essay Items.   Students with disabilities may have extreme difficulty with short-answer items because of the organization, reasoning, and writing skills required. For these reasons, complicated essay questions requiring long responses should be avoided. If you use an essay question, be sure students understand terms like *compare, contrast,* and *discuss.* Use a limited number of essay questions, and allow students to use outlines for their answers. Some students may need to record their answer rather than writing it; all students will need to have sufficient time.

Example

> *Poor:* Compare and contrast the Canadian and United States governments.
>
> *Improved: Compare* and *contrast* the Canadian and United States governments.
>
>   I. *Compare* by telling how the governments are *alike.* Give two examples.
> II. *Contrast* by telling how the governments are *different.* Give two examples.

If the short-answer question focuses on recall, you can adapt it in ways that will help students to organize their thoughts and not be overwhelmed.

Example (adapted from *Creating a Learning Community at Fowler High School,* 1993)

> *Poor:*
>
> Directions: On your own paper, identify the following quotations. Tell (1) who said it, (2) to whom it was said or if it was a soliloquy, (3) when it was said, and (4) what it means.
>
> But soft, what light through yonder window breaks?
> It is the east, and Juliet is the sun.
> Arise, fair sun, and kill the envious moon.
> (Include a series of several more quotes.)
>
> *Improved:*
>
> Directions: In the space provided, identify the following for each quotation.
>
> Tell   1. Who said it
>   2. To whom it was said or if it was a soliloquy
>   3. When it was said
>   4. What it means

Who said it; to whom it was said	*When it was said*
Juliet	When Tybalt kills Mercutio
Romeo	When Juliet waits for news from Romeo
Paris	
Mercutio	The balcony scene
The Prince	When Paris discusses his marriage with Friar

1. But soft, what light through yonder window breaks?
   It is the east, and Juliet is the sun.
   Arise, fair sun, and kill the envious moon.

Who said it   *To whom*   *When*   *What it means*

_____   _____   _____   _____

_____   _____   _____   _____

_____   _____   _____   _____

Multiple-Choice Items. If the test contains multiple-choice questions, have students circle the correct answer rather than writing the letter of the correct response next to the item or transferring the answer to a separate sheet. Arrange response alternatives vertically, and include no more than four alternatives for each question. Keep the language simple and concise, and avoid wording such as "a and b but not d," or "either a or c," or "none of the above" that weights the item more heavily for reasoning skills. Limit the number of multiple-choice items, and give students with disabilities plenty of time to complete the test. Other students may easily be able to answer one item per minute, but it will take exceptional students longer. Basically, you need to follow the suggestions listed in Chapter 6 and realize that poorly constructed and formatted items are likely to be more detrimental to students with disabilities.

Binary-Choice Items. True/false and other binary-choice items need to be stated clearly and concisely. Answers should be circled. Negatively stated items should be avoided. Sometimes students are asked to change false items to make them true, but this is not recommended for students with disabilities. Limit the number of items to from ten to fifteen.

Completion Items. These items can be modified to reduce the student's dependence on structured recall by providing word banks that accompany the items. The word bank is a list of possible answers that reduces dependence on memory. The list can be printed on a separate sheet of paper so that the student can move it up and down on the right side of the page. Also, provide large blanks for students with motor control difficulties.

Performance Assessments. The first accommodation to performance assessments may need to be in the directions. Students with disabilities need directions that clearly specify what is expected, with examples, and a reasonable time frame. Because these assessments involve thinking and application skills, it is important to be certain that students with disabilities are able to perform the skills required. The steps may need to be clearly delineated. Obviously, if some aspect of the performance requires physical skills or coordination that the disability prevents or makes difficult, assistance will need to be provided. If the performance requires group participation, you will need to closely monitor the interactions.

Portfolios.   In some ways, this type of assessment is ideal for students with disabilities because the assignments and products can be individualized to show progress. This means that you may need to adapt the portfolio requirements to fit well with what the student is capable of doing. In the portfolio you could include your reflection of how the student made progress despite the presence of the disability to demonstrate how the student was responsible for success.

Adaptations in Test Administration

Adaptations during test administration involve changes in procedures that lessen the negative effect of disabilities while the student is taking the test. Most of these procedural accommodations depend on the nature of the disability or difficulty, as summarized in Figure 11.5, and are based on common sense. For example, if the student has a visual problem, you need to give directions orally and check

Case Study for Reflection

Mr. Ashcraft is a seventh grade social studies teacher in a predominantly working-class school. He is a twelve-year veteran who has been recognized by fellow teachers, administrators, and parents as a good teacher. At the beginning of the school year, Mr. Ashcraft was confronted with four special education students in his fourth-period class. All were boys; one was bilingual, and two were diagnosed as having attention deficit disorders and learning disabilities. The fourth boy was extremely emotionally impaired, and this was his first time in a mainstreamed classroom. Although Mr. Ashcraft had no experience with any special population, he was selected to take these students because of his reputation as a good teacher and classroom manager.

Each of the four students posed unique assessment problems. With the help of one of the special education teachers and a counselor, Mr. Ashcraft learned some of the basic requirements of PL 101-476 (IDEA). He also learned some ways of adapting assessment instruments for these students. These methods included giving fewer problems, deleting a choice on multiple-choice tests, providing a word bank for fill-in-the-blank questions, and allowing students to skip certain sections altogether. He was also told he could give students oral tests and allow them to take tests before or after school.

Mr. Ashcraft was very concerned about this situation and felt he was in an awkward position. With no training in this area he felt unqualified to make assessments about these new students. He questioned the legitimacy of what he was doing. When he shared his concerns with the head of the special education department, he was told that mainstreaming students was the way things were going and he might as well get used to it.

Questions for Consideration
1. Are Mr. Ashcraft's assessment accommodations appropriate?
2. What additional assessment accommodations would you suggest to Mr. Ashcraft?
3. What can Mr. Ashcraft do to feel more confident in assessing these students?

FIGURE 11.5   Adaptations in Test Administration

Disability or Problem	Adaptations
Poor comprehension	1. Give test directions both orally and in writing. 2. Double-check student understanding. 3. Avoid long talks before the test. 4. Allow students to tape-record responses to essay questions or the entire test. 5. Correct open-ended responses for content only and not for spelling or grammar. 6. Provide examples of expected correct responses. 7. Remind students to check for unanswered questions. 8. Allow the use of multiplication tables or calculators for math tests. 9. Read the test aloud for students with reading comprehension difficulties. 10. Give an outline for essay question responses. 11. Give students an audio recording of instructions and questions. 11. Use objective items.
Auditory difficulties	1. Use written rather than oral questions. 2. Go slowly for oral tests, enunciating and sounding out distinctly. 3. Seat students in a quiet place for testing. 4. Stress the importance of being quiet to all students.
Visual difficulties	1. Give directions orally as well as in writing. 2. Give exam orally or tape recorded on audiocassette. 3. Allow students to take the test orally. 4. Seat the student away from visual distractions (e.g., windows and doors). Use a carrel or place desk facing wall. 5. Avoid having other students turn in papers during the test. 6. Meet classroom visitors at the door and talk in the hallway.
Time constraint difficulties	1. Allow more than enough time to complete the test. 2. Provide breaks during lengthy tests. 3. Give half the test one day, half the second day. 4. Avoid timed tests. 5. Give students with slow writing skills oral or tape-recorded tests.
Anxiety	1. Avoid adding pressure by admonishing students to "Hurry and get finished" or by saying, "This test will determine your final grade." 2. Do not threaten to use test results to punish students. 3. Do not threaten to use tests to punish students for poor behavior. 4. Give a practice test or practice items. 5. Allow students to retest if needed. 6. Do not threaten dire consequences if students do not do well. 7. Emphasize internal attributions for previous work. 8. Avoid having a few major tests; give many smaller tests. 9. Avoid norm-referenced testing; use criterion-referenced tests.
Embarrassment	1. Make the modified test closely resemble the regular test; use the same cover sheet. 2. Avoid calling attention to mainstreamed students as you help them. 3. Monitor all students the same way. 4. Do not give mainstreamed students special attention when handing out the test. 5. Confer with students privately to work out accommodations for testing. 6. Do not single out mainstreamed students when returning tests.
Variability of behavior	1. Allow retesting. 2. Allow student to reschedule testing for another day. 3. Monitor closely to determine if behavior is preventing best work.

Source: Adapted from Wood, J., *Adapting instruction to accommodate students in inclusive settings,* 4th edition, copyright © 2002, pp. 567–569. Adapted by permission of Pearson Education, Inc., Upper Saddle River, New Jersey.

carefully to determine if he or she has understood the questions. For students who are hindered by time constraints, provide breaks and make sure they have sufficient time to complete the test.

In general, it is best to place a Testing—Do Not Disturb sign on your classroom door to discourage visitors and other distractions. You will need to monitor these students closely as they take the test and encourage them to ask questions. It is also helpful to encourage them to use dark paper to underline the items they are currently working on (Lazzari & Wood, 1994).

Adaptations in Testing Site

You may find it necessary to allow students with special needs to take the test in a different location than the regular classroom. This alternative test site is often the resource room in the school or some other room that is quiet with fewer distractions. As long as someone can monitor the testing, the student will have more opportunities to ask questions and feel less embarrassed when asking for clarification or further explanation. You will want to work out the details of using an alternate testing site with the special education teacher.

If you are unsure about how you should accommodate students with special needs, check with the special education teacher in your school. This individual can help you more fully understand the strengths and limitations of each student, as well as the appropriateness of specific adaptations.

Grading and Reporting Accommodations

The purpose of grading is to provide an accurate indication of what students have learned. For students with special needs in inclusive settings, it is necessary to consider some adaptations to the grading procedures used for all students to make sure that student disabilities do not unduly influence the determination of the grade. This may present a dilemma for teachers. On the one hand, is it fair to use different grading standards and procedures for some students? On the other hand, is it fair to possibly penalize students by forcing an existing grading scheme on them that may have detrimental impacts? The ideal solution would be to keep the grading system for students with special needs the same as that used for other students and be sure that appropriate accommodations have been made in the assessment strategies to ensure that the information on which the grade is determined is not adversely affected by the disability. However, depending on the student's IEP, it may be necessary to adapt the grading system that is used.

Grading Accommodations

Several types of grading accommodations are appropriate for students with special needs (Mehring, 1995). These include IEP grading, shared grading, and contract grading.

IEP Grading.   The IEP grading system bases grades on the achievement of the goals and objectives stated in the student's IEP. The criteria needed to obtain satisfactory progress are stated in the IEP. It is problematic, however, to translate success in reaching IEP objectives to grades. One approach is to use the school district's performance standards to determine grades. For example, if the student has performed at the 90 percent proficiency level, as required by the IEP to demonstrate competence, and 90 percent translates to a B letter grade, then the student is assigned a B for that assessment. Another approach is to review the criteria in the IEP and match levels of performance with what other students need to demonstrate for different grades. If you decide, for instance, that the level of mastery a student with special needs demonstrates by achieving but not exceeding all IEP objectives is about the same level as that demonstrated by other students receiving Cs, then the grade for the student with special needs would also be a C. If the student exceeds stated IEP objectives, then a B or A may be appropriate.

Because the goal of inclusion is to make the educational experience of students with disabilities like that of other students, it is best if the grading procedures reflect the same criteria. You should avoid a process whereby the grade is determined merely on the percentage of IEP objectives obtained, because there is a tendency to inadvertently set low or easier objectives to help students obtain good grades (Cohen, 1983).

Shared Grading.   In shared grading, the regular classroom and special education or resource room teachers determine the grade together. The weight that each teacher provides for the grade should be agreed on at the beginning of the marking period. This usually reflects the extent to which each teacher is responsible for different areas of learning. Typically, the classroom teacher will have the most influence on the grades.

One advantage of this type of grading is that the special education or resource room teacher may be able to provide some insight that helps explain some bad grades and other mitigating circumstances related to the student's disability. Using this team approach also helps the classroom teacher determine appropriate criteria and standards for grading.

Contracting.   A contract is a written agreement between the regular classroom teacher and the student that specifies the nature of the work that the student must complete to achieve a particular grade. Teachers frequently use contracts for students with special needs because they can integrate IEP objectives and clearly state for the student and parents the type and quality of work to be completed. For older students, the contract should include options for achieving different grades. Contracts for elementary-level students should be simpler, with more general outcomes at a single level, as illustrated in Figure 11.6. Several components should be included in a contract, such as:

- a description of the work to be completed
- a description of criteria by which work will be evaluated
- signatures of the student, teacher, and other involved parties
- a time line for completion of the work

FIGURE 11.6 Sample Contract for Elementary Level Students

My Contract

If I . . .

- Take my belongings from my backpack and put them in my desk without being asked,
- Come to my reading group the first time it is called,
- Clean off my desk after snack and put all the garbage in the trash can,
- Raise my hand each time I want to answer, and
- Put all my finished papers in the "done" basket before lunch

. . . then I will receive a "plus" for the morning's work.

If I . . .

- Line up on the playground the first time the whistle is blown,
- Put all the classroom supplies back in the supply boxes after project time,
- Put all my finished papers in the "done" basket before I go home,
- Put my homework papers in my portfolio to take home, and
- Put my belongings in my backpack, get my coat from the cubby, and line up before my bus is called

. . . then I will receive a "plus" for the afternoon's work.

_____   _____
Student   Teacher

                    _____
                    Date

Source: Wood, J., _Adapting instruction to accommodate students in inclusive settings,_ 4th edition, copyright © 2002, p. 597. Adapted by permission of Pearson Education, Inc., Upper Saddle River, New Jersey.

Reporting Accommodations

Regardless of the grading system that you use, it will probably be necessary to supplement the regular progress report with additional information. This is typically done as a checklist or a narrative summary that interprets achievement in light of the student's disability. A checklist is convenient for showing progress in developmentally sequenced courses and can easily integrate IEP with course objectives to give a more complete report. The checklist states the objectives, and the teacher indicates if each has been mastered or needs further work.

A narrative summary helps you to give the student a still more personalized evaluation. Although such a report takes some time, it more fully explains why the teacher believes the student demonstrated certain skills, which skills were not mastered, and which need special attention. The narrative can also be used to report on behavioral performance, emotions, and interpersonal skills, as well as academic performance. Specific incidents or examples can be described. The following is an example of a progress report for an eighth-grade student with a learning disability (Mehring, 1995). Notice that the teacher has indicated areas of improvement, accommodations (typing), and areas that will be stressed in the future.

Alphonso has improved his ability to recognize and correct spelling errors. He has mastered the recognition and capitalization of proper nouns, names, titles, and buildings. He is not yet consistent in his capitalization of cities. Punctuation, especially the use of commas, is also an area in which Alphonso needs improvement. He has been using the computer to prepare drafts of his written products. This has made it easier for him to edit since his handwriting is laborious and illegible at times. The overall quality and length of his creative writings has improved significantly since the last reporting period. We will continue to focus on capitalization and punctuation throughout the next grading period. In addition, we will begin working on recognizing and correcting sentence problems (fragments, run-ons, unclear pronoun reference, and awkward sentences). (p. 17)

By focusing a supplemental progress report on the learning process, students will have a better idea about how they need to change to improve their performance. Students and parents need to know if a specific approach to learning needs to be modified or if something else needs to be further investigated.

Summary

The purpose of this chapter was to introduce you to the assessment adaptations needed to accommodate students with special needs in inclusive settings. Overall, suggestions made in other chapters apply to these students, but you need to keep some additional considerations in mind. In general, it is important to make sure that a student's disability does not influence his or her performance on tests and other types of assessments. Major points in the chapter include:

- Legal mandates in PL 101-476 (IDEA) require educational experiences, including assessment, to take place in the least restrictive environment.
- Regular classroom teachers are responsible for gathering information to identify students for special education services.
- The evaluation of students for identification must be nondiscriminatory—in the student's native language and not racially or culturally biased.
- Teacher observation is a major component in identification and writing the student's IEP.
- Teachers are responsible for setting individualized learning targets with appropriate assessments.
- Teachers are responsible for providing specific assessment information for referral and possible identification.
- Procedures are implemented to make identifying a student for special education services difficult.
- Students are identified as having one or more educational disabilities, based in part on careful teacher observation.
- Teachers are responsible for assessing the adaptive behaviors of students referred and identified as having mental retardation.
- Comprehension difficulties require adaptations in test directions.
- Auditory and visual difficulties require a minimum of distractions.

- Time constraint difficulties require longer testing time and frequent breaks in testing.
- Anxiety and embarrassment need to be minimized for students with special needs.
- The behavior of students with disabilities varies from day to day; this variation needs to be considered when observing and evaluating student behavior.
- Adaptations may need to be made to test directions, the format of the test, and the construction of different types of items.
- Adaptations may be needed during test administration and to the testing site.
- Grading students with special needs should include consideration of IEP objectives, opinions of other teachers working with the student, and contracting.
- Supplemental reports and feedback are helpful for focusing attention on IEP and learning process objectives.

SELF-INSTRUCTIONAL REVIEW EXERCISES

1. According to PL 94-142, what are the two essential responsibilities of regular classroom teachers concerning the assessment of students with special needs who are in inclusive settings?

2. Indicate whether each of the following statements represents nondiscriminatory assessment (Y for yes, N for no):

   a. A single procedure may be used for identification.
   b. Assessment is conducted by a multidisciplinary team.
   c. Assessments are conducted in English.
   d. The disability may not affect the scores students receive.
   e. Racial and cultural discrimination must be avoided.

3. Read the following scenario and indicate whether the teacher has properly followed the steps necessary to refer a student for identification.

   Mrs. Albert was immediately suspicious of Jane, thinking that she might have a learning disability. Jane did not achieve very well on written tests and seemed to have trouble concentrating. She was also distracted very easily. Mrs. Albert tried Jane in another reading group, but this did not seem to help. After looking at Jane's previous test scores, Mrs. Albert decided to refer her for identification.

4. Indicate whether each of the descriptions listed is characteristic of students with mental retardation (MR), emotional disturbance (ED), sensory impairment (SI), physical impairment (PI), or learning disability (LD).

   a. diabetes
   b. language deficit
   c. discrepancy between ability and achievement
   d. poor adaptive behaviors
   e. poor eyesight
   f. slow learning

5. Indicate whether each of the difficulties listed is characteristic of students with comprehension difficulties (C), sensory difficulties (SD), time constraint difficulties (TCD), anxiety (A), embarrassment (E), or variability of behavior (VB).

   a. gets sequence of steps wrong
   b. worries excessively about performance
   c. hands in an incomplete test with other students
   d. has trouble one day finishing a test, no trouble the next day
   e. takes longer to complete the test

6. Indicate whether each of the following test administration adaptations is considered good practice (Y for yes, N for no).

   a. making tests with fewer items
   b. closely monitoring students while they are taking a test
   c. modifying tests
   d. giving special attention when handing out tests
   e. using norm-referenced testing
   f. emphasizing internal attributions
   g. giving practice tests
   h. allowing students to take a written test orally
   i. using objective rather than essay items
   j. using normal seating arrangements
   k. checking student understanding of directions

7. Read the following scenario and indicate what was correct and what was incorrect or lacking in the teacher's assessment accommodations.

   Mr. Parvin was careful to read all the directions aloud, and he gave examples of how the students should answer each item. He prepared a separate set of directions for his students with special needs. He designed the test to make sure as many questions as possible were included on each page. He underlined key words in the short-answer questions and wrote objective items so that the students corrected wrong answers. Mr. Parvin did not permit questions once students began the test. He told students that they had to complete the test in thirty minutes, and he placed a sign on the door indicating that testing was taking place.

8. Ms. Ramirez has a learning-disabled student in her classroom. His name is Tyron. Ms. Ramirez has decided to use a contract grading procedure, and she wants to be able to report progress on the contract to Tyron's parents. How would Ms. Ramirez begin to develop her contract, and how would she report progress to his parents?

ANSWERS TO SELF-INSTRUCTIONAL REVIEW EXERCISES

1. Gathering information for identification and implementing the IEP.

2. a. N, b. Y, c. N, d. Y, e. Y.

3. Mrs. Albert did some things right but in general did not do enough to justify formal referral. She seems to have targeted behaviors that are characteristic of students

with a learning disability, and she did try one instructional intervention. However, more instructional interventions are needed to be sure that the problems could not be ameliorated in the class without referral. There is no indication that the teacher made any more structured, diagnostic assessments, and there is no evidence of any type of prereferral review. A serious oversight is that Mrs. Albert has not requested that outsiders review the situation.

4. a. PI, b. LD, c. LD, d. MR, e. SI, f. none.

5. a. C, b. A, c. E, d. VB, e. TCD.

6. a. N, b. Y, c. Y, d. N, e. N, f. Y, g. Y, h. Y, i. Y, j. N, k. Y.

7. Correct procedures included reading the directions aloud, giving examples, underlining key words, and placing a sign on the door. Incorrect procedures, from an adaptation perspective, included giving students with disabilities a separate set of directions (which may cause embarrassment), putting too much on each page of the test, asking students to correct wrong answers for objective items, not permitting questions during the test, and giving students what seems like a short time limit.

8. It would be best to begin with a clear indication of the work to be completed and how different grades will be assigned. A specific time line for completing the work should be included. Signatures of the student and parents are needed to ensure that all understand. The teacher's report should not simply indicate what grades are achieved, but should also include some personalized comments and suggestions.

SUGGESTIONS FOR ACTION RESEARCH

1. Interview two or three regular classroom teachers about the accommodations they make for students with special needs who are in their classes. Ask about their experience in gathering information for identification and setting learning targets, as well as about the assessment accommodations they have made. Compare their responses to suggestions in the chapter.

2. Interview two special education teachers. Ask them what they believe regular classroom teachers need to know to accommodate students with special needs in inclusive settings. In their work with regular classroom teachers, what do they see as the teachers' greatest weaknesses when making assessment accommodations?

3. Interview school division central office personnel who are responsible for students with special needs. What is the district's approach toward assessing students with special needs? What kind of support is provided for the teachers?

4. In a team with one or two other students, devise a plan for how you would accommodate the assessment of one or two students with special needs who have been placed in regular classrooms. You will need as much information about the students as possible, and it would be best if you could observe the students. Once the plan is complete, review it with the students' teacher(s) for feedback and suggestions.

CHAPTER

12 Grading and Reporting Student Performance

In the past few chapters we have seen how teachers can assess students on a variety of learning targets. As was pointed out in the model of classroom assessment presented in Chapter 1, now you need to do something with the assessments. Specifically, you will need to make professional judgments about the quality of student work, then translate that into grades and reports. We begin with a discussion of the importance of a teacher's professional judgment in the use of assessment, then we consider some specific approaches to marking, grading, and reporting.

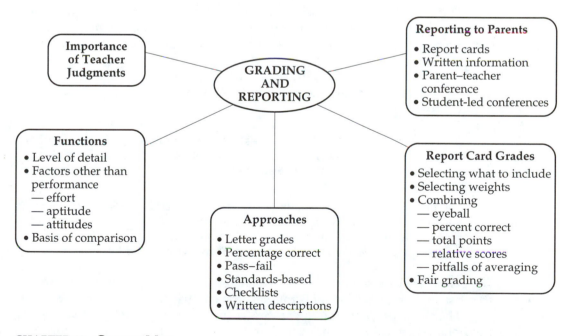

Importance of Teacher Judgments

GRADING AND REPORTING

Reporting to Parents
- Report cards
- Written information
- Parent–teacher conference
- Student-led conferences

Functions
- Level of detail
- Factors other than performance
  — effort
  — aptitude
  — attitudes
- Basis of comparison

Approaches
- Letter grades
- Percentage correct
- Pass–fail
- Standards-based
- Checklists
- Written descriptions

Report Card Grades
- Selecting what to include
- Selecting weights
- Combining
  — eyeball
  — percent correct
  — total points
  — relative scores
  — pitfalls of averaging
- Fair grading

CHAPTER 12   Concept Map

Teachers' Judgments

You are probably aware of several different objective approaches to grading, such as grading on the curve and assigning grades based on the percentage of test items answered correctly. But this doesn't begin to capture the complexity and difficulty of grading. In practice, teachers make a number of professional judgments about how to evaluate and grade students. Judgments are made before assessment (e.g., the difficulty of test items, what is covered on the assessment, whether extra credit items will be included), as well as after assessments are completed (e.g., scoring short-answer and essay items). Further judgments are made in combining scores of different assessments to determine grades (e.g., how assessments are weighted, how to handle borderline scores). Here are some typical questions teachers ask that are answered by using their judgment:

> Should effort and improvement be included in the grade?
> How should different assessments be weighted and combined?
> What distribution of grades should I end up with?
> What do I do if most of my students fail the test?
> Are my grades supposed to mean the same thing as other teachers' grades?
> Am I grading students too hard or too easy?
> What do I do with students who test well but don't hand in homework?
> Should student participation be included in the grade?

There are no straightforward, necessarily correct answers to these questions, and few school districts or schools provide teachers with much more than general guidelines and a grading scale. Consequently, grading practices vary considerably, even within the same school.

Also, unforeseen, unique situations may arise with students. These individual situations require teachers to use professional judgments. Consider the following scenarios (Brookhart, 1993):

> In your seventh grade social studies class, report card grades were based on quizzes, tests, and an out-of-class project which counted as 25% of the grade. Terry obtained an A average on his quizzes and tests but has not turned in the project despite frequent reminders.

> You are a biology teacher of a high school class which consists of students with varying ability levels. For this class you give two exams in each term. As you compute Bernie's grade for this term, you see that on the first exam, he obtained a score equivalent to a B, and on the second exam, a low A. (pp. 131, 133)

What grades would you give? Should Terry get a low grade even though he scores so high on tests? Should Bernie get an A because he showed improvement?

The evaluating and grading process requires you to make many *professional* decisions. These decisions are based on your personal value system toward a number of different issues. In the end, grading is more a reflection of this value system, of perceived importance or perspective, than it is based on following specific correct guidelines or rules. Essentially, you develop a philosophy of grading that translates into what you do. To develop your own personal grading plan, then, you need to consider and answer for yourself the following questions (Frisbie & Waltman, 1992):

What meaning should each grade symbol carry?
What should "failure" mean?
What elements of performance should be incorporated in a grade?
How should the grades in a class be distributed?
What should the components be like that go into a final grade?
How should the components of the grade be combined?
What method should be used to assign grades?
Should borderline cases be reviewed?
What other factors can influence the philosophy of grading? (p. 210)

These questions are best answered when they are based on an understanding of the different purposes or functions grades serve and the types of comparison standards that are used. In the end, you need to use methods and comparisons that best meet your major purpose. As we will see, grades often serve several purposes, which makes matters more complicated.

Let me make one point as clear as I can concerning professional judgments. These are *subjective* and *intuitive* in the sense that there is no single correct procedure or set of rules that take professional decision making out of the process. There is no completely objective procedure, nor should there be. You may use a grading scale, score student tests and performances, then mathematically calculate grades, but this is not a procedure that is necessarily correct because it appears to be objective. Think for a moment about a physician making a decision about whether a patient is sufficiently strong to endure an operation. In a sense, this is like grading. The doctor takes many measures, then examines them *in the light of his or her experience and knowledge* before giving a yes or no judgment. Could two physicians differ in their opinions about whether to operate, given the same information? Absolutely. Likewise, two teachers can differ on the meaning of students' performances. One teacher might look at the tests and conclude that the student has mastered a skill, while another teacher might conclude the opposite. In the end, it is your value system that makes the difference, and to be an effective teacher you need to understand the issues, make some informed judgments, and then be willing to have confidence in your decisions. Your goal is to use unbiased, thoughtful reasoning (Guskey & Bailey, 2001).

In Chapter 1 it was pointed out that teachers' assessment and grading decisions are heavily influenced by teacher beliefs and values about enhancing student learning and that these beliefs and values often conflict with external pressures such as mandated statewide testing, parental concerns, and district policies (McMillan, 2002b; McMillan & Workman, 1999). Teacher internal values and beliefs are essential because they provide a rationale for using grading practices that are most consistent with what is most important in the teaching/learning process. Thus, since teachers want all students to succeed, they may give extra credit to enable students to "pull up" low grades. Because of individual differences in students, teachers may use different types of assessments so everyone has a chance of obtaining a good grade. Performance assessments may be used because they motivate and engage students more effectively than multiple-choice tests and allow teachers to grade participation. Note in the following teacher responses how grading decisions are based on more encompassing beliefs and values about learning:

> To me grades are extremely secondary to the whole process of what we do. I have goals to what I want to teach, and I use assessment so that I know what I need to work on, what students have mastered, and what they haven't.

> I'm always trying to find some ways so that all the children can find success, not just Johnny and Suzy getting the A but also Sally and Jim can get an A also.

> Then I generally think of their effort, whether I feel they've really tried and whether they've turned in all their work. If they tried to make an effort to improve, I won't give them an F.

> When it's borderline, how hard has the child worked during the year?

External factors pressure teachers to adopt certain grading practices that focus on auditing and reporting student achievement, rather than promoting learning. Although teacher beliefs and values stress what is best for learning, these external pressures are usually more oriented to auditing student learning. Clearly, mandated statewide accountability testing has changed classroom assessment to be more aligned with the format of the statewide test, with consequences for grading as well. Teachers want "objective" evidence of student performance to defend grades to parents, and district policies may restrict the nature and use of different grading procedures. Practical constraints limit what teachers can realistically accomplish. Although it might be best to use many different samples of student performance for grades, it might not be feasible in light of other instructional needs. It is best to consider these external factors with your own beliefs and values about teaching and learning in mind. Recognize that tension may exist, but keep your grading decision making based primarily on what is best for student learning.

Functions of Marking, Grading, and Reporting

Why do teachers mark and grade student performances? The answer to this question is based on how the marks and grades are *used*. Are grades used to improve student learning or report student accomplishment? To rank order students (e.g., class rank) or to indicate progress toward clearly defined targets? To inform parents or evaluate curriculum? To evaluate teachers? For guidance and administrative uses? In most schools, marking, grading, and reporting serve a variety of functions. To consider these multiple uses and incorporate your own value system, it is helpful to separate what you do in the classroom from uses outside your class. That is, you mark papers and give students grades continually in class, and your use of grades in this context is probably quite different from what others may do with them.

Functions of Marking and Grading

What do you want your grades to mean to your students? How do you want them to be affected? Do you want to motivate students to improve? Do you want to point out strengths and weaknesses? How do you want your students to interpret the grades they receive on tests, papers, and projects? The vast majority of teachers want marks and grades to have a positive impact on student learning, motivation, affect, and other outcomes. Yet many use grading practices that do not have that effect. Suppose Mr. Wren decides to be "fair" to students by using the top score on a test as 100 and adjusts the percentage correct for all other students accordingly. Would it be fair if the class happened to have one or two exceptionally bright students? What might happen to student motivation in that class? This is one of many factors that will determine how grades are interpreted and thus affect students. Some other important influences include the level of detail communicated in the grade or mark about the student performance, whether factors other than performance are included, and the basis of comparison of the grades. We'll consider these with the assumption that the primary use of grades in the classroom should be to inform and motivate students.

Level of Detail Communicated.   One decision you will make about grading students is how much detail they will receive about their performance. Let me use my daughter as an example. When Ryann was in the sixth grade a few years ago, she spent several weeks putting together a report on Italy. In looking over the report, I thought she did an excellent job (of course there may be just a little bias here!). She got the paper back with a B+ on it and a short comment, "good work." She was somewhat disappointed, but more important, didn't know why she did not get a higher grade. There was no information about how the teacher had come to this conclusion. How did this affect her? She was sad and bewildered, in general a negative effect. An alternative could have been for the teacher to provide her with a detailed summary of how the teacher evaluated each section of the paper, so that she could better understand the strengths and weaknesses.

This example demonstrates the importance of level of detail. Whether you give grades or numbers, you have an option of giving a single indication or one that includes enough detail so that students know where they have made mistakes, where to improve, and what they have done well. This more detailed feedback has a positive effect on motivation, and it allows students to make more accurate connections between how they studied or prepared and their performance. At least when returning a conventional test with each item marked correct or incorrect, students can see which questions they missed and figure out their strengths and weaknesses. Unfortunately, for much student work, the level of detail is minimal. What students need is specific information based on the learning targets.

Factors Other Than Performance.   It's fairly obvious that the primary determinant of a mark or grade is the performance of the student. The more a student knows, understands, and can do, the better the grade. However, it's not as simple as it seems. First, there is the issue of whether *high* means in comparison to other students or in comparison to a well-defined learning target. We'll consider this factor in the next section. Second, when grades are determined solely on performance, there is a tendency to emphasize knowledge and simple understanding targets, in part because measures for these targets are easier to develop, and grades based on such measures are easier to defend. This may mean that deep understanding, reasoning, and product targets are mitigated. Third, what do you do with factors such as student effort, aptitude, improvement, and attitude? These are aspects of student performance that are important for most teachers, particularly when doing whatever they can to encourage and motivate students. In fact, many studies have documented that teachers tend to award a "hodgepodge grade of attitude, effort, and achievement" (Brookhart, 1993, p. 36; Cross & Frary, 1996; McMillan, 2001b; McMillan, 2002a; McMillan, Workman & Myran, 1998). A look at each of these factors is warranted.

Let's begin with student effort. There is a commonsense logic to why student effort should be considered when grading. Aren't students who try harder learning more, even if it doesn't show up on a test, paper, or project? More effort suggests more motivation and interest, and shouldn't we reward students when they are motivated and interested? Isn't it good to motivate low-achieving students who try hard? Don't we need to find something to praise low-achieving students for to keep them motivated? Isn't it good to focus students on an internal attributional factor that they can control to face subsequent learning tasks with more confidence? Isn't it true that we value effort as a society, so children should learn the importance of effort by seeing it reflected in their grades?

These may be compelling reasons to include effort in determining grades, but there are also some good reasons not to do so. First, different teachers operationalize effort differently, so it is something that varies from one teacher to another. Second, we don't have a satisfactory way to define and measure effort. It's true that we could define effort as "completing homework" or "participating in class discussion" or "being on-task," but each of these definitions is problematic. The one that could be easily and accurately measured, completing homework, is pretty shallow. Participation in class discussion is influenced by many factors, only one of which is controlled by each student. How do you know if a student is on-task? Sometimes it seems obvious, though students can fake this pretty well, and most of the time we either can't tell or can't systematically observe and record sufficiently to get a good measure. If students know they will be graded on effort, will they try to make you think that they are trying by how they act, when in fact it's a bluff and they really aren't trying?

Third, does including effort tend to favor more assertive students? What about students who are quiet? Could gender or racial/ethnic characteristics be related to the value of effort or expectations about showing effort? Certainly we would not want our grades to be affected by these characteristics. Fourth, how much would effort count? What amount of a grade or percentage of a score would be reasonable? We really don't know, and how would you keep the level of contribution the same for each student? Finally, are we sending students the wrong message if they learn that they can get by just by trying hard, even if the performance is less than satisfactory?

So what is the resolution? There seem to be some pretty good reasons for and against including effort. This is one of those areas of professional judgment that you'll need to make decisions about. But I do have some suggestions. If you want to include effort, use it for borderline cases. Never allow effort to become a major part of a mark or score. Second, report effort separately from performance. Do this often and allow students opportunities to disagree with your assessment. Try to define effort as clearly as possible, and stick to your definition. It should be shared with students, with examples. If you include effort for one student, it's only fair to include it for all students. Figure 12.1 summarizes arguments for and against the use of effort in grading.

A second factor that can easily influence grades and marks is student aptitude or ability. This reflects the student's potential or capability for learning. The argument for including aptitude goes something like this: If we can tailor assignments and grading to each student's potential, all students can be motivated and all students can experience success. Rather than grading only on achievement, which favors students who bring a higher aptitude for learning, grades reflect how well each student has achieved in relation to his or her potential. That is, each student is graded by comparing achievement to aptitude. Using this approach, we can better identify when students are over- or underachieving. High-aptitude students will be challenged, and low-aptitude students will have realistic opportunities for good grades.

However, this argument is based on knowing what aptitude is and being able to assess it. There has never been an agreed-upon definition of aptitude, though it often is used synonymously with general intelligence. Work by Sternberg (1986)

FIGURE 12.1   Arguments For and Against Using Effort in Grading

For	Against
• Students who try hard learn more	• Teachers operationalize effort differently
• Rewards motivation and engagement	• Hard to define and measure
• Rewards lower-achieving students for something	• Can be faked
• Rewards an internal attributional factor that is in control of the student	• Favors more assertive students
• Leads to higher grades	• Lack of consistency in how effort is weighted
	• Teaches students that they can get by with effort and not performance
	• Takes focus away from performance

and Gardner (1985) has challenged traditional definitions of intelligence and has shown that we are still a long way from adequately understanding something as complex as aptitude for learning. Furthermore, measuring aptitude is fraught with difficulties, not the least of which concerns cultural bias. Even if we had a proper definition and a good measure, there are insurmountable practical difficulties in trying to assess aptitude for each student and grade accordingly. Then there is the issue of explaining to high-aptitude students and their parents how they can get a higher score than low-aptitude students yet obtain a lower grade. Would you like to explain that? Some teachers essentially adopt two grading systems—one for low-aptitude students that emphasizes improvement, one for high-aptitude students based more on absolute achievement. The problem with this approach is that the meaning of the grades is different.

Thus, while there is no question that students do have different levels of ability, and you need to use this knowledge in instruction and for giving students feedback, you don't want to try to factor it into grades and marks. The only exception might be for borderline situations when giving semester grades. Even then, it would be better to use prior achievement than to use aptitude. Using prior achievement avoids the conceptualization and measurement problems associated with aptitude. This suggests another factor, improvement, that could be used for grading.

Because learning is defined as a change in performance, why not measure how much students know before and then after instruction? Students who show the most improvement, hence learning, would get the highest grades. Again, there are some serious limitations to this approach. What happens when students score high in the beginning, on the pretest, and don't have an opportunity to show improvement? What about student faking, in which students intentionally receive a low score on the pretest to more easily show improvement? Like trying to incorporate aptitude, keeping track of pre- and postinstruction scores for each student would not be very practical. But also like aptitude and effort, improvement can be a positive motivator for borderline situations.

A final factor to consider in classroom grading and marking is student attitudes. Shouldn't students with a positive attitude be rewarded? Suppose two students perform about the same and are between two grades. If one or both students have a very positive attitude, would that mean that they should get the higher grade? Like student effort, attitudes are important, and it would be nice if we could efficiently and accurately include this in grading. The reality is that attitudes are difficult to define and measure and are susceptible to student faking. So like the other "nonacademic" factors we have considered, it is generally not a good idea to try to use attitudes in grading. It is best if grades and marks are predominantly determined by student performance in relation to learning targets. If other factors are included, their influence should be minimal.

Basis of Comparison.   A major consideration in determining the meaning and method of grading is whether grades communicate comparisons with others or to predefined standards or levels of performance. Grading by comparison to the achievement of other students is referred to as **norm-referenced**. In the classroom, this means that the function of each student's grade is to indicate how the student performed in comparison with the other students in the class (or several classes in middle and high schools). This method is known popularly as *grading on the curve.* Certain proportions of students are given designated grades, regardless of the level of performance of the students. That is, a certain percentage of the class will receive As, Bs, Cs, Ds, and Fs. There is no indication of how much students master or what percentage of test items were answered correctly. A student can answer 70 percent of the items on one test correctly, and if that is the highest score, it will be an A. On another test, a 70 might be relatively low, receiving a C or D. It's also possible for a student to get a C for getting a 95 on a test if others received even higher scores.

In norm-referenced grading, the standard is a relative one that changes, depending on the composition of the class. It is done by rank ordering student performances from highest to lowest and then assigning grades based on a predetermined curve (e.g., top 10 percent will receive As, next 30 percent Bs, next 40 percent Cs, next 10 percent Ds, bottom 10 percent Fs). If you are in a high-ability class, it's usually more difficult to get a good grade.

Because norm-referenced grading is based on comparing students to each other, its major function is to show which are the highest- or best-performing students. In this sense, it sorts students, and because this is still a purpose of most schools, some kind of norm-referencing is often incorporated in grading. (Indeed, a definition of grades that includes C as average and B as above average is a norm-referenced type of comparison.) This could be done by adjusting curves based on student ability (e.g., honors track classes have a higher percentage of As than general track classes), by how difficult teachers make their tests, and by how tough teachers are in grading papers, projects, and other products.

One of the myths about norm-referenced grading is that you try to obtain a *curve* of student scores, usually something that looks like a normal curve (Figure 12.2a). Actually, this type of curved scores is not what you want, because at each cut point between different grades you have a maximum of students at the borderline between the grades. If your purpose is to conclude that some students clearly know more than others, you would want to obtain a sculpted curve of scores that looks like a wave in Figure 12.2b. Then each cut point at the bottom of the waves minimizes borderline scores and you will be more accurate in your conclusions. Although you probably won't be able to get scores that look like those in Figure 12.2b, look for naturally occurring breaks. For example, if seven students scored above 80 on a test of knowledge and the next few students scored between 60 and 70, those two groups of students likely have different amounts of knowledge. However, using this *gap* method of identifying grading categories is fairly arbitrary, and it is likely that the breaks might be at different locations if the data were recollected. Thus, you need to use clear, distinct breaks that are relatively large.

Another function of relative grading is to foster student competitiveness. It is clear that when students know that their grade is dependent on how others perform, a very competitive environment is created, which, in turn, usually has a negative impact on student effort, motivation, interpersonal relationships, and

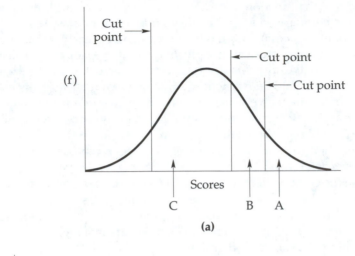

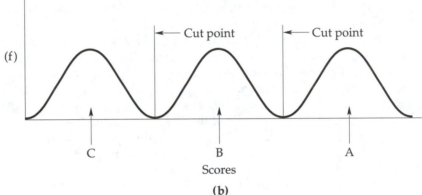

FIGURE 12.2   Normal and Sculpted Grading Curves

teacher communication. The motivation of students who continually score near the bottom is undermined. Student cooperation is reduced. For these reasons, as well as the capriciousness with which some teachers set curves (my son had a teacher who set the curve by the highest score—please don't do that!), most grading is now based on the absolute level of student performance, without any comparison to how others performed.

Grading that is determined by what level of performance is obtained is often called **standards-based** or **criterion-referenced**. There is no comparison with other students, so it is possible for all students to get the same grade. The most common method of using absolute levels of performance is called *percentage-based* grading. This is most typically used for objective tests, for which teachers assign a grade to a specific percentage of items answered correctly. Usually the school system establishes the scale, such as the following:

A   94–100   percent correct
B   86–93   percent correct
C   75–85   percent correct
D   65–74   percent correct
F   below 65 percent correct

The *standard* is supposedly set by the percent of correct items for each grade. Thus, a scale in which 96–100 is an A is often regarded as more stringent or tough than a scale with an A range of 90–100. I believe this is a myth, due to variation in item difficulty and the reality of needing to sort students. Let's examine item difficulty first.

Simply put, a score of 70 on a hard test means something different from a 70 on an easy test. Consequently, what is important is not only the percentage correct, but also how hard it is to get those items correct. Two teachers, given the same learning target, can easily come up with different assessments that are not the same in terms of difficulty. Suppose you are assessing student knowledge of different regions of the United States. One way to assess the target is to ask which states are in a region; you might say, for example, "Name three plains states." Another approach is to give a multiple-choice question:

Which of the following is a *plains* state?
a. New York
b. Maine
c. Florida
d. North Dakota

The target is the same, but the completion item is more difficult. How do you know how difficult a test is going to be before you give it to your students? This is a common situation that teachers must deal with. Estimating difficulty before the test depends on how others have performed and the capabilities of those students. For example, if you have a high-aptitude class that works hard to learn the content but then gets a low score on the test, then the test is probably pretty tough. On the other hand, if your low-aptitude class exerts minimum effort and does well, it's probably an easy test.

What happens when you don't have any prior experience, you give a test, and most students get a very low grade? In this circumstance either the students didn't know much or the test was not a fair assessment. Because you can't be sure which of these is true, you can justifiably make adjustments so that the distribution of scores reflects the range of likely student performance (but I wouldn't advocate adjusting high scores downward). As already indicated, some teachers do this by using the top score to signify 100 percent and recalculating all the students' scores with this new maximum number of possible correct answers. This is actually too arbitrary because the performance of a single student is too influential, but some adjustment may be needed. Yes, this is *subjective,* but no more so than your choice of item difficulty. Remember, your goal is to fairly evaluate student performance.

It's quite possible that a single test or assessment is not fair and that a reliance on the scores would be an injustice to students. In any event, it's not difficult for teachers to tailor item difficulty to their students so that a final distribution of grades meets normative standards or guidelines.

Then there is the reality of needing to sort students. Although theoretically all students can master learning targets and receive As, most teachers simply can't do this. Because we still use school to indicate to others which particular students, from the entire group of students, have performed best, the normative expectation is that teachers (especially middle and high school teachers) will give some As, a lot of Bs and Cs, a few Ds, and even some Fs. To meet this expectation, tests are devised so that not all students will do really well. That is, enough difficulty is built into the test so that not all students will get As. The reality is that most teachers, one way or another, combine absolute performance and sorting in the assigning of grades. This isn't bad or inappropriate, but it needs to be clarified for what it is so that whatever methods are used are fair to students. Recently we have been moving more and more to absolute standards and defining levels of standards in a way that still permits some sorting of students (some call this setting high standards), but sorting is still a function of schooling we need to deal with.

Another type of criterion-referenced performance standard is to spell out, in some detail, the specific behaviors students must perform to obtain a grade. This is used with performance assessments of skills and products. The scoring rubric and exemplars define the behaviors, and, on the basis of the teacher's observations, a grade is assigned to indicate which behaviors were demonstrated and hence which grade is received. In these systems, students' performances are compared only to the rubrics and exemplars, not to each other. A grade may be assigned to different levels, but it is more common to simply indicate the level achieved. As we will see in the next section, this leads to a different type of reporting system from the traditional A, B, C, D, and F.

Figure 12.3 summarizes differences between norm- and criterion-referenced approaches to assessment for marking and grading students.

Approaches to Marking and Grading

There are several ways to mark and grade student performance. We will consider the most common types of symbols or scores that are used, including letter grades, percentage correct, pass-fail grades, standards-based, checklists, and written descriptions. Most teachers use a combination of these in the classroom, even if final semester or course grades are determined by the district.

Letter Grades.   The most common way most teachers mark student performance on products other than objective tests is to give a letter grade. Traditionally, letter grades correspond to different adjectives, such as excellent or outstanding, good, average or acceptable, poor, and unsatisfactory, and often plus and minus symbols are used to provide finer distinctions. Letter grades provide a convenient, concise, and familiar approach to marking. In addition, grades are readily understood by students and parents to provide an overall indication of performance.

FIGURE 12.3   Characteristics of Norm- and Criterion-Referenced Assessment

	Norm-Referenced	Criterion-Referenced
Interpretation	Score compared to the performances of other students	Score compared to predetermined standards and criteria
Nature of Score	Percentile rank; standard scores; grading curve	Percentage correct; descriptive performance standards
Difficulty of Test Items	Uses average to difficult items to obtain spread of scores; very easy and very difficult items not used	Uses average to easy items to result in a high percentage of correct answers
Use of Scores	To rank order and sort students	To describe the level of performance obtained
Effect on Motivation	Dependent on comparison group; competitive	Challenges students to meet specified learning target
Strengths	Results in more difficult assessments that challenge students	Matches student performance to clearly defined learning targets; lessens competitiveness
Weaknesses	Grades determined by comparison to other students; some students are always at the bottom	Establishing clearly defined learning targets; setting standards that indicate mastery

The major limitation of grades is that they provide only a general indication of performance. There is nothing wrong with giving students an overall, summary judgment in the form of a grade. However, such a general mark, by itself, does not indicate anything about what was done correctly or incorrectly. Strengths and limitations are not communicated. There is also a tendency for teachers to be influenced by factors other than performance in coming up with a grade on papers, projects, and presentations (e.g., effort, work habits, attitude). Furthermore, because teachers differ in their value systems, the proportion of students getting each grade can vary. In one class, most students can get As and Bs, while in another class, most students receive Bs and Cs.

What you need to make clear to your students about grades is what each letter means, so that their interpretation is accurate, appropriate, and helpful. Does getting an A mean that I did outstanding work, or does it mean that I did best in the class? Does it mean that the teacher thinks I worked hard on this or that I can do it really well? Does getting a C mean that I did about as well as most students or that I did satisfactory work?

As you can see, there are a number of possible interpretations, depending on how much factors other than performance are included and the basis of comparison (norm- or criterion-referenced). In other words, grades can communicate effort, achievement, improvement, achievement in comparison to aptitude (some teachers grade high-aptitude students tougher), relative standing, or level of mastery. You need to be clear, first to yourself and then to your students, about what each letter grade means. Figure 12.4 presents different interpretations of grades.

Notice that it is possible to combine or mix norm- and criterion-referenced approaches (Terwilliger, 1989). What often occurs is that the higher grades tend to be norm-referenced and the lower ones criterion-referenced. That is, to get an A,

FIGURE 12.4 Different Interpretations of Letter Grades

Grade	Criterion-Referenced	Norm-Referenced	Combined Norm- and Criterion-Referenced	Based on Improvement
A	Outstanding or advanced: complete knowledge of all content; mastery of all targets; exceeds standards	Outstanding: among the highest or best performance	Outstanding: very high level of performance	Outstanding: much improvement on most or all targets
B	Very good or proficient: complete knowledge of most content; mastery of most targets; meets most standards	Very good: performs above the class average	Very good: better than average performance	Very good: some improvement on most or all targets
C	Acceptable or basic: command of only basic concepts or skills; mastery of some targets; meets some standards	Average: performs at the class average	Average	Acceptable: some improvement on some targets
D	Making progress or developing: lacks knowledge of most content; mastery of only a few targets; meets only a few standards	Poor: below the class average	Below average or weak: minimum performance for passing	Making progress: minimal progress on most targets
F	Unsatisfactory: lacks knowledge of content; no mastery of targets; does not meet any standards	Unsatisfactory: far below average; among the worst in the class	Unsatisfactory: lacks sufficient knowledge to pass	Unsatisfactory: no improvement on any targets

students need to perform better than most, but a failure judgment tends to be based on absolute standards. If a purely relative scale were used and the norming group were the class itself, some students would always fail, despite what might be a high level of performance (a better procedure is to use data from previous classes to set the norm from a larger group). Also, some students would always succeed. It is only with absolute scales that all students can either succeed or fail.

Percentage Correct. For objective tests, the most common approach to reporting performance is to indicate the percentage of items answered correctly. Thus, we often characterize our achievement as, say, getting a 75 or a 92 on a test. These numbers refer to the percentage of items or points obtained out of a possible 100. These scores are easy to calculate, record, and combine at the end of the grading period. Usually, letter grades are associated with ranges of scores, so it's really a letter grade system that gives students a finer discrimination in their performance. It is possible, if not very common, to grade everything with percentage correct, even papers and essay items.

One limitation of using percentage correct in marking and grading is that, like a letter grade, only a general indication of performance is communicated. Another disadvantage is that the discriminations that are suggested by a scale from 1 to 100 are much finer that what can be reliably assessed. Because of error in testing, there is no meaningful difference between scores differentiated by one or two points. That is, scores of 92 and 93 or 77 and 78 suggest the same level of student performance. In other words, the degree of precision suggested by percentage correct is not justified given the error that exists.

A third limitation is the tendency to equate percentage of items correct with percent mastered. As I have pointed out, items can differ tremendously in level of difficulty, so when students obtain a high percentage of correct answers, mastery may or may not be demonstrated, depending on the difficulty level of the assessment. Thus, it is probably incorrect to conclude that when a student obtains a 100 he or she knows 100 percent of the learning targets, or that a score of 50 corresponds to mastery of half of the targets.

Pass-Fail. The idea of making a simple dichotomous evaluation, such as pass versus fail or satisfactory versus needs improvement, is consistent with mastery learning. In these approaches to learning and instruction, students are assessed on each learning objective. The judgment is criterion-referenced and results in a mastery–no mastery decision. Typically, students work on each objective until they demonstrate mastery, then move on.

There is a certain appeal to this approach, especially at the early elementary level, but it doesn't reflect very well the actual levels of performance that students demonstrate. Basically, a two-category system is too simple. Most teachers find that at least three categories are needed, something like fail, pass, and excellent, or N (needs improvement), S (satisfactory), and O (outstanding). A related limitation is that when we use a dichotomous system, even less information is being communicated to students than when grades are used. Also, it is difficult to keep standards high with a pass-fail system. The tendency is to relax the standards so that most students will not fail. This tells students clearly what they need to do to avoid failure, but it doesn't tell them very much about what excellent or outstanding performance is like.

On the other hand, there is now considerable interest in assessing high schools on *mastery* of skills needed for the workplace and using the assessments for giving students a "certificate of initial mastery" (Rothman, 1995). In these efforts, there is a conscious attempt to keep the standards high.

Standards-Based. With the recent popularity of using standards and high-stakes testing in education, standards-based grading has emerged as a new and highly effective form of providing feedback to students and parents. Guskey and Bailey (2001) identify four steps in the development of standards-based grading:

1. Identify major learning goals and standards.
2. Establish performance indicators for the standards.
3. Identify benchmarks that indicate graduated levels of proficiency.
4. Develop reporting forms that indicate progress and final achievement toward meeting the standards.

The challenge with identifying the standards is to get them at the right level of specificity. Standards that are too detailed and numerous make reporting cumbersome and time-consuming for teachers, and too complex for parent understanding. Standards that are too general do not provide enough information to show strengths or weaknesses. One effective approach to get standards at the right level is to begin with broad ones (often these are required) and provide more specific standards under each one (see Figure 12.5). This allows parents and students to see overall performance as well as areas of strength and weakness.

The performance indicators are descriptors that indicate the status of student achievement in relation to the standard. The most common form is to use four descriptors: *beginning, progressing, proficient*, and *exceptional*. When the standard is behaviorally oriented, descriptors that indicate how often the standard was reached could be used, such as *seldom, sometimes, frequently*, or *consistently*. It is important for the descriptors to show graduated levels of proficiency to facilitate the reporting of progress as well as current status. By indicating progress, students and parents are able to gauge the amount of learning that has been demonstrated over the marking period. This is key information for understanding the link between student motivation and performance.

Checklists. A variation of the pass-fail approach is to give students a checklist of some kind to indicate their performance on each aspect of the learning target. The checklist has two or more categories. In a simple dichotomous checklist, the teacher might prepare a series of statements that describes aspects of the performance that the students need to include and places a check mark next to each one the teacher judges to be demonstrated. To indicate student affect, checks can be placed next to each one demonstrated. This shows what the student both has and has not done.

FIGURE 12.5 Elementary Reporting Form Illustrating a Grade for Achievement in the Subject Area with Separate Indicators for Process Skills

Mathematics Grade:	1st B	2nd	3rd	4th
Demonstrates understanding of concepts	3			
Demonstrates mathematical thinking	3			
Makes mental calculations and reasonable estimations	4			
Uses strategies to solve problems	3			
Collects, organizes, and analyzes data	2			
Demonstrates a knowledge of basic facts	3			
Computes accurately	3			
Completes assignments on time	4			

Key to Subject Area Grades:

A = Outstanding (90–100% Mastery of Subject Goals)
B = Very Good (80–89% Mastery of Subject Goals)
C = Satisfactory (70–79% Mastery of Subject Goals)
D = Experiencing Difficulty (Below 70% Mastery of Subject Goals)

Key to Skills Grades:

   4 = Consistently or Independently
   3 = Usually
   2 = Sometimes
   1 = Seldom
NE = Not Evaluated

Source: Gusky, T. R., & Bailey, J. M. (2001). *Developing grading and reporting systems for student learning.* Thousand Oaks, CA: Corwin Press, p. 150. Reprinted by permission of Corwin Press, Inc.

A more elaborate approach provides students with scales of performance. The teacher makes checks on the scale to indicate the level of performance. This is typical of making performance assessments products. The rubric that describes the scoring is used as the checklist. The advantage of this type of grading is that the students receive detailed feedback about what they did well and what needs improvement. The detail in the rubric helps students understand more precisely where they need to improve. The difficulty of this approach is developing the checklists and keeping the system practical. However, once you develop detailed lists, they are fairly efficient because you only make check marks. This can be done efficiently, even if there are several such statements for each student product. It is certainly more efficient than writing comments on papers, though some individualized comments are important as well.

Written Descriptions.   An alternative to giving only a grade or score is to mark students' work with written descriptions. The advantage of this approach is that the comments can be highly individualized, pointing out unique strengths and weaknesses, and can focus attention on important issues. Students appreciate the effort of teachers who take the time to make these comments. Of course, the time needed is a major disadvantage. Most teachers simply do not have sufficient time to give this level of feedback. Then there is the added complication of converting the descriptions into grades or scores for report cards. Here the advantage from one perspective becomes a disadvantage because the uniqueness of the descriptions makes it difficult to grade consistently and fairly.

Recently, assessment experts have focused attention on how marking and grading can improve instruction and student learning (Guskey, 1994; Guskey & Bailey, 2001). It is clear that from this perspective, detailed checklists, narratives, and marking based on prespecified criteria are preferred. To enhance student motivation, the grading needs to be specific. Relative comparisons among students should be avoided. But from a realistic perspective, your marking and grading also must be practical and result in accurate summaries for report cards. The challenge is to incorporate as much detail and reference to learning targets as possible when marking each piece of student work without being overwhelmed. Then you'll need to combine the marks into a final grade for the semester. At this point, the function of grading is reporting to others. We'll consider this function briefly before looking at some ways to come up with the final grade.

Determining Report Card Grades

Unit and semester grades are given by teachers to provide a single indicator of student performance. Recognizing that professional judgment is essential for determining final grades as well as marks and grades for individual assessments, you will need to make some decisions. These decisions can be summarized in the form of three steps:

1. Select what to include in the final grade.
2. Select weights for each individual assessment.
3. Combine weighted scores to determine a single grade.

Let's examine each of these steps.

Select What to Include in the Final Grade

This is where you will have a fair amount of leeway. It is up to you to determine which assessments will contribute to the final grade. As I have already suggested, it is best if you base final grades primarily on academic performance. But which performances should be included? Tests? Participation in class? Papers? Quizzes? Homework? Before selecting the assessments, think again about your overall learning goals. Your selection of what goes into the final grade should provide the most accurate information in relation to these goals. That is, the assessments selected should be closely aligned with the goals. If you have done a good job of basing your formal assessments on the learning targets, then each of these assessments will contribute meaningfully to the grade. It is less clear if pop quizzes, participation, and homework should be included.

On the one hand, pop quizzes, participation, and homework do focus on student performance, but is their purpose to give students feedback in a formative sense or reward student effort, or can they legitimately serve as documentation of student learning and understanding? If they are primarily formative in nature, to give students practice and feedback, they may be viewed more as instruction than assessment and should not be included in a final grade. Some teachers argue that pop quizzes are not fair to students, and some also contend that homework may not have been completed by the student. Many teachers realize that participation in class is influenced by group dynamics and personality. Other teachers view pop quizzes, participation, and homework as indicators of how much students are paying attention and learning in class and will use them to calculate final grades. The choice of whether to include these student performances is yours, and either choice is legitimate. Just be sure to make clear to students and parents what is going into the grade and why it is fair.

You will want to be especially careful in considering factors such as attendance, effort, and personal/social characteristics such as cooperativeness, participation, and work habits in determining grades. Specifically, you don't want nonacademic factors, which probably have little relationship to academic learning, to influence the final grade. Suppose a student is absent from school and misses a test. Does that mean a zero is appropriate? Even if the student has been expelled, giving a zero for not being present, and then inferring that the grade ultimately received reflects academic learning, is clearly a mistake. What about a student who, while in a cooperative learning group, doesn't participate very much or contribute to others' learning? Should that student's grade be penalized for displaying weak cooperative skills? Do you evaluate the quality or quantity of the participation? Should a student who continually says silly things be penalized?

I believe the best rule on these matters is this: If a grade is for academic performance in areas such as reading, science, mathematics, history, and the like, then the grade should be determined only by student academic performance. This is essentially a matter of maintaining appropriate validity so that your inferences about academic performance are reasonable. If cooperativeness and participation are important targets, report separate grades for each.

Finally, in planning the assessments that you will include, carefully consider how many are needed to give an accurate overall judgment of each student's performance. Would it be reasonable to base a semester grade on a single exam? How about a nine-week grade—would two tests and a paper be sufficient? Probably most would agree that a single assessment, alone, is definitely not sufficient. In the words of Grant Wiggins, "A single grade hides more than it reveals" (1998, p. 248). Three assessments for a nine-week grade is much better, but even that may not be enough.

The rule of thumb with respect to number of assessments needed is the more, the better, as long as assessment time does not interfere significantly with instructional time. So, although one or two assessments would probably be too few, you wouldn't want to give a test every day! Once again, your professional judgment is needed. I have found that at least one fairly major test or other assessment is needed about every two weeks. Many teachers are constrained by a fifty-minute or less class period, and it's difficult to sample two weeks of content in anything less than an hour of testing time. Besides, children have limited attention spans. If students lose interest or find it hard to concentrate, error is introduced into the assessment.

Select Weights for Each Assessment

Not only do you need to identify the assessments; you also need to decide how much each one will count in the final grade. Obviously, more important assessments are given greater weight. What determines if an assessment is important? You probably guessed it—more professional judgment! The most significant assessments are those that (1) correspond most closely to the learning goals and targets (content-related evidence for validity), (2) reflect instructional time, (3) are most reliable, and (4) are most current.

Because there are multiple learning targets in a unit or semester, you need to break out the percentage that each target contributes to the whole. I have illustrated this in Figure 12.6 in the form of a pie chart for a unit on the animal kingdom. You

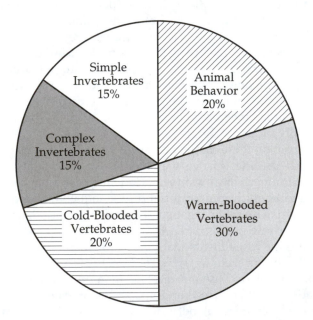

FIGURE 12.6   Percentage of Each Topic That Contributes to the Final Grade

can see that different percentages correspond to each topic. In this case, the overall goal is determined mostly by vertebrate animal characteristics and behaviors. Now you need to weigh your assessments to match these percentages so that the final grade reflects the relative contribution of each topic. This will provide good content-related evidence for validity, which is a primary concern. We'll look at some examples of how to do that in the next section. In this example, about 50 percent of what determines the final grade should be the assessments on vertebrates. This percentage is independent of the length of the book chapters, or assessments, or the instructional time devoted to each topic. What you are determining is solely the value of each of the topics.

Even though instructional time is not a factor in the first consideration of weights, it's still an important barometer of the amount of emphasis given to each topic. For that reason, I think it's only fair to take time devoted to instruction as a factor. As I have already emphasized, students need to know before an assessment is taken what will be covered. Often this includes topics or concepts that have not been discussed in class. Although there is nothing wrong with testing students on material they learn on their own, it's best if the weights reflect instructional focus. If you spent 50 percent of your nine weeks studying simple invertebrates, it probably wouldn't be fair to weight this topic at only 15 percent. Similarly, you might determine that you *intend* to weight vertebrates at 50 percent, but when you look back over the weeks you figure that only 25 percent of the students' time was spent learning about vertebrates. This would suggest that a more appropriate weight would be 30–35 percent, at most. Obviously you don't know for sure how much time you take until the instruction is completed. This means that your final determination of weights needs to be finalized close to the end of instruction as well. Weights should not be set in stone at the beginning of the unit.

Reliability is a factor in weighing because, *other things being equal,* especially validity, we want to put more weight on more accurate assessments. This will reduce the overall amount of error that is included in determining the grade. Although most teachers don't get specific numerical reliabilities, generally reliability increases with a greater number of items for each target and for objective items. But it is important to emphasize that the most important concern is validity; highly reliable assessments should never be given more weight than is appropriate, given the validity of the assessment.

If you test the same content more than once, as you would with a cumulative final exam, put more weight on the most current assessment. In fact, a later assessment on the same material might mean that the earlier assessment should be dropped. After all, if your goal is to communicate accurately the nature of a student's current performance, wouldn't the more recent assessment be better? From a practical standpoint, however, you'll find that it's difficult to simply discard an earlier test score. The best compromise is to weigh the cumulative exam more than each of the preceding ones so that final performance outweighs what students demonstrate at the beginning or middle of the unit.

Given these considerations, you now need to combine the assessments properly to obtain the final grade.

Combining Different Scores and Grades

The three basic approaches to combining scores and grades are the eyeball method, the percent correct method, and the total points method.

Eyeball Method.   The first one is what I call the *eyeball* method because the teacher simply reviews the scores and grades and estimates an average for them, without performing any calculations, to come up with what seems to be the correct grade. This has obvious disadvantages, not the least of which is the lack of objectivity. This method isn't recommended, but it does have one redeeming quality. With eyeballing the teacher asks, "All things considered and looking at the whole as more than the sum of each part, what is the most valid grade for this student?" The notion that it's important to consider everything together has some merit because it recognizes that teacher professional judgment is needed to give grades. At the other extreme, you have teachers who mindlessly calculate averages without any consideration of factors that might be important, such as student absenteeism, effort, and possible testing error. For example, what would you do if, after working closely with a fourth-grade student for several weeks, she failed a math exam when you knew for certain through classwork that she knew how to do the calculations? Would an F be a fair and accurate grade for this student? Just because the test says it's so, does that mean it *is*?

Percent Correct Method.   Because most teachers need to show some objective methods in their grading, scores and grades are typically combined into a single score that converts to a grade. Here you need to be sure that the calculations you use to combine the assessments are done correctly. Because most districts require teachers to use a percent correct scale in grading, we'll focus on combining scores to obtain a composite *percentage correct* score, which is readily converted to a grade.

Consider the example about a unit on animals (see Figure 12.6). If all you had for the final grade was a test for each of the topics, you would simply multiply the percentage of correct scores obtained by the percentages indicated in the chart, and then add the five products. To make matters simple, let's assume that you gave five 100-point tests, one for each topic. Here are the scores of two students on the five tests:

Test	LaKeith	Dion
1	70	85
2	65	90
3	80	88
4	75	93
5	83	95

You decide to weight each of the tests by the percentage indicated in the pie chart. This can be done by multiplying each test score by the percentage expressed as a decimal (e.g., 15 percent, .15; 20 percent, .20) and then adding the resulting products. In this example, LaKeith's composite score would be 75:

$$(70 \times .15) + (65 \times .15) + (80 \times .20) + (75 \times .30) + (83 \times .20) = 75.35.$$

Dion's composite score would be 91:

$$(85 \times .15) + (90 \times .15) + (88 \times .20) + (93 \times .30) + (95 \times .20) = 90.75.$$

These composite scores would then be converted to grades, depending on the grading scale.

In reality, most teachers have a variety of different types of scores and grades and tests with different numbers of items, so keeping track of these and doing the calculations can get fairly complex. One important principle in doing this is to first *convert each score or grade to the same scale*. If you are using the percent correct scale, this means converting each score, or grade, or other assessment to a percent correct score. For a test with 50 items, this means multiplying the raw score obtained by 2. For a test with 10 items, multiply the raw score by 10. What about grades for papers and essay items? Here you need to have a key so each grade is given a percent correct score. For example, an A paper is given a 96, an A– paper a 92, a B+ paper a 90, and so forth. If you are including homework in your grade and using a check, check minus, and check plus system, you need to find a way to convert these to result in a number between 0 and 100. In this case, you might decide that each check is a 90, a check plus is 100, and a check minus corresponds to 80.

Let's look at an example of how to do all of this in practice. Figure 12.7 illustrates part of Ms. Lopez's gradebook. The gradebook is a record of student accomplishments and performances throughout the grading period. In this case, you can see that there were two quizzes, a midterm exam, a final exam, a paper, and homework. For each test, Ms. Lopez records the raw score, records grades for papers, and places a check mark beneath each homework assignment completed. Ms. Lopez has decided that the final grade will be determined as follows:

> final exam, 40 percent
> midterm exam, 30 percent
> quizzes, 5 percent each
> papers, 15 percent
> homework, 5 percent

This means that the unit quizzes, together, will count 10 percent. She has set up her gradebook to efficiently convert the raw scores to the percent correct, weight them, then add them to arrive at composite scores. You will probably find it most convenient to prepare your own gradebook. A good procedure is to use a loose-leaf notebook with graph paper. You can customize the columns to meet your own requirements. Usually attendance and assessment scores and grades are recorded on separate pages.

In recent years, computerized grading software programs and electronic gradebooks have become very popular. The spreadsheet formats and database management systems make it easy and efficient to enter scores and calculate final grades and simplify record keeping, especially for middle and high school teachers who have large numbers of students. Many programs offer flexibility in combining and weighting different entries. Guskey (2002) points out, however, that the mathematical precision that is achieved does not necessarily bring greater objectivity, accuracy, or

Semester: Fall 2002

Unit: Plant Biology

Student	Quiz 1 (5%)			Quiz 2 (5%)			Midterm (30%)			Final Exam (40%)			Paper (15%)		Homework (5%)				Weighted Composite Score	Final Grade
	Raw Score	% Correct	Weighted Score	Raw Score	% Correct	Weighted Score	Raw Score	% Correct	Weighted Score	% Correct	Weighted Score	Grade	% Correct	Weighted Score	#1	#2	Average	Weighted Score		
Alex	23	92	4.6	19	95	4.75	47	94	28.2	88	35.2	A-	95	14.25	✓	✓	100	5	92	B+
Eric	20	80	4.0	17	85	4.25	42	84	25.2	92	36.8	B	89	13.35	✓	✓	100	5	88.6	B
Stacey	24	96	4.8	16	80	4.00	46	92	27.6	80	32.0	C+	82	12.30		✓	50	2.5	83.2	C+
Adam	18	72	3.6	20	100	5.00	48	96	28.8	75	30.0	B-	86	12.90	✓	✓	100	5	85.3	B-
Will	22	88	4.4	18	90	4.50	41	82	24.6	85	34.0	C+	82	12.30	✓	✓	100	5	84.80	C+
Ryann	23	92	4.6	19	95	4.75	43	86	25.8	90	36.0	B	89	13.35	✓	✓	100	5	89.5	B
Alik	25	100	5.0	18	90	4.50	45	90	27.0	98	39.2	A	98	14.70	✓	✓	100	5	95.4	A-
Tina	19	76	3.8	18	90	4.50	38	76	22.8	78	31.2	B	89	13.35		✓	50	2.5	78.15	C

FIGURE 12.7 Part of Ms. Lopez's Gradebook

fairness. He points out that these programs do not lessen the challenges teachers face when making decisions about what will be included and how each score or grade contributes to the final grade (e.g., how to handle zeros, averaging, improvement).

The first quiz had 25 items, so Ms. Lopez multiplied each raw score by 4 to obtain the percent correct number. The second quiz had 20 items, so she multiplied the raw scores by 5. Each midterm had 50 items, so she multiplied the scores for each by 2. The final exam had 100 points, so it did not need to be converted. She worked out a score for each grade that could be given to the papers, and she gave each completed homework check a 100. To obtain a grade for the homework, she added the scores (either 100 or 0) and then divided by the total number of homework assignments, in this case 2 (this number is small for space reasons; typically much more homework would be recorded). After she has calculated all the weighted scores, she adds them to determine the final unit grade for each student, using a common grading scale (A = 95–100, B = 85–94, C = 75–84, D = 65–74, F = below 65).

In Figure 12.8, the calculations are shown from the scores of two students in Ms. Lopez's class (see Figure 12.7), Eric and Tina. In these cases, the final unit grades are fairly clear, but what about Will? As you can see in Figure 12.7, he is a borderline student, and you will need to be prepared to deal with such cases. In Will's case, he's so close to a B (84.8), shouldn't the teacher "give" it to him? This is where you would need to think about the strongest information you have about Will's understanding of plant biology. His final was an 85, barely a B–, but both his midterm and paper grades were in the C range. Normally, these would be your best indicators of understanding the content, so from one perspective it would be justifiable to leave his final grade as a C+. On the other hand, if he had gotten only a couple more questions correct on any of the exams, his composite score would have been over 85. Isn't there enough error in those tests to justify giving him the benefit of the doubt and raising his grade to a B–? This is also a reasonable response. What will help in such cases is to think about your classroom interaction with Will and other students who obtained a B as a final grade. Was he as knowledgeable as the B students? If so, it would be reasonable to raise his grade. Were there any extenuating circumstances that would have influenced his work? Another approach I have found to work well is to grade

FIGURE 12.8   Calculation of Unit Final Grades

	Quiz 1	Quiz 2	Midterm	Final	Paper	Homework
Composite						
Eric	$20 \times 4 = 80$	$17 \times 5 = 85$	$42 \times 2 = 84$	92	B (89)	$\checkmark\checkmark$(100)
	$80 \times .05 = 4.0$	$85 \times .05 = 4.25$	$84 \times .3 = 25.2$	$92 \times .4 = 36.8$	$89 \times .15 = 13.35$	$100 \times .05 = 5$
	4.0 $+$	4.25 $+$	25.2 $+$	36.8 $+$	13.35 $+$	5 $= 88.6$
Tina	$19 \times 4 = 76$	$18 \times 5 = 90$	$38 \times 2 = 76$	78	B (89)	$\checkmark$ (50)
	$76 \times .05 = 3.8$	$90 \times .05 = 4.5$	$76 \times .3 = 22.8$	$78 \times .4 = 31.2$	$89 \times .15 = 13.35$	$50 \times .05 = 2.5$
	3.8 $+$	4.5 $+$	22.8 $+$	31.2 $+$	13.35 $+$	2.5 $= 78.15$

hard for each test and assignment, then give borderline students the higher final grade. What you want to be able to say with confidence is that the final grade is a fair and accurate indication of student performance on the learning goal.

Total Points Method.   If you don't like to calculate percentages, you can use the same approach by giving each assessment a number of points and adding the points obtained for all the assessments to get a total. The points should be assigned to each assessment to reflect their weight in determining the total. For example, we could use points for Ms. Lopez rather than percentages. If the final is to count as 40 percent of the grade, then 40 percent of the total number of points should be allocated to the final exam. If the final had 100 questions, and each item counted for one point, then there would need to be a grand total of 250 points possible. The remaining points could be allocated to each assessment based on the percentage times 250. Thus, each quiz would have 12.5 points, the midterm would have 75 points, and the paper would have 37.5 points.

You can see the disadvantage of this approach. Either you have to adjust the number of items to equal the points each assessment should provide, or you have to change the score of an assessment to reflect the points. This means that each quiz, in this case, would have a maximum of 12.5 points, regardless of the number of items. Obviously this is pretty cumbersome, so if the total points method is used, the assessments are carefully designed to avoid the recalculation of any individual assessment so that they can simply be added. However, this tends to constrain the nature of the assessments. Rather than have the method of combining scores drive the assessments, let each assessment be constructed to provide the best measure of student performance, and then combine. The percent correct approach is much better than total points for this reason.

Whether you use the percent correct or total points method, when you include many different assessments and mathematically combine them you are essentially taking the average of all the performances. While averaging is justified as a way to include all the assessments (and keep students motivated), there is a danger that *mindless* averaging will distort the student's true capabilities. For example, when a student evaluation system is designed to move students from novice to expert on an appropriate skill continuum, it may not make good sense to average performances during the entire period of learning (Wiggins, 1998). If a student begins as a novice and obtains a low score, should that score be averaged with a final "expert" performance to result in an average grade? What is critical is reporting student attainment of the skill in relation to the rubric and scoring criteria at the time of the report, regardless of earlier performances.

Combining Relative Scores and Grades.   If you happen to be one of a small percentage of teachers who grade using a norm-referenced approach, you have an additional step to take when combining scores. Because the emphasis is on relative standing, you need to take into account the degree or amount of difference between students on each assessment. This is because the contribution of each assessment is a function of the difference between students as well as the score. To illustrate with a simple example, suppose I give a midterm and all students obtain the same score. On the final, the scores are pretty well distributed. I want the midterm to count for 50 percent, so I weight it appropriately, multiply by the score, and then add the product to the final exam. This is, in reality, weighting the final exam at 100 percent. Because all students obtained the same score on the midterm, what is added to the final is the same for each student. Thus, the only variability I can get is what is provided by the final exam. Although you are unlikely to have a situation in which all students score the same on a test, differences in variation will affect the actual contribution of each assessment to the total.

There isn't space here to go into detail, with examples, of how to combine relative scores into a final grade. The suggested approach is to calculate linear transformations of each raw score to a standard score. You first figure the standard scores, then weight them, then add them together. The final determination of grades is made on the basis of what percentage of students should receive each grade.

Suggestions for Fair Grading

Teachers have an overriding concern for grading students fairly (Brookhart, 1993). This is good, and we have discussed many factors teachers need to consider to result in fair grading practices. These suggestions, and some new ones, are summarized in Figure 12.9 as do's and don'ts. A couple of issues deserve some additional attention.

One issue that many teachers disagree about is how to handle the zeros that students obtain when they do not hand in an assignment or are absent from class for some reason. To clarify the issue, you need to consider the effect of a zero on an average. If I have a zero for 20 percent of my grade because I didn't hand in any homework, I could have an 80 percent average on all the tests and flunk the class ($80 \times .80 = 64; 20 \times 0 = 0; 64 + 0 = 64$). Would this grade be a fair representation of what I knew, of how I performed? I think not! One of the worst offenses in grading is the indiscriminant use of zeros. It seems to me that you need to record a failure in this situation, but not give it a zero. Perhaps a 65 would be appropriate, but not completing an assignment does not mean zero achievement or learning. You may react by thinking that a score of 65 would encourage students not to do their work, because the penalty is not very severe. However, this is a motivational problem, and it shouldn't be solved by grading practices. Grades should reflect only performance in relation to learning targets. Another problem of averaging zeros is that student motivation may be negatively affected if it becomes impossible to achieve a passing grade. The likely result in this circumstance is that the student simply will not try to learn any more.

A second approach to zeros is to use them only for assessments that have a minuscule effect on the final grade. This is done by weighting the assessment very little. However, a better policy, from my perspective, is to avoid zeros altogether.

Another issue is the lowering of grades in response to student cheating. Obviously cheating is a very serious offense, and appropriate disciplinary action is warranted. However, lowering grades is not appropriate discipline because of the

FIGURE 12.9   Do's and Don'ts of Effective Grading

Do	Don't
Use well-thought-out professional judgments	Depend entirely on number crunching
Try everything you can to score and grade fairly	Allow personal bias to affect grades
Grade according to preestablished learning targets and standards	Grade on the curve using the class as the norm group
Clearly inform students and parents of grading procedures at the beginning of the semester	Keep grading procedures secret
Base grades on student performance	Base grades on intelligence, effort, attitudes, or motivation
Rely most on current information	Penalize poorly performing students early in the semester
Mark, grade, and return assessments to students as soon as possible and with as much feedback as possible	Return assessments weeks later with little or no feedback
Review borderline cases carefully; when in doubt, assign the higher grade	Be inflexible with borderline cases
Convert scores to the same scale before combining	Use zero scores indiscriminately when averaging grades
Weight scores before combining	Include extra credit assignments that are not related to the learning targets
Use a sufficient number of assessments	Rely on one or two assessments for a semester grade
Be willing to change grades when warranted	Lower grades for cheating, misbehaving, tardiness, or absence

extreme negative impact this may have on the grade. Suppose you give a zero to a student when he or she is caught cheating on a test. Does this score accurately represent the student's knowledge and performance? Here you are using grades to punish the student. It would be better to find another kind of punishment and retest the student.

Finally, it's important to be willing to change grades when justified. In the first place, mistakes are made in calculating grades. A possible hint of this occurs when a final grade for a student doesn't seem right. In this circumstance, go back over the calculations to be sure there are no mistakes. Second, students sometimes have legitimate arguments about a grade. It is possible to overlook things. In fact, this is probable when you grade a lot of assessments. Be willing to admit that you were wrong and record the best, most accurate score or grade.

Case Study for Reflection

By the end of the first nine-week marking period, Ms. Byrd, a new middle school English teacher, had collected and graded a substantial amount of student work, including 9 weekly tests, 12 quizzes, nearly 30 homework assignments, a writing journal, a research project, and several in-class assignments. When the time came to turn in student grades, she calculated individual student averages based on all the assignments and tests, the journal, and the research project. She weighted each grade recorded in her gradebook the same, but wasn't confident about how to translate journal and research project grades into numbers to get the overall average. Also, as she did the grades she found several students she thought should have done better and others who probably deserved a lower grade, but she went with the numbers.

Questions for Consideration
1. What suggestions do you have for Ms. Byrd to improve her grading practices?
2. What kind of parent reaction do you think she might get when the grades are sent home?

Reporting Student Progress to Parents

An important function of marks and grades is to provide information that can be shared with parents. We know that parents are critical to student learning, and effectively reporting student progress can help parents better understand their children and know what they can do to provide appropriate support and motivation. Reporting to parents can take many forms, including weekly or monthly reports, phone calls, letters, newsletters, conferences, and, of course, report cards. Although grades are the most common way by which parents keep abreast of student progress, what those grades communicate is usually limited.

Report Cards

The foundation for most reporting systems is the report card. This simple form is constructed to communicate to parents the progress of their children. Typically, either grades or numerical scores are provided, along with teacher comments or observations that relate to effort, cooperation, and other behaviors. To effectively communicate, parents must be able to understand what the grades and comments mean. The information needs to be accurately interpreted, and parents need to learn enough to guide improvement efforts. Some report cards are meant more for students than for parents. In this case, students need to interpret the information for self-evaluation.

Most report cards indicate only current status in different subjects, and they do not provide the detail needed for parents to know what to *do* with the information (see Azwell & Schmar, 1995; Guskey, 1996; Guskey and Bailey, 2001; and Wiggins,

1998, for alternatives to traditional report cards). Consequently, you'll probably need to supplement report cards with other forms of communication.

Written Information

One approach to reporting student progress is to provide some type of written report. This could be done weekly, biweekly, or monthly. In the progress report, include learning targets for the period, copies of rubrics and scoring criteria, student performances on individual assessments, descriptions of student motivation and affect, suggestions for helping the student, and grades if possible. Because this will take some time, it's best to have a standard form on which you can quickly record information. Older students can be taught to calculate their current grade average in the class. You will want to be sure to include some positive comments. It may be helpful to identify two or three areas that the parents could focus on until the next report. If possible, provide specific expectations for what you want parents to do at home to help. Be clear in asserting that parents need to be partners in the learning process. If these expectations can be individualized for each student, so much the better, but even a standard list of expectations is good.

Another type of written communication is the informal note or letter. Taking only a minute or two to write a personal note to parents about their child is much appreciated. It shows concern and caring. Begin such a note with something positive, then summarize progress and suggest an expectation or two.

Parent–Teacher Conferences

The parent–teacher conference is the most common way teachers communicate with parents about student progress. This is typically a face-to-face discussion, though phone conferences and calls can also be used. In fact, brief phone calls by the teacher to talk with parents, like informal notes, are very well received and appreciated, especially when the calls are about positive progress and suggestions rather than for disciplinary or other problems.

There are two types of parent–teacher conferences, based on two primary purposes. Group conferences, such as what occurs at back-to-school nights, are conducted in the beginning of the year to communicate school and class policies, class content, evaluation procedures, expectations, and procedures for getting in touch with the teacher. Individual conferences are conducted to discuss the individual student's achievement, progress, or difficulties. Parent–teacher conferences may be initiated by either the teacher or the parent, based on these purposes.

Parent–teacher conferences are required in most elementary schools. Middle and high school teachers find conferences much more difficult to conduct because of the number of students. But even if the conference is in the context of a back-to-school night, most of the suggestions in Figure 12.10 apply.

It is essential to plan the conference and to be prepared. This means having all the information well organized in advance and knowing what you hope to achieve from the conference. This will probably include a list of areas you want to cover

FIGURE 12.10 Checklist for Conducting Parent–Teacher Conferences

✓ Plan each conference in advance.
✓ Conduct the conference in a private, quiet, comfortable setting.
✓ Begin with a discussion of positive student performances.
✓ Establish an informal, professional tone.
✓ Encourage parent participation in the conference.
✓ Be frank in reviewing student strengths and weaknesses.
✓ Review language skills.
✓ Review learning targets with examples of student performances that show progress.
✓ Avoid discussing other students and teachers.
✓ Avoid bluffing.
✓ Identify two or three areas to work on in a plan of action.

and some questions to ask parents. If possible, you may be able to find out what parents would like to review before the conference. Examples of student work should be organized to show progress and performance in relation to learning targets. The conference is an ideal time for pointing out specific areas of strength and weakness that report card grades cannot communicate.

You want the conference to be a conversation, not a lecture. Listening to parents will help you understand their child better. Even though it is natural to feel anxious about meeting with parents, it's important to take a strong, professional stance. Rather than being timid, take charge. This should be done with a friendly and informal tone that encourages parents to participate. You'll want to be positive, but you need to be direct and honest about areas that need improvement. Keep the focus on academic progress rather than student behavior. I think it's always important to discuss student performance in reading, writing, and speaking. These language skills are essential and should be reviewed. Avoid discussing other students or teachers, and be willing to admit that you don't know an answer to a question. By the end of the conference you should identify, in consultation with the parents, a course of action or steps to be taken at home and at school. Guskey and Bailey (2001) suggest additional recommendations based on whether the time frame is before, during, or after the conference (see Figure 12.11).

Student-Led Conferences

A new kind of reporting to parents involves students as the leader in their own conferences. In a student-led conference, students lead parents through a detailed and direct review of their work. Teachers fill the role of facilitator by creating a positive environment in which the conferences can take place, and by preparing students. In order for students to take responsibility for leading a conference with their parents, they need to have reflected on and evaluated their performance. This is usually accomplished by some kind of portfolio assessment. In addition to promoting student responsibility, parents tend to be more involved.

FIGURE 12.11   Recommendations for Effective Parent–Teacher Conferences

Before the Conference . . .	During the Conference . . .	After the Conference . . .
• Encourage parents to review student work at home, note concerns or questions, and bring those to the conference.	• Provide child care, refreshments, and transportation, if needed.	• Provide parents with a telephone number and schedule of specific times so they may call you with concerns.
• Schedule times that are convenient for both working and nonworking parents.	• Show multiple samples of student work and discuss specific suggestions for improvement.	• Follow up on any questions or concerns raised during the conference.
• Notify parents well ahead of scheduled conference times.	• Actively listen and avoid the use of educational jargon.	• Plan a time to meet again, if necessary.
• Provide staff development for new teachers on the purpose for conferences, preparation, and scheduling.	• Communicate expectations and describe how parents can help.	• Encourage parents to discuss the conference with their child.
• Consider alternative locations, such as churches or community centers for parents' convenience.	• Develop a system for on-going communication with each parent that recognizes parents as partners.	• Ask parents for written evaluation of the conference and encourage them to make suggestions.
• Print conference schedules and materials in multiple languages, if necessary.	• Provide resources or materials that parents might use at home to strengthen students' skills.	• Debrief with colleagues to look for ways to improve future conferences.

Source: Gusky, T. R., & Bailey, J. M. (2001). *Developing grading and reporting systems for student learning.* Thousand Oaks, CA: Corwin Press, p. 188. Reprinted by permission of Corwin Press, Inc.

In a student-led conference, students are essentially telling a story about their learning. This helps parents see progress over time from the perspective of the student. In preparing for the conference, students must learn to describe and evaluate their work. This self-reflection promotes additional learning and gives students confidence that they are able to understand their capabilities and achievements. A sense of pride and ownership is developed in the student. See Bailey and Guskey (2001) for more details about setting up and conducting student-led conferences.

Summary

This chapter stressed the importance of a teacher's professional judgment when implementing a grading and reporting system. There is no completely objective procedure for grading. Grading is professional decision making that depends on the teacher's values and beliefs, experience, external pressures, and best subjective judgments. We reviewed the different functions of marking and grading and took a close look at how factors other than academic performance affect grades. The chapter examined the basis of comparison used in grading, as well as approaches to marking and grading. Approaches to combine assessments were presented, along with reporting procedures to parents. Important points include the following:

- In the classroom, the major function of marking and grading is to provide students with feedback about their performance.
- Teachers need to provide a sufficient level of detail for marking to be informative for students.
- In general, use effort, student aptitude, improvement, and attitudes as factors affecting grades only in borderline cases.
- Grades communicate comparison between student performance and the performance of other students (norm-referenced) or between student performance and predetermined standards (criterion-referenced).
- The major function of norm-referenced systems is to rank and sort students. Student competitiveness is fostered; most teachers find they must do some degree of sorting.
- The major function of criterion-referenced systems is to judge students in relation to established levels of performance.
- Percent correct is the most common type of criterion-referenced grading. Percentage correct depends on item difficulty.
- The goal in grading is to provide a fair and accurate record of student performance in relation to learning targets.
- Approaches to grading include using letters, percent correct measures, standards-based, pass-fail tests, checklists, and written descriptions.
- Determining report card grades requires professional decisions about what to include, how to weight each assessment, and how weighted assessments are combined.
- It is important to clarify the role homework will play in determining grades; nonacademic factors should only be included in borderline cases.
- Provide a sufficient number of assessments to obtain a fair and accurate portrait of the student.
- Weight each assessment by the contribution to the goal, instructional time, reliability, and recency. Give more recent, comprehensive assessments more weight.
- Put all assessments on the same scale before weighting and combining. Weight before combining.
- Consider variation of each assessment if combining relative comparisons.
- Be flexible with borderline cases; don't let numbers make what should be professional, subjective decisions.
- Do not use zeros indiscriminately when averaging scores.
- Grades should not be affected by inappropriate student behavior or cheating.
- Grades should be changed when warranted to reflect the most fair and accurate record of student performance.

- Reporting student progress to parents can be done by phone, with written materials, and in teacher–parent conferences.
- Reports to parents should be well prepared with samples of student work to illustrate progress and areas that need further attention.
- Teacher–parent conferences are informal, professional meetings during which teachers discuss progress with parents and determine action steps to be taken.
- Student-led conferences with parents promote student self-evaluation and parent involvement.

SELF-INSTRUCTIONAL REVIEW EXERCISES

1. Indicate whether each of the following refers to norm-referenced (NR) or criterion-referenced (CR) grading.

   a. used to show which students are the worst in a group
   b. average test scores are typically lower
   c. easily adapted from scoring rubrics
   d. uses percentile rank
   e. uses percent correct
   f. items tend to be easier
   g. determination of standards is subjective
   h. fosters student competitiveness

2. In what ways is teacher professional judgment important in determining the actual standard employed in grading and marking students?

3. What major limitation do most approaches to grading have in common? What can teachers do to avoid this limitation?

4. From the following scenario, summarize what Ms. Gallagher did wrong when she determined her report card grades.

   Ms. Gallagher calculated semester grades on the basis of a midterm, a comprehensive final exam, and student participation, which consisted of homework, class participation, and effort. Each component was worth 100 points; they were added and then divided by three to obtain the composite score, which was then translated to a grade.

5. Using the following grading scale and scores, what percent correct grade would Ralph and Sally receive?

   90–100 A, 80–89 B, 70–79 C, 60–69 D, <60 F
   Midterm # 1, 20 percent
   Midterm # 2, 20 percent
   Final exam, 30 percent
   Paper, 20 percent (A=100, A–=92, B+=88, B=85, B–=82, C+=78, C=75, C–=72)
   Participation, 10 percent (same scale as paper)

	Ralph	*Sally*
Midterm #1, 40 possible points	30 points	35 points
Midterm #2, 50 possible points	40 points	35 points

Final exam, 200 possible points	170 points	140 points
Paper	B+	C
Participation	A–	A

6. Shaunda is a sixth grader. She is the oldest in a low-income family of six. Because her parents are not home very much, Shaunda takes on responsibilities with her brothers and sisters. The family lives in a small home, so it's hard for Shaunda to get the privacy she needs to do her homework. Consequently, she often does not hand in any homework. She has a very positive attitude toward school and she is very attentive in class and tries hard to do well. Your class uses the following grading policy: in-class work accounts for 25 percent of the final grade; homework, 25 percent; and 50 percent for tests and quizzes. The grading scale in the school is 95–100, A; 85–94, B; 75–84, C; 65–74, D; <65, F. Shaunda's averages are in-class work, 85 percent; homework, 30 percent; and tests and quizzes, 70 percent. What overall composite percent correct would Shaunda have? What grade would you give her? Does the grade reflect her academic performance? Should the grading policy be changed?

7. Suppose you have a very capable student who does very well on tests (e.g., 95s) but very poorly on homework. He just doesn't want to do work he sees as boring. His homework scores pull his test scores down so that the overall average is B-. What final grade would you give?

ANSWERS TO SELF-INSTRUCTIONAL REVIEW EXERCISES

1. a. NR, b. NR, c. CR, d. NR, e. CR, f. CR, g. CR, h. NR.

2. The standard is set by how difficult the teacher makes the assessment items; scores essay, short-answer, and performance-based assessments; and sets the criterion level (e.g., the percentage correct).

3. The major limitation of letter grades, percent correct, and pass-fail approaches is that they provide only a general overview of performance. Supplemental information that details the strengths and weaknesses of the students is needed.

4. I hope you noticed immediately that Ms. Gallagher made several significant errors. First, there are too few assessments to determine a semester grade; many more are needed. Second, the three components should not be weighted equally. Because the final is comprehensive, it should count the most. The participation grade is weighted too heavily and should not combine academic work (homework) with nonacademic factors. The weighting makes it possible for students who have poor performance to do satisfactorily in the course. There is no indication of how much each of the separate participation components is counted. This example is pretty bad!

5. First, convert all scores to the same 100-point scale. Because the first midterm is worth 40 points, the score would be multiplied by 2.5, the second midterm score by 2, and the final exam divided by 2. Each of these scores is multiplied by the appropriate weight and then added.

   Ralph: $(30 \times 2.5 \times .2) + (40 \times 2 \times .2) + (170/2 \times .3) + (88 \times .2) + (92 \times .1) = 15 + 16 + 25.5 + 17.6 + 9.2 = 83.3 = B$

Sally: $(35 \times 2.5 \times .2) + (35 \times 2 \times .2) + (140/2 \times .3) + (75 \times .2) + (100 \times .1) = 17.5 + 14 + 21 + 15 + 10 = 77.5 = C+$

6. Shaunda's composite score would be figured as $(85 \times .25) + (30 \times .25) + (70 \times .5) = 21.25 + 7.5 + 35 = 63.75$. According to the grading scale, she would receive an F. This reflects the relatively high contribution of homework and the fact that she was not able to get much of it finished. However, her classwork and performance on tests tell a different story, and a more accurate grade would be a D. Suppose homework was 10 percent instead of 25 percent and classwork was 40 percent. Then her composite would be a 72, almost 10 points higher. Given her home situation, she certainly should not fail, and the grading scale needs to be changed to put more weight on academic performance. The relatively high percentage for in-class work, 25 percent, is subject to teacher bias and should be reduced.

7. Actual test performance should not be affected negatively by nonacademic factors such as effort and compliance. I'd use a policy that homework won't hurt a grade, but could improve it, and give the student an A. Obviously, the student did not really need the homework, which suggests a change in homework assignments.

SUGGESTIONS FOR ACTION RESEARCH

1. Create a grading plan that would make sense for a class you plan to teach. Include a statement of purpose and explain what would be included, how weights would be established, and the final grading scale. Then give the plan to other students and ask them to critique it. If possible, give the plan to a classroom teacher and see how realistic it is.

2. Interview teachers on the subject of grading. Do they use a norm-referenced or criterion-referenced approach or a combination? Ask them about the areas that require professional judgments, like what to do with borderline students, how zeros are used, how to apply extra credit, and the like. Ask them how they use grades to motivate students.

3. Observe a class when graded tests or papers are returned to students. What is their reaction? What do they seem to do with the information?

4. Conduct an experiment by giving some students just grades and other students grades with comments and suggestions for improvement. See if the students react differently. Interview the students to determine if the nature of the feedback affected their motivation.

5. Talk with some parents about their experiences with parent–teacher conferences. What did they get out of it? How could it have been improved? Were the suggestions in Figure 12.10 followed?

CHAPTER 13

Administering and Interpreting Standardized Tests

Standardized testing was considered in Chapter 4 in the context of instructional planning. In that chapter, we reviewed different types of standardized tests and scores to better understand students' initial levels of achievement and aptitude, strengths and weaknesses, and deficiencies in order to establish learning targets and plan an effective instructional program. In this chapter, we are concerned with other important uses of standardized tests by classroom teachers, including year-to-year program evaluation and interpreting standardized test scores to parents. We will also discuss your role in administering standardized tests. First, however, we need to review the statistical terms and numerical indices that are commonly used in creating and reporting standardized test scores. Although your reaction to the term *statistics* may include some anxiety, we will deal with a conceptual understanding that does not require advanced mathematical calculations.

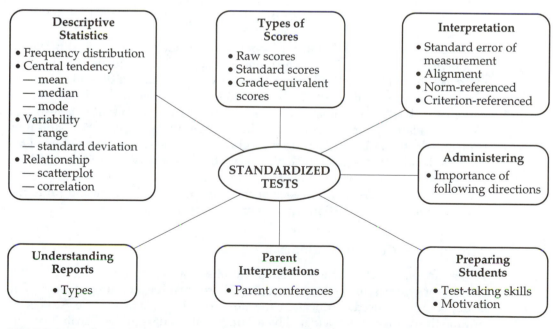

Descriptive Statistics
- Frequency distribution
- Central tendency
  — mean
  — median
  — mode
- Variability
  — range
  — standard deviation
- Relationship
  — scatterplot
  — correlation

Types of Scores
- Raw scores
- Standard scores
- Grade-equivalent scores

Interpretation
- Standard error of measurement
- Alignment
- Norm-referenced
- Criterion-referenced

STANDARDIZED TESTS

Administering
- Importance of following directions

Understanding Reports
- Types

Parent Interpretations
- Parent conferences

Preparing Students
- Test-taking skills
- Motivation

CHAPTER 13   Concept Map

Fundamental Descriptive Statistics

Descriptive statistics are used to describe or summarize a larger number of scores. The nature of the description can be in the form of a single number, such as an average score, a table of scores, or a graph. You have seen and read many of these kinds of descriptions (e.g., the average rainfall for a month, the median price of new homes, a baseball batting average). Descriptive statistics efficiently portray important features of a group of scores to convey information that is essential for understanding what the scores mean. For standardized tests, descriptive statistics are used as the basis for establishing, reporting, and interpreting scores.

Frequency Distributions

The first step in understanding important characteristics of a large set of scores is to organize the scores into a frequency distribution. This distribution simply indicates the number of students who obtained different scores on the test. In a simple **frequency distribution,** the scores are ranked, from highest to lowest, and the number of students obtaining each score is indicated. If the scores are organized into intervals, a *grouped frequency distribution* is used. Suppose, for example, that a test had eighty items. Figure 13.1 illustrates the scores received by twenty students, as well as simple and grouped frequency distributions that show the number of students obtaining each score or interval of scores.

Often the scores are presented graphically as a frequency polygon or histogram to more easily explain important features (Figures 13.2a and 13.2b). The **frequency polygon** is a line graph, which is formed by connecting the highest frequencies of each score. The **histogram** is formed by using rectangular columns to represent the frequency of each score.

For a relatively small number of scores, a frequency polygon is usually jagged, as shown in Figure 13.2a. For a large number of scores and test items, the line looks more like a smooth curve. The nature of the curve can usually be described as being *normal, positively skewed, negatively skewed,* or *flat.* Typically, for standardized tests, the curve very closely approximates a normal distribution (a symmetrical, bell-shaped curve) for a large group of students (e.g., for the norming group). If the distribution is **positively skewed,** or skewed to the right, most of the scores are piled up at the lower end and there are just a few high scores. For a **negatively skewed** distribution, it is just the opposite—most of the scores are high with few low scores (skewed to the left). In a flat distribution, each score is obtained with about the same frequency. Figures 13.3a–13.3d illustrate each of these types of curves.

Measures of Central Tendency

A measure of central tendency is a single number that is calculated to represent the average or typical score in the distribution. There are three measures of central tendency commonly used in education: the mean, median, and mode. The **mean** is the arithmetic average. It is calculated by adding all the scores in the distribution and

FIGURE 13.1   Frequency Distributions of Test Scores

Student	Score	Simple Frequency Distribution		Grouped Frequency Distribution	
		Score	f	Interval	f
Austin	96				
Tyler	94	96	1	92–96	3
Tracey	92	94	1	86–91	4
Karon	90	92	1	80–85	7
Hannah	90	90	2	74–79	3
Lanie	86	86	2	68–73	3
Allyson	86	84	3		
Felix	84	80	4		
Tryon	84	78	1		
Freya	84	74	2		
Mike	80	70	2		
Mark	80	68	1		
Ann	80				
Kristen	80				
Laura	78				
Megan	74				
Michelle	74				
Kathryn	70				
Don	70				
Jim	68				

then dividing that sum by the number of scores. It is represented by $\bar{X}$ or M. For the distribution of scores in Figure 13.1 the mean is 82.

$$\bar{X} = \frac{\Sigma X}{N}$$

where

$\bar{X}$ = the mean
Σ = the sum of (indicates that all scores are added)
X = each individual score
N = total number of scores

for Figure 13.1:

$$\bar{X} = \frac{1,640}{20}$$

$$\bar{X} = 82$$

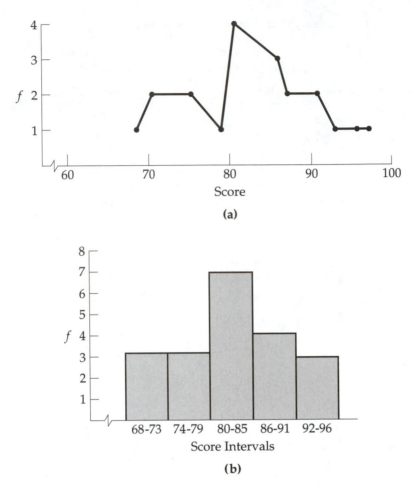

FIGURE 13.2   Frequency Polygon of Scores (a) and Histogram (b) from Figure 13.1

The **median,** represented by *mdn,* is the midpoint, or middle, of a distribution of scores. In other words, 50 percent of the scores are below the median, and 50 percent of the scores are above the median. Thus, the median score is at the 50th percentile. The median is found by rank ordering all the scores, including each score even if it occurs more than once, and locating the score that has the same number of scores above and below it. For our hypothetical distribution, the median is 82 (84 + 80/2; for an uneven number of scores it will be a single existing score).

The **mode** is simply the score in the distribution that occurs most frequently. In our distribution, more students scored an 80 than any other score, so 80 is the mode. It is possible to have more than one mode; in fact, in education, *bimodal distributions* are fairly common.

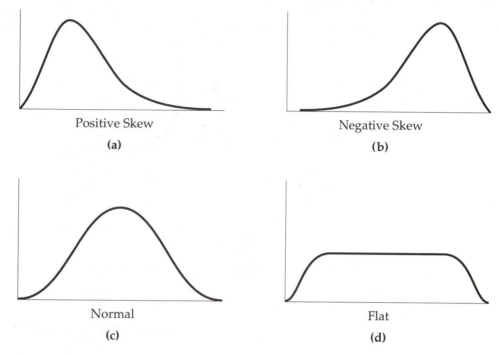

FIGURE 13.3   **Types of Frequency Distributions**

In a normal distribution, the mean, median, and mode are the same. In a positively skewed distribution, the mean is higher than the median (hence skewed positively), and in a negatively skewed distribution, the mean is lower than the median. This is because the mean, unlike the median, is calculated by taking the value of every score into account. Therefore extreme values affect the mean, whereas the median is not affected by an unusual high or low score.

Measures of Variability

A second type of statistic that is essential in describing a set of scores is a measure of variability. Measures of variability, or dispersion, indicate how much the scores spread out from the mean. If the scores are bunched together close to the mean, then there is little or a small amount of variability. A large or great amount of variability is characteristic of a distribution in which the scores are spread way out from the mean. Two distributions with the same mean can have very different variability, as illustrated in Figure 13.4.

To more precisely indicate the variability, two measures are typically used, the range and standard deviation. The **range** is simply the difference between the highest and lowest score in the distribution (in our example 28; 96 – 68). This is an easily calculated but crude index of variability, primarily because extremely

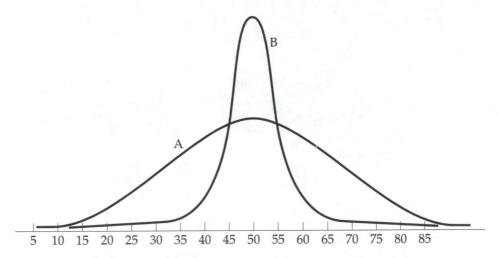

5   10   15   20   25   30   35   40   45   50   55   60   65   70   75   80   85

FIGURE 13.4   Distributions with the Same Mean, Different Variability

high or low scores result in a range that indicates more variability than is actually present.

A more complicated but much more precise measure of variability is standard deviation. The **standard deviation** (*SD*) is a number that indicates the *average* deviation of the scores from the mean. It is calculated by employing a formula that looks difficult but is relatively straightforward. These are the essential steps:

1. Calculate the mean of the distribution.
2. Calculate the difference each score is from the mean (these are called deviation scores).
3. Square each difference score (this makes all the deviation scores positive).
4. Add the squared difference scores.
5. Divide by the total number of scores in the distribution.
6. Calculate the square root of the result of step 5.

These steps are illustrated with our hypothetical set of test scores in Figure 13.5. Essentially, you simply calculate the squared deviation scores, find the *average* squared deviation score, and then take the square root to return to the original unit of measurement. In this distribution, one standard deviation is equal to 7.92. Unless you are using a normative grading procedure, standard deviation is not very helpful for classroom testing. However, because of the relationship between standard deviation and the normal curve, it is fundamental to understanding standardized test scores.

With a standardized test, the frequency distribution of raw scores for the norming group will usually be distributed in an approximately normal fashion. In

FIGURE 13.5   Steps in Calculating Standard Deviation

Score	(1) Deviation Score	(2) Deviation Score Squared	(3) Squared Deviation Scores Added	(4) Added Scores Divided by N	(5) Square Root
96	$96 - 82 = 14$	$14 \times 14 = 196$	+196		
94	$94 - 82 = 12$	$12 \times 12 = 144$	+144		
92	$92 - 82 = 10$	$10 \times 10 = 100$	+100		
90	$90 - 82 = 8$	$8 \times 8 = 64$	+ 64		
90	$90 - 82 = 8$	$8 \times 8 = 64$	+ 64		
86	$86 - 82 = 4$	$4 \times 4 = 16$	+ 16		
86	$86 - 82 = 4$	$4 \times 4 = 16$	+ 16		
84	$84 - 82 = 2$	$2 \times 2 = 4$	+ 4		
84	$84 - 82 = 2$	$2 \times 2 = 4$	+ 4		
84	$84 - 82 = 2$	$2 \times 2 = 4$	+ 4		
80	$80 - 82 = -2$	$-2 \times -2 = 4$	+ 4		
80	$80 - 82 = -2$	$-2 \times -2 = 4$	+ 4		
80	$80 - 82 = -2$	$-2 \times -2 = 4$	+ 4		
80	$80 - 82 = -2$	$-2 \times -2 = 4$	+ 4		
78	$78 - 82 = -4$	$-4 \times -4 = 16$	+ 16		
74	$74 - 82 = -8$	$-8 \times -8 = 64$	+ 64		
74	$74 - 82 = -8$	$-8 \times -8 = 64$	+ 64		
70	$70 - 82 = -12$	$-12 \times -12 = 144$	+144		
70	$70 - 82 = -12$	$-12 \times -12 = 144$	+144		
68	$68 - 82 = -14$	$-14 \times -14 = 196$	+196 = 1,256	$1,256/20 = 62.8$	$\sqrt{62.8} = 7.92$

a normal distribution, the meaning of the term *one standard deviation* is the same in regard to percentile rank, regardless of the actual value of standard deviation for that distribution. Thus, $+1SD$ is always at the 84th percentile, $+2SD$ is at the 98th percentile, $-1SD$ is at the 16th percentile, and $-2SD$ is at the 2nd percentile in every normal distribution. This property makes it possible to compare student scores to the norm group distribution in terms of percentile rank and to compare relative standing on different tests. For instance, suppose a norm group took a standardized test, and on the basis of their performance a raw score of 26 items answered correctly was one standard deviation above the mean for the norm group (84th percentile). When a student in your class gets the same number of items correct (26), the percentile reported is the 84th. Obviously, if the norm group were different and 26 items turned out to be at +2SD, then the student's score would be reported at the 98th percentile. You would also know that a score at one standard deviation on one test is the same in terms of relative standing as one standard deviation on another test. Most important for standardized tests, standard deviation is used to compute standard scores and other statistics that are used for interpretation and analysis.

Measures of Relationship

It is often helpful, even necessary, to know the degree to which two scores from different measures are related. Typically, this degree of relationship is estimated by what is called a *correlation coefficient*. Correlations are reported in standardized test technical manuals for validity and reliability. Also, an important principle in interpreting test scores, standard error of measurement, is determined from correlation.

Scatterplot.   The scatterplot, or *scattergram*, is a graphic representation of relationship. When used in education, a scatterplot can give you a descriptive picture of relationship by forming a visual array of the intersections of students' scores on two measures. As illustrated in Figure 13.6, each measure is rank ordered from

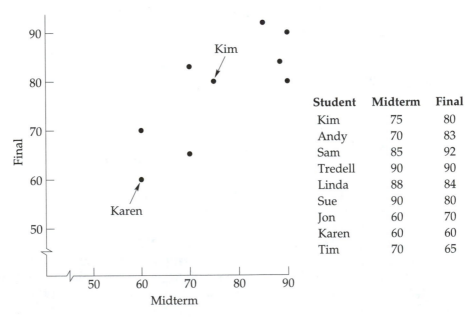

Student	Midterm	Final
Kim	75	80
Andy	70	83
Sam	85	92
Tredell	90	90
Linda	88	84
Sue	90	80
Jon	60	70
Karen	60	60
Tim	70	65

FIGURE 13.6   Scatterplot of Relationship between Two Tests

lowest to highest on a different axis. The two scores from each student are used to establish a point of intersection. When this is completed for all students, a pattern is formed that provides a general indication of the direction and strength of the relationship. The direction of the pattern indicates whether there is a positive, a negative, a curvilinear, or no relationship. It is positive if scores on one variable increase with increases in the other scores, and it is negative (inverse) if scores on one variable increase as scores on the other measure decrease. If the pattern looks like a U shape, it is curvilinear; and if it is a straight line or no particular pattern at all, there is little if any relationship.

Scatterplots help to identify intersections that are not typical, which lower the correlation coefficient, and to identify curvilinear relationships. However, these scatterplots are rarely reported in standardized test manuals. Typically, these manuals report the correlation coefficients.

Correlation Coefficient.   The **correlation coefficient** is a number that is calculated to represent the direction and strength of the relationship. The number ranges between −1 and +1. A high positive value (e.g., +.85 or +.90) indicates a high positive relationship, a low negative correlation (e.g., −.10 or −.25) represents a low negative relationship, and so forth. The *strength* of the relationship is independent from the *direction.* Thus, a positive or negative value indicates direction, and the value of the correlation, from 0 to 1 or from 0 to −1, determines strength. A perfect correlation is designated by either +1 or −1. As the value approaches these perfect correlations it becomes stronger, or higher. That is, a correlation is stronger as it changes from .2 to .5 to .6, and also as it changes from −.2 to −.5 to −.6. A correlation of −.8 is stronger (higher) than a correlation of +.7.

There are several different types of correlation coefficients. The most common one is the Pearson product-moment correlation coefficient. This is the one most likely to be used in test manuals. It is represented by *r.*

Four cautions need to be emphasized when interpreting correlations. First, correlation does not imply causation. Just because two measures are related, it does not mean that one *caused* the other. Other factors may be involved in causation, and the direction of the cause is probably not clear. Second, be alert for curvilinear relationships, because most correlation coefficients, such as the Pearson, assume that the relationship is linear. Third, also be alert to what is called **restricted range.** If the values of one measure are truncated, with a small range, it will in all likelihood result in a low correlation. Given a full range of scores, the correlation would be higher. Fourth, relationships expressed as correlation coefficients generally are less precise than the number would suggest. That is, a very high correlation of .80 does not mean that 80 percent of the relationship is accounted for. If you think of correlation as predicting one score from another score, you will see how relatively imprecise this can be. Examine the scatterplots of various correlations in Figure 13.7. You will see that in a moderate relationship (c), if you try to predict the value of variable *B* on the *y* axis, say, from a score of 10 for variable *A,* a range of approximately 5 to 20 is predicted.

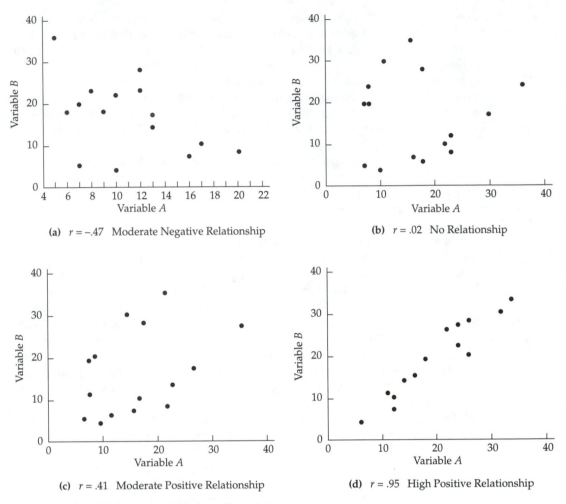

(a) $r = -.47$ Moderate Negative Relationship

(b) $r = .02$ No Relationship

(c) $r = .41$ Moderate Positive Relationship

(d) $r = .95$ High Positive Relationship

FIGURE 13.7   Scatterplots of Various Correlations

Types of Derived Standardized Test Scores

Three kinds of standardized test scores were introduced in Chapter 4: raw scores, percentile rank, and grade equivalent. Raw scores are simply the number of items answered correctly. Raw scores, by themselves, however, are not as versatile as other scores that are *derived* or *transformed* from these raw scores. One easily understood derived score, for example, is percent correct. Percentile rank and grade equivalent scores are also derived in the sense that they are computed from raw score distributions. There are additional derived scores that are commonly used with standardized tests, and we will consider these in this chapter, along with further discussion of percentile ranks and grade equivalents. Descriptions of the various types of standardized test scores that you will encounter are summarized in Figure 13.8.

Standard Scores

Standard scores are derived from raw scores in units based on the standard deviation of the distribution. They are obtained by using a linear transformation, which simply changes the value of the mean and one standard deviation, or a nonlinear, normalizing transformation based on the percentiles of the normal curve. Most standard scores reported with standardized tests are normalized, though we will briefly review two common linear transformations, z-scores and T-scores. The term *standard* in this context does not mean a specific level of performance or expectation. Rather, it refers to the standard normal curve as the basis for interpretation. Standard scores have equal units between different values, which allows for additional statistical procedures.

Z-Score. The simplest and most easily calculated standard score is the **z-score**, which indicates how far a score lies above or below the mean in standard deviation units. Since $1SD = 1$, a z-score of 1 is one standard deviation unit above the mean.

FIGURE 13.8   Types of Derived Standardized Test Scores

Type	Description
Percent Correct	Number of points obtained divided by the total number of points possible, and multiplied by 100
Percentile Rank	Percentage of norm group examinees who scored at or below the given score
Grade Equivalent	Score that indicates the median score of students in the norm group at the same grade and month
Standard Scores	
z-score	Score based on a distribution with mean of 0 and a standard deviation of 1
T-score	Score based on a distribution with a mean of 50 and a standard deviation of 10
NCE	Score based on a distribution with a mean of 50 and a standard deviation of 21.06
Stanine	Score based on dividing the normal distribution into nine parts; each score describes one part
Deviation I.Q.	Score based on a distribution with a mean of 100 and a standard deviation of 15 or 16
Scale	Unique scores to indicate growth over several years in relation to the norm group

The formula for computing z-scores is relatively straightforward if you know the value of one standard deviation:

$$z\text{-score} = \frac{X - \bar{X}}{SD}$$

where

X = any raw score
$\bar{X}$ = mean of the raw scores
SD = standard deviation of the raw score distribution

For example, a z-score for 90 in our hypothetical distribution would be 1.01 (90 – 82/7.92). If the raw score is less than the mean, the z-score will be negative (e.g., the z-score for 70 in our distribution of twenty students would be –1.01 (70 – 82/7.92).

If the z-score is a **linear transformation,** the distribution of z-scores will be identical to the distribution of raw scores. It is also possible to *normalize* the raw score distribution when converting to z-scores. This transforms the distribution to a normal one, regardless of what the raw score distribution looked like. If the raw score distribution is normal, then using the formula will also result in a normal distribution of z-scores. For most standardized tests, the standard scores are normalized. Thus, a z-score of 1 is at the 84th percentile, a z-score of 2 is at the 98th percentile, and so forth.

Because the z-score distribution has a standard deviation equal to 1, these scores can easily be transformed to other standard scores that will only have positive values (e.g., *T*-scores, NCEs, stanines, SAT scores).

T-*Score.*   **T-scores** are the same as z-scores except the *T*-score distribution has a different mean, 50, and a different standard deviation, 10. *T*-scores are obtained by using a simple formula to convert from z-scores:

$$T\text{-score} = 50 + 10(z)$$

Thus, a *T*-score of 60 is the same as a z-score of 1; both are at the 84th percentile. Like z-scores, *T*-scores may be straight linear transformations from the raw score distribution, or normalized.

Normal Curve Equivalent.   The **normal curve equivalent (NCE)** is a normalized standard score that has a mean of 50 and a standard deviation of 21.06. The reason for selecting 50 for the mean and 21.06 for the standard deviation was so that NCE scores, like percentiles, would range from 1 to 99. The percentiles of 1, 50, and 99 are equivalent to NCEs of 1, 50, and 99. However, at other points on the scale, NCEs are not the same as percentiles. For example:

NCE	Percentile
90	97
75	88
25	12
10	3

It is fairly easy to confuse NCEs with percentiles because they convert the same range of scores (1–99), especially for someone who is not familiar with measurement principles. Thus, you need to be careful when explaining what NCEs mean to parents. So why are NCEs used at all? Because they are standard scores (percentiles are not), they can, like other standard scores, be used statistically for research and evaluation purposes. For example, Chapter 1 programs have frequently used NCEs to report growth and improvement.

Stanines.   One popular type of standard score for standardized tests is the stanine. A **stanine** indicates about where a score lies in relation to the normal curve of the norming group. Stanines are reported as single-digit scores from 1 to 9. A stanine of 5 indicates that the score is in the middle of the distribution; stanines 1, 2, and 3 are considered below average; 7, 8, and 9 are above average; and stanines of 4, 5, and 6 are about average. Think of each stanine as representing a part of the normal curve, as illustrated in Figure 13.9. Although there is a precise, statistically determined procedure for determining stanines, it is practical to use the range from 1 to 9 as a simple, easily understood way to indicate relative standing. Each stanine covers a specific area of the normal curve in terms of percentiles:

Stanine	Percentile Rank	Stanine	Percentile Rank
9	96 or higher	4	23 to 39
8	89 to 95	3	11 to 22
7	77 to 88	2	4 to 10
6	60 to 76	1	Below 4
5	40 to 59		

Notice that there is a different percentage of scores in stanines 5, 6, 7, 8, and 9. This is because the width of the stanine is the same in relation to the curve of the normal distribution. Another way you can think about stanines is that they have a mean of 5, with a standard deviation of 2. Because they are normalized, stanines from conceptually similar but different tests can be compared, such as aptitude and achievement tests. Remember that meaningful differences in performance are indicated when the scores differ by at least two stanines.

A disadvantage of the stanine is that even though you know the area of the normal curve the score lies in, you don't know what part of this area the score is in. In this sense, stanines are less precise than percentile rank. For example, percentile scores of 42 and 58 have the same stanine score of 5. However when stanine scores differ by more than 1, it is probable that there is a meaningful difference between achievement in those areas. That is, if the reading stanine score is 5 and the mathematics stanine is 7, it is likely that the student is demonstrating stronger achievement in mathematics.

Scaled Score.   Most standardized tests use what is called a **scaled score** (also called the *level,* or *growth score*) to show year-to-year progress in achievement and to compare different levels of the same test. Each test publisher uses a different scale, ranging between 0 and 999. Higher scores are associated with higher grade levels. For example, the Iowa Test of Basic Skills uses a score of 200 to indicate the median performance of students in the fourth grade, 150 as the median for first graders, and 250 as the median for eighth graders. The complete scale, across grade levels, is as follows:

Grade:	K	1	2	3	4	5	6	7	8	9
SS:	130	150	168	185	200	214	227	239	250	260

Thus, the median performance for third graders is assigned a score of 185, and so on. *The Comprehensive Tests of Basic Skills,* Fourth Edition, uses a mean score of 707 for fourth-grade reading and 722 for fifth-grade reading. These median and mean scores, and associated standard deviations, provide anchors against which a student's progress can be compared. This makes it possible to use developmental standard scores to plot performance from year to year. However, because they are more abstract than other scores, they are relatively difficult to interpret.

Deviation IQ and Standard Age Scores. For many years, the results of IQ and general ability testing have been reported on a scale that has a mean of 100 and a standard deviation of 15 or 16. Originally, IQ scores were actual intelligent quotients, calculated by dividing mental age by chronological age and multiplying this ratio by 100. Today, IQ scores are determined like other derived standard scores. For each age group in a norming sample, the raw scores are converted to z-scores, then to deviation IQ scores by multiplying the z-score by 15 or 16 and adding that product to 100. Most test publishers refer to the student's "ability," "aptitude," or to "standard age" scores rather than IQ because *intelligence* today refers to many other traits besides academic ability or reasoning. Some of these tests have a standard deviation as small as 12 or as large as 20. This is one reason that it is inappropriate to compare the scores of two individuals who have taken different tests.

Other Standard Scores. The advantage of standard scores—being able to convert raw scores to scores directly related to the normal curve and percentile rank—is also a disadvantage from the standpoint that there are so many different standard scores. Some test publishers use unique standard scores. Once you understand the nature of the scores, you can readily interpret the results. But you may need to look in the technical manual of the test to know what the publisher has assigned as the mean and standard deviation.

Grade Equivalent Scores

Grade equivalents (GEs) were also introduced in Chapter 4. These scores are much like scale scores, except that the unit is expressed in grade levels and months. As pointed out earlier, GEs are useful only in indicating growth or progress; they should not be used for grade placement. In addition, most GEs are determined by interpolation. That is, a test may be given to beginning fourth graders, and the median score for that group will be assigned a grade equivalent of 4.0. The same test might be given to a beginning group of fifth graders, with the median score given a GE of 5.0. No other tests are given, but scores are still reported in months (e.g., 4.2 or 4.8). If the students in grades 4, month 2 and month 8 were not given the test, how was the median of each group determined? The answer is that the medians were interpolated, estimated, from existing scores. This means that the reported scores of, say, 4.1 or 4.6, are only estimates. For some tests, GEs are extrapolated beyond the grade levels actually tested. Thus, a test may be given to students in grades 3, 4, and 5, but GEs may range from 2.0 to 7.0 and beyond. Extrapolated scores are less accurate than interpolated ones, and they should be interpreted cautiously.

Figure 13.9 shows a normal distribution with the corresponding standard deviation units, percentiles, and selected standard scores.

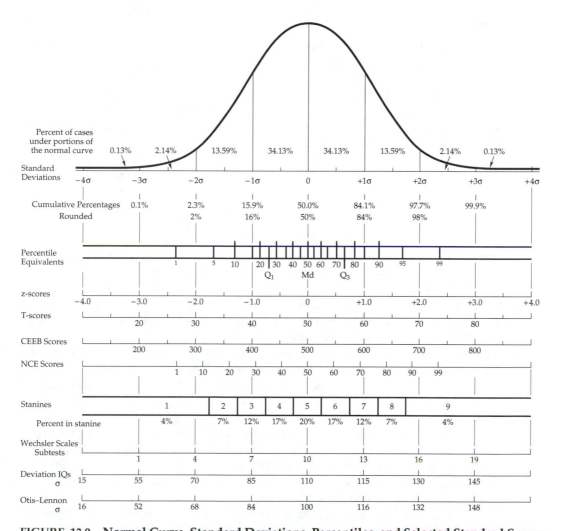

FIGURE 13.9   Normal Curve, Standard Deviations, Percentiles, and Selected Standard Scores

Source: Test service notebook no. 148, p. 2. Used courtesy of The Psychological Corporation. Harcourt Brace Jovanovich, Publishers. Reproduced by permission.

Interpreting Standardized Tests

Armed with a basic knowledge of important descriptive statistics and types of scores, you can now better understand how to interpret and use your students' *standardized test scores.* We begin our discussion with two more technical issues—standard error of measurement and alignment of the test with curriculum, teaching, and classroom assessments. Then we will look at issues involved in norm- and criterion-referenced interpretation before examining some actual standardized test score reports.

Standard Error of Measurement

As I have stressed throughout this book, every test has some degree of error. Chapter 3 introduced the relationship between error and reliability. Basically, as error increases, reliability decreases. But we can directly measure reliability only in a test; we cannot know what type or amount of error has influenced a student's score. Therefore we estimate the degree of error that is probable, given the reliability of the test. This degree of error is estimated mathematically and is reported as the **standard error of measurement (SEM).**

SEM is determined by a formula that takes into account the reliability and standard deviation of the test. If a student took a test many times, the resulting scores would look like a normal distribution. That is, sometimes the student would get "good" error and get a higher score, and sometimes the student would get "bad" error, resulting in a lower score. If we assume that the student's *true* score is the mean of this hypothetical distribution, then we can use this as a starting point for estimating the *actual* true score. From what we know about the normal curve and standard deviation, 68 percent of the time the actual true score would be between one standard deviation of the student's normal curve of many testings, and 96 percent of the time the actual true score would fall within two standard deviations of this distribution. We call the standard deviation of this hypothetical normal distribution the *standard error of measurement.*

For example, if a student's GE score on a test were 3.4, and the test had a standard error of measurement of .2, then we would interpret the student's true performance, with 68 percent confidence, to be 3.4 ±.2; and with 96 percent confidence, we would interpret the student's true score to be 3.4 ±.4. In other words, the standard error of measurement creates an interval, and it is within this interval that we can be confident that the student's true score lies. Different degrees of confidence are related to the number of standard errors of measurement included; these intervals can be thought of as **confidence bands.** Of course, we do not know *where* in the interval the score lies, so we are most accurate in interpreting the performance in terms of the interval, not as a single score.

The idea of interpreting single scores as bands or intervals has important implications. If you are drawing a conclusion about the performance of a single student, your thinking should be something like this: "Trevor's performance in mathematics places him between the 86th and 94th percentiles," rather than, "Trevor's score is at the 90th percentile." This will give you a more realistic and accurate basis for judging Trevor's real or actual level of performance. When comparing two scores from the same test battery, a meaningful difference in performance is indicated only when the intervals, as established by one standard error of measurement, do not overlap. Thus, it would be wrong to conclude that a student's language achievement score of 72 is *higher* than the reading score of 70 if the standard error is two or more. The same logic is needed for comparing ability with achievement or for comparing the scores of different individuals on the same test. That is, if the bands do not overlap, then you should conclude that there is no difference between the scores.

Fortunately, test publishers report standard errors of measurement to help you interpret the scores properly, and often they are displayed visually in the form of a shaded band surrounding the score. Unfortunately, there is usually a slightly different standard error of measurement for each subtest and for different ranges of scores. Thus, in the technical manual, there are tables of standard errors of measurement. I don't want to suggest that you consult these tables for each student and for each score. However, it may be helpful to use this information in decisions regarding referral for identification for special education, and for placement into special programs. Many standardized test reporting formats display the appropriate standard error of measurement on each student's report, although you will need to look at a key to know the exact nature of the band. Some tests use one SEM; others use the middle 50 percent.

Alignment

One of the most critical aspects of interpreting standardized test scores is to determine the extent to which the test content is aligned with the curriculum, with your teaching, and with your classroom assessments. This is particularly important given the recent standards-based emphasis for both curriculum and standardized tests. At a relatively simple level, you can review the test content and make judgments about how well that content matches the content in the curriculum. A more detailed analysis considers whether the emphasis given to different topics in your teaching matches the emphasis given on the test. Further alignment judgments can be made concerning the match between test format and content and the format and content of classroom assessments. Finally, a more sophisticated review of the items, instruction, and classroom assessments examines the cognitive level demanded. The cognitive level can vary according to one or more of the taxonomies that have been developed.

If the content, emphasis, and cognitive level of the standardized test match well with your instruction, the curriculum, and classroom assessment, then there is strong alignment. With strong alignment, the standardized test scores serve as a check on the effectiveness of the instruction. With weak alignment, scores on standardized tests have some implications, but because of a lack of emphasis on the same content and cognitive level, these implications are not as clear. For example, if we know that there is a good match, and the scores are low, there is reason to learn why. High test scores with a good match are validation that students are indeed learning the content as intended.

Interpretation of Norm-Referenced Standardized Tests

Most standardized tests are designed to provide norm-referenced interpretations. This allows you to compare performance to a well-defined *norming* or reference group and to determine relative strengths and weaknesses of students. When comparing an individual's performance to the norm group, the overall competence of this group is critical in determining relative position. Ranking high with a low-performing group may indicate, in an absolute sense, less competence than ranking low in a high-performing group. Thus, the exact nature of the norming group is important, and several types of norms can be used.

Types of Standardized Test Norms.   Norms are sets of scores. Each type of norm differs with respect to the characteristics of the students who comprise the norm group. The most commonly used type are *national norms*. These norms are based on a nationally representative sample of students. Generally, testing companies do a good job of obtaining national samples, but there is still variation from one test to another based on school cooperation and the cost of sampling. Also, most testing companies oversample minorities and other underrepresented groups. Thus, one reason that national norms from different tests are not comparable is that the sampling procedures do not result in equivalent norm groups. For example, you should never conclude that one student has greater knowledge or skill than another because her reading score on the Stanford Achievement Test is at the 90th percentile, compared to another student who scored at the 80th percentile on the Metropolitan Achievement Test (there would also be differences in the content of the items). On the other hand, most testing companies use the same norm group for both achievement and aptitude batteries, which allows direct achievement/aptitude and subtest score comparisons.

There are also many different *special group norms*. These types of norms comprise subgroups from the national sample. For example, special norms are typically available for large cities, high- or low-socioeconomic-status school districts, suburban areas, special grade levels, norms for tests given at different times of the year (usually fall and spring), and other specific subgroups. Whenever a special group norm is used, the basis for comparison changes, and the same raw score on a test will probably be reported as a different percentile rank. For instance, because both achievement and aptitude are related to socioeconomic status (higher socioeconomic status, higher achievement), school districts that contain a larger percentage of high-socioeconomic-status students than is true for the population as a whole (and hence the national norm group) almost always score above the mean with national norms. Conversely, districts with a high percentage of low-socioeconomic-status students typically have difficulty scoring above the mean. However, if the high socioeconomic status district is compared to suburban norms, the percentile ranks of the scores will be lower; for low-socioeconomic-status districts, the percentiles will be higher if the norm group is low-socioeconomic-status districts. Understandably, then, suburban districts almost always want to use national norms.

One common misconception is that students who test in the spring of the year obtain a higher percentile rank than students who test in the fall. However, each of these testing times has a separate norm group, so that a student is compared only to those in the norming group who took the test at the same time during the year. However, a grade equivalency or developmental score would be higher for students taking the spring test because they would, in fact, have greater knowledge than students in the same grade level in the fall.

Another type of norm is one that is for a single school district. These are called *local norms*. Local norms are helpful in making intraschool comparisons and in providing information that is useful for student placement in appropriate classes. These different types of norms make it very important for you to examine standardized test reports and know the type of norm that is used to determine percentile rank and standard scores.

Using Test Norms.   Once you understand clearly the type of norm group that is used, you will be in a position to interpret the scores of your students accurately. In making these interpretations and using the norms correctly, adhere to the following suggestions (summarized in Figure 13.10):

1. Remember That Norms Are Not Standards or Expectations.   Norm-referenced test scores show how a student compares to a reference group. The scores do not tell you how much the student knows in terms of specific learning targets, or how much students should know. Students who score below the norm (that is, below the mean score) may or may not be meeting your learning targets. That determination is criterion-referenced.

2. Match Your Intended Use of the Scores with the Appropriate Norm Group. As we have discussed, there are many different types of norms. You need to determine your intended use and then use the norm group that will provide you with the most valid comparison. For determining general strengths and weaknesses and aptitude/achievement discrepancies, national norms are appropriate. If you want to use the scores to select students for a special class, local norms are probably best. When you counsel a student regarding a career, national norms will not be as helpful as norms more specific to the field.

FIGURE 13.10   Checklist for Using Norm-Referenced Test Scores

✓ Are norms differentiated from standards and expectations?
✓ Is the type of norm matched with the intended use?
✓ Is the norm group sampling representative and well described?
✓ Are the test norms current?

3. Sampling for the Norm Group Should Be Representative and Well Described. You should supplement the test publisher's description of the norming group with an examination of the specific nature of the sampling that was used. This can be found in the technical manual for the test. Often, we need to be sure that specific subgroups are represented in the proper proportion. This determination will be possible only if the sampling procedures are clearly described and relevant characteristics of the sample are provided, such as gender, age, race, socioeconomic status, and geographic location.

4. If Possible, Use the Most Recently Developed Test Norms. Standardized test norms are developed on the basis of sampling one year, and this serves as the reference group for several more years. Thus, you may well use the same test that was normed in, say, 2001, with your students in 2005. This means that the performance of your students in 2005 is compared to how well students performed on the test in 2001. Over the years between the norming and current testing, the curriculum can change to be more consistent with the test, and there can be changes in your student population. These factors affect the current scores and make it possible for all school divisions to be rated above average. For the norming group, 50 percent of the students are below average. This distribution is set so that in the future more than 50 percent of the students could obtain a raw score higher than the mean raw score of the norming group. In general, the most current norms provide the most accurate information. You should be wary of using old test norms that have not been updated.

The Scholastic Assessment Test (SAT) provides an interesting illustration of how the date of the norming group makes an impact. Until 1995, the norming group for the SAT consisted of 10,000 college-bound students tested in 1941. Every year since then, each student who has taken the SAT has been compared to this 1941 norm group. This has resulted in a decline in SAT averages because the population of students taking the SAT recently has a much larger percentage of lower-ability students. Thus, this decline is a function of a population of students taking the SAT, which is different from the original norming group. Today, the SAT has been *renormed* to more adequately reflect the population of students who currently take the test.

Criterion-Referenced Interpretations

As we previously discussed, criterion-referenced interpretations compare student performance to established standards rather than to other students. Some standardized tests are only criterion-referenced (they may also be called objectives based, absolute, domain referenced, standards-referenced, or content referenced, though the technical meaning may differ). These tests are designed to provide a valid measure of skills and knowledge in specific areas. Most norm-referenced tests also provide criterion-referenced information by indicating the number of items answered correctly in specific areas, but because the primary purpose of these tests is to compare individuals, they typically do not provide information as meaningful as what criterion-referenced tests provide. Thus, you need to keep in mind that there is a difference between a criterion-referenced standardized test and criterion-referenced interpretations.

Whether the test is norm or criterion-referenced, it is important for each skill or area for which a score is reported to be described in detail. With delimited and well-defined learning targets, the score can more easily be interpreted to suggest some degree of mastery. Without a clearly defined target, such interpretation is questionable at best. Typically, criterion-referenced tests do the best job of this because it is essential to their primary purpose.

Your judgment concerning the degree of a student's mastery is usually based on the percentage of correctly answered items that measure a specific target. The meaning that is given to the percentage of correct answers is generally made by the teacher, based on a review of the definition of the target and the difficulty of the items. This involves your professional judgment; in some districts standards may be set by a team, a group of educators, or parents. An important aspect of making this decision is having a sufficient number of items to adequately measure the trait. Criterion-referenced tests are designed to have enough items for each score, but norm-referenced tests may or may not have enough items.

Although results are not reported as percentile ranks or standard scores, there may be information in the technical manual about the difficulty of items or average scores of various groups. This information is helpful when deciding the correspondence between the percentage of items answered correctly and mastery of the skill or content area. One approach to doing this is to set in your mind a group of "minimally competent" students in reference to the target, then see how many items these students answer correctly. If the mean number of correct answers is, say, seven of ten, then your "standard" becomes 70 percent of the items. It may be that the level is set in relation to a goal for students by the end of the year, or you may set standards based on how others have performed in the past. Regardless of the approach, the interpretation is largely a matter of your professional judgment, so think carefully about the criteria you use.

With these recommendations, keep the following suggestions in mind when making criterion-referenced interpretations from standardized tests (summarized in Figure 13.11):

1. Determine the Primary Purpose of the Test—Is It Norm- or Criterion-Referenced? Criterion-referenced tests are designed for criterion-referenced

FIGURE 13.11   **Checklist for Using Criterion-Referenced Test Scores**

✓ Is the primary purpose of the test norm- or criterion-referenced?
✓ Are measured targets delimited and clearly defined?
✓ Are there enough items to measure each target adequately?
✓ Is the difficulty level of the items matched with the learning targets?

interpretations. As long as the descriptions of the traits match your learning targets, these types of tests will provide the best information. Be wary of using norm-referenced tests for criterion-referenced interpretations.

2. Examine the Clarity and Specificity of the Definitions and Traits Measured.   For each score that is reported there needs to be an adequate definition of what is being measured. Norm-referenced tests tend to define what is measured more broadly, criterion-referenced tests more specifically. You may need to consult the technical manual to get sufficient detail of the definition to make a valid judgment about the match between what the tests says it is measuring and what you want measured. There should be good content-related evidence of validity to demonstrate an adequate sampling of content or skills from a larger domain.

3. Be Sure There Is a Sufficient Number of Items to Make a Valid Decision. The general rule is to have at least six to eight different test items for each target. For learning targets that are less specific, more than ten items may be needed. In some norm-referenced tests you may see skills listed with as few as three or four items. This is too few for making reasonable conclusions, especially if the items are objective, but it may suggest a need for further investigation.

4. Examine the Difficulty of Items and Match This to Your Standards.   Norm-referenced tests may not use easy items because they do not discriminate among students, while criterion-referenced tests tend to have easy items so that most students will do reasonably well. This means that the difficulty of the items may differ considerably with the same definition for the target. Inspect the items carefully and use your knowledge of their difficulty in setting standards.

Figure 13.12 summarizes differences between norm- and criterion-referenced interpretations.

FIGURE 13.12   Norm- and Criterion-Referenced Interpretations

Norm-Referenced	Criterion-Referenced
• Based on how an individual compares to others	• Based on performance compared to absolute levels or standards of proficiency
• Nature of comparison or "norm" group critical	• Needs clearly defined learning targets
• Provides percentile rank and standard scores	• How absolute levels are determined and who sets them are critical
• Allows comparisons between different subjects and different years	• Provides percentage correct and categorical designation (e.g., pass-fail)

Understanding Standardized Test Score Reports

When you first look at some standardized test score reports, they may seem to be very complicated and difficult to understand. This is because they are designed to provide as much information as possible on a single page. For a comprehensive battery, scores are often reported for each skill as well as each subskill. The best approach for understanding a report is to consult the test manual and find examples that are explained. Most test publishers do a very good job of showing you what each part of the report means.

There are also many different types of reports. Each test publisher has a unique format for reporting results and usually includes different kinds of scores. In addition, there are typically different formats to report the same scores. Thus, the same battery may be reported as a list of students in your class, the class as a whole, a skills analysis for the class or individual student, individual profiles, profile charts, growth scale profiles, and other formats. Some reports include only scores for major tests; others include subskill scores and item scores. Different norms may be used. All of this means that each report contains somewhat different information, organized and presented in dissimilar ways. You need to first identify what type of report you are dealing with, then find an explanation for it in an interpretive guide. After you have become acquainted with the types of standardized tests and reports used in your school, you will be in a position to routinely interpret them in accurate and helpful ways.

Figures 13.13 and 13.14 illustrate student reports for different standardized tests. For the Iowa Test of Basic Skills Performance Profile, various norm-referenced scores are summarized in the upper box for this third grader. The SS is the ITBS standard score, GE refers to Grade Equivalent, NS is the National Stanine, NCE is the Normal Curve Equivalent, and NPR is the National Percentile. The confidence bands indicate the standard error of measurement. You can see that Mary is pretty much average compared to the national norm group. She is strong in social studies and sources of information and relatively weaker in science and language, especially capitalization. The bottom of the profile provides more detailed information, showing how many items were attempted, the percentage correct, and the average percentage correct for the nation. This is a more criterion-referenced type of information and can be used to better understand overall performance.

In Figure 13.14 a slightly different report format is illustrated. In this report similar derived scores are shown. Within mathematics, because the bands for problem solving and procedures do not overlap, it can be concluded that Elizabeth is significantly weaker in procedures than problem solving and weaker in social studies than total reading. Similar to the ITBS Profile, content clusters are shown for more of a criterion-referenced interpretation. Also, this report includes an aptitude measure, the Otis-Lennon School Ability Test. These results indicate slightly higher nonverbal results than achievement results, which suggests that in some content areas Elizabeth's achievement scores could be expected to be higher.

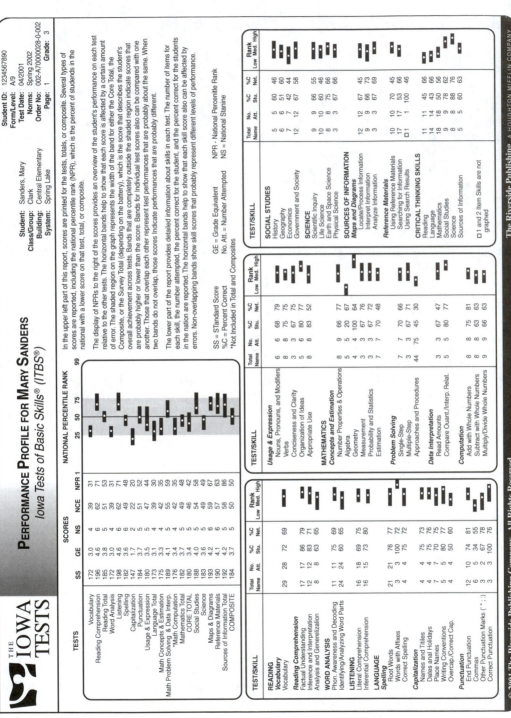

FIGURE 13.13 Individual Performance Profile

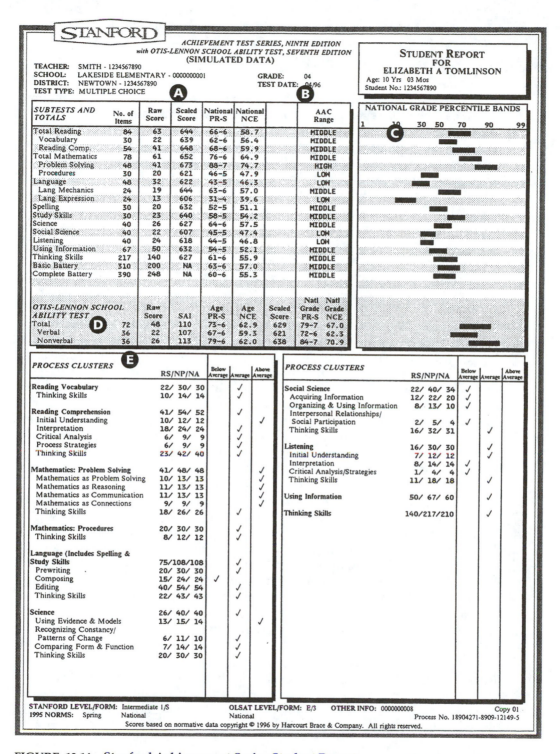

FIGURE 13.14   Stanford Achievement Series Student Report

Copyright © 1996 by Harcourt Educational Measurement. All rights reserved. Reproduced by permission.

Interpreting Test Reports for Parents

Most teachers interpret the results of standardized tests for parents, although research has shown that nearly half of our teachers feel unprepared to do this (Nolen, Haladyna, & Haas, 1989). Because you are in contact with students daily and are aware of their classroom performance, you are in the best position to communicate with parents regarding the results of standardized tests. You can determine what level of detail to report and how the results coincide with classroom performance. This is done most effectively face-to-face in the context of a teacher–parent conference, though many schools send written reports home without scheduling a conference. In such a conference, you can point out important cautions and discuss the results in a way that will make sense. Before the conference, you should review available information and prepare it to show student progress and areas of strength and weakness that may need specific action at home and school. This should include other examples of student work, in addition to the test results, to lessen the tendency to place too much value on test scores.

In preparing for the conference, keep in mind that most parents are interested in particular types of information. These include some indication of relative standing, growth since earlier testing, weaknesses, and strengths. For each of these areas you should present the relevant numbers, but be sure to include a clear and easy-to-understand narrative—using plain, everyday language—that explains the numbers. You should always include some explanation of norms and the standard error of measurement. It is important for parents to realize that, for most reports, the scores do not represent comparisons with other students in the class. Parents obviously don't need an extended explanation of error, but it's important for them to understand that the results represent *approximate* and not absolute or precise performance.

Of the different types of scores to report to parents, percentiles are most easily understood, even though some parents will confuse percentile with percentage correct. They may also think that percentile scores below 70 are poor because they are accustomed to grading systems in which 70 or below may mean failure. In fact, for most standardized tests, students will score in the average range if they answer 60 to 70 percent of the items correctly. Grade equivalents are commonly reported but easily misunderstood. Parents often think that GEs indicate in which grade a student should be placed. You will need to be diligent in pointing out that GEs are only another way of comparing performance to the norm group.

Some standardized tests have special reports that are prepared for parents. Although these are very informative, it is still important to supplement the scores with a note from the teacher indicating a willingness to confer with the parents, by phone or in person, to answer any questions and clarify the meaning of the results.

In summary, the following suggestions will help you interpret standardized test reports confidently and in a way that will accurately inform parents and help the student:

1. Understand the Meaning of Every Score Reported to Parents. It is embarrassing, not to mention unprofessional, not to know how to interpret each score on the report.

2. Examine Individual Student Reports Comprehensively before a Conference with Parents.   This will prevent you from trying to understand and explain at the same time.

3. Gather Evidence of Student Performance in the Classroom That Can Supplement the Test Scores.   This demonstrates your commitment to the preparation and careful analysis of each student's performance, and it provides more concrete examples of performance that parents can easily understand.

4. Be Prepared to Address Areas of Concern Most Parents Have, Such as Standing, Progress, Strengths and Weaknesses.   This may require you to review the student's previous performance on other standardized tests.

5. Be Prepared to Distinguish between Ability and Achievement.   Many parents want to know if their child is performing "up to their ability." You might even have a short written description of the difference to supplement your verbal explanation.

6. Explain the Importance of Norms and Error in Testing for Proper Interpretation.   This could include your knowledge of any extenuating circumstances that may have affected the student's performance.

7. Summarize Clearly What the Scores Mean.   Don't simply show the numbers and expect the parents to be able to understand. You will need to summarize in language that the parents can comprehend.

8. Try to Create a Discussion with Parents, Rather Than Making a Presentation to Them.   Ask questions to involve parents in the conference and to enhance your ability to determine if they in fact understand the meaning of the scores.

Case Study for Reflection

Mrs. Jones called right after the standardized test score reports were sent home. She wanted to know how her daughter, Ellen, could be scoring so high yet not be getting very good grades. In reviewing Ellen's scores, it turns out that she scored on the 80 and 90 national percentile range for most subjects, but her grades were Cs and Bs.

Questions for Consideration
1. How would you explain the meaning of Ellen's national percentile scores to her mother?
2. How would you explain the discrepancy between her grades and test score? What other information might be important in providing a reasonable explanation?
3. How would you prepare for a meeting with Mrs. Jones to discuss the scores and Ellen's grades?

Preparing Students to Take Standardized Tests

You want your students to perform as well as possible on standardized tests, and with high-stakes testing accompanying increased demands for accountability, it is important for every student to have a fair opportunity to do his or her best work. This is accomplished if students are properly prepared before taking the test, and this preparation will probably be your responsibility.

One area to address is making sure that students have good test-taking skills. These skills help to familiarize the students with item formats and give them strategies so that the validity of the results is improved. Students should be proficient with the test-taking skills listed in Figure 13.15.

You also want to set an appropriate classroom climate or environment for taking the test. This begins with your attitude toward the test. If you convey to students that you believe the test is a burden, an unnecessary or even unfair imposition, then students will also adopt such an attitude and may not try their best. Be happy with the test, convey an attitude of challenge and opportunity. Discuss with your students the purpose and nature of the test. Emphasize that it is most important for students to try to do their best, not just to obtain a high score. Tell the students how the tests will be used in conjunction with other information; this will reduce anxiety. You want to enhance student confidence by giving them short practice tests. These tests help to acquaint students with the directions and the types of items they will answer.

Student motivation is an important factor. Motivate your students to put forth their best effort by helping them understand how the results from the test will benefit them. Show how results can be used to improve learning and essential life skills, their knowledge of themselves, and planning for the future. Avoid comments that might make students concerned or anxious.

FIGURE 13.15 Important Test-Taking Skills

1. Listen carefully to directions; ask questions if directions are not clearly understood.
2. Read directions and all items slowly and carefully.
3. Look for key words.
4. Follow directions carefully.
5. Understand the concept of "best answer."
6. Establish a pace in answering items so that no items are unanswered.
7. Skip difficult items and return to them if time permits.
8. Do not omit items as long as guessing is not penalized; make an educated guess.
9. Eliminate alternatives on multiple-choice tests rather than looking for the correct answer.
10. Check to make sure answers and items match.
11. Check items if there is extra time.

Some of your students may be so anxious about the test that their anxiety seriously interferes with their performance. If you suspect that a student's performance is adversely affected by test anxiety, after you have done all you can to alleviate the fears, then you may want to have the student examined by a counselor to determine the extent of the problem. If necessary, appropriate counseling and desensitization exercises can be explored. At the very least, incorporate your awareness of the anxiety when interpreting the results of the test.

Of course, be sure that the physical environment for taking the test is appropriate. There should be adequate work space and lighting as well as good ventilation. The room should be quiet, without distractions, and the test should be scheduled to avoid events that may disturb the students. Students should be seated to avoid distractions and cheating. Morning testing is preferred. It is best to remove any visual aids that could assist students and to place a sign on the outside of the door, such as Testing—Do Not Disturb.

Figure 13.16 lists some do's and don'ts regarding the test preparation practices of teachers.

Administering Standardized Tests

Because most standardized tests are given in the classroom, you will most likely be responsible for administering them to your students. The most important part of

FIGURE 13.16   Do's and Don'ts of Standardized Test Preparation

Do	Don't
Improve student test-taking skills	Use the standardized test format for classroom tests
Establish a suitable environment	
Motivate students to do their best	Characterize tests as an extra burden
Use released items	Tell students important decisions are made solely on the basis of test scores
Explain why tests are given and how results will be used	Use previous forms of the same test
Give practice tests	Teach the test
Tell students they probably won't know all the answers	Have a negative attitude about the test
	Use items with a format that is identical to the test
Tell students not to give up	
Allay student anxiety	Limit instruction and classroom assessments to be aligned only with the test
Have a positive attitude about the test	

administering these tests is to *follow the directions carefully and explicitly*. This point cannot be overstated. You must adhere strictly to the instructions that are given by the test publisher. The procedures are set to ensure standardization in the conditions under which students in different classes and schools take the test. The directions indicate what to say, how to respond to student questions, and what to do as students are working on the test. Familiarize yourself with the directions before you read them to your students, word for word as specified. Don't try to paraphrase directions or recite them from memory, even if you have given the test many times.

During the test you may answer student questions about the directions or procedures for answering items, but you should not help students in any way with an answer or what is meant by a question on the test. Although you may be tempted to give students hints or tell them to "answer more quickly" or "slow down and think more," these responses are inappropriate and should be avoided. You need to suspend your role as classroom teacher for a while and assume the role of test administrator. This isn't easy, and you may well catch yourself with minor variations from the directions.

While observing students as they take the test, you may see some unusual behavior or events that could affect the students' performance. It is best to record these behaviors and events for use in subsequent interpretation of the results. Interruptions should also be recorded.

The test directions specify time limits for subtests. You must follow these strictly, including the instruction to collect completed answer sheets and tests promptly. Once the test is over, you will need to account for all copies to ensure test security. Some tests require that you write down the exact beginning and ending times.

Summary

The purpose of this chapter was to introduce you to the principles of standardized testing to enable you to administer such tests and interpret your students' scores. Although standardized testing may not directly influence your day-to-day teaching, you have a professional responsibility to interpret the scores from these types of tests accurately for yourself, students, and parents. The results of standardized tests, when used correctly, provide helpful information concerning the effectiveness of your instruction and progress of your students. Important points in the chapter include the following:

- Frequency distributions show you how scores are arrayed: normal, positively skewed, negatively skewed, flat.
- Measures of central tendency include the mean, median, and mode.
- Measures of variability, such as the range and standard deviation, provide numerical values for the degree of dispersion of scores from the mean.
- Standard scores, such as z, T, NCE, the developmental scale, and deviation IQ scores, are converted from raw scores into units of standard deviation.

- Grade equivalency scores indicate performance related to norming groups and should be cautiously interpreted.
- Scatterplots show relationships graphically as being positive, negative, or curvilinear.
- Correlation coefficients are numbers from –1 to 1 that indicate direction and strength of the relationship.
- Correlation does not imply causation.
- Standard error of measurement (SEM) expresses mathematically the degree of error to be expected with individual test scores; test results are best interpreted as intervals defined by the SEM.
- Percentile rank, standard scores, and grade equivalents for students are based on comparisons with the norming group.
- Alignment of the content, emphasis, and cognitive level of a test with instruction is needed for proper interpretation.
- Norm-referenced test scores provide external measures and help identify relative strengths and weaknesses.
- Different types of norms, such as national norms, special group norms, or local norms, influence the reported percentile ranks and other comparative scores.
- Norms are not standards or expectations; they should be recent, appropriate to your use, and based on good sampling.
- Criterion-referenced interpretations depend on the difficulty of the items and professional judgments to set standards.
- Good criterion-referenced judgments depend on well-defined targets and a sufficient number of test items to provide a reliable result.
- Standardized test reports vary in format and organization; consult the interpretive guide to aid in understanding.
- Adequate interpreting of standardized test scores to parents depends on your preparation, your full understanding of the meaning of the scores, your ability to translate the numerical results into plain language, and placing the scores in the context of classroom performance.
- Prepare your students for taking standardized tests by establishing a good environment, lessening test anxiety, motivating students to do their best, avoiding distractions, and giving students practice tests and exercises.

SELF-INSTRUCTIONAL REVIEW EXERCISES

1. For the following set of numbers, calculate the mean, median, and standard deviation. Also determine linear z- and T-scores for 18, 20, and 11.

   10, 17, 18, 15, 20, 16, 15, 21, 12, 11, 22

2. If you have a normal distribution of scores with a mean of 80 and a standard deviation of 6, what is the approximate percentile rank of the following scores: 86, 68, 83, and 71?

3. Given the following standardized test scores for Mary, an eighth grader, her mother believes that Mary is in the wrong grade. She believes Mary would be better off in the ninth grade. She also believes that the test scores seem to indicate that Mary is stronger in science than in language arts, mathematics, or social science. How would you respond to Mary's mother?

Test	NATL PR	Stanine	GE
Mathematics	75	6	9.2
Science	87	7	9.7
Social studies	80	7	9.4
Language arts	63	6	8.5
Study skills	72	6	9.0

4. Indicate whether each of the following suggested activities help or hinder student performance on a standardized test:

   a. Tell students their futures depend on their scores.
   b. To avoid making students anxious, do not tell them very much about the test.
   c. Make sure the room temperature is about right.
   d. Arrange desks so that students face each other in groups of four.
   e. Give students a practice test that is very similar in format.
   f. Tell students they probably won't be able to answer many of the questions.
   g. Teach to the test.
   h. Tell students you think the test is taking away from class time and student learning.

ANSWERS TO SELF-INSTRUCTIONAL REVIEW EXERCISES

1. $\bar{X} = 161/11 = 16.09$; $mdn = 16$. Rounding the mean to 16, the SD is 3.83. The z- and T-scores are as follows: 18: $z = 18 - 16/3.83 = .53$; $T = 50 + 10(.53) = 55.3$; 20: $20 - 16/3.83 = 1.05$; $T = 50 + 10(1.05) = 60.5$; 11: $11 - 16/3.83 = -1.31$; $T = 50 + 10(-1.31) = 36.9$.

2. The score of 86 is one standard deviation above the mean, so the percentile is the 84th; 68 is two standard deviations below the mean, so the percentile is the 2nd; 83 is one half of a standard deviation above the mean, so the percentile rank is between 50 (mean) and 84 (one SD); because 34 percent of the scores lie in this range, one half of 34 is 17, so 83 is at about the 67th percentile (50 + 17) (actually it would be a little greater than 17 because of the curve of the distribution, but 67 is a good approximation); using the same logic, 71, which is one and one half standard deviations below the mean, would be at approximately the 8th percentile (50 – 34 + 8).

3. Mary's mother is probably looking at the GEs and thinking that this means Mary should be in the ninth grade. This is not true. It's very possible that most of the students in the eighth grade have GEs of 9 or higher. It's true that Mary's science score is her highest, but, given a normal standard error of measurement that is about 6 percentile points, the confidence interval overlaps suggest that there is no meaningful difference between science (81–93) and social studies (74–86), but it could be concluded that the science score is definitely higher than the language arts (57–69). The stanines give you the impression that the scores on all the tests are about the

same, which is somewhat misleading. Yes, they are all well above the norm, but the science percentile score is at the top of stanine 7, while the language arts percentile is at the bottom of stanine 6. Refer to examples of reports in Chapter 4 for interpretation. Give examples of some test scores.

4. a. hinder, b. hinder, c. help, d. hinder, e. help, f. hinder, g. help, h. hinder.

SUGGESTIONS FOR ACTION RESEARCH

1. Observe a class in which students take a standardized test. If possible, take a copy of the test administration guidelines with you and determine how closely the teacher follows the directions. What has the teacher done to motivate the students and set a proper environment? Observe the students as they are taking the test. Do they seem motivated and serious? How quickly do they work?

2. Sit in on two or three teacher–parent conferences that review the results of standardized tests. Compare what occurs with the suggestions in the chapter. How well, in your opinion, does the teacher interpret the scores? Is the teacher accurate?

3. Interview some parents about standardized tests. What did they get from the reports? Which types of scores were most meaningful to them? Did the results surprise them? Were the results consistent with other performance, such as grades?

4. Interview some teachers about standardized testing. Ask them how they use the results of standardized tests to improve their instruction. Ask them to recall situations in which parents did not seem to understand the results of the test very well. Looking back, what could the teacher have done differently to enhance parent understanding?

APPENDIX A

The Scope of a Teacher's Professional Role and Responsibilities for Student Assessment

The scope of a teacher's professional role and responsibilities for student assessment may be described in terms of the following activities. These activities imply that teachers need competence in student assessment and sufficient time and resources to complete them in a professional manner.

Activities Occurring prior to Instruction

a. Understanding students' cultural backgrounds, interests, skills, and abilities as they apply across a range of learning domains and/or subject areas
b. Understanding students' motivations and their interests in specific class content
c. Clarifying and articulating the performance outcomes expected of pupils
d. Planning instruction for individuals or groups of students

Activities Occurring during Instruction

a. Monitoring pupil progress toward instructional goals
b. Identifying gains and difficulties pupils are experiencing in learning and performing
c. Adjusting instruction
d. Giving contingent, specific, and credible praise and feedback
e. Motivating students to learn
f. Judging the extent of pupil attainment of instructional outcomes

Activities Occurring after the Appropriate Instructional Segment (e.g., lesson, class, semester, grade)

a. Describing the extent to which each pupil has attained both short- and long-term instructional goals
b. Communicating strengths and weaknesses based on assessment results to students and parents or guardians
c. Recording and reporting assessment results for school-level analysis, evaluation, and decision making
d. Analyzing assessment information gathered before and during instruction to understand each student's progress to date and to inform future instructional planning
e. Evaluating the effectiveness of instruction
f. Evaluating the effectiveness of the curriculum and materials in use

Activities Associated with a Teacher's Involvement in School Building and School District Decision Making

a. Serving on a school or district committee examining the school's and district's strengths and weaknesses in the development of its students
b. Working on the development or selection of assessment methods for school building or school district use
c. Evaluating school district curriculum
d. Other related activities

*Activities Associated with a Teacher's Involvement
in a Wider Community of Educators*

a. Serving on a state committee asked to develop learning goals and associated assessment methods
b. Participating in reviews of the appropriateness of district, state, or national student goals and associated assessment methods
c. Interpreting the results of state and national student assessment programs

Source: Standards for Teacher Competence in Educational Assessment of Students (1990). American Federation of Teachers, National Council on Measurement in Education, National Education Association.

Standards for Teacher Competence in Educational Assessment of Students

Standard	*Skills*
1. Teachers should be skilled in *choosing* assessment methods appropriate for instructional decisions.	a. Use concepts of assessment error and validity. b. Understand how valid assessment supports instructional activities. c. Understand how invalid information can affect instructional decisions. d. Use and evaluate assessment options considering backgrounds of students. e. Be aware that certain assessment activities are incompatible with certain instructional goals. f. Understand how different assessment approaches affect decision making. g. Know where to find information about various assessment methods.
2. Teachers should be skilled in *developing* assessment methods appropriate for instructional decisions.	a. Be able to plan the collection of information needed for decision making. b. Know and follow appropriate principles for developing and using different assessment methods. c. Be able to select assessment techniques that are consistent with the intent of the instruction. d. Be able to use student data to analyze the quality of each assessment technique used.
3. The teacher should be skilled in administering, scoring, and interpreting the results of both externally produced and teacher-produced assessment methods.	a. Be skilled in interpreting informal and formal teacher-produced assessment results, including performances in class and on homework. b. Use guides for scoring essay questions, projects, response-choice questions, and performance assessments. c. Administer standardized achievement tests and interpret reported scores. d. Understand summary indexes, including measures of central tendency, dispersion, relationships, and errors of measurement. e. Analyze assessment results to determine student strengths and weaknesses. f. Use results appropriately and do not increase students' anxiety levels.

Standard	Skills
4. Teachers should be skilled in using assessment results when making decisions about individual students, planning teaching, developing curriculum, and making recommendations for school improvement.	**a.** Use accumulated assessment information to organize a sound instructional plan. **b.** Interpret results correctly according to established rules of validity. **c.** Use results from local, regional, state, and national assessments for educational improvement.
5. Teachers should be skilled in developing valid pupil grading procedures that use pupil assessments.	**a.** Devise, implement, and explain a procedure for developing grades. **b.** Combine various assignments, projects, in-class activities, quizzes, and tests into a grade. **c.** Acknowledge that grades reflect their own preferences and judgments. **d.** Recognize and avoid faulty grading procedures. **e.** Evaluate and modify their grading procedures.
6. Teachers should be skilled in communicating assessment results to students, parents, other lay audiences, and other educators.	**a.** Understand and be able to give appropriate explanations of how to interpret student assessments as moderated by student background factors such as socioeconomic status. **b.** Explain that assessment results do not imply that background factors limit a student. **c.** Communicate to parents how they may assess a student's educational progress. **d.** Explain the importance of taking measurement errors into account when making decisions based on assessment. **e.** Explain the limitations of different types of assessments. **f.** Explain printed reports of assessments at the classroom, school district, state, and national levels.
7. Teachers should be skilled in recognizing unethical, illegal, and otherwise inappropriate assessment methods and uses of assessment information.	**a.** Understand laws and case decisions that affect their classroom, school district, and state assessment programs. **b.** Understand the harmful consequences of misuse or overuse of various assessment procedures such as embarrassing students or violating a student's right to confidentiality. **c.** Understand that it is inappropriate to use standardized student achievement test scores to measure teaching effectiveness.

Source: Standards for Teacher Competence in Educational Assessment of Students (1990). American Federation of Teachers, National Council on Measurement in Education, National Education Association.

A P P E N D I X   B

The Student Evaluation Standards

Propriety

P   Propriety Standards   The propriety standards help ensure that student evaluations will be conducted legally, ethically, and with due regard for the well-being of the students being evaluated and other people affected by the evaluation results. These standards are as follows:

P1   Service to Students   Evaluations of students should promote sound education principles, fulfillment of institutional missions, and effective student work, so that educational needs of students are served.

P2   Appropriate Policies and Procedures   Written policies and procedures should be developed, implemented, and made available, so that evaluations are consistent, equitable, and fair.

P3   Access to Evaluation Information   Access to a student's evaluation information should be provided, but limited to the student and others with established legitimate permission to view the information, so that confidentiality is maintained and privacy protected.

P4   Treatment of Students   Students should be treated with respect in all aspects of the evaluation process, so that their dignity and opportunities for educational development are enhanced.

P5   Rights of Students   Evaluations of students should be consistent with applicable laws and basic principles of fairness and human rights, so that students' rights and welfare are protected.

P6   Balanced Evaluation   Evaluations of students should provide information that identifies both strengths and weaknesses, so that strengths can be built upon and problem areas addressed.

P7   Conflict of Interest   Conflicts of interest should be avoided, but if present should be dealt with openly and honestly, so that they do not compromise evaluation processes and results.

Source: The Joint Committee on Standards for Educational Evaluation (2003). *The Student Evaluation Standards.* Thousands Oaks, CA: Corwin Press.

Utility

U   Utility Standards   The utility standards help ensure that student evaluations are useful. Useful student evaluations are informative, timely, and influential. Standards that support usefulness are as follows:

U1   Constructive Orientation   Student evaluations should be constructive, so that they result in educational decisions that are in the best interest of the student.

U2   Defined Users and Uses   The users and uses of a student evaluation should be specified, so that evaluation appropriately contributes to student learning and development.

U3   Information Scope   The information collected for student evaluations should be carefully focused and sufficiently comprehensive, so that evaluation questions can be fully answered and the needs of students addressed.

U4   Evaluator Qualifications   Teachers and others who evaluate students should have the necessary knowledge and skills, so that evaluations are carried out competently and the results can be used with confidence.

U5   Explicit Values   In planning and conducting student evaluations, teachers and others who evaluate students should identify and justify the values used to judge student performance, so that the bases for the evaluations are clear and defensible.

U6   Effective Reporting   Student evaluation reports should be clear, timely, accurate, and relevant, so that they are useful to students, their parents/guardians, and other legitimate users.

U7   Follow-Up   Student evaluations should include procedures for follow-up, so that students, parents/guardians, and other legitimate users can understand the information and take appropriate follow-up actions.

Feasibility

F   Feasibility Standards   The feasibility standards help ensure that student evaluations can be implemented as planned. Feasible evaluations are practical, diplomatic, and adequately supported. These standards are as follows:

F1   Practical Orientation   Student evaluation procedures should be practical, so that they produce the needed information in efficient, nondisruptive ways.

F2   Political Viability   Student evaluations should be planned and conducted with the anticipation of questions from students, their parents/guardians, and other legitimate users, so that their questions can be answered effectively and their cooperation obtained.

F3   Evaluation Support   Adequate time and resources should be provided for student evaluations, so that evaluations can be effectively planned and implemented, their results fully communicated, and appropriate follow-up activities identified.

Accuracy

A   Accuracy Standards   The accuracy standards help ensure that a student evaluation will produce sound information about a student's learning and performance. Sound information leads to valid interpretations, justifiable conclusions, and appropriate follow-up. These standards are as follows:

A1   Validity Orientation   Student evaluations should be developed and implemented, so that interpretations made about the performance of a student are valid and not open to misinterpretation.

A2   Defined Expectations for Students   The performance expectations for students should be clearly defined, so that evaluation results are defensible and meaningful.

A3   Context Analysis   Student and contextual variables that may influence performance should be identified and considered, so that a student's performance can be validly interpreted.

A4   Documented Procedures   The procedures for evaluating students, both planned and actual, should be described, so that the procedures can be explained and justified.

A5   Defensible Information   The adequacy of information gathered should be ensured, so that good decisions are possible and can be defended and justified.

A6   Reliable Information   Evaluation procedures should be chosen or developed and implemented, so that they provide reliable information for decisions about the performance of a student.

A7   Bias Identification and Management   Student evaluations should be free from bias, so that conclusions can be fair.

A8   Handling Information and Quality Control   The information collected, processed, and reported about students should be systematically reviewed, corrected as appropriate, and kept secure, so that accurate judgments can be made.

A9   Analysis of Information   Information collected for student evaluations should be systematically and accurately analyzed, so that the purposes of the evaluation are effectively achieved.

A10   Justified Conclusions   The evaluative conclusions about student performance should be explicitly justified, so that students, their parents/ guardians, and others can have confidence in them.

A11   Metaevaluation   Student evaluation procedures should be examined periodically using these and other pertinent standards, so that mistakes are prevented or detected and promptly corrected, and sound student evaluation practices are developed over time.

APPENDIX C

National Content Standards Projects

Subject	Developers	Order Information*
Arts	The Consortium of National Arts Education Associations	*National Standards for Arts Education,* write MENC Publication Sales, 1806 Robert Fulton Dr., Reston, VA 22091, or call (800) 828-0229
Civics	The Center for Civic Education	*National Standards for Civics and Government,* write Center for Civic Education, 5146 Douglas Fir Rd., Calabasas, CA 91302-1467, or call (800) 350-4223
Economics	The National Council on Economic Education, the Foundation for Teaching Economics, the American Economics Association Committee on Economic Education, and the National Association of Economics Education	Write National Council of Economic Education, 1140 Avenue of the Americas, New York, NY 10036, or call (800) 338-1192.
English	National Council of Teachers of English and the International Reading Association	*Standards for the Assessment of Reading and Writing,* write National Council of Teachers of English, 1111 W. Kenyon Rd., Urbana, IL 61801-1096, or call (800) 369-6283.
Foreign languages	The American Council on the Teaching of Foreign Languages, the American Association of Teachers of German, the American Association of Teachers of French, and the American Association of Teachers of Spanish and Portuguese	Write to the American Council on the Teaching of Foreign Languages, 6 Executive Plaza, Yonkers, NY 10701, or call (914) 963-8830.
Geography	The National Council for Geographic Education, the National Geographic Society, the Association of American Geographers, and the American Geographical Society	*Geography for Life: National Geographic Standards 1994,* write National Council for Geographic Education, Jacksonville State University, 206A Martin Hall, Jacksonville, AL 36265-1602, or call (256) 782-5293.

Health	American Association for Health Education	*National Health Education Standards,* write American Association for Health Education, 1900 Association Dr., Reston, VA 22091, or call (800) 213-7193.
History	The National Center for History in the Schools at the University of California at Los Angeles	*National Standards for World History, National Standards for United States History,* and *National Standards for History for Grades K–4,* write Social Studies School Service, 10200 Jefferson Blvd., Room LA6, P.O. Box 802, Culver City, CA 90232-0802, or call (800) 421-4246.
Mathematics	The National Council of Teachers of Mathematics	*Curriculum and Evaluation Standards for School Mathematics, Professional Standards for Teaching Mathematics,* and *Assessment Standards for School Mathematics,* write N.C.T.M., 1906 Association Dr., Reston, VA 20191-1593, or call (800) 235-7566.
Physical education	The National Association for Sport and Physical Education	*Content Standards* and *Assessment Guide for School Physical Education,* write N.A.S.P.E., 1900 Association Dr., Reston, VA 22091, or call (800) 321-0789.
Science	The National Research Council, drawn from the National Academy of Sciences, the National Academy of Engineering, and the Institute of Medicine	*National Science Education Standards,* write National Academy Press, Box 285, Constitution Ave., NW, Washington, DC 20055, or call (800) 624-6242.
Social studies	The National Council for the Social Studies	*Expectations of Excellence: Curriculum Standards for Social Studies,* write NCSS Publications, P.O. Box 2067, Waldorf, MD 20604-2067.
Technology	International Society for Technology in Education	*National Technology Standards* ISTE 480 Charnelton St., Eugene, OR 97401-2626, or call (800) 336-5191.

*Internet addresses can be found at www.aclin.org/sarb/content

GLOSSARY

Adaptive behavior   being able to meet independence and social responsibility expectations for the age and context in which the behavior occurs.

Affect   *see* Affective.

Affective   beliefs and emotional feelings.

Alternative assessment   refers to a number of different kinds of assessments that are not traditional paper-and-pencil tests, such as performance and portfolio assessments.

Alternatives   refers to possible answers in a multiple-choice item.

Analytic scale   type of scoring in which separate scores are provided for each criterion used.

Anchor   examples of student responses, products, and performances that illustrate specific points on a scoring criteria scale.

Anecdotal observation   brief written notes or records of student behavior.

Aptitude test   type of standardized test that measures cognitive ability, potential, or capacity to learn.

Assessment   the process of gathering, evaluating, and using information.

Attitude   a predisposition to respond favorably or unfavorably to something; consists of affective, cognitive, and behavioral components.

Authenticity   describes instruction and assessment that are characterized by tasks that are similar to what is done or accomplished in real life.

Benchmark   content standard for particular grade levels or developmental levels.

Binary-choice item   type of selected-response item in which the respondent selects one of two possible answers.

Blueprint   *see* Test blueprint.

Central tendency error   Scoring bias in which students tend to be rated in the middle of the evaluation scale.

Classroom assessment   the collection, evaluation, and use of information for teacher decision making.

Classroom climate   *see* Classroom environment.

Classroom environment   feeling tones and nature of interpersonal interactions in a classroom.

Cognitive   mental processing that includes knowing, understanding, and reasoning.

Confidence bands   show the standard error of measurement for obtained scores.

Content-related evidence   type of evidence for validity in which judgments are made about the representativeness of a sample of items from a larger domain.

Content standards   describe what students should know and be able to do.

Construct-related evidence   type of evidence for validity that focuses on the meaning and definition of constructs that are assessed.

Constructed-response item type of item in which students create or produce their own answer or response.

Correlation coefficient a number between –1 and +1 that indicates the direction and strength of relationship between two measures.

Criteria categories of specific behaviors or dimensions used to evaluate students.

Criterion-referenced type of test score interpretation in which performance is compared to levels of established criteria.

Criterion-related evidence type of evidence for validity in which scores from an assessment are related to other measures of the same trait or future behavior.

Distractors Incorrect alternatives in a multiple-choice item.

Educational goal a general statement of what students should know and be able to do.

Educational objective a relatively specific statement of what students should know and be capable of doing at the end of an instructional unit.

Emotionally disturbed consistent, inappropriate behaviors and feelings not attributed to other disabilities that interfere with academic work.

Essay type of item in which students provide an extended or restricted written response to a question.

Evaluation interpretation of gathered information to make the information meaningful.

Exemplar *see* Anchor.

Expectation level of performance communicated to others.

Extended-type task a performance assessment task that may last days or weeks in which students provide extensive answers to tasks.

Feedback indicating verbally or in writing the correctness of an action, answer, or other response.

Formative assessment assessment that occurs during instruction to provide feedback to teachers and students.

Frequency distribution indicates the number of individuals receiving each score.

Frequency polygon shows the number of individuals receiving each score as a line graph.

Generosity error scoring bias in which teachers rate students higher than their performance deserves.

Goal *see* Educational goal.

Grade equivalent (GE) type of standardized test score that indicates performance in units of year and month of school as compared to the norm group.

Halo effect general impression influences scores or grades on subsequent assessments.

Histogram: graphic illustration of a frequency distribution, using bars to represent the frequency of each score or groups of scores.

Holistic scale type of scoring in which a single score is given for overall performance.

Individualized education program (IEP) plan for providing appropriate services to students with disabilities.

Instructional validity judgment of the extent of the match between what is taught and what is assessed.

Item analysis   review of pattern of responses to an objective item to determine the quality of distractors, discriminiation, and difficulty.

Learning disability   mental processing deficit that manifests as a significant discrepancy between aptitude and achievement.

Learning target   a description of performance that includes what students should know and be able to do and what criteria are used to judge the performance.

Linear transformation   derived scores that are consistent with the raw score distribution.

Likert scale   rating scale in which a respondent indicates the extent to which there is agreement or disagreement among a series of statements.

Mean   arithmetic average of all scores in a distribution.

Measurement   a systematic process of differentiating traits, characteristics, or behavior.

Median   the midpoint of a distribution, dividing it into an equal number of scores.

Mental retardation   poor aptitude and adaptive behaviors that result in slow learning.

Mode   the most frequently occurring score in a distribution.

Negatively skewed   a distribution in which the mean is lower than the median.

Nondiscriminatory   assessment in which the nature of the materials, questions, and procedures do not influence the results.

Normal curve equivalent (NCE)   derived normalized score with a mean of 50 and a standard deviation of 21.06.

Norm-referenced   a type of test interpretation in which relative standing is identified by comparing performance to how others (norm group) performed.

Objective   see Educational objective or Teaching objective.

Oral questioning   type of assessment in which the teacher asks questions orally.

Percentile rank   indicates the percentage of scores at or below the specified score.

Performance assessment   type of assessment in which students perform an activity or create a product.

Performance criteria   *see* Criteria.

Performance standard   a set of criteria designated to signify qualitatively different levels of performance.

Personal communication   student interactions with the teacher to provide assessment information.

Portfolio   a systematic collection of student products to assess progress.

Positively skewed   a distribution in which the mean is higher than the median.

Range   the difference between the highest and lowest score in a distribution.

Rating scale   a scale that contains gradations of the trait being assessed.

Readiness test   type of standardized aptitude test that identifies strengths and weaknesses of specific skills.

Reasoning   mental operation in which cognitive skills are combined with knowledge to solve a problem, make a decision, or complete a task.

Reliability   the consistency, stability, and dependability of scores.

Restricted range   a small range of scores.

Restricted-type task   performance assessment task in which the student provides a limited response to a task that is completed within a day, hour, or minutes.

Rubric   a scoring guide that uses criteria to differentiate between levels of student proficiency on a rating scale.

Scaled score   derived scores used in standardized testing to indicate growth in years.

Scatterplot   visual array of scores from two measures that illustrates possible relationships.

Selected-response item   type of item for which students select a response from possible responses that are provided.

Self-assessment   students reporting on or evaluating themselves.

Semantic differential   rating scale in which opposite adjectives are used and respondents check appropriate spaces between the adjectives.

Severity error   scoring bias in which teachers rate students lower than they should.

Sociogram   pictorial graph that shows how members of a group relate to one another.

Speeded tests   type of test in which students have a set, minimal amount of time to answer all questions.

Standard deviation   a number that indicates the average distance of scores from the mean.

Standard error of measurement (SEM)   estimate of the degree of error in obtained scores.

Standards   *see* Performance standards *or* Content standards.

Standards-based   *See* Criterion-referenced.

Stanine   derived score that indicates the approximate location of a score on the normal distribution.

Stem   question or phrase in a multiple-choice item that is answered by selecting from given alternatives.

Summative assessment   assessment that occurs at the end of an instructional unit to document student learning.

Table of specifications   *see* Test blueprint.

Target   *see* Learning target.

Teacher expectation   beliefs about what students are capable of knowing, understanding, and doing.

Teacher observation   method of gathering assessment information in which the teacher systematically or informally observes students.

Teaching objective   a description of the instructional plan.

Test   a formal, systematic procedure for assessment in which students respond to a standard set of questions.

Test battery   several standardized tests that are normed on the same sample.

Test blueprint   systematic presentation of the learning targets and nature of items in an assessment.

Test-retest   a stability estimate of reliability in which a group answers the same questions twice.

T-**score**   derived score with a mean of 50 and a standard deviation of 10.

Validity   the appropriateness and legitimacy of the inferences, claims, and uses made from test scores.

Values   end states of existence or desirable modes of conduct.

z-**score**   derived scores with a mean of 0 and a standard deviation of 1.

REFERENCES

Airasian, P. W. (2001). *Classroom assessment* (4th ed.). New York: McGraw-Hill.

Ames, C. A. (1990). Motivation: What teachers need to know. *Teachers College Record, 91,* 409–421.

Anderson, L. W. (1981). *Assessing affective characteristics in the schools.* Needham Heights, MA: Allyn & Bacon.

Anderson, L. W., & Krathwohl, D. R. (2001). *A taxonomy for learning, teaching, and assessing: A revision of Bloom's taxonomy of educational objectives.* New York: Longman.

Arter, J., & McTighe, J. (2001). *Scoring rubrics in the classroom: Using performance criteria for assessing and improving student performance.* Thousand Oaks, CA: Corwin Press.

Arter, J., & Spandel, V. (1992). Using portfolios of student work in instruction and assessment. *Educational Measurement: Issues and Practice, 11,* 36–44.

Arter, J. A. (1996). Establishing performance criteria. In R. E. Blum and J. A. Arter (Eds.), *Handbook for student performance assessment in an era of restructuring* (pp. VI-1:1–VI-2:8). Alexandria, VA: Association for Supervision and Curriculum Development.

Azwell, T., & Schmar, E. (1995). *Report card on report cards: Alternatives to consider.* Portsmouth, NH: Heinemann.

Bacon, M. (1993). *Restructuring curriculum, instruction, and assessment in the Littleton Public Schools.* Littleton, CO: Littleton Public Schools.

Bailey, J. M., & Guskey, T. R. (2001). *Implementing student-led conferences.* Thousand Oaks, CA: Corwin Press.

Beyer, B. K. (1985). Critical thinking: What is it? *Social Education, 22,* 270–276.

Billups, L. H., & Rauth, M. (1987). Teachers and research. In V. Richardson-Koehler (Ed.), *Educator's handbook.* White Plains, NY: Longman.

Black, P., & Wiliam, D. (1998). Assessment and classroom learning. *Assessment in Education, 5(1),* 103–110.

Bloom, B. S. (Ed.) (1956). *Taxonomy of educational objectives: The classification of educational goals. Handbook 1. Cognitive Domain.* New York: David McKay.

Braun, C. (1976). Teacher expectation: Sociopsychological dynamics. *Review of Educational Research, 46,* 185–213.

Brookhart, S. M. (1993). Teachers' grading practices: Meaning and values. *Journal of Educational Measurement, 30,* 123–142.

Brookhart, S. M. (1997). A theoretical framework for the role of classroom assessment in motivating student effort and achievement. *Applied Measurement in Education, 10,* 161–180.

Brookhart, S. M. (2001). Successful students' formative and summative uses of assessment information. *Assessment in Education, 8(2),* 153–169.

Brophy, J. E., & Alleman, J. (1991). Activities as instructional tools; A framework for analysis and evaluation. *Educational Researcher, 20,* 9–23.

Brophy, J. (1981). Teacher praise: A functional analysis. *Review of Educational Research, 51,* 5–32.

Brophy, J. E. (1998). *Motivating students to learn.* Boston: McGraw-Hill.

Burke, K. (1999). *How to assess authentic learning.* Arlington Heights, IL: SkyLight Professional Development.

Camp, R. (1992). Portfolio reflections in middle and secondary school classrooms. In K. B. Yancey (Ed.), *Portfolios in the writing classroom.* Urbana, IL: National Council of Teachers of English.

Chappuis, S., & Stiggins, R. J. (2002). Classroom assessment for learning. *Educational Leadership, 60(1),* 40–44.

Cohen, S. B. (1983). Assigning report card grades to the mainstreamed child. *Teaching Exceptional Students, 15,* 86–89.

Collins, A., & Dana, T. M. (1993). Using portfolios with middle grades students. *Middle School Journal, 25,* 14–19.

Creating a learning environment at Fowler High School. (1993). Syracuse, NY: Inclusive Education Project, Syracuse University.

Cross, L. H., & Frary, R. B. (1996) *Hodgepodge grading: Endorsed by students and teachers alike.* Paper presented at the annual meeting of the National Council on Measurement in Education, New York.

Davis, M. M. D. (1995). *The nature of data sources that inform decision making in reading by experienced second grade teachers.* Doctoral dissertation, Old Dominion University.

Doyle, W. (1986). Classroom organization and management. In M. C. Wittrock (Ed.), *Handbook of research on teaching* (3rd ed.). New York: Macmillan.

Ekman, P., & Friesen, W. V. (1969). The repertoire of nonverbal behavior: Categories, origins, usage, and coding. *Semiotica, 69,* 49–97.

Elawar, M. C., & Corno, L. (1985). A factorial experiment in teachers' written feedback on student homework: Changing teacher behavior a little rather than a lot. *Journal of Educational Psychology, 77,* 162–173.

Ennis, R. H. (1987). A taxonomy of critical thinking dispositions and abilities. In J. B. Baron and R. J. Sternberg (Eds.), *Teaching thinking skills: Theory and practice.* New York: W. H. Freeman.

Evertson, C., & Green, J. (1986). Observation as inquiry and method. In M. C. Wittrock (Ed.), *Handbook of research on teaching* (3rd ed., pp. 162–213). New York: Macmillan.

Feather, N. (Ed.). (1982). *Expectations and actions.* Hillsdale, NJ: Erlbaum.

Forsyth, D. R. (1999). *Our social world* (3rd ed.). Belmont, CA: Wadsworth.

Fraser, B. J. (1994). Research on classroom and school climate. In D. Gabel (Ed.), *Handbook of research on science teaching and learning.* New York: Macmillan.

Fraser, B. J. (1999). Using learning environment assessments to improve classroom and school climates. In H. J. Freiberg (Ed.), *School climate: Measuring, improving and sustaining health learning environments.* London: Falmer Press.

Frisbie, D. A., & Waltman, K. K. (1992). Developing a personal grading plan. *Educational Measurement: Issues and Practice, 11,* 35–42.

Gagne, E. D., Yekovich, C. W., & Yekovich, F. R. (1993). *The cognitive psychology of school learning* (2nd ed.). New York: HarperCollins.

Gardner, H. (1985). *Frames of mind: The theory of multiple intelligences.* New York: Basic Books.

Glatthorn, A. A. (1998). *Performance assessment and standards-based curricula: The achievement cycle.* Larchmont, NY: Eye on Education.

Gold, S. E. (1992). Increasing student autonomy through portfolios. In K. B. Yancey (Ed.), *Portfolios in the writing classroom.* Urbana, IL: National Council of Teachers of English.

Good, T. L., & Brophy, J. E. (2003). *Looking in classrooms* (9th ed.). New York: Longman.

Gordon, M. (1987). *Nursing diagnosis: Process and application.* New York: McGraw-Hill.

Gronlund, N. E. (1993). *How to make achievement tests and assessments* (5th ed.). Needham Heights: Allyn & Bacon.

Gronlund, N. E. (1995). *How to write and use instructional objectives* (5th ed.). New York: Macmillan.

Gullickson, A. R. (2003). *The student evaluation standards.* Thousand Oaks, CA: Corwin Press.

Guskey, T. R. (1994). Making the grade: What benefits students? *Educational Leadership, 52,* 14–20.

Guskey, T. R. (Ed.). (1996). *Communicating student learning: 1996 ASCD Yearbook.* Alexandria, VA: Association for Supervision and Curriculum Development.

Guskey, T. R. (2002). Computerized gradebooks and the myth of objectivity. *Phi Delta Kappan 83*(10), 775–780.

Guskey, T. R., & Bailey, J. M. (2001). *Developing grading and reporting systems for student learning.* Thousand Oaks, CA: Corwin Press.

Haertel, E. (1990). *From expert opinions to reliable scores: Psychometrics for judgment-based teacher assessment.* Paper presented at the annual meeting of the American Educational Research Association, Boston.

Hanna, G. S. (1993). *Better teaching through better measurement.* Orlando, FL: Harcourt Brace Jovanovich.

Hebert, E. A. (1998). Lessons learned about student portfolios. *Phi Delta Kappan, 79,* 583–585.

Hein, G. E., & Price, S. (1994). *Active assessment for active science: A guide for elementary school teachers.* Portsmouth, NH: Heinemann.

Herman, J. L., Aschbacher, P. R., & Winters, L. (1992). *A practical guide to alternative assessment.* Alexandria, VA: Association for Supervision and Curriculum.

Heubert, J. P., & Hauser, R. M. (Eds.). (1999). *High stakes testing for tracking, promotion, and graduation.* Washington, DC: National Academy Press.

Hill, B. C., Ruptic, C., & Norwick, L. (1998). *Classroom based assessment.* Norwood, MA: Christopher-Gordon.

Hohn, R. L. (1995). *Classroom learning and teaching.* White Plains, NY: Longman.

Hoy, L., & Greg, M. (1994). *Assessment in special education.* Pacific Groves, CA: Brooks/Cole.

Jackson, P. W. (1990). *Life in classrooms.* New York: Holt, Rinehart, and Winston.

Jamentz, K. (1994). Making sure that assessment improves performance. *Educational Leadership, 51,* 55–57.

Kendall, J. S., & Marzano, R. J. (1997). *Content knowledge: A compendium of standards and benchmarks* for *K–12 education*. Aurora, CO: Mid-continent Regional Educational Laboratory.

Kindsvatter, R., Wilen, W., & Ishler, M. (1996). *Dynamics of effective teaching* (3rd ed.). White Plains, NY: Longman.

Kissock, C., & Iyortsuun, P. T. (1982). *A guide to questioning: Classroom procedures for teachers*. London: Macmillan Press.

Knapp, M. L. (1996). *Nonverbal communication in human interaction* (4th ed.). New York: Holt.

Krathwohl, D. R., Bloom, B. S., & Masia, B. B. (1964). *Taxonomy of educational objectives, handbook II: Affective domain*. New York: David McKay.

Lambdin, D. V., & Walker, V. L. (1994). Planning for classroom portfolio assessment. *The Arithmetic Teacher, 41*, 318–324.

Lazzari, A. M., & Wood, J. W. (1994). *Test right: Strategies and exercises to improve test performance*. East Moline, IL: LinguiSystems.

Leathers, D. G. (1997). *Successful nonverbal communication: Principles and applications* (3rd ed.). New York: Macmillan.

Lickona, T. (1993). The return of character education. *Educational Leadership, 51*, 6–11.

Linn, R. L., & Gronlund, N. E. (2000). *Measurement and assessment in teaching* (8th ed.). Englewood Cliffs, NJ: Prentice-Hall.

Marsh, H. W., & Craven, R. (1997). Academic self-concept: Beyond the dustbowl. In G. D. Phye, (Ed.), *Handbook of classroom assessment: Learning, adjustment, and achievement*. San Diego, CA: Academic Press.

Martin-Kniep, (1998) Why am I doing this? *Purposeful teaching through portfolio assessment*. (1998). Portsmouth, NH: Heinemann.

Marzano, R. J. (1992). *A different kind of classroom: Teaching with dimensions of learning*. Alexandria, VA: Association for Supervision and Curriculum Development.

Marzano, R. J. (1996). Understanding the complexities of setting performance standards. In R. E. Blum and J. A. Arter (Eds.), *Handbook for student performance assessment in an era of restructuring* (pp. 1:6-1–1:6-8). Alexandria, VA: Association for Supervision and Curriculum Development.

Marzano, R. J. (2001). *Designing a new taxonomy of educational objectives*. Thousand Oaks, CA: Corwin Press.

Marzano, R. J., Brandt, R., & Hughes, C. S. (1988). *Dimensions of thinking: A framework for curriculum and instruction*. Alexandria, VA: Association for Supervision and Curriculum Development.

Marzano, R. J., & Kendall, R. S. (1996). *A comprehensive guide to designing standards-based districts, schools, and classrooms*. Aurora, CO: Mid-continent Regional Educational Laboratory.

Marzano, R. J., Pickering, D., & McTighe, J. (1993). *Assessing student outcomes: Performance assessment using the dimensions of learning model*. Alexandria, VA: Association for Supervision and Curriculum Development.

Mayer, R. E. (2002). *The promise of educational psychology: Vol. II. Teaching for meaningful learning*. Upper Saddle River, NJ: Merrill/Prentice Hall.

McMillan, J. H. (1980). Attitude development and measurement. In J. H. McMillan (Ed.), *The social psychology of school learning*. New York: Academic Press.

McMillan, J. H. (2001a). *Essential assessment concepts for teachers and administrators*. Thousand Oaks, CA: Corwin Press.

McMillan, J. H. (2001b). Secondary teachers' classroom assessment and grading practices. *Educational measurement: Issues and Practice, 20*(1), 20–32.

McMillan, J. H. (2002a). Elementary school teachers' classroom assessment and grading practices. *Journal of Educational Research 95*(4), 203–214.

McMillan, J. H. (2002b). *The impact of high-stakes external testing on classroom assessment decision-making*. Paper presented at the annual meeting of the American Educational Research Association, New Orleans.

McMillan, J. H., & Forsyth, D. R. (1991). What theories of motivation say about why learners learn. In R. J. Menges and M. D. Svinicki (Eds.), *College teaching: From theory to practice*. San Francisco: Jossey-Bass.

McMillan, J. H., Simonetta, L. G., & Singh, J. (1994). Student opinion survey: Development of measures of student motivation. *Educational and Psychological Measurement, 54*, 496–505.

McMillan, J. H., & Workman, D. (1999). *Teachers' classroom assessment and grading practices: Phase 2*. Richmond, VA: Metropolitan Educational Research Consortium.

McMillan, J. H., Workman, D., & Myran, S. M. (1998). *Teachers' classroom assessment and grading practices: Phase 1*. Richmond, VA: Metropolitan Educational Research Consortium.

McTighe, J., & Ferrara, S. (1998). *Assessing learning in the classroom*. Washington, DC: National Education Association.

Mehrabian, A. (1981). *Silent messages* (2nd ed.). Belmont, CA: Wadsworth.

Mehrens, W. A., & Lehmann, I. J. (1987). *Using standardized tests in education* (4th ed.). New York: Longman.

Mehring, T. A. (1995). Report card options for students with disabilities in general education. In T. Azwell & E. Schmar (Eds.), *Report card on report cards: Alternatives to consider.* Portsmouth, NH: Heinemann.

Morgan, N., & Saxton, J. (1991). *Teaching, questioning, and learning.* New York: Routledge.

National Council of Teachers of Mathematics (1995). *Assessment standards for school mathematics.* Reston, VA: National Council of Teachers of Mathematics.

National Council on Measurement in Education. (1995). *Code of professional responsibilities in educational measurement.* Washington, DC: Author.

National Forum on Assessment. (1995). *Principles and indicators for student assessment systems.* Cambridge, MA: National Center for Fair and Open Testing (FairTest).

National standards for civics and government. (1994). Calabasas, CA: Center for Civic Education.

National Standards for United States History: Exploring the American Experience (1994). Los Angeles, CA: National Center for History in the Schools.

Newmann, F. M. (1997). Authentic assessment in social studies: Standards and examples. In G. D. Phye (Ed.), *Handbook of classroom assessment: Learning, adjustment, and achievement.* San Diego, CA: Academic Press.

Nolen, S. B., Haladyna, T. M., & Haas, N. S. (1989). *A survey of Arizona teachers and administrators on the uses and effects of state-mandated standardized achievement testing* (Tech. Rep. No. 89–2). Phoenix, AZ: Arizona State University, West Campus.

Norris, S. P., & Ennis, R. H. (1995). *Evaluating critical thinking.* Pacific Grove, CA: Midwest Publications.

Oosterhof, A. C. (1987). Obtaining intended weights when combining students' scores. *Educational Measurement: Issues and Practices, 6,* 29–37.

Ormrod, J. E. (1999). *Human learning* (3rd ed.). Upper Saddle River, NJ: Merrill/Prentice-Hall.

Overton, T. (2003). *Assessing learners with special needs: An applied approach.* Upper Saddle River, NJ: Merrill/Prentice Hall.

Phye, G. D. (1997a). Classroom assessment: A multidimensional perspective. In G. D. Phye (Ed.), *Handbook of classroom assessment: Learning, adjustment, and achievement.* San Diego, CA: Academic Press.

Phye, G. D. (Ed.). (1997b). *Handbook of classroom assessment: Learning, adjustment, and achievement.* San Diego, CA: Academic Press.

Popham, W. J. (1994). *Anonymity-enhancement procedures for classroom affective assessment.* Paper presented at the annual meeting of the American Educational Research Association, New Orleans.

Popham, W. J. (2002). *Classroom assessment: What teachers need to know* (3rd ed.). Needham Heights, MA: Allyn & Bacon.

Porter, C., & Cleland, J. (1995). *The portfolio as a learning strategy.* Portsmouth, NH: Boynton/Cook.

Quellmalz, E. (1987). Developing reasoning skills. In J. B. Baron & R. J. Sternberg (Eds.), *Teaching thinking skills: Theory and practice.* New York: W. H. Freeman.

Quellmalz, E. S., & Hoskyn, J. (1997). Classroom assessment of reasoning strategies. In G. D. Phye (Ed.), *Handbook of classroom assessment: Learning, adjustment, and achievement.* San Diego, CA: Academic Press.

Raviv, A., Raviv, A., & Reisel, E. (1990). Teachers and students: Two different perspectives: Measuring social climate in the classroom. *American Educational Research Journal, 27,* 141–157.

Rickards, D., & Cheek, E., Jr. (1999). *Designing rubrics for K–6 classroom assessment.* Norwood, MA: Christopher-Gordon Publishers.

Rokeach, M. (1973). *The nature of human values.* New York: Free Press.

Roth, W. M. (2001). Gestures: Their role in teaching and learning. *Review of Educational Research, 71*(3), 365–392.

Rothman, R. (1995). The certificate of initial mastery. *Educational Leadership, 52,* 41–45.

Ryan, A. M., & Deci, E. L. (2000). Self-determination theory and the facilitation of intrinsic motivation, social development, and well-being. *American Psychologist, 55,* 68–78.

Salvia, J., & Ysseldyke, J. E. (2001). *Assessment* (8th ed.) Boston: Houghton Mifflin.

Scruggs, T. E., & Mastropieri, M. A. (1992). *Teaching test-taking skills: Helping students show what they know.* Cambridge, MA: Brookline Books.

Shepard, L. A. (2000). The role of assessment in a learning culture. *Educational Researcher 29*(10), 4–14.

Simpson, E. J. (1972). The classification of educational objectives in the psychomotor domain. *The psychomotor domain* (vol. 3). Washington, DC: Gryphon House.

Smith, J. K., Smith, L. F., & De Lisi, R. (2001). *Natural classroom assessment: Designing seamless instruction & assessment.* Thousand Oaks, CA: Corwin Press.

Spinelli, C. G. (2002). *Classroom assessment for students with special needs in inclusive settings.* Upper Saddle River, NJ: Merrill/Prentice Hall.

Stenmark, J. K. (1991). *Mathematics assessment: Myths, models, good questions, and practical suggestions.* Reston, VA: The National Council of Teachers of Mathematics.

Sternberg, R. J. (1986). The future of intelligence testing. *Educational measurement: Issues and practice, 5,* 19–22.

Stiggins, R. J. (1993). Teacher training in assessment: Overcoming the neglect. In S. Wise (Ed.), *Teacher training in assessment and measurement skills.* Lincoln, NE: Buros Institute.

Stiggins, R. J. (2001). *Student-centered classroom assessment* (3rd ed.). New York: Merrill.

Stiggins, R. J. (2002). Assessment crisis: The absence of assessment for learning. *Phi Delta Kappan, 83*(10), 758–765.

Stiggins, R. J., & Conklin, N. F. (1992). *In teachers' hands: Investigating the practices of classroom assessment.* Albany, NY: State University of New York Press.

Strickland, K., & Strickland, J. (1998). *Reflections on assessment: Its purposes, methods, and effects on learning.* Portsmouth, NH: Heinemann.

Terwilliger, J. S. (1989). Classroom standard setting and grading practices. *Educational Measurement: Issues and Practice, 8,* 15–19.

Tittle, C. K., Hecht, D., & Moore, P. (1993). Assessment theory and research for classrooms: From *Taxonomies* to constructing meaning in context. *Educational Measurement: Issues and Practices, 12,* 13–19.

Tombari, M. L., & Borich, G. D. (1999). *Authentic assessment in the classroom: Applications and practice.* Upper Saddle River, NJ: Merrill.

Valencia, S. W., & Calfee, R. (1991). The development and use of literacy portfolios for students, classes, and teachers. *Applied Measurement in Education, 4,* 333–345.

Wiggins, G. P. (1993). *Assessing student performance: Exploring the purpose and limits of testing.* San Francisco: Jossey-Bass.

Wiggins, G. P. (1998). *Educative assessment: Designing assessments to inform and improve student performance.* San Francisco, CA: Jossey-Bass.

Wiggins, G. P., & McTighe, J. (1998). *Understanding by design.* Washington, DC: Association for Supervision and Curriculum Development.

Witt, J. C., Elliott, S. N., Daly, E. J., III, Gresham, F. M., & Kramer, J. J. (1998). *Assessment of at-risk and special needs children* (2nd ed.). Boston: McGraw-Hill.

Wolf, D. P. (1989). Portfolio assessment: Sampling student work. *Educational Leadership, 46,* 35–39.

Wood, J. W., (2002). *Adapting instruction to accommodate students in inclusive settings* (4th ed.). Upper Saddle River, NJ: Prentice Hall.

Wurtz, E. (1993). *Promises to keep: Creating high standards for American students.* Report on the Review of Education Standards from the Goals 3 and 4 Technical Planning Group to the National Education Goals Panel, Washington, DC.

Wylie, R. C. (1989). *Measures of self-concept.* Lincoln: University of Nebraska Press.

INDEX